EUROPEAN UNION LAW

Second Edition

Alina Kaczorowska

Routledge
Taylor & Francis Group

LONDON AND NEW YORK

Second edition published 2011
by Routledge
2 Park Square, Milton Park, Abingdon, Oxon, OX14 4RN

Simultaneously published in the USA and Canada
by Routledge
270 Madison Avenue, New York, NY 10016

Routledge is an imprint of the Taylor & Francis Group, an informa business

© 2009, 2011 Alina Kaczorowska

The right of Alina Kaczorowska to be identified as author of this work has been asserted
by her in accordance with sections 77 and 78 of the Copyright, Designs and Patents Act 1988.

Previous editions published by Routledge-Cavendish

First edition 2009

Typeset in Times New Roman by
RefineCatch Limited, Bungay, Suffolk
Printed and bound in Great Britain by
MPG Books Ltd, Bodmin, Cornwall

British Library Cataloguing in Publication Data
A catalogue record for this book is available from the British Library

Library of Congress Cataloging in Publication Data
Kaczorowska, Alina.
  European Union law / Alina Kaczorowska. – 2nd ed.
    p. cm.
  1. Law—European Union countries.   2. European Union countries.   I. Title.
  KJE947.K333 2010
  341.242′2—dc22

                                              2010022057

ISBN13: 978–0–415–58253–7 (hbk)
ISBN13: 978–0–415–58246–9 (pbk)
ISBN13: 978–0–203–83736–8 (ebk)

OUTLINE CONTENTS

DETAILED CONTENTS

PREFACE

I am very happy to have had the opportunity of producing this second edition of *European Union Law* at a time when fascinating and exciting new developments have just occurred in the life of the EU. Whilst I like the idea of keeping this work up to date by publishing a new edition every two years my position with this second edition was that I had no choice but to write it! The entry into force of the Treaty of Lisbon on 1 December 2009 made so many huge changes in EU law that without the presence of this new edition I would have had to beg my publishers to withdraw the first edition from the market.

One of the merely practical changes is that almost every one of the articles in the Treaty on European Union and the Treaty establishing the European Community has been renumbered. Of course, I should not leave out the fact that almost every one of them has also been amended, repealed or replaced!

The renumbering of Treaty articles raises the matter of how to present case law decided prior to 1 December 2009. In this respect I have, when commenting on cases and when appropriate, chosen to refer to the article numbers extant at the time of the judgment, and to place new article numbers within square brackets immediately afterwards. I have also, wherever possible, avoided using old numbering in the book but where this has been unavoidable the new number has been placed in square brackets immediately after the old. The renumbering of articles is, however, inconsequential in comparison with the substantial and profound changes in EU law which this book examines in detail. They required the inclusion of new chapters in this edition on "The protection of human rights in the EU", "The Common Foreign and Security Policy" and on the "Values and objectives of the EU including the creation of an area of freedom, security and justice".

I would like to express my sincere appreciation and gratitude to my editor, Fiona Kinnear, who has been her usual helpful, kind, tactful and professional self. It has indeed been a pleasure to work with her, Holly Davis and other members of Routledge's personnel in the preparation of this edition.

Finally, my special thanks to someone who prefers not to be named but who has been my rock and my inspiration and who has spent hours assisting me with this book.

This book is up to date as at 1 May 2010.

Alina Kaczorowska

GUIDE TO THE COMPANION WEBSITE

www.routledge.com/textbooks/9780415582469

Visit *EU Law*'s Companion Website to discover a range of resources designed to enhance the learning and teaching experience for both students and lecturers.

On this accompanying website, you'll find the following resources:

Essay-style questions with suggested answers

Practice tackling essay-style questions on topics of EU Law that come up frequently in exams, and learn how to structure your answers and what to include with the suggested answers.

Diagrams

PowerPoints of the diagrams contained within the text are ideal for use in lectures or to help summarise and understand complex or important topics.

Weblinks

Probe deeper by using the website links provided which have been specifically selected to help you find authoritative and reliable sources for further study.

Updates

Keep on track with the latest developments in EU Law with the regular text updates.

TABLES OF EQUIVALENCES(¹)

Treaty on European Union

Old numbering of the Treaty on European Union	New numbering of the Treaty on European Union
TITLE I—COMMON PROVISIONS	TITLE I—COMMON PROVISIONS
Article 1	Article 1
	Article 2
Article 2	Article 3
Article 3 (repealed) (¹)	
	Article 4
	Article 5 (²)
Article 4 (repealed) (³)	
Article 5 (repealed) (⁴)	
Article 6	Article 6
Article 7	Article 7
	Article 8

(¹) Replaced, in substance, by Article 7 of the Treaty on the Functioning of the European Union ('TFEU') and by Articles 13(1) and 21, paragraph 3, second subparagraph of the Treaty on European Union ('TEU').
(²) Replaces Article 5 of the Treaty establishing the European Community ('TEC').
(³) Replaced, in substance, by Article 15.
(⁴) Replaced, in substance, by Article 13, paragraph 2.

(¹) Tables of equivalences as referred to in Article 5 of the Treaty of Lisbon. The original centre column, which set out the intermediate numbering as used in that Treaty, has been omitted.

xxi

Old numbering of the Treaty on European Union	New numbering of the Treaty on European Union
TITLE II—PROVISIONS AMENDING THE TREATY ESTABLISHING THE EUROPEAN ECONOMIC COMMUNITY WITH A VIEW TO ESTABLISHING THE EUROPEAN COMMUNITY	TITLE II—PROVISIONS ON DEMOCRATIC PRINCIPLES
Article 8 (repealed) ([5])	Article 9
	Article 10 ([6])
	Article 11
	Article 12
TITLE III—PROVISIONS AMENDING THE TREATY ESTABLISHING THE EUROPEAN COAL AND STEEL COMMUNITY	TITLE III—PROVISIONS ON THE INSTITUTIONS
Article 9 (repealed) ([7])	Article 13
	Article 14 ([8])
	Article 15 ([9])
	Article 16 ([10])
	Article 17 ([11])
	Article 18
	Article 19 ([12])

[5]   Article 8 TEU, which was in force until the entry into force of the Treaty of Lisbon (hereinafter 'current'), amended the TEC. Those amendments are incorporated into the latter Treaty and Article 8 is repealed. Its number is used to insert a new provision.

[6]   Paragraph 4 replaces, in substance, the first subparagraph of Article 191 TEC.

[7]   The current Article 9 TEU amended the Treaty establishing the European Coal and Steel Community. This latter expired on 23 July 2002. Article 9 is repealed and the number thereof is used to insert another provision.

[8]   — Paragraphs 1 and 2 replace, in substance, Article 189 TEC;
— paragraphs 1 to 3 replace, in substance, paragraphs 1 to 3 of Article 190 TEC;
— paragraph 1 replaces, in substance, the first subparagraph of Article 192 TEC;
— paragraph 4 replaces, in substance, the first subparagraph of Article 197 TEC.

[9]   Replaces, in substance, Article 4.

[10]   — Paragraph 1 replaces, in substance, the first and second indents of Article 202 TEC;
— paragraphs 2 and 9 replace, in substance, Article 203 TEC;
— paragraphs 4 and 5 replace, in substance, paragraphs 2 and 4 of Article 205 TEC.

[11]   — Paragraph 1 replaces, in substance, Article 211 TEC;
— paragraphs 3 and 7 replace, in substance, Article 214 TEC.
— paragraph 6 replaces, in substance, paragraphs 1, 3 and 4 of Article 217 TEC.

[12]   — Replaces, in substance, Article 220 TEC.
— the second subparagraph of paragraph 2 replaces, in substance, the first subparagraph of Article 221 TEC.

Old numbering of the Treaty on European Union	New numbering of the Treaty on European Union
TITLE IV—PROVISIONS AMENDING THE TREATY ESTABLISHING THE EUROPEAN ATOMIC ENERGY COMMUNITY	TITLE IV—PROVISIONS ON ENHANCED COOPERATION
Article 10 (repealed) ([13]) *Articles 27a to 27e (replaced)* *Articles 40 to 40b (replaced)* *Articles 43 to 45 (replaced)*	Article 20 ([14])
TITLE V—PROVISIONS ON A COMMON FOREIGN AND SECURITY POLICY	TITLE V—GENERAL PROVISIONS ON THE UNION'S EXTERNAL ACTION AND SPECIFIC PROVISIONS ON THE COMMON FOREIGN AND SECURITY POLICY
	Chapter 1—General provisions on the Union's external action
	Article 21
	Article 22
	Chapter 2—Specific provisions on the common foreign and security policy
	Section 1—Common provisions
	Article 23
Article 11	Article 24
Article 12	Article 25
Article 13	Article 26
	Article 27
Article 14	Article 28
Article 15	Article 29
Article 22 (moved)	Article 30
Article 23 (moved)	Article 31
Article 16	Article 32
Article 17 (moved)	*Article 42*

([13]) The current Article 10 TEU amended the Treaty establishing the European Atomic Energy Community. Those amendments are incorporated into the Treaty of Lisbon. Article 10 is repealed and the number thereof is used to insert another provision.

([14]) Also replaces Articles 11 and 11a TEC.

Old numbering of the Treaty on European Union	New numbering of the Treaty on European Union
Article 18	Article 33
Article 19	Article 34
Article 20	Article 35
Article 21	Article 36
Article 22 (moved)	*Article 30*
Article 23 (moved)	*Article 31*
Article 24	Article 37
Article 25	Article 38
	Article 39
Article 47 (moved)	Article 40
Article 26 (repealed)	
Article 27 (repealed)	
Article 27a (repealed) (^{15})	*Article 20*
Article 27b (replaced) (^{15})	*Article 20*
Article 27c (replaced) (^{15})	*Article 20*
Article 27d (replaced) (^{15})	*Article 20*
Article 27e (replaced) (^{15})	*Article 20*
Article 28	Article 41
	Section 2—Provisions on the common security and defence policy
Article 17 (moved)	Article 42
	Article 43
	Article 44
	Article 45
	Article 46
TITLE VI—PROVISIONS ON POLICE AND JUDICIAL COOPERATION IN CRIMINAL MATTERS (repealed) (^{16})	

(^{15})   The current Articles 27a to 27e, on enhanced cooperation, are also replaced by Articles 326 to 334 TFEU.
(^{16})   The current provisions of Title VI of the TEU, on police and judicial cooperation in criminal matters, are replaced by the provisions of Chapters 1, 5 and 5 of Title IV of Part Three of the TFEU.

Old numbering of the Treaty on European Union	New numbering of the Treaty on European Union
Article 29 (replaced) ([17])	
Article 30 (replaced) ([18])	
Article 31 (replaced) ([19])	
Article 32 (replaced) ([20])	
Article 33 (replaced) ([21])	
Article 34 (repealed)	
Article 35 (repealed)	
Article 36 (replaced) ([22])	
Article 37 (repealed)	
Article 38 (repealed)	
Article 39 (repealed)	
Article 40 (replaced) ([23])	*Article 20*
Article 40 A (replaced) ([23])	*Article 20*
Article 40 B (replaced) ([23])	*Article 20*
Article 41 (repealed)	
Article 42 (repealed)	
TITLE VII—PROVISIONS ON ENHANCED COOPERATION (replaced) ([24])	*TITLE IV—PROVISIONS ON ENHANCED COOPERATION*
Article 43 (replaced) ([24])	*Article 20*
Article 43 A (replaced) ([24])	*Article 20*
Article 43 B (replaced) ([24])	*Article 20*
Article 44 (replaced) ([24])	*Article 20*
Article 44 A (replaced) ([24])	*Article 20*
Article 45 (replaced) ([24])	*Article 20*

([17])   Replaced by Article 67 TFEU.
([18])   Replaced by Articles 87 and 88 TFEU.
([19])   Replaced by Articles 82, 83 and 85 TFEU.
([20])   Replaced by Article 89 TFEU.
([21])   Replaced by Article 72 TFEU.
([22])   Replaced by Article 71 TFEU.
([23])   The current Articles 40 to 40 B TEU, on enhanced cooperation, are also replaced by Articles 326 to 334 TFEU.
([24])   The current Articles 43 to 45 and Title VII of the TEU, on enhanced cooperation, are also replaced by Articles 326 to 334 TFEU.

Old numbering of the Treaty on European Union	New numbering of the Treaty on European Union
TITLE VIII—FINAL PROVISIONS	TITLE VI—FINAL PROVISIONS
Article 46 (repealed)	
	Article 47
Article 47 (replaced)	*Article 40*
Article 48	Article 48
Article 49	Article 49
	Article 50
	Article 51
	Article 52
Article 50 (repealed)	
Article 51	Article 53
Article 52	Article 54
Article 53	Article 55

Treaty on the Functioning of the European Union

Old numbering of the Treaty establishing the European Community	New numbering of the Treaty on the Functioning of the European Union
PART ONE—PRINCIPLES	PART ONE—PRINCIPLES
Article 1 (repealed)	
	Article 1
Article 2 (repealed) (^{25})	
	Title 1—Categories and areas of union competence
	Article 2
	Article 3
	Article 4
	Article 5

(^{25})   Replaced, in substance, by Article 3 TEU.

Old numbering of the Treaty establishing the European Community	New numbering of the Treaty on the Functioning of the European Union
	Article 6
	Title II—Provisions having general application
	Article 7
Article 3, paragraph 1 (repealed) ([26])	
Article 3, paragraph 2	Article 8
Article 4 (moved)	*Article 119*
Article 5 (replaced) ([27])	
	Article 9
	Article 10
Article 6	Article 11
Article 153, paragraph 2 (moved)	Article 12
	Article 13 ([28])
Article 7 (repealed) ([29])	
Article 8 (repealed) ([30])	
Article 9 (repealed)	
Article 10 (repealed) ([31])	
Article 11 (replaced) ([32])	*Articles 326 to 334*
Article 11a (replaced) ([32])	*Articles 326 to 334*
Article 12 (repealed)	*Article 18*
Article 13 (moved)	*Article 19*
Article 14 (moved)	*Article 26*
Article 15 (moved)	*Article 27*
Article 16	Article 14
Article 255 (moved)	Article 15

[26]   Replaced, in substance, by Articles 3 to 6 TFEU.
[27]   Replaced, in substance, by Article 5 TEU.
[28]   Insertion of the operative part of the protocol on protection and welfare of animals.
[29]   Replaced, in substance, by Article 13 TEU.
[30]   Replaced, in substance, by Article 13 TEU and Article 282, paragraph 1, TFEU.
[31]   Replaced, in substance, by Article 4, paragraph 3, TEU.
[32]   Also replaced by Article 20 TEU.

Old numbering of the Treaty establishing the European Community	New numbering of the Treaty on the Functioning of the European Union
Article 286 (moved)	Article 16
	Article 17
PART TWO—CITIZENSHIP OF THE UNION	PART TWO—NON-DISCRIMINATION AND CITIZENSHIP OF THE UNION
Article 12 (moved)	Article 18
Article 13 (moved)	Article 19
Article 17	Article 20
Article 18	Article 21
Article 19	Article 22
Article 20	Article 23
Article 21	Article 24
Article 22	Article 25
PART THREE—COMMUNITY POLICIES	PART THREE—POLICIES AND INTERNAL ACTIONS OF THE UNION
	Title I—The internal market
Article 14 (moved)	Article 26
Article 15 (moved)	Article 27
Title I—Free movement of goods	Title II—Free movement of goods
Article 23	Article 28
Article 24	Article 29
Chapter 1—The customs union	Chapter 1—The customs union
Article 25	Article 30
Article 26	Article 31
Article 27	Article 32
Part Three, Title X, Customs cooperation (moved)	Chapter 2—Customs cooperation
Article 135 (moved)	Article 33
Chapter 2—Prohibition of quantitative restrictions between Member States	Chapter 3—Prohibition of quantitative restrictions between Member States
Article 28	Article 34

Old numbering of the Treaty establishing the European Community	New numbering of the Treaty on the Functioning of the European Union
Article 29	Article 35
Article 30	Article 36
Article 31	Article 37
Title II—Agriculture	Title III—Agriculture and fisheries
Article 32	Article 38
Article 33	Article 39
Article 34	Article 40
Article 35	Article 41
Article 36	Article 42
Article 37	Article 43
Article 38	Article 44
Title III—Free movement of persons, services and capital	Title IV—Free movement of persons, services and capital
Chapter 1—Workers	Chapter 1—Workers
Article 39	Article 45
Article 40	Article 46
Article 41	Article 47
Article 42	Article 48
Chapter 2—Right of establishment	Chapter 2—Right of establishment
Article 43	Article 49
Article 44	Article 50
Article 45	Article 51
Article 46	Article 52
Article 47	Article 53
Article 48	Article 54
Article 294 (moved)	Article 55
Chapter 3—Services	Chapter 3—Services
Article 49	Article 56

Old numbering of the Treaty establishing the European Community	New numbering of the Treaty on the Functining of the European Union
Article 50	Article 57
Article 51	Article 58
Article 52	Article 59
Article 53	Article 60
Article 54	Article 61
Article 55	Article 62
Chapter 4—Capital and payments	Chapter 4—Capital and payments
Article 56	Article 63
Article 57	Article 64
Article 58	Article 65
Article 59	Article 66
Article 60 (moved)	*Article 75*
Title IV—Visas, asylum, immigration and other policies related to free movement of persons	Title V—Area of freedom, security and justice
	Chapter 1—General provisions
Article 61	Article 67 (^{33})
	Article 68
	Article 69
	Article 70
	Article 71 (^{34})
Article 64, paragraph 1 (replaced)	Article 72 (^{35})
	Article 73
Article 66 (replaced)	Article 74
Article 60 (moved)	Article 75
	Article 76

(^{33}) Also replaces the current Article 29 TEU.
(^{34}) Also replaces the current Article 36 TEU.
(^{35}) Also replaces the current Article 33 TEU.

Old numbering of the Treaty establishing the European Community	New numbering of the Treaty on the Functioning of the European Union
	Chapter 2—Policies on border checks, asylum and immigration
Article 62	Article 77
Article 63, points 1 et 2, and Article 64, paragraph 2 (³⁶)	Article 78
Article 63, points 3 and 4	Article 79
	Article 80
Article 64, paragraph 1 (replaced)	*Article 72*
	Chapter 3—Judicial cooperation in civil matters
Article 65	Article 81
Article 66 (replaced)	*Article 74*
Article 67 (replaced)	
Article 68 (replaced)	
Article 69 (replaced)	
	Chapter 4—Judicial cooperation in criminal matters
	Article 82 (³⁷)
	Article 83 (³⁷)
	Article 84
	Article 85 (³⁷)
	Article 86
	Chapter 5—Police cooperation
	Article 87 (³⁸)
	Article 88 (³⁸)
	Article 89 (³⁹)

(³⁶)   Points 1 and 2 of Article 63 EC are replaced by paragraph 1 and 2 of Article 78 TFEU, and paragraph 2 of Article 64 is replaced by paragraph 3 of Article 78 TFEU.
(³⁷)   Replaces the current Article 31 TEU.
(³⁸)   Replaces the current Article 30 TEU.
(³⁹)   Replaces the current Article 32 TEU.

Old numbering of the Treaty establishing the European Community	New numbering of the Treaty on the Functioning of the European Union
Title V—Transport	Title VI—Transport
Article 70	Article 90
Article 71	Article 91
Article 72	Article 92
Article 73	Article 93
Article 74	Article 94
Article 75	Article 95
Article 76	Article 96
Article 77	Article 97
Article 78	Article 98
Article 79	Article 99
Article 80	Article 100
Title VI—Common rules on competition, taxation and approximation of laws	Title VII—Common rules on competition, taxation and approximation of laws
Chapter 1—Rules on competition	Chapter 1—Rules on competition
Section 1—Rules applying to undertakings	Section 1—Rules applying to undertakings
Article 81	Article 101
Article 82	Article 102
Article 83	Article 103
Article 84	Article 104
Article 85	Article 105
Article 86	Article 106
Section 2—Aids granted by States	Section 2—Aids granted by States
Article 87	Article 107
Article 88	Article 108
Article 89	Article 109
Chapter 2—Tax provisions	Chapter 2—Tax provisions

Old numbering of the Treaty establishing the European Community	New numbering of the Treaty on the Functioning of the European Union
Article 90	Article 110
Article 91	Article 111
Article 92	Article 112
Article 93	Article 113
Chapter 3—Approximation of laws	Chapter 3—Approximation of laws
Article 95 (moved)	Article 114
Article 94 (moved)	Article 115
Article 96	Article 116
Article 97	Article 117
	Article 118
Title VII—Economic and monetary policy	Title VIII—Economic and monetary policy
Article 4 (moved)	Article 119
Chapter 1—Economic policy	Chapter 1—Economic policy
Article 98	Article 120
Article 99	Article 121
Article 100	Article 122
Article 101	Article 123
Article 102	Article 124
Article 103	Article 125
Article 104	Article 126
Chapter 2—monetary policy	Chapter 2—monetary policy
Article 105	Article 127
Article 106	Article 128
Article 107	Article 129
Article 108	Article 130
Article 109	Article 131
Article 110	Article 132

Old numbering of the Treaty establishing the European Community	New numbering of the Treaty on the Functioning of the European Union
Article 111, paragraphs 1 to 3 and 5 (moved)	*Article 219*
Article 111, paragraph 4 (moved)	*Article 138*
	Article 133
Chapter 3—Institutional provisions	Chapter 3—Institutional provisions
Article 112 (moved)	*Article 283*
Article 113 (moved)	*Article 284*
Article 114	Article 134
Article 115	Article 135
	Chapter 4—Provisions specific to Member States whose currency is the euro
	Article 136
	Article 137
Article 111, paragraph 4 (moved)	Article 138
Chapter 4—Transitional provisions	Chapter 5—Transitional provisions
Article 116 (repealed)	
	Article 139
Article 117, paragraphs 1, 2, sixth indent, and 3 to 9 (repealed)	
Article 117, paragraph 2, first five indents (moved)	*Article 141, paragraph 2*
Article 121, paragraph 1 (moved) *Article 122, paragraph 2, second sentence (moved)* *Article 123, paragraph 5 (moved)*	Article 140 (⁴⁰)
Article 118 (repealed)	
Article 123, paragraph 3 (moved) *Article 117, paragraph 2, first five indents (moved)*	Article 141 (⁴¹)

(⁴⁰)   — Article 140, paragraph 1 takes over the wording of paragraph 1 of Article 121.
       — Article 140, paragraph 2 takes over the second sentence of paragraph 2 of Article 122.
       — Article 140, paragraph 3 takes over paragraph 5 of Article 123.
(⁴¹)   — Article 141, paragraph 1 takes over paragraph 3 of Article 123.
       — Article 141, paragraph 2 takes over the first five indents of paragraph 2 of Article 117.

Old numbering of the Treaty establishing the European Community	New numbering of the Treaty on the Functioning of the European Union
Article 124, paragraph 1 (moved)	Article 142
Article 119	Article 143
Article 120	Article 144
Article 121, paragraph 1 (moved)	*Article 140, paragraph 1*
Article 121, paragraphs 2 to 4 (repealed)	
Article 122, paragraphs 1, 2, first sentence, 3, 4, 5 and 6 (repealed)	
Article 122, paragraph 2, second sentence (moved)	*Article 140, paragraph 2, first subparagraph*
Article 123, paragraphs 1, 2 and 4 (repealed)	
Article 123, paragraph 3 (moved)	*Article 141, paragraph 1*
Article 123, paragraph 5 (moved)	*Article 140, paragraph 3*
Article 124, paragraph 1 (moved)	*Article 142*
Article 124, paragraph 2 (repealed)	
Title VIII—Employment	Title IX—Employment
Article 125	Article 145
Article 126	Article 146
Article 127	Article 147
Article 128	Article 148
Article 129	Article 149
Article 130	Article 150
Title IX—Common commercial policy (moved)	*Part Five, Title II, common commercial policy*
Article 131 (moved)	*Article 206*
Article 132 (repealed)	
Article 133 (moved)	*Article 207*
Article 134 (repealed)	
Title X—Customs cooperation (moved)	*Part Three, Title II, Chapter 2, Customs cooperation*

Old numbering of the Treaty establishing the European Community	New numbering of the Treaty on the Functioning of the European Union
Article 135 (moved)	*Article 33*
Title XI—Social policy, education, vocational training and youth	Title X—Social policy
Chapter 1—social provisions (repealed)	
Article 136	Article 151
	Article 152
Article 137	Article 153
Article 138	Article 154
Article 139	Article 155
Article 140	Article 156
Article 141	Article 157
Article 142	Article 158
Article 143	Article 159
Article 144	Article 160
Article 145	Article 161
Chapter 2—The European Social Fund	Title XI—The European Social Fund
Article 146	Article 162
Article 147	Article 163
Article 148	Article 164
Chapter 3—Education, vocational training and youth	Title XII—Education, vocational training, youth and sport
Article 149	Article 165
Article 150	Article 166
Title XII—Culture	Title XIII—Culture
Article 151	Article 167
Title XIII—Public health	Title XIV—Public health
Article 152	Article 168
Title XIV—Consumer protection	Title XV—Consumer protection

Old numbering of the Treaty establishing the European Community	New numbering of the Treaty on the Functioning of the European Union
Article 153, paragraphs 1, 3, 4 and 5	Article 169
Article 153, paragraph 2 (moved)	*Article 12*
Title XV—Trans–European networks	Title XVI—Trans–European networks
Article 154	Article 170
Article 155	Article 171
Article 156	Article 172
Title XVI—Industry	Title XVII—Industry
Article 157	Article 173
Title XVII—Economic and social cohesion	Title XVIII—Economic, social and territorial cohesion
Article 158	Article 174
Article 159	Article 175
Article 160	Article 176
Article 161	Article 177
Article 162	Article 178
Title XVIII—Research and technological development	Title XIX—Research and technological development and space
Article 163	Article 179
Article 164	Article 180
Article 165	Article 181
Article 166	Article 182
Article 167	Article 183
Article 168	Article 184
Article 169	Article 185
Article 170	Article 186
Article 171	Article 187
Article 172	Article 188
	Article 189

Old numbering of the Treaty establishing the European Community	New numbering of the Treaty on the Functioning of the European Union
Article 173	Article 190
Title XIX—Environment	Title XX—Environment
Article 174	Article 191
Article 175	Article 192
Article 176	Article 193
	Titre XXI—Energy
	Article 194
	Title XXII—Tourism
	Article 195
	Title XXIII—Civil protection
	Article 196
	Title XXIV—Administrative cooperation
	Article 197
Title XX—Development cooperation (moved)	*Part Five, Title III, Chapter 1, Development cooperation*
Article 177 (moved)	*Article 208*
Article 178 (repealed) (⁴²)	
Article 179 (moved)	*Article 209*
Article 180 (moved)	*Article 210*
Article 181 (moved)	*Article 211*
Title XXI—Economic, financial and technical *cooperation with third countries (moved)*	*Part Five, Title III, Chapter 2, Economic, financial and technical cooperation with third countries*
Article 181a (moved)	*Article 212*
PART FOUR—ASSOCIATION OF THE OVERSEAS COUNTRIES AND TERRITORIES	PART FOUR—ASSOCIATION OF THE OVERSEAS COUNTRIES AND TERRITORIES
Article 182	Article 198
Article 183	Article 199

(⁴²)   Replaced, in substance, by the second sentence of the second subparagraph of paragraph 1 of Article 208 TFEU.

Old numbering of the Treaty establishing the European Community	New numbering of the Treaty on the Functioning of the European Union
Article 184	Article 200
Article 185	Article 201
Article 186	Article 202
Article 187	Article 203
Article 188	Article 204
	PART FIVE—EXTERNAL ACTION BY THE UNION
	Title I—General provisions on the union's external action
	Article 205
Part Three, Title IX, Common commercial policy (moved)	Title II—Common commercial policy
Article 131 (moved)	Article 206
Article 133 (moved)	Article 207
	Title III—Cooperation with third countries and humanitarian aid
Part Three, Title XX, Development cooperation (moved)	Chapter 1—development cooperation
Article 177 (moved)	Article 208 ([43])
Article 179 (moved)	Article 209
Article 180 (moved)	Article 210
Article 181 (moved)	Article 211
Part Three, Title XXI, Economic, financial and technical cooperation with third countries (moved)	Chapter 2—Economic, financial and technical cooperation with third countries
Article 181a (moved)	Article 212
	Article 213
	Chapter 3—Humanitarian aid
	Article 214
	Title IV—Restrictive measures

([43])   The second sentence of the second subparagraph of paragraph 1 replaces, in substance, Article 178 TEC.

Old numbering of the Treaty establishing the European Community	New numbering of the Treaty on the Functioning of the European Union
Article 301 (replaced)	Article 215
	Title V—International agreements
	Article 216
Article 310 (moved)	Article 217
Article 300 (replaced)	Article 218
Article 111, paragraphs 1 to 3 and 5 (moved)	Article 219
	Title VI—The Union's relations with international organisations and third countries and the Union delegations
Articles 302 to 304 (replaced)	Article 220
	Article 221
	Title VII—Solidarity clause
	Article 222
PART FIVE—INSTITUTIONS OF THE COMMUNITY	PART SIX—INSTITUTIONAL AND FINANCIAL PROVISIONS
Title I—Institutional provisions	Title I—Institutional provisions
Chapter 1—The institutions	Chapter 1—The institutions
Section 1—The European Parliament	Section 1—The European Parliament
Article 189 (repealed) ([44])	
Article 190, paragraphs 1 to 3 (repealed) ([45])	
Article 190, paragraphs 4 and 5	Article 223
Article 191, first paragraph (repealed) ([46])	
Article 191, second paragraph	Article 224
Article 192, first paragraph (repealed) ([47])	
Article 192, second paragraph	Article 225
Article 193	Article 226

[44] Replaced, in substance, by Article 14, paragraphs 1 and 2, TEU.
[45] Replaced, in substance, by Article 14, paragraphs 1 to 3, TEU.
[46] Replaced, in substance, by Article 11, paragraph 4, TEU.
[47] Replaced, in substance, by Article 14, paragraph 1, TEU.

Old numbering of the Treaty establishing the European Community	New numbering of the Treaty on the Functioning of the European Union
Article 194	Article 227
Article 195	Article 228
Article 196	Article 229
Article 197, first paragraph (repealed) ([48])	
Article 197, second, third and fourth paragraphs	Article 230
Article 198	Article 231
Article 199	Article 232
Article 200	Article 233
Article 201	Article 234
	Section 2—The European Council
	Article 235
	Article 236
Section 2—The Council	Section 3—The Council
Article 202 (repealed) ([49])	
Article 203 (repealed) ([50])	
Article 204	Article 237
Article 205, paragraphs 2 and 4 (repealed) ([51])	
Article 205, paragraphs 1 and 3	Article 238
Article 206	Article 239
Article 207	Article 240
Article 208	Article 241
Article 209	Article 242
Article 210	Article 243
Section 3—The Commission	Section 4—The Commission

([48])   Replaced, in substance, by Article 14, paragraph 4, TEU.
([49])   Replaced, in substance, by Article 16, paragraph 1, TEU and by Articles 290 and 291 TFEU.
([50])   Replaced, in substance, by Article 16, paragraphs 2 and 9 TEU.
([51])   Replaced, in substance, by Article 16, paragraphs 4 and 5 TEU.

Old numbering of the Treaty establishing the European Community	New numbering of the Treaty on the Functioning of the European Union
Article 211 (repealed) ([53])	
	Article 244
Article 212 (moved)	*Article 249, paragraph 2*
Article 213	Article 245
Article 214 (repealed) ([55])	
Article 215	Article 246
Article 216	Article 247
Article 217, paragraphs 1, 3 and 4 (repealed) ([56])	
Article 217, paragraph 2	Article 248
Article 218, paragraph 1 (repealed) ([57])	
Article 218, paragraph 2	Article 249
Article 219	Article 250
Section 4—The Court of Justice	Section 5—The Court of Justice of the European Union
Article 220 (repealed) ([58])	
Article 221, first paragraph (repealed) ([59])	
Article 221, second and third paragraphs	Article 251
Article 222	Article 252
Article 223	Article 253
Article 224 ([60])	Article 254
	Article 255
Article 225	Article 256
Article 225a	Article 257

([53])   Replaced, in substance, by Article 17, paragraph 1 TEU.
([55])   Replaced, in substance, by Article 17, paragraphs 3 and 7 TEU.
([56])   Replaced, in substance, by Article 17, paragraph 6, TEU.
([57])   Replaced, in substance, by Article 295 TFEU.
([58])   Replaced, in substance, by Article 19 TEU.
([59])   Replaced, in substance, by Article 19, paragraph 2, first subparagraph, of the TEU.
([60])   The first sentence of the first subparagraph is replaced, in substance, by Article 19, paragraph 2, second subparagraph of the TEU.

Old numbering of the Treaty establishing the European Community	New numbering of the Treaty on the Functioning of the European Union
Article 226	Article 258
Article 227	Article 259
Article 228	Article 260
Article 229	Article 261
Article 229a	Article 262
Article 230	Article 263
Article 231	Article 264
Article 232	Article 265
Article 233	Article 266
Article 234	Article 267
Article 235	Article 268
	Article 269
Article 236	Article 270
Article 237	Article 271
Article 238	Article 272
Article 239	Article 273
Article 240	Article 274
	Article 275
	Article 276
Article 241	Article 277
Article 242	Article 278
Article 243	Article 279
Article 244	Article 280
Article 245	Article 281
	Section 6—The European Central Bank
	Article 282
Article 112 (moved)	Article 283

Old numbering of the Treaty establishing the European Community	New numbering of the Treaty on the Functioning of the European Union
Article 113 (moved)	Article 284
Section 5—The Court of Auditors	Section 7—The Court of Auditors
Article 246	Article 285
Article 247	Article 286
Article 248	Article 287
Chapter 2—Provisions common to several institutions	Chapter 2—Legal acts of the Union, adoption procedures and other provisions
	Section 1—The legal acts of the Union
Article 249	Article 288
	Article 289
	Article 290 ([61])
	Article 291 ([61])
	Article 292
	Section 2—Procedures for the adoption of acts and other provisions
Article 250	Article 293
Article 251	Article 294
Article 252 (repealed)	
	Article 295
Article 253	Article 296
Article 254	Article 297
	Article 298
Article 255 (moved)	*Article 15*
Article 256	Article 299
	Chapter 3—The Union's advisory bodies
	Article 300
Chapter 3—The Economic and Social Committee	Section 1—The Economic and Social Committee

([61])   Replaces, in substance, the third indent of Article 202 TEC.

Old numbering of the Treaty establishing the European Community	New numbering of the Treaty on the Functioning of the European Union
Article 257 (repealed) ([62])	
Article 258, first, second and fourth paragraphs	Article 301
Article 258, third paragraph (repealed) ([63])	
Article 259	Article 302
Article 260	Article 303
Article 261 (repealed)	
Article 262	Article 304
Chapter 4—The Committee of the Regions	Section 2—The Committee of the Regions
Article 263, first and fifth paragraphs (repealed) ([64])	
Article 263, second to fourth paragraphs	Article 305
Article 264	Article 306
Article 265	Article 307
Chapter 5—The European Investment Bank	Chapter 4—The European Investment Bank
Article 266	Article 308
Article 267	Article 309
Title II—Financial provisions	Title II—Financial provisions
Article 268	Article 310
	Chapter 1—The Union's own resources
Article 269	Article 311
Article 270 (repealed) ([65])	
	Chapter 2—The multiannual financial framework
	Article 312
	Chapter 3—The Union's annual budget

([62])   Replaced, in substance, by Article 300, paragraph 2 of the TFEU.
([63])   Replaced, in substance, by Article 300, paragraph 4 of the TFEU.
([64])   Replaced, in substance, by Article 300, paragraphs 3 and 4, TFEU.
([65])   Replaced, in substance, by Article 310, paragraph 4, TFEU.

Old numbering of the Treaty establishing the European Community	New numbering of the Treaty on the Functioning of the European Union
Article 272, paragraph 1 (moved)	Article 313
Article 271 (moved)	*Article 316*
Article 272, paragraph 1 (moved)	*Article 313*
Article 272, paragraphs 2 to 10	Article 314
Article 273	Article 315
Article 271 (moved)	Article 316
	Chapter 4—Implementation of the budget and discharge
Article 274	Article 317
Article 275	Article 318
Article 276	Article 319
	Chapter 5—Common provisions
Article 277	Article 320
Article 278	Article 321
Article 279	Article 322
	Article 323
	Article 324
	Chapter 6—Combating fraud
Article 280	Article 325
	Title III—Enhanced cooperation
Articles 11 and 11a (replaced)	Article 326 (⁶⁶)
Articles 11 and 11a (replaced)	Article 327 (⁶⁶)
Articles 11 and 11a (replaced)	Article 328 (⁶⁶)
Articles 11 and 11a (replaced)	Article 329 (⁶⁶)
Articles 11 and 11a (replaced)	Article 330 (⁶⁶)
Articles 11 and 11a (replaced)	Article 331 (⁶⁶)
Articles 11 and 11a (replaced)	Article 332 (⁶⁶)

(⁶⁶)   Also replaces the current Articles 27a to 27e, 40 to 40b, and 43 to 45 TEU.

Old numbering of the Treaty establishing the European Community	New numbering of the Treaty on the Functioning of the European Union
Articles 11 and 11a (replaced)	Article 333 ([66])
Articles 11 and 11a (replaced)	Article 334 ([66])
PART SIX—GENERAL AND FINAL PROVISIONS	PART SEVEN—GENERAL AND FINAL PROVISIONS
Article 281 (repealed) ([67])	
Article 282	Article 335
Article 283	Article 336
Article 284	Article 337
Article 285	Article 338
Article 286 (replaced)	*Article 16*
Article 287	Article 339
Article 288	Article 340
Article 289	Article 341
Article 290	Article 342
Article 291	Article 343
Article 292	Article 344
Article 293 (repealed)	
Article 294 (moved)	*Article 55*
Article 295	Article 345
Article 296	Article 346
Article 297	Article 347
Article 298	Article 348
Article 299, paragraph 1 (repealed) ([68])	
Article 299, paragraph 2, second, third and fourth subparagraphs	Article 349
Article 299, paragraph 2, first subparagraph, and paragraphs 3 to 6 (moved)	*Article 355*

([67])   Replaced, in substance, by Article 47 TEU.
([68])   Replaced, in substance, by Article 52 TEU.

Old numbering of the Treaty establishing the European Community	New numbering of the Treaty on the Functioning of the European Union
Article 300 (replaced)	*Article 218*
Article 301 (replaced)	*Article 215*
Article 302 (replaced)	*Article 220*
Article 303 (replaced)	*Article 220*
Article 304 (replaced)	*Article 220*
Article 305 (repealed)	
Article 306	Article 350
Article 307	Article 351
Article 308	Article 352
	Article 353
Article 309	Article 354
Article 310 (moved)	*Article 217*
Article 311 (repealed) ([69])	
Article 299, paragraph 2, first subparagraph, and paragraphs 3 to 6 (moved)	Article 355
Article 312	Article 356
Final Provisions	
Article 313	Article 357
	Article 358
Article 314 (repealed) ([70])	

© **European Communities, http://eur-lex.europa.eu/**

([69])   Replaced, in substance, by Article 51 TEU.
([70])   Replaced, in substance, by Article 55 TEU.

TABLES OF CASES

l

EUROPEAN COURT OF JUSTICE (NUMERICAL)

THE GENERAL COURT (ALPHABETICAL)

OPINIONS OF THE EUROPEAN COURT OF JUSTICE

COMMISSION DECISIONS IN COMPETITION CASES (NON-MERGER)

COMMISSION DECISIONS IN MERGER CASES

JUDGMENTS OF THE EUROPEAN COURT OF HUMAN RIGHTS

JUDGMENTS AND OPINIONS OF THE INTERNATIONAL COURT OF JUSTICE AND THE PERMANENT COURT OF INTERNATIONAL JUSTICE

CASES FROM OTHER JURISDICTIONS

United Kingdom

USA

TABLES OF LEGISLATION

TREATIES, AGREEMENTS, CONVENTIONS, CHARTERS AND PROTOCOLS

TREATIES, AGREEMENTS, CONVENTIONS, CHARTERS AND PROTOCOLS

SECONDARY LEGISLATION

Regulations

1969

1969

1971

1975

1979

Directives

(Unless otherwise specified these are of the Council alone)

1964

2002

2003

Recommendations

Resolution of the Council

NATIONAL LEGISLATION

Austria

Belgium

Bulgaria

Chech Republic

Cyprus

Denmark

USA

TABLE OF ABBREVIATIONS

AC – Advisory Committee on Restrictive Practices and Dominant Positions

AAC – average avoidable cost

AC – Advisory Committee on Restrictive Practices and Dominant Positions

ACP – African, Caribbean and Pacific Countries

AEC - as efficient competitor

AG – Advocate General

AJDA – Actualité Juridique Droit Administratif

All ER – All England Law Reports

Antitrust L.J – Antitrust Law Journal

AVC – average variable cost

BSE – Bovine Spongiform Encephalopathy

CA – English Court of Appeal

CAP – Common Agricultural Policy

Cardozo J. Int'l & Comp – Cardozo Journal of International and Comparative Law

CARDS – Community Assistance for Reconstruction, Development and Stability in the Balkans

CCP – Common Commercial Policy

CCT – Common Customs Tariff

CE – Compulsory Expenditure

CE – Conseil d'Etat Français

CEE – Charge Having Equivalent Effect to a Customs Duty

CEEP – European Centre of Enterprises with Public Participation

CEPOL – European Police College

CFI – Court of First Instance

CFP – Common Fisheries Policy

CFSP – Common Foreign and Security Policy

Chi. J. Int'l L. – Chicago Journal of International Law

CIS – Confederation of Independent States

CIVCOM – Committee for Civilian Aspects of Crisis Management

CJQ – Civil Justice Quarterly

CLP – Current Legal Problems

CMLRev – Common Market Law Review

CMLR – Common Market Law Reports

CN – Combined Nomenclature

CoA – Court of Auditors

Colum. J. Eur. L. – Columbia Journal of European Law

COM – Proposed legislation and other Commission communications to the Council and/ or the other institutions, and their preparatory papers. Commission documents for the other institutions (legislative proposals, communications, reports, etc.)

Comp. L.J. – Competition Law Journal

Conn. J. Int'l L. – Connecticut Journal of International Law

CoR – Committee of the Regions

COREPER – Committee of Permanent Representatives

COSI – Standing Committee on Internal Security

CS Treaty– European Coal and Steel Community Treaty

CSDP – Common Security and Defence Policy

C-SIS – Central Schengen Information System

DCP – Draft Common Position

DG – Directorate General

Dick. L. Rev – Dickinson Law Review

DOs – designations of origin

DSB – WTO Dispute Settlement Body

Duke J. Comp. & Int'l L. – Duke Journal of Comparative and International Law

EA Treaty – European Atomic Energy Community Treaty

EC – European Community

EC Bull. – Bulletin of the European Communities

ECB – European Central Bank

ECHR – European Convention on Human Rights

ECJ – European Court of Justice

ECLR – European Competition Law Review

ECN – European Competition Network

ECOFIN – Economic and Financial Affairs Council

ECOSOC – United Nations Economic and Social Committee

ECR – European Court Reports

ECSC – European Coal and Steel Community

ECtHR – European Court of Human Rights

ECU – European Currency Unit

EEA – European Economic Area

EEAS – European External Action Service

EEC – European Economic Community

EEIG – European Economic Interest Grouping

EESC – European Economic and Social Committee

EDA – European Defence Agency

EFTA – European Free Trade Association

EGF – European Gendarmerie Force

EHRR – European Human Rights Reports

EIB – European Investment Bank

EJN – European Judicial Network

ELRev – European Law Review

ELJ – European Law Journal

EMCDDA – European Monitoring Centre for Drugs and Drug Addiction

EMS – European Monetary System

EMU – Economic and Monetary Union

EP – European Parliament

EPC – European Political Co-operation

EPL – European Public Law

EPO – European Patent Office

EPP – European Public Procecutor's Office

ERM I – Exchange Rate Mechanism established under the EMS

ERM II – Exchange Rate Mechanism established under the EMU

ERRF – European Rapid Reaction Force

ERTA – European Road Transport Agreement

ESCB – European System of Central Banks

ESDI – European Security and Defence Identity

ESDP – Common European Security and Defence Policy

ESIF – European Security and Intelligence Force

ETUC – European Trade Union Confederation

EU – European Union

EU BGs – European Union Battle Groups

EUSC – European Union Satellite Centre

EUISS – European Union Institute for Security Studies

EUMC – European Monitoring Centre for Racism and Xenophobia

EUMS – European Union Military Staff

Euratom – European Atomic Energy Community

Euro. C.J. – European Competition Law Journal

Eurojust – European Prosecutors Co-operation

Europol – European Police Office

Fordham Intl L.J. – Fordham International Law Journal

FRA – EU Agency for Fundamental Rights

FRG – Federal Republic of Germany

FSJ – Freedom, Security and Justice

Ga. J. Int'l & Comp. L. – Georgia Journal of International and Comparative Law

GATS – General Agreement on Trade in Services

GATT – General Agreement on Tariffs and Trade

GC – General Council

GDP – Gross Domestic Product

GDR – German Democratic Republic

German L. J. – German Law Journal

GFCT – German Federal Constitutional Tribunal

GIs – geographical indications

GNI – Gross National Income

GNP – Gross National Product

Harv.L.Rev – Harvard Law Review

HL – House of Lords

HR – High Representative of the Union for Foreign Affairs and Security Policy

HRs – human rights

Hum.Rts.L.Rev – Human Rights Law Review

ICJ – International Court of Justice

ICJ Rep. – Reports of Judgments, Advisory Opinions and Orders of the International Court of Justice

ICLQ – International and Comparative Law Quarterly

ICN – International Competition Network

IGC – Intergovernmental Conference

IIA – Inter-Institutional Agreement

ILO – International Labour Organisation

IMI – Internal Market Information System

Int'l J. Const. L. – International Journal of Constitutional Law

Int'l Rev.L. & Econ – International Review of Law and Economics

IPA – Instrument for Pre-accession Assistance

IPRs – Intellectual Property Rights

ISPA – Instrument for Structural Policies for Pre-Accession

J. Competition L. & Econ. – Journal of Competition Law & Economics

J. Contemp. Health L. & Pol'y – Journal of Contemporary Health Law and Policy

JCMS – Journal of Common Market Studies

JHA – Justice and Home Affairs

JORF – Journal Officiel de la République Française

JSA – Joint Supervisory Authority for the Schengen Information System

JV – Joint Venture

KNK – Kurdish National Congress

LIEI – Legal Issues of European Integration

LPP – Legal profession privilege

LRAIC – long-run average incremental cost

ME – European Mutual Society

MEP – Member of the European Parliament

MEQR – Measure Having Equivalent Effect to a Quantitative Restriction

MFF – Multiannual Financial Framework

MR – Merger Regulation

NATO – North Atlantic Treaty Organisation

NCA – National Competition Authority

NCE – Non-Compulsory Expenditure

NGO – non-governmental organisation

NHS – National Health Service

N-SIS – National Schengen Information System

Nw. J. Int'l L. & Bus. – Northwestern Journal of International Law and Business

nyr – not yet reported

OCT – Overseas Countries and Territories

OECD – Organisation for Economic Co-operation and Development

OEEC – Organisation for European Economic Co-operation

OFT – Office of Fair Trading

OHIM – Office for Harmonisation of the Internal Market

OJ – Official Journal of the European Union

OLAF – European Anti-Fraud Office

OMC – Open Method of Co-ordination

OPEC – The Organisation of Petroleum Exporting Countries

OSCE – Organisation for Security and Co-operation in Europe

OUP – Oxford University Press

Oxford J. Legal Stud. – Oxford Journal of Legal Studies

PCJI – Permanent Court of International Justice

PDO – Protected designation of origin

PGI – Protected geographical indication

PJCC – Police and Judicial Co-operation in Criminal Matters

PKK – Kurdish Workers' Party

PLI/Pat – Practising Law Institute

PSC – Political and Security Committee

PSCs – points of single contact

QB – Queen's Bench

QBD – Queen's Bench Division

Q.E. – written question addressed by an MEP to EU institutions

QMV – Qualified Majority Voting

QR – Quantitative restriction

R&D – Research and Development

RBFM – Reglement van het Beamtenfonds voor het Mijnbedrijf, the Regulation governing the relations between the Dutch social security authority and those insured by it

REITOX – European Information Network on Drugs and Drug Addiction

RFDA – Revue Française de Droit Administratif

RGM – relevant geographical market

RIAA – Reports of International Arbitral Awards

RIM – Rapid Intervention Mechanism

RIS – Review of International Studies

RPM – relevant product market

RRM – Rapid Reaction Mechanism

RTDE – Revue trimestrielle de droit européen

RTM – relevant temporal market

SAPARD – Special Accession Programme for Agriculture and Rural Development

SCE – European Co-operative Society

SE – Societas Europea

SEA – Single European Act

SEC – Commission's documents which cannot be classified in any of the other categories, i.e. a "sweeper up" of all other miscellaneous documents

SFOR – Stabilisation Force in Bosnia and Herzegovina

SGP – Stability and Growth Pact

SIRENE – Supplementary Information Request at the National Entries

SIS – Schengen Information System

SIS-II – second-generation Schengen Information System

SO – Statement of Objections

SSNIP – Small but Significant Non-Transitory Increase in Price

TECS – Europol computer system

TEU – Treaty on European Union

Tex. Int'l L.J – Texas International Law Journal

TFEU – Treaty on the Functioning of the European Union

ToA – Treaty of Amsterdam

ToL – Treaty of Lisbon

ToN – Treaty of Nice

TRIPs – Trade Related Aspects of Intellectual Property Rights Agreement

TTBER – Technology Transfer Block Exemption Regulation (Regulation 772/2004)

UKCLR – United Kingdom Competition Law Review

UN – United Nations

UNCTAD – United Nations Conference on Trade and Development

UNESCO – United Nations Educational, Scientific and Cultural Organisation

UNICE – Union of Industrial and Employers' Confederation of Europe

USFTC – United States Federal Trade Commission

VAT – Value Added Tax

WEU – Western European Union

WTO – World Trade Organisation

Yale L.J. – Yale Law Journal

YBEL – Yearbook of European Law

GLOSSARY OF FOREIGN WORDS

A fortiori – from the stronger, even more so, with even stronger reason

A posteriori – based on observation (i.e. empirical knowledge)

A priori – presupposed, based on deduction or hypothesis rather than experiment, the opposite of a posteriori

Ab initio – from the beginning

Acquis (of the EU) – the entire body of EU law accumulated thus far plus the political, procedural and institutional rules and practices which bind all the Member States together with the European Union

Acte clair – a clear act

Actio popularis – Action to obtain remedy by a person or a group in the name of the general public without being a direct victim or being authorised by a victim to represent him

Ad hoc – for this, for a particular purpose

Ad litem – for the lawsuit

Ad valorem – according to an object's value. Often used in connection with customs duties. Ad valorem duties are levied on products at certain rates per cent on their value

Amicus curiae – "friend of the court", a third party allowed to submit a legal opinion (in the form of an amicus brief) to the court

Bona fides – in (or with) good faith

Contra legem – against the law, interpretation contrary to the meaning of the relevant provision of law

Coup d'état – sudden takeover of the government of a country by elements from within that country (usually by the military), generally carried out by violent or illegal means

Damnum emergens – the loss suffered, as opposed to lucrum cessans

De facto – in fact, actually

De jure – by right, by law, according to law

De minimis – this term comes from the principle de minimis non curat lex – the law does not concern itself with trifles

Effet utile – this refers to the principle of efficiency/effectiveness. In the context of EU law it refers to the manner in which the ECJ interprets EU law. It consists of giving the EU objectives their fullest effect and maximum practical value

En banc – on a bench

Erga omnes – against everybody

Et seq. – and the following

Etc – et cetera – and others of like character; and so on; and so forth

Ex nunc – from now on, opposite to ex tunc

Ex officio – from office, by virtue of the office or position, by right of office

Ex parte – on one side only

Ex tunc – retrospectively, opposite to ex nunc

Exeptio non adimpleti contactus – the principle according to which performance of an obligation may be withheld by one party if the other party has itself failed to perform the same or a related obligation

Force majeure – greater force

Forum – the place where the court seised with the litigation is located

Ibid – an abbreviated form of "ibidem" – in the same place, in the same book, on the same page

In abstracto – theoretically, reasoning on general terms without taking account of a factual situation, opposed to in concreto

In camera – in private

In foro interno in foro externo – internal competences must be matched by external competences

Inter alia – among other things

Interim – in the meantime

Ipso facto – by the fact itself, by the mere fact

Jus cogens – compelling law, imperative, peremptory rules of international legal order

Law of the forum – the law of the place where the court seised with the litigation is located

Lex specialis derogat priori – a special statute overrules a general statute

Locus standi – recognised position, right to intervene, right to appear in court

Lucrum cessans – the loss of prospective profits

Nulla crimen sine lege – no crime without a pre-existing law making the act a crime

Nulla poena sine lege – no punishment without a pre-existing prohibitory rule of law

Obiter dictum – a remark in passing. Obiter does not form part of the ratio decidendi of a case and therefore creates no binding precedent, but may be used as persuasive authority in subsequent cases

Patere legem – comply yourself with the laws that you made for others

Per se – through itself, by himself or itself, in itself, taken alone, inherently, in isolation, without referring to anything else

Prima facie – at first sight, on the face of it, so far as can be judged from the first disclosure

Primus inter pares – first among equals

Prior – the former, earlier

Qua – considered as, in the capacity of

Raison d'être – reason for being

Ratio decidendi – the reason for deciding. The principle or principles of law on the basis of which a court decides the case before it

Ratio legis – the underlying principle, reasoning, grounds, scheme

Ratione loci – by reason of location

Ratione materiae – by reason of the matter involved

Ratione personae – by reason of the person concerned

Ratione temporis – by reason of time

Res judicata – when a matter has been finally adjudicated upon by a court of competent jurisdiction. It may not be reopened or challenged by the original parties or their successors in interest

Sensu stricto – strictly speaking

Stare decisis et non quieta movere – stand by decisions and do not move that which is quiet

Status quo ante – the way things were before

Sui generis – of its own kind, unique

Supra – above

Ubi jus, ibi remedium – where there is a right, there is a remedy

Ultra petitia – beyond, in excess of. When a Court rules beyond that which was requested by the parties

Ultra vires – beyond the powers

Via – by way of or by means of

Vice versa – the other way round

Vis-à-vis – in relation to

1

THE HISTORY OF EUROPEAN INTEGRATION

CONTENTS

SUMMARY

1. This chapter outlines the history of European integration from 1945 to 2010. It explains the main factors contributing to the creation of the first Community in 1951, that is, the European Coal and Steel Community (ECSC), and those relevant to the creation of the other two Communities in 1957, that is, the European Atomic Energy Community (Euratom) and the European Economic Community (EEC). It should be noted that under the Treaty of Maastricht the EEC was renamed to become the European Community (EC) and that under the ToL the EU succeeded and replaced the EC.

2. The European Coal and Steel Community Treaty (CS Treaty) was designed to provide a common market for coal and steel. It was concluded for a period of 50 years from its entry into force, and ceased to exist on its expiry on 23 July 2002. The Euratom was designed to create "the conditions necessary for the speedy establishment and growth of nuclear industries". Unlike the EC, which, after a bumpy start, became the main vehicle for European integration, both the ECSC and the Euratom achieved less prominence and became unimportant to the extent that the ECSC was allowed to expire without renewal (the areas of coal and steel are governed by the general principles applicable to the internal market) while the Euratom, after the entry into force of the ToL, continues its controversial and uninspiring existence as a separate Community, i.e. it has not become part of the EU.

3. The original EEC Treaty was amended on several occasions. One of the earliest amendments was the Single European Act (SEA), which laid the foundation for the completion of the internal market and created an impetus for further integration. Until the adoption of the SEA, the EC was, in practice, firmly based on inter-governmentalism – a unanimous vote in the Council being the rule for the adoption of any legislative act, even though the EEC Treaty permitted majority voting. The SEA introduced Qualified Majority Voting (QMV) in the Council in many areas; thus, a Member State could no longer veto legislation of which it disapproved in those areas. The change in the Council voting rules resulted in proliferation of Community legislation, which in turn gave the Commission many more opportunities to effect outcomes through policy implementation, in particular in respect of the creation of the internal market.

4. The Treaty on European Union (TEU) i.e. the Treaty of Maastricht was designed to create an "ever-closer union among the peoples of Europe" by adding two areas of inter-governmental co-operation, one on Common Foreign and Security Policy (CFSP) ("Pillar 2") and the other on Co-operation in Justice and Home Affairs (JHA) ("Pillar 3"), to the pre-existing Community structures. The three Pillars together made up the European Union (EU). However, the degree of integration was considerably less in the areas covered by Pillars 2 and 3 than under the EC Treaty, the content of which constituted the major part of Pillar 1.

5. Both the TEU and the EC Treaty were further revised by the Treaties of Amsterdam (ToA) and of Nice (ToN).

6. In order to simplify the existing treaties, to provide greater transparency in the EU's decision-making procedures and to further European integration, on 29 October 2004 the 25 heads of state or government of the Member States of the EU adopted the Treaty on European Constitution, which required ratification by all Member States in order to become a binding treaty. Voters in France and The Netherlands rejected the proposed EU constitution. As a result, the European Council Summit held in June 2007 decided to abandon this treaty and instructed the 2007 Inter-governmental Conference (IGC) to prepare a new Reform Treaty (which was subsequently called the Treaty of Lisbon (ToL)).

7. On 13 December 2007 the European Council signed the Treaty of Lisbon (ToL), which after being challenged in some Member States and initially rejected by the Irish people in a referendum held in July 2008 but subsequently accepted in a second referendum (which took place in October 2009), entered into force on 1 December 2009. The ToL is not an all-encompassing treaty as was the case of the failed Constitutional Treaty. Its sole purpose is to dramatically amend the existing treaties: the Treaty on European Union (TEU) and the EC Treaty which, under the ToL, was given a new name: the Treaty on the Functioning of the European Union (the TFEU). Both Treaties are of equal legal value. The ToL abolishes the Pillar structure but special procedures are provided for the CFSP (see Chapter 5). The ToL finally gets rid of the confusing distinction between the EC and the EU as the EU replaces and succeeds to the EC.

1.1 Introduction

With the entry into force of the Treaty of Lisbon (ToL) on 1 December 2009, the EU has commenced a new chapter in its existence. It can be said that under the ToL the EU is more democratic than some of its Member States, provides a very high level of protection of human rights to its citizens, gives its institutions the powers necessary to meet the 21st century challenges speedily and efficiently, dramatically improves the relationship between the Union and its citizens in that it brings the EU closer to ordinary people, and is well equipped to make a real impact on the international scene, i.e. to contribute to peace, security, the sustainable development of the Earth, eradication of poverty and the protection of human rights worldwide. The 27 States which are Members of the EU share the common values, which are expressly stated in Article 2 TEU, based on democracy, human rights and principles of social justice. However, there is also much diversity between the Member States, the most obvious being cultural and linguistic. This is reflected in the motto of the EU – "unity in diversity". Indeed, the EU, with its 494 million inhabitants, the world's third largest population after China and India, has found a way to accommodate diversity and to use it in a constructive way to achieve unity.

The ToL is not the final product of the EU. It is part of an ongoing process which started after WWII. In order to appreciate and understand the complexity of the EU it is necessary to examine its history and origins.

1.2 Europe after World War II (WWII)

Some 50 million people lost their lives during World War II, 60 million people of 55 ethnic groups from 27 countries were displaced, 45 million were left homeless, many millions were wounded and only some 670,000 were liberated from Nazi death camps.[1] The psychological devastation of survivors, the physical destruction, the genocide, slave labour, mass killing, mass rape, concentration camps and other horrors perpetrated during World War II exceeded anything ever experienced. After the war, Europe was in ruins and politically divided. Most Central and Eastern European countries were de facto occupied by the Soviet Union.

The rebuilding of Europe not only posed a formidable challenge but was also the catalyst that

---

1.   M. Kishlansky, P. Geary and P. O'Brien, *Civilization in the West*, Volume C, 1991, New York: Harper Collins, p 920, and W. L. Shirer, *The Rise and Fall of the Third Reich*, 1991, London: Mandarin, p 1139.

led to European unity. Many factors have contributed to a new perception of post-war Europe; one was the United States' vision of the post-war world and of the reconstruction of Europe.

Three factors determined the policy of the United States:

- Politics;

- Economics; and

- Humanitarianism.

As to the political factor, at the Conference at Yalta held in February 1945 Franklin D. Roosevelt, the president of the USA, Winston Churchill, the prime minister of the UK and Joseph Stalin, the first secretary of the Soviet Union, reached an agreement as to the fate of Eastern and Central Europe and Germany. At that time the Soviet Red Army had already conquered, or according to Stalin "liberated" from German occupation, most of the eastern part of Europe. Once the Red Army entered, it stayed. Stalin had no intention whatsoever of giving back one inch of "liberated" territory.[2]

At Yalta Roosevelt and Churchill seemed to accept Soviet domination of the countries under Soviet occupation, although Churchill pressed for free elections and democratic governments, in particular in Poland. This was promised by Stalin. All parties had agreed that the countries of Eastern and Central Europe would be democratic and would be friendly with the Soviet Union. However, the understanding of democracy was different for the USA and the UK, where it meant liberal democracy involving free elections and a multiparty system, than for the Soviet Union, where it meant "people's democracy", that is, power going to puppet governments created by the Soviet Union. Stalin did not keep the promise to allow free elections in Poland. Between 1945 and 1948 he installed Communist governments in all territories occupied by the Red Army. As a result, nine countries, which before 1939 had been independent, became incorporated into the Soviet Union (for example Latvia, Lithuania and Estonia) or became Soviet satellites. As Winston Churchill said in his speech in Missouri in 1946: "From Stettin in the Baltic to Trieste in the Adriatic an iron curtain has descended across the continent."[3] Indeed, Stalin had cut Eastern and Central European countries off from the rest of the world.

The reaction of the "free world" was contained in the Truman doctrine. Truman was vice president in Roosevelt's government and succeeded to the office of president of the USA upon the death of Roosevelt in 1945.

On 12 March 1947 President Truman announced to the US Congress his approach towards the Soviet Union. He said:

"At the present moment in world history nearly every nation must choose between alternative ways of life. The choice is too often not a free one … It must be the policy of the United States to support people who are resisting attempted subjugation by armed minorities or by outside pressure."[4]

His statement is known as the Truman Doctrine and considered by many as the beginning of a cold war, which officially ended in December 1989. During that period no direct fighting took

---

2.   M. Kishlansky *et al, Civilization in the West*, Volume C, 1991, New York: Harper Collins, pp 920–21.

3.   H. Middleton, *Britain and the World since 1750*, 1984, Oxford: Blackwell, p 93.

4.   M. Kishlansky *et al, Civilization in the West*, Volume C, 1991, New York: Harper Collins, p 928.

place between the USA and the Soviet Union, but they fought indirectly to keep their existing allies, and to acquire new allies worldwide.

Immediately after Truman's speech, he asked the US Senate for, and obtained, financial aid of US$400 million for Greece and Turkey in order to contain the expansion of communism in both countries. From that time the containment of communism played an important role in helping European reconstruction.

The United States had emerged from World War II richer and more powerful than ever. As a main supplier for the Allied Forces its industry and business boomed. It was the only major belligerent whose own soil, apart from Pearl Harbour, was not a site of conflict. In 1945–46, the US accounted for half of the gross world products of goods and services, and held two-thirds of the world's gold.[5] Therefore, for the Americans it was necessary to find new markets. Only a prosperous Europe could become a major market for American goods; thus American self-interest contributed to European recovery.

Lastly, there were also humanitarian considerations, which should not be minimised. The chaos facing post-war Europe was an obstacle to any significant progress towards political stability and economic prosperity and to the protection of basic rights. From 1945 to 1947 Europe did not make any significant progress in this direction.

1.3   The Marshall Plan

On 5 June 1947 at a Conference at Harvard University Truman's Secretary of State, George C. Marshall, announced the American plan for European reconstruction. In order to eliminate "hunger, poverty, desperation and chaos", the real enemies of freedom and democracy, and to restore "the confidence of the European people in the economic future of their own countries",[6] Marshall proposed cash grants to all European nations subject to two conditions:

■ European states were to co-operate in the distribution of American aid; and

■ They had to progressively abolish trade barriers.[7]

All European nations were invited to participate in the Marshall Plan, even the Soviet Union if it contributed some of its resources to the cause. Stalin called the Plan a capitalist plot and forced all countries under his control that had expressed interest in the Plan to withdraw. The British Foreign Secretary at that time, Ernest Bevin, told the UK Parliament that when the Marshall proposals were announced, he grabbed them with both hands. So did other European countries.

As a result of the Marshall Plan US$13.6 billion was transferred to Europe, in addition to US$9.5 billion in earlier loans and US$500 million in private charity.[8] The Marshall Plan was a huge success as it helped to restore Western European trade and production while controlling inflation. By 1951 Western Europe was booming. However, not only the Plan itself but, most importantly, the manner in which it was administered greatly contributed to the unity of Europe.

---

5.   M. Kishlansky *et al, Civilization in the West*, Volume C, 1991, New York: Harper Collins, p 920.
6.   J. A. Garraty with R. A. McCaughey, *The American Nation, A History of the United States Since 1865*, 7th ed, 1991, New York: Harper Collins, p 826.
7.   S. Hoffman and Ch. Maier, *The Marshall Plan: A Retrospective*, 1984, Boulder, CO: Westview Press, p 6.
8.   J. A. Garraty and R. A. McCaughey, *The American Nation, A History of the United States Since 1865*, 7th ed, 1991, New York: Harper Collins, p 826.

Initially, 16 European countries participated in the Plan: Austria, Belgium, Denmark, France, Greece, Iceland, Ireland, Italy, Luxembourg, The Netherlands, Norway, Portugal, Sweden, Switzerland, Turkey and the United Kingdom. West Germany joined the Plan later, and thus through economic co-operation West Germany was reconciled with other European countries.

Under the leadership of France and the United Kingdom, the Committee for European Economic Co-operation was set up, and later replaced by the permanent Organisation for European Economic Co-operation (OEEC), to plan and distribute American aid. The main features of the administration of the Plan were:

- Co-operation among its participants in order to stabilise their economies;

- Intensified planning at the inter-governmental level and thus development of a global approach toward economic recovery;

- Limited nationalisation in all participating States; and

- Co-operation between private and public sectors in order to free market forces, modernise production and raise productivity.

The success of reconstruction through centrally co-ordinated planning and co-operation made clear that the best way for Europe to recover its international prestige was to act as a single entity in world markets. As a result of economic co-operation within the framework of the Marshall Plan, various European organisations began to emerge in order to strengthen inter-governmental integration in political, military and economic matters. One of those organisations was the ECSC, established on the basis of the Schuman Plan.

1.4 The Schuman Plan

Robert Schuman, the French minister for foreign affairs,[9] followed the advice of Winston Churchill, who emphasised in his speeches that France should take Germany back into the community of nations.[10] Schuman was well qualified to take the first step in the normalisation of relations with Germany as, on the one hand, he took part in the First World War on the German side in a civilian capacity, his mother tongue was Luxemburgish (at the time considered a German dialect) and his language of education was standard German, and on the other hand, he became a French citizen in 1919 and during the Second World War fought in the French Resistance, was interrogated by the Gestapo and by extraordinary luck avoided being sent to the concentration camp at Dachau.

He believed that Europe was facing three problems:

- Economic dominance by the USA;

- Military dominance by the Soviet Union; and

- A possible war with rejuvenated Germany.

---

9. P. Gerbet, "La genèse du Plan Schuman, Dès origines à la déclaration du 9 mai 1950", (1956) Revue Française de Science Politique, pp 525 et seq.

10. Winston Churchill said: "I am going to say something that will astonish you. The first step in the re-creation of the European family must be a partnership between France and Germany", in M. Charlton, *The Price of Victory*, 1983, London: British Broadcasting Corporation, pp 38–9.

The Americans supported the idea of political and economic integration in Europe since it would, in the long term, reduce the cost of their obligations and commitments in Europe. Robert Schuman considered that the best way to achieve stability in Europe was to place the production of steel and coal (then two commodities essential to conduct a conventional war) under the international control of a supranational entity. The creation of a common market for steel and coal meant that interested countries would delegate their powers in those commodities to an independent authority.

On 9 May 1950 Robert Schuman announced his Plan, based on proposals put forward by Jean Monnet, an eminent French economist and the "father of European integration".[11] Although in Schuman's Plan only France and Germany were expressly mentioned, Schuman invited other European states to join, in particular Britain, Italy and the Benelux countries.

The Schuman Plan was enthusiastically accepted by Germany, and Konrad Adenauer, the chancellor of Germany, saw it as a breakthrough towards the beginning of German statehood and independence. Personally, Adenauer was in favour of closer relations with the West and of the abandonment of traditional German policy, which for centuries had concentrated on the East. The Schuman Plan was advantageous to both Germany and France, as for Germany it offered a way of regaining international respectability, and in the immediate future the opportunity to gain access to the Saarland, and for France, the opportunity to control the German economy.

The Schuman Plan attracted attention in many European countries. As a result, an international conference was held in Paris on 20 June 1950, attended by France, Italy, West Germany and the Benelux countries, to consider the Plan. Following from this, a Treaty creating the European Coal and Steel Community was signed on 18 April 1951 in Paris and it entered into force on 23 July 1952.

The Contracting Parties were: Belgium, France, Italy, Luxembourg, The Netherlands and West Germany.

The institutional structure of the ECSC was original in that it consisted of:

- The High Authority. This was made up of representatives of the Member States acting independently in the interests of the ECSC. The High Authority was in charge of the production and distribution of coal and steel, and was entrusted with supranational competencies, including the power to make legally binding "decisions" and "recommendations", directly applicable in Member States. (On supranationality see section 1.7);

- A Special Council of Ministers, a partly legislative, partly consultative body representing the interests of the Member States;

---

11. Jean Monnet (1888–1979) profoundly believed that peace and prosperity in Europe could only be achieved if European states formed a federation, or at least acted as one economic unit. He prepared the Schuman Declaration and, in 1952, became the first president of the High Authority of the ECSC. In 1955 he resigned from the office, but instead of retiring, he founded the Action Committee for the United States of Europe, a federalist movement which brought together eminent European politicians and trade union leaders who wanted to advance the idea of European integration. Monnet and his movement were driving forces behind all initiatives in favour of the European Union, including the creation of the Euratom, the common market, the European Monetary System, the European Council, British membership in the Community and direct elections to the European Parliament. The outstanding achievements of Jean Monnet were recognised by the European Council held in Luxembourg on 2 April 1976, which proclaimed him an "Honorary Citizen of Europe". For a short biography of Jean Monnet see: www.historiasiglo20.org/europe/monnet.htm (accessed 10/10/07).

■ The Common Assembly made up of MPs from Member States, with only supervisory and advisory functions; and

■ The Court of Justice responsible for ensuring "that in the interpretation and application of this Treaty . . . the law is observed."

The Treaty was concluded for a period of 50 years and expired on 23 July 2002. After its expiry the ECSC ceased to exist. To deal with the consequences of its disappearance a Protocol on the Financial Consequences of the Expiry of the CS Treaty and on the Research Fund for Coal and Steel was attached to the ToN (under the ToL it has become Protocol 37 attached to the Treaties). Pursuant to this Protocol the Council adopted a number of decisions to deal with the liquidation of the ECSC. On completion of liquidation, the net worth of the assets of the ECSC was transferred into "Assets of the Research Fund for Coal and Steel", the revenue from which is used to finance research in sectors related to the coal and steel industry. Since the expiry of the ECSC, coal and steel (being goods) are subjected to the rules in the Treaties.

Initially, the ECSC was very successful, and by 1954 all barriers to trade in coal, coke, steel, pig iron and scrap iron were eliminated between Member States. Trade in those commodities rose spectacularly and the common pricing policy and production limits set up by the High Authority, as well as common rules on competition, merger controls and so on, rationalised the production of steel and coal within a wholly integrated market. However, since 1980, for many reasons, the ECSC slowly declined.[12]

The CS Treaty put into practice the neofunctionalist theory (a variation of functionalism), implicit in the Schuman Declaration, and advocated by both Robert Schuman and Jean Monnet (see section 1.20).

1.5   The Messina Conference

In June 1955 in Messina (Sicily) the foreign ministers of the Contracting States of the ECSC decided to "pursue the establishment of a United Europe through the development of common institutions, a progressive fusion of national economies, the creation of a common market and harmonisation of social policies".[13] From this materialised two Treaties signed in Rome on 25 March 1957. The first established the European Economic Community (EEC) and the second the European Atomic Energy Community (Euratom). The Treaties came into force on 1 January 1958. In time they became known as "the Rome Treaties".

Both were concluded for an indeterminate period of time.

---

12.   See K. J. Alter "The Theory and Reality of the European Coal and Steel Community" in S. Meunier and K. McNamara (eds), *European Integration and Institutional Change in Historical Perspective*, 2007, Oxford: Oxford University Press. The author examines the 50 years of existence of the ECSC and rightly points out that the ECSC had neither created a common market in coal and steel, nor played a central role in the development of national coal and steel industries.

13.   Quoted by D. Lasok in D. Lasok "Law and Institutions of the European Union", 6th ed., 1994, London, Dublin, Edinburgh: Butterworths, p 19.

1.6   The European Atomic Energy Community (Euratom)

The main objective of the European Atomic Energy Community Treaty (EA Treaty) (as indicated in Article 1 EA) was to create "the conditions necessary for the speedy establishment and growth of nuclear industries".[14] Its tasks were laid down in Article 2 EA and encompass:

- The promotion of research and dissemination of technical information regarding atomic energy;

- The establishment of uniform standards for health and safety;

- The promotion of investment;

- The equitable supply of ores and nuclear fuels;

- The security of nuclear materials;

- The international promotion of peaceful uses of nuclear energy; and

- The creation of a common market in this area.

The institutional framework set up by the EA Treaty is identical to that of the EEC Treaty.

The Euratom's main success is in the area of non-proliferation of nuclear weapons. Apart from that, it has had no real impact on the nuclear industry, which remains within the national domain of each Member State, or on nuclear research, with the exception of nuclear fusion. Further, the EA Treaty has not evolved in the same way as did the EC Treaty. Its fundamental provisions have remained substantially unamended. As a result, the Euratom suffers many failings:

- Its objective of developing nuclear energy has become obsolete given that out of 27 Member States 11 never had any nuclear production at all, Italy has abolished it, and Belgium, Germany, Spain and Sweden are working on a phase-out;

- It shows a clear "democratic deficit" given the absence of any requirement for the Council to formally consult the European Parliament (EP) on measures adopted under the EA Treaty;

- It does not address a major concern of EU citizens relating to the impact of the development of the nuclear industry on public health and on the environment. A survey carried out in the EU showed that 61 per cent of the EU population consider that the use of nuclear energy should be reduced due to concerns surrounding nuclear waste and the danger of accidents.[15]

After the entry into force of the ToL, the Euratom continues its controversial and uninspiring existence as a separate Community, i.e. it has not become part of the EU.

1.7   The European Economic Community (EEC)

The European Economic Community became very much the most important Community of the three (the others being the ECSC and the Euratom) and the heart of European integration. The

---

14.   Article 1 EA.

15.   http://europa.eu/rapid/pressReleasesAction.do?reference=IP/07/280&format=HTML (accessed 11/10/07).

original Treaty mainly concerned economic co-operation between Member States, including the establishment of a common market. Additionally, it created the possibility of further co-operation in any area not covered by the Treaty of Rome but chosen by the Member States by common consent.[16] Although economic objectives were in the forefront, the Treaty of Rome also contained a political agenda. Articles 2 and 3 EC laid down the long-term objectives for the Community, that is, the co-ordination of economic and monetary policies leading to an economic and monetary union between the Member States.

The EEC's uniqueness and originality lay in its institutions, which have been reformed on many occasions, and are examined in detail in Chapter 6.

The first decade of the Community was exceptional in terms of economic growth, investment and internal integration. Small countries such as Belgium, Luxembourg and The Netherlands realised that their membership allowed them to have an influence, out of proportion with their size, upon international matters and international trade.[17]

Since the creation of the European Communities the idea of European integration has been very much alive, but its actual implementation has been beset with difficulties and controversies, the most important being the constant struggle between inter-governmentalism and supranationality.

Both are mechanisms of decision-making in international organisations. Essentially, supranationalism involves a great degree of transfer of sovereignty from individual states to transnational institutions.

Supranationality has been defined as involving:

"... states working with one another in a manner that does not allow them to retain complete control over developments. That is, states may be obliged to do things against their preferences and their will because they do not have the power to stop decisions. Supranationalism thus takes inter-state relations beyond co-operation into integration, and involves some loss of national sovereignty."[18]

Inter-governmentalism is described as:

"... arrangements whereby nation states, in situations and conditions they can control, cooperate with one another on matters of common interest. The existence of control, which allows all participating states to decide the extent and nature of this cooperation, means that national sovereignty is not directly undermined."[19]

Under this mechanism decisions are made by unanimity.

The vision of Europe and the shape of European integration depend upon the form of co-operation chosen by the Member States. Supranationality entails important restrictions on national sovereignty and, if successful, leads to the creation of a federal structure. By contrast, inter-governmentalism implies that the competencies of the Member States remain intact unless

---

16. Article 235 of the EC Treaty (Article 308 EC).
17. D. Armstrong, L. Lloyd and J. Redmond, *From Versailles to Maastricht. International Organisation in the Twentieth Century*, 1996, Basingstoke: Macmillan, pp 154–9.
18. N. Nugent, *The Government and Politics of the European Union*, 6th edition, 2006, Basingstoke: Palgrave Macmillan.
19. Ibid.

otherwise agreed. Its ultimate form is a confederation (as to both theories and their application in the context of the EU see Chapter 4.8).

1.8   The Luxembourg Accord

The first disagreement among the Member States occurred in 1965. It is known as the "empty chairs" crisis, as France refused to attend Council meetings from July 1965 to January 1966.

The then president of the French Republic, Charles de Gaulle, was in favour of inter-governmentalism and thus against increasing the powers of the Community. The immediate cause of the crisis was the Commission's package of proposals aiming at increasing the competencies of the Commission and of the EP. The Commission's proposal on the adoption of the financing arrangements for the Common Agricultural Policy (CAP) was accepted by France. The two remaining proposals were rejected. The first concerned new methods of financing the Community, aiming at ending national contributions towards the budget and replacing them with a system of "own resources" of the Community, mainly provided by the revenue from the common external tariff. This proposal was considered as essential by the Commission to give the institutions more independence from the Member States. The second proposal concerned increasing the involve-ment of the EP in decision-making procedures in general, and in budgetary matters in particular. It was supported by the EP and by The Netherlands.

The proposals were used by France to express its dissatisfaction in two areas. They were:

- First, that of the role of the Commission, which, under the presidency of Walter Hallstein, was accused by France of exceeding its competence by acting more like a supranational rather than an inter-governmental body;

- Second, that of the proposed major change in decision-making within the Council, which consisted of replacing unanimity with qualified majority voting. The EC Treaty provided that at the beginning of the final stage of the transitional period, which was approaching, the new voting system should apply.

In order to dramatise the situation, France decided not to attend the Council meetings (hence the empty chairs). Under pressure from French farmers, de Gaulle decided to negotiate with other Member States (the Commission was not invited). In January 1966 an informal agreement was reached, known as the Luxembourg Accord, which provided that:

"Where, in the case of a decision which may be taken by majority vote ... the Council, will endeavour ... to reach solutions which can be adopted by all the Members of the Council ... the French delegation considers that where very important interests are at stake the discussion must be continued until unanimous agreement is reached."[20]

Accordingly, unanimous voting was the main way of adopting EC legislation from 1966 until the adoption of the 1986 SEA.

The Luxembourg Accord marked a clear confirmation of inter-governmental co-operation and thus constituted a serious blow to supranationality, although the Accord has never been given

---

20.   J. Lambert, "The Constitutional Crisis, (1965–66)", 4 JCMS, p 226.

any legally binding status in EC law.[21] It was the main reason for years of stagnation of the Community, as it prevented progress towards further integration by giving priority to the national interests of the Member States.

1.9 The Merger Treaty

The idea of rationalising the institutional structure of the three Communities was first introduced by the Convention on Certain Institutions Common to the European Communities of 25 March 1957. The Convention provided for the establishment of a single Assembly (the EP), a single Court of Justice, and a single Economic and Social Committee for all three Communities.

Further rationalisation took place in April 1965 when the Treaty (known as the Merger Treaty) establishing a Single Council and a Single Commission of the European Communities was signed. The Treaty came into force on 13 July 1967. Under the Merger Treaty the three Communities shared the same institutions, although they remained legally independent and the competencies of the institutions were subject to the respective Treaties.

1.10 The 1969 Hague Summit

An important development in shaping future co-operation between Member States, outside the Communities' framework, took place at the proposal of Georges Pompidou, the successor to Charles de Gaulle. A meeting (which became known as The Hague Summit) was convened in The Hague in December 1969, to which Pompidou, more flexible in his approach towards the development of the Community (although as opposed to the construction of a supranational Europe as de Gaulle had been),[22] invited all heads of state or government of the Member States. The main decisions taken by The Hague Summit were to:

- Enlarge the Communities by admission of the UK, Denmark, Norway and Ireland (see Chapter 3.3.1);

- Establish European Political Co-operation (EPC);

- Adopt measures leading to Economic and Monetary Union (EMU) between Member States;

- Introduce regular meetings of foreign ministers of the Member States;

- Reform the CAP financing;

- Establish technical co-operation;

- Put development aid and social policy on the Community agenda;

- Create a European University.

---

21. In Case 68/86 *UK v Council* [[1988] ECR 855] the ECJ held that decision-making procedures in the Treaty "are not at the disposal of the Member States or of the institutions themselves".

22. H. Simonian, *The Privileged Partnership: Franco-German Relations in the European Community: 1968–1984*, 1985, Oxford: Oxford University Press, p 35.

In the immediate period after The Hague Summit the international oil crisis and the budgetary crisis within the Community stunted its growth for almost two decades. Nevertheless, during that period certain aspects of the agenda created by the ambitious decisions of The Hague Summit were further developed. Two of the decisions taken at The Hague Summit merit special attention: the establishment of European Political Co-operation and the initiatives aimed at creating an Economic and Monetary Union, the latter having become a reality under the SEA and TEU.

1.10.1   Establishment of European Political Co-operation (EPC)

The Hague Summit decided to examine the best ways of achieving progress in the establishment of a political union. In October 1970 the Davignon Report (named after its author, the political director of the Belgian Foreign Ministry) was adopted by the foreign ministers of the Member States as a basic strategy in this area, and was then approved by the Copenhagen Summit on 23 July 1973.[23] It proposed the harmonisation of foreign policy of the Member States outside the Community framework based upon regular exchanges of their respective views and, when possible, leading to a common position. It therefore recommended traditional inter-governmental co-operation in political matters without any supporting common structures. Some changes to EPC were tabled in a subsequent report, which was adopted by foreign ministers meeting in London on 13 October 1981.[24] The above-mentioned reports and the Solemn Declaration on European Union agreed at the Stuttgart Summit in 1983 constituted the foundation of EPC.[25] It was incorporated in Title III of the SEA[26] (see section 1.13.7) and can be viewed as the precursor to the more formalised co-operation in Common Foreign and Security Policy (CFSP) matters under the Treaty of Maastricht, although the CFSP, even under the ToL, is still essentially inter-governmental, rather than supranational (see Chapter 5).

1.11   The Community from 1970 to 1985 – years of stagnation

From 1970 to 1985 the Community was in a state of stagnation. This so-called "Eurosclerosis" can be explained partially by the difficult international situation, but more importantly by lack of desire on the part of the Member States for further integration. Instead of developing an effective strategy for dealing with common problems created by the oil embargo in 1973, each Member State decided to act on its own. As a result, the UK and France signed bilateral agreements with Iran and Saudi Arabia for oil supplies, while The Netherlands was left out in the cold with its supplies completely cut off by OPEC (The Organisation of Petroleum Exporting Countries).

National interests and national policies prevailed over Community objectives. The stagnation of the Community was exacerbated by three major unsolved issues: budgetary matters, the UK contribution to the Community budget and the reform of the CAP. However, during that period some positive developments took place. These included:

---

23.   (1973) Seventh General Report on the Activities of the European Communities, Brussels, Luxembourg, p 502 et seq.

24.   EC Bull. Supp. 3/81, point 14 et seq.

25.   EC Bull. 6/83, points 18–29.

26.   Article 30 SEA and Article 1 and 3 SEA Title I.

- The reform of the Community budget;

- The creation of "own resources" of the Community, aiming at replacing the system of national contributions;

- The first direct elections in June 1979 to the EP; and

- The formalisation by the Paris Summit in December 1974 of summit meetings of heads of state or government of the Member States as a European Council.

1.12   Relaunch of European integration

The early 1980s witnessed a new attitude of Member States towards the Community. The unexpected emergence of enthusiasm, optimism and commitment to European integration, and a political will on the part of Member States to further the development of the Community, are difficult to explain. The change in mood, although surprising, was nevertheless essential to the survival of the idea of European unity. Among the factors that contributed to the new approach were:

- The improvement of the international economic situation;

- The commitment of the new French president, François Mitterrand, to the development of the Community, strongly supported by the German chancellor, Helmut Kohl;

- The appointment on 1 January 1985 as president of the European Commission of Jacques Delors, who decided to accelerate the process of integration by submitting concrete projects; and

- The realisation by the Member States that only common action could improve the competitiveness of national economies and increase their share of world exports, especially vis-à-vis the USA, Japan and the newly industrialised countries.

A greater convergence in all fields within the framework of the Community was perceived to be the answer to the problems posed by growing interdependence of international trade. Furthermore, national solutions to international problems proved unrewarding. The economic turmoil of 1973, when Member States retreated to protective measures applied at national level, is the best example in this respect. As a result, some of the earlier proposals for reforming the Community were re-examined and are discussed below.

1.12.1   The Tindemans Report

In December 1974, Leo Tindemans, the Belgian prime minister, was asked by his European Council colleagues at a Paris Summit to prepare a report on a European Union. The Report (called "The Tindemans Report"), which he submitted in December 1975, set a bold agenda for economic, monetary and political integration headed by a supranational executive body accountable to a directly elected bicameral parliament.[27] The Report was considered very controversial and its implementation was never seriously examined. Its only practical result was an invitation to

---

27.   M. Holland, *European Community Integration*, 1992, London: Pinter, pp 60–68.

the Council and the Commission to prepare annual reports on progress towards the creation of a European Union.

1.12.2   The Three Wise Men Report

More realistic reforms were proposed in "The Three Wise Men" Report prepared at the request of the European Council of 1978 and submitted to it in October 1979.[28] This report emphasised the role of the European Council as a true contributor to the improvement of the decision-making procedures within the Community. It also examined the reasons for failures of the Community institutions to perform their tasks efficiently. It explained that the failures lay "rather in political circumstances and attitudes that sometimes produced conflicting conceptions of the right way forward, and sometimes produced no clear conceptions at all".[29] However, the Report did not produce any concrete results.

1.12.3   The Spinelli and Dooge Reports

Another important initiative was a Report containing proposals for institutional reforms submitted by Altiero Spinelli, a strong supporter of reform of the Community leading to closer integration, a former Commissioner for Industrial Policy and an MEP. The Report was endorsed by the EP, which set up an Institutional Committee, with Spinelli as a co-ordinating *rapporteur*, responsible for preparing a comprehensive draft regarding the creation of a European Union. The Spinelli Draft Treaty of European Union was adopted with enthusiasm by the EP on 14 February 1984 (out of 311 MEPs, 237 were in favour, 31 against and 43 abstained).[30] The Draft Treaty was strongly supported by President Mitterrand and indeed, at the Fontainebleau Summit in June 1984, under his initiative an ad hoc committee made up of representatives of the Member States, under the chairmanship of James Dooge,[31] was set up in order to examine the Draft. At the same time, the Fontainebleau Summit created the Adonnino Committee and entrusted it with the preparation of proposals concerning the free movement of persons within the Community with a view to establishing a "Europe of Citizens".[32] The final report of the Dooge Committee was presented at the Brussels Summit in March 1985,[33] and adopted by the majority of its members. The report recommended the introduction of the co-decision procedure designed to give more powers to the EP, the recognition of the European Council as a Community institution and the preparation of a new treaty on the European Union.

1.12.4   Lord Cockfield's White Paper

Lord Cockfield, the commissioner in charge of the internal market, volunteered to prepare a complete Internal Market Programme. His initiative was endorsed by Delors, who went on to

---

28.   A. N. Duff, "The Report of the Three Wise Men", (1981) 19 JCMS, p 237 et seq.
29.   Ibid., p 239.
30.   [1984] OJ C77 53.
31.   James Dooge was a former Irish Minister for Foreign Affairs and former leader of the Irish Senate (1973–77) and at that time was a member of the Irish Senate (Upper House of Parliament).
32.   XVIII General Report on the Activities of the European Communities, 1984, point 5.
33.   EC Bull. 3/85, points 3.5.1 et seq.

extend the initial proposal to cover all industries, including steel and coal.[34] The White Paper prepared by Cockfield identified the remaining barriers to trade within the Community and set up a timetable for their elimination by the end of 1992.

The White Paper and comments on the Dooge Committee Report from Member States were submitted to the Milan Summit in June 1985, which welcomed the White Paper and instructed the Council of Ministers to initiate a precise programme based on it. However, the main achievement of this summit was the decision of the heads of state or government to convene an IGC to revise the EEC Treaty, despite opposition from the UK, Denmark and Greece. The conference met in Luxembourg and in Brussels during the autumn of 1985. The outcome of the IGC was the Single European Act.

1.13　The Single European Act (SEA)

The SEA was signed on 17 and 28 February 1986 and came into effect on 1 July 1987. It was not very ambitious (which explains its acceptance by the Member States), but had much potential for expansion. Its main features are discussed below.

1.13.1　The strengthening of the concept of the internal market and a provision that it be completed by 31 December 1992

As a result of this, nearly 300 measures were enacted in order to create "an area without internal frontiers in which the free movement of goods, persons, services and capital is ensured" (Article 14 (2) EC – Article 26(2) TFEU).

1.13.2　The increase in the number of areas of qualified majority voting within the Council

It is interesting to note that this applied to two-thirds of the 300 measures necessary to create the internal market.

1.13.3　The extension of the legislative powers of the EP

A new co-operation procedure enhancing the participation of the EP in the decision-making procedures in 10 areas was introduced. This procedure, with many modifications over the years, is contained in Article 294 TFEU. It has been renamed under the ToL and is now referred to as the ordinary legislative procedure. Another new procedure, "the assent procedure" (under the ToL it is called the consent procedure), gave the EP an important new role in that the approval of the EP (by an absolute majority) was thereafter required for the admission of new members to the Community and in respect of conclusion of association agreements with third countries (see Chapter 7.3 and 7.4.1).

34.　Lord Cockfield, *The European Union. Creating the Single Market*, 1994, London: Wiley Chancery Law, pp 28–59.

1.13.4 The establishment of the European Council and the affirmation of its composition

This is discussed in Chapter 6.2.

1.13.5 The creation of the Court of First Instance in order to ease the workload of the ECJ

This is discussed in Chapter 6.6.10.

1.13.6 The extension of Community competencies to new areas

It must be remembered that in some areas the Community was already active in practice on the basis of general Treaty provisions, for example, the protection of the environment, research and regional policy, the protection of consumers and social cohesion.

1.13.7 The formalisation of the mechanism for European Political Co-operation (EPC)

This was initiated by The Hague Summit in 1969. EPC became recognised and incorporated into the structure of the Community in Title III of the SEA, but was not subject to judicial review by the ECJ. Title III SEA declared that Member States would endeavour jointly to formulate and implement a European foreign policy. Accordingly, EPC did not entail the transfer of any legal powers to Community institutions; it essentially formalised a forum for normal inter-state multi-lateral co-operation. The improvements to EPC effected by the SEA were:

- The distinction between foreign ministers' meetings within EPC and within the Council was abolished;

- An EPC secretariat was set up in Brussels;

- A mechanism was provided to convene emergency meetings of the Political Committee or foreign ministers of the Member States within 48 hours upon a request from at least three Member States;

- The Commission and the EP became associated with EPC; and

- The Commission and the Presidency of the Council became responsible for ensuring consistency between the external policies of the Community and policies agreed within the framework of EPC.

EPC resulted in adoption of common positions on many issues such as the Middle East, Eastern Europe and South Africa. However, on many occasions vague declarations after events had taken place and little direct action undermined the importance of EPC. The necessity of adopting a new approach to EPC was further highlighted when Member States were faced with the 1990 Gulf Crisis and the deteriorating situation in the former Yugoslavia.

In the 1990 Gulf Crisis, no agreement was reached among Member States on the use of force against Iraq. The position of Member States varied from immediate and unconditional support for the US military action (Prime Minister Margaret Thatcher of the UK was in Colorado with President Bush senior when the crisis arose and promised UK support) to the Irish policy of non-intervention based on neutrality.

In relation to the crisis in the former Yugoslavia, as Dinan stated: "Far from reflecting well on the Community, the Yugoslav War emphasised deep foreign policy differences between Member States and showed the limits of EC international action."[35]

Each international crisis revealed divergences in opinion between Member States and the impossibility of presenting a common front to the outside world. This had contributed to the incorporation of a Common Foreign and Security Policy into the TEU, although the CFSP was still placed on an inter-governmental level and was not communitarised at Maastricht, through the introduction of the Pillar structure. Under the ToL special rules apply to the CFSP (see Chapter 5).

1.13.8 The reformulation of the social policy of the Community

The preamble to the original EC Treaty set out as its main long-term objectives "the constant improvement of the living and working conditions" of the people of the Member States and underlined the commitment of the Community to the economic and social progress of the Member States by common action to eliminate the barriers which divided Europe. These objectives were implemented through the Social Fund established in 1958. Initially, it was assumed that under the EEC Treaty the social dimension of the internal market would flow indirectly from the establishment of the internal market, that is, its creation would provide the desired improvement in living and working conditions without the need for active intervention by the Community.[36]

The CS Treaty contained some social provisions designed to alleviate the effect of the reconstruction of the steel and coal industries for workers employed in these sectors.

In the period prior to the adoption of the SEA, the social policy of the Community lacked direction. It was mainly developed by the creative approach of the ECJ based on Article 12 EC (non-discrimination based on nationality – Article 18 TFEU), Article 141 EC (equal pay for men and women – Article 157 TFEU), Article 39 EC (free movement of workers – Article 45 TFEU), Article 42 EC (social security – Article 48 TFEU), and so on, and by some occasional intervention of the Community such as the adoption of the sex equality directives,[37] and of the First Social Action Programme of 1974. As to the Social Fund its main task, at that time, was to compensate for the difficulties that some social groups might experience resulting from structural changes due to the operation of the common market. During the 1960s, a period of economic boom and low unemployment, the Social Fund was mainly involved in the retraining of workers affected by structural changes. After the 1973 oil crisis its priority was to combat steadily growing unemployment. By 1986 16 million workers in the Community, that is, 16 per cent of its workforce, were out of work.[38] A new approach to the social policy was needed.

Jacques Delors, the then president of the Commission, with his French socialist background, was pushing for the development of a European social policy, and Member States, most of them then governed by social democratic governments, were in favour of integrating a social dimension into the creation of the internal market.[39] The amendments to the EC Treaty by the SEA that

35. D. Dinan, *Ever Closer Union?* 1994, London: Anne Rienner Publishers, p 489.

36. G. Scappucci, "Social and Employment Policy", in G. Glöckler, L. Junius, G. Scappucci, S. Usherwood and J. Vassallo (eds), *Guide to EU Policies*, 1998, London: Blackstone, pp 249–62.

37. Directives 75/117/EEC [1979] OJ L45/19; 76/207/EEC [1976] OJ L39/40; and 79/7/EEC [1979] OJ L6/24.

38. A. M. Williams, *The European Community*, 2nd ed, 1994, Oxford, UK and Cambridge, USA: Blackwell, pp 59 et seq.

39. This was acknowledged in the 1992 programme on the completion of the internal market.

related to this were, for example, insertion of Article 130a of the EC Treaty (Article 158 EC – Article 174 TFEU) on economic and social cohesion and Article 118b of the EC Treaty (Article 137 EC – 153 TFEU) which allowed the Commission to encourage social dialogue, but neither specified how this was to be achieved nor set any objectives that such a dialogue should pursue; Article 118a of the EC Treaty, which for the first time provided a legal basis for the adoption of directives to improve health and safety in the working environment, although harmonising measures were restricted to setting minimum requirements in this area. These Articles,[40] in conjunction with the new legislative procedure (that is, the co-operation procedure) under which a measure could be adopted by QMV in the Council, were used to create the social dimension of the Community.

It is important to note that at the Strasbourg summit in December 1989 all Member States except the UK adopted the Charter of the Fundamental Social Rights of Workers. The UK opposed it on the ground that over-regulation of the labour market would discourage the creation of jobs. The rejection by the UK of the Charter led to the adoption by the remaining Member States of a Protocol on Social Policy attached to the TEU.

1.13.9 Conclusions on the SEA

The impact of the SEA on European integration was both practical, in that it successfully created an internal market, which was officially completed on 31 December 1992, and psychological, in that it encouraged the Member States to pursue common objectives within the framework of the Community. It paved the way for the Treaty of Maastricht.

1.14   From the Single European Act to the Treaty of Maastricht (the Treaty on European Union (TEU))

The Commission stated that "if the programme [the SEA] succeeded, it would fundamentally alter the face of Europe".[41] This was especially true as the SEA contained a hidden agenda, that is, the creation of economic and monetary union, a necessary complement to the single market. However, in order to achieve the objectives set out in the SEA, it was necessary to deal first with persisting internal conflicts. These were dealt with by the adoption of the Delors I Package, a Commission proposal in 1987 for a radical reform of the Community's financial system for the period 1988–93. The Delors I Package introduced budgetary discipline, ended the "British rebate" saga,[42] reformed the CAP and provided for the Commission to put forward new initiatives. The

---

40.   In cases where measures went beyond the scope of Article 118b of the EC Treaty, the Community institutions tried to rely on Articles 100 and 235 of the EC Treaty (Articles 94 EC and 308 EC – Articles 115 and 352 TFEU).

41.   EC Bull. 6/85, point 18.

42.   The terms of EC membership were not favourable to the UK as it gained almost nothing from the CAP. Additionally, the British VAT contribution to the EC budget was very high due to high consumption levels in the UK. From 1 January 1973 to 31 December 1986 the UK's net contribution to the EC Budget was £7,772 million, which represented a net payment of £1.52 million per day of membership (I. Barnes and J. Preston, *The European Community*, 1988, London and New York: Longman, pp 5 et seq). The main issue was not that the UK contribution was too high, as it was similar to other Member States, but the imbalance between its contribution and its receipts from the EC Budget. This problem was acknowledged from the time of UK accession. However, when Margaret Thatcher became prime minister of the UK, which coincided with the end of the transitional

Commission under the presidency of Jacques Delors was committed to further integration with a view to introducing EMU. Its motto was "one market, one money".

The Hanover Summit of June 1988 reappointed Jacques Delors as president of the Commission. It also affirmed his vision of the Community by declaring that "in adopting the Single European Act, the Member States of the Community confirmed the objective of progressive realisation of economic and monetary union."[43] The Hanover Summit, most importantly, set up a Committee, chaired by Jacques Delors, to examine the measures necessary for the establishment of EMU. The task of this Committee was to prepare concrete stages leading towards monetary union for the Madrid Summit in June 1989. Jacques Delors, in his annual speech on 17 January 1989 to the EP, assessed progress in the completion of a single market and set the agenda for the newly appointed Commission, which was to promote the devolution of more power to the EP by the Member States and the creation of EMU by successive stages. His vision of the Community was clear: it was a "frontier free economic and social area on the way to becoming a political union",[44] although at this stage political union was not his priority. The Madrid Summit in June 1989 examined the Delors Report[45] without taking particular notice of the changing situation in Europe.[46]

The dismantling of the barbed wire border between Hungary and Austria on 2 May 1989 was the first tear in the "Iron Curtain" and started the sequence of events that led towards the next stage of integration in the 1990s.

The "German question" became the main preoccupation of Member States. The old political division between West and East was abolished; the Soviet Union was in a coma; the old order was shattered.

Under the pressure of events and uncertainty the Federal Republic of Germany (FRG) accelerated the reunification process. Helmut Kohl, in his ten-point programme on German reunification submitted to the Bundestag (the German Parliament) on 28 November 1989, underlined that German unity was entirely a German matter. Nevertheless, in six of the points he underlined FRG commitment to the Community, the necessity to embed inter-German relations in an all-European process, and the necessity for further strengthening the Community, especially in the light of the historic changes occurring in Europe.[47] The official policy of Germany on reunification echoed the famous call of Thomas Mann in 1953 "not a German Europe but for a European Germany".

---

period during which the UK did not pay its full contribution to the EC budget, the renegotiation of the UK financial contribution (which anyway was marginal compared to the UK budget as a whole) became the single preoccupation of the British Government. Thus, during the 1980s the main point on the UK agenda at each European Summit was to obsessively complain about the injustice of the UK's financial contribution in an aggressive and perhaps not the best diplomatic manner. This negative attitude of the UK contributed to the growing unpopularity of the UK within the Community and, at the same time, to the growing unpopularity of the Community with the British people. Finally, the European Summit meeting in Fontainebleau in June 1984 formalised a rebate for the UK from the EC budget as part of a package of EC budget reforms.

43. EC Bull. 6/88, point 1.1.14.
44. EC Bull. Supp. 11/89, point 18.
45. J. Delors, *Report on Economic and Monetary Union in the EC*, 1989, Luxembourg: Office for Official Publications of the European Communities.
46. Only a very brief discussion on the changes in the Soviet bloc, EC Bull. 6/89, Presidency Conclusion, point 1.1.16.
47. E. Kirchner, "Genscher and What Lies Behind Genscherism", (1990), 13 West European Politics, pp 159–77.

The idea of the likely hegemony of Germany within the Community, once reunited, haunted all European leaders.[48] Jacques Delors considered that German reunification was a matter the Germans had to deal with. In his annual speech on 17 January 1990 to the EP he presented his programme for the Commission's forthcoming year and emphasised that East Germany was a special case. He noted that reunification of Germany, although being left to the German nation, nonetheless must be achieved "through free self-determination, peacefully and democratically, in accordance with the principles of the Helsinki Final Act, in the context of an East–West dialogue and with an eye to European integration".[49] Indeed, at that time the Brandenburg Gate in Berlin was opened and the first democratic elections in the former German Democratic Republic (GDR) were announced. It was clear that, at that stage, nothing could really stop the inevitable reunion of the German nation.

President Mitterrand of France began to put pressure on other Member States to create a political union to counterbalance the implications of German reunification by closely linking the largest Member State with the Community in political matters.[50] The Extraordinary Summit held in Dublin on 28 April 1990 formally welcomed East German integration into the Community. In reply Helmut Kohl agreed to political union alongside EMU. The Dublin Summit asked foreign ministers to prepare proposals regarding co-operation between Member States in political matters for the Dublin Summit in June 1990. These were to constitute the basis of a second Intergovernmental Conference.[51]

The second Summit in Dublin on 25–26 June 1990 decided to convene two Intergovernmental Conferences on 14 December 1990, one on EMU and the other on political union. The two IGCs were intended to be parallel with ratification of both instruments taking place within the same time frame. In the course of negotiations two approaches emerged:

- The first favoured a "Three Pillars" structure, the so-called Temple, consisting of a main agreement based on the EC Treaty and two separate arrangements outside the main framework covering co-operation on Common Foreign and Security Policy and Justice and Home Affairs matters.

- The second proposal was more ambitious and suggested the "tree" model, a single "trunk" having several branches and treating integration in all three areas as a common foundation (the tree) with special arrangements in particular fields (the branches). The second project was strongly federalist and as such judged too controversial by the foreign ministers of the Member States to be submitted for consideration at Maastricht.

The deliberations of the IGCs were based on the first project with modifications introduced by

---

48. British Prime Minister Margaret Thatcher strongly opposed reunification of Germany and tried to convince Mitterrand that indeed, within the EC, Germany's hegemony would assert itself and that France and the UK should act together, as in the past, to prevent or at least slow the process of reunification. Mitterrand agreed with her but considered that the reunification was inevitable, and instead of prevention, it was better to strengthen the EC through further political integration. (Thatcher wanted to widen the EC to include Central European countries and thus counterbalance the excessive influence of a reunited Germany.) M. Thatcher, *The Downing Street Years*, 1993, New York: Harper Collins, pp 688–726.

49. EC Bull. Supp. 1/90, point 6.

50. A united Germany with its 77 million people, that is, 25 per cent of the entire population of the Community at that time, would account for 27 per cent of its GDP.

51. R. Corbett, "The Intergovernmental Conference on Political Union", (1992) 30 JCMS, p 274.

a second proposal made by The Netherlands on 8 November 1989, which provided for unanimous voting within the CFSP while submitting the implementation of adopted measures to a qualified majority vote. The Intergovernmental Conferences began on 15 December 1990. The Maastricht Summit held on 9 and 10 December 1991 approved the text of the TEU. The final version was signed on 7 February 1992 at Maastricht. It was agreed that the process of ratification should be completed by the end of 1992. Its entry into force was to coincide with the completion of a single market. In practice, the process of ratification was fraught with difficulties.

The TEU was rejected by Danish voters in a national referendum held on 2 June 1992 (the Edinburgh Summit in December 1992 reassured the Danes and in the second referendum held on 18 May 1993, 56.8 per cent voted in favour of the TEU[52]), and was challenged before the German Constitutional Court[53] and the English High Court in *R v Secretary of Foreign and Commonwealth Affairs, ex parte Rees-Mogg*.[54]

1.15 The Treaty of Maastricht and the European Union

To examine the main features of the TEU is not an easy task. As McAllister said:

> "Maastricht is like Janus. It faces both ways: towards inter-governmentalism, and towards some kind of 'federal vocation'. It is as ambiguous as the oracle of Delphi; as the Community itself. It reflects the extent to which the States are, and are not, able to agree."[55]

The Treaty itself was a lengthy document, badly drafted. It was divided into seven Titles, and there were 17 legally binding Protocols and 33 Declarations attached. The latter have an interpretive function, although declarations of this kind are generally not relied on by the ECJ in its interpretation of the Treaties.[56]

The Economist reported, half jokingly, that the negative referendum in Denmark and a very narrow majority vote in France regarding the ratification of the TEU could be explained by the fact that the governments of those countries gave their people the original version to read. The Economist contrasted this with Ireland, where the Irish Government published a booklet summarising the Maastricht Treaty in plain language and consequently won a two-thirds vote in favour.[57] The only justification for producing such a confusing legal document was that the TEU was a transitional treaty. It established a procedure for its own revision.

The TEU was based on the so-called "Temple" structure, which consisted of the following elements:

---

52.   D. Howarth, "The Compromise on Denmark and the Treaty on European Union: A Legal and Practical Analysis", (1994) 31 CMLRev, pp 765–805; D. Curtin, "The Constitutional Structure of the Union: A Europe of Bits and Pieces", (1993) 30 CMLRev, p 17.

53.   M. Herdegen, "Maastricht and the German Constitutional Court: Constitutional Restraints for an 'Ever Closer Union'", (1994) 31 CMLRev, pp 235–49.

54.   [1994] 1 All ER 457, QBD.

55.   R. McAlister, *From EC to EU, A Historical and Political Survey*, 1997, London: Routledge, p 225.

56.   L. Senden, *Soft Law in European Community Law*, 2004, Oxford: Hart Publishing, pp 374–80.

57.   Quoted by P. Demaret, "The Treaty Framework", in D. O'Keeffe and P. M. Twomey (eds), *Legal Issues of the Maastricht Treaty*, 1994, London: Wiley Chancery Law, p 3.

1.15.1 The roof of the Temple

The roof of the Temple consisted of common provisions which laid down the objectives of the EU. The main purpose of the TEU was to "establish the foundations of an ever closer union among the people of Europe". To attain this purpose, the TEU set the following general objectives for the EU:

- The promotion of economic and social progress and a high level of employment with a view to achieving balanced and sustainable development, through the establishment of an area without internal frontiers, through the strengthening of economic and social cohesion and through the establishment of economic and monetary union;

- The establishment of a single currency within the framework of economic and monetary union;

- The promotion of an international identity for the EU through implementation of a common foreign and security policy (CFSP) which might lead to a common defence policy (see Chapter 5));

- The establishment of citizenship of the EU (see Chapter 22);

- The development of closer co-operation in the fields of justice and home affairs (JHA) (see Chapter 2.4));

- The improvement in the effectiveness of the EU institutions mostly by extending the legislative powers of the EP (see Chapter 7.3 and 7.4));

- The extension of EU competences to new policies while reinforcing the existing ones (see Chapter 4);

- The affirmation of the commitment of the EU to the protection of human rights (see Chapter 9);

- The introduction of the principle of subsidiarity (see Chapter 4.4.1.1).

1.15.2 Three Pillars, each Pillar dealing with one of the three main areas of EU policy

1.15.2.1 Pillar 1

Pillar 1, or "The Community Pillar", covered all policies existing under the previous Treaties and introduced fundamental amendments to the EEC Treaty.

The European Economic Community was renamed by the TEU. The name "European Economic Community" was replaced by "European Community" (the EC) in order to underline the fundamental changes in objectives. The most important changes concerning the EC Treaty were:

- The recognition of the principle of subsidiarity, which operates to restrict the Community's involvement in national matters;

- The establishment of European citizenship, which creates new rights for the nationals of Member States (see Chapter 22);

- The redefinition of the objectives of the Community in areas such as health, education, training, industrial policy, telecommunications and energy networks, research and development, consumer protection, trans-European networks, and culture;

- The extension of EC competences in environmental protection and development aid for poor countries;

- The deepening of the Commission's accountability to the EP while extending the EP's participation in decision-making procedures (see Chapter 6.5.5.1);

- The establishment of European Economic and Monetary Union depending on the extent to which Member States' economies converge in terms of inflation, interest rates and other criteria laid down in the EC Treaty;

- The extension of the ECJ's powers in relation to Member States that refuse to comply with its judgments (see Chapter 15.5).

1.15.2.2 Pillar 2

Pillar 2, or "The Common Foreign and Security Policy Pillar", concerned inter-governmental co-operation on common foreign and security policy (CFSP) (see Chapter 5).

1.15.2.3 Pillar 3

Pillar 3, or "The Justice and Home Affairs Pillar", covered inter-governmental co-operation in the fields of justice and home affairs (JHA) (see Chapter 2.4). Under the TEU Pillar 3 consisted of determination of nine areas listed in Article K1 EU regarded as "matters of common interest" to the Member States. These essentially covered co-operation in criminal justice (and some civil justice matters) and co-operation in asylum, immigration and visa matters. Co-operation in these areas was enumerated as follows in the Treaty:

- Asylum policy (Art. K1(2));

- Rules governing the crossing by persons of the external borders of the Member States and the exercise of controls thereon (Art. K1(2));

- Immigration policy; policy regarding the conditions of entry, movement and residence of nationals of third countries; policy regarding combating illegal immigration, residence and work (Art. K1(3));

- Policy regarding combating drug addiction (Art. K1(4));

- Policy regarding combating fraud on an international scale as far as this is not covered by points 7–9 below (Art.K1(5));

- Judicial co-operation in civil matters (Art. K1(6));

- Judicial co-operation in criminal matters (Art K1(7));

- Customs co-operation (Art K1(8));

- Police co-operation for the purpose of preventing and combating terrorism, unlawful drug trafficking and other serious forms of international crimes, including, if necessary, certain aspects of customs co-operation, by way of the organisation of a Union-wide system of exchanging information within the European Police Office (Europol) (Art. K1(9)).

Under Article K9, the so called "passerelle" or "bridge" provision, the Council, acting unanimously on a proposal from the Commission or a Member State, was allowed to transfer items mentioned in Articles K1(1)–(6) from Pillar 3 to Pillar 1. The Council exercised this option. Apart from matters relating to police and judicial co-operation in criminal matters all matters relating to these areas were transferred to the EC Treaty. The ToL completed this process. It abolished the Pillar structure with the consequence that the entirety of Pillar 3 has become Title IV of the TFEU.

1.15.2.4   The Plinth of the Temple

The base of the Temple (its "plinth") consisted of the final provisions.

1.15.3   The difference between the Pillars

The difference between Pillar 1, on the one hand, and Pillars 2 and 3, on the other, is that Pillar 1 was based on the so-called "Community method" (now called "EU method"),[58] while Pillars 2 and 3 were based on inter-governmental co-operation. That is, as a matter of principle, unanimity was required for any measure adopted under Pillars 2 and 3.

1.16   The Treaty of Amsterdam (ToA)

The ToA was signed on 2 October 1997 and came into effect on 1 May 1999. It had three parts and substantially amended both the TEU and the EC Treaty. It simplified the latter, deleted obsolete provisions, updated others and renumbered almost all of them. All modifications were set out in an explanatory report prepared by the General Secretariat of the Council of the European Union.[59] The Treaty of Amsterdam was accompanied by 13 Protocols, 51 Declarations adopted by the Amsterdam Summit of June 1997 and eight unilateral Declarations submitted by individual Member States. The Treaty of Amsterdam entered into force on 1 May 1999 following its ratification by all the then 15 Member States of the European Union by 30 March 1999.

1.16.1   The main features of the ToA

The main features of the ToA were:

- The extension of the objectives of the EU and the EC. In respect of the EU, the objectives included the promotion of economic and social progress, the progressive establishment of the area of FSJ, further development of the concept of EU citizenship, and the strengthening of existing policies. In respect of the EC, the objectives were not changed, or greatly extended. However, a new obligation was imposed on the EC when adopting legislative measures. They must be assessed in the light of two considerations: the prohibition of

---

58.   The EU glossary provides the following definition of the "Community/EU method": "The Community method is based on the idea that the general interest of Union citizens is best defended when the Community institutions play their full role in the decision-making process, with due regard for the subsidiarity principle" see http://europa.eu/scadplus/glossary/communitisation_en.htm (1/5/10).

59.   [1997] OJ C353/1.

discrimination between men and women, and the protection of the environment. Further, the EC gained competence to adopt measures concerning entry to the territory of the EU of non-EU nationals, movement of persons, and the co-ordination of employment policies.

- The confirmation of the stability pact and the timetable for EMU;

- The suspension of rights of a Member State that violate basic human rights (see Chapter 3.2.2);

- The progressive creation of the area of FSJ for EU citizens (see Chapter 2.4);

- The extension of the scope of the principle of non-discrimination to prohibit discrimination based on "sex, racial or ethnic origin, religion or belief, disability, age, and sexual orientation";

- The protection of the processing of personal data and of the free movement of such data in respect of both individuals and Community institutions. This is embodied in Article 16 TFEU;

- The inclusion of a chapter on employment;

- The incorporation of the Social Charter into the EC Treaty. The UK decided to join the Social Protocol. As a result, it was incorporated into the Treaty provisions on social policy, education, training and youth (see Title X of the TFEU);

- The extension of the powers of the EP. The clear winner at the Amsterdam Summit was the EP. The co-decision procedure (under the ToL this procedure is called the ordinary legislative procedure) has been extended to 15 existing Treaty provisions concerning eight areas.

- Involvement of national parliaments in decision-making procedures. The ToA involved national parliaments in the legislative decision-making procedures in the EU in order to give them an opportunity to express their views on matters which might be of particular interest to them. It required the Commission to promptly forward all proposals to national parliaments. Subject to exceptions based on urgency, proposals could not be placed before the Council for six weeks after they were made available to national parliaments. Protocol 13 attached to the ToA set out the above rules (the current position is detailed in Chapter 4.4.1.2.2);

- The establishment of the principle of transparency (the current position is examined in Chapter 7.1.2.2);

- An explanation of the role and application of the principles of subsidiarity and proportionality. This is discussed in Chapter 4.4.1 and 4.4.2;

- The introduction of the concept of enhanced co-operation. The concept of enhanced co-operation permits differential integration, that is, in certain projects only some Member States participate. Before the adoption of the ToA, Member States were allowed various opt-outs, for example, participation in EMU or the Schengen system. The ToA formalised this type of arrangement and mainstreamed it to a greater degree. The procedure under the ToA was substantially amended by the ToN, and then by the ToL and accordingly is discussed in Chapter 4.7;

- The introduction of changes in the implementation of the CFSP (the CFSP is examined in Chapter 5;

- The incorporation of the Schengen acquis into the TEU (see Chapter 2.4.4).

1.17 The Treaty of Nice (ToN)

The European Council Summit held in Nice (December 2000) finally resolved the complicated legacy of the 1997 ToA. The "leftovers" of the 1997 Amsterdam Summit, that is, the long overdue changes to institutions and decision-making procedures (the most difficult areas to reform), had become of vital importance and urgency in the light of the then future enlargement of the EU. After 350 hours of negotiations in the IGC and five more days of hard bargaining within the Summit Meeting, the 15 heads of state or government agreed on the provisional text of the Treaty of Nice. The final text was signed on 26 February 2001 and the Treaty entered into force on 1 February 2003.

1.17.1 The most important changes to the ToA introduced by the ToN

These were:

- Reform of the institutions of the EU, including the redistribution of votes in the Council of the EU. The ToL has further reformed the EU institutions (see Chapter 6);

- Revision of the enhanced co-operation procedure which has been further revised by the ToL (see Chapter 4.7);

- The establishment of a new mechanism aimed at preventing infringements of human rights (see Chapter 3.2.2).

1.17.2 Issues not dealt with until the IGC of 2004

Irrespective of the vitriolic attack of the EP on the Treaty for being unambitious and shaped by narrow national interests, it is incontestable that the ToN paved the way for future enlargements of the EU. However, important issues were put off until 2004 when a new IGC was convened to deal with them. These issues were:

- The status of the Charter of Fundamental Rights of the European Union. Should it have binding force? If so, in what manner should this be achieved?

- Simplification and consolidation of the existing Treaties (the EU, EC and EA Treaties) into one Treaty, in order to make them clearer and more readable;

- The clear delimitation of competences between the EU and the Member States. This matter was raised by Chancellor Gerhard Schröeder. Indeed, this matter was of vital importance for powerful German Länders. (This issue had previously been highlighted by the Laeken Declaration in 2001);

- The role of national parliaments in the European system.

1.18 The constitution that never was

The Laeken Summit held in December 2001 adopted a "Declaration on the Future of the European Union", which committed the European Union to become more democratic, transparent and effective and to pave the way towards a Constitution of the European Union. The task of preparing a form of Constitution was conferred on a novel body – the Convention. The Laeken Summit appointed Mr Valéry Giscard d'Estaing, the former French president, as chairman of the Convention. Its 105 members represented governments and national parliaments of the Member States and candidate states, the European Parliament and the European Commission, that is, the main parties involved in the debate on the future of the European Union. The status of observers was given to 13 representatives of the European Economic and Social Committee, the Committee of the Regions, the European social partners (that is, bodies representing labour, such as the European Trade Union Confederation, and management, such as the European Confederation of Industries) and the European Ombudsman. The Laeken Declaration posed some 60 questions to be debated and considered by the Convention. These questions focused on the following topics:

- Better division and definition of competences in the European Union;

- Simplification of the Union's instruments, and assessment of their influence;

- Different aspects of the perceived democratic deficit of EU institutions;

- More democracy, transparency and effectiveness;

- Simplification of the existing treaties.

The opening meeting of the Convention took place on 28 February 2002. A draft of a Treaty establishing a Constitution for Europe was ready in July 2003. Subsequently it served as a basis for the 2003/2004 IGC. The final draft was approved by the Brussels Summit (June 2004) and signed in Rome on 20 October 2004 by the heads of state or government of the 25 Member States and the three candidate states (Bulgaria, Romania and Croatia). In order for the EU Constitution to enter into force, all Members of the EU had to ratify it either using the parliamentary method, that is, the treaty must be approved by the national parliament of a Member State, or by a referendum, in which case the treaty is submitted directly to citizens who vote for or against it. The method of ratification was left to the Member State. According to the EU Constitution, it was to enter into force on 1 November 2006. The deadline was not met because the peoples of France and The Netherlands rejected the Constitution on 29 May 2005 and 1 June 2005 respectively.

In this context the Brussels Summit held on 16 and 17 June 2005 decided that the date envisaged for the entry into force of the Constitution was not tenable, but the process of ratification was not abandoned. A year later the Vienna Summit agreed on "a period of reflection" with a view to deciding the best way forward with regard to institutional reforms. The Brussels Summit held in December 2006 decided to continue the period of reflection into 2007. By June 2007, the EU Constitution had been ratified by 18 Member States; others had put ratification on hold.

The European Council Summit held in June 2007 decided to abandon the constitutional project; however, as institutional reforms of the kind envisaged by the Constitutional Treaty were necessary, given that the EU, then comprising 27 Member States, could not function properly under the then current rules on governance, the European Council decided to convene an IGC and entrusted it with the preparation of a new treaty called the Reform Treaty (see immediately below).

It is submitted that the proposed Constitution was not a "tidying up exercise". It was a very ambitious piece of work that, for the first time, clearly defined the division of power between the

EU and Member States, and in doing so gave the EU greater powers, enhanced the role of the EP, bolstered democratic accountability and transparency by giving national parliaments an important role in the adoption of EU legislation, assigned to the Charter of Fundamental Rights its rightful place, and "melted" the EU's three Treaties into one.

1.19 The Treaty of Lisbon (ToL): the Treaty on European Union (TEU) and the Treaty on the Functioning of the European Union (TFEU)

On 13 December 2007 the European Council held in Lisbon approved the Reform Treaty, which replaced the abandoned Constitutional Treaty.[60] On that date the Reform Treaty became the Treaty of Lisbon (ToL), named as such because of its links with Lisbon. It was prepared under the presidency of Portugal, the relevant IGC was held in Lisbon, the informal meeting of the European Council held in Lisbon in mid-October 2007 gave its approval to the draft Reform Treaty and the signing ceremony took place in Lisbon in December 2007. The ToL entered into force on 1 December 2009.

1.19.1 The history of the ToL

For the first time in the history of the EC/EU the IGC convened to prepare a draft of what was then referred to as the Reform Treaty (now the Treaty of Lisbon) was, in the first instance, provided with extremely detailed instructions. These included, in effect, a final draft of the intended Treaty and the IGC was merely asked to produce a full draft document based precisely and specifically upon detailed wording (including punctuation!) supplied by the European Council meeting of 21/22 June 2007. The European Council gave the IGC a mandate that constituted "the exclusive basis and framework" for its activity and that "in the absence of indications to the contrary in this mandate" demanded that the text of the Treaties remain unchanged.[61]

It is clear that when considering the intended Reform Treaty the European Council did not wish the IGC to make any real contribution to the intended treaty but wished, in effect, (other than following the formal requirements in connection with the IGC) to deal with the matter all in one go in June 2007 and not to see any further debate as to the content of the intended treaty. It may be said that in this respect the European Council effected a very streamlined administrative process, avoiding delays and what could be regarded as unnecessary bureaucracy. On the other hand, one might be left wondering why the European Council did not adopt the same approach with the Reform Treaty as with the Constitutional Treaty (see the approach of the Laeken European Summit to the preparation of the Constitutional Treaty by the IGC in Chapter 1.18), given that the greater the number of participants involved, the more democratic legitimacy and credibility is afforded to a new Treaty.

The explanation provided by the European Council was that enough time had been spent on

---

60. An incomplete version of the ToL was published in the OJ ([2007] OJ C306/1). For a consolidated version see: Peadar ó Broin (ed.), Treaty of Lisbon 2007: Consolidated Version of the Treaties Amended by the Treaty of Lisbon, 2008, IEA Publication, free download at http://iiea.com/publicationxtest.php?publication_id=33 (accessed 18/02/08). This contains amended versions of each Treaty.

61. The Presidency Conclusion concerning the IGC Mandate, in particular point 5. Brussels European Council 21/22 June 2007.

the revision of the Treaties, including a reflection period of almost two years initiated by the European Council held in June 2005 and terminated by it in June 2007 with the announcement of the death of the Constitutional Treaty. During that time, according to the European Council, all important matters were subject to wide public debate, which prepared the ground for the Reform Treaty.[62]

In mid-October 2007 the draft Reform Treaty was submitted to the European Council, which, after making some concessions to Member States which were unhappy with some aspects of the new Treaty, ensured its signing as the Treaty of Lisbon on 13 December 2007 by the heads of state or government of the Member States.

1.19.2   The ratification of the ToL

All Member States (including The Netherlands and France, the two Member States that torpedoed the Constitutional Treaty) but Ireland, decided to effect ratification via parliament rather than to expose the ToL to the uncertainty of national referenda. Ireland was the only Member State that, by virtue of its Constitution, had to hold a referendum. On 12 July 2008, the Irish voters rejected the ToL. Subsequently, the Irish Government decided to hold a second referendum after obtaining the following assurances from the European Council held in June 2009.

- Each Member State will be represented in the Commission of the European Union by one commissioner of its own nationality;

- Irish neutrality will not be affected by EU law;

- Sensitive ethical issues such as abortion will be within the exclusive competence of Ireland;

- The system of direct taxation will remain within the exclusive competence of Ireland;

- Workers' rights and public services are and will remain valued and protected in Ireland and in the EU.

In the second referendum which took place in October 2009 Irish voters approved the ToL.

In Germany, the ToL was challenged before the German Federal Constitutional Court. In July 2009, the Court ruled that the ToL was compatible with the German Constitution. In particular, the Court held that the ToL did not transform the EU into a federal State, that EU citizenship did not replace national citizenship and that a Member State, under the ToL, was not required to provide troops for a European army. However, the Court held that a modification of domestic legislation ensuring greater participation of the German parliament in the control and supervision of EU affairs was required. The necessary legislation was subsequently adopted. In this judgment the German Federal Constitutional Court confirmed its position on the supremacy of EU law, i.e. that supremacy of EU law derives from the German act conferring power to the EU

---

62.   On this point it is interesting to note the following comment in "The Treaty of Lisbon: Implementing the Institutional Innovations", Joint Study, CEPS, EGMONT and EPC, p 145, November 2007, available at http:// www.epc.eu (see publications) (accessed 3/1/08): ". . . we are faced with complex, unreadable texts, negotiated in secrecy, far from public scrutiny."

and not from EU law itself and therefore has maintained its reservations on primacy of EU law over the German Constitution (see Chapter 13.11.1).[63]

The last hurdle to be jumped before ratification was that the President of the Czech Republic refused to sign the ToL, although the Treaty had been approved by the Czech Parliament, and declared to be in conformity with the Czech Constitution by the Czech Constitutional Court,[64] unless he obtained a guarantee that his country would not be exposed to massive property claims by Germans expelled from the then Czechoslovakia after World War II. In order to accommodate the Czech Republic, Protocol 30 "On the Application of the Charter of Fundamental Rights of the European Union to Poland and to the United Kingdom" was extended to the Czech Republic (see Chapter 9.4.4).

1.19.3   The position of the UK

The UK obtained many opt-outs in key areas. It is allowed (as is Ireland and Denmark) to decide whether to opt in or to opt out of policies relating to the whole area of FSJ. The UK also negotiated for itself and Poland Protocol 30 (which also applies to the Czech Republic, see immediately above) attached to the Treaties that provides that no "court can rule that laws, regulations or administrative practices or action" of the UK/Poland/the Czech Republic are inconsistent with the principles set out in the Charter of Fundamental Rights of the EU, and to avoid any doubts, the Protocol emphasises that the Charter creates no new rights enforceable in the UK/Poland/the Czech Republic (see Chapter 9.4.4). Additionally, the UK's previous opt-outs have been confirmed (for example, non-participation in the EMU and in the Schengen Agreement). The above, combined with the fact that unanimity of voting in the Council was retained in the CFSP, in direct taxation and in social security matters, made the ToL acceptable to the UK Government. Prime Minister Gordon Brown of the UK said that the ToL had not crossed "red lines" on major concerns for the UK, and therefore there would be no need to call a referendum.

1.19.4   The structure of the ToL

The ToL has only seven articles. The first two contain amendments to the TEU and the EC Treaty (now TFEU), and therefore are very lengthy. Article 3 ToL states that the ToL is concluded for an unlimited time; Article 4 ToL refers to Protocols 1 and 2 to be attached to the ToL; Article 5 ToL deals with the renumbering of articles, sections and titles of both the TEU and the TFEU; Article 6 ToL concerns the procedure for ratification of the ToL; and Article 7 ToL confirms that each official language in which the ToL was drafted is authentic and that Italy will be the depository of the ToL. Two Protocols, one Annex and the Final Act of the IGC are attached to the ToL. It is to be noted that 37 Protocols, two Annexes and 65 Declarations are attached to the TEU and TFEU and when appropriate to the EA Treaty. Technically, the TEU and the TFEU are part of the ToL and therefore Protocols and Declarations attached to them are also attached to the ToL. However, the ToL specifically provides that the two following Protocols are annexed to it, i.e:

---

63.   The full text of the judgment of the German Federal Constitutional Court in English is available at http:www.bverfg.de/entscheidungen/es20090630 2bve000208en.html (10/2/10)

64.   The full judgment was published in the *Irish Times* on 11 November 2008.

- Protocol No 1 amending the Protocols annexed to the Treaty on European Union, to the Treaty establishing the European Community and/or to the Treaty establishing the European Atomic Energy Community;

- Protocol No 2 amending the Treaty establishing the European Atomic Energy Community.

It can be seen from the above that the ToL is merely a "wrapping" or "introductory" Treaty. Its main purpose is to effect amendments of the TEU and the EC Treaty.

The IGC was mandated to base the ToL on the Constitutional Treaty but with the modifications specified in the mandate. Consequently, elements of that Treaty are present in the ToL. However, unlike the Constitutional Treaty, which proposed the melting of the three existing Treaties into one, the ToL only amends the current Treaties. It does this in the following ways:

- Article 1(3) TEU provides that the EU should be based on two Treaties: the Treaty on European Union (as amended) (TEU) and the Treaty on the Functioning of the European Union, which amends the EC Treaty and gives it a new name: the TFEU. Both Treaties are of equal legal value. The TFEU abolishes the Pillar structure which was introduced by the Treaty of Maastricht but special procedures are provided for the CFSP (see Chapter. 5). The ToL finally gets rid of the confusing distinction between the EC and the EU. Article 1 TEU specifies that "The Union shall replace and succeed the European Community".

  As a result of the above changes, only the EU has legal personality and thus is the only entity able to enter into international agreements, including those relating to membership of international organisations.

- The Euratom exists outside the ToL. It is "hanging on the side". Protocol 2 annexed to the ToL contains changes to the current EA Treaty and also provides that some provisions of both the TEU and the TFEU apply to the EA Treaty.

1.19.5 Brief assessment of the ToL

There has been much public debate on whether what was the proposed Constitution is really dead or whether the ToL has resurrected it by recycling and relabelling its provisions. In this respect it can be said that the ToL, instead of being an all-encompassing treaty as was the failed Constitutional Treaty, only amends the EU Treaty and the EC Treaty. The ToL avoids any reference suggesting ambition on the part of the EU to become a federation. The ToL does not use the word "constitution". Not only has terminology suggesting a state-like status for the EU been abandoned but also any reference to EU paraphernalia such as an anthem, a motto and a flag, although they will continue to be used. 16 Member States declared their adherence to these symbols in Declaration 52 attached to the Treaties.

The significance to be given to the ToL depends upon whether it is assessed from the point of view of a Eurosceptic or from that of an advocate of European integration. Nevertheless, both are likely to be disappointed by the ToL. Each amendment can be criticised by both. For example, for a Eurosceptic the fact that the Member States have agreed that QMV will apply to 44 further policies confirms the increasing loss of national sovereignty. An advocate of European integration, however, would criticise the ToL for extending QMV to many areas which have no impact on achieving a real union (for example, extension in respect of decisions on the methods used for gathering statistics in the eurozone, or concerning the composition of the CoR) while maintaining national vetoes in crucial areas such as direct taxation, defence and the CFSP.

If assessed in simple terms and dispassionately, the ToL effected the reforms necessary in the ever-enlarging EU, that is, it improves the efficiency of the decision-making process in the EU and makes the EU a very democratic entity.

Examples of the improvement of efficiency of the decision-making process in the EU are:

■ The ordinary legislative procedure has become the main legislative procedure for the adoption of legislative acts and has been extended to a further 44 areas;

■ Double majority voting in the Council, when it enters into force in 2014, will be more effective than the current weighted voting system;

■ The reduction in number of the members of the EP makes it less unwieldy;

■ The creation of the post of the High Representative of the Union for Foreign Affairs and Security Policy (HR) who combines the posts of Vice-President of the Commission and of High Representative for Foreign and Security Policy and has to ensure coherence and unity in respect of the EU's external action, as does the establishment of the post of president of the European Council;

■ The granting of legal personality to the EU.

Examples of the greater democratisation of the EU are:

■ The EP has gained new powers:
  ● legislative (as it has become a co-legislator);
  ● budgetary (as it has powers equal to that of the Council over the EU budget); and
  ● political (for example, it elects the President of the Commission);

■ The involvement of national parliaments in the functioning of the EU adds a new dimension to the application of the principle of subsidiarity and reinforces democratic control of the EU activities;

■ The social rights of EU citizens are better protected:
  ● First through the Charter of Fundamental Human Rights in the EU, which contains provisions on social rights that must be guaranteed by national courts and by the Court of Justice of the European Union (The CJEU);[65] and
  ● Second through the inclusion of a "social clause" that specifies that social requirements are to be taken into account in all EU policies;

■ The respect for fundamental human rights of EU citizens is enhanced through the conferment of binding legal status on the Charter of Fundamental Human Rights in the EU and the accession of the EU to the ECHR;

■ Natural and legal persons have gained broader access to the CJEU under Article 263 TFEU (see Chapter 16.2.3.3.3);

---

65.   This collective name covers three courts: the Court of Justice of the European Union colloquially known as the European Court of Justice (the ECJ); the General Court, which was previously known as the Court of First Instance (CFI) and specialised courts which were previously known as "judicial panels" (see Chapter 6.6).

■ The application of the "EU method" to measures relating to the establishment of an area of FSJ ensures judicial (exercised by the CJEU) and political (exercised by the EP and national parliaments) control over the adoption and implementation of such measures;

■ The ToL reinforces the principle of representative democracy, ensures transparency of the EU legislative process and the political participation of EU citizens in the process. Article 11 (4) TEU contains a new form of popular participation. Under this provision, one million or more of EU citizens, who are nationals of a significant number of Member States, may ask jointly the Commission to prepare a proposal for a legal act necessary to implement the objectives of the Treaties. This "citizens' initiative" has the potential to make a great impact on EU legislation;

■ The ToL clarifies the division of competences between the EU and the Member States so that under the ToL it is clearer in which areas a Member State has dominion, in which the EU is empowered to act alone and in which it shares competences with Member States;

■ The ToL provides procedures for Member States wishing to leave the EU.

1.20   Theories of integration

Three main theories have been presented to explain the process of integration. These are examined below.

1.20.1   Functionalism

Functionalism is a theory in international relations formulated by David Mitrany (1888–1975) in the 1930s and 1940s.[66] Functionalists believe that the state, as a form of social organisation, is obsolete and that world problems can only be solved through global integration entailing collective governance, that is, a world-government, and "material interdependence" between states. Such integration is difficult to achieve because it erodes a state's sovereignty. However, states are willing to work together on relatively small "functional" issues and integrate in limited functional, technical, and/or economic areas. Once they do this, they not only learn how to co-operate but most importantly realise the benefits flowing from integration. This is likely to result in integration achieved in one narrow area spilling over into broader areas with a view to achieving global peace and prosperity.

1.20.2   Neofunctionalism

Neofunctionalists focus on regional integration and not on global integration. According to neofunctionalists states begin by co-operating in limited functional or economic areas, but integration in one economic sector or area creates pressure for further economic integration within and beyond that sector/area.

Neofunctionalists consider that there are two kinds of "spillover":

---

66.   D. Anderson, "David Mitrany (1888–1975): An Appreciation of His Life and Work", (1998) 24 RIS, p 579.

- Functional, which concerns integration in a specific economic sector or specific issue-area which it is hoped will spill over into other areas; and

- Political, which leads to the creation of a supranational structure, that is, a federation of states.

Jean Monnet hoped that by integrating a sector vital to national interests, that is, coal and steel, which after World War II were the means of production of armaments, the "spillover" effect would be set in motion. Once the participating states realised the benefits of having the coal and steel sectors integrated, they would want to extend integration to other areas, with the final result being the establishment of a federal system. This was one of the reasons why the UK (which did not wish to become part of a federation) was not initially interested in participating in the ECSC.

1.20.3 Multilevel governance (MLG)

Without going into a debate on neofunctionalism, it is important to note that economic integration does not necessarily lead to political integration, as the latter obviously requires political will. However, while neofuntionalism may be useful in explaining the process of integration in the first 30 years of existence of the Communities, it fails to take account of the peculiarities of European integration since the late 1980s. Since then the creation of the EU by the Treaty of Maastricht has placed the ideological debate on a different plane as the EU is now perceived as a system of multilevel or network governance.[67] This theory, or as some call it, "an organising metaphor"[68] emphasises special features of the EU in that the EU is multidimensional, the degree of integration varies depending on the policy area and the governance of the EU is composed of multiple coexisting policy models. According to this theory the decision-making process is taken "across multiple territorial levels" and thus instead of focusing on "integration" one should focus on how various authorities, i.e. national, European, regional and local, private and public, participate in the decision-making process in the EU. According to this theory authority has gradually moved from national governments and has been dispersed among various private and public agents. However, there is fluidity between various levels of authority in that the authority may move between different levels and varies depending upon the policy area. Marks defined the MLG of the EU as "a set of overreaching, multi-level policy networks [where] . . the structure of political control is variable, not constant across policy space".[69] This theory is rather confusing but as Rosamond stated it "gives us a chance of being confused in a reasonably sophisticated way".[70]

---

67.   M. Jachtenfuchs, "Theoretical Perspective on European Governance", (1995) 1 ELJ, p 115, and "The Governance Approach to European Integration", (2001) JCMS p 245.
68.   B. Rosamond, "New Theories of European Integration", in M. Cini, N. Pérez-Solórzano Borragán (eds), *European Union Politics*, 3rd edition, 2010, Oxford: OUP, p 117.
69.   Ibid, 116.
70.   Ibid, 121.

AIDE-MÉMOIRE

EU BIG EVENTS AND BIG DATES

9 May 1950 – The Schuman Plan. R Schuman, the French foreign minister, proposed the creation of the European Steel and Coal Community.

18 April 1951 – Signature of the Treaty creating the European Coal and Steel Community (CS Treaty), which entered into force on **23 July 1952** and expired on **23 July 2002**.

25 March 1957 – Signature of the Treaty creating the European Economic Community (EC Treaty) and the European Atomic Energy Community (EA Treaty), both of which entered into force on **1 January 1958**.

14 January 1963 – France vetoed the accession of the UK to the Communities. The second application by the UK was submitted in 1967 and immediately rejected by France.

8 April 1965 – The Merger Treaty was signed merging the executive bodies of the three Communities (the CS, EC and EA) and creating a single Council and a single Commission. It entered into force on **13 July 1967**.

1 July 1965 – Beginning of the "empty chairs" crisis ended by the Luxembourg Accord of **January 1966**.

29 January 1966 – The Luxembourg Accord ends the first major political crisis in the EC. Under the agreement unanimity voting in the Council was agreed when "vital national interests" of a Member State were at issue.

1 July 1968 – Elimination of all customs duties in respect of industrial products, the creation of the Customs Union among Member States and the establishment of the Common Customs Tariffs for goods from outside the Community (see Chapter 18). This was achieved 18 months in advance of the agreed timetable.

1–2 December 1969 – The Hague Summit. The Member States decided to meet regularly at the level of heads of state or government. These informal meetings were recognised as a Community institution, that is, the "European Council", by the Paris Summit in December 1974.

24 April 1972 – Creation of the monetary "snake", which constituted the first stage towards the creation of the European Monetary Union.

1 January 1973 – Accession of Denmark, Ireland and the UK to the Communities (see Chapter 3.3.1).

7 July 1978 – Creation of the European Monetary System (EMS), replacing the monetary "snake". The Exchange Rate Mechanism (ERM) was launched on **13 March 1979**.

10 June 1979 – First direct elections of members of the EP by citizens of Member States based on universal adult suffrage.

1 January 1981 – Accession of Greece to the Communities (see Chapter 3.3.2).

14 June 1985 – The Schengen I Agreement was signed between Germany, France and the

Benelux countries aiming at abolishing the internal borders among them and creating a single external border, where checks for all the Schengen countries were to be carried out in accordance with a common set of rules.

1 January 1986 – Accession of Spain and Portugal to the Communities (see Chapter 3.3.3).

17 and 28 February 1986 – Signature of the Single European Act which entered into force on **1 June 1987**.

19 June 1990 – Signature of the Schengen II Agreement which aimed at eliminating frontier controls between the participating Member States. It entered into force on 26 March 1995.

3 October 1990 – Reunification of Germany (see Chapter 3.3.4).

7 February 1992 – Signature of the Treaty of Maastricht, which entered into force on **1 November 1993**, and which created the European Union.

31 December 1992 – The official completion of the internal market (see Chapter 17).

1 January 1995 – Accession of Austria, Finland and Sweden to the EU (see Chapter 3.3.5).

2 October 1997 – Signature of the Treaty of Amsterdam, which entered into force on **1 May 1999**.

1 January 1999 – The Euro became the currency for 11 Member States.

8 December 2000 – The European Council agreed on the Treaty of Nice, which was signed on **26 February 2001** and entered into force on **1 February 2003**.

18 July 2003 – Approval of a draft of a Constitutional Treaty by the Brussels European Council Meeting. The proposed EU Constitution was signed in Rome on **20 October 2004** by the heads of state or government of the 25 Member States and the three candidate states. **21/22/23 June 2007** – The European Council decided to abandon the Constitutional Treaty. As a result, it never came into force.

1 May 2004 – Accession of 10 Member States to the EU: Cyprus, The Czech Republic, Estonia, Hungary, Latvia, Lithuania, Malta, Poland, Slovakia and Slovenia (see Chapter 3.3.6).

3 October 2005 – Official accession negotiations with Turkey and Croatia commenced (see Chapter 3.3.9.1 and 3.3.9.3).

1 January 2007 – Accession of Bulgaria and Romania to the EU (see Chapter 3.3.7).

23 June 2007 – The 2007 IG commenced its work on the Reform Treaty (the Treaty of Lisbon – the ToL).

13 December 2007 – The European Council approved the Reform Treaty (the Lisbon Treaty) (see Chapter 1.19).

15 December 2007 – The Netherlands Antilles islands of Bonaire, Saabs, Sint Eustatius, Curaçao and Saint Martin became part of the EU (see Chapter 3.3.8).

1 December 2009 – the entry into force of the ToL.

RECOMMENDED READING

Books

Cini, M. and Pérez-Solórzano Borragán, N. (eds), *European Union Politics*, 3rd Edition, 2010, Oxford: OUP

Ott, A. and Vos, E. (eds), *Fifty Years of European Integration*, 2009, Cambridge: CUP

van Empel, M., *'From Paris to Nice': Fifty years of Legal Integration in Europe: International Pallas Conference, Nijmegen, May 24, 2002*, 2003, The Hague: Kluwer Law International

Vinen, R., *History in Fragments: Europe in the Twentieth Century*, 2002, London: Abacus

Articles

Birkinshaw, P., "A Constitution for the EU?" (2004) 10 (1) EPL, p 57

Curtin, D., "The Constitutional Structure of the Union: A Europe of Bits and Pieces", (1993) 30 CMLRev, p 17

Dougan, M., "The Treaty of Lisbon 2007: Winning Minds, not Hearts" (2008) 45 CMLRev, p. 617

Šlosarčík, I., "Czech Republic 2006–2008: On President, Judges and the Lisbon Treaty" (2010) 16 EPL, p 1

Ward, I., "Bill and the Fall of the Constitutional Treaty", (2007) 13/3 EPL, p 461

Ziller, J., "The German Constitutional Court's Friendliness towards European Law: On the Judgment of *Bundesverfassungsgericht* over the Ratification of the Treaty of Lisbon" (2010) 16 EPL, p 53

2

VALUES AND OBJECTIVES OF THE EU INCLUDING THE CREATION OF AN AREA OF FREEDOM, SECURITY AND JUSTICE (FSJ)

CONTENTS

SUMMARY

1. Article 2 TEU lists the values on which the EU is founded. They are:

   ▪ Respect for human dignity (a new value);

   ▪ Freedom (previously referred to as "liberty");

   ▪ Democracy;

   ▪ Equality (a new value);

   ▪ The rule of law;

   ▪ Respect for human rights, including the rights of persons belonging to minorities.

These values are common to all the Member States "in a society in which pluralism, non-discrimination, tolerance, justice, solidarity and equality between women and men prevail". The observance of EU values by the Member States is supervised by the EU which may intervene if a Member State violates them or even if there is merely a danger of them being breached. Under Article 7 TEU the EU may take measures such as a warning or suspension of the EU rights with regard to the offending Member State. Further, the accession of a State to the EU depends on that State's adherence to EU values.

2. The objectives that justify the EU's existence and its competences are listed in Article 3 TEU. They are clearly formulated and enhance the fact that economic objectives are as important as social, cultural, environmental and humanitarian objectives. The promotion of peace, the EU's values and the well-being of its people constitute the overreaching objectives of the EU. More specific objectives are:

A.   The creation of an area of FSJ;

B.   The establishment of the internal market which must pursue not only economic objectives but also social, cultural and environmental goals;

C.   The establishment of monetary and economic union (EMU);

D.   The reinforcement of the EU's presence on the international stage with a view to promoting its values and interests and contributing to the protection of EU citizens outside the EU.

2.1   Introduction

The ToL defines and provides a better comprehension than the previous treaties of why the Member States are together in the EU and of the values and objectives which are shared by EU citizens. Articles 2 to 7 and 47 TEU are essential as they define the EU itself, its values, objectives, relations with Member States and its legal personality. The Preamble to the ToL refers to "the cultural, religious and humanist inheritance of Europe, from which have developed the universal values of the inviolable and inalienable rights of the human person, freedom, democracy, equality and the rule of law". However, no specific religion is mentioned in the Treaties.

The striking features of the ToL's objectives are its emphasis on the respect, promotion and protection of human rights and the commitment of the EU to make itself more democratic and more relevant to its citizens.

2.2   The values on which the EU is founded

Article 2 lists the values on which the EU is founded. Some of them have never before been mentioned in the Treaties, i.e. the respect for human dignity and equality although the EU commitment to them has always been implicit. Article 2 TEU states that:

> "The Union is founded on the values of respect for human dignity, freedom, democracy, equality, the rule of law and respect for human rights, including the rights of persons belonging to minorities. These values are common to the Member States in a society in which pluralism, non-discrimination, tolerance, justice, solidarity and equality between women and men prevail."

These values are not declarations without commitment. They are enforceable in that if breached, or even if there is merely a danger of them being breached, the EU can take measures such as a warning to or suspension of the EU rights of the offending Member State (see Chapter 3). Additionally, in so far as candidate states are concerned, one factor in judging their suitability for membership will be whether or not they have demonstrated adherence to these values.

2.3   Over-reaching and specific objectives of the EU

The overreaching objectives of the EU changed with the coming into force of the ToL. Article 3(1) TEU lists as overreaching objectives: the promotion of peace, of the EU's values and of the well-being of its people. The specific objectives of the EU are set in Article 3 TEU as follows:

"2.   The Union shall offer its citizens an area of freedom, security and justice without internal frontiers, in which the free movement of persons is ensured in conjunction with appropriate measures with respect to external border controls, asylum, immigration and the prevention and combating of crime.

3.   The Union shall establish an internal market. It shall work for the sustainable development of Europe based on balanced economic growth and price stability, a highly competitive social market economy, aiming at full employment and social progress, and a high level of protection and improvement of the quality of the environment. It shall promote scientific and technological advance.

It shall combat social exclusion and discrimination, and shall promote social justice and protection, equality between women and men, solidarity between generations and protection of the rights of the child.

It shall promote economic, social and territorial cohesion, and solidarity among Member States.

It shall respect its rich cultural and linguistic diversity, and shall ensure that Europe's cultural heritage is safeguarded and enhanced.

4.   The Union shall establish an economic and monetary union whose currency is the euro.

5.   In its relations with the wider world, the Union shall uphold and promote its values and interests and contribute to the protection of its citizens. It shall contribute to peace, security, the sustainable development of the Earth, solidarity and mutual respect among peoples, free and fair trade, eradication of poverty and the protection of human rights, in particular the rights of the child, as well as to the strict observance and the development of international law, including respect for the principles of the United Nations Charter."

The above list clearly shows that the ToL assigns a very important place to non-economic objectives, i.e. to social and environmental objectives. Further, it mentions, for the first time, cultural objectives so that the EU is required to respect "rich cultural and linguistic diversity" and not only safeguard the cultural heritage of Europe but also develop it. Ambitious international objectives of the EU are contained in Article 3(5) TEU which are to be pursued in accordance with the principles of international law, including those contained in the UN Charter. The granting of international legal personality to the EU will allow the EU to play a greater role on the international stage.

2.4   Specific objective: the creation of an area of freedom, security and justice (FSJ)

The most important specific objective of the ToL is the creation of an area of FSJ. This ambitious political project confirms that the safety and well-being of EU citizens are at the centre of EU concerns. To achieve this objective the ToL incorporates the provisions of Pillar 3 created by the Treaty of Maastricht (including the Schengen system) into the TFEU and thus the "EU" method applies to them. As a result, the ordinary legislative procedure under which the Commission has exclusive right to initiate legislative proposals and legislation is adopted jointly by the EP and the Council voting by QMV, has become the rule in respect of the adoption of measures in the area of FSJ. There are, however, exceptions to this rule:

- In respect of measures concerning police and judicial co-operation the Commission shares the right to initiate legislative proposals with Member States. Under Article 76 TFEU a quarter of Member States may initiate a proposal;

- A unanimous vote in the Council is required in respect of measures concerning:
  - Passports, residence permits, and any other such documents (Article 77(3) TFEU);
  - Family law matters with cross-border implications (Article 81(3) TFEU);
  - The establishment of minimum rules concerning "other" (i.e not expressly mentioned in this article) aspects of criminal procedure (Article 82(2) (d) TFEU);
  - The identification of areas (these are areas which are not expressly mentioned in Article 83(1) TFEU) of serious crime for which the establishment of minimum rules is needed;
  - The establishment of a European Public Prosecutor's Office (Article 86(1) TFEU);
  - Operational co-operation between national law enforcement authorities (Article 87(3) TFEU) and the limitations under which such authorities may operate in the territory of another Member State (Article 89 TFEU).

Unanimity is required in the European Council in respect of any extension of the mandate of the European Public Prosecutor's Office (Article 86(4) TFEU).

In the areas where unanimity applies the EP is either consulted or required to give its consent.

The ECJ has jurisdiction over all measures relating to the creation of the area of FSJ, i.e over the whole area of FSJ. Pre-ToL jurisdictional restrictions have been removed. Additionally, under Article 263 TFEU, the ECJ has jurisdiction to review the legality of Council decisions adopted under the CFSP imposing sanctions on natural or legal persons. However, in the area of police and judicial co-operation in criminal matters, the pre-ToL legislation remains in force for a period of 5 years following the entry into force of the ToL unless repealed, amended or annulled mean-while (Article 10 of Protocol 36 on "Transitional Provisions" attached to the Treaties). In parallel, during the 5 year period following the entry into force of the ToL, the Commission will have no power to bring proceedings against a Member State under Article 258 TFEU in respect of breaches of such legislation. Further, Article 276 TFEU excludes jurisdiction of the ECJ to review the validity or proportionality of operations carried out by the police or other law enforcement agencies of a Member State, or the exercise of responsibilities incumbent of law and order and the safeguarding of internal security. This seems obvious given that the ECJ has never had jurisdic-tion to review internal situations. This restriction, however, does not prevent the ECJ from ruling on the validity of certain acts of national authorities in the light of EU law and on the interpret-ation of the relevant EU acts.

The extension of judicial control over the whole of the area of FSJ, in particular in respect of police and judicial co-operation in criminal matters (subject to the above mentioned exceptions), is essential to ensure the adequate protection of the human rights of the alleged offenders and the alleged victims. It is to be noted that a new urgent preliminary ruling procedure applies to extremely urgent cases relating to the area of FSJ. One type of which is expressly mentioned in

Article 267(4) TFEU which requires that the ECJ acts with the minimum of delay in a situation where a case pending before a referring court or tribunal of a Member State concerns a person in custody or deprived of liberty and the answer to the question raised in the referral will be decisive as to the assessment of that person's legal situation (see Chapter 10.2.1).

Under the ToL, national parliaments have been assigned an important role in the area of FSJ. Under Article 7(2) of Protocol 2 attached to the ToL they may use the "orange and yellow cards" procedure to ensure that a legislative proposal concerning the area of FSJ respects the principle of subsidiarity (see Chapter 4.4.1.2.2). Under Article 70 TFEU the national parliaments are to be informed of the results of evaluation of the implementation of measures adopted in the area of FSJ, in particular, of results of evaluation of the implementation of measures aimed at facilitating full application of the principle of mutual recognition in respect of judicial decisions and in respect of the activities of a standing committee to be established under Article 71 for the purpose of ensuring operational co-operation on internal security of the EU (Article 71 TFEU). National parliaments have also their input in the control (Article 88(2) TFEU) and evaluation of activities of Europol (Article 85(1) TFEU).

It is submitted that the application of the "EU method" to the area of FSJ will result in a higher degree of efficiency, legal certainty, accountability and democratic control being exercised by the EP and national parliaments.

2.4.1 Opt-out possibilities and other special arrangements applicable to the area of FSJ

The ToL has not eliminated the differing participation of the Member States in measures relating to the area of FSJ. On the one hand, it allows opt-out possibilities and, on the other, facilitates "enhanced co-operation" (see Chapter 4.7).

The pre-ToL opt-outs are respected and new ones have been granted to the UK, Ireland and Denmark. Under Protocol 21 attached to the Treaties "On the Position of the United Kingdom and Ireland in respect of the Area of Freedom, Security and Justice", the opt-out possibilities apply to the entire area of FSJ. Protocol 22 gives the same right to Denmark. As a result, each of the UK, Ireland and Denmark is entitled to decide which pieces of legislation relating to the area of FSJ it wishes to adopt on a case-by-case basis. Those three Member States may decide to opt-in during the decision-making stage or later when the measure has already been adopted. Protocol 21 details the consequences of non-participation of the UK and Ireland (the same applies to Denmark under Protocol 22) in the amendment of measures in the actual adoption of which either of the UK, Ireland and Denmark has decided to participate, and therefore is bound by the measure. Under Article 4a of Protocol 21 if the Council determines that non-participation by the UK and Ireland (this also applies to Denmark) makes the existing measure "inoperable", it may, by QMV, urge those Member States to indicate their desire to participate within two months. If the invitation to participate is not accepted by each of the UK, Ireland, or Denmark, after the expiry of that period or at the entry into force of the amending measure, whichever is later, the measure will cease to be binding for a non-participating Member State. Under Article 4a(3) of Protocol 21 the Council may, by QMV, decide that the non-participating Member State, bears the "direct financial consequences . . . necessarily and unavoidably incurred" resulting from the cessation of its participation in the existing measure. This solution, on the one hand, puts pressure on a non-participating State to participate in a measure, although that State cannot be forced to participate, but on the other, ensures that participating Member States can move forward by ejecting a non-participating Member State from the existing measure. Additionally, a non-participating Member State may be required to pay costs which are necessarily and unavoidably incurred as a direct consequence of its cessation of participation.

The opt-out possibilities from the Schengen system for the UK, Ireland and Denmark have been amended to match those contained in Protocol 21 for the UK and Ireland and Protocol 22 for Denmark. As a result, these Member States have complete freedom to decide whether to participate in the adoption of a new measure and in the amendment of a measure in which they have participated. The consequences of non-participation in the amendment of an existing measure are the same as under Protocol 21 for the UK and Ireland and Protocol 22 for Denmark.

Protocol 19 "On the Schengen Acquis Integrated into the Framework of the EU" also deals with the position of States which participate in the Schengen acquis but which are not Member States of the EU (see section 2.4.4.2). Those countries, at the time of writing, are: Iceland, Norway and Switzerland. They can participate in Council meetings when it deals with Schengen items and express their views on them but have no voting rights if the Council decides to proceed to formal adoption of proposed measures. They are bound by such measures.

2.4.2   The definition of the area of FSJ

The term "area" is flexible enough to encompass the following policies: asylum, immigration, border controls, judicial co-operation in civil matters, and judicial and police co-operation in criminal matters.

There is no definition of the concepts of "freedom", "security" and "justice". With regard to "freedom" Article 3(2) TEU makes reference to freedom of movement of persons thus ensuring that EU citizens are able to move across borders within the area without being subject to border controls. Further, paragraph 6 of the 1998 Vienna Action Plan, which was the first programme document adopted by the Council with a view to creating the area of FSJ, specifies that "freedom" means more than freedom of movement, it includes "freedom to live in a law-abiding environment in the knowledge that public authorities are using everything in their individual and collective power (nationally, at the level of the Union and beyond,) to combat and contain those who seek to deny or abuse that freedom" ([1999] OJ C19/1). Accordingly, the concept of freedom is linked to the concept of "security" in that it includes freedom from threats posed by criminals. It can be argued that the term "freedom" implicitly includes all freedoms which have been conferred on EU citizens, e.g. the freedom to work in a host Member State, the freedom to provide services, and the freedom to establish a business in a host Member State.

The concept of "security" has similar meaning as under national law. It means that the EU shall ensure that EU citizens enjoy a high level of internal security, i.e. freedom from crime. However, Article 72 TFEU assigns to the Member States the main responsibility for the maintenance of law and order and safeguarding of internal security and specifies that "national security remains the sole responsibility of each Member State". As a result, any action at EU level will be complementary and subject to the principle of subsidiarity.

The concept of "justice" was referred to in the Conclusions of the Tampere Presidency as aiming at ensuring that EU citizens "are not discouraged or prevented from exercising their rights"[71] by divergences and differences between national justice systems. The "justice" dimension of the area of FSJ is based on judicial co-operation between Member States. In order to remove

---

71.   Bull EU, 10-1999, para 28.

obstacles resulting from differences in national justice systems, the EU must ensure that either on the basis of the principle of mutual recognition or by means of harmonising legislation, judgments and other similar decisions in civil and criminal matters given in one Member State are recognised in another Member State and that EU citizens have access to justice in respect of matters with a cross-border dimension.

2.4.3 EU programmes implementing measures aimed at the creation of the area of FSJ

The European Tampere Council (October 1999) set an ambitious agenda for the creation of the area of FSJ. It adopted a five-year programme, called the Tampere Programme, defining the priority areas, specific objectives and a timetable for implementing these objectives. The Council set a "scoreboard" by which progress in these priority areas was to be assessed. In fact the "scoreboard" was regularly updated to monitor implementation of the relevant measures. The Tampere Programme expired in June 2004.[72] Subsequent programmes have been based on the principles established by the Tampere programme.

For 2004–09 The Hague Programme was agreed by the European Hague Council in November 2004. The Commission was given one year to prepare proposals for concrete actions and a timetable for their adoption and implementation. On 10 May 2005 the Commission submitted its Five Year Action Plan for Freedom Justice and Security.[73] It identified 10 key areas for priority action and made concrete proposals for action, with a timetable for their adoption and implementation.[74]

The Hague programme expired in 2010 and was replaced by the Stockholm programme, adopted by the European Council in December 2009. The Stockholm programme contains 170 initiatives to be translated into concrete proposals, which if adopted, should be implemented by the end of 2014. The Commission has prepared 10 proposals which cover all aspects of the area of FSJ, i.e. from proposals on fighting cybercrime, border control, and asylum, to proposals concerning the choice of law in divorce proceedings for a couple with differing nationalities.[75]

2.4.4 The Schengen acquis

Under Protocol 19 attached to the Treaties the Schengen acquis is integrated into the framework of the EU. Apart from opt-out possibilities granted to the UK, Ireland and Denmark and special arrangements for non-EU States participating in the Schengen system, the Schengen acquis applies to all Member States. There are no possibilities for opt-outs by candidate States when they join the EU.

---

72. For the assessment of the Tampere Programme by the Commission see: COM(2004) 4002 final.
73. See http://ec.europa.eu/justice_home/news/information_dossiers/the_hague_priorities/index_en.htm (accessed 10/12/2007).
74. For an assessment of the Hague programme see: Communication from the Commission to the Council, the European Parliament, the European Economic and Social Committee and the Committee of the Regions – Justice, freedom and security in Europe since 2005: an evaluation of The Hague programme and action plan {SEC(2009) 765 final} {SEC(2009) 766 final} {SEC(2009) 767 final}
75. See MEMO/10/139.

2.4.4.1   A brief history of the Schengen system

An agreement between France and Germany in July 1984 in Saarbrücken on the elimination of frontier controls between the two countries, which was intended as a way of strengthening Franco-German relations, gave birth to the Schengen system. The Benelux countries had already abolished border checks for their nationals. They decided to join the Franco-German project. It resulted in the adoption of the Schengen I Agreement on the gradual abolition of checks at common borders, which was signed on 14 June 1985, between the Benelux countries and France and Germany in Schengen, a small town in Luxembourg. It provided that border controls should be abolished on 1 January 1990 between territories of the Contracting Parties. In order to achieve this objective, working groups were established to draw up necessary measures on the relaxation of border controls such as the introduction of mixed checks at the borders, visual checks on EU nationals (based on a system whereby EU nationals might place a green sticker in the front window of their cars) and co-ordination of measures strengthening the control of external borders to keep out undesirables by harmonising visa controls, asylum and deportation policies. Issues relevant to internal security such as harmonisation of firearms and ammunition laws, police co-operation in combating illegal trading in drugs and serious international crimes were also addressed. The above work culminated in the adoption of the Schengen Implementing Convention on 19 June 1990 (Schengen II) between the same five Contracting States. This Convention entered into force on 26 March 1995.

In the relationship between the Schengen group and the EC, the Commission had the status of observer at the Schengen meetings. The Schengen system was subordinated to EC law by means of the compatibility requirement established in Article 134 of Schengen II, which stated that the Schengen provisions should apply only if they were compatible with EC law. For that reason it was quite easy to incorporate the Schengen system into the EC Treaty. The protocol attached to the ToA provided for the incorporation of the Schengen II agreement into the EU's legal framework. In order to do this, the Council of the European Union, which took over from the Executive Committee set up under the Schengen Agreement, adopted a number of decisions. On 1 May 1999 it established a procedure incorporating the Schengen Secretariat into the General Secretariat of the Council.[76] The elements of Schengen II which needed to be incorporated into the EC Treaty (the Schengen acquis) were defined by a Council decision adopted on 20 May 1999.[77]

Member States that joined the EU after 1 May 2004 are bound by the Schengen acquis, but certain provisions will apply to them only after abolition of border controls at their borders adjacent to States participating in the Schengen system. Such border controls will be abolished when a Member State has passed the preparedness test in respect of four areas: air borders, visas, police co-operation and personal data protection. Experts from the EU will assess the level of preparedness by means of questionnaires and visits to selected institutions and places of the country of assessment.

The incorporation of the Schengen system into the framework of the EU means that all principles of EC law are applicable to the Schengen acquis and that EU institutions are supervising its proper implementation.

---

76.   [1999] OJ L119/49.
77.   [1999] OJ L176/1.

2.4.4.2   Membership of the Schengen area

At the time of writing 25 States fully apply the Schengen acquis: 22 EU countries (Austria, Belgium, the Czech Republic, Denmark, Estonia, Finland, France, Germany, Greece, Hungary, Italy, Latvia, Lithuania, Luxembourg, Malta, Netherlands, Poland, Portugal, Slovakia, Slovenia, Spain, Sweden), and 3 non-EU countries: Norway, Iceland and Switzerland. Three Member States: Bulgaria, Cyprus and Romania have not yet met the criteria for participating although some Schengen acquis apply to them, e.g. they participate in the area of police and judicial cooperation and of external border controls. The UK and Ireland have decided to maintain border controls with other EU countries and are therefore outside the Schengen area. In March 1999 the UK asked to participate in some aspects of Schengen, namely police and legal co-operation in criminal matters, the fight against drugs and the Shengen Information System (see below). The Commission gave a favourable opinion on 21 July 1999 and the Council approved on 29 May 2000.[78] Ireland, because of the existence of a Common Travel Area with no border controls between Ireland and the UK, was unable to implement the Schengen Agreement without terminating the existing agreement with the UK. Ireland asked in June 2000 to participate in the same aspects of Schengen as the UK. The request was approved by the Council in 2002.[79]

2.4.4.3   The main features of the Schengen II agreement

The main features of the Schengen II agreement are:

A.   It creates a territory without internal borders. Between participating countries internal border posts have been closed (and often demolished). Inside the Schengen territory there are no road or rail identity checks. However, when travelling by air, passports or national ID cards must usually be shown. This is not required under the Schengen system but constitutes an international air security measure. There are passport checks between two EU Member States when one of them is a non-Schengen Member State, for example, between the UK and France. As to customs checks between Members of the EU, there are none, but between two Schengen Member States, one of which is not a Member State of the EU, customs controls remain;

B.   It introduces tight controls on non-EU nationals entering the Schengen territory. These are aimed at eliminating illegal immigration and combating crime. In this respect common rules for crossing external borders and uniform rules and procedures for controls have been adopted by the participating Member States, including harmonisation of rules regarding the conditions of entry and visas for non-EU nationals. A Community Code on the rules governing the movement of persons across borders has been adopted. Its latest version, at the time of writing, is contained in Regulation 810/2009[80] which provides an opportunity for a third country national to challenge the refusal of a visa and which establishes common fees for a visa. Its Articles 13, 14 and 15 set out numerous conditions to be satisfied by non-EU nationals when they are entering the Schengen area.

---

78.   [2000] OJ L131/43.
79.   [2002] OJ L 64/20.
80.   [2009] OJ L243/1. The regulation entered into force in April 2010.

A Shengen visa covers all Schengen territory. If non-EU nationals are considered to be unlawfully in one Schengen country, they are deemed to be illegally in all and will be expelled from Schengen territory;

C.   It strengthens the co-operation between police (including the rights of cross-border surveillance and hot pursuit), immigration, customs and judicial authorities of the participating Member States;

D.   It provides for common rules for asylum seekers;[81]

E.   It provides for separation in air terminals and ports of people travelling within the Schengen area from those arriving from elsewhere;

F.   It sets up a system, known as the Schengen Information System. This is referred to as SIS II. The previous system SIS I was replaced by SIS II by Regulation 1987/2006[82] because SIS I was designed to accommodate a maximum of 18 Member States and with the enlargement of the EU it needed a major overhaul. SIS II provides for a computerised exchange of information. SIS II allows the placing of alerts concerning persons (wanted, missing, foreign nationals banned from entering the EU and persons to be discreetly monitored by the relevant national authorities) together with a request that a specific action be taken if the person is found, and concerning lost and stolen property. The Schengen Member States supply/receive information through national networks (N-SIS II) which are connected online with a central system (C-SIS II), located in Strasbourg. C-SIS II is a hub which provides technical support for the system, that is, it works as an intermediary in the exchange of information.

Although the system is European, the information is national as each participating Member State decides what information it wishes to enter into the alert database.

Within SIS II, N-SIS II can exchange information directly with another N-SIS II without having to go through C-SIS II and can obtain additional or supplementary information to that provided by C-SIS II via the SIRENE (Supplementary Information Request at the National Entries) system, i.e. a human interface of SIS II. The service is available 24 hours a day, seven days a week. In each Schengen Member State there is a SIRENE – a point of contact in respect of SIS II alerts and post-hit procedure (that is, ensuring that appropriate action is taken) operated by staff who receive and transmit additional data, enforce "alerts" and assist SIS II users. The SIRENE offices are connected with each other via SISNET, a sophisticated telecommunication system which ensures that the exchanged information is adequately protected.

Requests for information through SIS II are verified and legally validated.

---

81.   The most important provisions relating to asylum are, inter alia, contained in Regulation 343/2003 (also known as Dublin II regulation) establishing the criteria and mechanisms for determining the Member State responsible for examining an asylum application lodged in one of the Member States by a third-country national ([2003] L222/3–23); Directive 2003/9 setting minimum reception conditions for asylum seekers ([2003] L31/18–25); Directive 2004/83 giving the definition of a refugee or person who may obtain subsidiary protection ([2004] L304/12–23); Directive 2005/85 on minimum standards on procedures for granting and withdrawing refugee status ([2005] L326/3–33); Regulation 2725/2000 on Eurodac, a Europe-wide fingerprint database for asylum seekers ([2000] L316/1–10) and Regulation 407/2002 implementing Eurodac ([2002] OJ L62/1–5).

82.   [2006] OJ L381/4.

Obviously, the electronic data exchange system is the most controversial aspect of the Schengen system as it raises issues relating to data protection and correctness of information. To answer these concerns safeguards have been put in place. First, the Schengen Implementing Convention contains very strict rules as to the categories of alerts that can be entered, the categories of persons who can access SIS II, the purpose for which personal data may be collected and the content of personal data. Second, monitoring of the proper application of the Convention's rules has been entrusted to an independent body, the Joint Supervisory Authority for the Schengen Information System (JSA), made up of two representatives of each Schengen Member State who are members of national bodies that are in charge of the protection of personal data. The JSA may visit sites and have access to all relevant documents.[83]

In respect of immigration, visas, asylum and checks at external borders many legislative acts have been adopted at EU level. It is outside the scope of this book to examine each of them. However, it must be noted that under the ToL the Member States have all necessary legal tools to develop a common asylum (Article 78(2) TFEU) and immigration policy (Article 79 TFEU) in accordance with the principle of solidarity (Article 89 TFEU).

2.4.5 Judicial co-operation in civil matters having cross-border implications

Judicial co-operation in civil matters is based on the principle of mutual recognition. Its objectives are listed in Article 81(2) TFEU. Some of them have already been achieved:

- The free movement of judgments in civil and commercial matters under Brussels I Regulation;[84]

- The free movement of orders on parental responsibility including orders concerning the return of the child in cases of child abduction within the EU under Brussels II Regulation;[85]

- The free movement of judgments, court settlements and authentic instruments on uncontested claims under Regulation 805/2004;[86]

- The free movement of insolvency orders under Regulation 1346/2000;[87]

- The possibility of a court in one Member State requesting the taking of evidence in civil and commercial matters by the competent court in another Member State under Directive 1206/2001.[88]

Effective access to justice has been improved under Directive 2003/8/EC[89] which establishes minimum common rules relating to legal aid for cross-border disputes and Directive 2004/80[90] relating

---

83. See: Schengen Information System SIS, http://www.europarl.europa.eu/comparl/libe/elsj/zoom_in/25_en.htm (accessed 10/12/07).
84. Regulation 44/2001 [2001] OJ L12/1.
85. Regulation 2201/2003 [2003] OJ L338/1.
86. [2004] OJ L143/15–39.
87. [2000] OJ L160/1.
88. [2001] OJ L174/1–24.
89. [2003] OJ L26/41–47.
90. [2004] OJ L261/15.

to compensation for crime victims which complements Framework Decision 2001/220/JHA on the Standing of the Victim in Criminal Proceedings.[91] Indeed for victims of crime it is vital that not only the offender is punished but also that they can obtain compensation for their suffering. The basic rule is that a victim should sue the offender for compensation. The minimum standard in exercising this right is provided for in the Decision on the Standing of the Victim in Criminal Proceedings.[92] The Decision imposes an obligation on a Member State to ensure that victims of crime can obtain a decision on compensation in the course of criminal proceedings and that the offender provides adequate compensation. However, it may occur that the offender has not been identified, or the offender has no assets or income. In such circumstances the Directive Relating to Compensation to Crime Victims[93] is of assistance. It sets up a system of co-operation among Member States to facilitate access to compensation. Under the Directive a Member State is obliged to set up a national scheme under which victims can obtain fair, easily accessible and appropriate compensation. A victim of crime in a cross-border situation will be compensated in accordance with the national rules of the Member State where compensation is sought.

Direct co-operation between judicial authorities of the Member States in civil and commercial matters has been established under Decision 2001/470/EC[94] as amended by Decision No 568/2009/EC[95] which created the European judicial network. It consists of contact points established in each Member State through which judicial authorities of Member States are in direct contact with each other. These contact points also provide the legal or practical information necessary to help authorities concerned to prepare an effective request for judicial co-operation.

Under the ToL the ordinary legislative procedure is used in the adoption of measures relating to civil and commercial matters with cross-border implications. However, in respect of measures concerning family law the Council is required to adopt acts by unanimity after consulting the EP (Article 81(3) TFEU). However, a passerelle clause under Article 81(3) TFEU allows the Council to switch to the ordinary legislative procedure for adoption of measures in aspects of family law to be determined by the Council. A decision by the Council to this effect must be notified to national parliaments. If none oppose it within 6 months of the date of notification, the Council may adopt the decision.

2.4.6 Co-operation between the judicial authorities of the Member States in criminal matters

The Tampere European Council (October 1999) endorsed the principle of the mutual recognition of judicial decisions as the foundation of judicial co-operation in both civil and criminal matters. The principle involves a great amount of trust on the part of one Member State in the judicial system of another. Under this principle, courts/relevant authorities in one Member State will recognise a judgment or other similar decision delivered in another Member State in conformity with the legislation of that other Member State.

The difference between mutual recognition and harmonisation is that:

---

91. [2001] OJ L82/1.
92. [2001] OJ L82/1.
93. [2004] OJ L261/15.
94. [2001] OJ L174/25–31.
95. [2009] OJ L168/35–40.

- Mutual recognition is a regulatory technique aimed at achieving an objective sought at EU level without the need to harmonise Member States' legislation, and thus national law and its peculiarities are maintained. It entails that a Member State will recognise a judgment, or other similar instrument delivered by the relevant authorities of another Member State, in accordance with the laws and regulations of that Member State;

- Harmonisation occurs when the same laws are adopted in all Member States. EU harmonising measures are regulations, directives and decisions. With regard to a regulation, it becomes part of national law at the date specified in that regulation. Consequently pre-existing national legislation which is incompatible with the regulation must be repealed. As to a directive, a Member State is required to achieve the objective it seeks to achieve within the time limit specified in the directive. If this objective has already been achieved, there is no need to legislate; otherwise a Member State must take all necessary measures, for example, it must enact national legislation, to comply with the relevant directive.

In respect of criminal law, taking account of the differences between the legal traditions and systems of the Member States, they are prepared to accept harmonising measures consisting of establishing common minimum standards. Thus, they do not wish to harmonise substantive/procedural criminal law beyond the degree required for successful mutual recognition of judgments and decisions delivered by the relevant authorities of other Member States. Article 82 TFEU reflects this reality. It deals with harmonisation of procedural criminal law. It states that any harmonising measure will be adopted "to the extent necessary to facilitate mutual recognition of judgments and judicial decisions and judicial co-operation in criminal matters having a cross-border dimension" and must take account of differences between legal traditions and criminal justice systems of the Member States. Such measures are to be adopted in accordance with the ordinary legislative procedure in respect of the following aspects of criminal procedure:

- Mutual admissibility of evidence;

- The rights of individuals in criminal procedure;

- The rights of victims of crime;

- Other aspects of criminal procedure which the Council may identify by a decision adopted by unanimity after obtaining consent from the EP.

An emergency brake procedure is provided in Article 82(3) TFEU in that if a Member State considers that a draft measure would affect fundamental aspects of its criminal justice system it may request that the draft measure be referred to the European Council. The ordinary legislative procedure is suspended and the European Council, within four months of this suspension, acting by consensus, may either refer the draft back to the Council, in which case the suspension is terminated and the Council may proceed with the adoption of the measure, or do nothing, or refer the draft back to the Commission, in which cases the draft is deemed not to be adopted. When a draft proposal is referred to the European Council, other States than the State that applied the brake, at least nine of them, may establish enhanced co-operation on the basis of the draft directive concerned during the suspension period or subsequently if the draft measure was not adopted by the Council. They may proceed after notifying the EP, the Council and the Commission. It is important to note that Article 82(2) TFEU states that the adoption of the minimum rules should not prevent Member States from maintaining or introducing a higher level of protection for individuals than that provided by the minimum rules.

At the time of writing the principle of mutual recognition of decisions in criminal matters has been implemented, inter alia, through:

■ The adoption of a Framework Decision on the European Arrest Warrant and the Surrender Procedures between Member States[96] aimed at shortening extradition procedures;

■ The adoption of a Framework Decision on the Execution in the European Union of Orders Freezing Property or Evidence;[97]

■ The adoption of Framework Decision 2008/978/JHA[98] on the European evidence warrant for the purpose of obtaining objects, documents and data for use in proceedings in criminal matters. The warrant allows prosecutors in EU Member States to collect and transfer evidence in cross-border cases.

Article 83 TFEU concerns harmonisation of substantive criminal law. Article 83(1) TFEU provides that the EP and the Council may, by means of directives adopted in accordance with the ordinary legislative procedure, establish minimum rules concerning the definition of criminal offences and the sanctions to be imposed for such offences. Only the most serious crimes with a cross-border dimension will be subject to EU legislation. These are listed in Article 83 TFEU as follows:

■ Terrorism;

■ Trafficking in human beings and sexual exploitation of women and children;

■ Illicit drug trafficking;

■ Illicit arms trafficking;

■ Money laundering;

■ Corruption;

■ Counterfeiting of means of payment;

■ Computer crime;

■ Organised crime.

The Council may, on the basis of a decision adopted by unanimity after obtaining consent from the EP, add to the list of crimes in the light of developments in crime.

Article 83(2) TFEU specifies an alternative basis for the adoption of harmonising measures which define criminal offences and sanctions where this is necessary to "ensure the effective implementation of Union policy in an area which has been subject to harmonising measures". The procedure to be used will be the same as that used for the adoption of the harmonising measure in question, i.e. if a harmonising measure was adopted under the ordinary legislative procedure, then a measure adopted under Article 83(2) TFEU, i.e. defining a criminal offence and sanctions, must also be adopted in accordance with the ordinary legislative procedure. Article 83(2) raises a question whether it constitutes the lex specialis on the basis of which the EU will be

---

96.   [2002] OJ L190/1.
97.   [2003] OJ L196/45.
98.   [2008] L350/72–92. The Decision will enter into force on 19 January 2011.

allowed to establish minimum rules relating to criminal offences in areas outside Title IV or whether that article applies only to Title IV. This matter is important for Member States which have secured for themselves opt-out possibilities from measures relating to the area of FSJ. So far the EU has established its competence to adopt rules relating to criminal offences in respect of environmental matters.[99]

An emergency brake is provided for in Article 83(3) TFEU in respect of measures to be adopted under Article 82(1) and 82(2) TFEU. However, when a Member State operates the emergency brake the remaining Member States, at least nine of them, may establish enhanced co-operation in respect of that measure under the same conditions as those specified in Article 82(3) TFEU (see above).

Prior to the entry into force of the ToL the Council adopted a number of framework decisions, joint actions and directives in order to approximate the definitions of certain serious offences such as terrorism, drug trafficking, counterfeiting the euro, money laundering, human trafficking, sexual exploitation of children and corruption in the private sector.

2.4.7   The European Prosecutors Co-operation (Eurojust)

This is a permanent body created in 2002 in order to reinforce the fight against serious crime. Eurojust is made up of 27 members (one from each Member State) who are experienced prosecutors, judges or police officers (The College of Eurojust). The objective of Eurojust is to facilitate the optimal co-ordination of actions for investigations and prosecutions regarding serious cross-border and organised crime, in particular by facilitating the execution of international mutual assistance requests and the implementation of extradition requests. Eurojust organises meetings between investigators and prosecutors from different Member States dealing with a particular crime, or with a specific type of criminality. It may also ask a Member State to start investigation or prosecution in respect of specific events. Eurojust actively co-operates with Europol and the European Judicial Network. Article 85 TFEU strengthens the role of Eurojust and assigns to it specific tasks such as:

"(a)   the initiation of criminal investigations, as well as proposing the initiation of prosecutions conducted by competent national authorities, particularly those relating to offences against the financial interests of the Union;

(b)   the coordination of investigations and prosecutions referred to in point (a);

(c)   the strengthening of judicial cooperation, including by resolution of conflicts of jurisdiction and by close cooperation with the European Judicial Network".

However, Eurojust has no power to carry out acts of judicial procedure when it initiates criminal investigations. Article 85(2) specifies that those acts should be carried out by the competent national officials.

2.4.8   The European Public Prosecutor's Office (EPP)

Article 86 TFEU provides for the possibility for the establishment of a European Public Prosecutor's Office responsible for investigating and prosecuting perpetrators of and accomplices in

---

99.   See Case C-176/03 *Commission v Council* [2005] ECR I-7879 and Case C-440/05 *Commission v Council* [2007] ECR I-9097.

offences against the financial interests of the EU. It remains to be seen whether the Council will consider it necessary to establish the EPP.

2.4.9   The Standing Committee on Internal Security (COSI)

Article 71 TFEU provides for the establishment of a standing committee on internal security. The abbreviation chosen for this new committee is COSI. COSI will be made up of representatives of the Member States which will decide whether to have one representative for all aspects of work of COSI or different representatives dealing with specific areas of the work of COSI. Its main task will be to facilitate, promote and strengthen the co-ordination of operational actions between Member States concerning internal security. It will regularly report to the Council which will, in turn, inform the EP and national parliaments of its activities. It will evaluate the efficiency of operational co-operation in order to identify any shortcomings and adopt recommendations to deal with them. If appropriate, COSI may involve other agencies and bodies, e.g. Eurojust, Europol, Frontex, in its work. Together with the Political and Security Committee (PSC), it will assist the Council in the implementation of the "solidarity clause" contained in Article 222 TFEU (see Chapter 8.3.3.1), i.e. to provide help and assistance if a Member State is the object of a terrorist attack or a victim of natural or man-made disaster.

2.4.10   The European Judicial Network (EJN)

This network was created in 1998 to improve judicial assistance, in particular in respect of serious crime. It is a decentralised network of contact points that advises and assists judicial authorities in criminal matters. The network comprises:

- The central authorities in each Member State responsible for international judicial co-operation; and

- One or more contact points, that is, persons appointed by the central authorities to facilitate judicial co-operation between Member States. The contact points are intermediaries providing legal and practical information, first to central authorities in their own Member State, second, to contact points in other Member States and third, to the local judicial authorities to help them to prepare a request for judicial co-operation in respect of serious crime or in respect of improving co-operation in general. The Commission is also a contact point for areas within its competence.

2.4.11   Police co-operation

Article 87 TFEU provides that common action in the field of police co-operation should include operational co-operation between police, customs and other specialised law enforcement authorities of the Member States to prevent, detect and investigate criminal offences, and to provide for exchange of information, joint training of police forces, and so on.

Police co-operation may take place between national police authorities and through the European Police Office (Europol), which was established in 1992 to deal with Europe-wide criminal investigations. It became fully operational on 1 July 1999. Europol has its headquarters in The Hague and its staff includes representatives of national law enforcement agencies (police, customs, immigration services, and so on). It has no executive powers and thus its officials are not entitled to conduct investigations or to arrest suspects. On 1 January 2010 Europol became an agency of the EU. As a result Article 88(2) TFEU became obsolete. Under this article the EP and the Council, acting in accordance with the ordinary legislative procedure, are empowered to determine the structure, operation and functioning of Europol. Decision 2009/371/JHA of 6 April 2009[100] which entered into force on 1 January 2010 deals comprehensively with the constitution and functions of Europol.

Europol is in charge of improving and developing co-operation between police forces in the following ways:

- By facilitating the exchange of information between national police forces;

- By providing expertise and technical support for investigations and operations carried out within the EU;

- By preparing intelligence analysis on the basis of information and intelligence provided by the Member States.

Europol's priorities are to co-ordinate Member States' actions against international money laundering, drug smuggling, illegal imports of nuclear materials, imports of stolen vehicles, illegal immigration networks, trafficking of human beings, sexual exploitation of children, money counterfeiting and terrorism. Europol's computer system (TECS) facilitates exchanges of information on persons suspected of criminal activities.

Article 89 TFEU provides for the possibility of police forces of one Member State operating in the territory of another Member State. Under Article 89 TFEU the conditions and limitation of the exercise of this possibility will be established by the Council, acting by unanimity after consulting the EP.

In the context of police co-operation the European Police College (CEPOL) must be mentioned. It is a police academy training senior and middle-rank police officers from the Member States. The emphasis is on the fight against cross-border and organised crime. CEPOL was set up in 2001 and is based at Bramshill, United Kingdom.

In respect of illegal drugs the European Monitoring Centre for Drugs and Drug Addiction (EMCDDA) was set up in February 1993. It collects, examines and compares data in this area and co-operates with European and international bodies. It has its own computer network, the European Information Network on Drugs and Drug Addiction (REITOX).

2.5   Specific objective: the creation of the internal market

Article 3(3) TEU states that the Union shall establish the internal market. It appears that under the ToL the emphasis is no longer merely on the establishment of the internal market but upon the observance of guidelines as to how that market should develop. These guidelines, being at the same time constraints, require that the internal market should ensure sustainable development of the EU, should not erode the European social model and while ensuring the existence of a highly competitive market economy should respond to environmental challenges by ensuring a high level of protection and improvement of the quality of the environment and should promote scientific and technological advances.

---

100.   [2009] OJ L121/37.

Non-economic objectives are to be pursued within the framework of the internal market such as:

- Promotion of scientific and technological advance;

- Combating of social exclusion and discrimination;

- Promotion of social justice and protection, equality between women and men, solidarity between generations and protection of the rights of the child;

- Promotion of economic, social and territorial cohesion, and solidarity among Member States;

- The respecting of the cultural and linguistic diversity of Europe and the safeguarding and developing of Europe's cultural heritage.

It is to be noted that although the objective to ensure "free and undisturbed competition" in the internal market has ceased to be an objective of the EU, this has no impact on EU competition policy. First, the importance of maintaining fair and undisturbed competition has been confirmed in Protocol 27 on the Internal Market and Competition attached to the Treaties and, second, the removal of this objective has been explained on the ground that free and fair competition is not an objective in itself but constitutes a means to an end, that is, the creation of the internal market (Chapter 26.1).

2.6   Specific objective: the establishment of Economic and Monetary Union (EMU)

Article 3(4) TEU provides that the EU shall establish "an economic and monetary union whose currency is the Euro".

One of the most controversial issues of European integration is certainly the creation of an economic and monetary union. The Treaty of Maastricht introduced Title VI containing provisions on the economic and monetary policy of the Union. Further a number of Protocols were attached to it introducing detailed provisions, including special arrangements (the so-called "opt-outs") for the UK and Denmark regarding their participation or not in the final stage of EMU, i.e. the adoption of the euro as a national currency. Neither the ToA nor the ToN nor the ToL make any significant changes in respect of EMU. The ToL confirms the general principles under which EMU is required to operate but reinforces the power of EU institutions, in particular the Commission, in respect of economic policies of the Member States.

The application of Treaty provisions relating to EMU depends on

- whether a Member State is classified as being a Member State with a derogation (i.e. derogation from EMU). There are two categories of Member States with derogation:

  - Those which have not yet satisfied the necessary conditions for the adoption of the euro;
  - Those which have secured for themselves opt-out possibilities from EMU, i.e. the UK and Denmark.

  To them various provisions on economic and monetary policy do not apply: e.g. certain parts of the Council's broad guidelines on economic policies; coercive measures applicable to a Member State which runs an excessive budgetary deficit; objectives and tasks relating to the ESCB, rules concerning the euro and other matters mentioned in Article 139(2) TFEU.

- Whether a Member State has adopted the Euro. If so, the Treaties provisions on EMU are fully applicable to it.

Sweden is in a special situation as it has satisfied the convergence criteria and thus can join the Eurozone but as a result of a negative referendum decided not to adopt the euro as its currency. Sweden is required to comply with the EMU provisions in the Treaties unless they are specifically addressed to the Member States which have adopted the Euro.

At the time of writing, 16 Member States have adopted the euro as their national currency. Those Member States are no longer able to control important aspects of their economic policy, especially by setting interest rates or devaluing their currency. This is the main disadvantage of EMU. However, this must be considered in the light of the growing interdependence and internationalisation of national economies. Does any country actually have any real economic sovereignty left to exercise? On the one hand, interest rates depend on market forces; on the other, devaluation of a national currency is a temporary measure which "backlashes" by creating inflationary consequences which lead to pressure for higher wages and so undermines the competitiveness of national products.

2.7 Specific objective: the affirmation and promotion of the EU's values worldwide and the protection of EU citizens outside the EU

Article 3(5) TEU defines the objectives of the EU with regard to the wider world.

The EU will, throughout the world, promote the values upon which it is based and reinforce the protection of EU citizens while they are outside the EU. The ToL expressly confirms the commitment of the EU to the eradication of world poverty and the protection of human rights worldwide, in particular the rights of the child. The international action of the EU is to be carried out in accordance with international law, including the principles contained in the UN Charter.

AIDE-MÉMOIRE

Values on which the EU is founded

- Respect for human dignity;

- Freedom;

- Democracy;

- Equality;

- The rule of law;

- Respect for human rights, including the rights of persons belonging to minorities.

Under Article 7 TEU any breach or a risk of breach of EU values by a Member State may entail a warning for the offending State or a suspension of rights deriving from EU membership. Further, the adherence to EU values is a necessary condition for admission of new States to the EU.

Objectives of the EU

Objectives of the EU are listed in Article 3 TEU as follows:

- The overreaching objectives of the EU are the promotion of peace, the EU's values and of the well-being of its people.

- Specific objectives:

  A. The creation of the area of FSJ;
  B. The establishment of the internal market which is to pursue the following goals:

     - Achieving sustainable development of Europe based on balanced economic growth and price stability, a highly competitive social market economy, aiming at full employment and social progress, and a high level of protection and improvement of the quality of the environment;
     - The promotion of scientific and technological advance;
     - The combatting of social exclusion and discrimination;
     - The promotion of social justice and protection, equality between women and men, solidarity between generations and protection of the rights of the child;
     - The promotion of economic, social and territorial cohesion, and solidarity among Member States;
     - The respecting of the cultural and linguistic diversity of Europe and the safeguarding and developing of Europe's cultural heritage;

  C. The establishment of EMU. At the time of writing 16 Member States have adopted the euro as their national currency;
  D. Confirmation and promotion of EU values and interests worldwide and contribution to the protection of EU citizens outside the EU.

RECOMMENDED READING

Books

Berglund, M., *Cross Border Enforcement of Claims in the EU: History, Present Time and Future*, 2009, London: KLI

Williams, A., *The Ethos of Europe*, 2010, Cambridge: CUP

Articles

Bantekas, I., "The Principle of Mutual Recognition in EU Criminal Law", (2007) 32/2 ELRev, p 365

Chia, J., "Immigration and its Imperatives", (2009) 15 ELJ, p 683

Dawes, A. and Lynskey, O., "The Ever-longer Arm of EC law: The Extension of Community Competence into the Field of Criminal Law" (2008) 45 CMLRev, p 131

Iglesias Sánchez, S., "Free Movement of Third Country Nationals in the European Union? Main Features, Deficiencies and Challenges of the new Mobility Rights in the Area of Freedom, Security and Justice" (2009) 15 ELJ, p 791

Murphy, C., "Fundamental Rights and Security: The Difficult Position of the European Judiciary" (2010) 16 EPL, p 289

Tulibacka, M., "Europeanization of Civil Procedures: In Search of a Coherent Approach" (2009) 46 CMLRev, p 1527

Von Bogdandy, A., "Founding Principles of EU Law: A Theoretical and Doctrinal Sketch" (2010) 16 ELJ, p 95

3

MEMBERSHIP OF THE EU

CONTENTS

SUMMARY

1. Important rights and obligations for the EU and for the Member States derive from the membership of the EU. All Member States are equal in that they enjoy the same privileges and have to fulfil the same obligations vis-à-vis each other and vis-à-vis the EU. Under the principle of equality, the EU is required to respect the national identity of the Member States and the essential functions of each Member State, in particular those which are intended to ensure the territorial integrity of the State, the maintenance of law and order and the safeguarding of national security. Member States are required to co-operate sincerely with EU institutions and with each other and in the spirit of solidarity assist each other in extreme circumstances such as natural or man-made disasters, terrorist attacks and armed aggression.

2. Membership of the EU is conditional upon satisfying the conditions for admission which are set out in Article 49 TEU. Membership may be suspended when a Member State disregards the basic values on which the EU is founded and it may be terminated under Article 50 TEU when a Member State expresses its wish to withdraw from the EU. There are no provisions in the Treaties dealing with the loss of membership by expulsion. Under Public International Law the absence of an express provision means that the EU has no power to expel its members.

3. At the time of writing, 27 European States are members of the EU, three more States have the status of candidate States, i.e. States with whom accession negotiations have been commenced following a decision adopted by the Council, and there are six potential candidate States. Since the establishment of the Communities, there have been five rounds of enlargement of the EU. Each of them is analysed in this chapter; and the enlargement policy towards states which are official candidates is discussed.

3.1   Introduction: the principle of equality, sincere co-operation and solidarity

The ToL contains a new provision emphasising that the EU should respect the equality of Member States before the Treaties and their national identities (Article 4(2) TEU). The principle of equality means that in the EU all Member States are equal[101] in that they enjoy the same privileges and have to fulfil the same obligations vis-à-vis each other and vis-à-vis the EU. Unlike certain international organisations (for example, UNESCO), no special status is granted to any Member State of the EU.

Under the principle of equality, EU law applies to all Member States without discrimination. Any difference in treatment is based on objective considerations and proportionate to the objectives that the EU seeks to achieve. However, under EU law the principle of equality does not entail that each Member State has the same voting power. Under the ToL the principle normally applied in international intergovernmental organisations that each member has one vote is an exception. The vast majority of legislative acts are adopted by the Council acting by QMV, which is currently determined on the basis of "weight" given to each Member State and which from 2014 will be based on the double majority of Member States and population (see Chapter 6.3.6.2.2). However, this "inequality" is compensated by the fact that the Council, when it adopts EU legislation by QMV acts together with the EP, which is directly elected by EU citizens and therefore the democratic control of any such act is ensured.

The EU must respect the national identity of the Member States, including local and regional identity. It is also obliged to respect the essential functions of each Member State, in particular those which are intended to ensure the territorial integrity of the State, the maintenance of law and order and the safeguarding of national security. Article 4(2) TEU specifies that national security "remains the sole responsibility of each Member State".

Under Article 4(3) TEU, the Member States are required to sincerely co-operate with the EU and with each other. This duty is not new. It requires the Member States to take all appropriate measures, whether general or particular, to ensure fulfilment of their obligations arising out of the Treaties or resulting from the acts of the EU institutions and to refrain from taking any measure which could jeopardise the attainment of the EU's objectives. If a Member State fails to fulfil this duty the Commission may commence proceedings against it under Article 258 TFEU (see Chapter 15.2.2). An aspect of the duty of sincere co-operation (which must always have been implicit within that duty), requiring each Member State to assist others in carrying out tasks which flow from the Treaties, is specifically spelt out in Article 4(3) TEU.

The ToL expressly recognises the principle of solidarity. Article 222 TFEU imposes a duty on a Member State and on the EU to assist a Member State in a situation where it is a victim of a terrorist attack or of a natural or man-made disaster. Further, the principle of solidarity is emphasised in the area of energy. Under Article 122(1) TFEU, if severe difficulties arise in the supply of certain products, in particular in the area of energy, the Council may, on a proposal from the Commission, acting in the spirit of solidarity, adopt appropriate measures. Another dimension of the principle of solidarity is the "mutual defence clause" inserted in Article 42(7) TEU. It states that if one Member State is a victim of armed aggression on its territory the others

---

101.   In this respect it is interesting to note what Jean Monnet said: "I have always realised that equality is absolutely essential in relations between nations, as it is between people." J. Monnet, *Memoirs*, 1978, London: Collins, p 97.

are obliged to provide it with help and assistance "by all means in their power" but in accordance with Article 51 of the UN Charter and subject to their commitments deriving from membership of NATO. Article 42(7) TEU entails that EU members, even if not members of NATO, are obliged to provide aid and assistance to a victim State.

It is important to note that:

A. Article 198 TFEU allows some Member States (Denmark, France, The Netherlands and the United Kingdom) to associate their overseas countries and territories (OCT) with the EU. These OCT are listed in Annex II to the Treaties (for example, some of the UK's OCT are Anguilla, the British Virgin Islands, the Cayman Islands and the Falklands Islands). Part IV of the TFEU Treaty applies to OCT only.

B. With respect to dependencies of EU Member States, various arrangements have been made. For example:

   ▪ To Greenland (a dependency of Denmark), which left the Communities in 1985, obviously the Treaties do not apply. Residents of Greenland, being Danish nationals, are, nevertheless, citizens of the EU but have no right to vote in elections to the EP. Protocol 34 "On Special Arangments for Greenland" attached to the Treaties regulates the treatment in the EU of fisheries products originating in Greenland.

   ▪ The situation of the Channel Islands and the Isle of Man, which are UK Crown dependencies, is regulated by Protocol 3 to the 1973 UK Treaty of Accession, which provides that only Community rules on the Common Customs Area and the Common External Tariff are applicable to them.

C. If a non-EU State has concluded an association agreement with the EU, for example on the basis of Article 217 TFEU, it remains outside the EU and therefore cannot be considered as a Member State.

3.2 Specific procedures applicable to membership of the EU: admission, suspension and withdrawal procedures

Three specific procedures apply to the membership of the EU. They are: the admission procedure, the suspension procedure and the withdrawal procedure.

3.2.1 The admission procedure

The requirements for admission are both substantive and formal. The substantive requirements were defined by the Copenhagen European Council Summit in June 1993. The ToL refers to them in Article 49 TEU. The formal requirements were changed by the ToL in that under Article 49 TEU the EP and national parliaments are to be notified of any application for EU membership submitted by a candidate state.

3.2.1.1 Substantive requirements

The Copenhagen Summit set out the following three substantive requirements that a candidate state must satisfy:

   ▪ Political requirements – a candidate state must be a state within the meaning of public international law, and must have stable institutions guaranteeing that the values on which the EU is founded are respected;

■ Economic requirements – a candidate state must have a functioning market economy and be able to cope with competitive pressures and market forces within the EU;

■ Legal requirements – a candidate state must be able to fulfil the obligations of EU membership, including acceptance of the objectives of political, economic and monetary union. This entails acceptance of the entire body of EU law known as the "*EU acquis*" which before the entry into force of the ToL was referred to as the "acquis communautaire".

In addition, Article 49 TEU sets out a fourth substantive requirement for admission to the EU, which was not expressly mentioned by the Copenhagen Summit. It is geographical in that a candidate state must be a European state. Each of the four requirements is considered below.

3.2.1.1.1   Political requirements

These are defined in Article 2 TEU, which states that:

"The Union is founded on the values of respect for human dignity, freedom, democracy, equality, the rule of law and respect for human rights, including the rights of persons belonging to minorities. These values are common to the Member States in a society in which pluralism, non-discrimination, tolerance, justice, solidarity and equality between women and men prevail."

A liberal-democratic model of government of a candidate state ensuring respect for the civil, political, economic and social rights of its citizens is a vital element of membership of the EU.[102] Therefore, only democratic states which respect human rights can apply for membership. All Member States of the EU, candidate states and potential candidate states must be contracting parties to the ECHR to which, under Article 6(2) TEU the EU itself will accede in due course.

3.2.1.1.2   Economic requirements

The level of economic development is crucial for the admission of a candidate state to the EU. This criterion is examined in respect of each enlargement later in this chapter.

3.2.1.1.3   Legal requirements

There are two legal requirements:

1. The first requirement is that a candidate state must be recognised as a state. Reference to the rules of public international law will clarify the legal status of the applying entity. In practice, since the Council must reach a unanimous decision regarding admission of a candidate state, if the latter is not recognised by any Member State, its application for admission will be rejected. So far, no irreconcilable problem has arisen in this area, although the candidacy of Cyprus posed delicate problems.

    The Republic of Cyprus, which came into being on 16 August 1960, is, de facto, divided into two sectors: Greek and Turkish. Turkey invaded the Northern part of Cyprus in 1974, as a response to the military coup d'état organised by the Greek Cypriot

---

102.   See S. Frowein, "The European Community and the Requirement of a Republican Form of Government", (1984) 82 Michigan Law Review, pp 1311 et seq.

right-wing paramilitary organisation, EOKA-B, backed up by the ruling Greek military junta in Greece, which overturned the democratically elected government of President Makarios. At that time Turkey claimed it was invading Cyprus to uphold its obligation under the 1960 Treaty of Guarantee "to re-instate the constitution of the Republic of Cyprus". In May 1983, the Rauf Denktash movement, which represents Turkish Cypriots, proclaimed the creation of the Turkish Republic of Northern Cyprus, recognised only by Turkey as an independent state.

The Republic of Cyprus has always been recognised by the international community as one country exercising sovereignty over the entire island. A political settlement between the Greek Cypriots and the Turkish Cypriots was not achieved before the Republic of Cyprus's accession to the EU. The Annan Plan, named after former Secretary General of the United Nations, Kofi Annan, proposed the establishment of a new state, the United Cyprus Republic, covering the entire island (apart from the British Overseas Base area). This State would be a confederation made up of two component states – the Greek Cypriot State and the Turkish Cypriot State – joined together by a minimal federal governmental apparatus. On 24 April 2004 the Plan was put before the two communities in a referendum for approval. While the proposal received a 65 per cent favourable vote from the Turkish community, the Greek Cypriot community rejected it by over 75 per cent. As a result, the Republic of Cyprus became a Member of the EU on 1 May 2004, but the Turkish sector, or the Turkish Republic of Northern Cyprus being under military control of Turkey, did not, in fact, join the EU. However, Turkish Cypriots, being citizens of the Republic of Cyprus, are EU citizens, and are entitled to vote in elections to the EP.

There are many factors which make the reunification of the island of Cyprus likely, such as the ongoing negotiations which started in 2008 between the President of the Republic of Cyprus and the leader of the Turkish Cypriots concerning such important matters as governance and power sharing, property, and the economy. Further, the opening of accession negotiations between the EU and Turkey (see section 3.3.9.3), will almost certainly force all interested parties to settle the problem of Cyprus peacefully.

2.   The second requirement is the acceptance by a candidate state of the EU acquis.[103] The EC acquis, according to the EP, constitutes a "criterion of global integration".[104] This term means, in the context of accession,[105] the acceptance by a new Member State, without reservation, and from the commencement of its formal membership, of the body of common rights and obligations that bind all EU Member States together – in other words, a candidate country must accept all of EU law and its basic political principles. In respect of the fifth enlargement (May 2004) the acquis communautaire (now the EU acquis) contained more than 80,000 pages of EU law. The acquis is constantly evolving and comprises:

---

103.   This term is usually used in French (see the English version of the TEU), although it can be translated into English as "Community patrimony" (or Community heritage).

104.   In its Resolution on the structure and strategy for the EU with regard to its enlargement adopted on 20/01/1993 the EP emphasised that all candidate states must accept the acquis communautaire, including the TEU and the objectives of further integration (A3-0189/92).

105.   On different aspects of the acquis communautaire see C. C. Gialdino, "Some Reflections on the Acquis Communautaire", (1995) CMLRev, pp 1089–121.

(a)   The normative acquis, such as:

- The founding Treaties and their amendments;
- Acts enacted by the institutions, such as regulations, directives, decisions, recommendations and opinions (Article 288 TFEU, Article 161 EA);
- Other acts whose adoption is provided for by the Treaties (for example, rules of procedures, and so on);
- Measures adopted in the area of the external relations of the EU – such as agreements entered into by the EU with one or more third states, with international organisations, or with a national of a third state;
- Other agreements the conclusion of which have been necessary to attain the objectives of the Treaties, for example, the Agreement of January 1957 establishing European Schools.

(b)   The political acquis, such as declarations, resolutions, principles and guidelines, and so on, adopted by the European Council, or the Council. Also included are common agreements of the Member States regarding the development and strengthening of the EU.

(c)   The judicial acquis, that is, the case law of the CJEU, which outlines the essential characteristics of the EU legal order (for example, direct effect, supremacy, unification, co-operation between the CJEU and national courts). It should, however, be noted that in the Acts of Accession there is no reference to specific case law for two reasons:

- The rulings of the ECJ are "acts" of the EU institutions and thus already part of the EU acquis; and
- It is unnecessary, and even dangerous, to "freeze" the case law of the CJEU for new members and, at the same time, allow its further development for older members. Indeed, the ECJ is not bound by its own decisions and it may always change the existing case law in order to promote new and essential objectives of the EU.

The acceptance of the EU acquis is a necessary condition for accession as it encompasses rights and obligations attached to the Union and its institutional framework. Candidate states must accept the acquis before they join the EU. Only in exceptional circumstances are exemptions, or derogations, granted to candidate states.

3.2.1.1.4   Geographical requirement

A candidate state must be a European state. This criterion can be explained by the fact that the EU wants to preserve the European identity of the Union.

In the Declaration on European Identity of 14 December 1973, the heads of state or government described the essential elements of European identity as "principles of representative democracy, of the rule of law, of social justice – which is the ultimate goal of economic progress – and of respect for human rights".[106] The Commission, in its report on "Europe and the Challenge of Enlargement", stated that:

---

106.   EC Bull. 12/73, point 130.

"The term 'European' has not been officially defined. It combines geographical, historical and cultural elements . . . and is subject to review. It is neither possible nor opportune to establish now the frontiers of the European Union, whose contours will be shaped over many years to come."[107]

At the time of writing, there are 50 states in Europe including the Vatican City. Some of them have had a short existence as states, having become independent as a result of the collapse of the Soviet Union and of the Yugoslav Federation, and through the division of Czechoslovakia into the Czech Republic and Slovakia.

Until now, only one non-European state has submitted an application for admission – Morocco in 1985 – which was rejected in 1987 by the Council as being incompatible with Article 237 EC Treaty [Article 49 TEU] because Morocco is not a European state.

3.2.1.2 Formal requirements

Article 49 TEU sets out the formal conditions for admission. This provision states that:

"Any European State which respects the values referred to in Article 2 and is committed to promoting them may apply to become a member of the Union. The European Parliament and national Parliaments shall be notified of this application. The applicant State shall address its application to the Council, which shall act unanimously after consulting the Commission and after receiving the consent of the European Parliament, which shall act by a majority of its component members. The conditions of eligibility agreed upon by the European Council shall be taken into account.

The conditions of admission and the adjustments to the Treaties on which the Union is founded, which such admission entails, shall be the subject of an agreement between the Member States and the applicant State. This agreement shall be submitted for ratification by all the contracting States in accordance with their respective constitutional requirements."

By virtue of Article 49 TEU a successful candidate state accedes to the EU, and therefore, by implication, to the Euratom.

The following stages in the procedure can be identified.

3.2.1.2.1 Submission of a formal application by a candidate state

The first step in the procedure consists of submitting a formal application for admission, in the form of a letter signed by the minister for foreign affairs of a candidate state, to the Presidency of the Council of the European Union. The application must be notified to the EP and national parliaments. Subsequently, the Council decides whether to initiate negotiations with the applicant state. This can take a considerable time. The Commission becomes involved and, after investigations, presents a "preliminary opinion", which either recommends the opening of negotiations or advises the Member States to wait until certain requirements are satisfied by an applicant state, or expresses its opposition to the admission. This opinion is not binding but is, nevertheless, of great influence. This influence is demonstrated by the fact that the Commission convinced the Member States to "freeze" the enlargement of the EC until the completion of the internal market.

The Council may take a position regarding the "preliminary opinion" of the Commission by adopting a "conclusion", which may confirm or ignore the Commission's opinion. In the case of

---

107.   EC Bull. 3/92, Supp., point 7.

Cyprus and Malta, the Council confirmed the favourable opinion of the Commission. However, in relation to Greek accession the Council ignored the negative opinion of the Commission.[108]

3.2.1.2.2   Negotiations

Negotiations commence with the so-called "screening", which consists of an analytical examination of the EU acquis. During that stage, which takes approximately one year, the Commission explains the acquis to the candidate state and, together with that state, evaluates its degree of preparedness. For the purposes of screening and the subsequent negotiations, the acquis is broken down into a number of chapters, each covering a specific policy area; for example, chapter 1 on the free movement of goods, chapter 2 on freedom of movement for workers, and so on. Thus, prior to actual, technical negotiations, the Commission establishes a "screening report" for each chapter of the acquis. In respect of each chapter, a candidate state submits its negotiating position, while the Commission prepares a Draft Common Position (DCP) for submission to the Council, which decides whether it can adopt a common position allowing opening of the chapters.

Some negotiations have been lengthy and complex (for example, with Spain, Portugal and Eastern and Central European countries), others swift and smooth (for example, with Austria, Finland, Norway and Sweden). Until the conclusion of negotiations admission is uncertain.

3.2.1.2.3   End of negotiations

Once negotiations are concluded on all chapters, a draft Accession Treaty that incorporates the result of the negotiations is agreed between the Council and the candidate state. The Draft Accession Treaty is subsequently submitted to the Commission and the EP. The opinion of the Commission is not binding, but in practice, as the Commission is fully involved in negotiations, its opinion is always followed. Since the adoption of the SEA, the EP, within the consent procedure, must give its consent to the accession of a candidate state by majority vote cast by a majority of its members. The first time this occurred was in 1994 when the EP assented to the admission of Austria, Finland, Norway and Sweden. During the proceedings leading to membership of these states, the EP was kept informed by the Council and by the Commission of the progress in negotiations, and expressed its comments in several resolutions.

The Treaty of Accession is usually very short. In the case of the UK it consists of three articles stating that the UK accedes to the three Communities and accepts all Community law. However, the Act of Accession, which is always annexed to the Treaty of Accession, is a voluminous document, often accompanied by protocols, annexes and declarations. Apart from declarations, all these documents are legally binding.

3.2.1.2.4   Ratification of the Treaty of Accession

The last stage concerns the ratification of the Treaty of Accession by the Member States and the candidate state in conformity with respective national constitutional rules. Often, a candidate state submits the final acceptance of its future membership to its people.

The Treaty of Accession enters into force only if all Member States ratify it. In the case of multiple candidatures, non-ratification by any one of the candidates does not affect the accession of others. In the case of Norway, its Government notified the EU that, as a result of a negative

---

108.   The Council, solely for political reasons, that is, to support nascent democracy in Greece, decided to accept the Greek application for admission: Opinion on the Greek Application for Membership, EC Bull. 2/76, Supp.

referendum, it would not ratify the Treaty of Accession. On 1 January 1995 the Council of the EU, including the then three new Member States, adopted a decision "adjusting the instruments concerning the accession of new Member States to the European Union",[109] and thus gave legal effect to the withdrawal of Norway from the process of accession.

From the signature of the Treaty of Accession to the actual accession a future Member State is kept informed, and is consulted at all levels and in all areas, and is also involved in the EU decision-making procedures, although it still has no right to vote. Its presence ensures that the existing Member States are fully aware of any difficulties and opposition to new measures, while permitting the new Member State to participate in developments which are taking place within the EU.

3.2.2 The suspension procedure

Under Article 7(1) TEU, the Council, acting by a majority of four-fifths of its members (excluding the defaulting Member State), on the basis of a reasoned proposal by one-third of the Member States, by the EP or by the Commission, and after obtaining consent of the EP, may determine the existence of a "clear risk of a serious breach" by a Member State of values on which the EU is based and which are set out in Article 2 TEU, and subsequently may address a recommendation to the Member State concerned. The defaulting State has the right to present its case before the determination is made. The Council is required to regularly verify that the grounds on which such a determination was made continue to apply.

It appears that if there is no adequate response from the Member State concerned, the procedure, set out in Article 7(2) TEU, for suspension of a defaulting Member State's rights deriving from EU membership will be used. Article 7(1) TEU contains an "early warning mechanism" and was introduced by the ToN.

There are two stages in the procedure under Article 7(2) TEU. The first relates to the determination of the existence of a serious and persistent infringement by a Member State of the fundamental values of the Union. The second relates to a decision either to suspend or not suspend EU membership rights, which may be taken by the European Council once the Council has determined the existence of a serious and persistent breach of Article 2 TEU.

3.2.2.1 First stage

Under Article 7(2) TEU the European Council (the defaulting Member State is excluded), acting unanimously on a proposal by one-third of the Member States or the Commission, and after obtaining the consent of the EP, may determine the existence of a serious and persistent breach by a Member State of the values on which the EU is founded. Such determination is made after giving an opportunity to the defaulting Member State to present its observations.

3.2.2.2 Second stage

Once the European Council has made the determination mentioned above, the Council may, acting by a qualified majority, decide to suspend certain rights of the defaulting Member State,

---

109.   [1995] OJ L1/221. A similar decision was taken by the Council when Norway, following a previous negative referendum (53.49 per cent against), failed to join the Communities in 1972.

including its right to vote in the Council. However, in applying Article 7(2) TEU the Council must take account of the possible consequences of such a suspension on the rights and obligations of natural and legal persons. During suspension, the defaulting Member State is bound to carry out its obligations flowing from the Treaties and the other Member States are bound to carry out their obligations to the defaulting Member State.

The Council, acting by a qualified majority vote, may decide subsequently to vary or terminate its decision, according to how the situation in the defaulting Member State evolves.

The ToL introduced a possibility for a defaulting Member State to challenge a determination made under Article 7(1) or 7(2) TEU but confined it to procedural aspects of such determination and imposed a strict time limit, in that the Member State concerned is required to bring proceedings before the ECJ within one month from the date of the adoption of an act by the Council or the European Council determining a breach of Article 7(1) or (2) TFEU. Under Article 267 TFEU, the ECJ is required to give a ruling within one month from the date of the commencement of the proceedings.

Article 7 of the TEU does not specify what would happen if a defaulting Member State were to continue violating Article 2 TEU in defiance of a decision adopted under Article 7(2) TEU. It is submitted that in such a situation general principles of public international law will apply to deal with a defaulting Member State.

So far, neither Article 7(1) nor Article 7(2) TEU has been used. However, the EU imposed diplomatic sanctions against Austria in February 2000, to express its condemnation of the election of Jörg Haider (the leader of the extreme right Austrian Freedom Party, known for his racist and xenophobic policies) as a government minister when his party, as a result of the 2000 election, joined a conservative-led Austrian Government. The sanctions consisted of freezing bilateral relations between Austria and 14 other Member States, and the suspension of all contacts at an inter-governmental level between Austria and the EU. The problem was settled when Mr Haider resigned from the Austrian Government, although his party did not follow his lead. Article 7 TEU could not have been used because Austria had not actually breached Article 7(1) TEU.

3.2.3 The withdrawal procedure

The ToL provides for voluntary withdrawal from the EU, which may take place at any time. A Member State that no longer wishes to be a member of the EU must notify the European Council of its desire to leave the EU. Following notification, the procedure set out in Article 50 TEU will be applied, consisting of conducting negotiations between the EU and the Member State concerned with a view to concluding a withdrawal agreement, specifying the arrangements for withdrawal and regulating the future relationship between the EU and the Member State concerned. The Council of the EU will conclude this agreement on behalf of the EU, acting by qualified majority voting (the Member State concerned is not allowed to vote), and after obtaining the consent of the EP.

The Member State concerned will cease to be a member of the EU at the date specified in the withdrawal agreement or, failing any agreement, two years after the notification to the European Council of its intention to withdraw unless the European Council, in agreement with the Member State concerned, unanimously decides to extend this period. Therefore, the withdrawal may enter into force even if the EU fails to give its consent.

The Member State concerned may always change its mind, or even rejoin the EU following the normal accession procedure contained in Article 49 TEU.

Until now no Member State has expressed a serious desire to leave the EU. The Community has twice dealt with a question of Member State secession, that is, when a part of an existing territory of a Member State has acquired political sovereignty or autonomy.

The first case concerns Greenland, which is the world's largest island that is not also considered a continent, and was an integral part of the Kingdom of Denmark at the time of the latter's accession to the Communities. No opposition was expressed to Greenland's subsequent withdrawal. The circumstances were as follows. In 1979 the government of Denmark granted home rule to Greenland; as a result Greenland remains under the Danish Crown and its inhabitants are still considered to be Danish citizens. The island enjoys autonomy in all matters but constitutional affairs, foreign relations and defence. In 1985 the people of Greenland decided in a referendum to withdraw from the European Communities, and negotiations were conducted between the Kingdom of Denmark and other Member States. As a result, the specific provisions for Greenland are set out in the Protocol on special arrangements for Greenland, annexed to the EC Treaty.

The second case concerns St Pierre and the Miquelon Islands. Their secession was considered as an internal matter for France and the Communities merely received notification from the French authorities.

3.3 Current and future membership of the EU

By the end of April 2010 five enlargements and one mini-enlargement had taken place. At the time of writing the EU covers almost all of Western and Central Europe and a substantial part of Eastern Europe. It has 494 million inhabitants, which is more than Russia and the USA put together.

3.3.1 First enlargement

On 1 January 1973 the UK, Denmark and the Republic of Ireland joined the Communities. Following a negative referendum, Norway did not accede. The reasons for accession of these three Member States were different, although the main consideration for Ireland and Denmark was to protect their existing economic links with the UK. Norway held a second referendum on the issue in 1994 and membership was rejected then too.

3.3.1.1 *Ireland*

In the Irish Republic 83 per cent of votes cast were in favour of accession. For Ireland membership of the EC was very attractive as it provided an opportunity to enter markets in the EC and thus reduce the traditional dependency upon the UK for export trade (70 per cent of exports were to the UK). Furthermore, as an agricultural country, Ireland could only gain from being a party to the CAP.

3.3.1.2 *Denmark*

Denmark, mainly an agricultural country, would clearly benefit from the CAP. Of its main commercial partners Germany was already a Member State, while the UK was about to join the EC. The advantages were carefully weighed by the Danes against the disadvantages, which would mainly be the severance of traditional links with other Nordic countries. In the national referendum, which took place after the negative vote in Norway, 63 per cent of Danish votes cast were in favour of accession.

3.3.1.3 The United Kingdom

The most controversial candidate was the UK.[110] However, after the departure from power of France's President de Gaulle, there was no opposition to UK membership. The accession negotiations lasted one year and focused on the following issues:

1. The length of the transitional period;

2. Agriculture. In the UK food was cheap due to imports from Commonwealth countries. The Heath government had two objectives in this respect: in the short term, to slow down the impact of the CAP by phasing it in as slowly as possible; and in the long term, to obtain compensation for the negative impact of the CAP by a satisfactory budgetary arrangement;

3. The UK's contribution to the Community budget. It was agreed that its contribution would be 8.64 per cent of the EC budget in 1973, increasing to 18.92 per cent in 1977, with limits on further increases in 1978 and 1979. There was no agreement regarding 1980;

4. New commercial arrangements with Commonwealth countries. The African, Caribbean and Pacific (ACP) countries were offered participation in the Yaoundé Convention (which was replaced by the Lomé Conventions and in 2000 by the Cotonou Agreement[111] and more recently by the Economic Partnership Agreements). In addition, the Community General System of Preferences was extended to Commonwealth countries. The question of exports of Caribbean sugar and New Zealand dairy products to the UK required special arrangements;

5. Fisheries. The first enlargement offered an opportunity for the EC to create a Common Fisheries Policy (CFP) based on free and equal access of the Member States to each other's waters; accordingly, UK participation in this policy was negotiated.

The accession negotiations were concluded in January 1972 when the Treaty of Accession of the four applying states was signed. The UK European Communities Act 1972 came into force on 1 January 1973. However, the UK Labour Party opposed the terms of entry and promised in its electoral campaign to "renegotiate" the Treaty of Accession. Indeed, once Labour were in power (1974–79), the question of the UK membership became a main item on the political agenda of the Labour government.[112] In the end UK membership was approved by the House of Commons (396 to 170) and by the people of the UK in a national referendum (67.2 per cent votes cast in favour).

---

110. The UK's application was rejected by France in 1963 and again in 1967.
111. The Cotonou Agreement, as were its predecessors, is the main element of the EU's development co-operation policy. It regulates trade between the EC and 79 ACP countries. Its main objectives are to reduce and eventually eradicate poverty in these countries whilst achieving sustainable development and their gradual integration into the global economy.
112. The question of "renegotiation" is examined in MSO, Membership of the European Community: Report on Renegotiation, Cmnd. 6003, March 1975.

3.3.2   Second enlargement

The second enlargement concerned Greece, which submitted its application on 12 June 1975. The negotiations were opened on 25 June 1975. On 23 May 1979 the Treaty of Accession and the Act of Accession were signed. Greece became a Member State on 1 January 1981.

Greece was the first Eastern European country to join the EC. Its heritage, resulting from centuries of Ottoman Turkish Empire rule, combined with its Orthodox Christianity, a legacy of the Byzantine Empire, set Greece apart from other Member States. For Greece, with its inefficient agriculture based mainly on small holdings with poor soil and low rainfall, its limited natural resources, weak industry and a fragile democracy as it emerged from years of dictatorship, the attraction of being a Member State was obvious. A transition period of five years was agreed in all areas, except tomatoes and peaches which were to be included in the CAP at the end of 1987.

3.3.3   Third enlargement

Portugal and Spain joined the EC on 1 January 1986. Portugal applied on 28 March 1977 and Spain applied on 28 July 1977. Both signed the Treaty of Accession on 12 June 1985. The end of military dictatorship in both countries enabled them to submit their applications for accession to the Communities.

The negotiations with Spain were protracted, as its proposed accession posed three major economic problems:

1.   Spanish agriculture and its competitiveness, especially against that of France and Italy, made its participation in the CAP very controversial.

2.   The Spanish fishing fleet was almost equal in size to that of the entire Community and therefore placed the CFP under strain.

3.   Spanish industry, especially cotton, woollen textiles, clothing and steel industries, due to low wages, threatened the position of other Member States and posed a challenge to the EC, which already had over-capacity problems in these sectors.

Portugal, a small and relatively poor country, posed no such threats to the economy of existing Member States. Its accession was delayed as a result of applying for membership at the same time as Spain. Furthermore, the negotiations with Spain and Portugal were halted when France decided that, before a new enlargement, budgetary matters within the EC should be settled. As a result, it was not until after the Fontainebleau Summit in 1984, which reached an agreement on contributions to the EC budget, that the accession negotiations with Spain and Portugal were resumed.

3.3.4   De facto enlargement: the case of the German Democratic Republic (GDR)

On 3 October 1990, in conformity with the West German Constitution, the former German Democratic Republic (GDR) became an integral part of the Federal Republic of Germany (FRG). On that date, by virtue of Article 299 EC, the territorial scope of application of EC Treaties was extended to the former East Germany.[113]

---

113.   See C. W. A. Timmermans, "German Unification and Community Law", (1990) 27 CMLRev, pp 437–49; C. Tomuschat, "A United Germany within the European Community", (1990) 27 CMLRev, pp 415–36.

It was not necessary to revise the EC Treaty, as the Federal Republic of Germany, the only legal government of Germany, always considered the GDR as part of its country when signing international treaties. However, Germany, taking into account the importance of the reunification and its impact on the German and EU economies, asked other Member States for approval, which was formally given by the Dublin European Council Summit on 28 April 1990. Additionally, the Dublin summit laid down transitional measures, allowing temporary derogations in the application of EC law to the territory of the GDR in certain areas such as competition policy and protection of the environment.

3.3.5   Fourth enlargement

On 1 January 1995 Austria, Finland and Sweden joined the EU.[114] Norway, although accepted by the Communities, did not accede, as a result of a negative referendum (its second such result, having held a previous referendum in 1972).

Austria submitted a formal application on 17 July 1989, Sweden on 1 July 1991, Finland on 18 March 1992 and Norway on 25 November 1992. Formal negotiations commenced on 1 February 1993.

All candidate states were EFTA[115] countries and Members of the European Economic Area.[116] As such, they already had considerable experience of working with the EC institutions and of the interpretation and application of EC law. Also, they had the appropriate "infrastructure", that is, staff, procedures and material support, to deal with negotiations with the EC. These went smoothly and the Treaty of Accession was signed on 24 June 1994. Thereupon, the candidate states had to renounce their EFTA membership and terminate all bilateral agreements between themselves and the Community, and all other international agreements incompatible with membership of the EU.

3.3.6   Fifth enlargement (Part I)

The fifth enlargement concerned Central and Eastern European states and Malta and Cyprus. The enlargement took part in two stages:

- On 1 May 2004 Cyprus, The Czech Republic, Estonia, Hungary, Latvia, Lithuania, Malta, Poland, Slovakia and Slovenia joined the EU;

- On 1 January 2007 Bulgaria and Romania joined the EU. As at 1 May 2004 neither of them was, according to the Commission, ready to become a member of the EU.

The fifth enlargement was the most challenging for the EU and for the candidate states. Apart from the two Mediterranean states, Cyprus and Malta, the applicants were Central and Eastern European states. Some of them were independent states for the first time in their history, for

---

114.   On the fourth enlargement see D. Booss and J. Forman, "Enlargement: Legal and Procedural Aspects", (1995) 32 CMLRev, pp 95–130.

115.   The European Free Trade Association, founded in 1960 by the UK, had established a free trade area among its member states. At the time of writing, EFTA members are: Iceland, Liechtenstein, Norway and Switzerland.

116.   See S. Peers, "An Even Closer Waiting Room? The Case for Eastern European Accession to the European Economic Area", (1995) 32 CMLRev, p 187.

example, Slovakia and Slovenia. All of them were establishing their freedom and independence after the collapse of Communism.

The accession process for the eight Central and Eastern European states was long, and even after their accession they were made subject to a lengthy transitional period. The most important restriction concerns the free movement of workers (see Chapter 23.4). Older Member States, fearing the influx of poorer, new EU citizens, were given an option to decide when, within seven years after the 2004 accession, to allow workers from new Member States to enter their labour market.

Only the UK, Ireland and Sweden, subject to some conditions relating to access to social benefits, decided to open up their job markets from the day of accession. From the same time Denmark accepted workers from new Member States on condition that they obtain a work permit in Denmark. In respect of participation in the CAP, farmers from new Member States will obtain full-scale support after a 10-year transitional period. However, the new Member States have also imposed some restrictions on older Member States. Some, fearing a massive loss of ownership of their agricultural land and property to rich nationals from older Member States, were allowed to decree a period during which sales to non-nationals would be subject to restrictions. Generally, the period is seven years, but for Poland it is 12 years.

The biggest problem for the EU related to the reconstruction and adjustment of the economies of the new Member States to the standards required by the Union. Indeed, at the time of enlargement on average the EU's 75 million new citizens earned only 40 per cent of the income enjoyed by people living in the older Member States.[117] The level of GDP for the new EU members varied from 35 per cent of the EU average in the case of Latvia to 74 per cent for Slovenia. During the accession period financial assistance to the new Member States was provided within the Phare (Poland and Hungary: Assistance for Restructuring their Economies) Programme aimed at reforming their economies; the ISPA (Instrument for Structural Policies for Pre-Accession) Programme, which provided support for the development of infrastructure; and the SAPARD (Special Accession Programme for Agriculture and Rural Development) Programme for modernisation of their agriculture. In total €3 billion a year was allocated among eight Central and Eastern European countries, whilst Cyprus and Malta received €95 million between them for the period 2000–04. Financial assistance continued to be provided for new Member States, worth €10 billion in 2004, €12.5 billion in 2005 and €15 billion in 2006.[118]

The Iron Curtain that descended across Europe after World War II "from Stettin in the Baltic to Trieste in the Adriatic", was finally lifted on 1 May 2004, and the new Member States have regained their rightful place in Europe, now a zone of peace, prosperity and stability.

According to the European Commission, so far the fifth enlargement has been very successful as it has fulfilled the favourable economic expectations of the EU.[119]

---

117. See http://europa/eu.int/abc/12lessons/print_index3_en.htm (accessed 10/12/2004).

118. More Unity and More Diversity, The European Union's Biggest Enlargement 2003. European Commission Publication, Luxembourg: Office for Official Publications of the European Communities.

119. See: the report prepared by the European Commission: The Enlargement, two years after: an economic evaluation, http://ec.europa.eu/economy_finance/index_en.htm (accessed 3/03/07). See also the Commission's official website on the impact of the 2004 enlargement: Enlargement, 3 Years After, at http://ec.europa.en/enlargement/5th_enlargement/index_en.htm (accessed 1/12/07).

3.3.7 Fifth enlargement (Part II)

Bulgaria and Romania signed Treaties of Accession on 25 April 2005. They joined the EU on 1 January 2007.

3.3.8 Mini-enlargements outside Europe

As a result of constitutional reforms which occurred in The Netherlands, on 15 December 2007 that country's Caribbean islands of Bonaire, Saba and Sint Eustatius became part of The Netherlands as the Kingdom Islands (with a status similar to that of Dutch municipalities), whilst Curaçao and Saint Martin became self-governing countries inside the Kingdom of The Netherlands. On that date all the above-mentioned Caribbean islands became part of the EU.

Previously, they were OCT of The Netherlands and thus EU law, apart from Part IV of the EC Treaty, did not apply to them. However, their inhabitants, being Dutch nationals, were citizens of the EU.

This was an enlargement taking place outside Europe.

In 2011, Mayotte, as a result of a referendum held in March 2009, will change its status from a French OCT to that of being France's 101st department. At that date, Mayotte will become part of France and therefore an outermost region of the EU.

3.3.9 Candidate countries

It is important to note that pre-accession financial aid has been rationalised by Regulation 1085/ 2006 establishing an Instrument for Pre-Accession Assistance (IPA),[120] which entered into force on 1 January 2007. IPA supersedes the five pre-existing pre-accession programmes: Phare, ISPA, SAPARD, Turkey instrument, and CARDS (Community Assistance for Reconstruction, Development and Stability in the Balkans). It establishes a coherent, unitary framework for financial assistance for both candidate and potential candidate countries. Under IPA an amount of €11,468 million is intended to be channelled over the period 2007–13 into helping such countries make necessary adjustments with a view to joining the EU.

At the time of writing Croatia, FYR Macedonia and Turkey have the status of candidate countries.

3.3.9.1 Croatia

On 3 October 2005 the EU opened accession negotiations with Croatia, which, at the time of writing, are near the final stage. The anticipated date for the accession of Croatia is 2012.[121]

3.3.9.2 FYR Macedonia

On 22 March 2004 FYR Macedonia applied to become an official candidate. In December 2005 upon the Commission's recommendation, the European Council approved FYR Macedonia as a candidate state. However, no date has been fixed for opening accession negotiations.

---

120. [2006] OJ L210/90.
121. Communication from the Commission COM(2009) 595 final.

3.3.9.3   Turkey

As a Member of NATO (the North Atlantic Treaty Organisation), Turkey has been patiently waiting for admission to the EU for many years.

Its first application for membership was lodged in April 1987. In December 1989 the Commission issued a negative opinion. It considered that the next step in Turkey's route to Brussels was a customs union with the Community. In January 1996 the customs union was agreed and this is in force. The main reason for the Commission's negative opinion was Turkey's poor human rights record. However, since a change of government in 1998, Turkey has started the process of democratisation.

Turkey was recognised as a candidate state in 1999. On 3 October 2005 the EU foreign ministers and the Turkish foreign minister reached agreement regarding the opening of official accession negotiations. This agreement was achieved after Austria, where 80 per cent of voters are against Turkey's accession, backed down from its demand for a "privileged relationship" with Turkey (meaning a second-class membership, rightly rejected by the Turks) as an alternative to membership. On 6 October 2005 the Commission, in its Communication to the Council and the EP,[122] recommended opening accession negotiations subject to some conditions. The Commission stated that Turkey sufficiently fulfilled the Copenhagen political criteria. It considered, however, that accession could not take place before 2014 and that negotiations should be carried out on the basis of a three-pillar strategy set out in the Communication. Since then negotiations have been opened on 11 chapters out of 33 chapters. The Commission, in its "Turkey 2009 Progress Report"[123] noted that Turkey fulfils the political criteria although it needs constitutional reforms and more efforts to ensure the adequate protection and enforcement of human rights including the rights of minorities. In respect of economic requirements, the Commission awarded Turkey the status of a "functioning market economy", confirming that Turkey will be able to cope with competitive pressure and market forces in the EU. It stated, though, that further steps should be taken towards structural reform of the Turkish economy in the long term.

The membership of Turkey poses great challenges to the EU. These are:

- Demographic (Turkey has 80 million inhabitants);

- Cultural (it is a secular country having a mainly Muslim population);

- Geopolitical (this will entail the re-evaluation by the EU of relations with the Middle East);

- Turkey continues to occupy the northern part of Cyprus, with 40,000 Turkish troops stationed on the island, and refuses to recognise Cyprus, a Member State of the EU. Until a solution is found to the Cyprus dispute, Turkey is unlikely to become a Member State.

Every challenge also being an opportunity, there are many arguments in favour of Turkey's accession. It would:

- Help to transform Turkey into a modern, well-functioning democracy, and thus extend peace, stability, prosperity, democracy, human rights and the rule of law not only across Europe but also into Asia;

---

122.   COM(204)656 final.
123.   SEC(2009) 1334.

- Strengthen the EU's external security, given that Turkey plays a moderating role in the unstable neighbouring region in the Middle East;

- Strengthen the EU's economy, given that Turkey has a very dynamic and rapidly growing economy;

- Ensure the security of energy supplies to the EU, since Turkey has at its border the most energy-rich regions on earth, which will thus constitute a corridor for road, rail, air and maritime pipeline connections between the EU and Turkey's southern neighbours;

- Reward Turkey for its support for NATO;

- Create a more multiracial and multi-religious EU;

- Reinforce secularism in Turkey (which has been a secular state since 1923); and

- Given that 23 per cent of the Turkish population is under the age of 15, to some extent respond to the problem of the increasingly aging population of the current EU.

3.3.10 Potential candidates

These are the Western Balkan states: Albania (applied on 28 April 2009), Montenegro (applied on 15 December 2008), Serbia (applied on 22 December 2009), Kosovo and Bosnia and Herzegovina. The last two, at the time of writing, have not formally applied. Each country has been promised the prospect of EU membership as and when they are ready. On 16 July 2009, Iceland applied for membership of the EU. Iceland is in a special position as it is a member of the EEA. On 24 February 2010, the Commission recommended the opening of negotiations with Iceland.

AIDE-MÉMOIRE

ENLARGEMENTS

First Enlargement: On 1 January 1973 Denmark, Ireland and the UK joined the Communities.

Second Enlargement: On 1 January 1981 Greece joined the Communities.

Third Enlargement: On 1 January 1986 Portugal and Spain joined the Communities.

De facto enlargement: On 3 October 1990 the former German Democratic Republic (GDR) became an integral part of the Federal Republic of Germany (FRG) and all three Community Treaties were extended to apply to the former GDR.

Fourth Enlargement: On 1 January 1995 Austria, Finland and Sweden joined the EU.

Fifth Enlargement (Part I): On 1 May 2004 the following states joined the EU: Cyprus, The Czech Republic, Estonia, Hungary, Latvia, Lithuania, Malta, Poland, Slovakia and Slovenia.

Fifth Enlargement (Part II): On 1 January 2007 Bulgaria and Romania joined the EU.

Mini-enlargement outside Europe: On 15 December 2008 The Netherlands Antilles

Caribbean islands of Bonaire, Saba and Sint Eustatius, Curaçao and Saint Martin became part of The Netherlands and consequently part of the EU.

Mayotte, as a result of a change of its status in France (from an OCT to a French department), will become part of the EU in 2011.

Candidate States: Croatia, FYR Macedonia and Turkey.

Potential Candidate States: Albania, Bosnia and Herzegovina, Montenegro, Serbia, Kosovo and Iceland.

RECOMMENDED READING

Books

Jacoby, W., *The Enlargement of the European Union and NATO. Ordering from the Menu in Central Europe*, 2006, Cambridge: CUP

Prechal, S., *Reconciling the Deepening and Widening of the European Union*, 2008, Cambridge: CUP

Tatham, A.F., *Enlargement of the European Union*, 2009, London: KLI

Article

Gialdino, C. C., "Some Reflections on the Acquis Communautaire", (1995) CMLRev, p 1089–121

4

COMPETENCES OF THE EU

CONTENTS

SUMMARY

1. Introduction. The ToL clarifies the distribution of power between the EU and the Member States. This is an important element in the democratisation of the EU and a clear response to the Member States complaints about "creeping competences drift" in favour of the EU.

2. The principal of conferral. The principle of conferral is contained in Article 5(2) TEU which provides that the EU can "act only within the limits of the competences conferred upon it by the Member States in the Treaties to attain the objectives set out therein. Competences not conferred upon the Union in the Treaties remain with the Member States". The principle of conferral guarantees that the EU cannot extend its competence at the expense of the Member States without their prior consent. Articles 3–6 TFEU provide lists of policy areas which are allocated either exclusively to the EU, or shared between the EU and the Member States or in which the Member States have exclusive competence and the EU can only provide support or co-ordination.

3. Exclusive competences of the EU. Article 3 TFEU provides a list of exclusive competences of the EU. It endorses the doctrine of implied powers established by the ECJ in the *ERTA* case in respect of external competences of the EU. Under this doctrine the EU's external competences extend to "the conclusion of an international agreement when this is within the framework of one of the Union's legislative acts or when it is necessary to help it exercise an internal competence or if there is a possibility of the common rules being affected or of their range being changed" (Article 3(2) TFEU). Under Article 47 TFEU the legal personality of the EC has been replaced with a new, single personality attributed explicitly to the EU. This will facilitate the conduct of external relations by the EU and enhance its external profile.

4. Competences shared between the EU and the Member States. Article 4 TFEU provides a non-exhaustive list of competences shared between the EU and the Member States. Areas not mentioned in Article 4 are within the shared competences if they are neither mentioned in Article 6 TFEU (which lists supporting, co-ordinating or supplementing competences of the EU) nor in Article 3 TFEU (which lists the exclusive competences of the EU). For the exercise of shared competences two principles are vital:

- the principle of subsidiarity under which in the areas of shared competences the EU can only intervene if certain objectives set out by the Treaties cannot be attained by the Member States and only if the EU can attain them with greater efficiency than the Member States; and

- the principle of proportionality according to which the EU's action, its content and form shall not exceed what is necessary to achieve the objectives of the Treaties.

Protocol 2 on the Application of the Principles of Subsidiarity and Proportionality attached to the Treaties establishes not only the conditions for the application of these principles but also a system for monitoring their application. Under the Protocol, national parliaments have been granted extensive powers to police the application of the principle of subsidiarity through the "yellow and orange cards" procedure.

5. Supportive competences. These refer to areas in which the Member States have not conferred competences on the EU but have decided to act through it. In these areas the EU supports, co-ordinates, encourages or complements measures taken at national level. Article 6 TFEU provides a list of areas in which the Member States have exclusive competence but the Union can provide support or co-ordination. It is to be noted that special rules are applicable to three areas, i.e. economic and employment policies and the CFSP.

6. The "flexibility clause" contained in Article 352 TFEU. The clause can be used to achieve the objectives of the Treaties as listed in Article 3 TEU but not to objectives of the CFSP. Its role has been marginalised by the facts that for the adoption of a measure under Article 352 TFEU the Council is required to obtain the EP's consent (previously under Article 308 EC the Council was required to consult the EP) and that its use is subject to the "yellow and orange cards" procedure available to national parliaments.

7. The exercise of Union competences by a limited number of Member States: the enhanced co-operation procedure. The ToL has further reformed the enhanced co-operation procedure to make it more attractive to the Member States, mainly by providing that when an enhanced procedure is in progress, the Council acting unanimously may adopt a decision, stipulating that it will act by QMV where the Treaty stipulates that the Council shall act unanimously. The only constraint imposed on the Council is that it must consult the EP. However, a new restriction is imposed as to initial authorisation in that the EP has to consent to this. In the past, the EP has not been very enthusiastic about the enhanced procedure.

8. The nature of the EU. The issue here is to determine whether the EU is an international organisation of a type similar to a confederation or an embryonic federal state or of a sui generis nature.

4.1   Introduction

The term "competence" refers to the responsibility for decision making in a particular policy area.

Since the inception of the EC important competences have been transferred to the EC/EU by Member States, which have had the effect of shrinking their individual spheres of competence, thus imposing limitations on their sovereignty. Since the establishment of the Community, its areas of competence have considerably expanded. This growth of Community competences, in particular in the circumstances where they were acquired through the creative interpretation of the EC Treaty by the ECJ, combined with the fact that the division of competences between the EC and the Member States was not clearly defined in the EC Treaty, became one of the most crucial issues in the debate about the future of the EU. In this debate the position of the parties concerned can be summarised as follows:

- The Member States feared that the system of delimitation of powers under the EC Treaty, based on the objectives to be achieved and means of achieving those objectives, made it very difficult to decide whether the Community's acts were within its competence or whether the Community exceeded its powers and by this encroached even further on national sovereignty. This fear was understandable in the light of the past record of the EC, but in recent years complaints about "creeping competences drift" in favour of the EC were less justified, given that the ambitious agenda of the EC (such as the creation of the internal market, EMU, and the area of FSJ) had required adoption of numerous measures which were necessary and directly linked to the successful implementation of the EC agenda. Nevertheless, the lack of clear boundaries between national and Community action reinforced the feeling of encroachment by the EC;

- EU citizens feared that the EC would acquire more and more powers without adequate democratic oversight;

- The EC feared that an irrevocable fixing of the Community competences would stall the dynamics of European integration, given that the Community may, as a result, not be free to respond to new challenges in ways which would allow its objectives to be fulfilled;

- Since 2000 the issue of division of competences has become part of the fundamental reform of the Union. The Declaration on the Future of Europe, issued by the Nice European Council and attached to the Treaty of Nice, called upon the 2004 IGC to address the issues of "how to establish and monitor a more precise delimitation of powers between the European Union and the Member States, reflecting the principle of subsidiarity".[124] In 2004 the IGC made proposals which were incorporated into the failed Constitutional Treaty, but have subsequently, with some amendments, found their place in the ToL. They are as follows:

---

124.   Declaration on the Future of Europe, para 5(1).

- The ToL codifies and describes the division of competences between the Union and the Member States (Article 2 TFEU). It clearly identifies policy areas in which the EU exercises exclusive, shared and supportive competences;
- The importance of the principle of conferral is emphasised in the Treaties as well as in Protocols and Declarations attached to them. Under this principle the EU exercises only the competences which Member States have conferred upon it with the result that competences not conferred upon it remain within the Member States;
- For the first time, the Treaties expressly provide for the possibility of reducing the competences of the Union, if appropriate. In this respect Article 48 (2) TEU specifies that proposals for the revision of the treaties "may, *inter alia*, serve either to increase or to reduce the competences conferred on the Union in the Treaties". Although it has always been possible for Member States to reduce competences of the EU, until now this has never been specified so clearly and, in fact, any revision of the treaties has been in favour of the development of the acquis communautaire (under the ToL this is referred to as the "EU acquis") and thus in favour of the extension of competences of the EC and the EU;
- With regard to areas of shared competences, Protocol 25 on the Exercise of Shared Competences attached to the Treaties envisages a situation where an EU institution decides to cease exercising its competence in a particular area. This occurs in particular when an EU institution decides to repeal a legislative act in order to comply with the principles of subsidiarity and proportionality. The Protocol states that the Council may, at the initiative of one or several of its members and in accordance with Article 241 TFEU, request the Commission to submit proposals for repealing a legislative act. In the area covered by the repealed legislative act Member States would regain their competence;
- National parliaments have been given an important role in policing the application of the principles of subsidiarity (section 4.4.1.2.2);
- The ToL establishes special rules with regard to three areas: economic and employment policies which are to be co-ordinated by Member States and the CFSP;
- The use of the "flexibility clause" contained in Article 352 TFEU has been marginalised (see section 4.6);
- Under Article 47 TEU, the EU has been granted legal personality. The EU, being the successor of the EC, has absorbed its legal personality. From now on there is only one legally recognised organisation, the EU, with a single legal personality. However, the granting of legal personality to the EU does not have any implications on the allocation of competences between the EU and the Member States. Declaration 24 attached to the Treaties confirms that "the fact that the European Union has a legal personality will not in any way authorise the Union to legislate or to act beyond the competences conferred upon it by the Member States in the Treaties".

Under the ToL the EU has not acquired any new exclusive competences although it has gained new shared and supporting competences. It is to be noted that prior to the entry into force of the ToL, the EU had already legislated in the majority of "new" areas on other legal bases. As a result, the ToL rather confirms the pre-existing competences of the EU than extends them. Entirely new competences, i.e. areas in which the EU had not acted or had no ability to act prior to the entry into force of the ToL, relate to: space policy; administrative co-operation aimed at improving the capacity of Member States, at their request, to implement EU law effectively; sport; crime prevention; establishment of a European Public Prosecutor; measures facilitating co-ordination and co-operation among Member States in respect of diplomatic and consular protection of EU citizens and the solidarity clause contained in Article 222 TFEU.

4.2   The principle of conferral

This principle is inherent to any legal person. It permits achievement of the objectives constituting the raison d'être of a legal person. In particular, it applies to international organisations or federal states. The principle of conferral is defined in Article 5 (2) TEU in the following terms:

> "Under the principle of conferral, the Union shall act only within the limits of the competences conferred upon it by the Member States in the Treaties to attain the objectives set out therein. Competences not conferred upon the Union in the Treaties remain with the Member States."

Article 4 TFEU expressly states that "competences not conferred upon the Union in the Treaties remain within the Member States" and that the Union "shall respect [Member States'] essential State function, including ensuring the territorial integrity of the State, maintaining law and order and safeguarding national security. In particular, national security remains the sole responsibility of each Member State".

The principle of conferral serves as both justification for an EU action, and as its legal basis. The principle is enforced, in the last resort, by the CJEU under Article 263 TFEU, which permits annulment of any measure adopted by EU institutions for lack of competence or infringement of essential procedural requirements.

Articles 2–6 TFEU identify three types of competences: exclusive, shared and supporting.

4.3   Exclusive competences of the EU

If the EU enjoys exclusive competence in a particular area, Member States are prevented from acting unilaterally or collectively in that area, irrespective of whether or not the EU has already acted, unless the EU has explicitly authorised them to adopt legally binding acts or measures implementing acts adopted by EU institutions (Article 2(1) TFEU). The principle of subsidiarity does not apply to areas in which the EU enjoys exclusive competences but the principle of proportionality does. Article 3 TFEU identifies areas which are within the exclusive competence of the EU. They are:

Under Article 3(1) TFEU:

- The Customs union;

- Those competition rules that govern the internal market;

- Monetary policy with regard to Member States that have adopted the euro;

- The conservation of marine biological resources under the common fisheries policy;

- The Common commercial policy.

Under Article 3(2) TFEU:

- The conclusion of an international agreement when this is within the framework of one of the Union's legislative acts or when it is necessary to help it exercise an internal competence or if there is a possibility of the common rules being affected or of their range being changed.

Article 3(2) TFEU endorses the peculiarity of external competences of the EU in that the EU enjoys not only express but also implied powers in respect of the conclusion of international agreements as specified in Title V of the TFEU. Under the ToL the EU was granted international personality enabling it to enter into international agreements with third States and international organisations.

4.3.1 Explicit powers

Explicit powers are those which are clearly defined in Treaty provisions or specified in one of the Union's legislative acts.

In external relations competences of the EU are expressly stated in the following articles:

- Article 207 TFEU on the Common Commercial Policy;

- Articles 132 and 219 TFEU on monetary policy of the EU;

- Article 186 TFEU on research;

- Article 191 TFEU on the protection of environment;

- Article 208 TFEU on development co-operation;

- Article 212 on economic and financial co-operation with third States;

- Article 217 TFEU on association agreements with one or more third States or international organisations.

4.3.2 Implied powers

Powers which do not result directly and expressly from a provision or a number of provisions of Treaties but from global and general objectives laid down by the Treaties as interpreted by the ECJ, are known as implied powers.

The doctrine of implied powers was recognised by the International Court of Justice in its *Advisory Opinion on Reparation for Injuries Suffered in the Service of the United Nations*,[125] and endorsed by the ECJ in Case 8/55 *Fédération Charbonnière de Belgique v High Authority*.[126] The ECJ has mainly applied it in relation to external competences of the Community, although the doctrine also has an internal dimension.

In the internal sphere the doctrine of implied powers relates to the powers of the EU institutions vis-à-vis Member States. In Joined Cases 281, 283–285 and 287/85 *Germany and Others v Commission*,[127] the ECJ held that when the Commission is under an obligation to carry out a specific task assigned to it by the EC Treaty, the Treaty confers on the Commission the necessary powers to carry out that task.

In the external sphere, the conditions under which the Community can rely on the doctrine of implied powers were established in Case 22/70 *Commission v Council (ERTA)*.[128]

---

125. (1949) ICJ Rep.174.
126. [1954–1956] ECR 292.
127. [1987] ECR 3203.
128. [1971] ECR 263.

THE FACTS WERE:

ERTA, a European agreement on the working practices of international road transport crews, was signed in Geneva on 19 January 1962. Amongst the signatories were five of the six original Member States. The agreement never came into force as it lacked sufficient ratifications. Consequently, negotiations took place starting in 1967. Meanwhile, at Community level Regulation 543/69 of 25 March 1969 was adopted with regard to the areas covered by the ERTA failed agreement. On 20 March 1970 the Council discussed the attitude to be taken towards the ERTA negotiations and adopted a resolution setting out the position. Subsequently, Member States conducted and concluded ERTA negotiations on the basis of the Council proceedings of 20 March 1970.

The Commission submitted an application for annulment of the Council resolution of 20 March 1970 on the grounds that:

- *the adoption of Regulation 543/69 transferred the competence for a common transport policy to the Community and consequently the Community was empowered to negotiate and conclude the agreement in question; and the Council, as it had no competence to adopt the resolution of 20 March 1970, had breached Articles 75 and 228 and 235 of the EC Treaty concerning the distribution of powers between the Council and the Commission and consequently the rights of the Commission to negotiate the agreement.*

Held:

The ECJ:

- Endorsed the doctrine of parallelism under which the external competences of the Community derive not only from express provisions of the Treaty, but may also derive from other provisions of the Treaty and from internal measures adopted within the framework of those provisions. The ECJ held that in order to determine in a particular case the Community competence to enter into international agreements "regard must be had to the whole scheme of the Treaty no less than its substantive provisions". As a result, the EC powers "arise not only from an express conferment by the Treaty . . . but may equally flow from other provisions of the Treaty and from measures adopted, within the framework of those provisions, by the Community institutions".

- Established that implied external powers are within the exclusive competence of the Community. The ECJ stated that where the Community had adopted Community rules within the framework of a common policy, the Member States are not allowed, individually or collectively, to enter into agreements with third states in the areas affected by those rules. The Court held that: "As and when such common rules come into being, the Community alone is in a position to assume and carry out contractual obligations towards third countries affecting the whole sphere of application of the Community legal system."

The two main facets of the *ERTA* judgment have been further explained in subsequent cases.

4.3.2.1   The doctrine of parallelism

The doctrine of parallelism means the internal competences of the Community should be matched by the external competences which may be conveniently expressed by the in foro interno in foro externo principle, that is, if the EC has powers in particular internal areas it should be entitled to extend them to external relations in those areas. Implied powers may be based on the provisions of the Treaty or upon measures adopted by Community institutions within the ambit of those provisions. In *Opinion 2/91 [Re ILO Convention 170]*,[129] the ECJ held that implied external powers may flow even from measures adopted under Article 308 EC [Article 352 TFEU].

The most controversial issue in relation to implied powers is whether the EU is empowered to exercise external powers in the absence of any internal measures. In this respect the ECJ has mitigated the *ERTA* principle according to which the Community cannot use an implied external competence in the absence of internal measures adopted in respect of a common policy.

In *Opinion 1/76 [Re Rhine Navigation Case]*,[130] the ECJ decided that when EC law has created powers for the Community within its internal system in order to attain a specific objective, the EC has authority to enter into international agreements necessary for the attainment of that objective, even in the absence of any internal measure. The Court stated that internal measures can be adopted on the occasion of the conclusion and implementation of an international agreement.[131] As a result, the participation of the EC in external relations based on implied powers is conditional upon the necessity to achieve a "specific objective" that cannot be attained without the participation of third states, and not on the existence of internal measures.

4.3.2.2   The nature of implied powers: exclusive or shared?

In the *ERTA* case the ECJ did not hesitate to state that external implied powers of the Community were exclusive. The implication of this statement is very important given that when the Community has exclusive powers, the Member States have no right, acting individually or even collectively, to undertake obligations with third countries which affect Community rules. In the 1970s the ECJ did not make any distinction between the existence and the nature of an external competence. Once the Court decided that the Community had implied competence, such a competence was automatically exclusive in nature. Since then, the ECJ has changed its approach. Now, the Court determines:

- First, whether the Community has competence in the relevant area, and if so, whether the competence is explicit or implied;

- Second, if the ECJ finds that the Community has implied competence, it determines its nature, that is, whether the relevant competence is exclusive or shared between the Community and the Member States. This determination of the nature of a competence is decided on a case-by-case basis. In *Opinion 1/03 relating to Competence of the Community to*

---

129.   [1993] ECR I-1061.
130.   [1977] ECR 741.
131.   "Open Skies" judgments: Case C-467/98 *Commission v Denmark* [2002] ECR I-9519; Case C-468/98 *Commission v Sweden* [2002] ECR I-9575; Case C-469/98 *Commission v Finland* [2002] ECR I-9627; Case C-471/98 *Commission v Belgium* [2002] ECR I-9681; Case C-472/98 *Commission v Luxembourg* [2002] ECR I-9741; Case C-475/98 *Commission v Austria* [2002] ECR I-9797; and Case C-476/98 *Commission v Germany* [2002] ECR I-9855).

conclude the forthcoming Lugano Convention on jurisdiction and the recognition and enforcement of judgments in civil and commercial matters,[132] the ECJ held that account must be taken of:

- Whether the relevant area is covered by the Community rules and also by the provisions of the intended agreement;
- The nature and content of those rules and those provisions with a view to ensuring that the agreement is not capable of undermining the uniform and consistent application of the Community rules and the proper functioning of the system which they establish;
- The current state of Community law in the area in question as well as its future development, in so far as that is foreseeable at the time of the judgment.[133]

On the basis of the above criteria an implied competence will be classified as exclusive in nature in the following situations:

1. Where internal EU rules are part of common rules, that is, where internal rules govern the entirety of the area in which the EU intends to conclude an international agreement. In such a situation only the EU is entitled to conclude an international agreement, otherwise the unity and the uniform application of EU law will be affected. The difficulty here is to decide whether or not the internal rules are part of common rules. This task is left to the ECJ.

2. Where the EU has achieved a complete harmonisation in the area in which the EU intends to conclude an international agreement. Any agreement in this area will necessarily affect the EU rules within the meaning of the *ERTA* judgment and, thus, only the EU has competence to conclude an international agreement. If the harmonisation is not complete, the ECJ will take account of the extent and the importance of harmonising rules. Thus, if harmonisation is limited to the establishment of a minimum standard in a particular area, the competence is shared with the Member States. However, if the relevant area is largely covered by EU rules with a view to achieving complete harmonisation, the Member States may not enter into international commitments outside the framework of the EU institutions, even if there is no contradiction between those commitments and the common rules.[134]

3. Where an internal legislative act has conferred on the EU exclusive external competence. This is a specific situation where "the Community has included in its internal legislative acts provisions relating to the treatment of nationals of non-member countries or expressly conferred on its institutions powers to negotiate with non-member countries, it acquires an exclusive external competence in the spheres covered by those acts."[135]

---

132. [2006] ECR I-1145.
133. *Opinion 2/91 [Re ILO Convention 170]* [1993] ECR I-1061.
134. *Opinion 2/91 [Re ILO Convention 170]* [1993] ECR I-1061.
135. *Opinion 1/94 [Re WTO Agreement]* [1994] ECR I-5267; *Opinion 2/92 [Re OECD National Treatment Instrument]* [1995] ECR I-521.

4.4   Competences shared between the EU and the Member States

Most competences are shared between the EU and the Member States. Under the principle of subsidiarity, in the areas of shared competences the EU can only intervene if certain objectives set out by the Treaties cannot be attained by the Member States and only if the EU can attain them with greater efficiency than the Member States. Further, any EU action in those areas must respect the principle of proportionality, i.e. such action "shall not exceed what is necessary to achieve the objectives of the Treaties".[136] Protocol 2 on the Application of the Principles of Subsidiarity and Proportionality attached to the Treaties establishes not only the conditions for the application of these principles but also a system for monitoring their application. Under the Protocol, national parliaments have been granted extensive powers to police the application of the principle of subsidiarity.

Article 2(2) TFEU states that in areas of shared competences Member States are allowed to act within the limitations imposed by the Treaty provisions as long as the EU is inactive or ceases to be active. Those limitations mean that a Member State cannot adopt measures contrary to the EU's principles and values, for example, in breach of the principle of non-discrimination on the ground of nationality,[137] or in breach of the principle of loyal co-operation as embodied in Article 4(3) TEU. Further, this provision clearly envisages a situation where the Union has decided to cease exercising its competence in a particular area in which case Member States will regain that area.

Some areas of shared competences are listed in Article 4 TFEU, others are those which are neither mentioned in Article 6 TFEU (which lists supporting, co-ordinating or supplementing competences of the EU) nor in Article 3 TFEU (which lists exclusive competences of the EU).

Article 4 TFEU provides the following non exhaustive list of areas falling within shared competences:

- The internal market;
- Social policy with regard to specific aspects defined in the Treaty;
- Economic and social cohesion;
- Agriculture and fisheries, excluding the conservation of marine biological resources;
- Environmental matters;
- Consumer protection;
- Transport;
- Trans-European networks;
- Energy;
- The area of freedom, security and justice;
- Common safety concerns in public health matters, for aspects defined in the TFEU.

Article 4(3) and (4) TFEU provides that in the areas of research, technological development and space and in the areas of development co-operation and humanitarian aid, the exercise of shared competences "shall not result in Member States being prevented from exercising theirs".

---

136.   Article 25 TFEU.
137.   Case 61/77 *Commission v Ireland* [1978] ECR 417.

4.4.1   The principle of subsidiarity

The principle of subsidiarity has a long history. It derives from the Catholic doctrine of Thomas Aquinas and has been used by the Roman Catholic Church, in particular by Pope Leo XIII in his Encyclical letter Rerum Novarum (1891),[138] Pope Pius XI in his Encyclical letter Quadragesimo Anno (1931)[139] and later by Pope John XXIII in his Pacem in Terris (1963)[140] to enhance the role of an individual in society in the context of a corporate state (especially a communist state). According to Pius XI:

> "It is an injustice, a grave evil and disturbance of right order for a larger and higher association to arrogate to itself functions which can be performed efficiently by smaller and lower societies."[141]

In the context of social organisation, the principle of subsidiarity means that decisions affecting individuals should always be taken at the lowest practical level, as closely as possible to the individuals concerned and that their initiatives should not be impeded by any authorities in those areas where individuals are the most competent to decide for themselves.

The principle of subsidiarity has its constitutional and political dimension in federations. It allocates powers between federal and local authorities in order to strike a balance between the needs of the federation and the protection of the interests of members of the federation, and thus decides which functions should be performed at the federal level, which should be shared between federal and local levels and which are within the exclusive competence of the latter.

4.4.1.1   The development of the principle of subsidiarity: from the SEA to the ToL

The principle of subsidiarity was implicit in Article 235 of the EC Treaty concerning the extension of competences of the Community. The SEA introduced it explicitly in relation to the protection of the environment. Article 130R(4) of the EC Treaty stated that the Community shall intervene in environmental matters ". . . to the extent to which the objectives referred to in paragraph 1 can not be attained better . . . at the level of the individual Member States".

For the first time, the principle of subsidiarity was expressly mentioned in the Treaty of Maastricht, i.e. in its Preamble, Articles A and B and in Article 5 EC. Its meaning, however, given its elusive nature and its political and legal connotations, was highly disputed. In order to clarify its meaning under EC law, the Lisbon European Council (June 1992)[142] asked each of the Commission and the Council to prepare a report on the procedural and practical steps needed to implement subsidiarity. The Edinburgh European Council (December 1992), on the basis of both of these reports and of other documents such as a draft Inter-Institutional Agreement on the

---

138.   http://www.vatican.va/holy_father/leo_xiii/encyclicals/documents/hf_l-xiii_enc_15051891_rerum-novarum_en.html (accessed 27/02/08).

139.   http://www.vatican.va/holy_father/pius_xi/encyclicals/documents/hf_p-xi_enc_19310515_quadragesimo-anno_en.html (accessed 27/02/08).

140.   http://www.vatican.va/holy_father/john_xxiii/encyclicals/documents/hf_j-xxiii_enc_11041963_pacem_en.html (accessed 27/02/08).

141.   Cited by J. Steiner, "Subsidiarity under the Maastricht Treaty", in D. O'Keefe and P. Twomey (eds), *Legal Issues of the Treaty of Maastricht*, 1994, London: Wiley Chancery Law, p 50. See also P. Carozza, "Subsidiarity as a Structural Principle of International Human Rights Law", (2003) 97(1) American Journal of International Law, pp 38–79.

142.   EC Bull. 6/1992, point 8.

Application of Article 5 EC submitted by the EP and a report from the president of the Commission regarding the Commission's review of existing and proposed legislation in the light of the principle of subsidiarity, adopted guidelines regarding the practical and procedural implications deriving from the principle of subsidiarity for EC institutions. Given the obvious link between the principle of subsidiarity and the principle of proportionality, the guidelines summarised and explained the procedural and practical steps necessary for implementation of both principles by the Community institutions.

The guidelines discussed above were incorporated into a Protocol on the Application of the Principles of Subsidiarity and Proportionality, which Protocol was annexed to the ToA. In the light of the fact that protocols annexed to a Treaty form an integral part of that Treaty, the Protocol conferred binding character on the principles of subsidiarity and proportionality and thus they have become subject to judicial review. The Protocol was complemented by the 1993 Inter-Institutional Agreement on Procedures for Implementing the Principle of Subsidiarity[143] between the Council, the EP and the Commission, requiring these institutions to respect the principle of subsidiarity and to take concrete steps to implement it. The Protocol set out three guidelines for the adoption of Community measures which will satisfy the requirement of subsidiarity at the EC level:

- The matter under consideration must have transnational aspects that cannot be properly regulated by an action taken by a Member State and requires a Community action;

- An action taken by a Member State alone, or an absence of a Community action, would conflict with the objectives of the EC Treaty;

- An action taken by the Community would produce clear benefits by reason of its scale or effects as compared with an action taken by an individual Member State.

The Protocol was based on the Edinburgh Conclusions[144] and confirmed the existing Community approach to the application of subsidiarity.

The requirements of the principle of subsidiarity have been accommodated by the new approach to EU patterns of governance introduced by the open method of co-ordination (OMC) created in the late 1990s. The 2000 Lisbon Council endorsed this method as being appropriate to help the Member States to develop national policies with a view to achieving the ambitious Lisbon Agenda that is making the EU the most competitive and dynamic knowledge-based economy in the world, capable of sustainable economic growth with more and better jobs and greater social cohesion by 2010. According to the European Council this method involves:

- Fixing guidelines for the Union combined with specific timetables for achieving the goals which they set in the short, medium and long terms;

- Establishing, where appropriate, quantitative and qualitative indicators and benchmarks against the best in the world and tailored to the needs of different Member States and sectors as a means of comparing best practice;

143. Its text in Europe, Documents, No. 1857, November 1993, p 44.
144. Overall Approach to the Application by the Council of the Subsidiarity Principle and Article 3b of the Treaty on European Union. Conclusion of the European Council, Edinburgh, December 1992, Annex 2 to Part A.

■ Translating these European guidelines into national and regional policies by setting specific targets and adopting measures, taking into account national and regional differences;

■ Periodic monitoring, evaluation and peer review organised as mutual learning processes.[145]

At the first glance it may seem that the OMC is similar to the procedures developed with regard to EU "soft law".[146] However, the similarity is illusory. The OMC is different from the pre-OMC soft law procedures and contents for the following reasons:

1. The OMC focuses on inter-governmental co-operation whereby the Council and the Commission determine the development and the content of the OMC and the ECJ has no input. Under the pre-OMC "soft law", the approach was supranational as the ECJ and the Commission determined its content. Due to recognition of "soft law" by the ECJ, it has become a source of Community law and has been included in the EU acquis.

2. Under the OMC the policy formulation and monitoring takes place at the highest political level (the Council and the European Council) while the monitoring of pre-OMC "soft law" was done through the peer review process at an administrative level, often on an ad hoc basis.

3. Pre-OMC soft law was used at random in relation to a particular policy area. The OMC is used systematically in relation to all policy areas with a view to achieving a common objective. It links not only national policies with each other and different Community policies one to the other but also national policies with Community policies. As S. Borrás and K. Jacobsson pointed out, the OMC provides: "The possibility for truly bottom-up political dynamics, which differ from the top-down structures of the previous law-making."[147]

4. The OMC is not confined to Member States but seeks the participation of all stakeholders, private and public. This was not the case of pre-OMC soft law as it did not seek the participation of social partners.

5. The OMC emphasises the mutual learning process through co-operation, exchange of knowledge and experiences. The pre-OMC soft law had no such objective.

---

145. Presidency Conclusions, p 37, available at http://www.europarl.europa.eu/summits/lis1_en.htm#d (accessed 10/11/07).

146. The term "soft law" has been used in public international law to describe international instruments which have no binding legal effects such as UN General Assembly resolutions and declarations, non-binding statements made by governments, codes of conduct issued by international organisations, etc. Under EU law "soft law" describes EU measures which have no binding legal force or whose binding legal force is less than absolute. These are recommendations, opinions, codes of conduct, guidelines, action plans, notices, collective recommendations, review and monitoring and benchmarking, etc. Soft law as opposed to "hard law" (i.e. binding rules) is seen as an attractive option for achieving specific objectives without being too heavy-handed.

147. S Borrás and K Jacobsson, "The Open Method of Co-ordination and New Governance Patterns in the EU", (2004) 11/2 Journal of European Public Policy, p 185, at 189.

4.4.1.2   Principle of subsidiarity under the ToL

The ToL recognises the importance of the proper application of the principle of subsidiarity and thus of drawing a clear demarcation line between the competences of a Member State and those of the EU. It ensures respect for the principle of subsidiarity in the following ways:

■ It identifies areas that are within the exclusive competence of the EU and its Member States;

■ It provides the following definition of the principle of subsidiarity in Article 5(3) TEU.

> "Under the principle of subsidiarity, in areas which do not fall within its exclusive competence, the Union shall act only if and insofar as the objectives of the intended action cannot be sufficiently achieved by the Member States, either at central level or at regional and local level, but can rather, by reason of the scale or effects of the proposed action, be better achieved at Union level."

It can be said that, on the basis of the above definition, the following criteria should be satisfied in order for the EU to take action in an area where it shares competences with the Member States:

■ The sufficiency criterion, that is, an action must be necessary in the sense that neither individuals alone nor Member States alone will achieve the objectives of the action;

■ The benefit criterion, that is, an action must bring added value over and above that which could be achieved by individuals or a Member State;

■ The close to the citizen criterion, which requires that decisions must be taken as closely as possible to the citizen;

■ The autonomy criterion, which requires that an action should secure greater freedom for the individual.

It is to be noted that Article 5(3) TFEU refers, for the first time, to the sub-State level, i.e. regional and local level.

4.4.1.2.1   The application of the principle of subsidiarity by the EU institutions

Under Article 1 of Protocol 2 on the Application of the Principles of Subsidiarity and Proportionaliy each EU institution is required to ensure "constant respect" for both principles. This is to be achieved as follows:

The European Commission

In order to satisfy the requirements of subsidiarity the Commission must:

■ Carry out wide consultations, where appropriate at regional and local level in respect of a proposed legislative act. If, in cases of exceptional urgency, the Commission fails to carry out such consultations it must give reasons for its decision in its proposal. Even prior to the entry into force of the ToL the Commission carried out wide consultations before putting forward any proposal for a legislative act. Since May 2006 the Commission has been sending new proposals and consultation papers to national parliaments with a view to inviting them to comment on whether those proposals conform to the requirements of subsidiarity and proportionality. The comments had been duly taken into consideration. When any national parliament submitted that the proposals were in breach of either or both principles, the Commission responded to these submissions individually. Under Protocol 2 a new procedure has been put in place allowing national parliaments to control the application of the principle of subsidiarity (see section 4.4.1.2.2).

- In the preamble to any legislation, where the EU does not have exclusive competence, the Commission has to justify the proposed legislation in the light of subsidiarity and proportionality. This justification will form part of the measure's legal basis. The Commission must show that it is more appropriate to act at EU level then at national level, using qualitative and if possible quantitative indicators.

- In accordance with the OMC, in secondary legislation the Commission gives preference to directives rather than regulations. Similarly, non-binding measures, such as recommendations, opinions and non-compulsory codes of conduct, are used when appropriate rather than binding measures. Further, the Commission relies on techniques of minimum standards and the principle of mutual recognition when appropriate. The principle of subsidiarity entails that co-operation between Member States should be encouraged by the Commission, which often supports, completes or supervises joint initiatives of the Member States.

- The Commission has been simplifying and updating the EU acquis.[148] Further, it has expressed its willingness to repeal legislative acts which are in breach of the principle of subsidiarity.

- The Commission is required to submit an annual report to the European Council, the EP, the Council and national parliaments on the application of Article 5 TEU. This annual report must also be forwarded to the ESC and the CoR.

The Council

The Council must examine each proposal submitted by the Commission and its own amendments to such proposals in the light of the principle of subsidiarity. However, the Council must not dissociate from its deliberations on the merits the application of the principle of subsidiarity. Both aspects must be examined at the same time.

The EP

The EP, having important legislative competences in many areas, is very much involved in the application of the principle of subsidiarity. The Inter-institutional Agreement on Procedures for Implementing the Principle of Subsidiarity provides that the EP must take into account the principle of subsidiarity and, in the light of Article 5 TEU, justify any amendment which substantially changes a proposal submitted by the Commission.

The ECJ

The principle of subsidiarity is not only a socio-political concept but also a fundamental principle of EU law. No special procedure has been established to bring an issue of subsidiarity before the ECJ, although a proposal that this should occur was made by the EP.[149]

The issue of subsidiarity is the most likely to arise in two types of proceedings before the CJEU:

- Under Article 267 TFEU, which enables national courts or tribunals, when they are faced with a question of interpretation of validity of EU law the resolution of which is necessary for them to give judgment, to refer that question to the ECJ under the preliminary ruling procedure;

---

148. COM(2006) 690.
149. A. G. Toth, "Is Subsidiarity Justiciable?" (1994) 19 ELRev, p 268, especially p 273.

▪ Under Article 263 TFEU, which concerns judicial review of acts of EU institutions, bodies, offices and agencies, an applicant may challenge the act itself by claiming that it was adopted in violation of the requirements laid down in Article 5 TEU. Article 8 of Protocol 2 extends the list of potential applicants under Article 263 to include the CoR in respect of legislative acts for the adoption of which the TFEU provides that it be consulted. However, national parliaments have no locus standi under Article 263 TFEU but a Member State may bring an action on behalf of its national parliament.

For the first time the issue of subsidiarity arose in Case C-84/94 *United Kingdom v Council [Re Working Time Directive]*.[150]

THE FACTS WERE:

The UK Government brought an action for annulment of Council Directive 93/104 concerning certain aspects of the organisation of working time. The UK Government argued that the Directive was adopted in breach of the principles of proportionality and subsidiarity as the Council failed to demonstrate that the objective of the Directive could better be achieved at Community level than at national level.

Held:

The ECJ held that the principle of subsidiarity can be relied upon by an applicant, although in this case it was invoked to support the main claim and not as an autonomous ground for annulment.

Comment:

The Court made a clear distinction between the principle of proportionality and the principle of subsidiarity.

With regard to the principle of subsidiarity the ECJ held that:

▪ the argument of the UK that the objective of the Directive would be better achieved at national level than at Community level concerned the principle of subsidiarity. The ECJ examined whether a measure adopted by a Member State would achieve the desired Community objective, concluding that this would not be the case and that an action at Community level was necessary since the objective of raising the level of health and safety that the Directive aimed to achieve "presupposes Community-wide action".

▪ Advocate General Léger emphasised that the principle of subsidiarity answers the question at which level, Community or national, the adoption of a legislative measure is more appropriate.

In respect of the principle of proportionality the ECJ held that:

---

150.   [1996] ECR I-5755.

> the argument of the UK that the Council could not adopt measures which were as general and as mandatory as those forming the subject-matter of the Directive must be examined in the light of the principle of proportionality. The ECJ examined whether less onerous, less restrictive measures adopted by the Community would achieve the aims pursued, that is, it verified "whether the means which it [the Directive] employs are suitable for the purpose of achieving the desired objective and whether they do not go beyond what is necessary to achieve it".
>
> On the basis of the above, the ECJ held that the measures adopted by the Directive were necessary and appropriate as they contributed directly to achieving the objective set out in the Directive and did not exceed what was necessary to achieve such objective.

While there is no doubt that the principle of subsidiarity is justiciable, it is a fact that as at the time of writing the ECJ has never annulled any EC/EU legislation on the ground that it was adopted in breach of that principle. In a judgment delivered by the Grand Chamber of the ECJ, in Joined Cases C-154/04 and C-155/04 *Alliance for Natural Health*,[151] the Court set out its position on the matter, which is that only in extreme circumstances will the Court find that the principle of subsidiarity has been breached. This approach is understandable in that the principle is, in reality, of a political nature. The ECJ has been reluctant to clearly state what subsidiarity really means in terms of the allocation of competences between the Community and the Member States. The ECJ's reluctance could additionally be explained by the fact that the concept of exclusive competences of the Community was manufactured by the ECJ itself as that concept had no legal basis in the original EC Treaty. In *Alliance for Natural Health* the ECJ held that:

" . . . the principle of subsidiarity does not call into question the powers conferred on the Community by the Treaty, as interpreted by the Court of Justice."

This is a reminder that the principle of subsidiarity is concerned with how power is exercised by the EU and not with the question of what powers are conferred on it. However, when the legitimacy of the decision-making process in the EU is challenged on the ground of subsidiarity, this necessarily involves the delicate task of defining areas of shared and exclusive competences. This is because subsidiarity does not apply to areas within the exclusive competence of the EU.

It is submitted that the attitude of the ECJ toward the principle of subsidiarity may change under the ToL, the reason being that the ToL clearly defines areas of exclusive competence of the EU. Therefore, the threat that the principle of subsidiarity will have a radical impact on judicial determination of the exclusive competences of the EU has been removed. Further, the establishment of a list of areas of shared competences under the ToL facilitates enquiries from the ECJ as to whether a particular legislative action on the part of the EU is necessary or the best one. Finally, the enhanced role of national parliaments and the Committee of the Regions (CoR) in the monitoring of the proper application of the principle of subsidiarity is conducive to making subsidiarity more intrusive as a general legal principle.

---

151. [2005] ECR I-6451.

4.4.1.2.2   The control of subsidiarity by national parliaments

Under Protocol 2 on the Application of the Principles of Subsidiarity and Proportionality a new procedure known as the "yellow and orange cards" has been introduced which gives national parliaments the opportunity to monitor the proper application of the principle of subsidiarity. Under Protocol 1 on the Role of National Parliaments in the European Union, all EU draft legislative acts must be forwarded to national parliaments. Within eight weeks of receipt of a draft legislative act or of any amendment to it, national parliaments may issue a reasoned opinion stating why what has been received does not comply with the principle of subsidiarity and indicate their opposition by voting against the proposal.

Each national parliament has been allocated two votes. If the parliament consists of two chambers or houses, each of them holds one of these votes. In a EU of 27 Member States, the total number of votes available is 54. If at least one third of those votes (18 votes) indicate that the principle of subsidiarity has not been complied with, the Commission, or the institution which initiated the proposed act, must review the proposal and decide whether it wishes to withdraw, amend or maintain it. A reason must be given to justify the decision.

In respect of a proposed legislative act concerning the area of FSJ originating from the Commission or a group of Member States, lower thresholds apply. The review procedure is triggered if at least one quarter of the votes of the national parliaments disagree with the proposal. This is the "yellow cards" procedure.

The "orange cards" procedure applies only to the ordinary legislative procedure (see Chapter 7.3). If at least a simple majority of votes cast by national parliaments (currently 28) indicate objections to a proposal, the Commission must review the proposal. If the Commission decides to maintain its proposal, it must issue a reasoned opinion stating why it considers that the proposal complies with the principle of subsidiarity. This reasoned opinion, together with reasoned opinions from the national parliaments, is then forwarded to the legislator (that is, the Council and the EP jointly), which decides the fate of the proposal. This means that if the Council by a majority of 55 per cent of its members and if the EP by a simple majority of the votes cast reject the proposal, it will not be given further consideration.

4.4.1.3   Assessment of the principle of subsidiarity

The concept of subsidiarity is indeed an elusive concept. It is submitted that its best definition is the following: "It is a principle for allocating power upwards as well as downwards, but it incorporates a presumption in favour of allocation downwards in case of doubt."[152] It is not tantamount to decentralisation and it admits degrees of exercise of powers. This entails that the decision should always be taken at the lowest practical level, thus leaving the EU to concentrate on the essential and vital objectives.

The principle of subsidiarity maintains the integrity of the EU while allowing the participation of national authorities in decision-making procedures provided they can exercise their functions satisfactorily. Subsidiarity maintains the balance of power between the EU and the Member

---

152.   The CEPR Annual Report, 1993, "Making Sense of Subsidiarity: How Much Centralization for Europe?", (1993) 4 Monitoring European Integration, p 4.

States, and imposes the burden of proof upon the EU institutions. Under the ToL the control of subsidiarity by national parliaments enhances the democratic legitimacy of the EU.

4.4.2 The principle of proportionality

Article 5 TEU states that:

> "Under the principle of proportionality, the content and form of Union action shall not exceed what is necessary to achieve the objectives of the Treaties."

The principle of proportionality was recognised by the ECJ in Case C8/55 *Fédération Charbonnière de Belgique v High Authority*[153] and has since become a general principle of EU law. It imposes a limitation upon the exercise of EU competences because it requires that:

- Any action of an EU institution should not go beyond what is necessary to achieve the declared, lawful objective;[154]

- The measure must be adequate and appropriate as to the legitimate objective to be attained;

- When an EU institution has a choice between a number of appropriate measures, it should choose the one which is the least burdensome and the least restrictive, and the disadvantages caused must not be disproportionate to the aims pursued;[155]

- Not only the content but also the form of Union action must comply with the requirement of proportionality.

Infringements of the principle of proportionality have been quite frequent. For example, in Case C-310/04 *Spain v Council*,[156] the ECJ held that the principle of proportionality was breached by the Council when it adopted the contested regulation amending the support scheme for cotton given that:

> "the Council . . . has not shown before the Court that in adopting the new cotton support scheme established by that regulation it actually exercised its discretion, involving the taking into consideration of all the relevant factors and circumstances of the case, including all the labour costs linked to cotton growing and the viability of the ginning undertakings, which it was necessary to take into account for assessing the profitability of that crop."

Consequently, the ECJ found that the principle of proportionality had been infringed and annulled the contested regulation.

4.5 Supportive competences of the EU

These refer to areas in which the Member States have not conferred competences on the EU but have decided to act through it. In these areas the EU supports, co-ordinates, encourages or

---

153. [1954–56] ECR 245.
154. Case 154/78 *Valsabbia* [1980] ECR 907.
155. Case C-331/88 *Fedesa* [1990] ECR I-4023.
156. [2006] ECR I-7285.

complements measures taken at national level. Article 6 TFEU provides the following list of areas in which the Member States have exclusive competence but the Union can provide support or co-ordination:

- Protection and improvement of human health;

- Industry;

- Culture;

- Tourism;

- Education, vocational training, youth and sport;

- Civil protection;

- Administrative co-operation.

In the above areas the EU may adopt incentive measures and make recommendations, but is prohibited from taking harmonising measures relating to national laws of Member States (Article 2(5) TFEU).

Under Article 5 TFEU the EU can only define "broad guidelines" in respect of economic and employment policies. As a result, in those areas the EU can define the framework of co-ordination between Member States but is prevented from taking any action which it is normally allowed to take in respect of areas in which it exercises supporting competences.

The CFSP is not included in Title I of the TFEU. The peculiarity of the CFSP necessitated the establishment of special rules as to the determination and the exercise of the competences by the EU and its Member States. These are set out in Article 24 TEU (see Chapter 5).

4.6 The "flexibility clause" contained in Article 352 TFEU

To ensure that the objectives of the internal market are met, Article 308 EC [its amended version is contained in Article 352 TFEU] allowed the Council, acting unanimously, on a proposal from the Commission, and after consulting the EP, to take measures it considered necessary, in a situation where the Community had no explicit or implied powers to act. In the 1970s and 1980s Article 308 EC was used to extend the competences of the Community without actually revising the EC Treaty. On the basis of Article 308 EC the Council adopted legislation in important areas not covered at that time by the EC Treaty, such as environmental protection, regional aid, research and technology. The Council leant, probably too frequently, upon Article 308 EC for two reasons:

- First, the Paris Summit held in October 1972 decided that in order to establish an economic and monetary union, as well as promote the social dimension of the Community, all provisions of the EC Treaty, including Article 308 EC, should be widely used. As a result, in the 1970s but mainly in the 1980s, the Council used Article 308 EC extensively and systematically. By 15 March 1992 677 measures, both internal and external, had been adopted on the basis of this article.

- Second, the Council could only adopt a measure on the ground of Article 308 EC if acting unanimously. This requirement ensured that no measure contrary to the interests of any Member State had any realistic chance of adoption. Thus, all extensions of competences under Article 308 EC were acceptable to all Member States.

However, the Commission was not happy about the extensive use of Article 308 EC by the Council because the use of this Article, in effect, involved revision of the EC Treaty outside the revision procedure specified in the EC Treaty. Further, revision of the EC Treaty by the Council undermined the democratic process within each Member State because the new competences had been given to the EC by the executive of each Member State, rather than by its legislative body or according to constitutional procedures used in a Member State. This democratic deficit was not compensated for by the fact that the EP was involved in the adoption of a measure, bearing in mind that the EP was only consulted under Article 308 EC. Resulting from the above, the ECJ imposed two conditions to be met in order to use Article 308 EC as the legal basis of a Community act.

▪ In Case 45/86 *Commission v Council [Re General Tariff Preferences]*,[157] the ECJ held that a measure could only be adopted under Article 308 EC if there was no other appropriate provision in the EC Treaty which would provide a legal basis for Community action. It could, however, have been used where powers existed elsewhere in the Treaty but were insufficient to attain the relevant Community objective.[158]

▪ In *Opinion 2/94 [Re European Convention on Human Rights]*,[159] the ECJ held that Article 308 EC could serve as justification for widening the scope of the EC's powers beyond the general framework set up by the Treaty provisions in general, and those provisions which referred to the EC's tasks and activities in particular. In this Opinion the issue was whether Article 308 EC could be used as a possible legal basis for the accession of the EC to the European Convention of Human Rights. The ECJ held that: "Article 235 of the EC Treaty [Article 308 EC], cannot be used as a basis for the adoption of provisions whose effect would, in substance, be to amend the Treaty without following the procedure which it provides for that purpose."

As can be seen from the above, the ECJ restored Article 308 EC to its initial role, that is, subject to the two above conditions, it could be used for filling gaps in the EC Treaty, but it could not be used for extending the areas of competence of the Community.

The ToL reduced the importance of the "flexibility clause" contained in Article 352 TFEU by making the following amendments to Article 308 EC:

▪ Article 352 TFEU can be used to achieve the objectives of the Treaties as listed in Article 3 TEU but will not apply to the CFSP;

▪ For the adoption of a measure under Article 352 TFEU the Council is required to obtain the EP's consent. Under Article 308 EC the Council was required to consult the EP;

▪ Under Article 352 TFEU, the Commission is required to "draw national Parliaments' attention to proposals based on this Article" so allowing them to use the "yellow and orange cards" procedure;

▪ Article 352 (3) TFEU specifies that "measures based on this Article shall not entail harmonisation of Member States' laws or regulations in cases where the Treaties exclude such harmonisation".

---

157. [1987] ECR 1493.
158. Case 45/86 *Commission v Council [Re General Tariff Preferences]* [1987] ECR 1493.
159. [1996] ECR I-1759.

Declarations 41 and 42 on Article 352 TFEU, attached to the Treaties, further limit the potential use of Article 352 TFEU. Declaration 41 excludes any action based on Article 352 TFEU in respect of the objectives of the Union set out in Article 3(1) TEU, i.e. concerning external action of the EU to promote peace, its values and the well-being of its peoples. This is because such action will be within the scope of the CFSP to which Article 352 does not apply. Declaration 42 states that Article 352 TFEU, being an integral part of an institutional system based on the principle of conferral, cannot be used to adopt measures whose effect would, in substance, amend the Treaties outside the procedures provided for that purpose. Declaration 42 reiterates the position taken by the ECJ in Opinion 2/94. Its main aim is to confirm the desire of the Member States to prevent any extension of the EU's competences.

4.7   Exercise of the Union's competences by a limited number of Member States: the enhanced co-operation procedure

The possibility for some Member States to establish closer co-operation between themselves, through the Community institutions and procedures, had been introduced by the ToA, and is known as "enhanced co-operation". The IGC, revising the ToA, decided that the conditions triggering enhanced co-operation needed substantial amendment. The ToA limited the use of enhanced co-operation to matters dealt with in Pillar 1 and in Pillar 3 (matters concerning police and judicial co-operation in criminal matters), imposed strict conditions for its use, and gave the right of veto to every Member State, even if that Member State did not wish to participate. Under the ToA the procedure was never used. The ToN profoundly revised the enhanced co-operation procedure in order to make it more attractive to Member States. The ToL has further reformed the procedure. Provisions relevant to enhanced co-operation are contained in Title IV of the TEU and Title III of Part Six of the TFEU.

In order to understand the implications of enhanced co-operation, a distinction must be made:

A.   Between co-operation among Member States within the institutional framework of the EU and outside that framework. With regard to the latter, each Member State, being a sovereign state, can enter into any international agreement with any other state, including another Member State, provided that such an agreement neither undermines the EU's objectives, nor compromises that Member State's obligations stemming from its membership of the EU. Examples of such agreements, which involve only a limited number of Member States, are: the agreement creating Eurocorps (see Chapter 5.5.1.1), and that creating the European Space Agency. The Treaties themselves allow for such agreements, e.g. Article 350 TFEU states that the Treaties shall not preclude the existence or completion of the Benelux Union in so far as the objectives of the Benelux Union are not attained by application of the Treaties.

B.   Between co-operation within the institutional framework of the EU which is "pre-defined" or "pre-determined" and enhanced co-operation as described in the ToL. "Pre-defined" or "pre-determined" co-operation within the institutional framework of the EU refers to a situation where the Treaties, a Protocol attached to them or secondary legislation set out rules and procedures for participation, or allow a Member State to "opt-out" of being a participant in that form of co-operation. The best examples are participation in the EMU, the Schengen acquis, or under Articles 114(4) and (5) TFEU, which allow a Member State to deviate from the application of EU law for certain specified reasons, in accordance with certain procedures. Enhanced co-operation refers to a situation where co-operation is not "pre-determined" or is pre-determined to a lesser degree. Thus, a group of Member States may be allowed to co-operate in certain permissible areas, but the manner in which they intend to co-operate and the details of arrangements they intend to enter into, still have to be addressed in the act establishing the co-operation. Further, under Article 20(4) TFEU acts adopted within the framework of enhanced co-operation do not form part of the EU acquis.

At the time of writing the mechanism of enhanced co-operation has never been triggered.

Enhanced co-operation is a mixed blessing. On the one hand, it introduces flexibility into the workings of the EU, as it allows co-operation among groups of Member States, as against amongst all Member States, on some projects, and on the other hand, it threatens the coherence of the EU. The danger is that enhanced co-operation allows for differential integration, that is, instead of all Member States moving towards the achievement of the EU's objectives at the same speed, some of them are allowed to move faster, and consequently some of them may never catch up. Further drawbacks are those of complexity and fragmentation of the EU's legal order.[160] Having said this in a Union of diverse members, diverse approaches may be seen as appropriate.

4.7.1 The main features of the enhanced co-operation procedure

They are:

- The TOL recognises the possibility of instituting enhanced co-operation in all areas of competences of the EU including the CFSP and within the CFSP the CSDP apart from areas in which the EU enjoys exclusive competences. Those are listed in Article 3 TFEU;

- Article 20 TEU provides that enhanced co-operation should further the objectives of the Union, protect its interests and reinforce its integration process whilst Article 326 TFEU states that the procedure must not undermine the internal market or the EU's economic, social and territorial cohesion; must not constitute a barrier to or discrimination in trade between the Member States and must not distort competition between them. Under Article 327 TFEU any enhanced co-operation must respect the competences, rights and obligations of non-participating Member States;

- Article 20(1) TEU specifies that enhanced co-operation may be undertaken only as a last resort, that is, when it has been established within the Council that the objectives of such co-operation cannot be achieved within a reasonable period by applying the relevant provisions of the Treaties;

- Article 328 TFEU requires that when enhanced co-operation is being established, it should be open to all Member States, at any time, provided that the Member State that wishes to participate complies with decisions taken within the established enhanced co-operation framework. The Commission and the participating Member States shall ensure that as many non-participating Member States as possible are encouraged to take part;

---

160. N. Walker, "Flexibility within a Metaconstitutional Framework", in G. de Búrca and J. Scott (eds), *Constitutional Changes in the EU: From Uniformity to Flexibility*, 2000, Oxford: Hart Publishing, p 10.

- Article 20(4) TFEU provides that acts adopted within the framework of enhanced co-operation do not form part of the EU acquis;

- Acts adopted within the framework of enhanced co-operation shall be applied by the participating Member States and their implementation shall not be impeded by non-participating Member States;

- In respect of enhanced co-operation which is in progress and which does not have military or defence implications, the Council acting unanimously may adopt a decision, stipulating that it will act by QMV where the Treaty stipulates that the Council shall act unanimously (Article 333 TFEU). The only constraint imposed on the Council is that it must consult the EP;

- Once enhanced procedure has been established, only participating Member States are entitled to vote in the Council on matters relating to that particular co-operation although all Members of the Council may take part in deliberations;

- Under Article 332 TFEU expenditure resulting from enhanced co-operation, other than administrative costs, shall be borne by the participating Member States, unless the Council acting unanimously, after consulting the EP, decides otherwise;

- Article 334 TFEU requires that the Council and the Commission ensure the consistency of activities decided upon within the framework of enhanced co-operation with other policies and activities of the EU.

The ToL's main innovation so far as enhanced co-operation is concerned is that it provides differing rules for the establishment of, and the participation in, enhanced co-operation in progress, depending on the policy areas. It establishes a general procedure in Article 329(1) TFEU and specific procedures in respect of three areas: the CFSP, the AFSJ and the CSDP.

4.7.2 General procedure for enhanced co-operation

Interested Member States (at the minimum, nine) are required to address a request to the Commission specifying the scope and objectives of their intended enhanced co-operation. The Commission may either submit a proposal for approval to the Council or may refuse to do this in which case a reason for refusal should be given. If the Commission decides to submit the proposal, the Council acting by QMV may grant authorisation to proceed after obtaining the consent of the EP.

With regard to any enhanced co-operation which is in progress, an interested Member State is required to notify the Commission of its intention to join. The Commission within four months of the date of receipt of the notification may, either confirm the participation of the Member State concerned, or decline the request in which case it should indicate arrangements to be adopted which would satisfy the conditions for participation and set a deadline for re-examining the request. On the expiry of that deadline, the Commission must re-examine the request. If the Commission still considers that the conditions for participation have not been fulfilled by the Member State concerned, it must forward the request to the Council which will take a final decision (Article 332 TFEU).

4.7.3   Enhanced co-operation in the CFSP

Under Article 329(2) TFEU, Member States (at a minimum, nine) may submit a request directly to the Council for authorisation to commence enhanced co-operation. The Council, after receiving an opinion from the HR on whether the enhanced co-operation is consistent with the EU's CFSP and from the Commission on its compatibility with other Union policies, acting unanimously, may give authorisation to proceed. The EP is only informed of the request.

An interested Member State is required to notify its intention to join any enhanced co-operation which is in progress to the Council, the HR and the Commission. However, only the opinion of the HR will be taken into account by the Council when it decides, by unanimity, on that Member State's participation. However, if the Council refuses the request it must indicate the arrangements to be adopted to fulfil the conditions for participation and set a deadline for re-examining the request.

4.7.4   Enhanced co-operation in the area of FSJ

The establishment of enhanced co-operation among at least nine Member States based on draft directives concerning police and judicial co-operation in criminal matters (Article 82(3) TFEU) or on directives establishing minimum rules concerning the definition of criminal offences and sanctions in the areas of particularly serious crimes with a cross-border dimension resulting from the nature or impact of such offences or from a special need to combat them on a common basis (Article 83(3) TFEU) involves only a notification to the EP, the Council and the Commission. No authorisation from the Council is required. The relaxed rules are justified by the fact that the adoption of a draft directive has been either suspended or blocked at the initiative of a Member State which has pulled the "emergency brake", i.e. decided that the adoption of the proposed measure would affect fundamental aspects of its criminal justice system (see Chapter 2.4.6).

4.7.5   Enhanced co-operation in the CSDP

There are the following types of enhanced co-operation in the CSDP.

4.7.5.1   *Permanent structured co-operation*

Under Article 42 TEU, "permanent structured co-operation" can be established by "those Member States whose military capabilities fulfil higher criteria and which have made more binding commitments to one another in this area with a view to the most demanding missions". There is no minimum threshold fixed in terms of the number of participating States (Article 46 TEU).

4.7.5.2   *The participation of Member States in missions outside the EU*

The EU may use Member States to carry missions outside the EU for peace-keeping, conflict prevention and strengthening international security in accordance with the principles of the United Nations Charter (Article 46 TEU).

4.7.5.3   Co-operation within the framework of the European Defence Agency

Co-operation between Member States wishing to be part of the European Defence Agency will be defined by the Council which will adopt, acting by a qualified majority, a decision defining the Agency's statute, seat and operational rules (Article 45(2) TEU).

4.8   Supranationality v inter-governmentalism: Is the EU a federation?

Many scholars have tried to conceptualise the EU legal order, the central question being: "Is the EU an international organisation of a type similar to a confederation or is it an embryonic federal state?"

Many issues make the debate difficult:

1.   The concept of a federation is complex: there are many definitions of federalism and many models of federal states. Examples are the USA, Canada, Germany, South Africa, Belgium and Switzerland. The issues are which variant of federalism should we use in a comparative reflection on the nature of the EU, and should we refer at all to the established models of federation for comparative guidance, given that the EU is unique and that European integration exhibits sui generis features?

2.   Should the debate be restricted to a legal or constitutional definition of a federation or should it encompass sociological, economic, political and cultural aspects?

3.   The EU is of a complex multidimensional nature.

4.   How relevant are the nineteenth-century definitions of "state", "sovereignty" and "treaty" to a conceptual discussion on the nature of the EU in the twenty-first century environment? Should we rethink or reformulate "old" definitions instead of trying to fit the EU into them? Or perhaps a new word is needed to describe the entity that is the EU?

The answers to the above questions are beyond the scope of this book. However, they illustrate some of the difficulties and challenges surrounding the debate and set it in context.

Having said the above, it may be useful to provide a basic, unsophisticated definition of a federation and a confederation.

4.8.1   Confederation

In a confederation two or more independent states unite for their mutual welfare and for the furtherance of their common aims. Usually they sign a treaty to this effect, which is often replaced by an agreed constitution. A central government is created that has certain powers, mostly in external affairs and defence. Component states retain their powers for domestic purposes. Often a common currency is introduced. The central government acts upon the member states, not upon the individuals. Each component state is fully sovereign and independent and thus possesses international legal personality. Each component state is free to leave the confederation.

Examples of confederations are: Switzerland (between 1291 and 1848), The Netherlands (between 1581 and 1795), the US (between 1776 and 1788) and Germany (between 1815 and 1866). While the EU in many respects does not fit into the definition of a confederation, it exhibits some of its features:

■   It is a union of states based on international treaties;

- It tried but failed to adopt a formal constitution. However, many scholars, including the author, accept that the EU already has a constitution, that is, the founding treaties as amended;

- Member States have delegated certain powers to EU institutions. Nevertheless, crucial areas, in particular foreign affairs and defence, are still within the individual realm of each Member State;

- Member States of the EU are allowed to have different forms of government;

- Each Member State is fully sovereign, independent and possesses international legal personality;

- There is a common currency although not all Member States have adopted it;

- A Member State is free to leave the Union if it so wishes. The right to withdraw is contained in Article 50 TEU;

- EU law is relevant to individuals, as they can bring claims in national courts based on EU law and can be direct addressees of measures taken by the EU institutions.

4.8.2   Federation

It is difficult to provide a definition of a federation without being too simplistic or too vague. Accordingly the following is far from being perfect.

In a federation two or more states unite to such an extent that they abandon their separate organisation as sovereign and independent states. Federations can be founded on international treaties, emerge as a result of decentralisation of a unitary state (for example, Belgium and Brazil) or be created by means of coercion (the USA). Governmental responsibilities are divided between the federal authority and the constituent members of the federation. Usually the federal government is entrusted with exclusive competence in foreign affairs, defence, immigration, citizenship, and so on, while member states have competence in respect of internal matters. Only the federal state possesses international personality and is regarded as a state under international law. There is a general principle that member states of a federation cannot enter into separate relations with foreign states, although some federal constitutions give member states a limited capacity to do this. The self-governing status of a component state is typically enshrined in a constitution and cannot be altered by a unilateral decision of the central government. Members have no right to leave a federation. Important features of a federation are the existence of a constitution, which is supreme, and of an independent arbiter of that constitution.

The EU exhibits the following federal features:

- It has supranational institutions:

    (a)   The Commission, which is independent, initiates legislation, acts as a watchdog to ensure the due application of EU law by all parties and is the executive of the EU. However, the Commission cannot be equated with a federal government because it is the European Council that gives the necessary political impetus to European integration, and the right to initiate legislation is not vested solely in the Commission;

    (b)   The EP: while the EP is democratically elected by EU citizens, it is less powerful than a national parliament. The EP cannot initiate legislation, is not the sole legislative body in the EU (see Chapter 6.5) and, unlike national parliaments, cannot impose taxes;

(c)　The ECJ: interprets EU law, rules on the validity of EU law, conducts judicial reviews of EU acts and monitors the uniform interpretation of EU law. Member States, EU institutions and, in limited circumstances, individuals have access to the ECJ. There is no doubt that the ECJ exercises an integrative influence on the EU, but the ECJ cannot be equated to a federal court and cannot be regarded as a supreme judicial arbiter in all matters because its role under EU law is different from that exercised by a federal court. In a federal state only the federal court (not a state court) can interpret the constitution, monitor the division of competences between the states and the centre, conduct judicial reviews and supervise a bill of rights. The ECJ does not directly supervise the division of competences between the EU and the Member States and the final arbitrator on human rights issues will be the ECtHR. Further, the ECJ is too inaccessible to citizens of the EU to be regarded as a federal court;

- EU law is supreme and thus prevails over the national law of a Member State (see Chapter 13);

- Individuals are subject to EU law;

- The direct effect of EU law ensures that individuals can rely on it in proceedings before national courts;

- The EU has created its own citizenship (see Chapter 22);

- It has a single currency, the euro;

- The division of competences between the EU and the Member States is based on the principles of conferral, subsidiarity and proportionality. In particular, the principle of subsidiarity is akin to a federation. However, the EU requires the consent of a majority of the Member States to legislate even in areas in which it enjoys exclusive competence. Thus the Member States retain control over the EU's actions;

- The Member States are responsible for the implementation of legislative measures adopted by the EU;

- The EU has its own resources and its own budget.

4.8.3　Conclusion

It is submitted that the EU is neither a federation nor a confederation. Its uniqueness lies in the fact that it encompasses some features of both to accomplish its objectives. It exhibits many federal features, while in the CFSP it exhibits features inherent to an international organisation of a type similar to a confederation. The EU is a new hybrid political and legal system that encompasses many of the political and legal advantages of a federal state while preserving the sovereignty of nation states. The preservation of sovereignty is particularly evident in areas of foreign policy, defence and taxation, which are typically within the competence of a federal state, but being particularly dear to many Member States, are within the exclusive competence of each of them.

Perhaps the best answer as to the identification of the nature of the EU is provided by Douglas-Scott in the following terms:

"In the end, it surely matters not whether we call the EU a federal system or not. It exhibits enough federal features to satisfy those who are determined to find it federal, and lacks some which would entitle purists to reject the title . . . The EU . . . is too sui generis, too complex, too multidimensional, to fit any such categorisation."[161]

AIDE-MÉMOIRE

Competences of the EU are exercised under the principal of conferral, i.e. the EU can exercise competences conferred on it by the Member States. Competences not conferred on the EU remain with the Member States. Under Article 241 TFEU there is the ability to separate competences, i.e. the possibility to give competences back to the Member States.

The TOL distinguishes three main types of competences

EXCLUSIVE	SHARED	SUPPORTIVE
Only the EU has competence to legislate in areas of its exclusive competence. The principle of proportionality applies but not the principle of subsidiarity	In the areas of shared competences both the EU and the Member States can legislate. The principle of subsidiarity and proportionality apply. Under Protocol 2 national parliaments control the application of the principle of subsidiarity through the "yellow and orange cards" procedure	In the areas of supportive competences Member States have exclusive competence but the EU can provide support and co-ordination (but not harmonisation)

---

161. S. Douglas-Scott, *Constitutional Law of the European Union*, 2002, Harlow: Pearson Longman, p 195.

COMPETENCES	POLICY AREAS
EXCLUSIVE THE EXHAUSTIVE LIST OF EXCLUSIVE COMPETENCES IS CONTAINED IN ARTICLE 3 TFEU	• THE CUSTOMS UNION • COMPETITION RULES NECESSARY FOR THE FUNCTIONING OF THE INTERNAL MARKET • MONETARY POLICY FOR MEMBER STATES WHICH HAVE ADOPTED THE EURO • CONSERVATION OF MARINE BIOLOGICAL RESOURCES UNDER THE COMMON FISHERIES POLICY • THE COMMON COMMERCIAL POLICY • CONCLUSION OF AN INTERNATIONAL AGREEMENT COVERED BY AN EXCLUSIVE INTERNAL COMPETENCE (THE ERTA CASE)
SHARED SOME ARE IDENTIFIED IN ARTICLE 4 TFEU, THE REMAINDER ARE DETERMINED ON THE BASIS OF ELIMINATION, I.E. A COMPETENCE IS SHARED IF IT IS NEITHER MENTIONED UNDER EXCLUSIVE NOR UNDER SUPPORTIVE COMPETENCE	• THE INTERNAL MARKET • SOCIAL POLICY FOR ASPECTS DEFINED IN THE TFEU • ECONOMIC, SOCIAL AND TERRITORIAL COHESION • AGRICULTURE AND FISHERIES, EXCLUDING CONSERVATION OF MARINE BIOLOGICAL RESOURCES • ENVIRONMENT • CONSUMER PROTECTION • TRANSPORT • TRANS-EUROPEAN NETWORKS • ENERGY • THE AREA OF FSJ • COMMON SAFETY CONCERNS IN PUBLIC HEALTH MATTERS IN RESPECT OF THE ASPECTS DEFINED IN THE TFEU • THE AREAS OF RESEARCH, TECHNOLOGICAL DEVELOPMENT AND SPACE BUT THE EU'S EXERCISE OF THAT COMPETENCE "SHALL NOT RESULT IN MEMBER STATES BEING PREVENTED FROM EXERCISING THEIRS" • THE AREAS OF DEVELOPMENT CO-OPERATION AND HUMANITARIAN AID BUT THE EU'S EXERCISE OF THAT COMPETENCE "SHALL NOT RESULT IN MEMBER STATES BEING PREVENTED FROM EXERCISING THEIRS"
SUPPORTIVE THE EXHAUSTIVE LIST OF SUPPORTIVE COMPETENCES IS CONTAINED IN ARTICE 6 TFEU	• PROTECTION AND IMPROVEMENT OF HUMAN HEALTH • INDUSTRY • CULTURE • TOURISM • EDUCATIONAL, VOCATIONAL TRAINING, YOUTH AND SPORT • CIVIL PROTECTION • ADMINISTRATIVE CO-OPERATION

NOTE: SPECIAL RULES APPLY TO ECONOMIC AND EMPLOYMENT POLICIES AND THE CFSP

RULES RELATING TO THE ESTABLISHMENT OF ENHANCED CO-OPERATION

	GENERAL ENHANCED CO-OPERATION	ENHANCED CO-OPERATION IN THE AREA OF FSJ IN CRIMINAL MATTERS	ENHANCED CO-OPERATION IN THE CFSP	ENHANCED CO-OPERATION IN THE CSDP (PERMANENT STRUCTURED CO-OPERATION)
AUTHORISING EU INSTITUTION	The Council	NOT REQUIRED	The Council	The Council
TYPE OF VOTE IN THE COUNCIL	QMV	N/A	Unanimity	QMV
MINIMUM NUMBER OF MEMBER STATES REQUIRED TO ESTABLISH ENHANCED CO-OPERATION	9	9	9	NO MINIMUM IS SET
TYPE OF PROCEDURE USED BY THE EP	CONSENT	THE EP MUST BE INFORMED	THE EP MUST BE INFORMED	N/A
PARTICIPATION OF THE COMMISSION	THE COMMISSION MAKES A PROPOSAL	THE COMMISSION MUST BE INFORMED	THE COMMISSION GIVES ITS OPINION	N/A
PARTICIPATION OF OTHER EU INSTITUTIONS OR BODIES	N/A	N/A	THE HR MUST GIVE HER OPINION	THE HR MUST GIVE HER OPINION

RECOMMENDED READING

Books

Bache, I. and Flinders, M. (eds), *Multi-level Governance*, 2004, Oxford: OUP

Birkinshaw P.J. and Varney, M., *The European Union Legal Order after Lisbon*, 2010, London: KLI

Konstadinides, T., *Division of Powers in European Union Law: The Delimitation of Internal Competences between the EU and the Member States*, 2009, London: KLI

Articles

Cardwell, P. J. and Kirkham, R., "The European Union: A Role Model for Regional Governance?", (2006) 12/3 EPL, p 403

Harbo, T-I., "The Function of the Proportionality Principle in EU Law", (2010) 16 ELJ, p 158

Meyring, B., "Intergovernmentalism and Supranationalism: Two Stereotypes for a Complex Reality", (1997) ELRev, p 221

Schütze, R., "On 'Federal' Ground: The European Union as an (Inter)national Phenomenon" (2009) 46 CMLRev, p 1069

5

THE COMMON FOREIGN AND SECURITY POLICY (CFSP)

SUMMARY

1. Introduction. Under the ToL the intrinsic dualism of the EU's foreign policy remains in that external action under the TFEU is conducted in accordance with the "EU method" and the CFSP is "subject to specific rules and procedures" (Article 24 TEU), i.e. the intergovernmental method. However, the ToL establishes new institutional arrangements and mechanisms aimed at enhancing the coherence and efficiency of EU external action.

2. Innovations introduced by the ToL aimed at improving the coherence of EU foreign policy. The main innovations are:

- The creation of the post of the High Representative of the Union for Foreign Affairs and Security Policy (HR);

- The establishment of the European External Action Service (EEAS);

- The ability for the European Council to make determinations of "strategic interests and objectives" for all EU external action;

- The creation of the post of the President of the European Council who exercises external representative responsibilities.

3. The principles and objectives of EU foreign action. The ToL refers to the EU's external action as comprising all its policies towards the wider world and sets out the principles and objectives applicable to all areas of EU foreign action whether provided for in the TFEU or the TEU. The principles are those which have inspired the creation, development and enlargement of the EU. The objectives are listed in Article 21(2) TEU.

4. The CFSP. The European Council and the Council are the main decision making bodies within the CFSP. The main role of the European Council is to "identify the Union's strategic interests, determine the objectives of and define general guidelines" for the CFSP as well as to decide on the EU strategy when facing international crises. The Council "shall frame the common foreign and security policy and take the decisions necessary for defining and implementing it on the basis of the general guidelines and strategic lines defined by the European Council". However, neither the European Council nor the Council are empowered to adopt legislative acts in respect of any CFSP matters. The European Council acts by unanimity, so does the Council, subject to exceptions concerning mainly decisions implementing the European Council guidelines and the potential use of the "passerelle clause". The Commission, resulting from the HR being ex officio Vice President of the Commission, is fully associated with the CFSP. It is the HR, not the Commission, who has the right to initiate proposals in the CFSP areas. The EP is consulted and kept informed. The ECJ has no jurisdiction under the CFSP but it is required to ensure that the CFSP does not encroach on other EU policies and vice versa, and has jurisdiction to review the legality of sanctions imposed against natural and legal persons under the CFSP. As to the Member States they are required to implement measures adopted by the Council, co-operate with each other and "actively and unreservedly in a spirit of loyalty and mutual solidarity" support the CFSP.

5. The Common Security and Defence Policy (CSDP). The ToL has:

- Extended and enhanced the objectives of the CSDP;

- Introduced the "mutual defence clause" and the "solidarity clause";

- Established new procedures to finance "urgent initiatives" under the CFSP, and in particular preparatory activities for CSDP missions, i.e. measures ensuring rapid access to the EU budget and the creation of a "start-up fund";

- Provided for the possibility of the Council to entrust the implementation of a CSDP operational task to a "coalition of willing and able States";

- Established the European Defence Agency (EDA);

- Introduced more flexibility as to the establishment and subsequent development of the "permanent structured co-operation";

- Expanded the Petersberg tasks to include joint disarmament operations, military advice and assistance tasks, conflict prevention and post-conflict stabilisation.

6. The Assessment of the CFSP. Under the ToL the CFSP has the potential to have a stronger political profile and an increased capacity to act consistently on the international stage. The main mechanism for ensuring this is the creation of the post of HR who has the necessary power under the Treaties, a substantial budget and a diplomatic corps, i.e. the EEAS, and who is empowered to speak on behalf of the EU, even in front of the UN Security Council.

5.1   Introduction

The EU is often described as an economic giant but a political dwarf. Its economic weight in the international arena has not been matched by an equal gravitas in international politics. This dichotomy can be explained by historical reasons. From its inception the Community was a "civilian power", that is, an organisation implicitly rejecting power politics and concentrating on the economic aspects of European integration.[162] In reality, it lacked military capacity to conduct a defence policy. This aspect of European affairs was developed mainly within the framework of NATO. The collapse of Communism, the reunification of Germany and the American policy of burden-shedding in military matters have changed perspectives on Europe's future foreign and defence policy. However, the realistic objective of the common foreign and security policy for the EU was and remains more to agree on a common position in international policy (that is, to speak with one voice) than to achieve a unified foreign policy conducted by supranational bodies, with the EU raised to the status of a superpower. This is because Member States are not currently willing, and may never be willing, to give up their exclusive power to conduct national and foreign policies as they wish. In particular, Member States which have a substantive military capability do not wish to lose the power and influence which that capability affords them in the international arena.

Prior to the entry into force of the ToL, the external action of the EU was conducted within Pillar 1 in accordance with the "Community method" [now "EU method"] and in Pillars 2 and 3 in accordance with the intergovernmental method (see Chapter 1.7). Although the ToL abolished the Pillar structure the distinction between the Community method and the intergovernmental method remains. Article 24 TEU states that the Common Foreign and Security Policy (CFSP) and its vital component, the European Security and Defence Policy (ESDP), which has been renamed by the ToL and is now called the Common Security and Defence Policy (CSDP), is "subject to specific rules and procedures", i.e. the intergovernmental method. This results in provisions relating to the EU foreign policy to be found in both the TFEU and the TEU. With regard to the TFEU, some foreign policies are expressly covered by its provisions, e.g. trade, development assistance, other forms of co-operation with third states, humanitarian aid, neighbouring policy, enlargement and diplomatic and consular protection of EU citizens when in a non EU country where their own state has no representation, others are based on the doctrine of implied powers (see Chapter 4.3.2). The TEU contains mainly rules concerning the CFSP including the CSDP.

One of the main objectives of the reform leading to the adoption of the ToL was to enhance the coherence of the EU's foreign policy, i.e. to make the EU's external action more efficient and effective within the existing division between intergovernmental CFSP and the Community areas of foreign policy. The option of applying the "Community method" to the CFSP was non-existent. For example the British Government clearly stated its position in its 2007 White Paper entitled "The Reform Treaty: The British Approach to the European Union Intergovernmental Conference" that a condition of signing of the ToL was "the maintenance of the UK's independent foreign and defence policy".[163] In those circumstances the ToL represents a step towards greater coherence both in terms of the location in the EU's Treaty architecture of provisions

---

162. P. Tsakaloyannis, "From Civilian Power to Military Integration", in J. Lodge (ed.), *The EC and the Challenge of the Future*, 1989, London: Pinter, p 243.

163. The Reform Treaty: The British Approach to the European Union Intergovernmental Conference, July 2007, CM 7174, 7.

relating to the external action of the EU and in terms of establishing new institutional arrangements and mechanisms with a view to maximising EU influence and presence on the global stage.

With regard to the ToL's architecture, a new Chapter I of Title V on "General provisions on the Union's external action" has been inserted into the TEU which sets out principles and objectives applicable to all provisions relating to EU external action irrespective of whether those provisions are located in the TFEU or the TEU. However, the splitting of provisions on the EU's external action into those governed by the "EU method" (which are located in the TFEU) and those to which the intergovernmental method applies (which are contained in the TEU) has not been complete. Some provisions of the TFEU are relevant to the CFSP (e.g. those relating to enhanced co-operation, those concerning the new "solidarity clause" (see Chapter 8.3.3) and the provisions on the imposition of economic sanctions on natural and legal persons) and vice versa.

With regard to institutional innovations the most important is the establishment of the post of a High Representative of the Union for Foreign Affairs and Security Policy (hereafter the HR) who ensures the uniform external representation of the EU, i.e. the HR is the single face and voice of the EU on the world political stage.

5.2   Innovations introduced by the ToL aimed at improving the coherence of EU foreign policy

The main innovations are: the creation of the post of the HR, the establishment of the European External Action Service (EEAS) and the ability for the European Council to make determinations of "strategic interests and objectives" for all EU external action. However, it is uncertain whether the allocation of external representative responsibilities to the President of the European Council in respect of the CFSP will contribute to the efficiency of the EU's external action although he will certainly ensure the continuity of all work of the European Council including that relating to the external affairs of the EU.

5.2.1   Creation of the post of the HR

The procedure for appointment of the HR is as follows: the European Council acting by a qualified majority, with the agreement of the President of the Commission, appoints the HR. Subsequently, the HR, the President of the Commission and the Commissioners must be approved by the EP by a vote of consent. The first HR, Baroness Catherine Ashton, was appointed in accord with this procedure in November 2009 for a five year term.

The holder of the post wears three hats:

- She is the Vice-President of the Commission and, as a member of the Commission, responsible for External Relations and European Neighbourhood Policy. The position of the HR in the Commission is very strong in that the HR is the only Vice-President and the only Commissioner who is appointed ex officio (although subject to the approval of the President of the Commission) and the only Commissioner who cannot be forced by the President of the Commission to resign. However, the EP has the right to apply a motion of censure on the entire Commission, including the HR. Further, the European Council, with the approval of the President of the Commission, may end the HR's term of office. It is to be noted that the HR is bound by Commission procedures to the extent that this is consistent with the tasks carried out by her within the CFSP. Under Article 18(4) TEU, the HR as a Commissioner, is "responsible within the Commission for responsibilities incumbent upon it in external relations and for co-ordinating other aspects of the Union's external action". This entails that she exercises authority over European Commission delegations (to more than 100 countries and many international organisations), which under the ToL, became EU delegations.

■ She replaces the High Representative for the Common Foreign and Security Policy, a post created under the Treaty of Amsterdam which was assigned to the Secretary General of the Council. The post of Secretary General of the Council has become a separate post from that of HR. Within the framework of the CFSP, the HR:

  ● Ensures unity, consistency and effectiveness of EU action relating to the CFSP acting in co-operation with the Council and the Commission;
  ● Assists the Council in all matters relating to the CFSP;
  ● If requested, acts on behalf of the Council in conducting political dialogue with third parties;
  ● Ensures the implementation of CFSP decisions together with the Council and the Member States;
  ● Refers any question, initiative or proposal on the CFSP to the Council;
  ● Represents the EU externally in all CFSP matters including before the UN Security Council;
  ● Regularly consults the EP;
  ● Has the right to propose the appointment of EU Special Representatives, who are accountable to her, with a mandate in relation to particular policy issues (Article 33 TEU);
  ● Is responsible for facilitating the harmonisation of Member States' views on the CFSP;
  ● Fulfils many other tasks which are set out in the aide-mémoire to this chapter.

■ She is the President of the Foreign Affairs Council. In this capacity, the HR has the right to make proposals to the Council and the right to convene extraordinary meetings of the Foreign Affairs Council at either her own initiative or that of a Member State. Views differ as to whether it is a good idea to submit proposals to a body which one chairs.

By merging three posts, the ToL ensures uniform external representation as well as greater coherence and unity in the conduct of EU foreign policy. However, some Member States fear that too much power has been vested on one individual. In this respect it can be said that with regard to the CFSP the HR only supervises the implementation of measures adopted by the European Council and the Council acting unanimously, This is clearly stated in Declaration 14 attached to the Treaties which provides that the provisions of the CFSP, including those relating to the new post of HR:

> . . . "will not affect the existing legal basis, responsibility and powers of each Member State in relation to the formulation and conduct of its foreign policy, its national diplomatic service, relations with third countries and participation in international organizations, including a Member State's membership of the Security Council of the UN."

Declarations 13 and 14 emphasise that the ToL will not give any new powers to the Commission or the EP, and that defence and security matters are within the exclusive competence of each Member State.

If the Member States do not all agree on a common policy with regard to a particular international issue, the HR will have no reason to exercise her power of implementation. However, if there is agreement between the Member States to present a common front on a particular issue, the voice of the HR (being the voice of 27 countries) will carry enormous weight.

5.2.2   Establishment of the EEAS

In order to assist the HR is performing her task, the ToL has created a new body, the European External Action Service (EEAS). This body, accountable to the HR, will be made up of officials from the relevant departments of the General Secretariat of the Council and of the Commission as well as diplomats from the Member States. The organisation, structure and functioning of the EEAS will be established by a decision of the Council, acting on a proposal from the HR after consulting the EP and obtaining consent from the Commission. The EEAS will also assist the President of the European Council, the President of the Commission and Commissioners in the area of external relations, and will work in close co-operation with the diplomatic services of Member States. The creation of the EEAS was as controversial as the creation of the post of HR, in that it has been submitted that the EEAS will, in fact, be the beginning of a European foreign service and thus will constitute a threat to the national foreign services of the Member States.

5.2.3   The power of the European Council to make determinations under Article 22 TEU

Under Article 22 TEU the European Council has the ability to make determinations of "strategic interests and objectives" for all EU external action. Such determinations may "concern the relations of the Union with a specific country or region or may be thematic in approach. They shall define their duration, and the means to be made available by the Union and the Member States" (Article 22(1) TEU). The determinations will be made by the European Council on a recommendation from the Council to which the HR for the CFSP and the Commission for non-CFSP foreign policy may submit joint proposals.

5.2.4   The powers of the President of the European Council in EU external action

One of the main tasks of the President of the European Council, a new position created by the ToL, is to "provide impetus" for the work of the European Council, to ensure "the preparation and continuity" of its work and to facilitate cohesion and consensus within the European Council. Thus he has a great influence on the work of the European Council in all areas of EU activity including its external action which are defined in Article 22 TEU. The President of the European Council is also entitled to convene extraordinary meetings to deal with new international developments. Further, without prejudice to the powers of HR, the President of the European Council ensures the external representation of the EU on issues concerning the CFSP. At the time of writing, it is uncertain whether the allocation of external representative responsibilities to the President of the European Council will enhance the coherence of EU external action or will became a source of confusion internally and externally and even a source of conflict between the HR and the President.

5.3   The principles and objectives of EU foreign action

Article 21 TEU sets out the principles which will guide the EU external action. These principles, inspired by the EU's creation, development and enlargement, are: democracy, respect for the rule of law, the protection of HRs, respect for human dignity, observance of the principles of equality and solidarity, and respect for the principles of the United Nations Charter and international law.

Under Article 21(2) the TEU lists the EU's objectives in its external relations. It states:

"The Union shall define and pursue common policies and actions, and shall work for a high degree of cooperation in all fields of international relations, in order to:

(a)   safeguard its values, fundamental interests, security, independence and integrity;

(b)   consolidate and support democracy, the rule of law, human rights and the principles of international law;

(c)   preserve peace, prevent conflicts and strengthen international security, in accordance with the purposes and principles of the United Nations Charter, with the principles of the Helsinki Final Act and with the aims of the Charter of Paris, including those relating to external borders;

(d)   foster the sustainable economic, social and environmental development of developing countries, with the primary aim of eradicating poverty;

(e)   encourage the integration of all countries into the world economy, including through the progressive abolition of restrictions on international trade;

(f)   help develop international measures to preserve and improve the quality of the environment and the sustainable management of global natural resources, in order to ensure sustainable development;

(g)   assist populations, countries and regions confronting natural or man-made disasters; and

(h)   promote an international system based on stronger multilateral cooperation and good global governance."

5.4   The Common Foreign and Security Policy (CFSP)

Specific provisions on CFSP are contained in Chapter 2 TEU. Section 1 of Chapter 2 deals with the CFSP (Articles 23–41 TEU), whilst section 2 applies to CSDP, the vital component the CFSP (Articles 42–47 TEU). The objectives for the CFSP are the same as those set out for all foreign EU action. Under Article 25 TEU they are to be pursued through:

"(a)   the general guidelines;

(b)   decisions defining:

(i)   actions to be undertaken by the Union;

(ii) positions to be taken by the Union;

(iii) arrangements for the implementation of the decisions referred to in points (i) and (ii);

and by

(c)   strengthening systematic cooperation between Member States in the conduct of policy."

5.4.1   The powers of the decision-making bodies under the CFSP

The main decision-making bodies within the CFSP are the European Council and the Council in its formation of the Foreign Affairs Council. The European Council "shall identify the Union's strategic interests, determine the objectives of and define general guidelines for the common foreign and security policy, including for matters with defence implications". At extraordinary meetings convened to deal with emergency situations, the European Council will have power to define the Union's strategy in respect of such situations (Article 26(1) TEU).

Under Article 26(2) TEU the Council "shall frame the common foreign and security policy and take the decisions necessary for defining and implementing it on the basis of the general guidelines and strategic lines defined by the European Council".

Under Article 31(1) TEU, neither the European Council nor the Council is empowered to adopt legislative acts in respect of CFSP matters.

Both the European Council and the Council act by unanimity except where the treaty specifically provides otherwise (Article 31 TEU). The main exceptions, under which the Council may act by QMV, are contained in Article 31(2) TEU and concern the following four types of decision:

- those which define an action or position on the basis of a decision of the European Council relating to the Union's strategic interests and objectives, as referred to in Article 22(1) TEU. In this situation the Council will implement any decision reached unanimously by the European Council;

- those which define an action or position on the basis of a proposal made by the High Representative "following a specific request from the European Council, made on its own initiative or that of the High Representative". In this situation the Council will act on the basis of a request unanimously agreed by the European Council;

- Those which implement a decision defining a Union action or position. The Council will vote by QMV in respect of a decision unanimously taken by the European Council;

- Those concerning the appointment of a special representative in accordance with Article 33 TEU. As above, the Council will implement a decision taken unanimously by the European Council.

In the above four situations the rule that decisions under the CFSP are taken unanimously is not challenged. The ToL only confirms the principle previously established under Pillar II that the Council is entitled to adopt implementing measures by QMV. Under Article 238(4) TFEU abstentions do not prevent a decision from being adopted by unanimity.

The list of exceptions set out in Article 31(2) TEU is not complete. There are the following additional exceptions which concern:

- Decisions relating to a "start-up fund" (Article 41(3) TEU) (see section 5.5);

- Decisions relating to the statute, seat and operational rules of the European Defence Agency (Article 45 TEU) (see section 5.5);

- Some decisions regarding Permanent Structured Co-Operation (see section 5.5);

- Decisions relating to procedural matters.

Further, Article 31(3) TEU contains a "passerelle" provision under which QMV may apply to matters not expressly mentioned under Article 31(2). However, only the European Council acting unanimously may decide to make use of the "passerelle" provision. Therefore, the "passerelle" provision is unlikely to be used. In the UK, the government is required to obtain approval of both Houses of Parliament before agreeing on the use of the "passerelle" provision.

Even in respect of exceptions set out in Article 31(2) TEU a Member State may object to the Council's voting by QMV. Article 31(2) contains "an emergency brake" procedure under which when a Member State considers that for vital and stated reasons of national policy the use of QMV is inappropriate, the vote will not be taken. The HR will intervene and will try to act as a broker, and if she fails, the matter will be referred to the European Council for a decision by unanimity.

A Member State may exercise "constructive abstention", that is, an abstention which does not hinder the adoption of the decision. If a Member State qualifies its abstention by a formal declaration, it is not obliged to apply the decision but must not act in a manner which will conflict with EU action taken pursuant to that decision. However, the rule of "constructive abstention" does not apply if the number of Member States abstaining in such a manner represents more than one third of the Member States comprising at least one third of the population of the EU, so the consequence here is that the decision is not adopted (Article 31(1) TEU).

5.4.2 The role of the Political and Security Committee (PSC)

The PSC is vital to the CFSP and the CSDP. The PSC is made up of permanent representatives of the Member States at ambassadorial level. The PSC meets two to three times a week. Under the CFSP, the PCS contributes to defining EU external policies and responses to international crises by delivering opinions to the Council at the request of the Council, the HR or on its own initiative. It also affects implementation of agreed policies, without prejudice to the powers of the HR.

5.4.3 Role of the Commission, the EP and the ECJ in the CFSP

The Commission is fully associated with the CFSP. The Commission and the HR may submit jointly proposals to the European Council concerning non-CFSP areas (Article 22 TEU). However, under the ToL the Commission has lost its right of initiative in respect of the CFSP in favour of the HR.

The EP is a consultative body under the CFSP. The HR is required to inform, and regularly consult with, the EP on the "main aspects and basic choices" of the CFSP and the CSDP and to ensure that the views of the EP are taken into account. The EP is entitled to ask the Council questions and to make recommendations to it and to the HR. It also holds twice a year an annual debate on progress in implementing the CFSP and CSDP (Article 36 TEU). As a result, democratic control by the EU of the CFSP is still weak as it consists mainly of consultations with the EP.

The ECJ has no jurisdiction in respect of matters covered by the CFSP. However, it has jurisdiction to ensure that the CFSP does not encroach on other EU policies and vice versa, i.e. that non-CFSP policies do not impinge on the CFSP (Article 40 TEU). Further, under Article 275 TFEU, the ECJ has jurisdiction to review the legality of sanctions against natural or legal persons imposed under the CFSP (Article 24(1) TEU).

5.4.4 Commitments of Member States under the CFSP

The ToL has strengthened the commitment of Member States to the achievement of the objectives of the CFSP. Article 24(3) TEU stresses that "The Member States shall work together to enhance and develop their mutual political solidarity. They shall refrain from any action which is contrary to the interests of the Union or likely to impair its effectiveness as a cohesive force in international relations".

The main commitment of the Member States within the CFSP is to implement measures adopted by the Council.

Member States have obligations vis-à-vis each other to consult and exchange information, especially when only some of them are members of international organisations or attend international conferences where decisions that potentially affect all of them may be taken.

Member States also have obligations vis-à-vis the Union. In this respect, the Member States must support the CFSP "actively and unreservedly in a spirit of loyalty and mutual solidarity" (Article 24(3) TEU). If a Member State is a member of an international organisation where decisions that potentially affect the Union may be taken, that Member State must defend the interests of the EU (Article 34(2) TEU). In the case of the Permanent Members of the UN Security Council, this must be achieved without compromising their responsibilities deriving from the UN Charter. Also, diplomatic and consular missions of Member States and EU delegations to third countries and to international organisations must co-operate in ensuring that the actions taken by the EU are complied with and implemented. Furthermore, they are required to exchange information, carry out joint assessments and contribute to the implementation of Article 20(2)(c) TFEU and Article 23 TEU, that is, to ensure diplomatic and consular protection of EU citizens in countries where their governments are not represented (see Chapter 22.4).

5.5   The Common Security and Defence Policy (CSDP)

It is important to emphasise the connection between the CSDP and other EU policies, in particular those relating to the creation of the area of FSJ. Many structures and mechanisms set up under one policy support, develop and enhance another. Consistency and efficiency require that whatever security, emergency or other serious problems arise in this area, the EU must tackle them using the full spectrum of its capabilities and resources. Article 21(3) TEU imposes an obligation on the Council and the Commission, assisted by the HR, to co-operate in order to ensure such consistency.

The CSDP, which is a vital component of the CFSP, has its own objectives in addition to those set out in respect of all EU external action. Article 42(2) TEU provides that "The common security and defence policy shall include the progressive framing of a common Union defence policy. This will lead to a common defence, when the European Council, acting unanimously, so decides." The main innovations of the ToL concerning the CSDP are:

- The inclusion of a form of mutual defence clause. If one Member State becomes a victim of armed aggression all other Member States are bound to aid and assist that victim State by all means in their power. However, such assistance must:

  - Be in conformity with Article 51 of the UN Charter which contains an exception to the prohibition of the use of force in international relations on the ground of self-defence;
  - Respect commitments of Member States which are members of the North Atlantic Treaty Organisation, which remains the basis of their collective defence and the forum for their implementation;
  - Be consistent with "the specific character of the security and defence policy of certain Member States" (Article 42(7) TEU);

- The inclusion of a "solidarity clause" contained in Article 222 TFEU. The clause does not specifically apply to the CSDP but is relevant in all situations where a Member State is the object of a terrorist attack or victim of a natural or man-made disaster. In those circumstances the EU and its Member States are required to assist the State concerned with all relevant means including military ones.

- The establishment of new procedures to finance "urgent initiatives" under the CFSP, and in particular preparatory activities for CSDP missions. Timely and appropriate levels of financing of such missions, as they are performed using capabilities provided by the Member States, are vital for their success. In order to ensure "rapid access" to the EU budget for missions financed by the EU, the Council will adopt a decision establishing the appropriate procedures. For missions which will not be financed from the Union budget, a new "start-up fund" will be established to which Member States will contribute. The details relating to the establishment, financing (in particular the amounts to be contributed to the fund) and functioning of the "start-up fund" will be provided by a Council decision. The "start-up fund" is seen by many as the first step towards the establishment of a common defence budget for the EU. Under Article 41(3) TEU, the HR is authorised to use the "start-up fund";

- The possibility for the Council to entrust the implementation of a CSDP operational task to a group of Member States which are "willing and have the necessary capacity" to accomplish it. The HR is to be associated with any such "coalition of the able and willing" among the Member States in terms of working out details concerning the management of the task in question;

- The establishment of the European Defence Agency (EDA) (which in fact was created in 2004!)[164] with a view to progressively improving the military capabilities of the Member States. Individual Member States will decide whether to join the EDA. The tasks of the EDA are set out in Article 45 TEU;

- The establishment of "permanent structured co-operation" which constitutes a specific form of enhanced co-operation in the areas covered by the CSDP;

- The expansion of the "Petersberg tasks" to include joint disarmament operations, military advice and assistance tasks, conflict prevention and post-conflict stabilisation (Article 43 TEU).

The CSDP has two dimensions: the defence dimension and the security dimension. They are examined below.

5.5.1 The defence dimension

When the Maastricht Treaty was negotiated the Member States agreed to include "the eventual framing of a common defence policy, which might lead to a common defence" in the scope of that Treaty. Under Pillar 2 of the TEU, the Western European Union was made responsible for ensuring a common defence policy.

The Western European Union (WEU) was founded on 6 May 1955 on the basis of the Brussels Treaty of 1948, which provided for collective defence and co-operation in economic, social and cultural matters. The WEU was only intended to strengthen security co-operation among its Contracting States and for that reason activities other than defence were subsequently transferred to the Council of Europe. As a result of the creation of NATO, the WEU lost its importance at

---

164. Under a Joint Action adopted by the Council on 12 July 2004 [2004] O J L45/17.

European level. However, there were many reasons for the EU's decision at Maastricht to re-energise the WEU:

■ Unlike NATO the WEU is a European organisation;

■ With the end of the cold war the USA had been seeking to reduce its military commitment in Europe;

■ Many Member States of the EU are not members of NATO; and

■ The crucial question regarding the relationship between NATO and the WEU had been solved, to the satisfaction of both organisations. The Member States agreed that the WEU should not undermine NATO and that its role should be limited to military operations outside the remit of NATO.

In June 1992, at a meeting near Bonn, the foreign ministers and defence ministers of the WEU countries had defined the future objectives of the WEU. These were called "Petersberg tasks" (named after the Hotel Petersberg where the meeting took place) and consisted of:

■ Conflict prevention tasks;

■ Humanitarian and rescue tasks;

■ Peacekeeping tasks; and

■ Tasks of combat forces in crisis management including peacemaking.

The ToA incorporated the Petersberg tasks into Title V of the TEU. Thus, all Member States whether or not members of WEU could participate in carrying out the Petersberg tasks.

In 1996, at a meeting in Berlin, NATO foreign ministers decided to build up the European Security and Defence Identity (ESDI) within the NATO structures rather than within the EU. This led to the establishment of close links with the WEU, which, under various agreements, was allowed to use NATO assets and capacities in its own military operations executed on behalf of the EU.

The Balkan War in 1995, and in particular NATO's intervention in Kosovo, changed the course of the EU defence policy. British Prime Minister Tony Blair and French President Jacques Chirac, for different reasons, recognised the necessity of setting up a new, genuine European defence strategy. In December 1998 at St Malo they issued a Declaration stating that:

"... the Union must have the capacity for autonomous action, backed by credible military forces, the means to decide to use them, and a readiness to do so, in order to respond to international crises."

The Cologne European Council (June 1999) endorsed the above Franco-British declaration and stated that the EU should have the ability to fulfil Petersberg tasks without prejudice to actions by NATO. The Cologne European Council outlined the ESDP [now the CSDP] and thus rejected the ESDI. The Council stated that the integration of the WEU into the EU, despite the previous arrangement, had to be abandoned as the Petersberg tasks would in future be carried out within the framework of the EU. As a result, the performance of the Petersberg tasks became part of the ESDP, and is now part of the CSDP.

The CSDP has three components: military, civilian and conflict prevention.

5.5.1.1 The military component

The content of this component was defined by the Helsinki European Council (December 1999). The Council agreed that:

- By 2003 Member States must, between them and co-operating on a voluntary basis in operations directed by the EU, be able to deploy within 60 days and to sustain for at least one year military forces of up to 50,000–60,000 persons in order to carry out the Petersberg tasks. This was the main objective of the military component and it was called a "Headline Goal";

- New political and military bodies and structures should be established to ensure the necessary political and strategic direction of the above operations;

- New arrangements should be made in order to ensure full consultation, co-operation and transparency between the EU and NATO;

- Appropriate arrangements should be put in place for non-European NATO members and other interested states to contribute to EU military crisis management.

Once the ambitious agenda of the Helsinki European Council was largely achieved, the European Council of June 2004 decided to further develop the EU's military crisis management capability by setting new "Headline Goal 2010". Under this document, the Member States made a commitment that by the year 2010, at the latest, they would be capable of responding "with rapid and decisive action applying a fully coherent approach to the whole spectrum of crisis management operations" and would redress shortfalls identified in the previous Headline Goal.[165]

The so-called "Headline Goal" has materialised as the European Rapid Reaction Force (ERRF). The formal agreement creating the ERRF was signed on 22 November 2004, and the ERRF was programmed to be fully operational by 2005. Informally, the ERRF, consisting of fewer than 50,000 soldiers, was put at the disposal of the EU much earlier. The first mission of the ERRF, known as "Operation Concordia", was launched on 31 March 2003 in the Former Yugoslav Republic of Macedonia and consisted of peacekeeping and other tasks necessary to control civil unrest in the FYR Macedonia. That mission was successfully accomplished and indeed, the list of completed and ongoing military EU operations is impressive.[166]

The ERRF is neither an EU army nor a standing army. Troops or units assigned by national armies to be part of the ERRF remain with their national armies, unless they are deployed by the EU. The commitment of national forces to any particular EU operation remains a sovereign decision of the Member State concerned.

Part of the military component (but this also can be part of the civilian component (see section 5.5.1.2)) is the European Union Battle Groups (EU BGs), which became operational on 1 January 2007. Each group comprises 1,500 combat soldiers. Larger Member States have their own battle groups while smaller Member States have created common groups. At the time of writing there are 18 groups which rotate every six months; two are always ready for immediate deployment. The EU BGs are at the disposal of the EU, can be deployed within five to ten days to deal with emergency situations when the UN or NATO cannot intervene quickly enough, and are

---

165. The Headline Goal 2010 together with the Council Declaration of 8 December 2008 on the Enhancement of the Capacities of the European Security and Defence Policy can be found at http://www.consilium.europa.eu/showPage.aspx?id=1349&lang=EN (20/3/10).

166. It can be found at http://www.consilium.europa.eu/showPage.aspx?id=268&lang=en (20/3/10).

sustainable for at least 30 days. They are intended to carry out the Petersberg tasks, in particular to undertake rapid response operations either for stand-alone operations or for the initial stage of larger operations. At the time of writing, EU BGs have never been employed. One of the main reasons is that for them to be deployed the unanimous approval of all 27 Member States is required.

In the context of the military component of the CSDP, it is appropriate to mention the Eurocorps which was born out of a Franco-German initiative and became operational in 1994.[167] It comprises one French and one German division, plus contingents from Belgium, Spain and Luxembourg, the so called "framework nations". In addition to the five "framework nations", a further seven countries, Austria, Greece, Italy, Poland, Romania, Turkey, and the USA, "the sending nations" have pledged troops or contribute operational staff. Eurocorps has approximately 60,000 soldiers of which about 1,000 are stationed at its headquarters, in Strasbourg. Eurocorps is not subordinate to any military organisation, although it has been certified by both the EU and NATO as satisfying the criteria for rapid reaction corps. Eurocorps is an army that could be placed at the disposal of any organisation, including NATO and the EU, and even a nation state, to perform humanitarian, peacekeeping and peace restoring missions. Eurocorps can also be employed in high-intensity combat operations. It participated in peacekeeping missions in Bosnia-Herzegovina, in Kosovo and in Afghanistan.

The issue of co-operation between the EU and non-European states which are members of NATO poses no major problem. Appropriate co-operation arrangements have been put in place.

5.5.1.2   The civilian component

This was developed by the Feira European Council of June 1999 and the Göteborg European Council of June 2001. It includes:

- Police-co-operation: the possibility of providing up to 5,000 policemen, including 1,000 within 30 days, for various policing tasks ranging from restoring order to the training of local police forces;

- Strengthening the rule of law: the possibility of providing up to 200 judges, prosecutors and other experts in this area;

- Civilian administration: the possibility of providing personnel to deal with various civilian aspects of crisis management such as help to guarantee free elections, or to reform the judicial, taxation or any other system of a requesting state, or to re-establish viable local administration;

- Civil protection to operate in emergency situations: the possibility of providing within three to seven hours two or three assessment teams consisting of 10 experts and of providing intervention teams consisting of 2,000 people.

All objectives of the civilian component have been achieved, the most important being the creation of the European Security and Intelligence Force (ESIF) consisting of up to 5,000 police to support peacekeeping missions, the Committee for Civilian Aspects of Crisis Management

---

167.   Jokingly its establishment was regarded either as "a French plot to winkle Germany out of NATO or a German plot to seduce France into NATO". See: G. Steil, "The Eurocorps and Future European Security Architecture", (1993) 2/2 European Security, pp 214–15.

(CIVCOM) in charge of gathering information, making recommendations and giving its opinion to the Political and Security Committee on civilian aspects of crisis management, and the police unit attached to the Council Secretariat and the Joint Situation Centre.

The European Gendarmerie Force (EGF),[168] which became fully operational on 20 July 2006, constitutes an important element of the civilian component. The EGF was created at the initiative of five Member States – France, Italy, The Netherlands, Portugal and Spain – with a view to handling crises that require management by police forces. The EGF is primarily at the disposal of the EU, but can also be deployed at the request of other international organisations, including NATO and the UN. It is based in Vicenza (Italy) in the "Generale Chinotto" barracks.

5.5.1.3   The conflict prevention component

The Göteborg European Council (June 2001) adopted the EU Programme for the Prevention of Violent Conflict. The HR plays an important role in this third component by ensuring consistency and effectiveness of all actions of the EU in respect of the regions concerned. If practicable, the EU must take measures with a view to enhancing the stability of a region and to creating a favourable political environment in it. In February 2001 the Commission set up a Rapid Reaction Mechanism (RRM) aimed at providing rapid financing for crisis management. The mechanism is used where there is a threat to public order or public security, or other similar circumstances which may destabilise a country.

5.5.2   The security dimension

The security dimension of the CSDP is based on the European Security Strategy agreed by the Brussels European Council in December 2003. It provides guidelines in respect of the EU's international security strategy, sets out the main priorities and determines the main threats to the EU's security such as terrorism, proliferation of weapons of mass destruction, regional conflicts, organised crime, and so on. The strategy was a response to the 9/11 terrorist attacks on targets in the USA, and to the conflict in Iraq.

5.5.3   The main political and military bodies established under the CSDP

These are:

- The Political and Security Committee (PSC). In respect of CSDP missions the PSC defines the strategic directions of the operations and interacts with the Military Committee of the EU and other relevant bodies, including the HR, who is required to stay in close and constant contact with the PSC (Article 43 TEU);

- The European Union Military Committee (EUMC) whose members are chiefs of defence of each Member State. Its role is to provide the PSC with consensus-based advice on military matters;

- The European Union Military Staff (EUMS) is made up of 140 officers from the Member States. They provide military advice and expertise with regard to execution of military crisis

---

168.   The agreement to create the EGF was signed on 17 September 2004.

management operations and perform three tasks, that is, early warning, situation assessment and strategic planning;

- The European Defence Agency;
- The EU Institute for Security Studies (EUISS);
- The European Union Satellite Centre (EUSC).

5.6   Assessment of the CFSP including the CSDP

The CFSP is based on the inter-governmental method. As a result it is subject to judicial review by the ECJ only in very limited circumstances and the involvement of the European Parliament is modest. Progress in the development of the CFSP has been hindered by the requirement of unanimity within the European Council and the Council on proposed measures. The ToL holds enormous potential for a more coherent external action of the EU. In particular, the creation of the new post of HR who has the necessary power, a substantial budget and a diplomatic corps, i.e. the EEAS, and who is empowered to speak on behalf of the EU, even before the UN Security Council, constitutes a step forward. It is submitted, however, that by allocating to the President of the European Council the external representation functions on issues concerning the CFSP, and in the light of the fact that the President of the European Commission it unlikely to abandon the EU's foreign policy entirely to the HR, the main objective of the reform consisting of achieving a more coherent and effective EU external action may be jeopardised. In any event, the Member States retain real power in all CFSP matters and it will depend on their political will as to whether or not the potential offered by the ToL is realised.

The military intervention of the USA, the UK and their allies in Iraq launched on 20 March 2003, despite the lack of authorisation from the UN Security Council, has shown a deep division between the Member States of the EU. However, when the EU speaks with one voice, it is a powerful voice. The EU can impose economic sanctions, and within the CSDP may intervene militarily against brutal regimes, although this is not the primary task of the military dimension of the EU.

The political weight of the EU, its credibility as the promoter of human rights and provider of humanitarian assistance whether in emergency situations or on a long-term basis, has been firmly established with the creation of the CSDP. In 2006 the EU sent 7,500 troops to support the UN peacekeeping force in South Lebanon subsequent to fighting between Hezbollah and the Israeli army, and sent 3,500 soldiers to the Democratic Republic of Congo to ensure security during parliamentary and presidential elections there. Soldiers and civilians from the EU are, at the time of writing, on peace-keeping, peace-building and conflict-prevention missions in Bosnia–Herzegovina, Kosovo, Moldova, the Ukraine, Afghanistan, Georgia, the Palestinian territories, Guinea Bissau and the Congo.

AIDE-MÉMOIRE

SPECIFIC TASKS PERFORMED BY THE HR

As the Vice-President of the Commission she:
- Is responsible for all tasks the Commission exercises in external relations (Article 18(4) TEU);

- Co-ordinates the Commission's external action work (Article 18(4) TEU).

As the HR for the CFSP, including the CSDP, she:
- Implements the CFSP (Articles 24(1), 27(2) and 32 TEU);

- Ensures, acting together with the Council, that the Member States support EU foreign policy and implement the CFSP (Article 24(3) TEU);

- Ensures unity, consistency and effectiveness of EU action relating to the CFSP acting in co-operation with the Council and the Commission (Article 26(2) TEU);

- Represents the EU externally on CFSP matters, including before the UN Security Council (Article 27(2) TEU);

- Conducts political dialogue with third parties, if requested (Article 27(2) TEU);

- Refers any question, initiative or proposal on the CFSP to the Council (Articles 30(1) and 42(4) TEU);

- Acts as a broker when a Member State decides to use the "emergency brake" procedure, i.e. it objects to the use of QMV by the Council (Article 31(2) TEU);

- Proposes the appointment of a special representative who will carry out his mandate under the authority of the HR (Article 33 TEU);

- Organises the co-ordination of Member States' actions in international organisations and at international conferences (Article 34(1) TEU);

- Consults and informs the EP on CFSP matters and ensures that the views of the EP are taken into account (Article 36 TEU);

- Requests an opinion from the Political and Security Committee (Article 38 TEU);

- Submits proposals on the new "start-up fund", and uses the fund under the authority of the Council (Article 41(3) TEU);

- Ensures co-ordination of the civilian and military aspects of CSDP missions acting under the authority of the Council and in constant contact with the Political and Security Committee (Article 43(2) TEU);

- Agrees with a "coalition of willing and able" Member States to which the Council entrusts a CSDP operational task on the management of that task (Article 44(1) TEU);

- Gives an opinion on the establishment of "permanent structured co-operation" under the CSDP (Article 46(2) TEU) and informs the Council and the EP on its development;

- Gives an opinion on whether a Member State should join a "permanent structured co-operation" in progress (Article 46(3) TEU);

- Makes recommendations to the Council for the opening of negotiations with a third state or an international organisation with a view to signing an agreement which has CFSP implications (Article 218(3) TFEU) and for the suspension of an existing agreement falling under the CFSP (Article 218(9) TFEU);

- Proposes CSDP missions (Article 42(4) TEU);

- Has responsibility, jointly with the Council, for the Political and Security Committee when the Committee directs CSDP crisis management operations (Article 38 TEU).

As the President of the Foreign Affairs Council (FA), she:
- Makes proposals to the FA Council (Article 27(1) TEU);

- Assists the FA Council (Article 21(1) TEU);

- Convenes extraordinary meetings of the FA Council (Article 30(2) TEU);

- Chairs meetings of the FA Council (Article 27(1) TEU).

AIDE-MÉMOIRE

**PROVISIONS OF THE TOL
ON EU EXTERNAL ACTION**

GENERAL PROVISIONS ON
THE EU EXTERNAL ACTION
ARE CONTAINED IN THE TOL

THEY ARE

TITLE V, CHAPTER 1 & OF THE TEU General provisions on the Union's External Action and Specific Provisions on the CFSP	PART V, TITLE I OF THE TEU General Provisions on the Union's External Action

SPECIAL PROVISIONS ON
THE EU EXTERNAL ACTION
ARE CONTAINED IN

THE TFEU Part V, Titles II, III, IV, V and VI + Article 3(2) which endorses the doctrine of implied powers	THE TEU Title V, Chapter 2: Specific Provisions on the CFSP Section 1: Common Provisions Section 2: Provisions on the CSDP

RECOMMENDED READING

Books

Cardwell, P.J., *EU External Relations and Systems of Governance: The CFSP, Euro-Mediterranean Partnership and Migration*, 2009, Abingdon: Routledge

Dashwood, A. and Maresceau, M. (eds), *Law and Practice of EU External Relations: Salient Features of a Changing Landscape*, 2008, Cambridge: CUP

De Vasconcelos, Á. (ed.), *What Ambitions for European Defence in 2020?*, 2009, Paris: European Union Institute for Security Studies

Grevi, G., Helly, D. and Keohane, D. (eds), *ESDP: The first 10 years (1999–2009)*, 2009, Paris: European Union Institute for Security Studies

Article

Neframi, E., "The Duty of Loyalty: Rethinking its Scope through its Application in the Field of EU External Relations" (2010) 47 CMLRev, p 323

6

THE INSTITUTIONAL FRAMEWORK OF THE EU

CONTENTS

SUMMARY

1. This chapter examines the main institutions of the EU. Article 13 TEU lists seven bodies that are entitled to be referred to as "EU institutions". They are: the EP, the European Council, the Council, the European Commission, the Court of Justice of the European Union (CJEU), the European Central Bank and the CoA.

2. Each of the seven EU institutions has a specific role to play in the functioning of the EU. The European Council shapes the future of the EU, the Council represents the interests of the Member States; the Commission, the interests of the EU; the EP, the interests of the people of the Member States; the CJEU ensures that in the functioning of the institutional system the law is observed; and the CoA is charged with supervision of the financial aspects of the EU. The European Central Bank defines and implements the monetary policy of the EU.

3. The division of functions between the seven institutions does not reflect the Montesquieu system of the "separation of powers" under which parliament is responsible for the performance of the legislative functions, government is responsible for executive functions and the courts are responsible for judicial functions.

In the EU legislative powers lie with the Council and the EP. The Commission is the "guardian of the Treaty" and as such supervises and, if necessary, enforces EU law. It also initiates and implements EU legislation. The EP, from being solely an advisory body, evolved into a directly elected body and under the ToL is a co-legislator and jointly with the Council adopts the EU budget. The CJEU (a collective name given to the ECJ, the General Court, formerly known as CFI, and specialised courts) ensures the observance of law in the implementation of the Treaties by the EU institutions, bodies and agencies and the Member States. Under Article 267 TFEU the ECJ and the General Court assist national courts in their difficult task of the interpretation of EU law, and thus ensure homogeneity and uniformity in its application in all Member States. The heads of state or government of the Member States, the President of the European Council and the President of the Commission form the European Council, which is crucial to the development of the EU as it provides the EU with political impetus on key issues.

6.1   Introduction

The seven main institutions mentioned in Article 13 TEU – the EP, the European Council, the Council, the European Commission, the Court of Justice of the European Union (CJEU), the European Central Bank and the CoA – form the basic structure of the institutional system of the EU. The ToL conferred the status of EU institutions on the European Council and the European Central Bank. The European Council which arose from the summit meetings of heads of state or government of the Member States was, until the entry into force of the ToL, a body of uncertain institutional status. Under the ToL the European Central Bank became an EU institution although its independence and special status continues.

To this basic institutional framework the following institutions and bodies must be added:

- Two main advisory bodies of the EU: the Economic and Social Committee and the Committee of the Regions to assist the Council and the Commission;

- Institutions necessary to carry out tasks peculiar to Economic and Monetary Union which are mainly relevant to the Member States which have adopted the euro as their national currency;

- The European Investment Bank which operates on a non-profit-making basis and grants loans and guarantees finance projects which contribute to the balanced and steady development of the internal market (Article 309 TFEU);

- Bodies which are within the scope of the Treaties and which assist the Council and the Commission in the accomplishment of their task: these are agencies, offices and centres, such as the European Environmental Agency, the European Training Foundation, the European Agency for the Evaluation of Medicinal Products, the Office for Veterinary and Plant Health Inspection and Control, the European Monitoring Centre for Drugs and Drug Addiction, Europol, Eurojust, the EU Agency for Fundamental Rights and the European Chemicals Agency.

Common rules apply to all institutions. They concern:

- The seats of the institutions;

- The languages of the institutions;

- The status of the staff of the EU.

These rules are examined below.

6.1.1   Seats of the institutions

Under Article 341 TFEU the seat of the EU institutions should be determined by common accord of the Member States. In practice, the determination of the permanent seats of the EU institutions has always been subject to fierce competition among the Member States. A Decision of 8 April 1965[169] provided a temporary solution by assigning the seats of the institutions among three different places: Luxembourg, Brussels and Strasbourg. This compromise gave rise to many political, financial and legal difficulties, especially with respect to where the sessions of the EP were to be held.[170] With a view to resolving matters, an agreement was reached at the Edinburgh Summit on 12 December 1992,[171] and subsequently adjusted by a European Council Decision adopted at the Brussels meeting on 29–30 October 1993,[172] which determined the seats of Community institutions. These pre ToL arrangements were confirmed by Protocol 2 attached to the Treaties and the EA Treaty "On the Location of the Seats of the Institutions and Certain Bodies, Offices, Agencies and Departments of the European Union". The Protocol allocates seats as follows:

- The Council has its seat in Brussels; however, during the months of April, June and October the Council meets in Luxembourg.

- The Commission has its seat in Brussels, although certain departments of the Commission, namely the administrative services of the EA, its Statistical Office and the Office for Official Publications, are located in Luxembourg.

- The CJEU, the CoA and the European Investment Bank have their seats in Luxembourg.

- The EP is required to hold 12 periods of monthly plenary sessions, including the budget session in Strasbourg each year but any additional plenary sessions are to be held in Brussels. The Committee of the EP is required to meet in Brussels. Its secretariat and departments are located in Luxembourg.

- The seat of the European Central Bank is located in Frankfurt.

- The seat of the CoR and the EESC is in Brussels.

- The European Police Office (Europol) has its seat in The Hague.

---

169.   [1967] OJ 152/18.
170.   Case 230/81 *Luxembourg v EP* [1983] ECR 255; Case 108/83 *Luxembourg v EP* [1984] ECR 1945; Cases 358/85 and 51/86 *France v EP* [1988] ECR 4821; Cases C-213/88 and C-39/89 *Luxembourg v EP* [1991] ECR I-5643 and Case C-345/95 *France v EP* [1997] ECR I-5215.
171.   [1992] OJ C341/1.
172.   [1993] OJ C323/1.

The Brussels European Council, in its Decision of 29 October 1993,[173] expressed a preference for the allocation of seats for various bodies and agencies in Member States which did not host any EU institutions. As a result, the European Environmental Agency is located in Copenhagen; the European Agency for Evaluation of Medicinal Products in London; the Agency for Health and Safety at Work in Bilbao; the Office for Harmonization in the Internal Market (Trade Marks, Designs and Models) in Alicante; the Office for Veterinary and Plant Health Inspection and Control in Dublin; the European Monitoring Centre for Drugs and Drug Addiction in Lisbon; Europol and Eurojust in The Hague; the European Police College (CEPOL) in Bramshill, UK; the EU Agency for Fundamental Rights in Vienna; and the European Chemicals Agency in Helsinki.[174]

6.1.2   Languages

Rules governing the languages of the institutions are determined by the Council, acting unanimously, but without prejudice to the provisions contained in the Rules of Procedure of the ECJ.[175] Regulation 1/1958 as amended[176] provides that the national languages of the Member States are official languages of the EU, all equal in rank and status.

As from 1 January 2007 there are 23 official languages. They are: Bulgarian, Czech, Danish, Dutch, English, Estonian, German, Spanish (its Castilian version), Finnish, French, Greek, Hungarian, Irish, Italian, Latvian, Lithuanian, Maltese, Polish, Portuguese, Romanian, Slovak, Slovene and Swedish.

The EU uses three alphabets: Cyrillic, Latin and Greek.

All language versions of the Treaties and of EU measures are equally authentic[177]. If there are any discrepancies between different language versions, they should be resolved without giving priority to any particular language.

It should be noted that by virtue of Council Conclusion "On the Official Use of Additional Languages within the Council and Possibly Other Institutions" adopted on 13 June 2005,[178] a Member State may conclude administrative arrangements with the Council and other institutions allowing its citizens to communicate with the Council, or the relevant institution, in languages other than those referred to in Regulation 1/1958 as amended.

Spain has concluded an administrative arrangement, such as mentioned above, with the Council[179] and the Commission[180] thereby allowing Spanish citizens to use, in addition to Castilian, three languages, that is, Basque, Catalan and Galician, which are recognised by Article 3(2) of the Spanish Constitution as official Spanish languages in the respective Autonomous Communities. The use of additional languages has two consequences:

---

173.   Decision of the Representatives of the Governments of the Member States on the Location of Seats of Certain Bodies and Departments, [1993] OJ C323/1.

174.   This agency became operational on 1 June 2007. See Commission Communication IP/07/745.

175.   Article 342 TFEU.

176.   [2003] OJ L236/33.

177.   Article 55 TEU.

178.   [2005] OJ C148/1.

179.   See Administrative Arrangement between the Kingdom of Spain and the Council [2006] OJ C/40/2.

180.   See Administrative Arrangement between the European Commission and the Kingdom of Spain [2006] OJ C73/14.

■ An individual who wishes to communicate in one of the additional languages does not write directly to the Council or the Commission, but to a body designated by the Spanish Government which translates the communication into Castilian and sends it to the relevant institution. The response from that institution is written in Castilian and forwarded to the designated body for translation into the relevant additional language and then sent to the individual concerned.

■ The cost of translating into an official language of the Member State is borne by the EU; the cost of translating into additional languages is borne by the Member State concerned.

The use of 23 official languages in the EU means that all official meetings are conducted in all official languages, which are translated from one to another simultaneously. Also, all official documents are in 23 languages, although French and English are imposed as working languages. All individual acts, that is, those addressed to Member States or to individuals, are written in the language of the relevant Member State. EU acts of general scope of application, for example regulations, are written in the 23 languages.

This use of multiple languages in the everyday running of the EU is necessary to ensure equality between Member States and transparency vis-à-vis the citizens of the EU. In addition, national authorities and courts, which often have to apply the EU acts directly to their nationals, must have the relevant text in their own national language. The principles of legal certainty and the protection of individual rights strengthen this requirement. Furthermore, conferring official status on 23 languages permits EU nationals to submit their complaints to a particular institution in their own language.

6.1.3   Common status applicable to staff of the EU

Protocol 7 "On the Privileges and Immunities of the European Union" attached to the Treaties and the EA Treaty replaced the Protocol on the Privileges and Immunities of the European Communities annexed to the Merger Treaty of 1965. Protocol 7 provides detailed rules concerning the privileges and immunities of the officials and other servants of the EU (Chapter V of Protocol 7) in that they should:

■ Be treated as officials of international organisations;

■ Be immune from legal proceedings in respect of acts performed in their official capacity;

■ Be exempt from national taxes on salaries, wages and emoluments paid by the EU;

■ Be entitled to the social security benefits established by the Treaties and the EA Treaty.

6.2   The European Council

The European Council plays a very important role in the institutional system of the EU. Until the entry into force of the ToL its exact institutional status within the Community was always subject to uncertainty.

The European Council originates from informal summit meetings of the heads of governments of the Member States and ministers of foreign affairs started in 1972. In Paris in December 1974 they officially agreed that "summit" meetings should thereafter be held on a regular basis. On 19 June 1983 in Stuttgart, the then 10 Heads of State and Government signed the Solemn Declaration on European Union. This specified the composition of the Council – that is, that it should comprise the heads of state or government and the president of the Commission, assisted by the ministers for foreign affairs of the Member States and a member of the Commission – and its main tasks.

Article 2 of the SEA brought the European Council within the framework of the Community but did not define its role or method of voting and did not subject its decisions to the possibility of judicial review by the ECJ. The TEU (before its amendment by the ToL) slightly clarified the European Council's role in Article 4 TEU, by providing that its main task was to give the EU "the necessary impetus for its development and shall define the general political guidelines thereof".

Under the ToL the European Council became a fully fledged EU institution. Article 13 TEU lists the European Council as one of the institutions of the EU. However, Article 15(1) TEU clearly states that the European Council is not allowed to adopt secondary legislation. Further, the ToL gave the European Council new powers (see below), created a full-time president of the European Council who replaces the six-monthly rotating EU presidency and provides in Article 262 TFEU that acts of the European Council which produce binding legal effects in relation to third parties are subject to judicial review by the ECJ. Under the ToL the European Council's political role remains unchanged, as is its exclusive competence to decide whether any revision of the Treaties is necessary.

The formula "heads of state or of government" is used to take into account the special constitutional position of the president of the French Republic who is the head of state and shares exercise of executive power with the head of government.

6.2.1   Main tasks

The importance of the European Council stems from the political role it plays in shaping the future of the EU. It exercises the following functions:

- It serves as a platform for the exchange of informal views and for unofficial discussions among the leaders of the Member States;

- It can examine any matter within the competence of the EU as well as any subject of common interest;

- It gives the necessary political impetus for the development of the EU;

- It settles sensitive matters and disputes which the EU institutions are not able to resolve, especially those referred by the Council;

- Within the framework of EU foreign action, including the CFSP, it defines principles and general guidelines;

- It decides whether a revision of the Treaties is required under either the ordinary revision procedure or the simplified procedures (see Chapter 8.2.5);

- It decides whether to use the "passerelle" clause contained in Article 48(7) TEU (see Chapter 8.2.5.2);

- It appoints the President of the European Council, selects the HR and the President of the European Commission;

- It decides on the list of Council configurations with the exception of the General Affairs and the Foreign Affairs Council and on the various configurations of the Presidency of the Council (see section 6.3) (Article 236 TFEU);

- It determines the existence of a serious and persistent breach by a Member State of the European Union's founding values (Article 7(2) TEU).

In the exercise of its supreme political power the European Council can be compared to holding a kind of presidential authority of the EU.

The real problem with the European Council is the continuing perceived democratic deficit in that the EP still has very limited control over the activities of the European Council, but there is an argument that the European Council has its own democratic legitimacy, since all the national heads of government are democratically elected.

All deliberations of the European Council are confidential. There is no record of informal exchanges of views between its members, the heads of state or government. However, when the European Council wishes to make a statement on matters of international concern or its discussions are aimed at reaching decisions, there is a written record of conclusions, and this is issued on the authority of the Presidency. Declarations and Conclusions of the European Council are adopted by common accord. Under the ToL the European Council can adopt decisions. They are usually implemented by the Council. Any act adopted by the European Council which produces binding legal effect on a third party may be reviewed by the ECJ under Article 263 TFEU.

6.2.2   Composition

Article 15(2) TEU specifies that the European Council should be made up of heads of state or government of the Member States, together with the President of the European Council and the President of the Commission. The HR should participate in the work of the European Council. When required, the members of the European Council may be assisted by a minister, and the President of the Commission may be assisted by a member of the Commission.

6.2.3   Functioning

Article 15(1) TEU confirms the previous arrangements regarding European Council meetings. It shall meet twice every six months although it can also meet in extraordinary sessions. All meetings are convened by its President,

Under Article 16(6) TEU preparation of European Council meetings is carried out by the General Affairs Council, in liaison with the President of the European Council and the Commission.

The European Council should not be confused with the Council, which is also an institution of the EU or the Council of Europe, which is not an EU institution but an inter-governmental organisation established in 1949, principally known for the creation, implementation and supervision of the European Convention on Human Rights (ECHR), although its mission is broader as it seeks not only to protect human rights, pluralist democracy and the rule of law, but also to develop Europe's cultural identity and diversity, and to find common solutions to the challenges facing European society, such as discrimination against minorities, xenophobia, intolerance, bioethics and cloning, terrorism, and so on. At the time of writing 47 European States are members of the Council of Europe and Contracting parties to the ECHR.

6.2.4   Voting

The European Council normally adopts measures by consensus (Article 15(4) TEU). If, in circumstances specified in the Treaties, a vote is taken by QMV, the President of the European

Council and the President of the Commission are not allowed to take part in the vote (Article 235(1) TFEU). There is the same definition of QMV for the European Council as for the Council. For the adoption of Rules of Procedure and other procedural matters the Council votes by a simple majority. When unanimity is required any abstentions do not prevent the adoption of a measure.

6.2.5   The President of the European Council

The post of full-time president of the European Council was created by the ToL. The President replaces the six-monthly rotating EU presidency. He is elected by the European Council acting by QMV. His term of office is two and a half years, renewable once. This post is permanent and its holder is required to be independent. In this respect Article 15(6) TEU states that the President of the European Council "shall not hold a national office". His main tasks are:

- to prepare the work of the European Council;

- to chair debates of the European Council;

- to try to facilitate consensus within the European Council;

- to ensure continuity of the work of the European Council;

- to deal with foreign policy issues at a heads of state level but without prejudice to the powers of the HR;

- to report to the EP after each of the meetings of the European Council.

The main reason for the creation of the post of the President of the European Council was to ensure coherence in the work of the European Council and continuity of its political agenda.

6.3   The Council of the European Union (the Council)

Following the entry into force of the Treaty of Maastricht, the Council of Ministers, which was referred to in the Treaties merely as "the Council", adopted Decision 93/591 on 8 November 1993,[181] in which it renamed itself. Since then its official name has been "the Council of the European Union". However, it is generally referred to as "the Council".

The Council, together with the EP, is the main legislative institution of the EU and defines and implements the EU's CFSP, based on the guidelines set by the European Council. It represents the national interests of each Member State and, being a purely inter-governmental body, its meetings risk degenerating into diplomatic conferences. However, it is also an EU institution, and thus it is required to promote the interests of the EU. This double function led the Council to be called "Janus-faced".[182] However, the impossible task of promoting simultaneously the two sets of interests, national and the EU's, is to some extent facilitated by the degree of convergence between the two.

---

181.   [1993] OJ L281/18.
182.   H. Smit and P. E. Herzog, *The Law of the European Economic Community – A Commentary on the EEC Treaty*, 1976, New York: Matthew Bender, Vol.4, pp 5–88.

6.3.1 Composition

By virtue of Article 16 TEU:

> "The Council shall consist of a representative of each Member State at ministerial level, who may commit the government of the Member State in question and cast its vote."

This formula, introduced by the TEU, allows Member States with a federal structure to be represented when the Council is examining matters which are within the exclusive competence of regional governments. So, for example, a minister of a Länder in Germany or of a region in Belgium, will attend such meetings instead of a minister in the federal government. In such a case, the regional minister is authorised to act on behalf of the Member State and thus commits the federal government both legally and politically.

The Council has no fixed composition and its membership varies according to the matters under discussion. However, there are always as many members as there are Member States. At meetings each minister is accompanied by a civil servant as part of a negotiating team. The Commission is also represented, although its influence depends upon the subject matter under discussion and the competences of the Commission in the area discussed. Since the entry into force of the ToL there are 10 different configurations of the Council of the EU:

- General Affairs;
- Foreign Affairs;
- Economic and Financial Affairs;
- Justice and Home Affairs;
- Employment, Social Policy, Health and Consumer Affairs;
- Competitiveness;
- Transport, Telecommunication and Energy;
- Agriculture and Fisheries;
- Environment;
- Education, Youth and Culture.

The General Affairs Council is specifically mentioned in Article 16(6) TEU. Its role is to ensure consistency in the work of different Council configurations, to prepare meetings of the European Council and to ensure the follow-up of these meetings, acting in co-operation with the Commission and the President of the European Council.

Under the ToL the European Council decides on the list of Council configurations with the exception of the General Affairs and the Foreign Affairs Council. However, irrespective of which configuration of the Council adopts a decision, that decision is always a Council decision without any mentioning of the configuration that has adopted it. The Council is a single body.

6.3.2 Competences

The main powers conferred on the Council are defined in Article 16 TEU. This provision states: "The Council shall, jointly with the European Parliament, exercise legislative and budgetary functions. It shall carry out policy-making and co-ordinating functions as laid down in the Treaties."

6.3.3 Presidency

Council meetings are chaired by a representative of the Member State holding the Council Presidency, which rotates every six months according to the order established by the European Council under Article 236 TFEU. Declaration 9 on Article 16(9) of the Treaty on European Union concerning the European Council Decision on the Exercise of the Presidency of the Council attached to the Treaties confirms the team presidencies, which were first established by the Council in 2006.[183] The team presidencies means that the Presidency of the Council, with the exception of the Foreign Affairs configuration, is held jointly by a pre-established team of three Member States for a period of 18 months. The teams are made up on a basis of equal rotation among the Member States, taking into account their diversity and geographical balance within the Union. Each member of a team holds the presidency for a six-month period in all configurations of the Council, with the exception of the Foreign Affairs configuration which has the HR as its permanent president. Members of the team, other than the one which holds the Presidency, assist the current Presidency in all its responsibilities on the basis of a common programme. Members of the team may decide alternative arrangements among themselves.

The main tasks of the Presidency are as follows:

1. The Member State which holds the Presidency chairs the Council meetings, and is responsible for preparing and organising the Council's work as efficiently as possible. It convenes Council meetings on its own initiative, or at the request of a Member State or of the Commission; determines its agenda; assists Member States to reach a compromise on EU issues; and decides on the time of voting. At the meetings of the Council, the Member State that holds the Presidency is represented in two capacities – as a Member State and as president of the Council. However, there are special arrangements for the Foreign Affairs Council which is permanently chaired by the HR;

2. It presides over bodies, such as COREPER, committees and organs of political co-operation. However, the Chair of the Political and Security Committee is held by a representative of the HR;

3. It represents the Council in dealings with institutions and bodies of the EU, such as the European Commission, the EP, the CoR and the EESC. In particular, it submits to the EP a work programme at the beginning of the Presidency, reports regularly to the EP and, at the end of the Presidency, presents a detailed report of its achievements, which report is discussed by the EP. It also acts on behalf of the Council in negotiations with the EP in the legislative process. However, in respect of foreign affairs the HR assumes all representative functions.

---

183. In September 2006, the Council made the following amendment to its Rules of Procedure: "Every 18 months, the three Presidencies due to hold office shall prepare, in close cooperation with the Commission, and after appropriate consultations, a draft programme of Council activities for that period". Point 2 of the Preamble to Council Decision 2006/683/EC/Euratom [2006] OJ L285/47.

4.   It prepares two programmes:

- The first sets out the main objectives for the work of the Council including the Presidency's particular priorities during the six-month period. The Member States are becoming more ambitious in determining the objectives they want to attain during the Presidency.[184] Each tries to make a lasting contribution to the development of the Union. In addition, they usually put on the agenda issues of vital national importance which are not necessarily considered as essential in the context of the EU;

- The second is prepared by the team Presidency and sets out a long-term programme for the forthcoming 18 months.

6.3.4   COREPER (the Committee of Permanent Representatives)

The Council is not a permanent body. Each meeting has to be prepared by civil servants acting within a number of committees, the most important being the Committee of Permanent Representatives (COREPER).[185]

This body was initially established on an informal basis to ensure the continuity of the Council's work. It was formally recognised by Article 4 of the Merger Treaty and is now defined in Article 16(7) TEU and Article 240 TFEU. COREPER is made up of permanent representatives of the Member States to the European Union. Each Member State has a permanent delegation in Brussels (similar to an embassy), which comprises national civil servants with ambassadorial rank. Article 16(7) TFEU sets out the tasks of COREPER. It states that:

"A Committee of the Permanent Representatives of the Governments of the Member States shall be responsible for preparing the work for the Council."

The main objective of COREPER is to prepare proposals, which are negotiated prior to the Council meeting, and thus avoid unnecessary discussion at ministerial level. There are two configurations of COREPER:

- COREPER I, made up of deputy permanent representatives, which concentrates on technical issues; and

- COREPER II, comprising the permanent representatives themselves, which focuses on general and political matters.

The Council forwards the matter to be discussed to COREPER I, which may create specialist or ad hoc committees, working groups, and so on, in order to examine it. They then refer the matter to COREPER II for further study. The Commission, and often the EP, is also involved in the discussion and negotiation of submitted proposals. The Council's agenda is divided into two parts: so-called "A" items and "B" items. If there is unanimous agreement in COREPER II on the proposal, it is put in Part A of the Council's agenda. Unless the Council opposes the proposal and

---

184.   For example, The Netherlands decided to finalise the IGC during its Presidency (from January 1997 to the end of June 1997). This objective was successfully achieved when the draft ToA was signed on 17 June 1997. Germany during its Presidency (from January to June 2007) finally settled the destiny of the previously proposed EU Constitution (see Chapter 1.18).

185.   Its name is the French acronym.

sends it back to COREPER, it will be adopted by the Council. If there is no agreement in COREPER II, the matter is put in Part B of the Council agenda for resolution.

The timetable for Council meetings is prepared in advance. Regular meetings are usually convened once per month; extraordinary sessions can take place at any time, but the agenda must be forwarded by the Presidency to the Member States at least 14 days in advance.

6.3.5 Sessions

The Council sessions are very frequent and often very long. Members of the Commission have access to the sessions and the right to speak. In the past the deliberations were held in camera. However, in order to ensure transparency the Edinburgh Summit of 11–12 December 1992 introduced the possibility of publicised debates.[186] The Council responded by amending its Rules of Procedure to provide for this to occur. The ToL has made the commitment of the Council binding in so far as deliberations and votes on draft legislative acts are concerned. However, in respect of non-legislative activities of the Council its deliberations and votes are still held in camera.

6.3.6 Voting

Votes in the Council are personal, although under the Council Rules of Procedure members of the Council may arrange to be represented at a meeting which they are not able to attend. Usually, they are replaced by a permanent representative or a deputy permanent representative of their Member State. However, their replacement has no right to vote. For that reason, under Article 239 TFEU another member of the Council (in addition to casting his or her own vote in accordance with his or her own wishes) votes (when requested), on behalf of and in accordance with the instruction of the absentee member. An attending member of the Council cannot act on behalf of more than one other member.

The Treaties provide three modes of voting:

- By simple majority;
- By qualified majority;
- By unanimity.

The choice of mode is not left to the Council; this is determined by the legal basis of the act in question. The Treaties normally require qualified majority voting or unanimity.

6.3.6.1 Simple majority

Simple majority voting, which was foreseen as a norm, is exceptional. Article 238(1) TFEU states that where the Council is required to vote by a simple majority, it shall act by a majority of its component members. The Council votes by a simple majority in respect of procedural matters including the adoption of its Rules of Procedure.

---

186. The first broadcast took place on 1 February 1993.

6.3.6.1.1   Unanimity

Unanimous voting, which was assigned a privileged place in the original Treaties, is now infrequent as a result of the revisions of the Treaties. Under the ToL unanimity continues to be required in relation to direct and indirect taxation, although Member States may decide to settle some tax issues (such as measures to tackle fraud) by majority voting. National vetoes remain, inter alia, with regard to foreign policy, certain aspects of social policy, culture, namely the aspects of Common Commercial Policy which affect cultural and audio-visual issues, constitutional and para-constitutional matters, and filling gaps in the Treaties with a view to attaining the objectives of the EU (Article 352 TFEU).

6.3.6.2   Qualified majority voting (QMV)

Qualified majority voting, which is the most frequently used mode of voting in the Council, was slow to take hold. This was because it took years for the Luxembourg Accord to fade away (see Chapter 1.8). The first change was made by the SEA which introduced QMV.

The current mode of voting (i.e. until 2014) is based on a "weight" given to each Member State, designed to ensure fairness in the decision-making process. The system of weighted votes reflects the size of a Member State and its demographic, economic and political "weight" within the EU. It has two objectives: first, to ensure that small Member States are not able to block a particular measure; and, second, to ensure that they have sufficient representation to avoid being systematically outvoted by the larger Member States. The ToL has introduced a new system of calculating QMV which will enter into force on 1 November 2014 and will be the only one applicable after 1 April 2017. The change ensures a more equitable and democratic voting system in the EU as it takes greater account of the size of the population of a Member State than the previous system.

6.3.6.2.1   Qualified majority voting until 31 October 2014

Under the ToL QMV is extended to 21 new areas and to 23 areas that under the pre-ToL Treaties required unanimity in the Council. However, the extension of QMV does not necessarily mean that the most important matters from the perspective of the Member States are subject to QMV. Certainly, the abolition of the veto in respect of police and judicial co-operation in criminal matters is the most dramatic, although the UK, Ireland and Denmark have negotiated opt-outs in these areas (see Chapter 2.4.1).

The number of votes each Member State can cast is as follows:

Germany, France, Italy and the United Kingdom – 29 each
Poland and Spain – 27 each
Romania – 14
The Netherlands – 13
Belgium, Greece, Hungary, Portugal, The Czech Republic – 12 each
Austria, Bulgaria, Sweden – 10 each
Denmark, Finland, Ireland, Lithuania, Slovakia – 7 each
Cyprus, Estonia, Latvia, Luxembourg, Slovenia – 4 each
Malta – 3

The total number of votes capable of being cast is 345.
For their adoption, acts of the Council require at least:

■ 255 votes in favour (out of 345, meaning 73.9 per cent) cast by the majority of members (i.e. at least 14 Member States out of 27) where the Treaty requires them to be adopted on a proposal from the Commission;

■ 255 votes in favour (out of 345 meaning 73.9 per cent) cast by at least two-thirds of members (at least 18 Member States out of 27) in cases where proposals originate from bodies other than the Commission.

A qualified majority vote must represent at least 62 per cent of the total population of the European Union.

If not all members participate in the vote,[187] for a proposal to pass the same proportion of weighted votes (73.9 per cent) and the same proportion of the population of the Member States (62 per cent) is required.

Under the above rules a proposal originating from the Commission will fail if there are 91 votes against, or if a majority of the Council members vote against it (i.e. 14 out of 27 Member States). A proposal which does not originate from the Commission will not pass if over one third of the members of the Council (10 out of 27 members) vote against it or Member States representing more than 38 per cent of the population of the EU vote against it.

6.3.6.2.2 The twofold majority QMV system to be used from 1 November 2014 to 31 March 2017 and exclusively from 1 April 2017

From 1 November 2014 the voting system in the Council based on the weighting of votes will be abolished. From that date, the ToL establishes a twofold majority. Normally (that is, if all members of the Council participate in the voting) that majority must comprise, for a proposal which originates from the Commission or from the HR:

■ First, at least 55 per cent of the Member States (that is, in an EU made up of 27 Member States at least 15 of those must be in favour); and

■ Second, the total population of the Member States forming the majority will have to account for at least 65 per cent of the population of the EU.

A blocking minority must include at least four Member States representing more than 35 per cent of the population of the EU. This is to ensure that the three Member States: the UK, Germany and France, which together represent more than 35 per cent of the population of the EU, acting in concert cannot block a proposal. A fourth Member State is needed to block the proposal, without which "the qualified majority shall be deemed attained" even if the population requirement of 65 per cent is not met. The requirement that at least four Member States are needed to prevent the adoption of a proposal will remain regardless of the future demographic changes in populations of the Member States.

If a proposal does not originate from the Commission or from the HR, the majority must comprise at least 72 per cent of the Member States (i.e. at least 20 Member States out of 27) representing at least 65 per cent of the population of the EU.

If not all members of the Council participate in voting, for a proposal to pass it needs, at least,

---

187. For example if a Member State secures for itself an opt-out or does not participate in enhanced co-operation it will not participate in the vote. However, if a Member State abstains, the calculation will be made according to the usual rules.

the same proportion of votes (55 per cent or 72 per cent) and the same percentage of the population of the Member States concerned (65 per cent) of the members taking part in the vote.

From 1 November 2014 to 31 March 2017 there will be two alternatives to the twofold majority voting:

- A Member State may, on the ground that the matter under consideration is of particular political sensitivity to that Member State, request that a measure be voted on in accordance with the qualified majority voting system as defined under the Treaty of Nice, i.e. the system in existence from the entry into force of the ToL until 1 November 2014;

- The ToL introduced an "Ioannina"[188] type compromise as follows: if the minority in the Council is significant in terms of number of Member States but insignificant in terms of ability to block the adoption of a measure, the Council will try to find a satisfactory solution while reserving the option to vote at any time. In order to trigger the Ioannina mechanism the group of Member States wishing to do this must represent either 75 per cent share of population necessary to constitute a blocking minority or three quarters of the number of Member States necessary to constitute a blocking minority. The Ioannina compromise is a deferral, not a veto. Its purpose is to give the Council more time to achieve broader support for a measure.

In order to assess the new voting system in the Council, it is important to note that in fact votes are rarely taken in the Council as almost all matters proceed by way of consensus. This is due to the fact first, that the Council traditionally seeks to achieve broad support for all measures and second, that consensus-building in the Council is greatly facilitated by the extensive preparatory process carried out by COREPER. Accordingly, it may be argued that the new voting system will have no significant impact on the work of the Council. Obviously, an opposite view can be expressed, that is, that the new system will have a great impact on decision-making in the Council, in that the lower threshold established for the adoption of a legislative measure, as compared to the current system, will force a Member State unhappy with an intended measure to join the majority of the Member States wishing to proceed with the proposal early in the negotiation process in order to retain some influence on the final outcome. It can also be said that the twofold majority voting system based on the population of a Member State is more democratic than the previous voting system. For example, the UK's voting power based on her share of population of the EU will be 12.3 per cent under the twofold majority system as compared to 8.4 per cent under the weighted votes system. It is also more efficient as it facilitates the formation of majorities and thus speeds the decision-making process.

6.3.6.2.3   The voting system to be used from 1 November 2017

The twofold majority voting system will apply from 1 November 2017. However, a new version of the Ioannina compromise, often referred to as the Ioannina II mechanism, may also be relied

---

188.   The Ioannina compromise was an agreement reached by foreign ministers of the Member States at a meeting held in 1994 in Ioannina (Greece) concerning the blocking minority subsequent to the fourth enlargement. It was decided that if members of the Council representing between 23 votes (the blocking minority prior to the fourth enlargement) and 26 votes (the blocking minority subsequent to the fourth enlargement) opposed the taking of a decision by the Council, it would seek to achieve a compromise, within a reasonable time, in that the opposed measure would only be adopted if at least 68 votes out of 87 were cast in favour. The Treaty of Nice did away with the Ioannina agreement.

upon by a significant number of Member States who oppose the adoption of a measure but on their own are insignificant in terms of ability to block its adoption. Under the Ioannina II mechanism a new threshold for triggering a deferral will apply in that either Member States opposing a proposal will have to have at least 55 per cent of the population necessary to constitute a blocking minority or they will have to represent at least 55 per cent of the Member States necessary to constitute a blocking minority.

6.4   The European Commission (the Commission)

Like the Council, the Commission was renamed following the entry into force of the Treaty of Maastricht. It is now the "European Commission", commonly referred to as "the Commission".

The Commission represents the interests of the EU. As a "revolutionary" body within the institutional system of the EU, it is also the most controversial institution. It exercises many functions, the most important is to "promote the general interest of the Union and take appropriate initiatives to that end" (Article 17 TEU). The Commission is:

■ The guardian of the Treaties;

■ The initiator of EU legislation;

■ The executive arm of the EU;

■ The representative of the EU in the international arena, except with regard to the CFSP and in other cases provided for in the Treaties.

The Commission employs about 25,000 European civil servants and is divided into departments called Directorates General (DGs). Each DG is responsible for a particular policy area and is headed by a Director General who is accountable to one of the commissioners. Overall co-ordination is provided by the Secretariat General, which also manages the weekly Commission meetings. The Secretariat General is headed by the Secretary General, who is answerable directly to the president.

The Commission divides its tasks among its members, and each commissioner is allocated one or more policy areas. Each commissioner has personal advisers who form his or her so-called Cabinet, which acts as a liaison between the commissioner and his or her Directorate(s) General. The chief of the Cabinet is usually the same nationality as the commissioner and deputises for him or her as necessary. The chief also meets weekly with other chefs de Cabinet in order to prepare the agenda for the Commission.

6.4.1   Composition

The Commission is made up of one commissioner per Member State. Attempts at reducing the number of commissioners failed. The European Council held in July 2009 provided legally binding assurances to the Irish Government prior to the second referendum concerning the ratification of the ToL by Ireland that Ireland and other Member States would be represented in the Commission by one commissioner of their nationality.[189] The provisions of the ToL relating to this matter are expected to be amended in the next accession treaty following the ToL.

---

189.   The European Council held in December 2009 confirmed this commitment.

Commissioners, other than the President of the Commission who is appointed in a different way (see below), are appointed as follows. The Council, by common accord with the person nominated as President of the Commission, adopts a list of persons whom it intends to appoint as members of the Commission. The list is established in accordance with a proposal submitted by each Member State. The president and the members of the Commission thus nominated are subject, as a body, to a vote of approval by the EP. After approval by the EP, the president and the other members of the Commission are appointed by the Council acting by QMV.

6.4.2   The President of the Commission

The ToL revised rules regarding the election of the President of the Commission and extends his powers over the Commissioners.

6.4.2.1   *The appointment of the President of the Commission*

Under Article 17(7) TEU, the President of the Commission is elected by the EP acting by a majority of its component members, based on a proposal from the European Council, which must by approved by QMV. In the choice of a candidate the European Council is required to take into consideration the result of the elections to the EP. If the candidate selected by the European Council fails to achieve EP approval, the European Council is required, within one month of the rejection of the previous candidate, to propose a new candidate, acting by QMV.

Under the ToL the EP will not only intensify its scrutiny over the Commission by electing its president but may also influence, to a great extent, the choice of the candidate for the presidency of the Commission. This may occur if, for example, the largest political group in the EP decides to tie its electoral campaign to a particular person as a candidate for the presidency of the Commission. In such a situation, it will be very difficult for the European Council not to nominate that person. The link between the elections to the EP and the choice of a candidate for the presidency of the Commission may also make elections to the EP more personalised and more important for voters. The consequence of this may be that, on the one hand, the Commission will acquire a new source of political legitimacy through the manner in which its president is elected, but on the other hand, if the president is too closely connected to a larger political group in the EP, questions may be raised as to his/her independence and objectivity.

An additional control of the EP over the Commission is that the President of the Commission and its commissioners, including the HR, as a body, are subject to a vote of consent by the EP. On the basis of this consent the Commission is appointed by the European Council, acting by a qualified majority.

6.4.2.2   *Powers of the President of the Commission*

Under Article 17(6) TEU the Commission works under the political guidance of its President who:

- Decides matters concerning the internal organisation of the Commission in order to ensure coherence, efficiency and the collegiality of Commission actions;

- Divides the tasks of the Commission among its members and is entitled to change the original allocation of tasks in respect of each commissioner in the course of the Commission's term of office, with the exception of the HR who is, ex officio, responsible for External Relations and European Neighbourhood Policy;

■ Appoints, from amongst the members of the Commission, Vice-Presidents but not the HR who is a Vice-President ex officio and whose appointment is subject to specific rules (see Chapter 5.2);

■ Can force a particular commissioner to resign. This possibility changes the relationship between the Commission and the EP. Under this arrangement it is unlikely that the EP will use its motion of censure, unless, based on the principle of collegiate responsibility of the Commission, the EP wants to remove the whole Commission. However, the President has no power to force the HR to resign but may make a proposal for her dismissal to the European Council which takes the final decision.

6.4.3   Conduct of Commissioners

The Commissioners must be chosen on the grounds of their general competence. Article 17(5) TEU specifies that only nationals of the Member States may be appointed as commissioners. Article 17(3) TEU provides that commissioners must act in the general interest of the EU and that their independence must be beyond doubt. In this respect they take a solemn oath before the ECJ. As Article 17(3) TEU provides, their independence requires that they "shall neither seek nor take instructions from any government or from any other body. They shall refrain from any action incompatible with their duties or the performance of their tasks". Under Article 245 TFEU each Member State undertakes to respect the independence of commissioners and not to seek to influence them in the performance of their tasks.

Under Article 245 TFEU commissioners are prohibited during their term from engaging in any other occupation, whether gainful or not, and from any action incompatible with their duties as commissioners. This excludes commissioners from being members of a national parliament or of the EP. However, academic activities, research and teaching are considered to be compatible with the status of commissioner.[190]

The scope of Article 245 TFEU was explained by the ECJ in Case C-432/04 *Commission v Cresson*,[191] in which in January 2003 the Commission brought proceedings against Mrs Edith Cresson, a member of the European Commission from 24 January 1995 to 8 September 1999.

THE FACTS WERE:

On 16 March 1999 the entire Commission presided over by Jacques Santer, including Mrs Cresson, collectively resigned but remained in office until 8 September 1999.

The subsequent Commission requested the ECJ to declare that Mrs Cresson's conduct as a commissioner amounted to favouritism, or if not that, then to gross negligence in breach of Article 213 EC [Article 245 TFEU] and consequently, to order that she be deprived wholly or partly of a pension or other benefits in its stead.

---

190.   For more on incompatibility see Q. E. No 2752/94 by F Herman, [1995] OJ C88/38.
191.   [2006] ECR I-6387.

The Commission alleged that Mrs Cresson showed favouritism to two of her close acquaintances, Mr Berthelot and Mr Riedinger.

In respect of Mr Berthelot, a 66-year-old dentist, when Mrs Cresson took office she wanted to employ him as her personal adviser. When this proved impossible because first, her Cabinet was already in place and all posts of personal adviser filled, and second, he was too old to be appointed temporarily, she used her influence to employ him as a visiting scientist, although in fact he worked exclusively as her personal adviser. Further, when Mr Berthelot's monthly allowance as a visiting scientist was reduced in order to take account of a pension which was paid to him in France, Mrs Cresson's Cabinet made 13 mission orders payable to Mr Berthelot for a sum of €6,900. The missions were fictitious, as was established during criminal proceedings carried out in Belgium in 1999 against Mrs Cresson. Also, at that time, Mr Berthelot's position as a visiting scientist was reclassified so that his monthly allowance was increased by approximately €1,000. When Mr Berthelot's contract as a visiting scientist expired he was offered another such contract, so that in total he was employed as a visiting scientist for 28 months although the Commission's rules provided for a maximum duration of 24 months. He did not, however, stay until the end of his contract. In December 1997 the contract was terminated at his request on medical grounds. Notwithstanding that, Mrs Cresson used her influence again to offer him a post of a special adviser from 1 January 1998. He rejected that offer. He died on 2 March 2000.

Mr Riedinger, a commercial lawyer, was offered three contracts by the Commission in 1995; at least two of these were offered at Mrs Cresson's express request. None of them was implemented and no payments were made.

Held:

The ECJ held that Mrs Cresson acted in breach of Article 213(2) EC [Article 245 TFEU] in relation to the appointment of Mr Berthelot and as regards the terms under which he worked. Accordingly, she was found liable for a breach of her obligations, which was of a certain degree of gravity. However, the Court did not impose any penalty on Mrs Cresson. In this respect the ECJ held that "having regard to the circumstances of the case, the finding of breach constitutes, itself, an appropriate penalty". The ECJ dismissed the charges against Mrs Cresson concerning the offers of work contracts for Mr Riedinger.

Comment:

The important points flowing from the above case are:

- The ECJ explained the scope of Article 213 EC [Article 245 TFEU] and confirmed that this provision constituted a proper legal base for proceedings against a commissioner. The ECJ gave a broad interpretation to the notion of "obligations arising from [a commissioner's office]". It stated that the members of the Commission are required to observe the highest standards of conduct. In particular, they have a duty to ensure that the general interest of the Community takes precedence at all times, not only over national interests, but also over personal interests. Although they have to conduct themselves in a manner which is beyond reproach, a certain degree of gravity of the conduct deviating from those standards is required for the conduct to be censured under Article 213(2) EC [Article 245 TFEU]. It is for the Court to decide, on a case by case basis, whether the conduct concerned only slightly deviated from those proper standards or whether it reached a degree of gravity which must be censured under Article 213(2) EC [Article 245 TFEU].

In respect of the penalty which may be imposed for a breach of the obligations arising from the office of commissioner, the ECJ distinguished between the penalty of compulsory retirement and a penalty in the form of deprivation of the right to a pension or other benefits instead. The penalty of compulsory retirement applies only where a breach has arisen, and continues during the term of office. The penalty of deprivation of benefits (pension or other) may be imposed irrespective of whether the breach occurs during or after the term of office and whether it was discovered or established during the term of office or after its expiry.

Following the resignation of the Commission presided over by Jacques Santer, the subsequent Commission adopted a very strict Code of Conduct[192] under which:

- a commissioner is required to act in accordance with the highest standards of public life;

- in order to avoid any conflict of interests, commissioners are subject to a one-year "cooling-off period" after leaving office, during which their prospective jobs may be vetoed by a special ethics committee.

Further, the Commission embarked on a broad reform programme based on the principles of independence, responsibility, accountability, efficiency and transparency to ensure that both the holders of high office and the servants of the EU are not only competent from a professional point of view, but also properly supervised.

6.4.4 Term of office

The term of office of commissioners was extended to five years by the Treaty of Maastricht in order to synchronise it with that of the EP. The mandate is renewable. Any vacancy, however arising, is filled for the remainder of the member's term of office by a new member appointed by common accord of the Member States. However, the Council may, acting unanimously, on a proposal from the President of the Commission, decide not to fill such a vacancy. In the event of any vacancy in the office of president his replacement should be appointed following the usual procedure (see section 6.4.2)[193]

If commissioners no longer fulfil the conditions required for the performance of their duties, or have been guilty of serious misconduct, the ECJ may, on application by the Council acting by a simple majority or the Commission, compulsorily retire them (Article 247 TFEU). At the time of writing, this possibility has been applied only once, and that was in a case of the total incapacity of a commissioner. In the event of any breach of obligations imposed upon commissioners, including those to behave with integrity and discretion even after they have ceased to hold office, sanctions may be imposed by the ECJ consisting of deprivation of pension rights or other benefits (see section 6.4.3). The EP also exercises some disciplinary power, but only over the entire Commission by submitting a motion of censure under Article 243 TFEU.

---

192. See Code of Conduct for Commissioners SEC (2004) 1487/2.
193. Article 246 TFEU.

6.4.5 Functioning: the principle of collegiality

The Commission is a collegiate body. This means that no member of the Commission is actually empowered to take any decision on his own and if a member has, in effect, made a decision, it expresses the position of the entire Commission.

The principle of collegiality is based on the equal participation of the commissioners in the adoption of decisions. The immediate consequence of this principle is that decisions should be the subject of collective deliberation and that all the members of the College of Commissioners bear collective responsibility at political level for all decisions adopted. Additionally, this principle means that each decision must be formally approved by the College. Failure to ensure this may render a measure invalid.[194] Apart from the exceptions provided in Articles 10 and 11 of the Commission's Rules of Procedure, the principle of collegiality requires that the Commission seeks a broad consensus among its members, although it may also submit the matter to a formal vote.[195] The president of the Commission is only primus inter pares; there is no casting vote.

The principle of collegiality is less formalistic than it appears on the surface, as explained in Case C-191/95 *Commission v Germany*.[196]

THE FACTS WERE:

The Commission decided to issue a reasoned opinion against the government of Germany for failure to provide for appropriate penalties in cases where companies limited by shares failed to disclose their annual accounts, as prescribed in particular by the First Company Directive 68/151/EEC of 9 March 1968 and the Fourth Company Directive 78/660/EEC of 25 July 1978. When Germany did not comply with the opinion, the Commission decided, in conformity with Article 226 EC [258 TFEU], to bring proceedings before the ECJ against the German Government. Both decisions were challenged by the German Government as not being the subject of collective deliberations by the College of Commissioners.

Held:

■ The ECJ held that the formal requirement for effective compliance with the principle of collegiality varies according to the nature and legal effect of the act. In the case of acts which have no binding legal effect, it is not necessary for the College "itself formally to decide on the wording of the acts which give effect to those decisions and put them in final form". In such circumstances it is sufficient if the information on which those decisions are based is available to the members of the College. In the present case, the measures in question had no binding legal effect and necessary information was available to the members of the College.

---

194. Case C-137/92P *Commission v BASF* [1994] ECR I-2555 in which the ECJ confirmed the decisions of the CFI regarding Cases T-79/89, T-84-86/89, T-91-92/89, T-94/89, T-96/89, T-98/89 *BASF* [1992] ECR II-315.
195. Under Article 250 TFEU a simple majority of its members is required.
196. [1998] ECR I-5449.

The principle of collegiality also entails that acts adopted by the College of Commissioners, in order to be binding on their addressees, must be authenticated by the signatures of the president of the Commission and of the executive secretary. The objective of authentication is to ensure that the text adopted by the College of Commissioners becomes fixed, so that in the event of a dispute it can be verified that the text adopted corresponds precisely to the text notified or published. In Joined Cases C-286 and 288P *Commission v Solvay*[197] the ECJ held that if an act adopted by the Commission has not been properly authenticated, the Community courts must, of their own motion, raise the issue and annul the act vitiated by that defect. This duty of the courts remains irrespective of whether or not the lack of authentication caused any harm to a party to the dispute.

6.4.6   Competences

The competences of the European Commission are described in Article 17(1) and (2) TFEU. Article 17(1) provides that:

"The Commission shall promote the general interest of the Union and take appropriate initiatives to that end. It shall ensure the application of the Treaties, and of measures adopted by the institutions pursuant to them. It shall oversee the application of Union law under the control of the Court of Justice of the European Union. It shall execute the budget and manage programmes. It shall exercise coordinating, executive and management functions, as laid down in the Treaties. With the exception of the common foreign and security policy, and other cases provided for in the Treaties, it shall ensure the Union's external representation. It shall initiate the Union's annual and multiannual programming with a view to achieving inter institutional agreements."

Article 17(2) confirms the Commission's right to initiate proposals for legislative acts and other acts unless the Treaties provide otherwise (see Chapter 7.2).

The role of the Commission under the CFSP is described in Chapter 5.4.3.

6.4.6.1   The European Commission as the "guardian of the Treaty"

The most important function of the Commission is to ensure that the provisions of the Treaties and the acts of the institutions are complied with by the Member States, any natural or legal person under the jurisdiction of a Member State and all EU institutions, bodies, offices and agencies. In order to fulfil this task the Commission has at its disposal important powers:

- The Commission is empowered to obtain any necessary information from Member States, individuals and undertakings. Member States have a duty to forward information required by the Commission, notify measures and projections of measures they intend to adopt, and provide explanations concerning any question of law or fact which the Commission considers important. This obligation derives either from specific provisions of the Treaties[198] or from measures adopted by the EU institutions,[199] or from Article 4(3) TEU which requires

---

197.   [2000] ECR I-2341.
198.   For example, Articles 114(5) and 117 TFEU.
199.   Especially the final provisions of directives which impose upon the Member States the obligation to notify the Commission of the adoption of implementing measures.

Member States to co-operate with the Commission in order to facilitate the achievement of the EU's tasks. The Commission may ask individuals and undertakings to forward information[200] and, under its investigative powers, to verify it. A request for information is often the first step in the Commission's investigation of an alleged infringement of EU law by an undertaking in competition matters.[201]

■ The Commission may take preventative actions. The Commission formulates recommendations and delivers opinions intended to ensure effective application of EU law in the future.

■ The Commission is empowered to enforce compliance with EU law. The obligation to observe EU law binds Member States, natural and legal persons, and the EU institutions, bodies and agencies. In respect of natural and legal persons, the Commission may impose pecuniary and/or administrative sanctions upon them in matters concerning the control of security under the EA Treaty and in competition issues under the TFEU. With regards to the Member States, under Article 258 TFEU the Commission may bring an action before the ECJ against a Member State in breach of EU law.[202] If any EU institution, body or agency violates EU law, the Commission may bring an action under Articles 263 or 265 TFEU; this is mostly applied in respect of the Council.[203]

■ The Commission may authorise, in certain circumstances, derogations from the provisions of the Treaties. Under the Acts of Accession and in respect of measures adopted by EU institutions in relation to international agreements the Commission is authorised to grant derogations. Under Articles 346 and 347 TFEU or Article 114(6) TFEU the Commission is empowered to authorise measures incompatible with the internal market. Such derogations may be authorised in cases where a Member State is faced with serious economic difficulties, internal disturbances and serious international tension, or if its essential interest of national security is in jeopardy.

■ In the context of EMU, the Commission monitors budgetary discipline in Member States in order to avoid excessive governmental deficits[204] and is empowered to supervise their balance of payments.[205]

6.4.6.2   *The European Commission as the initiator of legislative measures*

The general interest of the EU requires that the Commission's main objective is to foster European integration. Consequently, its right to initiate legislative measures in order to further develop the EU is well justified. Article 17(2) TEU confirms the Commission's virtual monopoly on the right to initiate proposals for both legislative and non-legislative acts (for exceptions see Chapter 7.2). However, the Commission's right to initiate legislation and other acts is not exercised lightly and is subject to many safeguards.

---

200. For example, Article 337 TFEU.
201. See Chapter 30.
202. See Chapter 15.
203. See Chapter 16.
204. Article 126 TFEU.
205. Articles 143 and 144 TFEU.

6.4.6.3   Executive powers of the Commission

Article 17 TEU states that the Commission shall exercise co-ordinating, executive and management functions, as laid down in the Treaties.

The administration of EU policies necessitates the adoption of numerous binding measures. In addition, the Commission implements the EU budget and administers four special funds: the European Social Fund, the European Development Fund, the European Agricultural Guidance and Guarantee Fund, and the European Regional Development Fund.

By virtue of Article 290 TFEU the Commission exercises delegated powers and under Article 291 implementing powers (see Chapter 8.5).

6.4.6.4   International functions of the Commission

The international functions of the Commission have been limited as a result of the establishment of the post of the HR and the post of the President of the European Council. In foreign affairs, with the exception of the CFSP, the Commission shares its tasks with the HR.

6.5   The European Parliament (EP)

The European Parliament, previously known as the Assembly of the European Communities, renamed itself in 1962 in order to emphasise the role it should play in the Community's policy-making process. Its role has indeed dramatically changed, as each revision of the original Treaties has substantially increased the EP's legislative powers, as follows:

- Initially the EP's powers were purely consultative;

- The SEA recognised the new name and introduced two legislative procedures: the assent and the co-operation procedures;

- The Treaty of Maastricht introduced the possibility for the EP to request the Commission to prepare a legislative proposal, and added a new procedure to those mentioned above: the co-decision procedure;

- The ToA extended the scope of application of the co-decision procedure;

- The ToN further extended the ambit of the co-decision and assent procedures;[206]

- The ToL increased the EP's competences in terms of its legislative and budgetary powers.

The ToL describes the EP as exercising legislative powers "jointly" with the Council. Indeed, under the ordinary legislative procedure (previously known as co-decision procedure), which is the predominant procedure for the adoption of EU legislative acts, the EP is put on an equal level with the EP (see Chapter 7.3) In quantitative terms, the EP has become a co-legislator with the Council in 44 new areas. Of particular importance is the application of the ordinary legislative procedure to the adoption of measures relating to the establishment of the area of FSJ. This means that the EP has become a co-legislator with regard to measures relating to frontier controls, asylum, immigration, judicial co-operation in criminal matters, minimum rules for the definition of and

---

206.   Legislative procedures are examined in depth in Chapter 7.

penalties in the areas of serious crime, incentive measures for crime prevention, Eurojust (European Prosecutors Co-operation), police co-operation, Europol and civil protection.

In budgetary matters, the distinction between Compulsory Expenditure and Non-Compulsory Expenditure was abolished by the ToL. The ordinary legislative procedure applies to both.

With regard to international agreements, under a new "consent" procedure (which is a new name given to the assent procedure) the EP's consent is needed for international agreements mentioned in Article 218(6) TFEU. In particular Article 218(6)(v) specifies that the consent of the EP is required for all international agreements in areas which are internally subject to the ordinary legislative procedure or where consent of the EP is needed. This means that if the ordinary legislative procedure applies to adoption of a measure relating to, say, asylum policy, an international agreement on asylum matters with third countries or an international organisation, must obtain the EP's consent.

Under the ordinary procedure for future revision of the Treaties, the EP is entitled to initiate such revision by submitting a proposal to that effect to the European Council. Additionally, the EP's consent is required if the European Council decides to convene a conference of representatives of national governments instead of convening a Convention with a view to revising the Treaties (see Chapter 8.2.5).

Some concerns have been voiced that the quantitative increase of the EP's competences may jeopardise the quality of its work and it has therefore been suggested that the EP should undertake an internal reform of its functioning, in particular with regard to legislative committees.

Also, the EP has gained additional political control over some EU institutions, in particular by being involved in the election of the president of the Commission, members of the Commission and the HR.

The EP, in comparison with other EU institutions in terms of attributed competences and the way it is constituted, has undergone great change since its inception. From 1979 it has been the only directly elected body in the Communities; hence, its claim to be a real parliament. Nevertheless, the EP, unlike national parliaments, is not a real, sovereign parliament as it has no power on its own to initiate and enact legislation or to impose taxes.

6.5.1   Election to the EP

In accordance with Council Decision 76/787 and the annexed Act on direct elections of 20 September 1976[207] adopted by the Council, the members of the EP are elected by direct universal suffrage.

Any national of a Member State who is qualified to vote in national elections may stand as a candidate for the EP. In Cases C-145/04 *Spain v UK*[208] and C-300/04 *Eman and Sevinger,*[209] the ECJ held that a Member State has exclusive competence to define the persons who are to be entitled to vote and to stand as a candidate in elections to the EP, but added that in exercising this competence, a Member State must comply with EU law, in particular, with the principle of equal treatment. As a result:

---

207.   [1976] OJ L278/1.
208.   [2006] ECR I-7917.
209.   [2006] ECR I-8055.

- In Case C-145/04 *Spain v UK*, it was found that the UK was entitled to confer the right to vote at EP elections on qualifying citizens of the Commonwealth residing in Gibraltar, who were neither British nationals nor citizens of the EU;

- In Case C-300/04 *Eman*, it was found that The Netherlands was in breach of the principle of equal treatment. This was because the Dutch Government did not objectively justify the difference in treatment between, on the one hand, Dutch nationals residing in a non-Member State, including those who had transferred their residence from The Netherlands Antilles and Aruba (a Dutch OCT associated with the EU) to a non-Member State and, on the other hand, Dutch nationals who moved from The Netherlands to reside in The Netherlands Antilles and Aruba. The former were entitled to vote and stand as a candidate in elections to the EP; the latter were refused the same entitlement. Thus, in both situations nationals of The Netherlands were living outside The Netherlands, but those living in OCTs were excluded from exercising their right to vote and to stand as candidates in elections to the EP.

Article 22(1) TFEU specifies that citizens of the EU residing in a Member State of which they are not nationals are entitled to vote in, and stand as candidates in elections to the EP in the Member State in which they reside under the same conditions as nationals of that Member State.

Employment by an EU institution is incompatible with membership of the EP, as is the holding of certain offices such as membership of national governments, or membership of national parliaments.

Directive 93/109/EC provided for a uniform electoral procedure[210] but did not introduce a uniform voting system in the Member States. In order to remedy this, Council Decision 2002/772/EC[211] provides that national electoral systems in respect of elections to the EP must meet the condition of proportional representation, which must be ensured either under a party list or a single transferable vote system. However:

- Member States may set a minimum threshold for the allocation of seats. At national level this threshold may not exceed 5 per cent of votes cast;

- Subdivision of an electoral area is allowed, provided that this will not generally affect the proportional nature of the voting system.

The first ever elections to the EP were held in 1979. Elections take place every five years.

6.5.2 Composition

The number of parliamentary seats is determined on the basis of the size of population in each Member State but, in the light of the wide differences between large and small Member States, this is not a strict mathematical formula. For example, Luxembourg has only 488,650 inhabitants, while the UK has 61 million. As a result, a compromise was reached which takes into consideration the size of the population in a Member State, while ensuring that the smallest Member States are adequately represented in the EP, and that its overall size does not produce an excessively large and unwieldy body. For that reason, under the ToL the maximum number of seats in

---

210. [1993] OJ L329/34.
211. [2002] OJ L283/1.

the EP is fixed at 750 plus the president of the EP. These seats are allocated to the Member States according to the principle of "degressive proportionality", with a minimum of 6 and a maximum of 96 seats.

The assignment of seats is as follows:

Germany	96
France	74
Italy and the UK	73 each
Spain	54
Poland	52
Romania	33
The Netherlands	26
Greece, Belgium, Portugal, The Czech Republic and Hungary	22 each
Sweden	20
Austria	19
Bulgaria	18
Slovakia, Denmark, Finland	13 each
Ireland and Lithuania	12 each
Latvia	9
Slovenia	8
Estonia, Cyprus, Luxembourg and Malta	6 each
Total	751

Members of the EP enjoy certain privileges and immunities, which are listed in Chapter III of Protocol 7 on the Privileges and Immunities of the European Union annexed to the Treaties. They are:

- Freedom of movement when they travel to or from the place of meeting of the EP;

- Immunity from any form of inquiry, detention or legal proceedings in respect of opinions expressed or votes cast in the performance of their duties;

- During a session of the EP they are, in their home Member State, granted the same immunities as are members of their national parliaments, and enjoy immunity from any measures of detention and from legal proceedings in the territory of any other Member State. However, the immunity can be waived by the EP if a member commits a criminal offence. It is interesting to note that the EP has modified its Rules of Procedure following the problem raised by the personal bankruptcy of Bernard Tapie, a member of the EP, in order to regulate this kind of situation in the future. In the absence of a uniform electoral procedure at EU level, this matter is governed in each Member State by its national electoral laws.[212]

General conditions governing the performance of the duties of MEPs are set out in Decision 2005/684/EC, Euratom adopted by the EP on 28 September 2005.[213] The decision, which entered into force on 14 July 2009, provides for a uniform salary system and a system for the reimburse-

---

212. On the consequences of the absence of uniform electoral procedure see: Case 294/83 *Parti Ecologiste "Les Verts" v EP* [1986] ECR 1339.
213. [2005] OJ L262/1.

ment of expenses. Its Article 10 states that the amount of the salary of a MEP shall be 38 per cent of the basic salary of a judge at the ECJ.

6.5.2.1 The EP and its political groups

Unlike national parliaments, the EP is not divided into a government and an opposition. MEPs sit in multinational groups based on political affiliation and not in national groups. A political group must have at least 25 members representing between them at least one-quarter of the Member States. Discipline within the political groups is lax, and national delegations and individual MEPs are free to switch allegiances as they wish. An MEP who does not belong to any political group is known as a non-attached MEP.

At the time of writing, the EP is organised into seven political groups as follows:

- Group of the European People's Party (Christian Democrats);

- Group of the Progressive Alliance of Socialists and Democrats in the European Parliament;

- Group of the Alliance of Liberals and Democrats for Europe;

- Group of the Greens/European Free Alliance;

- European Conservatives and Reformists Group;

- Confederal Group of the European United Left/Nordic Green Left;

- Europe of Freedom and Democracy Group.

6.5.2.2 The EP and the European political parties

The ToA recognised the importance of European political parties in Article 191 EC. The revised version of Article 191 EC is contained in Article 10(4) TEU which states that "Political parties at European level contribute to forming European political awareness and to expressing the will of citizens of the Union". Under Article 224 TFEU the Council and the EP acting in accordance with the ordinary legislative procedure are allowed to adopt regulations governing political parties at European level, and in particular the rules regarding recognition of political parties at European level and their funding.

The Declaration on Article 191 EC [Article 10(4) TEU], attached to the ToN, clarified the scope of the paragraph: it neither involves the transfer of powers from a Member State to the EU, nor affects relevant national constitutional provisions. The funding of political parties at European level from the EU budget must not be used for direct or indirect funding of national political parties. Furthermore, the funding rules apply on the same terms to all political parties represented in the EP. Regulation 2004/2003 on the funding of political parties at European level[214] sets out rules for obtaining funding for such a party from the EU. A group of MEPs representing national parties hostile to the EU (Eurosceptics) brought an action for annulment of the Regulation, arguing that it was undemocratic and discriminatory. The action was dismissed by the CFI (now the General Court).[215]

---

214. [2003] OJ L297/1.
215. Case T-13/04 *Bonde and Others v EP and Council*, Order of 11 July 2005 (unpublished).

6.5.3 Organisation

From its inception the EP has considered itself a parliament. At that time it was the Assembly of the ECSC and it adopted rules of procedure similar to those of any parliament. Parliamentary status was recognised by the Treaties of Rome and enhanced by the universal suffrage to the EP. Under Article 232 TFEU the EP adopts its own Rules of Procedure. However, the power of the EP is limited by the obligation to respect the allocation of competences between the EU institutions as determined by the Treaties.[216]

The EP elects the president, 14 vice presidents and 6 quaestors for two and a half years. In doing this account is taken of the need to ensure an overall fair representation of Member States and political views.

The president chairs debates, exercises an administrative and disciplinary function similar to those of a leader of any national parliament, and represents the EP in international relations, on ceremonial occasions and in administrative, legal and financial matters. At the beginning of every European Council meeting the president sets out the EP's point of view and its concerns as regards the items on the agenda and other subjects. He also signs the EU budget. He is allowed to delegate his powers to the vice presidents. The quaestors are responsible for administrative and financial matters directly concerning members of the EP.

The president, vice presidents and quaestors (who have observer status) form the Bureau of Parliament, which is responsible for the organisation and administration of the EP. The Conference of Committee Chairs is made up of the president of the EP and the chairperson of each political group. Its main tasks are as follows:

- It takes decisions on the organisation of the EP's work and matters relating to legislative planning;

- It is responsible for matters relating to relations with the other institutions and bodies of the EU, with the national parliaments of Member States, with non-member countries and with non-Union institutions and organisations;

- It decides on the composition and competences of committees, such as committees of inquiry, joint parliamentary committees, standing delegations and ad hoc delegations (see below);

- It submits proposals to the Bureau of Parliament concerning administrative and budgetary matters relating to the political groups.

The Secretary General of the EP and the Secretariat of the EP assist the EP in administrative and organisational matters.

6.5.3.1 EP Committees and delegations

Under its Rules of Procedure, the EP may establish permanent, temporary, specialised, general and joint committees. Such committees may examine particular topics in detail, prepare opinions at the request of the Council and prepare resolutions concerning new initiatives of the EP. Additionally, the EP may set up standing inter-parliamentary delegations.

---

216. This was emphasised by the ECJ in Case 294/83 *Parti Ecologiste "Les Verts"* [1986] ECR 1339.

6.5.3.1.1   Permanent committees

There are 20 permanent committees, which meet once or twice per month in Brussels; each of them deals with a specific aspect of EU activities.[217] Their role is to draft, adopt and amend legislation. They also consider proposals from the Council and the Commission. They are of particular importance as they streamline the work of the EP. They prepare reports for debates in the EP, and liaise with the Commission and the Council between parliamentary sessions. They can meet at any time at the request of their chairman, or the president of the EP. The members of committees are elected on the basis of proposals submitted by political groups. Political and geographical factors, and representations by the parliamentary political groups within a committee, are also taken into consideration. In principle, each MEP is a sitting member of one permanent committee, and an advisory member-suppliant of another.

6.5.3.1.2   Temporary committees

On a proposal from the Conference of Presidents, the EP may at any time create temporary committees, whose powers, composition and term of office are defined at the same time as the decision to create them is taken. Their term of office may not exceed 12 months, except where the EP extends that term beyond 12 months.

6.5.3.1.3   Committee of Inquiry

Article 226 TFEU permits the EP to set up a temporary Committee of Inquiry to investigate, without prejudice to the powers conferred by the Treaties on other EU institutions and bodies, alleged contraventions and maladministration in the implementation of EU law, except where the alleged facts are being examined before a court and while the case is still subject to legal proceedings.[218] The request to set up a Committee of Inquiry must specify precisely the subject of the inquiry and include a detailed statement of the grounds for it. A Committee of Inquiry must conclude its work with the submission of a report within not more than 12 months of its creation. The EP may twice decide to extend this period by three months. Therefore, a Committee of Inquiry can sit for a maximum of 18 months.

6.5.3.1.4   Joint parliamentary committees

The EP may set up joint parliamentary committees with the parliaments of states associated with the EU or states with which accession negotiations have been initiated.

6.5.3.1.5   Subcommittees

Subject to prior authorisation by the Conference of Presidents, a standing or temporary committee may, in the interests of its work, appoint one or more subcommittees, of which it shall at the same time determine the composition and area of responsibility. Subcommittees shall report to the committee that set them up.

---

217.   There are 17 Internal Affairs Committees and 3 External Affairs Committees. The External Committee on Foreign Affairs has two subcommittees: one on Human Rights and one on Security and Defence.

218.   On the right to petition the EP see Chapter 22.6.

6.5.3.1.6   Standing inter-parliamentary delegations

Inter-parliamentary delegations may be set up on a proposal from the Conference of Committee Chairs. Their main role is to establish and maintain relations with parliaments of non-Member States. Their competence and the number of their members are determined by the EP.

All EP bodies, particularly the committees, shall co-operate with their counterparts at the Parliamentary Assembly of the Council of Europe in fields of mutual interest, with the aim of improving the efficiency of their work and avoiding duplication of effort.

6.5.4   Sessions

Article 229 TFEU provides that:

> "The European Parliament shall hold an annual session. It shall meet, without requiring to be convened, on the second Tuesday in March.
>
> The European Parliament may meet in extraordinary part-session at the request of a majority of its component Members or at the request of the Council or of the Commission."

In Case 101/63 *Wagner v Fohrmann and Krier*,[219] the ECJ held that the EP is in session from the opening until the close of the annual session. Each annual session follows immediately the preceding session. Thus, in practice the EP is always in session. Despite this the EP is on holiday in August. The annual calendar of the EP provides for:

- 12 four-day plenary sessions in Strasbourg and six additional two-day plenary sessions in Brussels;

- Two weeks a month for meetings of parliamentary committees and inter-parliamentary delegations;

- One week a month for political group meetings; and

- Four weeks a year where MEPs concentrate exclusively on constituency work.

The sessions are open to the general public.

6.5.5   Competences

Under the original Treaties the EP was only a supervisory and advisory body. The EP's fight for power, strengthened by direct elections, resulted in the acquiring of many important competences. There are five main functions which the EP exercises at present:

- Democratic supervision of EU institutions;

- Adoption of the EU budget jointly with the Council;

- Adoption of EU legislation jointly with the Council;

- Participation in the external relations of the EU;

- Protection of human rights within and outside the EU.

---

219.   [1964] ECR 195.

6.5.5.1 Democratic supervision of EU institutions

The EP exercises democratic supervision over the Commission by: electing the president of the Commission and approving the Commission, as a body; by discussing in an open session the Commission's annual legislative and work programme, an annual general report on the activities of the EU and an annual general report on the application of EU law; by the possibility of using a motion of censure and by other means of general control. Further, the EP controls the exercise of delegated powers by the Commission (see Chapter 8.5.2). The political control of the EP extends over other institutions such as the Council, the European Council and the bodies in charge of political co-operation and of economic and monetary matters.

General and permanent democratic supervision is exercised by the EP over the Commission, the Council and other institutions and bodies by various means.

6.5.5.1.1 The EP has power to ask the Commission and the Council questions on any topic (Article 230 TFEU) and the HR on matters relating to the CFSP

These questions may take various forms: written, oral without debates, oral with debates, question times, and so on:

- Written questions: the Commission and the Council are obliged to answer such questions within three weeks if they are "priority" questions (they require immediate answer but not detailed research), and six weeks if not. Written questions can also be addressed to the ECB. Written questions, and answers to them, are published in the Official Journal;

- Oral questions without a debate, which must first be approved by the Bureau of Parliament, may be put to the Council and the Commission during the plenary session;

- Oral questions with a debate may only be put by a parliamentary committee, a political group or at least 40 MEPs. Sometimes they lead to a Resolution adopted by the EP;

- Question time, which is modelled on the British parliamentary tradition, was introduced in 1973: in each plenary session a period of time is especially set aside for questions to be put to individual commissioners regarding current affairs. The questions are brief and precise, and so are the answers. After each answer any member of the EP may ask an additional question and, if necessary, at the request of 29 MEPs the question time may lead to a debate.

The possibility of asking questions ensures a follow-up of the legislative and administrative activities of the Commission and the Council, and imposes an obligation to justify them before the EP.

6.5.5.1.2 Resolutions

Resolutions are adopted by the EP following a general debate based on a motion tabled by an MEP and a relevant parliamentary committee. Resolutions express the position of the EP on important issues with a view to influencing the Commission or the Council, but are not binding.

6.5.5.1.3 Reports, programmes of actions, and so on

Another general method of political control involves the EP's right to examine annual and period reports, programmes of action, and so on, submitted by various bodies, including:

A.   **The Commission.** By virtue of Article 233 TFEU, the Commission must submit an annual report on the activities of the EU to the EP. The Commission has, on its own initiative, decided to annex its annual work programme to these reports. In February each year both are discussed by the EP and commented upon in a resolution on the general policy of the EU. Further, the Commission is required to submit an annual report on the implementation of the budget and only the EP can adopt a decision on the granting of discharge to the Commission in respect of the implementation of the budget. In addition to general reports, the Commission is required to submit reports on particular topics, e.g. in respect of progress achieved by the EU in social matters under Article 159 TFEU.

B.   **The Council.** At the beginning of each Presidency the president of the Council presents a work programme for its Presidency to the EP and launches a debate on it with MEPs. At the end of each Presidency a final report is submitted to the EP on the outcomes achieved. Ministers from the Council often participate in debates before the EP and may, at any time, ask the president of the EP for permission to make a statement.

C.   **The European Council.** Each summit meeting commences with a declaration by the president of the EP setting out the position of the EP on topics to be discussed by the European Council, notice of which has been previously forwarded to the EP. At the end of each summit meeting the president of the European Council presents the EP with a report on the outcome of its activities. Also, the European Council is required to submit a written annual report to the EP on progress achieved by the EU. Within the framework of the CFSP the EP may put questions and make recommendations to the Council, and the HR. It also holds a debate twice a year on progress in implementing the CFSP, including CSDP (Article 36 TEU).

D.   **The European Central Bank.** The president of the ECB is required to submit an annual report to the EP in plenary session.

6.5.5.1.4   Legislative initiative of the EP

By virtue of Article 225 TFEU the EP is entitled to call on the Commission to submit a legislative proposal to the Council on matters on which it considers that the EU is required to act in order to implement the Treaties. The Commission does not have to comply but if it decides not to proceed must inform the EP of the reasons.

6.5.5.1.5   Permanent committees

Parliamentary permanent committees may invite members of the Commission to present legislative proposals and answer questions. The Commission has always accommodated the EP committees. It would seem that as a result of this course, a permanent control by EP committees over the activities of the Commission has been developed.

6.5.5.1.6   Committee of Inquiry

The EP may, at the request of one-quarter of its members, establish a temporary Committee of Inquiry to investigate alleged contraventions or maladministration in the implementation of EU law. Such a body ceases to exist on the submission of its report.

6.5.5.1.7 Petitions to the EP

By virtue of Article 24 TFEU every citizen of the EU has the right to petition the EP. This right is further expanded in Article 227 TFEU, which provides that any citizen of the EU, and any natural or legal person residing or having its registered office in a Member State, has the right to address, individually or in association with other citizens or persons, a petition to the EP on a matter which comes within the EU's field of activity and which affects him, her or it directly (this topic is discussed in Chapter 22.6).

6.5.5.1.8 Appointments and approval of appointments

The EP appoints an ombudsman, who deals with complaints by a natural or a legal person residing or having its registered office in a Member State with a view to achieving an amicable solution (see Chapter 22.7). Such complaints concern instances of maladministration in the activities of the EU institutions or bodies.

The EP elects the president of the Commission,[220] and by a vote of consent approves the Commission as a body. This includes approval of the HR who is ex officio the vice-president of the Commission. The extensive interviews of candidates to be Commissioners conducted by the EP in relation to the nomination of the members of the Commission appointed in 2009 demonstrate that the power is far from being theoretical.

The EP must be consulted in respect of the appointment of the president, the vice-president and the members of the Executive Board of the European Central Bank.

6.5.5.1.9 Motion of censure

The EP may force the entire Commission, as a collegiate body, to resign but not its president, nor a particular commissioner. In order to avoid abuse, Article 234 TFEU laid down stringent requirements as to a motion of censure:

- A time of reflection of at least three days after the motion has been tabled is required;

- Provided that at least 50 per cent of MEPs have voted and that a two-thirds majority of the votes cast is in favour, the motion of censure will be carried;

- The vote must be open.

A motion of censure is an exceptional measure; if successfully carried out, it may lead to a serious crisis in the EU without achieving the desired objective, which normally is the removal of one or two commissioners but not the entire College of Commissioners. The final result of a successful motion of censure is doubtful. Commissioners are nominated by the Member States and thus nothing would prevent a Member State from nominating the same persons, although without the approval of the EP it is difficult to envisage how the Commission would operate.

Notwithstanding the above, Article 234 TFEU provides a powerful weapon for the EP in the complex political interaction between the three institutions: the EP, the Council and the Commission. For example, the use of a motion of censure as mentioned above, although not carried, was one of the main factors leading to the resignation of the Commission presided over by Jacques Santer. On 16 March 1999, for the first time in the history of the EU, the president of the Commission, Jacques Santer, was, together with all commissioners, forced to resign. Under the

---

220. Articles 17(3) and 7 TEU.

principle of collegiate responsibility the entire Commission, including its president, was in effect dismissed. Mismanagement, fraud, the awarding of financial contracts and other irregularities committed by some commissioners were confirmed by the "comité de sages" set up jointly by the EP and the Commission following an EP resolution on 14 January 1999 on improving the financial management of the Commission. The resignation occurred shortly after the EP failed to pass a motion of censure to dismiss the Commission (293 votes in favour to 232 against with 27 abstentions).

6.5.5.1.10 Proceedings before the ECJ

The EP is a privileged applicant under Article 263 TFEU, and as such automatically has standing to challenge the legality of any reviewable act adopted by EU institutions, bodies and agencies. In practice, the EP has brought many proceedings challenging the legality of acts adopted by the Council. Under Article 265 TFEU the EP is entitled to bring an action against EU institutions or bodies for illegal inaction (see Chapter 16.4). Further, the EP may ask the ECJ for an opinion with regard to the compatibility of an envisaged international agreement with the provisions of the Treaties under Article 218(11) TFEU.

6.5.5.2   *Participation in the adoption of the EU budget*

Until 1969 the Communities were funded through direct financial contributions from the Member States based on their Gross National Income (GNI). In 1969, as a result of an agreement between Member States, the "own resources" were introduced which provides the EU with its own independent source of revenue. The "own resources" of the EU are made up of:

- 1 per cent of VAT on goods and services in the EU (about 12 per cent of revenue);

- Customs duties (from the common customs tariff applied to trade with third countries) (about 11 per cent of revenue);

- Agricultural import levies and duties (about 1 per cent of revenue);

- "Gross National Income (GNI) resource". This refers to the contribution made by each Member State based on its share of the Community's total GNI, capped at 1.27 per cent. This accounts for 76 per cent of revenue;

- Miscellaneous resources such as taxes paid by the staff on their salaries, contributions from third countries to EU programmes and fines imposed for breaches of EU law. This amounts to about 1 per cent of the budget.

The total EU revenue for 2010 amounted to some €141.5 billion, representing around 1 per cent of the 27 Member States GNI which, in turn, is equivalent to about €235 Euro per head of the population. The EU budget is not allowed to be in deficit, i.e. the expenditure must not exceed the revenue. In comparison with the EU expenditure, the UK expenditure for 2010 was £704 billion.[221] The EU budget is mainly spent on EU citizens, directly or indirectly, on helping less developed countries around the world and on humanitarian aid to help non-EU countries

---

221.   Availble at http:///budget.treasury.gov.uk (15/2/10).

afflicted by natural disasters and other crisis situations. Only around six cents in every euro are spent on running the EU, i.e. to cover expenses relating to the staff and building costs.

Before the Budgetary Treaties of 1970 and 1975 were adopted, the EP was only consulted on the Communities' budget. Under the Budgetary Treaties and until the entry into force of the ToL, the EU budget was divided into Compulsory Expenditure (CE), which related to those items resulting from Treaty obligations or secondary legislation, mainly the financing of the CAP, the CFP and the expenditure resulting from international agreements and Non-Compulsory Expenditure (NCE) which covered other items such as social and regional policy, research and aid, and so on. The EP had the last word on "Non-compulsory expenditure" and had the right to reject the budget as a whole. Under the ToL, the EP has an equal right to the Council to adopt the entire annual EU budget of the EU. However, before any annual budget is drafted it must accord with the multiannual financial framework (MFF) which is adopted by the Council acting unanimously after obtaining the consent of the EP. The MFF determines:

> "the amounts of the annual ceilings on commitment appropriations by category of expenditure and of the annual ceiling on payment appropriations. The categories of expenditure, limited in number, shall correspond to the Union's major sector activity."

At the time of writing, the MFF in force covers the period from 2007 to 2013.

The following stages in the budgetary procedure are described in Article 310 TFEU:

1. The Commission prepares a preliminary draft, based on estimates of expenditure submitted by each institution, which is placed before the EP and the Council no later than 1 September for the following financial year (from 1 January to 31 December).

2. The Council is entitled to make amendments and adopts its reasoned position on the draft budget which is forwarded to the EP for its first reading no later than 1 October.

3. The EP has 42 days to accept, or amend the budget. Inaction amounts to the acceptance of the submitted draft budget. If the EP approves the Council's position, the budget can be adopted. If the EP amends, by a majority of its component members, the draft budget the altered draft is sent to the Council and to the Commission. The Council may, within 10 days, accept the amendments and adopt the budget. If the Council refuses to accept the EP's amendments, the president of the EP and the president of the Council must immediately set up the Conciliation Committee.

4. The Conciliation Committee is made up of members of the Council or their representatives and an equal number of MEPs. The Committee has 21 days to agree on a joint text which must be approved by QMV of the members or representatives of the Council and by a majority of the MEPs. The Commission acts as a broker between the two delegations. If the Conciliation Committee fails to agree a joint text, the Commission has to submit a new draft budget. If the joint text has been agreed, the EP and the Council have 14 days to approve or reject it. If the EP adopts the budget, it is adopted even if the Council rejects the joint text. Only if both the EP and the Council reject the draft budget is it definitely rejected, with the result that the Commission must prepare a new draft budget.

If, at the beginning of the financial year, the budget has not been adopted, a sum equivalent to no more than 1/12 of the budget appropriations for the preceding financial year may be spent each month. The inconvenience this creates for the institutions is significant, as the previous year's budget continues to operate on a one-twelfth for each month basis. This means that the institutions cannot exceed the previous year's limits, although Article 315 TFEU permits an increase in expenditure on the approval of the Council and the EP.

6.5.5.3 Participation in legislative procedures

Unlike national parliaments the EP is neither entitled to initiate legislative measures, nor to adopt them on its own accord. Under the ToL the EP legislative powers have been considerably extended. It, acting jointly with the Council, adopts the vast majority of EU legislation (see Chapter 7.3).

6.5.5.4 Participation in the revision of Treaties

Under the ordinary procedure for future revision of the Treaties (see Chapter 8.2.5.1), the EP is entitled to initiate such revision by submitting a proposal to that effect to the European Council. Additionally, the EP's consent is required for a decision of the European Council to convene a conference of representatives of national governments instead of convening a Convention with a view to revising the Treaties (see Chapter 8.2.5.1).

6.5.5.5 Participation in the external relations of the EU

With regard to international agreements, under the "consent procedure" (which is a new name given to the assent procedure) the EP's consent is needed in respect of all agreements listed in Article 218(6)(a) which includes agreements in areas which are internally subject to the ordinary legislative procedure, i.e. if the ordinary legislative procedure applies to adoption of a measure relating to, say, asylum policy, an international agreement on asylum matters with third countries or an international organisation must obtain the EP's consent.

6.5.5.6 Protection of Human Rights within and outside the EU

The EP plays an important role as a defender and protector of human rights within and outside the EU. In this respect, the EP:

- May initiate a proposal concerning the determination that there is a clear risk of a serious breach by a Member State of the values on which the EU is founded, and its consent is required for the making of such a determination (Article 7(1) TEU). Further, under Article 7(2) TEU, the EP's consent is needed to make a determination of the existence of a serious and persistent breach by a Member State of the values on which the EU is founded (see Chapter 3.2.2);

- Prepares two annual reports on the human rights situation, one relating to countries outside the EU, and the other in respect of rights enshrined in the Charter of Fundamental Rights;

- Conducts debates and adopts resolutions regarding breaches of human rights worldwide. At each of its monthly part-sessions, the EP puts aside time to discuss breaches of human rights, democracy and the rule of law. Often these debates lead to adoption of a resolution condemning governments which are violating human rights;

- When informed by the Council that the EU has suspended an agreement with a third country because that country violates human rights, uses all methods at its disposal to put pressure on that country to rectify the situation;

▪ Established the Sakharov Prize for Freedom of Thought in 1988. The prize is awarded to individuals or organisations who – like Andrei Sakharov – have made a substantial contribution to the struggle for respect of human rights.

6.6 The Court of Justice of the European Union (CJEU)

Under the ToL all EU courts are referred to as the "Court of Justice of the European Union". This collective name covers three courts: the Court of Justice of the European Union which was previously known as the Court of Justice of the European Communities and is colloquially known as the European Court of Justice (the ECJ); the General Court, which was previously known as the Court of First Instance (CFI) and specialised courts which were previously known as "judicial panels". At the time of writing there is only one specialised court in existence, i.e. the European Union Civil Service Tribunal.

The main task of the ECJ and the General Court is to ensure that in the interpretation and application of the Treaties the law is observed (Article 19(1) TEU).

Article 19(3) TEU states that the CJEU shall:

"(a)   rule on actions brought by a Member State, an institution or a natural or legal person;
(b)   give preliminary rulings, at the request of courts or tribunals of the Member States, on the interpretation of Union law or the validity of acts adopted by the institutions;
(c)   rule in other cases provided for in the Treaties".

6.6.1 The ECJ – its composition

Article 19(1) TEU specifies that the ECJ shall consist of one judge from each Member State. This allows the ECJ to have a judge who is an expert in the national law of a Member State, and who speaks the language of that Member State.

The ECJ is assisted by 11 Advocates General (A-G). The ToL increased the number of A-G from 8 to 11[222] with the result that Poland has acquired a permanent A-G and the number of A-G involved in the rotating system has been increased from three to five. Judges and A-G are appointed by the Member States by common accord. The ToL introduced a new procedure as to the appointment of judges and A-G. Under Article 255 TFEU, a new panel will be established to give an opinion on candidates' suitability to perform the duties of judges and A-G before the governments of the Member States make the appointment. The Panel consists of seven persons selected from former members of the ECJ and the General Court, members of national supreme courts and lawyers of recognised competence, one of whom is proposed by the EP. Although the Panel only gives an opinion, which the Member States may choose not to follow, it is difficult in practice to envisage an appointment which goes against the opinion of the Panel, in particular when one of the members of the Panel is nominated by the EP.

The number of A-G may be increased by the Council acting unanimously, at the request of the ECJ, especially in order to ease the Court's workload or to accommodate a Member State that

---

222.   See Declaration 38 attached to the Treaties on Article 252 TFEU regarding the number of A-G in the CJEU.

considers that it is under-represented in the ECJ. Further, under Article 13 of Protocol 3 on the Statute of the CJEU attached to the Treaties, the ECJ may request the EP and the Council, acting in accordance with the ordinary legislative procedure, to appoint assistant rapporteurs, whose independence is beyond doubt and who possess the necessary legal qualifications, to ease the workload of judges in particular when they act as judges-rapporteurs.

Article 253 TFEU provides that the judges and the A-G are chosen from persons "whose independence is beyond doubt and who possess the qualifications required for appointment to the highest judicial offices in their respective countries or who are jurisconsults of recognised competence". The inclusion of jurisconsults allows academics, civil service lawyers and jurists, that is, lawyers without professional qualification, to be appointed even though in their own country they would not be eligible for the highest judicial offices.

The originality of the composition of the ECJ is emphasised by the presence of A-G, who are members of the Court. By virtue of Article 252 TFEU, the function of an A-G is as follows:

"It shall be the duty of the Advocate-General, acting with complete impartiality and independence, to make, in open court, reasoned submissions on cases which, in accordance with the Statute of the Court of Justice of the European Union, require his involvement."

Advocates General are required to be neutral as between the applicant and the defendant. They represent the interests of justice. They review the factual and legal aspects of a case, and must reach a conclusion which constitutes their recommendation of how the ECJ should decide the case. The conclusion is very detailed and often suggests original and new legal approaches to the disputed matter, but is not binding on the CJEU. Even if rejected in a particular case, the opinion of an A-G may be later reconsidered in a similar case since it often indicates the direction in which EU law should evolve. Furthermore, the opinion is very useful to help understanding of the case as the judgments of the CJEU are very short. Since 2003 A-G give an opinion only if the ECJ considers that a particular case raises a new point of law.

The posts of A-G are allocated as follows: one from each of the six largest Member States – Germany, France, Italy, Spain, the UK and Poland – and the remaining five positions rotate in alphabetical order between the 21 smaller Member States.

6.6.2   Term of office

Judges and A-G are appointed for six years, which term is renewable without any limitation. Usually, they hold the office for two terms. In order to ensure continuity in the work of the ECJ there is a rolling programme of replacement of some of the judges and A-G every three years.

Under Protocol 7 on the Privileges and Immunities of the European Union and Protocol 3 on the Statute of the CJEU judges and A-G:

- Have privileges and immunities similar to other officials of the EU;

- Are immune from legal proceedings in respect of acts performed in their official capacity, including words spoken or written, but this immunity may be waived by the ECJ;

- In criminal proceedings in any of the Member States, provided immunity is waived, must be tried only by the court competent to judge the members of the highest national judiciary.

Before taking up a post at the ECJ, each judge or A-G must take a solemn oath that they will perform their duties impartially and conscientiously and preserve the secrecy of the deliberations of the Court. The independence of judges or A-G requires that they cannot hold any political or administrative post during their term of office, or engage in any occupation incompatible with their mandate, unless an exceptional exemption is granted by the ECJ. They must behave with integrity and discretion both during and after their term of office.

Judges or A-G may resign, but should hold their office until their successor is appointed. Usual disciplinary measures apply to both judges and A-G. A unanimous opinion of all judges of the ECJ and A-G (other than the person concerned) is required in order to decide that one of them no longer fulfils the required conditions or meets the obligations arising from his or her office and thus should be disciplined, dismissed or deprived of his or her right to pension or other benefits. Under Article 6 of Protocol 3 when the person concerned is a member of the General Court or of a specialised court, the ECJ is required to consult the relevant court before taking a decision.

6.6.3 Organisation

The ECJ remains permanently in session, although hearings do not usually take place during judicial vacations. The duration of judicial vacations is determined by the ECJ in the light of the needs of the Court's business. In case of urgency, the president may convene the ECJ during vacations.

The president of the ECJ is elected for a period of three years (which is renewable) by the judges of the ECJ from among their own number by an absolute majority in a secret ballot. The president:

- Directs the judicial business and administration of the Court;

- Chairs hearings and deliberations;

- May order interim measures (Article 243 TFEU);

- May suspend the application of a contested act (Article 278 TFEU);

- May suspend enforcement of decisions of the Council or the Commission imposing a pecuniary obligation on persons other than Member States (Article 299 TFEU);

- May grant or refuse (by reasoned order) a request for expedited or accelerated procedure.

The registrar of the ECJ is appointed for six years (after which reappointment is allowed) by the ECJ after consultation with the A-G. The registrar's main tasks are as follows:

- To be in charge of the day-to-day administration of the ECJ, financial management and accounts;

- To assist the ECJ in the acts of procedure, that is, the acceptance, transmission and custody of documents;

- To be present in person or by a substitute at all hearings of the ECJ as a Chamber and all meetings of the ECJ, apart from disciplinary proceedings and matters outside its competence;

- To act as Guardian of the Seals, in charge of archives and of the publication of the decisions rendered by the ECJ;

- To supervise the officials and other employees attached to the ECJ – they being accountable to the registrar under the authority of the president of the ECJ.

Each judge and A-G is assisted by three referendaires; usually they have the same nationality as their senior and form their Cabinet. They are lawyers, usually with a Doctorate in Law. They prepare pre-trial studies on the legal aspects of the case at issue and assist in the drafting of judgments and opinions.

6.6.4 Functioning

The quorum for the Full Court is 15 judges, for chambers of three or five judges the quorum is three, and for the Grand Chamber it is nine. The decisions of the ECJ will be valid only when an uneven number of judges sit in deliberation. For that reason, additional judges have been appointed at times when there was an even number of Member States. The president has no casting vote.

The ECJ may sit as a Full Court, in a Grand Chamber (13 judges) or in chambers of three or five judges. It sits in a Grand Chamber when a Member State or an EU institution, which is a party to the proceedings, so requests, or when the complexity or importance of the matter so requires. The Court sits as a Full Court in exceptional cases listed in the Court's Statute, that is:

- When the European Ombudsman, or a commissioner or a member of the Court of Auditors must be compulsorily retired or deprived of their right to pension or other benefit; or

- Where the case under consideration is of exceptional importance in terms of its legal implications for the EU.

A party to the proceedings cannot apply for a change in composition of the ECJ on the basis that there is a judge who has the nationality of that party, or that there is no judge from the Member State of that party. In order to ensure that there is no conflict of interest, a judge or an A-G is not permitted to take part in a case in which they have previously participated as agent or adviser, or in which they have acted for one of the parties or in any other capacity. Also, the president of the ECJ may, for some special reason, decide that a judge or A-G should not take part in the disposal of a particular case.

6.6.5 Procedure

A distinction must be made between the procedure in direct actions (which do not involve proceedings in national courts, but only before the CJEU, that is, the ECJ and the General Court) and the procedure in references for a preliminary ruling. In both procedures there are two stages: written and oral. It is to be noted that in respect of the expedited/accelerated procedure, urgent preliminary rulings procedure and simplified procedure shorter deadlines apply and the written stage may be abandoned.

6.6.5.1   Steps in the written procedure

In both types of action once the application is filed with the registrar, the president of the ECJ appoints from among the judges a judge-rapporteur, who prepares a preliminary report on the case. If an A-G is appointed, both he and the judge-rapporteur monitor the progress of the case.

6.6.5.1.1   In direct actions

- Direct actions begin when an application from a claimant is received by the registrar. The application should contain the name and permanent address of the parties, the subject-matter of the dispute, the legal arguments invoked by the applicant and the form of the order sought. It must be lodged within the time limit prescribed for such action by the Treaty.

▧ The defendant is notified and has one month to submit a written defence. Subsequently, each party may submit one further written pleading, that is, the applicant may reply to the defendant's submission, and the defendant may lodge a rejoinder, that is, a reply to the applicant's reply to the defence. As a result, there are usually two written pleadings from each party (but not in respect of special procedures – see below).

6.6.5.1.2   In preliminary rulings

▧ The preliminary ruling procedure begins with a national court sending its request for a preliminary ruling to the ECJ.

▧ On its receipt the registrar makes arrangements for the request to be translated into all official languages of the EU. It is then served on the parties to the main proceedings. The Member States and EU institutions are also notified. The registrar publishes a notice in the Official Journal specifying the subject-matter of the request and the names of the parties.

▧ From the date of publication of the notice the parties and all interested Member States and EU institutions have two months to submit their written observations.

6.6.5.1.3   Common features

After the written part is closed, the parties are asked whether they wish to have a hearing and if so, why. They must reply within one month. Subsequently, the ECJ decides, on the basis of a report submitted by the judge-rapporteur and views expressed by the A-G, whether any preparatory inquiries, the ordering of the examination of particular witnesses, the ordering of experts' reports, inspection of a place, and so on, are needed and whether a hearing should be held for oral argument. If so, the judge-rapporteur prepares a report for hearing which is made public.

6.6.5.2   Steps in the oral procedure

▧ These commence with the reading of the preliminary report of the judge-rapporteur, which will have been forwarded to the parties before the opening of the oral stage and comprises a summary of the case. The report includes the legal arguments invoked by the parties, and the factual situation based on the evidence presented during the written stage and preparatory enquiry.

▧ The next step is the hearing of the parties through their representatives; the Court may also examine experts and witnesses. Under Article 27 of Protocol 3 annexed to the Treaties the ECJ may impose pecuniary penalties on defaulting witnesses. The Court may also order a witness or an expert to be heard before a judicial authority of his place of permanent residence. Under Article 30 of Protocol 3 any violation of an oath by a witness or expert must be treated in the same manner as if this had occurred before one of the courts of the Member State concerned with jurisdiction in civil proceedings. At the request of the ECJ, the Member State concerned shall prosecute the offender before its competent court.

▧ At the conclusion of the oral stage the representatives of the parties make closing speeches to the Court, first the claimant and then the defendant.

■ Some weeks later, the A-G delivers his/her opinion. Usually, this ends the oral proceedings (although it is still possible in certain circumstances to reopen the oral procedure) and the ECJ proceeds to deliberate on the case. The ECJ may decide, after hearing the A-G, to deliver judgment without an opinion. This occurs when the case does not raise new questions of law.

The Court's deliberations are based on a draft judgment prepared by the judge-rapporteur. They are and must remain confidential. Neither the A-G, nor translators, nor legal secretaries are present. During the deliberations the judges will try to reach a consensus on the matter. If no consensus is achieved, then the decision is reached by a majority vote. There are no dissenting or separate opinions. The judgment is a single collegiate judgment. It must state the reasons on which it is based, and must be signed by all judges who took part in the deliberations. It is delivered in open court and is binding from that date.

6.6.6   Special forms of procedure

These are:

■ **The simplified procedure.** This is used in references for preliminary rulings. If a question referred is identical to a question already answered by the ECJ, or an answer to it admits no reasonable doubt or may be easily inferred from existing case law, the ECJ may deliver its judgment by reasoned order;

■ **The expedited/accelerated procedure.** This is used with regard to very urgent cases. An application for this procedure allows the prioritisation of cases and, if granted, the avoidance of various procedural stages. On the application of one of the parties or a court seeking a preliminary ruling, the president of the ECJ decides whether the case requires the use of this procedure;

■ **The urgent preliminary rulings procedure** which applies only to preliminary rulings in the area of FSJ (see Chapter 10.2.1);

■ **A procedure established under Article 20 of the Statute of the CJEU** under which cases may be determined without an Opinion of an A-G where they do not raise any new point of law. In 2009 about 52 per cent of cases were decided without an Opinion of the A-G;[223]

■ **Applications for interim measures.** Under Articles 278 and 279 TFEU the CJEU may grant interim measures. Article 279 TFEU allows the court to prescribe any necessary interim measures in cases pending before it while Article 278 TFEU relates to interim measures in respect of an EU measure, the validity of which is being disputed in proceedings pending before the court. A party to the proceedings may ask the president of the ECJ (if a case is before the ECJ) or the president of the General Court (if a case is before the General Court) to grant interim measures consisting of the suspension of the operation of the EU measure which forms the subject matter of the action, or any other interim measure if there is a risk to the applicant of serious and irreparable harm, and where damages would not be an adequate remedy.

---

223.   The 2009 Report of the CJEU is available at its official website.

6.6.7 Jurisdiction of the ECJ

There are three categories of proceedings which can be brought before the ECJ: contentious, non-contentious and consultative.

6.6.7.1 Contentious proceedings

The ECJ has jurisdiction in the cases which are the most important from the EU perspective. Accordingly, in contentious matters it has jurisdiction in respect of:

- Actions under Articles 258 and 259 TFEU against a Member State for failure to fulfil its obligation (see Chapter 15);

- Actions (including the imposition of financial penalties) under Article 260 TFEU against a Member State for failing to comply with an earlier judgment of the ECJ (see Chapter 15.5);

- Actions brought in relation to disputes arising from the agreement on the setting-up of the European Economic Area;

- Actions for annulment under Articles 263 TFEU brought by a Member State against the EP and/or against the Council (with the exception of measures adopted by the Council in respect of State aid, dumping and implementing powers which fall within the jurisdiction of the General Court) or brought by one EU institution against another;

- Actions for failure to act under Article 265 TFEU. The ECJ shares its jurisdiction with the General Court. It has jurisdiction in respect of the same categories of actions as those relating to actions for annulment;

- Actions brought under Article 271 TFEU against a Member State for failure to fulfil its obligation under the Statute of the European Investment Bank and the European Central Bank;

- Disputes between Member States which relate to the subject matter of the Treaties if the Member States concerned have concluded a special agreement conferring jurisdiction on the ECJ in respect of such a dispute (Article 274 TFEU);

- Exceptions set out in the Treaties concerning the CFSP. In CFSP matters the ECJ has jurisdiction only in exceptional circumstances, i.e., it ensures that measures adopted under the CFSP have not encroached on non-CFSP policies of the EU and vice versa, i.e. that non-CFSP policies do not impinge on the CFSP (Article 40 TEU), and reviewing the legality on sanctions against natural or legal persons imposed under the CFSP (Article 24(1) TEU);

- Legality of an act which has determined that that there is a clear risk of a serious breach by a Member State of the EU values or indeed, that there is a serious and persistent breach by a Member State of the values on which the EU is founded but only in respect of procedural stipulations contained in Article 7 TEU. Only the Member State concerned by the determination may make a request and this must be made within one month from the date of such determination (Article 269 TFEU);

- Review, in exceptional circumstance, of decisions of the General Court on appeals from the European Union Civil Service Tribunal;

- Appeals from judgments of the General Court on points of law only.

6.6.7.2   Non-contentious proceedings

In non-contentious proceedings, that is, the preliminary reference procedure (see Chapter 10), the ECJ rules on questions of EU law which have arisen in a national court or tribunal concerning the interpretation of EU law and of acts of the EU institutions, and the validity of such acts. Judgment on the principal issue is given by a national court, and the ECJ answers only the referred questions. Since the abolition of the Pillar structure the ECJ has jurisdiction to give preliminary rulings in the whole of the area of freedom, security and justice. However, some temporal and substantive restrictions have been imposed (see Chapter 10.2).

6.6.7.3   Consultative proceedings

Unlike its name, the consultative jurisdiction of the ECJ always results in binding decisions. It is not necessary that a dispute exists on the matter brought to the attention of the ECJ, although in practice this is often the case.

The consultative jurisdiction exists in respect of both the EU and the Euratom: Article 218(11) TFEU and Articles 103 and 104 EA. In the case of the EU it arises in the context of international agreements between the EU and a third country, or countries or international organisations. The Council, the Commission, the EP or a Member State may ask the ECJ for its opinion as to whether the envisaged agreement is compatible with the provisions of the Treaties. If the ECJ considers that the agreement in question is contrary to EU law, the only possibility for that agreement to enter into force, apart from its renegotiation, is to revise the Treaties. The consultative jurisdiction of the ECJ has become quite popular in recent years.

6.6.8   Incidental matters

There are a number of specific issues in respect of the procedure before the ECJ which need to be mentioned: the parties to the proceedings, the language of the proceedings, the costs and the intervention of third parties. These are dealt with below.

6.6.8.1   Parties to the proceedings

The parties must be represented:

- EU institutions, bodies and agencies and the Member States must be represented by an agent appointed for the particular case;

- Individuals and undertakings must be represented by a lawyer authorised to practice before a court of a Member State. However, a lawyer cannot represent himself. In Cases C-174 and C-175/96P *Orlando Lopes*,[224] the ECJ rejected an application submitted by a Portuguese lawyer (who refused to be represented by another lawyer) on the ground that no one is permitted to represent him or herself. University teachers, who are nationals of a Member State whose law accords them the right of audience (for example, Germany) may represent clients before the ECJ. They enjoy rights and immunities necessary to the independent exercise of their duties.

---

224.   Case C-174/96P [1996] ECR I-6401 and Case C-175/96P [1996] ECR I-6409.

6.6.8.2 Language

The ECJ is multilingual and may conduct proceedings in any official language. Only one language may be used as the procedural language in a particular case. All procedure is then conducted in the chosen language: written pleadings, examination of witnesses, and so on.

In the case of an individual, or an undertaking or a Member State, the language of the procedure is the language of the defendant. If an EU institution, body or agency is a party to the proceedings, the applicant may choose the language of the procedure. The Rules of Procedure allow for some flexibility in respect of the choice of the procedural language in that any derogation from the rules applicable to the choice of the procedural language is decided by the president of the ECJ or the General Court and not by the courts themselves, unless the other party to the proceedings opposes such derogation.

In the case of a preliminary ruling the procedural language is that of the court or tribunal which referred the question to the ECJ. However, at the well justified request of one of the parties to the main proceedings before a national court, and provided the views of the other party and the A-G are duly taken into account, the president of the ECJ may authorise the use of another language in the oral procedure.

6.6.8.3 Costs

The ECJ does not charge parties for its services, although in exceptional circumstances they may be required to pay some fees, for example, for the translation of certain documents. However, the ECJ determines which party should pay the costs of the proceedings. Usually it is the losing party; however, the ECJ may decide otherwise.

It is interesting to note that the Rules of Procedure of the ECJ have adopted the German, English and Italian system in respect of fees paid to a lawyer of the winning party. Thus, the losing party pays the fees of the experts, witnesses, their own lawyer and the lawyer of the other party.

Usually, the ECJ does not fix the costs of the proceedings. This question is normally left to the parties, although in the case of a disagreement, the party concerned may apply to the ECJ which will settle the matter by an order.

Legal aid is available. An application for legal aid with supporting documents may be lodged with the judge-rapporteur, whose chamber takes a final decision on the matter.

6.6.8.4 Intervention of a third party

The ECJ permits the intervention of a third party in proceedings which have already commenced. Member States and EU institutions may intervene without establishing an interest in the result of the case. Other EU bodies, offices and agencies of the Union can intervene if they establish an interest in the result of a case brought before the ECJ. Individuals and undertakings are required to justify their intention to intervene and cannot intervene in cases between Member States, between EU institutions and between Member States, and between EU institutions (Article 40 of Protocol 7 attached to the Treaties).

Individuals and undertakings may obtain necessary information concerning the case from the Official Journal (OJ). The registrar must publish a notice in the OJ, which specifies the date on which the application was lodged, gives the names and the addresses of the parties, indicates the subject matter of the dispute, the form of the order sought by the parties and contains a brief statement of the pleas in law on which the application is based. The application to intervene must be limited to supporting the form of order sought by one of the parties and must be lodged within one month of publication of the notice in the OJ. In other words, an intervening party cannot submit a new form of order.

6.6.9   Revision and interpretation of judgments

There is no appeal from judgments rendered by the ECJ. However, in two situations a judgment of the ECJ may be revised:

- Article 42 of Protocol 3 provides that: "Member States, institutions, bodies, offices and agencies of the Union and any other natural or legal persons may, in cases and under conditions to be determined by the Rules of Procedure, institute third-party proceedings to contest a judgment rendered without their being heard, where the judgment is prejudicial to their rights";

- An application for revision of a judgment by a party to the proceedings will be admissible "on discovery of a fact which is of such a nature as to be a decisive factor, and which, when the judgment was given, was unknown to the Court and to the party claiming the revision".[225] The application must be lodged within 10 years from the date of the judgment and within three months of discovery of the previously "unknown" fact.[226]

A party to proceedings before the ECJ or an EU institution, provided it demonstrates an interest in the decision, may ask the ECJ for the interpretation of a judgment if its meaning or scope gives rise to uncertainty.[227] In Case 5/55 *Assider*,[228] the ECJ emphasised that:

"the only parts of a judgment which can be interpreted are those which express the judgment of the Court in the dispute which has been submitted for its final decision and those parts of the reasoning upon which this decision is based and which are, therefore, essential to it . . . the Court does not have to interpret those passages which are incidental and which complete or explain the basic reasoning."

Thus, only the operative part of the judgment, i.e. the ratio decidendi, will be interpreted by the ECJ. A request for interpretation may concern the effect of the judgment, but not its application or the legal implications arising from it.[229]

6.6.10   The General Court (previously known as the Court of First Instance (CFI))

The General Court, formerly known as the Court of First Instance, was created to ease the workload of the ECJ, and enable the ECJ to concentrate on its fundamental tasks without affecting the effectiveness and the quality of the Community judicial system. The CFI [the

---

225.   Article 44 of Protocol 3 "on the Statute of the Court of Justice of the European Union" attached to the Treaties.
226.   Case 1/60 *Acciaieria Ferriera di Roma v High Authority* [1960] ECR 165.
227.   Article 40 of the Protocol on the Statute of the ECJ.
228.   [1954–56] ECR 135.
229.   Case 9/81 *Court of Auditors v Williams* [1982] ECR 3301.

General Court] was established by Council Decision 88/591 of 24 October 1988 in accord with the provisions of the SEA.[230]

In accordance with Article 48 of Protocol 3 attached to the Treaties, the General Court is made up of 27 judges. They are nominated by the common accord of the Member States, one from each Member State. Judges are appointed for a renewable term of six years and a partial replacement takes place every three years. They are subject to the same rules with regard to nomination, privileges, immunities and disciplinary measures as are judges of the ECJ. However, it is not necessary for judges of the General Court to possess the qualifications required for appointment to the highest judicial offices in their respective countries, but only those for the exercise of judicial office.

There are no A-G appointed to assist the General Court, but in some cases a judge is called upon to perform the task of an A-G.

The General Court sits in chambers of three judges or five judges and in a Grand Chamber of 13 judges. If an important and complex legal matter is under consideration the General Court may sit in plenary session.

In order to ease the workload of the General Court, under the Council Decision of 26 April 1999 (which entered into force on 1 July 1999), it is permitted to sit "when constituted by a single judge". However, a judge of the General Court may sit as a single judge only in cases which do not raise any difficulties in law or in fact, which are of limited importance, and which do not involve any special circumstances.

The General Court has its own registrar, appointed by its judges, who is in charge of the judicial and practical organisation of the Court. The procedure before the General Court is the same as before the ECJ.

Under Article 256 TFEU the General Court has jurisdiction in respect of:

- Actions or proceedings referred to in Articles 263, 265, 268, 270 and 272 TFEU with the exception of those which are within the jurisdiction of specialised courts and those reserved to the ECJ under Protocol 3 annexed to the Treaties;

- Appeals from the specialised courts. At the time of writing, this applies to appeals from the European Union Civil Service Tribunal, being the only specialised court;

- Disputes concerning the application of EU competition law to undertakings;

- Actions based on arbitration clauses contained in a contract entered into by, or on behalf of the EU under Article 272 TFEU;

- Requests for interim measures under Article 279 TFEU.

6.6.11 Specialised courts

Article 257 TFEU provides for the establishment of specialised courts which are also referred to as judicial panels. Under this provision the EP and the Council may, acting in accordance with the ordinary legislative procedure, establish specialised courts which are to be attached to the General Court. A specialised court may be established on a proposal from the Commission after consultation with the ECJ or at the request of ECJ after consultation of the Commission.

---

230.   [1988] OJ L319/1.

Members of a judicial panel are appointed by the Council acting unanimously, after obtaining an opinion from a panel established under Article 255 TFEU.

The General Court acts in an appellate capacity in respect of decisions delivered by judicial panels. An appeal to the ECJ from the General Court is allowed only in cases where there is a serious risk that the unity or consistency of EU law will be affected.

The first panel was established by Council Decision 2004/752/EC/Euratom[231] in respect of cases concerning EU staff. This panel is called the European Union Civil Service Tribunal. It became operational in December 2005. The Tribunal is made up of seven judges. At the time of writing the creation of a second panel, an EU Patent Tribunal, is being examined.

6.7   The Court of Auditors (CoA)

The Court of Auditors calls itself "the financial conscience" of the EU. It was established by the Treaty of Brussels of 22 July 1975, constituted in 1977 and recognised as a Community institution by the Treaty of Maastricht. The ToA enlarged the scope of the Court's audit to Pillars 2 and 3 of the EU and thus the Court became an EU institution. The ToA confirmed the Court's locus standi under Article 230 EC [Article 263 TFEU] for the purpose of protecting its prerogatives with regard to other EU institutions. Its role continues unchanged by the ToL.

The CoA has no judicial functions, thus it is not really a court but an independent auditing body, the EU's financial watchdog. In order to fulfil its tasks the CoA has extensive investigative powers, that is, it can investigate the paperwork of any person or organisation handling EU income or expenditure. However, it has no power to prosecute those responsible for irregularities.[232] In a situation where irregularities are suspected the CoA prepares a written report and, depending upon who is thought to be responsible for them, submits it either to the Commission or to the relevant Member State. If the CoA suspects fraud, corruption, or other illegal activity, it transfers the case to the European Anti-Fraud Office (OLAF).

The CoA is composed of 27 members, one from each Member State. . Each member must either have belonged to a national external audit body or be "especially qualified" to carry out the audit. Their independence must be beyond doubt. They are nominated by Member States and appointed by the Council, acting by QMV after consulting the EP, for a six-year renewable term.

The usual limitations and arrangements aimed at ensuring the independence of the members of the CoA, as well as privileges, immunities, disciplinary measures, and so on, apply to them. The members, who sit as a college, elect a president for three years (renewable) to chair the Court's meetings, to ensure that the Court's decisions are properly implemented and to represent the Court in all its external relations. The CoA is independent of the other EU institutions and national governments.

6.7.1   Main tasks

The main tasks of the CoA are:

- To audit all the revenue and expenditure of the EU;

---

231.   [2004] OJ L333/7.

232.   It is to be noted that the EU has no power to institute criminal proceedings; these would be a matter for national authorities.

- To ensure that the financial affairs of the EU are properly managed, especially that all revenue has been received, and all expenditure incurred in a lawful and regular manner;

- At the end of a fiscal year to produce annual accounts which, together with the replies of the institutions, are published in the Official Journal;

- To prepare special reports and opinions at the request of the EU institutions. The Court must be consulted on any proposal for EU legislation of a financial nature and on proposals for measures relating to the fight against fraud. Its reports and opinions are not legally binding;

- On its own initiative, to draft reports on the financial implications of certain programmes or measures envisaged by the Community;

- To assist the EP and the Council in exercising their powers of control over the implementation of the EU budget.

6.8   The European Central Bank (ECB)

This is the central bank for the EU's single currency. It is in charge of the formulation and implementation of the monetary policy of the EU. Under the ToL it became an EU institution (Article 13 TEU and Article 282 TFEU). However, it occupies a special place in the institutional framework of the EU in that being part of the European System of Central Banks (the ESCB which comprises the ECB and the national central banks of all Member States irrespective of whether or not they have adopted the euro) its main objective is to ensure price stability rather than to participate in achieving all of the objectives of the EU. It has, unlike other EU institutions, legal personality. Its activities are not funded from the EU budget but are financed from contributions by national central banks of the Member States. This entails, inter alia, that if the ECB is found liable, the ECB itself is liable and must pay compensation to the injured party from its own resources (Article 340(3) TFEU).

6.9   Advisory bodies of the EU: The European Economic and Social Committee (EESC) and the Committee of the Regions (CoR)

These are examined below.

6.9.1   The European Economic and Social Committee (EESC)

The EESC was established by the 1957 Treaty of Rome in order to involve economic and social interest groups in the establishment of the internal market, to provide institutional machinery for briefing the Commission and the Council on social and economic matters and to give to these groups a share in the decision-making processes of the Community.

Under Article 301 TFEU the number of members of the EESC shall not exceed 350. Its members are representatives of various categories of economic and social activity. These include farmers, producers, workers, dealers, craftsmen, professionals, as well as representatives of the general public from all Member States. They are appointed by the Council, acting by QMV after consulting the EP, for a five-year renewable term.

The EESC is divided into three groups:

- "Employers", comprising the representatives of employers' organisations and chambers of commerce;

- "Workers", comprising trade union representatives; and

- "Various Interests", made up of representatives of small businesses, farmers, professionals, craftsmen, environmental and consumer groups, and so on.

The members of each group are allocated between six working sections, each in charge of a specific policy area. The EESC is an advisory body entrusted with the task of expressing the opinions of these sections in respect of legislative measures prepared by the Council and the Commission. Its opinions are non-binding.

The EP may also consult the EESC if it deems such consultation appropriate. Consultation of the EESC is however compulsory for the Commission with regard to proposals in areas such as CAP, the right of establishment, the mobility of labour, transport, approximation of laws, social policy, the European Social Fund and vocational training, the guidelines and incentives for employment, the social legislation resulting from agreements between management and labour, measures implementing Article 157 TFEU and measures relating to public health (Article 168(4) TFEU). In other areas consultation is optional. The EESC may issue opinions on its own initiative.

The Committee has played a very constructive role within the EU as it represents the citizens of the EU and their interests, and thus constitutes a step towards a people's union.

6.9.2   The Committee of the Regions (CoR)

Under Article 305 TFEU the number of members of the CoR shall not exceed 350. The exact composition of the CoR will be determined by the Council, acting unanimously on a proposal from the Commission. The CoR consists of representatives of regional and local bodies of the Member States. Their terms of appointment, office, privileges, and so on, are similar to those of the EESC (above). The Treaty of Nice requires members of the Committee of the Regions to be elected members of regional or local authorities, or to be politically answerable to an elected assembly. They are appointed by the Council acting by a qualified majority, after consulting the EP, on the basis of proposals submitted by the Member States.

The Committee of the Regions was created to allow the regions and local authorities to influence and participate in the Community legislative process.

Under the ToL the Commission must consult the CoR in many areas, including all areas of compulsory consultation provided for the EESC, i.e. matters involving, inter alia, the protection of the environment, the Social Fund, vocational training, cross-border co-operation and transport. The Commission, the EP and the Council may also consult the Committee in other areas.

If the EESC is consulted pursuant to Article 304 TFEU (compulsory consultation), the Committee of the Regions must be informed by the Commission or by the Council of the request for an opinion. The CoR may issue an opinion on the matter if specific regional interests are involved. The CoR may also provide an opinion on its own initiative but, as is the case of the EESC, its opinions are not binding. If the Council or the Commission fixes a time limit for the submission of an opinion by the CoR or the EESC, this must not be less than one month from the notification of the request. The absence of an opinion will not prevent the Council or the Commission from taking further action.

The CoR gained additional powers under the ToL. The CoR has the right to start proceedings before the ECJ:

■ when it considers that the principle of subsidiarity has been violated by a legislative act for the adoption of which it was "compulsorily" consulted (Article 8 of Protocol 2 on the Application of the Principles of Subsidiarity and Proportionality attached to the Treaties);

■ to defend its prerogatives (Article 263 TFEU).

6.10 Other institutions, bodies, offices and agencies

The TEU provided for the creation of new institutions within the framework of EMU: the European Central Bank, the European Monetary Institute and the European System of Central Banks. Their role has been strengthened by the ToA, the ToN and the ToL.

Among other EU bodies mention should be made of specialised advisory committees created on the ground of Article 242 TFEU. These include, inter alia, the Committee of Transport under Article 99 TFEU; the Economic and Finance Committee under Article 134 TFEU and the Committee on the European Social Fund under Article 163 TFEU.

Additionally, there are a number of EU agencies, each of which has a separate legal personality. They are created by EU secondary legislation to carry out specific technical, scientific or managerial tasks. Examples of agencies are: the European Environmental Agency, the European Training Foundation, the Office for Veterinary and Plant Health Inspection, and so on.

AIDE-MÉMOIRE

PART I

THE MAIN EU INSTITUTIONS AND THEIR FUNCTIONS

The European Council

It is the ultimate political decision-maker in the EU. It comprises the heads of state or government, the President of the European Council and the President of the Commission. The HR participates in the work of the European Council. It meets four times a year in Brussels and publishes conclusions after each meeting. Do not confuse with the Council of Europe, which is an entirely separate organsiation from the EU and is no part of the EU.

Main functions:

■ Shapes the future of the EU;

■ Gives the necessary impetus for the development of the EU;

■ Settles sensitive matters which the Council is not able to resolve;

■ Constitutes a platform for the exchange of informal views;

■ Identifies the strategic interests of the EU foreign action including the CFSP;

■ Takes decisions concerning the revision of the Treaties;

■ Participates in the appointment of senior EU officials;

■ Authorises the use of "passerelle" provisions.

It does not adopt legislative acts but may adopt decisions and guidelines.

The President of the European Council. The post of full-time President of the European Council was created by the ToL. He is elected by the European Council acting by QMV. His term of office is two and a half years, renewable once. This post is permanent and its holder is required to be independent. His main tasks are to:

- Prepare the work of the European Council;

- Chair debates of the European Council;

- Try to facilitate consensus within the European Council;

- Ensure continuity of the work of the European Council;

- Deal with foreign policy issues at a heads of state level but without prejudice to the powers of the HR;

- Report to the EP after each meeting of the European Council.

The European Commission

Represents the interests of the EU and is made up of 27 commissioners, i.e. one from each Member State.

Main functions:

- Guardianship of the Treaties;

- Initiates legislative measures;

- Drafts and implements the EU budget;

- Exercises executive powers;

- Carries out some international functions;

The Council of the European Union

Represents the national interests of the Member States – it is made up of government ministers from the Member States.

Main functions:

- Jointly with the EP adopts EU legislation and the EU budget;

- Ensures co-ordination of economic policies of the Member States;

- Frames the CFSP and takes the decisions necessary for defining and implementing it on the basis of the general guidelines and strategic lines defined by the European Council;

- Concludes international agreements.

The European Parliament

The EP is the parliamentary body of the EU and represents the interests of EU citizens. Its members are directly elected by them once every five years.

Main functions:

- Jointly with the Council adopts EU legislation and the EU budget;

- Exercises democratic supervision over all EU institutions including the election of the President of the Commission;

- Elects the European Ombudsman;

- May at the request of one-quarter of its members, establish a temporary Committee of Inquiry to investigate alleged contraventions or maladministration in the implementation of EU law;

- Participates in the conduct of external relations.

The Court of Justice of the European Union (The CJEU)

This collective name covers three courts: the Court of Justice of the European Union, colloquially known as the European Court of Justice (the ECJ); the General Court, which was formerly known as the Court of First Instance (CFI) and specialised courts which were previously known as "judicial panels". At the time of writing there is only one specialised court: the European Union Civil Service Tribunal.

The ECJ and the General Court are made up of 27 judges, one from each Member State.

Main function:

- Ensures that in the interpretation and application of the Treaties the law is observed.

The Court of Auditors

The EU financial watchdog, made up of 27 members, one from each Member State.

Main function:

- Ensures that the financial affairs of the EU are properly managed.

The European Central Bank (ECB)

This is the central bank for the EU's single currency.

Main function:

- Formulates and implements the monetary policy of the EU.

PART II

Special note about the three councils (two of them have been mentioned in Part I)
The European Council. It is made up of heads of state or government of all EU countries, the President of the European Council and the President of the European Commission. It meets, four times a year, in Brussels. The meetings agree on overall EU policy, and review progress in attainment of EU objectives. Generally gives impetus to the EU. It is the highest level policy-making body in the EU. Its meetings are called "summits".

The Council of the European Union. Jointly with the EP adopts EU legislation and the EU budget. It has no fixed composition. Its membership varies according to the matter under consideration. It consists of representatives of each Member State at ministerial level authorised to commit the government of that state. It is generally referred to as "the Council".

The Council of Europe. This is an inter-governmental organisation created in 1949 which has a membership of 47 European states. It is not an EU institution at all! Its main objectives are:

- The promotion of European unity by proposing and encouraging European action in economic, social, legal and administrative matters;

- The promotion of human rights, fundamental freedoms and pluralist democracy;

- The development of a European cultural identity.

It is best known for its human rights activities including elaboration of the European Convention for the Protection of Human Rights and Fundamental Freedoms (ECHR) and supervision of its application.

DO NOT CONFUSE THE THREE COUNCILS!

RECOMMENDED READING

Books

Arnull, A., *The European Court of Justice*, 2nd edition, 2006, Oxford: OUP

Burrows, N. and Greaves, R., *The Advocate General and EC Law*, 2007, Oxford: OUP

Coen, D. and Richardson, J. (eds), *Lobbying the European Union: Institutions, Actors, and Issues*, 2009, Oxford: OUP

Moury, C. and De Sousa, L. (eds) *Institutional Challenges in Post-Constitutional Europe: Governing Change*, 2009, Abingdon: Routledge

Schmitt, H. (ed), *European Parliament Elections after Eastern Enlargement*, 2010, Abingdon: Routledge

Articles

Chiti, E., "An Important Part of the EU's Institutional Machinery: Features, Problems and Perspectives of European Agencies" (2009) 46 CMLRev, p 1395

Kraemer H., "The European Union Civil Service Tribunal: A New Community Court Examined After Four Years of Operation" (2009) 46 CMLRev, p 1873

Lang, J. T., "Checks and Balances in the European Union: The Institutional Structure and the 'Community Method' ", (2006) 12 EPL, p 127

Tsadiras, A., "The Position of the European Ombudsman in the Community System of Judicial Remedies", (2007) 32/5 ELR, p 607

7

LEGISLATIVE PROCEDURES IN THE EU

SUMMARY

1. Introduction. One of the main objectives of the reform of the EU was to simplify the EU's legislative process and to make it more transparent and democratic. The ToL responded to this in many ways:

- It has simplified the law making process by establishing an ordinary legislative procedure (which was previously known as the co-decision procedure) as a standard procedure for adopting legislative acts. This procedure ensures that the EP is put on an equal footing with the Council with the result that no act can be adopted without both bodies' agreement. The word "ordinary" emphasises that this procedure has become the predominant way of adopting EU legislation. The remaining procedures are called "special procedures". Two of them involve the EP, i.e. the consent procedure (which was previously known as the assent procedure) and the consultation procedure.

- It has reinforced the principle of representative democracy by extending the application of the ordinary legislative procedure to approximately 40 new areas of EU policies. As a result the ordinary legislative procedure, under which the EP, the only body in the EU directly elected by EU citizens, legislates jointly with the Council, applies to approximately 83 areas of EU policy. Additionally, under the "passerelle" provisions (i.e. bridging provisions which allow switching from special legislative procedures to the ordinary procedure, without the necessity to use the IGC mechanism requiring ratification by all Member States) there is the opportunity for the EP prerogatives to be further extended. It is to be noted that the EP as well as being now involved in the ordinary legislative procedure was formerly and remains involved in special procedures under which it is either consulted or gives its consent to legislative proposals. The principle of representative democracy has been reinforced not only by the above but also by the fact that under the ToL national parliaments, which are directly elected by EU citizens in their own States, are very much involved in the EU legislative process and have the power to block the adoption of legislative proposals through the use of the "yellow and orange cards" procedure (see Chapter 4.4.1.2.2).

■ It has reinforced the participatory democracy by:

● Imposing a duty on all EU institutions to give EU citizens and their representative associations the opportunity to make known and publicly exchange their views;

● Requiring that the Commission conducts broad consultations with parties concerned to ensure that the EU's actions are coherent and transparent;

● Giving EU citizens an opportunity to submit proposals direct to the Commission for adoption of legal acts necessary to implement the Treaties. The modality and conditions of the exercise of the citizens' initiative are to be determined under the special procedure provided for in Article 25 TFEU but one condition has been expressly stated in Article 11(4) TEU, i.e. the initiative must be supported by no less than one million EU citizens who are nationals of a substantive number of Member States. The Commission decides whether to act on the proposal;

■ It has enhanced the importance of the principle of transparency in two ways, first, by ensuring the broadest possible access to documents of all EU institutions the details of which are to be determined by an EU regulation and second, by requiring the EP to meet in public and the Council to "open" its deliberations and votes on draft legislative acts to the public.

2. Legislative proposals. These are normally initiated by the Commission, although in exceptional cases the initiative is shared with the HR in respect of non-CFSP foreign policies, the implementation of the "solidarity clause" (Article 222(3) TFEU), and the imposition of economic sanctions under Article 215(1) TFEU. Further, in respect of measures concerning judicial and police cooperation in criminal matters not only the Commission but also a quarter of the Member States have the right to initiate proposals (Article 76 TFEU). The Council (under Article 241 TFEU) and the EP (under Article 225 TFEU) are entitled to ask the Commission to prepare any proposals considered desirable for the attainment of the objectives of the Treaty and under Article 11(4) TEU no fewer than one million EU citizens, who between them are nationals of a substantive number of Member States, may ask the Commission to prepare a proposal for a legal act necessary to implement the Treaties. However, neither the EP, nor the Council, nor EU citizens can force the Commission to act. Under the Better Regulation programme and in conformity with Article 11(2) and (3) the Commission's approach to legislative proposals involves the widest possible consultation with all interested parties and the economic, social and financial assessment of the impact of legislative proposals.

The legal basis of a proposal, that is, the relevant article of the EU Treaty, determines which EU institutions are involved in its adoption and under which procedure that occurs.

3. The ordinary legislative procedure: Article 294 TFEU. Under the ToL the ordinary legislative procedure has become a standard procedure for the adoption of EU legislative acts. It is described in Article 294 TFEU. It involves the tripartite participation of the Commission, the Council and the EP.

4. Special legislative procedures. Some special legislative procedures involve the participation of the EP, others allow the Commission and the Council to act jointly, or only the Commission to act alone. Two special procedures in which the EP is involved are:

▪ The consultation procedure under which the Council is required to consult the EP but is not bound by the EP's opinion.

▪ The consent procedure under which the Council has to obtain the EP's assent before adopting a legislative act. The EP can accept or reject a proposal but cannot amend it.

7.1 Introduction

Pre-ToL legislative process of the EU was very complicated for two reasons:

▪ Revisions of decision-making procedures, made in order to give more powers to the EP, had led to extremely complex compromises.

▪ Tension between inter-governmentalism and supranationality in the context of a democratic deficit, which the EP (the only body in the EU elected directly by EU citizens) claimed to be able and entitled to legitimately overcome, was reflected in the process.

Resulting from their complexity the pre-ToL legislative procedures were criticised for being too bureaucratic, secretive and difficult to understand. Further, they contributed to the EC's democratic deficit. The ToL responded to this criticism in many ways as outlined below.

7.1.1 Simplification of the EU legislative process

This was achieved by establishing the ordinary legislative procedure (which was previously known as the co-decision procedure) as the standard procedure for adopting legislative acts. This procedure ensures that the EP is put on an equal footing with the Council with the result that no act can be adopted without both bodies' agreement. The word "ordinary" emphasises that this procedure has become the predominant way of adopting EU legislation. The remaining procedures are called "special procedures". Two of them involve the EP, i.e. the consent procedure (which was previously known as the assent procedure) and the consultation procedure. Other examples of special procedures are those involving:

▪ the Council and the Commission (e.g. Article 31 TFEU on the adoption of measures relating to the Common Customs Tariff);

▪ the Commission, the Council and the social partners (e.g. Articles 154 and 155 TFEU relating to adoption of measures concerning the definition of European social standards);

▪ only the Commission in the adoption of legislative measures (e.g. Article 106(3) TFEU concerning adoption of measures relating to undertakings with a special position).

7.1.2 The ToL has introduced many innovations aimed at reducing or even eliminating democratic deficit in the EU's legislative process

With regard to innovations aimed at reducing or even eliminating democratic deficit in the EU's legislative process two strands can be identified, one which reinforces the principle of representative democracy and the other which goes beyond representative institutions and ensures the transparency of the EU legislative process and the political participation of EU citizens in that process. Articles 10 and 11 TEU encompass both strands.

7.1.2.1   Enhancement of democratic representation by the ToL

So far as the enhancement of democratic representation is concerned the principle of democracy finds its most important expression in representative institutions. Under the ToL, the EP, whose members are directly elected by EU citizens, has seen its prerogatives enlarged. The ordinary procedure applies to virtually all areas in which the Council takes decisions by QMV. This represents approximately 40 new areas, including agriculture, fisheries, structural funds and vital policies covered by the area of FSJ, such as frontier controls, immigration, judicial co-operation in criminal matters, minimum rules for the definition of and the penalties in areas of serious crime, incentives for crime prevention, Eurojust, police co-operation, Europol and civil protection. As a result, under the ToL the ordinary procedure applies to approximately 83 areas including 33 to which prior to the entry into force of the ToL the co-decision (now the ordinary procedure) applied. Further, the ToL contains so called "passerelle" or bridging clauses which will allow switching from special legislative procedures to the ordinary legislative procedure without the necessity to use the IGC mechanism requiring ratification by all Member Sates. There are two types of "passerelle" provisions:

- A general "passerelle" provision contained in Article 48(7) TEU which allows the European Council, acting unanimously, after obtaining the consent of the EP (which shall be given by a majority of its component members) to authorise the application of the ordinary procedure for any area or case, provided that no national parliament opposes the proposed switch within six months of being notified of the European Council initiative;

- Specific "passerelle" provision. The following "passerelle" provisions contemplate the possibility of switching from the special procedure to the ordinary procedure:

  - Under Article 81 TFEU the Council, acting unanimously, may propose a change from the special procedure to the ordinary procedure for the adoption of measures in the area of judicial co-operation in civil matters concerning family law with cross-border implications. A proposal must be notified to national parliaments and any of them may oppose the change within six months.
  - No right of veto is given to national parliaments when the change of procedures concerns: certain fields of social policy (Article 153(2) TFEU); certain areas of environmental policy (Article 192(2) TFEU); and in respect of certain policies concerning the area of FSJ. In all these cases the Council must act unanimously.

The EP is also involved in special procedures in which it is either consulted or gives its consent. The ToL further enhances the principle of representative democracy by involving national parliaments in the EU legislative process. Their role is described in Article 12 TEU and certainly the most valuable contribution of national parliaments is the possibility of using the "yellow and orange cards" procedure (see Chapter 4.4.1.2.2) to ensure that legislative proposals adopted by the Commission are compatible with the principle of subsidiarity. It is also important to note that the members of the European Council and the Council, who represent national governments at the EU level, are directly elected by EU citizens and democratically accountable either to their national parliaments, or to their citizens.

As to participatory democracy, Article 11(2) imposes on EU institutions an obligation to give citizens and their representative associations the opportunity to make known and publicly exchange their views in all areas of Union action. Article 11(3) TEU requires that the Commission conducts broad consultations with parties concerned in order to ensure that the Union's actions are coherent and transparent. The best form of ensuring a broad consultation on vital EU legislative initiatives is to use referenda. Although this has been suggested for some time it has never been used. However, Article 11(4) TEU provides for a new form of popular participation. Under this provision no less than one million EU citizens, who are between them nationals of a significant number of Member States, may ask the Commission to prepare a proposal for a legal act necessary to implement the Treaties. The citizens' initiative has the potential of making a great impact on EU legislation but its use must respect the principle of equality enshrined in Article 9 TEU so that legislative initiatives exercised by a strong and well organised group will not frustrate the will of the majority of EU citizens. The Commission decides whether to act on the proposal.

7.1.2.2   The principle of transparency

The fundamental importance of the principle of transparency, which emerged in the early 1990s in the EU, was recognised by the ToA and is confirmed in Article 1 TEU which states that: "This Treaty marks a new stage in the process of creating an ever closer union among the peoples of Europe, in which decisions are taken as openly as possible [i.e. transparently] and as closely as possible to the citizen". In general, the application of the principle of transparency takes two forms, the right of access to documents of the EU institutions, and the public nature of the legislative process.

7.1.2.2.1   Access to documents

Article 1 TEU has been further detailed in Article 15 TEU. The main innovation is that new general rules on access to documents to all EU institutions will be adopted to ensure that all EU institutions conduct their work as openly as possible "in order to promote good governance and ensure the participation of civil society" and that all persons, natural and legal, not only EU citizens will have the right to consult documents which are in possession of all EU institutions. At the time of writing Regulation (EC) 1049/2001,[233] which needs to be amended, is the main legislation which contains rules on principles, conditions and limits on the right of access to documents of the EP, the Council and the Commission. Although most EU institutions, agencies and bodies have adopted rules similar to those contained in Regulation 1049/2001, there are some exceptions in that the European Council and the ECJ, at the time of writing, have never adopted rules relating to access to their documents. However, Article 15(3) TEU specifies that for the ECJ, European Central Bank, and the European Investment Bank, rules on access will be confined to areas in which they "exercise their administrative tasks" although those bodies may, at their own initiatives give access to other documents. Under Article 15(3) TEU the new regulation on access to documents will take priority over the more specific rules concerning access to documents adopted by EU institutions, bodies, offices and agencies. This provision also requires that the EP and the Council must ensure the publication of documents relating to the legislative procedures.

---

233.   [2001] OJ L 145/43.

Accordingly, it seems that both institutions must ensure the greatest possible access to such documents.

7.1.2.2.2 Public nature of the legislative process

The ToL's innovation on the public nature of the legislative process is that under Article 15(2) TEU the EP is required to meet in public whilst the Council under Article 15(2) and Article 16(8) TEU is required to meet in public when it deliberates and votes on a draft legislative act.

7.1.3   Conclusion

It is submitted that the ToL recognises and addresses the need to bridge the gap between the administration, which is often seen as opaque and impersonal, and its citizens to ensure that the EP (which directly represents EU citizens at Union level) and national parliaments (which directly represents EU citizens at national level) play an ever increasing role in the EU legislative process.

It is important to note that the ToL does not define legislative acts but it is clear that the concept of legislative acts refers to acts which have been adopted under the ordinary procedure or special procedures but not to delegated acts or implementing acts (see Chapter 8.5).

7.2   Legislative proposals

While the legislative process is usually initiated by the Commission, this may also be done jointly by the Commission and the HR in respect of non-CFSP foreign matters, the implementation of the "solidarity" clause (Article 222(3) TFEU), and the imposition of economic sanctions under Article 215(1) TFEU.

In respect of measures concerning judicial and police co-operation in criminal matters not only the Commission but also a quarter of the Member States have the right to initiate proposals (Article 76 TFEU).

It should be noted that the Council (under Article 241 TFEU) and the EP (under Article 225 TFEU) are entitled to ask the Commission to prepare any proposals considered desirable for the attainment of the objectives of the Treaties. The Commission is not obliged to agree to the request, but it might be politically difficult for it to refuse.

The ToL gives the right to one million or more EU citizens acting together to ask the Commission to prepare a proposal in respect of a matter within the competence of the Commission if that matter, according to those citizens, requires EU legislation for the purpose of implementing the Treaties. The procedure and conditions for the exercise of this citizens' initiative are to be determined by the Council after obtaining the consent of the EP.

Once the Commission decides that a legislative act is needed in any particular area, the appropriate Directorate General formulates a broad outline of an envisaged proposal for approval by the relevant commissioner who, all being well, submits it to the College of Commissioners (that is, the commissioners acting together). If the College agrees that the proposal is worth pursuing and the timing is right, it is then subject to further consideration as outlined below.

Under the Better Regulation programme[234] launched in 2002 (and revised in November

---

234.   The main objectives of the EU's Better Regulation programme are to cut red tape, improve the quality of EC legislation, reinforce respect for, and the effectiveness of EC legislation, and modernise and simplify the existing

2006[235]), addressed to all EU institutions and to the Member States, which was aimed at simplifying and improving the regulatory environment, and the Inter-Institutional Agreement (IIA) on Better Lawmaking signed by the EP, the Council and the Commission in 2003,[236] the Commission adopted a new approach to legislative proposals:

- First, the Commission assesses the economic, social and environmental impact of legislative proposals with a view to eventual achievement of the best results, and to minimising any negative aspects. Further, in 2006, the president of the Commission set up an Impact Assessment Board (which is accountable to him and which is independent of Commission departments), which examines draft impact assessments and provides opinions on their quality.

- Second, draft proposals are submitted to the widest possible consultation with all interested parties, including governmental authorities, professional bodies, experts, consumer groups and the Commission's own Legal Service. This requirement of consultation has been strengthened by the principle of subsidiarity. The consultation exercise often leads to redrafting, or even abandonment, of a proposal.

- Third, in 2005 the Commission introduced a common methodology, which forms part of the impact assessments,[237] for assessing administrative costs arising from a proposal.

- Fourth, the Commission regularly screens legislative proposals pending before the legislator to ensure that they are still relevant and up to date.

- Fifth, the Commission tries to find alternatives to laws and regulations, for example, by reliance on co-regulation (consisting of entrusting the social partners and non-governmental organisations with the achievements of EU objectives) and self-regulation (consisting of freely given commitments by private bodies to solve problems between themselves in a specific sector). This is in accordance with the requirements of the OMC.

If a draft proposal passes the impact assessment and other above-mentioned requirements, it is submitted to the College of Commissioners, which decides by a simple majority vote whether or not it should proceed. If the decision is in the affirmative, the proposal is translated into all official languages of the EU, submitted to the Council, the EP and national parliaments, and published in the OJ. However, if a proposal concerns areas in which the Commission is empowered to legislate alone, it is simply translated and published in the OJ. There is no need to send it to any other institution or to national parliaments.

Upon receipt of a proposal, the Council normally sends it to COREPER, or in rare cases to a

---

legislation while ensuring the requirements of the principles of subsidiarity and proportionality are respected. The programme covers policy-making, from its conception through implementation to enforcement. For more details see the Better Regulation website: http//ec.europa.eu/governance/better_regulation/index_en.htm (accessed 12/07/07).

235.   COM(2006) 689 final.

236.   [2003] OJ C321/1.

237.   On 9 March 2007 the European Council, on the basis of a Communication submitted by the Commission, approved the Action Programme for Reducing Administrative Burdens. Its main objective is to reduce the administrative burden of existing regulations in the EU. The Council has fixed a reduction target of 25 per cent of the administrative burden, to be achieved jointly by the EU and Member States by 2012. European Council Summit, 8/9 March 2007, Conclusion, para 25.

specialised committee (for example, the Special Committee on Agriculture or the Political Committee), for further study. All items on the Council's agenda, apart from those prepared by specialised committees, are examined by COREPER, unless the Council (by unanimity) or COREPER (by simple majority) decides otherwise. Accordingly, in the majority of cases the Commission's proposal is submitted to COREPER (see Chapter 6.3.4).

The Commission forwards proposals to the EP. A proposal is first examined by an MEP working in one of the parliamentary committees, who prepares a report. Subsequently, the relevant parliamentary committee considers the report, and may amend or change it. The report is then submitted to the EP, which in plenary session takes a vote on the report, rejecting or adopting it. By so doing, the EP gives its opinion on the proposal.

In conformity with Article 4 of Protocol 2 attached to the ToL, the Commission must forward directly to national parliaments all draft legislative acts and all amended drafts at the same time as they are sent to the EP and the Council. Similarly, the EP is required to send its draft legislative acts and its amended drafts to national parliaments. As to the Council, it must send to national parliaments draft legislative acts and amended drafts originating from a group of Member States, the Court of Justice, the European Central Bank or the European Investment Bank.

The legal basis adopted by the Commission will determine which procedure is to be used. Under the ToL, it is usually the ordinary legislative procedure.

7.3   The ordinary legislative procedure: Article 294 TFEU

Within the ordinary procedure the EP stands on an equal footing with the Council, as the procedure involves joint decision-making between them. Under the ToL the ordinary procedure applies to 83 areas of EU policies. The ordinary procedure, which was introduced by the Treaty of Maastricht under the name of co-decision procedure, was very complex. The ToA simplified it and the ToL, without making any substantive changes, renamed it. The procedure is still very complex. It involves co-operation between the Commission, the Council and the EP. For that reason in 2007 the three institutions adopted a Joint Declaration on Practical Arrangements for the Co-decision Procedure which remains in force and applies to the ordinary legislative procedure.[238]

Under the ordinary procedure national parliaments act as "watchdogs", i.e. decide whether a draft legislative act accords with the requirements of the principle of subsidiarity. The CoR and the ESC must be consulted if the Treaties so provide and may also submit opinions if they consider appropriate.

The ordinary procedure may be extended to new areas under the "passerelle" provisions (see section 7.1.2.1) and may also be suspended in some circumstances, i.e. under the "emergency brake" procedure. In respect of certain matters concerning the creation of the area of FSJ (see Chapter 2.4) and social security (Article 48 TFEU), a member of the Council may oppose the use of the ordinary procedure if it considers that proposed draft legislation would affect fundamental aspects of the legal system of the Member State he represents. In such a situation the procedure is suspended and the matter is referred to the European Council which, within four months, may either refer the matter back to the Council and thus terminate the suspension of the ordinary procedure or take no action or request the Commission to prepare a new proposal. If the

---

238.   [2007] OJ C145/5. The Declaration replaced the previous one adopted in 1999.

European Council takes no action the legislation originally proposed is deemed not to have been adopted.

The ordinary procedure is described in Article 294 TFEU. The various stages in the co-decision procedure can be summarised as follows:

7.3.1 Proposal

The Commission forwards a proposal to the EP, the Council and national parliaments.

7.3.2 First reading

A. First, the EP acting by simple majority delivers its opinion which:

- May approve the proposal without amendments; or
- May contain amendments.

B. Then, the Commission may:

- Incorporate any EP amendments into its original proposal if it is of a view that they improve the proposal or are likely to facilitate agreements between the EP and the Council and then resubmit the amended proposal to the Council; or
- Retain the original proposal without incorporating any amendments.

C. Then, the Council may by QMV:

- Accept the Commission's proposal and, provided that the EP did not make any amendments, it can adopt the act; or
- Accept by QMV the Commission's proposal with amendments proposed by the EP having been incorporated into the proposal by the Commission. The act can then be adopted; or
- Adopt a common position:
  - Rejecting any or all amendments made by the EP. In this situation the Council forwards the common position to the EP together with a statement of reasons;
  - Rejecting the Commission's proposal, which proposal was not amended by the EP, but the Council wants to make changes to it.

7.3.3 Common position

If the Council has adopted a common position, the Commission sends a communication to the EP explaining why it supports or opposes the common position, together with the text of the common position. If relevant, the Commission comments on the Council's view on the EP's amendments.

7.3.4 Second reading

A. The EP. It has three months (which may be extended by one month) to express its opinion on the Council's common position. Within that time the EP may:

- Make amendments (including repeating those rejected by the Council at the first reading) by an absolute majority of its component members. The amended text is forwarded to the Council and the Commission; or
- Approve the Council's common position (by simple majority). The act can be adopted; or

- Take no action. The act can be adopted; or
- Reject the Council's common position by an absolute majority. The act is deemed not to have been adopted. The procedure ends.

B.   The Commission. It must deliver an opinion on any of the EP's amendments. If the Commission gives a negative opinion on at least one amendment, the Council will have to act by unanimity if it wishes to accept the EP's overall position.

C.   The Council. It has three months (which may be extended by one month) following the receipt of the EP's amendments to:

- Approve them either by QMV or by unanimity (if the Commission has delivered a negative opinion). The act can be adopted;
- Reject the EP's amendments to its common position. In this situation the president of the Council and the president of the EP will set up a Conciliation Committee within six weeks of the rejection of the amendments by the Council (this may be extended by two weeks).

7.3.5   The conciliation stage

A Conciliation Committee is made up of an equal number of representatives of the EP (the EP delegation) and of the Council (the Council delegation) and the Commissioner in charge of the dossier who acts as a broker between the two delegations. Its purpose is to produce a joint text – a compromise between the position of the Council and the EP on disputed points – within six weeks (which may be extended by two weeks) from the setting-up of the Conciliation Committee. The joint text must be approved by both delegations as follows:

- The Council delegation by QMV or unanimity depending upon the subject matter of the proposal;
- The EP delegation by simple majority.

If the Conciliation Committee fails to produce a joint text, the procedure ends. The act is deemed not to have been adopted.

7.3.6   Third reading

If the Conciliation Committee agrees on a joint text, it must be adopted within six weeks (which may be extended to eight weeks) by both the EP and the Council:

- The EP must adopt the joint text by a majority of the votes cast;
- The Council must adopt the joint text by QMV.

If either institution fails to adopt the joint text within the prescribed time limit, the act is deemed not to have been adopted. The procedure ends.

7.4   Special legislative procedures

Some special legislative procedures involve the participation of the EP; others allow the Commission and Council to act jointly, or only the Council or the Commission to act alone. Special procedures which involve the EP are the consent procedure and the consultation procedure.

7.4.1   The consent procedure

Under the consent procedure, introduced by the SEA, the Council acts on a proposal of the Commission after receiving consent from the EP. The specificity of the consent procedure is that the EP can only vote on the entire proposal, without the possibility of making any amendments. Usually, the Council is required to act by unanimity, but QMV is sufficient for the conclusion of international agreements referred to in Article 218(8) TFEU. The EP acts by a majority of the votes cast, except for a decision upon an application for membership of the EU where an absolute majority is required.

Examples of provisions which require adoption of legislative acts in accordance with the consent procedure are:

- Article 7(2) TEU, concerning sanctions imposed on a Member State for a serious and persistent breach of fundamental human rights;

- Article 49 TEU, concerning the accession of new members to the EU;

- Article 223(1) TFEU, concerning proposals on a uniform procedure for elections to the EP;

- Article 218 TFEU concerning the conclusion of association agreements, an agreement on EU accession to the ECHR; agreements establishing a specific institutional framework by organising co-operation procedures; agreements having important budgetary implications for the EU and other specific international agreements to which either the ordinary legislative procedure applies or the consent of the EP is required;

- Article 311 TFEU, under which the EP must give its consent to the adoption of implementing measures for the EU's own resources system by the Council;

- Article 25 TEU, under which the Council is required to obtain the consent of the EP in respect of the adoption of measures aiming at strengthening the rights of EU citizens or adding new rights.

It is to be noted that under Article 226 TFEU, the EP has the right to initiate and to have the last word on the adoption of regulations defining its investigative powers concerning alleged contraventions or maladministration in the implementation of EU law. Such regulations are to be adopted in accordance with the special legislative procedure, after obtaining the consent of the Council and the Commission.

7.4.2   The consultation procedure

Under the original Treaty the consultation procedure was the only legislative procedure involving the participation of the EP. It requires the Council to obtain the opinion of the EP.

This procedure starts with the submission of a formal proposal by the Commission to the Council. The latter must ask the EP for its opinion on the proposal. The Council is not obliged to follow the opinion delivered by the EP but it must receive it. The EP has a duty to co-operate loyally with other EU institutions, and especially to deliver its opinion within a reasonable time in order to allow the Council to adopt a measure within the required time frame.[239]

---

239.   Case C-65/93 *EP v Council* [1995] ECR I-643.

What occurs when the EP fails to deliver its opinion was explained by the ECJ in Cases 138 and 139/79 *Roquette*.[240]

THE FACTS WERE:

The Council adopted Regulation 1293/79 on the basis of Article 43(2) EC [replaced by Article 20 TFEU], which required the consultation of the EP, but without receiving an opinion from the EP. The Council argued that it requested the opinion but the EP did not reply and thus, by its own conduct, and knowing the urgency of the matter, the EP made it impossible for the Council to comply with the consultation requirement.

Held:

The ECJ held that when the Treaty provides for the consultation of the EP, this requirement must be strictly complied with, since "due consultation of the Parliament in the cases provided for by the Treaty . . . constitutes an essential formality disregard of which means that the measure concerned is void". The arguments of the Council would have been accepted if it had exhausted all existing procedural possibilities provided by Community law[241] to force the EP to deliver its opinion, which was not the case in *Roquette*.

If the Council or the Commission amends its initial proposal substantially, the EP must be consulted a second time, unless the modification matches the amendments suggested by the EP.[242]

7.4.3   The Council's power to legislate alone

Procedures where the Council can legislate without the participation of the EP are relics of the early days of the Communities and apply to very limited areas.

Under these procedures the Council can adopt laws proposed by the Commission, or acting on its own initiative, without the participation of any other institution. Examples of these procedures are:

- Article 26 TFEU in respect of fixing the common customs duties;

- Article 108(2) TFEU in respect of compatibility of grants of aid by the Member States with EU competition law;

- Some aspects of the Common Commercial Policy (Article 207(3) TFEU).

---

240.   [1980] ECR 3333.

241.   For example, the Council may request emergency procedures which are envisaged in the EP Rules of Procedure or an extraordinary session of the EP provided for in Article 196 EC.

242.   Case 41/69 *Chemiefarma* [1970] ECR 661; Case 1253/79 *Battaglia* [1982] ECR 297; Case C-65/90 *EP v Council* [1992] ECR I-4593; Joined Cases C-13/92 to C-16/92 *Driessen en Zonen and Others v Minister van Verkeer en Waterstaat* [1993] ECR I-4751; Case C-408/95 *Eurotunnel SA and Others v SeaFrance* [1997] ECR I-6315.

7.4.4 The Commission's own powers of legislation

The Commission has independent but limited power to legislate without the participation of any other EU institution. This power is operable only in cases where specific articles of the Treaty so authorise.

Under the ToL the Commission is empowered to enact legislative measures of general scope of application in limited areas, that is, concerning monopolies and concessions granted to companies by Member States (Article 106(3) TFEU)) and concerning the right of workers to remain in a Member State after having been employed there (Article 45(3)(d) TFEU). It appears that the Commission has rarely used this free-standing power to adopt legislative measures.[243] However, the Commission has been very much involved in issuing individual measures (that is, decisions) addressed to Member States, undertakings and individuals, mainly in competition and state aid matters.

7.4.5 The procedure relating to the social partners dialogue between management and labour: Articles 154 and 155(2) TFEU

The dialogue between the social partners, that is the two sides of industry – management and labour – at both national and EU levels, constitutes an indispensable component of the European social model. It concerns the discussions, consultations, negotiations and joint actions undertaken by the social partner organisations.

The Treaty of Amsterdam introduced in Articles 138 and 139 EC [Articles 154 and 155(2) TFEU] procedures which involve the participation of the social partners in the adoption of legislative measures relating to the definition of European social standards.

Under Article 154 TFEU the Commission is required to consult the social partners twice on any measure in the field of social policy:

■ First, before submitting any proposal, on the desirability of EU action in the relevant area; and

■ Second, when, after the first consultation, the Commission still considers that EU action in the relevant field is advisable, on the content of the envisaged proposal.

The social partners give their opinion, or recommendation, on the proposed measure and may also decide to initiate the Article 155(2) TFEU procedure leading to the conclusion of contractual agreements between them. The purpose of such agreements is to establish minimum standards in the relevant area of social policy. The agreements are legally binding once implemented. They can be implemented in two ways:

■ The social partners may ask the Council to adopt a decision (which normally takes the form of a directive) on a proposal submitted by the Commission;

■ The social partners may make their national member organisations responsible for implementing the agreement in line with the relevant national procedures and practices. These are known as "autonomous agreements" as the social partners themselves are responsible for implementing and monitoring these agreements.

Under 155(2) TFEU, the EP must be kept informed.

---

243. For example, only two directives have been adopted using this procedure: one on transparency between Member States and companies (Dir. 80/723 [1980] OJ L195/35) and the other on competition in the telecommunications sector (Dir. 88/301 [1988] OJ L131/73).

AIDE-MÉMOIRE

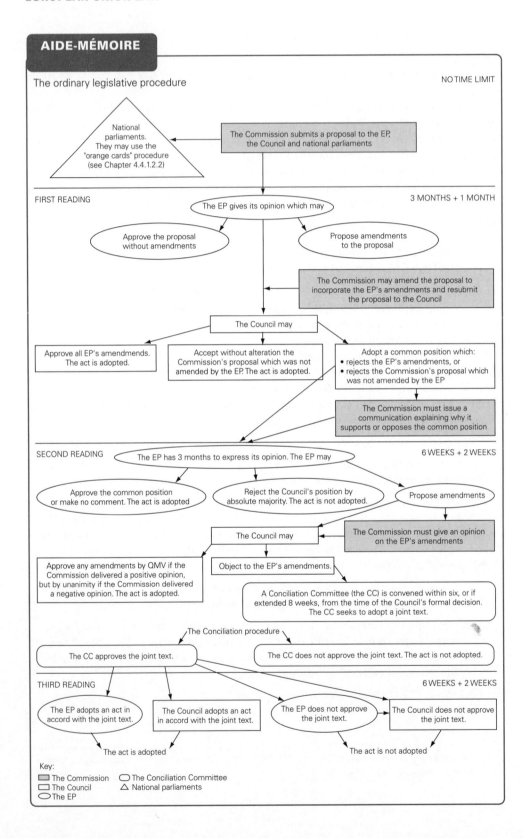

The ordinary legislative procedure

NO TIME LIMIT

National parliaments. They may use the "orange cards" procedure (see Chapter 4.4.1.2.2)

The Commission submits a proposal to the EP, the Council and national parliaments

FIRST READING

3 MONTHS + 1 MONTH

The EP gives its opinion which may

Approve the proposal without amendments

Propose amendments to the proposal

The Commission may amend the proposal to incorporate the EP's amendments and resubmit the proposal to the Council

The Council may

Approve all EP's amendmends. The act is adopted.

Accept without alteration the Commission's proposal which was not amended by the EP. The act is adopted.

Adopt a common position which:
• rejects the EP's amendments, or
• rejects the Commission's proposal which was not amended by the EP

The Commission must issue a communication explaining why it supports or opposes the common position

SECOND READING

6 WEEKS + 2 WEEKS

The EP has 3 months to express its opinion. The EP may

Approve the common position or make no comment. The act is adopted

Reject the Council's position by absolute majority. The act is not adopted.

Propose amendments

The Commission must give an opinion on the EP's amendments

The Council may

Approve any amendments by QMV if the Commission delivered a positive opinion, but by unanimity if the Commission delivered a negative opinion. The act is adopted.

Object to the EP's amendments.

A Conciliation Committee (the CC) is convened within six, or if extended 8 weeks, from the time of the Council's formal decision. The CC seeks to adopt a joint text.

The Conciliation procedure

The CC approves the joint text.

The CC does not approve the joint text. The act is not adopted.

THIRD READING

6 WEEKS + 2 WEEKS

The EP adopts an act in accord with the joint text.

The Council adopts an act in accord with the joint text.

The EP does not approve the joint text.

The Council does not approve the joint text.

The act is adopted

The act is not adopted

Key:
◼ The Commission   ◯ The Conciliation Committee
▢ The Council   △ National parliaments
◯ The EP

RECOMMENDED READING

Books

O'Brennan, J. and Raunio, T., (eds) *National Parliaments within the Enlarged European Union. From 'Victims' of Integration to Competitive Actors?*, 2009, Abingdon: Routledge

Sieberson, S.C., *Dividing Lines between the European Union and Its Member States*, 2008, Cambridge: CUP

Articles

Adamski, D., "How Wide is 'the Widest Possible'? Judicial Interpretation of the Exceptions to the Right of Access to Official Documents Revisited" (2009) 46 CMLRev, p 521

Alemanno, A., "The Better Regulation Initiative at the Judicial Gate: A Trojan Horse within the Commission's Walls or the Way Forward?" (2009) 15 ELJ, p 382

Cuesta Lopez, V., "The Lisbon Treaty's Provisions on Democratic Principles: A Legal Framework for Participatory Democracy" (2010) 16 EPL, p 123

De Leeuw, M.E., "Openness in the Legislative Process in the European Union", (2007) 32/3 ELR, p 295

8

SOURCES OF EU LAW

SUMMARY

This chapter examines the sources of EU law. The Treaties do not contain any express provision classifying sources of EU law, nor do they establish the hierarchy of such sources. In the absence of any clarification on either of these points, other factors, such as indications provided by the Treaties, practices established by the EU institutions and the Member States, and judgments rendered by the ECJ, assist in the identification of the following sources of EU law:

1. Primary sources. These are composed of the law in the founding Treaties: the EC and the EA Treaties as amended by subsequent Treaties; protocols and annexes attached to these Treaties which form an integral part of them; and acts of accession of new Member States. Primary sources are at the pinnacle of the hierarchy of EU law.

2. General principles of EU law. This refers mainly to a body of unwritten principles which underpin the EU legal order. However, exceptionally some principles are expressly mentioned in the Treaties and are therefore clearly primary sources. The CJEU has recourse to general principles in order to supplement other sources of EU law. They rank below the primary sources but above all other sources, unless they are already included in the primary sources.

3. External sources which derive from international agreements concluded between the EU and third states or international organisations. The EU has legal personality and as such is empowered to enter into international agreements. By virtue of Article 216(2) TFEU such international agreements are binding on the EU and the Member States and form an integral part of EU law. In the hierarchy of sources they rank below primary sources and general principles of EU law but above secondary sources.

4. Secondary sources. These are legislative and non-legislative acts which the relevant EU institutions are empowered to adopt. Three types – regulations, directives and decisions – are binding; the remainder – recommendations and opinions – have no binding legal force. Secondary sources which are binding rank in importance below primary sources, general principles of EU law and law stemming from international agreements. The ToL establishes a hierarchy of secondary sources in that a distinction is made between those binding acts which are adopted on the basis of the Treaties, and which are referred to in Article 289 TFEU as legislative acts, and those binding acts which are adopted on the basis of secondary acts, i.e. on the basis of legislative acts. These non-legislative acts are either delegated or implementing acts.

5. EU acts not expressly mentioned in Article 288 TFEU. These are acts of a binding and non-binding nature, none of which are mentioned in Article 288 TFEU. Their ranking in importance, provided they are of a binding nature, depends on their object and material content.

6. Case law of the ECJ. There is no doctrine of precedent under EU law. However, for many reasons, the most important being legal certainty, the ECJ is reluctant to depart from the principles laid down in earlier cases. Thus, previous case law is important as it provides guidelines for subsequent cases which raise the same or similar issues, but previous judicial decisions are not regarded as a complete statement of law and are not binding on national courts or on the ECJ. Thus, they are not regarded as a source of EU law.

8.1 Introduction

The classification of sources of EU law can be based on various criteria. It is possible to distinguish between:

- Written and unwritten sources;

- Internal and external sources;

- Primary and secondary sources;

- Sources mentioned by the Treaties and those which have been introduced by practice;

- Sources, in the strict sense, of EU law which comprise primary and secondary sources, and sources in a broad sense covering all rules applicable to the EU legal order written and unwritten, external and internal.

In order to simplify the classification of sources of EU law, the following typology is suggested:

1. Primary sources, which are contained in the founding Treaties as amended, protocols and annexes attached to them, and acts of accession of new Member States;

2. General principles of EU law including those which ensure the protection of fundamental human rights;

3.   External sources which derive from international agreements concluded between the EU and third countries or international organisations;

4.   Secondary sources, which are listed in Article 288 TFEU, i.e. regulations, directives and decisions. The ToL makes a distinction between legislative acts adopted by EU institutions on the basis of Treaties and non-legislative acts which are adopted on the basis of legislative acts, i.e. delegated and implementing acts;

5.   Some atypical acts, i.e. which do not take the form of regulations, directives or decisions, may have binding effect. Some of them are mentioned in the Treaties, others have their origin in the practice of EU institutions.

The case law of the ECJ merits special attention. It is not regarded as a source of EU law but, in practice, the ECJ, in order to ensure coherence and consistency of its case law, relies on earlier cases to decide subsequent cases which raise the same or similar issues.

8.2   Primary sources of EU law

The primary sources of EU law comprise the two founding Treaties remaining in force (the ECSC Treaty is no longer in force as it has expired), as amended over the years, protocols and annexes attached to the founding treaties and their amendments and acts of accession of new Member States to the existing Communities and to the EU. Further, under Article 6(1) TEU the Charter of Fundamental Rights of the European Union is regarded as a primary source of EU law (see Chapter 9.4).

8.2.1   The founding treaties and their amendments

The two founding treaties are:

■ The Treaty of Rome of 25 March 1957 establishing the European Economic Community (EEC); it entered into force on 1 January 1958;

■ The Treaty of Rome of 25 March 1957 establishing the European Atomic Energy Community (Euratom); it entered into force on 1 January 1958.

Both founding treaties were concluded for an unlimited period and have been amended many times.

As at the time of writing, the last amendments to the founding treaties took place in December 2009 when the Treaty of Lisbon (ToL) entered into force. The purpose of this Treaty was to amend the Treaty on European Union (TEU) and the EC Treaty which was renamed to become the Treaty on the Functioning of the European Union (TFEU). As a result, the ToL itself is not designed to have a lasting existence of its own. It does not constitute a third treaty. It contains only seven articles, however, the first two are very long as they contain amendments to the TEU and the TFEU (see Chapter 1.19.4). The Euratom exists outside the ToL. It is "hanging on the side". Protocol 2 annexed to the ToL contains changes to the EA Treaty and also provides that some provisions of both the TEU and the TFEU apply to the EA Treaty.

The founding Treaties, as amended, are considered to be "the constitutional Treaties". The idea that the founding Treaties establishing the three Communities are different from classical international treaties was recognised by the ECJ in Case 26/62 *Van Gend en Loos*,[244] in which the Court held that "this Treaty is more than an agreement which merely creates mutual obligations between the Contracting States" and that "the Community constitutes a new legal order of international law", which creates rights and obligations not only for the Member States but more importantly for their nationals "which become part of their legal heritage".

The constitutional nature of the founding Treaties, as well as the legal implications deriving from their peculiar status under public international law, has been progressively developed by the ECJ. In Case 294/83 *Les Verts*,[245] the ECJ considered the EC Treaty as the "basic constitutional Charter" of the Community, and in *Opinion 1/91 [Re First EEA Agreement]*[246] refused to inter-pret international agreements in the same manner as the EC Treaty because of the peculiar nature of the EC Treaty.

The two treaties on which the EU is founded are the TEU and the TFEU. Article 1 TEU states that "The Union shall be founded on the present Treaty and on the Treaty on the Functioning of the European Union (hereinafter referred to as "the Treaties"). Those two Treaties shall have the same legal value". The equality between the TEU and TFEU means that neither is subordinate to the other. Indeed, the separation of the two treaties is formal rather than substantive in that both Treaties constitute one text and no hierarchy as to their importance is established. The fusion of the EU and the European Community as well as the suppression of the pillar structure has resulted in the disappearance of any frontiers between the two Treaties although special rules still apply to the CFSP (see Chapter 5). The CJEU has jurisdiction to interpret both treaties, with exceptions concerning matters covered by the CFSP. Despite the fact that neither Treaty prevails the TEU, which contains provisions on principles, values, fundamental human rights, objectives of the EU, and provisions on the institutional framework of the EU, is essential to the interpretation of both Treaties, in particular the TFEU which contains detailed provisions on the functioning of the EU. The same legal standing as that of the Treaties is granted to the Charter of Fundamental Rights in the European Union in the light of which all provisions of both Treaties are to be interpreted subject to Protocol 30 (see Chapter 9.4).

8.2.2 Protocols and annexes to the Treaties

In accordance with Article 2(2) of the Vienna Convention of 23 May 1969 on the Law of Treaties, protocols and Annexes to the founding Treaties, or to Treaties amending the founding Treaties, have the same legal effect as the Treaties themselves. This is embodied in Article 51 TEU, which states that:

"The Protocols and Annexes to the Treaties shall form an integral part thereof."

There are 37 Protocols and 2 Annexes attached to the Treaties. The ECJ has confirmed many times the binding force of Protocols and Annexes.[247]

---

244. *NV Algemene Transport- en Expeditie Onderneming van Gend & Loos v Netherlands Inland Revenue Administration* [1963] ECR 3.
245. [1986] ECR 1339.
246. [1991] ECR 6079.
247. Case 149/85 *Wybot* [1986] ECR 2391; Case 314/85 *Foto-Frost* [1987] ECR 4199; Case 260/86 *Commission v Belgium* [1988] ECR 955.

The protocols could have been incorporated into the Treaties. However, their existence means that the Treaties themselves avoid being too lengthy.

8.2.3   Declarations annexed to the Treaties

Sixty five Declarations have been annexed to the Treaties. Declarations are of various kinds: they may be made by the Conference which adopted the Treaty, by Member States, or by a Member State or EU institutions expressing their intention or views on a particular point. Declarations annexed to the Treaties are not legally binding as, unlike the Annexes and Protocols, they have not been incorporated into the Treaties by express provisions. In fact they are annexed to the Final Acts of the Conferences adopting them, and not directly to the Treaties. Under Article 31 SEA, and Article L TEU, declarations annexed to those two Treaties were expressly excluded from the jurisdiction of the ECJ. Accordingly, the ECJ has no power to interpret them.

Whether a unilateral declaration made by a Member State can give rise to EU obligations is debatable. In international law some declarations produce legal effects (for example, when a Member State issues a protest objecting to an act or action carried out by another Member State or recognises a particular situation, or renounces a right), and some are sources of obligations (for example, when a Member State promises to do something or to abstain from doing something). This is illustrated in the *Nuclear Tests Case*,[248] where a unilateral declaration made by France that it would cease conducting atmospheric nuclear tests was considered by the ICJ as giving rise to an obligation because, first, it was made publicly and, second, France had the clear intention to be legally bound by it.

It is submitted that the specific nature of EU law prevents declarations from acquiring any legal effect, or giving rise to an obligation: first, they cannot be classified as EU acts; second, they have not been incorporated into the Treaties; and third, they cannot restrict, exclude or modify the legal effect of the Treaties. In C-354/04P *Gestoras Pro Amnistia and Others v Council*,[249] the ECJ refused to give any legal effect to a declaration. In Case C-49/02 *Heidelberger Bauchemie*,[250] the ECJ held that declarations cannot be used to interpret a provision of secondary legislation, unless a specific reference is made in the wording of the relevant provision.[251]

It should be noted that, unlike the ICJ with regard to the UN Charter, the ECJ has compulsory jurisdiction to resolve any dispute between Member States falling within the scope of the Treaties and to provide clarifications on a particular point of law. Accordingly, the ECJ is the final arbiter on the rights and obligations of a Member State and would, if required, define them irrespective of the content of any declaration made by a Member State.

8.2.4   Acts of accession

Acts of accession are legally binding. They are similar, from the point of view of the legal effect they produce, to the Treaties.

---

248. *Nuclear Tests (Australia v France)* (1974) ICJ Rep., p 253.
249. [2007] ECR I-1579.
250. [2004] ECR I-6129.
251. Case C-292/89 *The Queen v Immigration Appeal Tribunal, ex parte Gustaff Desiderius Antonissen* [1991] ECR I-745; and Case C-329/95 *Administrative proceedings brought by VAG Sverige AB* [1997] ECR I-2675.

8.2.5   Revision of Treaties: Article 48 TEU

The ToL sets out two revision procedures: the "ordinary revision procedure" and the "simplified revision procedure".

8.2.5.1   The ordinary revision procedure (Article 48(1)–(5) TEU)

There are two versions of the ordinary revision procedure. Under Article 48(1)–(5) TEU both versions start with the submission of a proposal for amendments to the Treaties by any Member State, the EP, or the Commission, to the Council. The next step is for the Council to submit the proposal to the European Council and to notify it to national parliaments. If the European Council decides that the proposed amendments are worthy of consideration it has two options. It may either convene a Convention or may decide that the proposed amendments do not justify the establishment of a Convention and can be dealt with by a conference of representatives of the governments of the Member States.

- In the first version of the ordinary revision procedure, the European Council adopts, by a simple majority, a decision, after consulting the EP and the Commission, to convene a Convention to examine the proposal. The Convention is made up of representatives of the national Parliaments, of the heads of state or government of the Member States, of the European Parliament and of the Commission. The European Central Bank is consulted in the case of institutional changes in the monetary area. The Convention is convened by the President of the European Council to prepare draft amendments to the Treaties. The Convention is required to adopt by consensus a recommendation to a conference of representatives of the governments of the Member States which will make final amendments to the amendments agreed by the Convention.

  The convention system has been used on two occasions: to draft the Charter of Fundamental Rights and to prepare the Constitutional Treaty. The main advantages of convening a convention are that this ensures a wide input into the revision process and makes it transparent.

- In the second version of the ordinary revision procedure, i.e. when amendments are regarded by the European Council as not being sufficiently important to convene a Convention, the European Council may decide by a simple majority, after obtaining the consent of the EP, to convene a conference of representatives of the governments of the Member States and to give them instructions as to the required amendments.

  In both versions the amendments enter into force if ratified by all the Member States in accordance with their respective constitutional requirements.

Article 48(1)–(5) TEU amended the pre-ToL revision procedure in the following ways:

- It provides for the establishment of an IGC (called a "Convention") when proposed amendments to the Treaties are considered by the European Council as fundamentally affecting the Treaties;

- National parliaments must be notified of any proposal for amendment of the Treaties;

- The EP has gained new powers under this procedure, i.e. it can initiate a proposal for amendments and its consent is required if the European Council decides not to convene a Convention;

■ Article 48(5) TEU states that if two years after the signature of a treaty amending the Treaties, four-fifths of the Member States have ratified it but one or more Member States have difficulties in proceeding with ratification, the matter should be referred to the European Council. However, the ToL does not specify how the European Council will then deal with the matter.

8.2.5.2 Simplified revision procedures (Article 48(6) and (7) TEU)

Article 48(6) and (7) TEU sets out two new simplified procedures for revision of the Treaties which are also known as "self-amending" provisions or "passerelle" provisions which translates into English as "bridging" provisions. "Passerelle" provisions are those which allow the reduction of procedural requirements or the making of adjustments or amendments to the Treaties without the necessity to have recourse to formal Treaties revision procedures as described in Article 48(1)–(5) TEU (above).

■ The first is described in Article 48(6) TEU. A Member State, the EP or the Commission may submit to the European Council a proposal for revising all or some of the provisions of Part III of the TFEU on the internal policies of the EU. The European Council may decide to make such an amendment after consulting the EP and the Commission and, if relevant, the ECB. However, the amendment must be approved by the Member States in accordance with their respective constitutions. Consequently, voting in national parliaments or, if required under national law, referenda, will be necessary for any amendment to become binding. Further, the amendment must not increase the competences of the EU.

■ The second is described in Article 48(7) TEU. It allows Member States to abolish vetoes in all areas in which unanimity is required if the European Council agrees unanimously to do this. The only exception concerns defence matters. Further, the European Council may, acting unanimously, allow the Council to apply the ordinary legislative procedure, instead of a special legislative procedure provided for the adoption of legislative acts in the relevant area. In addition, to the requirement of unanimity in the European Council, national parliaments must be notified and must give their approval. If any of them opposes the European Council decision within six months of the date of such notification, the decision must not be adopted. Further, a decision under Article 48(7) TEU may be adopted after obtaining the consent of the EP, based on a majority of its component members. Article 48(7) TEU contains a general "passerelle" provision on the basis of which special "passerelle" type-procedures may be used in respect of specific areas, e.g. under Article 312(2) TFEU the European Council may, unanimously, adopt a decision authorising the Council to act by QMV when adopting a multiannual financial framework. "Passerelle" provisions, because they can significantly alter the provisions of the Treaties, are controversial in a situation where national parliaments have no right to veto the proposed change, e.g. Article 153(2) TFEU under which the Council may change the requirements for adoption of decisions in certain areas of social policy from special legislative procedures to the ordinary legislative procedure.

8.2.6 Ranking of primary sources in the hierarchy of sources of EU law

The primary sources are at the top of the hierarchy of sources of EU law; their supremacy means that all other sources of EU law are subordinate.

The superiority of the primary sources over other sources of EU law is strengthened by the prohibition of any revision of the Treaties, either by an act or a practice of the EU institutions or the Member States, outside the procedures set out in the Treaties themselves. In Case 43/75 *Defrenne*,[252] the ECJ rejected the possibility of revision of the Treaties based on Article 39 of the 1969 Vienna Convention on the Law of Treaties, which provides that a revision of a particular treaty may result from a common accord of all contracting parties. The Court held that a modification of the Treaty can take place, without prejudice to other specific provisions contained in the Treaty, only on the grounds of Article 236 of the EC Treaty (Article 48 TEU).

Since 1957 it has been well established that the Member States are not permitted to act by a common agreement to revise the Treaties outside the existing procedures and therefore exclude the EU institutions from participating in these procedures.[253]

8.3 General principles of EU law

In "judicial legislation" a special place is given to the general principles of EU law. These are unwritten rules of law which a judge of the ECJ has to find and apply but not create. General principles have a triple role to play. They are applied to:

- Avoid denial of justice;

- Fill what would otherwise be gaps in EU law;

- Strengthen the coherence of EU law.

The general principles of EU law consist mainly of principles of administrative justice and of the protection of fundamental human rights.

Article 340(2) TFEU expressly allows judges of the ECJ to apply general principles common to the laws of the Member States to determine the non-contractual liability of the EU. However, the ECJ has not limited the application of the general principles to this area but has applied them to all aspects of EU law.

In formulating general principles the ECJ draws inspiration from many sources including the following major sources:

- Public international law and its general principles inherent in all organised legal systems;

- National laws of the Member States by identifying general principles common to the laws of the Member States;

- EU law by inferring the general principles from the nature of the EU;

- Fundamental human rights.

These sources are examined below.

---

252.   [1976] ECR 455.

253.   The conclusion of agreements with third countries which would alter the provisions of the Treaties is included: see Opinion 1/91 [EEA Agreement I] [1991] ECR I-6079 and Opinion 1/92 [EEA Agreement II] [1992] ECR I-2821.

8.3.1 Public international law and its general principles inherent in all organised legal systems

The creation of a new international legal order by the Community did not preclude the ECJ from making reference to the general principles of public international law. The ECJ has endorsed some of them, for example, the principle of compatibility of successive conventional obligations;[254] the right of nationals to enter and remain in the territory of their own country;[255] the rule of customary international law concerning the termination and the suspension of a treaty by reason of a fundamental change of circumstances;[256] and rejected others as contrary to this new legal order. For example, the principle of reciprocity, especially under its form of the exeptio non adimpleti contactus (the principle according to which performance of an obligation may be withheld if the other party has itself failed to perform the same or a related obligation) was considered by the ECJ as incompatible with the EU legal order.[257]

8.3.1.1 The principle of legal certainty

The most important principle of public international law recognised by the ECJ is the principle of legal certainty which is in itself vague. In the context of EU legislation it means that the law must be certain, that is, clear and precise,[258] and its legal implications foreseeable, especially in its application to financial matters.[259] Further, all EU acts aimed at producing legal effects must be adopted on a proper legal basis.[260] At national level it means that national legislation implementing EU law must be worded in such a way as to be clearly understandable to those concerned as to the content of their rights and obligations.[261] The ECJ has given a concrete scope of application to the principle of legal certainty in order to escape its tautological nature and to clarify its content. As a result, under the principle of legal certainty, the following rules have been established by the ECJ:

- the principle of non-retroactivity of administrative acts;[262]

- the principle of good faith which requires that EU institutions in administrative and contractual matters act in conformity with that principle;[263]

- the principle of patere legem[264] (under this principle an authority which has made law for others must itself comply with that law);

- the principle of vested or acquired rights;[265]

---

254. Case 10/61 *Commission v Italy* [1962] ECR 1.
255. Case 41/74 *Van Duyn* [1974] ECR 1337.
256. Case C-162/96 *Racke* [1998] ECR I-3655.
257. Joined Cases 90 and 91/63 *Commission v Belgium and Luxembourg* [1964] ECR 625.
258. Case C-110/03 *Belgium v Commission* [2005] ECR I-2801.
259. Case 325/85 *Ireland v Commission* [1987] ECR 5041.
260. Case C-325/91 *France v Commission* [1993] ECR I-3283.
261. Case 257/86 *Commission v Italy* [1988] ECR 3249; Case C-376/02 *Stichting "Goed Wonen" v Staatssecretaris van Financiën* [2005] ECR I-3445.
262. Case 234/83 *Gesamthochschule Duisburg v Hauptzollamt München – Mitte* [1985] ECR 327.
263. Joined Cases 43/59, 45/59 and 48/59 *Eva von Lachmüller and Others v Commission* [1960] ECR 463.
264. Case 38/70 *Deutsche Tradax* [1971] ECR 145; Case 68/86 *UK v Council* [1988] ECR 855.
265. Case 100/78 *Rossi* [1979] ECR 831; Case 159/82 *Verli-Wallace* [1983] ECR 2711.

■ the principle of legitimate expectations which means that "those who act in good faith on the basis of law as it is or seems to be should not be frustrated in their expectations". This principle has given rise to many cases in the context of commercial activities of individuals and undertakings.

8.3.1.2 Procedural rights

Another category of general principles taken from public international law concerns the procedural rights necessary to safeguard the protection of substantive rights, such as the right to defence and especially to a fair hearing in administrative proceedings,[266] including the right to be heard before the Commission in competition cases in the stage of the preliminary enquiry[267] and before the CJEU[268] and the refusal to recognise the possibility of an extraordinary appeal without any written text.[269]

8.3.2 General principles common to the laws of the Member States

It is not necessary that a general principle is recognised by the legal systems of all Member States. It is sufficient if a given principle is common to several national legal systems, although "non-negligible divergences" constitute an obstacle to its recognition.[270] Advocate General Slynn in Case 155/79 *AM and S v Commission* explained the manner in which the ECJ discovers unwritten principles of EC law by citing H. Kutscher, a former judge of the ECJ. He explained:

"... when the Court interprets or supplements Community law on a comparative law basis it is not obliged to take the minimum which the national solutions have in common, or their arithmetic mean or the solution produced by a majority of the legal systems as the basis of its decision. The Court has to weigh up and evaluate the particular problem and search for the 'best' and 'most appropriate' solution. The best possible solution is the one which meets the specific objectives and basic principles of the Community ... in the most satisfactory way."[271]

Therefore, the discovery of general principles common to the Member States is based on a comparative study of national laws of the Member States but avoids any mechanical or mathematical approach leading to the lowest common denominator. To the contrary, the spirit of national laws, their evolution and general features are taken into consideration by the ECJ. The general tendency, or sometimes lack of general tendency, may also inspire the judges.

In the process of discovery of general principles, the ECJ is entitled to choose the most appropriate from the point of view of the objectives of EU law, but subject to the principle in *Hoechst*[272] that the substance of fundamental human rights is left untouched. It has, for example,

---

266. Case 7/69 *Commission v Italy* [1970] ECR 111; Case 17/74 *Transocean Marine* [1974] ECR 1063, Case 85/76 *Hoffmann-La Roche* [1979] ECR 461; Case 53/85 *AKZO Chemie* [1986] ECR 1965.
267. Case 374/87 *Orkem* [1989] ECR 3283.
268. Joined Cases 42 and 49/59 *SNUPAT* [1961] ECR 53.
269. Case 12/68 *X v Audit Board of the European Communities* [1970] ECR 291.
270. Joined Cases 46/87 and 227/88 *Hoechst* [1989] ECR I-2859.
271. [1982] ECR 1575 at 1649.
272. Joined Cases 46/87 and 227/88 [1989] ECR I-2859.

recognised a principle which is rejected by all Member States but one[273] and rejected a principle common to national laws of all Member States but incompatible with the requirements of EU law.[274] Once the ECJ incorporates a national principle into EU law, it becomes an independent, autonomous principle which may have a different meaning from the one known to national laws. Among the principles common to the national laws of the Member States the ECJ has discovered and adopted the following:

- The principle of equality before economic regulation;[275]

- The principle of the hierarchy of legal measures which allows distinguishing between legislative acts and measures necessary to their implementation;[276]

- The principle of the prohibition of unjust enrichment;[277]

- The principles of non-contractual liability of the EU institutions, bodies, offices and agencies;[278]

- The principle of confidentiality of written communications between lawyer and client,[279] but it applies only in the context of an independent lawyer, not in the relationship of an in-house lawyer;[280]

- The principle of access to the legal process;[281]

- The principle of the protection of business secrets of an undertaking;[282]

- The principle of the retroactive application of a more lenient penalty in favour of natural and legal persons who have earlier incurred a more severe penalty.[283]

8.3.3   General principles inferred from the nature of the EU

The ECJ has inferred from the specific nature of the Communities/EU and from the objectives and the context of the Treaties a certain number of principles. Some of them are well rooted in EU law, others are more dubious. In this respect the ECJ in Case C-353/92 *Greece v Council*[284] rejected the principle of EU preference which was acknowledged as a general principle of EU law in previous decisions.[285] This rejection demonstrates that the list of general principles is not exhaustive or definitive.

General principles inferred from the nature of the EU can be divided into two categories. The

---

273.   Case 9/69 *Sayag* [1969] ECR 329.

274.   Case 26/67 *Danvin* [1968] ECR 315.

275.   Case 8/57 *Groupement des Hauts Fourneaux et Aciéries Belges v High Authority* [1957–58] ECR 245.

276.   Case 25/70 *Köster* [1970] ECR 1161.

277.   Case 26/67 *Danvin* [1968] ECR 315. Also, see Chapter 16.5.6.4.

278.   Joined Cases 83 and 94/76, 4, 15 and 40/77 *Bayerische HNL* [1978] ECR 1209.

279.   Case 155/79 *AM & S* [1982] ECR 1575.

280.   See Chapter 30.

281.   Case 222/84 *Johnston* [1986] ECR 1651.

282.   Case 53/85 *AKZO Chemie* [1986] ECR 1965; Case C-36/92P *SEP* [1994] ECR 1911.

283.   Joined Cases 387/02, 391/02 and 403/02 *Criminal Proceedings against Berlusconi and Others* [2005] ECR I-3565.

284.   [1994] ECR I-3411.

285.   Case 5/67 *Beus* [1968] ECR 83.

first concerns institutional and constitutional law of the EU; the second relates to principles which are inherent to the creation of the internal market.

8.3.3.1   General principles reflecting institutional and constitutional law of the EU

These principles are:

■ The principles of direct effect, direct applicability, supremacy of EU law, effectiveness of EU law and the principle of the liability of Member States in damages for breaches of EU law vis-à-vis individuals. They derive from the objectives of the Treaties and have been developed by the ECJ to promote effective enforcement of EU law within the national legal systems of the Member States. These principles are examined in depth in this book (see Chapters 11, 12, 13, 14);

■ The principle of solidarity.[286] Solidarity is required in the internal and external relations of the Member States. The Treaty of Maastricht developed the principle of solidarity and recognised it as binding. Instances where the principle of solidarity is of particular relevance have been detailed by the ToL. Under Article 222 TFEU in all situations where a Member State is the object of a terrorist attack or victim of a natural or man-made disaster other Member States and the EU are required to assist and help the Member State concerned. Under Article 42(7) TEU when a Member State is the victim of armed aggression on its territory, the other Member States have the duty to aid and assist the Member State concerned by all means in their power in accordance with Article 51 of the UN Charter and subject to their international commitments (see Chapter 5.5). Apart from the exceptional situations described above, the principle of solidarity means that all Member States should contribute to the harmonious development of the Union and thus the principle of solidarity strengthens economic and social cohesion within the EU and the commitment of all Member States to the foreign policy of the EU;

■ The principle of loyal co-operation between EU institutions and Member States, and between Member States themselves based on Article 4(3) TEU (see Chapter 15.2.3.2);

■ The principle of subsidiarity (see Chapter 4.4.1);

■ The principle of conferral (see Chapter 4.4);

■ The principle of effective judicial protection of citizens of the EU (see Chapter 16.2.3.3.3);

■ The principle of equality. This is a principle of fundamental importance to the EU. It entails not only the equality between Member States (see Chapter 3.1) but also equality in the treatment of EU citizens. Article 9 TEU states: "In all its activities, the Union shall observe the principle of the equality of its citizens, who shall receive equal attention from its institutions, bodies, offices and agencies". The Treaties prohibit all forms of discrimination (direct and indirect) based on nationality.[287] This is recognised by Article 18 TFEU. Article 19 TFEU extends the principle of non-discrimination to prohibit discrimination based on sex,

---

286.   Case 39/72 *Commission v Italy* [1973] ECR 101.
287.   Case 155/80 *Oebel* [1981] ECR 1993.

racial or ethnic origin, religion or belief, disability, age[288] and sexual orientation. Article 2 TEU provides that equality between women and men constitutes a fundamental value on which the Union is founded;

- The principle of proportionality. This was known only to German law but has become a general principle of Community law since it responds to the needs of the EU legal order.

This principle was applied in Case 11/70 *Internationale Handelsgesellschaft*,[289] in which the ECJ held that: "A public authority may not impose obligations on a citizen except to the extent to which they are strictly necessary in the public interest to attain the purpose of the measure."

This means that if the burdens imposed on addressees of a measure are clearly out of proportion to the objective which an EU measure seeks to achieve, the measure will be annulled. The principle of proportionality requires that the measure must be appropriate and necessary in order to achieve the objective legitimately pursued. When there is a choice between several appropriate measures, the measure which is least onerous, which causes least hardship or impediment, must be selected; and the disadvantages caused must not be disproportionate to the aims pursued. This principle has been extensively used in all areas of EU law, in particular in the context of the establishment of the internal market.

The importance of the principle of proportionality is confirmed in Article 5(1) TEU. Even with the incorporation of the principle into the Treaties, the creative role of the ECJ can still be felt: as proportionality is a relative concept. It is up to the Court to determine whether a measure is disproportionate or otherwise. In particular, in areas where EU institutions enjoy a large measure of discretion, which involves political, economic and social choices on their part, and in which they are called upon to undertake complex assessments (such as measures taken under the CAP or measures relating to the protection of public health), the Court will tend not to interfere unless there is blatant and obvious infringement of the principle, that is, if a measure is manifestly inappropriate as to the objective pursued. For example, in Joined Cases C-453/03, C-11/04, C-12/04 and C-194/04 *ABNA*[290] the ECJ annulled a provision of an EC directive as being disproportionate. According to that provision, manufacturers of compound animal feed, at the customer's request, were obliged to indicate the quantitative composition of the feed. The manufacturers argued that the disclosure of the formulas for the composition of their products would put them at risk of such formulas being used by their competitors and thus would have deleterious effect on their investments, research and innovation. The ECJ agreed.

8.3.3.2   General principles reflecting the neo-liberal philosophy of the internal market

The principles of the free movement of goods, people, services and capital, the principle of the homogeneity of the internal market, the principles relating to competition law, and so on, are closely related to the proper functioning of the internal market.

---

288. Case C-144/04 *Mangold* [2005] ECR I-9981.
289. [1970] ECR 1125.
290. [2005] ECR I-10423.

8.3.4   The fundamental principles of human rights

The protection of fundamental human rights is examined in Chapter 9. It is important to note that the ECJ has found sources of inspiration in establishing the extent of protection of human rights under EU law in constitutional traditions common to the Member States,[291] the ECHR and other international conventions which the Member States have ratified.[292]

The ECJ has recognised, inter alia, the following rights:

▨ The right to equal treatment, including non-discrimination based on nationality or gender;[293]

▨ The right to human dignity;[294]

▨ The right to exercise economic and professional activities, although this may be legitimately restricted in the light of the social function of the protected activity;[295]

▨ The right to respect for an individual's private and family life,[296] home[297] and correspondence as set out in Article 8 of the ECHR, but this does not exclude the interference of public authorities under the conditions defined by law and necessary to ensure public security and the economic welfare of a country or actions exercising the enforcement powers of the Commission in competition matters;[298]

▨ The right to property,[299] but commercial interests in which the risk factor is inherent to the substance are not protected;[300]

▨ The right to medical secrecy;[301]

▨ The right of association;[302]

▨ The right to free speech;[303]

▨ The right to religious freedom;[304]

---

291. Case 11/70 *Internationale Handelsgesellschaft* [1970] ECR 1125.
292. Such as the International Covenant on Civil and Political Rights in Case C-249/96 *Lisa Jacqueline Grant v South-West Trains Ltd* [1998] ECR I-621; The European Social Charter and the ILO Convention no. 111 concerning discrimination in respect of employment and occupation in Case 149/77 *Defrenne* [1978] ECR 1365.
293. Case 149/77 *Defrenne*, ibid.
294. Case C-36/02 *Omega* [2004] ECR I-9609.
295. Case 4/73 *Nold* [1974] ECR 491; Case 44/79 *Liselotte Hauer v Land Rheinland-Pfalz* [1979] ECR 3727; Case 234/85 *Staatsanwaltschaft Freiburg v Franz Keller* [1986] ECR 2897; Joined Cases C-90 and C-91/90 *Neu* [1991] ECR I-3617; Case C-210/03 *Swedish Match* [2004] ECR I-11893.
296. Case C-60/00 *Carpenter* [2002] ECR I-6279.
297. Case C-94/00 *Roquette Frères* [2002] ECR I-9011.
298. Case 136/79 *National Panasonic* [1980] ECR 2033; Case C-404/92P *X v Commission* [1994] ECR I-4737; Case C-76/93P *Scaramuzza* [1993] ECR I-5173.
299. Case 44/79 *Hauer* [1979] ECR 3727.
300. Joined Cases 154, 205, 206, 226 to 228, 263 and 264/78, 39, 31, 83 and 85/79 *Valsabbia* [1980] ECR 907.
301. Case C-62/90 *Commission v Germany* [1992] ECR I-2575; Case C-404/92P *X v Commission* [1994] ECR I-4737.
302. Case 175/73 *Union Syndicale and Others v Council* [1974] ECR 917.
303. Case C-260/89 *Elliniki* [1991] ECR I-2925; Case C-23/93 *TV 10 SA* [1994] ECR I-4795; Case C-112/00 *Schmidberger* [2003] ECR I-5659.
304. Case 130/75 *Prais* [1976] ECR 1589.

■ The principle of non-retroactivity of penal measures;[305]

■ Procedural rights such as the right to defence, access to the court, to a fair hearing.[306]

8.3.5 Ranking of general principles of EU law

In the hierarchy of sources, general principles are as important as founding Treaties, especially the fundamental principles which are expressly acknowledged by Article 2 TEU, and which must be respected by the European Union and all its institutions. The ECJ recognises other general principles in so far as they are compatible with the founding Treaties and fundamental human rights.

8.4 External sources which derive from international commitments of the EU

By virtue of Article 216(2) TFEU international agreements entered into by the EU with third countries or international organisations are binding upon the EU institutions and the Member States. This provision rejects the general principle of public international law according to which only contracting parties to an international agreement are bound by it.

In Case 181/73 *Haegeman v Belgium*,[307] the ECJ held that the provisions of international agreements, from their entry into force, form an integral part of the Community legal order. Advocate General Rozes stated in Case 270/80 *Polydor Limited v Harlequin Records Shops Limited*[308] that an act by which the Council expresses the willingness of the Community to be bound by an international agreement, if such an act is adopted, neither modifies the nature, nor legal effects of an international agreement but has only "instrumental" character.

If an international agreement to which the EU is a contracting party provides for the establishment of a body empowered to supervise or monitor its proper functioning, or its uniform application in all contracting states, then any decisions adopted by such a body also form an integral part of the EU legal order.[309] The same applies to "recommendations" of such bodies because of their "direct link" with an international agreement.[310]

The ECJ accepts the supremacy of international agreements concluded between the EU and third states or international organisations because their conformity with the Treaties can be verified either prior to or after their conclusion. With regard to the prior verification, under Article 218(11) TFEU, a Member State, the EP, the Council or the Commission may ask the ECJ for an opinion as to the compatibility of an envisaged agreement with the Treaties. If the ECJ's opinion is adverse, the envisaged agreement will not enter into force unless it is amended or the Treaties are revised. Once an international agreement has been concluded, its validity can be challenged under Articles 263 and 267 TFEU.[311]

---

305. Case 63/83 *Kirk* [1984] ECR 2689.
306. Case T-47/03 *Sison* [11/07/07] nyr and T-327/03 *Stichting Al-Aqsa v Council* [11/07/07] nyr.
307. [1974] ECR 449.
308. [1982] ECR 329.
309. Case 87/75 *Bresciani* [1976] ECR 129; Case C-192/89 *Sevince* [1990] ECR I-3461; Case C-69/89 *Nakajima* [1991] ECR I-2069.
310. Case C-188/91 *Deutsche Shell* [1993] ECR I-363.
311. Opinion 1/75 *Local Cost Standard* [1975] ECR 1355.

8.4.1 Ranking of international agreements concluded by the EU with third countries in the hierarchy of sources of EU law

In the hierarchy of sources of EU law, international agreements concluded between the EU and third countries or international organisations are situated below primary sources and general principles of EU law, but above secondary sources.

In Case 40/72 *Schröeder KG v Germany*,[312] the ECJ held that international agreements and all acts of the EU institutions adopted in relation to their conclusion prevail over secondary sources of EU law. As a result, all unilateral measures such as regulations, directives and decisions must be interpreted in conformity with international agreements. Any conflicting secondary legislation may be annulled by the ECJ by virtue of Article 263 TFEU.[313] Also any breach of an international agreement by EU institutions may give rise to liability for damages under Article 340(2) TFEU.[314]

Direct effect of international agreements is discussed in Chapter 12.6.

8.5 Secondary sources of EU law

Under the Treaties, Member States have conferred important legislative powers on the EU institutions which enable them to implement the provisions of the Treaties and thus give full effect to EU law and policies.

The ToL is the first Treaty which makes a reference to legislative acts adopted by EU institutions. Previously, the founding Treaties carefully avoided any mention of "law-making powers" or "legislation" in relation to EU institutions. However, the ECJ did not hesitate to refer expressly to "legislative powers of the Community" in Case 106/77 *Simmenthal*[315] and the "legal system of the Treaty" in Case 25/70 *Köster*.[316]

The ToL rationalises, simplifies and provides for the hierarchy of secondary sources. It retains regulations, directives and decisions as legally binding instruments for legislative acts and for non-legislative acts. In this respect Article 288 TFEU states that the EU institutions "shall adopt regulations, directives, decisions, recommendations and opinions". However, the same provision expressly states that recommendations and opinions have no binding force, and thus they are neither legal acts nor considered as sources of EU law.

Article 289(3) TFEU states that "legal acts adopted by legislative procedure shall constitute legislative acts". As a result, acts adopted in accordance with the ordinary legislative procedure and special legislative procedures are to be regarded as legislative acts. Legislative acts are to be distinguished from non-legislative acts which are of two kinds:

- Delegated acts. Under Article 290(1)TFEU "A legislative act may delegate to the Commission the power to adopt non-legislative acts of general application to supplement or amend certain non-essential elements of the legislative act".

- Implementing acts. They are described in Article 290 (2) TFEU as follows: "Where uniform conditions for implementing legally binding Union acts are needed, those acts shall confer

---

312. [1973] ECR 125.
313. Case C-188/88 *NMB v Commission* [1992] ECR I-1689.
314. Case 181/73 *Haegeman v Belgium* [1974] ECR 449.
315. [1978] ECR 629.
316. [1970] ECR 1161.

implementing powers on the Commission, or, in duly justified specific cases and in the cases provided for in Articles 24 and 26 of the Treaty on European Union, on the Council".

The ToL therefore establishes a hierarchy of secondary sources of EU law in that a distinction is made between those binding acts which are adopted on the basis of the Treaties, and which are referred to in Article 289 TFEU as legislative acts and those binding acts which are adopted on the basis of secondary acts, i.e. on the basis of legislative acts. These non-legislative acts are either delegated or implementing acts.

It is to be noted that there is a difference between a delegated act and an implementing act in that:

▪ Separate Treaties provisions are applicable to each of them and each has its own definition on the basis of which it is clear that they are mutually exclusive, i.e. the same act cannot be at the same time a delegated and an implementing act.

▪ The scope of each act is different. With regard to a delegated act it is of general application to supplement or amend certain non-essential elements of a legislative act. As to an implementing act its adoption is required because there is a need for uniform conditions for the implementation of a legally binding act.

▪ Different powers are exercised by the Commission when it adopts a delegated act and when it adopts an implementing act. The delegation of powers is always discretionary and the institution which has delegated its powers can always revoke the delegation. The Commission, when exercising its delegated powers is allowed not only to amend a legislative act but also "supplement" it. This clearly involves the exercise of "quasi legislative" powers by the Commission. As to an implementing act it is purely executive. Normally, Member States are required to implement legally binding acts of the EU but in the circumstances described in Article 291(2) TFEU, i.e. "where uniform conditions for implementing legally binding Union acts are needed, those acts shall confer implementing powers on the Commission", the Commission is required to act, i.e. its intervention is compulsory.

▪ Under Article 291 TFEU implementing acts may be either of individual or general scope of application depending upon the circumstances. This is not the case of delegated acts which are always of a general scope and thus the Commission is not allowed to adopt a delegated act relating to a measure of an individual nature.

▪ In respect of delegated acts, the exercise of the delegated power by the Commission is controlled by the legislator, i.e. the EU institution which has adopted the basic legislative act which is to be amended or supplemented by the Commission. The legislator can revoke the delegation or oppose the entry into force of the delegated act. So far as implementing acts are concerned, the power of control is exercised by the Member States.

In order to distinguish implementing acts from legislative acts and delegated acts, the word "implementing" must be inserted in the title of implementing acts and the word "delegated" in the title of delegated acts. Whether the distinction in the title of the act will be sufficient to avoid confusion so far as EU citizens are concerned remains to be seen. The use of the same nomenclature, i.e. regulations, directives and decision for acts which can be of a legislative or non legislative nature and in respect of implementing and delegated acts, challenges the principle of transparency. However, it also can be said that the introduction of different nomenclature for different acts would make the system of secondary acts of the EU very complex.

8.5.1 Legislative acts

Article 289 TFEU specifies that legislative acts are those which are adopted by the ordinary or special legislative procedure. Article 289(4) TFEU, however, provides an important clarification. Some acts which are adopted on the basis of the Treaties in accordance with special rules provided for in the Treaties are to be regarded as legislative acts despite the fact that they have not been adopted in accordance with the ordinary or special legislative procedures.

8.5.2 Delegated acts – Comitology

Prior to the entry into force of the ToL, by virtue of Article 202 EC [replaced in substance by Article 16(1) TEU and Articles 290 and 291 TFEU] the Council was empowered "to confer on the Commission . . . powers for the implementation of the rules which the Council lays down. . .". Accordingly, the Commission possesses delegated powers, which in practice means that while the Council adopts a framework act (usually a regulation), for example in relation to CAP, the Commission is in charge of the details and, for example, must fix the quotas, determine the price, and so on, through regulations or decisions.

The above delegated implementing power exists in respect of a wide range of policies such as EMU, the common market, social policy, asylum policy, CAP and CFP. The Commission must act within the limits of the authority delegated by the Council. The ECJ has given a broad interpretation to such delegated implementation powers by recognising the wide discretion of the Commission, including the ability to impose sanctions and to authorise derogations.[317]

In order to ensure that the Commission exercises implementing powers in accordance with the Council's instructions, a system of procedural mechanisms, the so called "comitology", has been established by the Member States. This first appeared as a necessary safeguard to the introduction of the CAP in 1962. At that time it was considered politically unacceptable that the Commission alone should implement delegated legislation. A supervision committee was set up comprising national civil servants and presided over by a non-voting Commission representative. With time, the system flourished and was extended to many areas. It was recognised by the SEA in Article 202 EC and legitimised by the ECJ in Case 25/70 *Köster*.[318] Comitology has become one of the hallmarks of EU administration.

Under the comitology system, the Commission is required to consult the relevant committee before adopting implementing measures. If the relevant committee disagrees with the Commission, an implementing measure is referred back to the Council for review.

Comitology has three main justifications:

- It has eased the workload of the Council. Had the Council been required to deal with the technical details of all its numerous legislative acts and subsequent modifications of those acts, it would have been engulfed and incapable of exercising its substantial and vital tasks;

- The Council has retained the opportunity to supervise the manner in which the delegated powers are exercised by the Commission. This has been achieved by the fact that the Commission has to consult the relevant committee before adopting an implementing measure. In

---

317. Case 41/69 *Chemiefarma* [1970] ECR 661 note 8; Case 57/72 *Westzucker* [1973] ECR 321; Case 230/78 *Eridania* [1979] ECR 2749; Joined Cases C-296/93 and C-307/93 *France and Ireland v Commission* [1996] ECR I-795.
318. [1970] ECR 1161.

the case of rejection of such a measure by the committee, the proposal is sent back to the Council;

▪ Member States have been given an opportunity to directly participate in the implementation of acts of the Council. This, on the one hand, enhances the democratic nature of the EU and, on the other, ensures that national interests are protected and duly taken account of when the Commission adopts implementing measures. In this respect, it is important to note that often technical details have great impact on the relevant sector of the national economy and by allowing a Member State to have its say on the matter confidence in the implementation process is enhanced.

The main criticisms of comitology before the adoption of Council Decision 1999/468[319] (see below) were:

▪ Lack of transparency. Prior to that 1999 Decision, basic information on committees was unavailable even to other EU institutions. No list of committees existed, nor were names of participants or details of their functions available;

▪ Complexity. The number of committees was growing pathologically and their choice of procedure was not on any predetermined basis;

▪ Most importantly, the EP had no supervisory powers over committees. Once the EP acquired important legislative powers, in particular under the Treaty of Maastricht, it argued that the system needed to be open at least to its scrutiny.

The necessity to rationalise comitology, and to respond to the EP's demand to be involved in the scrutiny of implementing legislation, prompted the Council to establish principles and rules governing comitology. Council Decision 1999/468[320] reduced the number of committee procedures to three – advisory, management and regulation – set out criteria which should be used to determine which of these procedures should apply in a particular case, set out rules of procedure for the committees and gave the EP certain rights to information and scrutiny. However, the EP remained dissatisfied, as under the 1999 Decision it had no power to oppose or influence the adoption of implementing measures. Pressure from the EP led to the adoption of Decision 2006/512/EC,[321] which amended the 1999 Decision and which addressed the main grievances of the EP. A new regulatory procedure "with scrutiny" was added to the three existing procedures under which the EP has not only the power of scrutiny but also the right to veto. The procedure is still complex and time-consuming and its further reform has been provided for in the ToL.

The ToL introduced Article 290 TFEU to deal with the exercise of delegated powers of the Commission. At the time of writing the Commission has submitted a proposal[322] to reform comitology in accordance with the requirements set out in Article 290 TFEU. Those requirements are:

▪ The act which expressly provides for the exercise of delegated powers by the Commission must be of general application;

---

319.   [1999] OJ L 184/23.
320.   Ibid.
321.   [2006] OJ L200/11.
322.   COM(2010)83 final.

- The Commission is allowed to amend or supplement certain non-essential elements of a legislative act. Article 290(1) TFEU states that essential elements of the legislative acts can never be subject to delegation;

- The EU institution which delegates its power to the Commission must define the objective, content, scope and duration of the delegation of power. As a result, the delegation must be clear, precise and detailed. Although Article 290 TFEU does not specify any time limit as to the duration of the delegation the possibility of revocation of the delegation entails that when the Commission is not acting appropriately the delegating institution may put an end to the powers it has delegated to the Commission;

- Article 290(2) TFEU specifies two methods of control that the delegating institution may use: first it may revoke the delegation and second it may oppose the entry into force of the delegated act. The right to revoke is an extreme measure and will rarely be exercised. The most likely situation is when new circumstances undermine the basis of the delegation of power. The second method of scrutiny of delegated acts takes place once the delegated act is notified to the legislator, i.e. the EP and the Council if the basic legislative act was adopted in accordance with the ordinary procedure. Article 290(2)(b) TFEU states that the delegated act may enter into force only if no objection has been made by the EP or the Council within a period set by the legislative act. The consequence of an objection is that the delegated act will not enter into force. This entails that the Commission may adopt a new act, amend the existing act, submit a proposal for a new legislative act, or do nothing. In order to revoke an act or to oppose its entry into force the EP must act by a majority of its component members and the Council by QMV.

8.5.3 Implementing acts

Implementing acts are purely executive acts. Article 291(2) TFEU specifies that the Commission or, in special circumstances, the Council may exercise implementing powers only when the basic legislative act so provides and only "where uniform conditions for implementing legally binding Union acts are needed". The power of control of the manner in which the Commission exercises the implementing power is granted to Member States. Article 291(3) TFEU states that the EP and the Council, acting by means of regulations in accordance with the ordinary legislative procedure, will establish the rules, principles and mechanisms which will allow the Member States to control the exercise by the Commission of implementing powers.

8.5.4 Classification of secondary sources

The ECJ confirmed that the classification of a particular act, that is, whether it should be considered as a regulation, directive or decision, depends upon its content, not its nomenclature, and it has often reclassified an act.[323]

The choice of a particular form – regulation, directive or decision – for a specific act is determined by reference to a provision of the Treaties which constitutes its legal basis. In Case 20/

---

323. Joined Cases 16/62 and 17/62 *Confédération Nationale des Producteurs de Fruits* [1962] ECR 471, Case 25/62 *Plaumann* [1963] ECR 95.

59 *Italy v High Authority*,[324] the ECJ held that if the form is expressly provided in a provision of the Treaty, the competent authority has no choice but to enact it accordingly. The question whether a less prescriptive measure can be adopted than that required by a particular provision (for example, instead of adopting a regulation the Council adopts a directive even though a particular provision provides for the former) must be answered in the negative. If there is no indication as to what kind of measure should be adopted, or a particular provision leaves the choice open,[325] the EU institution invested with power to adopt the measure must decide which one is the most appropriate to achieve the objective prescribed by the provision in question[326] and act in accordance with the principle of proportionality.[327] This choice is, nevertheless, subject to judicial review by the ECJ under Article 263 TFEU (see Chapter 16).

8.5.5 Formal and substantive requirements for the adoption of secondary acts

Some formal and substantive requirements must be satisfied for a measure to be legally binding.

8.5.5.1 *Formal requirements*

Formal requirements with regard to legislative acts refer to the authority in the Treaties permitting adoption of a measure, and the manner in which it should be notified to addressees. As to non-legislative acts, implementing acts and delegated acts these must refer to the legislative acts on the basis of which they have been adopted.

8.5.5.1.1 Statement of reason/s

Article 296 TFEU provides that measures must "state the reasons on which they are based and shall refer to any proposals, initiatives, recommendations, requests or opinions required by the Treaties".

The objective of this requirement was explained by the ECJ in Case 24/62 *Germany v Commission*[328] as permitting:

■ The parties concerned by any particular measure to defend their rights;

■ The CJEU to exercise its supervisory functions; and

■ All Member States and all EU nationals to ascertain the circumstances in which the EU institutions apply the provisions of the Treaties.

Every measure must indicate the detailed reasons for its enactment.[329] These must be clear and unequivocal,[330] taking into account the context and the other rules applicable to the subject-

---

324. [1960] ECR 325.
325. For example, Article 103 TFEU or Article 46 TFEU, which provide for regulations or directives, or refer only to "measures" in general as in Article 77 TFEU.
326. Joined Cases 8–11/66 *Cimenteries* [1967] ECR 75.
327. Article 296(1) TFEU.
328. [1963] ECR 63.
329. For example, Case C-27/90 *SITPA v Oniflhor* [1991] ECR I-133; Case C-69/89 *Nakajima All Precision Co. Ltd v Council* [1991] ECR I-2069; Case C-353/92 *Greece v Council* [1994] ECR I-3411.
330. Case 1/69 *Italy v Commission* [1969] ECR 277.

matter. They must also be precise if the adoption of a measure is subject to the assessment of an economic situation by an EU institution.[331]

A less detailed statement of reasons is accepted if the applicant who wishes to challenge the validity of a measure under Article 263 TFEU has contributed to, or participated in, the procedure leading to the adoption of that measure,[332] or if the measure derives from a constant practice of EU institutions,[333] but any change in that practice requires more detailed explanations as to its legal basis and the objectives which the measure aims to achieve.

The CJEU is entitled to raise, of its own motion, the absence of or insufficiency of "reasons for enactment" of EU acts challenged before it.[334] Such absence or insufficiency may result in the annulment of a measure by the CJEU.

8.5.5.1.2 Legal basis

The choice of a legal basis for non-legislative acts poses no problem as they must be based on a relevant legislative act. However, in respect of legislative measures the determination of their legal basis is not easy, especially in the context of the involvement of the EP in the legislative procedures of the EU. There are, however, three main principles which assist the relevant institutions in choosing the appropriate legal basis for a legislative act. These are:

- The choice must be based on objective criteria which are amenable to judicial review by the CJEU, including in particular the aim and the content of the act.[335] This ensures legal certainty;

- If a EU measure pursues a twofold purpose or has a twofold component and if one of these is identifiable as the main or predominant purpose or component, whereas the other is merely incidental, the act must be based on a single legal basis, namely that required by the main or predominant purpose or component.[336] This is referred to as the theory of "principal and accessory";

- Exceptionally, if a EU measure simultaneously pursues several objectives which are inseparably linked and are of equal importance, that is, without one being secondary and indirect in relation to the other, the measure may be based on several legal bases.[337]

The application of the above principles is illustrated by Joined Cases C-164/97 and C-165/97 *EP v Council*.[338]

---

331. Case 24/62 *Germany v Commission* [1963] ECR 143.
332. Case 13/72 *The Netherlands v Commission* [1973] ECR 27; Case 1252/79 *SpA Acciaierie e Ferriere Lucchini v Commission* [1980] ECR 3753.
333. Case 73/74 *Groupement des Fabricants de Papiers Peints de Belgique and Others v Commission* [1975] ECR 1491; Case 102/87 *France v Commission* [1988] ECR 4067.
334. Case T-471/93 *Tiercé Ladbroke SA v Commission* [1995] ECR II-2537.
335. Case C-269/97 *Commission v Council* [2000] ECR I-2257; Case C-300/89 *Commission v Council* ('*Titanium dioxide*') [1991] ECR I-2867; Case C-336/00 *Huber* [2002] ECR I-7699; Case C-176/03 *Commission v Council* [2005] ECR I-7879.
336. Case C-42/97 *Parliament v Council* [1999] ECR I-869; Case T-99/05 *Spain v Commission* [judgment of 10/05/07] nyr. However, the relevant case can be found on the official website of the Community Courts: http://www.curia.europa.eu/en/transitpage.htm.
337. Case C-336/00 *Huber* [2002] ECR I-7699; Case C-281/01 *Commission v Council* [2002] ECR I-2049; *Opinion 2/00 [Re Cartegena Protocol]* [2001] ECR 1-9713; Case C-178/03 *Commission v EP and Council* [2006] ECR I-107.
338. [1999] ECR I-1139.

THE FACTS WERE:

The EP brought proceedings against the Council for annulment of Regulations 307/97 and 308/97 concerning the protection of forests against pollution and fire. The EP argued that both Regulations were adopted on an inappropriate legal basis, that is, Article 37 EC [amended by Article 43 TFEU under which the ordinary legislative procedure applies] instead of Article 175 EC [amended by Article 192 TFEU which provides for the ordinary legislative procedure to be used]. Consequently, the EP's prerogatives in respect of the procedure involving its participation in the drafting of legislation were undermined. The adoption on the basis of Article 37 EC meant that the EP was merely consulted, while Article 175 EC provided for the use of the co-operation procedure defined by Article 252 EC [this procedure was abolished by the ToL].

Held:

The ECJ annulled both Regulations. The Court confirmed that the choice of legal basis for a measure must be based on objective factors which are amenable to judicial review, taking into account, in particular, the aim and content of the measure. The ECJ stated that when the aims of contested regulations are partly agricultural and partly of a specifically environmental nature then, in order to determine the appropriate legal basis, the Council has to apply the theory of the "principal and accessory"[339] unless the measure is intended to pursue both objectives, in which case the measure must be based on the two legal bases.[340] However, the adoption of measures on two legal bases is precluded if those two legal bases are incompatible.[341]

The ECJ decided that the main objective of both regulations was the protection of forests intended to ensure that the natural heritage represented by forest ecosystems is conserved. Although the measures referred to in the regulations may have certain positive repercussions on the functioning of agriculture, those consequences were incidental to the primary aim of the Community schemes for the protection of forests. For that reason the regulations should have been adopted on the basis of Article 175 EC [Article 192 TFEU] instead of Article 37 EC [Article 43 TFEU].

In the context of the establishment of the internal market Article 95(1) EC [Article 114 TFEU] served as a legal basis for numerous EC measures. This provision was rather vague as it stated that the Council, after consulting the EP and acting by QMV, may adopt measures having as their object the improvement of the conditions for the establishment and functioning of the internal market. Not surprisingly, Member States have often considered that the choice of Article 95(1) EC as a legal basis for a particular measure was inappropriate

In 2002, the ECJ elucidated the meaning of Article 95(1) EC [Article 114 TFEU]. It held that

---

339. Case 70/88 *EP v Council* [1991] ECR I-4529.
340. See Case C-360/93 *EP v Council* [1966] ECR I-1195.
341. Case C-300/89 *Commission v Council* [1991] ECR I-2867.

this article is not a "catch-all-provision" allowing the Council to legislate as it wishes.[342] A measure adopted on the basis of Article 95 EC [Article 114 TFEU] "must genuinely have as its object the improvement of the conditions for the establishment and functioning of the internal market". Article 95(1) EC [114 TFEU] does not confer general legislative powers on EU institutions but a specific power to adopt measures intended to improve the functioning of the internal market. Consequently, the choice of Article 95 EC [114 TFEU] cannot be justified by the fact that there is a mere finding of disparity between national rules, nor by the fact that there is an abstract risk of obstacles to the freedom of movement, nor by the fact that there is a risk of distortion of competition.[343] Otherwise a judicial review of compliance with the requirement of EU law for a proper legal basis might be rendered nugatory. The ECJ emphasised that Article 95(1) EC [Article 114 TFEU] can only be used as a legal basis to prevent future obstacles to trade resulting from disparity of national laws, and the emergence of such obstacles must be likely.[344]

Under the TFEU, further clarifications are provided in that:

■ Article 114(2) TFEU excludes from the scope of Article 114 TFEU measures relating to fiscal provisions, the free movement of persons and the rights and interests of employed persons;

■ Article 114(1) TFEU states that the ordinary legislative procedure is to be used for the adoption of measures which have as their object the establishment and functioning of the internal market and that the EP and the Council must consult the EESC. Consequently, an abuse of Article 114 TFEU is less likely to occur under the TFEU than was the case under the EC Treaty given the involvement of the EP and the EESC in the adoption of measures under Article 114 TFEU.

8.5.5.1.3 Publication of a measure

In Case 98/78 *A. Racke v Hauptzollamt Mainz*,[345] the ECJ held that the fundamental principles of the Community legal order require that an act emanating from public authorities cannot produce legal effect unless it comes to the knowledge of its addressees.

Depending upon the form of a measure, it must be either published in the Official Journal of the European Union or notified to its addressee.[346] Article 297 TFEU provides that all legislative acts must be published in the OJ whilst non-legislative acts adopted in the form of a regulation, a directive or a decision are to be published in the OJ if:

■ They take the form of regulations or directives addressed to all Member States; or

■ They take the form of decisions which do not specify to whom they are addressed.

The OJ constitutes an important source of information on all aspects of EU activities, including

---

342. Case C-491/01 *The Queen and Secretary of State for Health, ex parte: British American Tobacco (Investments) Ltd and Others* [2002] ECR I-11453.
343. Case C-376/98 *Germany v EP and Council* [2000] ECR I-8419.
344. Case C-350/92 *Spain v Council* [1995] ECR I-1985; Case C-377/98 *The Netherlands v EP and Council* [2001] ECR I-7079; Joined Cases C-434/02 *Arnold André GmbH* [2004] ECR I-11825 and C-210/03 *Swedish Match* [2004] ECR I-11893; Case C-380/03 *Germany v EP and Council* [2006] ECR I-11573.
345. [1979] ECR 69.
346. Case 185/73 *Hauptzollamt Bielefield* [1974] ECR 607.

EU legislation. It is published on most weekdays, simultaneously in all official languages; each version has the same pagination.

- Under the 'L' series legislation, treaties, the budget and all binding acts are published;

- The 'C' series comprises miscellaneous information and notices such as draft legislation prepared by the Commission, common positions adopted by the Council and minutes of the plenary sessions of the EP;

- The 'S' series is devoted to the specialised use of firms competing for public contracts;

- An annex to the OJ contains the reports of debates of the EP.

Under Article 297 TFEU measures not required to be published in the OJ must be notified to their addressees:

- To natural or legal persons residing within the EU, by registered letter or delivery with acknowledgment;[347]

- To natural or legal persons residing outside the EU, through diplomatic channels, that is, ambassadors accredited to the EU institutions;

- To Member States, through their permanent representatives in Brussels.

8.5.5.1.4   Date of entry into force of a measure

The date of entry into force of a particular measure may be specified in the measure itself. If a measure is notified, it enters into force on the day of its notification, unless otherwise provided for in the measure; and if published, and in the absence of any specification, it is deemed by virtue of Article 297 TFEU to become operative 20 days after its publication. This applies to both legislative and non-legislative acts.

The ECJ held in Case 98/78 *Racke*[348] that the day of publication does not mean the day on which the OJ is available in the territory of each Member State but the day when it is available at the seat of the Office for Official Publications of the EU at Luxembourg. Unless proved to the contrary, this is, for evidential purposes, taken to be the day the OJ containing the text of the act in question was published.

In relation to an act which requires publication, a specific date is usually fixed for its entry into force. This is done to avoid the risk of its immediate entry into force, without any transition period, undermining the principles of legal certainty and legitimate expectation.[349] In Case 17/67 *Firma Max Neumann v Hauptzollamt Hof/Saale*[350], the ECJ held that only in a case of extreme necessity may an act enter into force immediately, that is, on the day of its publication in the OJ. The institutions concerned must have serious reasons to believe that delay between the date of the publication of an act and its entry into force would cause prejudice to the EU, and that its immediate entry into force is necessary to prevent speculation or a legal void.

---

347. Decision 22/60 of the High Authority of 7/09/1960, [1960] OJ B/1248.
348. [1979] ECR 69.
349. Case 74/74 CNTA [1975] ECR 533.
350. [1967] ECR 441.

8.5.5.2   Substantive requirements

In respect of substantive requirements, the ECJ rejected the retroactive application of secondary legislation, apart from in exceptional cases when the objective to be achieved by a measure requires this. In such cases the legitimate expectations of the persons concerned by that measure must be respected.[351]

The ECJ has also confirmed the right of an EU institution to withdraw or to abrogate a measure, but in doing so laid down certain conditions. When a measure creates individual rights, withdrawal is permitted: within a reasonable time (approximately six months); solely for reasons of illegality;[352] and public and private interests must be duly taken into account.[353] When a measure does not afford rights to individuals, it may be withdrawn within a reasonable time (according to the ECJ this seems to be between two and three years).[354]

8.5.6   Regulations

Regulations are the most important form of EU acts. They ensure uniformity of solutions on a specific point of law throughout the EU. They apply erga omnes (in relation to everyone) and simultaneously in all Member States. Article 288 TFEU defines regulations in the following terms:

> "A regulation shall have general application. It shall be binding in its entirety and directly applicable in all Member States."

A regulation is comparable to a statutory law in England. Its main features are discussed below.

8.5.6.1   A regulation has general application

The ECJ in Case 101/76 *Koninklijke Scholten Honing v Council and Commission*[355] explained this feature of a regulation by stating that it applies "to objectively determine situations and produces legal effects with regard to persons described in a generalised and abstract manner". Regulations are expressed in general, abstract terms, and the mere fact that it is possible to determine the number, or even identity, of the persons affected by a measure does not call into question its nature as a regulation, provided that the class of those potentially within its scope of application is not closed at the time of its adoption.[356]

---

351.   Case 98/78 *Racke* [1979] ECR 69; Case 14/81 *Alpha Steel Ltd. v Commission* [1982] ECR 749; Case C-248/89 *Cargill v Commission* [1991] ECR I-2987 and Case C-365/89 *Cargill* [1991] ECR I-3045.
352.   Joined Cases T-79, 84–86, 91–92, 94, 96, 98, 102 and 104/89 *BASF* [1992] ECR II-315.
353.   Joined Cases 42 and 49/59 *SNUPAT* [1961] ECR 53; Joined Cases 53 and 54/63 *Lemmerz-Werke* [1963] ECR 239; Case 15/85 *Consorzio Cooperative d'Abruzzo* [1987] ECR 1005.
354.   Case 14/61 *Koninklijke* [1962] ECR 253.
355.   [1977] ECR 797.
356.   Case 231/82 *Spijker Kwasten* [1983] ECR 2559.

8.5.6.2 A regulation is binding in its entirety

This means that its incomplete[357] or selective[358] implementation is prohibited under EU law. Also, its modification or adjunction, or the introduction of any national legislation capable of affecting its content or scope of application, is contrary to EU law.[359]

The above well-established principles acquire a special importance in the case of an incomplete regulation. EU regulations are incomplete if they require Member States to adopt necessary measures to ensure their full application. Sometimes this requirement is expressly stated in a regulation itself, as for example the obligation to adopt laws, regulations or administrative provisions in order to ensure its efficient application.[360] Sometimes a reference is made to Article 4(3) TEU which provides that Member States shall take all necessary measures to fulfil their obligations arising from the Treaties. National measures are subordinated to the provisions contained in a regulation and must neither alter them nor hinder their uniform application throughout the EU.[361]

In circumstances described in Article 291 TFEU, the Commission is required to adopt implementing measures.

8.5.6.3 Regulations are directly applicable in all Member States

This means that they become part of the national law of the Member States at the date of their entry into force. Their implementation into national law is not only unnecessary but, more importantly, prohibited by EU law,[362] except in so far as implementation may be required by an incomplete regulation.

The direct effect of regulations is examined in Chapter 12.3.

8.5.7 Directives

Directives are defined in Article 288 TFEU in the following terms:

> "A directive shall be binding, as to the result to be achieved, upon each Member State to which it is addressed, but shall leave to the national authorities the choice of form and methods."

Directives are used to harmonise national legislation, regulations and administrative provisions. Unlike regulations, they require co-operation between the EU and the Member States. They respect the autonomy of national institutional and procedural systems while imposing upon the Member States the obligation of achieving a necessary result and thus directives establish the same legal regime in all Member States with regard to the relevant legal matter. A directive was once described as being able to "intrigue, derange, devise, all this is due to its peculiarity".[363]

There are three main features of directives.

---

357. Case 39/72 *Commission v Italy* [1973] ECR 101.
358. Case 18/72 *NV Granaria* [1972] ECR 1163.
359. Case 40/69 *Hauptzollamt Hamburg-Oberelbe v Firma Paul G. Bollmann* [1970] ECR 69.
360. Case C-52/95 *Commission v France* [1995] ECR I-4443; Case 128/78 *Commission v United Kingdom [Re Tachographs]* [1979] ECR 419.
361. Case C-290/91 *Johannes Peter v Hauptzollamt Regensburg* [1993] ECR I-2981.
362. Case 39/72 *Commission v Italy* [1973] ECR 101.
363. R. Kovar, "Observations sur l'intensité normative des directives", in F. Capotorti, C. D. Ehlermann *et al.* (eds), *Du droit international au droit de l'intégration. Liber Amicorum Pierre Pescatore*, 1987, Baden-Baden: Nomos, p 359.

8.5.7.1   Unlike regulations, directives have no general application

Directives are binding only on their addressees, that is, a particular Member State, or some Member States, or all of them. However, they have general scope of application when they are addressed to all Member States. In Case 70/83 *Gerda Kloppenburg v Finanzamt Leer*,[364] the ECJ classified EC directives addressed to all Member States as acts having general application. In such a situation, they require that a certain result must be obtained throughout the EU within a specific time limit.

8.5.7.2   Article 4(3) TFEU imposes on an addressee Member State an obligation to achieve the objective of a directive but leaves the choice of measures, procedures, methods, and so on, necessary to achieve that result to its discretion

In order to achieve the prescribed result directives are often very precise and detailed. For that reason, directives often leave little or no choice as to their implementation. Accordingly, in many cases, directives must be implemented into national law as they stand.

In Case 38/77 *Enka*,[365] the ECJ held that it follows from Article 249 EC [Article 288 TFEU] that discretion left to the Member States as to the choice of form and methods is subject to the result that the Council or the Commission intended to obtain. Thus, if necessary, an addressee Member State may be left without any margin of discretion as to the manner of implementation of a directive.[366]

The essential objective of directives is to achieve the prescribed result. This means that the national law of the Member State must be in conformity with the prescribed results once the time limit for the implementation of a directive expires. For that reason sometimes no changes are necessary at the national level, if under national law the prescribed result has already been achieved. Nevertheless, in the majority of cases an addressee Member State has to implement a directive into national law. The ECJ held that it is not necessary to copy the text of a directive into a national text. This seems, however, to be the best way to avoid any disputes.[367] Partial or selective implementation of a directive is contrary to EU law. Also, its implementation cannot be limited to a certain territory of a Member State. In Case C-157/89 *Commission v Italy*,[368] the ECJ held that a Member State cannot invoke the autonomy of some of its regions in order to avoid implementation of some provisions of a directive.

The choice of methods and forms of implementation of directives has been restricted by the ECJ. The Court held that they must ensure legal certainty and transparency.[369] In Case 102/79

---

364. [1984] ECR 1075.

365. [1977] ECR 2203.

366. This position has been confirmed in other cases: Case 102/79 *Commission v Belgium* [1980] ECR 1473; Case 150/88 *Kommanditgesellschaft in Firma Eau de Cologne & Parfümerie-Fabrik, Glockengasse n. 4711 v Provide Srl* [1989] ECR 3891; Case C-29/90 *Commission v Greece* [1992] ECR 1971.

367. Case 252/85 *Commission v France* [1988] ECR 2243; Case C-360/87 *Commission v Italy* [1991] ECR I-791; Case C-190/90 *Commission v The Netherlands* [1992] ECR I-3265; Case C-217/97 *Commission v Germany* [1999] ECR I-5087.

368. [1991] ECR I-57, also Case C-33/90 *Commission v Italy* [1991] ECR I-5987.

369. Case C-131/88 *Commission v Germany* [1991] ECR I-825; Case C-58/89 *Commission v Germany* [1991] ECR I-4983.

Commission v Belgium,[370] the ECJ held that a simple administrative practice, or an internal circular, is not sufficient to ensure legal certainty,[371] since such methods are easily modified by national administrations and lack adequate publicity.

In the UK EU directives are usually implemented by statutory instruments under the 1973 European Community Act but sometimes by an Act of Parliament.

8.5.7.3 *It is clear from the wording of Article 288 TFEU that an addressee Member State is responsible for the implementation of directives into national law*

Usually directives provide for a specific time limit within which they must be brought into effect in the territories of the Member States. It is very important to note that directives enter into force at the date specified by them, or if no date is specified, then 20 days after publication, but they produce their full legal effect after the expiry of a fixed time limit which varies depending upon the subject-matter of the directive. In most cases the time limit is no more than two years.

Before the expiry of the time limit some obligations may arise for a Member State (see Chapter 11.4), but not for individuals, as the ECJ held in Case 80/86 *Criminal proceedings against Kolpinghuis Nijmegen BV*.[372] However, once the time limit has expired, the situation changes dramatically.[373] In Case 270/81 *Felicitas*,[374] the ECJ held that the general principle is that in all cases when a directive is correctly implemented into national law, it produces legal effects with regards to individuals through the implementing measures adopted by the Member State concerned. An individual is entitled to base a claim upon a directive despite the directive having been incompletely or incorrectly implemented by a Member State. It is important to note that directives do not have horizontal direct effect (but see exceptions in Chapter 12.4.1.5) Non-implementation of a directive within a prescribed time limit produces the following results:

- It becomes directly applicable upon the expiry of the time limit;[375]

- If its provisions are directly effective, an individual may rely on them in proceedings before a national court upon the expiry of the time limit;

- The Commission may bring an action under Article 258 TFEU against the Member State concerned for breach of EU law.[376] It is to be noted that the Commission may also bring proceedings when, during the transposition period, a Member State has adopted national measures liable seriously to compromise the result prescribed by the directive;[377]

- An individual may, upon the expiry of the time limit, sue a defaulting Member State for damages, provided certain conditions are satisfied[378] (see Chapter 14).

It is important to note that all directives, in their final provisions, impose on the Member State

---

370. [1980] ECR 1473; see also Case C-360/88 *Commission v Belgium* [1989] ECR 3803.
371. Case C-58/89 *Commission v Germany* [1991] ECR I-4983.
372. [1987] ECR 3969.
373. On direct applicability and direct effect of directives see Chapters 11 and 12.
374. [1982] ECR 2771.
375. Case 148/78 *Ratti* [1979] ECR 1629.
376. See Chapter 15.
377. Case C-422/05 *Commission v Belgium* [2007] ECR I-4749.
378. Joined Cases C-6/90 and C-9/90 *Andrea Francovich and Danila Bonifaci and Others v Italy* [1991] ECR I-5357.

concerned an obligation to provide a list of measures which have been taken in order to implement them. This facilitates the task of the Commission regarding the determination of conformity of national law with EU law in the area covered by the relevant directive. When a Member State does not notify the Commission, or provides an incomplete notification, it is in breach of Article 4(3) TEU even if it has taken all necessary measures, and the Commission is empowered to bring an action before the ECJ[379] by virtue of Article 258 TFEU.

8.5.8 Decisions

Decisions have no general scope of application unless addressed to all Member States. They may be addressed to a particular Member State, or to any legal or natural person or they may have no addressees. The effect of a decision is specified in Article 288 TFEU, which states that:

> "A decision shall be binding in its entirety. A decision which specifies those to whom it is addressed shall be binding only on them."

This definition covers both decisions which are addressed to specified parties and decisions which have no particular addressees. With regard to decisions specifying their addressee the ECJ in Case 54/65 *Compagnie des Forges de Châtillon, Commentry & Neuves-Maisons v High Authority*[380] described it as:

> "A measure emanating from the competent authority, intended to produce legal effects and constituting the culmination of procedure within that authority, whereby the latter gives its final ruling in a form from which its nature can be identified."

Decisions which are addressed to particular persons are similar to administrative acts issued by national authorities. In most cases, decisions are issued by the Commission in competition matters, or by the Council if a Member State fails to fulfil EU obligations.

Decisions which have addressees are binding in their entirety, which means that they may prescribe not only a particular result to be achieved but also the form and methods necessary to achieve it. This distinguishes them from directives, which are merely binding as to the result to be achieved. A decision may be very detailed.

Decisions are directly effective vis-à-vis their addressees only; but in certain cases, that is, if a person (natural or legal) proves that he/she/it has locus standi under Article 263 TFEU, that person may bring annulment proceedings under Article 230 EC as well as claim damages under Article 340(2) TFEU.[381]

Decisions which are not addressed to any particular addressee are, for example, decisions adopted in the framework of trade policy, e.g. for the adoption of an action programme. Further under the CFSP decisions are the main binding measures adopted by the European Council and the Council. There are three main types of decisions under the CFSP, decisions on the strategic interests and objectives of the Union, decisions defining a Union action and decisions defining a Union position (see Chapter 5).

---

379. See Chapter 15.
380. [1966] ECR 185.
381. See Chapter 16.

8.5.9   Non-binding acts: recommendations and opinions

Article 288 TFEU expressly provides that recommendations and opinions have no binding force. Although they are not sources of EC law, their importance should not be underestimated, in particular in respect of recommendations adopted by the Council or the Commission which invite Member States to adopt a specific line of conduct.

Recommendations and opinions are adopted in areas in which the EU has no legislative powers, or when a transitional period is necessary in order to achieve a certain stage at which the EU institutions would be empowered to adopt binding measures. A recommendation is often an instrument of indirect action of EU institutions intended to prepare the next stage of development in a particular area. In Case 322/88 *Grimaldi*,[382] the ECJ held that recommendations are not devoid of all legal effect. National judges are obliged to take them into consideration in the interpretation of EU law.

In opinions, EU institutions express their views on a given question.

8.5.10   Ranking of secondary sources in the hierarchy of sources of EU law

Secondary sources of EU law are, in the hierarchy of sources, classified after primary sources, general principles of EU law, and international agreements concluded between the EU and third states or international organisations.

8.6   EU acts not expressly mentioned in Article 288 TFEU

There are sources of EU law, not mentioned in Article 288 TFEU, which are strictly speaking not secondary sources but some of which, nevertheless, may produce binding legal effects.[383] In this category two kinds of act can be distinguished. First, acts which are mentioned in the Treaties; and second, acts which are not mentioned in the Treaties.

8.6.1   Acts which are mentioned in the Treaties

The Treaties expressly mention the following acts:

- Those which despite their name, are of different legal nature from those listed in Article 288 TFEU, e.g. directives adopted by the Council on the basis of Article 218(2) TFEU, which are addressed to the Commission or to the HR to give instructions in connection with negotiating international agreements to be concluded between the EU and third countries or between the EU and international organisations;

- Interinstitutional agreements. Under Article 295 TFEU the EP, the Council and the Commission are allowed to make arrangements for co-operation with each other, in particular by concluding interinstitutional agreements which may be of a binding nature;

- General guidelines adopted by the European Council for the CFSP. These are referred to in Article 25(a) TEU;

---

382.   [1989] ECR 4407.
383.   See European Parliament, Report Kirk-Reay, Doc. 148/78 of 30.5.1978.

- Internal rules of procedure which regulate the composition, functioning and procedures of each EU institution. They are binding on the institution concerned. The rules of procedure of the CJEU are special in that they are binding on both the courts and the parties to the proceedings.

- Recommendations and opinions that one EU institution addresses to another, some of them are binding, some are not.

8.6.2 Acts not mentioned by the Treaties

These are: resolutions, deliberations, conclusions, communications and common declarations of two or more EU institutions adopted by various EU institutions. The EP has expressed its concern as to the increasing number of atypical acts (i.e those which take a form not mentioned in the Treaties) adopted by EU institutions outside the EC Treaty.[384] The ToL responded by, first, simplifying the nomenclature of secondary sources of EU law and second by stating in Article 296(3) TFEU that "When considering draft legislative acts, the European Parliament and the Council shall refrain from adopting acts not provided for by the relevant legislative procedure in the area in question".

In principle acts not mentioned by the Treaties are not legally binding, but the ECJ has, on rare occasions, held that where the institution concerned has expressed its intention to be bound by them, such acts may produce legal effects.[385]

8.7 The contribution of the ECJ to the creation of sources of EU law: interpretation of EU law and the case law of the ECJ

The special position of the ECJ as a law-maker requires some explanation.

The ECJ as an EU institution enjoys a special status given that:

- Until the establishment of the General Court (formerly known as the CFI), the ECJ was the one and only judicial institution in the Community. Its authority is similar to that of national supreme courts, such as the Supreme Court of the United Kingdom, or the Cour de Cassation in France. There in no control over and no appeal against its decisions. The creation of the General Court has not changed the position of the ECJ. However, the latter constitutes an appellate court on points of law from the decisions of the General Court.

- The ECJ's mission is not only to apply the law expressly laid down by, or under, the Treaties but, more importantly, to promote continuous development of EU law, to supplement its provisions, and to fill gaps in the Treaties. Bingham J in *Customs and Excise Commissioners v Samex SpA* has described this as a ". . . creative process of supplying flesh to a sparse and loosely constructed skeleton".[386]

---

384. See Report Burger, EP Doc. Session 215/68–69 of 12.03.1969.
385. E.g. Proceedings of 20 March 1970 in Case 22/70 *Commission v Council [ERTA]* [1971] ECR 263, or in Case C-25/94 *Commission v Council* [1996] ECR I-1469, an arrangement between the Council and the Commission which clearly stated that the two institutions intended to enter into a binding commitment towards each other.
386. [1983] 3 CMLR 194.

8.7.1   Methods of interpretation in EU law

The ECJ, in order to carry out its tasks, relies on a variety of methods of interpretation and a number of interpretive devices. The interpretation of EU law is based on Article 31 of the 1969 Vienna Convention on the Law of Treaties, which provides that interpretation should be based on the ordinary meaning of the terms of a treaty in the context and in the light of its object and purpose. However, the ECJ has given priority to interpretation "in the general context" (the systematic method) "and in the light of its object and purpose" (the teleological method) over the literal interpretation of the Treaties.[387]

In Case 283/81 *Srl CILFIT and Lanificio di Gavardo SpA v Ministry of Health*,[388] the ECJ emphasised the particular difficulties in the interpretation and application of EU law. EU legislation is drafted in several languages and each version is authentic. Thus, the comparison of different versions is sometimes necessary. Furthermore, EU law uses terminology and refers to legal concepts which are peculiar to it. The EU meaning of legal concepts often differs from the meaning under the national laws of the Member States. In *CILFIT* the ECJ summarised the complexity of the interpretation of EU law in the following terms:

> ". . . every provision of the Community law [EU law] must be placed in its context and interpreted in the light of the provisions of Community law [EU law] as a whole, regard being had to the objectives thereof and to its state of evolution at the date on which the provision in question is to be applied."

In addition to the above, the ECJ relies on other methods of interpretation depending upon the case and the degree to which the provision to be interpreted is ambiguous, obscure or imprecise. The most characteristic features of interpretation of EU law by the ECJ are:

- The wide eclecticism of the methods used to interpret EU law combined with the willingness to draw from each of them the maximum effectiveness;

- The consideration given to the originality and autonomy of EU law vis-à-vis international law and national laws of the Member States;

- The consideration given to the need to maintain the coherence of the EU legal system;

- The consideration given to the need to ensure the unity and homogeneity of EU law.

These considerations and methods require and, at the same time, allow the ECJ to become a law-maker. Whether this "judicial legislation" should be criticised or considered as an asset is a different matter.[389] Its use of the concept of effectiveness provides a good example. In public international law the concept of effectiveness is applied by an international judge when confronted with two possible interpretations of a legal provision, one which confers some meaning on it, and the other which renders it devoid of any significance. The judge gives priority to the former. The ECJ not only sets aside the interpretation which renders a provision devoid of its effective-

---

387.   The method used by the ECJ has been described as being "meta-teleological", see M. Lasser, *Judicial Deliberations: A Comparative Analysis of Judicial Transparency and Legitimacy*, 2004, Oxford: Oxford University Press; H. Rasmussen, *On Law and Policy of the European Court of Justice: A Comparative Study in Judicial Policy Making*, 1986, Dordrecht: Martinus Nijhoff; and M. Maduro, *We, the Court*, 1998, Oxford: Hart Publishing.

388.   [1982] ECR 3415.

389.   See R. Lecourt, *L'Europe des Juges*, 1976, Bruxelles, Bruylant; I. Ward, *A Critical Introduction to European Law*, 2nd ed., 2003, London: Butterworths, pp 97–101.

ness, but more importantly rejects any interpretation which results in limiting or weakening the effectiveness of that provision.[390]

In interpreting EU law, the ECJ takes into consideration the evolving nature of the EU and thus interprets EU law in the light of new needs which did not exist at the time of ratification of the founding Treaties.

The ECJ has inferred from EU law the existence of external competences of the EU based on parallel internal competences and the doctrine of EU acquis.

Also, such fundamental principles as supremacy of EU law, direct applicability, direct effect of EU law and a Member State's liability in tort have been established by the ECJ.

None of the fundamental principles mentioned above were contained or provided for in the founding Treaty entered into in 1957 by Belgium, France, Germany, Italy, Luxembourg and The Netherlands, or in the subsequent amendments to that Treaty. They were progressively inferred by the ECJ, and each of them provided an integrationist impetus that appeared, at different times, to be lacking on the part of different Member States.

Resulting from what many perceived to be the ECJ's apparent political activism, it was accused of "running wild" and thus of contravening one of the basic principles of liberal democracy, that is, that of judicial neutrality and independence.[391] Democracy requires that law is created by democratically accountable politicians, not judges. The Court itself made little effort to justify its activism and few seem to have cared that, since its inception, the "Supreme Court" of the new Europe has, in addition to pursuing its primary purpose, been pursuing a virtually political agenda. For some, the Court's activism has been necessary and desirable; for others it has been inexcusable.

It is certainly true, however, that without the ECJ having been active in promoting legal integration through the introduction of the aforementioned fundamental principles, the EU would not be the great power which it is today. In the submission of the author, it is fascinating that whilst the political elite of Europe, during the last half of the twentieth century, failed to develop any unified vision as to how Europe would look at the beginning of the twenty-first century, the judges of the ECJ followed a constant course for 50 years which in many ways has made Europe what it is today.

8.7.2 Precedent in EU law

Under EU law there is no doctrine of precedent. The previous case law of the ECJ is neither binding on the General Court, nor on national courts, nor on itself. The EU legal system follows civil law systems in its approach to precedent. However, there are a number of arguments in favour of the recognition of the binding nature of previous judgments of the ECJ. These are set out below:

- The ECJ, having a major role to play in the development of the EU legal order (which according to its judgment in Case 26/62 *Van Gend & Loos* [392] "constitutes a new legal order of international law"), will depart from its previous case law only in exceptional circumstances, and after considering all legal implications;

- The ECJ has gradually built coherent, stable and consistent case law that can serve as a

---

390. Case C-437/97 *Evangelischer Krankenhausverein Wien v Abgabenberufungskommission Wien and Wein & Co. HandelsgesmbH v Oberösterreichische Landesregierung* [2000] ECR I-1157.
391. I. Ward, *A Critical Introduction to European Law*, 2nd ed., 2003, London: Butterworths, pp 97–101.
392. [1963] ECR 3.

yardstick for other European courts, national courts, litigants and their counsel and the ECJ is unlikely to frustrate their expectations, without mature reflection;

- The principle of legal certainty which requires that law must be reasonably predictable, so that citizens may arrange their affairs in full knowledge of the legal consequences, and the principle of equality, which requires that like situations must be treated in like manner, necessitate that some recognition is given to the binding nature of previous law. Thus previous judgments of the ECJ, which have formulated general propositions about law, are expected to be followed because of the need for legal certainty and equality;

- It can be said that the ECJ judgment in Case 283/81 *Srl CILFIT and Lanificio di Gavardo SpA v Ministry of Health*,[393] in which the Court stated that national courts of final instance are not obliged to refer a question relating to the interpretation of EC law to the ECJ if they consider that, in the light of the previous case law, the answer is obvious, constitutes an implicit recognition of the binding nature of previous decisions of the ECJ;

- By departing from its previous case law, the ECJ would, to some extent, undermine its own authority;

- The ECJ, while delivering a new judgment, makes reference in the text of that judgment to previous relevant cases which raise the same or similar issues;

- The doctrine of precedent is not as rigid as it may appear in that if it seems that a previous case was wrongly decided, the courts will use every effort to distinguish the circumstances of the current case from those of the previous case, so allowing themselves not to follow the previous case. Further, in countries where the doctrine of stare decisis is recognised,[394] supreme courts are allowed to deviate from the existing case law if circumstances so require. In England the House of Lords made a declaration in 1966 stating that its decisions, although binding upon all lower courts, are not binding on itself;

- The acceptance of the binding nature of ECJ judgments may even be acceptable to civil law countries. Although civil law countries have no doctrine of stare decisis, most of them accept the doctrine of jurisprudence constant (consistent case law), according to which a long series of previous decisions applying a particular rule of law carries great weight and may be determinative in subsequent cases.[395]

It is submitted that although the case law of the ECJ is not formally recognised as a source of EU law, its importance should not be underestimated. The ECJ has gradually built a coherent and consistent body of case law but none of it is cast in stone. Accordingly, whilst it is necessary to preserve the integrity of law, it is also necessary, in exceptional circumstances, to change the direction, and to depart from pre-existing rules.

In practice, the ECJ has been very reluctant to depart from its earlier case law. In the first 35 years of its existence the ECJ avoided any express departure from its earlier decisions. It was in Case C-10/89 *CNL SUCAL v HAG GF (HAG II)*[396] that the ECJ, for the first time, overturned its

---

393. [1982] ECR 3415.
394. The legal term *stare decisis et non quieta movere* means "stand by decisions and do not move that which is quiet".
395. See R. Youngs, *English, French and German Comparative Law*, 1998, London: Cavendish, p 50 et seq.
396. [1990] ECR I-3711.

previous judgment delivered 16 years earlier in Case 192/73 *Van Zuylen v HAG (HAG I)*[397] and stated that the previous judgment was wrongly decided. Subsequently, the ECJ has given judgments conflicting with its earlier judgments.[398]

Notwithstanding the above, it can be said that, overall, the ECJ has been able to strike a delicate balance between the need to adapt EU law to the changing objectives of the EU and the need to ensure that its case law is consistent, stable and reasonably certain.

AIDE-MÉMOIRE

HIERARCHY OF SOURCES OF EU LAW

 1st — PRIMARY SOURCES: THE TEU + THE TFEU + PROTOCOLS AND ANNEXES ATTACHED TO THE TREATIES + ACTS OF ACCESSION OF MEMBER STATES + THE CHARTER OF FUNDAMENTAL RIGHTS OF THE EU

 2nd — GENERAL PRINCIPLES OF EU LAW: SO FAR AS THEY ARE NOT ALREADY INCLUDED IN THE PRIMARY SOURCES

 3rd — INTERNATIONAL AGREEMENTS WITH THIRD STATES AND INTERNATIONAL ORGANISATIONS ENTERED INTO BY THE EU

 4th — SECONDARY SOURCES: LEGISLATIVE ACTS: REGULATIONS + DIRECTIVES + DECISIONS
THEY ARE LEGISLATIVE ACTS IF THEY ARE ADOPTED ON THE BASIS OF THE TREATIES IN ACCORDANCE WITH THE ORDINARY LEGISLATIVE PROCEDURE OR SPECIAL LEGISLATIVE PROCEDURES

 5th — SECONDARY SOURCES: NON-LEGISLATIVE ACTS: REGULATIONS + DIRECTIVES + DECISIONS
THEY ARE NON-LEGISLATIVE ACTS IF THEY ARE ADOPTED ON THE BASIS OF LEGISLATIVE ACTS.
THEY ARE OF TWO KINDS: DELEGATED ACTS (ART. 290 (1) TFEU AND IMPLEMENTING ACTS (ART. 290(2) TFEU)

ACTS NOT EXPRESSLY MENTIONED IN ART. 288 TFEU (ATYPICAL ACTS) THEIR RANKING, PROVIDING THEY ARE OF BINDING NATURE, DEPENDS ON THEIR OBJECT AND MATERIAL CONTENT

---

397. [1974] ECR 731,
398. For example: Cases 115 and 116/81 *Adoui and Cornuaille* [1982] ECR 1665 in relation to Case 41/74 *Van Duyn v Home Office* [1974] ECR 1337; Case 34/79 *Henn and Darby* [1979] ECR 3795 in relation to Case 121/85 *Conegate Limited v HM Customs & Excise* [1986] ECR 1007; Case 302/87 *EP v Council (Comitology)* [1988] ECR 5615 in relation to Case C-70/88 *EP v Council (Chernobyl)* [1990] ECR I-2041; see also Joined Cases C-267 and 268/91 *Criminal proceedings against Bernard Keck and Daniel Mithouard* [1993] ECR I-6097 (Chapter 20).

RECOMMENDED READING

Books

Bernitz, U., Nergelius, J. and Cardner, C., *General Principles of EC Law in a Process of Development*, 2008, London: KLI

Everson, M. and Eisner J., *The Making of a European Constitution: Judges and Law Beyond Constitutive Power*, 2007, London: Routledge Cavendish

Lasser, M., *Judicial Deliberations: A Comparative Analysis of Judicial Transparency and Legitimacy*, 2004, Oxford: Oxford University Press

Raitio, J., *The Principle of Legal Certainty in EC Law*, 2003, The Hague: Kluwer Academic Publishers

Senden, L., *Soft Law in European Community Law*, 2004, Oxford: Hart Publishing

Tridimas, T., *The General Principles of EU Law*, 2nd edition, 2007, Oxford: Oxford University Press

Article

Hofmann, H., "Legislation, Delegation and Implementation under the Treaty of Lisbon: Typology Meets Reality" (2009) 15 ELJ, p 482

9

PROTECTION OF HUMAN RIGHTS IN THE EU

SUMMARY

1. Introduction. The ToL not only confirms previously acknowledged fundamental human rights as general principles of EU law, but also recognises them as basic values on which the EU is founded (Article 2 TEU). The ToL reiterates and extends previous commitments of the EU to the protection of HRs, makes the Charter of Fundamental Rights of the European Union a binding instrument, and provides for the accession of the EU to the ECHR.

2. The recognition by the ECJ of HRs as fundamental principles of EU law. After an initial refusal, the ECJ has recognised fundamental HRs as forming part of the general principles of EU law. This was necessary to ensure that legitimacy, supremacy and uniform application of EU law would not be endangered by the ECJ's refusal to take account of constitutional traditions of the Member States and their international commitments to the protection of HRs deriving mainly from their accession to the ECHR. The ECJ, by recognising HRs as being part of the general principles of EU law, has established a standard of protection of HRs at the EU level which accords both with national values and the ECHR and, at the same time, ensures the achievement of the objectives of the EU.

3. Political acceptance of fundamental HRs: from the Treaty of Maastricht to the ToL. The recognition of fundamental HRs as general principles of EC law gained political acceptance, first of EC institutions, which in 1977 issued a Joint Declaration on Fundamental HRs and second, of the Member States, which endorsed the ECJ's approach to the protection of HRs in the amendments to the Treaty of Rome. The Member States have progressively introduced various mechanisms to enhance the respect of the EC and the Member States for fundamental HRs. For example, the ToA introduced a mechanism for subjecting to sanctions Member States guilty of a "serious and persistent breach" of the principles, including respect for human rights (Article 7 TEU), on which the EU is founded. With time, however, the political agenda of EU institutions and some Member States became more ambitious. It focused on two methods of introducing and enhancing HRs protection under EU law: first, via the adoption of a separate EU bill of rights which materialised with the adoption of the Charter of Fundamental Rights of the European Union and second, via accession of the EU to the ECHR. This was achieved by the ToL.

4. The Charter of Fundamental Rights of the European Union. The Charter was adopted to increase the visibility of HRs protection within the EU. It was first "solemnly proclaimed" by the EP, the Council and the Commission at the European Council meeting in Nice in 2000 and although the Charter had no binding force until the entry into force of the ToL, it had a considerable impact on EU law. Under the ToL the Charter has become a binding document and has the same legal value as the TEU and TFEU. Thus the Charter has become a primary source of EU law. The Charter is confined to the catalogue of existing rights, it does not create new rights. Each of its 50 articles relates to "rights, freedoms and principles" contained in six Titles:

- Dignity (1);

- Freedoms (II);

- Equality (III);

- Solidarity (IV);

- Citizens Rights (V);

- Justice (VI).

These "rights, freedoms and principles" are taken from the ECHR, the European Social Charter, the Community Charter of Social Rights of Workers, common constitutional traditions of the Member States, judgments of the ECJ and ECtHR, and international human rights conventions of the UN, the Council of Europe and the ILO to which the Member States are contracting parties.

The Charter clearly sets out its scope of application in "horizontal" articles, i.e. Articles 51–54. Article 51(1) states that the Charter is addressed to the institutions, bodies and agencies of the EU and the Member States "only when they are implementing EU law". Article 51(1) also provides that in its application the principle of subsidiarity must be respected. Articles 6(1) TEU and Article 51(2) of the Charter confirm that the Charter neither extends the scope of application of EU law, nor creates any new competences for the EU, nor any new tasks for the Union. A consequence of this is that the EU will not be able to legislate to vindicate a right set out in the Charter unless the power to do so is set out in the Treaties themselves. Individuals will not be able to take a Member State to court because it has failed to uphold the rights in the Charter unless the right involved derives from national measures implementing EU law.

Despite the assurances contained in Article 6(1) TEU and Article 51(2) of the Charter and in other "horizontal provisions" of the Charter some Member States, in particular the UK and Poland, feared that the Charter and its interpretation by the ECJ might spread to unrelated areas of national law, which is clearly precluded by Article 51(1) of the Charter as it requires a link between national law and EU law for the application of the Charter, and feared that the Charter drafted in an opaque language might create "new rights" which are not provided for by national or international sources. The UK and Poland secured the adoption of Protocol 30 on the application of the Charter in their respective countries, and in December 2009 this was extended by the European Council to the Czech Republic. It is submitted that the Protocol does not constitute an opt-out of the Charter for the UK, Poland and the Czech Republic but rather states the understanding of those Member States with regard to issues which are perceived by them as unclear.

5. The accession of the EU to the European Convention on Human Rights. Article 6(2) TEU provides that the EU shall accede to the ECHR. When this has occurred the ECtHR will be the final authority in the area of HRs, not only in the 47 European States which are contracting parties to the ECHR but also in the EU. The accession will ensure that:

- There is one consistent standard of protection of HRs in Europe;

- Member States will not find themselves accountable for breaches of the ECHR by the EU as occurred in *Matthews v UK*;

- The EU will be able to defend itself before the ECtHR in cases where the EU is directly or indirectly involved and have a judge in the ECtHR who will provide the necessary expertise on EU law.

6. The EU Agency for Fundamental Rights (FRA). The FRA, a successor of the European Monitoring Centre on Racism and Xenophobia, was created in 2007. Its main task is to provide advice and assistance to the EU institutions and to the Member States when implementing EU law, with a view to supporting them when they take measures or formulate policies which are within their respective competences and which have human rights implications. Thus the FRA protects fundamental HRs standards in general rather than being directly involved in the protection of individuals by dealing with individual complaints. Its importance is enhanced by the fact that it can give opinions on legislative proposals and their compatibility with human rights standards. However, instead of formulating opinions on all legislative proposals and their implications on the protection of human rights, it is allowed to act only if requested by the EP, the Council or the Commission. Thus, its actual influence on the standard of protection of fundamental HRs in the EU is limited and will depend on whether the FRA will successfully establish its reputation and standing by preparing high quality expert opinions.

9.1 Introduction

The extent and the quality of protection of fundamental HRs in the EU has changed dramatically with the entry into force of the ToL. Under Article 2 TEU, which lists the values on which the Union is founded, respect for human rights, including the rights of persons belonging to minorities, has been recognised as being one of them. The great innovations of the ToL in respect of the protection of HRs are as follows:

- Under Article 6(1) TEU, the Charter of Fundamental Rights of the European Union, as adopted at Strasbourg on 12 December 2007, has become legally binding and has the same legal value as the TFEU and TEU;

■ Under Article 6(2) TEU the EU will become a contracting party to the ECHR.

Additionally, the EU confirms its previous commitments to the protection of HRs, inter alia, in Article 6(3) which states that fundamental HRs, as guaranteed by the ECHR and as they result from the constitutional traditions common to the Member States, constitute general principles of the Union's law.

The above innovations mark the move of the EU towards the creation of a Union of fundamental rights, a move which emphasises that appropriate protection of HRs in the EU will contribute to the solidification of the achievements of integration rather than threaten its objectives.

9.2   The recognition by the ECJ of HRs as fundamental principles of EU law

At their inception the Communities focused on economic objectives. This, and the existence of the ECHR explain why the matter of HRs was initially relatively neglected.

The ECJ was, nevertheless, confronted with fundamental HRs issues quite early in its life. The cases which arose before the ECJ concerned alleged contradictions between obligations imposed by the High Authority of the ECSC and the rights granted to undertakings under their national constitutional law. On the one hand, the rights and freedoms contained in national constitutions were superior to any other sources of law, and their observance was imposed on any relevant public authorities of the various Member States in their dealings with the public, but it would be impossible to permit national constitutional laws to prevail over Community law without compromising the latter's uniform application throughout the Community. On the other hand, the founding Treaties neither contained any reference to HRs nor imposed on EC institutions any requirement to observe these rights. It was the task of the ECJ to find a solution to this legal impasse. For the first time, in Case 1/58 *Friedrich Stork & Cie v High Authority*,[399] the ECJ, when determining the relationship between fundamental HRs and Community law, refused to allow the examination of Community law in terms of its compliance with fundamental human rights and freedoms contained in national constitutions. The ECJ justified its decision on the ground that its task was to apply the law of the Community, not the national laws of Member States.

The criticism expressed by Member States, and especially the German Federal Constitutional Tribunal, together with the establishment of the principle of supremacy of EC law led the ECJ to alter its position on the above in an obiter statement in Case 29/69 *Stauder*[400] in which it held that fundamental HRs constituted general principles of Community law and as such were protected by the ECJ. This position was further elaborated in Case 11/70 *Internationale Handelsgesellschaft*[401] when the Court emphasised that:

---

399.   [1959] ECR 17, also Joined Cases 36, 37, 38–59 and 40/59 *Präsident Ruhrkolen-Verkaufsgesellschaft mbH and Others v High Authority* [1960] ECR 423 where the ECJ refused to invalidate Community law on the grounds of national law, even where contained in the constitution.
400.   [1969] ECR 419.
401.   [1970] ECR 1125.

"The protection of such rights, whilst inspired by the constitutional traditions common to the Member States, must be ensured within the framework of the structure and objectives of the Community."

This solution was considered as insufficient. In order to increase the protection of fundamental HRs, the ECJ decided to make reference to international conventions in this area, especially to the ECHR to which all Member States are contracting parties. In Case 4/73 *Nold*[402] the ECJ held:

". . . international treaties for the protection of human rights on which the Member States have collaborated or of which they are signatories, can supply guidelines which should be followed within the framework of Community law."

The ECJ has, however, emphasised that the protection of human rights is not absolute, and ". . . far from constituting unfettered prerogatives, [it] must be viewed in the light of the social function",[403] and thus it is legitimate that "these rights should, if necessary, be subject to certain limits justified by the overall objectives pursued by the Community, on condition that the substance of these rights is left untouched".[404]

It can be said that the recognition of fundamental HRs by the ECJ was necessary because of:

▪ The extension of the competences of the EC;

▪ The emergence of the principle of supremacy of EC law which entails that EC law prevails over all national law, including constitutional provisions guaranteeing fundamental HRs. Therefore, Member States, in particular Germany and Italy could not accept the supremacy of EC law without any guarantees of protection of HRs on the part of the EC;

▪ The necessity of ensuring that the protection of fundamental HRs would not jeopardise the achievement of objectives set out in the treaties.
The establishment of an EC standard of protection of fundamental HRs by the ECJ, which was inspired by the constitutional traditions of the Member States[405] and international HRs treaties to which Member States are contracting parties,[406] allowed the ECJ to examine Community acts in the light of their compatibility with fundamental HRs but subject to restrictions justified by objectives pursued by the Community. These restrictions, as the ECJ held in Case 44/79 *Hauer*,[407] must not however, constitute a disproportionate and intolerable interference with fundamental HRs.

Despite the above limitations, the ECtHR in the *Bosphorus* case[408] held that the standard of protection of HRs within the EU was satisfactory in terms of substantive guarantees and procedural mechanisms controlling their observance. In this case, the ECtHR declined to re-examine the issue of violation of the ECHR on the ground that it had already been examined by the ECJ in

---

402. [1974] ECR 491.
403. Case 11/70 *Internationale Handelsgesellschaft* [1970] ECR 1125.
404. Case 265/87 *Schräder* [1989] ECR 2237.
405. Case 11/70 *Internationale Handelsgesellschaft* [1970] ECR 1125.
406. Such as the International Covenant on Civil and Political Rights in Case C-249/96 *Lisa Jacqueline Grant v South-West Trains Ltd* [1998] ECR I-621; The European Social Charter and the ILO Convention no. 111 concerning discrimination in respect of employment and occupation in Case 149/77 *Defrenne* [1978] ECR 1365.
407. Case 44/79 *Liselotte Hauer v Land Rheinland-Pfalz* [1979] ECR 3727.
408. *Bosphorus v Ireland* (2006) 42 EHRR 1.

a reference for a preliminary ruling from the Irish Supreme Court. This conclusion was reached after the ECtHR reviewed the system of protection of HRs in the EU and the treatment of the *Bosphorus* case as contained in the Opinion of the Advocate General and by the ECJ. The ECtHR was satisfied that the EU protects HRs in a manner which can be regarded as at least equivalent to that established under the ECHR.[409]

The ECJ has recognised numerous HRs as general principles of EU law (see Chapter 8.3.4). However, the ECJ in Case C-249/96 *Grant v South-West Trains Ltd*[410] explained the limitations on the power to act in the field of human rights as follows: "Although respect for the fundamental rights which form an integral part of those general principles of law is a condition of the legality of Community acts, those rights cannot in themselves have the effect of extending the scope of the Treaty provisions beyond the competences of the Community". As a result the EU can protect human rights within the limits of powers conferred on it by the Treaties. Accordingly, review by the ECJ of the Member States' compliance with the HRs standard is only possible when the matter is within the scope of EU law. In Case C-299/95 *Kremzow v Austria*,[411] the applicant claimed that his right to free movement was infringed when he was unlawfully imprisoned for murder. The ECJ held that there was no connection between his situation and the EC Treaty provisions on the free movement of persons. As a result, the ECJ had no jurisdiction to review national measures in the light of their compatibility with the HRs standard as the circumstances of the case fell outside the scope of EC law. This approach has been confirmed in Article 51(2) of the Charter of Fundamental Rights of the European Union (see section 9.4.3).

In addition, in Case 5/88 *Wachauf*[412] the ECJ held that the protection of fundamental HRs is imposed not only on EC institutions, especially when they adopt binding measures, but also on the Member States in their application of such measures. Thus, national authorities in applying EU law must ensure "as far as possible" that HRs are protected.[413]

9.3   Political acceptance of fundamental HRs: from the treaty of Maastricht to the ToL

The importance of fundamental HRs prompted the Council, the Commission and the European Parliament to sign a Joint Declaration on 5 April 1977 which expressed their attachment to the protection of HRs. Although the Declaration was solely a political statement, it suggested a new approach, that is, the need for the Community to incorporate the ECHR into EC law. This initiative was blocked by the Member States at the Maastricht Conference and, finally, in Opinion 2/94 the ECJ held that the EC had no competence to accede to the ECHR without revising the Treaty.[414]

---

409.   In para 155 of the judgment the ECtHR stated that "equivalent" meant the same as "comparable" and that any requirement that the organisation's protection be "identical" rather than "comparable" could run counter to the interests of international co-operation.
410.   [1998] ECR I-621.
411.   [1997] ECR I-2629.
412.   [1989] ECR 2609.
413.   C-351/92 *Graff* [1994] ECR I-3361.
414.   [1996] ECR I-1759.

Notwithstanding the above, the Member States did endorse the approach of the ECJ to the protection of fundamental HRs. For the first time the Treaty of Maastricht recognised fundamental HRs as guaranteed by the ECHR and, resulting from the constitutional traditions common to the Member States, as fundamental principles of EU law. Further, the Treaty of Maastricht incorporated three provisions relating to the protection of human rights. These provisions:

- Provided that matters of common interest in Co-operation in the Fields of Justice and Home Affairs shall be dealt with in accordance with the requirements of the ECHR and the 1951 Convention on the Status of Refugees (Article 63(1) EC–Article 78(1) TFEU);

- Provided that Community policy in the field of development co-operation "shall contribute to the general objective of developing and consolidating democracy and the rule of law, and that of respecting human rights and fundamental freedoms" (Article 177(2) EC – its substantially revised version is contained in Article 208 TFEU);

- Introduced the possibility of suspending certain rights of a Member State when the Council determines the existence of "serious and persistent violation" of human rights by that Member State (Articles 7(2) and (3) TEU).

The ToN added a new paragraph to Article 7 TEU allowing the Council to determine the existence of a "clear risk of a serious breach" of human rights by a Member State and to address appropriate recommendations to that prospectively defaulting Member State (Article 7(1) TEU).[415]

With time, the political agenda of EC institutions and some Member States was more ambitious. It focused on two methods of introducing and enhancing HRs protection under EC law: first, via the adoption of a separate EU bill of rights and second, via accession of the EU to the ECHR. This was achieved by the ToL.

9.4   The Charter of Fundamental Rights of the European Union

The origin and main features of the Charter are examined below.

9.4.1   The Charter's origin and impact on EU law prior to the entry into force of the ToL

The idea of creating an EU Charter of Fundamental Rights was put forward by the German EU Presidency in early 1999. This idea was approved by the Cologne Council of June 1999 which mandated the drafting of a Charter to the Convention. The composition of that Convention and its tasks were established by the Tampere European Council (December 1999). This was to be "a task of revelation rather than creation, of compilation rather than innovation".[416] The Convention was made up of 15 personal representatives of the heads of state or government of the Member States, 16 members of the European Parliament, and 30 members of national parliaments. The Convention commenced its work in November 1999, electing as its chairman the

---

415.   See Chapter 3.2.2.

416.   See the Commission Communication on the Charter of Fundamental Rights of the European Union, para 7. COM(2000) 559.

former president of the Federal Republic of Germany Roman Herzog. It completed its work on 20 October 2000 and sent its draft Charter to the European Council together with non binding Explanations for each article of the draft Charter.

At the Nice European Council (December 2000), the Council, the EP and the Commission jointly made a solemn Declaration to respect the Charter. The Nice European Council welcomed this Declaration of commitment by these three institutions but decided to consider the question of the Charter's legal status during the general debate on the future of the European Union, which was initiated on 1 January 2001. During that process, the Charter was revised in parallel with the drafting of a Constitutional Treaty. The revised version was then incorporated as Part Two of the draft Constitutional Treaty. The revision was necessary to respond to concerns of the UK. During the negotiations leading to the adoption of the ToL further amendments were made to "horizontal" provisions of the Charter (i.e. Articles 51 to 54 of the Charter which clarify its scope and applicability) and to its Explanations. This resulted in the Charter (as amended) being "solemnly proclaimed" for the second time by the EP, the Commission and the Council on 12 December 2007.[417]

Until the entry into force of the ToL the Charter was not binding, but even as a non-binding document, had a substantial impact on EU law. This is in the light of the fact that the three institutions which proclaimed the Charter had committed themselves to respect it. In particular, the Commission decided that any proposed legislative or regulatory act adopted by it should be subject to a compatibility check with the Charter.[418] Since the establishment of the Fundamental Rights Agency (see section 9.6) the Commission has referred its legislative proposals to the Agency for examination of their compatibility with the Charter. The EP did not hesitate to challenge EC legislative acts before the ECJ on the ground of their incompatibility with HRs, including those confirmed by the Charter,[419] and the ECJ has referred to the Charter in numerous judgments.[420]

9.4.2   The Content of the Charter

The Charter confirms that HRs are indivisible, interrelated and interdependent. It contains civil, cultural, economic, political and social rights. Its catalogue of rights is more extensive than that contained in the ECHR which lists only civil and political rights. Each of 50 "rights, freedoms and principles" contained in six Titles: Dignity (I); Freedoms (II); Equality (III); Solidarity (IV); Citizens' Rights (V); and Justice (VI) are taken from the ECHR, the European Social Charter, the Community Charter of Social Rights of Workers, common constitutional traditions of the Member States, judgments of the ECJ and ECtHR, and international human rights conventions of the UN, the Council of Europe and the ILO to which Member States are contracting parties. Articles 51–54 of the Charter, the so called "horizontal provisions", clarify the applicability and the scope of the rights, freedoms and principles set out in the Charter. Its Titles are as follows:

---

417.   The text of the amended Charter and its revised Explanations can be found in [2007] OJ C303/1 and C/303/17.

418.   The Commission Communication on Compliance with the Charter of Fundamental Rights in Commission legislative proposals: Methodology for Systematic and Rigorous Monitoring, COM (2005) 172.

419.   See Case C-540/03 *EP v Council* [2006] ECR I-5769.

420.   For the first time the ECJ made reference to the Charter in Case C-540/03 *EP v Council* [2006] ECR I-5769. Subsequently, the ECJ has frequently referred to the Charter, e.g. see Case C-303/05 *Advocaten voor de Wereld VZW v Leden van de Ministerraad* [2007] ECR I-3635.

Title I: **Dignity**, affirms the protection of the dignity of the person, the right to life, the right to the integrity of the person, freedom from torture and inhuman or degrading treatment or punishment and the prohibition of slavery and forced labour;

Title II: **Freedoms**, guarantees the right to liberty and security, respect for private and family life, protection of personal data, the right to marry and found a family, freedom of thought, conscience and religion, freedom of expression and information, freedom of assembly and association, freedom of the arts and sciences, the right to education, freedom to choose an occupation and the right to engage in work, freedom to conduct a business, the right to property, the right to asylum and protection in the event of removal, expulsion or extradition;

Title III: **Equality**, guarantees equality before the law, non-discrimination, cultural, religious and linguistic diversity, equality between men and women, the rights of the child, the rights of the elderly and social and occupational integration of persons with disabilities to ensure their independence and participation in the life of the community;

Title IV: **Solidarity**, provides for workers' rights to information and consultation within the undertaking, collective bargaining and action, access to placement services, protection in the event of unjustified dismissal, fair and just working conditions, prohibition of child labour, protection of young people at work, family and professional life, social security and social assistance, health care, access to services of general economic interest, environmental protection and consumer protection;

Title V: **Citizens' rights**, guarantees the right to vote and stand as a candidate at elections to the EP and at municipal elections if they reside in a host Member State, the right to good administration, the right of access to documents and to the ombudsman, the right to petition the EP, freedom of movement and residence, and the right to diplomatic and consular protection;

Title VI: **Justice**, assures the right to an effective remedy and a fair trial, the presumption of innocence and the right of defence, the principles of legality and proportionality of criminal offences and penalties, and the right not to be tried or punished twice in criminal proceedings for the same criminal offence.

Article 52 on the scope of guaranteed rights provides that any limitations imposed on the exercise of the rights and freedoms contained in the Charter must be provided by law and respect the essence of those rights and freedoms. Subject to the principle of proportionality any limitation may be imposed, but only if it is necessary and genuinely meets objectives of general interest recognised by the EU or the need to protect the rights and freedoms of others.

Article 52 of the Charter provides some guidance on how to interpret the rights contained in the Charter. In particular it states that where Charter rights correspond to the ECHR rights, the meaning and scope of the rights shall be the same as those laid down by the ECHR. As to rights resulting from constitutional traditions common to the Member States, Article 52(4) provides that those rights are to be interpreted in harmony with those traditions. Article 52(6) provides that full account is to be taken of national laws and practices when articles to the Charter make reference to national law. Article 52(7) requires courts of the Union and the Member States to give "due regard" to the Revised Explanations accompanying the Charter. Article 52(5) explains the difference between "rights" and "principles" (see section 9.4.3.1).

Articles 53 and 54 provide that nothing in the Charter shall be interpreted as restricting fundamental rights, and that the Charter shall not be interpreted as providing a right to engage in activity which aims to destroy or limit the rights set out in the Charter.

9.4.3   The binding nature of the Charter of Fundamental Rights of the European Union

Under Article 6(1) TEU the Charter of Fundamental Rights, as amended in 2007, is a binding document and has the same legal value as the Treaties. Thus the Charter has become a primary source of EU law. The Charter clearly sets out its scope of application in "horizontal" articles. Article 51(1) states that the Charter is addressed to the institutions, bodies and agencies of the EU and the Member States "only when they are implementing EU law". Thus, the Charter does not apply to purely domestic law. A link between a national situation and EU law must be established for the Charter to be applicable. Article 51(1) also provides that in the application of the Charter the principle of subsidiarity must be respected. Article 6(1) TEU and Article 51(2) of the Charter confirm that the Charter neither extends the scope of application of EU law, nor creates any new competences for the EU, nor any new tasks for the Union. A consequence of the situation confirmed by Article 6(1) TEU and Article 51(2) of the Charter is that the EU will not be able to legislate to vindicate a right set out in the Charter unless the power to do so is set out in the Treaties themselves. And individuals will not be able to take a Member State to court because it has failed to uphold the rights in the Charter unless the Member State in question was implementing EU law. As a result, the Charter may be relied upon to challenge EU legislation which does not comply with the provisions of the Charter but cannot be used to challenge national legislation for non-compliance with the Charter unless the legislation in question is implementing EU law.

Despite the assurances contained in Article 6(1) TEU and Article 51(2) of the Charter and in other "horizontal provisions" of the Charter, some Member States, in particular, the UK and Poland feared that the Charter and its interpretation by the ECJ might spread to unrelated areas of national law. Such spreading is, however, clearly precluded by Article 51(1) of the Charter which requires a link between national law and EU law for the application of the Charter. There were also fears that the Charter having been drafted in an opaque language raises uncertainties as to:

- The legal implications of a distinction between "rights, freedoms and principles";

- Whether the Charter creates new rights or whether it merely confirms existing rights.

During the negotiations leading to the adoption of the ToL, the UK and Poland secured the adoption of Protocol 30 on the application of the Charter in their particular country. The European Council held in December 2009[421] agreed to a demand made by the President of the Czech Republic to extend the application of Protocol 30 to the Czech Republic. Indeed, the Czech President, Mr Klaus, after the second Irish referendum, which gave the green light to the ToL,

---

421.   Council of the European Union (1 December 2009), *Brussels European Council 29/30 October 2009: Presidency Conclusions*, 15265/1/09 REV 1, available at http://www.consilium.europa.eu/uedocs/cms_data/docs/pressdata/en/ec/110889.pdf (14/3/10).

refused to sign the Treaties unless his country could became a party to the Protocol. The explanation of Mr Klaus was that the application of the Charter could lead to a flood of property claims by Germans expelled from the Czech Republic after World War II.

The protocol raises an issue as to whether it constitutes an opt-out from the Charter so far as the UK, Poland and the Czech Republic are concerned, or whether is it a kind of "interpretative device" which will have no impact on the application of the Charter to the three States concerned.

9.4.3.1 The legal implications of a distinction between "rights, freedoms and principles"

The determination of the meaning of "freedoms" poses no difficulties. Title II of the Charter, which contains a list of "freedoms" in the majority of its articles actually uses the word "rights", e.g. Article 6 refers to the right to liberty and security, Article 7 refers to the right to respect for private and family life, Article 11 refers to the right to freedom of expression. However, it is uncertain whether the freedom of the arts and sciences contained in Article 13 contains a right or a principle. It seems that "freedoms", although a separate category under the Charter, either refer to rights or principles.

The distinction between rights and principles is controversial. Views differ as to the meaning of "principles". According to Lord Goldsmith QC, who was the UK representative on the Convention which drafted the 2000 version of the Charter, "rights" refer to "individually justiciable classic rights" mainly civil and political rights, whilst principles express "aspirations and objectives for what Government should do". On the legal plane the difference entails that principles are not justiciable in the same way as classical rights as they "only give rise to rights to the extent that they are implemented by national law or, in those areas where there is such competence, by Community law".[422] Whether the distinction made by Lord Goldsmith is correct will, at same stage, be clarified by the ECJ but in the light of the Revised Explanations it seems that some economic rights are justiciable (see below).

The Charter and its Revised Explanations provides some clarification as to the meaning of "principles". Article 52(5) of the Charter explains that principles set out in the Charter "may be implemented by legislative and executive acts" of the EU and the Member States when implementing EU law. They "shall be judicially cognizable only in the interpretation of such acts and in the ruling on their legality". On the basis of Article 52(5) of the Charter it can be said that this provision confirms that principles, alone, cannot give rise to directly enforceable rights but they may impact on the interpretation of the nature and scope of rights afforded by the EU or national implementing legislation and even on their validity. With regard to validity of EU law or national law implementing EU law, a declaration of invalidity made by the ECJ in respect of EU law, or by a national court dealing with national law implementing EU law, may, nevertheless, affect directly enforceable rights, i.e. if the relevant law is invalid so are any "rights" which it had sought to create.

The Revised Explanations give some examples of principles: Article 25 on the rights of the elderly, Article 26 on the integration of persons with disabilities and Article 37 on environmental

---

422. Paper by the Rt Hon Lord Goldsmith QC presented to the Henrich Böll Stiftung 2001, "A Charter of Rights, Freedoms and Principles" para 35 available at http://www.gruene-akademie.de/download/europa_goldsmith.pdf (14/3/10).

protection. However, the Revised Explanations provide that some articles may contain elements of rights and principles, e.g. Article 23 on equality between men and women, Article 33 on family and professional life and Article 34 on social security and social assistance. As a result, some social and economic rights may not be mere principles but may confer justiciable rights on individuals. It is submitted that the Charter does not indicate how to distinguish between rights and principles although it clearly distinguishes between justiciable rights and principles. The latter are justiciable only in the circumstances identified under Article 52(5) of the Charter.

9.4.3.2   The issue of whether the Charter contains new rights or whether it merely confirms existing rights

The Charter in its preamble "reaffirms" that it contains existing rights rather than creates new rights. The Revised Explanations provide a source for each of the Charter rights based on the constitutional traditions and international treaties to which Member States are contracting parties, including the ECHR, the Social Charter of the Union, and the case law of the ECtHR and the ECJ. Consequently, if the original source of a right is binding on a Member State, the simple restatement of that right in the Charter cannot deprive the underlying right of its binding legal status.

From the point of view of the UK, the right of collective bargaining and action embodied in Article 28 of the Charter gives rise to the concern that the Charter creates a new free-standing right. This Article states:

> "Workers and employers, or their respective organizations, have, in accordance with Union law and national laws and practices, the right to negotiate and conclude collective agreements at the appropriate levels and, in cases of conflicts of interest, to take collective action to defend their interests, including strike action."

At the time of writing, under UK law there is no specific right to strike. Consequently, the issue arises whether Article 28 introduces a new, free-standing right to strike in UK law. In this respect the Revised Explanations relating to Article 28 provide that this provision is based on Article 6 of the European Social Charter which provides for a right to collective bargaining, points 12–14 of the Community Charter of the Fundamental Social Rights of Workers which concern collective action and Article 11 ECHR which was interpreted by the ECtHR as encompassing the right to collective action.[423] However, Article 11 ECHR contains rights which are not absolute and thus may be limited by national law.

It is submitted that in any event the right to strike has been recognised under EU law. In Case C-438/05 *International Transport Workers' Federation and Finnish Seamen's Union v Viking Line ABP and OÜ Viking Line Eesti*[424] and Case C-341/05 *Laval un Partneri Ltd v Svenska Byggnadsarbetareförbundet and Others*[425] the ECJ not only recognised the right to strike but also provided an insight into how this right is to be interpreted under EU law.

---

423. *Scmidt and Dahlström v Sweden* (application No 5589/72) judgment of Feb 1976, Series A, No 21 at para 36.
424. [2007] ECR I-10779.
425. [2007] ECR I-11767.

THE FACTS WERE:

In Case C-438/05 International Transport Workers' Federation and Finnish Seamen's Union v Viking Line ABP and OÜ Viking Line Eesti, a Finnish maritime transport undertaking wished to establish itself in Estonia and in that connection to register one of its vessels in Estonia. The Finnish undertaking wanted to take advantage of cheaper labour in Estonia but was opposed by a Finnish trade union affiliated to a federation of trade unions based in the UK, and supported by the workers' federation, which threatened to organise strikes and boycotts had the undertaking concerned failed to apply the collective agreement applicable in Finland to the crew of the vessel which would fly the Estonian flag.

In Case C-341/05 Laval un Partneri Ltd v Svenska Byggnadsarbetareförbundet and Others, a Latvian construction company wanted to post its workers at one of its Swedish subsidiaries but was opposed by Swedish trade unions which sought an assurance from the Latvian undertaking that it would apply the relevant Swedish collective agreement to its posted workers to ensure that they would be paid the same wages as Swedish workers covered by the collective agreement.

In both above cases negotiations with the relevant union failed and the unions exercised their right of collective action, in particular the right to strike with a view to forcing the undertakings concerned to sign and implement the collective agreements. The referring courts asked the ECJ whether collective action constituted a restriction contrary to Articles 43 and 49 EC [Articles 49 and 56 TFEU] and if so, whether such a restriction could be justified under EC law.

Held:

The ECJ rejected arguments relating to non application of Articles 43 and 49 [Articles 49 and 56 TFEU] to the cases under consideration. First, it stated that the fact that Article 137(5) EC [Article 153(5) TFEU] which explicitly excludes from the scope of Community law the right to strike and to lock-out does not mean that collective action falls outside the scope of Community law relating to free movement. Second, the ECJ rejected the argument according to which the right to take collective action, including the right to strike, concerns the exercise of fundamental rights and thus falls outside the scope of Article 43 EC [Article 49 TFEU]. The ECJ emphasised that the right to take collective action, recognised by international conventions, is also recognised under Community law as it forms an integral part of the general principles of Community law. However, this right is not absolute but subject to restrictions and limitations and as such needs to be reconciled with other fundamental rights and principles protected under the EC Treaty in the light of the principle of proportionality.

Comment:

The application of Articles 43 and 49 EC [Articles 49 and 56 TFEU] to trade union organisations posed no problem. In accordance with the previous case law of the ECJ both articles are horizontally directly effective and thus apply to private persons such as trade union organisations and to measures adopted by such organisations.

The ECJ, not surprisingly, held that collective action taken by trade unions with a view to compelling the undertakings concerned to sign and implement the relevant collective agreements constituted an obstacle to the exercise of the right of establishment and the right to provide services by the undertakings concerned, given that the contents of the collective agreements were liable to deter those undertakings from exercising their rights under the EC Treaty. However, the ECJ emphasised that a restriction of this kind may be justified by an overriding reason of public interest, such as the protection of workers in the host Member State against possible social dumping, provided that it is established that the restriction is suitable to achieve the legitimate objective pursued and does not go beyond what is necessary to achieve that objective. Consequently, collective action taken by trade union organisations is, in principle, justified under Articles 43 and 49 EC [Articles 49 and 56 TFEU] on the ground of the protection of workers provided that such collective action is within the limits imposed by the principle of proportionality. Obviously, when such actions are directly discriminatory, they may be justified only on the grounds of public policy, public security or public health.

In Case C-341/05 *Laval un Partneri Ltd*, the ECJ held that the restriction imposed by the relevant trade union was directly discriminatory because it failed to take into account, irrespective of their content, collective agreements to which undertakings that posted workers to Sweden were already bound in the Member State in which they were established, in so far as under Swedish rules they were treated in the same way as national undertakings which had not concluded a collective agreement. The ECJ found that those directly discriminatory measures could not be justified on grounds of public policy, public security or public health.

In Case C-438/05, the ECJ was more lenient than in Case C-341/05. It left to the referring court the task of assessing whether the collective action taken by the relevant trade union was in conformity with the principle of proportionality.

In the light of the above judgments it is clear that Article 28 of the Charter of Fundamental rights of the European Union does not create a free-standing right to strike. However, it is also clear that the right to strike has been recognised by the ECJ as forming part of the general principles of EU law and thus was recognised before the entry into force of the Charter. It is also clear from the case law of the ECJ that this right must be exercised in accordance with EU law and national law. In the Finnish case the ECJ made an express reference to Article 28 of the Charter to limit the scope of the right in that the ECJ acknowledged that the right to strike may not be relied upon "where the strike is *contra bonos mores* or is prohibited under national law or Community law".[426]

9.4.4 Protocol 30 on the application of the Charter to Poland, the UK and the Czech Republic

Protocol 30 contains two provisions. Its Article 1(1) states that the Charter does not extend the ability of the ECJ or any court or tribunal in the UK, Poland or the Czech Republic "to find

---

426.   Supra note 424. *International Transport Workers' Federation, Finnish Seamen's Union*, para 44.

the laws, regulations or administrative provisions, practices or action" of the UK, or Poland or the Czech Republic inconsistent with the Charter. Article 1(2) provides that (in order to dissipate any doubt) nothing in Title IV of the Charter, which concerns the "solidarity" rights, creates justiciable rights applicable in the UK, Poland or the Czech Republic except in so far as such rights are provided for by the laws and practices of the Member State concerned.

Article 2 states that to the extent that a provision of the Charter refers to national laws and practices, it shall apply to the UK, Poland and the Czech Republic only to the extent that the rights or principles it contains are recognised by the law and practices of the UK, Poland or the Czech Republic.

Views differ as to the legal effect of the Protocol. It is submitted that the Protocol is part of the Treaties and thus cannot be disregarded by the EU courts and institutions, or national courts of the Member States. Its Article 1(1) seems to repeat that the Charter does not create new rights. As to existing national law if it is inconsistent with the Charter it is automatically inconsistent with EU law or international law and sometimes with both. Thus this provision reiterates the content of Article 51 of the Charter.

In respect of Article 1(2) of Protocol 30 it can be said that this provision confirms the distinction between rights and principles which Article 52(5) and its Explanations endorse. It clarifies any doubts as to Title IV in that it confirms that Title IV sets out only principles, not justiciable rights. On the basis of Article 1(2) it is unlikely that any Article set out in Title IV will be found to contain justiciable rights in respect of any Member States but certainly not in respect of the UK, Poland or the Czech Republic because such a finding would be inconsistent with the express wording of Article 1(2) of Protocol 30.

With regard to Article 2 of Protocol 30, it confirms what Article 52(6) of the Charter states, i.e. that "full account" of national laws and practice should be taken into account where there is reference to them in the Charter.

It is submitted that Protocol 30 does not constitute an opt-out of the Charter. Its wording suggests that it states the position of the UK, Poland and the Czech Republic on the points mentioned above but it does not constitutes any "opt-out". Nothing in the Protocol suggests that the Charter is non binding in respect of the UK, Poland and the Czech Republic. However, it is not impossible that the interpretation of the Charter in respect of these three Member States may differ as compared with other Member States but this will depend upon whether the ECJ decides that the Charter rights and the general principles of EU law are the same; if so, there is no difference between the Charter and the general principles with the consequences that the Protocol will be meaningless. However, if the ECJ decides that the general principles of EU law are not identical to the rights contained in the Charter, the Protocol will be of relevance in that national courts and the ECJ will be prevented from assessing national law in terms of its compatibility with the Charter. It seems, however, that even if the Charter rights and the general principles of EU law were somehow found to be different from each other, the ECJ will develop its case law in the direction of ensuring their convergence. It seems that the main objective of the Protocol is to ensure that if the Charter indeed creates new rights, the Protocol ensures that so far as the UK, Poland and the Czech Republic are concerned the Charter must be interpreted as not creating any new rights. Further, it is to be noted, as the Protocol confirms in its preamble, that it is without prejudice to other obligations devolving upon Poland and the UK under the TFEU, the TEU and Union law generally. Therefore, Article 6(3) TEU ensures that on the basis of general principles of EU law any EU or UK, or Polish or Czech implementing legislation can be challenged on the ground of infringements of fundamental HRs. Those principles exist independently from the Charter with the consequence that when the ECJ decides that a Charter right constitutes a general principle of EU law, any protection afforded under the Protocol will be removed.

9.5   The accession of the EU to the European Convention on Human Rights (ECHR)

Article 6(2) TEU states that the EU shall accede to the ECHR. Protocol 8 "Relating to Article 6(2) of the Treaty on European Union on the Accession of the Union to the European Convention on the Protection of Human Rights and Fundamental Freedoms" attached to the Treaties provides that any agreement relating to the acession must make provision for preserving the specific characteristics of the Union and EU law and ensure that the accession neither affects the competences of the Union nor the powers of its institutions nor the situation of Member States in relation to their commitments under the ECHR, in particular in respect of Protocols attached to the ECHR to some of which only some Member States are contracting parties, nor the obligation of the Member States to submit a dispute concerning the interpretation or application of the Treaties to the ECJ.

An accession agreement, as any international agreement, will be concluded in conformity with the requirements set out in Article 218 TFEU. However, Article 218(8) TFEU specifically mentions that an agreement on accession of the EU to the ECHR must be concluded unanimously by the Council and will enter into force after being approved by the Member States in accordance with their respective constitutional requirements. Pursuant to Article 218(6)(a)(ii) TFEU, the Council is required to obtain the consent of the EP for concluding the agreement on EU accession.

Under Article 218(2) TFEU the Council authorises the opening of negotiations on the recommendation of the Commission, adopts a negotiating directive, authorises the signing of agreement and concludes it. Under Article 218(10) TFEU the EP must be fully informed of all stages of the negotiations. At the time of writing, the Commission has submitted to the Council its draft negotiating directive.[427] At this early stage many issues are uncertain but it is clear that the EU will not become a Member of the Council of Europe and that the possibility of the ECJ to refer a question on the interpretation of the ECHR to the ECtHR within a formal mechanism similar to a preliminary ruling procedure existing under Article 267 TFEU, is unlikely to be accepted by the EP.[428]

The accession of the EU to the ECHR creates an interesting situation. On the one hand, EU law is not prevented from guaranteeing HRs more generously than the ECHR; on the other hand, there is an implication that when the matter in question has any human rights implications the EU will surrender its autonomy in the interpretation of EU law to another international body, i.e. the ECtHR.

The accession of the EU to the ECHR may create some difficulties, bearing in mind that EU law restricts certain rights on the grounds of the overriding interests of the EU, and that the ECJ and the ECtHR have differing views on the interpretation of the extent of certain rights, e.g. in

---

427.   See IP/10/291 and MEMO/10/84.

428.   See the Draft Opinion of the EP Committee on Foreign Affairs for the EP Committee on Constitutional Affairs on institutional aspects of the accession of the EU to the ECHR, 2009/2241 (INI) of 9/2/10 available at http://www.europarl.europa.eu/meetdocs/2009_2014/documents/afet/pa/804/804460/804460en.pdf (22/4/10).

respect of enforcement of EU competition law, on the right not to incriminate oneself, on the scope of legal privilege, and on the extent of the right to inviolability of premises and other places including private homes. Nevertheless, the provisions of the ECHR and their interpretation by the ECtHR should hold sway as the proposed Article 6(3) TEU clearly states that the fundamental rights as enshrined in the ECHR constitute general principles of EU law.

It is submitted that the accession of the EU to the ECHR constitutes the best way of enhancing the legal protection of HRs in the EU legal order and is a sign of self-confidence and maturity on the part of the EU, as it shows the world the EU's readiness for its institutions to be monitored, by an outside body, on HRs issues. Further, the *Bosphorus* case [429] clearly indicates that scrutiny by the ECtHR of ECJ judgments will occur only exceptionally. Additional advantages can be summarised as follows:

▪ The EU's accession to the ECHR will ensure that there is the same standard of protection of fundamental human rights throughout Europe;

▪ Member States will not be held accountable for breaches of HRs by EU institutions. In *Matthews v UK*,[430] the ECtHR found the UK in breach of Article 3 of Protocol 1 to the ECHR by denying the applicant, a Gibraltar national, the right to vote in the direct elections to the EP. The exclusion was based on the EC Act on Direct Elections of 1976 which was annexed to Council Decision 76/787,[431] and which had status equivalent to a Community treaty and as such could not be challenged before the ECJ because the ECJ has no jurisdiction to review EU treaties. Similarly, in *Cantoni v France*,[432] although the ECtHR found no violation of Article 7 of the ECHR it held that the fact that Article L. 511 of the French Public Health Code was based almost word for word on Directive 65/65 did not remove that Article from the ambit of Article 7 of the ECHR;

▪ The EU will participate in the judicial system established by the ECHR in that it will be able to defend itself when a case concerns directly or indirectly the EU and will have its own judge in the ECtHR who will provide the necessary expertise on EU law.

The relationship between the ECJ and the ECtHR is to be defined but according to the statement made by Mr Holovaty, Vice Chairperson of the Committee of Legal Affairs and Human Rights of the Council of Europe's Parliamentary Assembly,[433] the accession will not jeopardise the autonomy of the ECJ. The ECJ will be treated by the ECtHR as any "domestic court", akin to constitutional or supreme courts of a contracting State to the ECHR, over which the ECtHR will exercise "external restraint".

---

429. See also *DH & Others v Czech Republic* (application No. 57325/00, judgment of 13 November 2007, para 187.
430. [1999] 28 EHRR 361.
431. [1976] OJ L278/1.
432. 22 October 1996.
433. His speech is available at: http://www.assembly.coe.int/CommitteeDocs/2010/intervention_Holovaty_%20E.pdf (10/4/10). On the relationship between the Council of Europe and the EU see: Report prepared by the Prime Minister of Luxembourg at the request of Heads of State and Government of Member States of the Council of Europe entitled: "Council of Europe-European Union: A Sole Ambition for the European Continent" which can be found at: http://www.gouvernement.lu/salle_presse/actualite/2006/04/11conseil_europe/english_mod.pdf (10/4/09).

9.6   The EU Agency for Fundamental Rights (FRA)

On 1 March 2007 the European Monitoring Centre for Racism and Xenophobia (EUMC) became the EU Agency for Fundamental Rights. The FRA builds upon the EUMC's work and has its seat in Vienna. The creation of the FRA was applauded by those who had been disappointed by the fate of the Charter of Fundamental Rights and by delays in accession of the EU to the ECHR, but criticised by those who had seen its existence as an unwelcome interference in the activities of the Council of Europe.

The work of the FRA is determined on the basis of a five-year Multiannual Framework adopted by the Council after consultation with the EP.[434]

An examination of Regulation 168/2007, which established the FRA,[435] reveals that the role assigned to the FRA is modest and its powers rather restricted. Its main task is to provide assistance and expertise to the EU and its Member States on human rights matters.

The disappointing aspects are:

- It is not empowered to monitor the situation in the Member States for the purposes of Article 7 TEU;

- It is restricted to the territory of the EU. In respect of official candidate states the FRA can only act if invited by the relevant association council, acting unanimously, and only in so far as the relevant council decides that the involvement of the FRA is necessary to facilitate implementation of the EU acquis;

- It has no teeth. It can neither carry out EU policy enhancing the protection of human rights, nor give judgements or opinions in respect of violations of human rights, nor bring to the attention of the EU, or its citizens, infringements of fundamental rights, in particular within the procedure set up in Article 7 TEU;

- Article 4(2) of Regulation 168/2007 expressly states first, that the FRA has no locus standi under Article 263 TFEU, that is, it cannot challenge the legality of EU measures before the ECJ, and second, it is not allowed to deal with the question of whether a Member State has failed to fulfil an obligation within the meaning of Article 258 TFEU;

- It has no competence to deal with individual complaints;

- Its opinions have no binding force;

- It can only give opinions on legislative proposals and their compatibility with human rights standards at the request of the EP, the Council or the Commission. Thus, instead of formulating opinions on all legislative proposals and their implications on the protection of human rights, it is allowed to act only if requested.

The main tasks of the FRA are described in Article 4 of Regulation 168/2007. These are:

- To provide advice and assistance to the EU's institutions and to the Member States when implementing EU law, with a view to supporting them when they take measures or formu-

---

434.   [2007] OJ L53/1.
435.   See the official website of the FRA at http://www.fra.europa.eu (accessed 12/4/10).

late policies within their respective competences having human rights implications. The FRA fulfils this task through:

(i) Formulating conclusions and opinions, on its own initiative, or at the request of the EP, the Council or the Commission;

(ii) Presenting an annual report on its activities;

(iii) Highlighting examples of good practice;

(iv) Preparing thematic reports on issues of particular importance to EU policies;

- To collect, record, analyse and disseminate relevant, objective, and comparable information on matters related to human rights protection. Information may be communicated to the FRA by the Member States, the EU institutions and bodies, national bodies, NGOs (non-governmental organisations) and international organisations, in particular the Council of Europe;

- To carry out academic research, which includes setting up academic networks;

- To develop a communication strategy in the area of human rights as a basis for a dialogue with civil society in order to raise public awareness of human rights;

- To co-operate closely with:

  - Member States, via National Liaison Officers and national human rights institutions;
  - EU institutions and bodies;
  - Civil society through the Fundamental Rights Platform – a co-operation network providing a mechanism for exchange of information and expertise on human rights issues;
  - International organisations, namely the Organisation for Security and Co-operation in Europe (OSCE) and the UN bodies active in the field of human rights;

- To co-ordinate its activities with the Council of Europe in order to avoid duplication, to ensure that its activities are complementary and provide added value to the activities of the Council of Europe. An important point is that the Council of Europe appoints an independent person to the Management Board of the FRA, who also participates in meetings of the Executive Board of the Council of Europe.

AIDE-MÉMOIRE

THE PROTECTION OF FUNDAMENTAL HRs IN THE EU IS BASED ON

THE CHARTER OF FUNDAMENTAL RIGHTS OF THE EUROPEAN UNION. THE CHARTER IS BINDING AND HAS THE SAME LEGAL VALUE AS THE TFEU AND THE TEU. ITS PROVISIONS ARE ADDRESSED TO THE INSTITUTIONS, BODIES AND AGENCIES OF THE EU AND THE MEMBER STATES WHEN THEY ARE IMPLEMENTING EU LAW. THE CHARTER ONLY CONFIRMS THE EXISTING RIGHTS AND DOES NOT CREATE NEW RIGHTS. ITS BENEFICIARIES ARE EU CITIZENS AND ALL PERSONS RESIDING WITHIN THE TERRITORY OF THE EU. EACH OF THE 50 ARTICLES OF THE CHARTER'S "RIGHTS, FREEDOMS AND PRINCIPLES" ARE CONTAINED IN SIX TITLES AS FOLLOWS:

THE ECHR
THE EU WILL ACCEDE TO THE ECHR (ART. 612) TEU.
AS A RESULT THE ECtHR WILL BE THE FINAL AUTHORITY ON HRs MATTERS IN THE EU

THE GENERAL PRINCIPLES OF EU LAW WHICH INCLUDE FUNDAMENTAL HRs AS GUARANTEED BY THE ECHR AND AS THEY RESULT FROM THE CONSTITUTIONAL TRADITIONS COMMON TO THE MEMBER STATES (ART. 613 TEU)

DIGNITY THIS CONCERNS	FREEDOMS THIS CONCERNS	EQUALITY THIS CONCERNS	SOLIDARITY THIS CONCERNS	CITIZENS' RIGHTS THIS CONCERNS	JUSTICE THIS CONCERNS
• HUMAN DIGNITY • THE RIGHT TO LIFE • THE RIGHT TO INTEGRITY OF PERSON • FREEDOM FROM TORTURE AND INHUMAN OR DEGRADING TREATMENT OR PUNISHMENT • PROHIBITION OF SLAVERY	• RIGHT TO LIBERTY AND SECURITY • RESPECT FOR PRIVATE AND FAMILY LIFE • FREEDOM OF THOUGHT, CONSCIENCE AND RELIGION • FREEDOM OF EXPRESSION AND INFORMATION • FREEDOM OF ASSEMBLY AND ASSOCIATION • FREEDOM OF ARTS AND SCIENCE • THE RIGHT TO EDUCATION • FREEDOM TO CHOOSE AN OCCUPATION AND RIGHT TO ENGAGE IN WORK • FREEDOM TO CONDUCT BUSINESS • RIGHT TO PROPERTY • RIGHT TO ASYLUM • PROTECTION IN THE EVENT OF REMOVAL, EXPULSION OR EXTRADITION	• NON DISCRIMINATION • CULTURAL AND LINGUISTIC DIVERSITY • EQUALITY BETWEEN MEN AND WOMEN • THE RIGHTS OF THE CHILD • THE RIGHTS OF THE ELDERLY • INTEGRATION OF PERSONS WITH DISABILITIES	• WORKERS' RIGHT TO INFORMATION AND CONSULTATION WITHIN THE UNDERTAKING • RIGHT OF COLLECTIVE BARGAINING AND ACTION • RIGHT OF ACCESS TO PLACEMENT SERVICES • PROTECTION IN THE EVENT OF UNFAIR DISMISSAL • FAIR AND JUST WORKING CONDITIONS • PROHIBITION OF CHILD LABOUR AND PROTECTION OF YOUNG WORKERS • PROTECTION OF FAMILY AND PROFESSIONAL LIFE • ENTITLEMENT TO SOCIAL SECURITY AND SOCIAL ASSISTANCE • ACCESS TO AND BENEFIT OF HEALTH CARE • ENVIRONMENTAL PROTECTION • CONSUMER PROTECTION	• RIGHT TO VOTE AND STAND AS CANDIDATES AT ELECTIONS TO THE EP • RIGHT TO VOTE AND STAND AS CANDIDATE AT MUNICIPAL ELECTIONS AT THE PLACE OF RESIDENCE • RIGHT TO GOOD ADMINISTRATION • RIGHT TO ACCESS A DOCUMENT • RIGHT TO REFER TO THE EU OMBUDSMAN • FREEDOM OF MOVEMENT AND RESIDENCE • RIGHT TO DIPLOMATIC AND CONSULAR PROTECTION OUTSIDE THE EU	• RIGHT TO AN EFFECTIVE REMEDY AND TO FAIR TRIAL • RIGHT TO BE PRESUMED INNOCENT UNTIL PROVEN GUILTY AND RIGHT TO DEFENCE • PRINCIPLES OF LEGALITY AND PROPORTIONALITY OF CRIMINAL OFFENCES AND PENALTIES • RIGHT NOT TO BE TRIED OR PUNISHED TWICE IN CRIMINAL PROCEEDINGS FOR THE SAME OFFENCE

RECOMMENDED READING

Books

Andreangeli, A., *EU Competition Enforcement and Human Rights*, 2008, Cheltenham: Edward Elgar Publishing Ltd

Hervey, T. and Kenner, J. (eds), *Economic and Social Rights Under the EU Charter of Fundamental Rights*, 2nd edition, 2006, London: Hart Publishing

Articles

Albi, A., "Ironies in Human Rights Protection in the EU: Pre-Accession Conditionality and Post-Accession Conundrums", (2009) 15 ELJ, p 46

Costello, C., "The Bosphorus Ruling of the European Court of Human Rights: Fundamental Rights and Blurred Boundaries in Europe", (2006) 6 HumRts L Rev, p. 87

Greer, S. and Williams, A., "Human Rights in the Council of Europe and the EU: Towards 'Individual', 'Constitutional' or 'Institutional' Justice?", (2009) 15 ELJ, p 462

Harpaz, G., "The European Court of Justice and its Relations with the European Court of Human Rights: The Quest for Enhanced Reliance, Coherence and Legitimacy", (2009) 46 CMLRev, p 105

Kühling, J., "Fundamental Rights", in A. von Bogdandy and J. Bast, *Principles of European Constitutional Law*, 2nd edition, 2010, Oxford: Hart Publishing

Van den Berghe, F., "The EU and Issues of Human Rights Protection: Some Solutions to More Acute Problems?", (2010) 16 ELJ, p 112

Von Bernstorff, J., and von Bogdandy, A., "The EU Fundamental Rights Agency within the European and International Human Rights Architecture: The Legal Framework and Some Unsettled Issues in a New Field of Administrative Law", (2009) 46 CMLRev, p 1035

Wouters, J., "The EU Charter of Fundamental Rights – Some Reflections on its External Dimension", (2001) 8 MJ 3

10

PRELIMINARY RULINGS: ARTICLE 267 TFEU

CONTENTS

SUMMARY

1. Article 267 TFEU states that the Court of Justice of the European Union (CJEU) is empowered to give preliminary rulings on the interpretation of the Treaties and the validity and interpretation of acts of the EU institutions, bodies, offices or agencies. Article 256(3) TFEU specifies that not only the ECJ but also the General Court shall have jurisdiction to give preliminary rulings in the areas determined by the Statute of the CJEU. However, at the time of writing, the ECJ has not made any arrangements to share its jurisdiction with the General Court and consequently, the ECJ alone is empowered to give preliminary rulings.

2. Under the ToL, the ECJ's jurisdiction to give preliminary rulings has been extended to the whole of the area of FSJ. However, this is subject to a temporal limitation in that in the field of police and judicial co-operation in criminal matters in respect of measures which were adopted before the entry into force of the ToL the ECJ's jurisdiction will commence five years after the entry into force of the ToL, on 1 December 2014, but if any particular measure (adopted before the entry into force of the ToL) is amended before the expiry of that period then that measure will be within the jurisdiction of the Court from the time of amendment. The temporal restriction does not apply to Member States which, prior to entry into force of the ToL, made a Declaration under Article 35(1) EU (since repealed) allowing their courts to make requests for a preliminary ruling in this area. There is a new urgent preliminary ruling procedure which enables the ECJ to deal speedily with referrals for a preliminary ruling in extremely urgent cases, e.g. when a person whose legal situation is to be assessed by the referring court on the basis of the answer from the ECJ is in custody or deprived of liberty.

3. Under the preliminary ruling procedure national courts and tribunals may refer questions on the interpretation of EU law. However, courts and tribunals against whose decisions there is no judicial remedy must, as a rule, refer such questions to the ECJ unless the ECJ has already ruled on the relevant point of EU law or unless the correct interpretation is obvious. As to validity of EU measures all national courts and tribunals must refer to the ECJ if in doubt as to the validity of the relevant measure.

4. Three aspects of jurisdiction of the ECJ under Article 267 TFEU are examined;

- The first concerns matters that can be referred. In this respect not all EU law is capable of being referred to the ECJ. The ECJ is precluded from giving preliminary rulings on the validity of primary sources (as opposed to their interpretation), on the validity of its own judgments, on matters excluded by Article 276 TFEU and on the CFSP matters;

- The second concerns national courts and tribunals which can make a request for a preliminary ruling. In this respect, only courts and tribunals which exercise a judicial function under state authority are regarded as "courts and tribunals" within the meaning of Article 267 TFEU. On this ground private arbitrators have been refused recognition as a court or tribunal;

- The third concerns territorial jurisdiction. The ECJ has broadly interpreted the territorial scope of Article 267 TFEU to include within its jurisdiction referrals from courts and tribunals situated outside the territory of the EU but having important connections with some Member States.

5. The ECJ has rarely refused to give a preliminary ruling. This may, however, occur when there is no genuine dispute between the parties to national proceedings, when a referred question has no relevance to the main dispute, or when a referring court has not provided sufficient factual and legal background in its reference.

6. A preliminary ruling on the interpretation of EU law is binding on the referring court and has retroactive effect unless the ECJ decides otherwise. A preliminary ruling on the validity of EU law entails that if the ECJ declares an act invalid all national courts and tribunals, not only the referring court, have to set aside that act. Although the ECJ has no power to replace an invalid act it has authorised itself to replace invalidated provisions by appropriate alternatives while the adoption of required measures by the institution concerned is awaited.

10.1   Introduction

Article 267 TFEU states:

"The Court of Justice of the European Union shall have jurisdiction to give preliminary rulings concerning:

(a)   the interpretation of the Treaties;

(b)   the validity and interpretation of acts of the institutions, bodies, offices or agencies of the Union;

Where such a question is raised before any court or tribunal of a Member State, that court or tribunal may, if it considers that a decision on the question is necessary to enable it to give judgment, request the Court to give a ruling thereon.

Where any such question is raised in a case pending before a court or tribunal of a Member State against whose decisions there is no judicial remedy under national law, that court or tribunal shall bring the matter before the Court.

If such a question is raised in a case pending before a court or tribunal of a Member State with regard to a person in custody, the Court of Justice of the European Union shall act with the minimum of delay."

Under Article 267 TFEU, the CJEU is entitled to give preliminary rulings. Further, Article 256 TFEU provides that the General Court may deliver preliminary rulings in areas to be specified by the Statute of the Court of Justice of the European Union. At the time of writing, no such specification has been made and it seems unlikely that the ECJ will relinquish its exclusive jurisdiction to give preliminary rulings.[436] However, if the situation changes in the future, the ECJ will, by virtue of Article 258(3) TFEU, have power to review a preliminary judgment of the General Court in a situation where there will be a serious risk of the unity or consistency of EU law being affected by such a judgment. Further, if the General Court were to have jurisdiction to give preliminary rulings, under Article 258(3) TFEU, it would be entitled to refer a request for a preliminary ruling to the ECJ in respect of cases which would require a decision of principle likely to affect the unity or consistency of EU law.

10.1.1   Co-operation between national courts and the ECJ within the preliminary ruling procedure

The preliminary ruling procedure constitutes the main form of co-operation between national courts and the ECJ. In Case 16/65 *Schwarze*,[437] the ECJ emphasised this aspect of preliminary rulings by stating that on the basis of the mechanism of co-operation established in what is now Article 267 TFEU, national courts and the ECJ, within their respective competences, are called upon to contribute directly and reciprocally to render a judgment. Indeed, under Article 267 TFEU the ECJ is not a court of appeal.[438] It assists national courts to reach a correct decision from the point of view of EU law.

---

436.   See The Information Note on References from National Courts for a Preliminary Ruling issued by the ECJ [2009] OJ C297/1. para 3.

437.   [1965] ECR 877; Case C-343/90 *Lourenço Dias* [1992] ECR I-4673; Case C-314/01 *Siemens and ARGE Telecom* [2004] ECR I-2549.

438.   See K. Alter, *Establishing Supremacy of European Law*, 2003, Oxford: Oxford University Press.

Article 267 TFEU allows national courts, when applying EU law, to adjourn the proceedings pending before them, and to seek advice from the ECJ on the interpretation or validity of EU law. The contribution of the ECJ to a final judgment is incidental since it only elucidates referred issues, and it is the national court that delivers the judgment.

Proceedings under Article 267 TFEU are not adversarial, and the parties to the original proceedings are not involved, although Article 23 of the Statute of the CJEU offers them the opportunity to make written and oral observations.

10.1.2   The main purpose of preliminary rulings

The main reason for preliminary rulings lies in the peculiarity of EU law. The principle of supremacy requires that EU law is uniformly applied in all Member States, that is, that EU law has the same meaning and effect throughout the EU. Thus, the main objective of Article 267 TFEU is to ensure that all national courts applying EU law, which they do independently from one another and are always more or less influenced by their own legal system, will reach the same solution on a point concerning EU law. In Case 166/73 *Rheinmühlen*,[439] the ECJ held that:

> "Article [267 TFEU] is essential for the preservation of the Community character of the law established by the Treaty and has the object of ensuring that in all circumstances this law is the same in all States of the Community."

At the same time the mechanism under Article 267 TFEU ensures that national courts are not placed in a position of subordination vis-à-vis the ECJ, since in a certain sense it is a dialogue between ECJ judges and a national judge. They must co-operate, not encroach upon one another's jurisdiction, as national law and the EU law are two separate legal systems.

The preliminary ruling procedure has greatly contributed to the development of EU law. The most important and fundamental principles of EU law, such as the principle of direct effect and the principle of supremacy of EU law, have been enunciated within the framework of the preliminary ruling procedure.

Article 267 TFEU also contributes to the legal protection of individuals. It allows them, via national courts, to have access to the ECJ.

10.1.3   Jurisdiction of the ECJ under Article 267 TFEU

The ECJ has jurisdiction both to interpret EU law and to assess the validity of EU acts adopted by EU institutions, bodies and agencies. As a result, it exercises two different functions under Article 267 TFEU, although both contribute to define the scope of application of EU law. The interpretation of EU law under Article 267 TFEU has become the main activity of the ECJ. In respect of the validity of EU measures national courts have no jurisdiction to declare an EU act invalid. Only the ECJ can make a declaration of its invalidity. National courts must refer to the ECJ whenever there is a reasonable doubt as to the validity of an EU act at issue.

There are certain conditions under Article 267 TFEU common to the exercise of both functions which must be satisfied before the ECJ can accept a reference. They concern:

---

439.   [1974] ECR 33.

■ The provisions of EU law capable of being referred to the ECJ;

■ The body allowed to refer to the ECJ;

■ The territorial jurisdiction of the ECJ under Article 267 TFEU.

10.2   The extension of the preliminary ruling procedure to the whole area of FSJ

Under the ToL, the ECJ has gained jurisdiction to give preliminary rulings in respect of the whole of the area of FSJ. Prior to the entry into force of the ToL there were the following limitations provided for in Articles 68 EC and 35(1) EU (both Articles were repealed by the ToL):

■ Whilst Article 68 EC (introduced by the ToA) extended the jurisdiction of the ECJ to Title IV, which deals with Visa, Asylum, Immigration and Other Policies related to the Free Movement of Persons, this was subject to the important limitation that only national courts or tribunals against whose decisions there was no judicial remedy in national law could seek a preliminary ruling. Further, under Article 68(2) EC the ECJ had no interpretive jurisdiction in respect of measures or decisions taken pursuant to Article 62(1) EC (that is, measures on the crossing of external borders of the Member States, measures relating to the maintenance of law and order and the safeguarding of internal security). Article 68(3) EC provided that the Council, the Commission or any Member State may refer a question of interpretation to the ECJ, but in such a case the ruling given by the ECJ shall not apply to judgments of courts or tribunals of the Member States which "have become res judicata".[440]

■ Article 35(1) EU provided for the jurisdiction of the ECJ to give preliminary rulings on the validity and interpretation of measures adopted under Title VI EU (Pillar 3 in respect of police and judicial co-operation in criminal matters), but only in cases where the Member State concerned had made a declaration under Article 35(2) EU (repealed by the ToL) that it accepted the jurisdiction of the ECJ under Article 35(1) EU (repealed by the ToL). A Member State making a declaration under Article 35(2) EU could specify either that any court or tribunal may request a preliminary ruling or that such requests may be made only by its courts of final instance.

The ToL, whilst removing the above restrictions has imposed a temporary limitation on the jurisdiction of the ECJ.

Under Article 10 of Protocol 36 on Transitional Provisions of the Treaty of Lisbon, in the area of police and judicial co-operation in criminal matters, the ECJ will have no jurisdiction to give preliminary rulings in respect of measures adopted before the entry into force of the ToL for a period of five years following the entry into force of the ToL. However, if any particular measure, adopted before the entry into force of the ToL, is amended before the expiry of that period then that measure will be within the jurisdiction of the Court from the time of amendment. The temporal restriction does not apply to Member States which, prior to entry into force of the ToL,

---

440.   The EP in its legislative resolution of 25 April 2007 on the draft Council decision adopting the provisions concerning the jurisdiction of the ECJ in fields covered by Title IV of Part Three of the EC Treaty (COM (2006) 0346) recommended that the ECJ should apply the standard procedure of Article 234 EC to matters covered by Title IV without any restriction, i.e. contained in Article 68(2) EC (A6–0082/2007).

made a Declaration under Article 35(1) EU (since repealed) allowing their courts to make requests for a preliminary ruling in this area. It is to be noted that the temporal limitation does not affect the ECJ having jurisdiction to give preliminary rulings on the interpretation and validity of measures concerning the whole area of FSJ adopted subsequent to the entry into force of the ToL.

An additional limitation is contained in Article 276 TFEU under which the ECJ has no jurisdiction to give preliminary rulings on the validity or proportionality of operations carried out by the police or other law-enforcement services of a Member States or the exercise of the responsibilities incumbent upon Member States in respect of the maintenance of law and order and the safeguarding of internal security. This is less controversial than it looks given that the ECJ has never had jurisdiction to review internal situations. However, nothing will prevent the ECJ from giving a preliminary ruling on the compatibility of certain acts of national authorities with EU law or interpretation of the relevant EU acts.

Preliminary rulings concerning the resolution of legal issues relating to the area of FSJ, pose a special problem for the ECJ in terms of the duration of preliminary ruling proceedings. At the time of writing the average duration of the preliminary reference procedure is about 17 months.[441] For cases concerning the area of FSJ the ECJ must respond quickly in order to comply with Article 6 ECHR and to ensure that the interests of justice are met. In addition, national courts are often required, either under EU law or under national law, to deliver a judgment within a very strict time limit or to give priority treatment to cases involving asylum, immigration, and/or matrimonial matters and matters of parental responsibility, European arrest warrants, and so on. In order to respond to those concerns, a new urgent preliminary ruling procedure was established. It is governed by Article 23a of Protocol 3 and Article 104b of the Rules of Procedure of the ECJ. This procedure is additional to the expedited or accelerated procedure (see Chapter 6.6.6).

10.2.1 The urgent preliminary ruling procedure

Council Decision 2008/79/EC[442] amending the Protocol on the Statute of the Court of Justice authorised the ECJ to introduce a new procedure enabling the Court to deal expeditiously and appropriately with requests for preliminary rulings in matters relating to the area of FSJ. The new procedure entered into force on 1 March 2008. It is difficult to list all cases in which the procedure will be used but Article 267(4) TFEU provides one example, i.e. the urgent preliminary ruling procedure is to be used in a situation where a case pending before a court of tribunal or a Member State concerns a person in custody or deprived of liberty and the answer to the question raised in the referral is decisive as to the assessment of that person's legal situation. Other examples are proceedings relating to parental authority or custody of children (see below).

The main features of the urgent preliminary ruling procedure are:

- In the written stage of the procedure only the parties to the main proceedings, the Member State of the court which has made the reference, the European Commission, and the Council and the EP (if either or both of them adopted the challenged measure) are entitled

---

441. According to the 2009 Report of the CJEU the average duration of a preliminary ruling procedure was 17.1 months in 2009 and 16.8 months in 2008, p 4. The Report is available at http://curia.europa.eu/jcms/jcms/ Jo2_7000 (7/4/10).

442. [2008] OJ L24/42.

to make written submissions. These must be in the language of the case and made within a very short period of time of receipt of the notice of the referral. Further in some cases the written procedure may be omitted. In the oral stage of the proceedings, other interested parties, in particular Member States other than that of the referring court, can make oral observations on the questions referred by the national court and on the written observations submitted by the authorised parties;

- A special Chamber within the ECJ has been established to screen and process referrals made under the urgent procedure. If the Chamber decides that a request for a preliminary ruling should be dealt with under the urgent procedure, the Chamber will give its ruling shortly after the hearing, and after hearing the A-G;

- The procedure is, for the most part, carried out electronically. As far as possible, all procedural documents are allowed to be submitted and served by fax or e-mail;

- The ECJ may, on its own motion, decide to deal with a referral under the urgent procedure.

In Case C-195/08 *PPU Inga Rinau*[443] the ECJ, for the first time, rendered a judgment under the urgent procedure. The referral was made in proceedings between Mrs Rinau and Mr Rinau regarding the return to Germany of their daughter Luisa, who had been retained in Lithuania by Mrs Rinau. The ECJ was asked to interpret Council Regulation 2201/2003 on jurisdiction and the recognition and enforcement of judgments in matrimonial matters and on matters of parental responsibility. The referral was received at the ECJ on 14 May 2008 and the judgment was rendered on 11 July 2008. Accordingly, in less than two months the ECJ dealt with the referral. This shows that the new procedure made a good start.

10.3   The subject-matter jurisdiction of the ECJ under Article 267 TFEU

Under Article 267 (1) TFEU national courts may request the ECJ to give preliminary rulings on the following matters.

10.3.1   Interpretation of primary sources of EU law

These include: the founding Treaties as amended; protocols; annexes to the Treaties; and acts of accession to the Communities and the EU.[444]

10.3.2   Interpretation and validity of secondary legislation

Article 267(1)(a) TFEU states that the ECJ has jurisdiction to give preliminary rulings in respect of the validity and interpretation of acts of the EU institutions, bodies, offices or agencies. In Case 9/70 *Franz Grad*,[445] the ECJ held that all acts adopted by EC institutions, without distinction, are capable of being referred under Article 234 EC [Article 267 TFEU]. This comprises not only

---

443.   [2008] ECR I-5271.
444.   Case 812/79 *Burgoa* [1980] ECR 2787.
445.   [1970] ECR 825.

acts expressly mentioned in Article 288 TFEU, or in the Treaties, but all other acts adopted outside its framework, for example, resolutions of the Council.[446].

National courts may also refer questions concerning EU law which is not directly effective. This is so since determining the exact meaning of national law which they have to apply, and which implements EU directives or decisions addressed to a Member State, may pose difficult interpretation problems,[447] or may give rise to doubts as to its validity.[448]

The ECJ has jurisdiction to interpret non-binding acts such as recommendations[449] and opinions. The validity of non-binding acts is decided by national courts.

10.3.3 Interpretation and validity of international agreements concluded between the EU and third countries

In Case 181/73 *Haegemann*,[450] the ECJ held that international agreements concluded by the EC [the EU] are to be considered as acts adopted by the EC institutions within the meaning of Article 234 EC [Article 267 TFEU]. The treatment of international agreements as EU acts is very important since this approach ensures uniformity in their interpretation and application throughout the EU. However, national courts or tribunals of third countries, which countries are contracting parties to those agreements, are neither allowed to refer to the ECJ under Article 267 TFEU, nor are they bound by its judgments.

The jurisdiction of the ECJ to give preliminary rulings extends to decisions adopted by bodies created by international agreements with a view to ensuring proper application of their provisions.[451] For example, in Case C-188/91 *Deutsche Shell*[452] the ECJ held that non-binding recommendations adopted by a Joint Committee established under the Convention on a Common EEC/ EFTA Transit Procedure, because of their direct link to the Convention, were part of the EU legal order, so that the ECJ had jurisdiction to give a preliminary ruling on their interpretation.

10.3.4 Matters excluded from referral

The ECJ is precluded from giving preliminary rulings on the following:

- The validity of primary sources, taking into account their constitutional nature, cannot be determined by the ECJ;

- Validity of judgments of the ECJ;[453]

- Matters specified in section 10.2:

---

446. Case 59/75 *Manghera* [1976] ECR 91.
447. Case 111/75 *Mazzalai* [1976] ECR 657.
448. Case 5/77 *Tedeschi* [1977] ECR 1555.
449. Case 113/75 *Frecassetti* [1976] ECR 983; Case C-322/88 *Grimaldi* [1989] ECR 4407.
450. [1974] ECR 449, which concerned an association agreement between the EEC and Greece. The *Haegemann* jurisprudence has been confirmed in many cases, for example in Case 52/77 *Cayrol* [1977] ECR 2261 concerning the association agreement between the EEC and Spain, and Case 65/77 *Razanatsimba* [1977] ECR 2229 concerning the Lomé Convention.
451. Case C-192/89 *Sevince* [1990] ECR I-3461 and Case C-188/91 *Deutsche Shell* [1993] ECR I-363.
452. [1993] ECR I-363.
453. Case 69/85 *Wünsche* [1986] ECR 947.

● Provisions relating to the CFSP and acts adopted on the basis of those provisions. This exclusion is subject to two exceptions in that the ECJ has jurisdiction:

○ to decide whether measures adopted under the CFSP have encroached on other policies of the EU and vice versa, i.e. whether measures adopted in non-CFSP policies have impinged on other areas of EU;

○ to review the legality of decisions providing for restrictive measures against natural or legal persons adopted by the Council on the basis of Chapter 2 of Title V TEU.

In respect of both exceptions proceedings for annulment of the above measures under Article 263 TFEU will be the appropriate way to challenge them, although if there are national implementing measures, it seems obvious that a national court or tribunal will be entitled to make a referral to the ECJ concerning issues covered by the above exceptions.

10.4   National courts and tribunals that can refer to the ECJ under Article 267 TFEU

Article 267 TFEU specifies that only courts and tribunals may ask for preliminary rulings. This prevents the parties to a dispute referring directly to the ECJ. If a contract concluded between private parties specifies that any dispute on a point of EU law should be referred to the ECJ, it will decline jurisdiction. Private parties cannot impose jurisdiction under Article 267 TFEU upon the ECJ.[454]

In most cases the question of whether a particular body is a court or a tribunal is self-evident although in some circumstances even a court recognised as such under national law may not be regarded as a court within the meaning of Article 267 TFEU (see Case C-96/04 *Standesamt Stadt Niebüll*[455] below). Uniformity in the application of EU law requires that the definition of a court or a tribunal for the purposes of Article 267 TFEU is independent of national concepts and has an autonomous, EU meaning. The case law of the ECJ has gradually determined the criteria permitting identification of a body which is to be regarded as "a court or a tribunal". It emerges from the case law[456] of the ECJ that the following criteria are relevant in determining whether or not a body making a reference is a court or tribunal for the purposes of Article 267 TFEU:

▪ Whether the body is established by law;

▪ Whether it is permanent;

▪ Whether its jurisdiction is compulsory;

▪ Whether its procedure is adversarial;

▪ Whether it applies rules of law;

▪ Whether it is independent;

▪ Whether it is called upon to give a decision of a judicial nature.

---

454.   Case 44/65 *Hessische Knappschaft* [1965] ECR 965; Case 93/78 *Mattheus* [1978] ECR 2203.
455.   [2006] ECR I-3561.
456.   Case C-54/96 *Dorsch Consult* [1997] ECR I-4961; Case C-516/99 *Schmid* [2002] ECR I-4573; Case C-182/00 *Lutz and Others* [2002] ECR I-547; Case C-96/04 *Standesamt Stadt Niebüll* [2006] ECR I-3561.

On the basis of the above criteria the ECJ decided:

■ In Case 61/65 *Vaassen-Göbbels*,[457] that a Dutch social security arbitration tribunal could refer since:

  ● its members and the Chairman were appointed by the Dutch Minister for Social Affairs and Public Health who also laid down the rules of procedure;
  ● it was a permanent body which settled disputes under Article 89 of the RBFM;[458]
  ● the procedure was adversarial;
  ● the jurisdiction of the social security arbitration tribunal was compulsory in all disputes involving the social security authority and the insurer;
  ● it was bound to apply rules of law and not equity.

■ In Case C-24/92 *Corbiau*,[459] that the director of taxation (Directeur des Contributions) in Luxembourg was not a court or tribunal and could not refer to the ECJ. This was so because he was not a third party to the proceedings (so he was not independent) as there was an institutional link between the Luxembourg tax authorities (which made the decision challenged by Corbiau) and the director of those authorities.

■ In Case 138/80 *Borker*,[460] that the Paris Conseil de l'Ordre des Avocats à la Cour de Paris (Paris Bar Council) was not a court or tribunal within the meaning of Article 267 TFEU because that body was not exercising any judicial function. In fact the body "made a request for a declaration relating to a dispute between a member of the Bar and the Courts or tribunals of another Member State".

■ In Case 246/80 *Broekmeulen*,[461] that the Appeals Committee for General Medicine, which was established by the Royal Netherlands Society for the Promotion of Medicine (and not considered as a court or tribunal under Dutch law), was a court or a tribunal for the following reasons:

  ● The national authorities appointed the chairman and one-third of the members of the Society body, so constituting a significant degree of involvement of The Netherlands public authorities in its composition;
  ● The procedure was adversarial;
  ● There was no appeal from the Appeals Committee to the courts;
  ● Any general practitioner, whether Dutch or from another Member State, intending to establish himself/herself in The Netherlands, was compelled to have his/her status recognised by the Society. In the case of refusal the Appeals Committee was competent in the last resort to decide the question of his/her registration as a doctor.

■ In Case C-134/97 *Victoria Film A/S*,[462] that the Skatterättsnämnden (Swedish Revenue

---

457. [1966] ECR 261.
458. Reglement van het Beamtenfonds voor het Mijnbedrijf, the Regulation governing the relations between the social security authority and those insured by it.
459. [1993] ECR I-1277.
460. [1980] ECR 1975.
461. [1981] ECR 2311.
462. [1998] ECR I-7023.

Board), which assesses the situation of an applicant from the point of view of internal taxation and delivers only preliminary decisions prior to binding decisions of the Swedish tax authorities, was not a court or a tribunal within the meaning of Article 267 TFEU. It exercised administrative authority, without at the same time being called on to decide a dispute. In this respect the ECJ held that:

> "Skatterättsnämnden does not . . . have as its task to review the legality of the decisions of the tax authorities but rather to adopt a view, for the first time, on how a specific transaction is to be assessed to tax. Where, upon application by a taxable person, Skatterättsnämnden gives a preliminary decision on a matter of assessment or taxation, it performs a non-judicial function which, moreover, in other Member States is expressly entrusted to the tax authorities."

Thus, if a body exercises only administrative functions and is not called upon to give a decision of a judicial nature, it is not regarded as a court or tribunal within the meaning of Article 267 TFEU.[463]

■ In Case C-53/03 *Synetairismos Farmakopoion Aitolias & Akarnanias (Syfait) and Others v GlaxoSmithKline plc and Others*,[464] that the Greek Competition Authority (the Epitropi Antagonismou) was not a court or tribunal as it was not an independent body because:

● The lawfulness of its decisions was, subject to some limitations, reviewed by the Minister for Development;
● Its members, although independent in the exercise of their duties, could be dismissed or their appointment could be terminated without any special safeguards; and
● It was not called upon to give a decision of a judicial nature.

■ In Case C-96/04 *Standesamt Stadt Niebüll*,[465] that a German local court (Amtsgericht) was not a court or tribunal within the meaning of Article 267 TFEU.

THE FACTS WERE:

The German Registry Office brought proceedings before a local court in order to transfer the right to determine a child's surname to one of his parents. The child in question, Leonhard Matthias, was born in Denmark to a married couple Dorothee Paul and Stefan Grunkin, both German nationals. Under Danish law the child was given the double-barrelled surname composed of his father's and mother's surnames. The German authorities refused to recognise the child's surname on the ground that under German law a child is not allowed to bear a double-barrelled surname. The child's parents challenged that refusal before the German courts. Their action was dismissed at final instance by the German Constitutional Court. In the meantime the parents divorced, but refused to change their child's surname as required

---

463. See Case C-192/98 *Azienda Nazionale Autonoma della Steade*, Order [1999] ECR I-8583; and Case C-440/98 *Radiotelevisione Italiana SpA*, Order [1999] ECR I-8597 in which referrals from the Italian Corte dei Conti were rejected on similar grounds.
464. [2005] ECR I-4609.
465. [2006] ECR I-3561.

by German law. The Registrar's Office in Niebüll brought the matter before the local court, which decided to refer to the ECJ questions on the compatibility of the German law with Articles 12 and 18 EC [Articles 18 and 21 TFEU].

Held:

The ECJ held that:

■ The referring court, although it was a court under German law, was not a court or tribunal within the meaning of Article 234 EC [Article 267 TFEU] on the ground that the court was exercising administrative authority, without at the same time being called on to decide a dispute.

Comment:

There was no dispute before the local court leading to a decision of a judicial nature as the dispute between the parents and the German authorities was settled at the last instance by the German Constitutional Court, and there was no dispute between the parents as they refused to change their child's surname. This case emphasises the importance of the functional criterion in the determination of the concept of "court or tribunal" in that an entity which is entitled to refer to the ECJ must exercise a judicial function, i.e. must be required to give a decision of a judicial nature. This was confirmed in Case C-497/08 *Amiraike Berlin GmbH*,[466] in which the Amtsgericht Charlottenburg, a German court recognised as such under German law, made a referral to the ECJ at the stage of national proceedings when it was exercising administrative functions consisting of the appointment of the liquidator of a company, without any dispute being raised before it and thus without being called to give a decision of a judicial nature.

■ In Case 14/86 *Pretore di Salò v Persons Unknown*,[467] that an Italian Pretore, a magistrate who initially acts as a public prosecutor and then as an examining magistrate, and thus exercises not only a judicial function but also other tasks, was a court or tribunal for the purposes of Article 267 TFEU. The ECJ accepted the referral on the ground that the request emanated from a body that acted in the general framework of its task of judging, independently and in accordance with the law, despite the fact that certain functions performed by that body were not strictly speaking of a judicial nature.[468]

■ In Case C-74/95 and C-129/95 *Criminal Procedures against X*,[469] the ECJ refused to accept a referral from an Italian public prosecutor. Advocate General Ruiz Jarabo Colomer stressed that the main task of the Procura della Repubblica is to submit evidence during the trial and thus it is a party to the proceedings. Further, it does not exercise judicial functions and as such should not be regarded as a court or a tribunal under Article 267 TFEU.

---

466. Judgment of 12/1/10 (NYR).
467. [1987] ECR 2545.
468. Confirmed in Case 318/85 *Greis Unterweger* [1986] ECR 955; Case C-393/92 *Almelo* [1994] ECR I-1477.
469. [1996] ECR I-6609.

10.5 Arbitration

The ECJ makes a distinction between private and public arbitration. The ECJ has always refused referrals from arbitrators dealing with private disputes but accepted them when public authorities have been involved in arbitration.

10.5.1 Private arbitration

Referrals in private arbitration have been examined by the ECJ many times. One of the first cases was Case 102/81 *Nordsee Deutsche Hochseefischerei GmbH v Reederei Mond.*[470]

THE FACTS WERE:

The parties to the disputed contract inserted an arbitration clause into the original contract providing that any disagreements between them on any question arising out of the contract would be resolved by an arbitrator and that all recourse to the ordinary courts was excluded. When a problem concerning the performance of that contract by a number of German shipbuilders arose, an arbitrator was appointed by the Chamber of Commerce of Bremen in accordance with the contract, after it became apparent that the parties could not agree on the appointment. During the arbitration proceedings a number of questions concerning the interpretation of EC law arose. The arbitrator asked the ECJ to give a preliminary ruling.

Held:

The ECJ refused to recognise the arbitrator as a court or tribunal for two reasons:

- First, that the parties to the dispute freely selected arbitration as a way of resolving any dispute between them;

- Second, that German public authorities were neither involved in the choice of arbitration by the parties nor were they "called to intervene automatically in the proceedings before the arbitrator".

Comment:

The ECJ emphasised that if private arbitration raises questions concerning Community law [EU law], national courts may have jurisdiction to examine those questions:

- In the framework of assistance they provide for arbitral tribunals, especially in the context of certain judicial measures which are not available to the arbitrator; or

- When determining and interpreting the law applicable to the contract under consideration; or

- Within the framework of control which they exercise in relation to arbitration awards.[471]

---

470.   [1982] ECR 1095.
471.   Case C-393/92 *Almelo* [1994] ECR I-1477.

It is submitted that the refusals to recognise an arbitrator as a court or tribunal under Article 267 TFEU (one of the more recent, at the time of writing, being in Case C-125/04 *Denuit and Cordenier v Transorient Mosaïque Voyages and Culture SA*[472]) should be reconsidered by the ECJ, which should take account of the advantages that arbitration offers to businessmen, namely:

- Choice of arbitrators;

- Confidentiality of proceedings;

- More speedy and less expensive proceedings as compared to those conducted before national courts.

If the refusal of the ECJ to recognise arbitrators as courts or tribunals is maintained, the attractiveness of arbitration will be substantially reduced.

10.5.2 Public arbitration

If public authorities are involved in arbitration, the situation is very different from that concerning private arbitration. For example, in Case 109/88 *Handels-og Kontorfunktionaerernes Forbund I Danmark v Dansk Arbejdsgiverforening*,[473] a Danish Industrial Arbitration Board was recognised as a court or tribunal within the meaning of Article 234 EC [Article 267 TFEU] because its jurisdiction was imposed upon the parties if they could not agree on the application of a collective agreement, its composition and procedure were governed by Danish law, and its award was final.

10.6 The territorial jurisdiction of the ECJ under Article 267 TFEU

Article 267 TFEU provides that only courts and tribunals of the Member States may ask for preliminary rulings. As a result, courts located in third countries, or international courts, are not permitted to refer under Article 267 TFEU.

The ECJ has given a wide interpretation to the territorial scope of application of Article 267 TFEU as it has accepted a reference:

- From a court situated in the Isle of Man, which is outside the system of British courts,[474] on the ground that the UK under its Act of Accession is responsible for the Isle of Man's external relations;

- From an administrative court of Papeete in Polynesia. In this case, the government of the UK argued that the court of Papeete was not within the jurisdiction of France, as it was situated in a French overseas department and that under Article 299(3) EC [Article 349 TFEU] it was outside the territorial scope of application of EU law. The ECJ held that this court under French law was taken to be a French administrative court, and that the question

---

472. [2005] ECR I-923. See also: Case C-126/97 *Eco Swiss China Time Ltd v Benetton International NV* [1999] ECR I-3055, in which the case had to reach the Supreme Court of The Netherlands before the questions on EC law were referred to the ECJ.

473. [1989] ECR 3199.

474. Case C-355/89 *Barr* [1991] ECR I-3479.

referred was within the jurisdiction of the ECJ as it concerned the application of the special conditions on association of overseas territories which included French Polynesia.[475]

10.7 Preliminary rulings on the interpretation of EU law

The ECJ has stated on many occasions that where the questions submitted concern the interpretation of EU law, the Court is in principle bound to give a ruling.[476]

The ECJ interpretation comprises:

- The determination of the exact meaning and scope of application of the provisions of EU law as well as the concepts which those provisions expressly or implicitly describe,[477] for example the concept of non-discrimination;

- The determination whether or not EU regulations need to be further completed or specified by national legislation;[478]

- The determination of the application of the provisions of EU law ratione materiae, ratione personae, ratione temporis, the legal effect they produce and especially whether or not they are directly effective;

- The determination of the meaning and legal implications of the principle of supremacy of EU law vis-à-vis national laws of the Member States;

- The interpretation of acts adopted not only by the EU institutions but also by EU bodies, offices and agencies.

Under Article 267 TFEU, the role of the ECJ is to interpret EU law, not national law. Therefore, the question of interpretation of, and the validity of, national law is outside the ECJ's jurisdiction.[479] However, the ECJ will accept reference in respect of purely internal matters in a situation where a provision of national law is based on or makes a reference to EU law. This was held by the ECJ in Joined Cases C-297/88 and C-197/89 *Dzodzi*.[480] Important limitations on the *Dzodzi* approach were imposed in Case C-346/93 *Kleinwort Benson*,[481] in which the ECJ held that with regard to wholly internal situations it would accept referrals only if two conditions were satisfied:

- The reference by national law to the provision of EU law must be "direct and unconditional"; and

- The application of a provision of EU law must be "absolutely and unconditionally" binding on the national court.

---

475. Cases C-100/89 and C-101/89 *Kaefer and Procacci v France* [1990] ECR I-4647; also Case C-260/90 *Leplat* [1992] ECR I-643.

476. Case C-326/00 *IKA* [2003] ECR I-1703; Case C-145/03 *Keller* [2005] ECR I-2529; Case C-419/04 *Conseil Général de la Vienne v Directeur Général des Douanes et Droits Indirect* [2006] ECR I-5645.

477. Case 10/69 *Portelange* [1969] ECR 309.

478. Case 94/71 *Schlüter* [1972] ECR 307.

479. For example Case 75/63 *Unger* [1964] ECR 177; Case 188/86 *Lefèvre* [1987] ECR 2963; Case 20/87 *Gauchard* [1987] ECR 4879; Case 152/83 *Demouche* [1987] ECR 3833; Case C-347/89 *Eurim-Pharm* [1991] ECR I-1747.

480. [1990] ECR I-3763, see also Case C-231/89 *Gmurzynska-Bscher* [1990] ECR I-4003.

481. [1995] ECR I-615.

However, the above conditions have not been observed by the ECJ in subsequent cases despite repeated requests from As-G.[482] Accordingly, the ECJ accepts requests for a preliminary ruling also where national law makes indirect and implicit references to EU law.

It is important to note that subsequent to the judgment in Case C-448/98 *Guimont*[483] (for facts and comments on *Guimont* see Chapter 20.6), the ECJ is willing to accept referrals concerning purely internal situations in the context not only of the free movement of goods, but also in relation to the free movement of capital and services where the referred case raises the issue of reverse discrimination, if its reply "might be useful" to the referring court.[484] The *Guimont* variation of the *Dzodzi* approach has been criticised as increasing the risk of wasting the resources of the litigants, of national courts and of the ECJ itself, given that when a referring court is not required to establish whether under national law reverse discrimination is prohibited, in many cases the ECJ will deliver a purely theoretical ruling.[485]

10.7.1 Difficulties in distinguishing between the interpretation and the application of EU law

A problem with the interpretation of EU law under Article 267 TFEU is that it is not easy to draw a line between the interpretation and the actual application of EU law. Under Article 267 TFEU the ECJ has jurisdiction to interpret EU law in abstracto and objectively. However, the necessity to assist national courts in rendering a judgment in a particular case requires that ECJ judges give their decision within the context of the law and facts of the case. Accordingly, the boundary between interpretation and application is fluid and varies depending upon the degree of precision of the question asked by national courts, the complexity of the factual and legal context of the dispute, and so on. For that reason, the ECJ is in a difficult position because:

- On the one hand, if its judgments are in fact not preliminary rulings but rulings on the merits, which has occurred on numerous occasions, the ECJ instead of interpreting EU law, is applying it and thus is encroaching upon the jurisdiction of national courts and undermining the division of competences between national courts and the ECJ. This is contrary to the spirit and the terms of Article 267 TFEU.

- On the other hand, if the preliminary ruling is too general, or the interpretation of a provision of EU law is too abstract, the national judge would have a large measure of discretion, so that the preliminary ruling may, instead of clarifying a particular question, obscure it even more. This situation calls into question the main objective of Article 267 TFEU, that is, to ensure uniformity of application of EU law throughout the EU.

---

482. E.g. in Case C-306/99 *BIAO* [2003] ECR I-1, A-G Jacobs called upon the ECJ to "affirm the criteria which is laid down in Kleinwort Benson".

483. [2000] ECR I-10663.

484. With regard to Article 30 TFEU, the ECJ held that when national authorities impose charges on goods crossing internal/regional borders the situation is within the scope of EC law, i.e. this is a breach of Article 25 EC [Article 30 TFEU], and consequently any referral relating to such situations will be accepted (see Case C-363/93 *Lancry* [1994] ECR I-3957 and Case C-72/03 *Carbonati Apuani* [2004] ECR I-8027). The *Guimont* approach has been applied to the free movement of capital (Case C-515/99 *Reisch* [2002] ECR I-2157) and to freedom to provide services (Case C-6/01 *Anomar* [2003] ECR I-8621).

485. See C Ritter, "Purely Internal Situations, Reverse Discrimination, Guimont, Dzodzi and Article 234", (2006) 31/5 ELRev, p 690.

It is not easy for the ECJ to reach a decision which is neither too precise nor too general, and indeed, some decisions of the ECJ under Article 267 TFEU have left no doubts as to the outcome of the case.[486]

10.7.2 Admissibility of referrals raising identical or similar questions to those already answered in previous judgments

The ECJ has always refused to regard its preliminary rulings on the interpretation of EU law as irrevocable. Accordingly, the ECJ may modify its interpretation of EU law and thus national courts are entitled to bring the same, or a similar matter (although based on different facts or supported by new legal arguments[487]), before the ECJ by way of a subsequent reference for a preliminary ruling. For that reason a new referral (or a referral concerning the same or similar question) cannot easily be dismissed. For example, in Case 28/67 *Molkerei-Zentrale*,[488] the ECJ examined at length new arguments invoked against its previous interpretation.

If the referred question is identical to one already decided, the ECJ may accept the preliminary question, but refer to the previous rulings and deal with the referral by means of a reasoned order. For example, in Case C-291/04 *Schmitz*,[489] in which the Police Tribunal of Neufchâteau referred questions identical to questions answered by the ECJ in Joined Cases C-151/04 *Nadin, Nadin-Lux SA*, C-152/04 *Durré*,[490] the ECJ dealt with the case by issuing a reasoned order.[491] Further, under the Rules of Procedure, the ECJ is entitled to dispose of a referral from national courts by means of a reasoned order, where the answer to a preliminary question can clearly be deduced from the existing case law.

10.7.3 Distinction between discretionary and compulsory reference by national courts to the ECJ

There are two possible approaches to ensuring uniformity in the application of EU law:

- The first, consisting of compulsory referrals to the ECJ each time a national court or tribunal has difficulties with the interpretation of EU law. This would be inconvenient in terms of the duration of proceedings and the heavy workload imposed upon the ECJ.

- The second, consisting of granting an unlimited discretion to national courts (whatever their position in the hierarchy of the national judicial system) as to whether or not to refer to the ECJ. However, to grant such discretion to national courts would jeopardise the homogeneity of EU law.

---

486. Case 33/65 *Dekker* [1965] ECR 905; Case 82/71 *Sail* [1972] ECR 119; Case C-213/89 *R v Secretary of State for Transport ex parte Factortame* (1) [1990] ECR I-2433; Case 222/84 *Johnston* [1986] ECR 1651; Case C-292/93 *British Telecom* [1996] ECR I-1631; Case C-224/01 *Köbler* [2003] ECR I-10239.

487. In Case 22/78 *ICAC* [1979] ECR 1168 the ECJ upheld its previous ruling on the ground that the new referral did not demonstrate any new factual or legal circumstances which would lead to a different interpretation.

488. [1968] ECR 143.

489. Order [2006] ECR I-59.

490. [2005] ECR I-11203.

491. Case 44/65 *Hessische Knappschaft* [1965] ECR 965.

EU law rejected both of the above approaches. Article 267 TFEU represents a compromise between them. Accordingly, national courts or tribunals against whose decisions there is no judicial remedy under national law "shall bring" a question of interpretation of EU law before the ECJ, while other national courts or tribunals have unfettered discretion in matters of referrals.

The idea behind this compromise is that, on the one hand, in the case of obviously wrong decisions of lower courts on a point of EU law, an appeal to a superior court will rectify that mistake. On the other, the obligation to refer imposed on the courts of last resort will prevent a body of national law, that is, not in accordance with EU law, from being established in a Member State.[492]

10.7.4 Discretion of national courts and tribunals to refer: Article 267(2) TFEU

The lower courts within the meaning of Article 267(2) TFEU have an unfettered discretion to refer to the ECJ. Article 267 TFEU recognises the exclusive jurisdiction of national courts to decide whether to refer.

A national judge has the sole discretion as to whether to refer. The ECJ has emphasised many times that national courts have the best knowledge of the case and that, taking into account their responsibility for rendering correct judgments, they, alone, are competent to assess the relevance of the question of EU law raised in the dispute and the necessity of obtaining a preliminary ruling.[493] Neither the parties to the dispute, nor their legal representatives, nor any other public authorities, which under certain national legal systems may interfere in the proceedings, can force a national court to refer. On the contrary, a national judge may decide to refer even if the parties to the dispute have not raised the issue,[494] or not to refer even if so requested by one of them,[495] or both as in Joined Cases C-320/94 and C-328/94 *Reti Televise Italiana*.[496] In Case C-85/95 *J Reisdorf*,[497] the ECJ held that parties may not challenge as irrelevant to the dispute a question referred by a national judge to the ECJ.

National procedural rules cannot impose restrictions on the court's discretion to make a referral. In Joined Cases 146/73 and 166/73 *Rheinmühlen*,[498] the ECJ emphasised that "a rule of national law whereby a court is bound on points of law by the rulings of a superior court cannot deprive the inferior courts of their power to refer to the ECJ questions of interpretation of Community law involving such rulings."[499]

National courts may refer a question at any stage of the proceedings. The ECJ, in Case 70/77 *Simmenthal*,[500] held that the proper administration of justice requires that a question should not be referred prematurely. However, it is outside the jurisdiction of the ECJ to specify at which

---

492. Case C-393/98 *Gomes Valente* [2001] ECR I-1327; Case C-99/00 *Lyckeskog* [2002] ECR I-4839; Case C-495/03 *Intermodal Transport* [2005] ECR I-8151.

493. For example in Case 53/79 *ONPTS v Damiani* [1980] ECR 273; Case 26/62 *Van Gend en Loos* [1963] ECR 3.

494. Case 126/80 *Salonia* [1981] ECR 1563.

495. Case C-152/94 *Van Buynder* [1995] ECR I-3981.

496. [1996] ECR I-6471.

497. [1996] ECR I-6257.

498. [1974] ECR 33 see also Case C-312/93 *Peterbroeck* [1995] ECR I-4599.

499. See also Case C-210/06 *Cartesio* [2008] ECR I-9641.

500. [1978] ECR 1453.

particular point of the proceedings the national courts should ask for preliminary rulings.[501] However, in order to facilitate the tasks of national courts and tribunals, the ECJ issued an Information Note on References from National Courts for a Preliminary Ruling.[502]

It emerges from the case law that the ECJ's acceptance or rejection of a request for a preliminary ruling will depend on:

- The existence of a genuine dispute;

- The relevance of the referred question to the dispute at issue;

- The proper determination of the factual and legal context of the dispute by the referring court.

10.7.5 Existence of a genuine dispute

In Case 104/79 *Foglia v Novello*,[503] the ECJ refused to give a preliminary ruling on the ground that there was no genuine dispute between the parties to national proceedings.

THE FACTS WERE:

Foglia, an Italian wine merchant, entered into a contract with Novello, an Italian national, for the delivery of liqueur wine to a person residing in France. The parties inserted an express clause providing that Novello would not pay any unlawfully levied taxes. The French authorities imposed a tax on the importation of the wine to France, which Foglia paid, although his contract with a shipper also provided that he should not be liable for any charges imposed in breach of the free movement of goods. Foglia brought proceedings against Novello, who refused to reimburse the French tax levied on Foglia.

Held:

The ECJ declined to exercise jurisdiction on the ground that there was no real dispute in the case. It held that:

"It . . . appears that the parties to the main action are concerned to obtain a ruling that the French tax system is invalid for liqueur wine by the expedient of proceedings before an Italian court between two private individuals who are in agreement as to the result to be obtained and who have inserted a clause in their contract in order to induce the Italian court to give a ruling on the point. The artificial nature of this expedient is underlined by the fact that Foglia did not exercise its rights under French law to institute proceedings over the consumption tax although it undoubtedly has an interest in doing so in view of the clause in the contract by which it was bound and moreover by the fact that Foglia paid the duty without protest."

---

501. Joined Cases 36 and 71/80 *Irish Creamery Milk Suppliers Association* [1981] ECR 735; Case 72/83 *Campus Oil* [1984] ECR 2727.
502. [2009] OJ C297/1.
503. [1980] ECR 745.

Comment:

Both parties had the same interest in the outcome of the dispute. This was to obtain a ruling on the invalidity or otherwise of the French legislation, since under their contracts they were not liable to pay for any unlawful charges imposed by France. Their action was a collusive and artificial device aimed at obtaining a ruling and not a genuine dispute which the ECJ could settle.

When the Italian court subsequently asked the ECJ to provide clarification of its preliminary judgment in Case 104/79 *Foglia v Novello*, the ECJ accepted the second reference but once again declined, on the same grounds,[504] to give a preliminary ruling.

Whether or not a real dispute exists is determined from the point of view of Article 267 TFEU. Thus, neither the fact that the parties challenge national legislation of one Member State before a court of another Member State, nor their agreement to "organise" proceedings before a national court leading to the preliminary ruling (as was the case of Foglia), is sufficient to prevent a real dispute from being dealt with by the ECJ.[505] This is illustrated by Case C-150/88 *Eau de Cologne v Provide*.[506]

THE FACTS WERE:

A German manufacturer of Eau de Cologne brought an action against an Italian company, Provide, following Provide's refusal to accept products and make payments on the ground that the packaging of the products was incompatible with Italian law and therefore the products could not be marketed in Italy, although the packaging was in conformity with EC law [EU law].

Held:

The ECJ accepted the referral from a German court, despite the fact that the compatibility of Italian law with EU law was at issue.

The decision of the ECJ in *Foglia and Novello* has been much criticised,[507] but the ECJ has reaffirmed its position.[508] In subsequent cases the ECJ has provided further guidance as to the existence of a genuine dispute.[509] In Case 93/78 *Mattheus*,[510] the ECJ declined to exercise its jurisdiction because the referred question concerned not the interpretation of EU law in force, but the opinion of the Court on the enactment of future laws. The ECJ has also refused to answer

---

504. Case 244/80 *Foglia v Novello II* [1981] ECR 3045.
505. Case C-412/93 *Leclerc-Siplec* [1995] ECR I-179; Case C-415/93 *Bosman* [1995] ECR I-4921.
506. [1989] ECR 3891.
507. See E Bebr, "The Possible Implications of Foglia v Novello II", 19 CMLRev, 1982, p 421; D Wyatt, "Foglia (No.2): The Court Denies it Has Jurisdiction to Give Advisory Opinions", (1982) 7 ELRev, 186.
508. Case 98/85 *Bertini* [1986] ECR 1885; Case C-231/89 *Gmurzynska* [1990] ECR I-4003.
509. See Case C-96/04 *Standesamt Stadt Niebüll* [2006] ECR I-3561 (section 10.4).
510. [1978] ECR 2203.

general or hypothetical questions.[511] In Case C-83/91 *Meilicke v ADV/ORGA FA Meyer*,[512] the question of compatibility of the German legal theory of disguised non-cash subscription of capital with the Second Company Law Directive was considered hypothetical, as it was irrelevant to the dispute in question.

Another aspect concerning the existence of an actual dispute was examined by the ECJ in Case C-159/90 *Society for the Protection of Unborn Children (Ireland) v Grogan*.[513]

THE FACTS WERE:

The plaintiff asked the Irish High Court for an injunction prohibiting Irish student organisations from distributing information concerning abortion clinics in the UK, as contrary to the Irish Constitution. The High Court, in the context of interlocutory proceedings, referred to the ECJ the question of whether the prohibition of the distribution of information on abortion was in breach of EC law, in particular of its provisions on the free movement of services. In the meantime the decision to refer was appealed to the Irish Supreme Court, which granted the injunction, but did not quash the part of the High Court referral regarding the issue whether the defendants were entitled under the Community provision on the freedom to provide services to distribute the information on abortion clinics in the United Kingdom.

Held:

The ECJ found a very diplomatic solution to the highly sensitive issue. The ECJ refused to give a preliminary ruling on the ground that it had no jurisdiction to hear a referral when the proceedings before the referring court were already terminated.

10.7.6 Relevance of a referred question to the main dispute

The relevance of a referred question to the actual dispute was for the first time clearly assessed in Case 126/80 *Salonia*.[514] In this case, the ECJ held that it could reject a reference, since the national court was seeking to obtain a preliminary ruling on the interpretation of EU law quite clearly not relevant to the actual case.

Subsequently, the ECJ declined its jurisdiction to answer a question which had no connection with the subject matter of the main action,[515] or as the ECJ held in Case C-18/93 *Corsica Ferries*,[516] which "does not respond to the objective need to resolve the main action", or to assess the validity of EU acts which do not apply to a particular dispute.[517]

The above approach is mitigated by the ability of the ECJ to reformulate the question referred

---

511. Case C-343/90 *Dias* [1992] ECR I-4673.
512. [1992] ECR I-4871.
513. [1991] ECR I-4685.
514. [1981] ECR 1563.
515. Case C-343/90 *Dias* [1992] ECR I-4673; Cases C-332, 333 and 335/92 *Eurico Italia* [1994] ECR I-711.
516. [1994] ECR I-1783.
517. Case C-297/93 *Grau Hupka* [1994] ECR I-5535.

by a national court,[518] or to take into consideration a provision of EU law which the national court did not mention in its referral.[519] Furthermore, in Case C-67/96 *Albany* ([1999] ECR I-5751), and in Joined Cases C-115/97 to C-117/97 and Case C-357/97 *Brentjevis Handelsonderneming BV*[520] the ECJ stated that there is a presumption that a referred question is relevant to the main dispute.

10.7.7 Determination of the factual and legal context of the dispute

A request for a preliminary ruling should state:

- ▦ All the relevant facts with clarity and precision;

- ▦ The legal context of the dispute;

- ▦ The reasons which compelled the judge to ask for a referral and the arguments submitted by the parties to the dispute.[521]

The ECJ has underlined that a well drafted referral contributes to a better comprehension of the factual and legal context of the dispute and thus assists the Member States and the EU institutions in the preparation of their observations and the ECJ in giving a useful reply.

In early cases the ECJ held that it was not its task to verify the facts and the qualification of the legal nature of the referred question.[522] In later cases the ECJ declined to exercise its jurisdiction for lack of relevant information.[523] More recent cases demonstrate that the insufficient contextualisation of a dispute will lead to the rejection of referrals as being manifestly inadmissible.[524]

The strict requirement of contextualisation of a dispute is of lesser importance in areas in which the facts are not that essential, for example, if the referred question concerns the validity of EU acts. In Case C-295/94 *Hüpeden*[525] and Case C-296/94 *Pietsch*[526] a national court formulated the referred question in very lucid but very brief terms – Is the provision X of Regulation Y valid? The ECJ accepted the referral. In Case C-316/93 *Vaneetveld*,[527] the ECJ held that, despite insufficient information submitted by the national court on the legal and factual context of the dispute (which was less imperative in this case as the subject-matter concerned technical points), it was able to formulate a useful reply.

It is interesting to note that the facts of a case, as described by a national court, have been

---

518.   Case 35/85 *Tissier* [1986] ECR 1207; Case C-315/92 *Clinique* [1994] ECR I-317.

519.   Case C-151/93 *Voogd Vleesimport en Export BV* [1994] ECR I-4915.

520.   [1999] ECR I-6025.

521.   See para 21–24 of the 2009 Information Notice.

522.   Case 20/64 *Albatros* [1965] ECR 29; Case 5/77 *Tedeschi* [1977] ECR 1555.

523.   Joined Cases C-320–322/90 *Telemarsicabruzzo* [1993] ECR I-393.

524.   For example, the ECJ issued an order of manifest inadmissibility of referrals for lack of information in Case C-378/93 *La Pyramide SARL* [1994] ECR I-3999; Case C-458/93 *Mostafa Saddik* [1995] ECR I-511; Case C-167/94 *Juan Carlos Grau Gomis* [1995] ECR I-1023; Case C-307/95 *Max Mara* [1995] ECR I-5083; Case C-101/96 *Italia Testa* [1996] ECR I-3081; Case C-191/96 *M Modesti* [1996] ECR I-3937; Case C-196/96 *Lahlou Hassa* [1996] ECR I-3945; Case C-158/99 *Corticeira Amorim-Algarve Ltd*, order of 2/7/1999 [unpublished].

525.   [1996] ECR I-3375.

526.   [1996] ECR I-3409.

527.   [1994] ECR I-763.

accepted by the ECJ even though they may be inexact or even erroneous! This occurred in Case C-352/95 *Phytheron International SA.*[528]

THE FACTS WERE:

A national court submitted not only insufficient information (as it did not mention who was the holder of a disputed trade mark in France and in Germany), but also provided the ECJ with erroneous factual and legal information, as it stated that the place where the product was manufactured was in Turkey when in fact it was in Germany.

Held:

The ECJ gave a preliminary ruling on the basis of the facts as stated in the order for reference and not as they transpired to be in the course of the proceedings before it.

Comment:

The preliminary ruling was irrelevant to the main dispute. The ECJ justified its decision to give a preliminary ruling on the grounds of legal certainty and the right to defence. In particular, it took account of the fact that the holder of the disputed trade mark was not a party to the main dispute and therefore could not submit his arguments to the ECJ. Further, the ECJ emphasised that: "to alter the substance of questions referred for a preliminary ruling would be incompatible with the Court's function under Article 177 of the Treaty [Article 267 TFEU] and with its duty to ensure that the Governments of the Member States and the parties concerned are given the opportunity to submit observations under Article 20 of the Statute of the Court, bearing in mind that, under that provision, only the order of the referring court is notified to the interested parties".[529]

This approach was confirmed in Case C-223/95 *Moksel*,[530] in which a German court erroneously described the factual situation of the dispute. The ECJ held that the separation of functions between national courts and the ECJ within the framework of Article 267 TFEU requires that it is the task of a national court to determine the particular factual circumstances of each case, and the ECJ has jurisdiction solely to give a ruling on the interpretation and the validity of EU law on the basis of the facts submitted by the national court.

10.7.8 Mandatory referral by national courts of last resort: Article 267(3) TFEU

The ECJ has clarified the exact meaning of Article 267(3) TFEU, which states that if a question of interpretation of EU law "is raised in a case pending before a court or tribunal of a Member State, against whose decision there is no judicial remedy under national law, the court or tribunal shall bring the matter before the Court".

---

528.   [1997] ECR I-1729.
529.   Joined Cases 141–143/81 *Holdijk* [1982] ECR 1299.
530.   [1997] ECR I-2379.

10.7.8.1 Definition of "courts or tribunals" against whose decision there is no judicial remedy

The ECJ decided that the concept of courts "against whose decision there is no judicial remedy under national law" (that is, under national law there is no right of appeal against their decisions) comprises not only final appellate courts in each Member State, but also all courts which decide a case in the last instance. In Case 6/64 *Costa v ENEL*,[531] the Giudice Conciliatore in Milan was the court of last instance because of the small sum of money involved in the dispute, that is, £1 which Costa refused to pay. This demonstrates that any court or tribunal against whose decision in a given case there is no judicial remedy falls within the scope of Article 267(3) TFEU, although in other cases an appeal would be possible against decisions of that court and tribunal.

The uncertainty as to whether a national court, against whose decision an appeal is possible, but only with leave to appeal having been granted by a higher court or the lower court itself, is a "final court" within the meaning of Article 267 TFEU was answered in Case C-99/00 *Kenny Roland Lyckeskog*.[532] In this case the ECJ held that the final appellate court is to be regarded as a court of last instance. As a result, the lower court is not regarded as the final court unless the lower court itself decides whether to grant leave.

10.7.8.2 Conditions relating to mandatory reference by national courts of last resort

At first glance, it seems that the terms of Article 267(3) TFEU are imperative and that they impose an obligation upon the courts of last instance to ask for a preliminary ruling each time the interpretation of EU law is at issue. This impression is, however, not correct, in that the ECJ has, over the years, come to recognise three exceptions.

In Joined Cases 28–30/62 *Da Costa*,[533] the ECJ held that Article 267(3) TFEU "unreservedly" requires the courts of last resort to refer, but recognised the first exception. It is not necessary to refer if the ECJ has already interpreted the same question in an earlier case since ". . . the authority of an interpretation under Article 234 [Article 267 TFEU] already given by the Court may deprive the obligation [to refer] from its purpose and thus empty it of its substance". Such is the case especially when the question raised is materially identical to a question which has already been the subject of a preliminary ruling. The ECJ may still accept such a reference, as exemplified in *Da Costa* where the question asked was identical to that raised in Case 26/62 *Van Gend en Loos*.[534]

The second exception was recognised in Case 83/78 *Pigs Marketing Board*[535] in which the ECJ held that the court should assess the relevance of the question raised before it in the light of the necessity to obtain a preliminary ruling.

The above two exceptions were restated and a third exception was developed in Case 283/81 *CILFIT Srl v Ministro della Sanità*[536] in which the extent of the discretion of courts of last resort was fully explained.

---

531. [1964] ECR 614.
532. [2002] ECR I-4839.
533. [1963] ECR 31.
534. [1963] ECR 3.
535. [1978] ECR 2347.
536. [1982] ECR 3415.

THE FACTS WERE:

The Italian Ministry of Health imposed an inspection levy on imports of wool coming from other Member States. An Italian importer of wool challenged the levy. The Italian court considered that the case law on this matter was reasonably clear, but as a court of final instance, it was uncertain whether or not it should refer the question of the legality of this fixed health inspection levy to the ECJ. The Italian court asked the ECJ whether it was obliged to refer under Article 234 EC [Article 267 TFEU] when EC law was sufficiently clear and precise and there were no doubts as to its interpretation.

Held:

The ECJ held that:

■ The courts of last resort, like any other courts or tribunals, have the discretion to assess whether a referral is necessary to enable them to give judgment. They are not obliged to refer if a question concerning the interpretation of EC law [EU law] raised before them is not relevant to the dispute, that is, if it can in no way affect the outcome of the case.

■ The principle set out in *Da Costa* applies. Accordingly, if the ECJ has already dealt with a point of law at issue, even though the questions are not strictly identical, the court of last resort is not obliged to refer.

■ There is no obligation to refer if "the correct application of Community law [EU law] may be so obvious as to leave no scope for any reasonable doubt as to the manner in which the question raised is to be resolved. However, before it comes to the conclusion that such is the case, the national court or tribunal must be convinced that the matter is equally obvious to the courts of the other Member States and to the Court of Justice (ECJ)."

In *CILFIT* the ECJ endorsed the French doctrine of acte clair. According to that doctrine, the court before which the exception prejudicielle (a question concerning the interpretation of a particular provision) is raised, must refer it to a competent court in order to resolve that question, but only if there is real difficulty concerning its interpretation, or if there is a serious doubt in this respect. Having said this, if the provision in question is clear, and if its meaning is obvious, the court should apply it immediately.

It stems from *CILFIT* that it is not necessary for a court of last resort to refer to the ECJ:

■ If the question of EU law is irrelevant to the dispute;

■ If the question of EU law has already been interpreted by the ECJ even though it may not be identical. However, this does not mean that national courts, whatever their position in the hierarchy of national courts, are prevented from referring an identical or a similar question to the ECJ. In *CILFIT* the ECJ clearly stated that all courts remain entirely at liberty to refer a matter before them if they consider it appropriate to do so;

■ If the correct application of EU law is so obvious as to leave no scope for reasonable doubt. This follows from the French doctrine of acte clair. However, the ECJ added that before a national court concludes that such is the case, it must be convinced that the question is equally obvious to courts in other Member States and to the ECJ itself. Furthermore, the ECJ added three requirements, which a national court must take into consideration, when deciding whether the matter is clear and free of doubts. These are:

- It must assess whether the matter is equally obvious to the courts of the other Member States in the light of the characteristic features of EU law and especially the difficulties that its interpretation raises, that is, that it is drafted in several languages and all versions are equally authentic;
- It must be aware that EU law uses peculiar terminology and has legal concepts which have different meanings in different Member States;
- It must bear in mind that every provision of EU law must be placed in its context and interpreted in the light of the provisions of EU law as a whole, its objectives, and the state of its evolution at the date on which that provision is to be applied.

With regard to courts within the scope of Article 267(2) TFEU the ruling in *CILFIT* assists them in deciding whether to refer, while under Article 267(3) TFEU it imposes a duty on courts of last resort to refer to the ECJ if there are any reasonable doubts as to the meaning of a provision of EU law.

In practice the endorsement by the ECJ of the doctrine of acte clair has sensibly extended the discretion of the courts of last resort. It has also increased the risk of conflicting decisions being rendered by the highest courts in each Member State. On many occasions national courts have decided not to refer to the ECJ on the basis of this doctrine and have imposed their own interpretation of EU law, and have thus prevented the ECJ from expressing its views.[537]

In the judgment in Case C-224/01 *Gerhard Köbler v Austria*[538] (for facts see Chapter 14.4) the ECJ clearly established that a Member State may be liable for failure of its courts of final instance to refer a case to the ECJ for a preliminary ruling. This will certainly curb the tendency of such courts to abuse the doctrine of acte clair. In *Köbler* the acknowledgment of the principle of state liability for judicial decisions of a national court adjudicating at last instance came as no surprise. This is so given previous judgments of the ECJ, in particular in Joined Cases C-46 and 48/93 *Brasserie du Pêcheur and Factortame*,[539] and in Case C-392/93 *British Telecommunications*.[540]

In *Köbler* the ECJ made a very important clarification as to state liability for loss or damage caused by a decision of a national court adjudicating at last instance. It held that non-compliance by the court in question with its obligation to make a reference for a preliminary ruling under the third paragraph of Article 267 TFEU constituted one of the decisive factors in determining whether or not the breach of EU law was sufficiently serious as to justify the award of damages to the applicants. In this respect, Advocate General Léger in his Opinion went further. He emphasised the role that this obligation plays in the exercise of the right to obtain a judicial determination in the light of Article 6(1) of the ECHR. According to him:

"... the obligation to make a reference for a preliminary ruling tends to form part of the analysis of the 'right to challenge a measure before the courts' (or the 'right to obtain a judicial determination'). According to the settled case-law of the European Court of Human Rights, although [t]he right to have a preliminary question referred to ... the Court of Justice is not absolute ..., it is not

---

537. For example, in *R v Secretary of State for the Home Department (ex parte Sandhu)* ([1982] 2 CMLR 553) the House of Lords refused to refer to the ECJ, although the question whether a divorced Indian husband of a British national, who was threatened with deportation from the UK, was entitled to stay in the UK on the basis of Directive 68/360 was far from being clear and free of doubts at that time.
538. [2003] ECR I-10239.
539. [1996] ECR I-1029.
540. [1996] ECR I-1631; see also Case C-302/97 *Konle* [1999] ECR I-3099 and Case C-424/97 *Haim* [2000] ECR I-5123.

completely impossible that, in certain circumstances, refusal by a domestic court trying a case at final instance might infringe the principle of fair trial, as set forth in Article 6(1) of the Convention, in particular where such refusal appears arbitrary."

Although the ECJ did not refer to Article 6(1) of the ECHR in the context of the duty of a national court to make a reference for a preliminary ruling as explained in *CILFIT*, the Court has, nevertheless, in this case reinforced this obligation in respect of a supreme court deciding a case at last instance. However, with the accession of the EU to the ECHR, the argument of A-G Léger regains its full strength. Further, on the authority of the ECJ judgment in Case C-154/08 *Commission v Spain*[541] (see Chapter 15.2.2.3), in which the ECJ held that Spain was in breach of EU law when its Supreme Court made an error of law by incorrectly interpreting the Sixth VAT Directive (the Supreme Court had no doubt as to the correct interpretation of the Directive and thus did not make a referral to the ECJ for a preliminary ruling), it is clear that national law, including a national constitution, cannot shield a Member State from incurring liability when its Supreme Court commits errors in interpreting EU law.

10.7.9 Procedure under Article 267 TFEU

The procedure under Article 267 TFEU is not adversarial and, in reality, constitutes a dialogue between national courts or tribunals and the ECJ. Until a preliminary ruling is given, the ECJ will stay in touch with the referring court to which it will send copies of the relevant documents, such as observations submitted by Member States and EU institutions.

In Case 13/61 *Bosch*[542] the ECJ held that no particular form is required for the reference, but emphasised in Case 101/63 *Wagner*[543] that the referring court is free to formulate it in direct and simple form.

In Case 72/83 *Campus Oil*,[544] it was recognised that national rules of procedure in this area should not inhibit lower courts, which have unfettered discretion under Article 234(2) EC to refer. However, it is outside the jurisdiction of the ECJ to verify whether the decision to refer was taken in conformity with national procedural rules.[545]

In Cases 146 and 166/73 *Rheinmühlen*,[546] the ECJ held that an order for reference is subject to the remedies normally available under national law.

Once the ECJ is seised by the referring court, it has jurisdiction to give a preliminary ruling until the withdrawal of the reference by the referring court.[547] In Case C-194/94 *CIA Security International SA, Signalson SA et Secutitel SA*,[548] the ECJ rejected the submission of the original parties that a modification of national law applicable to the dispute, subsequent to the referral, rendered the preliminary ruling unnecessary. The ECJ held that this question should be assessed by the referring court, which was solely competent to decide whether or not a preliminary ruling

---

541. Judgment of 12/11/09 (NYR).

542. [1962] ECR 45.

543. [1964] ECR 195.

544. [1984] ECR 2727.

545. Case 65/81 *Reina* [1982] ECR 33; Case C-10/92 *Balocchi* [1993] ECR I-5105, confirmed in Case C-39/94 *Syndicat Français de l'Express International* [1996] ECR I-3547.

546. [1974] ECR 33 and 139.

547. Case 106/77 *Simmenthal* [1978] ECR 629.

548. [1996] ECR I-2201.

was still required in order to enable it to give judgment. In Case 31/68 *Chanel*,[549] the ECJ held that, when in a matter of which it is seised it is informed by the referring court or the superior court that an appeal has been lodged in the national court against the national decision, proceedings in the case before the ECJ should be postponed until the decision of the referring court is confirmed by a superior court and, if it is overturned, the ECJ must set aside the proceedings under Article 267 TFEU.

The procedure for the ECJ is set out in Title III of the Protocol 3 on the Statute of the ECJ annexed to the Treaties, and in the Rules of Procedure of the ECJ.[550]

In Article 267 TFEU proceedings the emphasis is on written pleadings more than on the oral procedure. The stages of the proceedings are dealt with in Chapter 6.6.5.

The oral and written pleadings of the parties must be limited to the legal context as determined by the referring court.[551] The parties are neither allowed to change the content of the question formulated by a national judge, nor to add their own questions,[552] nor declare the referral without object.[553] Furthermore, the original parties are not entitled to challenge the jurisdiction of the ECJ,[554] nor involve in the proceedings persons other than those specified in Article 23 of the Protocol 3. This rule also applies to the EU institutions, bodies, offices and agencies, Member States participating in the proceedings[555] and to third States when they are allowed to make submissions, i.e. when a preliminary ruling raises an issue covered by an agreement concluded by a third State with the EU.[556]

The reference procedure is time-consuming as it takes 17–18 months. For that reason in some cases preliminary rulings have been used as tactical devices. The best example is provided by the Sunday trading cases[557] in which the referral to the ECJ permitted the defendant companies to trade on Sundays while awaiting the preliminary rulings. Over a number of years the defendants who were in breach of the Shops Act argued that the Act was contrary to provisions of EU law on the free movement of goods.

10.7.10 Effect of preliminary rulings concerning the interpretation of EU law

The Treaties are silent on the legal effect of preliminary rulings concerning the interpretation of EU law. In Joined Cases 28–30/62 *Da Costa*,[558] the ECJ defined the legal effects of preliminary rulings. It stated that the referring court is bound by the interpretation given by the ECJ, either in reply to the question or when it decides an identical question.

The ratio legis (the underlying principle) of proceedings under Article 267 TFEU requires that the preliminary ruling is taken into consideration by the referring court. However, this obligation is limited. Only if the ruling permits the referring court to resolve the dispute at issue is such a

---

549.   [1970] ECR 403. Ord.
550.   [2005] OJ L288/51.
551.   Case 62/72 *Bollman* [1973] ECR 269.
552.   Case 247/86 *Alsatel* [1988] ECR 5987.
553.   Case 5/72 *Fratelli Grassi* [1972] ECR 443.
554.   Case C-364/92 *SAT* [1994] ECR I-43.
555.   Case 39/75 *Coenen* [1975] ECR 1547.
556.   Article 23 of Protocol 3.
557.   One of them was Case 145/88 *Torfaen Borough Council v B & Q plc* [1989] ECR 3851 (see Chapter 20.9), also A Arnull, 'What Shall We Do on Sunday?', 16 ELRev. p.112.
558.   [1963] ECR 31.

ruling binding on it. Otherwise, the referring court may refer the same question in a second referral as happened in *Foglia v Novello (No 2)*.[559]

Preliminary rulings have retroactive effect, that is, they apply from the entry into force of the provision in question. In Case 52/76 *Benedetti v Munari*,[560] the ECJ held that:

"... the rule as ... interpreted may, and must, be applied by the courts even to legal relationships arising and established before the judgment ruling on the request for interpretation."

The retroactive effect of a preliminary ruling, that is, from the entry into force of the provision in question, has two main drawbacks. First, national rules on the limitation period differ from one Member State to another and, consequently, the outcome of a preliminary ruling may have different implications for litigants in different Member States. Second, a preliminary ruling may have a serious impact on the public finances of Member States in a situation where reimbursement of unlawful amounts paid by claimants or likely to be paid by a Member State resulting from its unlawful conduct may cause serious economic repercussions for that Member State. For that reason in some cases the ECJ decided to take into consideration the fact that the retrospective effect of its judgment may cause serious problems in respect of bona fide legal relationships established before the preliminary ruling,[561] and restricted its temporal effects with effect from the date of the decision onwards (that is, the prospective effect). Thus, the exception to the principle of retroactivity suffers important limitations:

- Only the ECJ may decide not to apply its judgment retroactively and the limitation of the temporal effect of its rulings must be confined to the case in which the particular ruling was given, and must not extend to any subsequent cases;

- Only in exceptional circumstances will the ECJ impose limitations on the temporal effect of a judgment, bearing in mind that such limitations are contrary to the principle of legal certainty. Two conditions must be satisfied before a limitation can be imposed:

  - Those concerned should have acted in good faith;
  - There should be a risk of serious practical difficulties if the effects of a judgment are not limited in time.[562]

For example, in Case 309/85 *Barra v Belgium*[563] the ECJ refused to restrict the temporal effect of its earlier ruling in Case 293/83 *Gravier v Belgium*.[564] As a result, illegal fees charged by the Belgian authorities for vocational training courses for nationals from other Member States were reimbursed to those persons who were entitled to claim reimbursement before the delivery of the

---

559. Case 244/80 [1981] ECR 3045.
560. [1977] ECR 163.
561. For example Case 43/75 *Defrenne* [1976] ECR 455; Joined Cases 66, 127 and 128/79 *Salumi* [1980] ECR 1237; Case 61/79 *Denkavit Italiana* [1980] ECR 1205; Case 24/86 *Blaizot* [1988] ECR 379; Case C-57/93 *Vroege* [1994] ECR I-4541; Cases C-197/94 and C-252/94 *Société Bautiaa* [1996] ECR I-505; Case C-262/88 *Douglas Harvey Barber v Guardian Royal Exchange Assurance Group* [1990] ECR I-1889; Case C-184/04 *Uudenkaupungin Kaupunki* [2006] ECR I-3039.
562. Case C-402/03 *Skov and Bilka* [2006] ECR I-199; Case C-184/04 *Uudenkaupungin Kaupunki* [2006] ECR I-3039.
563. [1988] ECR 355.
564. [1985] ECR 593.

ruling in *Gravier*. However, in Case 24/86 *Blaizot*[565] and Case 43/75 *Defrenne*[566] the ECJ decided to give prospective effect to the rulings. This meant that the rulings applied only to those persons who had commenced proceedings prior to the ECJ's rulings and for everyone else the ruling applied only from the date it was given. In *Blaizot* the ECJ held that university education was within the scope of the Treaty if it constituted vocational training. As a result, illegal fees charged for university courses by Belgium were only reimbursed to students who had already brought proceedings before Belgian courts and could not be charged to future students. In *Defrenne* claims for backdated pay could only be made by those who had already started legal proceedings or submitted an equivalent claim prior to the date of the ruling. The differences in salary between male stewards and female air hostesses were to be abolished prospectively.

The exceptional nature of a temporal restriction on retroactivity of preliminary rulings was emphasised in Joined Cases C-290/05 *Nádashi* and C-333/05 *Németh*.[567]

THE FACTS WERE:

Hungarian authorities, in breach of Article 110 TFEU, imposed a registration duty on used motor vehicles from other Member States which did not take into account the depreciation in value of such vehicles as compared to similar used vehicles which had already been registered in Hungary. The Hungarian authorities pleaded serious difficulties, namely the administrative costs involved in case-by-case examination necessary to reimburse the excess tax, the cost of which would, according to the Hungarian Government, probably exceed the total amount to be reimbursed, and the difficulties involved in identifying persons entitled to be reimbursed.

Held:

The ECJ refused to limit the temporal effect of its judgment. The court ruled that the condition relating to the risk of difficulties was not satisfied because:

▪ The amounts to be reimbursed were not so high as to cause serious economic repercussions for Hungary; and

▪ Under EC law a Member State is required to reimburse excess amounts paid by the person concerned in accordance with national procedural rules, which rules should respect the principles of equivalence and effectiveness. Therefore, administrative costs involved must be assumed by the Member State.

---

565.   [1988] ECR 379.
566.   [1976] ECR 455.
567.   [2006] ECR I-10115.

10.7.10.1 The implications of retroactive effect of preliminary rulings on the finality of decisions of a national administrative body or a national court. The principle of res judicata and its limitations

It emerges from the case law (see Chapter 13.9) of the ECJ that:

▪ A judicial decision which has become final after all rights of appeal have been exhausted, or after the expiry of the time limit provided for appeal proceedings, can no longer be challenged.[568] This is subject to the exception set out in in Case C-119/05 *Ministero dell'Industria, del Commercio e dell'Artigianato v Lucchini SpA.*[569] In *Lucchini* the ECJ held that a national judgment which had became res judicata but was in flagrant violation of the division of competences between the Community [the EU] and a Member State as it encroached on exclusive competences of the Commission exercised under Article 88 EC [Article 108 TFEU], was in breach of EC law and could no longer enjoy the status of res judicata.

▪ An administrative decision which has satisfied the requirements set out in Case C-453/00 *Kühne & Heitz NV v Productschap voor Pluimvee en Eieren*, becomes res judicata, that is, can no longer be called into question.[570]

It is to be noted that although a national court or an administrative body which had rendered a decision, which in the light of a subsequent judgment of the ECJ, was in breach of EU law, it is not required (subject to the above exceptions), to reopen national proceedings in order to comply with EU law, individuals have not been left without a remedy. They may rely on a preliminary ruling of the ECJ in national proceedings to establish Member State liability for infringement of EU law and thus obtain compensation for damage caused to them by a mistaken judicial or administrative decision which under national law has become res judicata.

10.8 Preliminary rulings on the validity of EU law

The question of the validity of acts adopted by EU institutions, bodies, offices and agencies may also be referred to the ECJ. However, as already noted the ECJ can neither rule on the validity of the Treaties (taking into account their constitutional nature), nor on matters covered by Articles 275 and 276 TFEU. Further, the ECJ will refuse to give preliminary rulings concerning the validity of its own judgments.[571]

10.8.1 Requirements in referrals on validity of EU acts

Lower courts have discretion as to whether to refer to the ECJ in a situation where the validity of an EU measure is contested. Normally, they will make a reference for a preliminary ruling if they have serious doubts as to the validity of the relevant EU measure.

---

568. Case C-234/04 *Kapferer v Schlank and Schick GmbH* [2006] ECR I-2585.
569. [2007] ECR I-6199.
570. Confirmed in Joined Cases C-392/04 and C-422/04 *i-21 Germany GmbH and Arcor AG & Co.KG v Germany* [2006] ECR I-8559.
571. Case 69/85 *Wünsche* [1986] ECR 947.

With regard to courts against whose decisions there is no judicial remedy under national law, in Case C-344/04 *International Air Transport*[572] the ECJ confirmed that a court of final resort is required to refer only where it considers that one or more arguments for invalidity of the EU act which have been put forward by the parties or otherwise raised by its own motion are well founded. Consequently, they have discretion and will refer only if the case raises any real doubt as to the validity of the relevant EU act.

The leading case on referrals to the ECJ on the validity of EU acts is Case 314/85 *Foto-Frost v Hauptzollamt Lübeck-Ost.*[573]

THE FACTS WERE:

Foto-Frost applied to a German municipal court to declare a decision issued by the Commission invalid on the grounds that the decision was in breach of requirements set out in a Council regulation which delegated authority to the Commission to adopt decisions. The German court requested a preliminary ruling as to whether it could review the validity of the decision in question.

Held:

The ECJ held that "national courts have no jurisdiction themselves to declare the acts of Community institutions invalid". The ECJ justified its decision on the following grounds:

- For the uniformity of Community law it is especially important that there are no divergences between Member States as to the validity of EC acts, since this would jeopardise the very unity of the Community [the EU] legal order as well as detract from the fundamental requirement of legal certainty.

- The coherence of the system requires that where the validity of measures is challenged before national courts, the jurisdiction to declare an act invalid must be reserved to the ECJ. The ECJ drew a comparison between its exclusive jurisdiction under Article 230 EC [Article 263 TFEU] and its jurisdiction to give preliminary rulings on the validity of EU acts under Article 234 EC [Article 267 TFEU].

Comment:

This case confirmed that the ECJ has exclusive jurisdiction to declare an EU act invalid. Accordingly, whilst national courts may consider the validity of EU acts and may declare them valid, they must, if they have doubts as to their validity, make reference under Article 267 TFEU.[574]

In Case C-461/03 *Schul*,[575] the ECJ had an opportunity to extend the principles set out in the

---

572.   [2006] ECR I-403.
573.   [1987] ECR 4199.
574.   Joined Cases C-304/04 and C-305/04 *Jacob Meijer and Eagle International Freight BV v Inspecteur van de Balastingdienst-Douanedistrict Arnhem* [2005] ECR I-6251.
575.   [2005] ECR I-10513.

CILFIT judgment to the question concerning the validity of EU measures but refused to change its position set out in *Foto-Frost*. It justified the refusal on the following grounds:

- Even if, at first glance, it may appear that provisions of EU law, which have been declared invalid by the ECJ, are comparable to the challenged provisions, the latter may have a different legal and factual context;

- The possibility of a national court ruling on the invalidity of a EU measure would be liable to jeopardise the essential unity of the EU legal order and undermine the fundamental requirement of legal certainty. Indeed, national courts in various Member States may have differing opinions as to the validity of a given measure;

- The coherence of the system of judicial protection instituted by the Treaties would be undermined given that Article 267 TFEU constitutes, as do Articles 263 and 277 TFEU, a means of reviewing the legality of EU measures. The Treaties entrusted such review to the ECJ, not to national courts.

10.8.2 Indirect challenge to EU measures under Article 277 TFEU

In Case C-188/92 *TWD Textilwerke Deggendorf GmbH*,[576] the ECJ excluded, in certain circumstances, the possibility of referring a question of validity. In this case the ECJ precluded a beneficiary of state aid (who was the subject of a decision adopted on the ground of Article 88 EC [Article 108 TFEU] and who could have challenged its validity, but let the prescribed time limit under Article 230 EC [Article 263 TFEU] elapse) from challenging the validity of measures implementing a decision adopted by national authorities in proceedings before a national court. This means that when an applicant does not bring an action for annulment of an act within the prescribed time limit, national courts are precluded from making a reference to the ECJ under Article 267 TFEU in respect of the validity of such an act. However, when a beneficiary of state aid has not been identified by a measure and has not been notified of that measure, the referral is admissible even though the beneficiary's action for annulment under Article 263 TFEU has been dismissed.[577]

In Case C-408/95 *Eurotunnel SA and Others v SeaFrance*[578] the ECJ clarified its decision in Case C-188/92 *TWD*. If an EU act is addressed to natural or legal persons, they will be precluded from challenging the validity of that act by way of a preliminary ruling. They have to bring an action for annulment pursuant to Article 263 TFEUwithin the prescribed time limit.

In *Eurotunnel* the ECJ extended its solution regarding regulations to directives.[579] In that case the challenged provisions of directives:

- Were addressed in general terms to Member States;

- Offered an option to the Member States, which by its very nature, precluded the applicants from being directly concerned by the directives;

---

576. [1994] ECR I-833. See also Case C-441/05 *Roquette Frères* [2007] ECR I-1993.
577. Joined Cases C-346/03 and C-529/03 *Atzeni and Others* [2006] ECR I-1875.
578. [1997] ECR I-6315.
579. Case C-241/95 *Accrington Beef* [1996] ECR I-6699. In some cases the ECJ has accepted an action for annulment challenging EC directives addressed to the Member States provided the applicant was directly and individually concerned: Case C-298/89 *Gibraltar* [1993] ECR I-3605; Case C-10/95P *Asocarne* [1995] ECR I-4149.

■ Were not directly applicable to the applicants.

10.8.3 Effect of a preliminary ruling on validity of EU acts

The peculiarity of the legal effects of preliminary rulings on the validity of EU acts derives from their close connection with the effects of actions for annulment under Article 264 TFEU, and from the distinction between a preliminary ruling confirming the validity of the act concerned, and a ruling declaring that act invalid.

If the ruling of the ECJ confirms the validity of an EU act, the referring court, as well as all other courts and tribunals within the meaning of Article 267 TFEU, may apply the act or, if they believe that it is invalid, refer again to the ECJ under Article 267 TFEU.

If the ECJ declares the challenged act invalid, the situation is different. In Case 66/80 *International Chemical Company*,[580] the ECJ held that although the preliminary ruling declaring an act invalid was addressed to the referring national court, it constituted at the same time sufficient justification for all other national judges to consider the act in question invalid in respect of judgments they may render. However, the ECJ added that its declaration in respect of the invalidity of an act should not prevent national courts from referring again the question already decided by the ECJ if there are problems regarding the scope or possible legal implications of the act previously declared invalid.

The extent of the ECJ's liberal approach in this area is illustrated in Case 32/77 *Giuliani*,[581] in which the ECJ agreed to answer the question whether it continued to maintain its position in respect of an act previously declared invalid. The Court's willingness to deal with the issue is justified by the fact that an EU act declared invalid under Article 267 TFEU nevertheless remains in force. Only the institution, body, office or agency that adopted the act in question is empowered to annul or modify it. It is also liable to compensate for any damage caused by the act. In addition, only national authorities are entitled to nullify a national provision which was adopted in order to implement or to apply the invalid act.[582]

It is important to note that the ECJ may declare only part of an act invalid.[583] The analogy with the effects of a successful action for annulment under Article 264 TFEU is obvious. For that reason, the ECJ decided that it is empowered to specify the consequences deriving from the invalidity of an act. These are as follows:

1. First, the ECJ held that it has jurisdiction to limit the temporal effect of preliminary rulings.

   In principle, all preliminary rulings have retroactive effect, including those confirming, or denying the validity of EU acts.[584] The ECJ has applied, by analogy, Article 264 TFEU in the context of Article 267 TFEU. In Case 112/83 *Produits de Maïs*,[585] the ECJ held that the maintenance of the coherence of the Community legal order provides sufficient justification for the application of Article 231 EC [Article 264 TFEU] in the

---

580. [1981] ECR 1191.
581. [1977] ECR 1863.
582. Case 23/75 *Rey-Soda* [1975] ECR 1279.
583. Case 130/79 *Express Dairy Food* [1980] ECR 1887.
584. Joined Cases 117/76 and 16/77 *Rückdeschel* [1977] ECR 1753.
585. [1985] ECR 719.

context of Article 234 EC [Article 267 TFEU]. Initially, the ECJ decided that if a regulation was invalid with effect from the date of the decision but only as to the future, the referring court was barred from drawing any consequences from the ECJ's declaration of invalidity of the act, even for the parties to the main actions in which the question of validity arose.[586]

This above approach was strongly criticised by national courts which considered that the ECJ had encroached upon their jurisdiction, since under Article 234 EC [Article 267 TFEU] national courts have to apply EC law to the main dispute.[587] The justification provided by the ECJ was based on the principle of legal certainty. The strong opposition of national courts was, however, taken into account by the ECJ in Case C-228/92 *Roquette*,[588] in which it held that the exceptional prospective effect of a preliminary ruling should not deprive those who had commenced proceedings before the date of the ECJ's judgment confirming invalidity of an act, or who had made an equivalent claim, of the right to rely on that invalidity in the main proceedings. For that reason, in many cases the ECJ has applied the solution it adopted in *Defrenne*, that is, temporal limitations are not imposed upon the parties to the main action nor on those who had instituted legal proceedings or made an equivalent claim prior to the date of the judgment.[589]

2. Second, the ECJ has authorised itself to replace invalidated provisions by appropriate alternatives while the adoption of required measures by the institution concerned is awaited.[590]

3. Third, the ECJ has reserved to the EU institution, body, office or agency concerned the exclusive right to draw conclusions from the invalidity of its act and take the necessary measures to remedy the situation.[591]

10.9 Interim relief

In the context of validity of EU acts the matter of interim measures arises with particular intensity. This matter may also have some importance in relation to the interpretation of EU law. Indeed, sometimes for a party to the proceedings the question of interim relief is vital if his rights under EU law are to have any substance.

Under Article 267 TFEU, an interim measure may be ordered by the CJEU or a national court for the period between seisure of the court and its final decision.

In Cases C-143/88 and C-92/89 *Zuckerfabrik Südderdithmarschen v Hauptzollamt Itzehoe*[592] the ECJ established the conditions for obtaining interim relief.

---

586. Case 4/79 *Providence Agricole de Champagne* [1980] ECR 2823.
587. For example, the judgment of 26 June 1985 of the French Conseil d'Etat in *ONIC v Société Maïseries de Beauce*, AJDA, 1985 p.615, concl. Genevois, and the judgment of 21 April 1989 of the Italian Constitutional Court in Fragd, RDI, 1989, p. 103.
588. [1994] ECR I-1445.
589. Case 41/84 *Pinna* [1986] ECR 1.
590. Case 300/86 *Van Landschoot* [1988] ECR 3443.
591. Case 124/76 *Moulins et Huileries de Point-à-Mousson* [1977] ECR 1795.
592. [1991] ECR I-415.

THE FACTS WERE:

The referring court asked the ECJ to assess the validity of a regulation and to determine whether that court had jurisdiction to suspend a national administrative act based on that regulation.

Held:

The ECJ held that, provided that a ruling had been sought from the ECJ, a national court should suspend the application of a national measure implementing an EC act [EU act] until the ruling of the ECJ was known. Such suspension is permitted only if certain stringent conditions are satisfied. These are as follows:

- A preliminary ruling on the issue of validity has been sought from the ECJ;

- There must be a serious doubt as to the validity of the EU act;

- The matter must be urgent;

- There must be a risk to the applicant of serious and irreparable harm, that is, damages would not be an adequate remedy;

- The interests of the EU must have been duly taken into account by the national court concerned.

In Case C-213/89 *R v Secretary of State for Transport, ex parte Factortame (No. 1),*[593] the ECJ held that if national law prevents the court from granting interim relief, such a rule of national law should be set aside. In that case this led to the interim suspension of the operation of a statute, a remedy which until then was not available to national courts.

In Case C-465/93 *Atlanta Fruchthandelsgesellschaft v BEF,*[594] the ECJ first, restated and clarified the conditions under which a national court may grant interim relief and, second, ruled that national courts may grant not only negative (that is suspensory) but also positive (that is creating a new legal position) interim measures. In this case the issue was whether or not a national court is allowed, in certain circumstances, to grant interim relief from the application of an EC act.

THE FACTS WERE:

Council Regulation 404/93 provided for a revised system of import quotas for bananas from non-traditional African, Caribbean and Pacific (ACP) countries. The German Federal Food Office (BEF) granted Atlanta such revised/reduced quotas. Atlanta challenged the regulation and asked for interim relief. The German court asked the ECJ whether it could, while awaiting a preliminary ruling, temporarily resolve the disputed legal position by an interim order, and, if so, under what conditions and whether a distinction should be made between an interim

---

593.   [1990] ECR I-2433.
594.   [1995] ECR I-3761.

order designed to preserve an existing legal position and one which was intended to create a new legal position.

Held:

The ECJ held that it has jurisdiction under Article 234 EC [Article 267 TFEU] to order any necessary interim measures. In relation to the first question the ECJ held that:

"The interim legal protection which the national courts must afford to individuals under Community law must be the same, whether they seek suspension of enforcement of a national administrative measure adopted on the basis of a Community regulation or the grant of interim measures settling or regulating the disputed legal positions or relationships for their benefit."

Comment:

In this case the ECJ added the following conditions to those laid down in *Zuckerfabrik*:

- The national court must justify why it considers that the ECJ should find the measure invalid;
- The national court must take into consideration the extent of the discretion allowed to EU institutions with regard to the adoption of the challenged measure;
- The national court must assess the EU interest in the light of the impact of suspension on the EU legal regime, that is, it must consider, on the one hand, the cumulative effect which would arise if a large number of courts were also to adopt interim measures for similar reasons and, on the other, those special features of the applicant's situation which distinguish the applicant from the other operators concerned;
- If the grant of interim relief represents a financial risk for the EU, the national court must require the applicant to provide adequate guarantees, such as the deposit of money or other security;
- The national court must take into account any previous Article 263 TFEU judgments concerning the disputed legislation.

AIDE-MÉMOIRE

THE PRELIMINARY RULINGS PROCEDURE UNDER ARTICLE 267 TFEU

1. The preliminary ruling procedure is, in effect, a dialogue between national courts and the ECJ on:

The interpretation of:

- Primary sources of EU law (Case 812/79 *Burgoa*);
- Secondary sources of EU law including those adopted by bodies, offices and agencies of the EU (Case 9/70 *Franz Grad*);
- International agreements concluded between the EU and a third country (181/73 *Haegemann*).

But the above are subject to the exception contained in Article 10 of Protocol 36 on Transitional Provisions of the ToL.

The validity of:

- Secondary sources;

- International conventions concluded between the EU and third countries.

But the ECJ has **no jurisdiction** to give preliminary rulings on:

- Validity of primary sources;

- Validity of judgments of the ECJ;

- Matters covered by Articles 275 and 276 TFEU;

- Validity and interpretation of national law and compatibility of national law with EU law (subject to exceptions set out in Joined Cases C-297/88 and C-197/89 *Dzodzi*).

2. Advantages of the preliminary rulings procedure:

- It constitutes a main form of co-operation between the ECJ and national courts as equals. For national courts, when they are faced with a question of EU law the resolution of which is necessary to give judgment, the preliminary ruling procedure provides an opportunity to seek guidance on such a question from the ECJ. The request is for assistance, not an appeal – it is an advisory jurisdiction only.

- For citizens of the EU and legal persons, Article 267 TFEU provides an opportunity, albeit limited, to indirectly challenge the legality of EU acts.

- For the ECJ the preliminary ruling procedure provides an opportunity to develop EU law given that the most important and fundamental principles of EU law, such as the principle of direct effect and the principle of supremacy of EU law, have been enunciated by the ECJ using the preliminary ruling procedure.

- For the EU the procedure is vital as it ensures that EU law has the same meaning and effect in all Member States of the EU.

3. Jurisdiction

Meaning of a court or tribunal (Case 61/65 *Vaassen-Göbbels*)

The following criteria are relevant in determining whether or not a body making a reference is a court or tribunal for the purposes of Article 267 TFEU:

- Whether the body is established by law;

- Whether it is permanent;

- Whether its jurisdiction is compulsory;

- Whether its procedure is adversarial;

- Whether it applies rules of law;

- Whether it is independent;

- Whether it is called upon to give a decision of a judicial nature.

Interpretation of EU law
A referral is generally inadmissible if:

- No question of EU law arises;

- The question is of obvious irrelevance;

- The dispute is spurious;

- There is lack of relevant factual or legal information;

- A prior ruling has been made by the ECJ on the same issue, but the ECJ may decide to deal with the referral by a reasoned order.

Validity of EU acts
A national court must refer to the ECJ if in doubt (C-344/04 *International Air Transport*). Only the ECJ can declare an act void (Case 314/85 *Foto-Frost*).

Obligation or discretion to refer on interpretation of EU law
National courts or tribunals adjudicating at last instance, **as a rule, must** refer but this is subject to the doctrine of **acte clair** (Case 283/81 *CILFIT*). Other courts can exercise their discretion.

4. Effect of a preliminary ruling

- On interpretation of EU law: it is binding on a referring court (Joined Cases 28–30/62 *Da Costa*) and has retroactive effect (Case 52/76 *Benedetti*), but the ECJ may restrict its temporal effects (Cases 24/86 *Blaizot*);

- On validity: not only a referring court but all national courts should set aside an invalid act, but the ECJ can replace invalidated provisions with appropriate alternatives while the adoption of required measures by the institution concerned is awaited (Case 66/80 *International Chemical Company*).

RECOMMENDED READING

Books
Broberg, M. and Fenger, N., *Preliminary References to the European Court of Justice*, 2010, Oxford: OUP

Obradovic, D., and Lavranos, N. (eds), *Interface between EU Law and National Law: Proceedings of the Annual Colloquium of the G. K. van Hogendorp Centre for European Constitutional Studies*, 2007, Groningen: European Law Publishing

Sinaniotis, D., *Interim Protection of Individuals before the European and National Courts*, 2006, The Hague: Kluwer Law International

Articles
Anagnostaras, G., "Preliminary Problems and Jurisdiction Uncertainties: The Admissibility of Questions Referred by Bodies Performing Quasi-Judicial Functions", (2005) 30 ELRev, p 878

Broberg, M., "*Acte Clair* revisited: Adapting the *Acte Clair* Criteria to the Demands of the Times", (2008) 45 CMLRev, p 1383

Broberg, M., "Preliminary References by Public Administrative Bodies: When Are Public Administrative Bodies Competent to Make Preliminary References to the European Court of Justice?", (2009) 15 EPL, p 207

Komárek, J., "In the Court(s) We Trust?: On the Need for Hierarchy and Differentiation in the Preliminary Ruling Procedure", (2007) 32/4 ELRev, pp 467–491

Ritter, C., "Purely Internal Situations, Reverse Discrimination, Guimont, Dzodzi and Article 234", (2006) 31/5 ELRev, p 690

Waldhoff, C., "Recent Developments Relating to the Retroactive Effect of Decisions of the ECJ", (2009) 46 CMLRev, p 173

11

DIRECT APPLICABILITY OF EU LAW

CONTENTS

SUMMARY

1. Direct applicability is a doctrine well known to public international law. It concerns the manner of incorporation of international law into municipal law. This varies greatly from one Member State to another. This chapter focuses on the doctrine of direct applicability of EU law which regulates the relationship between EU law (a species of international law) and the national laws of the Member States in terms of how EU law is put into effect in the domestic legal systems of the Member States.

2. In the EU context, direct applicability means that rules of EU law must be fully and uniformly applied in all Member States from the date of their entry into force and for so long as they continue to be in force. Direct applicability of EU law ensures that EU law is incorporated into the municipal law of the Member States without the need for its specific implementation, that is, there is no need (as there is in dualist countries like the UK) to pass an Act of Parliament to give effect to it. However, not all EU law is directly applicable.

3. The founding Treaties, their amendments duly ratified, protocols and conventions attached to them are directly applicable.

4. With regard to secondary sources, regulations and decisions are directly applicable, but in respect of directives the views diverge. Some argue that they are directly applicable, others reject that view. This controversy is examined in this chapter in the light of the judgment of the ECJ in *Wallonie* and in Case C-422/05 *Commission v Belgium*.

5. In respect of international agreements concluded between the EU and third countries or international organisations, a distinction must be made between international agreements which become part of EU law without any need for adoption of EU legislation, and international agreements which require adoption of implementing measures by the appropriate EU institutions or by the Member States. While the first mentioned international agreements are directly applicable, the direct applicability of the second mentioned agreements depends on the type of secondary legislation which is adopted to give effect to such agreements, that is, is it a regulation, a directive or a decision?

11.1   Introduction

EU law is neither foreign nor external to the legal systems of the Member States. To the contrary, it forms an integral part of national laws. Its peculiar position is due to the manner in which it is put into effect in the national legal order of the Member States.

Direct applicability is a doctrine well known to public international law. However, public international law does not regulate the conditions in which provisions of international treaties become part of municipal laws in order to be applied by national courts. It is left to each country to decide on the relationship between international and municipal law. In this respect there are two theories: dualist and monist.

▪ Under the dualist theory international law and municipal law are independent and separate systems. As a result, an international treaty duly ratified produces legal effect only at the international level, that is, it is only binding on the contracting states. In order to be applied by national courts it is necessary, by a second step, to pass enabling legislation, so that it can take effect at the national level. However, once an international provision is implemented into national law, it is applied by national courts as any other municipal provision, not as an international one.

▪ In the monist view the unity between international and municipal law means that international law automatically becomes law within a contracting state. It is directly applicable. There is no need for enabling legislation as a treaty becomes an integral part of the national law of a contracting state once the procedure for its ratification is completed. An international provision is applied by municipal courts as such and not as a provision of domestic law.

EU law has enunciated its own doctrine of direct applicability. In Case 28/67 *Firma Molkerei*[595] the ECJ held that direct applicability ensures that the provisions of Community law are incorporated into the national legal order of the Member States without the need for their implementation, i.e. for the passing of enabling legislation. In Case 106/77 *Simmenthal*,[596] the ECJ held that direct

---

595.   [1968] ECR 143.
596.   [1978] ECR 629.

applicability means that rules of Community law must be fully and uniformly applied in all Member States from the date of their entry into force and for so long as they continue to be in force.

EU law, due to its specificity, gives preference to the monist theory. In this respect, Article 288 TFEU provides that regulations are directly applicable in all Member States. More importantly, the preference for the monist theory derives from the nature of the EU. Only a monist system is compatible with the idea of European integration. In Case 6/64 *Costa v ENEL*[597] the ECJ emphasised its peculiar nature by stating:

> "By contrast with ordinary international treaties, the Treaty has created its own legal system which, on the entry into force of the Treaty, became an integral part of the legal systems of the Member States and which their courts are bound to apply."

As a result, EU law cannot tolerate national divergences as to Member States relations vis-à-vis EU law, since the dualist system jeopardises the attainment of the objectives of the Treaties and is contrary to the spirit and objectives of EU law. Member States may preserve the dualist system in relation to international law, but it is excluded in relations between EU law and national law. As a result, EU law becomes an integral part of national law without any need for its formal enactment, and national judges are bound to apply it. Further, it occupies a special place in the domestic legal systems of the Member States as it is applied as EU law and not as municipal law. Direct applicability depends on the source of EU law; for some sources it is automatic and general in scope, for others it is conditional and limited.

It is important to note that the doctrine of direct applicability is distinct from the doctrine of direct effect (see Chapter 12). The doctrine of direct effect concerns the enforceability or otherwise of EU law before national courts. In the early years of the Community the terms "direct applicability" and "direct effect" were not always used correctly, that is, they were often mistaken for each other and some authors challenged the distinction between them.[598] The correct view is that each doctrine is distinct and has a different meaning under EU law.[599]

11.2 Direct applicability of the Treaties

The original signatories of the three founding Treaties ratified them according to national constitutional procedures. In monist countries, such as France, the Treaties were incorporated into municipal law on the basis of their ratification.[600] In dualist countries, such as Belgium, Germany and Italy, it was necessary for national parliaments to intervene in order to supply the national legal basis for the Treaties and thus recognise their binding effect in municipal law:

▪ First, by authorising their government to ratify them; and

▪ Second, by incorporating them into domestic law in a legislative form similar to a British Act of Parliament.

---

597.   [1964] ECR 585.
598.   D. Wyatt, "Directly Applicable Provisions of EEC Law", (1975) 125 New Law Journal, p 485, esp. pp 576 and 577.
599.   J. P. Warner, "The Relationship between European Community Law and the National Laws of Member States", (1977) 93 Law Quarterly Review, p 8; T. Winter, "Direct Effect and Direct Applicability: Two Distinct and Different Concepts in Community Law", (1972) 9 CMLRev, p 425.
600.   *Loi of 2 August 1957* and a *Decret d'application* of 28 January 1958. JORF of 22.2.1958.

In Joined Cases 9/65 and 58/65 *San Michele*[601] the ECJ refused to acknowledge any conditions for implementation of the Community Treaties into the municipal law of the Member States and held that the Treaties are binding and should be applied by national judges not as internal law but as Community law.

For Member States which have subsequently joined the Communities and the EU, the principle of direct applicability of the Treaties was obvious and the case law of the ECJ clarified this point beyond any doubt. Since membership is conditional upon the acceptance of the EU acquis, the various accession acts have expressly recognised the direct applicability of EU law. In the United Kingdom section 2(1) of the European Communities Act 1972 recognises direct applicability of Community law. It provides that:

"All such rights, powers, liabilities, obligations and restrictions from time to time created or arising by or under the Treaties, as in accordance with the Treaties are without further enactment to be given legal effect or used in the United Kingdom shall be recognised and available in law, and enforced, allowed and followed accordingly; and the expression 'enforceable Community right' and similar expressions, shall be read as referring to one to which this subsection applies."

Section 2(2) of the Act further confirms that Community law forms an integral part of the law of the United Kingdom.

Although Community law is incorporated into the law of the UK by means of implementing legislation, more specifically by the European Communities Act 1972, it does not emanate from the British Parliament and cannot be applied by British courts as municipal law. Upon their ratification, the Treaties automatically became law in the UK from the perspective of EU law. Implementing legislation was not necessary, but the UK, as a dualist country, decided that upon accession to the Communities, from a purely national perspective it was necessary to make Community law applicable within the national legal system by means of an Act of Parliament.

In Ireland the Treaties were implemented by an act of parliament very similar to the 1972 UK European Communities Act. Its Article 2 provides expressly that from 1 January 1973 the Treaties, as well as measures adopted by EC institutions, shall be binding and form an integral part of Irish law.

In Denmark Article 3 of the law of 11 October 1972 relating to the Accession of Denmark to the European Communities introduced the Treaties directly into national law without any implementing measures, although Denmark is also a dualist country.

11.3   Direct applicability of regulations

The direct applicability of regulations is expressly recognised in Article 288 TFEU. In the United Kingdom their direct applicability is recognised by section 2(1) of the European Communities Act 1972. Not only are any implementing measures unnecessary, they are regarded as obstructing the direct applicability of EU regulations. In Case 34/73 *Variola*[602] the ECJ was asked whether provisions of a regulation can be implemented into Italian law by internal measures reproducing the contents of that regulation in such a way as not to affect its substance. The ECJ held that:

---

601.   [1967] ECR 1; Ord. [1967] ECR 259.
602.   [1973] ECR 981.

"By virtue of the obligations arising from the Treaty and assumed on ratification, Member States are under a duty not to obstruct the direct applicability inherent in regulations and other rules of Community law."

The Constitutional Court of Italy recognised the statement of the ECJ in the *Frontini* case.[603] It held that it derived from the logic of the Community system that regulations should not, as directly applicable legislative acts, be subject to national implementing measures capable of modifying them, imposing conditions as to their entry into force, substituting them, derogating from them or abrogating them, even partially.

In monist countries direct applicability of regulations is self-evident. In France, in case *Syndicat des Hautes Graves de Bordeaux*[604] the French Conseil d'Etat (highest administrative court) in its Decision of 22 December 1978 held that regulations, by virtue of Article 249 EC [Article 288 TFEU], become from their publication an integral part of national law of the Member States. The French Constitutional Court also confirmed this.[605]

11.4 Direct applicability of directives

Directives are addressed to the Member States i.e. to one of them, some of them, or all of them. Article 288 TFEU provides that Member States are under an obligation to achieve the objectives set out in EU directives. Procedures and methods necessary to attain these objectives are left to the discretion of the Member States addressed.

Whether directives are directly applicable is a matter of controversy. For English scholars directives are not directly applicable since they require implementing measures.[606] Others, especially from monist Member States, argue that Member States only have powers to implement directives, which is quite different from the incorporation of international treaties into municipal law.[607] They make a distinction between the competence d'execution and the competence of reception. Member States exercise the former in relation to directives but not the latter. Those scholars refuse to accept that until directives are transposed into municipal law, they do not exist from a legal point of view. In this respect, Judge P. Pescatore said that a directive cannot be considered as "a judicial non-entity from an internal viewpoint".[608]

The question of direct applicability of directives was considerably clarified by the ECJ in Case C-129/96 *Inter-Environnement Wallonie ASBL v Région Wallonne*.[609]

---

603. [1974] 2 CMLR 372.

604. R.526, RTDE, 1979.717. Concl. Genevois.

605. Decisions of 30 December 1977, RTDE, 1979, 142, note G. Isaac and J. Molinier.

606. See for example J. Tillotson, *European Community Law*, Second Edition, 1996, London: Cavendish, p 69.

607. For example R. Kovar, "La contribution de la cour de justice à l'edification de l'ordre juridique communautaire", (1993) 4/1 Recueil de l'Académie de droit européen, p 57 et seq.

608. P. Pescatore, "A non-être juridique du point de vue interne", in *L'effet des directives communautaires: une tentative de démythification*, 1980, Paris: Dalloz, p 171.

609. [1997] ECR I-7411; the judgment in the *Wallonie* case was confirmed by the ECJ Case C-157/02 *Rieser Internationale Transporte* [2004] ECR I-1477.

THE FACTS WERE:

Inter-Environnement Wallonie ASBL, a non-profit-making organisation, applied to the Belgian Conseil d'Etat for the annulment of a Walloon Regional Council Decree which expressly purported to implement Directive 75/442 on hazardous waste, as amended by Directive 91/689, and which was issued during the period prescribed for the transposition of Directive 91/689. The applicant argued that the Decree was contrary to the Directive as it did not include within its definition of waste a substance or object which directly or indirectly forms an integral part of an industrial production process. The Belgian Conseil d'Etat asked the ECJ, inter alia, whether Articles 10 and 249 EC [Articles 4(3) and 288 TFEU] preclude Member States from adopting national legislation contrary to a non-implemented directive before the period for its transposition has expired.

Held:

The ECJ confirmed three important points:

- First, the Court held that directives enter into force at the date of their notification to their addressees and not at the end of the transposition period laid down in the directive itself;

- Second, the ECJ confirmed that although a directive enters into force upon its notification to a Member State concerned, it only becomes legally effective from the expiry of the implementation period;

- Third, prior to the judgment in this case it had been well established that before the expiry of the prescribed time limit, no obligations or rights arise from a directive for a Member State or for individuals (Case 148/78 *Ratti*[610]). For that reason, it had been widely assumed that until the transposition of directives into national law, or the expiry of the time limit prescribed for their implementation, they do not exist from a legal point of view, that they are not considered directly applicable. The judgment of the ECJ in the above case has challenged those assumptions. The ECJ held that by virtue of Articles 10 EC and 249 EC [Article 4(3) and 288 TFEU] Member States have the obligation to refrain from adopting and bringing measures into force during a directive's transposition period if such measures are likely to seriously compromise the result required by the directive.

The principle established by the ECJ in *Wallonie* was applied by the French Conseil d'Etat (highest administrative court in France) in Case No 269814 *M. Sueur et autre* of 29 October 2004.[611] In this case two EC directives, which were both in force, but for one of which the time limit prescribed for its implementation had not yet expired, set out rules which were incompatible with each other. The French Conseil d'Etat decided that during the period when both the directives were simultaneously in force, a Member State could either:

---

610.   [1979] ECR 1629.
611.   See (2004) Europe, No. 12, para 391,11.

- Adopt measures compatible with the older directive, subject to the requirement that such measures would not seriously undermine the achievement of the objectives of the new directive; or

- Adopt measures which were incompatible with the older directive but aimed at achieving the result required by the new directive.

The limitation imposed upon the legislative freedom of a Member State during the prescribed transposition period can be explained only if directives are directly applicable. In this respect the Commission stated in the *Wallonie* case that on the basis of Articles 10 EC and 249 EC [Article 4(3) and 288 TFEU] a Member State has a kind of standstill obligation, which means that during the implementation period no national measures should be adopted (whether or not they intend to implement the directive) which "increase the disparity between the national and Community rules". Consequently, the Member States must refrain from jeopardising the achievement of one or more of the objectives of the directive. Further, the adoption of such a measure would create legal uncertainty for individuals.

The standstill obligation is legally enforceable. For the first time, in Case C-422/05 *Commission v Belgium*[612] the ECJ declared Belgium in breach of Articles 10 EC and Article 249 EC [Article 4(3) and Article 288 TFEU] for adopting national measures almost at the end of a transitional period (three months before its expiry) which were liable to seriously compromise the result prescribed by the directive in question.

It is submitted that the fact that a Member State can be declared in breach of its obligations under EU law for adopting national measures incompatible with the requirements of a relevant directive during the period allowed for its transposition, demonstrates that directives are in general terms directly applicable from the time of their notification to a Member State concerned. Further, the obligation imposed on a Member State during the transposition period to abstain from adopting national measures which have (as the Commission emphasised in this case) "a lasting negative impact on the conditions for the transposition and application of the Directive" intensifies as the time for transposition of a directive draws near. The above case confirms that directives not only have legal existence during the transposition period but may give rise to binding obligations with regard to the Member States. The above judgment of the ECJ shows that the role played by directives in the framework of the Community legal system is more important than, at first glance, Article 249 EC [Article 288 TFEU] may suggest.

The issue whether individuals can rely on directives before the expiry of the transposition period to challenge national rules, whether intended to implement the directive or not, which conflict with the requirements laid down in provisions of the directive has been answered in the affirmative by the ECJ. In particular, they can have legitimate claims against their Member States in a situation where it is obvious, as it was in Case C-422/05 *Commission v Belgium*, that it would be highly unlikely for a Member State to meet the deadline for transposition of the directive as it had introduced national rules fundamentally contrary to the requirements of the directive almost at the end of the transposition period. Further, in Case C-246/06 *Velasco Navarro v Fogasa*,[613] the ECJ held that during the period falling between the date of the entry into force of a directive, i.e. the date of its notification to the Member State concerned, and the deadline for

---

612.   [2007] ECR I-4749.

613.   [2008] ECR I-105 see also Case C-81/05 *Cordero Alonso* [2006] ECR I-7569.

its transposition, a national court is obliged to interpret national law which is within the scope of the directive in compliance with general principles and fundamental rights recognised in the EU legal order.

Following from all the above, it can be said that directives are directly applicable from the moment of their notification to the Member State concerned and as such form an integral part of national law before the expiry of the time limit prescribed for their implementation.

11.5   Direct applicability of decisions

Decisions are directly applicable, irrespective of whether they are addressed to a Member State or to a natural or to a legal person. The same principle applies to decisions which have no identified addressees.

11.6   Direct applicability of international agreements concluded between the EU and third countries, and between the EU and international organisations

By virtue of Article 216(2) TFEU international agreements concluded between the EU and third countries, or international organisations, are binding on EU institutions, and on Member States.[614]

International agreements normally specify the conditions for their entry into force. Some international agreements become part of EU law without any need for EU legislation; others require adoption of implementing measures by the appropriate EU institutions and, in some instances, by the Member States.

For an international agreement that does not require adoption of any implementing measures, the EU act which authorises its conclusion and the expression of the EU's consent to be bound by it have the effect of incorporating the agreement into EU law. It is directly applicable. In practice, often a decision or a regulation adopted by the Council reproducing in its annexe the text of an agreement is published in the OJ.

With regard to an international agreement that requires adoption of implementing measures, it is for the Commission to ensure that the appropriate secondary legislation is adopted in good time so that the EU obligations stemming from an international agreement are fulfilled. In some cases, implementing measures may be required not only at EU level but also, in conformity with the principle of subsidiarity, at national level. If an international agreement is implemented by means of a regulation or a decision, it is directly applicable. However, if the EU adopts a directive, the controversy as to its direct applicability persists (see above).

If national implementing measures are required to give effect to an international agreement, such an agreement will become part of national law of the relevant Member State in accordance with the terms specified in the implementing legislation.

---

614.   There is no similar provision in the EA Treaty, but is seems certain that the same principle applies to the EA Treaty. See: D. Lasok and J. Bridge, *Law and Institutions of the European Union*, 6th edition, 1994, London/Dublin/ Edinburgh: Butterworths, p 73.

AIDE-MÉMOIRE

DIRECT APPLICABILITY OF EU LAW

The doctrine of direct applicability of EU law regulates the relationship between EU law (a species of international law) and national laws of the Member States in terms of how EU law is put into effect in the domestic legal systems of Member States.

In the EU context, direct applicability means that directly applicable rules of EU law must be fully and uniformly applied in all Member States from the date of their entry into force and for so long as they continue to be in force. There is no need for their implementation, that is, there is no need (in dualist countries like the UK) to pass an Act of Parliament to give effect to them.

The following sources of EU law are directly applicable:

- The Treaties, Protocols and Annexes attached to them and The Charter of Fundamental Rights of the European Union;

- Regulations;

- Decisions; and

- International agreements concluded between the EU and third countries, and between the EU and international organisations, that do not require the adoption of legislative measures at EU or national level.

Direct applicability of international agreements, which require the adoption of secondary legislation at EU level, depends on the type of secondary legislation: a regulation (see above), a directive (see below), or a decision (see above).

Directives – direct applicability has been subject to controversy, but some clarifications were provided by the ECJ in the *Wallonie* case and in Case C-422/05 *Commission v Belgium*. There is no doubt, however, that a directive, during the period between its entry into force and the end of the transposition period normally specified in that directive, has legal existence and may give rise to obligations for the Member State concerned.

RECOMMENDED READING

Book

Falkner, G., Treib, O., Hartlapp, M. and Leiber, S., *Complying with Europe: EU Harmonization and Soft Law in the Member States*, 2005, New York: Cambridge University Press

Article

Winter, T., "Direct Effect and Direct Applicability: Two Distinct and Different Concepts in Community Law", (1972) 9 CMLRev, p 425

12

DIRECT EFFECT OF EU LAW

CONTENTS

SUMMARY

1. This chapter examines the concept of the direct effect of EU law, which was established by the ECJ in Case 26/62 *Van Gend en Loos*, in which the Court held that: "Community law [EU law] . . . not only imposes obligations on individuals but it is also intended to confer upon them rights which national courts must protect."

Direct effect means that some provisions of EU law may give rise to rights which individuals (natural and legal persons) can enforce before national courts. These rights flow directly from EU law and are entirely independent of national law. Indeed, an individual can rely on directly effective provisions of EU law in the absence of, or against a national provision.

2. In order to produce direct effect, a provision of EU law must be clear, precise and unconditional and must confer rights on individuals. Thus, its application must not depend upon the adoption of further implementing measures, either at the national or the EU level (the direct effect test).

3. EU law makes a distinction between horizontal and vertical direct effect. Vertical direct effect refers to a situation where an individual is allowed to rely on a provision of EU law in national proceedings against a Member State or its emanations. Horizontal direct effect concerns a situation where an individual is allowed to invoke a provision of EU law in national proceedings against another individual (that is, a natural or legal person). In practice, this distinction is very important since it considerably limits the scope and the effectiveness of EU law in the case of a provision which may produce only vertical direct effect.

4. Provisions of the Treaties and of regulations may be both horizontally and vertically directly effective.

5. Directives are more problematic. Subject to the direct effect test, provisions of directives can only produce vertical direct effect and only after the time limit for their implementation has expired. If the provisions of an EU directive are sufficiently precise and unconditional, although that directive is not implemented within the prescribed period, an individual may rely upon them once the prescribed time limit has elapsed.

A Member State which has failed to transpose a directive within the prescribed time limit cannot rely on an unimplemented directive in proceedings against individuals.

In order to alleviate the negative consequences of the denial of horizontal direct effect for directives, the ECJ has developed four approaches:

- It has extended the concept of a Member State by introducing the autonomous EU concept of a public body;

- It has imposed the duty on national courts to interpret national law in conformity with EU law. This is referred to as indirect horizontal effect;

- It has allowed individuals to rely on a directive to determine whether the national legislature, in exercising its choice as to the form and methods for implementing the directive, has kept within the limits of its discretion set out in the directive;

- It has allowed individuals to rely on a directive in proceedings against a State or its emanations despite the fact that such an action affects the rights of individuals who are not part of the vertical relationship, i.e. a relation between a State and the claimant. This is referred to as "triangular" horizontal effect.

It is submitted that the ECJ is in the process of developing a fifth approach allowing individuals, in some exceptional circumstances, to rely on directives in proceedings against other individuals. As at the time of writing two such circumstances have been identified. They are:

A. On the authority of Case C-443/98 *Unilever*, in the situation where the relevant directive does not create any new laws, rights or obligations for individuals, that is, as the ECJ held in that case, the relevant provision of the directive "does not in any way define the substantive scope of the legal rule on the basis of which the national court must decide the case before it".

The above can be called "a procedural" direct horizontal effect.

B. On the authority of Case C-144/04 *Mangold* de facto direct horizontal effect has been recognised by the ECJ in a situation where there is a need to ensure the full effectiveness of the principle of non-discrimination on grounds of age, as given expression in Directive 2000/78.

Additionally, individuals who have suffered damages resulting from a Member State's breach of EU law can claim compensation under the *Francovich* remedy (see Chapter 14).

6. A decision addressed to a Member State can only produce vertical direct effect. A decision addressed to a natural or a legal person can produce both vertical and horizontal direct effect.

7. Provisions of international agreements concluded between the EU and third countries or international organisations, subject to the test for direct effect, can produce vertical direct effect. It is uncertain whether or not provisions of international agreements can be horizontally directly effective as there is no judicial authority on this point.

12.1   Introduction

Under public international law, some provisions of international treaties may confer rights on, or impose obligations on individuals. This possibility was recognised for the first time by the Permanent Court of International Justice (PCIJ) in the Case *Concerning Competences of the Courts of Danzig*[615] in which it was held that an exception to the principle of individuals not being subject to public international law arises if the intention of the contracting parties was to adopt a treaty which creates rights and obligations for them capable of being enforced by municipal courts. The PCIJ emphasised that this intention must be express and not inferred from the treaty since this kind of international treaty constitutes an exception to a general principle. Such treaties are classified under public international law as "self-executing". They automatically become part of the national law of the contracting parties and are directly enforceable in national courts.

The *Danzig* exception that an international treaty can confer rights on individuals enforceable in municipal courts has become a principle of EU law. In Case 26/62 *Van Gend en Loos*,[616] the ECJ held that Community law [EU law] is directly effective and thus creates rights and obligations for EU nationals enforceable before national courts. In doing this, the Court ignored the *Danzig* requirements that in order for an international treaty to be directly effective, an express provision in the treaty or a clear intention of the contracting parties in this respect is necessary.

THE FACTS WERE:

In 1960 Van Gend imported urea-formaldehyde, a chemical product, into The Netherlands from Germany. In December 1959 The Netherlands enacted legislation which modified the Benelux tariff system, and which brought into effect the Brussels Convention on Nomenclature unifying the classification of goods for customs purposes. Under the new nomenclature Van Gend's product was reclassified. This resulted in an increase in the duty payable on urea-formaldehyde to 8 per cent on an ad valorem *basis as compared to 3 per cent payable previously under Dutch law. On 14 January 1958 the EEC Treaty came into force. Its Article 12 [repealed] provided that:*

"Member States shall refrain from introducing between themselves any new customs duties on imports or exports or any charge having equivalent effect, and from increasing those which they already apply in their trade with each other."

Van Gend challenged the increase as contrary to Article 12 of the EC Treaty [repealed]. When his claim was rejected by the customs inspector, he appealed to the Dutch Tariecommissie

---

615.   Advisory Opinion of 3 February 1928, Series B, No. 15, esp. 17.
616.   [1963] ECR 3.

(Customs Court) in Amsterdam. Under Article 234 EC [Article 267 TFEU] the Customs Court submitted two questions to the ECJ:

- *first, whether Article 12 of the EC Treaty [repealed] could create rights for individuals as claimed by Van Gend; and*

- *second, provided the answer to the first question was in the affirmative, whether the modification in customs duties was prohibited by Article 12 of the EC Treaty [repealed].*

The Governments of Belgium, Germany and The Netherlands submitted additional memoranda to the ECJ claiming that first, Article 12 of the EC Treaty [repealed] created obligations for Member States and not rights for individuals and second, that if a breach of EC law occurred, the proceedings should solely be based on Articles 226 and 227 EC [258 and 259 TFEU].

Held:

The Court stated that direct effect is derived from the peculiar nature of Community law [EU law] and relied on three particular arguments to support its decision. The arguments were:

- First, the objectives of the EC Treaty imply that the Treaty itself is "more than an agreement which created mutual obligations between the contracting states" as it establishes the Community which "constitutes a new legal order of international law . . . the subjects of which comprise not only Member States but also their nationals".

- Second, it stems from the Treaty's preamble, which refers to the Member States, to its people and to the institutional system of the Community, that EC law affects both the Member States and their citizens. It also requires the co-operation of the Member States in the functioning of the Community through its institutions such as the European Parliament (EP) and the Economic and Social Committee.

- Third, the Court invoked an argument drawn from Article 234 EC [Article 267 TFEU] (under which national courts may request from the ECJ a preliminary ruling on the interpretation and validity of EC law), that the Member States "have acknowledged that Community law has an authority which can be invoked by their nationals before those courts and tribunals".

From all these arguments the ECJ inferred that Community law [EU law] "independently of the legislation of Member States . . . not only imposes obligations on individuals but is also intended to confer upon them rights which become part of their legal heritage".

Comment:

The rejection of the aforementioned requirements of the *Danzig* exception was clear-cut when the ECJ stated that: "Those rights arise not only where they are expressly granted by the Treaty, but also by reason of obligations which the Treaty imposes in a clearly defined way upon individuals as well as upon the Member States and upon the institutions of the Community." Therefore, the fact that the addressees of the provisions of the EC Treaty are the Member States "does not imply that their nationals cannot benefit from this obligation".

To the contrary, the Treaty confers rights upon EU nationals not only when its provisions expressly so provide but also when its provisions impose clearly defined obligations upon the Member States.

Additionally, the direct effect of EU law ensures its effectiveness since, as the ECJ held in *Van Gend*, "The vigilance of individuals concerned to protect their rights amounts to an effective supervision in addition to the supervision entrusted by Articles [226 and 227 EC-Articles 258 and 259 TFEU] to the diligence of the Commission and of the Member States."

12.1.1 Criteria of direct effect

It was left to the ECJ to determine the conditions under which a provision of EU law becomes directly effective. The criteria that emerged from decisions of the ECJ rendered mostly under Article 234 EC [Article 267 TFEU] are simple. A provision of EU law, in order to produce direct effect, must be:

- sufficiently clear and precise;[617] and

- unconditional in that it is capable of judicial application without any need for adoption of further implementing measures, either at national or EU level.[618]

The ECJ has subsequently clarified these requirements:

- First, it held that lack of clarity or precision did not hinder a provision from producing direct effect if that provision may be clarified or defined in more precise terms by means of interpretation by the CJEU or a national judge;[619]

- Second, a condition attached to a provision which suspends its application does not nullify its direct effect but merely delays it, until the realisation of the condition or the expiry of the time limit;[620]

- Third, a provision is considered as unconditional, despite the requirement for adoption of some implementing measures on the part of a Member State or an EU institution, if neither a Member State nor an EU institution has discretion to adopt those measures. In Case 57/65 *Lütticke*,[621] the ECJ held that in order to implement Article 90(3) EC [110(3) TFEU], the Member States had no discretionary powers and thus decided this provision was directly effective. In Case 8/81 *Becker*,[622] the ECJ held that if implementation measures concern

---

617. Case 148/78 *Ratti* [1979] ECR 1629; Case 8/81 *Becker* [1982] ECR 53. The phrase "clear and precise" was examined in depth in Case C-236/92 *Comitato di Coordinamento per la Difesa della Cava v Regione Lombardia* [1994] ECR I-483.

618. Case 203/80 *Casati* [1981] ECR 2595; also Case 8/81 *Becker* [1982] ECR 53; Case 43/75 *Defrenne* [1976] ECR 455.

619. Case 27/67 *Fink Frucht* [1968] ECR 223; Case 43/75 *Defrenne* [1976] ECR 455; Case C-262/88 *Barber* [1990] ECR I-1889.

620. Case 2/74 *Reyners* [1974] ECR 631; Case 59/75 *Manghera* [1976] ECR 91.

621. [1966] ECR 205.

622. [1982] ECR 53.

solely procedural matters, a provision in question is still considered as unconditional and as such may be enforced before national courts;

- Fourth, a provision must be capable of creating rights for individuals. In almost all cases brought before the ECJ an individual has claimed a right conferred upon him/her by EU law and thus his/her direct interest in the application of the relevant directive was self-evident. This interest to bring a claim has been generously interpreted by the ECJ. In Joined Cases C-87/90, C-88/90 and C-89/90 *A. Verholen and others v Sociale Verzekeringsbank Amsterdam*[623] the ECJ stated that an individual may rely on Directive 79/7 before a national court if he bears (i.e. suffers) the effects of a discriminatory national provision regarding his spouse, who was not a party to the proceedings, provided that his spouse comes within the scope of the directive.

12.1.2   Vertical and horizontal direct effect

Vertical direct effect refers to a situation where an individual (that is, a natural or legal person) is allowed to rely on a provision of EU law in national proceedings against a Member State or its emanations.

Horizontal direct effect concerns a situation where an individual (that is, a natural or legal person) is allowed to invoke a provision of EU law in national proceedings against another individual.

If a provision of EU law is only vertically directly effective, an individual is barred from commencing proceedings based on that provision against another individual before a national court. This may produce unfair results, as explained below.

12.2   Direct effect of the Treaties

The ECJ in *Van Gend en Loos* (see above) held that direct effect of the provisions of the EC Treaty is not automatic since the provisions need to be clear, precise and unconditional. It further established that Article 12 of the EC Treaty [repealed] satisfied those conditions and therefore was vertically directly effective. The question whether provisions of the EC Treaty other than Article 12 could produce vertical direct effect was answered by the ECJ in Case 57/65 *Alfons Lütticke v Hauptzollampt Saarlouis*.[624]

THE FACTS WERE:

Lütticke imported whole milk powder from Luxembourg on which the German customs authorities levied duty and a turnover tax. Lütticke claimed that the imported product should be exempt from turnover tax as domestic natural milk and whole milk powder were exempt under the Turnover Tax Law. The Finanzgericht des Saarlands referred to the ECJ under Article 234 EC [Article 267 TFEU] the question whether Article 90 EC [Article 110 TFEU],

---

623.   [1991] ECR I-3757.
624.   [1966] ECR 205.

which prohibits the imposition of such taxes, has direct effect and so confers rights upon individuals which a national court must protect.

Held:

The ECJ held that Article 90 EC [Article 110 TFEU] does produce such direct effect and consequently creates individual rights which must be enforced by national courts. Therefore, all doubts as to the vertical direct effect of Treaty provisions were dispelled.

The question of whether or not Treaty provisions can produce horizontal direct effect was decided by the ECJ in Case 43/75 *Defrenne v SABENA*.[625]

THE FACTS WERE:

Miss Defrenne, who was employed as an air hostess by the Belgian airline company SABENA (a private company), claimed for losses she sustained in terms of the lower pay she received compared with male cabin stewards doing the same work. The Cour de Travail referred to the ECJ, within the preliminary ruling procedure, the question of whether she could rely on Article 141 EC [Article 157 TFEU], which prohibits all discrimination between men and women workers, and thus requires that they receive equal pay for performing the same task in the same establishment or service. The wording of Article 141 EC [Article 157 TFEU] clearly indicated that further measures were necessary to implement this article.

Held:

The ECJ held that in her case it was easy to apply Article 141 EC [Article 157 TFEU] as the facts clearly showed that she was discriminated against. It stated that: ". . . the prohibition of discrimination between men and women applies not only to the action of public authorities, but also extends to all agreements which are intended to regulate paid labour collectively, as contracts between individuals".

Comment:

In cases of discrimination which cannot be easily identified it may be necessary for the EU or the Member States to adopt implementing measures.

The case law of the ECJ has gradually identified those provisions of the Treaties which have both direct vertical and horizontal effect, those which have only direct vertical effect and those which do not produce direct effect.

---

625. [1976] ECR 455.

12.3   Direct effect of regulations

Provisions of regulations may produce both vertical and horizontal direct effect. Whether or not a particular provision has direct effect is a matter for the proper construction of that provision in the light of the criteria for direct effect set out by the ECJ. The vertical direct effect of regulations was recognised in Case 93/71 *Leonesio v Italian Ministry of Agriculture*.[626]

THE FACTS WERE:

Under Council Regulation 2195/69 relating to a scheme to reduce dairy herds and over-production of dairy products, payments to farmers who slaughtered their dairy cows should be made within two months. The Italian Government delayed implementation of the scheme until the introduction of necessary budgetary provisions (part of the cost was paid by national authorities). Leonesio slaughtered her dairy cows and did not receive payment within the two-month period. Leonesio brought an action before a national court against the Italian Ministry of Agriculture for payments.

Held:

The ECJ held that:

"Regulations were of direct effect, creating a right in the applicant Leonesio to a payment which could not be conditional or altered by national authorities, and which was immediately enforceable in the national courts."

Horizontal direct effect of regulations was confirmed by the ECJ in Case C-253/00 *Antonio Muñoz Cia SA v Frumar Ltd*.[627]

12.4   Direct effect of directives

Three main arguments have been invoked against direct effect of directives:

- First, Article Article 288 TFEU provides that only regulations are directly applicable. On this basis it was argued that directives can neither be directly applicable nor directly effective;

- Second, directives have no general application. Article 288 TFEU clearly states that they are addressed only to the Member States and leaves to them the form, methods and procedures necessary to attain the objectives pursued by the relevant directive. Therefore, directives cannot create rights for individuals since they are not addressees of directives. According to this argument individual rights can only be conferred by national measures implementing directives;

- Third, the difference between regulations and directives disappears if the latter can produce direct effect. This equality between them, from a legal point of view, is incompatible with

---

626.   [1972] ECR 287. Similar conclusions were reached by the ECJ in Case 43/71 *Politi* [1973] ECR 1039.

627.   [2002] ECR I-7289.

the Treaties given that their provisions expressly provide that only directives are appropriate to harmonise specific areas of EU law.

The ECJ's arguments in favour of conferring on directives the ability to produce direct effect are as follows:

- The refusal to confer on directives the ability to produce direct effect is incompatible with Article 288 TFEU, which states that directives have binding force. Consequently, individuals should invoke them in appropriate circumstances;

- The principle of effectiveness, which has been applied by the ECJ in order to promote effective enforcement of EU law within the legal systems of the Member States,[628] requires recognition of the direct effect of directives, which entails their application by national courts;

- It is inferred from Article 288 TFEU, which makes no distinction between various legislative acts adopted by EU institutions in the circumstances where a national court decides to refer a question relating to interpretation or validity of those acts to the ECJ, that no distinction should be made between directives and other secondary legislation in terms of their ability to produce direct effect. Consequently, Article 267 TFEU implies that individuals should be allowed to rely on provisions of directives in proceedings before national courts.

Based on the above arguments, the ECJ has recognised that directives can be directly effective.

The ECJ first invoked the possibility that directives may produce direct effect in Case 9/70 *Franz Grad*.[629] In this case the question concerned direct effect of a Council decision, but the ECJ stated that other measures mentioned in Article 249 EC [Article 288 TFEU] may produce direct effect, inter alia, directives.

In Case 33/70 *SACE*,[630] the ECJ was asked to give its ruling on the combined effect of directly effective provisions of the EC Treaty and of the directive implementing them. The Court's judgment indicated the possibility of a directive having direct effect.

The first decision of the ECJ in which direct effect of a directive was expressly recognised was Case 41/74 *Van Duyn*.[631]

THE FACTS WERE:

Miss Van Duyn, a Dutch national, arrived at Gatwick Airport on 9 May 1973. She intended to work as a secretary at the British headquarters of the Church of Scientology of California. The British immigration authorities refused her leave to enter on the grounds of public policy. Although it was not unlawful to work for the Church of Scientology, the UK Government warned foreigners that the effects of the Church's activities were harmful to the mental

---

628. See R. Ward, "National Sanctions in EC law: A Moving Boundary in the Division of Competence", (1995) 1 ELJ, p 205.
629. [1970] ECR 825. On direct effect of EC decisions see section 12.5.
630. [1970] ECR 1213.
631. [1974] ECR 1337.

health of those involved. Miss Van Duyn challenged the decision of the immigration authorities on two grounds:

- Article 39 EC [Article 45 TFEU] which grants workers the right of free movement between
  Member States subject to its paragraph 3, which imposes limitations on grounds of public
  policy, public security or public health; and

- Article 3(1) of Directive 64/221 [Article 27(2) of Directive 2004/38], which further implements Article 39(3) EC [Article 45(3) TFEU] and which provides that measures taken by
  Member States regarding public policy must be "based exclusively on the personal conduct of the individual concerned".

Miss Van Duyn claimed that Article 3(1) of Directive 64/221 was directly effective and that the
refusal to allow her to enter the UK was not based on her conduct but on the general policy of
the British Government towards the Church of Scientology.

The English High Court asked the ECJ whether both Article 39 EC [Article 45 TFEU] and
Directive 64/221 were directly effective.

Held:

The ECJ held that both produced direct effect. In particular, the ECJ held that "given the
nature, general scheme and wording [of Article 3(1) of Directive 64/221] its effectiveness
would be greater if individuals were entitled to invoke it in national courts". Therefore, based
on the principle of effectiveness, the ECJ decided that Article 3(1) of Directive 64/221 was
directly effective.

The case law of the ECJ regarding directives has further elucidated the concept of direct effect.
Six main points of guidance have appeared:

1. The general principle is that directives should be correctly implemented into national law,
   so that individuals can rely on their provisions before national courts through the
   national implementing measures.[632] As a result, there should be no need to verify whether
   a provision of a directive satisfies the three criteria for direct effect, that is, it must be
   clear, precise and unconditional. In this way, an individual should have the benefit of
   rights conferred by directives in the manner envisaged by Article 288 TFEU. Therefore,
   the question of direct effect should not arise since the correct transposition of provisions
   of directives means that they are part of national law.

   The question of whether a directive has been correctly implemented into national law
   concerns, in reality, the conformity of national law with EU law, and not the question of
   direct effect. Thus, any relevant provision of a directive implemented into national law
   can be invoked in any dispute (including a dispute between individuals) in order to verify
   whether national authorities have implemented it in accordance with requirements
   specified in the directive.[633] Furthermore, implementing measures may be called into
   question in the process of interpretation of national law in conformity with EU law. In

---

632. Case 270/81 *Felicitas* [1982] ECR 2771.
633. Case 51/76 *Nederlandse Ondernemingen* [1977] ECR 113, at para 24.

this respect, in Case 14/83 *Von Colson and Kamann*[634] the ECJ held that national courts in applying national law, and especially its provisions implementing directives, have a duty to interpret national law in the light of the text and objectives of the directive in question in order to achieve the results envisaged in Article 288 TFEU. This case has established the doctrine of indirect horizontal direct effect (see section 12.4.1.2).

2. In order to curtail non-implementation of directives by Member States within the specific time limit, usually laid down in the measures themselves, the ECJ held in Case 148/78 *Publico Ministero v Ratti*[635] that, provided the provisions of a directive are sufficiently precise and unconditional, their non-implementation within the prescribed period does not affect their direct effect.

THE FACTS WERE:

Ratti was selling solvents and varnishes. He fixed labels to certain dangerous substances in conformity with Directives 73/173 and 77/728, but contrary to Italian legislation of 1963. He was prosecuted by Italian authorities for breach of Italian legislation. Directive 73/173 had not been implemented in Italy, although the time limit prescribed for its implementation had elapsed on 8 December 1974. Also Directive 77/728 had not been transposed into Italian law but the time limit for its implementation had not then yet expired. The Milan Court asked the ECJ under Article 234 EC [Article 267 TFEU] which set of rules should be applied, national law or Directives 73/173 and 77/728.

Held:

The ECJ held that if the provisions of a directive are sufficiently precise and unconditional, although that directive is not implemented within the prescribed period, an individual may rely upon them.

3. A Member State which has failed to transpose a directive within the prescribed time limit cannot rely on it in proceedings against individuals.[636]

4. In the context of criminal proceedings against individuals the ECJ has consistently ruled that a directive cannot, of itself and independently of national implementing measures, impose obligations on an individual and therefore it cannot be relied upon in proceedings against individuals.[637] The ECJ emphasised that in such a situation a directive cannot have the effect of determining or aggravating the liability in criminal law of persons who have infringed its provisions.[638]

---

634. [1984] ECR 1891; also Case 31/87 *Beentjes* [1988] ECR 4635; Joined Cases C-397 to C-403/01 *Pfeiffer* [2004] ECR I-8835.

635. [1979] ECR 1629.

636. Case 80/86 *Kolpinghuis Nijmegen* [1987] ECR 3969; Joined Cases C-397 to C-403/01 *Pfeiffer* [2004] ECR I-8835.

637. Joined Cases C-397/01 to C-403/01 *Pfeiffer and Others* [2004] ECR I-8835; Joined Cases 387/02, 391/02 and 403/02 *Criminal Proceedings against Berlusconi and Others* [2005] ECR I-3565.

638. Case 80/86 *Kolpinghuis Nijmegen* [1987] ECR 3969; Case C-60/02 *X* [2004] ECR I-651.

5. Directives can only produce vertical direct effect. This has been confirmed many times by the ECJ, despite contrary opinions of Advocates General.[639] In Case C-91/92 *Faccini Dori*, the ECJ held:

    "The effect of extending that case law [on vertical direct effect] to the sphere of relations between individuals would be to recognise a power in the Community to enact obligations for individuals with immediate effect, whereas it has competence to do so only where it is empowered to adopt regulations."[640]

    The above is a very valid reason, but the main argument against attributing direct horizontal effect to directives is that direct effect is intended to force a Member State to comply with its EU law obligations in order to ensure that individuals derive benefits from EU law. For that reason directives should not apply to their detriment. That is why the principle of horizontal direct effect does not apply to relations between individuals.

6. As Advocate-General Ruiz-Jarabo Colomer stated in his Opinion in Joined Cases C-152/07 to C-154/07 *Arcor AG & Co. KG* (C-152/07), *Communication Services TELE2 GmbH* (C-153/07) *Firma 01051 Telekom GmbH* (C-154/07) *v Germany*:[641]

    "The doctrine of direct effect operates on a vertical, one-way plane (from an individual to the State), in that traffic in the opposite direction (reverse vertical relationships) and perpendicular routes which would enable a directive to be relied on between individuals (horizontal direct effect) are both prohibited."

    Notwithstanding this, in some exceptional cases the ECJ allowed directives to produce horizontal direct effect (see section 12.4.1.5).

Conclusion

It can be seen from the above that direct effect of a directive becomes an issue only if the implementing measures adopted by a Member State are incompatible with its provisions[642] or insufficient[643] or, as in *Ratti*, when a Member State fails to implement a directive within the prescribed time limit.

12.4.1 Mitigating the lack of horizontal direct effect of directives

The refusal to give horizontal direct effect to directives means that even if conditions for direct effect are satisfied, an individual cannot rely on them in proceedings brought against another

---

639. Conclusions of Van Gerven in Case C-271/91 *Marshall* [1993] ECR I-4367 at 4381; Jacobs in Case C-316/93 *Vaneetveld* [1994] ECR I-763 at 765; Lenz in Case C-91/92 *Faccini Dori* [1994] ECR I-3325.
640. Para 24 [1994] ECR I-3325, confirmed many times: Case C-472/93 *Luigi Spano and Fiat Geotech* [1995] ECR I-4321; Joined Cases C 397/01 to C 403/01 *Pfeiffer* [2004] ECR I-8835; Joined Cases 387/02 391/02 and 403/02 *Criminal Proceedings against Berlusconi and Others* [2005] ECR I-3565; Case C-80/06 *Carp* [2007] ECR I-4473
641. [2008] ECR I-5959.
642. Case 38/77 *Enka* [1977] ECR 2203; Case 103/88 *Fratelli Constanzo* [1989] ECR 1839.
643. Case 36/75 *Rutili* [1975] ECR 1219.

individual.[644] As a result, individuals cannot enforce their rights because the other party involved is an individual.[645] This is obviously an unjust and unfair situation since, for example, if individuals are employed in the public sector, they may bring proceedings against their employer based on the direct effect of a directive, but if those individuals work in the private sector, they have no remedy based on direct effect of a directive against their employer.[646] Thus, if a Member State fails to properly implement a directive, those who have a legitimate claim under the directive can only enforce their rights against a public body or its emanations, not against another individual. However, such individuals are not left without remedy. They can bring proceedings against a Member State for damages resulting from incorrect implementation of a directive (see Chapter 14).

In order to overcome the practical implications deriving from refusal to confer horizontal direct effect on directives, the ECJ has developed four approaches, and is possibly developing an additional approach. These are:

1. Under the first approach, the ECJ has extended the meaning of a Member State, or its emanations.

2. Under the second approach, the ECJ has imposed a duty on national courts to interpret national law in conformity with EU law. The result of this duty is the creation of what is known as indirect horizontal effect.

3. Under the third approach, an individual is allowed to rely on a directive in proceedings against another individual or a Member State, in order to determine whether the national legislature, in exercising its choice as to the form and methods for implementing the directive, has kept within the limits of its discretion set out in the directive.

4. Under the fourth approach, the ECJ allows an individual to bring proceedings against a State in a situation where such an action affects the rights of individuals who are not part of the vertical relationship.[647] This is referred to as "triangular" horizontal effect.

5. With regard to the possible fifth approach it is uncertain whether there is a fifth emerging way in which the ECJ attempts to remedy the lack of horizontal direct effect of directives. Case law on this topic is confusing. It is submitted, however, that the ECJ has allowed individuals in some exceptional circumstances to rely on directives in

---

644. "Individual" means not only any natural or legal person (see Case 138/86 *Direct Cosmetics* [1988] ECR 3937) but also any legal subject, whether private or public (see for example, Joined Cases C-487/01 and C-7/02 *Gemeente Leusden* [2004] ECR I-5337) who may be "concerned" by the relevant provision. On this topic see S. Prechal, *Directives in EC Law*, 2nd edition, 2005, Oxford: Oxford University Press, p 238.

645. On this question see S. Prechal, "Remedies after Marshall", (1990) CML Rev, p 451.

646. For example, in Case 152/84 *Marshall v Southampton and South West Area Health Authority* [1986] ECR 723, the claimant succeeded in her equal pay claim against a public heath authority based on Directive 76/207/EEC, whilst in *Duke v GEC Reliance Ltd* [1988] 1 All ER 626, the claimant failed in a similar claim brought against a private company.

647. Case C-201/02 *Wells* ([2004] ECR I-723) and Joined Cases C-152/07 to C-154/07 *Arcor* [2008] ECR I-5959.

proceedings against another private party.[648] Only time will tell whether or not the ECJ maintains the thrust of these judgments.

12.4.1.1 The first approach: The extensive interpretation given by the ECJ to the meaning of a State or the emanations of a State

On the basis of the vertical direct effect of directives, individuals have directly enforceable rights on which they may rely in an action against a Member State in proceedings before national courts. Bearing in mind that any action against a Member State is in fact taken against a body of the relevant Member State, the question arises as to what bodies are considered as belonging to the Member State. In general, the answer is rather simple. The dichotomy of public/private bodies is known in all Member States. Nevertheless, the ECJ, in order to maximise the effect of directives, introduced an autonomous meaning of public body in Case 152/84 *Marshall v Southampton and South West Hampshire Area Health Authority (AHA) (Teaching) (No.1).*[649]

THE FACTS WERE:

Miss Marshall, an employee of AHA, was required to retire at the age of 60, while for her male colleagues the retirement age was 65. She was dismissed at 62. Miss Marshall, who wished to remain in employment, argued that the British Sex Discrimination Act 1975, which excluded from its scope of application provisions in relation to death and retirement, was contrary to Council Directive 76/207 on Equal Treatment. The UK had adopted this Directive but had not amended the 1975 Act, considering that discrimination in retirement ages was allowed. The Court of Appeal asked the ECJ under Article 234 EC [Article 267 TFEU] whether the dismissal of Miss Marshall was unlawful, and whether she was entitled to rely upon Directive 76/207 in national courts.

Held:

The ECJ answered both questions in the affirmative. It held that AHA was a public body regardless of the capacity in which it was acting, that is, public authority or employer. It emphasised that:

"The argument submitted by the United Kingdom that the possibility of relying on provisions of the directive against the respondent *qua* organ of the State would give rise to an arbitrary and unfair distinction between the rights of State employees and those of private employees, does not justify any other conclusion. Such a distinction may easily be avoided if the Member State concerned has correctly implemented the directive into national law."

Subsequently, the ECJ has elucidated the concept of "a State" and given to it a wide

---

648. See I. Ward, *A Critical Introduction to European Law*, 2nd edition, 2003, London: LexisNexisButterworths, pp 78–80.
649. [1986] ECR 723.

interpretation.[650] In Case C-188/89 *Foster and Others v British Gas plc*[651] the ECJ provided a definition of a body which is an emanation of a Member State. It is a body:

"... whatever its legal form, which has been made responsible pursuant to a measure adopted by a public authority, for providing a public service under the control of that authority and had for that purpose special powers beyond those which resulted from the normal rules applicable in relations between individuals".

It results from that definition that three criteria should be satisfied in order to consider an entity as an emanation of a Member State. These are:

- It must be made responsible for providing a public service;

- It must provide that service under the control of the Member State; and

- It must have special powers to provide that service, beyond those normally applicable in relations between individuals.

This test has been applied by national courts, inter alia British courts, to determine whether an organisation can be considered to be an emanation of the Member State.

In *Doughty v Rolls Royce*,[652] the Court of Appeal decided that although Rolls Royce was 100 per cent owned by the Member State, as the Member State was its sole shareholder and thus any services it provided were under control of the Member State, it did not fulfil the remaining criteria established in *Foster*. As a result, Doughty, in a very similar situation to Miss Marshall, could not invoke Directive 76/207 and was barred from commencing proceedings against Rolls Royce.

The opposite conclusions were reached by the ECJ in Case C-157/02 *Rieser Internationale Transporte GmbH v Asfinag*.[653]

THE FACTS WERE:

Asfinag, an Austrian undertaking, which under a licence concluded with the Austrian Government was responsible for the construction, operation, maintenance and financing of Austrian motorways and expressways and was allowed to impose tolls and user charges in order to finance itself, argued that it was not a public body within the meaning of EU law.

---

650. The following bodies have been regarded as emanations of a Member State: Tax authorities – Case 8/81 *Becker* [1982] ECR 53; Police authorities – Case 222/84 *Johnston* [1986] ECR 1651; Health Boards – Case 152/84 *Marshall*, supra note 649; local government bodies – Case 103/88 *Fratelli Constanzo* [1989] ECR 1839; professional bodies established by statutory instruments – Joined Cases 266–7/87 *The Royal Pharmaceutical Society of Great Britain* [1989] ECR 1295; and a body set up by the German Government to promote German agriculture and the German food industry, but which carried out its activity through a private company whose organs were set up in accordance with private law rules and financed by compulsory contributions paid by undertakings in the German agriculture and food sector – Case C-325/00 *Commission v Germany* [2002] ECR I-9977.
651. [1990] ECR I-3313.
652. [1992] 1 CMLR 1045.
653. [2004] ECR I-1477.

Held:

The ECJ held that Asfinag was a public body.

Comment:

The ECJ based its reasoning on the facts that the Austrian state:

- was the sole shareholder of Asfinag;

- had the right to check all measures taken by the company and its subsidiaries;

- could require any information at any time;

- imposed objectives in terms of the organisation of traffic, safety and construction;

- approved the annual budgets of Asfinag; and

- fixed the amount of the tolls to be levied.

Accordingly, Asfinag satisfied all three criteria set out in *Foster*.

One explanation why *Doughty v Rolls Royce* and *Rieser Internationale* might be distinguished is that in *Rieser Internationale*, there was a closer connection with an activity that is normally primarily a matter for the state – that is, the construction of motorways, whereas Rolls Royce concerned an activity that is normally carried out in the private sector.

12.4.1.2 The second approach: Interpretation of national law in conformity with EU Law by national courts: indirect horizontal effect

National judges are required to interpret national law in conformity with EU law. This principle, which is often called "indirect horizontal effect", constitutes a logical consequence of the supremacy of EU law and applies in relation to all EU law irrespective of whether a provision of EU law is directly effective. National law, whether enacted before or after the entry into force of the Treaties in the relevant Member State, must conform to EU law. In Case 14/83 *Von Colson and Kamann*,[654] the ECJ emphasised that national judges are obliged to interpret national law in the light of the text and objectives of EU law, which in this particular case was a directive. This solution is based on two premises:

- First, on Article 4(3) TEU, which imposes upon the Member States a duty of loyal and active co-operation. Article 4(3) TFEU provides that Member States must take all appropriate measures, whether general or particular, to fulfil their obligations arising out of the Treaties and resulting from measures adopted by EU institutions. They must facilitate accomplishment of the tasks of EU institutions. This means that the Member States must adopt implementing measures vis-à-vis the Treaties and acts of EU institutions.

- Second, in Case 30/70 *Scheer*,[655] the ECJ held that under Article 10 EC [Article 4(3) TFEU]

---

654. [1984] ECR 1891.
655. [1970] ECR 1197.

the Member States have a duty to do whatever possible to ensure the effectiveness of the provisions of EU law. According to the ECJ Article 10 EC [Article 4(3) TFEU] applies to all national bodies, including national courts, which have a duty to ensure that national law conforms to EU law, and thus the requirement of the principle of effectiveness is satisfied, that is, rights vested in individuals by EU law are protected by national courts. The combined effect of Article 288 TFEU, Article 4(3) TEU and the principle of effectiveness secures adequate enforcement of any obligations imposed on individuals.

The possibility of obliging national courts to interpret national law in conformity with Community law was mentioned for the first time in Case 111/75 *Mazzalai*,[656] in which the ECJ approved the conclusion of Advocate General Darmon, who said that the interpretation of a directive in the light of EC law may be useful for national judges in order to ensure that their interpretation conforms to the requirements of Community law. However, it was two decisions of the ECJ rendered the same day, Case 14/83 *Von Colson and Kamann*[657] and Case 79/83 *Harz*,[658] that provided a new solution to the problem of mitigating the effect of the vertical/horizontal public/private dichotomy of directives.

THE FACTS WERE:

Von Colson and Harz, both females, argued that they were discriminated against on grounds of gender when applying for a job: Von Colson in the public service when she applied for the post of prison social worker, and Harz in the private sector when she applied to join a training programme with a commercial company. Under German law implementing Council Directive 76/207, although it was accepted that Von Colson and Harz had been discriminated against unlawfully, they were entitled to receive only nominal damages, that is, reimbursement of their travel expenses. They claimed that such implementation was contrary to Article 6 of Directive 76/207, which provides that:

"Member States shall introduce into their national legal systems such measures as are necessary to enable all persons who consider themselves wronged by failure to apply to them the principle of equal treatment . . . to pursue their claims by judicial process after possible recourse to other competent authorities."

Both applicants argued that the remedy under German law was inadequate and that they should be offered the post or receive substantial damages. Under Article 234 EC [Article 267 TFEU] the German labour court referred to the ECJ the following questions: whether Article 6 of Directive 76/207 was directly effective, and whether under that Directive Member States were required to provide for particular sanctions or other legal consequences in cases of discrimination on grounds of sex against a person seeking employment.

---

656. [1976] ECR 657, para 10.
657. [1984] ECR 1891.
658. [1984] ECR 1921.

Held:

The ECJ held that:

- national law must be interpreted in such a way as to achieve the result required by the directive regardless of whether the defendant was a Member State or a private party;

- sanctions for discrimination were left to national law. The Court stated that, on the one hand, the employer is not obliged to offer a contract of employment to an applicant being discriminated against on the ground of gender but, on the other hand, the principle of effectiveness requires that compensation must, in any event, be adequate to the damage sustained and must amount to more than purely nominal compensation. The German Labour Court subsequently found that it had power to award damages to both plaintiffs not exceeding six months gross salary.

Comment:

In both cases the interpretation of national law in conformity with the Directive resulted in providing an efficient remedy to the applicants tantamount to conferring on Article 6 of Directive 76/207 horizontal direct effect.

A further issue that arose in the case law was whether interpretation in conformity with Community law was restricted to national law implementing measures or extended to all law. The answer was provided by the ECJ in Case C-106/89 *Marleasing*.[659]

THE FACTS WERE:

Under the Spanish Civil Code a company could be nullified on the grounds of "lack of cause". Marleasing claimed that the defendant company was established in order to defraud its creditors, that the founders' contract was a sham and since the contract of associations was void for "lack of cause", it, as one of the creditors could recover its debt personally from those behind the scheme. The defendants argued that under Article 11 of the EC First Company Directive 68/151, which provided an exhaustive list of the grounds on which the nullity of a company may be declared, lack of cause was not mentioned. Directive 68/151 had not been implemented in Spain, although the prescribed time limit for its implementation had elapsed. The Spanish court asked the ECJ, within the preliminary ruling procedure, whether Article 11 of Directive 68/151 was directly effective, and whether it prevented a declaration of nullity on grounds other than those listed in that provision.

---

659.   [1990] ECR I-4135.

Held:

The ECJ held:

- that directives could not produce horizontal direct effect, thus the defendant could not rely on Article 11 in proceedings against another individual. Also Article 11 of Directive 68/151 exhaustively listed the grounds of nullity and did not include the grounds on which Marleasing relied;

- that based on its judgment in *Von Colson* a Spanish court was obliged "so far as was possible" to interpret national law, whether it pre-dated or post-dated the directive, in the light of EC law.

Comment:

The obligation of interpretation of national law "so far as possible" in conformity with EU law meant that a Spanish court had to interpret Spanish law in such a way as to disregard provisions of the Spanish Civil Code which predated Directive 68/151, so the duty of interpretation extended to all national law.

12.4.1.2.1 Limitations imposed on the Marleasing doctrine

Marleasing is a very controversial case. On the one hand, the judgment states that the obligation to interpret national law in conformity with EU law is demanded only "as far as possible"; on the other hand, it does not require a national judge to interpret a national provision in the light of the directive. It simply strikes down a conflicting national provision which was never intended to implement the directive.[660] This seems, in fact, to apply the concept of direct effect under a different name. The ECJ has, however, elucidated the meaning of *Marleasing* in Case C-334/92 *Wagner Miret v Fondo de Garantia Salarial*.[661]

THE FACTS WERE:

Wagner Miret was employed as a senior manager in a Spanish company that became insolvent. Under Directive 80/987 Member States were required to set up a fund to compensate employees should their employer became insolvent. Spain had established such a fund, but it did not apply to senior management staff.

Held:

The ECJ held that:

- Directive 80/987 was not precise enough to produce direct effect and that Spanish law clearly limited access to the fund.

---

660. See also Case C-472/93 *Luigi Spano and Fiat SpA* [1995] ECR I-4321 and Case C-449/93 *Rockfon* [1995] ECR I-4291.
661. [1993] ECR I-6911.

> Spanish law could not be interpreted in such a way as to include senior management staff within the group of people to be compensated from that fund as that law clearly excluded higher management staff from claiming from the fund payment of amounts owing by way of salary.

In Joined Cases C-397–403/01 *Pfeiffer*,[662] the ECJ held that when domestic provisions, which have been specifically enacted for the purpose of transposing a directive and are intended to confer rights on individuals (that is having direct effect) are incompatible with the directive, a national court must presume that the Member State had the intention of fulfilling the obligations arising from the directive and therefore is bound to interpret national law, so far as possible, in the light of the wording and the purpose of the directive concerned in order to achieve the result sought by the directive. The national court must take into consideration the whole body of rules of national law, not only the provisions of national law implementing the directive, and must select, from the interpretative methods recognised by national law, the one which allows it to construe the challenged provision of national law in such a way as to ensure that the directive is fully effective. As a result, the national court must do whatever lies within its jurisdiction to ensure that the objective of the directive is achieved.

However, the duty to interpret national law in conformity with EU law is not absolute so as to require interpretation of national law contra legem, but only "so far as possible". In this context a question arises as to the meaning of the words "so far as possible", that is, as to the limit of a national court's obligation to interpret national law in the light of the wording and the purpose of the directive in order to achieve the results prescribed in Article 288 TFEU. It is submitted that the limits can be identified as follows:

1. First, in *Wagner Miret* the ECJ accepted that the contested directive could not be interpreted so as to include the applicant within its scope of application. In subsequent cases the ECJ confirmed that national courts are not required to interpret national law contra legem.[663]

2. Second, in Case 80/86 *Kolpinghuis Nijmegen*,[664] the ECJ established that the uniform interpretation of Community law must be qualified in criminal proceedings, if the effect of interpreting national legislation in the light of the directive would be to impose criminal liability on individuals in circumstances where such liability would not arise under the national legislation taken alone. In this case, the ECJ held that the obligation for a national judge to make reference to the terms of the directive, when he interprets relevant provisions of national law, is limited by general principles of Community law, and especially by the principle of legal certainty and non-retroactivity.

In Joined Cases C-74/95 and C-129/95 *Criminal Proceedings against X*[665] an Italian judge, within the preliminary ruling proceedings under Article 234 EC [267 TFEU],

---

662. [2004] ECR I-8835.
663. Case C-192/94 *El Corte Ingles* [1996] ECR I-1281; Case C-111/97 *EvoBus Austria* [1998] ECR I-5411; Case C-81/98 *Alcatel Austria* [1999] ECR I-7671.
664. [1987] ECR 3969.
665. [1996] ECR I-6609.

asked the ECJ to interpret some provisions of Directive 90/270 on the minimum safety and health requirements for work with display screens.[666] The Italian court did not exclude the possibility that the interpretation provided by the ECJ might, in due course, have determined or aggravated the liability of individuals in breach of that directive, although Italian law, which implemented its provisions, did not provide for any penal sanctions. The ECJ held that:

> "...the obligation on the national court to refer to the content of the directive when interpreting the relevant rules of its national law is not unlimited, particularly where such interpretation would have the effect, on the basis of the directive and independently of legislation adopted for its interpretation, of determining or aggravating the liability in criminal law of persons who act in contravention of its provisions."[667]

The ECJ explained that the principle of legality in relation to crime and punishment and especially the principle of legal certainty, its corollary, precludes bringing criminal proceedings in respect of conduct not clearly defined as culpable by law. In support of its decision the ECJ referred to the general principles of law which result from the common constitutional tradition of the Member States and Article 7 of the ECHR.

In Joined Cases 387/02, 391/02 and 403/02 *Criminal Proceedings against Berlusconi and Others*,[668] the ECJ confirmed that in the context of criminal proceedings against an individual a directive cannot of itself, and independently of national legislation adopted by a Member State for its implementation, have the effect of determining, or increasing the criminal liability of the accused person who has infringed its provisions.

3.   Third, it appears that in a situation where national law imposes civil liability on a private party, the ECJ does not impose on national courts any obligation to avoid interpreting national law in conformity with EU law.

4.   Fourth, initially the ECJ rejected the idea that national courts have a duty to interpret national law in conformity with EU law before the expiry of the transposition period of a directive. In Case C-212/04 *Adeneler*,[669] the ECJ held that:

> "where a directive is transposed belatedly, the general obligation owed by national courts to interpret domestic law in conformity with the directive exists only once the period for its transposition has expired" (para 115).

However, in Case C-246/06 *Velasco Navarro (Josefa) v Fondo de Garantía Salarial (Fogasa)*[670] the ECJ held that although an individual cannot rely on a provision of a directive with regard to events occurring before the end of the transposition period fixed for that directive (in this case the period fixed ended on 8 October 2005), a national court is, nevertheless, obliged to interpret national law in conformity with fundamental principles of EU law from the date of entry into force of the directive (i.e. in this case from 8 October 2002) in order to ensure that the principle of non-discrimination, being a

---

666.   [1990] OJ L156/1.
667.   [1997] ECR I-7411.
668.   [2005] ECR I-3565.
669.   [2006] ECR I-6057.
670.   [2008] ECR I-105.

fundamental principle of EU law, is respected. The ECJ stated that during the period falling between the date of the entry into force of Directive 2002/74[671] (i.e. from 8 October 2002) and the deadline for transposition of that directive (i.e. 8 October 2005) the relevant national law was de facto within the scope of the directive and thus within the scope of EU law and consequently should be interpreted in the light of the general principles of EU law, one of which is the principle of non-discrimination.

- The obligation arises only when the national provision in question is to any extent open to interpretation, that is, it is unclear or ambiguous. National courts will refuse to interpret national provisions contra legem;
- The principle of legal certainty, in the sense of legal predictability of law, often prevents national judges from construing national rules in conformity with EU law.[672]

12.4.1.2.2 The Marleasing doctrine in the United Kingdom – an example of the application of that doctrine

In *Webb v EMO Air Cargo (No. 2)*,[673] the first relevant British case after *Marleasing*, the House of Lords asked the ECJ for some clarification under Article 234 EC [Article 267 TFEU] on the question of interpretation of national law in conformity with EC law, and especially on its application to pre-dating national legislation.

THE FACTS WERE:

Mrs Webb was offered a temporary job to replace an employee, who was on maternity leave. Before her employment commenced, she discovered that she was pregnant. As a result she was, in effect, dismissed. She argued that this was unlawful under Directive 76/207 which prohibits discrimination based on sex. The House of Lords, when called upon to interpret the Sex Discrimination Act 1975 which implemented Directive 76/207, asked the ECJ under Article 234 EC [Article 267 TFEU] proceedings whether Mrs Webb's dismissal was contrary to Directive 76/207.

Held:

The ECJ held that Mrs Webb's dismissal was in breach of Directive 76/207.

Comment:

As a result of the ECJ's judgment, the House of Lords had to interpret the Sex Discrimination Act 1975 as required by Directive 76/207. The House of Lords interpreted Section 5(3) of the Act which provided that in order to determine discrimination, a comparison between the treatment of women and men must be based on similar "relevant circumstances", as

---

671.   [2002] OJ L270/10,
672.   E.g. The Hoge Raad in Case *Michelin v Michels*, Rechtspraak NJB 1994/2, p.14.
673.   [1995] 4 All ER 577.

meaning that "relevant circumstances" meant in the case of Mrs Webb's unavailability for work due to pregnancy, and not as previously stated by the House of Lords as simply her unavailability to work. The House of Lords held that a male employee could not be dismissed on those grounds, and thus Mrs Webb's dismissal was discriminatory.

The House of Lords in the *Webb* case, and British courts[674] in subsequent cases, have clearly accepted the decision of the ECJ in *Marleasing*, that is, that national legislation must be interpreted in conformity with EU law.

12.4.1.3 Third approach aimed at alleviating the lack of direct horizontal effect of directives: the level of discretion available to Member States under the relevant directive

For the first time, in Case 51/76 *Verbond van Nederlandse Ondernemingen*[675] the ECJ decided that individuals could rely on provisions of a directive in proceedings before national courts in order to determine whether the national legislature, in exercising its choice as to the form and methods for implementing the relevant directive, had kept within the limits of its discretion set out by that directive. Thus, the Court focused on the level of discretion available to Member States under the directive, instead of applying the usual test for direct effect. The Court based its reasoning on the principle of effectiveness of Community law and the requirements of Article 249 EC [Article 288 TFEU]. This reasoning was confirmed in Case C-287/98 *Luxembourg v Linster*.[676]

THE FACTS WERE:

Luxembourg had expropriated plots of land owned by the claimants in order to build a motorway. The claimants argued that the expropriation was in breach of Directive 85/337/EEC on the assessment of the effects of certain public and private projects on the environment,[677] as the project had not been preceded by an environmental impact study or a public inquiry as required by the Directive.

Held:

The ECJ held that individuals are allowed to rely on provisions of a directive, irrespective of whether those provisions are directly effective or not, to verify whether the national

---

674. For example: *Braymist Ltd v Wise Finance Co Ltd* [2002] Ch 273; *Director-General of Fair Trading v First National Bank* [2002] 1 AC 481.
675. [1977] ECR 113; see also Case C-72/95 *Kraaijeveld and Others* [1996] ECR I-5403; Case C-435/97 *WWF and Others v Autonome Provinz Bozen and Others* [1999] ECR I-5613.
676. [2000] ECR I-6917.
677. [1985] OJ L 175/40.

legislature, in exercising its choice as to the form and methods for implementing the directive, had kept within the limits of its discretion set by the directive. It was for the referring court to decide whether the requirements of Directive 85/337/EEC had been met by the national authorities.

Under the third approach mentioned earlier in this chapter, in a situation where the prescribed time limit for implementation of a directive has expired, an individual can rely on its provisions in proceedings before a national court against another individual or against a Member State to challenge national implementing measures. It is the task of a national court to determine whether the disputed national measure falls outside the margin of discretion which the directive leaves to the Member State.

12.4.1.4   The fourth approach under which the ECJ allows an individual to bring proceedings against a State in a situation where such proceedings affect the rights of individuals who are not part of the vertical relationship – "triangular" horizontal effect

In Case C-201/02 *Wells*,[678] the ECJ held, for the first time, that "adverse repercussions on the rights of third parties, even if the repercussions are certain, do not justify preventing an individual from invoking the provisions of a directive against the Member State concerned" (paragraph 57). In *Wells*, the claimant was allowed to rely on Directive 85/337 to force a Member State to carry out an environmental impact assessment, as provided for in the directive, resulting in a temporary (or, depending on the results of that assessment, even permanent) cessation of the working of a quarry, located near Ms Wells' dwelling-house. In *Wells*, the ECJ held that the obligation in question was not imposed on the quarry owners but on a Member State and thus the argument submitted by the UK, which was described by the ECJ as an "inverse direct effect" of the provisions of that directive in relation to the quarry owners, was rejected. The ECJ confirmed that directives can produce "trangular" horizontal effect in Joined Cases C-152/07 to C-154/07 *Arcor*.[679]

THE FACTS WERE:

The cases related to the liberalisation of telecommunications markets based on EC Directives, which in Germany were implemented on 1 August 1996 by the German Law on Telecommunications. Before the liberalisation Deutsche Telekom enjoyed a legal monopoly in Germany in the retail provision of fixed-line telecommunications services. Since liberalisation, Deutsche Telekom has had to compete with alternative operators with regard to local network access services. Abusive practices of Deutsche Telekom with regard to its competitors had been condemned by a Commission decision and this condemnation was confirmed by the CFI [the General Court] in Case T-271/08 Deutsche Telekom AG v Commission.[680]

---

678.   [2004] ECR I-723.
679.   [2008] ECR I-5959.
680.   [2008] ECR II-477.

The claimants, Arcor AG and others, all operators of public telecommunications networks in Germany offering their customers a carrier selection service through interconnection to the local network of Deutsche Telekom, brought proceedings before a national court challenging the decision of the German Federal Agency for Electricity, Gas, Telecommunications, Post and Rail Networks ("the regulatory authority") which approved a connection charge of €0.004 per minute in respect of call charges for the provision of calls originating in Deutsche Telekom's national telephone network. The decision had been adopted on 29 April 2003 by the regulatory authority and was justified on the ground that revenues from end users accruing to Deutsche Telekom, an undertaking in a dominant position, did not cover all the costs of activating the local loop[681] with the result that in the absence of a connection charge there would have been a deficit.

As a result of the Commission decision finding Deutsche Telekom AG in breach of Article 82 EC [Article102 TFEU],[682] the German regulatory authority, by decision of 23 September 2003, revoked the decision of 29 April 2003, on the ground that Deutsche Telekom no longer had any connection cost deficit, since an increase in the price paid by end-users for provision of the local loop had been approved in the interim. However, as the decision had no retrospective effect, the claimants brought proceedings challenging the connection charges before the relevant German court which upheld their claims. Germany and Deutsche Telekom brought an appeal against this decision. The referring court asked the ECJ, inter alia, the question whether in circumstances where proceedings adversely affect a third party (i.e. Deutsche Telekom, not a party to the proceedings) the claimants (Arcor AG and others) were allowed to rely on a directive against a Member State (i.e. the German regulatory authority).

Held:

The ECJ held that the claimants could rely on the relevant EC directives. It stated that:

"It is clear that Deutsche Telekom is a third party in relation to the dispute before the referring court and is capable only of suffering adverse repercussions because it levied the connection charge at issue in the main proceedings and because, if that charge were removed, it would have to increase its own subscribers' rates. Such a removal of benefits cannot be regarded as an obligation falling on a third party pursuant to the directives relied on before the referring court by the appellants in the main proceedings."

Comment:

The ECJ clearly established that the relevant provisions of directives satisfied the test for direct effect and that Deutsche Telekom, a third party in relation to the dispute before the

---

681. The term "local loop" refers to the physical circuit connecting the network termination point at a subscriber's premises to the main distribution frame or equivalent facility in the fixed public telephone network.

682. Decision 2003/707/EC (Case COMP/C-1/37.451, 37.578, 37.579 – *Deutsche Telekom AG* ([2003] OJ L 263/9) fining Deutsche Telekom €12 600 000 for abusing its dominant position by operating abusive pricing in the form of a "margin squeeze" by charging its competitors (inter alia, the claimants in the commented cases) prices for wholesale access that were higher than its prices for retail access to the local network. The decision of the Commission was confirmed by the CFI [the General Court] in Case T-271/03 *Deutsche Telekom AG v Commission* [2008] ECR II-477.

referring court, would suffer adverse financial consequences and probably would have to increase its own subscribers' rates. However, it is also clear that in those circumstances the loss of unlawful benefits cannot be equated to the creation of a new obligation on a third party, i.e. Deutsche Telekom. As Advocate General Colomer stated in his Opinion:

> "There is no room for disharmony in the repertoire of Community case-law, although, in cases such as the present one, it will yield to the melody of triangular relationships."

Indeed, Deutsche Telekom would not suffer genuine damage by being prevented from imposing unlawful charges.

12.4.1.5 The fourth approach: exceptional circumstances under which directives may produce horizontal direct effect

It is submitted that, so far, the ECJ has developed two exceptions to the principle that directives cannot produce horizontal direct effect. The first exception can be called "a procedural" direct horizontal effect and the second can be called direct horizontal effect based on fundamental principles of EU law. Both are examined below.

12.4.1.5.1 Procedural direct horizontal effect of directives

This exception was established in Case C-443/98 *Unilever Italia SpA v Central Food SpA*.[683]

THE FACTS WERE:

Directive 83/189, which lays down a procedure for the provision of information in the field of technical standards and regulations,[684] was adopted in order to remove technical obstacles to the free movement of goods. Under the Directive Member States are required to notify the Commission of any national draft technical regulations within the scope of the Directive, the reason being that other Member States and the Commission then have an opportunity to assess the compatibility of any relevant draft technical regulation with Article 28 EC [Article 34 TFEU]. Under the Directive, subsequent to notification, the notifying Member State is required to suspend the enactment procedure of a relevant draft regulation for an initial period of three months, which period may be extended in various ways. One of them is provided for in Article 9(3) of Directive 83/189, according to which the suspension period mentioned above may be extended by 12 months following the date of notification if the Commission expresses its intention to propose an EU measure in the area covered by the proposed national draft technical regulation.

Italy prepared a draft regulation concerning labelling indicating the geographical origin of various kinds of olive oil. Italy notified its draft law to the Commission. Following this, the

---

683.   [2000] ECR I-7535.
684.   [1983] OJ L 109/8.

Commission published in the OJ a notice indicating that the three months period of suspension applied to the Italian draft law. Before the end of the suspension period the Commission informed the Italian Government that it intended to legislate in the area covered by the draft law and therefore required Italy to suspend for one year enactment of its draft law. Despite this the Italian Parliament continued the enactment procedure. In response the Commission stated that should Italy enact the draft law, the Commission would start proceedings against Italy under Article 226 EC [Article 258 TFEU] and would declare the new Italian law unenforceable against individuals. Despite this, Italy enacted its draft legislation. Four months later the Commission adopted Regulation 2815/98 concerning marketing standards for olive oil[685] which, in particular, laid down rules governing the designation of origin of virgin and extra virgin olive oils on their labels or packaging.

After the entry into force of the new Italian legislation, but before the adoption of Regulation 2815/98, Unilever, an Italian company, delivered to a warehouse of Central Food, also an Italian company, 648 litres of extra virgin olive oil. Central Food refused to pay for these goods on the ground that the olive oil was not labelled in accordance with the new Italian law. Unilever started proceedings against Central Food for payment of sums due under the contract, arguing that the legislation did not apply as it was in breach of Directive 83/189 and that Unilever's products were labelled in conformity with the preceding (and still in force) legislation. The Italian Pretore di Milano referred the matter to the ECJ.

Held:

The ECJ held that the Italian court was required, in civil proceedings between individuals concerning contractual rights and obligations, to refuse to apply the new Italian legislation. Consequently, the ECJ, by allowing Unilever to rely on Article 9(3) of Directive 83/189, attributed to this provision horizontal direct effect.

Comment:

The ECJ explained that the principle that directives cannot produce horizontal direct effect does not apply where a national technical regulation was adopted in breach of Articles 8[686] and 9 of Directive 83/189 and thus it is affected by a substantial procedural defect. This was because, as the ECJ held:

> "Directive 83/189 does not in any way define the substantive scope of the legal rule on the basis of which the national court must decide the case before it. It creates neither rights nor obligations for individuals."

It flows from the above that the exception, which can be called "procedural direct horizontal effect", applies in a situation where a directive is of a procedural nature, that is, it neither creates new law, nor any rights nor any obligations for individuals. The result in *Unilever* was that the preceding Italian law was applicable to the dispute as the new Italian law was rendered inapplicable by the ECJ and there was no valid Community legislation on the matter

---

685.   [1998] OJ L 349/56.
686.   See Case C-194/94 *CIA Security v Signalson and Securitel* [1996] ECR I-2201.

(Regulation 2815/98 was not adopted at the relevant time). The judgment may seem unfair in relation to Central Food, but the company has a very powerful remedy at its disposal: the *Francovich* remedy. Italy was in blatant breach of EC law, and the breach was sufficiently serious to guarantee an award of damages to Central Food if it suffered loss.

12.4.1.5.2 De facto direct horizontal effect based on the need to ensure the full effectiveness of the principle of non-discrimination on grounds of age, as given expression in Directive 2000/78

The above was established in Case C-144/04 *Werner Mangold v Rüdiger Helm.*[687]

THE FACTS WERE:

In 2003 Mr Mangold, a German national aged 56, entered into an employment contract with Mr Helm, a lawyer practising in Germany. The employment was to be for six months only. This was in accordance with a special provision of German law which had been enacted with a view to facilitating employment of employees older than 52 and which specifically provided for six-month fixed-term contracts. A few weeks after commencing employment, Mr Mangold brought proceedings against his employer before a German Labour Court (Arbeitsgericht) claiming that the national law was contrary to Directives 1999/70 (which gives effect to the framework agreement on fixed-term work entered into by ETUC, UNICE and CEEP) and Directive 2000/78 (which establishes a general framework for combating discrimination on the grounds of religion or belief, disability, age or sexual orientation as regards employment and occupation, with a view to putting into effect in the Member States the principle of equal treatment). Accordingly, he argued that the clause fixing the term of his employment was void.

Neither directive makes a specific reference to the prohibition of discrimination based on age. Further, at the time of the proceedings the transitional period for the implementation of Directive 2000/78 had not expired.

Held:

The ECJ held that that the principle of non-discrimination, being a general principle of EC law, the source of which could be found in recitals 1 and 4 of the preamble to the directive and in various international instruments and in the constitutional traditions common to the Member States allowed Mr Mangold to challenge the German legislation because that legislation did not take account of other factors (such as an earlier contract of employment of indefinite duration concluded with the same employer) but imposed the conclusion of fixed-term contracts of employment once the worker had reached the age of 52. The ECJ considered that observance of the general principle of equal treatment, in particular in respect of age, could not depend on the expiry of the period for the transposition of a directive which directive

---

687.   [2005] ECR I-9981.

intended to lay down a general framework for combating discrimination on the grounds of age.

Comment:

The ECJ allowed Mr Mangold, in fact, to rely on the relevant provision of the directive on the ground that the provision in question embodied one of the fundamental principles of EC law: the prohibition of discrimination based on age. However, the ECJ did not mention the issue of horizontal direct effect.

The above judgment has been very controversial. Its exact meaning was unclear. In this circumstance, in Case C-555/07 *Seda Kücükdeveci v Swedex GmbH & Co. KG*,[688] a national court, within the preliminary rulings procedure, asked the ECJ to elucidate its judgment in *Mangold*.

FACTS:

Ms Kücükdeveci had been employed by Swedex GmbH & Co. KG since 1996, at which time she was 18 years old, and was dismissed by her employer in 2006. She challenged the dismissal on the ground that the calculation of the period of notice applicable to her dismissal was contrary to Directive 2000/78. Indeed, under German law, only periods of employment completed after the age of 25 were taken into account in calculating the notice period. At the time of proceedings Directive 2000/78 was in force in Germany.

Held:

The ECJ held that the principle of non-discrimination on grounds of age as given expression by Council Directive 2000/78 must be interpreted as precluding national legislation, such as that at issue in the main proceedings, which provides that periods of employment completed by an employee before reaching the age of 25 are not taken into account in calculating the notice period for dismissal.

Comment:

The ECJ tried to wriggle out of giving the answer to the question referred by reminding the referring court of its obligation to interpret national law in conformity with EU law. However, this option was not available to the referring court because in its referral it stated that the relevant national law was clear and precise and thus not open to an interpretation in conformity with Directive 2000/78. The answer of the ECJ to the referring court in respect of the implications of its judgment in *Mangold* was as follows:

"It must be recalled here that, . . ., Directive 2000/78 merely gives expression to, but does not lay down, the principle of equal treatment in employment and occupation, and that the principle of non-discrimination on grounds of age is a general principle of European Union law in that it constitutes a specific application of the general principle of equal treatment" (para 50).

---

688.   Judgment of 19/1/10 (NYR).

The above paragraph may be interpreted in many ways. However, the following points seem obvious:

1. The ECJ did not relax its position with regard to the refusal of accepting direct horizontal effect of EU directives;

2. The ECJ confirmed that the principle of non-discrimination on the ground of age constitutes a general principle of EU law and that Directive 2000/78 makes this principle real and more specific;

3. With the entry into force of Directive 2000/78 the national legislation at issue in the main proceedings, which concerns a matter governed by that directive (in this case the conditions of dismissal) was brought within the realm of EU law;

4. The ECJ did not follow the proposal submitted by A-G Bot who, on the one hand, argued against conferring on the principle of non-discrimination on grounds of age an autonomous scope because the major disadvantage of that approach would be to deprive Directive 2000/78 of all useful effect and on the other, refused to challenge the lack of horizontal direct effect of directives. A-G Bot explained in para 70 of his Opinion that: ". . . a directive which has been adopted to facilitate the implementation of the general principle of equal treatment and non-discrimination cannot reduce the scope of that principle. The Court should therefore, as it has done in regard to the general principle of Community law itself, accept that a directive intended to counteract discrimination may be relied on in proceedings between private parties in order to set aside the application of national rules which are contrary to that directive."

It is submitted that the judgment of the ECJ is fully justified. A national court is required under national law to respect fundamental principles of national law and consequently to invalidate any clause in a contract of employment which is contrary to public policy or to the basic principles of society. Mr Mangold should have been protected under German constitutional law. As this did not occur, the ECJ decided that Mr Mangold should be protected under EU law. This is well justified under the principle of supremacy of EU law. Where national law does not provide the same protection as EU law and the matter is within the scope of the Treaties, EU law should intervene. The justification based on supremacy of EU law is a logical consequence of the judgment of the ECJ in *Simmenthal*. Under this approach EU law prevails over conflicting national law irrespective of whether the proceedings are between a private party and a State or between two private parties. However, this approach should be used when it is impossible for a national court to interpret national law in conformity with EU law. Additionally, this approach is justified by Article 4(3) TEU which imposes on a Member State the obligation to ensure that its national law is in conformity with EU law. This approach, however, was not applied by the ECJ which based its judgment on the principle of effectiveness.

The above judgments raises the question of whether the ECJ will apply the ratio decidendi of *Mangold* and *Kücükdeveci* to proceedings between private parties in situation where directives contribute to ensuring observance of fundamental rights. In this respect, A-G Bot noted that bearing in mind the ever increasing intervention of EU law in relations between private persons the ECJ will inevitably be asked to provide guidance to national courts. He ended his Opinion by saying:

". . . the Court must, in my view, think now about whether the designation of rights guaranteed by directives as fundamental rights does or does not strengthen the right to rely on them in proceedings between private parties. The present case offers the Court an opportunity to set out the answer which it wishes to give to that important question".

However, on this occasion the ECJ declined the invitation to clarify its position on this important matter.

12.5   Direct effect of decisions

Under Article 288 TFEU, two kinds of decisions can be adopted by EU institutions, those which identify their addressees and those which have no addressees. Article 288 TFEU states that a decision which specifies those to whom it is addressed shall be binding only on them. It is submitted that both kinds of decisions may create rights and obligations for individuals or Member States and may produce direct effect. As a result, irrespective of whether a decision identifies its addressee or not, it may be directly effective if it satisfies the criteria for direct effect. Accordingly, the pre-ToL case law on direct effect of decisions remains unchanged.

In Case 9/70 *Franz Grad v Finanzamt Traunstein*[689] the ECJ recognised that the combined effect of a Treaty provision, a directive and a decision may have direct effect and therefore create rights for individuals enforceable before national courts.

THE FACTS WERE:

Council Decision 65/271 of 13 May 1965 placed the German Government under an obligation to introduce a common VAT system for road haulage, abolish specific taxes in existence and not to introduce new ones thereafter. A harmonising Directive laid down the deadline for the implementation of Decision 65/271. In addition, Article 25 EC [Article 30 TFEU] prohibited introduction of any new customs duties or charges having equivalent effect. However, in this case the German Government levied a tax on the carriage of a consignment of preserved fruit from Hamburg to Austria. The claimant, a haulage contractor, challenged the tax as contrary to Decision 65/271. The court, Finanzgericht Munchen, made reference for a preliminary ruling to the ECJ to determine whether the decision produced direct effect.

Held:

The ECJ held that the decision did have direct effect and thus conferred individual rights which must be protected in national courts. The ECJ emphasised that ". . . it would be incompatible with the binding effect attributed to decisions by Article [249 EC- Article 288 TFEU] to exclude in principle the possibility that persons affected might invoke the obligation imposed by a decision". The ECJ decided that the obligation in question was sufficiently clear and unconditional to produce direct effect. The ECJ based its reasoning exclusively on the principle of effectiveness.

---

689.   [1970] ECR 825.

In Case C-156/91 *Hansa Fleisch*,[690] the above approach was confirmed in relation to a decision standing alone. Additionally, decisions adopted by a body created by an international treaty concluded between the EU and third countries may produce direct effect.[691]

A decision addressed to a legal or natural person may produce horizontal direct effect. For example, a decision adopted by the Commission regarding an undertaking in breach of competition law may be relied on by another undertaking, which is a victim of anti-competitive practice of the former. Under Article 299 TFEU, decisions which impose pecuniary obligations on persons other than States are enforceable in accordance with the national procedures of the Member State of the addressee. However, a decision addressed to a Member State can only produce vertical direct effect. The justification for the rejection of horizontal direct effect is the same as in the case of directives.[692]

12.6 Direct effect of international agreements concluded between the EU and third countries, and the EU and international organisations

The ECJ has the same approach towards international agreements concluded between the EU and third countries as monist countries. The best summary of the case law of the ECJ in respect of the direct effect of international agreements concluded between the EU and third countries or international organisations is given in the conclusion of A-G M Darmon in Case 12/86 *Demirel*.[693] He emphasised that a provision of an agreement concluded between the Community [the EU] and third countries may be considered as producing direct effect when, in relation to its terms, object and nature, it contains a clear and precise obligation which is not subordinated to the intervention of any subsequent act. This means, for example, that a provision of an international agreement, which may be drafted in terms identical to a provision of EU law (which is recognised as capable of producing direct effect), may not be regarded as directly effective since the object and nature of the agreement will determine whether the relevant provision of the agreement can produce direct effect. Consequently, the test for direct effect of international agreements to which the EU is a party is stricter than the normal test of direct effect for EU law in general, in that, for such international agreements, the alleged direct effect must be consistent with the system and context of the treaty, as well as satisfying the other standard conditions for direct effect.[694]

This principle of direct effect of international agreements was established in Cases 21–24/72 *International Fruit Company N.V. and Others v Produktschap voor Groenten en Fruit*.[695]

---

690. [1992] ECR I-5567.
691. For example, a decision adopted by the Association Council EEC-Turkey: Case C-192/89 *Sevince* [1990] ECR I-3461; Case C-237/91 *Kazim Kus* [1992] ECR I-6781; Case C-171/95 *Recep Tetik* [1997] ECR I-329.
692. Case C-80/06 *Carp* [2007] ECR I-4473.
693. [1987] ECR 3719.
694. See Case C-308/06 *The Queen on the application of: International Association of Independent Tanker Owners (Intertanko), International Association of Dry Cargo Shipowners (Intercargo), Greek Shipping Co-operation Committee, Lloyd's Register, International Salvage Union v Secretary of State for Transport* (judgment of 3/06/08) and Ch. Timmermans, "The International Lawyer and the EU", in C. Wickremasinghe (ed.), *The International Lawyer as Practitioner*, (British Institute of International and Comparative Law), 2000, London at p 95.
695. [1972] ECR 1219.

THE FACTS WERE:

The claimant challenged import licensing and quota regulations imposed by Regulations 459/ 70, 565/70 and 686/70 upon importers as being contrary to Article XI GATT. Under Article 234 EC [Article 267 TFEU] the ECJ was asked whether those Regulations could be relied upon by the claimants.

Held:

The ECJ held that in order to produce direct effect, the provisions of an international agreement must be capable of conferring rights on individuals before they can be invoked. Article XI GATT did not create rights for individuals. As a result, EC regulations could not be affected by Article XI GATT.

This case was the first in the consistent line of refusals by the ECJ to give direct effect to GATT/WTO (World Trade Organisation) agreements. The ECJ's intransigence has continued, notwithstanding the criticism of many Advocates General in their Advisory Opinions,[696] and despite the declaration of the Dispute Settlement Body of the WTO that EC legislation implementing these agreements is in breach of certain WTO rules.[697]

In Case 87/75 *Bresciani*,[698] the ECJ allowed individuals to rely on the provisions of an international agreement concluded between the Community and third countries. In Case 104/81 *Kupferberg*,[699] the ECJ held that neither the nature, nor the structure of an international agreement can prevent an individual from relying on its provisions in proceedings before national courts.

Notwithstanding the above, the direct effect of provisions in free trade,[700] co-operation[701] and association[702] agreements has been recognised by the ECJ.

The form in which an international agreement is introduced into EU law, that is, whether by a decision or by a regulation adopted by the Council, is not taken into consideration by the ECJ in determining whether any of its provisions produce direct effect.

With regard to horizontal direct effect of international agreements, it is rare that an international agreement is concluded with the intention of conferring rights and duties on natural or legal persons. It seems that this is the main reason why there is no case law on this topic, although in Case 270/80 *Polydor Ltd v Harlequin Records Shops*[703] the question of whether an international agreement can produce horizontal direct effect was asked but not answered by the ECJ.

---

696.   S. Griller, "Judicial Enforceability of WTO Law in the European Union", Annotation to Case C-149/96 *Portugal v Council*, [2000] 3 J. Int. Economic Law, pp 441–72.

697.   Case C-377/02 *Léon Van Parys NV v Belgisch Interventie- en Restitutienbureau* [2005] ECR I-1465; see also Chapter 14.

698.   [1976] ECR 129.

699.   [1982] ECR 3641.

700.   Case 104/81 *Kaupferberg* [1982] ECR 3641.

701.   Case C-103/94 *Zoulika Krid* [1995] ECR I-719.

702.   Case 87/75 *Bresciani* [1976] ECR 129 (Yaoundé Convention); Case 17/81 *Pabst* [1982] ECR 1331 (association agreement between the EEC and Greece); Case 438/00 *Kolpak* [2003] ECR I-4135 (association agreement between the Communities and Slovakia).

703.   [1982] ECR 329.

AIDE-MÉMOIRE

DIRECT EFFECT

This means that some provisions of EU law may confer on individuals rights which they can enforce directly before national courts. Individuals can rely upon a directly effective provision of EU law in the absence of, or against a national provision (Case 26/62 *Van Gend*).

CRITERIA FOR DIRECT EFFECT – THE DIRECT EFFECT TEST

A provision of EU law in order to be directly effective must satisfy three criteria:

- It must be clear and precise;

- It must be unconditional, which means that there is no need for the adoption of further implementing measures at either national or community level; and

- It must be capable of creating rights for individuals.

VERTICAL AND HORIZONTAL DIRECT EFFECT

Vertical direct effect refers to a situation where an individual, that is, a natural or legal person, is allowed to rely on a provision of EU law in national proceedings against a Member State or its emanations.

Horizontal direct effect concerns a situation where an individual is allowed to invoke a provision of EU law in national proceedings against another individual.

DIRECT EFFECT OF EU LAW

Provisions of the Treaties may be both vertically (Case 26/62 *Van Gend*) and horizontally (Case 43/75 *Defrenne*) directly effective.

Provisions of regulations may be both vertically (Case 93/71 *Leonesio*) and horizontally (C-253/00 *Antonio Muñoz*) directly effective.

Provisions of directives can only produce **vertical** direct effect (Case 41/74 *Van Duyn*) and only after the time limit for their implementation has expired (Case 148/78 *Ratti*). A Member State which has failed to implement a directive within the prescribed time limit cannot rely on it in proceedings against individuals (Case 80/86 *Kolpinghuis Nijmegen*).

As a principle, provisions of directives have **no horizontal direct effect** (Case C-91/92 *Faccini Dorî*).

The ECJ has developed four approaches in order to overcome the negative practical implications deriving from the lack of horizontal direct effect of EC directives:

- It has extended the concept of a Member State by introducing the autonomous EU concept of a public body (Case C-188/89 *Foster*).

- It has imposed a duty on national courts to interpret national law in conformity with EU law (Case 14/83 *Von Colson*) subject to two limitations:

  - interpretation contra legem is not required (Case C-334/92 *Wagner Miret*);

- interpretation of EU law must be qualified in criminal proceedings, where the effect of interpreting national legislation in the light of the directive would be to impose criminal liability in circumstances where such liability would not arise under the national legislation taken alone (Case 80/86 *Kolpinghuis Nijmegen*).

- Individuals can rely on a directive to determine whether or not the national legislature, in exercising its choice as to the form and methods for implementing the directive, has kept within the limits of its discretion set out in the directive (Case 51/76 *Verbond van Nederlandse Ondernemingen*).

- Individuals may rely on a directive in proceedings against a State or its emanation despite the fact that such an action affects the rights of individuals who are not part of the vertical relationship. This is referred to as the "triangular" horizontal effect (C-201/02 *Wells* and Joined Cases C-152/07 to C-154/07 *Arcor*).

EXCEPTIONAL CASES WHERE A DIRECTIVE CAN HAVE HORIZONTAL DIRECT EFFECT

- "Procedural" direct horizontal effect (Case C-443/98 *Unilever*);

- De facto direct horizontal effect based on the need to ensure the full effectiveness of the principle of non-discrimination on grounds of age, as given expression in Directive 2000/78 (Case C-144/04 *Mangold* and Case C-555/07 *Seda Kücükdeveci*).

Provisions of decisions:

- Addressed to individuals can produce both vertical and horizontal direct effect;

- Addressed to a Member State or to Member States can produce vertical direct effect (Case 9/70 *Franz Grad*) but not horizontal direct effect. The justification for the rejection of horizontal direct effect is the same as in the case of directives.

Provisions of international agreements concluded between the Communities and third countries or international organisations can produce vertical direct effect, but the test is stricter than the normal test for direct effect of EU law in general, in that the alleged direct effect must be consistent with the system and context of the international treaty, as well as satisfying the other standard conditions for direct effect (Cases 21–24/72 *International Fruit Company*). It is uncertain whether or not provisions of international agreements can be horizontally directly effective as there is no judicial authority on this point.

RECOMMENDED READING

Books

Prechal, S., *Directives in EC Law*, 2nd edition, 2005, Oxford: Oxford University Press

Vereecken, M. and Nijenhuis, A. (eds), *Settlement Finality in the European Union: The EU Directive and its Implementation in Selected Jurisdictions*, 2005, The Hague: Kluwer Law International

Articles

Betlem, G., "The Doctrine of Consistent Interpretation – Managing Legal Uncertainty", (2002) 22 Oxford J. Legal Stud., p 397

Král, R., "Questioning the Limits of Invocability of EU Directives in Triangular Situations", (2010) 16 EPL, p 239

Lohse, E. J., "Fundamental Freedoms and Private Actors – towards an 'Indirect Horizontal Effect' ", (2007) 13/1 EPL, p 159

Prescatore, P., "The Doctrine of Direct Effect: An Infant Disease of Community Law", (1983) 8 ELRev, p 155

Tridimas, T., "Black, White, and Shades of Grey: Horizontality of Directives Revisited", (2002) 21 YBEL, p 327

13

SUPREMACY OF EU LAW

CONTENTS

SUMMARY

1. This chapter focuses on the principle of the supremacy of EU law over the national laws of the Member States. The founding Treaties and their amendments are silent on the issue of priority between national and Community law [EU law]. However, the ToL, without directly mentioning the principle of supremacy, in Declaration 17 has confirmed that in accordance with the case law of the ECJ "the treaties and the law adopted by the Union have primacy over the law of Member

States". The ECJ had no hesitation in declaring that EU law must take priority over, and supersede any national provision which clashes with EU law. This was established in Case 6/64 *Costa v ENEL*, in which the ECJ held:

"... the law stemming from the Treaty, an independent source of law, could not, because of its special and original nature, be overridden by domestic provisions, however framed, without being deprived of its character as Community law and without the legal basis of the Community itself being called into question."

2. Primacy, at least as asserted by the ECJ, is over both ordinary national law and national constitutional law of Member States, even when national constitutional law relates to the protection of human rights or to the internal structure of the Member State. However, as there is no case law of the ECJ on measures adopted under the CFSP and given that the ECJ, as a matter of principle, has no jurisdiction in respect of such measures, it is uncertain whether the principle of primacy applies to them.

3. It flows from the principle of supremacy that a national court is bound to enforce EU law and give full effect to it, if necessary refusing on its own motion to apply any conflicting provision of national legislation in a situation where the issue of EU law has been pleaded by the parties to the proceedings. In such a situation when faced with a national provision which clashes with EU law, a national court should apply EU law and should not wait for annulment or repeal of inconsistent national law by domestic legislatures or constitutional organs. However, the duty of national courts to raise points of EU law of their own motion, i.e where the parties to the proceedings have failed to raise points of EU law, is subject to the principle of national procedural autonomy.

4. International agreements concluded before accession of a Member State to the EU prevail over EU law. Article 351(1) and (2) TFEU endorses this principle. However, a Member State has the duty to eliminate any incompatibility of such an agreement with EU law. International agreements entered into by a Member State subsequent to its accession to the EU are invalid if they conflict with EU law. This is in accordance with the principles of public international law that subsequent international agreements should not affect earlier agreements.

5. In Joined Cases C-402/05 P and C-415/05 P *Kadi*, the ECJ held that although the CJEU has no jurisdiction to review the legality of measures adopted by the UN Security Council, in fact, it did review them. The ECJ held that EU law prevails over binding measures adopted by the UN Security Council if such measures are in breach of fundamental principles of EU law.

6. The principle of res judicata overrides the principle of supremacy of EU law but not in all circumstances. In Case C-119/05 *Lucchini* the ECJ held that this principle must not be applied in so far as it prevents the recovery of Member State aid granted in breach of EU law. It remains to be seen whether the *Lucchini* exception will be extended to other circumstances. The consequences of giving the principle of res judicata such a special place in the EU legal order are attenuated in that individuals can claim compensation under the Francovich principles in a situation where a judgment rendered against them has become res judicata, but is subsequently found to be contrary to EU law.

7. The doctrine of supremacy necessarily limits the sovereign rights of the Member States. Some Member States continue to struggle to accept the principle of supremacy of EU law.

13.1 Introduction

There is no mention of the supremacy of Community law [EU law] in the founding Treaties. The absence of any express provision is not, however, a gap in Community law but a result of diplomacy and caution. Indeed, an express provision would have confirmed the federal nature of the Community and thus dissuaded some Member States from acceding to the Communities. For that reason less controversial phraseology was used, for example, in Article 249 EC [Article 288 TFEU], which confers binding effect upon measures adopted by EU institutions, and in Article 10 EC [Article 4(3) TFEU], which requires that Member States abstain from taking measures capable of compromising the attainment of the objectives of the Treaties. However, the ToL, without any express provision having been inserted into the Treaties to this effect, in Declaration 17 confirms the case law of the ECJ on the principle of supremacy. Declaration 17 quotes an Opinion of the Council Legal Service on the Primacy of EC Law of 22 June 2007 which states that: "The fact that the principle of primacy will not be included in the future treaty shall not in any way change the existence of the principle and the existing case-law of the Court of Justice". Therefore, Declaration 17 does not make any changes as to the existence and meaning of the principle of supremacy, it simply confirms the current position of the ECJ on this matter.

The supremacy of EU law, according to the ECJ, is based on the fact that, contrary to ordinary international treaties, the founding Treaties have created their own legal system. In Case 6/64 *Flaminio Costa v ENEL*[705] the ECJ held that: "The Treaty has created its own legal system which on the entry into force of the Treaty, became an integral part of the legal systems of the Member States". According to the ECJ the supremacy results from the peculiar nature of the EU and not from concessions made by constitutional laws of the Member States. For that reason, the primacy of EU law does not depend on which theory each Member State applies in order to determine the relationship between national and international law.

From the perspective of the ECJ the supremacy of EU law is unconditional and absolute. All EU law prevails over all national laws. This means that national laws are subservient to all sources of EU law, that is, subservient to:

- The provisions of the Treaties, and Protocols and Annexes attached to them;

- Secondary legislation (that is, regulations,[706] directives,[707] and decisions[708]). However, as the ECJ has no jurisdiction over matters relating to the CFSP, with the exceptions set out in Article 275 TFEU (see Chapter 5.4.3) and in the absence of pre-ToL case law on this matter, it is uncertain whether the principle of primacy applies to measures adopted under the CFSP. It can be argued that in the light of Declaration 17, the principle of supremacy does not apply to measures adopted under the CFSP with the exception of those specified in Article 275 TFEU;

- The general principles of EU law;[709] and

---

705.   [1964] ECR 585.
706.   Case 43/71 *Politi* [1971] ECR 1039; Case 84/71 *Marimex* [1972] ECR 89.
707.   Case 158/80 *Rewe* [1981] ECR 1805; Case 8/81 *Becker* [1982] ECR 53.
708.   Case 130/78 *Salumificio de Cornuda* [1979] ECR 867.
709.   Case 5/88 *Wachauf* [1989] ECR 2609.

▪ International agreements concluded between the EU and third countries[710] or international organisations.

13.2   The establishment of the doctrine of supremacy of EU law by the ECJ

The issue of priority between Community law [EU law] and national law of the Member States arose before national courts in the early years of the Community. National courts referred to the ECJ for clarifications, under the procedure laid down in Article 234 EC [Article 267 TFEU]. The ECJ took it upon itself to firmly establish the principal of supremacy of Community law as a necessary condition for the existence of the Community itself and its peculiar nature in the international legal order.

Two years after the 1962 judgment in *Van Gend en Loos*,[711] the ECJ was ready to spell out the full implications of its judgment in that case and to enunciate the principle of supremacy of EC law over the national laws of the Member States. This it did in Case 6/64 *Costa v ENEL*.[712]

THE FACTS WERE:

Costa was a shareholder of a private undertaking nationalised by the Italian Government on 6 September 1962. When subsequently assets of many private undertakings (including that in which Costa held shares) were transferred to ENEL, a company which was created by the Italian Government for the purposes of the nationalisation, Costa, who was also a lawyer, refused to pay an electricity bill for £1 sent by ENEL and was accordingly sued by ENEL. He argued, inter alia, that the nationalisation legislation was contrary to various provisions of the EC Treaty. The Milanese Giudice Conciliatore referred the matter to the ECJ under Article 234 EC [Article 267 TFEU]. The Italian Government claimed that the referral was "absolutely inadmissible" since a national court, which is obliged to apply national law, cannot avail itself of Article 234 EC [Article 267 TFEU]. In the meantime the Italian Constitutional Council decided in favour of national legislation by applying the dualist theory.

Held:

The ECJ held that membership of the Community entailed a permanent limitation of the sovereign rights of the Member States to the extent that national law enacted subsequent to the accession of a Member State to the Community could not be given effect if and so far as it was contrary to Community law. The ECJ held ". . . the law stemming from the Treaty, an independent source of law, could not, because of its special and original nature, be overridden by domestic legal provisions, however framed, without being deprived of its character as Community law and without the legal basis of the Community itself being called into question".

---

710.   Case 38/75 *Nederlandse Spoorwegen* [1975] ECR 1439; Cases 267–269/81 *SPI and SAMI* [1983] ECR 801.
711.   [1963] ECR 3.
712.   [1964] ECR 585.

Comment:

To justify the supremacy of EC law, the ECJ based its reasoning on the following three arguments:

- first, the direct applicability and direct effect of Community law would be meaningless if Member States were permitted, by subsequent legislation, to unilaterally nullify the effects of EC law by means of a legislative measure which would prevail over Community law. The Court held that: "The Treaty has created its own legal system which on the entry into force of the Treaty, became an integral part of the legal systems of the Member States and which their courts are bound to apply". According to the ECJ the integration into the laws of each Member State of provisions which derive from the Community, and more generally the terms and the spirit of the Treaty, make it impossible for the Member State, as a corollary, to accord precedence to a unilateral and subsequent measure over a legal system accepted by them on a basis of reciprocity. Furthermore, the ECJ stated that: "The precedence of Community law is confirmed by Article 249 EC [Article 288 TFEU], whereby a regulation 'shall be binding' and 'directly applicable in all Member States'. This provision, which is subject to no reservation, would be quite meaningless if a State can unilaterally nullify its effects by means of a legislative measure which could prevail over Community law."

- second, by transferring certain competences to the Community institutions the Member States have limited their sovereignty. The ECJ held that: "By creating the Community of unlimited duration . . . and more particularly real powers stemming from a limitation of sovereignty or a transfer of powers from the Member States to the Community, the Member States have limited their sovereign rights, albeit within limited fields, and have thus created a body of law which binds both their nationals and themselves."

- third, the need to maintain the uniformity of application of Community law. This ensures homogeneity of the Community legal order. In this respect the ECJ held that: "The executive force of Community law cannot vary from one Member State to another in deference to subsequent domestic laws, without jeopardising the attainment of the objectives of the Treaty set out in Article 3(2) EC [repealed] and giving rise to the discrimination prohibited by Article 12 EC [Article 18 TFEU]."

The position of the ECJ has not changed since its decision in *Costa*. If anything, the ECJ has become increasingly radical in confirming the obvious implications of the supremacy of EU law vis-à-vis the Member States.[713] Indeed, whatever the reaction of the Member States and no matter how long it took to gain full recognition of this principle by the Member States, for the EU supremacy is a necessary requirement of its existence.

It is correct to say that in order to achieve the objectives of the founding Treaties, to uniformly

---

713. See Chapter 14.4, the 2006 judgment of the ECJ in Case C-173/03 *Traghetti del Mediterraneo SpA v Italy* ([2006] ECR I-5177), in which the Court confirmed that a Member State is liable for damage caused to an individual by a manifest infringement of Community law attributable to a Supreme Court of that Member State, and Section 13.9 Case C-119/05 *Lucchini* in which the ECJ qualified its earlier judgment in Case C-234/04 *Kapferer*.

apply EU law throughout the EU,[714] to ensure the proper functioning of the internal market, and for the EU to become a fully integrated structure, the supremacy of EU law must be respected by the Member States. Otherwise, the EU will cease to exist as we currently understand it.[715]

13.3   Supremacy of EU law over national constitutional law of the Member States

The ECJ confirmed that a provision of national constitutional law cannot be invoked in order to nullify the application of EU law given that this is contrary to the EU public order, and, further, this position of the ECJ remains unchanged when fundamental human rights enshrined in the Constitution of a Member State are at issue.

This point was dealt with in Case 11/70 *Internationale Handelsgesellschaft.*[716]

THE FACTS WERE:

EC regulations set up a system of export licences, guaranteed by a deposit, for certain agricultural products. The system required that products be exported during the validity of a licence; otherwise the deposit would be forfeited. The plaintiffs lost a deposit of DM17,000 and argued that the system introduced by EC regulations and run by the West German National Cereals Intervention Agency was in breach of the fundamental human rights provisions contained in the German Constitution, in particular the principle of proportionality. The Frankfurt Administrative Court referred to the ECJ under Article 234 EC [Article 267 TFEU] to determine the validity of one of the two regulations in question.

Held:

The ECJ confirmed the supremacy of Community law over national constitutional law in the following terms: "... the law stemming from the Treaty, an independent source of law, cannot because of its very nature be overridden by rules of national law, however framed, without being deprived of its character as Community law and without the legal basis of the Community itself being called in question. Therefore, the validity of a Community measure or its effect within a Member State cannot be affected by allegations that it runs counter to either fundamental rights as formulated by the constitution of that Member State or the principles of a national constitutional structure".

In this case, the ECJ declared the regulation in question as valid and the system of deposit as an appropriate method of attaining the objectives relating to the common organisation of the agricultural markets.

It is worth noting that the ECJ held that fundamental human rights, taking into account their importance, cannot be disregarded by the EU. Respect for them forms an integral part of the

---

714.   In Joined Cases C-143/88 and C-92/89 *Zuckerfabrik Suderdithmarschen* the ECJ held that uniformity of application of EC law constitutes a fundamental requirement of the Community legal order [1991] ECR I-415 at para 26.

715.   As the ECJ explained in Case 14/68 *Walt Wilhelm* [1969] ECR 1.

716.   [1970] ECR 1125.

general principles of EU law and the protection of such rights must be ensured within the framework of the structure and objectives of the EU (see Chapter 9). It is submitted that one of the motivations for the development of human rights jurisprudence by the ECJ was the need to respond to challenges to the supremacy doctrine by national constitutional courts on the issue of the adequacy of the protection given to fundamental rights by EU law. However, with the accession of the EU to the ECHR the protection of fundamental human rights by the EU will be subject to supervision of the ECtHR and thus reservations made by constitutional courts of some Member States to the supremacy of EU law, i.e. they reserved to themselves the right to review the constitutionality of EU law in particular, its compliance with fundamental human rights enshrined in their national constitutions,[717] will be pointless. Further, Declaration 17, although a non binding instrument, clearly affirms the position of the Member States on primacy of EU law over national law at every level, including constitutional law of the Member States taking into account that the position of the ECJ on the supremacy of EU law is clear and unambiguous. Consequently, it remains to be seen whether the pre-ToL controversy relating to the supremacy of EU law in all circumstances and over all national law will persist under the ToL.

13.4 Supremacy of EU law over national law enacted prior and subsequent to a Member State's accession to the EU

If there is a conflict between EU law and national law enacted prior to a Member State's accession to the EU, then it must be resolved in favour of EU law. All pre-dating national law is deemed to be abrogated, or at least devoid of its legal effect, in so far as it is contrary to EU law. For reasons of legal certainty an express repeal of conflicting pre-existing national law is desirable, and in some circumstances required under EU law.[718]

Where there is conflict between EU law and national law enacted subsequent to the accession of a Member State to the EU, the former prevails. This was established in Case 6/64 *Costa v ENEL*.[719]

13.5 Supremacy of EU law and international agreements entered into by a Member State

A distinction must be made between international agrrements entered into by a Member State prior to, and subsequent to its accession to the EU.

13.5.1 Agreements concluded prior to accession to the EU

International agreements concluded before accession of a Member State to the EU prevail over EU law. Article 351(1) and (2) TFEU endorses this principle. It provides that:

"The rights and obligations arising from agreements concluded before 1 January 1958 or, for acceding States, before the date of their accession, between one or more Member State on the one

717. C. Grabenwarter, "National Constitutional Law Relating to the European Union", in A. von Bogdandy and J. Bast, *Principles of European Constitutional Law*, 2010, Oxford: Hart, pp 85–91.
718. Case 167/73 *Commission v France* [1974] ECR 359.
719. [1964] ECR 585.

hand, and one or more third countries on the other, shall not be affected by the provisions of this Treaty.

To the extent that such agreements are not compatible with the Treaties, the Member State or States concerned shall take all appropriate steps to eliminate the incompatibility established. Member States shall, where necessary, assist each other to this end and shall, where appropriate, adopt a common attitude."

The scope of Article 351 TFEU was examined by the ECJ in Case C-466/98 *Commission v UK*.[720]

THE FACTS WERE:

This case concerned "open sky" agreements concluded between many EU Member States and the USA. The UK Government concluded the first agreement with the USA in 1946. This was the Bermuda I Agreement, which was amended in 1977 by the Bermuda II Agreement. In 1992, the USA Government offered the UK (and other Member States) the possibility of concluding a bilateral "open sky" agreement revising the Bermuda II Agreement. In 1995, the UK signed such an agreement ignoring the Commission's letter of formal notice stating that negotiation and conclusion of agreements in the area of air transport was within the exclusive competence of the Commission.

According to the UK, as the rights and obligations conferred in the Bermuda I Agreement were not substantially changed by the Bermuda II Agreement, the Bermuda II Agreement, although concluded four years after accession of the UK to the Communities, constituted a continuation of the Bermuda I Agreement and therefore could not be considered as a new agreement. It was therefore within the scope of Article 307 EC [Article 351 TFEU], that is, the UK Government argued that the Bermuda II Agreement was protected by para 1 of Article 307 EC [Article 351 TFEU].

Held:

The ECJ found that the Bermuda II Agreement was a new agreement, mainly on the basis that its preamble expressly stated that the Bermuda II Agreement was replacing the Bermuda I Agreement in order to respond to the development of traffic rights between the USA and the UK. This necessity to adjust the Bermuda I Agreement to new circumstances demonstrated that the Bermuda II Agreement was a new agreement creating new rights and obligations between the contracting parties and as such was outside the scope of para 1 of Article 307 EC [Article 351 (1) TFEU].

Although insulating some aspects of pre-EU treaties (such as those aspects entailing obligations to other States) from challenge because of incompatibility with EU law, Article 351 TFEU also seeks to prevent a Member State from relying on previous international agreements in order to escape its obligations imposed by the Treaties. In Case 10/61 *Commission v Italy*,[721] the ECJ held that Italy could not invoke GATT (a pre-accession agreement) provisions on customs duties to

---

720.   [2002] ECR I-9427.
721.   [1962] ECR 1.

escape the obligations of the EC Treaty relating to intercommunity exchanges[722] because Article 351 TFEU only guarantees the rights held by third countries under pre-accession agreements. Also, Article 351 TFEU imposes an important limitation on a Member State's obligations arising out of an international agreement concluded prior to its accession, in that the EU as such cannot be bound by such an agreement vis-à-vis third countries.[723]

In practice, the principle contained in Article 351 TFEU poses difficult problems for national judges in the case of a conflict between international agreements and EU law. This problem is best illustrated by the contradictions between the Conventions of the International Labour Organisations and the EC Directive relating to the night work of women.[724]

International agreements concluded between the Member States before their accession to the Communities or the EU, but which remain in force subsequent to the accession, are usually subject to special provisions of the Treaties.[725]

13.5.2 Agreements concluded subsequent to accession

In accordance with the principles of public international law, subsequent international agreements should not affect earlier agreements. Therefore, international agreements concluded by Member States after their accession to the Communities or the EU will be disregarded if incompatible with EU law. Therefore the issue of supremacy does not arise as such agreements are invalid under EU law.

13.6 Supremacy of EU law and binding resolutions of the UN Security Council (UNSC)

The background to the issue of validity of UNSC resolutions under EU law is that the UNSC itself and its Sanctions Committee (which was set up to ensure that Members of the UN were implementing UNSC resolutions) identified some terrorist organisations and persons involved in terrorist activities and placed them on a UN list (that is, the affected persons list). Members of the UN were required to ensure that funds controlled by those individuals or entities (for example, Osama bin Laden, al-Qaeda, the Taliban) are frozen. The Member States of the EU decided to take collective action pursuant to the UNSC resolutions. Accordingly, the Council adopted a number of Common Positions under Pillar 2 and Pillar 3, on the basis of some of which further implementing measures (for example, regulations) were adopted. To these regulations a list of persons, entities and bodies affected by the freezing of funds was attached. The list was updated by the SC Sanctions Committee and the Commission was empowered to amend or supplement those lists accordingly.

The Council placed on the above-mentioned list not only persons and entities identified by the

---

722. Also, in Case C-144/89 *Commission v UK* [1991] ECR I-3533 the ECJ held that the provisions on the CFP could not be replaced by conventional rules emanating from an international convention entered into by the UK prior to the accession to the Communities with regard to other Member States.

723. Case 812/79 *Burgoa* [1980] ECR 2787.

724. Case C-345/89 *Stoeckel* [1991] ECR I-4047; Case C-158/91 *Jean-Claude Levy* [1993] ECR I-4287; Case C-13/93 *ONEM* [1994] ECR ECR I-371.

725. For example, Article 350 TFEU concerning the customs union between Belgium and Luxembourg as well as the Benelux Union.

UNSC but also others identified on the basis of information from Member States. A number of individuals and entities whose names were put on the list brought proceedings to annul the Council's and Commission's implementation of the SC resolutions on the ground that their human rights had been breached in various ways, in particular, the right to a fair hearing.

The CFI (the General Court), in dealing with cases concerning the affected person, made a distinction between a situation where the applicant was placed on the affected persons list by the UNSC or the UNSC Sanctions Committee and a situation where inclusion of a person or entity on the list was decided completely autonomously by the Council on the basis of information supplied by one or more Member States.

- In the first situation, the CFI [the General Court] decided that it had no jurisdiction to review the legality of the UNSC resolution directly or indirectly, although it had jurisdiction to determine whether UNSC resolutions were in conformity with jus cogens.[726] Its conclusion was that given the procedural guarantees contained in UNSC resolutions, fundamental human rights were sufficiently protected when assessed in the light of jus cogens.[727] Accordingly, the CFI [The General Court] upheld the validity of the relevant EC regulations.

- In the second situation involving the exercise of the Community's own powers, entailing a discretionary appreciation by the Community of who should be on the list, the Community institutions were bound to comply with the requirements of fundamental human rights. The CFI [the General Court] found that the contested Community legislation did not contain a sufficient statement of reasons and that it was adopted in the course of a procedure during which the applicant's right to a fair hearing was not observed. As a result, the CFI [the General Court] annulled the relevant Community acts in so far as they concerned the applicants.[728]

On appeal, the ECJ confirmed judgments of the CFI [the General Court] in respect of the annulment of measures involving the exercise of the Community's own powers but refused to uphold the validity of EU measures implementing resolutions adopted by the UNSC under Chapter VII of the UN Charter, i.e. resolutions which under Article 103 of the UN Charter are binding on all members of the UN and prevail over any conflicting international agreements.

In Joined Cases C-402/05 P and C-415/05 P *Kadi and Al Barakaat International Foundation v Council of the European Union and Commission of the European Communities*[729] the ECJ decided that the EU was not bound by the UN Charter and secondary UN law in circumstances where secondary UN law was adopted in breach of fundamental principles of EU law, i.e. in breach of

---

726. Jus cogens are imperative, peremptory rules of international legal order. They are superior to any other rules of international law. They are so fundamental that they bind all states and do not allow any exception. A peremptory rule is defined in Article 53 of the 1969 Vienna Convention on the Law of Treaties as: ". . . a norm accepted and recognised by the international community of States as a whole as a norm from which no derogation is permitted and which can be modified only by a subsequent norm of general international law having the same character."

727. Case T-306/01 *Yusuf and Al Barakaat International Foundation v Council and Commission* [2005] ECR II-3533 and Case T-315/01 *Kadi v Council and Commission* [2005] ECR II-3649, see Posch (A), The Kadi Case: Rethinking the Relationship between EU Law and International Law? (2009) 15 Colum.J.Eur.L, 1.

728. Case T-228/02 *Organisation des Modjahedines du Peuple d'Iran v Council* [2006] ECR II-4665; Case T-47/03 *Jose Maria Sison v Council* [2007] ECR II-73 and Case T-327/03 *Stichting Al-Aqsa v Council* [2007] ECR II-79.

729. [2008] ECR I-6351. The position taken by the ECJ has been confirmed in many cases, e.g. Case C-399/06 P and Case C-403/06 P *Faraj Hassan and Chafiq Ayadi v Council and the Commission* [judgment of 3/12/09 (nyr)].

fundamental human rights, in particular, the right to fair trial. The ECJ held that neither the ECJ nor the CFI (the General Court) has jurisdiction to review the lawfulness of resolutions adopted by the UNSC "even if that review were to be limited to the examination of that resolution with jus cogens" and that no judgment of the CJEU can challenge the primacy of obligations deriving from the UN Charter, even if that judgment finds EU measures implementing a UNSC resolution as being contrary to the higher rule of law of the EU legal system. However, the ECJ has jurisdiction to review the validity of any EU act, including that giving effect to a binding UN resolution, in the light of fundamental principles of EU law. The ECJ emphasised that such a review:

> "must be considered to be the expression, in a Community based on the rule of law, of a consti-tutional guarantee stemming from the EC Treaty as an autonomous legal system which is not to be prejudiced by an international agreement" (para 316).

The ECJ found that the UN resolution, which left no discretion to the Member States as to its implementation, "patently" violated the right of defence, in particular the right to be heard, and the right to effective judicial review of those rights in respect of the persons concerned. As a result, the ECJ annulled the challenged measure (i.e. Regulation 881/2002).

Two conclusions flow from the *Kadi* case, first that the protection of fundamental human rights in the EU is of the highest importance in that the EU will give preference to the protection of fundamental human rights even if this means a breach of the UN Charter. In this respect Advo-cate General Maduro in his Opinion in *Kadi* stated that "[M]easures which are incompatible with the observance of human rights . . . are not acceptable in the Community".[730] The second conclu-sion is that the EU legal system is autonomous with regard to international legal order, i.e. EU law prevails over binding measures adopted by the UNSC if such measures are in breach of funda-mental principles of EU law.

13.7 Supremacy of indirectly effective EU law

The combined effect of the judgment of the ECJ in Joined Cases C-6/90 and C-9/90 *Francovich v Italian State* and *Bonifaci v Italian State*,[731] which established Member States' liability in tort (see Chapter 14.2), and of the judgment in Case 14/83 *Von Colson and Kamann*[732] (see Chapter 12.4.1.2), which requires national courts to interpret national law in conformity with EU law, is that all EU law, irrespective of whether or not it is directly effective, overrides national law inconsistent with EU law. Prior to the above judgments, it was generally considered that only directly effective EC law was superior to national law. This view had been reached as a result of two circumstances:

- Either all or a vast majority of previous judgments of the ECJ on the supremacy of Com-munity law had, by chance, concerned directly effective Community provisions; and

- An individual could only rely on directly effective Community law in proceedings before national courts.

The obligation to interpret national law in conformity with EU law covers all EU law, whether

---

730. (2008) 3 CMLR 41.
731. [1991] ECR I-5357.
732. [1984] ECR 1891.

or not directly effective. However, this obligation has its limitation in that national judges are required to interpret national rules conflicting with provisions of EU law only "as far as possible". This means that national courts are not required to interpret national law contra legem unless conflicting national provisions impose criminal sanctions on EU citizens. Accordingly, if "consistent interpretation" is not possible, an individual is not without a remedy. He has the right to claim compensation under the *Francovich* principle (see Chapter 14).

The principle of direct effect is not important in relation to Member State liability in tort. In Cases C-46 and 48/93 *Brasserie du Pêcheur* and *R v Secretary of State for Transport, ex parte Factortame (No 3)* [733] the ECJ held that the right to damages was independent of the direct effect of the Community law in question. The Court held that:

> "The right of individuals to rely on directly effective provisions before national courts is only a minimum guarantee and is not sufficient in itself to ensure the full and complete implementation of Community law. That right, whose purpose is to ensure that provisions of Community law prevail over national provisions, cannot, in every case, secure for individuals the benefit of the rights conferred on them by Community law and, in particular, avoid their sustaining damage as a result of a breach of Community law attributable to a Member State."

The above judgment confirms that individuals' EU rights, including the right to damages, must prevail over all acts of Member States, legislative, executive or judicial.

The principle of supremacy entails the following consequences for national courts:

- If a claimant relies on EU law to "exclude" a national provision which is contrary to a provision of EU law, and if the claim is successful, a national court must disapply the inconsistent national provision. With regard to directives, it is irrelevant whether or not the provision at issue is directly effective. A national provision inconsistent with EU law is invalid but is not superseded by the relevant provision of EU law, the result being that there is a gap in national law. This was confirmed by the ECJ in Case C-287/98 *Luxembourg v Berthe Linster and Others*. [734]

- If a claimant relies on EU law to "substitute" a relevant provision of EU law for a national provision, the national court will replace the inconsistent national provision by the relevant provision of EU law, but only if such a provision of EU law is directly effective. Indeed, if a provision of EU law is not clear, precise and unconditional (that is, not directly effective), how can it replace the existing national law? In these circumstances it seems that individuals may be left in the position of being unable to enforce their rights deriving from EU law, although they will normally have a claim under the *Francovich* principle.

In both above situations individuals can use EU law to offset the adverse consequences in terms of the effectiveness of EU law in two ways:

- They may rely on the duty imposed on national courts to interpret national law in conformity with EU law to fill the gap in national law; or

- They may use EU law to claim compensation under the *Francovich* principle.

In the light of the above it is arguably irrelevant whether or not EC law is directly effective,

---

733.   [1996] ECR I-1029.
734.   [2000] ECR I-6917.

given that individuals' EU rights, including the right to damages, must prevail over all acts of Member States, legislative, executive or judicial. The *Francovich* principle allows an individual to seek damages against a Member State in a situation where a failure by national law to comply with EU law did not satisfy the conditions for the invocation of direct effect but the claimant satisfies the conditions established in *Francovich*.

13.8   Supremacy of EU law as a challenge to national courts

Supremacy of EU law creates problems for national courts, in particular in a situation where a national judge has no power under national law to declare a statute void. This issue was examined in Case 106/77 *Amministrazione delle Finanze v Simmenthal.*[735]

THE FACTS WERE:

Simmenthal imported a consignment of beef from France to Italy. He was asked to pay for veterinary and public health inspections carried out at the frontier. He paid, but sued in the Italian court for reimbursement of the money paid out, arguing that the fees charged were contrary to Community law. After reference to the ECJ, which held that the inspections were contrary to Article 30 EC [Article 35 TFEU] as being equivalent in effect to a quantitative restriction and that the fees were consequently unlawful under Article 25 EC [Article 30 TFEU] being charges equivalent to customs duties, the Italian court ordered the Italian Ministry to repay the fees. The ministry refused to repay, claiming that the national statute of 1970 under which Simmenthal was liable to pay fees was still preventing any reimbursement and could only be set aside by the Italian Constitutional court. The matter was referred once again to the ECJ under Article 234 EC [Article 267 TFEU].

Held:

The ECJ held that:

- in the event of incompatibility of a subsequent legislative measure of a Member State with Community law, every national judge must apply Community law in its entirety and must set aside any provision of national law, prior or subsequent, which conflicts with Community law;

- national courts should not request or await the prior setting aside of an incompatible national provision by legislation or other constitutional means, but of their own motion, if necessary, refuse the application of conflicting national law and instead apply Community law.

In Joined Cases C-10/97 to C-22/97 *Ministero Delle Finanze v IN.CO.GE.'90 Srl and Others*[736] the ECJ clarified its judgment in *Simmenthal*.

---

735. [1978] ECR 629.

736. [1998] ECR I-6307.

The obligation to give full effect to EU law and thus to protect rights which that law confers upon individuals empowers national judges to suspend, as an interim measure, the application of national law which they suspect to be in conflict with EU law although to do so may be contrary to national law.[738] Similarly, administrative authorities are required to set aside any national provision incompatible with EU law.[739] In relation to sanctions, especially of a penal nature, imposed under national law but incompatible with EU law, those sanctions are considered as being devoid of any legal effect.[740]

However, the ECJ has refused to acknowledge the logical consequences of its judgment in *Simmenthal* in that it has not imposed on national courts a general duty to apply EU law ex officio, i.e when parties to the proceedings did not raise points of EU law. Instead, the ECJ has relied on the principle of autonomy of national procedural law (see below) to determine, on a case-by-case basis whether, in the circumstances of each case, a national court is required to apply EU law on its own motion. Under this approach the respect for autonomy of procedural law of each Member State is subject to the principle of equivalence (i.e. that national procedural rules applicable to a claim under EU law must not be less favourable than those governing similar domestic actions), the principle of effectiveness (i.e. that national procedural rules must not render practically impossible or excessively difficult the exercise of rights conferred by EU law) and the principle of proportionality.

In Case C-312/93 *Peterbroeck*[741] and in Joined Cases C-430–431/93 *Van Schijndel*,[742] the ECJ held that in order to comply with the principles of equivalence and effectiveness a national procedural rule must be assessed by reference to the role it plays in the proceedings, their progress and their special features, viewed as a whole, before the various national courts. Further basic

---

737. See also Case 34/67 *Lück* [1968] ECR 245.
738. Case C-213/89 *Factortame* [1990] ECR I-2433.
739. Case 103/88 *Fratelli Costanzo* [1989] ECR 1861.
740. Case 88/77 *Schonenberg* [1978] ECR 473; Case 269/80 *Tymen* [1981] ECR 3079; Joined Cases C-338/04, C-359/04 and C-360/04 *Placanica* [2007] ECR I-1891.
741. [1995] ECR I-4599.
742. Joined Cases C-430/93 and C-431/93 *Jeroen van Schijndel and Johannes Nicolaas Cornelis van Veen v Stichting Pensioenfonds voor Fysiotherapeuten* [1995] ECR I-4705.

principles of national procedural law such as the protection of the right of defence, the principle of legal certainty and the proper conduct of procedure must be taken into account in order to assess whether a procedural rule complies with the principles of equivalence and effectiveness. The application of the above test is not easy for national courts with the consequence that they often make a reference for a preliminary ruling to the ECJ. Further in Case C-446/98 *Fazenda Pública v Câmara Municipal do Porto*[743] the ECJ stated that in "certain cases" national courts are required to make a reference for a preliminary ruling. It emerges from the case law of the ECJ that a national court is obliged to apply EU law ex officio:

- When national public policy rules require ex officio application of national law EU law equivalent to the national law must be applied ex officio. For example, in Joined Cases C-222/05 to C-225/05 *Van der Weerd*,[744] national rules relating to public policy concerned the powers of administrative bodies and the court itself and provisions relating to admissibility. The provisions of EU law relevant to the dispute, i.e. Directive 85/511, were not of a similar importance in the Community legal order and therefore a national procedural rule did not breach the principle of equivalence. As a result, the referring body had no obligation to apply on its own motion the relevant EU law. Obviously, in each Member State the requirement of public policy may be defined differently with the consequence that in some Member States where the concept of public policy is defined in broader terms than those in *Van der Weerd* a national court may be required to apply Directive 85/511 ex officio. This approach challenges the uniformity in the application of EU law;

- In Case C-126/97 *Eco Swiss*[745] and in Joined Cases C-295/04 to C-298/04 *Manfredi*[746] the ECJ ruled that Articles 81 and 82 EC [Articles 101 and 102 TFEU] are matters of public policy which must be automatically applied by the national court. The implication of these rulings is that the EU has developed the concept of EU public policy although its content has not been clearly defined by the ECJ. Further, the ECJ has not, so far, specified the extent of the duty to apply EU law ex officio in that it is not clear whether a national court must only raise, ex officio, the point of EU law or whether it is required to broaden the dispute which is before the court and/or supplement the facts;

- A national judge has a duty to apply EU law, ex officio, in a situation where only the application of EU law can ensure the protection of rights conferred on individuals by EU law.[747] However, depending upon the circumstances of the case, the obligation imposed on a national court to raise a point of EU law on its own motion is subject to the following limitation: if the parties have had a real opportunity to raise a plea based on EU law before a national court but missed it there is no obligation for a national court to raise the point of EU law ex officio irrespective of the importance of the relevant provision of EU law in the EU legal order. Indeed, the national courts should not be obliged to stand in the shoes of

---

743. [2000] ECR I-11435.
744. Joined Cases C-222/05 to C-225/05 *J. van der Weerd and Others v Minister van Landbouw, Natuur en Voedselkwaliteit* [2007] ECR I-4233.
745. Case C-126/97 *Eco Swiss China Time Ltd v Benetton International NV* [1999] ECR I-3055.
746. Joined Cases C-295/04 to C-298/04 *Vincenzo Manfredi and Others v Lloyd Adriatico Assicurazioni SpA and Others* [2006] ECR I-6619.
747. Case C-240/98 *Océano Grupo Editorial SA v Roció Murciano Quintero* [2000] ECR I-4941.

incompetent lawyers representing the parties.[748] In *Van der Weerd*, the ECJ held that the claimant had had this opportunity and therefore the principle of effectiveness did not require the referring court to examine of its own motion, a plea based on EU law.

The case law of the ECJ is very liberal with regard to the application of EU law ex officio by national courts in that in many cases it accepts that no such obligation exists under EU law. In Case *Van Schnidel*, the ECJ decided that in the particular circumstances of that case (i.e. in civil proceedings in which a judge was allowed to act on his own motion only in exceptional cases where the public interest required his intervention), EU law did not require the national court to raise of its own motion an issue concerning EU law. In Case C-455/06 *Heemskerk*[749] the ECJ held that the referring court had no duty to raise, ex officio, the relevant EU law in a situation where to do this would be in breach of a national procedural rule which prohibited *reformatio in pejus*, i.e. a rule stating that the person bringing an appeal must not be placed in a less advantageous position than that in which he would have found himself in the absence of an appeal. This was despite the fact that the ex officio application of EU law would have corrected a misapplication of EU law by the relevant national authorities and would have resulted in the recovery of the export refund granted from EU funds which seemed to have been paid unduly to the claimant. Accordingly, the ECJ refused to condemn a national procedural rule, even though the ex officio application of EU law would have ensured the protection of the financial interests of the EU. The ECJ's approach, based on the principle of autonomy of national procedural law, to the ex officio application of EU law undermines the principle of supremacy of EU law, which should ensure that EU law prevails irrespective of whether or not the parties to proceedings have raised the issue of EU law before national authorities. It also jeopardises the uniform application of EU law in that, depending on national procedural rules, which differ from one Member State to another, national courts will reach different decisions depending on whether they are allowed or willing to apply EU law on their own motion. Finally, the test of lawfulness of national law which, on the one hand, seeks to ensure respect for procedural autonomy of national rules and, on the other, the effective protection of rights conferred under EU law, is very complex and allows many justifications (e.g. the protection of the rights of defence, the principle legal certainty, and the proper conduct of procedure) for avoiding the application of EU law.

13.9 The principle of res judicata as the limit of the doctrine of supremacy of EU law

In 2006 the ECJ dispelled one of the then remaining uncertainties relating to the supremacy of EU law. This was the issue of whether or not under Community law there was an obligation for a national court to review, and possibly set aside, a judgment which had became final and thus had acquired the status of res judicata, but was contrary to a subsequent judgment of the ECJ. This was examined in Case C-234/04 *Kapferer v Schlank and Schick GmbH*.[750]

---

748.   Case C-312/93 *Peterbroeck, Van Campenhout & Cie SCS v Belgian State* [1995] ECR I-4599.

749.   C-455/06 *Heemskerk BVFirma Schaap v Productschap Vee en Vlees* [2008] ECR I-8763.

750.   [2006] ECR I-2585.

THE FACTS WERE:

In 2000 Ms Kapferer, an Austrian national residing in Austria, in her capacity as a consumer received a letter from Schlank and Schick GmbH, a German company making mail order sales in Austria and elsewhere, informing her that she had won a prize of €3,906.16 in cash. The award of that prize was subject to a "test order" without obligation. She sent the "test order" to Schlank and Schick, but it was impossible to establish whether she had actually placed an order for products at that time. Two years later, not having received the prize Ms Kapferer instituted proceedings in the Austrian District Court under the Austrian Consumer Protection Law for an order directing Schlank and Schick GmbH to pay her the prize, plus interest.

The main argument submitted by Schlank and Schick GmbH, that the District Court (a court of first instance) had no jurisdiction under Regulation 44/2001 to adjudicate the case, was dismissed by that court. As to the substance, the District Court dismissed Ms Kapferer's claim. Unsurprisingly, Schlank and Schick GmbH did not appeal and the judgment of the court of first instance became final (res judicata). After the judgment became final, Ms Kapferer appealed against the judgment to the Landesgericht Innsbruck (the Regional Court for Innsbruck). The appellate court had doubts as to the international jurisdiction of the court of first instance and decided to refer to the ECJ a question of whether or not it had a duty under Article 10 EC [Article 4(3) TFEU] to reopen and set aside a final and conclusive judgment on international jurisdiction if that judgment were proved to be in breach of Community law.

Held:

The ECJ held that a national court is not required to disapply its internal rules of procedure in order to review and set aside a final judicial decision, even if that decision is contrary to Community law. This indicates that the principle of res judicata prevails over the principle of supremacy of Community law.

The judgment in *Kapferer* was necessary to clarify the previous judgment of the ECJ in Case C-453/00 *Kühne & Heitz*.[751] The referring court in *Kapferer* was uncertain as to the meaning of the ECJ's judgment in *Kühne & Heitz*, in particular whether it was required to transpose the principles laid down in that judgment to the case before it.

In Case C-453/00 *Kühne & Heitz*:

THE FACTS WERE:

A Council Regulation of 1975 on the common organisation of the market in poultry meat set out a system of payments to producers exporting to non-Member States, known as "refunds". The amount of "refund" depended upon the custom tariff classification of the exported products. Kühne & Heitz, a Dutch company, exported quantities of poultry meat and was initially granted the refunds, but subsequently its products were reclassified and a claim

---

751.   [2004] ECR I-837.

for reimbursement of sums paid was made by the Dutch authorities. Kühne & Heitz unsuc-cessfully appealed against the reimbursement request. The appellate body did not refer any question of interpretation of the customs nomenclature to the ECJ for a preliminary ruling.

Three years later in Case C-151/93 Criminal Proceedings against M. Voogd Vleesimport en -export BV[752] *the ECJ gave an interpretation of the relevant provision of the 1975 Regula-tion in line with that submitted by Kühne & Heitz to the Dutch appellate body three years earlier. Relying on the ECJ's later judgment, Kühne & Heitz sought a review of the customs classification of the goods and, as a consequence, recovery of the refunds which it had reimbursed. The Dutch Administrative Court referred the matter to the ECJ.*

Held:

The ECJ held that if:

- national law confers on an administrative body competence to reopen a decision in ques-tion, which has become final; and

- the administrative decision became final only as a result of a judgment of a national court against whose decisions there is no judicial remedy; and

- judgment was based on an interpretation of Community law which, in the light of a sub-sequent judgment of the ECJ, was incorrect and which was adopted without a question being referred to the ECJ for a preliminary ruling in accordance with the conditions pro-vided for in Article 234 EC; and

- the person concerned complained to the administrative body immediately after becoming aware of that judgment of the ECJ;

the administrative body concerned was, by virtue of Article 10 EC [Article 4(3) TFEU], under a duty to review its decision in order to take account of the interpretation of the relevant provision of EC law given in the meantime by the ECJ.

Comment:

The Advocate General, in his Advisory Opinion in *Kühne & Heitz*, based his reasoning on the principle of supremacy of Community law over national law. He argued that in order to ensure the full operation of Community law and its uniform application, the principle of supremacy of EC law requires that any rule of national law, which prevents any administrative body from re-examining its decision which has become final, should be disregarded.

The ECJ totally ignored the Advocate General's Advisory Opinion, but both the Advocate General and the ECJ reached the same conclusion. However, the ECJ confined its judgment to the facts of the case and therefore refused to establish a general rule under EC law which would require a national body to re-examine its final decision in order to make it consistent with subsequent judgments of the ECJ, although it did establish such a general rule in a subsequent judgment in Joined Cases C-392/04 and C-422/04 *i-21* and *Arcor*,[753] i.e. it con-

---

752.   [1994] ECR I-4915.
753.   [2006] ECR I-8559.

firmed that an administrative body responsible for the adoption of an administrative decision incompatible with EC law is under an obligation to review and possibly to reopen that decision if the four conditions set out *Kühne & Heitz* are fulfilled.

The ECJ distinguished its decision in *Kapferer* from its decision in *Kühne & Heitz*. The ECJ explained that the situation in *Kapferer* was different from that in *Kühne & Heitz*, because the judgment in *Kapferer* had become res judicata and the four conditions set out in *Kühne & Heitz* were not satisfied, whereas they were in *Kühne & Heitz*.

The judgment in *Kapferer*, which imposes an important limitation on the scope of the principle of supremacy of EU law, is well justified for the following reasons:

- The principle of res judicata is of great importance to national legal systems as it ensures both the stability of law and legal relations, and the sound administration of justice.

- Prior to the entry into force of the ToL, the Member States clearly stated their position as to the importance of the principle of res judicata. Article 68(3) EC (repealed), which allowed the Council, the Commission or a Member State to request a preliminary ruling on matters dealt with under Title IV, stated that such a ruling should not apply to judgments of national courts which have become res judicata. Thus, it would be incongruous for the ECJ to take a totally opposed stand to that clearly expressed by the Member States.

- Despite the fact that the principle of res judicata overrides the principle of supremacy of EU law, in practice individuals have not been left without a remedy in a situation where a judgment, which had become res judicata and was subsequently found to be contrary to EU law, was rendered against them. In *Kühne & Heitz* the ECJ emphasised that proceedings resulting in a judicial decision, which has acquired the status of res judicata, and proceedings seeking to establish the liability of a Member State are fundamentally different one from another in terms of purpose and of parties involved. Indeed, the main objective of proceedings seeking to establish Member State liability for infringement of EU law is for individuals concerned to obtain compensation for damage caused to them by a mistaken judicial decision and not to revise a judgment delivered by a court adjudicating at last instance. Consequently, the principle of res judicata does not call into question the principle of Member State liability.

In Case C-119/05 *Lucchini*,[754] however, the ECJ imposed an important restriction on the primacy of the principle of res judicata over the principle of supremacy of EU law. In this case the ECJ held that in a situation where a Member State granted aid to an undertaking in breach of a Commission decision declaring all the aid applied for to be incompatible with the internal market, a judgment delivered by a national court which confirmed entitlement to the grant of the aid (and which made no reference to EC law or the relevant Commission decision) should be set aside as contrary to EC law. This was notwithstanding the fact that under national law the national judgment had become res judicata. The ECJ justified this on the following grounds:

---

754. [2007] ECR I-6199.

- First, that the national courts had no jurisdiction to decide whether the state aid applied for by the claimant was compatible with the internal market. By virtue of Article 88 EC [Article 108 TFEU] the Commission has exclusive competence to decide on such matters, and its decisions are subject to judicial review under Article 230 EC [Article 263 TFEU];

- Second, national courts have no jurisdiction to declare an EC act invalid. In this case the relevant act was the decision of the Commission, on the basis of which national implementing measures were taken. This matter is within the exclusive competence of the ECJ (see Chapter 10.8);

- Third, neither the Italian court of first instance, nor the Italian appellate court had referred to the applicable provisions of EC law or to the Commission's decision.

On the basis of the above the ECJ could have stated that, irrespective of the fact that the national judgment had became res judicata, that judgment had no effect on the matter of recovery of state aid as it neither concerned the validity of the aid nor its compatibility with the requirements of the internal market. Instead, the ECJ chose to rely on the principle of supremacy of EU law. The Court held that according to well-established EC law, national courts must give full effect to the provisions of EC law and, if necessary, of their own motion set aside any provision of national law, including the relevant provision of the Italian Civil Code containing the principle of res judicata, which is contrary to EC law.

The implications of this case are uncertain. On the one hand, it can be said that the circumstances of this case were exceptional and thus the judgment should be confined to this case alone; on the other hand, it is not certain that the judgment should not be applied to other cases where national authorities are encroaching (and probably deliberately so) on the exclusive competences of the Commission. Indeed, had the ECJ recognised the primacy of the principle of res judicata over the obligation of recovery of state aid granted in breach of EC law, it would have allowed a flagrant violation of the division of competences between the EU and the Member States.

13.10 The principle of supremacy of EU law in the UK

The European experience regarding the principle of supremacy of EU law shows that Member States may not be keen on this principle, and an example of this is the UK where for many years the British judiciary had difficulty in reconciling the irreconcilable, that is, in reconciling the principal of supremacy of EU law with Dicey's model of Parliamentary sovereignty according to which:

- British courts may not question the validity of Parliamentary legislation;

- There are no limits to the legislative power of Parliament subject to the exception that Parliament cannot limit its own powers for the future. This means that no legislation enacted by Parliament is irreversible and that a later Act of Parliament impliedly repeals an earlier Act in so far as they are inconsistent.

The breakthrough came in *Factortame (No.2)*,[755] in which the UK Law Lords accorded primacy to Community law [EU law]. In this respect, Lord Bridge said:

---

755. [1991] 1 AC 603, at 658.

"If the supremacy, within the European Community, of Community law over national law of Member States was not always inherent in the EEC Treaty it was certainly well-established in the jurisprudence of the European Court of Justice long before the United Kingdom joined the Community. Thus, whatever limitation of its sovereignty Parliament accepted when it enacted the European Communities Act 1972 it was entirely voluntary. Under the terms of the Act of 1972 it has always been clear that it was the duty of a United Kingdom court, when delivering final judgment, to override any rule of national law found to be in conflict with any directly enforceable rule of Community law."

Thus, the British judiciary has qualified the doctrine of Parliamentary sovereignty, but in the UK the debate continues as to whether the primacy of EU law flows from the political choice made by the UK Parliament in 1972, or whether it derives from EU law.

In any event, under EU law there should be no difficulties in the UK with recognition of the supremacy of EU law because:

▪ When a state accedes to the EU, it must accept the EU acquis. At the time of accession of the UK, the principle of supremacy was already well rooted in Community law;

▪ Section 2(4) of the European Communities Act 1972 provides that "any enactment passed or to be passed shall be construed and have effect subject to the foregoing provisions of this Section". As a result, all legislative acts enacted subsequent to the European Communities Act 1972 are subject to EU law and thus any conflict between EU law and subsequent national legislation should be resolved in favour of the former on the grounds of supremacy of EU law;

▪ Grabenwarter pointed out that UK scholars emphasise that "British constitutional law hardly contained any provisions which could infringe EC law".[756]

13.11 The principle of supremacy in Member States other than the UK

Only two of the original six Member States Luxembourg and the Netherlands[757], accepted the reasoning of the ECJ and recognised the supremacy of EU law based on the peculiar nature of the EU legal order.[758] It is outside the scope of this book to deal in detail with the acceptance or otherwise of the principle of supremacy of EU law by Member States other than the UK. In general, the Member States are willing to accept the principle of supremacy of EU law over their ordinary national law. The problem lies in the relationship between national constitutional law and EU law. This is examined below with regard to two Member States, one being an original Member State (Germany), and the other being a "new" Member State which acceded to the EU in 2004 (Poland).

---

756. C. Grabenwarter, "National Constitutional Law Relating to the European Union", in A. von Bogdandy, and J. Bast, *Principles of European Constitutional Law*, 2nd edition, 2010, Oxford: Hart, p 89.

757. Decision *Metten v Minister van Financiën* of 7 July 1996, NJB-katern (1995) 426.

758. See M. Thill, "La Primauté et l'Effet Direct du Droit Communautaire dans la Jurisprudence Luxembourgeoise", [1990] RFDA 978.

13.11.1 Germany

The recognition of the supremacy of EU law over fundamental human rights as enshrined in the German Constitution was and still is the main challenge for the German Federal Constitutional Tribunal (GFCT). In its judgment of 29 May 1974 *Solange I* (in German Solange means "as long as"),[759] the GFCT held that as long as there is a hypothetical conflict between Community law [EU law] and the guarantees of fundamental rights in the German Constitution, the rights as embodied in the German Constitution would override Community law [EU law]. In a judgment of 22 October 1986 (*Solange II*)[760] the GFCT qualified its judgment in *Solange I* by stating that the ECJ had demonstrated that Community law [EU law] ensures efficient protection of fundamental human rights equal to the protection guaranteed by the German Constitution and therefore the GFCT would not exercise its jurisdiction as specified in *Solange I* as long as the ECJ maintains high standards for protection of fundamental human rights.

Subsequently, in *Brunner and Others v The European Union Treaty*[761] the GFCT had to deal with a case in which the constitutionality of the TEU was challenged. The GFCT rendered a long judgment in which it held that the supremacy of Community law [EU law] was conditional. The GFCT ruled that it was empowered to ensure that Community institutions and bodies are acting within the limits of powers granted to them under the EC Treaty and thus do not jeopardise the constitutional rights of German inhabitants. Accordingly, the GFCT reserved to itself ultimate jurisdiction to determine the validity of EU law in the light of the human rights protections set out in Germany's Basic Law. It has been suggested that the GFCT's later decision in the *Bananas* case[762] represents a retreat from *Brunner*, but there does not seem to be any tangible incompatibility between the two cases, and the reservation/qualification in *Brunner* to Germany's acceptance of the supremacy doctrine still seems to represent a potential challenge to supremacy in a future fundamental rights cases. This was confirmed by the GFCT in its judgment of 30 June 2009[763] in which the GFCT made its position of primacy very clear when assessing the compatibility of the ToL with the German Constitution. It stated that primacy of EU law derives from the German act conferring powers to the EU, and not from EU law, and that it will intensify its control over EU acts to ensure that they comply not only with common European human rights standards, but also that EU institutions when adopting EU acts have respected the substantive scope of the powers that have been delegated to them. The Court proposed the establishment of a special procedure according to which its competence to rule on such disputes would be immune from any challenge.

13.11.2 Poland

The position of the Polish Constitutional Tribunal is clear. EU law prevails over all national law except the Polish Constitution.[764] Accordingly if there is an inevitable conflict between EU law

---

759. *Internationale Handelsgesellschaft mbH v Einfuhr- und Vorratstelle für Getreide und Futtermittel* [1974] 2 CMLR 540.
760. *Re Wünsche Handelsgesellschaft* [1987] 3 CMLR 225.
761. [1994] 1 CMLR 57.
762. Bundesverfassungsgericht, 7 June 2000, 2 BvL 1/97.
763. The full text of the judgment of the German Federal Constitutional Court in English is available at http:www.bverfg.de/entscheidungen/es20090630 2bve000208en.html (10/2/10)
764. Judgment of the Polish Constitutional Tribunal of 11/05/2005 available at http://www.trybunal.gov.pl/OTK/teksty/otkpdf/2005/K_18_04.pdf (accessed 12/12/09).

and the Polish Constitution, i.e. a conflict which cannot be resolved even by interpretation in favour of EU law, it will be resolved by either the making of an amendment to the Polish Constitution or the withdrawal of Poland from the EU. This approach was tested when the Polish Constitutional Tribunal[765] found that national law implementing the Framework Directive on the European Arrest Warrant was incompatible with the Polish Constitution (which prohibits the extradition of Polish citizens) and that the time limit for implementation of the Directive had elapsed. The Polish Constitutional Tribunal was willing to delay annulment of the contested law in order to give time for the Polish legislature to make necessary amendments to the Polish Constitution.

AIDE-MÉMOIRE

SUPREMACY OF EU LAW

This means that EU law takes priority over, and supersedes any national law (Case 6/64 *Costa v ENEL* and Declaration 17 attached to the Treaties which confirms the position of the ECJ on supremacy of EU law).

CLASH BETWEEN NATIONAL LAW AND EU LAW

In the event of a conflict between EU law and national law, the conflicting domestic provisions must be set aside. A national court must not request or await the prior setting aside of an incompatible national provision by legislation or other constitutional means but must do this of its own motion (Case 106/77 *Simmenthal*). However:

- A Member State is not required to nullify conflicting national law, which may continue to apply to situations outside the scope of EU law (Joined Cases C-10/97 to C-22/97 *Ministero Delle Finanze*).

- There is no general duty imposed on national courts to apply EU law ex officio (i.e. when the parties to the proceedings have not raised points of EU law) (Case C-312/93 *Peterbroeck* and in Joined Cases C-430–431/93 *Van Schijndel*).

THE RELATIONSHIP OF SUBORDINATION BETWEEN EU LAW AND NATIONAL LAW

All EU law, irrespective of whether or not it is directly effective, prevails over all national law, even that relating to the protection of human rights and to the internal structure of the Member States (Case 11/70 *Internationale Handelsgesellschaft*), although not every Member State has accepted this principle without qualification. This means that national laws, from the perspective of EU law, are subservient to all sources of EU law, that is, subservient to:

- the provisions of the Treaties;

- secondary legislation. However, as the ECJ has no jurisdiction over matters relating to

---

765. W. Sadurski, " 'Solange Chapter 3': Constitutional Courts in Central Europe – Democracy – European Union", EUI Working Paper, Law, No. 2006/40 and K. Kowalik-Bańczyk, "Should We Polish It Up? The Polish Constitutional Tribunal and the Idea of Supremacy of EU Law", (2005) 6/10 German Law Journal, available at http://www.germanlawjournal.com/past_issues_archive.php?show=10&volume=6 (accessed 16/09/07).

the CFSP, with the exceptions set out in Article 275 TFEU (see Chapter 5) and in the absence of pre-ToL case law on this matter, it is uncertain whether the principle of supremacy applies to measures adopted under the CFSP;

- general principles of EU law; and

- international agreements concluded between the EU and third countries/international organisations.

LIMIT OF THE SUPREMACY OF EU LAW

- The principle of res judicata overrides the principle of supremacy of EU law (Case C-234/04 *Kapferer*) but not in all circumstances (Case C-119/05 *Lucchini*);

- International agreements entered prior to the accession of a Member State to the EU prevail over EU law. However, a Member State has the duty to ensure that any conflict between such agreements and EU law is eliminated. Further, in accordance with public international law, if obligations arising from EU law conflict with rights held by a Member State, under a pre-accession agreement, the Member State must refrain from exercising such rights to the extent necessary for the performance of its EU obligations. As a result, Article 351 TFEU only guarantees the rights held by third countries under pre-accession agreements (Case 10/61 *Commission v Italy*).

RECOMMENDED READING

Books

Alter, K., *Establishing the Supremacy of European Law: The Making of an International Rule of Law in Europe*, 2nd edition, 2003, Oxford: Oxford University Press

Barents, R., *The Autonomy of Community Law*, 2003, The Hague: Kluwer Law International

Articles

Lenaerts, K. and Corthaut, T., "Of Birds and Hedges: The Role of Primacy in Invoking Norms of EU Law", (2006) 31 ELRev 289

Schmid, C., "All Bark and No Bite: Notes on the Federal Constitutional Court's 'Banana Decision' ", (2001) 7 ELJ 95

14

LIABILITY OF A MEMBER STATE FOR DAMAGE CAUSED TO INDIVIDUALS BY AN INFRINGEMENT OF EU LAW

CONTENTS

SUMMARY

1. The principle of Member State liability was established in Joined Cases C-6 and 9/90 *Francovich v Italy* and *Bonifaci v Italy* in which the ECJ stated that "a principle of State liability for damage to individuals caused by a breach of Community law for which it [a Member State] is responsible is inherent in the scheme of the Treaty".

2. In subsequent cases the ECJ has clarified the conditions which must exist for a Member State to incur liability. These are that:

■ The rule of law which has been infringed must confer rights on individuals;

■ The breach must be sufficiently serious to merit an award of damages; and

■ There must be a direct causal link between the Member State's breach of EU law and the loss suffered by the applicant.

3. A Member State is liable regardless of the organ of the Member State whose act or omission infringed EU law. Accordingly, a Member State may be liable for damage caused to an individual by a manifest infringement of EU law attributable to a supreme court of that Member State. It can also be held accountable for wrongful acts of its organs or its officials when they act beyond their capacity, but to all appearances as competent officials or organs.

4. The application by national courts of the conditions for liability is illustrated in the *Factortame* cases, the most important cases in terms of the impact of EU law on UK law.

5. The scope of the principle of national procedural autonomy, and its limits, are of great practical importance in respect of all claims based on EU law which are adjudicated by national courts. This matter is of even greater importance with regard to claims concerning Member State liability for damage caused to individuals, given that the principle of national procedural autonomy entails that a claim for reparation must be made in accordance with the domestic rules on liability. However, the principle of Member State liability has eroded the principle of procedural autonomy to the point where it requires a Member State to create a new remedy in damages, if an equivalent remedy does not exist under national law, to give effect to EU law.

14.1   Introduction

The principle that a Member State should be liable in damages to individuals who have suffered loss as a result of that Member State's infringement of EU law is today one of the cornerstones of EU law. Its origin can be found in Case 60/75 *Russo v Aima*,[766] in which the ECJ held that a Member State should pay compensation for damage caused by its own breach of Community law, but referred to national law to lay down the necessary conditions applicable to liability in tort.

The main justifications for the introduction of the above principle into EU law mentioned by the ECJ in Joined Cases C-6/90 and C-9/90 *Francovich v Italian State and Bonifaci v Italian State*[767] were the supremacy of EC law, the necessity of ensuring the effectiveness of EC law and the requirements of Article 10 EC [Article 4(3) TFEU]. The less obvious reason, and not mentioned in these cases, is that in the late 1980s many Member States delayed the implementation of directives which were mainly used to complete the internal market. At that time there was no effective remedy, bearing in mind that penalties against defaulting Member States were only introduced in 1993 by the Treaty of Maastricht in Article 228(2) EC [Article 260(2) TFEU].

The best way to ensure implementation of a directive was to allow individuals to enforce their rights before national courts, that is, to permit them to sue a defaulting Member State for loss that they had suffered, especially in cases where directives were not directly effective, or when individuals had no remedy based on indirect horizontal effect (see Chapter 12.4.1.2).

It can be said that in order to increase pressure on the Member States to implement directives and, at the same time, to ensure that rights conferred by EU law on individuals were adequately protected at national level, the ECJ established the principle of non-contractual liability of a Member State – which does not depend on the criteria for direct effect being present.

14.2   The establishment of the principle of Member State liability

In Joined Cases C-6/90 and C-9/90 *Francovich v Italian State and Bonifaci v Italian State*[768] the ECJ established the principle of Member State liability.

---

766.   [1976] ECR 45.
767.   [1991] ECR I-5357.
768.   [1991] ECR I-5357.

THE FACTS WERE:

In the Francovich case, as a result of the bankruptcy of his employer, Francovich lost 6,000,000 lira. In due course he sued his former employer but could not enforce judgment as the employer had become insolvent. He decided to commence proceedings against the Italian state for sums due, or for compensation in lieu, under Council Directive 80/987, which was not implemented in Italy although the prescribed time limit had already elapsed. Directive 80/987 on protection of employees in the event of the insolvency of their employers required that the Member State set up a scheme under which employees of insolvent companies would receive at least some of their outstanding wages.[769] In Case 22/87 Commission v Italy the ECJ under Article 226 EC [Article 258 TFEU] held Italy in breach of EC law for non-implementation of Directive 80/987. The Italian court made reference to the ECJ under Article 234 EC [Article 267 TFEU] to determine whether the provision of the Directive in relation to payment of wages was directly effective, and whether the Italian state was liable for damages arising from its failure to implement the Directive.

Held:

The ECJ held that the provision in question was not sufficiently clear to be directly effective, but made the following statement in relation to the second question: "It is a general principle inherent in the scheme of the Treaty [that] a Member State is liable to make good damage to individuals caused by a breach of Community law for which it is responsible."

In this case the ECJ upheld the claim against the Italian Government and established three conditions necessary to give rise to liability in the case of total failure of a Member State to implement a directive. They are as follows:

1.   The result required by the directive must include the conferring of rights for the benefit of individuals;

2.   The content of those rights must be clearly identifiable by reference to the directive; and

3.   There must be a causal link between the breach of the Member State's obligation and the damage suffered by the individual.

The three above-mentioned conditions have been further clarified in subsequent cases.

14.3   The development of the principle of Member State liability

In *Francovich* the ECJ left many matters unclear. These matters were clarified in Joined Cases C-46/93 and C-48/93 *Brasserie du Pêcheur SA v Germany and R v Secretary of State for Transport, ex parte Factortame Ltd and Others (Factortame (No. 3)).*[770]

---

769.   Council Directive 80/987 was implemented in the United Kingdom in the Employment Protection (Consolidation) Act 1978 as amended. It set up the Redundancy Fund, which provides payments for employees of insolvent companies.

770.   [1996] ECR I-1029.

THE FACTS WERE:

Case C-46/93 Brasserie du Pêcheur SA v Germany

Brasserie, a French brewer, brought proceedings in a German court against Germany for losses it had suffered as a result of a ban imposed by the German authorities on beer which did not comply with the purity standards imposed by the German Biersteuergesetz (Law on Beer Duty). Brasserie was forced to cease exporting beer to Germany. In Case 178/84 Commission v Germany[771] the ECJ had already ruled that such a ban was incompatible with Article 28 EC [Article 34 TFEU].

Case C-48/93 R v Secretary of State for Transport ex parte Factortame (for more detailed facts see section 14.5).

The UK Government had enacted the Merchant Shipping Act 1988, which made the registration of fishing vessels dependent upon conditions as to their owner's nationality, residence and domicile, so depriving Factortame, a Spanish owned company, of its right to fish within the UK's quota under the terms of the Common Fisheries Policy. Factortame brought an action before the English High Court seeking damages for losses it had suffered as a result of the enactment of the Merchant Shipping Act 1988. In previous judgments (Case C-221/89 Factortame (No. 2)[772] and Case C-246/89 Commission v United Kingdom[773]) the ECJ had held such legislation contrary to EC law.

Held:

The ECJ held that Member States would be liable under Community law for breaches of EC Treaty and Community measures in certain circumstances. These are:

1. The rule of law which has been breached must be one which is intended to confer rights on individuals.

2. The breach must be sufficiently serious to merit an award of damages. To be held liable a Member State must have "manifestly and gravely" disregarded its obligation. To assess whether this condition is satisfied, national courts should take into consideration a number of factors such as:

    ▪ the clarity and precision of the EC rule breached;
    ▪ the element of discretion in the adoption of legislative acts by national authorities;
    ▪ whether the infringement was intentional or accidental;
    ▪ whether any error of law was excusable;
    ▪ whether any action or advice on the part of the Commission had contributed to the breach.

3. There must be a direct causal link between the Member State's default and the loss suffered by the claimant.

---

771. [1987] ECR 1227.
772. [1991] ECR I-3905.
773. [1991] ECR I-4585.

Additionally, the ECJ abolished the disparity between the conditions governing liability of Community institutions based on Article 288(2) EC [340(2) TFEU], and the conditions under which a Member State may incur liability for damage caused to individuals in like circumstances. In this respect the ECJ stated:

"the conditions under which the state may incur liability for damage caused to individuals cannot, in the absence of particular justification, differ from those governing the liability of the Community in like circumstances. The protection of the rights of individuals derived from Community law cannot vary on whether a national authority or a Community institution is responsible for the damage."[774]

In subsequent cases the ECJ further clarified the scope of the principle of Member State liability as follows:

1. The apparent disparity between the second condition laid down in *Francovich* and the second condition set out in *Brasserie* and *Factortame* has been explained by the ECJ when it held that both are "in substance . . . the same since the condition that there should be a sufficiently serious breach, although not expressed in *Francovich*, was nevertheless evident from the circumstances of the case".[775] Indeed, non-implementation of a directive within the required time limit constitutes a sufficiently serious breach. Thus, for claimants like *Francovich*, the second condition, which is the most difficult to evidence, is automatically met when a Member State fails to transpose the relevant directive within the prescribed time limit.

2. The conditions for Member State liability apply to all breaches of EU law, whether legislative, executive or administrative. A Member State is liable regardless of the organ of the Member State whose act or omission has breached EU law. Also, it is irrelevant whether the provision in question is directly effective or not. The ECJ emphasised that direct effect constitutes a minimum guarantee and thus *Francovich* liability is a necessary corollary of the principle of effectiveness of EU law.

3. In Case C-470/03 *AGM COS.MET Srl v Suomen Valtio, Tarmo Lehtinen*,[776] the ECJ endorsed the principle of public international law according to which a Member State can be held accountable for wrongful acts of its organs or its officials when they act beyond their capacity but to all appearances as competent officials or organs.[777] In this case the ECJ held that a Member State can be liable in a situation where a public official makes what are in fact personal statements, but which give the persons to whom they are addressed the impression that they express an official position taken by the Member State. The Court emphasised that the decisive factor for statements of an official to be attributed to the Member State is whether the persons to whom those statements are addressed can reasonably suppose, in the given context, that they are positions taken by the official with the authority of his office. When a Member State is found liable in such a

---

774.   Case C-46/93 *Brasserie du Pêcheur v Germany* [1996] ECR I-1029, para 51.

775.   Joined Cases C-178/94, C-179/94, C-188/94, C-189/94 and C-190/94 *Dillenkofer and Others* [1996] ECR I-4845.

776.   [2007] ECR I-2749.

777.   See *The Jessie* (1921) RIAA 57 and *The Wonderer* (1921) RIAA 68.

situation, EU law does not preclude an official from being held liable in addition to the Member State, but does not require this.

4. An applicant suing a Member State need not prove that the authorities were at fault. The ECJ stated that "reparation for loss or damage cannot be made conditional upon fault (whether intentional or negligent) going beyond that of a sufficiently serious breach of Community law".[778]

5. The ECJ has placed the onus upon national courts to uphold rights flowing from EU law under national rules governing public liability in tort. It has imposed upon those courts the duty to "verify whether or not the conditions governing state liability for a breach of Community law are fulfilled". National courts must ensure that the protection of EU rights is given equal status and is not less favourable than the protection afforded to similar rights arising under domestic law. National courts must not impose any procedure that makes it more difficult, or even impossible, for an individual to rely upon those rights (see section 14.6).

6. In a Member State with a federal structure the reparation of damage is not necessarily ensured by the central government of that Member State, but may instead be provided by the government of the relevant member of the federal structure.[779]

7. In Member States in which some legislative and administrative tasks are devolved to territorial bodies possessing a certain degree of autonomy, or to any other public body legally distinct from the Member State, reparation of damage caused by such a body to individuals may be made by that body.[780]

14.3.1 The first condition for Member State liability – the breached provision must confer rights on individuals

According to the case law of the ECJ, the purpose of the legal rule infringed must be to grant rights to the individual, the content of which can be identified with sufficient precision on the basis of the relevant provision of EU law.

To be unconditional and sufficiently precise in the above context requires that the words of a provision relied upon by the claimant define with sufficient clarity the identity of the persons entitled to the benefit from that right, and to ascertain whether the claimant is such a beneficiary, the extent and content of that right and the identity of the legal body charged with protecting that right.[781]

14.3.2 The second condition for Member State liability – the breach of EU law must be sufficiently serious to merit an award of damages

The most difficult criterion set out for the determination of Member State liability is that relating to "a sufficiently serious breach" of EU law. In respect of what is to be regarded as a sufficiently

---

778. Case C-46/93 *Brasserie du Pêcheur SA* [1996] ECR I-1029, paras 75–80.
779. Case C-302/97 *Konle v Austria* [1999] ECR I-3099.
780. Case C-424/97 *Haim II* [2000] ECR I-5123.
781. Case C-6/90 *Francovich* [1991] ECR I-5357.

serious breach, the ECJ held that " 'where a Member State was not called upon to make any legislative choices and possessed only considerably reduced, or even no discretion, the mere infringement of Community law may be sufficient to establish a sufficiently serious breach".[782] Thus, the condition requiring a sufficiently serious breach of EU law implies manifest and grave disregard by the Member State for the limits set on its discretion. What exactly "sufficiently serious" or "manifest and grave" means can only be gleaned from looking at the subsequent decisions of the ECJ.

One of them is Case 392/93 *R v HM Treasury ex parte British Telecommunications plc*,[783] which concerned the failure to properly implement Article 8(1) of Directive 90/531. In this case the ECJ found that:

- The Member State concerned had a wide discretion of power in the field in which it was acting;

- The wording of the provisions of the original directive was imprecise and as a result was capable of being interpreted in the manner implemented;

- Implementation had been carried out after taking legal advice as to the meaning of the directive;

- There was no ECJ case law on the subject;

- There was no objection from the Commission as to the interpretation applied.

In the light of the above, there was not a sufficiently serious breach of EU law.

In Case C-5/94 *Hedley Lomas*,[784] which concerned the UK authorities' refusal, in breach of a directive, to grant an export licence, the ECJ stated that "where the Member State was not called upon to make any legislative choices and possessed only considerably reduced, or even no discretion, the mere infringement of community law may be sufficient to establish a sufficiently serious breach". Accordingly, the UK was found in breach of EU law.

In Cases C-178, 179 and 189/94 *Dillenkofer*,[785] the ECJ held that non-implementation of a directive within the prescribed time limit constitutes, per se, a serious breach of EU law, and consequently gives rise to a right of reparation for individuals suffering injury.

In Case C-140/97 *Rechberger*,[786] Austria incorrectly implemented Article 7 of Directive 90/314, which, the ECJ held, left no discretion to a Member State in its implementation. Thus, Austria "manifestly and gravely" disregarded the limits of its discretion and therefore was held liable.

In Case C-278/05 *Robins and Others v Secretary of State for Work and Pensions*,[787] the ECJ held that under Article 8 of Directive 80/987/EEC on the protection of workers in the event of the employer's insolvency, Member States enjoy considerable discretion for the purposes of determining the level of protection of entitlement to pension benefits.

---

782. Case C-5/94 *R v Minister of Agriculture, Fisheries and Food ex parte Hedley Lomas (Ireland) Ltd* [1996] ECR I-2553. See also Case C-319/96 *Brinkmann* [1998] ECR I-5255.

783. [1996] ECR I-1631.

784. Case C-5/94 *R v Minister of Agriculture, Fisheries and Food ex parte Hedley Lomas (Ireland) Ltd* [1996] ECR I-2553.

785. [1996] ECR I-4845.

786. [1999] ECR I-3499.

787. [2007] ECR I-1053.

14.3.3 The third condition for Member State liability – there must be a direct causal link between the breach EU law and the loss suffered by an individual

In Joined Cases C-46/93 and C-48/93 *Brasserie du Pêcheur and Factortame (No. 3)*,[788] the ECJ held that it is for the national courts to determine whether there is a direct causal link between the breach of the obligation resting on the Member State and the damage sustained by the injured parties. This is largely a question of fact. Thus national procedural rules are relevant as to the establishment of the causal link, the quantification of loss and the type of damage which can be recoverable (see section 14.6).

14.4 A breach of EU law by a Supreme Court of a Member State

In Case C-224/01 *Gerhard Köbler v Austria*[789] the ECJ, for the first time, had to decide whether the principle of Member State liability, set out in Joined Cases C-6/90 and C-9/90 *Francovich and Bonifaci*[790] and explained in subsequent cases, is also applicable in a situation where the infringement of EC law is attributable to a supreme court of a Member State.

THE FACTS WERE:

Under Austrian Salary law a university professor, on completion of 15 years' service as a professor at Austrian universities, was eligible for a special length-of-service increment to be taken into account in the calculation of his retirement pension.

Since 1986 Mr Köbler had been employed, under a public law contract with the Austrian state, as an ordinary professor in Innsbruck (Austria). Before 1986 Mr Köbler taught at universities in various Member States. When in 1996 Mr Köbler applied to the competent Austrian authorities for the special length-of-service increment, his request was refused on the ground that he had not completed 15 years' exclusively at Austrian universities.

Mr Köbler challenged the above decision before the Verwaltungsgerichtshof (Austrian Supreme Administrative Court) as contrary to Article 39 EC [Article 45 TFEU] and Regulation 1612/68. The Verwaltungsgerichtshof decided to ask the ECJ for a preliminary ruling. Subsequent to the judgment of the ECJ in Case C-15/96 Schöning-Kougebetopoulou[791] *delivered on 15 January 1998, the Austrian Supreme Administrative Court was asked by the Registrar of the ECJ whether it deemed it necessary to maintain its request for a preliminary ruling. The Supreme Administrative Court requested the parties to the national proceedings to give their views on the matter, emphasising that, at first glance, the legal issue submitted for a preliminary ruling had been resolved in the light of the judgment of the ECJ in Case C-15/96 Schöning-Kougebetopoulou, in a way favourable to Mr Köbler. On 24 June 1998, the Austrian Supreme Administrative Court withdrew its request for a preliminary ruling and, by a judgment of the same day, dismissed Mr Köbler's application on the ground that the special*

---

788.   [1996] ECR I-1029, at paragraph 65.
789.   [2003] ECR I-10239.
790.   [1991] ECR I-5357.
791.   [1998] ECR I-47.

length-of-service increment was a loyalty bonus and as such could be objectively justified under the provisions on the free movement of workers by a pressing public-interest reason!

In response Mr Köbler brought proceedings before the Landesgericht für Zivilrechts-sachen Wien (Regional Civil Court in Vienna) against the Republic of Austria for reparation of the loss he allegedly suffered as a result of non-payment to him of the special length-of-service increment. He claimed that the judgment of the Austrian Supreme Administrative Court of 24 June 1998 was in breach of directly applicable Community law as it had disregarded the judgment of the ECJ in Case C-15/96 Schöning-Kougebetopoulou. In these circumstances the Austrian Regional Civil Court decided to refer the matter to the ECJ for a preliminary ruling on a number of questions.

Held:

The ECJ confirmed that the principle of Member State liability applies to judicial decisions of a national court adjudicating at last instance.

The ECJ examined the conditions necessary to establish the liability of a Member State:

- In respect of the first condition which requires that the legal rule infringed must confer rights on individuals, the ECJ without any hesitation decided that Article 39 EC [Article 45 TFEU] and Article 7(1) of Regulation 1612/68 were intended to confer rights on individuals.

- From the context of the case it appears that the second condition which requires that the breach in question must be sufficiently serious was also satisfied, taking into account that:

  - The Austrian Supreme Administrative Court in its order for reference of 22 October 1997 stated that: ". . . the special length-of service increment for ordinary university professors is in the nature of neither a loyalty bonus nor a reward, but is rather a component of salary under the system of career advancement" but came to the opposite conclusion when delivering its judgment of 24 June 1998.
  - The Verwaltungsgerichtshof misinterpreted the judgment of the ECJ in Case C-15/96 *Schöning-Kougebetopoulou* in which the ECJ held that a national measure which makes a worker's remuneration dependent on his length of service, but excludes any possibility for comparable periods of employment completed in the public service of another Member State to be taken into account, was in breach of EC law.
  - In the light of the above and given that the ECJ did not rule on the issue of whether or not such a national measure could be justified under EC law in *Schöning-Kougebetopoulou*, the Verwaltungsgerichtshof should have maintained its request for a preliminary ruling as the requirements set out in Case 283/81 *CILFIT* were not fulfilled.

So, on the substantive issue, the ECJ held in effect that the Austrian Supreme Administrative Court (Verwaltungsgerichtshof) had prima facie breached EC law (contrary to the ECJ's decision in *Schöning-Kougebetopoulou*) by not treating Mr Köbler's work experience in universities in other EU Member States as reckonable for the purpose of the 15-year increment to be used when calculating his pension. On the procedural issue of whether a preliminary reference should have been made to the ECJ by the Verwaltungsgerichtshof, the ECJ held that the Verwaltungsgerichtshof should have made such a reference in order to determine whether there was any possible justification (that is, any exception/derogation) under EC law for the Austrian policy.

Despite all the above, the ECJ found that the breach of EC law by the Verwaltungs-gerichtshof was not sufficiently serious as to give rise to liability on the part of the Austrian state! This conclusion of the ECJ is contrary to the opinion expressed by the Advocate General, who felt that the Verwaltungsgerichtshof made an inexcusable error when it dismissed the application of Mr Köbler.

Comment:

It is submitted that the ECJ, when it failed to qualify the breach as being sufficiently serious, also failed in one of its main functions, that is, to protect the rights of individuals conferred upon them by Community law [EU law]. It is interesting to note that in the above judgment the ECJ emphasised the role of the judiciary in the protection of rights derived by individuals from Community rules. In particular, the ECJ stated that:

"... [where] an infringement of those rights by a final decision of such a court (a court of a Member State adjudicating at last instance) cannot thereafter normally be corrected, individuals cannot be deprived of the possibility of rendering the State liable in order in that way to obtain legal protection of their rights".

It is not clear why this reasoning did not operate to entitle Mr Köbler to damages.

Two arguments submitted to the ECJ against the extension of the principle of Member State liability to national courts adjudicating at last instance in a situation (where incorrect decisions taken by such courts have caused damage to individuals) were particularly interest-ing: one based on the principle of res judicata is discussed in Chapter 13.9; the other, based on the independence of the judiciary, is examined below.

In its judgment the ECJ noted that there is a basic difference between Member State responsibility and the personal liability of the judges and because of this difference, Member State liability for judicial decisions, taken by national judges adjudicating at last instance, contrary to Community law, "does not appear to entail any particular risk that the independ-ence of a court adjudicating at last instance will be called into question". This point is not well explained.

It is submitted that better explanations could have been given to support the extension of Member State liability to national courts deciding in the last instance. These are that:

- The objective of ensuring the independence and authority of the judiciary has not been considered as hindering the introduction in most Member States of proceedings aimed at redressing the malfunctioning of civil or administrative courts, even if such courts are the highest courts in a Member State.

- In respect of miscarriages of justice in penal proceedings, most Member States have set up special procedures allowing for the revision of final judgments. Consequently, Member States should not introduce double standards, one where national law in concerned, and one where EC law is concerned.

- The situation already exists in many Member States whereby the duty of judges of supreme courts of a Member State to be impartial is not undermined despite the fact that if their decisions relating to the interpretation and the application of the European Conven-tion on Human Rights is wrong, then their government may pay compensation to such citizens as have suffered as a result of those wrong decisions.

The judgment in Köbler was further clarified in Case C-173/03 *Traghetti del Mediterranes SpA (TDM) v Italy.*[792]

THE FACTS WERE:

In 1981 TDM, an Italian maritime transport undertaking, brought proceedings before an Italian court against its competitor, Tirrenia di Navigazione (Tirrenia), seeking compensation for damage that Tirrenia caused it between 1976 and 1980 as a result of charging fares below the cost price on the maritime cabotage market between mainland Italy and the islands of Sardinia and Sicily. According to TDM, the conduct of Tirrenia constituted unfair competition and abuse of a dominant position in breach of Article 82 EC. The charging of low fares was made possible by subsidies granted to Tirrenia by the Italian authorities, which subsidies, according to TDM, were in breach of Articles 90 and 92 EC [Articles 110 and 112 TFEU].

TDM's claim was dismissed by all Italian courts, as was its request submitted to national courts for a preliminary ruling under Article 234 EC [Article 267 TFEU]. When, in the last resort, the Italian Supreme Court (the Italian Corte Supreme di Cassazione) dismissed the claim, TDM (in fact, its administrator as TDM was put into liquidation during the national proceedings) brought proceedings against the Italian state before the Tribunale di Genova seeking reparation for damage caused to it by the judgment of the Italian Supreme Court, in particular by the Italian Supreme Court's erroneous interpretation of EC law and its refusal to make a reference for a preliminary ruling under Article 234 EC [Article 267 TFEU]. The Tribunale di Genova decided to refer to the ECJ as it was uncertain about the effect of Köbler on Italian legislation, which limited liability of the Supreme Court as follows:

1.   It excluded liability in connection with the interpretation of provisions of law or assessment of facts or evidence in the exercise of judicial functions by the Supreme Court;

2.   It limited liability to cases of intentional fault or serious misconduct.

Held:

The ECJ held that:

▪ The exclusion of liability was contrary to EC law. The Court emphasised that such exclusion would amount to depriving the principle of Member State liability of all practical effect and lead to a situation where individuals would have no judicial protection if a national court adjudicating in the last instance committed a manifest error whilst interpreting provisions of law or assessing facts and evidence.

▪ The limitation of liability solely to cases of intentional fault and serious misconduct would be in breach of EC law if it leads to exclusion of liability in cases where a manifest infringement of the applicable law has been committed. In this respect the ECJ stated that it had clearly indicated in *Köbler* that liability for an infringement of EC law resulting from a judgment of a supreme court occurs only in exceptional cases where the court has manifestly infringed Community law. The following factors should be taken into account in

---

792.   [2006] ECR I-5177. See also Case C-154/08 *Commission v Spain* [judgment of 12/11/09 (NYR)] (see Chapter 15.2.2.3).

deciding whether or not a supreme court of a Member State has manifestly infringed EC law:

- The degree of clarity and precision of the rule infringed;
- Whether the error of law was excusable or inexcusable;
- The position taken, where applicable, by a Community institution on the disputed matter;
- Non-compliance with the obligation to make a reference for a preliminary ruling.

The ECJ concluded that while a Member State is allowed to impose conditions as to liability for infringement of Community law by its supreme court, under no circumstances may such conditions be stricter than those for a manifest infringement of Community law as defined in *Köbler*. Accordingly, a condition based on a concept of intentional fault or serious misconduct that goes beyond manifest disregard of Community law is contrary to EC law as it would call into question the right to reparation founded on the Community legal order.

14.5   The application of the principle of State liability in the UK – the Factortame case

The leading case on this topic is *R v Secretary of State for Transport, ex parte Factortame Ltd and Others (No. 5)*,[793] in which the House of Lords (now the Supreme Court) applied the three conditions for liability and found the UK liable. This case is one of the numerous Factortame cases concerning the UK Merchant Shipping Act 1988, which made the registration of fishing vessels in the UK dependent upon conditions as to the nationality, residence and domicile of their owners.

THE FACTS WERE:

According to the UK Merchant Shipping Act 1988 a vessel could be registered as British if it was British owned, and it was British owned if both the legal owners and not less than 75 per cent of the beneficial owners were qualified persons or qualified companies. Being regarded as a "qualified person" was conditional upon being a British citizen resident and domiciled in the UK and in order to be a "qualified company", it was necessary to be incorporated in the UK and to have the relevant percentage of shares owned and the relevant percentage of its directors as "qualified persons".

Factortame, being a Spanish owned company, could not register, and not being registered, was prevented from fishing within the UK's quota under the terms of the common fisheries policy. Factortame sought an interim order from the national court, which would result in the suspension of operation of the relevant provisions of the Act. In proceedings before the English courts, the House of Lords held that the applicants would suffer irreparable damage if the interim relief which they sought was not granted. Notwithstanding this, the House of

---

793.   [1999] 3 CMLR 597.

Lords found that English courts had no jurisdiction to grant such relief, as the remedy was barred by statute. The House of Lords referred to the ECJ the matter of whether or not this rule of national law set out in the statute should be set aside. The ECJ answered in the affirmative (Case C-213/89 R v Secretary for Transport, ex parte Factortame Ltd (No. 1)).[794] In Case C-221/89 Factortame (No. 2)[795] the ECJ held such legislation as contrary to EC law; this was confirmed in Case C-246/89 Commission v United Kingdom.[796]

After the preliminary rulings delivered by the ECJ in Joined Cases C-46/93 and C-48/93 Brasserie Du Pêcheur SA v Federal Republic of Germany and R v Secretary of State for Transport, ex parte Factortame Ltd and Others (No. 3),[797] the question for the domestic courts was to determine whether the UK's breaches of EC law were sufficiently serious as to entitle the claimants to compensation.

The UK Divisional Court held that the UK's breach of EC law was sufficiently serious to give rise to liability in damages to individuals, who suffered loss as a consequence of that breach. The Court of Appeal upheld the decision of the Divisional Court in R v Secretary of State for Transport, ex parte Factortame Ltd (No. 4).[798] The Secretary of State appealed to the House of Lords. He argued that:

- The UK had a wide measure of discretion in dealing with a serious economic problem. Therefore, it could not be said that when exercising its discretion, the UK manifestly and gravely disregarded its powers; and

- No liability could be imposed on the UK even if there was a breach of EC law, since the breach was excusable for a number of reasons: first, the law in this area was unclear until the ECJ had given judgments; second, the conduct of the UK could be objectively justified on substantial grounds taking into account that, on the one hand, under the common fisheries policy the quotas allocated to Member States were to be protected by them and, on the other hand, under international law it is a state's prerogative to decide who should be entitled to register a vessel and fly its flag.

Held:

The House of Lords held:[799]

1. With regard to the condition of nationality, that the legislation was in breach of EC law [Article 12 EC – Article 18 TFEU] and that this breach was sufficiently serious to give rise to liability in damages to individuals who suffered loss as a consequence.

   The judgment of the House of Lords is not surprising. In *Factortame (No. 3)* the ECJ had already dealt with arguments invoked in *Factortame (No. 5)* by the Secretary of State. In this respect Lord Slynn said:

---

794. [1990] ECR I-2433.
795. [1991] ECR I-3905.
796. [1991] ECR I-4585.
797. [1996] ECR I-1029.
798. [1998] EULR 456.
799. *Regina v Secretary of State for Transport, Ex Parte Factortame Ltd and Others (Factortame No. 5)* [1999] 3 CMLR 597.

"It was obvious that what was done by the Government was not done inadvertently. It was done after anxious consideration and after taking legal advice. . . . The shortness of the transitional period, the fact that there was no way in domestic law of challenging the statute, and that the respondents were obliged not merely to avoid being removed from the old register but to apply to be put on the new register all emphasised the determination of the Government to press ahead with the scheme despite the strong opposition of the Commission and the doubts of its officials.

Therefore, it seems clear that the deliberate adoption of legislation which was clearly discriminatory on the ground of nationality was a manifest breach of fundamental Treaty obligations."

Lord Hope emphasised that if in the present case damages were not to be held to be recoverable, it would be hard to envisage any case, short of one involving bad faith, where damages would be recoverable.

All Law Lords agreed that the breach of Community law by the UK was sufficiently serious to entitle the respondents to compensation for damage directly caused by that breach.

2. In respect of the domicile condition, the House of Lords agreed that it should be treated in the same way as nationality. Thus, that condition was also considered breached and the breach as being sufficiently serious.

3. In relation to the residence condition, Lord Slynn held that, on the one hand, the condition was excusable taking into account the aim of the legislation which was to protect the livelihood of British fishing communities, but, on the other hand, it was not, taking into account that this condition was applied not only to fishermen but also to shareholders and directors of companies owning fishing vessels. Consequently, the condition of residence could not be justified where the discrimination was so obvious. Further, the British Government all along took the view that the residence condition in itself was not sufficient to achieve its objective and so, taken separately, could not be justified.

Comment:

The *Factortame* cases made a great impact on the law of the UK for three reasons:

- The UK expressly recognised the principle of supremacy of EC law;

- For the first time since 1688, that is, prior to the Bill of Rights, the British judiciary is able to overturn the will of the legislature, even though it has knowledge of its express wish;

- The UK courts, including the House of Lords, for the first time ever applied the conditions for Member State liability.

14.6 National procedural autonomy and the principle of Member State liability

In the absence of uniform EU procedural rules, it is for the domestic legal system of each Member State to designate the courts and tribunals having jurisdiction in respect of claims based on EU law and to lay down the procedural rules governing actions for safeguarding rights which individuals derive from EU law. This is known as the principle of national procedural autonomy, which was recognised by the ECJ in Case 33/76 *Rewe-Zentralfinanz eG et Rewe-Zentral AG v Landwirtschaftskammer für das Saarland*.[800] In Case 158/80 *Rewe-Handelsgesellschaft Nord mbH et Rewe-Markt Steffen v Hauptzollamt Kiel*,[801] the ECJ stated that, as a matter of principle, a Member State is not obliged to invent special remedies to give effect to EC law [EU law].

Procedural rules are very important as they concern such matters as causation, remoteness of damage, interim relief, limitation periods, quantum of damages, burden of proof, evidence, locus standi, and so on. Leaving such important matters to be decided by national procedural rules which, on the one hand, are different in different Member States, and on the other hand, do not take into account the peculiarity of EU law, could undermine the extent of the protection of the rights conferred by EU law on individuals, prejudice legal certainty and justice, and call into question the authority of EU law.

The ECJ has been very aware of the above implications of the principle of procedural autonomy on the uniform application and effectiveness of EU law. The Court's call for the adoption of legislation harmonising the most important aspects of procedural law not having been answered by the EU legislature,[802] the Court has developed its own way of dealing with this matter.

On the basis of Article 10 EC [Article 4(3) TEU], which requires Member States to take all necessary measures to achieve the objectives set in the Treaties and to abstain from adopting any measures which may jeopardise their achievement, the ECJ has gradually limited the scope of the principle of procedural autonomy. The first limitations were imposed by three principles:

- That of equivalence or non-discrimination, which requires that under national procedural rules claims based on EU law must not be treated less favourably than those relating to similar domestic claims.[803]

- That of effectiveness, which requires that the application of domestic rules and procedures must not render the protection of individuals' EU rights practically impossible or excessively difficult.[804] The ECJ stated that in order to decide whether or not a national procedural provision renders the exercise of rights conferred upon individuals impossible or excessively difficult, reference must be made to the role of that provision in the procedure, its progress and its special features, viewed as a whole, before the various national courts. In that context, it is necessary to take into consideration, where relevant, the principles which form the basis of the national legal system, such as the protection of the rights of the defence, the principle of legal certainty and the proper conduct of the proceedings.[805]

- That of proportionality (see Chapter 8.3.3.1).

Subsequently, the intrusion of the ECJ into the autonomy of procedural rules, based on the above principles, has increased as evidenced by, inter alia, the following cases:

---

800.   [1976] ECR 1989.
801.   [1981] ECR 1805.
802.   See A. Arnull, *The European Union and its Court of Justice*, 1999, Oxford: Oxford University Press, p 151.
803.   Supra note 801.
804.   Case 45/76 *Comet* [1976] ECR 2043.
805.   Case C-312/93 *Peterbroeck* [1995] ECR I-4599; Joined Cases C-430/93 and C-431/93 *Van Schijndel* [1995] ECR I-4705; Case C-129/00 *Commission v Italy* [2003] ECR I-14637; Case C-222/05 *Van der Weerd* [2007] ECR I-4233.

■ In Case 106/77 *Simmenthal*,[806] a national court was required to set aside national law incompatible with EC law without requesting or waiting for the legislature or other branches of government to set aside an incompatible national provision by legislation or other constitutional means.

■ In Case 14/83 *Von Colson and Kamann*,[807] on the basis of the principle of effectiveness a national court was required to ensure that compensation was adequate to the injury sustained and amounted to more than purely nominal compensation, and further that the penalty for a breach of Community law was adequate and proportional so as to deter breach of obligations imposed in the context of the Equal Treatment Directive.

■ In Case C-177/88 *Dekker*,[808] a national court was required to disregard a national procedural rule which made the employer's liability for breach of the principle of equal treatment subject to proof of fault attributable to the employer.

■ In some cases (i.e. Case C-208/90 *Emmott*;[809] Case C-246/96 *Magorrian*[810] and Case C-295/04 *Vincenzo Manfredi*[811]), a national court was required to disregard the limitation period imposed under national law. In the light of subsequent cases, however, it appears that a Member State is entitled to determine limitation periods and to provide for rules concerning the interruption or suspension of those periods, but subject to compliance with the principles of equivalence and effectiveness[812] and subject to exceptional situations, such as in *Emmott*. In Case C-445/06 *Danske Slagterier v Germany*,[813] the ECJ provided three important clarifications as to the limitation period imposed under national law in respect of actions for compensation based on the *Francovich* remedy.

● The first issue was whether the limitation period begins to run only upon the directive in question being fully and correctly transposed into national law, or whether, in accordance with German law, when the first injurious effects have already been produced and further injurious effects are foreseeable. The ECJ held that the rule in *Emmott* applies to exceptional circumstances, i.e. when the time-limit has already expired prior to the establishment of a situation incompatible with EU law and thus the time-limit is set in such a manner as to deprive the injured parties of any opportunity whatsoever to rely on their rights before national courts. Therefore, in was in the light of the circumstances in *Emmott* that the ECJ stated that, until such time as a directive has been properly transposed, a defaulting Member State may not rely on an individual's delay in initiating proceedings. In *Danske* the situation was different in that the existence of the time-limit did not produce a result similar to that in *Emmott* and therefore there was no breach of the principle of effectiveness. Accordingly, the ECJ held that EU law does not preclude

---

806. [1978] ECR 629.
807. [1984] ECR 1891.
808. [1990] ECR I-3941.
809. [1991] ECR I-4269.
810. [1998] ECR I-7153.
811. [2006] ECR I-6619.
812. Case C-261/95 *Palmisani* [1997] ECR I-4025; Case C-542/08 *Friedrich G. Barth v Bundesministerium für Wissenschaft und Forschung* [judgment of 15/4/10 (nyr)].
813. [2009] ECR I-2119.

the commencement of the limitation period being fixed at the time when the first injurious effects have been produced, even if that date is prior to the correct transposition of the relevant directive.

● The second issue was whether the 3-year limitation period imposed under German law was in conformity with the principle of effectiveness. The ECJ decided that, in principle, such a time-limit is not liable to make it in practice impossible or excessively difficult to exercise the rights conferred by EU law and therefore is compatible with the principle of effectiveness. However, the ECJ added that in order to serve their purpose of ensuring legal certainty, limitation periods must be fixed in advance.[814]

● The third issue was whether the limitation period can be interrupted or suspended by proceedings brought by the Commission under Article 226 EC [Article 258 TFEU] against the Member State concerned in a situation where there is no effective legal remedy in the State in question to compel it to transpose a directive. The ECJ decided that the limitation period for claims seeking to establish State liability in relation to loss and damage arising from the inadequate transposition of a directive is not interrupted or suspended where the Commission brings infringement proceedings under Article 226 EC [Article 258 TFEU] against the State concerned. In this respect the ECJ held that:

"An individual may therefore bring an action seeking reparation under the detailed rules laid down for that purpose by national law without having to wait until a judgment finding that the Member State has infringed Community law has been delivered. Consequently, the fact that institution of infringement proceedings does not have the effect of interrupting or suspending the limitation period does not make it impossible or excessively difficult for individuals to exercise the rights which they derive from Community law" (para. 39).

■ In *Danske* the ECJ clarified the issue of whether a national rule under which an obligation to pay compensation does not arise if the injured party has willfully or negligently failed to avert the damage by not utilising an available legal remedy was in breach of the principles of equivalence and effectiveness. The referring court asked the ECJ to clarify the meaning of paragraph 84 contained in *Brasserie du Pêcheur and Factortame* according to which national courts were allowed to inquire whether a claimant showed reasonable diligence in order to avoid the loss or damage, or limit its extent and, in particular, to assess whether the claimant had availed himself in time of all the legal remedies. The answer from the ECJ was that:

"It would. . . ., be contrary to the principle of effectiveness to oblige injured parties to have recourse systematically to all the legal remedies available to them even if that would give rise to excessive difficulties or could not reasonably be required of them" para. 62.

As a result, a national rule that imposes on the claimant the obligation to use legal remedies available to him under national law is not contrary to EU law provided that the recourse to the legal remedies can reasonably be required of the claimant. It is for the referring court to determine in the light of the circumstances of the case whether the utilisation of the legal remedy is reasonable.

■ In Case C-271/91 *Marshall v Southampton and South West Area Health Authority II,*[815] a

---

814. Case C-62/00 *Marks & Spencer* [2002] ECR I-6325.
815. [1993] ECR I-4367.

national court was required to award the claimant full and adequate compensation and thus disregard any national rule setting a maximum limit on the recoverable quantum of damage for sex discrimination.

■ In Case C-213/89 *R v Secretary of State for Transport, ex parte Factortame Ltd and Others (No. 2)*,[816] a national court was required to grant interim relief to the claimants, although under national rules it had no jurisdiction to do so as this remedy was barred by statute.

■ In Case C-118/08 *Transportes Urbanos y Servicios Generales SA v Administración del Estado*,[817] the ECJ held that differing procedural rules concerning an action to establish State liability depending on whether the action is based on a breach of EU law or on a breach of a constitutional provision were in breach of the principle of equivalence. In this case, under Spanish procedural rules a claimant in an action to establish State liability based on a breach of EU law was required to exhaust all remedies, whether administrative or judicial, against the administrative measure which had caused him harm and which has been adopted pursuant to legislation contrary to EU law. No such requirement was imposed on a claimant in actions to establish State liability based on a breach of a provision of the Spanish Constitution. The principle of equivalence could only be breached if both actions were similar to each other. In dealing with this point the ECJ compared both actions in terms of their purpose and essential characteristics and came to the conclusion that they were indeed similar. Accordingly, the Spanish procedural rules were in breach of the principle of equivalence.

The gradual limitation of the scope of the principle of procedural autonomy reached its apogee in *Francovich and Bonifaci v Italy*, in which the ECJ imposed, for the first time, on the Member State an obligation to create a specific damages action if an equivalent action has been unknown to national law. Thus, the statement in Case 158/80 *Rewe* that there was no obligation imposed on the Member States to create new remedies has been qualified by the development of the principle of Member State liability.[818]

It results from the above that due to the requirements of EU law, the procedural conditions for obtaining compensation have, to a great extent, been modified/amended/disregarded to ensure that an appropriate remedy is available to an individual whose EU rights have been infringed by a Member State. The equivalence and effectiveness principles have been used to achieve some consistency in the remedies available at national level. In some exceptional cases the principle of effectiveness has led to the creation of a wholly new remedy, that is, the so called *Francovich* remedy.

It is important to add that the duty imposed on national courts to interpret national law in conformity with EU law means that national judges are obliged to creatively construe domestic procedural rules in order to give effect to EU law and, thus, to contribute to reformulation of the parameters of national remedial regimes.

National courts are still struggling to give the appropriate form and substance to an action in tort against a Member State or its emanations, in particular given that damages principles, as opposed to remedies, are still underdeveloped at the EU level. On the one hand, more clarification

---

816.   [1990] ECR I-2433.
817.   Judgment of 26/1/10 (nyr).
818.   This was confirmed in Case C-432/05 *Unibet* [2007] ECR I-2271.

is needed from the ECJ as to the ambit of the remedy in damages, and on the other hand, national law needs to find ways, acceptable to EU law, to incorporate this remedy into national procedural law. Notwithstanding this, it can be said that the principle of procedural autonomy, when it comes to the need to ensure the complete and effective protection of individuals' EU rights, only operates to the extent that the existing procedural rules can indeed guarantee the attainment of the specific objectives pursued by the EU legal order.

AIDE-MÉMOIRE

NON-CONTRACTUAL LIABILITY OF A MEMBER STATE

A Member State may be held liable for damage caused to individuals (Joined Cases C-6/90 and C-9/90 *Francovich and Bonifaci v Italian State*). The ECJ set out the three conditions under which a Member State may incur such liability (Joined Cases C-46/93 and C-48/93 *Brasserie du Pêcheur and Factortame*). The first two conditions are determined by reference to EU law, but the third condition is a matter of domestic procedural rules as it concerns causation, quantification of loss and heads of loss. The three conditions are:

The rule of law, which has been infringed, must be one which is intended to confer rights to individuals

A national judge must ascertain, from the wording of the provision, the identity of the persons entitled to benefit from the right in question, whether the claimant is such a beneficiary, the extent and content of the right and the identity of the legal body charged with protecting that right. Such a provision need not be directly effective.

The breach must be sufficiently serious to merit an award of damages

The establishment of the existence of a sufficiently serious breach will differ depending on the margin of discretion enjoyed by the national authorities in the field where the violation was committed:

- If the breach took place in an area where the Member State enjoys considerable freedom of action, liability will only arise when the circumstances under which the national authorities acted, and especially the degree of clarity and precision of the provision infringed, clearly point towards the implication that their conduct was intentional and thus inexcusable (Joined Cases C-46/93 and C-48/93 *Brasserie du Pêcheur/Factortame (No. 3)*);

- If the breach took place in an area where the Member State enjoyed little or no discretion at all, a breach will automatically be considered as sufficiently serious, without requirement of any further proof to that effect (Case C-5/94 *Hedley Lomas*; Cases C-178, 179 and 189/94 *Dillenkofer*).

There must be a direct causal link between the Member State's default and the loss suffered by the applicant

Under the principle of national procedural autonomy this matter is to be determined by reference to national procedural rules (Case 33/76 *Rewe-Zentralfinanz*). To ensure that remedies are available at national level to individuals suing a Member State for damages resulting from a breach of EU law by that Member State, the principle of procedural autonomy is subject to:

■ The principle of equivalence or non-discrimination, which requires that under national procedural rules claims based on EU law must not be treated less favourably than similar domestic claims;

■ The principle of effectiveness, which requires that the application of domestic rules and procedures must not render the protection of individuals' EU rights practically impossible or excessively difficult;

■ The requirement that, if an equivalent remedy does not exist under national law, a new damages remedy must be created by a Member State (Joined Cases C-6/90 and C-9/90 *Francovich and Bonifaci v Italian State*);

■ The requirement that national law must be interpreted in conformity with EU law (Case 14/83 *Von Colson*).

The liable party

A Member State is liable regardless of the organ of the Member State (legislative, executive or administrative) whose act or omission infringed EU law. Thus, a Member State may be liable for damage caused to an individual by a manifest infringement of EU law attributable to a supreme court of that Member State (Case C-224/01 *Köbler*, Case C-173/03 *Traghetti*) or for wrongful acts of its organs or its officials when they act beyond their capacity but to all appearances as competent officials or organs (Case C-470/03 *AGM COS.MET*).

RECOMMENDED READING

Book

Hofstötter, B., *Non-Compliance of National Courts: Remedies in European Community Law and Beyond*, 2005, The Hague: Asser Press

Articles

Beutler,B., 'State liability for breaches of Community law by national courts: Is the requirement of a manifest infringement of the applicable law an insurmountable obstacle?' (2009) 46 CMLRev, p 773

Briza, P., "Lucchini SpA – Is There Anything Left of the *Res Judicata* Principle?" (2008) 27(1) CJQ, p 40 (Comment on Case C-119/05 Ministero dell'Industria del Commercio e dell'Artigianato v Lucchini SpA)

Granger, M.-P. F., "National Applications of Francovich and the Construction of a European Adminstrative *Ius Commune*", ELRev 2007, 32(2), p 157

Meltzer, D. J., "Member State Liability in Europe and the United States", (2006) 4 Int'l J. Const. L, p 39

15

ENFORCEMENT OF EU LAW – ACTIONS AGAINST MEMBER STATES

SUMMARY

1. This chapter examines the main actions aimed at ensuring compliance by Member States with their EU obligations. The fact that the EU can enforce compliance with its rules through effective sanctions against a Member State in breach of its obligations confers a unique status on EU law. The effectiveness of its enforcement mechanisms far exceeds that of public international law.

2. The most important and most frequently used action is provided for and defined in Article 258 TFEU. It allows the Commission to bring proceedings against a Member State for failure to fulfil an obligation under the Treaties. The Commission, as the "guardian of the Treaties", has a wide discretion and can set aside the proceedings at any stage, or continue them even if a defaulting Member State has terminated the breach but did so after the expiry of the time limit fixed in the reasoned opinion.

A. To ensure effectiveness of Article 258 TFEU, the ECJ has construed the notion of failure broadly. Such a failure may result from an action, an omission or a failure to act by a Member State.

B. The defendant in the proceedings is a Member State and it is a national government which appears before the ECJ. A Member State may be held responsible for a failure attributable to any national body, including a national parliament, its judiciary, any private or semi-private body which it controls as well as actions of private individuals if it was in a position to prevent or terminate the conduct which breached EU law.

C. The obligation which a Member State has allegedly failed to fulfil must be well determined, in that Article 258 TFEU requires that a Member State must be in breach of a specific and precise obligation, which exists at the time the Commission starts the Article 258 TFEU procedure.

D. The procedure itself reflects the philosophy of Article 258 TFEU, that is, that the action should not be brought unless there is no other possibility of enforcing EU law. The use of non-contentious means in the proceedings under Article 258 TFEU constitutes one of its dominant features. Two phases can be identified in the procedure: the informal phase and the formal phase. During the informal stage, the Commission invites the Member State concerned to provide explanations, comments and relevant information with a view to discussing and settling the matter. If this fails, the Commission may proceed to the formal stage consisting of an administrative phase and a judicial phase. During the administrative phase the Commission continues the dialogue with the Member State concerned, and if necessary issues a letter of formal notice, which defines the subject-matter of the dispute and sets a reasonable period in which the alleged failure must be corrected. If, after the expiry of that period, the Member State persists in its failure, the Commission may issue a reasoned opinion, setting out the legal arguments supporting its view that the Member State has failed its obligations arising out of the Treaties, fixing a new time limit within which the alleged breach must be remedied, and indicating appropriate measures which should be taken to remedy the breach. If the Member State concerned still persists in its failure, the Commission may bring proceedings before the ECJ.

E. The ECJ will dismiss an application under Article 258 TFEU if the Commission has not complied with the procedural requirements imposed by that provision. In particular:

  ▪ If the time limit fixed by the Commission either in the letter of formal notice or in the reasoned opinion is not reasonable;
  ▪ If the complaints and legal arguments in the application under Article 258 TFEU are not identical to those invoked in the letter of formal notice and the reasoned opinion;
  ▪ If the Commission has failed to indicate what measures the Member State is required to take in order to comply with its obligation.

  As to defences which a Member State may invoke, other than as above, they are rarely successful. This is mainly because the ECJ has, on the one hand, rejected defences recognised under public international law, such as reciprocity and necessity, as being unsuitable to the EU legal order, and, on the other hand, restrictively interpreted circumstances likely to exonerate a defaulting Member State.

3. Actions under Article 259 TFEU, where one Member State decides to bring proceedings before the ECJ against another Member State, are rare. This is because the political implications of such an action may damage friendly relations between the Member States involved. Consequently, Member States prefer that the Commission acts against the defaulting State under Article 258 TFEU.

4. A judgment of the ECJ declaring a failure of a Member State to fulfil a Treaty obligation is declaratory in nature. The defaulting Member State is required to take all necessary measures to comply with that judgment within the shortest possible period.

5. The Commission may request that the ECJ impose pecuniary sanctions on the defaulting Member State in the following situations:

■ If a Member State fails to comply with a judgment of the ECJ declaring that Member State in breach of EU law, the Commission may bring proceedings for the imposition of pecuniary sanctions. To that effect the Commission may start new proceedings under Article 258 TFEU. However, the ToL removes the requirement that the Commission submits to the defaulting Member State a "reasoned opinion". This considerably speeds up the new proceedings. Nevertheless, Article 260(2) ensures that the Member State concerned has the opportunity to submit its observation before the Commission commences Article 260(2) proceedings.

■ Under Article 260(2) TFEU the Commission may, in its application to the ECJ which asks for a finding of failure, when a Member State has failed to notify to it measures transposing a directive adopted under a legislative procedure, request the ECJ to impose a pecuniary penalty. In such a situation the Commission is not required to wait until a Member State concerned fails to comply with a judgment of the ECJ to propose a pecuniary penalty.

The Commission is required to propose the amount of penalty, but the ECJ is not bound by it. The amount of penalty – which may take the form of a lump sum, a daily payment or both – depends on the seriousness of the breach, the duration and the need to ensure that the penalty is a deterrent to further infringements. However, when the Commission asks for the imposition of a pecuniary penalty in its application for a finding of a failure to notify to it measures transposing a directive, and the ECJ finds that there has been an infringement, the ECJ may impose the financial penalty proposed by the Commission but the amount of such penalty should not exceed that specified by the Commission. The Member State concerned has an obligation to pay on the date set by the ECJ in its judgment.

15.1 Introduction

The availability of an action for failure to fulfil an obligation arising from the Treaties, which may be brought against a defaulting Member State, enhances the originality of the EU legal order. The fact that the EU can enforce compliance with its rules through effective sanctions against a Member State which is in breach of its obligation confers a unique status on EU law.

A comparison between public international law and EU law in respect of Member State responsibility for infringement of its international obligations demonstrates that there are a number of features which enhance the originality of EU law:

■ First, in Case 7/71 *Commission v France*[819] the ECJ held that the liability of a Member State is not, for the purposes of enforcement procedures, conditional upon the existence of loss suffered by another Member State.

---

819. [1971] ECR 1003.

■ Second, the principle of public international law under which no liability is placed upon a Member State unless it is at fault is rejected by EU law. In Case 25/59 *The Netherlands v High Authority*[820] the ECJ held that an action under Article 258 TFEU aims at ensuring that the interests of the EU prevail over the inertia and resistance of a Member State.

■ Third, some defences which a Member State may plead under public international law have been rejected by the ECJ as being incompatible with the EU legal order.[821]

■ Fourth, an action for failure to fulfil a Treaty obligation may have a broad context: in that the judgment of the ECJ is not only rendered against the defaulting Member State, but often also determines the exact scope of an obligation imposed upon that Member State.[822] This accords with the fact that uniformity in the application of EU law constitutes one of the main objectives of the enforcement action under Article 258 TFEU.

■ Fifth, the peculiarity of the EU legal order is emphasised by the Commission's powers to initiate proceedings against a defaulting Member State in its role as the "guardian of the Treaties". Article 17(1) TEU specifies that the Commission "shall oversee the application of Union law under the control of the CJEU". Thus, contrary to the rules of public international law, an EU institution, and not the other Member States,[823] has the principle responsibility for ensuring that the Member States comply with EU law.

■ Sixth, the ECJ has exclusive, mandatory and unreserved jurisdiction in all types of actions for failure by a Member State to fulfil an obligation. Under Article 344 TFEU the ECJ has exclusive jurisdiction to settle disputes between Member States concerning the interpretation or application of the Treaties.[824]

■ Seventh, the system of pecuniary sanctions which may be imposed upon a defaulting Member State, which refuses to comply with a judgment of the ECJ, or which has been found by the ECJ in breach of its obligation to notify measures transposing a directive adopted in accordance with legislative procedures to the Commission, constitutes a forceful means to bring about a change in that Member State's conduct. For the first time in Case C-387/97 *Commission v Greece*[825] the ECJ ordered a Member State to pay €20,000 per day of non-compliance with its judgment. The purpose of the imposition of financial penalties is not to seek to punish the defaulting Member State but to induce it to comply with the judgment of the ECJ and, in a wider context, to reduce the possibility of similar breaches being committed again.

---

820. [1960] ECR 355.
821. For example the defence based on necessity in Case 7/61 *Commission v Italy* [1961] ECR 317, or reciprocity in Joined Cases 90 and 91/63 *Commission v Belgium and Luxembourg* [1964] ECR 625; Case 232/78 *Commission v France* [1979] ECR 2729.
822. Case 7/71 *Commission v France* [1971] ECR 1003.
823. Under Article 259 TFEU Member States are also empowered to bring an action against each other for an alleged breach of EU law but only after the matter has been laid before the Commission.
824. See Case C-459/03 *Commission v Ireland* [2006] ECR I-4635.
825. [2000] ECR I-5047.

The jurisdiction of the ECJ in respect of actions for failure to fulfil obligations has been extended under the ToL. The ECJ has, in addition to the pre-ToL jurisdiction over the law of the European Community, gained jurisdiction over all of the area of FSJ. However, in respect of measures concerning police and judicial co-operation in criminal matters (i.e. Framework decisions) adopted prior to the entry into force of the ToL, Protocol 9 on Transitional Provisions attached to the Treaties establishes special rules. It shields them from the jurisdiction of the ECJ and from enforcement action of the Commission under Article 258 TFEU for a period of five years after the entry into force of the ToL. If any such measure is amended before the expiry of that period then that measure will be within the powers of EU institutions from the time of amendment.

It is to be noted that some provisions of the Treaties provide for simplified proceedings against a Member State who has failed to fulfil its obligations deriving from the Treaties. The common point of these procedures is the possibility for the Commission or a Member State to bring the matter directly before the ECJ in a much shorter period of time than under Article 258 or 259 TFEU. Usually the administrative stage takes a different, simplified form, and the Commission is not bound to deliver a reasoned opinion. Those procedures are described, inter alia, in Articles 108(2), 114(9) and 348 TFEU and include the Rapid Intervention Mechanism examined in Chapter 20.12.

15.2 Action against a Member State by the Commission under Article 258 TFEU

Article 258 TFEU states:

> "If the Commission considers that a Member State has failed to fulfil an obligation under the Treaties, it shall deliver a reasoned opinion on the matter after giving the State concerned the opportunity to submit its observations.
>
> If the State concerned does not comply with the opinion within the period laid down by the Commission, the latter may bring the matter before the Court of Justice of the European Union."

The case law of the ECJ has clarified terms used in Article 258 TFEU, in particular it has defined:

- The notion of "failure of a Member State to fulfil an obligation under the Treaties";

- The concept of a Member State as a defendant;

- The kind of obligation which is likely to give rise to an action under Article 258 TFEU.

Article 258 TFEU sets out a procedure to be followed by the Commission, which gives the Member State an opportunity, on the one hand, of remedying the breach before the action is brought before the ECJ, and on the other hand, to present its defence to the Commission's complaint. If the Commission still considers that a Member State is in breach of its obligation, it may institute proceedings before the ECJ. At the judicial stage, it is extremely difficult for a Member State to justify its failure to comply with EU law. Various imaginative defences have been pleaded, and the great majority of them have been summarily rejected by the ECJ.

The above topics are dealt with below.

15.2.1   Definition of a failure of a Member State to fulfil an obligation under the Treaties

A failure by a Member State to fulfil an obligation is assessed in the light of the nature and scope of that obligation[826] and may result from an action, or from an omission, or a failure to act.[827] In Case 301/81 *Commission v Belgium*,[828] the ECJ held that in order to constitute a failure to fulfil an obligation it is not necessary to prove opposition, or inertia, on the part of a Member State.

The failure under Article 258 TFEU:

■ May consist of some action taken by a Member State, such as the application of national law incompatible with EU law, the adoption of a legislative act contrary to EU law,[829] or an express refusal to fulfil an obligation imposed by EU law. In Case C-459/03 *Commission v Ireland*,[830] the ECJ found Ireland in breach of Article 226 EC [258 TFEU], when Ireland brought proceedings against the UK before an arbitration tribunal established in accordance with the dispute settlement procedure set out under the UN Convention on the Law of the Sea, without having first informed and consulted the relevant EU institutions. The Court ruled that the provisions of the Convention invoked by Ireland were part of Community law, as a result of transfer of these matters to the Community, and consequently the ECJ had exclusive jurisdiction to deal with any disputes relating to their interpretation or application.

■ May arise from a failure to act. In many cases under Article 226 EC [258 TFEU] the Commission initiated proceedings against a Member State for non-implementation of EU directives within the prescribed time limit. Under the ToL, the Commission's powers to force Member States to implement EU directives have been strengthened in that under Article 260(3) TFEU the Commission may propose the imposition of pecuniary penalties in the initial infringement proceedings, i.e. in its application to the ECJ in which it asks for a finding of a failure.

In respect of an administrative practice contrary to EU law, such a practice must be, to some degree, of a consistent and general nature in order to amount to a failure to fulfil obligations for the purposes of Article 258 TFEU.[831] Such a practice can give rise to Article 258 TFEU proceedings, even if the applicable national law itself complies with EU law.[832]

15.2.2   Member States as defendants

Proceedings under Article 258 are brought against the defaulting Member State. The failure within the meaning of Article 258 TFEU arises regardless of the national body which is at the origin of the action or inaction.

---

826.   Case 31/69 *Commission v Italy* [1970] ECR 25.
827.   Case C-265/95 *Commission v France* [1997] ECR I-6959.
828.   [1983] ECR 467.
829.   Case C-157/89 *Commission v Italy* [1991] ECR I-57.
830.   [2006] ECR I-4635.
831.   Case C-387/99 *Commission v Germany* [2004] ECR I-3751; Case C-494/01 *Commission v Ireland* [2005] ECR I-3331; Case C-287/03 *Commission v Belgium* [2005] ECR I-3761.
832.   Case C-278/03 *Commission v Italy* [2005] ECR I-3747; Case C-441/02 *Commission v Germany* [2006] ECR I-3449.

15.2.2.1 Constitutionally independent branches of the Member State

In Case 77/69 *Commission v Belgium*,[833] the ECJ held that a Member State is liable for a failure attributable to its constitutionally independent body. In this case, the Belgian government[834] tried to plead in its defence the independence of the Belgian parliament, which could not be forced by the government to adopt a required legislative act. The ECJ answered that:

"... the liability of a Member State under Article [258 TFEU] arises whatever the agency of the State whose action or inaction is the cause of the failure to fulfil its obligations, even in the case of a constitutionally independent institution."

In Cases 227–230/85 *Commission v Belgium*,[835] the ECJ emphasised that the national division of competences between central and regional authorities which, especially in the context of a federal state, may result in a large measure of autonomy being conferred on the local or regional authorities, would not constitute a sufficient defence for a Member State, even if the local or regional authorities are solely empowered to implement necessary local legislation, and have failed to do so.

15.2.2.2 Private or semi-public bodies

A failure to fulfil an obligation under the Treaty by any private or semi-public body, which is controlled by a Member State, is imputable to that Member State.

In Case 249/81 *Commission v Ireland [Re Buy Irish Campaign]*,[836] Ireland was held liable for financing through the Irish Goods Council, a government sponsored body, a campaign to "Buy Irish" which promoted Irish products to the disadvantage of imports, although the Irish Goods Council could not adopt binding measures and the campaign was a failure.

15.2.2.3 A Member State's judiciary

It results from the case law of the ECJ that a Member State is liable under Article 258 TFEU if the failure is imputable to its court or a tribunal.

In Case C-129/00 *Commission v Italy*,[837] the Commission complained that the Italian Supreme Court (Corte Suprema di Cassazione) was mainly responsible for erroneous interpretation of Community law, which interpretation had been followed by a substantial proportion of Italian courts. The ECJ declared that Italy was in breach of EC law by failing to amend the relevant legislation, which was construed and applied by the Italian courts including its Supreme Court, in a manner inconsistent with EC law. In his Advisory Opinion delivered in this case Advocate General Geelhoed emphasised the relevance of the judgment of the ECJ in Case C-224/01 *Gerhard Köbler v Austria*[838] to the procedure under Article 226 EC [258 TFEU] (see Chapter 14.4).

---

833. [1970] ECR 237; also Case 8/70 *Commission v Italy* [1970] ECR 961.
834. The term "government" means the executive.
835. [1988] ECR 1; see also Case C-57/89 *Commission v Germany* [1991] ECR I-883; Case C-47/99 *Commission v Luxembourg* [1999] ECR I-8999.
836. [1982] ECR 4005.
837. [2003] ECR I-14637.
838. [2003] ECR I-10239.

He suggested the application of the following criteria to decide whether or not judicial decisions of national courts incompatible with EU law amount to a failure on the part of a Member State to fulfil its obligations under the Treaties. They are as follows:

- Whether judgments incompatible with EU law delivered by national courts adjudicating at last instance are regarded by inferior courts as a judicial authority in the national legal order;

- Whether judicial decisions contrary to EU law are important in numerical terms and in terms of their judicial authority, that is, for example are not isolated or numerically insignificant judicial decisions and have been confirmed by supreme courts in appeal proceedings;

- How substantial is the impact of judicial decisions incompatible with EU law on the achievement of the objectives sought by EU law which have been infringed by national decisions incompatible with it. In particular, whether judicial decisions incompatible with EU law produce harmful effects in respect of economic operators who have to carry out their economic activities in more difficult conditions than their competitors or other persons who are in a similar situation in other Member States.

It seems that the Commission's reluctance to initiate proceedings against a Member State for breach of EU law by its highest courts is a thing of the past.[839] In Case C-154/08 *Commission v Spain*,[840] the Commission brought proceedings against Spain for the infringement of EU law by its Supreme Court which erroneously interpreted the Sixth VAT Directive, Directive 77/388/EEC. The Spanish Supreme Court had no doubt as to the interpretation of the Directive and thus did not make a preliminary ruling to the ECJ. The three criteria stated above were satisfied, in that the judgment of the Spanish Supreme Court was followed by the Spanish national tax administration and other Spanish courts, and had considerable impact on economic operators in Spain. The Spanish Government argued that, as the independence of the Spanish Supreme Court was protected by the Spanish Constitution, it could not remedy the breach. The ECJ swiftly rejected this line of defence by stating that, in accordance with its earlier case law, in particular Case C-219/00 *Commission v Italy*, a Member State may be held responsible for action or inaction of any of its agencies including a constitutionally independent institution such as its supreme court. For the first time ever, the ECJ declared that a Member State was in breach of EU law as a result of a Supreme Court judgment. Neither in *Köbler*, nor in Case C-129/00 *Commission v Italy* (above), nor in Case C-173/03 *Traghetti del Mediterranes SpA (TDM) v Italy*,[841] did the ECJ make any direct statements condemning the highest national courts for their failure to comply with EU law. Therefore the importance of the judgment in Case C-154/08 *Commission v Spain* is that the ECJ condemned the ruling of the supreme court of a Member State itself and not the conduct of the national administration based on an erroneous ruling of a supreme court as occurred in Case C-129/00 *Commission v Italy*. The implication of Case C-154/08 *Commission v Spain* is that the

---

839. The Commission initiated proceedings against the French Cour de Cassation and the German Bundesfinanzhof (the highest court in financial matters), but both cases were settled. See question EQ No. 1907/85 [1986] OJ C137/7.
840. Judgment of 12/11/09 (nyr).
841. [2006] ECR I-5177.

Commission may bring proceedings against a Member State once a national court of last instance closes a case and gets it wrong. The above judgment should be applauded but one wonders to what extent the initiation of proceedings under Article 258 TFEU against a supreme court of a Member State, which inevitably undermines the authority of the court in question, may damage the spirit of co-operation between the ECJ and national courts and thus, whether, in the long run, it may produce more harm than good.

It is important to note that in Case C-154/08 *Commission v Spain*, the ECJ seems to approve the criteria set out by Advocate General Geelhoed in *Köbler* (see above) when it stated that isolated or numerically insignificant judicial decisions which have not been confirmed by supreme courts in appeal proceedings may not necessarily amount to a failure on the part of a Member State to fulfil its obligations under the Treaties.

15.2.2.4 Private individuals

A Member State may be responsible for actions of its nationals, if it is in a position to prevent or terminate such an action. In Case C-265/95 *Commission v France*[842] the ECJ found France liable for not taking all measures necessary to prevent its citizens from obstructing the free movement of fruits and vegetables within the internal market (see Chapter 20.2.4).

15.2.3 Determination of the kind of obligation which is likely to give rise to an action under Article 258 TFEU

Failure to fulfil an obligation under the Treaties entails that there is an obligation imposed by the Treaties. The obligation must be well determined, that is, Article 258 TFEU requires that a Member State must be in breach of a pre-existing, specific and precise obligation.[843]

The term "an obligation under this Treaty" is widely interpreted. It comprises obligations imposed:

- By the Treaties, protocols, annexes and all other primary sources;

- By EU secondary legislation – regulations,[844] decisions[845] and directives;[846]

- By binding acts, not expressly mentioned in Article 289 TFEU,[847] adopted by EU institutions;

- By international agreements concluded between the EU and third countries which by virtue of Article 216(2) TFEU "are binding upon institutions of the Union and on Member States".[848] In Case C-239/03 *Commission v France*,[849] the ECJ confirmed that Member States

---

842. [1997] ECR I-6959.
843. Case 7/71 *Commission v France* [1971] ECR 1003.
844. Case 33/69 *Commission v Italy* [1970] ECR 93; Case 8/70 *Commission v Italy* [1970] ECR 961.
845. Cases 6 and 11/69 *Commission v France* [1969] ECR 523.
846. The majority of proceedings under Article 258 TFEU concern EU Directives.
847. Case 141/78 *France v UK* [1979] ECR 2923.
848. Case 104/81 *Kaupferberg* [1982] ECR 3641; Cases 194 and 241/85 *Commission v Greece* [1988] ECR 1037; Case C-228/91 *Commission v Italy* [1993] ECR I-2701.
849. [2004] ECR I-9325.

are obliged to comply with obligations arising from mixed agreements, that is, agreements concluded jointly by the Community and its Member States with non-Member States in the areas in which the EC and the Member States share competences. The ECJ ruled that mixed agreements have the same status as purely community agreements in so far as their provisions are within the scope of Community competences.[850]

Non-compliance by a Member State with a ruling of the ECJ under Article 258 TFEU constitutes a breach of EU law by that Member State, which is dealt with under Article 260 TFEU.

15.2.3.1   General principles of EU law

It is submitted that the failure of a Member State to fulfil its obligations arising from general principles of EU law may also give rise to liability of a Member State under Article 258 TFEU:

- First, the ECJ has underlined in many cases that general principles of EU law form an integral part of EU law.

- Second, general principles may be invoked in proceedings against EU institutions, bodies, offices and agencies under Articles 263 TFEU, 265 and 340(2) TFEU. By analogy, the Commission should be allowed to rely upon them to bring proceedings against a Member State under Article 258 TFEU.

- Third, in Case C-260/89 *ERT*,[851] the ECJ held that the general principles of EU law are binding on the EU institutions and on the Member States when acting within the scope of EU law.

So far as the author is aware, no case has been brought against a Member State on this basis.

15.2.3.2   Obligations arising from Article 4(3) TEU [Article 10 EC]

Article 4(3) TEU provides that:

"Pursuant to the principle of sincere cooperation, the Union and the Member States shall, in full mutual respect, assist each other in carrying out tasks which flow from the Treaties.

The Member States shall take any appropriate measure, general or particular, to ensure fulfilment of the obligations arising out of the Treaties or resulting from the acts of the institutions of the Union.

The Member States shall facilitate the achievement of the Union's tasks and refrain from any measure which could jeopardise the attainment of the Union's objectives."

Article 4(3) first indent expressly recognises the principle of mutual sincere co-operation which has always been implied. Indents 2 and 3 of Article 4(3) TEU contain a revised version of Article 10 EC, which has been successfully used as a legal basis by the Commission in actions for failure to fulfil obligations.

---

850.   See, to that effect, Case 12/86 *Demirel* [1987] ECR 3719 and Case C-13/00 *Commission v Ireland* [2002] ECR I-2943.

851.   [1991] ECR I-2925.

Initially, Article 10 EC was considered to be an interpretive device requiring Member States to act in good faith. Gradually, its scope of application has been extended:

- First, Article 10 EC has served to strengthen the binding effect of Community obligations imposed upon the Member States.

- Second, the ECJ has imposed, by virtue of Article 10 EC, the obligation on national courts to interpret national law in conformity with Community law.

- Third, Article 10 EC has become an independent and autonomous source of obligation. As a result, a breach of Article 10 EC [Article 4(3) TEU indents 2 and 3] gives rise to liability of the Member States under Article 226 EC [Article 258 TFEU].

In Case C-137/91 *Commission v Greece [Re Electronic Cash Registers]*[852] the ECJ explained the autonomous function of Article 10 EC [Article 4(3) TEU indents 2 and 3].

THE FACTS WERE:

Greek law enacted in 1988 required the use of electronic cash registers by certain retailers. However, the approval of such registers was conducted by national authorities, which refused to certify any register containing less than 35 per cent "add-on value" from Greece. Other Member States complained to the Commission that this policy was contrary to the free movement of goods. During the investigation the Commission sent two faxes to the Greek Permanent Representation in Brussels asking for more information. None came. The Commission considered that lack of response constituted an infringement of Article 10 EC. In those circumstances, the Commission issued a formal notice under Article 226 EC [Article 258 TFEU] against Greece, but the latter did not submit any observation on the alleged incompatibility of Greek law with Community law. Finally, the Commission delivered its reasoned opinion. No reply was received by the Commission, which then decided to bring proceedings before the ECJ.

The Government of Greece challenged the Commission proceedings. It claimed that it gave the Commission all necessary information concerning the legislation in question at a meeting in Athens in September 1990 and a year later sent the Commission the text of a new Act. According to the Greek Government there was no reason for providing additional information required by the Commission as the latter was fully aware of the situation before the action under Article 226 EC [258 TFEU] was brought. The Commission argued that the Greek Government provided the required information two years after it was requested and that at that stage the time limit fixed by the reasoned opinion had elapsed.

Held:

The ECJ held that Greece had violated Article 10 EC [Article 4(3) indents 2 and 3 TEU]. The ECJ stated that "the failure to reply to the Commission's questions within a reasonable period made the task which it has to perform more difficult and therefore amounts to a violation of the obligation of co-operation laid down in Article [10 EC]".

---

852.   [1992] ECR I-4023.

It emerges from the case law of the ECJ that Article 10 EC [Article 4(3) indents 2 and 3 TEU] imposes a positive duty on Member States to co-operate with the Commission in its investigations into alleged violations of EU law. Failure to do so is in itself sufficient to give rise to liability of a Member State under Article 258 TFEU,[853] regardless of whether a Member State refuses, or simply ignores the request of the Commission for information,[854] or omits to forward necessary indications allowing the Commission to exercise its role of "guardian of the Treaties",[855] or otherwise violates its obligation of loyal co-operation.[856]

Perhaps the strongest ever condemnation of a Member State for failure to co-operate with the Commission was pronounced by the ECJ in Case C-82/03 *Commission v Italy*.[857] The ECJ shared the frustration of the Commission concerning the lack of co-operation on the part of Italy. The Court stated that: "Article 10 EC [Article 4(3) indents 2 and 3 TEU] makes it clear that the Member States are required to cooperate in good faith with the enquiries of the Commission pursuant to Article 226 EC [258 TFEU], and to provide the Commission with all the information requested for that purpose". The ECJ concluded that the persistent silence of the Italian Government, and its refusal to forward information requested by the Commission, were contrary to the spirit and the wording of Article 10 EC [Article 4(3) indents 2 and 3 TEU] and as such amounted to failure to fulfil its obligations.

15.2.4 The procedure which the Commission must observe in the pursuance of its tasks under Article 258 TFEU

The Commission is the master of proceedings under Article 258 TFEU. It enjoys a broad discretion and may stop proceedings at any stage. The Article 258 TFEU procedure consists of an informal phase and a formal stage. The latter comprises an administrative and a judicial stage.

15.2.4.1 Informal phase

In the informal phase the Commission enjoys a double discretion:

- First, it decides whether or not a Member State is in breach of an obligation; and

- Second, it assesses various aspects of the situation in question, especially by placing it in the political context, in order to determine whether to commence proceedings against the defaulting Member State.

In many cases the Commission may decide not to act when faced with sensitive political issues. For example, the UK was in breach of EC law for more than 20 years by not introducing national

---

853. See also Case C-33/90 *Commission v Italy* [1991] ECR I-5987; Case C-65/91 *Commission v Greece* [1992] ECR I-5245.

854. Case 272/86 *Commission v Greece* [1988] ECR 4875; Case C-375/92 *Commission v Spain* [1994] ECR I-923.

855. For example, Case C-40/92 *Commission v UK* [1994] ECR I-989.

856. For example, in Case C-459/03 *Commission v Ireland* [2006] ECR I-4635, Ireland was in breach of Article 10 EC [Article 4(3) TFEU] for bringing proceedings against the UK under the dispute settlement procedure laid down in the UN Convention on the Law of the Sea, without informing and consulting the relevant Community institutions, and for ignoring the Commission's request to suspend these proceedings.

857. [2004] ECR I-6635.

legislation required by the ECJ subsequent to its ruling in *Van Duyn*.[858] Advocate General Roemer in Case 7/71 *Commission v France*[859] suggested that in certain circumstances the Commission should abstain from initiating proceedings under Article 226 EC [Article 258 TFEU], i.e:

▪ When there is a possibility of reaching a settlement;

▪ When the effect of the breach of EU law is minor;

▪ When the proceedings of the Commission would exacerbate a major political crisis in the defaulting Member State, especially in the context of a minor violation of EU law by that Member State; and

▪ When there is a possibility that the provision in question would be modified or annulled in the near future.

All complaints of breaches of EU obligations are registered by the General Secretariat of the Commission, and are the subject of reports concerning the situation of the alleged violations of the Treaties. These reports are periodically examined by the chief of the private office, or Cabinet, of each commissioner, and their observations are forwarded to the Commission. Once there is sufficient evidence that a Member State is in breach of EU law, the appropriate Directorate General commences proceedings.

At the informal stage the Commission invites the Member State concerned to provide some explanations and the Member State is reminded that it has an obligation to co-operate under Article 4(3) indents 2 and 3 TEU.[860] The request for information takes the form of a "letter pre-258 proceedings". It fixes a time limit for the reply. Usually the Commission and representatives of the Member State discuss the matter. Sometimes the negotiations between them take a considerable amount of time; sometimes both parties will settle the matter immediately. The length of time spent during the informal phase is of some importance, especially when the Commission decides to take formal proceedings against the defaulting Member State. Usually the longer the period of time spent on the informal proceedings, the more easily the ECJ will accept a short deadline for compliance imposed by the Commission in the formal proceedings.

The existence of informal proceedings emphasises the non-punitive nature of Article 258 TFEU. The objective of the provision is to terminate the violation of EU law, and not to exacerbate the dispute. However, if no settlement is possible, the Commission will start the formal phase.

15.2.4.2 Administrative stage (Pre-litigation procedure)

The pre-litigation procedure fulfils two main objectives: it gives the Member State concerned the opportunity to comply with its obligations under EU law, and to avail itself of its right to defend itself against charges formulated by the Commission.[861] During the pre-litigation procedure the Commission is required to perform two acts, that is, sending the letter of formal notice and preparing the reasoned opinion.

---

858. The violation was finally rectified by the Immigration (European Economic Area) Order 1994, SI 1994 no. 1895.
859. [1971] ECR 1003.
860. Case 147/77 *Commission v Italy* [1978] ECR 1307.
861. Case 293/85 *Commission v Belgium* [1988] ECR 305; Case C-439/99 *Commission v Italy* [2002] ECR I-305; Case C-431/02 *Commission v UK* (judgment of 12/10/2004, unpublished).

15.2.4.2.1 Letter of formal notice

In Case 51/83 *Commission v Italy*,[862] the ECJ held that the letter of formal notice constitutes an essential formal requirement under Article 258 TFEU and its omission would result in the inadmissibility of an action under this Article.

The letter of formal notice determines the scope of the case and cannot be widened, even at the stage of the reasoned opinion.[863] It invites a defaulting Member State to submit its observation on the disputed matters. It guarantees the right of defence to the Member State concerned, although the Member State is not obliged to reply. Usually the Commission gives a defaulting Member State two months to reply, but in urgent matters this time limit may be shortened.

The procedure may be terminated if the Commission is convinced that, in the light of the explanations provided by the Member State, there is no violation of EU law, or if the failure is corrected immediately. Otherwise, after the expiry of the time limit fixed in the letter of formal notice, the Commission will normally issue a reasoned opinion.

15.2.4.2.2 Reasoned opinion

The main difference between the letter of formal notice and the reasoned opinion is that the former "is intended to define the subject-matter of the dispute and to indicate to the Member State ... the factors enabling it to prepare its defence",[864] while in the reasoned opinion the Commission must establish the legal arguments in respect of the alleged failure of a Member State to fulfil its obligation under the Treaties.[865]

The reasoned opinion must contain a cogent and detailed exposition of the reasons which led the Commission to the conclusion that a Member State has failed to fulfil its obligation under the Treaties.[866]

The reasoned opinion invites the defaulting Member State to cease the infringement and indicates the appropriate measures that should be taken to that end.[867] It also fixes a time limit for the Member State concerned to comply – usually two months, but in urgent cases this period may be shortened. The time limit cannot be changed by the ECJ,[868] although it will be taken into account when the ECJ determines whether the Commission had given a "reasonable time" to comply with the reasoned opinion. In Case 74/82 *Commission v Ireland*,[869] the ECJ viewed with disapproval the period of five days given in the reasoned opinion to Ireland to amend its legislation, which had been in force for more than forty years. There was no urgency and this period was considered by the ECJ as unreasonable, although the action was not dismissed. The ECJ took into consideration the fact that the Commission issued its reasoned opinion on 9 November 1981 and referred to the ECJ on 19 February 1982, which means that the Irish had two and a half months to deal with the matter, and took the view that in the light of this a period of five days was not

---

862. [1984] ECR 2793.

863. Case 51/83 *Commission v Italy* [1984] ECR 2793.

864. Case 51/83 *Commission v Italy* [1984] ECR 2793.

865. In Case 7/61 *Commission v Italy [Re Pigmeat case]* [1961] ECR 317 the ECJ held that "the opinion referred to in Article [226] of the Treaty [Article 258 TFEU] must . . . contain a sufficient statement of reasons to satisfy the law".

866. Case C-207/96 *Commission v Italy* [1997] ECR I-6869; Case C-439/99 *Commission v Italy* [2002] ECR I-305.

867. Case 7/61 *Commission v Italy* [1961] ECR 317; Case 70/72 *Commission v Germany* [1973] ECR 813.

868. Case 28/81 *Commission v Italy* [1981] ECR 2577; Case 29/81 *Commission v Italy* [1981] ECR 2585.

869. [1984] ECR 317.

unreasonable. Thus, as the Court noted, the Commission's regrettable behaviour did not affect the admissibility of the action.

In Joined Cases 142 and 143/80 *Amministrazione delle Finanze dello Stato v Essevi SpA and Carlo Salengo*,[870] in proceedings under Article 234 EC [267 TFEU], the ECJ held that the Commission is not the final arbitrator as to the determination of the rights and obligations of the Member States. The legality or otherwise of conduct of a Member State can only be appraised by a judgment of the court. Accordingly, even if a Member State has complied with the reasoned opinion, this does not mean that the Member State concerned is immune against future claims that it is still in violation of EU law. However, if the Member State concerned complies with the reasoned opinion within the prescribed time limit, the Commission is barred from bringing proceedings before the ECJ.[871] Otherwise, the Commission may commence the next step in the proceedings under Article 258 TFEU, that is, bring the matter before the ECJ.

The discretion that the Commission enjoys under Article 258 TFEU applies throughout the proceedings, and the ECJ has no jurisdiction to consider whether the exercise of that discretion is appropriate.[872] The wide discretion of the Commission is justified by the fact that under Article 258 TFEU the Commission has no obligation to act.[873]

In Case 7/71 *Commission v France*,[874] the ECJ held that the proceedings under Article 226 EC [258 TFEU] are not confined to a pre-established time limit "since, by reason of its nature and its purpose, this procedure involves a power on the part of the Commission to consider the most appropriate means and time-limits for the purposes of putting an end to any contravention of the Treaty". This aspect of the Commission's discretion is enhanced by the possibility of bringing proceedings against a defaulting Member State, even when the latter has complied with the reasoned opinion but after the expiry of the time limit specified in it.

The issue of whether a Member State has failed to fulfil its obligation is determined by reference to the situation prevailing in that Member State at the end of the time limit set out in the reasoned opinion and not by reference to the time when proceedings were brought before the ECJ.[875] As a result, the Commission may bring proceedings many years after the expiry of the time limit fixed in the reasoned opinion, and irrespective of whether or not the alleged infringement has been brought to an end.[876] In Case 7/61 *Commission v Italy*,[877] the ECJ recognised that the Commission may many years later, have an interest in determining whether a violation of EU law has occurred. In Case 39/72 *Commission v Italy*[878] the ECJ held that its ruling in such a case may be useful, especially in order to establish the basis of the Member State's liability vis-à-vis other Member States, the EU and the individuals concerned. Further, if the Commission decides to bring proceedings many years after the expiry of a deadline specified in the reasoned opinion it

---

870. [1981] ECR 1413.
871. Case C-200/88 *Commission v Greece* [1990] ECR I-4299.
872. Case C-236/99 *Commission v Belgium* [2000] ECR I-5657; Case C-383/00 *Commission v Germany* [2002] ECR I-4219.
873. See Case 48/65 *Alfons Lütticke* [1966] ECR 19 and Chapter 16.4.3.1.
874. [1971] ECR 1003.
875. Case C-143/02 *Commission v Italy* [2003] ECR I-2877; Case C-446/01 *Commission v Spain* [2003] ECR I-6053.
876. Case C-519/03 *Commission v Luxembourg* [2005] ECR I-3067 and Case C-562/07 *Commission v Spain* [judgment of 6/10/09].
877. [1961] ECR 317.
878. [1973] ECR 101.

does not have to show an interest to bring proceedings or to state the reasons why it is bringing an action for failure to fulfil obligations since the subject-matter of the action as it is to be found in the application corresponds to the subject-matter of the dispute as stated in the letter of formal notice and in the reasoned opinion.[879]

It is important to note that neither the formal letter of notice, nor the reasoned opinion, have binding legal effect. For that reason they cannot be challenged under Article 263 TFEU. In Case 48/65 *Alfons Lütticke*[880] the ECJ stated that the reasoned opinion was merely a step in the proceedings.

15.2.5   The procedure before the ECJ

The ECJ will first assess whether the Commission has complied with the procedural requirements imposed by Article 258 TFEU. This is necessary to ensure that a defaulting Member State's rights to defence are protected. The ECJ will dismiss an application under Article 258 TFEU in the following circumstances:

15.2.5.1   *If the time limit fixed by the Commission either in the letter of formal notice or in the reasoned opinion is not reasonable*

In Case 293/85 *Commission v Belgium [Re University Fees]*,[881] which concerned the compliance of Belgium with the ECJ ruling in *Gravier*, Belgium was given only eight days to reply to the letter of formal notice and 15 days to comply with the reasoned opinion. The ECJ held that these time limits were insufficient for Belgium given the complexity of the matter.[882]

The ECJ will take into account many factors in deciding whether or not the time limit fixed by the Commission may be considered as reasonable. In Case 85/85 *Commission v Belgium*,[883] the ECJ held that a period of 15 days was reasonable in the light of the considerable length of time taken by the informal proceedings.

15.2.5.2   *If the complaints and legal arguments in the application under Article 258 TFEU are not identical to those invoked in the letter of formal notice and the reasoned opinion*[884]

The case law of the ECJ demonstrates that historically the Court applied the requirement that the letter of formal notice and the reasoned opinion must contain identical complaints and legal argument rigorously. This was done, on the one hand, to protect the defaulting Member State

---

879.   Case C-333/99 *Commission* v *France* [2001] ECR I-1025; Case C-474/99 *Commission* v *Spain* [2002] ECR I-5293; and Case C-33/04 *Commission* v *Luxembourg* [2005] ECR I-3067.

880.   [1966] ECR 19.

881.   [1988] ECR 305.

882.   In Case 293/83 *Gravier* v *City of Liege* [1989] ECR 593, the ECJ held that the fees (so called "minerval") imposed upon EU nationals studying in Belgium were discriminatory and in breach of Article 49 EC [Article 56 TFEU], which ensures the free movement of services throughout the Community.

883.   [1986] ECR 1149, see also Case 74/82 *Commission* v *Ireland* [1984] ECR 317 already examined in this chapter.

884.   For example, Case C-210/91 *Commission* v *Greece* [1992] ECR I-6735, Case C-157/91 *Commission* v *The Netherlands* [1992] ECR I-5899; Case C-296/92 *Commission* v *Italy* [1994] ECR I-1.

against new complaints and legal arguments of the Commission and, on the other hand, to counterbalance the discretion which the Commission enjoys under Article 226 EC [Article 258 TFEU].[885] However, it seems that the ECJ changed its position in the mid 1990s.[886] In Case C-433/03 *Commission v Germany*,[887] the ECJ stated that it is not necessary that the statement of the subject matter of proceedings set out in the reasoned opinion matches exactly that contained in the application under Article 226 EC [Article 258 TFEU] lodged with the ECJ. What counts is that the subject matter of the proceedings has not been extended or altered in either document.[888] In Case C-433/03 *Commission v Germany*, the Commission added to the strength of its application by referring to the then recent case law relevant to the proceedings. The ECJ agreed that this addition did not change the substance of the complaint and accordingly rejected Germany's argument that the Commission should have sent Germany a further reasoned opinion setting out the recent changes in the case law before starting the infringement proceedings before the ECJ.

15.2.5.3   If the Commission fails to indicate what measures a Member State is required to take in order to comply with its obligation

In Case C-431/02 *Commission v UK*,[889] the Commission in all relevant documents, that is, in the letter of formal notice, in the reasoned opinion and in the application under Article 226 EC [Article 258 TFEU], failed to identify what exact measures the UK was required to take to comply with Directive 75/442/EEC in respect of its implementation in Gibraltar. While acknowledging the physical and legal impossibility of the UK complying with the standards relating to the packaging and labelling of hazardous waste required under the Directive in respect of Gibraltar, the Commission stated that the UK had to find an appropriate solution, but without indicating exactly what that solution might comprise. The ECJ dismissed the action against the UK on the ground that the Commission failed to identify and explain in a cogent and detailed manner what measures the UK was required to take in order to comply with its obligations under the above Directive.

The burden of proof is placed on the Commission. In Case 300/95 *Commission v UK*,[890] the ECJ provided clarification in respect of the Commission's obligation to prove its allegation that a Member State is in breach of Article 258 TFEU.

THE FACTS WERE:

The Commission argued that the United Kingdom was in violation of Article 7 of Council Directive 85/374 on product liability, as it implemented the Directive without transposing its text verbatim. The UK Government argued that it had correctly implemented the Directive

---

885.   Case C-191/95 *Commission v Germany* [1998] ECR I-5449, Case C-365/97 *Commission v Italy* [1999] ECR I-7773.
886.   Case C-375/95 *Commission v Greece* [1997] ECR I-5981; Case C-105/02 *Commission v Germany* [2006] ECR I-9659.
887.   [2005] ECR I-6985.
888.   Case C-279/94 *Commission v Italy* [1997] ECR I-4743; Case C-52/00 *Commission v France* [2002] ECR I-3827; Case C-139/00 *Commission v Spain* [2002] ECR I-6407.
889.   Judgment of 12 October 2004, unpublished.
890.   [1997] ECR I-2649.

given that it is left to the discretion of the Member State to decide as to the form and methods of implementation of directives. What counts is that the objectives of the directive are attained. According to the UK the objectives were attained. The Commission considered that this was not the case, since the British courts had to interpret Article 7 of Directive 85/374 contra legem in order to achieve the objectives of that directive.

Held:

The ECJ rejected the application submitted by the Commission. The ECJ held that in order to assess the scope of national legislative or administrative provisions, the Commission must take into account the way that national courts interpret those provisions in practice. Thus, the Commission must not only establish that a Member State is in breach of EC law, but must also prove that national courts, in practice, interpret the provision in question contrary to EC law.

The ECJ reminded the Commission that in order to establish the failure of a Member State to fulfil its obligations, the Commission could not base its application under Article 226 EC [Article 258 TFEU] on a supposition or a simple allegation.[891]

Comment:

It seems that the ECJ has established a presumption that national courts interpret national law in conformity with EU law, which is, in any event, required under EC law.[892]

It is submitted that the ECJ's dicta, which confers on national courts the role of the guardian of EU law, is contrary to the principle of legal certainty, especially when national courts have to interpret a provision of national law which implements EU law contra legem in order to attain the objectives required by a directive.

In the judicial stage the ECJ fully investigates the merits of the case, and the Member State may invoke new arguments in its defence.[893] The ECJ decides the matter taking into consideration the situation as it was at the expiry of the time limit fixed in the reasoned opinion[894] and it cannot take account of any subsequent changes.[895] Obviously in some cases, changes in national legislation between the expiry of the period of compliance fixed by the reasoned opinion and the lodging of an application with the ECJ may be so fundamental as to render the judgment of the ECJ otiose. This occurred in Case C-177/03 *Commission v France*,[896] in which the ECJ emphasised that:

"In such situations, it may be preferable for the Commission not to bring an action but to issue a

---

891. Case C-62/89 *Commission v France* [1990] ECR I-925; Case C-159/94 *Commission v France* [1997] ECR I-5815; Case C-431/02 *Commission v UK* (judgment of 12/10/2004, unpublished); Case C-441/02 *Commission v Germany* [2006] ECR I-3449.

892. See Case 14/83 *Von Colson and Kamann* [1984] ECR 1891; Case C-91/92 *Faccini Dori* [1994] ECR I-3325.

893. Contrary to the opinion of the Commission, the ECJ confirmed in Case C-414/97 *Commission v Spain* [1999] ECR I-5585 that the Member State's right to defence entails that new arguments may be invoked before the ECJ.

894. Case C-200/88 *Commission v Greece* [1990] ECR I-4299; Case C-133/94 *Commission v Belgium* [1996] ECR I-2323; Case C-310/03 *Commission v Luxembourg* [2004] ECR I-1969; Case C-312/03 *Commission v Belgium* [2004] ECR I-1975.

895. Case C-211/02 *Commission v Luxembourg* [2003] RCR I-2429.

896. [2004] ECR I-11671.

new reasoned opinion precisely identifying the complaints which it intends pursuing, having regard to the changed circumstances" (para 21).

The ECJ may, in the light of the legal arguments submitted by both parties during the proceedings under Article 258 TFEU, give an interlocutory ruling, inviting the Commission and the Member State concerned to find a solution ensuring the effective application of EU law, but as with any interlocutory decision, the proceedings can be reopened if necessary.[897] Additionally the Commission is entitled to request interim measures.

15.2.6 Defences

The ECJ has strictly interpreted the defences available to Member States. The philosophy of Article 258 TFEU requires that the defaulting Member State put an end to the violation of EU law as soon as possible, and thus some defences recognised under public international law have been rejected by the ECJ.

Josephine Steiner has rightly pointed out that "Many defences to an action under Article [258 TFEU] have been attempted; few have succeeded."[898] She added that the best defence for a defaulting Member State is to deny the obligation. The claim of a procedural irregularity in the adoption of an EU measure also constitutes an excellent defence. However, the strict approach in the interpretation of defences offers little hope for a defaulting Member State. Even the fact that the time limit prescribed in the secondary legislation has not yet expired may not be invoked. In Case C-422/05 *Commission v Belgium*,[899] the ECJ declared, for the first time ever, that a Member State may be in breach of Articles 10 EC and Article 249(3) EC [Articles 4(3) TEU indents 2 and 3 and Article 288 TFEU] for adopting national measures almost at the end of a transitional period (three months before its expiry) which were liable to seriously compromise the result prescribed by the directive in question (see Chapter 13.4).

15.2.6.1 Successful defences

The following defences have been accepted by the ECJ.

15.2.6.1.1 Unlawful obligation

The best defence for the Member State concerned is to bring an action for annulment under Article 263 TFEU against the challenged measure. The ECJ has permitted a defaulting Member State to call into question the validity of an EU act in Article 226 EC [Article 258 TFEU] proceedings. It seems quite strange that a defaulting Member State may challenge the validity of EU acts in proceedings under Article 258 TFEU in view of the fact that Member States have privileged locus standi under Article 263 TFEU to challenge the validity of any EU act, which would seem to give them an adequate alternative remedy in this context. Indeed, initially the court insisted on use being made of Article 230 EC [Article 263 TFEU] by a Member State.[900] There is no clear justification for the change of attitude of the ECJ, but it seems that the reason may be

---

897. Case 170/78 *Commission v UK* [1980] ECR 415; Case 149/79 *Commission v Belgium* [1980] ECR 3881.

898. J. Steiner, *EC Law*, 4th edition, 1994, London: Blackstone, p 347.

899. [2007] ECR I-4749.

900. For example, Case 20/59 *Italy v High Authority* [1960] ECR 325.

provided by Article 241 EC [Article 277 TFEU] which allows the challenging of EU legislation indirectly through the medium of attacking implementing measures adopted on the basis of that legislation and thus, at least theoretically, an escape from the strict deadline of Article 263 TFEU (see Chapter 16.3). However, with regard to Article 258 TFEU proceedings the ECJ has limited the opportunity of a Member State to rely on the unlawfulness of an EU act to two situations:

- The first was discussed by the ECJ in Case 226/87 *Commission v Greece*,[901] in which the ECJ stated that a Member State may call into question the legality of a decision if such a decision is affected by evident and serious vices which render it "non-existent". With regard to regulations, in Case 116/82 *Commission v Germany*[902] the ECJ accepted that the illegality of regulations may be invoked as a defence to proceedings under Article 226 EC [Article 258 TFEU].

- The second exception was established in Case 6/69 *Commission v France*,[903] in which the French Government successfully proved that the decision in question was adopted in an area in which the Member State had exclusive competence.

15.2.6.1.2 *Force majeure*

Another possibility for a Member State is to invoke force majeure, although, at the time of writing, this defence has never been successfully pleaded. The reason for this is that the ECJ has always interpreted this concept strictly. The definition of force majeure was provided in Case 296/86 *McNicoll v Ministry of Agriculture*[904] in proceedings under Article 230 EC [263 TFEU], and has been transposed to proceedings under Article 226 EC [Article 258 TFEU].[905] In that case the ECJ held that:

> ". . . whilst the concept of *force majeure* does not presuppose an absolute impossibility of perform-
> ance, it nevertheless requires that non-performance of the act in question be due to circumstances
> beyond the control of persons pleading *force majeure*, that the circumstances be abnormal and
> unforeseeable and that the consequences could not have been avoided through the exercise of all
> due care."

As a result, what are considered under national law as exonerating circumstances, such as unforeseeable and irresistible political events – namely the dissolution of a national parliament, political difficulties, governmental crises, delays in the legislative procedure, social and economic disorders, and so on – were rejected by the ECJ.[906] Consequently, it is very difficult for a Member State to successfully plead this defence although in Case 101/84 *Commission v Italy [the Traffic Statistics case]*[907] the Government of Italy was close to succeeding.

---

901. Case 20/59 *Italy v High Authority* [1960] ECR 325.
902. [1986] ECR 2519, also Case C-258/89 *Commission v Spain* [1991] ECR I-3977.
903. [1969] ECR 523.
904. [1988] ECR 1491.
905. Case 145/85 *Denkavit* [1987] ECR 565; Case C-105/02 *Commision v Germany* [2006] ECR I-9659.
906. See K. D. Magliveras, "Force Majeure in Community Law", 15 ELR, 1990, p 460.
907. [1985] ECR 2629.

THE FACTS WERE:

The Italian Government argued that following a bomb attack by the Red Brigade (a terrorist organisation) on the Ministry of Transport's data-processing centre, which destroyed its register, it was impossible to comply with EC Directive 78/546 which required the Member State to forward statistical data in respect of the carriage of goods by road.

Held:

The ECJ held that the delay of four-and-a-half years between the terrorist attack and the implementation of the directive was too long to exonerate Italy. In this respect the ECJ held that:

"... although it is true that the bomb attack, which took place before 18 January 1979, may have constituted a case of *force majeure* and created insurmountable difficulties, its effect could only have lasted a certain time, namely the time which would in fact be necessary for an administration showing a normal degree of diligence to replace the equipment destroyed and to collect and prepare the data."

15.2.6.1.3 Uncertainty as to the exact meaning of the obligation

Under Article 258 TFEU the Commission must determine with precision, or at least sufficiently from a legal point of view, the obligation which a Member State has failed to fulfil.[908] This requirement has been used by the Member States as a defence under Article 258 TFEU.

Initially, the ECJ recognised this defence only if uncertainty as to the exact meaning of the obligation concerned its essential aspect.[909] Gradually, however, the ECJ has accepted that even in proceedings under Article 226 EC [Article 258 TFEU] Member States are entitled to elucidation by the ECJ as to the exact scope of the obligations they are supposed to fulfil, especially in the event of divergent interpretations.[910] The extent of the ECJ's acceptance of this defence is still difficult to determine. In this respect, in Case C-133/94 *Commission v Belgium*[911] the Government of Belgium pleaded, inter alia, the obscurity and ambiguity of a provision concerning the concept of "chemical installation" under Council Directive 85/337/EEC on environmental impact assessments. The Commission implicitly agreed with Belgium as the Commission subsequently decided to define the precise meaning of that concept. Notwithstanding this, the ECJ held Belgium in breach of Article 226 EC [Article 258 TFEU].

15.2.6.2 Unsuccessful defences

The ingeniousness of the Member States in constructing defences to Article 258 TFEU proceedings is astonishing. Over the years they have attempted to plead almost every justification imaginable for their failure to fulfil their obligations under the Treaty.

The following are examples of the most popular unsuccessful defences.

---

908. Case 20/59 *Italy v High Authority* [1960] ECR 325.
909. Case 26/69 *Commission v France* [1970] ECR 565; Case 70/72 *Commission v Germany* [1973] ECR 813.
910. Case 7/71 *Commission v France* [1971] ECR 1003.
911. [1996] ECR I-2323.

15.2.6.2.1 Defence based on reciprocity

This defence is recognised under public international law but rejected by EU law as contrary to the spirit and objectives of the EU legal order.[912] A Member State cannot withhold its own performance even if either an EU institution or another Member State has failed to perform its obligations. This was examined in Cases 90 and 91/63 *Commission v Luxembourg and Belgium [Re Import of Powdered Milk Products]*.[913]

THE FACTS WERE:

Luxembourg and Belgium argued that the their action would have been legal if the Commission had introduced certain measures, which it was authorised to enact, and that under public international law if one party fails to perform its obligation, the other is entitled to withhold its own performance.

Held:

The ECJ held that:

"In fact the Treaty is not limited to creating reciprocal obligations between the different natural and legal persons to whom it is applicable, but establishes a new legal order which governs the powers, rights and obligations of the said persons, as well as the necessary procedures for taking cognizance of and penalizing any breach of it. Therefore, except where otherwise expressly provided, the basic concept of the Treaty requires that the Member States shall not take the law into their own hands. Therefore, the fact that the Council failed to carry out its obligations cannot relieve the defendants from carrying out theirs."

Comment:

The position of the ECJ is fully justified because:

The Treaties prohibit unilateral retaliatory actions on the part of a Member State against another Member State or an EU institution. Under the Treaties unlawful actions or omissions either of Member States or EU institutions are investigated and properly dealt with.[914] Thus, there is neither the need, nor any justification, for permitting Member States to "take the law into their own hands".

The exception of non-performance, known as the *exceptio non inadempleti contractus*, a doctrine according to which performance of an obligation may be withheld if the other party has itself failed to perform the same or a related obligation, is justified in international law given that the international legal order is based on consent and reciprocity and that there is no international court that exercises permanent and mandatory jurisdiction in respect of disputes between sovereign states. However, it would not be appropriate to apply the doctrine in the

---

912. G. Conway, "Breaches of EC Law and the International Responsibility of Member States", (2002) 13 European Journal of International Law, p. 679; B. Simma and D. Pulkowski, "Of Planets and the Universe: Self-Contained Regimes in International Law", (2006) 17(3) European Journal of International Law, pp 483–529.
913. [1964] ECR 625.
914. Case C-359/93 *Commission v The Netherlands* [1995] ECR I-157.

realm of the EU legal order, because of the mandatory and exclusive jurisdiction of the ECJ, which deals with disputes relating to the interpretation and application of EU law. The ECJ alone decides whether a Member State has complied with obligations arising out of EU law.

The rejection of defences based on reciprocity entails that:

1. Any unilateral action of a Member State aimed at correcting the effect of a violation of EU law by another Member State is prohibited.

    If a Member State considers that another Member State has failed to fulfil its obligations under EU law, that Member State may bring an action under Article 259 TFEU against the defaulting Member State, or ask the Commission to act under Article 258 TFEU.

    In Case 232/78 *Commission v France [Re Restrictions on Imports of Lamb]*[915] the ECJ held that:

    > "A Member State cannot under any circumstances unilaterally adopt, on its own authority, corrective measure or measures to protect trade designed to prevent any failure on the part of another Member State to comply with the rules laid down by the Treaty."

    This statement was repeated almost word for word by the ECJ in Case C-14/96 *Paul Denuit*,[916] in which a Belgian judge, although under Article 234 EC [Article 267 TFEU] proceedings, asked the ECJ whether Belgium was entitled to take unilateral measures against Member States which were in breach of Council Directive 89/552 establishing a single audiovisual area in the EC, especially to oppose the retransmissions to the territory of Belgium of programmes broadcast by the national broadcasting body of another Member State which did not comply with certain provisions of the Directive.[917]

2. A Member State cannot invoke in its defence that another Member State is also in breach of the same obligation, even though the Commission has not initiated proceedings against that other Member State.[918]

3. Neither the Member State which is an alleged victim of the violation of EU law by another Member State, nor any other Member State is allowed to plead that violation in its defence.[919]

4. A Member State cannot rely in its defence under Article 258 TFEU on the fact that an EU institution has acted unlawfully or failed to act when it was under a duty to act. Articles 263 and 265 TFEU provide in such a case an appropriate procedure for the very purpose of rectifying those problems[920] (see Chapter 16). In Case C-359/93 *Commission v*

---

915. [1979] ECR 2729.
916. [1997] ECR I-2785.
917. See also: Joined Cases 142–143/80 *Esssevi* [1981] ECR 1413; Case C-11/95 *Commission v Belgium* [1966] ECR I-4115; Case C-118/03 *Commission v Germany* [unpublished].
918. Case 232/78 *Commission v France [Re Restrictions on Imports of Lamb]* [1979] ECR 2729.
919. Case 52/75 *Commission v Italy* [1976] ECR 277.
920. Cases 90 and 91/63 *Commission v Belgium and Luxembourg* [1964] ECR 625.

The Netherlands,[921] the ECJ held that this defence would also be rejected when an EU institution fails to comply with its own obligations under the Treaty subsequent to a failure by a Member State.

15.2.6.2.2 Defence based on necessity

This defence, rejected by the ECJ, is recognised under public international law, which sets out stringent criteria for such a defence to be accepted, i.e. there must be exceptional circumstances of extreme urgency, the status quo ante (the situation which previously existed) must be re-established as soon as possible, and the State concerned must act in good faith.[922]

In Case 7/61 *Commission v Italy [The Pigmeat case]*,[923] Italy banned all imports of pork into Italy from other Member States in order to avert an economic crisis. The ECJ held that with respect to emergency situations the appropriate remedy was laid down in Article 226 (now repealed) and, for reasons similar to those under the principle of reciprocity, declared the unilateral action by Italy to be in breach of EU law.

15.2.6.2.3 Defence based on the peculiarity of national systems, especially their constitutional, administrative and institutional organisation

This defence was rejected by the ECJ in Case 77/69 *Commission v Belgium*.[924]

THE FACTS WERE:

The Government of Belgium argued that its attempts to pass the necessary amendments to legislation relating to the tax on wood were fettered by the Belgian parliament, a body which the government had no power to compel to act. A draft to amend a discriminatory tax scheme on wood was submitted to the Belgian parliament, but had fallen with the dissolution of parliament.

Held:

The ECJ held that the Member State was liable under Article 226 EC [Article 258 TFEU] whenever an agent of the Member State, including a constitutionally independent institution, fails to fulfil its obligation arising from EU law.

15.2.6.2.4 Defence based on the division of powers between central and regional authorities

This defence was rejected in Case 1/86 *Commission v Belgium [Re Failure to Implement Directives]*.[925]

---

921.   [1995] ECR I-157.
922.   The defence of necessity was successfully invoked by the UK when it bombed the *Torrey Canyon*, a ship flying the Liberian flag which was grounded outside the British territorial waters as it represented a threat of an ecological disaster, but this defence failed in the *Rainbow Warrior* case [1990] 82 ILR 499.
923.   [1961] ECR 317.
924.   [1970] ECR 237.
925.   [1987] ECR 2797.

THE FACTS WERE:

The Belgian Government stated that it was constitutionally unable to compel some of its regions to comply with a judgment of the ECJ requiring the implementation of a number of EC directives within the prescribed time limit. The Belgian Government claimed that it had nether power to compel regional authorities (in this case in the Walloon and Brussels regions) to implement Community legislation where the Directives were, despite the efforts of regional governments, not wholly implemented, nor to substitute them for local legislation.

Held:

The ECJ held that:

"... each Member State is free to delegate powers to its domestic authorities as it considers fit and to implement Directives by means of measures adopted by regional or local authorities. That division of powers does not however release it from the obligation to ensure that the provisions of the Directive are properly implemented in national law .... a Member State may not plead provisions, practices or circumstances existing in its internal legal system in order to justify failure to comply with its obligations under Community law."

15.2.6.2.5 Defence based on breach of EU law by its institutions and on circumstances existing in the EU legal order

This defence was rejected in Case C-263/96 *Commission v Belgium*.[926]

THE FACTS WERE:

Belgium argued that delays in the adoption of further implementing measures by the EU institutions justified non-implementation of Directive 89/106 on construction products, and that Belgium's failure did not adversely affect the creation of the internal market in construction products, taking into account the fact that the market, due to the delays on the part of the EU, had not yet been established. The Belgian Government also argued that Directive 89/106 had been modified by subsequent directives on several occasions, and that its final version was in the process of preparation.

Held:

The ECJ rejected all defences submitted by Belgium. It held that non-adoption of further implementing measures on the part of the EU institutions could not justify a failure to implement the directive. Further, the ECJ rejected the defence based on circumstances existing in the EU legal order. In this respect, the ECJ emphasised that the obligation of implementation which results from Article 249 EC [288 TFEU] cannot be modified according to the circum-

---

926. [1997] ECR I-7453.

stances, even though the difficulties have their source in the EU legal order. The ECJ underlined that the obligations arising out of the EC Treaty are assessed objectively, that is, they are not conditional upon the existence of loss, and therefore a Member State may not rely on the argument that the failure to adopt measures to transpose a directive had no adverse impact on the functioning of the internal market or of that directive.

Comment:

In this case, the failure to fulfil the obligation resulted solely from non-implementation of the directive within a prescribed time limit. This shows that a directive must be implemented within the required time limit, regardless of the fact that it may be subject to future modifications and amendments.

15.2.6.2.6 Defence based on political and economic difficulties experienced by a Member State, or specific local conditions

Political difficulties cannot be pleaded in order to justify a failure to comply with obligations resulting from EU law. In Case 8/70 *Commission v Italy*,[927] a defence based on a ministerial crisis in Italy was rejected. Indeed, in the light of the political turbulence in Italy after World War II, the acceptance of this defence would have paralysed the operation of EU law in that country.

Interesting arguments relating to political difficulties were submitted by the UK in Case 128/78 *Commission v UK [Re Tachographs]*.[928]

THE FACTS WERE:

The Commission brought an action against the UK for failure to comply with Regulation 1463/70 relating to the introduction of tachographs in commercial vehicles. By this regulation tachographs were made compulsory, and had to replace the use of individual record books. They were strongly opposed by the trade unions in the UK ("the spy in the cab"). The Government of the UK suggested that the installation and use of tachographs should be on a voluntary basis. It argued that the resistance from the trade unions would lead to political difficulty, would result in strikes in the transport sector and thus seriously damage the whole economy of the UK.

Held:

The ECJ held that Regulation 1463/70 was, as is any other regulation, binding in its entirety on the Member State, and thus its incomplete or selective application would breach EU law. In addition, the ECJ stated that it was inadmissible for a Member State to disapply those provisions of the regulation which it considered contrary to national interests. Practical difficulties in the implementation of an EU measure cannot permit a Member State to unilater-

---

927. [1970] ECR 961.
928. [1979] ECR 419.

ally opt out of fulfilling its obligations, since the EU institutional system ensures that due consideration is given to them in the light of the principles of the internal market and the legitimate interests of the other Member States. As a result, the ECJ rejected the possibility of political difficulties as a justification for non-compliance with Regulation 1463/70.

Defences based on economic difficulties,[929] or threats of social troubles, or specific local conditions[930] were rejected by the ECJ. In Case C-45/91 *Commission v Greece*,[931] the Greek Government tried to justify its failure to implement the directive on the safe disposal of toxic waste, on the ground of "opposition by the local population". This argument was rejected and the ECJ repeated that a Member State cannot rely on an internal situation to justify its failure to fulfil its obligations under the Treaties.

15.2.6.2.7 Defences based on the minimal effect of the violation of EU law

There is no de minimis rule under Article 258 TFEU. The scale, or the frequency of the infringement cannot justify the failure of a Member State to fulfil its obligations under the Treaties. In Case C-105/91 *Commission v Greece*,[932] the Greek Government admitted that its scheme on taxation of foreign vehicles was unlawful and discriminatory, but argued that the Greek vehicles which were eligible for tax concessions represented no more than 10 per cent of the internal demand, and thus there was no manifest discrimination. This argument was rejected.

It is to be noted that in some areas of EU law, in particular in EU competition law, the de minimis rule is accepted (see Chapter 26.6.3).

15.2.6.2.8 Defence based on the argument that administrative practices ensure that national law in breach of EU law is not applied in fact

This defence was relied upon by the French Government in Case 167/73 *Commission v France [Re French Merchant Seamen]*.[933]

THE FACTS WERE:

The French Government attempted to justify the existence of national law (the French Code Maritime enacted in 1926), which was in breach of EU law, on the basis that it was no longer enforced in practice. The Code required a ratio of three Frenchmen to one foreigner for certain jobs on French merchant ships. This provision was in breach of Article 39 EC [Article 45 TFEU] and EC Regulation 1612/68.

---

929. Case 70/86 *Commission v Greece* [1987] ECR 3545.
930. Case C-56/90 *Commission v United Kingdom [Re Bathing Water Directive]* [1993] ECR I-4109; Case 339/87 *Commission v The Netherlands [Re Protection of Wild Birds]* [1990] ECR I-851.
931. [1992] ECR I-2509.
932. [1992] ECR I-5871.
933. [1974] ECR 359. See also Case C-531/03 *Commission v Germany* [Judgment of 10/03/2005] unpublished.

Held:

The ECJ held that although according to the French Government this provision was a second-ary hindrance since it was not applied in practice by the French Administration, and that there was in addition a ministerial circular to this effect, the uncertainty resulting from its continued existence constituted itself a hindrance incompatible with the requirements of the free movement of workers.

Comment:

It is interesting to mention that France did not comply with the decision of the ECJ. As a result, the Commission, after more than twenty years, brought proceedings against France. In Case C-334/94 *Commission v France*[934] the French Government repeated the same argu-ments as 20 years before with the knowledge that since 1973 the ECJ had confirmed in many cases that neither a ministerial circular nor an administrative practice, even though long-established, are adequate measures to ensure the proper application of EC law. Obviously France was, once again, found in breach of EC law.

15.2.6.2.9 Defence based on direct effect of EU law

This defence was invoked in Case 167/73 *Commission v France*.[935] It failed as the ECJ held that it was likely to confuse EU citizens and create legal uncertainty. It is, however, an interesting defence given that, on the one hand, the supremacy of EU law ensures that in the case of a conflict between EU law and national law the former will prevail and, on the other hand, that an indi-vidual may rely on directly effective provisions of EU law in proceedings brought before a national court.

After some hesitation,[936] the ECJ, in Case C-433/93 *Commission v Germany*,[937] held that under Article 249(3) EC [Article 288 TFEU] the application of a directive must be ensured by imple-menting measures adopted by a Member State independently of the possible direct effect of its provisions. In Case C-253/95 *Commission v Germany*,[938] the ECJ added that direct effect is invoked only in special circumstances, in particular when a Member State has not taken the necessary implementing measures as required under the directive, or if it has adopted implementing meas-ures but they have not conformed to the directive. The ECJ emphasised that direct effect consti-tutes a minimum guarantee resulting from the binding nature of the obligation imposed upon a Member State by a directive, and is insufficient in itself to ensure its full and complete application.

---

934.   [1996] ECR I-1307.
935.   [1974] ECR 359.
936.   In Case 29/84 *Commission v Germany [Re Nursing Directive]* ([1985] ECR 1661) the ECJ held that a defence based on direct effect of Community law might be accepted provided that three conditions were satisfied: administrative practice must fully ensure the application of Community law, there must be no legal uncertainty concerning the legal situation which the directive regulates and individuals concerned must be aware of their rights. In this case those conditions were not satisfied.
937.   [1995] ECR I-2303.
938.   [1996] ECR I-2423.

15.3 Action against a Member State by another Member State under Article 259 TFEU

For the Member States an alternative to proceedings under Article 258 TFEU is provided in Art 259 TFEU which states that:

> "A Member State which considers that another Member State has failed to fulfil an obligation under the Treaties may bring the matter before the Court of Justice of the European Union.
>
> Before a Member State brings an action against another Member State for an alleged infringement of an obligation under the Treaties, it shall bring the matter before the Commission.
>
> The Commission shall deliver a reasoned opinion after each of the States concerned has been given the opportunity to submit its own case and its observations on the other party's case both orally and in writing.
>
> If the Commission has not delivered an opinion within three months of the date on which the matter was brought before it, the absence of such opinion shall not prevent the matter from being brought before the Court."

Article 259 TFEU recognises the autonomous right of any Member State to act against another Member State that has failed to fulfil its obligations arising from EU law.

A Member State is not required to justify its interest to act and thus may bring an action against the defaulting Member State if it believes that the general interests of the EU necessitate such action, or if it considers that the illegal conduct of another Member State affects its own vital interests.

The Commission is very much involved in the proceedings:

- First, before a Member State brings an action against another Member State, the Commission must be informed; and

- Second, the Commission must proceed in exactly the same manner as under Article 258 TFEU, that is, it investigates the matter, gives both parties an opportunity to submit their arguments orally and in writing, and finally delivers a reasoned opinion within three months of the date on which the matter was brought.

The involvement of the Commission serves two purposes:

- The Commission acts during the period of three months as an intermediary between the Member States concerned; it attempts to settle the case and find an acceptable solution. The period of three months is a "cooling off" period during which the Commission endeavours to resolve the matter in the light of the EU interest;

- The participation of the Commission in proceedings under Article 259 TFEU emphasises its privileged role as the "guardian" of the Treaties and the exceptional nature of an action by one Member State against another.

The case law in respect of Article 227 EC [Article 259 TFEU] confirms the benefit of the Commission's involvement. Actions under this Article are extremely rare and, in general, seldom reach the ECJ. Up to the time of writing the ECJ has delivered a handful of judgments under Article 227 EC [Article 259 TFEU], e.g. Case 141/78 *France v UK [Re Fishing Mesh]*[939] and Case C-388/95 *Belgium v Spain*.[940]

---

939.   [1979] ECR 2923.
940.   [2000] ECR I-3123.

Disputes between Member States concerning the application of the Treaties are, for political reasons, dealt with under Article 258 TFEU. This solution is advantageous to the Member States for three reasons:

■ The Member State concerned avoids unnecessary confrontations with another Member State while achieving the objectives sought, that is, compelling the defaulting Member State to comply with EU law;

■ The Commission bears the burden of proof and conducts the investigations; and

■ The Member State concerned may participate in the Article 258 TFEU proceedings. Under Article 40 of the Statute of the CJEU, a Member State, or any EU institutions, may intervene to support or reject the application of the Commission in the case brought before the ECJ.[941]

15.4 Effect of a ruling confirming a failure of a Member State to fulfil its EU obligations

There is no express provision in the Treaties regarding the legal effect of ECJ rulings under Article 258 TFEU. However, it results from Article 260(1) TFEU that they are declaratory in nature.
Article 260(1) TFEU states that:

"If the Court of Justice of the European Union finds that a Member State has failed to fulfil an obligation under the Treaties, the State shall be required to take the necessary measures to comply with the judgment of the Court."

The defaulting Member State must comply with the judgment, including paying or contributing to the applicant's costs if so ordered. Further, if the Commission in its application for finding a failure of a Member State to notify national measures implementing a directive adopted in accordance with legislative procedures has asked the ECJ to impose pecuniary penalties and if the ECJ has found an infringement and agreed to impose the proposed penalties, the payment obligation takes effect on the date set by the Court in its judgment. If the application is dismissed, the applicant may be ordered to pay or contribute to the defendant's costs.

If the application is successful, the defendant is required to take all necessary measures in order to remedy the failure and its consequences, both in the past and in the future.[942] Furthermore, national courts and national authorities of the defaulting Member State are required to disapply any national law declared incompatible with EU law and to take all appropriate measures to ensure the effective application of the latter.[943]

For individuals there are important consequences flowing from a ruling under Article 258

---

941. In such a case the ECJ grants or refuses leave to intervene in support of the order sought by the Commission or the Member State concerned. For example in Case C-80/92 *Commission v Belgium* ([1994] ECR I-1019), the ECJ granted the UK leave to intervene in support of the form of order sought by the Commission; in Case C-246/89 *Commission v UK [Re Nationality of Fishermen]* ([1991] ECR 1-4585) the ECJ granted leave to Spain to intervene in support of the form of order sought by the Commission and to Ireland to intervene in support of the form of order sought by the UK. However, private parties are not permitted to intervene.

942. Case 70/72 *Commission v Germany* [1973] ECR 813.

943. Case 48/71 *Commission v Italy* [1972] ECR 527.

TFEU. In Joined Cases 314–316/81 and 83/82 *Procureur de la République v Waterkeyn*[944] the ECJ held that:

"... if the Court finds in proceedings under Articles [226] to [228 EC] [Articles 258 to 260 TFEU] ... that a Member State's legislation is incompatible with the obligations which it has under the Treaty the courts of that State are bound by virtue of Article 228 [258 TFEU] to draw the necessary inferences from the judgment of the Court. However, it should be understood that the rights accruing to individuals derive, not from that judgment, but from the actual provisions of Community law having direct effect in the internal legal order."

Another important consequence is that individuals who have suffered loss resulting from the infringement of EU law by the relevant Member State may, in national proceedings, rely on the ECJ's judgment confirming that infringement. Such a ruling of the ECJ often provides sufficient evidence for national courts to decide whether the second condition relating to a Member State's liability, that is, requiring a sufficiently serious breach of EU law, has been satisfied.

The Treaties do not specify a time limit for compliance with a judgment rendered under Article 258 TFEU. However, the ECJ has imposed strict conditions in this respect. In Case 69/86 *Commission v Italy*[945] the ECJ held that:

"Article [228 EC] [Article 260 TFEU] does not specify the period within which a judgment must be complied with. However, it is beyond dispute that the action required to give effect to a judgment must be set in motion immediately and be completed in the shortest possible period."

The ECJ is not a federal court and thus is not empowered to annul national law incompatible with EU law,[946] or to compel a defaulting Member State to comply with the Court's judgment by granting an injunction, or to order a Member State to take specific measures.[947] The ECJ may, however, impose pecuniary penalties.

15.5 Pecuniary sanctions under Article 260 (2) and (3) TFEU

Non-compliance with judgments rendered under Article 226 EC [Article 258 TFEU] became a serious problem in the late 1980s. At this time, when the Commission started to pursue defaulting Member States more vigorously than previously, it discovered that Member States were very reluctant to co-operate with the Commission on many matters. Until the entry into force of the Treaty of Maastricht the excessive delays and flagrant refusals on the part of defaulting Member States to comply with judgments of the ECJ were not subject to any penalties. The Commission, as the guardian of the Treaties, was bound to take the necessary steps to compel the defaulting Member State to remedy the breach,[948] which steps consisted of commencing second proceedings based on Article 226 EC [258 TFEU] for breach of Article 228 EC [260 TFEU].[949] In those

---

944. [1982] ECR 4337.
945. [1987] ECR 773. See also Case 169/87 *Commission v France* [1988] ECR 4093 and Case C-334/94 *Commission v France* [1996] ECR I-1307, which probably set a record – more than 20 years of non-compliance! (That is, between the judgment of the ECJ in the original infringement proceedings given on 4 April 1974 and the subsequent proceedings based on Article 228 EC.)
946. For example Case 6/60 *Humblot* [1960] ECR 559.
947. Case C-104/02 *Commission v Germany* [2005] ECR I-2689.
948. Case 281/83 *Commission v Italy* [1985] ECR 3397.
949. Case 48/71 *Commission v Italy* [1972] ECR 527.

circumstances, a more radical approach was necessary. The Treaty of Maastricht introduced the possibility for the ECJ to impose pecuniary penalties on Member States which refused to comply with its judgments. The ToL has further reformed the system of imposition of pecuniary penalties in Article 260(2) and (3) TFEU.

Article 260(2) and (3) TFEU states that:

"1.   If the Court of Justice of the European Union finds that a Member State has failed to fulfil an obligation under the Treaties, the State shall be required to take the necessary measures to comply with the judgment of the Court.

2.   If the Commission considers that the Member State concerned has not taken the necessary measures to comply with the judgment of the Court, it may bring the case before the Court after giving that State the opportunity to submit its observations. It shall specify the amount of the lump sum or penalty payment to be paid by the Member State concerned which it considers appropriate in the circumstances.

   If the Court finds that the Member State concerned has not complied with its judgment it may impose a lump sum or penalty payment on it.

   This procedure shall be without prejudice to Article 259.

3.   When the Commission brings a case before the Court pursuant to Article 258 on the grounds that the Member State concerned has failed to fulfil its obligation to notify measures transposing a directive adopted under a legislative procedure, it may, when it deems appropriate, specify the amount of the lump sum or penalty payment to be paid by the Member State concerned which it considers appropriate in the circumstances.

   If the Court finds that there is an infringement it may impose a lump sum or penalty payment on the Member State concerned not exceeding the amount specified by the Commission. The payment obligation shall take effect on the date set by the Court in its judgment."

The ToL has responded to the main criticism concerning the system of imposition of pecuniary penalties in that it has shortened the stages that lead to such imposition as follows:

■ When the Commission brings proceedings for the imposition of pecuniary sanctions following non-compliance of a Member State with an earlier judgment of the ECJ finding that Member State in breach of EU law, the Commission is not required to submit to the defaulting Member State a "reasoned opinion" as was the case before the entry into force of the ToL. The removal of the reasoned opinion requirement speeds up the procedure and avoids the unnecessary repetition of the Commission's work given that the failure has already been declared in the original proceedings on the same legal basis. However, Article 260(2) ensures that the Member State concerned has the opportunity to submit its observation before the Commission commences Article 260(2) proceedings.

■ Under Article 260(2) TFEU the Commission may, in its application to the ECJ which asks for a finding of failure, when a Member State has failed to notify to it measures transposing a directive adopted under a legislative procedure, request the ECJ to impose a pecuniary penalty. In such a situation the Commission is not required to wait until a Member State concerned fails to comply with a judgment of the ECJ to propose a pecuniary penalty. This possibility should be welcome as it:

● concerns a failure which is obvious and therefore there is no need for the Commission to wait until the defaulting Member State fails again to comply with the initial judgment of the ECJ before any pecuniary penalty can be imposed;

- puts more pressure on the Member States to implement EU directives;
- ensures that the amount of pecuniary penalty imposed by the ECJ will not be higher than that proposed by the Commission.

In a Communication of December 2005,[950] which replaced two previous Communications[951] on the topic, the Commission specified its policy under Article 228 EC [Article 260 TFEU] and defined the method of calculating pecuniary sanctions. The communication was the response of the Commission to the judgment of the ECJ in Case C-304/02 *Commission v France* (see below). The Communication provides that the Commission in all cases under Article 228 EC [260 TFEU] will ask the ECJ to impose both a daily penalty payment and a lump sum on a defaulting Member State and sets out the following detailed mode of calculation of penalties applicable to all types of non-compliance with an original judgment.

With regard to the determination of the amount of the daily penalty:

- It is based on the "basic uniform lump sum" of €600 per day of delay;

- The basic lump sum is adjusted by two co-efficient multiplicands: one takes account of the gravity of the infringement and the other of the period of non-compliance. For example, the Commission considers as very serious the breach of the principle of non-discrimination, and as serious the infringement of provisions ensuring the four freedoms.[952] The first multiplicand is within the scale from 1 to 20, and the second from 1 to 3 calculated at a rate of 0.10 per cent per month from the date of delivery of the Article 258 TFEU judgment.

- In order to make the penalty a real deterrent to non-compliance with the judgment, the Commission established a special invariable factor "n" for each Member State, which takes into consideration the financial capacity of the defaulting Member State, which is calculated on the basis of the GNP of each Member State, combined with the weighting of voting rights in the Council.

To calculate an amount of a daily penalty payment the co-efficient for seriousness and for duration are multiplied by the "n" factor of the relevant Member State. As to a lump sum, a minimum amount has been set for each Member State.

Prior to the adoption of the 2005 Communication two cases decided under Article 228(2) EC [260 TFEU] attracted attention: first, Case C-387/97 *Commission v Greece*,[953] because in that case, for the first time ever, the ECJ ordered a Member State to pay daily penalty payments for non-compliance with its initial judgment[954] and second, Case C-304/02 *Commission v France*[955] in which the ECJ ordered France to pay both a lump sum penalty and a daily penalty payment not merely one or the other.

In Case C-387/97 *Commission v Greece*, the ECJ ordered Greece to pay to the Commission (into the account "EC own resources") a penalty payment of €20,000 for each day of Greece's delay in implementing the measures necessary to comply with the judgment in Case C-45/91

---

950. SEC(2005) 1658.
951. One of 5/06/96 and one of 28/02/97.
952. Agence Europe Nr. 6742, 6.6. 1996.
953. [2000] ECR I-5047.
954. Case C-45/91 *Commission v Greece* [1992] ECR I-2509.
955. [2005] ECR I-6263.

Commission v Greece, commencing from notification of the judgment in Case C-387/97 *Commission v Greece* and continuing until the judgment in Case C-45/91 had been complied with.

The ECJ is not bound by the figure suggested by the Commission. It may increase or reduce the figure or may decide not to impose any penalty at all as only it is entitled, in each case, to decide what is just, proportionate and equitable.[956] The ToL introduced one limitation on the ECJ's powers in that under Article 260(2) TFEU proceedings the ECJ, on finding the infringement, may impose a lump sum or penalty payment not exceeding the amount specified by the Commission.

In Case C-304/02 *Commission v France*[957] the ECJ ordered France to pay:

- A penalty payment of €57,761,250 for each period of six months of non-compliance with the initial judgment (Case C-64/88 *Commission v France*) starting from delivery of the judgment in Case C-304/02 *Commission v France* and continuing until the day on which the breach of obligations in the initial judgment was brought to an end; and

- A lump sum of €20,000,000 for France's persistent non-compliance with the initial judgment.

The imposition of both a daily penalty payment and a lump sum sends a clear message to Member States which persist in ignoring the Court's judgments: the price to pay may be very high! In Case C-304/02 *Commission v France* the duration of the infringement was considerable (more than ten years), as was the seriousness of the breach (failure to comply with the technical measures of conservation of fishery resources prescribed by the rules of the Common Fisheries Policy (CFP), in particular the requirements regarding the minimum size of fish allowed to be caught, which failure constituted a serious threat to the maintenance of certain species and certain fishing grounds and jeopardised pursuit of the fundamental objective of the CFP).

AIDE-MÉMOIRE

PROCEDURE UNDER ARTICLE 258 TFEU

Relating to a Member State's failure to fulfil an obligation under the Treaties
Member State: any national body including parliament (Case 77/69 *Commission v Belgium*); the judiciary (Case C-129/00 *Commission v Italy* and Case C-154/08 *Commission v Spain*); any private or semi-private body which the Member State controls (Case 249/81 *Commission v Ireland Re Buy Irish Campaign*), private individuals if the Member State was in a position to prevent, or terminate their conduct which had breached EU law (Case C-265/95 *Commission v France*).

Failure: any shortcoming relating to fulfilment of obligations arising from the Treaties. It may result from an action, or from an omission, or a failure to act of the Member State concerned.

---

956. For example, in Case C-119/04 *Commission v Italy* ([2006] ECR I-6885) the ECJ did not impose any penalty because Italy provided evidence that it had complied with the initial judgment albeit after the date on which the Commission had issued its reasoned opinion.

957. [2005] ECR I-6263.

Obligation under the Treaties: a specific and precise obligation, which exists at the time the Commission starts the Article 258 TFEU procedure (Case 7/71 *Commission v France*).

Procedure:

1. Informal phase: Pre-258 Proceedings Letter.

2. Formal phase:
   - Administrative stage (pre-litigation procedure):
     - Letter of Formal Notice (Case 51/83 *Commission v Italy*);
     - Reasoned Opinion (Case 7/61 *Commission v Italy [Re Pigmeat case]*).
   - Judicial stage: the Commission brings proceedings before the ECJ.

Applicant: The Commission   **Defendant:** a Member State

Defences:

Procedural defences:

- The time limit fixed by the Commission either in the letter of formal notice or in the reasoned opinion is not reasonable (293/85 *Commission v Belgium [Re University Fees]*);

- The complaints and legal arguments in the application under Article 258 TFEU are not identical to those invoked in the letter of formal notice and the reasoned opinion (Case C-433/03 *Commission v Germany*);

- The Commission has failed to indicate what measures a Member State is required to take in order to comply with its obligation (Case C-431/02 *Commission v UK*).

Substantive defences:
Successful or potentially successful defences:

- Unlawful obligation (Case 226/87 *Commission v Greece* and Case 6/69 *Commission v France*);

- Force majeure (Case 101/84 *Commission v Italy*);

- Uncertainty as to the meaning of the obligation (Case C-133/94 *Commission v Belgium*).

Unsuccessful:

- Reciprocity (Cases 90 and 91/63 *Commission v Luxembourg and Belgium [Re Import of Powdered Milk Products]*);

- Necessity (Case 7/61 *Commission v Italy [Pigmeat case]*);

- Peculiarity of a national system (Case 77/69 *Commission v Belgium*);

- Difficulty existing in the EU legal order (Case C-263/96 *Commission v Belgium*);

- Political difficulties (Case 8/70 *Commission v Italy*);

- Economic difficulties (Case 70/86 *Commission v Greece*);

■ Minimal effect of the violation (Case C-105/91 *Commission v Greece*);

■ Administrative practices (Case 167/73 *Commission v France [Re French Merchant Seamen]*);

■ Direct effect of EU law (Case 167/73 *Commission v France*).

Effect of a judgment:

Effect of a judgment against the defendant: it must comply with the judgment including paying or contributing to the applicant's costs if so ordered (Article 260(1) TFEU and Case 70/72 *Commission v Germany*). Under Article 260(3) TFEU the Commission may ask the ECJ to impose pecuniary penalties in the initial judgment establishing a failure of a Member State to notify to the Commission national measures transposing a directive adopted under legislative procedures.

Effect of a judgment against the applicant: the application is dismissed but the applicant must pay or contribute to the defendant's costs if so ordered.

If the defendant refuses to comply with the judgment, the Commission may start new proceedings under Article 258(1) TFEU and the ECJ may impose pecuniary sanctions – either a lump sum or a daily penalty payment or both (Article 260(2) TFEU) (Case C-304/02 *Commission v France*). Under Article 260(2) TFEU the Commission is not required to submit a "reasoned opinion" to the Member State concerned, as was the case before the entry into force of the ToL. This speeds up the proceedings.

PROCEDURE UNDER ARTICLE 259 TFEU

Applicant: a Member State   **Defendant:** a Member State

Procedure:

1. The Commission must be informed by the applicant and subsequently acts as an honest broker;

2. Cooling off period of three months;

3. If no settlement is reached within three months, the applicant may start proceedings before the ECJ and the usual Court proceedings will follow (Case 141/78 *France v The United Kingdom [Re: Fishing Mesh]*).

Effect of a judgment:

Effect of a judgment against the defendant: it must comply with the judgment including paying or contributing to the applicant's costs if so ordered.

Effect of a judgment against the applicant: the application is dismissed but the applicant must pay or contribute to the defendant's costs if so ordered;

Non-compliance with a judgment under Article 259 TFEU has never occurred, but the Article 259 TFEU procedure is seldom used!

RECOMMENDED READING

Book

Tallberg, J., *European Governance and Supranational Institutions: Making States Comply*, 2003, London: Routledge

Articles

Conway, G., "Breaches of EC Law and the International Responsibility of Member States", (2002) 13, European Journal of International Law, p 679

Kilbey, I., "Financial penalties under Article 228(2) EC: Excessive complexity?", (2007) 44 CMLRev, pp 743–59

Prete, L, and Smulders, B., "The Coming of Age of Infringement Proceedings", (2010) 47 CMLRev, p 9

16

DIRECT ACTIONS AGAINST EU INSTITUTIONS, BODIES, OFFICES AND AGENCIES

SUMMARY

1. This chapter outlines the various forms of the so-called direct action, which involves bringing proceedings directly before the CJEU against EU institutions, bodies, offices or agencies. Direct actions can be divided into three categories:

- First, actions which challenge the legality of an act adopted by EU institutions, bodies, offices or agencies either by doing this directly under Article 263 TFEU or indirectly under Article 277 TFEU. The latter allows applicants (in support of an action challenging implementing measures addressed to them) to plead the illegality of the general measure upon which the implementing measures are based;

- Second, actions which seek to compel an EU institution, body, office or agency to adopt a measure, or to take a decision defining its position in circumstances where it has a legal duty to take a particular action. Such a decision may then be challenged under Article 263 TFEU;

- Third, actions seeking compensation for damage caused by EU institutions, bodies, offices or agencies or their servants under Article 340(2). However, if the ECB is found liable, bearing in mind that it is an independent EU institution financed by contributions from national central banks of the Member States, in accordance with Article 340(3) TFEU, the

ECB itself is liable (not the EU) and must pay compensation to the injured party from its own resources.

2. With the entry into force of the ToL, the CJEU's jurisdiction under Article 263 TFEU was substantially extended, including over the whole area of FSJ but subject to some restrictions concerning matters specified in Articles 269 TFEU, 40 TEU and 274 TFEU.

3. Article 263 TFEU specifies the conditions for admissibility of an action for annulment and the grounds for annulment. Articles 264 and 266 TFEU specify what the outcome of a successful action will be.

A. Any act adopted by an EU institution, body, office or agency which produces binding legal effect in relation to third parties, irrespective of its form and name, can be reviewed under Article 263 TFEU.

B. There are three categories of applicants under Article 263 TFEU:

- Privileged applicants: the Council, the EP, the Commission and the Member States. They can bring an action for annulment against all reviewable acts and are not required to justify their interest to act. The only condition that they have to satisfy is to bring proceedings within the time limit set out in Article 263(5) TFEU;

- Semi-privileged applicants, such as the CoA, ECB and CoR, can only challenge acts which encroach on their prerogatives. They must respect the deadline set out in Article 263(5) TFEU;

- Non-privileged applicants: natural and legal persons. A prerequisite for starting an action under Article 263 TFEU is that such persons must show an interest in seeking the annulment of the contested act. Such an interest must be actual and present, not merely hypothetical. In almost all actions for annulment the legal interest is obvious as the effects of the contested act bring about a detrimental change in the applicant's legal position. Prior to the entry into force of the ToL non-privileged applicants were rarely successful, apart from a situation where they were direct addressees of a decision, i.e. a classic judicial review situation. Otherwise they had to satisfy the admissibility threshold by establishing that they were directly and individually concerned by a decision addressed to "another person" or that an act in the form of a regulation or a directive, i.e. an act of general application was in fact a decision addressed to them. To establish an individual concern was extremely difficult in respect of acts of general application because a non-privileged applicant had to show that the effect of such an act was so peculiar to him, and to him alone, that he was individually distinguished by the measure from everybody else. The ToL facilitates access to the CJEU for non-privileged applicants in that it makes a distinction between challenges concerning regulatory acts and non-regulatory acts. In respect of regulatory acts, i.e those which do not entail any implementing measures, non-privileged applicants have to prove only that they are directly concerned by the act. This is fairly easy to establish (see below). However, in respect of non-regulatory acts the pre-ToL requirements for locus standi still stand.

  The main difficulty with Article 263 TFEU is that neither this article nor the Treaties provide any definition of the concept of a "regulatory act". It is submitted that the most plausible interpretation of the concept of "a regulatory act" is that only non-legislative acts, i.e. acts other than those adopted in accordance with the ordinary legislative procedure and special legislative procedures, are to be regarded as regulatory acts.

To be directly concerned applicants must show that the contested measure affects their legal position and that the measure leaves no discretion to its addressee as to its implementation. Therefore, it is the action or inaction of the addressee that is of direct concern to applicants, not the decision itself.

With regard to individual concern, which an applicant is still required to establish in respect of non-regulatory acts, the Plaumann test applies under which the applicant must show that he is affected by the contested measure by reason of certain attributes which are peculiar to him or by reason of circumstances which differentiate him from all other persons. The very strict interpretation of "individual concern" was widely criticised. As a result, the ECJ, with time, has relaxed this strict interpretation in cases:

- Concerning the existence of non-contentious procedures which involve, more or less, direct participation of applicants in the adoption of measures, for example, Member State aid, competition law, anti-dumping rules;
- Where the applicants have differentiated themselves from others by being holders of intellectual property rights in the circumstances where the challenged measure has prevented them from using their trademark or other protected right;
- Where an EU institution has a duty to take account of the consequences of its intended act on the position of individuals;
- Where the political interests of the EU so require.

The relaxation of excessive rigidity in the interpretation of the concept of individual concern has not, however, been sufficient. In many cases applicants have alleged a denial of justice, that is, that they have no effective judicial protection under their national laws of the rights deriving from the EU legal order. The ECJ has not been sympathetic to them and has nipped in the bud any attempt by the General Court to change the strict approach to the interpretation of Article 263 TFEU, as evidenced by Case C-50/00P *Unión de Pequeños Agricultores*. The Court has consistently held, without ever examining the effectiveness of either EU or national systems of legal remedies available to individuals, that applicants are sufficiently protected as long as they have access to a court, whether a national court or the CJEU. Consequently, if an action is inadmissible under Article 263 TFEU, it is the task of Member States, by virtue of Article 4(3) TEU, to ensure adequate judicial protection of rights deriving from the EU legal order. This obligation has been enshrined in Article 19(1) TEU.

C. Principles of legal certainty and equality in the administration of justice require that an action for annulment commences within two months of publication/notification of the contested measure. The time limit is rigorously enforced and the only excuses accepted by the CJEU are force majeure or exceptional circumstances. If an act is not challenged within the two months period, it is thereafter immune from annulment.

D. Article 263(2) TFEU sets out the grounds for annulment of EU acts. They are:

- Lack of competence;
- Infringement of an essential procedural requirement;
- Infringement of the Treaties or any rule of law relating to their application; and
- Misuse of powers.

E. If an action for annulment is successful, the CJEU, by virtue of Article 264 TFEU, will declare the contested act void. The declaration applies erga omnes, that is, anybody, not only the parties to the proceedings, can rely on its unlawfulness and the institution which adopted it is, under Article 266 TFEU, required to take all necessary measures to comply with the judgment. In exceptional circumstances the CJEU may declare all or some provisions of the annulled act to be operative until a competent institution adopts an act which will replace the one struck down by the Court.

4. Article 277 TFEU complements Article 263 TFEU. The former's plea of illegality can only be invoked as an ancillary plea, that is, as a means by which applicants, in support of an action challenging implementing measures addressed to them or to a third person, plead the illegality of the general measure upon which the implementing measures are based. For that reason the plea is referred to as an indirect action, that is, it challenges indirectly the validity of a measure on the basis of which a subsequent measure has been taken. The main features of the plea of illegality are:

A.   A plea of illegality is not explicitly time-barred but it cannot be used to circumvent the requirements of Article 263 TFEU. Accordingly, if the applicant is the addressee of an individual act but has not challenged it within the time limit set out in Article 263 TFEU, a claim under Article 277 TFEU will be inadmissible. Further, based on the judgment of the ECJ in Case C-188/92 *TWD Textilwerke* in which the Court held that in circumstances where the time limit for a direct action under Article 263 TFEU has elapsed, and the applicant had locus standi to bring a direct action under Article 263 TFEU but neglected to do so within the time limit prescribed by that Article the Court will consider as inadmissible proceedings under Article 267 TFEU.

B.   Any act of general application adopted by an EU institution, body, office or agency is reviewable under Article 277 TFEU.

C.   As Article 277 TFEU states that "any party" may bring proceedings under this article it seems that no limitations are imposed as to the potential applicants.

D.   The grounds for an action under Article 277 TFEU are the same as for an action under Article 263 TFEU.

E.   The effect of a successful action is that the general act, which may be called a parent act, is rendered inapplicable only to the applicant's case and the implementing measure is annulled in so far as the applicant is concerned. Although the parent act is still valid and immune from annulment, in practice the relevant institution, which has adopted the parent act, will amend or repeal it under Article 266 TFEU.

5. The purpose of an action for failure to act under Article 265 TFEU is to compel the relevant EU institution, body, office or agency to act in circumstances where it has a legal duty to do this.

A.   Potential defendants are EU institutions, bodies, offices and agencies.

B.   There are three categories of applicants:
   ▪ Privileged applicants: EU institutions (but not the CJEU) and Member States;
   ▪ Semi-privileged applicants: the ECB, the CoA and the CoR. They have locus standi to raise an action for failure to act in respect of areas within their respective fields of competence;
   ▪ Non-privileged applicants: any natural or legal person. They have locus standi under Article 265 TFEU but only if the relevant EU institution, body, office or agency has

failed to adopt a measure which they are legally entitled to claim. This means that they have to satisfy the same requirements for locus standi as under Article 263 TFEU. However, they cannot rely on Article 265 TFEU to circumvent the time limit set out in Article 263(5) TFEU.

C.   The procedure comprises two stages:

  ■ The administrative stage during which the applicant must call upon the relevant institution to act. Following this, the institution has two months to act in accordance with the request or to define its position, that is, to issue a statement of its views on a particular matter, its proposal for action, or, in the case of refusal, the reason for not taking a particular action. Consequently, the institution that has been called upon to act defines its position not only when it acts in accordance with the wishes of the applicant but also when it states that it is not going to act, or adopts a measure which is different from that desired or considered necessary by the applicant. A disappointed applicant may rely on Article 263 TFEU to challenge the position taken by the relevant institution but cannot take any further action under Article 265 TFEU.

  ■ The judicial stage. If the EU institution, body, office or agency that has been called upon to act fails to define its position within two months of being so requested, the applicant has a further two months within which it may bring an action for failure to act before the CJEU.

D.   By virtue of Article 266 TFEU the effect of a successful action under Article 265 TFEU is that the defaulting institution will be required to take the necessary measures to remedy its failure in conformity with the judgment of the CJEU. If it fails, a repeat action may be brought under Article 265 TFEU.

6. Article 340 TFEU deals with liability of the EU. Article 340(1) TFEU governs contractual liability of the EU and provides that such liability shall be governed by the law applicable to the contract. The EU's contracts will normally contain a clause of choice of law. Under Article 272 TFEU the CJEU has jurisdiction over contractual arbitration clauses in contracts concluded by or on behalf of the EU, whether that contract is governed by public or private law.

7. Article 340(2) TFEU deals with non-contractual liability of the EU, which must make good any damage caused by its institutions and by its servants in the performance of their duties. In Case 5/71 *Schöppenstedt* the ECJ held that an action in damages is autonomous and thus an applicant is not required to proceed first under Articles 263 or 265 TFEU.

A.   Applicants under Article 340(2)and (3) TFEU: any natural and legal person (including associations, but they are subject to the conditions set out in Case T-304/01 *Abad Pérez*) as well as a Member State.

B.   Defendants: any EU institution, but not the ECJ, nor the General Court. In addition, an action may be brought against the EIB, the ECB and any body, office or agency created on the basis of the Treaties which acts on behalf of the EU.

C.   Three basic conditions for establishing non-contractual liability of the EU, based on laws common to the Member States, were set out by the ECJ in Case 4/69 *Lütticke*:

  ■ A wrongful act or omission by an EU institution or its servants; and
  ■ Damage to the applicant; and
  ■ A causal link between the two.

In Case C-352/98 *Laboratoires Pharmaceutique Bergaderm*, the ECJ abandoned a distinction between conditions governing EU liability for failures of administration and conditions for liability for the adoption of wrongful acts having legal effect or wrongful omissions to adopt a binding act when under a duty to do so. The Court held that the decisive test when considering liability of an EU institution is the degree of discretion that institution enjoyed when adopting the allegedly wrongful act, irrespective of whether or not the act was of an administrative nature or constituted a legislative measure and whether or not it was an individualised act or a normative act of general application. At the time of writing the conditions for EU liability are:

- With regard to the first condition set out in Case 4/69 *Lütticke*, that is, unlawfulness of the conduct. This requires that the applicant establishes the existence of a sufficiently serious breach of a superior rule of law intended to confer rights on individuals:
  - To establish the existence of a sufficiently serious breach, the applicant must prove that an EU institution "manifestly and gravely disregarded the limits of its discretion". This is assessed in the light of criteria similar to those relating to non-contractual liability of a Member State for damage caused to individuals by an infringement of EU law;
  - A superior rule of law is, for example, a provision of the Treaties, or a general principle of EU law;
  - The requirement that a superior rule of law must be intended to confer rights on individuals does not mean that the rule must have the protection of individuals exclusively as its object. It suffices that it has a beneficial effect on the protection of individuals in general.
- The second condition set out in Case 4/69 *Lütticke*, that is, damage. This must be certain and specific, but does not need to be quantifiable.
- The third condition set out in Case 4/69 *Lütticke*, that is, the existence of a causal connection between the conduct and the damage in question. The damage must not be too remote, and must be a sufficiently direct consequence of the conduct of the relevant institution.

D. In Case C-47/07 *Masdar*, the ECJ decided that a claim based on unjust enrichment may be brought under Article 340(2) TFEU. The only requirement that the applicant must satisfy is the proof of enrichment of the defendant for which there is no valid legal basis and the impoverishment of the applicant which is linked to that enrichment.

E. In Joined Cases C-120/06 P and C-121/06 P *FIAMM*, the ECJ rejected the possibility that the EU may be held liable for lawful acts that may cause damage.

F. Under Article 46 of the Statute of the CJEU there is a five-year limitation period running from the day the damage materialised, not from the time of the fact or event giving rise to the damage. It may be suspended by:

- Proceedings brought by the applicant before the CJEU, or
- A preliminary request addressed by the applicant to the relevant institution, but only if followed by an application under Articles 263 TFEU or 265 TFEU and within the time limit set out in these provisions.

16.1   Introduction

By virtue of Article 5(2) TEU all EU institutions are required to act within the limits of the powers conferred upon them by the Treaties. EU law provides a number of mechanisms with a view to ensuring that EU institutions, bodies, offices and agencies function properly and do not exceed their powers. In this respect the CJEU exercises jurisdiction similar to that exercised by the administrative courts in the Member States.

The EU recognises the following actions against EU institutions, bodies, offices and agencies:

- Actions under Article 263 TFEU for annulment of EU acts;

- Actions under Article 265 TFEU for failure to act against EU institutions, bodies, offices or agencies;

- The so-called plea of illegality, defined in Article 277 TFEU; and

- Actions for damages caused by EU institutions to individuals involving non-contractual liability of the former under Articles 268 and 340(2) TFEU. However, if the ECB is found liable, bearing in mind that it is an independent EU institution financed by contributions from national central banks of the Member States, in accordance with Article 340(3) TFEU, the ECB itself is liable (not the EU) and must pay compensation to the injured party from its own resources.

The ToN limited the ECJ's jurisdiction in respect of actions brought under Articles 263 and 265 TFEU to the most important cases, that is, those brought by privileged and semi-privileged applicants.

The important feature of the above actions is that natural and legal persons are allowed to bring them before the CJEU. Under the ToL access to the CJEU has been widened although there are still uncertainties as to the extent to which the new rules improve individuals' access to justice within the EU (see section 16.2.3.3.3). For that reason, for individuals considering attacking EU acts under Article 263 TFEU, an action in a national court may be more appropriate provided implementing measures have been adopted at national level. If action is to be taken in a national court, a natural or legal person should bring an action for judicial review of national measures implementing the contested EU act,[958] as the contested act itself is immune from challenge in this way. Bearing in mind that only the ECJ is entitled to declare an EU act as invalid, a national court will almost certainly refer the issue of validity of an EU act, where this is in doubt, to the ECJ under Article 267 TFEU, and meanwhile will suspend the operation of a national measure based on the contested EU act. The final result may be a declaration of invalidity of the EU act by the ECJ, and thus a natural or legal person may achieve the objective of successfully challenging the legality of an EU act in an indirect manner.

With the entry into force of the ToL, the CJEU's jurisdiction under Article 263 TFEU has, in addition to areas previously covered by EC law, been extended as follows:

A.   In respect of the area of FSJ, the CJEU has jurisdiction over all acts adopted by EU institutions, bodies, offices and agencies. This is subject to two limitations:

- A temporal limitation in that in the field of police and judicial co-operation in criminal matters in respect of measures which were adopted before the entry into

---

958.   The word "act" refers to any legislation or administrative decision of a EU institution, body, agency or office.

force of the ToL the CJEU's jurisdiction will commence five years after the entry into force of the ToL but if any particular measure (adopted before the entry into force of the ToL) is amended before the expiry of that period then that measure will be within the jurisdiction of the Court from the time of amendment;

■ A pre-ToL limitation in that the ECJ has no jurisdiction to review the validity and proportionality of operations carried out by police and other enforcement agencies with a view to maintaining law and order and the safeguarding of the internal security of a Member State (see Chapter 10.2).

B. Under the ToL, the ECJ has jurisdiction to assess the lawfulness of procedural aspects of a determination made by the European Council or the Council that a clear risk has been identified of serious infringement by a Member State of values on which the EU is founded. Proceedings may be brought by the Member State against whom the determination has been made within one month from the date of that determination. The ECJ must give its ruling within one month from the date of request (Article 269 TFEU).

C. Member States are empowered to bring an action for annulment of an EU act which according to their national parliament, or one of its parliament's chambers, does not comply with the principle of subsidiarity. Although such an action is brought by a Member State it may also be simply "notified" by a Member State, as the actual applicant is the national parliament or a chamber of that parliament. Further, the CoR can bring an action for annulment based on the infringement of the principle of subsidiarity, but only in respect of acts on which it is required to be consulted.

D. With regard to the CFSP the CJEU has no jurisdiction. However, this is subject to two exceptions:

■ Under Article 40 TEU, the ECJ has jurisdiction to ensure that the implementation of the CFSP does not impinge on non-CFSP polices of the EU and vice versa, i.e. that measures adopted in non-CFSP matters do not encroach on CFSP matters;

■ The ECJ has jurisdiction to review the legality of decisions providing for restrictive measures against natural or legal persons adopted by the Council on the basis of Chapter 2 of Title 5 of the TEU (see Chapter 13.6).

16.2   Action for annulment under Article 263 TFEU

Article 263 TFEU provides:

"The Court of Justice of the European Union shall review the legality of legislative acts, of acts of the Council, of the Commission and of the European Central Bank, other than recommendations and opinions, and of acts of the European Parliament and of the European Council intended to pro-duce legal effects *vis-à-vis* third parties. It shall also review the legality of acts of bodies, offices or agencies of the Union intended to produce legal effects *vis-à-vis* third parties.

It shall for this purpose have jurisdiction in actions brought by a Member State, the European Parliament, the Council or the Commission on grounds of lack of competence, infringement of an essential procedural requirement, infringement of the Treaties or of any rule of law relating to their application, or misuse of powers.

The Court shall have jurisdiction under the same conditions in actions brought by the Court of

Auditors, by the European Central Bank and by the Committee of the Regions for the purpose of protecting their prerogatives.

Any natural or legal person may, under the conditions laid down in the first and second paragraphs, institute proceedings against an act addressed to that person or which is of direct and individual concern to them, and against a regulatory act which is of direct concern to them and does not entail implementing measures.

Acts setting up bodies, offices and agencies of the Union may lay down specific conditions and arrangements concerning actions brought by natural or legal persons against acts of these bodies, offices or agencies intended to produce legal effects in relation to them.

The proceedings provided for in this Article shall be instituted within two months of the publication of the measure, or of its notification to the plaintiff, or, in the absence thereof, of the day on which it came to the knowledge of the latter, as the case may be."

An action for annulment is similar to what is known under the law of England and Wales (and also recognised in Scottish law) as an application for judicial review.

The requirements imposed by Article 263 TFEU are examined below. They concern:

- Acts which can be reviewed;

- Applicants permitted to act on the basis of Article 263 TFEU;

- The grounds for annulment;

- The time limit for bringing an action for annulment.

16.2.1   Reviewable acts

Under Article 263 TFEU the following legislative and other acts are reviewable:

- Acts of the Council, the Commission and of the European Central Bank other than recommendations and opinions;

- Acts adopted jointly by the EP and the European Council intended to produce legal effects with regard to third parties;

- Acts of bodies, offices or agencies of the EU intended to produce legal effects vis-à-vis third parties.

The simplicity of the above list is illusive. In fact matters are complex and need to be examined from the point of view of the author of the act and with regard to the nature of the act.

16.2.1.1   Author of the act

The principle that only acts adopted by the EU institutions, bodies, offices or agencies are reviewable is self-evident but poses many challenges in practice. These are examined below.

16.2.1.1.1   Acts adopted by Member States

Acts adopted by a particular Member State or Member States are outside the scope of Article 263 TFEU – national measures impacting on EU law are dealt with through the preliminary reference procedure under Article 267 TFEU. In practice, however, it is not always easy to determine whether a particular act should be considered as adopted by a EU institution or a Member State.

For example, in Case C-97/91 *Oleificio Borelli SpA v Commission*[959] the ECJ held that it had no jurisdiction to rule on lawfulness of an opinion unfavourable to the applicant adopted by the relevant national authorities, which opinion led up to the Commission's decision refusing to grant aid to the applicant. Thus, a national measure is not reviewable under Article 263 TFEU despite the measure having been adopted pursuant to an EU act.

Sometimes Member States act within the Council, but outside its competence as a EU institution. The question of how to determine whether an act, irrespective of its form and name, adopted by the Council is an act of the Council or an act adopted by the Member States meeting within the framework of the Council (that is, as an international conference) was resolved in Case 22/70 *Commission v Council [ERTA]*.[960] In this case the ECJ had to decide, inter alia, whether deliberations concerning the European Road Transport Agreement (ERTA) were reviewable under Article 263 TFEU. The ECJ held that the "status" of an act depends on the determination of who, at the relevant time, had competence to negotiate and conclude it. The legal effect of the deliberations varies depending upon whether they are considered as an act within the competence of the EU, or as an expression of policy co-ordination between the Member States in a specific area. The ECJ decided that the deliberations in this case belonged to the first category, as the EU had competence to negotiate and conclude the ERTA. Accordingly, they were reviewable under Article 263 TFEU. In Joined Cases C-181/91 and C-248/91 *EP v Council and Commission*,[961] where the facts were different from those in the *ERTA* case, the ECJ held inadmissible for the purposes of Article 263 TFEU an act adopted on the proposal of the Commission by "the Member States meeting within the Council" granting emergency aid to Bangladesh. This was because the EU had no exclusive competence in the area of humanitarian aid.

16.2.1.1.2 Acts adopted by the European Council

Under the ToL, The European Council has become a fully fledged EU institution authorised to adopt binding acts. As a result, those of its acts which are intended to produce binding effects vis-à-vis third parties are reviewable under Article 263 TFEU.

16.2.1.1.3 Acts adopted under delegated powers

If one EU institution delegates certain powers to another EU institution, the question arises: who is the author of the act? In this respect, the case law of the ECJ is well established – the author of the act is the institution which has delegated its competences. Although the author of the act is always the delegating institution, an action against the delegate institution is admissible as being brought against the delegating institution.[962] This is illustrated in Cases T-253/02 *Chafiq Ayadi*[963] and T-49/04 *Faraj Hassan v Council and Commission*.[964]

---

959. [1992] ECR I-6313.
960. [1971] ECR 263 (for facts see Chapter 4.3.2).
961. [1993] ECR I-3685.
962. Joined Cases 7/56 and 3/57 to 7/57 *Algera and Others v Common Assembly of the ECSC* [1957–58] ECR 39; Joined Cases 32/58 and 33/58 *SNUPAT v High Authority* [1959] ECR 127; and Joined Cases T-369/94 and T-85/95 *DIR International Film and Others v Commission* [1998] ECR II-357.
963. [2006] ECR II-2139.
964. [2006] ECR II-52.

If a certain task is delegated to a particular person, e.g. if the Commission empowers one of the commissioners to inform the addressee that an act has been adopted by the Commission, that act is deemed to emanate from the Commission.[965]

Under the ToL the identification of the author of the act becomes easier in that all non legislative acts adopted in the form of a regulation, directive or a decision should specify in their title that they are delegated acts and should mention the name of the institution which effected the delegation.

16.2.1.1.4 Acts adopted by the EP

Until the entry into force of the Treaty of Maastricht acts adopted by the EP were not formally reviewable. In practice, however, the ECJ, had, in a number of decisions, recognised that acts of the EP were reviewable:

■ In Case 230/81 *Luxembourg v EP*,[966] deliberations of the EP concerning the change of its seat were challenged by Luxembourg. The ECJ held the action admissible on the grounds that the deliberations concerned all three Communities and based its decision on Article 38 CS which permits a challenge to acts of the Parliament;

---

965. Case 48/69 *ICI* [1972] ECR 652. The ECJ accepted the validity of the delegation of signature.
966. [1983] ECR 255.

■ In Case 294/83 *"Les Verts" v Parliament*,[967] the ECJ could not make reference to Article 38 CS (as it had in Case 230/81 *Luxembourg v EP*) because the applicant was a legal person and as such its action for annulment was ruled out under both the CS and the EC Treaties. Despite this, the ECJ recognised the reviewability of acts emanating from the EP and explained that since the EC is a Community based on the rule of law, neither the Member States, nor Community institutions, can escape the control of the conformity of their acts with the basic constitutional charter, that is the EC Treaty. This full recognition of acts of the EP as reviewable constituted an example of judicial revision of the Treaty. This revision was well justified, taking into account the evolution of the EP from an advisory and supervisory body to a body increasingly involved in the decision-making procedures. It was also arguably necessary in the light of the principle of effectiveness to ensure the control of the legality of the EP's acts, in particular those intended to produce legal effect vis-à-vis a third party, although a formal amendment to the EC Treaty might have been the better way to achieve this.

The case law of the ECJ shows that reviewable acts of the EP comprise not only acts adopted by the EP as an institution, but also by its organs, such as its Bureau for the allocation of funds amongst political parties,[968] or the Declaration of the President of the European Parliament regarding the adoption of the EU budget.[969]

Acts which are not considered as reviewable under Article 263 TFEU include: an act establishing a parliamentary commission of inquiry,[970] the waiver of immunity[971] or acts emanating from the EP's political parties or political groups.[972]

16.2.1.1.5 Acts adopted by bodies, offices or agencies of the EU

The ToL, for the first time, expressly recognised that not only acts adopted by the EU institutions but also those adopted by EU bodies, offices or agencies, provided they produce binding legal effects vis-à-vis third parties, are reviewable under Article 263 TFEU. However, before the entry into force of the ToL, the Community courts [the CJEU] recognised the possibility of challenging the validity of acts emanating from bodies, offices or agencies of the EU. The Courts accepted for review, inter alia, acts adopted by the European Investment Bank under Article 237 EC [Article 271 TFEU];[973] the European Investment Fund; the Board of Appeal of the Community Trade Mark Office under Article 63 of Council Regulation 40/94;[974] the Community Plant Variety Office and its Board of Appeal under Article 73 and 74 of Council Regulation 2100/94[975] and the European Agency for Reconstruction.[976] Further, in Cases C-193 and 194/87 *Maurissen v CoA*,[977] the ECJ accepted an action for annulment brought by a legal person against the CoA.

---

967. [1986] ECR 1339.
968. [1986] ECR 1339.
969. Case 34/86 *Council v Parliament* [1986] ECR 2155; Case C-284–90 *Council v Parliament* [1992] ECR I-2328.
970. Case 78/85 *Groupe des Droites Européennes v EP* [1986] ECR 1754 (Ord.).
971. Case 149/85 *Roger Wybot v Edgar Faure and Others* [1986] ECR 2391.
972. Case C-201/89 *Jean-Marie Le Pen and the Front National v Detlef Puhl and Others* [1990] ECR I-1183.
973. In Case T-460/93 *Tete v EIB* [1993] ECR II-1257.
974. [1994] OJ L11/1.
975. [1994] OJ L227/31.
976. Case T-411/06 *Sogelma v European Agency for Reconstruction* [2008] ECR II-2771.
977. [1990] ECR I-95.

16.2.1.1.6 International agreements concluded between the EU and third countries

These are considered as acts emanating from EU institutions.[978] It is submitted that this situation ignores the distinction between international agreements themselves, and acts adopted by EU institutions regarding the conclusion or application of such agreements. In the first case, the ECJ should not exercise jurisdiction under Article 263 TFEU because international agreements are not acts of EU institutions; they are international treaties within the meaning of public international law. However, in the second case, the ECJ should be, and is, empowered to annul, for example, a decision of the Commission concerning the conclusion of an agreement with a third country,[979] or a decision regarding the application of an international agreement,[980] because those acts emanate from EU institutions and as such should be and are reviewable under Article 263 TFEU.

16.2.1.1.7 Decisions of the European Economic Area (EEA) Joint Committee

The EEA Joint Committee is an organ set up under the EEA Agreement, and thus is not an EU institution. Therefore, its acts are not reviewable under Article 263 TFEU.[981]

16.2.2 Nature of the act

The ECJ has considerably extended the category of reviewable acts. In Case 22/70 *Commission v Council [ERTA]*,[982] it held that not only acts listed in Article 249 EC [Article 288 TFEU] can be challenged under Article 230 EC [Article 263 TFEU] but also any act which has binding legal effects, whatever its nature and form. The ToL confirms this development as Article 263 TFEU states that all acts adopted by EU institutions, bodies, offices or agencies which produce legal effects vis-à-vis third parties are reviewable.

The content and scope of application of an act are the decisive factors, not its form and name. The case law of the ECJ clarified this point in relation to borderline cases. The following acts are considered as reviewable under Article 263 TFEU:

- Deliberations of the Council in ERTA;[983]

- A communication of the Commission which by means of interpretation of a directive introduces new obligations;[984]

- A Code of Conduct adopted with a view to co-ordinating management of structural funds, but published in the section "Communication and information" of the Official Journal;[985]

- A letter from the Commission;[986]

- A decision orally communicated to the applicant;[987]

---

978. Case 181/73 *Haegeman* [1974] ECR 449.
979. Case C-327/91 *France v Commission* [1994] ECR I-3641.
980. Case 30/88 *Greece v Commission* [1989] ECR 374.
981. Case T-376/04 *Polyelectrolyte Producers Group v Council and Commission* [2005] ECR II-3007 (Ord).
982. [1971] ECR 263.
983. [1971] ECR 263.
984. Case C-325/91 *France v Commission* [1993] ECR I-3283.
985. Case C-303/90 *France and Belgium v Commission* [1991] ECR I-5315.
986. Case 1/57 *Usines à Tubes de la Sarre* [1957–1958] ECR 105.
987. Cases 316/82 and 40/83 *Kohler v CoA* [1984] ECR 641; Case T-3/93 *Air France* [1994] ECR II-121.

- An official declaration made by the Commissioner in charge of competition matters declaring the EU Merger rules inapplicable to the acquisition of Dan Air by British Airways;[988]

- A letter from the Commission stating reasons for rejecting a complaint under competition law;[989]

- A letter from the Director General of the Directorate General for Agriculture of the Commission informing a Member State of the reduction of advanced funds in respect of the financing of rural developments from the European Guidance and Guarantee Fund.[990]

The ECJ has held that the following acts are not reviewable under Article 263 TFEU:

- All acts which only confirm an existing situation, since they do not modify the legal position of the applicant;[991]

- All acts which set up a global policy of the EU in a specific subject area, that is, establishing programmes of the EU, since they envisage future measures and thus do not change the current legal situation of the applicant;[992]

- All internal measures adopted by EU institutions which produce legal effects only vis-à-vis that institution, such as instructions, internal rules, circulars, and so on.[993] However, these may be challenged indirectly, provided they produce binding legal effect, if an individual decision was based on such internal measures;[994]

- All preparatory acts of EU institutions, since the challengeable act must be a final statement of an institution's position, not merely an interim position.[995] In Case 60/81 *IBM v Commission*,[996] the Commission decision to commence proceedings against IBM, and a statement of objections to its marketing practices as being incompatible with Articles 81 and 82 EC [Articles 101 and 102 TFEU] (which was annexed to the decision), was considered as a step in the proceedings. The idea behind this rule is that work of EU institutions would be paralysed if preparatory acts were reviewable. However, an action for annulment of such acts is allowed if they produce binding effects or if they constitute a final position in ancillary proceedings, which would result in the adoption of a final decision. This distinction is difficult to apply in practice, especially in cases concerning competition law, state aid and anti-dumping measures – for example, a decision to forward documents to a complaining undertaking,[997] a decision to deny access to a file in an anti-dumping case,[998] a decision

---

988.   Case T-3/93 *Air France* [1994] ECR II-121.
989.   Case T-37/92 *BEUC* [1994] ECR II-285.
990.   Case C-249/02 *Portugal v Commission* [2004] ECR I-10717.
991.   Joined Cases 42 and 49/59 *SNUPAT* [1961] ECR 53; Case T-106/05 *Evropaiki Dinamiki* [2006] ECR II-82.
992.   Case 9/73 *Schlüter* [1973] ECR 1135; Case C-142/95P *Associazione Agricoltori della Provincia di Rivigo* [1996] ECR I-6669.
993.   Case 20/58 *Phoenix-Rheinrohr* [1959] ECR 75; Case C-322/91 *TAO* [1992] ECR 1–6373 (Ord).
994.   Joined Cases 32 and 33/58 *SNUPAT v High Authority* [1959] ECR 127.
995.   Case T-175/96 *Berthu* [1997] ECR II-811; Case T-376/04 *Polyelectrolyte Producers Group v Council and Commission* [2005] ECR II-3007 (Ord.).
996.   Case 60/81 *International Business Machines Corporation v Commission* [1981] ECR 2639; Case C-282/95P *Guérin* [1997] ECR I-1503.
997.   Case 53/85 *AKZO Chemie* [1986] ECR 1965; Case T-46/92 *Scottish Football Association* [1994] ECR II-1039.
998.   Case C-170/89 *BEUC* [1991] ECR I-5709.

to refuse to initiate proceedings under Article 86 EC [Article 106(2) TFEU][999] or Article 88(2) EC [Article108(2) TFEU] concerning state aid.[1000] All were regarded as reviewable, but a letter refusing to protect confidentiality of documents forwarded to the Commission by the applicant was not considered as a reviewable act;[1001]

■ A decision of the Commission to refuse to initiate proceedings against a Member State which is allegedly in breach of EU law under Article 258 TFEU. In Case 48/65 *Lütticke*,[1002] the ECJ held that a part of the procedure prior to bringing the Member State before the ECJ constitutes a stage which is designed to invite the Member State to fulfil its obligations arising out of the Treaties. At this stage of Article 258 TFEU proceedings, the Commission states its position by issuing an opinion. Such an opinion cannot produce binding legal effects. This position of the ECJ has been confirmed in many cases;[1003]

■ Regulation 2187/93, which was adopted by the Council in order to comply with ECJ rulings concerning the illegality of Council Regulations allocating milk quotas.[1004] It contained a proposal for compensation for approximately 12,000 farmers who were entitled to damages by virtue of Article 288(2) EC [Article340(2) TFEU].

In Case T-541/93 *Connaughton* and Case T-554/93 *Murray*,[1005] the applicants brought an action for annulment of Articles 8 and 14 of Regulation 2187/93, which provided that the acceptance of compensation by a farmer precluded him from any other action, irrespective of its nature, against any EC institutions. The CFI [the General Court] held that the Regulation in question was only a proposal and, as such, did not produce legal effects. Consequently, it was not considered as a reviewable act within the meaning of Article 230 EC [Article 263 TFEU]. The CFI [the General Court] emphasised that once the proposal was accepted, it would produce legal effects vis-à-vis the applicant, but not before;

■ A decision of the Commission to bring a civil action before courts in the USA against certain manufacturers of tobacco products in the USA for their alleged involvement in smuggling cigarettes into the EU and thus causing the EU a loss of customs and tax revenue which are part of "own resources" of the EU.[1006] The ECJ held that the decision did not produce binding legal effects as it did not change the legal position of the likely defendants in proceedings in the USA.

16.2.3 Applicants under Article 263 TFEU

Article 263 TFEU establishes three categories of applicants:

■ Privileged applicants, who may bring an action for annulment against all reviewable acts and are not required to justify their interest to act;

---

999. Case C-313/90 *CIRFS* [1993] ECR I-1125.
1000. Case C-312/91 *Spain v Commission* [1992] ECR I-4117; Case C-47/91 *Italy v Commission* [1992] ECR I-4145.
1001. Cases T-90/96 and T-136/96 *Automobiles Peugeot* [1997] ECR II-663.
1002. [1966] ECR 19.
1003. Case C-87/89 *Sonito v Commission* [1990] ECR I-1981; Case C-247/90 *Emrich* [1990] ECR I-3913; Case T-479 and 559/93 *Bernardi* [1994] ECR II-1115.
1004. For example, Case C-104/89 *Mulder* [1992] ECR I-3061.
1005. [1997] ECR II-563.
1006. Case C-131/03P *R.J. Reynolds Tobacco Holdings, Inc. and Others v Commission* [2006] ECR II-7795.

- Semi-privileged applicants, such as the CoA, the ECB and the CoR which may only challenge acts in order to defend their prerogatives;

- Non-privileged applicants, who, apart from a situation where they are addressees of a decision, must establish that they are directly and individually concerned by a non-regulatory act and directly concerned by a regulatory act which does not entail any implementing measures.

16.2.3.1 Privileged applicants

Under Articles 263 TFEU the Council, the EP, the Commission and the Member States are privileged applicants. They may challenge any reviewable acts and they have unrestricted locus standi.

In relation to the Commission the privileged status is justified on the basis that the Commission is the guardian of the Treaties, as specifically provided in Article 17(1) TEU.

The extension of this privileged status to the Council is a logical consequence of its position within the institutional framework of the EU.

The Member States as contracting parties to the Treaties are particularly interested in defending their rights against unlawful measures adopted by the EU institutions, bodies, offices or agencies. A Member State under its unrestricted locus standi may challenge an act addressed to another Member State[1007] or even an act which was adopted with its consent.[1008] The only condition for privileged applicants is that they must challenge an act within the time limit set out in Article 263(5) TFEU.

The EP was initially denied locus standi, but became a semi-privileged applicant under the Treaty of Maastricht and finally acquired the status of a privileged applicant under the ToN.[1009] The current status of the EP is well justified given that it has become a co-legislator and the fact that it is the only directly elected body of the EU.

16.2.3.2 Semi-privileged applicants

These are the CoA, the ECB and the CoR. These institutions have locus standi for the purpose of protecting their prerogatives.

16.2.3.3 Non-privileged applicants

Non-privileged applicants under Article 263 TFEU are natural or legal persons. Unless they are addressees of a decision, they have many hurdles to jump over to establish locus standi under Article 263 TFEU.

16.2.3.3.1 Interest to act

Applicants under Article 263 TFEU must first justify their interest in seeing the contested measure annulled. Such an interest must be present and actual, not merely hypothetical. In Case

---

1007. Case 6/54 *The Netherlands v High Authority* [1954–1956] ECR 103.
1008. Case 166/78 *Italy v Council* [1979] ECR 2575; Italy had voted in favour of the measure in the Council.
1009. Case C-70/88 *EP v Council* [1990] ECR I-2041.

T-141/03 *Sniace SA v Commission*,[1010] the CFI [the General Court] held that this requirement constitutes a prerequisite for any action for annulment. This prerequisite is usually not mentioned, given that in 99 per cent of cases the interest of an applicant to bring an action for annulment is self-evident.

Non-privileged applicants are required to show that an EU act has affected their rights protected under the EU law "at present". As a result, an interest regarding a future legal situation which might happen, which is uncertain or subject to changes in circumstances in law or in fact, is outside the scope of Article 263 TFEU.[1011] Further, applicants are required to prove that the contested measure has had a detrimental effect on their personal situation.[1012] Accordingly, applicants cannot challenge a decision which is favourable to their interests.[1013]

The ECJ has been very liberal in the assessment of the interest to act under Article 263 TFEU. The ECJ considered admissible an application where the contested decision had already been complied with by its addressee at the time when the action for annulment was brought[1014] or where the contested measure had already been annulled.[1015] However, very strict requirements as to the admissibility of applications in relation to the nature of the act and to the situation of the applicant vis-à-vis the act have more than balanced the favourable approach of the CJEU to the concept of the interest to act.

16.2.3.3.2 Locus standi of associations

An association has locus standi in the following situations:

■ Where the relevant EU act has granted it procedural rights to that effect, for example, the Merger Regulation;[1016]

■ Where it represents its members which themselves are either directly concerned by a regulatory act which does not entail any implementing measures or directly and individually concerned by a non-regulatory act;

■ Where the relevant EU act affects an association's own interests so as to distinguish it individually;[1017]

■ Where the role of the applicant association in the preparation of the challenged acts was substantial.[1018]

1010. [2005] ECR II-1197, see also Case T-167/01 *Schmitz-Gotha Fahrzeugwerke GmbH v Commission* [2003] ECR II-1873 (Ord).

1011. For example, Case T-138/89 *NBV* [1992] ECR II-2181.

1012. This is assessed favourably to the applicants in Case 77/77 *Benzine en Petroleum Handelsmaatschappij* [1978] ECR 1513.

1013. Ibid.

1014. Case T-46/92 *Scottish Football Association v Commission* [1994] ECR II-1039; Cases T-480 and 483/93 *Antillean Rice* [1995] ECR II-2305.

1015. Case 76/79 *Könecke* [1980] ECR 665.

1016. T-12/93 *Vittel* [1995] ECR II-1247.

1017. Joined Cases T-481–484/93 *Vereniging van Exporteurs in Levende Varkens and Others v Commission* [1995] ECR II-2941.

1018. Cases 67/85, 68/85 and 70/85 *Van der Kooy* [1988] ECR 219; Case C-313/90 *CIRFS and Others v Commission* [1993] ECR I-1125; Case T-122/96 *Federolio* [1997] ECR II-1559; Joined Cases T-481–484/93 *Exporteur in Levende Varkens* [1995] ECR II-2941.

On the basis of the above, associations such as Greenpeace[1019] and a European economic interest group representing producers of coagulants and synthetic flocculants[1020] were refused locus standi under Article 263 TFEU, the reason being that had they had this standing, an actio popularis would have been introduced which is contrary to the philosophy of Article 263 TFEU.

16.2.3.3.3 Reviewable acts

Non-privileged applicants can always challenge a decision addressed to them. This is a classic judicial review situation and thus needs no further explanation. In respect of acts which are not decisions addressed to an applicant the establishment of locus standi under Article 263 TFEU is not easy. Prior to entry into force of the ToL, non-privileged applicants could satisfy the admissibility threshold by establishing that they were directly and individually concerned by a decision addressed to "another person" or that an act in the form of a regulation or a directive, i.e. an act of general application, was in fact a decision addressed to them. To establish individual concern was extremely difficult in respect of acts of general application because a non-privileged applicant had to show that the effect of such an act was so peculiar to him, and to him alone, that he was individually distinguished from everybody else by the act.

The ToL facilitates access to the CJEU for non-privileged applicants in that it makes a distinction between challenges concerning regulatory and non-regulatory acts. In respect of regulatory acts which do not entail any implementing measures non-privileged applicants need only to prove that they are directly concerned by the act. This is fairly easy to establish (see section 16.2.3.3.4). However, in respect of non-regulatory acts the pre-ToL requirements for locus standi still stand.

The main difficulty with Article 263 TFEU is that neither this article nor the Treaties provide any definition of the concept of a "regulatory act". Two plausible interpretations of the concept of regulatory acts can be submitted.

- The first interpretation is that a regulatory act is an act of general application which produces legal effects, regardless of its legislative nature. As a result, all regulations would be regulatory acts.

- The second interpretation is that only non-legislative acts, i.e. acts other than those adopted in accordance with either the ordinary legislative procedure or special legislative procedures are to be regarded as regulatory acts.

It seems that the second interpretation is more plausible because under the first interpretation non-privileged applicants would have almost unrestricted access to the CJEU with the result that the CJEU would be flooded with applications and the EU institutions would spend most of their time and resources defending the legality of acts they have adopted. However, under this interpretation the right to effective judicial remedy under Article 263 TFEU would be ensured in that the situation that occurred in Case T-177/01 *Jégo-Quéré v Commission*[1021] would be avoided. In this case the CFI [the General Court] decided that the applicant was individually concerned by a measure of general application which did not necessitate any implementing measures at national level, and therefore the applicant could not initiate proceedings before the national courts, despite

---

1019. Case C-321/95 *Stichting Greenpeace Council (Greenpeace International) and Others v Commission* [1998] ECR I-1651.

1020. Case T-376/04 *Polyelectrolyte Producers Group v Council and Commission* [2005] ECR II-3007 (Ord.).

1021. [2002] ECR II-2365.

the fact that the measure in question (by restricting his rights or by imposing obligations on him) affected his legal position in a manner which was both definite and immediate. Indeed, the only way in which the applicant could gain access to a national court was to knowingly infringe the contested measure. In that case, the CFI [the General Court] emphasised that individuals cannot be required to breach the law in order to have access to justice. However, in Case C-50/00P *Unión de Pequeños Agricultores (UPA) v Council*,[1022] the ECJ rejected the judgment of the CFI [the General Court] in Case T-177/01 *Jégo-Quéré*. In *UPA* it was clear that the appellant did not enjoy effective judicial protection under EU law. The ECJ, however, did not accept that the appellant had no legal remedies (that is, that it was suffering a denial of justice) under EU law. Instead the ECJ stated that there was another way of ensuring the effectiveness of the appellant's right to judicial protection, that is, under national law. In paragraph 41 of the judgment the ECJ stated that:

"... it is for the Member States to establish a system of legal remedies and procedures which ensure respect for the right to effective judicial protection."

This solution is enshrined in Article 19(1) TEU.

The second interpretation of "regulatory acts" under Article 263 TFEU is supported by many arguments:

▪ The Treaties make a distinction between legislative and non-legislative acts and therefore it is logical to assume that non-legislative acts, i.e. delegated and implementing acts are to be regarded as regulatory acts;

▪ The recognition by the ToL of the EP as a co-legislator ensures democratic control over legislative acts of the EU and therefore, the imposition of restrictions on access to the CJEU under Article 263 TFEU is justified. As a result, in respect of legislative acts the applicants would be required to establish that they are directly and individually concerned by them;

▪ It is logical to assume that the reference to regulatory acts (which acts do not entail any implementing measures) concerns non-legislative acts given that non-legislative acts by their very nature contain implementing measures;

▪ To avoid a situation similar to that which occurred in Case T-177/01 *Jégo-Quéré* Article 19(1) TEU states that "Member States shall provide remedies sufficient to ensure effective legal protection in the fields covered by Union law". As a result, it is the responsibility of the Member States, not the EU, to ensure that their citizens have the right to effective legal remedy. If a Member State fails to do this, the Commission may commence Article 258 TFEU proceedings, and an applicant may start proceedings against the defaulting Member State before a national court based on the *Francovich* remedy;

▪ In practice, legislative acts which do not require implementing measures are rare.

Whichever interpretation is given to the concept of "regulatory acts" access to the CJEU has been improved under the ToL in that for regulatory acts which do not entail implementing measures the requirement to establish individual concern has been dropped. The ToL, irrespective of the interpretation which the ECJ will finally give to the concept of "regulatory acts", will improve

---

1022. [2002] ECR I-6677.

individuals' access to justice within the EU. This can be exemplified by Case T-47/95 *Terres Rouges Consultant SA and Others v Commission*,[1023] In this case the largest importers of bananas from Côte d'Ivoire (who between them imported 70 per cent of Côte d'Ivoire's production and amongst whom was Terres Rouges Consultant, who imported bananas from that country only), were denied individual concern in respect of a Regulation adopted by the Commission, which substantially restricted the quantity of bananas which Côte d'Ivoire could export in order to comply with the requirement of GATT and international agreements concluded between the Community and certain South American countries. The CFI [the General Court] held that the fact that a restricted number of traders imported a large proportion of Côte d'Ivoire's bananas did not amount to circumstances differentiating them from other importers. Had the ToL been applicable to this case, the applicant would have been required to establish only direct concern, which would have been fairly straightforward taking into account that the challenged regulation was an implementing regulation which did not require any further implementing measures.

16.2.3.3.4 Challenges of both regulatory and non-regulatory acts by non-privileged applicants under Article 263 TFEU: the concept of direct concern

In respect of both regulatory acts which do not require any implementing measures and non-regulatory acts a non-privileged applicant is required to establish that he is directly concerned by the relevant act.

In order to establish direct concern, applicants must show that the relevant measure directly affects their legal situation and that the addressee of that measure has no discretion in implementing it, i.e. such implementation must be purely automatic and resulting from EU rules without the application of other intermediate rules.[1024]

The best way to illustrate this point is to examine Case 123/77 *UNICME and Others v Council*.[1025]

THE FACTS WERE:

Under a Council regulation, only holders of an import licence issued by the Italian Government were allowed to import Japanese motorcycles. The applicants, Italian importers of such motorcycles and their trade association, UNICME, challenged the regulation.

Held:

The ECJ held that the applicants were not directly concerned because the Italian Government had discretion as to the grant of import licences. As a result, they were concerned not by the Regulation, but by the subsequent refusal of import licences by the Italian authorities.

If a Member State has no discretion as to the application of an EU measure, applicants can claim that they are directly concerned. For example, in Joined Cases 41–44/70 *International Fruit*

1023. [1997] ECR II-481.

1024. Case C-404/96 P *Glencore Grain v Commission* [1998] ECR I-2435; Case C-486/01 P *National Front v Parliament* [2004] ECR I-6289; Case C-15/06 P *Regione Siciliana v Commission* [2007] ECR I-2591.

1025. [1978] ECR 845.

Co v Commission[1026] the granting of import licences for dessert apples, which was based on an EU rule, was modified by a Commission regulation. The latter imposed on the Member States specific rules for dealing with such licences. As a result, national authorities had no discretion in the matter.

If a Member State first decides how to deal with a particular issue and then asks the Commission to confirm that decision, as occurred in Joined Cases 106 and 107/63 *Toepfer*,[1027] the applicant is directly concerned (once the decision of the national authority has been confirmed by the Commission) because a Member State must follow a confirmation by the Commission.

One exception to the above rule was established in Case 11/82 *Piraïki Patraïki v Council*,[1028] in which the ECJ held that an applicant satisfies the requirement relating to direct concern in a situation where the likelihood of the addressee of the relevant measure not giving effect to it is purely theoretical and the addressee's intention to act in conformity with it is not in doubt.

THE FACTS WERE:

The Commission gave permission to the French Government to impose quotas on imports of yarn from Greece. Although the French authorities had discretion as to whether or not to impose quotas, in the light of previous restrictions imposed on such imports and of a request to use the quotas submitted to the Commission by the French Government, which was granted, it was highly unlikely, or as the ECJ held "purely theoretical", that the French authorities would not exercise their discretion to impose quotas.

Held:

The ECJ held that the possibility that a Member State might decide not to make use of the authorisation obtained from the Commission was entirely theoretical, since there could be no doubt as to the intention of the Member State to act in accordance with the authorisation. Accordingly, the link between the applicant and an EU act was not severed by a mere possibility that a Member State may not take authorised measures, which in this case was highly unlikely. Therefore the applicants were directly concerned by the measure.

It is to be noted that the ECJ has always refused to recognise that a region of a Member State could claim to be directly concerned by an EU measure. In Case C-15/06P *Regione Siciliana v Commission*,[1029] the CFI [the General Court] decided that Sicily, a region of Italy which possesses legal personality under national law, was directly concerned by a Commission decision withholding the assistance granted to Italy to build a dam in Sicily and requesting reimbursement of sums already paid in the light of delays and irregularities in the implementation of aid. Both the CFI [the General Court] and ECJ agreed that the region of Sicily was individually concerned given the financial implications of the request for reimbursement, but the ECJ agreed with the Commission

---

1026. [1971] ECR 411.
1027. [1965] ECR 405.
1028. [1985] ECR 207, see also Case 62/70 *Bock* [1971] ECR 897; Case 29/75 *Kaufhof* [1976] ECR 431; Case T-85/94 *Branco* [1995] ECR II-45.
1029. [2007] ECR I-2591.

that the region was not directly concerned because the aid was granted to Italy, not to the region, and that the Italian Government enjoyed discretion, first as to whether to grant assistance to the region and second, as to the repayment of the sums due from the state budget. The argument put forward by the region based on lack of effective judicial protection was given short shrift. Indeed, the Italian Government, as a privileged applicant and direct beneficiary of aid, could have brought proceedings for annulment of the contested decision under Article 263 TFEU.

16.2.3.3.5 Challenges of non-regulatory acts by non-privileged applicants: the concept of individual concern

Article 263 TFEU requires that an applicant who wishes to challenge a non-regulatory act must prove that he is both directly and individually concerned by that act. Obviously, there is no problem if such an act is specifically addressed to him. In all other cases he must prove that a decision addressed to "another person" or that the act in the form of a regulation or a directive, i.e. an act of general application, is in fact a decision addressed to him.

16.2.3.3.5.1 A decision in a form of a regulation, which must be of direct and individual concern to the applicant

The difference between a regulation and a decision was explained by the ECJ in Cases 41–44/70 *International Fruit Company and Others v Commission*.[1030] The ECJ held that the essential features of a decision result from the limitation of its addressees, while a regulation has essentially a general scope of application as it is applicable not to a limited number of addressees, named or otherwise individually identified as in the case of a decision, but to a category of persons envisaged in abstracto and in their entirety.

The case law of the ECJ, as to circumstances where a decision is disguised by being presented as a regulation, has evolved:

- Initially, the ECJ considered that this situation might occur where an entire regulation is, in fact, a decision adopted by an EC institution with the exclusive or main purpose of evading a procedure specifically prescribed by the Treaty for dealing with the applicant, that is, the regulation was adopted by an EC institution in misuse of its powers;[1031]

- Subsequently, the ECJ accepted that a true regulation may be addressed to specific persons;[1032]

- Later, the ECJ recognised that a regulation may, in fact, be a bundle of decisions addressed to each applicant;[1033]

- Finally, in Case C-309/89 *Codorníu SA v Council*[1034] the ECJ recognised that one and the

---

1030. [1971] ECR 411.
1031. Joined Cases 16 and 17/62 *Confédération Nationale des Producteur de Fruits et Légumes and Others v Council* [1962] ECR 471.
1032. Case 30/67 *Industria Molitoria Imolese and Others v Council* [1968] ECR 115. The ECJ held that: "a measure which, taken as a whole, has the characteristics of a regulation, may nevertheless contain provisions addressed to specific persons in such a way as to distinguish them individually", p. 121.
1033. Cases 41–44/70 *International Fruit Company v Commission* [1971] ECR 411.
1034. [1994] ECR I-1853.

same provision of a regulation may have, at the same time, both general and individual scope of application.

Initially, the ECJ considered that a provision of a regulation could not, at the same time, have both general and individual scope of application.[1035] However, under the influence of the so-called theory of "hybrid regulations" developed by Advocates General, in particular Verloren Van Themaat in Joined Cases 239 and 275/82 *Allied Corporation and Others v Commission*,[1036] and which applied mostly to anti-dumping cases, the ECJ changed its position. In *Codorníu* the ECJ recognised that the same provisions of a regulation may have, at the same time, general and individual scope of application. In this case the ECJ held that although the regulation was "by nature and by virtue of its sphere of application of a legislative nature", this did not prevent it from being of individual concern to some of those who were affected. Thus, it seems that the ECJ accepts that an act of general application may also affect the interests of an individual. However, the ECJ emphasised that neither the fact that a provision of a regulation may, in practice, affect its addressees differently one from another,[1037] nor the fact that it is possible to determine the number or even the identity of the persons affected by a regulation[1038] call into question its nature as a regulation, as long as it is possible to establish that it applies by virtue of an objective legal or factual situation defined by that regulation.

16.2.3.3.5.2 A decision addressed to a person other than the applicant, which is of direct and individual concern to the applicant

The ECJ has interpreted the notion of a decision addressed to a person other than the applicant very broadly. Such a person may be not only a natural or legal person, but also a Member State[1039] or a third country.[1040]

16.2.3.3.5.3 Provisions of a directive which can be equated with a decision

With regard to directives, the ECJ has accepted that an action for annulment of a directive can be admissible provided that the directive contains provisions which can be equated with a decision, and that the applicant is directly and individually concerned by them.[1041]

In Joined Cases T-172/98 and T-175/98 to T-177/98 *Salamander*[1042] the CFI emphasised that successful actions for annulment of directives will be rare, given that by their very nature directives are measures of general application requiring the Member State to take implementing measures

---

1035. Case 45/81 *Alexander Moksel Import-Export GmbH & Co. Handels-KG v Commission* [1982] ECR 1129.

1036. [1984] ECR 1005.

1037. Case 6/68 *Zuckerfabrik Watenstedt* [1968] ECR 409.

1038. Joined Case 789 and 790/79 *Calapk* [1980] ECR 1949.

1039. In most cases an individual applicant challenges a decision addressed to the Member State, for example Case 25/62 *Plaumann* [1963] ECR 95. See the case law on individual and direct concern examined in this chapter.

1040. Case C-135/92 *Fiscano AB* [1994] ECR I-2885 in which the ECJ considered that a Swedish company was individually and directly concerned by a decision addressed by the Commission to the Government of Sweden (at that time Sweden was not a Member State of the EU).

1041. Case C-298/89 *Government of Gibraltar v Council* [1993] ECR I-3605; Case C-10/95P *Asocarne* [1995] ECR I-4149.

1042. [2000] ECR II-2487. See also Case T-298/04 *Efkon AG v EP and Council* [2008] ECR II-7 (Ord) in which the CFI [the General Court] confirmed the possibility for an applicant to bring an action for annulment of a directive. However, the applicant failed the Plaumann test in that it could not establish that it was individually concerned by the relevant provision of the directive. On appeal, the ECJ confirmed the judgment of the CFI [the General Court] (Case C-146/08 P *Efkon Ag v EP and Council* [2009] ECR I-49 (Ord)).

and thus it will be the Member State's implementing measure that will produce legal effects in relation to third parties, not the directive itself.

16.2.3.3.5.4 The concept of individual concern

The most confusing and complicated question under Article 263 TFEU is the issue of individual concern, mostly because of inconsistency in the decisions of the CJEU in this area. Individual concern was defined by the ECJ in Case 25/62 *Plaumann & Co. v Commission*.[1043]

THE FACTS WERE:

Plaumann was an importer of clementines. Under the Common Customs tariff he paid 13 per cent customs duty, as did any importer of clementines from outside the Community. The Government of Germany asked the Commission for authorisation under Article 25(3) EC Treaty (repealed) to suspend this duty. The Commission refused and issued a decision in this respect. Plaumann challenged this decision.

Held:

The ECJ held that Plaumann was not individually and directly concerned by the Commission's decision, although he was affected, as any importer of clementines, by the decision. His commercial activities were such that they could, at any time, be practised by any person, and thus he did not distinguish himself from others in relation to the challenged decision. The ECJ stated that individual concern can be established if persons other than the addressees of the decision demonstrate "that the decision affects them by reason of certain attributes which are peculiar to them or by reason of circumstances in which they are differentiated from all other persons".[1044]

In the above case the applicant was considered as being a member of an "open class", that is, anyone may, at any time, practice the commercial activity in question and potentially join the group of producers of particular goods.

In Cases 106 and 107/63 *Alfred Toepfer and Getreide-Import Gesellschaft v Commission*[1045] the ECJ explained the circumstances in which an applicant will be regarded as belonging to a "fixed" group and therefore individually concerned within the meaning of Article 263(4) TFEU.

THE FACTS WERE:

On 1 October 1962, being the day on which the German authorities mistakenly reduced the levy for imports of maize from France to Germany, Toepfer applied for a licence to import maize from France to Germany. The German intervention agency realised the mistake and refused to grant licences from 2 October 1962. Three days later the Commission confirmed

---

1043. [1963] ECR 95.
1044. [1963] ECR 95, at 107.
1045. [1965] ECR 405.

> *this ban on the grant of licences and authorised the German authority to reimpose the full levy. Toepfer challenged the Commission's decision on the grounds that he was individually and directly concerned.*
>
> *Held:*
>
> The ECJ held that the applicant was individually concerned because the number and identity of those individually concerned "had become fixed and ascertainable before the contested decision was made". They were a "closed group": the decision affected their interests and position in a way significantly different from other importers who might wish to apply for a licence after the decision of the German authorities but during the remaining period of the ban. Therefore, only those who applied on 1 October were individually concerned since from 2–4 October applications were refused and on 4 October the Commission issued its decision. As a result, Toepfer was within the closed group who applied on 1 October; the larger group, that is, those who applied between 2–4 October was open since they were refused licences and could reapply thereafter without loss to them as the levy would be the same after 2 October.

Similarly, in Case 62/70 *Bock v Commission*,[1046] the ECJ held that Bock was individually concerned by a decision adopted by the Commission because when he applied for a licence to import Chinese mushrooms, the German authorities refused to grant it and asked the Commission to confirm their decision, which the Commission did. The decision was issued to deal with Bock's application. Accordingly, he belonged to an ascertainable and fixed group of importers at the time of the adoption of that decision.

The fact that the identities of the economic operators to whom a measure applies were known to the Commission at the time a measure was adopted is not on its own sufficient to establish individual concern. What is required is that the measure affects applicants in a special way, that is, distinguishes them from all other persons by reason of certain attributes which are peculiar to them or by reason of their peculiar circumstances.[1047]

The ECJ restrictively interprets "certain peculiar attributes" or "circumstances which differentiate" a person from others when challenging a decision addressed to another person, or a regulation in the form of a decision. As a result, the ECJ refused to recognise that a person was individually concerned in the following situations:

- In the *Plaumann* case where the decision concerned specific activities, that is, importing of clementines;

- Where the number of the affected persons was limited;[1048]

1046. [1971] ECR 897.
1047. Joined Cases C-15/91 and C-108/91 *Buckl* [1992] ECR I-6061; Case C-213/91 *Abertal* [1993] ECR I-3177; Case C-309/89 *Codorníu* [1994] ECR I-1853; Case T-476/93 *FRSEA and FNSEA v Council* [1993] ECR II-1187; and Case T-472/93 *Campo Ebro* [1995] ECR II-421.
1048. In *Plaumann* there were 30 importers of clementines. A similar situation arose in Case T-11/99 *Firma Léon Van Parys NV v Commission* [1999] ECR II-1355.

▨ Where an undertaking was the only one concerned by a measure in a particular Member State;[1049]

▨ Where an undertaking operated in a determined zone and the regulation expressly applied to that geographically delimited zone;[1050]

▨ Where an undertaking was a direct competitor of another undertaking to which the decision was addressed;[1051]

▨ Where the number of undertakings concerned was limited to three undertakings in a Member State, but potential competitors would not be in a position to enter the market for at least two years;[1052] and

▨ Where an undertaking was the largest importer of the relevant product in two Member States.[1053]

The ECJ's unrealistic approach to the concept of individual concern based on the assumption that as long as any person at any time may practice a particular activity, or become a member of a particular class of producers, has been subject to criticism. The ECJ responded by relaxing its very strict interpretation of Article 263(4) TFEU as discussed below.

16.2.3.3.5.5   EU policy areas characterised by the existence of non-contentious procedures which involve, more or less, direct participation of undertakings in the adoption of measures

If applicants assist the Commission in the preparation of a measure then their association with the adoption of the measure differentiates them from others and their individual concern is self-evident.[1054] This mostly occurs in competition, anti-dumping and state aid cases.

For example, if a complaint is lodged against a competitor for an alleged breach of Articles 101 and 102 TFEU, which leads to a decision of the Commission exempting the competitor by virtue of Article 101(3) TFEU, or confirming that there was no breach of competition rules on its part, then the complaining undertaking is individually concerned by the decision addressed to the competitor,[1055] not because it is in a relationship of competition with the competitor but because it initiated the proceedings which resulted in the adoption of the measure.

Similarly, a decision of the Commission upon receiving a complaint to refuse the opening of proceedings under Article 108(2) TFEU concerning aid granted to an undertaking by a Member State may be challenged by the undertaking which made the complaint to the Commission[1056]

1049. Case 231/82 *Spijker Kwasten* [1983] ECR 259; Case 97/85 *Union Deutsche Lebensmittelwerke GmbH and Others v Commission* [1987] ECR 2265.

1050. Case 30/67 *Industria Molitaria Imolese and Others v Council*, supra note 1032.

1051. Case 10 and 18/68 *Eridania* [1969] ECR 459.

1052. Case 101/76 *KSH NV v Council and Commission* [1977] ECR 797.

1053. Case C-209/94 *Buralux* [1996] ECR I-615.

1054. Case T-125/96 *Boehringer Ingelheim Vetmedica GmbH* [1999] ECR II-3427.

1055. Case 26/76 *Metro SB-Großmärkte* [1977] ECR 1875; Joined Cases 142 and 156/84 *BAT and and R. J. Reynolds Industries Inc. v Commission* [1986] ECR 1899.

1056. Case 169/84 *Cofaz* [1986] ECR 391, Case C-198/91 *William Cook* [1993] ECR I-2487, Case C-225/91 *Matra* [1993] ECR I-3203.

provided that the complaining undertaking's position in the market has been significantly affected by the contested measure.[1057]

With regard to dumping,[1058] in Case 264/82 *Timex Corporation v Council*[1059] the applicant challenged a regulation which was adopted because of Timex's complaints concerning cheap mechanical watches coming from the Soviet Union. The regulation imposed an anti-dumping duty taking into account information forwarded by Timex. However, Timex then claimed that the new duty was too low. The ECJ held that because the regulation was based on Timex's situation, Timex was individually concerned.

In Case C-358/89 *Extramet Industrie SA v Council*,[1060] the economic analysis of the situation of the applicant Extramet (it was the largest importer and end-user of the product on which anti-dumping duty was imposed and it had difficulty in obtaining supplies from alternative sources) and of its degree of dependence vis-à-vis the effect that the regulation had on the market (its business depended on imports of the product) differentiated it from other undertakings so as to allow it to claim individual concern.[1061] This was despite the fact that Extramet was not involved in the preparation of the contested decision and the Commission was not aware of its particular situation when establishing the existence of dumping.

It is interesting to note that in Joined Cases T-528/93, T-542/93, T-543/93 and T-546/93 *Metropole Télévision SA and Others v Commission*,[1062] the Commission argued that the applicant was not individually concerned as it did not participate in the preparation of the measure. The CFI [the General Court] replied that effective participation in the adoption of a measure cannot be required in order to establish an individual concern as it would amount to the introduction of an additional requirement which is not provided for in Article 230 EC [Article 263 TFEU]. Therefore, the CFI [the General Court] rightly indicated that participation in the adoption of a measure constitutes solely a factor facilitating the recognition of individual concern, but it is not a necessary requirement.

16.2.3.3.5.6 Relaxation of the restrictive interpretation of requirements relating to individual concern in cases where the relevant EU institution has a duty to take account of the consequences of the intended act on the position of the applicant

The restrictive interpretation of requirements relating to individual concern has been relaxed in cases where the relevant EU institution has a duty, that is, provisions of EU law impose an

---

1057. Case T-117/04 *Vereniging Werkgroep Commerciële Jachthavens Zuidelijke Randmeren and Others v Commission* [2006] ECR II-3861.

1058. In the context of the internal market, dumping occurs when a non-EU undertaking sells its products below domestic market prices, which are at the same time below the real cost of goods. This strategy is used to penetrate the market and eliminate competitors. An undertaking affected by such conduct of a foreign undertaking may complain to the Commission, which may adopt a provisional regulation and request the Council to issue a definite regulation imposing an anti-dumping duty to counterbalance the competitive advantage of the foreign undertaking and which is determined in the light of the effect of the dumping on EU undertakings, especially the one that lodged the complaint.

1059. [1985] ECR 861.

1060. [1991] ECR I-2501.

1061. See A. Arnull, "Challenging EC Anti-dumping Regulations, The Problem of Admissibility", European Competition Law Review, 1992, p 73.

1062. [1996] ECR II-649.

obligation on that institution to take account of the consequences of the intended act on the position of individuals.

The above is exemplified in Case C-152/88 *Sofrimport SARL v Commission*.[1063]

THE FACTS WERE:

In conformity with a regulation Sofrimport shipped apples from Chile. This regulation was amended to the effect that it suspended import licences for Chilean apples. When the amended regulation came into force, apples being imported by Sofrimport were in transit. The French authorities refused to issue an import licence to Sofrimport and the latter challenged the regulation.

Held:

The ECJ held that an earlier regulation imposed a duty upon the EC authorities to take into consideration the case of goods in transit when adopting a new regulation, and consequently importers with goods in transit constituted a fixed and ascertainable group and could be considered as individually concerned.

Similar circumstances occurred in Joined Cases T-480/93 and T-483/93 *Antillean Rice Mills NV and Others v Commission*.[1064] In these cases the applicants' shipment of rice was in transit when the contested decision was adopted by the Commission and in addition, as a result of a meeting between The Netherlands' permanent representative's office and the Commission, in which the applicants had participated, the Commission was aware of the particular situation. These factors differentiated the applicants from other existing and future exporters of rice. Consequently, they were considered as being individually concerned.

It can be seen from the above that when a provision of EU law imposes a duty on the Commission to take account of the peculiar situation of the applicant,[1065] such a situation will be regarded as constituting "specific circumstances" within the meaning of the case law of the ECJ.

16.2.3.3.5.7 *Applicants who differentiate themselves from others by being holders of intellectual property rights*

The restrictive interpretation of the requirement of individual concern has been relaxed in respect of applicants who differentiate themselves from others by being holders of intellectual property rights in a situation where an act of general application "expropriates" the intellectual property right from the applicants, i.e. it prevents an applicant from using intellectual property rights in the course of its business.

The leading case on the above is Case C-309/89 *Codorníu SA v Council*.[1066]

1063. [1990] ECR I-2477.
1064. [1995] ECR II-2305.
1065. See also Case 11/82 *Piraïki Patraïki and Others v Commission* [1985] ECR 207 (section 16.2.3.3.4); Case 62/70 *Bock* [1971] ECR 897; Case 29/75 *Kaufhof AG v Commission* [1976] ECR 431; Case T-85/94 *Branco v Commission* [1995] ECR II-45.
1066. [1994] ECR I-1853.

THE FACTS WERE:

Codorníu, a Spanish producer of quality sparkling wines, had been the holder of a graphic trade mark since 1924 for one of its wines designated as "Gran Cremant de Codorníu". In certain regions of France and Luxembourg the word "cremant" was also used for a certain quality of wine. The producers in those countries asked the Community to adopt a regulation which would reserve the word "cremant" only for their sparkling wine. Council Regulation 2045/89 restricted the use of the word "cremant" to wines originating in France and Luxembourg in order to protect the traditional description used in those areas. Codorníu challenged the regulation.

Held:

The ECJ held that Codorníu was differentiated from other producers of wine since it had registered and used the word "cremant" since 1924. Although Regulation 2045/89 was a "true" regulation, it did not prevent it from being of individual concern to Codorníu, which was badly affected by the regulation. Also, the restriction of the word "cremant" to wine originating from a certain region of France and Luxembourg could not be objectively justified and, in addition, was contrary to Article 12 EC [Article 18 TFEU] which prohibits discrimination based on nationality.

Comment:

The implications of *Codorníu* are twofold:

■ The ECJ accepted that the provision of a regulation could be, at the same time, of a general and individual scope of application; and

■ The ECJ recognised that the protection of intellectual property rights may confer on the holder of those rights locus standi under Article 263 TFEU in specific circumstances.

The meaning of "specific circumstances" was explained, inter alia, in Case T-30/07 *Denka International BV v Commission*.[1067]

THE FACTS WERE:

The applicant, Denka International BV ("Denka"), a manufacturer of dichlorvos, an insecticide, for which it holds a patent and which it sold under the trade mark "Denkarepon", brought an action for partial annulment of Commission Directive 2006/92/EC of 9 November 2006 which amended annexes to Council Directives 76/895/EEC, 86/362/EEC and 90/642/EEC as regards maximum residue levels for captan, dichlorvos, ethion and folpet ([2006]OJ L 311/31). This directive modified the maximum residue level for dichlorvos from the previously applicable 2 mg/kg to a new residue level of 0.01 mg/kg. The change of the maximum level for dichlorvos resulted in the applicant being unable to sell dichlorvos because the new maximum residue

---

1067. [2008] ECR II-101 (Ord).

level was so low that it made unlikely any demand for the product. Denka claimed, inter alia, that it was in a situation similar to that of the applicant in the Codorniu case. It submitted that it was individually concerned by the contested directive by reason of being a holder of a patent and a trade mark for dichlorvos in that the use of the trademark had been greatly affected by the directive.

Held:

The CFI [the General Court] held that the existence of legal protection for a trademark is not, in itself, capable of distinguishing the applicant from all other manufacturers and distributors of dichlorvos.[1068] The CFI [the General Court] explained why the situation of Denka differed from that of the applicant in Case *C-309/89 Codorniu v Council.* In *Codorniu*, the contested regulation reserved the description "crémant" to an identified class of producers, even though the applicant had registered that same designation as a trade mark and had used it over a long period before the adoption of the contested regulation. For that reason, as the CFI [the General Court] stated, Codorniu was:

> "... clearly distinguished from all other economic operators. Rather than the enjoyment in the abstract of an intellectual right, it was the specificity of the designation which that right protected and which the contested measure had, in a way, expropriated from the applicant that gave rise to the solution adopted in *Codorniu v Council.*"

Comment:

In *Denka*, the contested directive neither aimed to reserve a specific intellectual right to certain operators to the detriment of the applicant, nor affected the substance of a specific trademark used by the applicant. Therefore, Denka was not in a situation comparable to that of an undertaking such as Codorniu, which exploited a trade mark for sparkling wines, but rather in a situation comparable to that of champagne producers. Indeed, as the Commission submitted, the contested directive had not prevented Denka International BV from using its trademark "Denkarepon" with regard to its products. Obviously, the judgment of the General Court would have been different had Denka been able to register its products under the trademark "Dichlorvos" and had so done!

16.2.3.3.5.8 *Relaxation of the restrictive interpretation in cases where political interests of the EU are at issue*

The restrictive interpretation of the requirement of individual concern has been relaxed where political interests of the EU are at issue.

One of the rare cases where the ECJ was prepared to relax its strict interpretation of the concept of individual concern was Case 294/83 *Parti Ecologiste "Les Verts" v EP*,[1069] in which the French Ecology Party challenged a decision of the EP's Bureau relating to financing of the electoral campaign preceding the 1984 EP elections.

The ECJ held that the French Ecology Party was individually concerned because:

1068. Case T-196/03 *European Federation for Cosmetic Ingredients v EP and Council* (Ord) [2004] ECR II-4263.
1069. [1986] ECR 1339.

"A political grouping which, unlike its rivals, is not represented in the European Parliament but which is able to put up candidates in the direct elections to the Parliament must, in order to avoid inequality in the protection afforded by the Court to groupings competing in the same elections, be regarded as being both directly and individually concerned."

The French Ecology Party failed the *Plaumann* test because it could neither be differentiated by reason of its peculiar attributes, as it was one of a potentially very wide group of political parties, nor by reason of circumstances as it had not decided whether to field candidates in the election. Had it not put up candidates for the EP elections, it would not have been affected by the decision at all and would have no interest to challenge the contested measure. The ECJ's judgment can be explained by political considerations, namely to ensure the widest possible participation of political parties in elections to the EP, and thus enhance the democratic legitimacy of the EU.

16.2.4   Grounds for annulment

Article 263(2) TFEU sets out the grounds for annulment of EU acts. These are:

- Lack of competence;
- Infringement of an essential procedural requirement;
- Infringement of the Treaties or any rule of law relating to their application; and
- Misuse of powers.

The CJEU has to apply the first two grounds ex officio in any event,[1070] but the last two only if invoked by the applicant. It is very important to claim all possible, and perhaps all conceivable grounds, because introduction of new grounds after the expiry of the time limit is not permitted. Further, the CJEU is empowered to specify and further crystallise the grounds invoked by the applicant.[1071]

16.2.4.1   Lack of competence

This ground is similar to substantive ultra vires in British administrative law, which occurs when the administration acts beyond its powers. EU institutions, bodies, offices or agencies have only the powers conferred upon them by the Treaties.

It was expected that this ground would be invoked often, especially by the Member States for the encroachment of EU law upon the national competences of the Member States. This has not materialised. As a result, this ground is rarely used, mostly because the applicants prefer to base their claims on the infringement of the Treaties.[1072] Lack of competence is mainly relied upon in cases challenging the legal basis of EU acts.[1073]

1070. Case 1/54 *France v High Authority* [1954–56] ECR 1.

1071. Case 4/73 *Nold* [1974] ECR 491.

1072. For example, see Joined Cases 3–18/58, 25/58 and 26/58 *Barbara Erzbergbau AG and others v High Authority* [1960] ECR 173.

1073. Case C-350/92 Spain v Council [1995] ECR I-1995; Case C-84/94 *UK v Council [Working Time Directive]* [1996] ECR I-5758; Case C-249/02 *Portugal v Commission* [2004] ECR I-10717.

16.2.4.2   Infringement of an essential procedural requirement

Infringement of an essential procedural requirement is analogous to procedural ultra vires. It occurs when an EU institution, body, office or agency fails to comply with a mandatory procedural requirement in the adoption of a measure, for example if the Council fails to consult the EP when the Treaty requires mandatory consultation of the EP prior to the adoption of a measure. The ECJ has annulled acts which provided for optional consultation of the EP where the Council did not give enough time to the EP to issue its opinion,[1074] or when the EP was not reconsulted when an act of the Council substantially altered an original proposal submitted to the EP.[1075] When an EU institution fails to comply with its own internal Rules of Procedure, the ECJ will annul the act in question.[1076]

Failure to provide reasons for an act as required by Article 296 TFEU is most often invoked under this ground.[1077]

16.2.4.3   Infringement of the Treaties or any rule of law relating to their application

This is the most often invoked ground. It encompasses not only infringements of the provisions of the Treaties but of all sources of EU law, including the general principles of EU law[1078] and infringements of international agreements concluded between the EU and third countries.[1079]

16.2.4.4   Misuse of powers

The ECJ has adopted the same definition of misuse of powers as under French administrative law (*detournment de pouvoir*).[1080] Misuse of powers is analogous to the English doctrine of improper purpose. In order to rely on this ground, the applicant must prove that an EU institution, body, office or agency has used its powers for objectives other than those provided for by the Treaties. Thus, a legitimate power has been used for an illegal end, or in an illegal way.

This ground is often invoked, but rarely successful because of the burden of proof it imposes on the applicant, who must prove, first, the actual subjective intention of an EU institution when it acted, and second, that an act was adopted with the exclusive purpose of achieving objectives other than prescribed by the Treaties, or evading a procedure specifically provided by the Treaties for dealing with the circumstances of the case.[1081] The second element is particularly difficult to establish given the multiplicity of objectives which an EU institution may legitimately pursue when adopting an act. Misuse of powers was successfully invoked in the context of a dispute

---

1074. Case 138/79 *SA Roquette Frères* [1980] ECR 3333.
1075. Case 41/69 *ACF Chemiefarma* [1970] ECR 661 and Case C-388/92 *EP v Council* [1994] ECR I-2067.
1076. Case C-137/92P *Commission v BASF (PCV)* [1994] ECR I-2555.
1077. Case 24/62 *Germany v Commission [Brennwein]* [1963] ECR 63; Case T-102/03 *CIS v Commission* [2005] ECR II-2357.
1078. Case 62/70 *Bock* [1971] ECR 897; Case 17/74 *Transocean Marine* [1974] ECR 1063; Case C-212/91 *Angelopharm GmbH v Freie Hansestadt Hamburg* [1994] ECR I-171; implementing measures based on secondary legislation but in breach of the latter – Case 25/70 *Köster* [1970] ECR 1161; Case 30/70 *Scheer* [1970] ECR 1197.
1079. Joined Cases 21–24/72 *International Fruit Company* [1972] ECR 1219.
1080. Case 2/57 *Compagnie des Hauts Fourneaux de Chasse v High Authority* [1957–58] ECR 199.
1081. Case C-331/88 *Fedesa* [1990] ECR I-4023.

between the EU and its staff when the EU servants proved that an EU institution acted in bad faith.[1082]

16.2.5 Time limit for an action for annulment under Article 263 TFEU

The time limit is two months and begins to run from the date of publication of an act in the Official Journal, or from its notification to the applicant.[1083] If the act was published, by virtue of Article 81 of the Rules of Procedure of the ECJ,[1084] the commencement of the time limit is extended by 14 days. Additionally, if an applicant is at a distance from the CJEU, the time is further extended by a single period of 10 days.[1085] Therefore, the time limit for an applicant from the UK is two months, plus 14 days, plus 10 days, provided the contested act was published in the OJ.[1086]

In the absence of publication or notification the time limit starts to run on the day when the act comes to the knowledge of the applicant, in the sense that it knows its essential content including the grounds on which it has been adopted.[1087] This is subject to an exception; if the party knows about the existence of the relevant act concerning it but has no precise knowledge of its content, that is, of its essential aspects, it is for that party to request from the relevant institution the full text of that act within a reasonable period.[1088] The CFI [the General Court] considered the period of 15 days as being reasonable in Joined Cases T-432/93, T-433/93 and T-434/93 *Socurte and Others v Commission*[1089] and of three weeks in Case T-465/93 *Murgia Messapica v Commission*,[1090] but the ECJ rejected a delay of two months in Case C-102/92 *Ferriere Acciaierie Sarde SpA v Commission*.[1091] However, there could be cases where a much longer period would be considered reasonable as the test is what is reasonable in all the circumstances.

The time limit is rigorously enforced by the CJEU. Once it elapses, the application is deemed inadmissible[1092] and the act becomes immune from annulment. This is justified by the principle of legal certainty and equality in the administration of justice.[1093]

In Joined Cases 25 and 26/65 *Simet and Others v High Authority*,[1094] the ECJ accepted an exception based on force majeure to the strict observance of the time limit. In Case T-218/01 *Laboratoire Monique Rémy SAS v Commission*,[1095] the CFI [the General Court] emphasised that

---

1082. In Joined Cases 18 and 35/65 *Gutmann* [1966] ECR 61, a Community official was allegedly transferred to Brussels in the interest of the service but in fact it was a disciplinary transfer; Case 105/75 *Giuffrida* [1976] ECR 1395.

1083. In Case 76/79 *Könecke* [1980] ECR 665, the ECJ held that the time limit starts to run the day after the notification takes place.

1084. [2009] OJ L24/8.

1085. Ibid

1086. This period includes official holidays, Saturdays and Sundays, and is not suspended during judicial vacations of the CJEU. If the period ends on Saturday, Sunday or an official holiday, it is extended until the end of the first following working day: Art. 80(1) (d) (e) and Art. 80(2) of the Rules of Procedure of the ECJ [2009] OJ L24/8.

1087. Case T-468/93 *Frinil* [1994] ECR II-33.

1088. Joined Cases T-485/93, T-491/93, T-494/93 and T-61/98 *Dreyfus* [2000] ECR II-3659.

1089. [1995] ECR II-503.

1090. [1994] ECR II-361.

1091. [1993] ECR I-801.

1092. For example, Case 108/79 *Belfiore* [1980] ECR 1769.

1093. Case 209/83 *Valsabbia* [1984] ECR 3089.

1094. [1967] ECR 113. See also Case T-106/05 *Evropaiki Dinamiki* [2006] ECR II-82 (Ord.).

1095. [2002] ECR II-2139 (Ord.).

apart from force majeure, only exceptional circumstances make an action admissible by derogation from the time limit set out in Article 230 EC [Article 263 TFEU]. An example of this is when the conduct of the relevant EU institution gives rise to pardonable confusion in the mind of a party acting in good faith and exercising all the diligence required of a normally prudent person. Both points were illustrated in Case T-12/90 *Bayer AG v EC Commission.*[1096]

THE FACTS WERE:

The Commission sent notification to the applicant company fining it for a number of infringements of Article 81 EC [Article 101 TFEU]. The company brought an action under Article 230 EC [Article 263 TFEU] to have the Commission's decision judicially reviewed. In response, the Commission argued that the application was inadmissible as it was time-barred under both Article 230 EC [Article 263 TFEU] and the ECJ's rules of procedure.

The applicant argued that the action was not time-barred, and relied on three separate contentions to support this argument. First, it was submitted that the Commission was guilty of a number of irregularities in the notification. In particular, the Commission notified the decision to the company's registered office and not to the company's legal department with which it had conducted all previous correspondence. Second, the company claimed that its internal organisational breakdown was an excusable error. Finally, the applicants pleaded force majeure in order to justify the delay in submitting the application under Article 230 EC [Article 263 TFEU].

Held:

The CFI [the General Court] rejected all three arguments. The Court held that in the notification the Commission complied with the necessary formalities contained in its rules of procedure as it sent the decision by registered letter with postal acknowledgment of receipt. The letter duly arrived at Bayer's registered office. Both the arguments relating to excusable error and force majeure were also rejected. The Court held that the delay had been caused by fault on the part of the applicants. Bayer could not claim that it committed any excusable error. In this respect, the fact that the Commission sent a letter to the applicant's registered office, whereas it had previously addressed all its communications directly to the applicant's legal department, could not constitute an exceptional circumstance since this is a normal procedure. The inadequate functioning of the applicant's internal organisation was the reason why the letter was not forwarded to the legal department. This circumstance could not be considered as unforeseeable and force majeure since in order to establish the existence of force majeure, there must "be abnormal difficulties, independent of the will of the person concerned and apparently inevitable, even if all due care is taken".

It is to be noted that in Case C-229/05P *Osman Ocalan*[1097] the applicant, Mr Serif Vanley, who missed the deadline for lodging an application at the Registry of the CFI [the General Court],

---

1096. [1991] ECR II-219, upheld by the ECJ in Case C-195/91P *Bayer* [1994] ECR I-5619.
1097. [2007] ECR I-439.

argued that the formalistic approach to the time limit should be relaxed in a situation where a case concerns serious breaches of fundamental human rights. This was rejected by the ECJ.

16.2.6 Effect of annulment

The effect of annulment is described in Article 264 TFEU, which provides:

> "1. If the action is well founded, the Court of Justice of the European Union shall declare the act concerned to be void.
>
> 2. However, the Court shall, if it considers this necessary, state which of the effects of the act which it has declared void shall be considered as definitive."

The effect of annulment is that an act is void. The judgment of the CJEU applies erga omnes,[1098] that is, it can be relied upon by everybody, not only the parties to the proceedings.

A successfully challenged act is void immediately, that is, from the day on which the ECJ renders its decision. This means that the act in question is devoid of past, present and future legal effects.

In respect of judgments rendered by the General Court the act is void from the expiry of the time limit for appeal, or from the time the appeal was rejected.

A decision of annulment has a retroactive effect, subject to Article 264(2) TFEU. In the latter case the CJEU may declare some or all of its provisions to be operative. Use of the declaratory power of the CJEU may be justified for a number of reasons, such as the need for legal certainty,[1099] respect for legitimate expectation, or the need to suspend the effects of annulment until a competent institution adopts an act which will replace the one struck down by the CJEU.[1100]

Under Article 266 TFEU a decision of annulment imposes upon the EU institution whose act has been declared void an obligation "to take the necessary measures to comply with the judgment of the Court of Justice of the European Union". If that institution refuses to comply with the decision of the CJEU, the aggravated party may bring an action under Article 265 TFEU, and, if appropriate, commence an action for damages under Article 340(2) TFEU.

In Case C-310/97P *Commission v Assidomän Kraft Products AB and Others*[1101] the ECJ provided important clarifications concerning the effect of its own judgment annulling a decision adopted by the Commission.

THE FACTS WERE:

This case closed the saga of the Wood Pulp Cartel cases,[1102] *in which the Commission found more than forty suppliers of wood pulp in violation of EU competition law, despite the fact that most of the relevant undertakings were not resident within the EU. Fines were imposed on*

1098. Case 3/54 *Assider* [1954–56] ECR 63.
1099. Case C-21/94 *EP v Council* [1995] ECR I-1827.
1100. Case C-65/90 *EP v Council* [1992] ECR 4616; Case 275/87 *Commission v Council* [1989] ECR 259.
1101. [1999] ECR I-5363.
1102. Joined Cases C-89/85, C-104/85, C-114/85, C-116/85, C-117/85, C-125/85, C-126/85, C-127/85, C-128/85 and C-129/85 *A. Ahlström Osakeyhtiö and Others v Commission [Re Wood Pulp Cartel]* [1993] ECR I-1307.

36 of the undertakings for violation of Article 81 (1) EC [Article 101(1) TFEU]. Among those fined were nine Swedish undertakings, which paid their fines (the case took place before Sweden joined the EU). Subsequently, 26 of the undertakings appealed to the ECJ against the decision. They challenged the Commission's finding that they breached competition law through concertation of prices for their products by means of a system of quarterly price announcements. However, the nine Swedish undertakings that had already paid fines, including AssiDomän, decided not to participate in the annulment proceedings. The ECJ annulled the decision of the Commission that the undertakings concerned infringed Article 81 (1) EC [Article 101(1) TFEU] through concertation of prices for their products on the grounds that the Commission had not provided a firm, precise and consistent body of evidence in this respect. As a result, the ECJ annulled or reduced the fines to €20,000 imposed on the undertakings which had instituted proceedings.

AssiDomän, Kraft Products and other undertakings, which did not join in the annulment proceedings, asked the Commission to refund to each of them the fine that they had paid to the extent that they exceeded the sum of €20,000. The Commission refused to refund them on the grounds that it had already complied with the ECJ order by reducing the fines in respect of the undertakings participating in the proceedings, and that the decision of the ECJ had no necessary impact on the fines imposed upon the Swedish undertakings. The undertakings concerned challenged that decision, first before the CFI [the General Court] and, subsequently before the ECJ.

Held:

The ECJ held that the Swedish undertakings were not entitled to have the fines reduced. The court justified its judgment on two grounds: first, the ECJ cannot rule ultra petita, that is, the scope of the annulment which it pronounces may not go further than that sought by the applicant and thus unchallenged aspects concerning other addressees did not form part of the matter to be tried by the ECJ. Second, although the authority erga omnes exerted by an annulling judgment attaches to both the operative part and the ratio decidendi of the judgment, it cannot entail annulment of an act not challenged before the ECJ but alleged to be vitiated by the same illegality. Consequently, Article 233 EC [Article 266 TFEU] cannot be interpreted as requiring the institution concerned to re-examine identical or similar decisions allegedly affected by the same irregularity addressed to addressees other than the applicant.

Comment:

The judgment of the ECJ is fully justified in so far as the Commission's decision is regarded as a bundle of individual decisions against each participating undertaking, and not as a single decision addressed to all of them. This solution was confirmed in Joined Cases C-238/99P et seq. *Limburgse Vinyl Maatschappij NV and Others [Re PVC Cartel (No II)] v Commission,*[1103] in which a number of undertakings successfully challenged the Commission's decision on the ground that it had not been signed by the appropriate persons. The ECJ held that the challenged decision was binding on those undertakings who had not appealed, but it was void in respect of undertakings that lodged the appeal.

1103. [2002] ECR I-8375.

Although the solution consisting of considering the Commission's decision as a bundle of separate decisions addressed to each participating undertaking penalises undertakings which decided not to appeal, it is, at the same time, fair. Undertakings may decide not to challenge a Commission decision in competition matters for a number of reasons, the most important being that the appeal procedure involves considerable investment in terms of time and money. Hindsight is very useful but the fact is that if an undertaking has chosen to economise by not spending time and money on an appeal and the judgment of the court in similar matters arrives after the limitation period has expired, it will be too late to jump on the bandwagon. Conversely, if the outcome turns out to be against the appellant, the decision not to participate will have been well justified.

16.3 Pleas of illegality under Article 277 TFEU

Article 277 TFEU provides:

"Notwithstanding the expiry of the period laid down in Article 263, sixth paragraph, any party may, in proceedings in which an act of general application adopted by an institution, body, office or agency of the Union is at issue, plead the grounds specified in Article 263, second paragraph, in order to invoke before the Court of Justice of the European Union the inapplicability of that act."

The procedure under Article 277 TFEU complements the procedure under Article 263 TFEU. The plea of illegality can only be invoked as an ancillary plea, that is, as a means by which applicants, in support of an action that challenges implementing measures addressed to them or to a third person (in which latter case applicants must show that they are directly and individually concerned so far as non-regulatory acts are concerned and directly concerned with regard to regulatory acts which do not entail implementing measures), plead the illegality of the general measure upon which the implementing measures are based. For that reason, it is referred to as an indirect action, that is, it challenges indirectly the validity of a measure on the basis of which a subsequent measure has been adopted. In practice, the plea of illegality is mostly used to challenge individual decisions based on EU regulations whose validity is called into question.[1104]

Unlike actions under Article 263 TFEU, the plea of illegality is not time-barred[1105] (but see below regarding the link the ECJ has made with Article 263 TFEU by saying Article 277 cannot be used to circumvent requirements of Article 263 TFEU).

The grounds for an action under Article 277 TFEU are the same as for an action for annulment under Article 263 TFEU, that is, lack of competence, infringement of an essential procedural requirement, infringement of the Treaty or any rule of law relating to its application, and misuse of powers.

The main feature of the plea of illegality is that, subject to certain conditions, it allows avoidance of the stringent requirements imposed under Article 263 TFEU for access to the CJEU in

---

1104.   Joined Cases 275/80 and 24/81 *Krupp Stahl AG v Commission* [1981] ECR 2489.
1105.   Joined Cases 25 and 26/65 *Simet* [1967] ECR 113; Case C-289/99P *Schiocchet* [2000] ECR I-10279.

terms of locus standi and the time limit. The ECJ held in Joined Cases 87, 130/77, 22/83, 9 and 10/84 *Vittorio Salerno and Others v Commission and Council*[1106] that:

> "The sole purpose of art [277 TFEU] is to protect parties against the application of an unlawful regulation where the regulation itself can no longer be challenged owing to the expiry of the period laid down in art [263 TFEU]. However, in allowing a party to plead the inapplicability of a regulation, art [277 TFEU] does not create an independent right of action; such a plea may only be raised indirectly in proceedings against an implementing measure, the validity of the regulation being challenged in so far as it constitutes the legal basis of that measure."

Thus, the plea of illegality constitutes an alternative way of judicially reviewing EU acts, and so permits any person to raise indirectly the question of the validity of an EU act. This point is well illustrated by Case 92/78 *Simmenthal.*[1107]

THE FACTS WERE:

Simmenthal, an Italian meat importer, claimed that the fees for health and sanitary inspection carried out at the Italian border were unlawful on several counts, inter alia, he challenged under Article 230 EC [Article 263 TFEU] a decision adopted by the Commission and, in support of that challenge, he relied on Article 241 EC [Article 277 TFEU] to challenge a number of regulations and notices, especially the notices of invitation to tender of 13 January 1978, upon which that decision was based, and which he could not challenge directly due to the expiry of a two-month time limit.

Held:

The ECJ held that the notices of invitation to tender were general acts "which determine in advance and objectively, the rights and obligations of the trader who wishes to participate", and as acts of general application cannot be challenged under Article 230 EC [Article 263 TFEU]. Only the challenged decision, which was adopted in consequence of the tender, and not the notices of invitation to tender themselves, could be of direct and individual concern to Simmenthal, and thus reviewable under Article 230 EC [Article 263 TFEU]. However, Simmenthal was allowed to challenge indirectly under Article 241 [Article 277 TFEU] the regulations and the notices of invitation to tender of 13 January 1978 (although as the ECJ stated the notices of invitation were not in the strict sense measures laid down by regulation).

16.3.1 Requirements imposed by Article 277 TFEU

Article 277 TFEU imposes some requirements relating to the type of acts that can be challenged and relating to persons who can claim locus standi. These are examined below.

1106. [1985] ECR 2523.
1107. [1979] ECR 777.

16.3.1.1   Reviewable acts

Article 277 TFEU provides that any act of general application adopted by an EU institution, body, office or agency may be challenged. The pre-ToL version of Article 277 TFEU limited the reviewable acts to regulations adopted jointly by the EP and the Council, and regulations of the Council, of the Commission, or of the ECB. However, even before the entry into force of the ToL the ECJ had interpreted this provision broadly. As a result, an applicant was allowed to rely on the plea of illegality not only against regulations adopted by the above-mentioned institutions, but also against any act of general application capable of producing legal effects similar to those produced by regulations.

16.3.1.2   Applicants

Article 277 TFEU cannot be used to circumvent the requirements of Article 263 TFEU. For that reason, the addressees of individual acts who have not challenged them within the time limit prescribed by Article 263(5) TFEU are not permitted to rely on the plea of illegality,[1108] apart from the case of an individual decision being null and void,[1109] or being a part of a "complex procedure comprising a number of interdependent acts", as for example in Case 16/64 *Gertrud Rauch v Commission*[1110] concerning the recruitment of an EU official.

The Commission and some Advocates General have suggested that Article 277 TFEU should not be construed as giving locus standi to Member States, the reason for these suggestions being that Member States are privileged applicants under Article 263 TFEU[1111] and therefore should not be allowed to rely on Article 277 TFEU, as such reliance might encourage them to ignore certain apparently illegal regulations and thus not challenge them within the time limit imposed by Article 263 TFEU. The position of the ECJ is unknown as it has not dealt with the matter. In Case 32/65 *Italy v Council and Commission*,[1112] the Advocate General in his opinion was of the view that Member States should be allowed to rely on the plea of illegality. However, the ECJ decided the case without considering the matter of a plea of illegality. As Article 277 TFEU states that "any party" may bring Article 277 TFEU proceedings it seems that there are no limitations in respect of applicants.

It is uncertain, although in general the ECJ seems rather unenthusiastic about it, whether a Member State may invoke the plea of illegality within the framework of enforcement proceedings under Article 258 TFEU.[1113]

EU institutions, unlike Member States and individuals, are not required to prove their interest when invoking pleas of illegality.

1108.   In Case 156/77 *Commission v Belgium* ([1978] ECR 1881) the ECJ held that Article 241 EC [277 TFEU] can never be relied upon by a Member State when it is an addressee of a decision, given that the purpose of Article 241 EC [277 TFEU] is to allow the challenge of a regulation not of a decision (para 22).

1109.   Joined Cases 1/57 and 14/57 *Société des Usines à Tubes de la Sarre v High Authority* [1957–58] ECR 105.

1110.   [1965] ECR 135.

1111.   See G. Bebr, "Judicial Remedy of Private Parties Against Normative Acts of the EEC: the Role of the Exception of Illegality", (1966) 4 CMLRev, p 7.

1112.   [1966] ECR 389.

1113.   Joined Cases 6 and 11/69 *Commission v France* [1969] ECR 523; Case 156/77 *Commission v Belgium* [1978] ECR 1881.

16.3.2 Exclusive jurisdiction of the CJEU under Article 277 TFEU

The CJEU has exclusive jurisdiction over pleas of illegality.[1114] This bears closer examination.

- First, national courts have no jurisdiction to deal with a plea of illegality. There is, however, an indirect possibility based on Article 267 TFEU for an applicant to rely on a plea of illegality in national proceedings when challenging national measures introduced to implement an EU act.[1115] As national courts have no jurisdiction to declare an EU act void, and provided they have reasons to believe that the EU act is invalid, they will under Article 258 TFEU ask the ECJ to determine the validity of such an act.

- Second, in Case C-188/92 *TWD Textilwerke Deggendorf GmbH v Bundesrepublik Deutschland*,[1116] as confirmed in Case C-178/95 *Wiljo NV v Belgium*,[1117] the ECJ established a firm principle that once the time limit for a direct action under Article 263 TFEU elapses, the CJEU will consider as inadmissible proceedings under Article 267 TFEU in relation to an applicant who had locus standi to bring a direct action under Article 263 TFEU, but neglected to do so within the time limit prescribed under Article 263(5) TFEU. The ECJ justified its decision on the basis of the principle of legal certainty. In *TWD*, the applicant was individually and directly concerned by a decision addressed to a third party. The above solution is even more obvious vis-à-vis a direct addressee of a decision.

16.3.3 Effect of a successful action under Article 277 TFEU

If the applicant is successful, the general act, which may be called a parent act, is rendered inapplicable only to that applicant's case. The implementing measure is annulled in respect of the applicant, but the parent act is still in force since it cannot be declared void as it is immune from direct challenge under Article 263 TFEU by lapse of time. In practice, the institution which adopted the parent act will amend or repeal that act under Article 266(1) TFEU, as it is under a legal obligation to comply with a judgment of the ECJ.

16.4 Action for failure to act under Article 265 TFEU

When an EU institution, body, office or agency has a positive obligation to act, that is, it must adopt certain measures required by the Treaties but fails to do so, Article 265 TFEU confers jurisdiction upon the CJEU to compel such an institution to act.

Article 265 TFEU states:

"Should the European Parliament, the European Council, the Council, the Commission or the European Central Bank, in infringement of the Treaties, fail to act, the Member States and the other institutions of the Union may bring an action before the Court of Justice of the European Union to have the infringement established. This Article shall apply, under the same conditions, to bodies, offices and agencies of the Union which fail to act.

1114. Joined Cases 31/62 and 33/62 *Milchwerke* [1962] ECR 501; Joined Cases 31 and 33/62 *Wöhrmann* [1962] ECR 501.
1115. Case 216/82 *Universität Hamburg v Hauptzollamt Hamburg-Kehrwieder* [1983] ECR 2771.
1116. [1994] ECR I-833.
1117. [1997] ECR I-585; Case C-408/95 *Eurotunnel SA v SeaFrance* [1997] ECR I-6315.

The action shall be admissible only if the institution, body, office or agency concerned has first been called upon to act. If, within two months of being so called upon, the institution, body, office or agency concerned has not defined its position, the action may be brought within a further period of two months.

Any natural or legal person may, under the conditions laid down in the preceding paragraphs, complain to the Court that an institution, body, office or agency of the Union has failed to address to that person any act other than a recommendation or an opinion."

The action under Article 265 TFEU is similar to the historic English writ of mandamus or, in Scotland, to the petition for an order requiring the specific performance of a statutory duty.

An action for failure to act is separate and different from an action for annulment, and has its own specific requirements, even though in Case 15/70 *Chevalley v Commission*[1118] the ECJ held that an action under Article 232 EC [Article 265 TFEU] provides an applicant with a method of recourse parallel to that of Article 230 EC [Article 263 TFEU]. The relationship between Articles 230 and 232 EC [Articles 263 and 265 TFEU] was explained by the ECJ in Joined Cases 10 and 18/68 *Società "Eridania" Zuccherifici Nazionali and Others v Commission*.[1119]

THE FACTS WERE:

The Commission had adopted a decision granting aid to three Italian sugar refineries. This decision was contested by other sugar producers before the Commission, which refused to annul its decision. This resulted in an action both for annulment under Article 230 EC [Article 263 TFEU] and for failure to act under Article 232 EC [Article 265 TFEU] brought by the other producers.

Held:

The ECJ held that the applicants could not succeed under Article 232 EC [Article 265 TFEU], since the refusal of the Commission to annul its decision was tantamount to an act rather than a failure to act. Also, the applicants were prevented from bringing an action under Article 230 EC [Article 263 TFEU] as they were not able to prove that they were directly and individually concerned by the decision. The ECJ emphasised that Article 232 EC [Article 265 TFEU] should not be used to circumvent the requirements set out in Article 230 EC [Article 263 TFEU].

Article 265 TFEU imposes its own conditions as to a potentially defaulting institution, body, office, or agency, the applicant, and the procedure. These matters are examined below.

16.4.1 Defaulting institution

Under the ToL an action for failure to act may be brought against any EU institution, body, office or agency.

1118. [1970] ECR 975.
1119. [1969] ECR 459.

16.4.2   Applicants

There are three categories of applicants: privileged, semi-privileged and non-privileged.

16.4.2.1   Privileged applicants

Article 265 TFEU provides that Member States and the other institutions of the EU are privileged applicants. They may bring an action before the ECJ to establish that a defendant institution has failed to act. They may require that the defendant institution adopts any act: regulations, directives, decisions and even a proposal concerning the EU budget,[1120] provided that EU law imposes a duty to act. The EP, which was initially excluded from bringing an action for annulment under Article 263 TFEU, has always been included in the list of privileged applicants under Article 265 TFEU. In Case 13/83 *EP v Council*[1121] the ECJ formally recognised the right of the EP to bring an action under Article 265 TFEU.

16.4.2.2   Semi-privileged applicants

The ECB, the CoA and the CoR are semi-privileged applicants. They have locus standi to raise an action for failure to act in respect of areas within their respective fields of competence.

16.4.2.3   Non-privileged applicants

Non-privileged applicants are natural and legal persons complaining that "an institution, body, office or agency has failed to address to that person any act other than a recommendation or an opinion".

The literal interpretation of this formula implies that applicants may only challenge a failure of an institution to adopt an act addressed to them, that is, an individual decision. This would have limited their locus standi under Article 265 TFEU even more than under Article 263 TFEU. Fortunately, the ECJ has interpreted Article 265 TFEU broadly by treating actions for failure to act as the same as actions for annulment in respect of locus standi of non-privileged applicants. This was clearly confirmed in Case 246/81 *Lord Bethell v Commission*.[1122]

THE FACTS WERE:

Lord Bethell, a member of the EP and chairman of the Freedom of the Skies Committee, complained to the Commission about anti-competitive practices of a number of European airlines in relation to passenger fares. He argued that the Commission was under a duty to submit proposals under Article 82 EC [Article 102 TFEU] to curtail those practices. Unsatisfied with the answer from the Commission, he brought an action for failure to act against the Commission under Article 232 EC [Article 265 TFEU], claiming that the Commission's reply

---

1120.   Case 302/87 *EP v Council* [1988] ECR 5637.
1121.   [1985] ECR 1513.
1122.   [1982] ECR 2277.

amounted in fact to a failure to act, and alternatively under Article 230 EC [Article 263 TFEU] arguing that the answer should be annulled.

Held:

The ECJ held that the application of Lord Bethell would be admissible only if the Commission "having been duly called upon . . . has failed to adopt in relation to him a measure which he was legally entitled to claim by virtue of the rules of Community law". Lord Bethell, although indirectly concerned by the measure as a user of the airlines and chairman of the Freedom of the Skies Committee which represented users, was, nevertheless, not in the legal position of a potential addressee of a decision, which the Commission had a duty to adopt with regard to him. His application under Article 230 EC [Article 263 TFEU] was rejected for the same reason. The analogy between locus standi of non-privileged applicants under Article 230 and 232 EC [Articles 263 and 265 TFEU] was thus confirmed by the ECJ.

The similarity between Articles 263 and 265 TFEU means that an application under Article 265 TFEU is admissible if the applicants are addressees of a prospective measure or if they are directly and individually concerned by a non-regulatory measure which an EU institution has failed to adopt,[1123] or if they are directly concerned by a regulatory measure which does not entail implementing measures.

16.4.3   Procedure under Article 265 TFEU

The procedure under Article 265 TFEU comprises two stages: an administrative stage and a judicial stage. The latter takes place before the CJEU. The procedure is examined below.

16.4.3.1   Administrative stage

An action for failure to act may be brought before the CJEU only if the institution, body, office or agency concerned has been called upon to act by the applicant, who has notified it of the complaint, and indicated what precise measures it wishes that institution to take.[1124]

There is no specific time limit for the submission of a complaint, but in Case 59/70 *The Netherlands v Commission*[1125] the ECJ held that the right to notify the Commission of its omission, or failure to act, should not be delayed indefinitely and that the complaint should be lodged within a "reasonable time". This decision was rendered in relation to the CS Treaty, but it seems that this solution can be transposed to the ToL.

Once the institution concerned is notified of the complaint, it has two months to define its position. The main problem is to determine what is meant by the phrase "define its position". The ECJ has gradually clarified this phrase.

The Court held that the institution defined its position if it had adopted any act, apart from a

---

1123.   See Joined Cases 97/86, 99/86, 193/86 and 215/86 *Asteris E.A. v Commission* [1988] ECR 2118; Case T-166/98 *Cantina Sociale Di Doliniova Soc. Coop. Rl and Others v Commission* [2004] ECR II-3991.

1124.   Joined Cases 114–117/79 *Fournier and Others v Commission* [1980] ECR 1529.

1125.   [1971] ECR 639.

reply asking the applicant to wait (which could not be considered as an answer[1126]), or referring to a position previously taken. For example, when the Commission sends a letter refusing to start proceedings against a competitor undertaking, it defines its position.[1127] However, refusal to take measures, which are required under a specific procedure, amounts to a failure to act; for example, an applicant is entitled to an answer, even one stating the refusal of the Commission to act.[1128] When an institution adopts a different act from that which was requested by the applicant,[1129] it also defines its position.

Refusal to act by the institution concerned is not necessarily tantamount to a failure to act. The institution concerned must be legally bound under EU law to act. Conversely, if it has discretion in this respect, an action for failure to act is not admissible. This point is illustrated by Case 48/65 *Alfons Lütticke GmbH v Commission*.[1130]

THE FACTS WERE:

Lütticke argued that a German tax on the importation of milk powder was contrary to Article 90 EC [Article 110 TFEU]. He asked the Commission to take enforcement action against Germany under Article 226 [Article 258 TFEU]. The Commission replied that the tax was not contrary to EC law, and, as a result, it did not intend to take action under Article 226 EC [Article 258 TFEU]

Held:

The ECJ held that first, by refusing to act, the Commission defined its position, and second, under Article 226 EC [Article 258 TFEU] the Commission enjoyed a large measure of discretion whether or not to start proceedings. Thus, the applicant could not force the Commission to act since he was not legally entitled to a particular measure. The Commission had no duty to act in respect of his request.

Once the institution concerned defines its position, the proceedings under Article 265 TFEU are terminated. If an applicant is legally entitled to a specific measure and unhappy about the answer it obtained from a particular institution, it may then bring proceedings against that institution under Article 263 TFEU to annul the decision adopted in its case.

It is interesting to note that unsuccessful applicants under Article 265 TFEU, that is, those who are told by the ECJ that the institution in question did define its position, have often asked the ECJ to transform their action under Article 265 TFEU into an action under Article 263 TFEU. The ECJ has always refused. Its refusal may have serious consequences for the applicant if the

---

1126. This happens usually when the Commission conducts further investigations concerning the matter: Joined Cases 42 and 49/59 *SNUPAT* [1961] ECR 53.

1127. Case 125/78 *GEMMA* [1979] ECR 3173.

1128. Case T-28/90 *Asia Motor France SA and Others v Commission* [1992] ECR II-2285; Case T-32/93 *Ladbroke Racing Ltd v Commission* [1994] ECR II-1015.

1129. Case C-107/91 *ENU v Commission* [1993] ECR I-599; Case C-25/91 *Pesqueras Echebastar SA v Commission* [1993] ECR I-1719.

1130. [1966] ECR 19.

time limit of two months provided under Article 265 TFEU has already expired, since it would mean that the time limit for bringing an action under Article 263 has also expired.[1131]

16.4.3.2　Judicial stage

If the institution concerned does not define its position within two months, the applicant has another two months to bring proceedings before the CJEU. The applicant is required to submit an application limited to the points it raised in the original complaint to the institution concerned.[1132] The time limit is strictly enforced by the CJEU.[1133]

If after the commencement of an action under Article 265 TFEU, but before the judgment of the CJEU, the institution in question defines its position, the application is considered as admissible but "without object".[1134] This solution seems unfair to the applicant, especially if it envisages bringing an action under Article 340(2) TFEU against the institution concerned. The ECJ justified its position by stating that in such circumstances a judgment under Article 265 TFEU would have no effect with respect to the defaulting institution.

The consequence of a successful action under Article 265 TFEU is that the ECJ declares the failure to act of the institution concerned, which under Article 266 TFEU "shall . . . take the necessary measures to comply with the judgment of the Court of Justice of the European Union" within a reasonable period of time.[1135]

16.5　Action for damages: non-contractual liability of the EU under Article 340(2) TFEU

The exclusive jurisdiction of the CJEU over disputes relating to non-contractual liability of the EU is based on Article 268 TFEU which provides:

"The Court of Justice of the European Union shall have jurisdiction in disputes relating to compensation for damage provided for in the second and third paragraphs of Article 340."

The General Court has jurisdiction in actions for damages brought by individuals while the ECJ exercises jurisdiction in actions commenced by Member States.

Article 340(2) and (3) TFEU states:

"(2) In the case of non-contractual liability, the Union shall, in accordance with the general principles common to the laws of the Member States, make good any damage caused by its institutions or by its servants in the performance of their duties.

(3) Notwithstanding the second paragraph, the European Central Bank shall, in accordance with

---

1131.　Case T-28/90 *Asia Motor France SA and Others v Commission* [1992] ECR II-2285.

1132.　Joined Cases 24 and 34/58 *Chambre Syndicale de la Sidérurgie de l'Est de la France and Others v High Authority* [1960] ECR 281; Cases 41 and 50/59 *Hamborner Bergbau AG, Friedrich Thyssen Bergbau AG v High Authority* [1960] ECR 493.

1133.　Cases 5–11/62 and 13–15/62 *San Michele and Others v High Authority* [1962] ECR 449; Case C-25/91 *Pesqueras Echebastar SA v Commission* [1993] ECR I-1719.

1134.　Case 302/87 *EP v Council* [1988] ECR 5615; the Council submitted the project of the Community budget after the EP submitted its application under Article 232 EC [Article 265 TFEU].

1135.　Case 13/83 *EP v Council* [1985] ECR 1513.

the general principles common to the laws of the Member States, make good any damage caused by it or by its servants in the performance of their duties."

Non-contractual liability of the EU is the corollary of the transfer of certain powers to the EU institutions by Member States, which requires that individuals are protected against unlawful conduct of the EU. Article 340(3) TFEU reiterates the pre-ToL case law of the ECJ under which the Court allowed proceedings against the ECB.

It is important to note that in Case 169/73 *Compagnie Continentale France v Council*[1136] the ECJ held that when it is a provision of the Treaty which causes damage to the applicant, there will be no liability on the part of any EU institution unless otherwise specified by the Treaties, because Treaties are agreements concluded between Member States, i.e. the author of the act is not the EU but the Member States.

16.5.1   The autonomous nature of an action under Article 340(2) TFEU

In the majority of cases an action for damages is based on the illegality of EU acts. As a result of alleged illegality being at issue, an action for damages under Article 340(2) TFEU may be an effective way of getting round the time limit of two months imposed by Articles 263 and 265 TFEU, with the additional benefit for natural and legal persons of the possible receipt of compensation.

In Case 5/71 *Schöppenstedt*[1137] the ECJ held that an action for damages under Article 288(2) EC [Article 340(2) TFEU] is autonomous as it has a special role to play within the system of remedies. The difference between an action for annulment and an action for damages is that the latter is intended not to nullify a particular measure, but to make good damage caused by an EU institution in the exercise of its functions.

The autonomous nature of an action under Article 340(2) TFEU is subject to one exception. If an action for damages would have the same effects as an action for annulment, but the applicant did not institute the latter within the prescribed time limit, the former will be inadmissible. Therefore, if an application under Article 340(2) TFEU is intended in fact to nullify an individual decision which has become definitive (that is, immune from annulment due to the expiry of the time limit provided for in Article 263(5) TFEU), or otherwise designed to provide a means of escaping the restrictions imposed by Article 263 TFEU, it will be rejected.[1138]

The above point is illustrated in Case T-91/05 *Sinara Handel GmbH v Council and Commission*.[1139]

1136.   [1975] ECR 117; Case T-113/96 *Dubois et Fils* [1998] ECR II-125, confirmed by the ECJ in Case C-95/98P *Dubois et Fils* [1999] ECR I-9835.

1137.   [1971] ECR 975.

1138.   Case 175/84 *Krohn* [1986] ECR 753; Case T-514/93 *Cobrecaf* [1995] ECR II-621; Case T-547/93 *Orlando Lopes v ECJ* [1996] ECR II-185; Case T-47/02 *Manfred Danzer v Council* [2006] ECR II-1779.

1139.   [2007] ECR II-245 (Ord).

THE FACTS WERE:

The applicant sought reimbursement of an amount precisely equal to the anti-dumping duty it paid to the national customs authorities pursuant to the relevant regulation, which the applicant alleged was unlawful. It argued that the amount claimed represented its loss of profit. The Commission submitted that the applicant was in fact seeking the nullification of the legal effects of the relevant regulation and that its claim was not for loss of profit but for repayment of the anti-dumping duties.

Held:

The CFI [the General Court] dismissed the application. It held that because the "damage, as identified and quantified by the applicant, must, in reality, be regarded as arising directly, necessarily and exclusively from the payment of the sum owed in respect of the anti-dumping duties imposed", the action was in fact a claim for repayment and as such within the exclusive jurisdiction of national courts.

The judgment of the CFI [the General Court] is in conformity with the principle that the CJEU has no jurisdiction to entertain actions for recovery of amounts wrongfully charged by a national administration on the basis of EU measures which are subsequently declared invalid. Therefore, the applicants should have brought proceedings before a national court as explained in section 16.5.5.2).

Unlike a judgment under Article 263 TFEU which is valid erga omnes,[1140] a judgment under Article 340(2) TFEU produces binding legal effects solely in relation to the applicant.

An action for damages is also independent from an action for failure to act under Article 265 TFEU.[1141]

16.5.2 Parties to proceedings under Article 340(2) TFEU

Applicants: any natural and legal person as well as a Member State may bring an action under Article 340(2) TFEU provided it is for loss resulting from unlawful, conduct of the EU institutions, or from a wrongful act of its servants in the performance of their duties.

Associations have a standing under Article 340(2) TFEU if either:

- They can establish a particular interest of their own distinct from that of their individual members; or

- A right to compensation has been assigned to them by their members.[1142]

Defendant: an action may be brought against the EU institution or institutions responsible for causing damage.[1143] In most cases, the defendant is either the Commission, or the Council, or

---

1140. See also Case T-489/93 *Unifrut Hellas EPE* [1994] ECR II-1201.
1141. Case 4/69 *Lütticke* [1971] ECR 325; Case 134/73 *Holtz and Willemsen* [1974] ECR 1.
1142. Case T-304/01 *Abad Pérez* [2006] ECR II-4857.
1143. Case 63 and 69/72 *Werhan* [1973] ECR 1229.

both, in respect of an allegedly wrongful act adopted by the Council acting on a proposal submitted by the Commission. Actions against the EP are rare, but its activities may cause damage to a natural or a legal person.[1144] Under the ToL more actions against the EP are expected in the light of the facts that the EP has become a co-legislator in respect of acts adopted in accordance with the ordinary legislative procedure and that it often participates in special legislative procedures. Prior to the entry into force of the ToL the ECJ broadly interpreted the notion of "an institution" and this interpretation which went beyond the list established in Article 7 TEU. It permitted the bringing of actions against the EIB,[1145] the ECB and the EU Ombudsman.[1146] although it rejected the bringing of an action against the European Council.[1147] However, under the ToL, the European Council, being an EU institution, is within the scope of Article 340(2) TFEU. It should be noted that it results from Article 340(2) TFEU that the CJEU has jurisdiction over all bodies, agencies or offices created on the basis of the Treaties which act on behalf of the EU.

While in theory an action against the ECJ is possible, in practice the ECJ cannot be a judge and a party in the same proceedings. Actions brought by staff against the CJEU arising from contracts of employment are dealt with under Article 270 TFEU by the EU Civil Service Tribunal (see Chapter 6.6.11).

The procedure under Article 340(2) TFEU is within the exclusive competence of the CJEU and therefore, national courts are prohibited from intervening in that procedure. In Case C-275/00 *First and Franex*,[1148] a Belgian court by interlocutory order commissioned an expert report concerning the assessment of the alleged damage caused by the way in which the Commission dealt with the dioxin crisis in the EU with a view to using the report against the Commission in Article 340(2) proceedings. The ECJ held it has "exclusive jurisdiction to prescribe, with regard to one of the institutions of the European Community, any interim measure or measure of inquiry, such as commissioning an expert report whose purpose is to establish the role of that institution in the events which allegedly caused damage, for the purposes of an action which may be brought against the European Community to establish its non-contractual liability".

16.5.3 Time limit

The admissibility of an action for damages is subject to a time limit. Under Article 46 of the Statute of the CJEU the proceedings under Article 340(2) TFEU "shall be barred after a period of five years from the occurrence of the event giving rise thereto". This unclear provision has been explained by the ECJ as meaning that an applicant may bring an ction under Article 340(2) TFEU within five years from the day the damage materialised.[1149]

It is logical to require that the limitation period cannot begin to run before all the requirements governing the obligation to make good the damage are satisfied. However, the fact that the applicant considers that it has not yet got all necessary evidence to prove, to the requisite legal standard, that all conditions set out in Article 340(2) TFEU are satisfied cannot prevent the

---

1144. T-203/96 *Embassy Limousine v EP* [1998] ECR II-4239.

1145. Case 370/89 *SGEEM* [1992] ECR I-6211.

1146. Case T-209/00 *Lamberts v Ombudsman* [2002] ECR II-2203, confirmed by the ECJ in Case C-234/02P *European Ombudsman v Lamberts* [2004] ECR I-2803.

1147. Case T-346/03 *Krikorian* [2003] ECR II-6037, confirmed by the ECJ in Case C-18/04P (unpublished).

1148. [2002] ECR I-10943.

1149. Case T-174/00 *Biret International v Council* [2002] ECR II-17.

limitation period from running. Only the CJEU can decide whether or not the conditions for liability are satisfied.[1150]

The time limit starts to run from the day the damage has materialised, not the time of the occurrence of the event, or the fact giving rise to the damage.[1151] The running of time is interrupted by:

- Proceedings brought by the applicant before the CJEU; or

- A preliminary request addressed by the applicant to the relevant institution, but only if followed by an application under Articles 263 or 265 TFEU and within the time limit set out in those provisions.[1152]

However, neither commencement of proceedings before a national court,[1153] nor an exchange of communications between the applicant and the relevant EU institution, interrupts the running of time.[1154]

16.5.4 Distinction between liability of the EU and liability of its servants

The EU must make good any damage caused by its institutions and by its servants in the performance of their duties. Liability of the EU for unlawful acts is dealt with in section 16.5.6.3. As to liability of the EU for acts of its servants, this is based on the concept of fault (*faute personnelle*), which is the wrongful act or omission of the servants of the EU acting in the course of their duty.

In Case 9/69 *Claude Sayag v Jean-Pierre Leduc and Others*,[1155] the ECJ held that the EU is liable only for those acts of its servants, which by virtue of the internal and direct relationship constitute the necessary extension of the tasks conferred on the EU institutions. This restrictive approach entails that if the conduct of a servant which gave rise to damage was performed outside the course of his duties, that is, on a "frolic of his own", the EU will not be liable. The remedy of a person suffering damage in such a situation is to commence action against the servant before a national court, which has jurisdiction ratione loci, and liability will be determined under the law of the forum. Conversely, if a wrongful act or omission was committed by an employee acting in the course of his duties, the victim should commence proceedings against the EU before the General Court, and liability will be determined according to EU law. If there is joint liability of a servant and the relevant EU institution, then the EU, after compensating the victim, may bring an action against the servant in order to recover all or part of any compensation paid to the victim.

16.5.5 Distinction between liability of the EU and liability of the Member States

Very often the EU institutions confer upon national authorities the task of applying or implementing EU measures. When the conduct of the national authority causes damage to individuals, the question arises: who is liable, the Member State, or the EU? The best solution for applicants

---

1150. Case C-282/05P *Holcim (Deutschland) AG v Commission* [2007] ECR I-2941.
1151. Case 256/80 *Birra Wührer* [1982] ECR 85; Case 145/83 *Adams* [1985] ECR 3539.
1152. T-174/00 *Biret* [2002] ECR II-17. See also Case T-106/98 *Fratelli Murri v Commission* [1999] ECR II-2553.
1153. Case C-136/01 *Autosalone Ispra dei Fratelli Rossi v European Atomic Energy Commission* [2002] ECR I-6565.
1154. Case T-166/98 *Cantina Sociale di Dolianova Soc.Coop.Rl. and Others v Commission* [2004] ECR II-3991.
1155. [1969] ECR 329.

would be to permit them to claim compensation for their loss at their option, either before national courts or before the CJEU. Unfortunately, this option is rejected by EU law because:

- First, an EU judge does not have jurisdiction to decide cases against the Member States in tort, nor do national judges have jurisdiction to decide cases against the EU;

- Second, the division of competences between the EU and the Member States in general, and in relation to a disputed matter in particular, prohibits encroachment on each other's sphere of competence.

For the above reasons, three situations can be distinguished. These are examined below.

16.5.5.1 Liability for wrongful or negligent implementation or application by national authorities of lawful EU acts

In this case, an action for damages should be brought against national authorities before national courts according to national procedure, and the conditions of liability should be determined by national administrative law. In Case 101/78 *Granaria*,[1156] the ECJ held that the question of compensation for loss incurred by individuals caused by a national body or by agents of the Member States, resulting from either their infringement of EU law or an act or omission contrary to national law while applying EU law, is not covered by Article 340(2) TFEU and has to be assessed by national courts according to the national law of the Member State concerned. However, the requirements of the principle of non-contractual liability must be respected.

16.5.5.2 Liability of national authorities in the case of correct application or implementation of unlawful EU acts

When national authorities have correctly applied or implemented an EU measure, there is no fault on the part of the Member State concerned. As a result, the EU is liable for damage resulting from an unlawful act, but national courts have jurisdiction, exceptionally in respect of actions concerning monetary compensation. This exception was explained by the ECJ in Case 96/71 *Haegeman v Commission*.[1157]

THE FACTS WERE:

Haegeman, a Belgian company, which imported wine from Greece (at that time Greece was not a Member State), was required to pay a countervailing charge imposed by a Council regulation. Belgian authorities collected monies which went to the EC's funds. The applicant alleged that the relevant regulation was unlawful and that it had suffered damage as a result of its existence.

1156. [1979] ECR 623.
1157. [1972] ECR 1005.

Held:

The ECJ held that for the applicant the proper forum was in a national court, as the monies were collected by national authorities and thus the applicant was in a direct relationship with them, not with the Council. If the applicant sought to challenge the relevant regulation, national courts could refer the matter under Article Article 234 EC [Article 267TFEU], since only the ECJ has jurisdiction to declare an EC act void.

If a measure is declared void by the CJEU, a national court will award compensation for the total damages suffered by the successful claimant. The sum awarded will be paid from national funds but national authorities can obtain reimbursement from EU funds.[1158]

The exclusive jurisdiction of national courts in actions for monetary compensation, where national authorities are not at fault, entails that such actions if brought before the CJEU will usually be declared inadmissible by the CJEU. Exceptions to this rule which allow the applicant to bring an action directly before the CJEU, are:

- On the authority of Case 175/84 *Krohn*,[1159] in a situation where the wrongful act is entirely attributable to an EU institution which has directly, exclusively and effectively exercised the power of decision without any involvement of national authorities, that is, national authorities had no discretion whatsoever in the matter;

- If it is impossible for national courts to order payments in the absence of EU provisions authorising national authorities to pay the claimed amount;[1160]

- If an action before national courts will, for procedural or other reasons, not result in the payment of the alleged damages.[1161]

It should be noted that in all actions, which do not involve payments of money, the CJEU has jurisdiction.[1162]

16.5.5.3   Joint liability of the EU and a Member State

In Joined Cases 5, 7 and 13 to 24/66 *Kampffmeyer*,[1163] the ECJ held that if there is joint liability of the EU and a Member State for an unlawful act, the applicant must first bring an action before national courts. Subsequently, a national court must refer the case under Article 267 TFEU to the

---

1158. J. A. Usher, *Legal Aspects of Agriculture in the European Community*, 1988, Oxford: Oxford University Press, pp 104–106, 150–51.

1159. [1986] ECR 753.

1160. For example, Joined Cases 64 and 113/76, 167 and 239/78, 27,28 and 45/79 *Dumortier Frères* [1979] ECR 3091; Case 5/71 *Schöppenstedt* [1971] ECR 975; Case T-166/98 *Cantina Sociale di Dolinova Soc. Coop. RI and Others v Commission* [2004] ECR II-3991.

1161. Case 281/82 *Unifrex* [1984] ECR 1969; Case 81/86 *Buizen* [1987] ECR 3677; Case T-167/94 *Nölle* [1995] ECR II-2589; Case T-195/00 *Travelex Global and Financial Services Ltd and Interpayment Services Ltd v Commission* [2003] ECR II-1677.

1162. Case 126/76 *Dietz* [1977] ECR 2431; Case C-282/90 *Industrie- en Handelsonderneming Vreugdenhil BV v Commission* [1992] ECR I-1937; Case C-104/89 and C-37/90 *Mulder* [1992] ECR I-3026.

1163. [1967] ECR 245.

ECJ, which, if it finds the measure unlawful, will annul the contested act. After its annulment, the national court will assess only the liability of the Member State and award damages corresponding to the damage caused by the national authorities of that Member State. The next step for the applicant will be to bring an action before the General Court to determine the liability of the EU, and obtain an award of damages.

It is submitted that the solution adopted in relation to the division of responsibility between the EU and the Member State is too complex, time-consuming and confusing. Further, in cases where neither national courts nor the CJEU have jurisdiction to decide a particular case, a denial of justice may result.[1164] However, under Article 19(1) TEU Member States are required to provide remedies sufficient to ensure effective legal protection of individuals in the fields covered by EU law. Therefore, they will be responsible, in the last resort, to ensure that individuals are adequately compensated in cases where the EU refuses to do so.

16.5.6 Conditions for liability under Article 340(2) TFEU

Article 340(2) TFEU contains general guidance concerning non-contractual liability of the EU, and leaves the ECJ to determine specific rules in this area. Indeed, Article 340(2) TFEU is unique as it requires the ECJ to establish the conditions of liability based on "general principles of the laws of the Member States". This means that general principles of laws of the Member States regarding liability of public authorities are relevant. Furthermore, it is not necessary that a particular rule is recognised in all Member States since this would lead to a lowest common denominator and thus ensure the minimum protection for victims of wrongful conduct of the EU.

The ECJ's approach is selective and based on a comparative study of national legal systems in the context of the specific requirements of EU law. This approach leaves the ECJ a considerable margin of appreciation in the selection of general principles appropriate to the peculiar needs of the EU. This is necessary taking into account the complexity of actions for damages based on Article 340(2) TFEU. On the one hand, the ECJ exercises its jurisdiction in relation to non-contractual liability in the context of disputes involving the economic policies of the EU and thus must take into account the legal and financial implications of its judgments when awarding damages to an applicant or determining unlawful conduct on the part of the EU institutions and, on the other hand, the ECJ must often resolve the delicate question of delimitation of competences between the EU and the Member States.

In Case 4/69 *Lütticke v Commission*[1165] the ECJ identified, on the grounds of general principles common to the Member States, the conditions necessary to establish EU liability as being:

- Unlawful conduct on the part of the EU;

- Damage to the applicant; and

- A causal link between the conduct of the EU institution and the alleged damage.

Initially the ECJ developed two regimes relating to EU liability under Art 340(2) TFEU:

- One concerning general liability relating to a failure of administration; and

- The other specifically regarding the liability of the EU for legislative acts.

1164. The best illustration is provided by Case C-55/90 *Cato* [1992] ECR I-2533.
1165. [1971] ECR 325.

In Case C-352/98 *Laboratoires Pharmaceutique Bergaderm SA v Commission*[1166] the ECJ merged the two regimes. However, the ECJ has rejected the possibility that the EU may be held liable for lawful acts that may cause damage to applicants.

For historical reasons, and in order to facilitate the understanding of the case law prior to *Bergaderm*, a short summary of the past interpretation of Article 340(2) TFEU is provided below.

16.5.6.1   Liability for administrative acts: past approach

When applicants claimed failure of administration they had to prove:

- The wrongful conduct of the institution;

- The existence of damage; and

- A causative link between the two.

Failure of administration comprises all defects in the organisation and the functioning of the service such as "defaulting organisations of the service",[1167] "negligence in the management",[1168] inappropriate supervision,[1169] breach of the principle of confidentiality of information obtained by the Commission,[1170] forwarding of erroneous information by the EU institutions,[1171] and breach of the provisions relating to hygiene and security at work.[1172] The case law of the ECJ makes no distinction in the degree of fault like, for example, under French law where there is a difference between simple and serious fault. The EU is liable in damages in cases of inexcusable errors or manifest and grave lack of diligence.

16.5.6.2   Liability for legislative acts: past approach

In determining liability the ECJ took into account the fact that the activities of EU institutions concerned more and more economic administration and less pure administration. The former is characterised by the exercise of a wide discretion by the EU institutions as they have to make choices of economic policies. Such factors as the complexity inherent in economic choices, difficulties in the application and interpretation of legislative measures in this area, and the wide margin of discretion exercised by the EU institutions had led the ECJ to find liability of EU institutions only in exceptional cases.

In Case 83/76 *Bayerische HNL v Council and Commission*[1173] the ECJ emphasised that ". . . exercise of the legislative function must not be hindered by the prospect of action for damages whenever the general interest of the Community requires legislative measures to be adopted which may adversely affect individual interests" and that "in a legislative context . . . the Community

---

1166.   [2000] ECR I-5291.

1167.   Case 23/59 *FERAM* [1959] ECR 245.

1168.   Case 9/56 *Meroni* [1957–1958] ECR 133.

1169.   Joined Cases 19/60, 21/60, 2/61 and 3/61 *Société Fives Lille Cail and Others v High Authority* [1961] ECR 281.

1170.   Case 145/83 *Adams* [1985] ECR 3539.

1171.   Joined Cases 19, 20, 25 and 30/69 *Richez-Parise* [1970] ECR 325; Case 169/73 *Compagnie Continentale France v Council* [1975] ECR 117.

1172.   Case 308/87 *Grifoni* [1990] ECR I-1203.

1173.   [1978] ECR 1209.

cannot incur liability unless the institution concerned has manifestly and gravely disregarded the limits on the exercise of its powers."[1174]

The ECJ stated in Case 5/71 *Schöppenstedt*:[1175]

"When legislative action involving measures of economic policy is concerned, the Community does not incur non-contractual liability for damage suffered by individuals as a consequence of that action, by virtue of the provisions contained in Article [340], second paragraph, of Treaty [TFEU], unless a sufficiently flagrant violation of a superior rule of law for the protection of the individual has occurred."[1176]

This is referred to under EU law as the "Schöppenstedt formula". The formula requires proof of three conditions with regard to legislative acts adopted by the EU. These conditions are:

- There must be a breach of a superior rule of law;

- The breach must be sufficiently serious;

- The superior rule must be one for the protection of the individual.

In addition, all conditions relating to non-contractual liability in general have to be satisfied, that is:

- Unlawful conduct on the part of the EU;

- Damage to the applicant; and

- A causal link between the conduct of the EU institution and the alleged damage.

The Schöppenstedt formula highlights the fact that EU institutions were especially protected against actions in damages under Article 340(2) TFEU for the very simple reason that all legislative acts entail that their authors enjoy a large margin of discretion. Indeed, it is not important whether a legislative act concerns economic policies sensu stricto or other areas such as transport, social policy and so on; what is important is that an institution has discretion and must exercise it in the interests of the EU. It must make choices in devising EU policies in the areas of competence of the EU in order to attain the objectives which are essential for integration of national policies and especially to harmonise national laws in specific areas.[1177] This is regardless of the fact that the relevant legislative measures may adversely affect individual interests. The threat of numerous applications for damages should not be allowed to hinder the EU in its policy making. For that reason the requirements contained in the Schöppenstedt formula were very restrictive and rigorous.

It can be seen from the above that when applicants were seeking to establish EU liability for failure of administration, their task was less onerous than in cases where applicants were seeking to establish liability of the EU for wrongful acts having legal effect.[1178]

1174. Ibid., at 1229.
1175. [1971] ECR 975.
1176. [1971] ECR 975.
1177. Case C-63/89 *Les Assurances du Crédit SA and Compagnie Belge d'Assurance Crédit SA v Council* [1991] ECR I-1799.
1178. Case T-203/96 *Embassy Limousines* [1998] ECR II-4239.

16.5.6.3   The current rules on liability of the EU under Article 340(2) TFEU

In the judgment in Case C-352/98 *Laboratoires Pharmaceutique Bergaderm SA v Commission*[1179] the ECJ merged the two regimes relating to non-contractual liability of the EU, i.e. one concerning general liability relating to a failure of administration; and the other specifically regarding the liability of the EU for legislative acts. The Court held that the decisive test when considering liability of an EU institution is the degree of discretion that an EU institution enjoyed when adopting the allegedly wrongful act, irrespective of whether the act was of an administrative nature or constituted a legislative measure[1180] and whether or not it was an individualised act or a normative act of general application.[1181]

The above approach focuses on the discretionary or non-discretionary nature of the wrongful act or conduct. The choice of focus shows that the Court has aligned the conditions under which the EU may be liable with those applicable to non-contractual liability that a Member State incurs for damages caused to individuals.

These conditions are:

▪ Unlawfulness of conduct. This requires that the applicant establishes the existence of a sufficiently serious breach of a rule of law intended to confer rights on individuals; and

▪ The existence of damage; and

▪ The existence of a causal connection between the conduct and the damage in question.

All conditions governing the EU's liability must be satisfied. If one of them is not fulfilled, the application is dismissed in its entirety without the necessity for the CJEU to examine the remaining conditions for such liability.[1182]

Conditions for liability of the EU for lawful acts are examined below.

16.5.6.3.1 Unlawfulness of the conduct which requires that the applicant must establish the existence of a sufficiently serious breach of a rule of law intended to confer rights on individuals

16.5.6.3.1.1 Breach of a rule of law

The rule breached must occupy a fundamental place in the EU legal order. It may relate to provisions of the Treaties, or to the general principles of EU law. This requirement has as its objective the exclusion of claims founded upon minor illegality.

Case 74/74 *CNTA v Commission*[1183] concerned a regulation which entered into force immediately after its publication, and which did not provide for a transitional period and abolished compensation for the effect of exchange rate fluctuations in the trade in colza and rapeseed. In this case the ECJ held the regulation to be legal but contrary to the principle of legitimate expectations (this being a general principle of EU law) in relation to undertakings which had already obtained

---

1179. [2000] ECR I-5291.

1180. As decided in Case T-285/03 *Agraz* [2005] ECR II-1063.

1181. Case C-390/94P *Antillean Rice* [1999] ECR I-769.

1182. Case C-146/91 KYDEP [1998] ECR II-4073.

1183. [1975] ECR 533, also Case 97/76 *Merkur Außenhandel GmbH & Co. KG v Commission* [1977] ECR 1063; Joined Cases C-104/89 and C-37/90 *Mulder and Others v Council and Commission* [1992] ECR I-3061.

export licences fixing the amount of compensation in advance and had concluded contracts prior to the abolition of the compensation scheme.

In the *Second Skimmed Milk Powder Case*[1184] the ECJ held that a regulation concerning the compulsory purchase of Community stocks of skimmed milk powder was contrary to the principle of non-discrimination[1185] and in Case 114/76 *Bela-Mühle Josef Bergmann KG v Grows-Farm GmbH & Co. KG*,[1186] which concerned the same regulation, the ECJ held that the regulation was also disproportionate as to the objective to be achieved.

Among other general principles recognised by the ECJ in the context of actions for damages are: the principle of the protection of acquired rights;[1187] the principle of proportionality;[1188] the principle of non-retroactivity;[1189] the principle of care and of sound administration;[1190] and the principle of equal treatment in the award of public contracts.[1191]

16.5.6.3.1.2 The rule must confer rights on individuals

This condition requires that the rule has as its object and as its effect the protection of rights of individuals. It is not, however, necessary that the rule does not have exclusively as its object the protection of individuals. It is sufficient that it has an effect on the protection of individuals in general. In Joined Cases 5, 7 and 13–24/66 *Kampffmeyer*,[1192] the ECJ held that the failure of the Commission to investigate fully the protective measures concerning the imposition of a levy on maize had infringed a rule of law which was of a general nature as it referred to the free trade in maize and the support of the maize market, but was, nevertheless, for the protection of individuals.

This condition excludes such rules as those regarding the decision-making procedure, for example, non-consultation of the EP in the adoption of a measure which was required by that procedure or absence of a proposal from the Commission or non-respect of the division of competences between EU institutions.[1193]

16.5.6.3.1.3 The breach must be sufficiently serious

The decisive test in determining whether or not an EU institution "manifestly and gravely disregarded the limits of its discretion" is the seriousness of the breach. This is assessed in the light of criteria in effect the same as those relating to non-contractual liability of a Member State for damage caused to individuals by an infringement of EU law. The criteria are:

1184. Joined Cases 83 and 94/76 and 4, 15, 40/77 *Bayerische HNL* [1978] ECR 1209.

1185. There are many cases concerning the principle of non-discrimination and equality: Case 238/78 *Ireks-Arkady* [1979] ECR 2955; Joined Cases 116 and 124/77 *Amylum* [1979] ECR 3497; Joined Cases 64 and 113/76, 167 and 239/78, 27, 28 and 45/79 *Dumortier Frères* [1979] ECR 3091.

1186. [1977] ECR 1211.

1187. Joined Cases 95 to 98/74, 15 and 100/75 *Union Nationale des Coopératives Agricoles de Céréales and Others v Commission and Council* [1975] ECR 1615.

1188. Joined Cases 63–69/72 *Wilhelm Werhahn Hansamühle and Others v Council* [1973] ECR 1229.

1189. Case 71/74 *Nederlandse Vereniging voor de Fruit- en Groentenimporthandel v Commission* [1975] ECR 1095.

1190. Case T-231/97 *New Europe Consulting and Brown v Commission* [1999] ECR II-2401; Case T13/99 *Pfizer Animal Health v Council* [2002] ECR II-3305; Case T-285/03 *Agraz* [2005] ECR II-1063.

1191. Case T-145/98 *ADT Projekt* [2000] ECR II-387; Case T-160/03 *AFCon Management Consultants and Others v Commission* [2005] ECR II-981.

1192. [1967] ECR 245.

1193. Case C-282/90 *Industrie- en Handelsonderneming Vreugdenhil BV v Commission* [1992] ECR I-1937.

- The clarity and precision of the EU rule breached;

- Whether the infringement was intentional or accidental;

- Whether any error of law was excusable;

- The degree of discretion enjoyed by the EU institution concerned;

- The "complexity of the situations to be regulated"; and

- The difficulties in the application or interpretation of the relevant text.

Accordingly, when an EU institution has only considerably reduced, or even no discretion, the mere infringement of EU law may be sufficient to establish the existence of a sufficiently serious breach.[1194]

With regard to irregularity in administering EU matters giving rise to liability, this is assessed by comparison with the conduct in similar circumstances of a normal prudent and diligent administration.[1195]

Should the Court find that the institution had limited or no discretion when adopting the act, this alone would not suffice to establish the existence of a sufficiently serious breach of EU law. The criteria set out above, such as the complexity of a situation to be regulated and the difficulties in the application or interpretation of the relevant text, will be taken into consideration.

Many claims have been rejected on the ground that the case at issue was so complex that an EU institution's violation of EU law could not be considered as being sufficiently serious.[1196]

It appears that in respect of competition cases, claims based on non-contractual liability of the Commission will often, or perhaps always, be dismissed on the basis of the complexity/difficulties in applying the relevant provisions of EC law. In Case T-28/03 *Holcim (Deutschland) AG v Commission*,[1197] the CFI [the General Court] refused to hold the Commission liable despite the fact that the Court recognised that the Commission's discretion, while adopting a decision finding Holcim in breach of Article 81(1) EC [Article 101(1) TFEU], was reduced. The refusal was on the ground that the case was extremely complex as it involved investigation into almost the entire European cement industry and the Commission had great difficulties in applying Article 81(1) EC [Article 101(1) TFEU] given the numerous factual elements of the case. On appeal, the ECJ held that the matter of complexity was a factual matter and thus it was for the CFI [the General Court] alone to determine it.[1198]

It should be said that the change of approach of the CJEU in application of the Schöppenstedt formula has not eliminated the requirement that only grave illegality will permit the applicants to successfully claim damages under Article 340(2) TFEU.

1194. Case C-321/00P *Commission v Camar and Tico* [2002] ECR I-11355; Case C-472/00P *Commission v Fresh Marine* [2003] ECR I-7541; Case T-285/03 *Agraz* [2005] ECR II-1063.

1195. Case T-225/99 *Comafrica* [2001] ECR II-1975.

1196. Case C-198/03P *Commission v CEVA Santé Animale SA and Pfizer Enterprises Sarl* [2005] ECR I-6357.

1197. [2005] ECR II-1357.

1198. Case C-282/05 *Holcim (Deutschland) AG* [2007] ECR I-2941. Such matters may be discussed in the context of appeal proceedings only where the applicant alleges that the CFI has distorted the facts. This was not alleged in this case.

16.5.6.3.2 Damage

The damage suffered must be actual and certain,[1199] regardless whether it is present or future.[1200] It must not be purely hypothetical[1201] or speculative.[1202] In Case C-243/05P *Agraz*,[1203] the ECJ ruled that uncertainty regarding the exact quantification of damage would not preclude a finding that the damage alleged by the applicant was sufficiently certain. Thus, in a situation where the damage alleged is real and actual but there is uncertainty as to the extent of damage, the condition relating to certainty of damage is satisfied.

Compensation may be obtained for all damage suffered, which comprises damnum emergens (the actual loss) and lucrum cessans (the income/profit which would have been earned/made). Advocate General Capatori said in Case 238/78 *Irex-Arkady*[1204] that damage "covers both a material loss . . . a reduction in a person's assets and also the loss of an increase in those assets which would have occurred if the harmful act had not taken place".

Thus, compensation for loss is intended to provide, so far as possible, restitution for the victim.[1205]

As to the actual amount of damages, this is generally negotiated between the parties. However, if they cannot reach agreement, the CJEU will determine the amount.[1206]

It is for applicants to produce the evidence with regard to the facts and the extent of the loss which they claim to have suffered.[1207]

16.5.6.3.2.1 Duty to mitigate loss

There is a duty to mitigate loss. In Joined Cases C-104/89 and 37/90 *Mulder*[1208] the ECJ reduced the damages which might otherwise have been awarded by the amount of profit which the producers could have reasonably earned from alternative activities, although the ECJ made no suggestion as to alternative activities, but the term "reasonable" implies that fundamentally different activities from their usual business were not considered as alternatives.

16.5.6.3.2.2 Contributory negligence

EU law recognises contributory negligence. If applicants have contributed through their own negligence to the resulting damage, the amount of damages will be reduced proportionally. In Case 145/83 *Adams v Commission*[1209] the ECJ held that Adams contributed through his negligence to the resulting damage and reduced the awarded amount by half.

1199. Case 51/81 *De Franceschi SpA Monfalcone v Council and Commission* [1982] ECR 117; Case T-478/93 *Wafer Zoo v Commission* [1995] ECR II-1479; Case C-243/05P *Agraz SA and Others v Commission* [2006] ECR I-10833.

1200. Case 33/59 *Compagnie des Hauts Fourneaux de Chasse v High Authority* [1962] ECR 381; Case 51/81 *De Franceschi SpA Monfalcone v Council and Commission* [1982] ECR 117.

1201. Case 54/65 *Compagnie des Forges de Châtillon, Commentry & Neuves-Maisons v High Authority* [1966] ECR 185; Case 4/65 *Société Anonyme Métallurgique Hainaut-Sambre v High Authority* [1965] ECR 1099.

1202. Joined Cases 54–60/76 *Compagnie Industrielle et Agricole du Comté de Loheac and Others v Council and Commission* [1977] 645; Case 74/74 CNTA [1975] ECR 533.

1203. [2006] ECR I-10833.

1204. [1979] ECR 2955.

1205. Case C-308/87 *Grifoni v EAEC* [1994] ECR I-341; Case C-295/03P *Alessandrini Srl and Others v Commission* [2005] ECR I-5673.

1206. Joined Cases C-104/89 and C-37/90 *Mulder* [2000] ECR I-203; Case T-260/97 *Camar* [2005] ECR II-2741.

1207. Case 26/74 *Roquette Frères* [1976] ECR 677; Case T-184/95 *Dorsch Consultant* [1998] ECR II-667.

1208. [1992] ECR I-3061.

1209. [1985] ECR 3539.

THE FACTS WERE:

Adams was employed by the Swiss-based multinational Hoffmann-La Roche. He forwarded confidential information to the Commission concerning breaches of Article 82 EC [Article 102 TFEU] by his employer, who, as a result, was heavily fined. During the proceedings Hoffmann-La Roche asked the Commission to disclose the name of the informant. The Commission refused, but forwarded to Hoffmann-La Roche certain documents which enabled them to identify Adams as the source of the leaked information. The forwarding of the relevant information was contrary to the duty of confidentiality contained in Article 214 EC [Article 17(3) and Article 7 TEU]. In the meantime Adams moved to Italy where he set up his own business. Hoffmann-La Roche used its international connections to destroy the business established by Adams in Italy. The Commission failed to inform Adams that his former employer was planning to persecute him. On his return to Switzerland Adams was arrested by the Swiss police for economic espionage and held in solitary confinement. His wife committed suicide. Adams brought proceedings before the ECJ against the Commission for loss of earnings and loss of reputation as a result of his conviction and imprisonment.

Held:

The ECJ held that the Commission was liable for the breach of duty of confidentiality as it allowed Adams to be identified as an informer, and awarded Adams £200,000 in damages for his mental anguish and lost earnings, and £176,000 for costs, half of what he had demanded. The reason for the reduction was Adams' contributory negligence. The ECJ held that Adams contributed to the resulting damage by failing to warn the Commission that he could be identified from the confidential documents, and by failing to enquire about progress of the proceedings, especially before returning to Switzerland.

16.5.6.3.3 The existence of a causal connection

A direct causal link must be established between the damage suffered and the unlawful conduct.[1210] The burden of proof is on the applicant.[1211]

In Joined Cases 64/76 and 113/76, 239/78, 27, 28 and 45/79 P *Dumortier Frères SA and Others v Council*,[1212] the ECJ held that there is no obligation to compensate all prejudicial consequences, however remote, resulting from the unlawful legislative act.

THE FACTS WERE:

A regulation which abolished production refunds for maize grits but not for maize starch, both used in brewing and baking and thus in direct competition with each other, was successfully challenged by the producers of maize grits. As a result of the successful action under Article

---

1210. Case 18/60 *Worms* [1962] ECR 195.
1211. Case 40/75 *Produits Bertrand* [1976] ECR 1.
1212. [1979] ECR 3091.

> *230 EC [Article 263 TFEU], the producers of maize grits brought an action under Article 288(2) EC [Article 340(2) TFEU]. They claimed compensation in relation to loss of refunds prior to the adoption of the regulation, lost sales and the closure of factories by two producers and the bankruptcy of a third.*
>
> *Held:*
>
> The ECJ held that the regulation was contrary to the principle of non-discrimination and equality, affected a limited and clearly defined group (that is, the producers of maize grits) and the damage exceeded the bounds of the inherent economic risks in this sector of business.
>
> The ECJ awarded damages only in relation to the loss of refunds. The reduction in sales was not considered as resulting from the abolition of refunds since the producers had increased the price of maize grits and had thus passed the loss to their purchasers. The closing of factories and the bankruptcy were not a sufficiently direct result of the withdrawal of refunds. Damage that is too remote will not give rise to the right of reparation.

16.5.6.4   Unjust enrichment and actions under Article 340(2) TFEU

In Case C-47/07 P *Masdar (UK) Ltd v Commission*,[1213] the ECJ ruled that a claim based on unjust enrichment can be brought under Article 340(2) TFEU.

The ECJ stated that although a claim based on unjust enrichment does not fall under the rules governing non-contractual liability in the strict sense, it nevertheless cannot deny legal redress to persons who have suffered a loss which has increased the wealth of another person solely on the ground that there is no express provision under the Treaties for pursuing that type of action.

The conditions for liability set out under Article 340(2) TFEU do not apply to an action for unjust enrichment. The only requirement that a claimant must satisfy is the proof of enrichment of the defendant for which there is no valid legal basis and the impoverishment of the applicant which is linked to that enrichment.

The ECJ decided to create the new action on two bases:

- An action for unjust enrichment is recognised by national laws of the Member States;

- Any denial of access to the CJEU in a situation where the EU has been unjustly enriched to the detriment of an applicant would be contrary to the principle of effective judicial protection laid down in the case law of the ECJ and enshrined in Article 47 of the Charter of Fundamental Rights of the European Union.

16.5.6.5   The rejection by the ECJ of non-contractual liability of the EU for damage caused by lawful EU acts

For a number of years there have been doubts as to whether the EU can be held liable under Article 340(2) TFEU for lawful acts in a situation where such acts have caused damage to

---

1213. [2008] ECR I-9761.

individuals. The CFI [the General Court] in Cases T-69/00 *FIAMM v Council and Commission*,[1214] T-151/00 *Le Laboratoire du Bain v Council and Commission*,[1215] T-301/00 *Groupe Fremaux SA and Palais Royal Inc v Council and Commission*,[1216] T-320/00 *CD Cartondruck AG v Council and Commission*,[1217] Case T-383/00 *Beamglow Ltd v EP, Council and Commission*[1218] and T-135/01 *Giorgio Fedon & Figli SpA and Others v Council and Commission*,[1219] decided that, in some exceptional circumstances, such liability may arise. The special circumstances referred to the requirement that the damage must be unusual, i.e it must exceed the limits of the economic risks inherent in the sector concerned, and special in nature, i.e. the EU measure must affect a limited and clearly defined group in a disproportionate manner by comparison with other operators. However, in the above mentioned cases the CFI [the General Court] decided that the first requirement was not satisfied. On appeal, the ECJ rejected the possibility that the EU can be held liable for lawful acts adopted by an EU institution.

The main justification provided by the ECJ for the rejection of the principle of non-fault liability of the EU for legislative acts was that no such principle is recognised by the vast majority of legal systems of the Member States. Indeed, as the Commission pointed out even in the Member States where the principle of non-fault liability is recognised, its application is confined to exceptional circumstances, and apart from France, limited solely to administrative acts. Under French law the recognition of non-fault liability for legislative acts is justified by the fact that the French Conseil d'État (Council of State – the highest administrative court in France) has no jurisdiction to review the constitutionality of national legislation and is subject to strict conditions requiring that the damage must be unusual, special, serious and direct, that the challenged legislature is not pursuing the common good and that the legislature has not ruled out compensation as a matter of principle. According to the Commission and the Council the principle of non-fault liability for legislative acts adopted by EU institutions should not be incorporated into EU law because first, it is not a "general principle common to the laws of the Member States" and second, under EU law, contrary to French law, the CJEU has jurisdiction to review EU acts in the light of the Treaties and fundamental principles of EU law and therefore EU law provides for the possibility of the liability of the EU to be put in issue if those higher-ranking norms are infringed.

Are the above justifications convincing? The Advocate-General, in his Opinion in *FIAMM*, submitted excellent arguments in favour of the recognition of the principle of non-fault liability in EU law, namely, that it is well established that no mechanical approach is taken to the selection of general principles of EU law. Therefore it is of no importance how many Member States adhere to the relevant principle. What is important is that the principle is appropriate to the needs and specific features of the EU legal system. According to the Advocate-General non-fault liability of the EU for both legislative and administrative acts adopted by EU institutions responds to the particular requirements of the EU legal order for the following reasons:

1214. [2005] ECR II-5393.
1215. [2005] ECR II-23.
1216. [2005] ECR II-25.
1217. [2005] ECR II-27.
1218. [2005] ECR II-5459.
1219. [2005] ECR II-29.

- It serves the interests of justice as it would offset the severity of the conditions relating to the establishment of non-contractual liability of the EU for unlawful acts.

- It meets the requirements of good governance as it would force the relevant EU institutions to be very careful when exercising their discretion to adopt legislative acts, which would be lawful but which may cause particularly serious damage to citizens of the EU.

The above are, certainly, very convincing arguments.

AIDE-MÉMOIRE

1. Actions for annulment under Article 263 TFEU

"Act" means any act (not only acts listed in Article 288 TFEU) which has binding legal effects in relation to third parties, whatever its nature and form, adopted by the defendant institution, body, office or agency.

Time limit

The proceedings must be commenced within **two months** of the publication of the act, or its notification to the applicant, or, in the absence thereof, of the day on which it came to the applicant's knowledge. This is strictly enforced: the only exceptions are based on force majeure and exceptional circumstances (Case T-12/90 *Bayer AG*).

Grounds for annulment

- lack of competence (occurs when the administration acts beyond its powers);

- infringement of an essential procedural requirement (takes place where the relevant EU institution fails to comply with a mandatory procedural requirement in the adoption of the measure);

- infringement of the Treaties (refers not only to the provisions of the Treaties but to all sources of EU law including general principles of EU law);

- misuse of powers (occurs when a legitimate power is used for an illegal end, or in an illegal way).

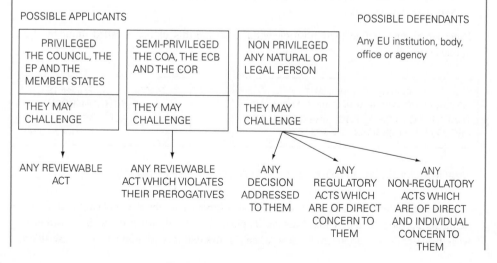

POSSIBLE APPLICANTS

POSSIBLE DEFENDANTS

| PRIVILEGED THE COUNCIL, THE EP AND THE MEMBER STATES | SEMI-PRIVILEGED THE COA, THE ECB AND THE COR | NON PRIVILEGED ANY NATURAL OR LEGAL PERSON | Any EU institution, body, office or agency |

THEY MAY CHALLENGE — THEY MAY CHALLENGE — THEY MAY CHALLENGE

ANY REVIEWABLE ACT

ANY REVIEWABLE ACT WHICH VIOLATES THEIR PREROGATIVES

ANY DECISION ADDRESSED TO THEM

ANY REGULATORY ACTS WHICH ARE OF DIRECT CONCERN TO THEM

ANY NON-REGULATORY ACTS WHICH ARE OF DIRECT AND INDIVIDUAL CONCERN TO THEM

2. Plea of illegality under Article 277 TFEU

Can only be invoked as an ancillary plea, that is, to challenge a measure implementing an EU act (for example, a decision which implements a regulation), not the act itself.

Time limit

No time limit, but the plea of illegality cannot be used to circumvent the requirements of Article 263 TFEU (Case 156/77 *Commission v Belgium*). If it is raised in preliminary ruling proceedings, the ECJ will decline to deal with the referral in a situation where an applicant who had locus standi to bring a direct action under Article 263 TFEU neglected to do so within the time prescribed under Article 263(5) TFEU (Case C-188/92 *TWD Textilwerke*).

Ground: THE SAME AS UNDER ART. 263 TFEU

POSSIBLE APPLICANTS ANY NATURAL OR LEGAL PERSON AND ANY MEMBER STATE	POSSIBLE DEFENDANTS ANY EU INSTITUTION, BODY, OFFICE OR AGENCY

Outcome of a successful action

The implementing measure is annulled in respect of the applicant but the act itself is still in force.

3. Action for failure to act under Article 265 TFEU

"Failure" exists only if an EU institution, body, office or agency has a duty to act deriving from EU law.

Time limit

- To request the defaulting institution to act: no specific time limit but the request must be made within a reasonable time (Case 59/70 *The Netherlands v Commission*);

- To start judicial proceedings: two months from the expiry of the two-month period during which the defendant was called upon to act (Joined Cases 5-11/62 and 13-15/62 *San Michele*), but failed.

Defendants: must define their position within two months of being called upon by the applicant to act.

POSSIBLE APPLICANTS SO FAR AS POSSIBLE APPLICANTS AND ACTS THAT THEY CAN CHALLENGE ARE CONCERNED ART. 265 TFEU MIRRORS ART. 263 TFEU	POSSIBLE DEFENDANTS ANY EU INSTITUTION, BODY, OFFICE OR AGENCY

APPLICANTS HAVE TO GO THROUGH THE FOLLOWING STAGES:

Administrative stage: the defendant must be called upon to act by the applicant and has to define its position. The defendant defines its position not only when it acts in accordance with the wishes of the applicant but also when it states that it is not going to act (Case 48/65

Alfons Lütticke), or adopts a measure which is different from that desired or considered necessary by the applicant (Case C-25/91 *Pasqueras Echehaster SA*). A disappointed applicant may rely on Article 263 TFEU to challenge the position taken by the relevant institution but cannot take any further action under Article 265 TFEU.

Judicial stage: If the defendant fails to act within two months from being called upon, the applicant has a further two months within which to bring proceedings before the CJEU.

Outcome of a successful action

Declaration of the CJEU that the defendant has failed to act. Under Article 266 TFEU the defendant must take the necessary measures to comply with the judgment within a reasonable period of time (Case 13/83 *EP v Council*).

4. Action for damages: non-contractual liability of the EU under Article 340(2) TFEU

The EU must make good any damage caused by its institutions and by its servants in the performance of their duties (Case 9/69 *Sayag*).

Time limit

Five years from the day the damage materialised, not the time of the occurrence of the event or fact giving rise to damage (Case 256/80 *Birra Wührer*). It may be suspended by:

- Proceedings brought by the applicant before the CJEU, or

- A preliminary request addressed by the applicant to the relevant institution, but only if followed by an application under Article 263 or 265 TFEU and within the time limit set out in those provisions (Case C-282/05P *Holcim*).

Conditions for liability

- Unlawfulness of the conduct of an EU institution, body, office or agency; and

- The existence of damage; and

- The existence of a causal link between the conduct and the damage.

POSSIBLE APPLICANTS ANY NATURAL OR LEGAL PERSON	POSSIBLE DEFENDANTS ANY EU INSTITUTION, BODY, OFFICE OR AGENCY

Outcome of a successful action

Damages are awarded to the applicant.

Miscellaneous matters

A. Claims based on unjust enrichment

They may be brought under Article 340(2) TFEU. The only requirement is that the applicant proves enrichment of the defendant without any valid legal basis and his improvishment deriving from the enrichment of the defendant (Case C-47/07 *Mosdar*).

B. No Liability of the EU for lawful acts

The ECJ rejected the possibility that the EU may be required to compensate for damage caused by its institutions in the absence of unlawful conduct on their part (Joined Cases C-120/06P and C-121/06 P FIAMM).

RECOMMENDED READING

Books

Biondi, A. and Farley, M., *The Right to Damages in European Law*, 2009, London: KLI

Gordon, R., *EC Law in Judicial Review*, 2007, Oxford: Oxford University Press

Ward, A., *Judicial Review and the Rights of Private Parties in EU Law*, 2nd edition, 2007, Oxford: Oxford University Press

Articles

Bebr, G., "Judicial Remedy of Private Parties against Normative Acts of the European Communities: The Rule of the Exception of Illegality", (1966) 4 CMLRev, p 7

Hilson, C., "The Role of Discretion in EC Law on Non-Contractual Liability", (2005) 42 CML Rev, p 677

Wils, W., "Concurrent Liability of the Community and a Member State", (1992) 17 ELRev, p 191

17

AN INTRODUCTION TO THE INTERNAL MARKET OF THE EU

The creation of a common market where goods, people, services and capital move freely was one of the main objectives of the EEC Treaty. The SEA gave a new impetus to the achievement of this objective. The SEA replaced the term "common market" by "an internal market" and defined it as:

> "...an area without internal frontiers in which the free movement of goods, persons, services and capital is ensured in accordance with the provisions of the Treaty" (Article 14 EC – Article 26(2) TFEU).

Based on a White Paper prepared by Lord Cockfield, when he was the member of the European Commission with responsibility for the internal market, more than 300 measures were introduced to bring the national markets of all Member States into one economic area without internal frontiers. This internal market was officially completed on 31 December 1992.

While the EC had competence to take all appropriate measures with the aim of establishing the internal market, those measures were difficult to determine in advance. During the period leading to the completion of the internal market the Community harmonised the laws in the Member States which directly affected the establishment and the proper functioning of the internal market. In this respect Article 308 EC (its amended version in contained in Article 352 TFEU – see Chapter 4.6), Articles 94 and 95 EC [Article 114 and 115 TFEU]) were most frequently used. However, the approach under Article 94 EC [Article 114 TFEU), consisting of legislative harmonisation of national technical standards across the Community, was too slow to achieve the objective of creating the internal market.

For that reason a new approach to technical harmonisation and standards was defined by a Council Resolution of 7 May 1985.[1220] Directives adopted under the new approach set out "essential requirements" such as safety requirements or other requirements in the general interests, and attestation procedures on the basis of which it is determined whether the product in question meets these requirements. If so, it carries a CE mark. A Member State cannot, on technical grounds, refuse access to a national market for such a product. The new approach constitutes a straightforward application of the principle of mutual recognition (see below).

After more than 15 years of experience, the new approach had proved to be an effective instrument for the achievement of the internal market.[1221] Consequently, the Commission made new proposals with a view to enhancing the implementation of the new approach.

1220. [1985] OJ C136/1.
1221. Communication from the Commission to the Council and the EP "Enhancing the Implementation of the New Approach Directives", COM(2003) 240 final.

The new approach focuses on two issues:

■ The prevention of new technical barriers to trade between the Member States. The EU tries to tackle this problem by exchanging information on national measures allowed under Article 36 TFEU using a procedure established under Decision 3052/95[1222] and Directive 98/48/EC[1223] as amended many times. The Directive requires the Member States to notify their draft technical regulations to the Commission and to the other Member States, thus providing the Commission with an opportunity to verify their conformity with EU law and, if necessary, to exercise its right to impose a standstill. Failure of a Member State to notify a national measure derogating from the principle of the free movement of goods constitutes a substantial procedural defect which renders a national measure unenforceable against individuals.[1224]

■ Harmonisation of European standards by European standardisation bodies.
  There are three standardisation bodies: the European Committee for Standardisation; the European Committee for Electrotechnical Standardisation; and the European Telecommunications Standards Institute.

The Commission's long-term plans and ambitions regarding the development of the internal market were outlined in its Communication of 20 November 2007,[1225] and revised in 2008 to respond to the worldwide financial crises.[1226] The Commission intends to take necessary measures to ensure that the benefits of globalisation are extended to all EU citizens, to give more power to consumers, to provide better and clearer information about the internal market to EU citizens, to ensure that EU citizens have effective remedies where required, to encourage development of small businesses, to stimulate innovation, to help maintain high social and environmental standards and to ensure safer financial products, e.g. bank accounts, savings, investment products and payments.

The free movement of goods is the foundation of the EU internal market. It involves:

■ The elimination of customs duties and charges having an equivalent effect (Articles 28–30 TFEU);

■ The elimination of quantitative restrictions and all measures having equivalent effect (Articles 34 and 35 TFEU), although exceptions are allowed under the Treaties and on the grounds of mandatory requirements established by the case law of the ECJ;

■ The prohibition of discriminatory internal taxation upon goods of other Member States (Article 110 TFEU);

■ The prohibition of state aid and subsidies[1227] unless authorised by the Commission;

■ The combating of domestic bias in public procurement of both goods and services. Member

---

1222. [1995] OJ L321/1.
1223. [1998] OJ L217/18. This directive repealed Directive 83/189 [1983] OJ L109/8.
1224. Case C-194/94 *CIA Security International* [1996] ECR I-2201; Case C-303/04 *Lidl Italia Srl v Comune di Stradelle* [2005] ECR I-7865.
1225. IP/07/1728 entitled "Commission Unveils its Vision for a Modern Single Market for All".
1226. IP/08/2000.
1227. Articles 107 and 109 TFEU.

States often favour national contractors in major public contracts for the supply of goods, work and services to public authorities and public utilities. The EU has adopted a number of measures to combat domestic bias.

The free movement of people and services allows EU nationals to work as employees or self-employed persons anywhere in the EU. There are still some obstacles to the exercise of the right to free movement of workers, the right of establishment and the provision of services, especially in relation to the recognition of professional qualifications. However, the creation of the area of FSJ within the EU greatly facilitates the free movement of persons.

Under the freedom of establishment and the freedom to provide services self-employed persons enjoy rights similar to those of workers. The right of establishment means that any EU national is entitled to set up in whichever Member State he wishes and to conduct business under the conditions laid down for nationals of that Member State. Exercise of the right of establishment and the right to provide services is also granted to companies and firms established in Member States of the EU. The free movement of services is hindered by the fact that the service sector is difficult to deregulate, but the adoption of Directive 2006/123/EC on Services in the Internal Market (see Chapter 24.2) will certainly contribute to the removal of obstacles to both the freedom of establishment and the freedom to provide services.

The ability for capital to move freely has been successfully accomplished. Directive 88/361[1228] eliminated all restrictions on movement of capital and ensured access to the financial systems and products of all Member States.

Common competition rules ensure that neither companies (through anti-competitive conduct or unlawful mergers) nor the Member States (through the granting of aid and subsidies) can distort competition within the internal market.

The EU has, to a great extent, harmonised rules on intellectual property rights, which are vital for the creation of the internal market given their impact on the free movement of goods and the maintenance of undistorted competition.

A single currency, which at the time of writing has been adopted by 16 Member States and six non-Member States (Andorra, San Marino, Monaco and the Vatican City on the basis of formal arrangements with the EU, Montenegro and Kosovo as de facto national currency, without any arrangements being made with the EU) facilitates trade between Member States and constitutes a powerful symbol of European integration. All "new" Member States are required to adopt the euro once they fulfil the convergence criteria. "Old" Member States – the UK and Denmark – on the basis of derogations, decided not to join the Eurozone. Sweden, as a result of a national referendum, although no specific opt-out is provided for it, has voluntarily excluded itself from the EMU and does not participate in ERM II.

The rules of the four freedoms are extended to three out of the four European Free Trade Association countries (Iceland, Norway and Lichtenstein) through the creation of the European Economic Area.

The EU is the third biggest internal market in the world, after China and India. Three principles have played a key role in the establishment of the internal market:

1.   The principle of non-discrimination embodied in Article 18 TFEU which prohibits "any discrimination on grounds of nationality". This principle has been generously

---

1228.   [1988] OJ L178/5.

interpreted by the ECJ as including the prohibition of direct discrimination and indirect discrimination. The latter is based on grounds other than nationality but, in practice, results in less favourable treatment of persons, goods, capital and services in a host Member State. The CJEU has applied the principle to all aspects of the internal market and in many cases the principle has been used as a basis for a remedy of last resort to enforce rights of EU citizens and undertakings.

2. For the ECJ the principle of non-discrimination is a starting point in eliminating obstacles to the four freedoms. The Court has not only condemned any discrimination, either direct or indirect, but has gone beyond discrimination to hold non-discriminatory obstacles as contrary to the Treaty provisions on free movement. Accordingly, all measures which are non-discriminatory but hinder access to the market are prohibited.

3. The principle of mutual recognition was introduced by the ECJ in Case 120/78 *Rewe-Zentral AG v Bundesmonopolverwaltung für Branntwein* (known as the *Cassis de Dijon* case)[1229] in the context of the free movement of goods. Under the *Cassis de Dijon* approach it means that a product lawfully produced and marketed in one Member State must be accepted in the other Member States even if it does not match technical or other specifications of those Member States. The principle of mutual recognition is not absolute, however, as Member States are allowed to exclude such a product from their national market on the grounds of derogations set out in the Treaties and on the basis of mandatory requirements aimed at protecting vital public interests.[1230]

The principle of mutual recognition has gradually been applied to aspects of the internal market other than the free movement of goods, namely the free movement of services and the recognition of the qualifications of EU citizens. The main advantage of the application of the principle of mutual recognition is that it guarantees the achievement of the objectives of the internal market without the need to harmonise Member States' national legislation and thus maintains the diversity of products and services within the internal market. The Commission identified the main problems with the application of the principle, clarified its meaning, incorporated it as a main tool of the internal market strategy 2003–2006 and recognised it as the cornerstone of Directive 2006/123/EC on Services in the Internal Market.

It is important to mention the creation of "SOLVIT", an online network which assists EU citizens and undertakings to find out-of-court solutions to problems relating to any aspect of the internal market. Each Member State has its "SOLVIT centre" which attempts to find a solution within a 10-week deadline, free of charge. The suggested solution is not binding but in many cases solves problems regarding the misapplication of internal market law by public authorities of the Member State concerned. SOLVIT and other networks, for example, FIN-NET, which seeks to solve problems in the cross-border financial services sector, enhance the fight of the EU against obstacles erected by Member States to the realisation of the internal market.

1229. [1979] ECR 649.
1230. See: The Commission's interpretative Communication on Facilitating the Access of Products to the Market of Other Member States: the Practical Application of Mutual Recognition, [2003] OJ C265/1.

RECOMMENDED READING

Books for Chapters 18–21

Barnard, C., *The Substantive Law of the EU. The Four Freedoms*, 2nd edition, 2007, Oxford: Oxford University Press

Davies, G., *European Union Internal Market Law*, 2006, London: Routledge Cavendish

Davies, M., *Nationality Discrimination in the European Internal Market*, 2003, The Hague: Kluwer Law International

Shuibhne, N. (ed.), *Regulating the Internal Market*, 2006, Cheltenham: Edward Elgar

Tryfonidou, A., *Reverse Discrimination in EC Law*, 2009, London: KLI

Articles

Dougan, M., "Minimum Harmonization and the Internal Market", (2000) 37 CMLRev, p 853

Möstl, M., "Preconditions and Limits of Mutual Recognition", (2010) 47 CMLRev, p 405

Weatherill, S., "New Strategy for Managing the EC's Internal Market", (2000) 53 CLP, p 595

18

THE CUSTOMS UNION AND THE PROHIBITION OF CUSTOMS DUTIES AND ALL CHARGES HAVING EQUIVALENT EFFECT TO CUSTOMS DUTIES (CEE)

CONTENTS

SUMMARY

1. Article 28 TFEU provides for the establishment of a customs union between the Member States covering all trade in goods. Goods are not defined in the Treaties but the ECJ has defined them as all products which have a monetary value and which may be the object of commercial transactions.

2. The precondition for the creation of the internal market was the establishment of a customs union amongst the Member States. This was done in two stages. The first was the creation of a tariff union which was completed in 1968. At that stage all customs duties and other restrictions were abolished and a common customs tariff was applied to goods coming from third countries. However, customs formalities remained in place, mainly because of the way the VAT, excise duties and statistical data were collected between the Member States. It was not until 31 December 1992 that the second stage was completed with the customs union itself coming into being and all "customs" checks at the internal borders of the EU being abolished.

3. Any customs union has two dimensions: internal, which involves the creation of a single customs territory between the participating states in which there are no customs duties or other restrictions on trade between the participating states, and external, which requires that the same customs duties and trade regulations apply to trade with all non-participating states. The external aspects of the customs union within the EU are based on the Common Customs Tariff and the Common Commercial Policy. The internal aspects of the customs union are covered by Articles 28–30 TFEU.

4. Article 30 TFEU prohibits a Member State from maintaining customs duties on goods imported from other Member States; on its exports; and on goods from third countries released by a Member State for free circulation in the EU; as well as from introducing any charges having equivalent effect to customs duties (CEE).

5. The concept of a CEE is an autonomous EU legal concept. It has been defined by the ECJ as covering any pecuniary charge, however small and whatever its designation and mode of application, which is imposed unilaterally on goods by reason of the fact that they cross a frontier, including a regional and internal frontier, even if it is not discriminatory, protectionist or imposed for the benefit of the Member State.

6. CEEs are prohibited unless they fall within the two exceptions to the prohibition set out in Article 30 TFEU, i.e. the prohibition does not apply:

▪ When the payment is consideration for a service actually rendered to the importer or exporter. However, such a service must genuinely benefit the importer, must provide a specific benefit to him, rather than be imposed for reasons of the general interest, and the sum charged for the service must be proportionate to the cost of the service.

▪ To payments for a service which is required under EU law or under international law. In such a situation a Member State is allowed to charge for that service provided the amount charged does not exceed the real cost of providing the service.

18.1   Introduction – the definition of goods

Article 28 TFEU provides that the customs union between the Member States covers all trade in goods. The ECJ has defined "goods" as all products which have a monetary value and which may be the object of commercial transactions.[1231] This definition includes:

▪ Waste. In Case C-2/90 *Commission v Belgium*,[1232] the ECJ refused to make a distinction between recyclable waste which has commercial value and non-recyclable waste which has no intrinsic value. Accordingly, there are now in free circulation between Member States not only goods which have commercial value but also goods which are capable of generating costs for undertakings;[1233]

▪ Consumer goods including medical products;[1234]

▪ Gold and silver collectors' coins provided they are not currently in circulation as legal tender;[1235]

1231. Case C-97/98 *Jägerskiöld* [1999] ECR I-7319.
1232. [1992] ECR I-4431.
1233. Case C-277/02 *EU-Wood-Trading GmbH v Sonderabfall-Management-Gesellschaft Rheinland-Pfalz mbH* [2004] ECR I-11957.
1234. Case 215/87 *Schumacher* [1989] ECR 617.
1235. Case 7/78 *R v Thompson* [1978] ECR 2247.

- Goods and materials supplied in the context of the provision of services;[1236]

- Electricity and gas;[1237]

- Goods originating in non-Member States which have completed customs formalities at the external frontier of the EU and are in free circulation between Member States.

When goods are ancillary to a main activity, they are covered by provisions of the Treaties other than those relating to the free movement of goods. Accordingly, advertisement materials, lottery tickets which are sold in one Member State for a lottery organised in another Member State[1238] and the supply of goods such as car body parts, oils, and so on, for repair of vehicles[1239] in another Member State do not fall within the definition of "goods" but are covered by the provisions of the Treaties relating to the free movement of services. Further, shares, bonds and other securities which can be valued in money and form the subject of commercial transactions are dealt with under the rules relating to the free movement of capital rather than the free movement of goods.

18.2   Customs union, its external and internal aspects

Any customs union has two dimensions: internal, which involves the creation of a single customs territory between the participating states in which there are no customs duties or other restrictions on trade between the participating states, and external, which requires that the same customs duties and trade regulations apply to trade with all non-participating states.

Article 28(1) TFEU regulates both external and internal aspects of the customs union. It states that:

> "The Union shall comprise a customs union which shall cover all trade in goods and which shall involve the prohibition between Member States of customs duties on imports and exports and of all charges having equivalent effect, and the adoption of a common customs tariff in their relations with third countries."

The external aspects of the customs union within the EU are based on the Common Customs Tariff and the Common Commercial Policy. The internal aspects of the customs union are covered by Articles 28–30 TFEU.

18.2.1   External aspects of the customs union within the EU

The external aspects of the customs union within the EU are based on:

- The Common Customs Tariff (CCT); and

- The Common Commercial Policy (CCP).

1236. Case 45/87 *Commission v Ireland [Re: Dundalk Water Supply]* [1988] ECR 4929.
1237. Case C-159/94 *Commission v France* [1997] ECR I-5815.
1238. Case C-275/92 *Schindler* [1994] ECR I-1039; Case C-6/01 *Anomar* [2003] ECR I-8621.
1239. Case C-55/93 *Van Schaik* [1994] ECR I-4837.

The first important step in shaping the external dimension of the customs union took place on 1 July 1968 with the establishment of a CCT for industrial products coming from outside the Community. The CCT sets a specific rate of customs duty for each of the various products identified in a special nomenclature.[1240]

Under the CCP the Member States fix the tariff rates for customs charges due on goods imported into the EU. The system was substantially reformed in 1988 when the Combined Nomenclature (CN) was introduced by virtue of Council Regulation 2658/87 ([1987] OJ L256/1). The CN is based on the International Convention on the Harmonised Commodity Description and Coding System and thus it uses the same nomenclature as the main commercial partners of the EU. The CN includes both the requirements of the CCT and the external trade statistics of the EU. Under Regulation 2658/87, each year a new regulation is adopted which applies from 1 January and which updates the CN and the rates of duty of the CCT.

Alongside the CN, the EU applies the integrated Community tariff TARIC (known as a "working tariff") which is a data bank for use by national customs authorities. TARIC contains all the information on third countries' duty rates, including preferential rates, and on all measures adopted by the EU relating to its CCP in this area, that is, general measures which relate to the CN, and specific measures such as tariff suspensions, anti-dumping and countervailing measures, bans on imports, tariffs quotas, export prohibitions, and so on.

In order to further unify the rules and procedures in respect of trade with non-Member States, the Council adopted Regulation 2913/92 on 12 October 1992. This established the Community Customs Code (CCC)[1241] which consolidated all of the EU customs legislation into a single text and set up a framework for the EU's import and export procedures. The most important provisions of the Community Customs Code relate to the Common Customs Tariff, the tariff classification of goods, the value of goods for customs purposes, the origin of goods, customs debts and their recovery, the appeal procedure against decisions of the customs authorities, and so on.

In order to impose an EU tariff duty on a product coming from outside the EU, the following steps are taken:

- The product must be classified in the CN.

- The product's origin must be determined. The tariff to be applied, if any, depends on the origin of the product (EU origin v non-EU origin; preferential origin v non-preferential origin, and so on). Article 23 of the Community Customs Code (CCC) deals with this matter.

- The product must be valued. The value needs to be determined to assess ad valorem duties. The value is determined in accordance with the principles contained in the WTO Customs Valuation Agreement, which were implemented by Chapter 3 of the CCC. The preferred method of valuation is based on the transaction value of the imported goods, that is, the price actually paid or payable by the importer.

- The tariff itself is applied in accordance with Article 20(1) of the CCC.

1240. Under Article 31 TFEU, the CCT must be fixed by the Council acting by a qualified majority on a proposal from the Commission.

1241. [1992] OJ L302/1. It entered into force on 1 January 1994 and has subsequently been amended on many occasions.

EU customs law is administrated by national customs authorities. They are the gatekeepers of the EU. They collect customs duties and transfer them to the EU (minus 10 per cent which covers the administration expenses of national customs authorities). These customs duties represent the "own resources" of the EU. The Customs Code Committee, consisting of representatives of Member States and chaired by a representative of the Commission, supervises the functioning of the entire system.

18.2.2 Internal aspects of the customs union within the EU

The customs union was completed on 1 July 1968 between the six founding Member States. From 1968 until the creation of the internal market on 31 December 1992 importers were required to complete numerous forms and documents at national borders for such purposes as gathering statistics, collecting taxes and enforcing security measures.

With the completion of the internal market in 1992, all formalities at national borders were abolished and the European Community became a territory without internal borders. Spot checks may still take place for drugs and immigration purposes, but routine border checks were abolished. This brought new challenges for customs officials in all Member States in respect of ensuring efficient and high-quality controls at the external borders. The accession of 10 new Member States on 1 May 2004 highlighted these challenges.

The strategy of the EU for the Customs Union was first outlined in Decision 253/2003,[1242] which established an action programme for customs in the EU up to 2007, known as "Customs 2007". Decision 624/2007[1243] has replaced the "Customs 2007" programme with a new programme known as "Customs 2013". The main objectives of the "Customs 2013" programme are:

- The development of a pan-European electronic customs environment;

- The implementation of a modernised customs code;

- The development of customs co-operation between the EU customs authorities and third countries in the field of supply chain security (security of transport of the world's cargo);

- Exchanges of information and best practice with the customs administrations of non-member countries, in particular candidate states and states which are neighbours of the EU.

"Customs 2013" is complemented by "Fiscalis 2008–2013",[1244] an action programme intended to improve the functioning of the taxation system in the internal market, and covers VAT and excise duties, direct taxation and taxes on insurance premiums.

Having said all the above, the main provision of the Treaties which prohibits customs duties on imports and exports or any charges having equivalent effect between Member States still remains, that is, Article 30 TFEU. The main reason for its retention is that despite customs duties on imports and exports having disappeared, it is always possible for a Member State to unilaterally impose charges which, although at first glance are not customs duties, are in fact equivalent to them.

1242. [2003] OJ L51/23.
1243. [2007] OJ L154/25.
1244. Decision 1482/2007/EC [2007] OJ L330/1.

18.3   Meaning of charges having equivalent effect to customs duties (CEE)

Article 30 TFEU prohibits not only customs duties but also any CEE. The prohibition of CEEs prevents Member States trying to get around Article 30 by relabelling or disguising what are in fact still customs charges/taxes.

There is no definition of "charges having equivalent effect to customs duties" in the Treaties. In Case 24/68 *Commission v Italy [Re Statistical Levy]*,[1245] the ECJ defined CEE as:

> "any pecuniary charge, however small and whatever its designation and mode of application, which is imposed unilaterally on goods by reason of the fact that they cross a frontier and which is not a custom duty in the strict sense . . ., even if it is not imposed for the benefit of the State, is not discriminatory or protective in effect and if the product on which the charge is imposed is not in competition with any domestic product."

The case law shows that a CEE has the following characteristics:

1.   It must be a pecuniary charge.[1246] Other obstacles are within the scope of the provisions relating to non-tariff barriers on the free movement of goods.

2.   Its amount is irrelevant. Even a small charge[1247] or a charge below the direct and indirect costs of services provided by the customs authorities[1248] is prohibited by Article 30 TFEU.

3.   It may result not only from a measure imposed by a Member State or other public authorities but also from an agreement concluded between individuals as exemplified in Case 16/94 *Dubois et Fils SA and General Cargo Services v Garoner (GA) Exploitation SA*.[1249]

THE FACTS WERE:

Dubois and General Cargo, who were forwarding agents, refused to pay a "transit charge" imposed on them by GE, the owner of an international road station near Paris where the customs authorities held offices. GE imposed the charge for vehicles completing customs clearance on their station in order to offset the costs of having the customs authorities on their premises. Dubois and General Cargo argued that a "transit charge" was in breach of Article 25 EC [30 TFEU].

Held:

The ECJ held that the "transit charge" was within the scope of Article 25 EC [Article 30 TFEU], i.e. it was a CEE even though it was not imposed by a Member State but resulted from an agreement concluded between a private undertaking (GE) and its customers (Dubois and General Cargo).

1245.   [1969] ECR 193.
1246.   Case 46/76 *Bauhuis v Netherlands* [1977] ECR 5.
1247.   Case 24/68 *Commission v Italy [Re Statistical Levy]* [1969] ECR 193.
1248.   Case C-111/89 *Bakker Hillegom* [1990] ECR I-1735.
1249.   [1995] ECR I-2421.

4.   The designation and mode of application of a charge is irrelevant for the application of Article 30 TFEU. Thus, it is considered as a CEE whether it is called a special charge,[1250] or a "price supplement",[1251] or a fee levied in order to defray the costs of compiling statistical data,[1252] or otherwise.

5.   Its beneficiaries or its destination are irrelevant. The leading authorities on this point are Joined Cases 2 and 3/69 *Sociaal Fonds v Brachfeld and Chougol Diamond Co.*[1253] In that case Belgium imposed a levy on imported diamonds which was not protectionist (Belgium is not a producer of diamonds) but was designed to provide social security benefits for workers in the diamond industry. The ECJ held that the levy was contrary to Article 25 EC [Article 30 TFEU]. In Joined Cases C-441 and 442/98 *Kapniki Mikhaïlidis AE and Others*,[1254] the imposition of a charge, the proceeds of which were to provide social benefits for workers in the tobacco industry, was condemned by the ECJ. Also, a charge made to protect the historical and artistic heritage of a Member State has been found unlawful.[1255]

In Case C-173/05 *Commission v Italy*,[1256] Sicily imposed a tax for environmental purposes.

THE FACTS WERE:

Sicily imposed an environmental tax on the ownership of a gas pipeline during the time when gas was actually in the pipeline. The pipeline was carrying gas from Algeria to Italy for distribution and consumption there, and for onward export to other Member States. The owners were described as those who carry on at least one of the activities of transportation, distribution, sales or purchasing of gas. The purpose of the tax was to fund investments to reduce and prevent environmental risks linked to the presence of the pipeline in Sicily. The gas was imported from Algeria to the EU on the basis of a Co-operation Agreement concluded between Algeria and the EC.

According to the Commission the real purpose of the fiscal imposition was to tax the transported product, namely gas, and not to tax the infrastructure itself (for environmental reasons) given that the tax was payable by owners who carry on one of the activities of transportation, distribution, sale or purchasing of the gas only when gas was in the pipeline and that the basis of assessment for the tax was the volume of the gas contained in the pipeline.

1250. Joined Cases 2 and 3/62 *Commission v Luxembourg* [1962] ECR 425.

1251. Case 77/76 *Fratelli Cucchi v Avez SpA* [1977] ECR 987.

1252. Case 24/68 *Commission v Italy [Re Statistical Levy]*, supra note 1245.

1253. [1969] ECR 211.

1254. [2000] ECR I-7145.

1255. Case 7/68 *Commission v Italy* [1968] ECR 617; C-72/03 *Carbonati Apuani* [2004] ECR I-8027.

1256. [2007] ECR I-4917.

Held:

The ECJ held that the Sicilian tax was in fact a CEE. The ECJ emphasised that the event giving rise to the tax was the actual presence of the gas in the infrastructure. Thus, the tax was charged on goods (the gas) and not on the ownership of infrastructure.

The purpose of the tax was irrelevant since a charge under Article 25 EC [Article 30 TFEU] cannot be justified whatever its purpose or the destination of the revenue from it. The tax was not imposed at the frontier but at a later stage. It was called an "environmental tax" but was in fact a CEE.

6.   It must be imposed by the reason of or on the occasion of the crossing of a frontier by goods, but the time and the place of imposition is not relevant. In Case 78/76 *Firma Steinike und Weinlig v Bundesamt für Ernährung und Forstwirtschaft*,[1257] the ECJ held that a charge need not be levied at a border in order to be a customs charge or CEE. Even a regional frontier is included. This was examined in Joined Cases C-363 and C-407–411/93 *Lancry and Others v Direction Générale des Douanes and Others.*[1258]

THE FACTS WERE:

A charge called "dock dues" was imposed on all goods imported, irrespective of their country of origin, including France itself, into French overseas territories. The purpose of "dock dues" was to raise revenue in order to encourage the local economy. Lancry, who imported flour into Martinique from France, challenged "dock dues" as contrary to Article 25 EC [Article 30 TFEU].

Held:

The ECJ held that a charge levied at a regional frontier is within the scope of Article 25 EC [Article 30 TFEU]. This article expressly refers to intra-state trade because it is presumed that there are no internal obstacles to trade within Member States. The abolition of internal charges is a pre-condition of the creation of the customs union between Member States. The charge imposed at a regional frontier constituted "at least as serious" an obstacle to the free movement of goods as a charge levied at national frontiers. Indeed, regional customs frontiers undermine the unity of the Community customs territory.

7.   Article 30 TFEU encompasses charges imposed at any stage of production or marketing.[1259]

1257. [1977] ECR 595.

1258. [1994] ECR I-3957; see also Case C-293/02 *Jersey Produce Marketing Organisation* [2005] ECR I-9543 and Case C-72/03 *Carbonati Apuani* ([2004] ECR I-8027) in which the ECJ held that a charge imposed by the municipality of Carrara on marble excavated within the municipality when that marble was transported to other municipalities in Italy or to other Member States was a CEE.

1259. Case 78/76 *Steinike und Weinlig v Germany* [1977] ECR 595.

8.   Compensatory taxes are also CEE. This was established in Cases 2 and 3/62 *Commission v Luxembourg [Re Gingerbread]*.[1260]

THE FACTS WERE:

The governments of Luxembourg and Belgium imposed a special import duty on imported gingerbread in order to compensate for the price difference between domestic gingerbread and imported gingerbread. Domestic gingerbread was more expensive as a result of high internal rates of taxation on rye, an ingredient of gingerbread.

Held:

The ECJ held that a special import duty levied on imported gingerbread was a CEE. Indeed, the objective of the tax was not to equalise the taxes on gingerbread but to equalise the price of it!

18.4   Categories of charges

There are three categories of charges: charges imposed solely on imported goods, charges imposed on both domestic and imported goods and charges imposed solely on domestic goods. Each category must be examined in the light of Article 30 TFEU.

18.4.1   Charges imposed solely on imported goods

If a charge is imposed only on imported products and does not fall within the exceptions to the prohibition laid down in Article 30 TFEU, it is clearly in breach of that article. There are no justifications for it.

18.4.2   Charges imposed on both domestic and imported goods

It is important to establish whether such a charge is imposed in the same way on domestic products and on imported products and to assess its purpose.

In Case 29/72 *Marimex SpA v Italian Minister of Finance*,[1261] a charge imposed on both domestic and imported meat in respect of veterinary inspections carried out in Italy in order to verify whether meat satisfied health standards required by Italian legislation was held unlawful by the ECJ. This was on the ground that inspections of imported meat were conducted by a body different from that inspecting domestic meat and each body applied criteria different from those applied by the other.

Even if charges imposed on both domestic and imported products are applied in the same way and according to the same criteria, they may be CEEs if the proceeds of the charge are to benefit

---

1260.   [1962] ECR 425.
1261.   [1972] ECR 1309; Case 132/78 *Denkavit v France* [1979] ECR 1923.

domestic products exclusively. This was decided in Case 77/72 *Capolongo v Azienda Agricola Maya*.[1262]

THE FACTS WERE:

Italy imposed a charge on all egg boxes, domestic and imported, in order to finance the production of paper and cardboard in Italy. The charge constituted a part of an overall charge on cellulose products.

Held:

The ECJ held that although the charge applied without discrimination to both domestically produced and imported egg boxes, it was to benefit domestic manufacturers alone and as such was discriminatory and constituted a CEE.

In Case 77/76 *Fratelli Cucchi v Avez SpA*,[1263] the ECJ set out the criteria which should be applied in order to assess whether a particular charge that is applied indiscriminately on both domestic and imported products is contrary to Article 30 TFEU or is within the scope of other Articles of the Treaties. In this case the same charge was levied on domestic and imported sugar, but its proceeds were intended to finance "adaptation aids" to the Italian beet producers and the sugar-processing industry. The ECJ held that such a charge would be a CEE if all the following criteria were met:

- If it had the sole purpose of financing activities for the specific advantage of domestic products;

- If the domestic products on which a charge was imposed and the domestic products which were to benefit from it were the same; and

- If the charge imposed on the domestic products was "made up" in full. That is, if, in fact, by way of a tax refund or otherwise domestic producers did not pay any charge at all.

When applying the above-mentioned criteria due regard must be had to other provisions of the Treaties, in particular to Article 110 TFEU, which prohibits direct and indirect discriminatory internal taxation, and to Article 107 TFEU on state aid. If domestic products benefit only partially from the proceeds of the charge, that charge may constitute a discriminatory tax in breach of Article 110 TFEU. Also a charge may, in fact, be a form of state aid prohibited under the Treaties.

18.4.3 Charges imposed exclusively on domestic goods

It is unusual for a Member State to discriminate against goods produced domestically and thus afford preferential treatment to imported goods, but such reverse discrimination was examined by the ECJ in Case 222/82 *Apple and Pear Development Council v K J Lewis*.[1264]

1262. [1973] ECR 611; Cases C-78–83/90 *Compagnie Commerciale de l'Ouest* [1992] ECR I-1847.
1263. [1977] ECR 987.
1264. [1983] ECR 4083.

THE FACTS WERE:

The Apple and Pear Development Council, a semi-public body, was set up in England and Wales to conduct research, to provide information, to collect statistics and to promote the consumption of apples and pears in England and Wales. A domestic levy was imposed on apples and pears grown in England and Wales to finance the Council's activities. Lewis, a grower of apples and pears, refused to pay the compulsory levy as being contrary to EC law.

Held:

The ECJ found that as the levy did not apply to imported products, it was compatible with Article 25 EC [Article 30 TFEU].

The lenient approach of the ECJ to charges imposed solely on domestic products[1265] changed in Joined Cases C-441/98 and C-442/98 *Kapniki Mikhaïlidis AE and Idrima Kinonikon Asphalise (IKA)*.[1266]

THE FACTS WERE:

Mikhaïlidis, a Greek public limited company, carried on business in the tobacco sector. Mikhaïlidis brought proceedings against IKA (a Greek social security institution which paid pensions and lump-sum compensation to insured persons and pensioners of the Tobacco Workers' Insurance Funds) for the refund of charges paid by Mikhaïlidis on the export of tobacco from Greece to Member States and non-Member States between 1990 and 1995. The charges were in fact (under different guises) imposed unilaterally on both domestic tobacco products being exported and on domestic tobacco products intended for the domestic market, and were credited to IKA for the benefit of the Tobacco Workers' Pension Branch. Mikhaïlidis argued that the charges were incompatible with Community law as being charges having equivalent effect to customs duties on export. IKA claimed that the charges levied were in fact a tax imposed on domestic tobacco products irrespective of whether or not exported in accordance with objective criteria and within the framework of the Greek general system of taxation.

Held:

The ECJ applied exactly the same approach to charges imposed exclusively on domestic products, as to charges imposed exclusively on imported products. The ECJ held that "it follows from the general and absolute nature of the prohibition of all customs duties applicable to goods moving between Member States that customs duties are prohibited".

The ECJ held that had a charge been imposed by reason of the fact that goods had crossed

---

1265. See: Cases 13 and 71/80 *Irish Creamery Milk Suppliers' Association v Ireland* [1981] ECR 735.
1266. [2000] ECR I-7145.

a frontier, the charge would have had equivalent effect to a customs duty and as such would be in breach of Articles 23 and 25 EC [Articles 28 and 30 TFEU].

Comment:

IKA and the Greek Government argued that the charge escaped classification as a CEE because it was in fact a tax within the meaning of Article 90 EC [Article 110 TFEU]. The ECJ left it to the referring court to decide whether this was the case but specified that before such a conclusion could be reached by the referring court, it would be necessary for the disputed charge to relate to a general system of internal dues. It said that in order to be so classified, "the charge to which exported tobacco product is subject must impose the same duty on both domestic products and identical exported products at the same marketing stage and the chargeable event triggering the duty must also be identical in the case of both products". It seems that in the above case the disputed charge would not be classified as an internal tax. Nevertheless this question was referred back to the Greek court.

18.5 Exceptions to the prohibition

A pecuniary charge is deemed to escape the prohibition embodied in Article 30 TFEU if it is levied for a service genuinely rendered to the trader or a service required under EU law/international law. Both exceptions, as any exceptions to a general rule, have been strictly interpreted by the CJEU.

18.5.1 A service rendered to the trader

Member States have tried to justify the imposition of charges on a number of grounds, the most popular being that a charge is in fact a fee paid for a service rendered to the trader. The first time this "justification" was invoked was in Joined Cases 52 and 55/65 *Commission v Germany*.[1267] The ECJ defined fees levied by Germany on importers for the provision of an import licence as a CCE on the ground that it did not bring any benefit to the importer.

The ECJ has gradually specified strict conditions which, if they apply cumulatively, allow a charge to escape the prohibition of Article 30 TFEU. A charge levied on goods by reason of the fact that they cross a frontier is not a CEE if it constitutes consideration for a specific service actually and individually rendered to the trader and the amount demanded is proportionate to the cost of supplying such a service. Therefore a charge will be lawful if it satisfies the three criteria examined below.

18.5.1.1 The service must be of genuine benefit to the trader

The condition that a service must provide a genuine benefit to the trader is very difficult to satisfy, taking into account the strict interpretation by the ECJ of a "genuine benefit". This is illustrated in Case 132/82 *Commission v Belgium [Re Storage Charges]*.[1268]

1267. [1966] ECR 159.
1268. [1983] ECR 1649.

THE FACTS WERE:

The Belgian authorities introduced a system whereby goods in Community transit could undergo customs clearance either at the border or in assigned warehouses within Belgium. If customs clearance in a warehouse was selected by the trader, the customs authorities imposed storage charges on the goods.

The Commission took exception to the levying of these costs, alleging that they were charges having an equivalent effect to customs duties and as such were prohibited under the EC Treaty. The Commission brought proceedings against Belgium before the ECJ.

Held:

The ECJ held that charges which are levied as part of the process of customs clearance on Community goods or goods in free circulation within the Community constitute CEEs, if they are imposed solely in connection with the completion of customs formalities. The ECJ accepted that the use of a public warehouse in the interior of the country offered certain advantages to importers. Nevertheless, given that such advantages were linked solely with the completion of customs formalities (which, whatever the place, were always compulsory) and that the storage charges were payable equally when the goods were presented at the public warehouse solely for the completion of customs formalities, even though they had been exempted from storage and the importer had not requested that they be put in temporary storage, the ECJ ruled that they were in breach of Article 25 EC [Article 30 TFEU].

18.5.1.2   The service must provide a specific benefit to the trader

The service must be specific. This means that the trader must obtain a definite specific benefit, enhancing his personal interest, not the general interest of all traders operating in the particular sector of the economy. This criterion was explained, for the first time, in Case 63/74 *W. Cadsky SpA v ICE*.[1269]

THE FACTS WERE:

Cadsky exported vegetables from Italy to Germany. The Italian Government imposed a mandatory quality control on products crossing the Italian frontier for which it charged exporters. Cadsky paid but later brought proceedings for recovery of sums paid. The Italian Government argued that the challenged fees represented payment for a service rendered to the trader since quality control constituted recognition of the quality of its products abroad, and in addition contributed to the improvement of the reputation of Italian vegetables in external markets, and thus enhanced the competitiveness of Italian products.

1269. [1975] ECR 281.

Held:

The ECJ held that the charge did not constitute payment for a service rendered to the operator, because a general system of quality control imposed on all goods did not provide a sufficiently direct and specific benefit to the trader. The benefit related to the general interest of all Italian vegetable exporters and, consequently, the individual interest of each of them was so ill-defined that a charge could not be regarded as consideration for a specific benefit actually and individually conferred.

Another leading case on this topic is Case 24/68 *Commission v Italy [Re Statistical Levy]*.[1270]

THE FACTS WERE:

The Italian Government imposed a levy designed to finance the gathering of statistics on all imports and exports. It argued that the statistical service was for the benefit of importers and exporters.

Held:

The ECJ held that the advantage provided to importers was too general and uncertain to be considered as a service rendered to the trader.

Member States have often tried to justify charges in respect of health inspections, arguing that they provide a benefit to the trader consisting of recognising the quality of imported goods. This justification has been rejected by the ECJ.

In Case 39/73 *Rewe-Zentralfinanz GmbH v Direktor der Landwirtschaftskammer Westfalen-Lippe*,[1271] charges imposed in relation to health inspections on apples were considered as a CEE on the grounds that the inspections were not carried out for the specific benefit of the trader but for public benefit as a whole.

In Case 87/75 *Bresciani v Amministrazione Italiana delle Finanze*,[1272] the ECJ held that charges in respect of veterinary inspections carried out on imported raw cowhides were a CEE since the inspection was mandatory under Italian law, and thus did not provide a specific service to the importer and all importers were obliged to submit to the inspection. In addition they were conducted in the general interest and thus the inspection fees should be paid by the beneficiaries, that is, the general public, which benefits from the free movement of goods.

The individualisation of the benefit as a condition justifying a charge was also evident in Case 340/87 *Commission v Italy*.[1273]

1270. Supra note 1245.
1271. [1973] ECR 1039.
1272. [1976] ECR 129.
1273. [1989] ECR 1483.

THE FACTS WERE:

The Italian customs authorities offered traders, at their request, an opportunity to complete customs formalities outside business hours in exchange for payment. The working hours of the Italian customs officials were only six hours a day. This was contrary to Directive 83/643 (then in force), which required customs posts to be open for at least 10 hours a day without interruption from Mondays to Saturdays, and at least six hours without interruption on Sundays.

Held:

The ECJ held that Italy was in breach of EC law by imposing fees on traders for administrative and customs formalities which were partially carried out during normal opening hours of customs posts. The opening hours for customs posts, being harmonised under an EC Directive, could not be considered as a specific service rendered to the trader. In addition, for a charge to escape the prohibition of Article 25 EC [Article 30 TFEU] it is necessary for the service provided to be genuine and individualised. In this case the last criterion was not satisfied.

A more recent case on this topic is Case C-389/00 *Commission v Germany*.[1274]

THE FACTS WERE:

The German authorities imposed on exporters of waste a compulsory contribution to a solidarity fund set up under the 1989 Basle Convention on the Control of Transboundary Movements of Hazardous Wastes and their Disposals as implemented by the relevant EC legislation. The contribution was designated to guarantee the financing of the return of waste into Germany in the event of illegal or incomplete exports, in circumstances where the party responsible was not in a position to bear those costs or could not be identified. The German Government argued that this service conferred a real benefit on exporters, since the subsidiary guarantee taken on by the state allowed them to penetrate the markets of the other Member States and also of the other contracting parties to the Basle Convention.

Held:

The ECJ emphasised that the Basle Convention imposed the same obligations on all Member States in pursuit of a general interest, namely protection of health and the environment, and the compulsory contribution fund did not confer on exporters of waste established in Germany any specific or definite benefit. They have the same opportunities as their competitors established in other Member States. Thus, nothing was given in return for their contribution. The charge was a CEE.

1274. [2003] ECR I-2001.

18.5.1.3 The sum charged must be proportionate to the cost of the service

The third criterion is that the sum charged for the service must be proportionate to the cost of the service. This criterion was explained by the ECJ in Case 170/88 *Ford España v Spain*.[1275]

THE FACTS WERE:

Ford España received a bill for clearing cars and goods through customs equal to 1.65 per cent of the declared value of cars and other goods imported into Spain. The Spanish Government argued that the sum represented fees for services rendered to Ford España.

Held:

The ECJ accepted that in this case the service was genuine and the benefit was of the required specific nature. Nevertheless, the charge was in breach of Article 25 EC [Article 30 TFEU] as it was based not on the cost of the service but on the value of the goods and as such was not commensurate with the service.[1276]

The position seems to be that only if a trader requests a service of his own volition will it be accepted as a benefit by the ECJ.

18.5.2 A mandatory service

If a service is required under EU law or under international law, that is, mainly on the basis of an agreement to which the EU is a contracting party, a Member State is allowed to charge for that service provided the amount charged does not exceed the real cost of providing the service.[1277] This exception was examined by the ECJ in Case 18/87 *Commission v Germany [Re Animals Inspection Fees]*.[1278]

THE FACTS WERE:

Measures were brought into effect throughout the European Community by Council Directive 81/389 which permitted Member States to carry out veterinary inspections on live animals transported into or through their national territories. Certain German provinces, known as Länder, charged fees for the cost of conducting those inspections. The charges imposed were justified, according to the German Government, to cover the actual costs incurred in maintaining the inspection facilities. The Commission argued that these charges amounted to charges having an equivalent effect to customs duties and could not be justified under the Directive. Accordingly, the Commission brought an action against Germany before the ECJ.

1275. [1989] ECR 2305.
1276. See also Cases 52 and 55/65 *Germany v Commission* [1966] ECR 159; Case 39/73 *Rewe-Zentralfinanz v Landwirtschaftskammer Westfalen-Lippe* [1973] ECR 1039.
1277. Case 46/76 *Bauhuis v Netherlands* [1977] ECR 5; Case 1/83 *IFG v Freistaat Bayern* [1984] ECR 349.
1278. [1988] ECR 5427.

Held:

The ECJ held that charges imposed in relation to health inspections required by Community law [EU law] are not to be regared as CEE if the following conditions are satisfied:

1. They do not exceed the actual costs of the inspections in connection with which they are charged;

2. The inspections are obligatory and uniform for the relevant products in the Community;

3. The inspections are prescribed by Community law in the general interests of the Community;

4. The inspections promote the free movement of goods, in particular by neutralising obstacles which could arise from unilateral measures of inspection adopted in accordance with Article 30 EC [Article 36 TFEU].

The ECJ held that the charges imposed for health inspections were not a CEE as they satisfied the above-mentioned criteria. The ECJ specified that the negative effect that such a fee may have on intra-Community trade could be eliminated only by virtue of Community provisions providing for the harmonisation of fees, or by imposing the obligation on the Member States to bear the costs entailed in the inspections, or, finally, by establishing that the costs are to be paid out of the Community budget.

Comment:

With respect to point 2, Directive 81/389 imposed on all Member States exporting and importing live animals an obligation to carry out veterinary inspections, and therefore the inspections were mandatory and uniform for all the animals concerned in the Community;

With respect to point 3, the inspections were prescribed by Directive 81/389. The objective of the Directive was the protection of live animals during international transport. As a result, inspections were carried out in the general interest of the Community and were not a specific interest of individual Member States;

With respect to point 4, Directive 81/389 harmonised the laws of the Member States regarding the protection of animals in international transport. The standardisation of the inspections promoted the free movement of goods, taking into account that it eliminated the possibility for a Member State to adopt measures restricting trade on grounds of the protection of the health and life of animals by virtue of Article 30 EC [Article 36 TFEU].

AIDE-MÉMOIRE

CUSTOMS UNION – ARTICLE 28 TFEU

The customs union has two dimensions:

- Internal: all customs duties and CEEs between the participating states are prohibited.

- External: the same customs and trade regulations apply throughout the EU to trade with third countries.

A Combined Nomenclature (CN) sets out rules for determining the classification of goods and is based on the 1988 Convention on the Harmonised Commodity Description and Coding System administered by the World Customs Organisation.

The Community Customs Code (CCC) consolidates all of the Community customs legislation into a single text and sets up a framework for the Community's import and export procedures.

A Common Customs Tariff (CCT) is applied to goods coming in to any port of the EU from outside the EU.

PROHIBITION OF CUSTOMS DUTIES AND CHARGES HAVING EQUIVALENT EFFECT TO CUSTOMS DUTIES UNDER ARTICLE 30 TFEU

Definition of "charges having equivalent effect" (Case 24/68 *Commission v Italy [Re Statistical Levy]*)

- any pecuniary charge (Case 46/76 *Bauhuis*);

- however small (Case 24/68 *Commission v Italy*);

- imposed not only by public authorities of a Member State but also arising from an agreement concluded between individuals (Case 16/94 *Dubois*);

- whatever its designation (Case 24/68 *Commission v Italy [Re Statistical Levy]*);

- whatever its purpose (Joined Cases 2 and 3/69 *Sociaal Fonds*);

- whatever its mode of application (Case 78/76 *Firma Steinike*);

- imposed on goods;

- by reason of the fact that they cross a border including a regional border (Joined Cases C-363 and C-407–411/93 *Lancry*) or an internal border (Case C-72/03 *Carbonati Apuani*).

NB. Compensatory taxes are also regarded as CEE (Cases 2 and 3/62 *Commission v Luxembourg [Re Gingerbread]*).

Three categories of charges

Under Article 30 TFEU, any CEE even if non-discriminatory or non-protectionist, or its purpose is to be commended is prohibited unless it comes within the narrow exceptions set out below.

1. **Charges imposed solely on imported goods:** always in breach of Article 30 TFEU unless they come within the narrow exceptions set out below.

2. **Charges imposed on both domestic and imported goods:** must be applied in the same way and according to the same criteria (Case 29/72 *Marimex*). They are CEEs, if:
   - their sole purpose is to finance activities for the specific advantage of domestic products;
   - the domestic products on which a charge is imposed and the domestic products which are to benefit from it are the same; and

- the charge imposed on domestic products is made up (that is, "reimbursed") in full (Case 77/76 *Fratelli Cucchi*);

unless they are within the exceptions set out below. If they are not CEEs they are to be examined under Article 110 TFEU or Article 107 TFEU.

3. **Charges imposed exclusively on domestic goods:** are CEEs if they fall more heavily on domestic goods intended for export than on domestic goods intended for a domestic market (Cases C-441/98 and C-442/98 *Kapniki Mikhaïlidis*).

Exceptions to the prohibition:
1. If the charge represents a fee for a service rendered to the trader but:
    - the service must be of genuine benefit to the trader (Case 132/82 *Commission v Belgium [Re Storage Charges]*);
    - the service must provide a specific benefit to the trader (Case 63/74 *Cadsky*);
    - the sum charged must be proportionate to the cost of the service (Case 170/88 *Ford España*).

2. If the charge represents a fee for a mandatory service required under EU or international law (Case 18/87 *Commission v Germany [Re Animals Inspection Fees]*).

RECOMMENDED READING

Book

Barnard, C., *The Substantive Law of the EU: The Four Freedoms*, Oxford: Oxford University Press, 2007

Article

Barents, R., "Charges of Equivalent Effect to Customs Duties", (1978) 15 CMLRev, p. 415

19

DISCRIMINATORY INTERNAL TAXATION

SUMMARY

1. Article 110 TFEU allows Member States to retain different internal tax regimes but prohibits the imposition of taxation which discriminates between domestic products and imported products, or which affords indirect protection to domestic products.

2. Under Article 110 TFEU, all discrimination, whether direct, indirect or reverse, is prohibited. Direct discrimination based on the origin of the product is plainly incompatible with the requirements of the internal market, and thus can never be justified. However, indirect discrimination, where differential tax treatment of imported products is based on criteria other than the origin of the product, although generally prohibited, may be justifiable where it is based on objective criteria and is effected in order to achieve acceptable social, environmental or economic aims (but the Court tends not to accept purely economic justifications). The list of objective justifications is rather vague and open-ended but not inconsistent with allowed justifications in other areas of free movement. Reverse discrimination refers to a situation where domestic products intended for export are taxed more highly than the same or similar domestic products intended for a domestic market. This is prohibited under Article 110 TFEU.

3. Article 110 TFEU has two paragraphs, each of which contains a separate prohibition. Article 110(1) TFEU deals with imported products which are so similar to domestic products that they require the same tax treatment. It prohibits any taxation which directly or indirectly discriminates against imported products. Two criteria are used in order to assess similarity of domestic and imported products. The first refers to the objective characteristics of domestic and imported products in terms of their origin, method of production, organoleptic qualities, and so on, and the second takes into account consumers' views as to whether both products meet the same needs. If both criteria are answered in the affirmative, the products are similar. If not, Article 110(2) TFEU is likely to apply. If a Member State breaches Article 110(1) TFEU, the remedy consists of equalising taxes between similar domestic and imported products.

4. Article 110(2) TFEU deals with imported products, which although not similar to domestic products, are nevertheless in competition with domestic products. Article 110(2) TFEU prohibits taxation that affords indirect protection to domestic products and thus ensures that domestic products are not protected from competitive pressures by the internal system of taxation. In order to assess whether products are in competition in the same market, not only present but also future consumer habits are analysed. Even partial, indirect and potential competition is taken into account. If a Member State infringes Article 110(2) TFEU, it must remove the protectionist taxes. The result of this is likely to be that products in competition will continue to be taxed at different rates from each other but the difference will be less substantial than previously.

5. A situation where imported products are neither similar to nor in competition with domestic products is outside the scope of Article 110 TFEU. However, if tax levied on a unique product is so high as to constitute an obstacle to the free movement of goods, Article 34 TFEU may apply.

6. A proper classification of a fiscal imposition will determine whether such an imposition should be challenged under Article 110 TFEU in conjunction with other articles of the Treaties or whether it falls solely within the scope of Article 110 TFEU or Article 30 TFEU. Indeed, the relationship between Article 110 TFEU and Article 30 TFEU poses a considerable difficulty, even now, and even for the highest national courts. This is so, because Articles 110 and 30 TFEU are complementary as they both deal with fiscal charges, but are mutually exclusive in that the same fiscal charge cannot belong to both categories at the same time. In order to draw a demarcation line between Articles 110 and 30 TFEU some useful "hints" are provided in section 19.6.1.

7. Each Member State has exclusive competence with regard to direct taxation, that is, in respect of taxes on personal income or company profits. As to indirect taxation (that is, taxes imposed on products/services) Member States are free to choose the tax systems they consider most appropriate and according to their preferences, but in doing so are not allowed to discriminate against products from other Member States, and they are subject to EU rules on VAT, excise duties and other EU measures adopted with a view to ensuring that the internal market is not adversely affected by disparities in national tax systems. EU competences in matters of taxation are set out in Articles 110–113 TFEU.

19.1 Introduction

Article 110 TFEU provides:

> "No Member State shall impose, directly or indirectly, on the products of other Member States any internal taxation of any kind in excess of that imposed directly or indirectly on similar domestic products.

Furthermore, no Member State shall impose on the products of other Member States any internal taxation of such a nature as to afford indirect protection to other products."

Fiscal barriers to trade may result not only from customs duties and charges having equivalent effect to them but also from the imposition on imported products of national taxes with which domestic products are not burdened. Article 110 TFEU guarantees that this will not happen. Its main objective is to ensure that the internal taxation system of a Member State makes no distinction between domestic and imported products. This was clearly stated by the ECJ in Case 252/86 *Bergandi*[1279] in which it was held that Article 90 EC [Article 110 TFEU] "must guarantee the complete neutrality of internal taxation as regards competition between domestic products and imported products".

Article 110 TFEU does not prohibit internal taxation. A Member State is free to set up a system of taxation which it considers as the most appropriate in respect of each product. The ECJ held in Case 90/79 *Commission v France [Re Levy on Reprographic Machines]*[1280] that a genuine tax is a measure relating to a system of internal dues applied systematically to categories of products in accordance with objective criteria irrespective of the origin of the products. Included in the concept of a tax are: tax refunds,[1281] stamp duties,[1282] countervailing charges[1283] and excise duties.[1284]

Article 110 TFEU applies only to products from Member States and to products originating in non-Member States which are in free circulation in the Member States[1285] and not to products imported directly from non-Member States.[1286] Further, Article 110 TFEU applies to a tax imposed not only on a specific product but also on a specific activity of an undertaking connected with that product, e.g. the transportation of the relevant product, in so far as the tax produces direct[1287] or indirect[1288] discriminatory effect on imported products. In Case C-221/06 *Stadtgemeinde Frohnleiten*,[1289] the ECJ rejected the argument submitted by the Austrian authorities that a tax imposed on the deposit of waste at a waste disposal site concerned the supply of services by the operator of the waste depositing facilities and thus should be examined in the light of the provisions of the TFEU relating to the free movement of services rather than in the light of the prohibition of discriminatory taxation set out in Article 110 TFEU. It held that what is relevant for the application of Article 110 TFEU is the effect of the tax, whether direct or indirect, on the cost of national and imported products. Any discriminatory effect which undermines the equal treatment of domestic products and imported products is prohibited under Article 110 TFEU.

In order to reduce the risk of the application of discriminatory internal taxation in respect of products from other Member States, the ECJ, in one of its earliest judgments, recognised that

---

1279. [1988] ECR 1343.
1280. [1981] ECR 283.
1281. Case 148/77 *H. Hansen jun. & O. C. Balle GmbH & Co. v Hauptzollamt de Flensburg* [1978] ECR 1787.
1282. Case 77/69 *Commission v Kingdom of Belgium* [1970] ECR 237.
1283. Supra note 1281.
1284. Case 170/78 *Commission v UK* [1980] ECR 417; Case C-167/05 *Commission v Sweden* [2008] ECR I-2127.
1285. Joined Cases 37/73 and 38/73 *Indiamex and De Belder* [1973] ECR 1609.
1286. Case C-130/92 *OTO* [1994] ECR I-3281; Case C-90/94 *Haahr Petroleum* [1997] ECR I-4085.
1287. Case 20/76 *Schöttle* [1977] ECR 247 and *Haahr Petroleum*, ibid.
1288. Case C-221/06 *Stadtgemeinde Frohnleiten Gemeindebetriebe Frohnleiten GmbH v Bundesminister für Land- und Forstwirtschaft, Umwelt und Wasserwirtschaft* [2007] ECR I-9643.
1289. Ibid.

Article 110 TFEU is directly effective. In Case 57/65 *Lütticke GmbH v Hauptzollamt*,[1290] the ECJ held that Article 90 EC [Article 110 TFEU] is clear, unconditional and not qualified by any condition, or subject to the requirement of legislative intervention on the part of Community institutions. Consequently it is of direct effect in the relationship between a Member State and an individual.

Article 110 TFEU covers all taxation procedures, including tax exemptions and grants of reduced rates of taxation, even if such tax advantages benefit only a small proportion of domestic products or are granted for special social reasons.[1291]

Under Article 110 TFEU, the fact that an imported product is subject to heavier taxation than a domestic product, even if that product seems identical to the domestic product, is not in itself an indication that there is a breach of Article 110 TFEU. This was explained by the ECJ in Case 140/79 *Chemial Farmaceutici SpA v DAF SpA*.[1292]

THE FACTS WERE:

Italian legislation imposed a heavier tax on synthetic alcohol, an imported product which was not produced in significant quantities in Italy, than on alcohol produced by fermentation which was produced domestically. Alcohol produced by fermentation, which is produced by distilling agricultural products (such as cereals, fruit, beet and molasses) and synthetic alcohol, which is derived from petroleum, are chemically identical and fully interchangeable. The Italian authorities submitted that the tax on synthetic alcohol was justified on the ground of an economic decision taken by the Italian Government to favour the manufacture of alcohol from agricultural products and, correspondingly, to restrain the processing into alcohol of petroleum in order to reserve petroleum for other more important economic uses.

Held:

The ECJ held that there was no breach of Article 90 EC [Article 110 TFEU].

Comment:

There was no breach of Article 90 EC [Article 110 TFEU] because:

- the tax differentiation was based on objective criteria, i.e. based on different raw materials used in the production of both products and on the differing production process;

- the taxation system pursued a legitimate objective, i.e. an industrial policy consisting of the promotion of the distillation of agricultural products rather than petroleum derivatives for which more important uses were envisaged by the Italian Government;

- the Italian tax system was non-discriminatory in that importers of alcohol obtained by fermentation were treated in the same way as Italian producers of alcohol by fermentation, and additionally, although the tax imposed on synthetic alcohol hindered its import-

---

1290. [1966] ECR 205, see also Case 10/65 *Deutschmann v Germany* [1965] ECR 469.
1291. Case 148/77 *H. Hansen jun. & O. C. Balle GmbH & Co. v Hauptzollamt de Flensburg* [1978] ECR 1787.
1292. [1981] ECR I.

ation from other Member States, it, at the same time, hindered the establishment of profitable production of synthetic alcohol in Italy;

■ the Italian tax system was not protectionist given that there was almost no production of synthetic alcohol in Italy.

Article 110 TFEU makes a distinction between similar products and products in competition. Under Article 110(1) TFEU any tax which discriminates directly or indirectly against an imported product which is similar to a domestic product is prohibited. If such discrimination occurs, a Member State must equalise the taxes. Article 110(2) TFEU condemns any fiscal protectionism on the part of a Member State in a situation where an imported product is in competition with a domestic product. If a breach of Article 110(2) occurs, a Member State is required to remove any protectionist element incorporated into the tax – this does not always lead to the imposition of the same tax on competing domestic and imported products.

19.2   Article 110(1) TFEU: the meaning of similar products

Article 110(1) TFEU prohibits the imposition of a higher rate of taxation on imported products than on similar domestic products. In this context it is necessary to define the concept of similarity. In Case 168/78 *Commission v France*,[1293] the ECJ emphasised that similarity should be assessed widely on the ground of analogy and comparability of uses rather then strict identity. Two criteria are applied in order to determine similarity within the meaning of Article 110(1) TFEU:

■ The first criterion refers to the objective characteristics of domestic and imported products. In Case 243/84 *John Walker*,[1294] the ECJ had to decide whether whisky and fruit liqueur wines were similar products for the purposes of Article 90(1) EC [Article 110 TFEU]. The ECJ specified the objective characteristics as relating to origin, production and organoleptic qualities, in particular the taste and alcohol content of these products. In both products the same raw material – alcohol – was found, but its content in whisky was twice that in liqueur wines. However, the production and organoleptic qualities were very different. For that reason the Court held that they were not similar products within the meaning of Article 90(1) EC [Article110 TFEU].

■ The second criterion is that if it is shown that domestic and imported products share the same objective characteristics, their similarity must be determined from the point of view of consumers. In Case 45/75 *Rewe-Zentrale*,[1295] the ECJ held that products are similar from the point of view of consumers if they are considered by them as having similar characteristics and meeting the same needs. The assessment of similarity is normally based on the Small but Significant and Non-transitory Increase in Price test (the SSNIP test (see Chapter 28)). according to which if a substantial number of consumers are likely to switch to an imported product if the price for the domestic product increases by 5 to 10 per cent (this is a small but

---

1293. [1980] ECR 347.
1294. [1986] ECR 875.
1295. [1976] ECR 181.

significant increase) the imported product and domestic product are regarded as similar products, i.e the imported product is a substitute of a domestic product from the point of view of consumers.

In Case 106/84 *Commission v Denmark*,[1296] the ECJ applied both criteria in respect of wine made from the grape and wine made from other fruits. They share the same objective characteristics as both are made from agricultural products, have the same alcohol content and are produced by means of the same process of fermentation. Also from the point of view of consumers they satisfy the same needs and are highly substitutable. The ECJ held that wines made from the grape and wines made from other fruits were similar products.

19.3   Direct, indirect and reverse discrimination

Three types of discrimination can be identified. These are dealt with below.

19.3.1   Direct discrimination

Direct discrimination based on nationality of a product is easy to spot. For that reason there are only a limited number of cases in which the ECJ has dealt with direct discrimination against imported products. It happened, however, in Case 57/65 *Alfons Lütticke GmbH v Hauptzollamt Sarrelouis*.[1297]

THE FACTS WERE:

Lütticke imported whole milk powder from Luxembourg, on which German customs levied duty and a turnover tax. Lütticke challenged the claim for payment of turnover tax on the ground that domestic natural milk and whole milk powder were exempt from it.

Held:

The ECJ condemned the German tax.

The ECJ insists on equal treatment of domestic and imported products, even though in some instances an internal tax may be beneficial to most importers and disadvantageous only to a few of them. This is illustrated in Case 127/75 *Bobie Getränkevertrieb v Hauptzollamt Aachen-Nord*.[1298]

THE FACTS WERE:

German legislation on beer provided for a rate of taxation for domestic beer, which rate increased in proportion to the output of the various breweries (from DM12 to DM15 per

---

1296. [1986] ECR 833.
1297. [1966] ECR 205.
1298. [1976] ECR 1079.

hectolitre) and for a different rate of taxation for imported beer, which was taxed at a flat rate (DM14.40 per hectolitre). The objective of the variable domestic rate was to ensure the survival of small German breweries. A large brewer importing beer from another Member State was better off as compared to a large German brewer, as the former paid DM0.60 less per hectolitre of beer. However, a small brewer importing beer from another Member State was at a disadvantage as compared to a German brewer of a similar size, being taxed at DM14.40 rather than DM12 per hectolitre.

Held:

The ECJ held that the German legislation on the taxation of beer was in breach of Article 90 EC [Article 110 TFEU]. The Court rejected the argument of Germany that the overall effect of a national taxation system should be taken into consideration. The ECJ emphasised that any discrimination is incompatible with Article 90 EC [Article 110 TFEU] and thus two different systems of taxation, one which applies to domestic products and another which deals with similar imported products, cannot be justified. Despite the fact that the tax system applied to imported products ensured broad equivalence, it nevertheless, in some cases, placed importers at a comparative disadvantage. The Court stated that a Member State must choose a system, whichever it considers the most appropriate, in respect of all similar taxed products. In this case the German Bundesfinanzhof rejected the argument of the claimant that all imported beer should be taxed at a flat rate of DM12 per hectolitre. It stated that the variable rate should be upheld but applied indiscriminately to all domestic and imported beer.

Article 110 TFEU also ensures that if treatment that would otherwise be preferential is given to domestic products, it must be extended to similar imported products. This issue was examined in Case 21/79 *Commission v Italy [Re Regenerated Oil]*.[1299]

THE FACTS WERE:

Italy levied lower charges on regenerated oil than on ordinary oil on the grounds of protection of the environment, except that this advantage was not available to imported regenerated oil. Italy justified this on the basis that it was impossible to distinguish, by means of the then experimental testing methods, whether imported oil was of primary distillation or regenerated. Italy argued that taking into account the very high production costs of regenerated oils as compared to oils of primary distillation and the impossibility of distinguishing them, many importers would claim improperly the benefit of the lower tax rates and thus avoid paying the higher rates of tax imposed on ordinary oils. This would lead to tax evasion in respect of imported products.

Held:

The ECJ held that imported products should not, in any way, be prevented from obtaining the same tax advantages as products produced in Italy. It was for the importers who wished to

---

1299. [1980] ECR 1, see also Case 148/77 *Hansen v Hauptzollampt Flensburg* [1978] ECR 1787 and Case 26/80 *Schneider-Import* [1980] ECR 3469.

enjoy the lower tax rate to prove that the oils imported were regenerated. Although the Italian authorities were entitled to require some evidence that removed the risk of tax evasion, they could not set standards of proof higher than necessary. The ECJ held that, for example, certificates issued by appropriate authorities of the exporting Member State should provide sufficient evidence.

In Case 28/67 *Firma Molkerei-Zentrale Westfalen/Lippe GmbH v Hauptzollamt Paderborn*,[1300] the ECJ held that the tax imposed on similar products must take into account the stage of development or construction at which the product is imported. Thus a Member State, when deciding upon the rate of taxation in respect of an imported product, must take into consideration all taxes levied on domestic products at earlier stages of their production, including taxes levied on raw materials and semi-finished products. However, the ECJ emphasised that the importance of these taxes diminishes proportionally as the previous stages of production and distribution become more remote.

Discriminatory conditions attached to the application of a tax are in breach of Article 110 TFEU. In Case 55/79 *Commission v Ireland*,[1301] the ECJ held that a tax which was applied without distinction to both imported and domestic products according to the same criteria but which provided for several weeks' grace in paying the amount due for domestic producers while requiring importers to pay it immediately on importation, was directly discriminatory and thus in breach of Article 90 EC [Article 110 TFEU].

In Case 15/81 *Schul*,[1302] the ECJ condemned a Member State for imposing its VAT without taking into consideration the residual part of VAT which was incorporated in the value of the product at the time of importation and already paid in the exporting Member State.

In Case 299/86 *Drexl*,[1303] the ECJ condemned a national law that imposed more severe penalties on undertakings in breach of VAT regulations on imported products than on undertakings in breach of VAT regulations on domestic products.

19.3.2 Indirect discrimination

Direct discriminatory taxation is easy to detect in the light of the strict prohibition embodied in Article 110 TFEU. As a result, Member States have tended to try to conceal by subtle means discriminatory internal taxes imposed on imported products. This was examined in Case 112/84 *Humblot v Directeur des Services Fiscaux*.[1304]

1300. [1968] ECR 143.
1301. [1980] ECR 481.
1302. [1982] ECR 1409 and 47/84 *Schul* [1985] ECR 1491.
1303. [1988] ECR 1213.
1304. [1985] ECR 1367.

THE FACTS WERE:

Under French law annual tax on cars differentiated between cars below 16 hp (horse power) (the tax rate was progressively increased up to a maximum of FF1,100) and above 16 hp (a flat rate tax of FF5,000 was applied). France did not manufacture cars above 16 hp. Consequently, all French-made cars were subject to a maximum tax of FF1,100 but all imported cars more powerful than 16 hp were subject to a higher tax. Humblot, who bought a Mercedes in France, challenged the French law.

Held:

The ECJ held that the French law was in breach of Article 90 EC [Article 110 TFEU] as it was protectionist and discriminatory in respect of cars imported from other Member States. It indirectly discriminated against imported cars, although there was no formal distinction between imported and domestic cars.

Both the rate of direct and indirect internal taxation on domestic and imported products and also the basis of assessment and rules regarding the imposition of the tax are important in determining whether there is a breach of Article 110 TFEU. This is exemplified by Case C-375/95 *Commission v Greece*.[1305]

THE FACTS WERE:

The Commission brought proceedings against Greece for introducing and maintaining in force the following national rules contrary to Article 90 EC [Article 110 TFEU]:

1. *Article 1 of Greek Law 363/1976 as amended by Law No 1676/1986 related to a special consumer tax applicable to imported used cars, under which in the assessment of their taxable value only 5 per cent reduction of the price of equivalent new cars was permitted for each year of age of the used cars and the maximum reduction was fixed at 20 per cent of the value of equivalent new cars.*

2. *Article 3(1) of Law No 363/1976, which was replaced by Article 2(7) of Law 2187/1994, concerning the determination of the taxable value of cars in order to levy the flat-rate tax, added a special duty which contained no reduction for used cars.*

3. *Article 1 of Law No 1858/1989 as amended many times regarding the reduction of a special consumer tax for anti-pollution technology cars applied only to new cars and not to imported used cars with the same technology.*

The Commission stated that the Greek Government was in breach of Article 90 EC [Article 110 TFEU] since the above-mentioned legislation created a system of internal taxation that indirectly discriminated against used cars imported from other Member States in comparison with used cars bought in Greece.

1305. [1997] ECR I-5981.

Held:

The ECJ held that the national rules for calculating special consumer tax and flat-rate added duty in order to determine the taxable value of imported used cars were in breach of Article 90 EC [Article110 TFEU].

The special consumer tax applicable only to imported used cars was in breach of Article 90 EC [Article 110 TFEU]. The ECJ rejected the argument submitted by Greece that the special consumer tax was also applied to domestic used cars when they were first purchased within the country, and that part of it remained incorporated in the value of those cars. The ECJ emphasised that the special consumer tax on imported used cars was usually higher than the proportion of the tax still incorporated in the value of used cars already registered and purchased on the Greek market, taking into account that the annual depreciation in the value of cars is considerably more than 5 per cent, that depreciation is not linear, especially in the first years when it is much more marked than subsequently, and, finally, that vehicles continue to depreciate more than four years after being put into circulation;

The ECJ condemned a special consumer tax for anti-pollution technology cars, which was applied only to new cars and not to imported used cars with the same technology, as being in breach of Article 90 EC [Article 110 TFEU].

Following the above case, the ECJ has dealt with many cases concerning discriminatory taxes imposed on second-hand cars imported from other Member States. More recently, courts of the Member States which joined the EU on and after 1 May 2004 have been faced with this "old problem".[1306]

In Case C-387/01 *Harald Weigel and Ingrid Weigel v Finanzlandesdirektion für Vorarlberg*,[1307] the ECJ confirmed that a national tax system that is liable to eliminate a competitive advantage held by imported products over domestic products would breach Article 110 TFEU.

THE FACTS WERE:

Mr and Mrs Weigel, both German nationals, transferred their residence from Germany to Austria subsequent to the appointment of Mr Weigel as director of the Vorarlberger Landes-bibliothek (Public Library) in Austria. Each spouse imported a car into Austria as personal property. In Austria they were required to register their cars and subsequently to pay the Austrian fuel consumption tax which comprised: the NoVA tax (the standard fuel consumption tax (Normverbrauchsabgabe)) and the NoVA surcharge tax (which represented a surchage of 20 per cent of the NoVA tax). Both were imposed upon the first-time registration of a motor vehicle in Austria but in different circumstances: the NoVA tax was a standard tax; the NoVA surcharge tax was applied in special circumstances (see below). Mr and Mrs Weigel jointly challenged the imposition of the tax.

1306. Joined Cases C-290/05 and C-333/05 *Nádasdi and Németh* [2006] ECR I-10115; Case C-313/05 *Brzezinski* [2007] ECR I-513.
1307. [2004] ECR I-4981.

Held:

The ECJ held that the NoVA tax was manifestly of a fiscal nature and as such should be assessed in the light of Article 90 EC [Article 110 TFEU]. The Court, relying on its previous case law regarding the taxation of imported cars, found that the NoVA tax was imposed without making any distinction between imported used cars and used cars bought in Austria.[1308] Both were subjected to the same tax. Thus, the NoVA tax was not in breach of Article 90 EC [Article 110 TFEU].

The NoVA surchargeTax was in breach of Article 90 EC [Article 110 TFEU] because it imposed a heavier tax burden on imported products than on domestic products. This tax, in practice, was always applied to imported used cars but never to second-hand domestic cars and only in exceptional circumstances to new cars registered for the first time in Austria (for example, in respect of a car privately assembled by an enthusiast). The actual objective of the tax, as the ECJ pointed out, was to eliminate a competitive advantage held by imported products over domestic products rather than to prevent the distortion of competition as claimed by the Austrian Government.

19.3.3 Reverse discrimination

It is extremely rare that a Member State imposes higher taxes on domestic goods than on identical or similar imported goods. This may, for example, occur if a Member State intends to discourage export of a valuable scarce commodity,[1309] and indeed there are other possible circumstances.

In Case C-234/99 *Niels Nygård v Svineafgifsfonden, and Ministeriet for Fødevarer, Landbrug og Fiskeri*,[1310] the ECJ clearly stated, for the first time, that Article 110 TFEU also applies to discriminatory taxes imposed on domestic goods for export.

THE FACTS WERE:

Under Danish law a production levy was charged for every pig bred and slaughtered in Denmark, irrespective of whether it was intended for the domestic market or for export. The same levy was also charged for every pig bred in Denmark and exported live. A part of the revenue generated by the levy was allocated to the financing of the production of pigs in

---

1308. Case C-375/95 *Commission v Greece* [1997] ECR I-5981 and Case C-393/98 *Ministério Público and António Gomes Valente v Fazenda Pública* [2001] ECR I-1327.

1309. Case 142/77 *Larsen and Kjerulff* [1978] ECR 1543.

1310. [2002] ECR I-3657, see also Case C-517/04 *Visserijbedrijf D.J.Koornstra & Zn vof v Productschap Vis* ([2006] ECR I-5015), in which the ECJ held that a charge levied on traders in The Netherlands for landing shrimp with fishing vessels registered in The Netherlands, set up for the purpose of financing shrimp sieves and peelers in The Netherlands, and which charge made no distinction as to whether shrimp were intended for the national market or for export in an unprocessed state, was in breach of Article 90 EC [Article 110 TFEU] in so far as the fiscal burden it imposed on the product processed or marketed on the national market was neutralised by the advantages which the charge was used to finance, while the charge on the products exported in an unprocessed state constituted a net burden. However, the ECJ left it to the referring court to decide whether the charge was indeed a CEE or whether it was a tax under Article 90 EC [110 TFEU].

Denmark and so benefited those exporting pigs. The remainder of the revenue generated by the levy was allocated to the financing of the slaughtering of pigs and of the processing of pig meat in Denmark and its sale on the domestic and export markets, and so did not bring any benefit to exporters of pigs. The levy scheme was, pursuant to Article 88(3) EC [Article 108(3) TFEU], notified and approved by the Commission as being lawful state aid.

Mr Nygård, a pig breeder established in Denmark, exported to Germany live pigs intended for slaughter between 1 August 1992 and 1 July 1993. Under German law he was required to pay a production levy in Germany for each pig supplied to the abattoirs. He paid the German production levy, but refused to do so in Denmark. The Danish Levy Fund commenced proceedings against Mr Nygård before the District Court in Skjern (Denmark). The Danish Court ordered Mr Nygård to pay the full amount of the production levy in respect of the exported pigs and interest. Mr Nygård appealed to the Vestre Landsret from the judgment of the District Court arguing, among other things, that the levy constituted discriminatory taxation prohibited under Article 90 EC [Article 110 TFEU]. The Vestre Landsret referred the matter to the ECJ.

Held:

The ECJ held that the levy in question should be classified as discriminatory internal taxation prohibited by Article 90 EC [Article 110 TFEU] to the extent to which the advantage deriving from the use made of its revenue compensated in part for the charge imposed on pigs produced for slaughter in Denmark, thereby placing at a disadvantage the production of pigs for live export to other Member States.

Comment:

The ECJ justified the extension in this case of the prohibition set out in Article 90 EC [Article 110 TFEU] to exported goods by reference to Case 142/77 *Larsen et Kjerulff*,[1311] which case previously stood alone and which provides that Article 90 EC [Article 110 TFEU] "must be interpreted as also prohibiting any tax discrimination against products intended for export to other Member States".

This broad interpretation of Article 90 EC [Article 110 TFEU] can probably be explained by the fact that, notwithstanding the silence of the Treaties in this respect, Article 110 TFEU should be interpreted as a separate but complementary provision to Article 30 TFEU and therefore should seek to:

"fill in any breaches which a fiscal measure might open in the prohibitions laid down, by prohibiting the imposition on imported products of internal taxation in excess of that imposed on domestic products."[1312]

Notwithstanding this reasoning, it remains that the ECJ's teleological interpretation of Article 90 EC [Article 110 TFEU], that is, based on the objective of the achievement of the internal market, is very far away from the literal interpretation of Article 90 EC [Article 110 TFEU]!

1311. [1978] ECR 1543.
1312. Cases 2–3/69 *Sociaal Fonds v Brachfeld and Chougol Diamond Co* [1969] ECR 211.

The neutrality of the internal taxation system is not challenged when lower taxes are imposed on goods for export than on other domestic goods since it does not create an obstacle to the free movement of goods. Only domestic goods destined for the home market are affected.

19.3.4 Objective justification

Differential taxation of products, which may serve the same economic ends, is not prohibited under Article 110 TFEU in so far as it is justified on the basis of objective criteria. However, direct discrimination based on the nationality of the product can never be objectively justified.

In Case C-375/95 *Commission v Greece*[1313] (see section 19.3.2), the ECJ held that national rules granting tax advantages (that is, reducing the special consumer tax) which applied only to new anti-pollution technology cars and not to imported second-hand cars with the same technology, could not be objectively justified under Article 90 EC [Article 110 TFEU]. A Member State cannot confer tax advantages on low emission cars while refusing those advantages to cars satisfying the same criteria from the other Member States without offending against the prohibition on discrimination laid down in Article 90 EC [110 TFEU]. Therefore, the imported used cars were discriminated against on the ground of nationality. This is always unlawful. Differential taxation where the criterion for charging a higher rate is the importation itself and where domestic goods are by definition excluded from the heavier taxation is always in breach of Article 110 TFEU.

Indirect discrimination, even if it results in discrimination against imported products, may be justified if it is based on objective criteria. The ECJ has taken a liberal approach in respect of these criteria. They may be based on the nature of the use of the raw materials, the processes employed in the production or manufacturing of goods, or they may refer to general objectives of economic and social policy of a Member State such as the protection of the environment or the development of regional policy, so far as those policies are compatible with EU law. The leading case on this topic is Case 196/85 *Commission v France*.[1314]

THE FACTS WERE:

France levied lower taxes on sweet wines produced in a traditional and customary fashion in certain regions of France than on imported liqueur wines (also sweet). The tax differentiation was not directly discriminatory as all similar wines, irrespective of the country of origin, could qualify for the lower rate of taxation. It was for France to justify the indirect discrimination. In this respect France showed that natural sweet wines were produced in areas of low rainfall and poor soil, whose economy depended on wine production. France argued that its regional policy was to encourage production in poor growing areas and thus develop those regions, and that this tax concession was open to all EU producers.

Held:

The ECJ accepted that a lower taxation levy on French sweet wines was objectively justified.

1313. [1997] ECR I-5981.
1314. [1987] ECR 1597.

Similarly, in Case 21/79 *Commission v Italy*,[1315] the Italian Government imposed a tax on imported and domestic cars based on their capacity to pollute, which was objectively justified on the ground of the protection of environment, although in the particular circumstances it imposed a heavier burden on imported cars than on domestic cars.

It can be seen from the above that the list of objective justifications is rather vague and open-ended, but not inconsistent with justifications allowed in other areas of free movement.

19.4   Article 110(2) TFEU: the meaning of products in competition

The concept of "products in competition" is wider than the concept of "similar products". In Case 170/78 *Commission v UK [Re Tax on Beer and Wine]*,[1316] the ECJ explained the scope of the application of Article 90(2) EC [Article 110(2) TFEU] in respect of "products in competition". It was one of many so-called "spirit cases".

THE FACTS WERE:

The UK maintained different levels of internal taxation for beer (£0.61 per gallon) and wine (£3.25 per gallon). Wine was mostly imported while beer was predominantly a domestic product. The Commission decided that this tax difference amounted to discrimination against imported wine and that by increasing the tax on wine, the British Government was encouraging consumers to buy beer. The UK argued that the two products were not inter-changeable and therefore there was no breach of Article 90 EC [Article 90 TFEU].

Held:

The ECJ held that that in order to determine the existence of a competitive relationship, it is necessary to take into account not only the present state of the market but also "possible developments regarding the free movement of goods within the Community and the further potential for substitution of products for one another which might be revealed by intensification of trade".

The ECJ stated that wine and beer were, to a certain extent, substitutable as they were capable of meeting the same needs of consumers. To measure the degree of substitutability, consumers' habits in a Member State, or in a particular region, should be taken into account, although these habits should not be regarded as immutable. Indeed, the tax policy of a Member State should not crystallise consumers' habits and thus consolidate an advantage gained by domestic producers. The Italian Government submitted that it was appropriate to compare beer with the most popular, lightest and cheapest wine because those products were in real competition. The ECJ agreed and held that the decisive competitive relationship between beer and wine must be established by reference to the lightest and cheapest wine. Those products were in competition. Consequently, the ECJ found the UK in breach of Article 90(2) EC [Article 110(2) TFEU].

1315. [1980] ECR 1.
1316. [1983] ECR 2265.

Comment:

Following the decision of the ECJ the UK removed the unlawful element of protection by adjusting tax rates for beer upwards and for wine downwards, but there were still different rates applied to both products.

This case and many others show that often there is not only a potential market for an imported product competing with a domestic product, but also that while such a market may exist, it is often suppressed by an unfair tax system.

Case C-167/05 *Commission v Sweden*[1317] illustrates the stages which the ECJ follows in the application of Article 110(2) TFEU.

THE FACTS WERE:

The Commission brought proceedings against Sweden for breach of Article 90(2) EC [Article 110(2) TFEU] on the basis that by applying a system of internal taxes under which strong beer (in excess of 3.5 per cent alcohol per volume), which was mainly produced in Sweden, was indirectly protected, as compared with the lightest, least expensive and the most popular wine (around 11 per cent alcohol per volume) mainly imported from other Member States. When Sweden acceded to the EU its excise duty on strong beer and light wine was almost identical. In 1997 Sweden reduced excise duty on beer by 40 per cent to respond to the substantial increase in cross-border trade in beer between Sweden and Denmark. Following the Commission's investigation, in 2001, Sweden reduced excise duty on wine by 18.8 per cent per volume. According to the Commission despite the reduction in excise duty on wine, it was subject to higher excise duty than beer by more than 20 per cent, and the Swedish tax system in respect of beer was therefore protectionist.

Held:

The ECJ held that the difference in the tax treatment of beer and wine was not such as to afford indirect protection to Swedish beer. This was because, first, the difference between the selling prices of a litre of strong beer and a litre of wine was virtually the same before and after taxation, and second, the Commission did not submit any statistical information showing that variations in the price of those products were likely to bring long-term changes in consumer habits in favour of wine and to the detriment of beer. The ECJ emphasised that certain sensitivity on the part of consumers to short-term changes in the prices of products in competition was not sufficient to evidence that the difference in the tax treatment of those products was liable to influence consumer behaviour.

Comment:

The ECJ followed three stages in order to establish whether Sweden was in breach of Article 110(2) TFEU. These were:

1317.   [2008] ECR I-2127.

First, the ECJ had to establish a competitive relationship between an imported product and a domestic product. In conformity with the case law of the ECJ an imported product and a domestic product are in such a relationship if they are substitutable, i.e. they are capable of meeting the same needs of consumers. This is established on the basis of the SSNIP test. In this case, the ECJ agreed with the Commission and Sweden that lighter and less expensive wines (appox. 11 per cent alcohol per volume) were comparable to beer having alcohol strength of around 5 per cent per volume.

Second, The ECJ examined the tax arrangements for each product in order to identify differences between the tax burden in terms of price, alcohol content and volume. In respect of products in competition this is not difficult given that they are dissimilar and therefore subject to different tax arrangements. In the commented case, the ECJ found that the alcohol strength by volume of the beverage, a factor used by the Swedish authorities for the basis of assessment of excise duty, was the most pertinent criterion. On this basis the ECJ decided that wine which was in competition with strong beer was subject to higher taxation than strong beer. In this respect the ECJ stated that: ". . ., it emerges from a comparison of the levels of taxation in relation to alcoholic strength that a wine with an alcoholic strength of 12.5% vol., which is in competition with strong beer, is subject to taxation per percentage of alcohol by volume which exceeds by approximately 20% per litre the taxation on strong beer (SEK 1.77 as against SEK 1.47), and that that difference increases to 36% in the case of a wine with an alcoholic strength of 11% vol. (SEK 2 as against SEK 1.47) and to 50% in the case of a wine with an alcoholic strength of 10% vol. (SEK 2.208 as against SEK 1.47)" (para 50).

Third, once the ECJ found that there were differences in tax arrangements between light wine and strong beer, it examined the alleged protectionist consequences deriving from these differences. In accordance with the case law of the ECJ, not only the direct and actual but also the indirect and potential protectionist effect is taken into account. In order to assess the alleged protectionist effect, in Case C-167/05 *Commission v Sweden* the ECJ examined the impact of taxation by reference to the difference between the final selling prices of the products and the impact of that difference on consumers' choice, both at the level of an individual consumer and the collective tendencies of consumers. In respect of the impact of price difference on a choice of an individual consumer the ECJ considered the final selling prices between a litre of strong beer and a litre of wine which were in competition with each other and compared the relationship between them with the relationship that would apply if the tax rates applied to beer were applied to wine. The ECJ found that the relationship between final selling prices of beer and wine was one to two point one (1:2.1) and then found that this ratio was not high enough to change the attitude of an individual consumer. With regard to collective consumer tendencies the ECJ found that the Commission had failed to prove a long-term change in consumer habits in favour of beer. In this respect the Commission submitted inconclusive evidence[1318] which

---

1318. The Commission relied on statistical data produced by Systembolaget (a Swedish undertaking which has a monopoly on sales of alcoholic beverages in Sweden) showing that at the time of accession of Sweden to the EU

according to the ECJ showed a certain sensitivity of Swedish consumers to prices but not long-term changes in consumer habits.

19.5 Unique products

It may occur that an imported product is unique in the sense that there is neither a similar domestic product nor a domestic product in competition with the imported product.

In Case 193/79 *Cooperativa Cofruta v Amministrazione delle Finanzo dello Stato*,[1319] Italy claimed that bananas were such unique products.

THE FACTS WERE:

Italy imposed a high tax on bananas. Italy is not considered to be a producer of bananas (its production is so insignificant that it was not taken into consideration). Accordingly, the Italian Government argued that bananas were neither similar to nor in competition with any domestic product.

Held:

On the grounds that a consumption tax was imposed on other exotic products such as coffee, cacao, and so on, in order to raise revenue for the state, the ECJ decided that bananas formed part of a broader Italian taxation system which was based on objective criteria unconnected with the origin of the product. The ECJ considered that bananas were, nevertheless, in competition with other table fruits. Taking into account the high tax imposed on bananas as compared to other table fruits, the ECJ concluded that Italy indirectly protected domestic table fruits by setting such a high rate of taxation on bananas. Consequently, Italy was held in breach of Article 90(2) EC [Article 110(2) TFEU].

Where there are no competing national products a tax imposed by a Member State on imported unique products is outside the scope of Article 110 TFEU, but may be caught by Article 34 TFEU,[1320] which prohibits quotas and equivalent restrictions on trade between Member States (see Chapter 20). This situation occurred in Case C-383/01 *De Danske Bilimportører v Skatteministeriet, Told-og Skattestyrelsen*,[1321] in which the ECJ had an opportunity to condemn a tax in the light of Article 28 EC [Article 34 TFEU] for the first time, but declined to do so.

---

the sales volumes of beer and wine in Sweden were relatively similar and that, after the reduction by 40 per cent of excise duty on beer, sales of wine dropped by 3.7 per cent, whilst sales of beer rose by 8.9 per cent. After the reduction in 2001 sales of wine increased by 11 per cent, which was the highest increase seen between 1995 and 2004. However, the data also showed that alongside that increase in wine sales, sales of beer increased by a much higher percentage.

1319. [1987] ECR 2085.
1320. Case C-47/88 *Commission v Denmark* [1990] ECR I-4509.
1321. [2003] ECR I-6065.

THE FACTS WERE:

De Danske, a Danish association of car importers, purchased a new Audi vehicle for a total price of €67,152, including €40,066 in registration duty. De Danske paid the duty but subsequently requested repayment from the Danish tax authorities, arguing that the excessive level of the registration duty made it impossible to import motor vehicles to Denmark under normal commercial conditions, and that the duty was imposed to benefit domestic purchasers of previously registered used vehicles, which according to Danish law are regarded as Danish products and therefore exempt from registration duty.

The Danish tax authorities refused any repayment. They argued that as there is no production of motor vehicles in Denmark, they are allowed to impose any amount in respect of registration duty. Further, they stated that the registration duty was not obstructing the free movement of goods given that during the period from 1985 to 2000, the total number of registered vehicles in Denmark rose from 78,453 to 169,492.

Held:

The ECJ held that the Danish registration duty was of a fiscal nature and thus a part of a general system of internal dues on goods. The Court explained that Article 90 EC [Article 110 TFEU] could not be used to censure the excessiveness of the level of taxation adopted by a Member State in the circumstances where there were no similar or competing domestic products and the challenged tax had no discriminatory or protective effect. Accordingly, the Danish registration duty imposed on new cars was not covered by the prohibition set out in Article 90 EC [Article 110 TFEU]. Further, based on the high and increasing number of registrations of new cars in Denmark, the ECJ found that the Danish tax was not impeding the free movement of goods and thus should not be classified as a measure having equivalent effect to a quantitative restriction within the meaning of Article 28 EC [Article 34 TFEU].

The above judgment confirms the ECJ's tendency to shy away from applying Article 34 TFEU to an apparently excessive tax imposed by a Member State in a situation where the product is unique.

19.6 The relationship between Article 110 TFEU and other provisions of the TFEU relating to the free movement of goods

19.6.1 The relationship between Articles 110 and 30 TFEU

The connection between Article 110 TFEU and Article 30 TFEU is very close, given that Article 110 TFEU supplements the provisions of the Treaties on the abolition of customs duties and charges having equivalent effect. However, Articles 30 and 110 TFEU operate at different levels.

Article 30 TFEU aims at ensuring that fiscal impediments are eliminated when products of Member States are crossing each others' national borders, while the purpose of Article 110 TFEU is to make sure that, whatever the internal tax system of a Member State, it does not discriminate directly or indirectly against products from other Member States. A fiscal charge is either a customs duty or a CEE or part of a general system of internal taxation. For that reason Article

110 and Article 30 TFEU are complementary, yet mutually exclusive.[1322] So, an imposition cannot, at the same time, be contrary to both Article 30 and Article 110 TFEU. Although in many cases it is difficult to distinguish between charges having equivalent effect and discriminatory internal taxation, there are some helpful clues which may render it less difficult. These are set out below:

- The determination of whether a charge is imposed only on imported products or on both domestic and imported products. If a fiscal charge is imposed exclusively on imported products, it is likely to be a charge equivalent to a customs duty. If a fiscal charge is levied on both domestic and imported products, it is more likely to be part of internal taxation.

- Definitions provided by the ECJ of a charge and of a tax:

  - The ECJ defined a charge having equivalent effect to a customs duty as encompassing any pecuniary charge, however small and whatever its designation and mode of application, that is imposed unilaterally on domestic or imported goods by reason of the fact that they cross a frontier.[1323]
  - In Case 90/79 *Commission v France [Re Levy on Reprographic Machines]*,[1324] the ECJ held that a genuine tax is a measure relating to a system of internal dues applied systematically to categories of products in accordance with objective criteria irrespective of the origin of the products. Therefore, if a charge is part of internal taxation and is based on criteria that are objectively justified by the nature of the products, their quality or their function rather than the fact of crossing a national border, it will be considered under Article 110 TFEU.

- The destination of the proceeds of the charge. In Case 77/76 *Fratelli Cucchi v Avez*,[1325] the ECJ stated that if a charge is imposed on both domestic and imported products but:

  (i)   has the sole purpose of providing financial support for the specific advantage of domestic products;
  (ii)   the domestic taxed products and the benefiting domestic products are the same; and
  (iii) the charge imposed on the domestic products is made good in full to domestic producers;

  that charge is to be considered as a CEE under Article 30 TFEU. However, if there is a partial compensation, a charge is not purely a customs duty or CEE and so the charge comes under Article 110 TFEU, and as such is prohibited in so far as it discriminates against the imported products or affords protection to domestic products. Indeed, in Case C-266/91 *Celbi*,[1326] the ECJ held that if the revenue from such a charge is used only partially to provide advantages to domestic products, the charge will constitute discriminatory

---

1322. Case 10/65 *Deutschmann v Germany* [1965] ECR 469; Case 57/65 *Lütticke* [1966] ECR 205; Case C-90/94 *Haahr Petroleum* [1977] ECR I-4085; Case C-234/99 *Nygård* [2002] ECR I-3657; Case C-387/01 *Weigel* [2004] ECR I-4981.

1323. Case 46/76 *Bauhuis v Netherlands* [1977] ECR 5; Case 132/78 *Denkavit v France* [1979] ECR 1923; Case 18/87 *Commission v Germany* [1988] ECR 5427; Case 340/87 *Commission v Italy* [1989] ECR 1483; Case C-130/93 *Lamaire NV v Nationale Dienst voor Afzet van Land- en Tuinbouwprodukten* [1994] ECR I-3215.

1324. [1981] ECR 283.

1325. [1977] ECR 987.

1326. [1993] ECR I-4337.

taxation contrary to Article 110 TFEU. The ECJ emphasised that "the criterion of the offsetting of the burden on domestic products is to be construed as requiring financial equivalence, to be verified over a reference period, between the total amount of the charge imposed on domestic products and the advantages exclusively benefiting those products."

■ The event that has triggered the imposition. If the charge is imposed by reason of the product crossing the border of the Member State, that is, it is an import/export, it is an unlawful charge under Article 30 TFEU. Any other operative event indicates that the imposition should be regarded as part of a general system of internal dues on goods and hence should be examined in the light of Article 110 TFEU. For example, in Case C-387/01 *Weigel*,[1327] the referring court had doubts as to whether the tax imposed on Mr and Mrs Weigel constituted a customs duty or a charge having equivalent effect to a customs duty, or whether the tax constituted discriminatory internal taxation. The ECJ, by relying on its previous case law, eliminated the application of Articles 23 EC [Article 28 TFEU] and 25 EC [Article 30 TFEU].[1328] The Court pointed out that the tax was imposed not just because the vehicle had crossed a border of a Member State but because the vehicle was required to be registered for the first time in a host Member State. Therefore the tax was manifestly of a fiscal nature and as such should be assessed in the light of Article 90 EC [Article 110 TFEU].

If a charge is incompatible with Article 110 TFEU, it is prohibited only to the extent to which it discriminates against imported products,[1329] whereas a charge under Article 30 TFEU is unlawful in its entirety.

19.6.2 The relationship between Articles 110 TFEU and 107 TFEU

Article 107 TFEU concerns state aid. In Case 73/79 *Commission v Italy*,[1330] the ECJ held that Articles 87 [Article 107 TFEU] and 90 EC [Article 110 TFEU] are complementary and may be applied cumulatively.

When a charge is applied without discrimination to domestic and imported products but the revenue from it is appropriated wholly to domestic products and thus fully offsets the burden of the charge imposed on them, this may constitute state aid in breach of Article 107 TFEU. It is for the Commission to decide whether that is the case.

19.6.3 The relationship between Articles 110 TFEU and 34 TFEU

Article 110 TFEU and Article 34 TFEU are mutually exclusive.[1331] However, internal taxes, which are outside the scope of Article 110 TFEU because there are no comparable domestic products,

---

1327. [2004] ECR I-4981.
1328. Case C-383/01 *De Danske Bilimportører v Skatteministeriet, Told- og Skattestyrelsen* [2003] ECR I-6065.
1329. Case 68/79 *Just* [1980] ECR 501; Case C-72/92 *Scharbatke* [1993] ECR I-5509.
1330. [1980] ECR 1533.
1331. Case 74/76 *Ianelli and Volpi* [1977] ECR 557; Cases C-78 to 83/90 *Compagnie Commerciale de l'Ouest* [1992] ECR I-1847.

may be in breach of Article 34 TFEU if the charges levied on imported products are so excessively high as to constitute an obstacle to the free movement of goods.[1332]

19.7   Repayment of unlawful fiscal impositions

Unlawful fiscal impositions, whatever their name, that is, charges, levies, supplementary payments, must be repaid. Under the principle of autonomy of national procedural rules it is for the domestic legal system of each Member State to lay down procedural rules applicable to actions for recovery of sums unduly paid under Articles 30 and 110 TFEU. Such rules, however, are subject to the principle of equivalence and the principle of effectiveness.[1333]

In accordance with the principle that a person should not be unduly enriched at the expense of another, when a trader has paid an unlawful charge and subsequently passed the cost on to another person, he is not entitled to claim reimbursement from the relevant national authorities.[1334] However, if the charge has been transferred only in part to another party, the trader can still claim reimbursement of the amount not transferred. In Case C-192/95 *Comateb*,[1335] the ECJ made important clarifications in this area. It held:

- First, that even if under national law there is a legal obligation, enforceable by a penalty, to include a charge in the sale of goods price, that is, to pass the charge on to a purchaser, this does not give rise to a presumption that the entire charge has been passed on;

- Second, that the purchaser to whom the charge was passed on is entitled to claim reimbursement either from the trader or from the relevant national authority;

- Third, irrespective of whether a trader has passed a charge on to a purchaser, the trader is still entitled to claim damages caused by an unlawful charge. This is particularly so when, as a result of the unlawful charge, the trader's products are more expensive than other similar products so that purchasers are few. Consequently, when the increased price of imported goods results in a reduction of sales, and thus of profits, a Member State may be liable. If domestic law provides for such a remedy, the domestic court must give effect to the trader's claim; if not, the trader can rely on the *Francovich* remedy (see Chapter 14).

19.8   Harmonisation of taxation within the European Union

At the time of writing Member States are enjoying sole responsibility for and dominion over direct taxation, that is, in respect of taxes on personal income and on company profits. EU taxation policy is confined to indirect taxation such as Value Added Tax (VAT) and excise duties, and measures within its competence which are intended to ensure that the internal market is not adversely affected by the disparity of national tax systems, for example, with regard to company taxation.

1332.   Case 47/88 *Commission v Denmark* [1990] ECR I-4509; Case C-383/01 *De Danske Bilimportører v Skatteministeriet, Told- og Skattestyrelsen* [2003] ECR I-6065.
1333.   Case C-312/93 *Peterbroeck* [1995] ECR I-4599; Case C-212/94 *FMC* [1996] ECR I-389.
1334.   Case 199/82 *San Giorgio* [1983] ECR 3595.
1335.   [1997] ECR I-165.

The Commission, without further encroaching on the fiscal sovereignty of the Member States, has made many proposals and taken many initiatives to reduce the harmful effect of the existing disparity between national tax systems, but so far to no avail.[1336] The main objective of the Commission's approach is not to replace the existing national systems by an EU-wide harmonised tax system, but to achieve the following objectives:

- To remove double taxation, which adversely affects many EU citizens and undertakings. For example, in *Weigel* the ECJ recognised that the challenged legislation "is likely to have a negative bearing on the decision of migrant workers to exercise their right to freedom of movement". This statement was further explained by the ECJ in the following manner:

  "... the Treaty offers no guarantee to a worker that transferring his activities to a Member State other than the one in which he previously resided will be neutral as regards taxation. Given the disparities in the legislation of the Member States in this area, such a transfer may be to the worker's advantage in terms of indirect taxation or not, according to circumstance. It follows that, in principle, any disadvantage, by comparison with the situation in which the worker pursued his activities prior to the transfer, is not contrary to Article 39 EC [Article 45 TFEU] if that legislation does not place that worker at a disadvantage as compared with those who were already subject to it."[1337]

- To reduce costs incurred by taxpayers subject to more than one tax system.

- To protect Member States' tax bases by preventing inadvertent non-taxation and abuse.

AIDE-MÉMOIRE

Article 110 TFEU

Article 110 TFEU allows each Member State to set up its systems of internal taxation as it considers appropriate but prohibits three kinds of discrimination by way of taxation:

- **Direct discrimination** against imported products based on their nationality. This is always unlawful and can never be justified (Case 57/65 *Lütticke GmbH v Hauptzollamt*);

- **Indirect discrimination** against imported products based on factors other than nationality (Case 112/84 *Humblot v Directeur des Services Fiscaux*). This may be justified by objective criteria (Case 196/85 *Commission v France*);

- **Reverse discrimination** against domestic products intended for export which are more heavily taxed than domestic products intended for a domestic market (Case C-234/99 *Niels Nygård*).

1336. See Commission's Memo/06/499 of 19/12/06 on a proposal on an EU co-ordinated approach to national direct tax systems. For example, the 1997 package of proposals entitled "Towards Tax Co-ordination in the European Union – A Package to Tackle Harmful Tax Competition" never materialised as a result of its rejection by the UK at the Helsinki European Council (December 1999).

1337. See also Case C-365/02 *Lindfors* [2004] ECR I-7183.

SIMILAR PRODUCTS, PRODUCTS IN COMPETITION AND UNIQUE PRODUCTS

Under Article 110 TFEU:

- **Similar products** must pay the same tax rate as each other (Article 110(1) TFEU). Similarity is assessed on the basis of two criteria:
  - the objective characteristics of the products (243/84 *John Walker*);
  - their substitutability from the point of view of consumers (Case 45/75 *Rewe-Zentrale*).

  An imported product is regarded as similar to a domestic product if it satisfies both the above criteria.

- **Products in competition** may suffer different tax rates but a Member State must remove any unlawful element of protection by adjusting tax rates upwards for domestic products and downwards for imported products (Article 110(2) TFEU). In assessing the competitive relationship between domestic and imported products, it is important to consider both the present state of the market and also its possible future development, including the further potential for substitution of products for one another. Thus, the consolidation of consumer habits in any Member State should not be encouraged by the tax policy of that Member State (Case 170/78 *Commission v UK [Re Tax on Beer and Wine]*).

Three stages in the application of Article 110(2) TFEU can be identified:

- First, it must be established that there is a competitive relationship between an imported product and a domestic product. In conformity with the case law of the ECJ an imported product and a domestic product are in such a relationship if they are substitutable, i.e. they are capable of meeting the same needs of consumers.

- An examination of the tax arrangements for each product is required in order to identify differences between them. In respect of products in competition this is not difficult given that they are dissimilar and therefore subject to different tax arrangements.

- If there are differences between tax arrangements, it is necessary to examine the alleged protectionist consequences deriving from differences between the tax arrangements for domestic and imported products. Not only direct and actual but also indirect and potential protectionist effect is taken into account. In order to assess the alleged protectionist effect, the ECJ examines the impact of taxation by reference to the difference between the final selling prices of the products and the impact of that difference on consumers' choice, both at the level of an individual consumer and the collective tendencies of consumers.

- **Unique products** (that is, those which are neither similar to nor in competition with any domestic product) may pay any tax rate, but any excessive imposition may be caught by Article 34 TFEU as a measure having equivalent effect to a quantitative restriction (C-383/01 *De Danske*). This has never occurred!

> **THE FOLLOWING CRITERIA MAY BE HELPFUL IN DISTINGUISHING BETWEEN A CHARGE UNDER ARTICLE 30 TFEU AND A TAX UNDER ARTICLE 110 TFEU**
>
> - Whether an imposition is levied only on imported products or on both imported and domestic products. If it is imposed only on an imported product, it is more likely to be a charge rather than a tax;
>
> - The definition of a charge (Case 24/68 *Commission v Italy [Re Statistical Levy]*) and of a tax (Case 90/79 *Commission v France [Re Levy on Reprographic Machines]*) provided by the ECJ;
>
> - The destination of the proceeds of the imposition (Case 77/76 *Fratelli Cucchi*);
>
> - The event that has triggered the imposition. If the imposition is triggered by reason of the product being imported/exported, it is an unlawful charge. Any other event suggests that the imposition is a tax.

RECOMMENDED READING

Books

Barnard, C., *The Substantive Law of the EU. The Four Freedoms*, 2nd edition, 2007, Oxford: Oxford University Press

Davies, G., *European Union Internal Market Law*, 2006, London: Routledge Cavendish

Davies, M., *Nationality Discrimination in the European Internal Market*, 2003, The Hague: Kluwer Law International

Shuibhne, N. (ed.), *Regulating the Internal Market*, 2006, Cheltenham: Edward Elgar

Articles

Danusso, M. and Dention, R., "Does the European Court of Justice Look for a Protectionist Motive under Article 95 [Article 90 EC]?", (1990) 1 LIEI, p 67

Easson, A., "The Spirits, Wine and Beer Judgments: A Legal Mickey Finn?" (1980) 5 ELRev, p 318

Graetz, M. J., and Warren, Jr., A. C., "Income Tax Discrimination and the Political and Economic Integration of Europe", (2006) 115 Yale L.J., p 1186

Snell, J., "Non-Discriminatory Tax Obstacles in Community Law", (2007) 56 ICLQ, p 339

20

QUANTITATIVE RESTRICTIONS (QRs) AND MEASURES HAVING EQUIVALENT EFFECT ON IMPORTS AND EXPORTS (MEQRs) – ARTICLES 34 AND 35 TFEU

CONTENTS

SUMMARY

1. Article 34 TFEU prohibits quantitative restrictions (QRs) both total and partial on imports, and measures having equivalent effect to them (MEQRs) between Member States. Article 35 TFEU extends the prohibitions to exports. These prohibitions are subject to Article 36 TFEU, which sets out grounds on which a Member State may justify national rules contrary to Articles 34 and 35 TFEU and subject to exceptions developed by the case law of the ECJ.

2. Article 34 TFEU is addressed to Member States as it applies to measures adopted by them. The ECJ has broadly interpreted both the concept of a Member State and the concept of measures adopted by it. The concept of a Member State includes all public bodies, emanations of a Member State and private bodies controlled by a Member State. The concept of measures refers to binding rules adopted by a Member State, as well as simple incentives and constant administrative practices. Failure to take measures, when necessary, makes a Member State responsible for the conduct of individuals which breaches EU law, if that Member State is in a position to prevent or terminate such conduct.

3. EU institutions are required to respect the prohibitions set out in Article 34 TFEU.

4. The Treaties neither define QRs nor MEQRs. While QRs are easy to define as they refer to classical bans and quotas prohibiting or limiting importation by amount or by volume, MEQRs are more problematic. Directive 70/50/EEC provided some guidance for the first time as to the meaning of MEQRs. The Directive divided MEQRs into two categories: distinctly and indistinctly applicable measures:

- Distinctly applicable measures are those which make a distinction between imported and domestic products in such a way that they "hinder imports which could otherwise take place, including measures which make importation more difficult or costly than disposal of domestic goods" (Article 2(1) of the Directive);

- Indistinctly applicable measures are those which apply to imported and domestic products alike, but their restrictive effect on the free movement of goods "exceeds the effect intrinsic to trade rules", that is, they in fact hinder intra-Community trade (Article 3 of the Directive).

5. The ECJ established its own definition of MEQRs in Case 8/74 *Procureur du Roi v Dassonville*. Known as the Dassonville formula, it describes MEQRs as any trading rules enacted by Member States which are capable of hindering directly or indirectly, actually or potentially, trade between Member States. This very broad formula encompasses not only rules which have restrictive effect, however small, but also those which are capable of potentially hindering trade between Member States. In *Dassonville* the ECJ did not make a distinction between distinctly and indistinctly applicable measures as it focused on the restrictive effects of a measure rather than its form. However, the Court accepted that in respect of indistinctly applicable measures "reasonable" restrictions may be outside the scope of Article 28 EC [Article 34 TFEU]. This line of reasoning was further developed in Case 120/78 *Rewe-Zentral v Bundesmonopolverwaltung für Branntwein* (otherwise and generally known as the *Cassis de Dijon* case).

6. In *Cassis de Dijon* the ECJ focused on indistinctly applicable measures. Such measures, although non-discriminatory, i.e. make no distinction as to the origin of a product, can constitute a real hindrance to trade between Member States. Article 3 of Directive 70/50 clearly envisaged this possibility. In addition, the *Dassonville* formula encompasses such measures given that it covers any measures which could have or do have an adverse effect on trade regardless of the motives, whether discriminatory or not, for their introduction.

The main aspects of the *Cassis de Dijon* case are:

- The ECJ confirmed that Article 34 TFEU applies to non-discriminatory national measures which hinder trade between Member States. They do so, because they are different from rules applicable in the Member State of origin of the relevant product;

- It introduced the rule of mutual recognition, that is, a presumption that goods which have been lawfully produced and marketed in one Member State can be introduced without further restrictions into other Member States. Thus, it is for the Member State of importation, and not for a trader, to prove otherwise. The principle of mutual recognition is often contrasted with harmonisation, as mutual recognition permits national differences to remain and as such is seen as a new way of facilitating integration;

- It introduced the rule of reason, under which a Member State is permitted to use measures which are reasonable (that is, "mandatory requirements") to protect its vital public interests in a manner which conforms with EU law, but only in the absence of common harmonising rules in the relevant area. Mandatory requirements include the effectiveness of commercial transactions, the protection of public health, the fairness of commercial transactions and the defence of the consumer. The list is not exhaustive and since the *Cassis de Dijon* case a number of new mandatory requirements have been accepted by the ECJ;

- It assigned to the principle of proportionality a vital role with regard to the application of the rule of reason in that indistinctly applicable measures enacted by a Member State must have effects which are proportionate to the aims they seek to achieve.

7. Subsequent to the *Cassis de Dijon* case, the scope of Article 28 EC [Article 34 TFEU] seemed limitless as it prohibited all national rules hindering trade between Member States, including not only those relating to product specification but also those relating to their marketing. In Joined Cases C-267 and 268/91 *Criminal Proceedings against Keck and Mithouard* the ECJ made a dramatic about-turn and stated that "contrary to what has been previously decided", rules affecting "selling arrangements" were outside the scope of Article 28 EC [Article 34 TFEU] provided that:

- They apply indistinctly to all traders operating within the territory of a Member State;

- They affect in the same manner, in law and in fact, the marketing of both domestic and imported products even though they may have some impact on the overall volume of sales.

8. The main problems with the *Keck* approach are:

- There is no clear definition of selling arrangements, and thus it is difficult to distinguish between indistinctly applicable rules which relate to the characteristics of the product (which are within the scope of Article 34 TFEU) and those which relate to selling arrangements (which are outside the scope of Article 34 TFEU).

- There is uncertainty as to how to determine, in practice, whether or not national rules in fact affect the marketing of imported products and domestic products in the same manner.

The growing case law of the ECJ on selling arrangements has, to some extent, reduced the first problem. As to the second, it flows from the post-*Keck* cases, in particular from Case 405/98 *Konsumentombudsmannen v Gourmet International Products AB* (the *Gourmet* case), that the ECJ has introduced the "market access" test in order to determine factual discrimination between domestic and imported products. Thus, in order to escape the application of Article 34 TFEU, national rules prohibiting certain selling arrangements "must not be of such a kind as to prevent access to the market by products from another Member State or to impede access any more than they impede the access of domestic products". This test is not easy to apply; nevertheless, it is submitted that from the post-*Keck* case law and the reasoning of the ECJ in *Gourmet* some conclusions may be drawn, i.e:

▪ A reduction in the volume of sales of a particular product after the introduction of a national measure is not decisive in assessing whether or not such a measure is preventing or impeding access of that product to the market in the Member State any more than for domestic products;

▪ In the assessment of the degree of severity of a restriction imposed by national rules, a decisive criterion is whether or not other forms of marketing/advertising of the imported products are available to importers, and if so, to what extent such alternatives will make the marketing/advertising of the product more onerous and more expensive for importers than if the restriction had not been imposed.

9. It emerges from Case C-110/05 *Commission v Italy* and Case C-142/05 *Åklagaren* that the access to the market test seems to have become essential in the assessment of national measures under Article 34 TFEU irrespective of whether they are product related or concern selling arrangements. Although the legal implications of the above cases are uncertain it seems that the access to the market test set out in *Gourmet* is likely to be modified and indeed, the distinction between product related restrictions and those concerning selling arrangements may lose its importance or even disappear.

10. In Case C-205/07 *Gysbrechts*, the ECJ broadened the scope of application of Article 35 TFEU. According to *Gysbrechts* it is no longer necessary to prove that a national measure has protective effects, i.e. provides a particular advantage for domestic products intended for a domestic market at the expense of domestic products intended for export. What is relevant is whether a national measure discriminates in fact against exported products and thus has a greater "actual effect" on export of goods than on the marketing of the goods in the domestic market.

11. To deal speedily and efficiently with grave disruptions to the free movement of goods, which cause serious and continuing losses to the individuals affected, Regulation 2679/98 established a Rapid Intervention Mechanism (RIM). Under the Regulation, the Commission is required to act immediately when there is a threat or a major obstacle to the free movement of goods and the Member State concerned is required to correct the situation within a very short time limit. If the failure persists, the Commission may bring proceedings against the Member State concerned before the ECJ in a much shorter time period than under the Article 258 TFEU procedure.

20.1 Introduction

The elimination of non-tariff barriers to the free movement of goods is governed by Articles 34 to 36 TFEU. Article 34 TFEU provides that:

"Quantitative restrictions on imports and all measures having equivalent effect shall be prohibited between Member States."

Article 35 TFEU repeats the same prohibition in respect of exports. Article 36 TFEU contains exceptions to the prohibitions laid down in Articles 34 and 35 TFEU (see Chapter 21). Articles 34 and 35 TFEU are vertically directly effective[1338] but do not produce horizontal direct effect.

1338. In respect of Article 34 TFEU, see Case 74/76 *Ianelli v Volpi SpA V Diutta Paola Meroni* [1977] ECR 557; for Article 35 TFEU, see Case 83/78 *Pigs Marketing Board (Northern Ireland) v Redmond* [1978] ECR 2347.

Article 28 EC [Article 34 TFEU] has been used by the ECJ as the principal tool for the removal of all barriers to the free movement of goods. Its scope of application has been gradually extended in order to respond to the development of the Community and its changing economic objectives.

It is important to note that Articles 34 to 36 TFEU only apply when there are no exhaustive harmonising measures in the relevant area at the EU level, i.e. when there is no secondary legislation adopted by EU institutions fully harmonising the relevant aspect of EU law (normally an EU regulation, or directive). When there is harmonising EU legislation any national measure must be assessed in the light of the relevant secondary legislation and not in the light of the Treaties,[1339] i.e. the principle of lex specialis applies.

Article 34 TFEU is very short. Nevertheless, it covers a number of concepts. These are examined below.

20.2   The concept of "measures taken by the Member States"

Article 34 TFEU is addressed to the Member States and concerns measures taken by them. The ECJ has broadly interpreted the concept of "a State" and the concept of "measures taken" by a Member State.

- The concept of a Member State includes not only any public body but also its emanations and private bodies controlled by it.

- The concept of "measures adopted by Member States" covers not only binding rules, but also simple incentives[1340] and constant administrative practice generally based on an individual decision.[1341] Also, a Member State may be responsible for the conduct of its citizens who obstruct the free movement of goods, if it is in a position to prevent or terminate such conduct. In such a situation, a Member State's failure to take appropriate measures constitutes a breach of Article 34 TFEU read in conjunction with Article 4(3) TEU.

20.2.1   Measures taken by any public body, whether legislative, executive or judicial

This refers to measures taken by any public authority.

20.2.2   Measures taken by semi-public bodies[1342]

In Case 266/87 *R v Royal Pharmaceutical Society of Great Britain, ex parte Association of Pharmaceutical Importers and Others*,[1343] the ECJ had to decide whether a measure adopted by a professional body such as the Pharmaceutical Society of Great Britain may come within the scope of Article 28 EC [Article 34 TFEU].

1339. Case C-309/02 *Radlberger Getränkegesellschaft mbH & Co., S. Spitz KG v Land Baden-Württemberg* [2004] ECR I-11763.
1340. Case 249/81 *Commission v Ireland [Re Buy Irish Campaign]* [1982] ECR 4005.
1341. Case C-41/02 *Commission v The Netherlands* [2004] ECR I-11375.
1342. Case 222/82 *Apple and Pear Development Council v K J Lewis Ltd* [1983] ECR 4083.
1343. [1989] ECR 1295.

THE FACTS WERE:

The Royal Pharmaceutical Society of Great Britain is a professional body established to enforce rules of ethics for pharmacists throughout the UK. This organisation convenes periodic meetings of a committee which has statutory authority to impose disciplinary measures on pharmacists found to have violated the rules of professional ethics. The Society enacted rules which prohibited a pharmacist from substituting one product for another that has the same therapeutic effect but bears a different trade mark when doctors prescribe a particular brand of medication. Pharmacists were therefore required to dispense particular brand name products when these were specified in prescriptions. This rule was challenged as being a MEQR prohibited by Article 28 EC [Article 34 TFEU].

Held:

The ECJ held that Article 28 EC [Article 34 TFEU] applies not only to rules enacted by the Member States but also encompasses rules adopted by a professional body such as the Royal Pharmaceutical Society of Great Britain, which exercises regulatory and disciplinary powers conferred upon it by statutory instrument. The ECJ stated that professional and ethical rules adopted by the Society, which required pharmacists to supply under a prescription only a particular brand name drug, may constitute MEQRs in breach of Article 28 EC [Article 34 TFEU].

Comment:

In this case the measures were justified under Article 30 EC [Article 36 TFEU].

20.2.3 Measures taken by private companies supported financially or otherwise by a Member State when carrying out activities contrary to Article 34 TFEU

This is illustrated by Case C-325/00 *Commission v Germany*.[1344]

THE FACTS WERE:

Germany argued that a German fund set up by the German Government to promote German agriculture and the German food industry, but which carried out its activity through the CMA – a private company whose organs were set up in accordance with private law rules and financed by compulsory contributions paid by undertakings in the German agriculture and food sector – was not a public body.

Held:

The ECJ held that CMA, although set up as a private body, established on the basis of law and bound by its Articles of Association, originally approved by the German public authorities, and

---

1344. [2002] ECR I-9977, see also Case 249/81 *Commission v Ireland [Re Buy Irish Campaign]* [1982] ECR 4005.

financed by compulsory contributions, must be distinguished from bodies set up by producers on a voluntary basis. Accordingly the CMA was a public body as it did not enjoy the same freedom as regards the promotion of national products as would producers or their associations based on voluntary membership. The scheme established by the CMA consisting of awarding a quality label to national products satisfying certain requirements (the CMA label) and subsequently advertising such products by emphasising their German origin was condemned by the ECJ as encouraging consumers to buy products with the CMA label to the exclusion of imported products.

20.2.4   Conduct of individuals who violate Article 34 TFEU

Until 1995 it had always been accepted that the prohibition contained in Article 28 EC [Article 34 TFEU] concerned an action taken by the Member State and not passivity or inaction on its part. However, the ECJ decided otherwise in Case C-265/95 *Commission v France*.[1345]

THE FACTS WERE:

For a decade the Commission received complaints regarding the passivity of the French Government in the face of acts of violence and vandalism committed by French farmers, such as interception of lorries transporting agricultural products from other Member States and destruction of their loads, threats against French supermarkets, wholesalers and retailers dealing with those products, damage to such products when on display in shops, and so on. The Commission, supported by the Governments of Spain and the UK, stated that on a number of occasions the French authorities showed unjustifiable leniency vis-à-vis the French farmers, for example, by not prosecuting the perpetrators of such acts when their identity was known to the police, since often the incidents were filmed by television cameras and the demonstrators' faces were not covered. Furthermore, the French police were often not present on the spot even though the French authorities had been warned of the imminence of demonstrations, or they did not interfere, as happened in June 1995 when Spanish lorries transporting strawberries were repeatedly attacked by French farmers at the same place over a period of two weeks and the police who were present took no protective action. The Government of France rejected the arguments submitted by the Commission as unjustified.

Held:

The ECJ held that France was in breach of its obligations under Article 28 EC [Article 34 TFEU], in conjunction with Article 10 EC [Article 4(3) TFEU], and under the common organisation of the markets in agricultural products for failing to take all necessary and proportionate measures in order to prevent its citizens from interfering with the free movement of fruit and vegetables.

1345. [1997] ECR I-6959.

Comment:

This is one of the landmark decisions of the ECJ. It held that Article 28 EC [Article 34 TFEU] is also applicable where a Member State abstains from taking the measures required in order to deal with obstacles to the free movement of goods, which obstacles are not created by the Member State.

Abstention thus constitutes a hindrance to the free movement of goods, and is just as likely to obstruct trade between Member States as is a positive act. However, Article 28 EC [Article 34 TFEU] in itself is not sufficient to engage the responsibility of a Member State for acts committed by its citizens, but is so when read in the light of Article 10 EC [Article 4(3) TEU], which requires the Member States not merely themselves to abstain from adopting measures or engaging in conduct liable to constitute an obstacle to trade, but also to take all necessary and appropriate measures to ensure that the fundamental freedom regarding the free movement of goods is respected on their territory.

Notwithstanding the fact that the ECJ recognises that a Member State has exclusive competences in relation to the maintenance of public order and the safeguard of internal security, it assesses the exercise of that competence by a Member State in the light of Article 28 EC [Article 34 TFEU]. As a result, the ECJ stated that the French authorities failed to fulfil their obligations under the Treaty on two counts: first, they did not take necessary preventive and penal measures; second, the frequency and seriousness of the incidents, taking into account the passivity of the French authorities, not only made the importation of goods into France more difficult but also created a climate of insecurity that adversely affected the entire intra-Community trade.

The implications of Case C-265/95 *Commission v France* were highlighted in Case C-112/00 *Eugen Schmidberger, Internationale Transporte und Planzüge v Austria.*[1346]

THE FACTS WERE:

Eugen Schmidberger, a German undertaking transporting timber and steel between Germany and Italy via the Brenner motorway, brought proceedings before the Austrian courts against the Republic of Austria, claiming that the Austrian authorities were in breach of Articles 28 and 29 EC [Articles 34 and 35 TFEU] as they failed to ban a demonstration organised by an Austrian environmental organisation, the Transitforum Austria Tirol (TAT), on the Brenner motorway that resulted in the complete closure of that motorway for almost 30 hours. TAT organised the demonstration in order to draw public attention to problems caused by the increase in traffic on the Brenner motorway and to call upon the Austrian authorities to take the necessary measures to deal with these problems; it had obtained authorisation from the local authorities to hold the demonstration on the Brenner motorway. Eugen Schmidberger sought compensation for losses suffered as a result of the closure of the Brenner motorway, claiming that Austria's failure to ban the demonstration constituted a sufficiently serious

---

1346. [2003] ECR I-5659.

breach of EC law for which Austria should be liable. The Austrian Government contended that the claim should be rejected on the grounds that the decision to authorise the demonstration was made after careful examination of the facts, that all known users and other parties likely to be affected by the closure of the motorway were informed in advance, that the demonstration was peaceful and did not result in traffic jams or other incidents, that the obstacle that it created was neither serious not permanent and that the demonstrators were entitled to exercise their freedom of expression and freedom of assembly, rights which are fundamental in a democratic society and enshrined in the ECHR and the Austrian Constitution.

Held:

The ECJ recognised that the closure of the motorway constituted an obstacle to the free movement of goods but accepted that the fact that the authorities of a Member State did not ban a demonstration in circumstances such as those of the main case was not incompatible with Articles 28 EC and 29 EC [Articles 34 and 35 TFEU] read together with Article 10 EC [Article 4(3) TEU].[1347]

Comment:

The ECJ made a distinction between Case C-265/95 *Commission v France* and the *Schmidberger* case. The Court emphasised that although in both cases the free movement of goods was obstructed, there were important differences between the circumstances of the respective cases in terms of the geographical scale and the intrinsic seriousness of the disruptions caused by individuals, as well as the manner in which the national authorities had acted in order to deal with these disruptions. The ECJ pointed out that the demonstration in Austria took place after being duly authorised by the relevant national authorities, was limited to a single occasion, was of short duration, and its objective was to allow citizens to exercise their fundamental rights to express publicly their views on a matter which was of importance to them and to society. Furthermore, the Austrian authorities limited as far as possible the disruption to road traffic, taking into consideration that they had taken appropriate measures to ensure that the demonstration passed off peacefully and without any serious incidents, all parties likely to be affected were informed in advance and advised to take alternative routes specially designed for this occasion. In contrast, in Case C-265/95 *Commission v France* the French authorities did not take any measures when faced with serious and repeated disruptions of the free movement of goods by its nationals, which disruptions were of such seriousness as to create a general climate of insecurity undermining the free movement of goods.

The decisions of the ECJ in the above cases have far-reaching implications. They mean that a Member State may be liable under Article 34 TFEU linked with Article 4(3) TEU if it does not prevent or adequately punish any conduct of its economic operators which is capable of hindering the free movement of goods. Therefore, a Member State is forced to intervene in situations where, for example, private individuals decide to promote domestic products to the detriment of those from other Member States or otherwise obstruct trade between Member States.

1347. For examination in depth of the justification provided by the Austrian Government. See paras 65–94 of the judgment.

20.3 Measures taken by EU institutions

The prohibition of QRs and of MEQRs applies not only to national measures but also to measures adopted by the EU institutions. In Case 15/83 *Denkavit Nederland*,[1348] the ECJ held that measures adopted by Community institutions are capable of falling foul of Articles 28 and 29 EC [Article 34 and 35 TFEU]. In Case C-114/96 *René Kieffer and Romain Thill*,[1349] the ECJ held that Community acts of general application may hinder trade between Member States.

20.4 The definition of QRs and MEQRs under Article 34 TFEU

The Treaties neither define QRs nor MEQRs. There is no problem in defining QRs as these have been in use for centuries. They restrict importation and exportation by amount or by volume. The most common restrictions on the physical quantity of imports or exports are quotas and bans. In Case 2/73 *Risetia Luigi Geddo v Ente Nazionale Risi*,[1350] the ECJ defined them as any measures which amount to a total or partial restraint on imports, exports or goods in transit. A total restraint refers to a ban. In Case 7/61 *Commission v Italy [Re Ban on Pork Imports]*,[1351] the ECJ condemned such a ban as contrary to Article 28 EC [Article 34 TFEU].

In respect of MEQRs the first official, but still incomplete, definition was given in 1967 by the Commission in response to a parliamentary question.[1352]

Under pressure from the Member States and the EP, the Commission decided to provide guidance as to the meaning and scope of "measures having equivalent effect" in Directive 70/50,[1353] which was adopted on the basis of the then Article 33(7) of the EC Treaty and therefore applicable only to measures to be abolished during the transitional period that ended in 1968. It has, however, provided important clarification of the notion of "measures having equivalent effect" and at the time of writing continues to be considered as a non-binding guideline to the interpretation of Article 28 EC [Article 34 TFEU]. Article 2(3) of the Directive gives a generic definition of MEQRs and divides them into two categories:

- **First, "measures, other than those applicable equally to domestic or imported products"**, that is **"distinctly applicable"** measures that "hinder imports which could otherwise take place, including measures which make importation more difficult or costly than the disposal of domestic production" (Article 2(1) of the Directive);

- **Second, "measures which are equally applicable to domestic and imported products"**, that is **"indistinctly applicable"** measures (Article 3 of the Directive). These measures are in breach of Article 28 EC "where the restrictive effect of such measures on the free movement of goods exceeds the effects intrinsic to trade rules". This occurs "where the restrictive effects on the free movement of goods are out of proportion to their purpose" or "where the same objective can be attained by other means which are less of a hindrance to trade". Accord-

---

1348. [1984] ECR 2171 and in Case C-51/93 *Meyhui NV v Schott Zwiesel Glaswerke AG* [1994] ECR I-3879.
1349. [1997] ECR I-3629.
1350. [1973] ECR 865.
1351. [1961] ECR 317.
1352. Written Question, M Delinger [1967] OJ 59.
1353. [1970] OJ L13/29.

ingly, such measures are lawful if they satisfy the requirements of the principle of proportionality.

20.5   Article 34 TFEU: the Dassonville formula

The ECJ provided its own definition of MEQRs in Case 8/74 *Procureur Du Roi v Dassonville*.[1354]

THE FACTS WERE:

Traders imported Scotch whisky into Belgium. The whisky had been purchased from a French distributor and had been in circulation in France. However, the Belgian authorities required a certificate of origin, which could only be obtained from British customs and which had to be made out in the name of the importers, before the goods could be legally imported into Belgium. As no certificate of origin could be obtained for the consignment, the traders went ahead with the transaction. They were charged by the Belgian authorities with the criminal offence of importing goods without the requisite certificate of origin. The defendants claimed that the requirement of a certificate of origin in these circumstances was tantamount to an MEQR and therefore was prohibited by Article 28 EC [Article 34 TFEU]. The Belgian court referred to the ECJ for a preliminary ruling on this question.

Held:

The ECJ held that the Belgian regulation constituted a MEQR because it potentially discriminated against parallel importers (that is, traders who are not authorised/approved dealers of a manufacturer of a product or of the holders of intellectual property rights over it, but who lawfully purchase it in a Member State where the price is lower and sell it in another Member State where the price obtainable for the same product is higher) who would be unlikely to be in possession of the requisite documentation.

In *Dassonville*, the ECJ defined the concept of measures having an equivalent effect to quantitative restrictions on imports as being all trading rules enacted by Member States which are capable of hindering directly or indirectly, actually or potentially, trade between Member States. This is known as the "Dassonville formula". The formula is very broad; the effect of national measures, including their potential effect,[1355] is decisive in determining whether they should be considered as MEQRs, regardless of the motive (discriminatory or not) for their introduction. Even if national measures have no significant effect on trade, they are still in breach of Article 34 TFEU. This is illustrated in Joined Cases 177 and 178/82 *Jan Van der Haar*.[1356]

1354.   [1974] ECR 837.
1355.   Case 249/81 *Commission v Ireland [Re Buy Irish Campaign]* [1982] ECR 4005.
1356.   [1984] ECR 1797.

> ### THE FACTS WERE:
>
> *Dutch excise law regulating the resale of tobacco products restricted imports of these products to a very small degree and provided for alternative ways of marketing them.*
>
> *Held:*
>
> The ECJ held the Dutch rules breached Article 28 EC [Article 34 TFEU]. The ECJ emphasised that Article 28 EC [Article 34 TFEU] does not recognise the de minimis rule as it:
>
> > "does not distinguish between measures . . . according to the degree to which trade between Member States is affected. If a national measure is capable of hindering imports it must be regarded as having an effect equivalent to a quantitative restriction, even though the hindrance is slight and even though it is possible for imported products to be marketed in other ways."

It is to be noted that the ECJ, although it has many times confirmed that the de minimis rule does not apply under Article 28 EC [Article 34 TFEU], had in some cases held that a national rule was outside the scope of Article 28 EC [Article 34 TFEU] because its restrictive effect on trade between Member States was too uncertain and indirect.[1357]

In *Dassonville* the ECJ did not make a distinction between distinctly and indistinctly applicable measures as it focused on the restrictive effects of a measure rather than on its form. However, the ECJ has encompassed within the formula both distinctly applicable measures, which affect imports only, and indistinctly applicable measures, which affect both imported and domestic products. The latter, without making a distinction between imported products and domestic products, may result in making imports more difficult or more expensive, that is, they relate to material discrimination rather than formal discrimination.

In paragraph 6 of the judgment the Court accepted that "reasonable" restrictions imposed by indistinctly applicable measures may be outside the scope of Article 28 EC [Article 34 TFEU]. In this respect, the Court stated that in the absence of Community harmonising measures guaranteeing for consumers the authenticity of a product's designation of origin, a Member State is allowed to take measures to prevent unfair practices to protect consumers, subject to the condition that such measures are reasonable. This line of reasoning was further developed in Case 120/78 *Rewe-Zentral v Bundesmonopolverwaltung für Branntwein* (the *Cassis de Dijon* case).[1358]

Discrimination against imported products may be formal (direct) or material (indirect).

- ■ Formal discrimination occurs when national measures treat similar situations in different ways that result in the hindering of trade between Member States, for example, when they impose certain customs formalities, mandatory inspections or licensing requirements that result in additional costs and delays for importers, but do not apply to domestic producers.

- ■ Material discrimination takes place when a national measure theoretically treats different situations in the same way but in practice imposes additional costs for the importer and thus

---

1357. Case C-93/92 *CMC Motorradcenter GmbH v Pelin Baskiciogullari* [1993] ECR I-5009; Case C-379/92 *Criminal Proceedings against Matteo Peralta* [1994] ECR I-3453; Case C-44/98 *BASF AG v Präsident des Deutschen Patentamts* [1999] ECT I-6269.

1358. [1979] ECR 649.

constitutes an obstacle to the free movement of goods (for example, the imposition of requirements concerning the packaging or the content of imported products). A national measure based on an apparently neutral criterion will amount to material discrimination if only domestic products can satisfy that criterion. This is illustrated by Case 45/87 *Commission v Ireland*.[1359]

THE FACTS WERE:

The Dundalk District Council laid down certain specifications concerning a tender for the construction of the Dundalk water supply scheme that included a clause stipulating that the materials used must be certified as complying with a national technical standard, that is, asbestos cement pressure pipes had to be "certified as complying with Irish Standard Specification 188:1975 in accordance with the Irish Standards Mark Licensing Scheme of the Institute for Industrial Research and Standards". Not surprisingly, only one Irish company could satisfy the requirement set out in the clause.

Held:

The ECJ held that the specification constituted a MEQR and therefore was in breach of Article 28 EC [Article 34 TFEU] as it excluded the use of asbestos cement pipes manufactured to an alternative standard providing equivalent guarantees of safety, performance and reliability.

20.6 Article 34 TFEU: internal situations

Purely domestic situations are outside the scope of Article 34 TFEU because it intends to protect only trade between Member States.[1360] However, a surprising development took place in Case C-448/98 *Criminal Proceedings against Jean-Pierre Guimont*.[1361]

THE FACTS WERE:

Mr Guimont, the technical manager of the Laiterie d'Argis located in Vaucluse in France, refused to pay a fine imposed by the Directorate for Competition, Consumer Affairs and Prevention of Fraud of the Department of Vaucluse for holding for sale, selling or offering Emmenthal cheese without rind contrary to the French law which expressly required that cheese bearing the designation "Emmenthal" must have, inter alia, "a hard, dry rind, of a colour between golden yellow and light brown". When Mr Guimont refused to pay the fine, criminal proceedings were brought against him before the Tribunal de Police (Local Criminal Court) of Belley. Mr Guimont argued that the French legislation was in breach of Article 28 EC

1359. [1988] ECR 4929.
1360. Case 98/86 *Mathot* [1987] ECR 809.
1361. [2000] ECR I-10663.

[Article 34 TFEU]. The Tribunal de Police asked the ECJ to answer whether or not this was the case.

Held:

The ECJ decided to accept the reference for a preliminary ruling (although the matter was purely internal). Because its reply "might be useful" to the referring court "if its national law were to require, in proceedings such as those in this case, that a national producer be allowed to enjoy the same rights as those which a producer of another Member State would derive from Community law in the same situation", i.e. if national law prohibits reverse discrimination.

Comment:

Surprisingly, the answer of the ECJ was based on the Dassonville formula, that is, that Article 28 EC [Article 34 TFEU] applies to any measure of a Member State which is capable, directly or indirectly, actually or potentially, of hindering trade between Member States, although the situation was purely internal.

The Governments of Germany, The Netherlands and Austria, together with the Commission, supported Mr Guimont. Their argument was based on the decision of the ECJ in Joined Cases C-321–324/94 *Pistre and Others*,[1362] in which the Court held that Article 28 EC [Article 34 TFEU] cannot be considered inapplicable simply because all facts of the specific case before the national court are confined to a single Member State. However, in *Guimont* the ECJ provided a justification for its solution in *Pistre*. The ECJ stated that ". . . It should be noted that the *Pistre* judgment concerned a situation where the national rule in question was not applicable without distinction but created direct discrimination against goods imported from other Member States", that is, the rule was distinctly applicable. However in *Guimont* the rule in question was indistinctly applicable. For that reason the ECJ explained in *Guimont* that in the situation where a national rule is indistinctly applicable, Article 28 EC [Article 34 TFEU] applies "only in so far as it applies to situations that are linked to the importation of goods in intra-Community trade". There was no importation of goods in *Guimont* and accordingly the ECJ should have declined to answer the preliminary question. Nevertheless, the ECJ decided to answer the question referred to it by the Tribunal de Police (Local Criminal Court) of Belley for (in the Court's words) the following reason:

> "In this case it is not obvious that the interpretation of Community law requested is not necessary for the national court. Such a reply might be useful to it [the referring court] if its national law were to require, in proceedings such as those in this case, that a national producer must be allowed to enjoy the same rights as those which a producer of another Member State would derive from Community law in the same situation."

The above statement means that the ECJ would accept a reference for a preliminary ruling with regard to purely internal situations if its reply "might be useful". This would be so in a situation where national law prohibits reverse discrimination. In such a situation national law

---

1362. [1997] ECR I-2343.

must be interpreted in conformity with EU law. The outcome of this case is that if the relevant national law prohibits reverse discrimination (for example, Article 3 of the Italian Constitution as interpreted by the Italian Constitutional Court prohibits reverse discrimination[1363]), claimants such as Mr Guimont will be successful in their claim; otherwise they will not be able to challenge a national rule that is indistinctly applicable, if there is, under national law, no redress against reverse discrimination.

Two conclusions can be drawn from *Guimont*:

- First, the ECJ, without interfering in the internal competences of Member States, reminded national courts that if reverse discrimination is illegal under national law, the *Guimont* approach applies and the ECJ will accept a referral from a national court if its reply "might be useful". However, it is the task of national courts, not the ECJ, to verify whether there is a rule under national law prohibiting reverse discrimination and thus the ECJ might deliver purely hypothetical preliminary rulings, wasting the time and money of the applicants, and both its own resources and those of the national courts (see Chapter 10.6).

- The second concerns the flexibility of the ECJ in interpreting the concept of a "purely domestic situation". This is exemplified in Case C-71/02 *Herbert Karner Industrie-Auktionen GmbH v Troostwijk GmbH*,[1364] in which the only external element was that Troostwijk GmbH, an Austrian undertaking whose main activities consisted of purchasing the stock of insolvent companies and selling it by auction, advertised the auction in question on the Internet among other means.

Karner vigorously argued that the reference from an Austrian court should not be accepted by the ECJ given that the dispute before the referring court related to a purely internal situation, as both parties to the proceedings were established in Austria, the goods in question were acquired following a case of insolvency which took place in the territory of Austria and the relevant Austrian legislation concerned forms of advertising in Austria. This was not the view of the ECJ, which, for the first time, expressly recognised that an indistinctly applicable national measure applied within the context of a purely domestic dispute may still fall within the scope of Article 28 EC [Article 34 TFEU].

The disappointing aspect of the judgment in *Karner* is that the ECJ failed to justify its judgment. One can only speculate on this issue. Perhaps the ECJ, without any express reference in its judgment, considers that the existence of the internet and the opportunity to use it as a means of conveying information has already abolished the border between what should be regarded as a matter of purely domestic significance and what should be regarded as a matter which has an EU dimension.

1363. A. Tryfonidou, "Carbonati Apuani SRL v Comune di Carrera: Should we Reverse 'Reverse Discrimination' "? (2005) 16 King's College L.J., p 373.
1364. [2004] ECR I-3025.

20.7 Article 34 TFEU: national measures indistinctly applicable to domestic and imported goods – the Cassis de Dijon approach

The ECJ was very aware that in the absence of Community rules, it was for Member States to lay down the conditions on access to national markets for imported products. A decision needed to be made as to the extent to which national legislation was to be tolerated. This matter was examined in Case 120/78 *Rewe-Zentral AB Bundesmonopolverwaltung Für Branntwein* (the *Cassis De Dijon* case).[1365]

THE FACTS WERE:

German legislation governing the marketing of alcoholic beverages set a minimum alcohol strength of 25 per cent per litre for certain categories of alcoholic products. This regulation prohibited an importer from marketing Cassis de Dijon, a French liqueur with an alcohol strength of between 15 and 20 per cent, in Germany. The German Government invoked human health and consumer protection concerns as the justification for the prohibition. The importer challenged the German legislation in the German court, which then referred the matter to the ECJ for a preliminary ruling.

Held:

The ECJ laid down a number of fundamental principles in respect of indistinctly applicable measures as follows:

- It confirmed that Article 28 EC [Article 34 TFEU] applies to non-discriminatory national measures which hinder intra-Community trade. They do so because they are different from rules applicable in the Member State of origin of the relevant product;

- It introduced the principle of mutual recognition, that is, a presumption that goods which have been lawfully produced and marketed in one Member State can be introduced, without further restrictions, into other Member States. This entails that it is for the Member State of importation, and not for a trader, to prove otherwise;

- It introduced the rule of reason, under which a Member State is permitted to use measures which, although within the Dassonville formula, will not infringe Article 28 EC [Article 34 TFEU] if they are necessary to protect its vital public interests (they are often referred to as "mandatory requirements" or as requirement of overriding public interest) applied in conformity with EC law, and in the absence of common harmonising rules in the relevant area. These mandatory requirements include the effectiveness of commercial transactions, the protection of public health, the fairness of commercial transactions and the defence of the consumer. The list of mandatory requirements is not exhaustive.

- It stated that the principle of proportionality is vital to the application of the rule of reason. Accordingly, indistinctly applicable measures enacted by a Member State must have effects which are proportionate to the aims they seek to achieve.

1365. [1979] ECR 649.

On the basis of the above principles, the ECJ held that the German Government's argument that alcoholic beverages with a low alcohol content may more easily induce a tolerance towards alcohol than alcoholic beverages with a higher alcohol content could not be accepted, taking into account that in the German market consumers could buy an extremely wide range of weak or moderately alcoholic products, most of them in a diluted form.

The defence based on the protection of consumers against unfair practices on the part of producers and distributors of alcoholic beverages by means of fixing minimum alcohol content was also rejected. In this respect the ECJ emphasised that this objective could be ensured by requiring the importers to display an indication of origin and the alcohol content on the packaging of products. Therefore the German Government did not provide any valid reason why alcoholic beverages lawfully produced and marketed in France should not be introduced into Germany. As a result, the unilateral requirement imposed by Germany of minimum alcohol content for the purposes of the sale of alcoholic beverages constituted a measure equivalent to a quantitative restriction and as such was incompatible with Article 28 EC [Article 34 TFEU].

The impact of the *Cassis de Dijon* judgment on the development of the free movement of goods is overwhelming.[1366] It can be said that the judgment provided the necessary legal tool to ensure free trade in the internal market:

- First, by putting the onus of proof on a Member State to justify a national measure, it has encouraged traders to challenge any attempt to restrict their commercial freedom;

- Second, it makes the scope of Article 28 EC [Article 34 TFEU] seem limitless as it prohibits all national rules hindering trade between Member States, including not only those relating to product specification but also those relating to their marketing.

20.7.1   The implications of the Cassis de Dijon case

Subsequent case law of the ECJ has clarified the principles laid down in *Cassis de Dijon*. The implications of the *Cassis de Dijon* case are dealt with below.

20.7.1.1   *The opportunity offered by the ECJ to Member States to justify national measures on the grounds of mandatory requirements has often been relied upon*

In the absence of EU rules in a particular area, a national measure that applies without discrimination to both domestic and imported products may escape the Article 34 TFEU prohibition if it is considered as being necessary in order to satisfy mandatory requirements. In *Cassis de Dijon* the

---

1366. "The decision in *Cassis* reinvigorated Article [28EC] [Article 34 TFEU] in an area where it had previously had minimal impact and where it had been widely assumed legislative harmonization of divergent national rules was required to eliminate obstacles to interstate trade. *Cassis de Dijon* is crucial to the integration of the market through the application of Article [28 EC] [Article 34 TFEU] by the courts", S. Weatherill and P. Beaumont, *EC Law*, 2nd edition, 1995, London: Penguin Books, p 494.

ECJ stated that mandatory requirements may relate in particular to the effectiveness of fiscal supervision, the protection of public health, the fairness of commercial transactions and the defence of the consumer. This list is not exhaustive. Therefore, it is always possible for a Member State to justify national legislation on the grounds of mandatory requirements which are not mentioned in *Cassis de Dijon*. Contrary to Article 36 TFEU, which contains an exhaustive list of possible justifications to the prohibition laid down in Article 34 TFEU, under *Cassis de Dijon* Member States are offered a wider choice. Subsequent case law of the ECJ shows that a number of mandatory requirements have been added to those enumerated in *Cassis de Dijon*. The following defences have been put forward by Member States.

20.7.1.1.1 The protection of consumers and the protection of public health

The ECJ has always strictly interpreted additional justifications available to Member States under the rule of reason. Only exceptionally have Member States been successful in this respect. Among cases in which the ECJ held that national measures may be necessary to protect consumers, it is interesting to mention Case 6/81 *BV Industrie Diensten Groep v J.A. Beele Handelmaatschappij BV*.[1367]

THE FACTS WERE:

Two Dutch undertakings were selling cable ducts; one imported them from Sweden and the other from Germany. The Swedish cable ducts were previously protected by a patent in Germany, The Netherlands and elsewhere; the German cable ducts were first imported into The Netherlands after the patent had expired. The first undertaking selling Swedish ducts wanted to stop the other undertaking from selling the German cable ducts in The Netherlands on the ground that they were a precise imitation of the Swedish cable ducts.

Held:

The ECJ held that national legislation prohibiting slavish imitations of products of a third party was justified on the ground that such slavish imitations were likely to confuse the consumers as to which products were genuine and which were imitations.

However, in Case 16/83 *Prantl*[1368] the ECJ held that when there was a close resemblance between a German bottle known as a bocksbeutel, in which expensive wine from a particular region of Germany was sold, and an Italian bottle traditional to Italy, in which cheap imported Italian wine was sold, Germany could not rely on the protection of consumers to prohibit the sale of the Italian wine in Germany. The ECJ emphasised that as long as the Italian bottle was traditional to Italy and not an imitation of the German bottle, there was no reason to prohibit its sale in Germany.[1369] The above judgments were delivered before the EC adopted common rules on

---

1367. Case 6/81 *Beele* [1982] ECR 707.
1368. [1984] ECR 1299.
1369. Contrast with Case C-317/91 *Deutsche Renault AG v Audi AG* [1993] ECR I-6227.

many aspects of the protection of intellectual property rights, in particular relating to the concept of confusion (see Chapter 21.6.2.2).

Another successful national limitation (that is, claim to a mandatory requirement) was invoked in Case 220/81 *Criminal Proceedings against Timothy Frederick Robertson and Others.*[1370]

THE FACTS WERE:

Criminal proceedings were commenced against Mr Robertson in Belgium for selling silver-plated cutlery from other Member States whose hallmarks were in breach of Belgian legislation. Under that legislation the sale in Belgium of silver-plated articles not stamped either with a Belgian hallmark or a hallmark of the Member State of exportation containing information equivalent to that provided by the Belgian hallmarks was prohibited.

Held:

The ECJ held that hallmarks must be intelligible to consumers of the Member State of importation and thus accepted the defence submitted by Belgium.

In most cases the ECJ held that national measures intended to protect consumers were not necessary and that the objectives pursued by national measures could be achieved by other means that would be less of a hindrance to trade between Member States, e.g. the *Cassis de Dijon* case itself.

In Case 207/83 *Commission v UK [Re Origin Marking of Retail Goods],*[1371] the issue was of whether origin-marking requirements imposed on all goods, whether imported or domestic, was a MEQR.

THE FACTS WERE:

Under UK legislation certain textiles, electrical and other goods offered for retail sale had to be marketed with or accompanied by an indication of their origin. The UK argued that for consumers it was necessary to have a clear indication of the country of origin of goods as it gave an indication of their quality.

Held:

The ECJ held that such a requirement merely enabled consumers to assert any prejudice they might have against foreign goods. UK legislation was contrary to Article 28 EC [Article 34 TFEU] as it slowed down the economic interchange between Member States. The ECJ held that manufacturers were free to indicate the country of origin but should not be compelled to do so.

1370. [1982] ECR 2349.
1371. [1985] ECR 1201.

20.7.1.1.2 The protection of the environment

In Case 302/86 *Commission v Denmark [Re Returnable Containers]*,[1372] the ECJ held that the protection of environment is a mandatory requirement which may restrict the scope of application of Article 28 EC [Article 34 TFEU].

THE FACTS WERE:

Under Danish law beer and soft drinks were required to be marketed only in containers that could be reused. Distributors of such products had to establish deposit-and-return schemes and recycle the containers. The containers had to be approved by the Danish National Agency for the Protection of Environment. The Danish Government acknowledged that these requirements were unduly onerous to foreign manufacturers and for that reason permitted the use of non-approved containers subject to very strict limits (3 000 hectolitres a year per foreign products). The Commission challenged these requirements as contrary to Article 28 EC [Article 34 TFEU].

Held:

In this case, the ECJ extended the list of mandatory requirements laid down in *Cassis de Dijon* to encompass the protection of the environment. However, in this particular case the ECJ rejected the justification submitted by the Danish Government based on the protection of the environment. The ECJ stated that the requirement for approval of the containers to be carried out solely by the Danish Agency was disproportionate and the concession for limited quantities was insufficient to remedy the violation of Article 28 EC [Article 34 TFEU].

The ECJ reached similar conclusions:

- In Case C-463/01 *Commission v Germany*,[1373] in which the ECJ condemned the German deposit system for non-reusable packaging as failing to comply with the principle of proportionality;

- In Case C-320/03 *Commission v Austria*,[1374] in which the ECJ condemned a ban on heavy trucks (more than 7.5 tonnes) using the A12, a major motorway between Germany and Italy (a major artery for transport of goods), in order to improve air quality in the Inn Valley through which the motorway passes, as disproportionate to the objective it sought to achieve.

20.7.1.1.3 The protection of the socio-cultural identity of a Member State

This justification was accepted by the ECJ in Cases 60 and 61/84 *Cinéthèque SA v Fédération Nationale des Cinémas Français*.[1375]

1372. [1988] ECR 4607.
1373. [2004] ECR I-11705.
1374. [2005] ECR I-9871.
1375. [1985] ECR 2605.

THE FACTS WERE:

French legislation prohibited the marketing of videos of films during the first year of the film's release, irrespective of whether the film was made in France or elsewhere, on the ground of the protection of the French film industry.

Held:

The ECJ held that the protection of cultural activities constitutes a mandatory requirement and that the French legislation was not in breach of Article 28 EC [Article 34 TFEU].

In Case 169/91 *Stoke-on-Trent City Council v B&Q Plc*,[1376] the ECJ recognised national and regional socio-cultural characteristics as a mandatory requirement covered by the rule of reason.

20.7.1.1.4 The improvement of working conditions

In Case C-312/89 *Union Départmentale des Syndicats CGT de L'Aisne v SIDEF Conforama*,[1377] the ECJ held that the protection of the working conditions of workers may constitute a mandatory requirement.

20.7.1.1.5 The maintenance of press diversity

In Case C-368/95 *Vereinigte Familiapress Zeitungsverlags- und vertriebs GmbH v Henrich Bauer Verlag*,[1378] the ECJ held that maintenance of press diversity may constitute an overriding requirement justifying a restriction on free movement of goods.

20.7.1.1.6 The prevention of fraud

In Case C-426/92 *Germany v Deutsches Milch-Kontor GmbH*,[1379] the ECJ recognised that the prevention of fraud constituted a legitimate concern of a Member State and as such may constitute a mandatory requirement.

20.7.1.1.7 The protection of young persons, i.e. below the age of 15

In Case C-244/06 *Dynamic Medien Vertriebs GmbH v Avides Media AG*,[1380] the ECJ held that the prohibition of e-mail order sales of image store media containing games which may be dangerous to young persons without prior examination by the relevant national authorities in the importing State may be justified by mandatory requirements in the public interest.

20.7.1.1.8 The protection of fundamental human rights

In Case C-112/00 *Eugen Schmidberger*, the ECJ accepted that the objective of safeguarding the protection of fundamental rights guaranteed under Articles 10 and 11 of the ECHR was a mandatory requirement.

1376. [1992] ECR I-6635.
1377. [1991] ECR I-997.
1378. [1997] ECR I-3689.
1379. [1994] ECR I-2757.
1380. [2008] ECR I-505.

In this case the task of the ECJ was not easy as the Court had to reconcile the requirements of fundamental human rights, namely the right to freedom of expression and the right to freedom of assembly as guaranteed respectively by Articles 10 and 11 of the ECHR, with the requirements of one of the fundamental freedoms of EC law, the free movement of goods. The ECJ accomplished this task with great wisdom. The ECJ recognised that neither of the relevant rights was absolute. The principle of the free movement of goods is subject to derogations set out in Article 30 EC [Article 36 TFEU] and to the overriding requirements of public interest under the rule of reason, as explained and developed by the ECJ since its judgment in *Cassis de Dijon*. Similarly Articles 10 and 11 of the ECHR may be subject to derogations justified by objectives in the public interest. In order to decide whether Member State interference with these rights can be justified, the ECtHR applies a four-tier test deciding:

- First, whether there has been interference by Member State authorities with the rights guaranteed under Articles 10 and 11 of the ECHR;

- Second, whether the interference has been "prescribed by law";

- Third, whether a Member State has pursued a legitimate aim while interfering with the exercise of the above rights; and

- Fourth, whether such interference is "necessary in a democratic society".

The ECJ applied the above test. In respect of the fourth tier, the ECJ assessed "what is necessary in a democratic society" in the light of the principle of proportionality and referred not only to its own case law but also to the judgments of the ECtHR.[1381]

20.7.1.2 A national measure indistinctly applicable to both domestic and imported products may be justified under the rule of reason in so far as it is proportional to the objective which such a national measure seeks to achieve

The principle of proportionality has played an essential role in excluding national measures when the objective they sought could be achieved by less stringent means. It has been applied in particular in relation to the use of generic names, presentation of products and the advertising of products. In Case 261/81 *Walter Rau Lebensmittelwerke v De Smedt*,[1382] national rules imposing certain requirements concerning the presentation of the product were examined.

THE FACTS WERE:

Under Belgian law margarine could only be sold in cube-shaped boxes in order to distinguish it from butter.

1381. Case C-368/95 *Familiapress* [1997] ECR I-3689; Case C-60/00 *Carpenter* [2002] ECR I-6279, and Eur. Court HR, *Steel and Others v. The United Kingdom* judgment of 23 September 1998, Reports of Judgments and Decisions 1998-VII, § 101.
1382. [1982] ECR 3961.

Held:

The ECJ held that the requirement was disproportionate since consumers would be sufficiently protected by appropriate labelling of the product. The ECJ emphasised that appropriate labelling would achieve the same objective as national measures with less hindrance to trade between Member States.

20.7.1.3 The principles laid down in Cassis de Dijon were established in order to remedy the absence of EU rules in a particular area

In a field in which the EU shares competences with Member States, once it legislates in a particular area Member States are precluded from enacting any legislative measures in that area which conflict with EU law. When national laws of the Member States have been harmonised at EU level, the legality of additional requirements imposed by a Member State in the harmonised area depends upon whether or not the EU harmonisation is complete or partial. This question arose in Case 29/87 *Dansk Denkavit v Ministry of Agriculture*.[1383]

THE FACTS WERE:

Directive 70/524 was enacted to harmonise all the national laws of the Member States with regard to both the presence of additives in, and the labelling requirements for, feed-stuffs. However, Danish importers of animal feed-stuff were required by Danish national law to obtain approval from the Danish authorities prior to import. In particular, foreign feed-stuffs were required to comply with certain procedural and labelling requirements which exceeded those specified in the Community directive harmonising procedures for such imports throughout the Community.

Held:

The ECJ held that Directive 70/524 was intended to harmonise all the material conditions for marketing feed-stuffs, including the identification of additives and their purity. Consequently, a Member State was prohibited from imposing additional health inspections not provided for by the Directive itself. As a result the justification based on the protection of public health was rejected by the ECJ.

However, sometimes it is difficult to distinguish which aspects have been harmonised and which are still within the competence of a Member State. This is well illustrated in Case C-162/97 *Gunnar Nilsson, Per Olov Hagelgren, Solweig Arrborn*.[1384]

1383. [1988] ECR 2965.
1384. [1998] ECR I-7477.

20.7.1.4   The principle of mutual recognition

The principle of mutual recognition sets out a presumption that goods which have been lawfully produced and marketed in one Member State can be introduced, without further restrictions, into other Member States. This entails that it is for the Member State of importation, and not for a trader, to prove otherwise. The principle of mutual recognition plays a vital role in respect of non-harmonised areas of EU law. The implementation of this principle has been enhanced by

Regulation 764/2008 laying down procedures relating to the application of certain national technical rules to products lawfully marketed in another Member State.[1385]

20.8 Article 34 TFEU: types of measures having equivalent effect to quantitative restrictions

These types of MEQRs are identified below.

20.8.1 National measures encouraging discrimination

Discrimination based on the nationality of goods is considered to be the worst type of discrimination. This is illustrated in Case 249/81 *Commission v Ireland [Re Buy Irish Campaign]*.[1386]

THE FACTS WERE:

The Irish Goods Council conducted a campaign to promote Irish products called "Buy Irish". The objectives of the campaign were set by the Irish Ministry of Industry, which also financed the campaign.

Held:

The ECJ held that the campaign was in breach of Article 28 EC [Article 34 TFEU] as it sought to substitute domestic goods for imported goods in the Irish market and thus check the flow of imports from other Member States. This was so notwithstanding the fact that the campaign was a failure and that the Irish Government adopted non-binding measures in promoting Irish products. The ECJ stated that the decisions of the Irish Council of Goods were capable of influencing the conduct of traders and consumers in Ireland.

A national scheme under which quality labels are awarded and subsequently affixed only to national products, even though a national producer can choose whether or not to apply for that label, constitutes a MEQR if the label underlines the national origin of the relevant product and thus encourages consumers to buy national products to the exclusion of imported products. Such a scheme was condemned in Case C-325/00 *Commission v Germany*.[1387] On the same ground in Case C-255/03 *Commission v Belgium*,[1388] the ECJ condemned a scheme set up by the Walloon Government instituting a "Walloon label of quality" attesting that the product on which it appeared was manufactured in Wallonia and that it possessed certain qualities and characteristics qualifying it for the award of the label. The Commission objected to any reference on the label to the geographical origin of the product. The ECJ agreed with the Commission.

1385. [2008] OJ l218/21.
1386. [1982] ECR 4005.
1387. [2002] ECR I-9977.
1388. [judgment of 17/06/2004 unpublished].

20.8.2 National measures which give preference to domestic products or confer some advantages on domestic products

The ECJ considers national measures which give preference to domestic products or confer some advantages on domestic products as discriminatory and thus they amount to MEQRs. This is exemplified in Case 72/83 *Campus Oil*.[1389]

THE FACTS WERE:

Irish legislation imposed on importers of petroleum products an obligation to acquire a certain percentage of their requirements from a state-owned refinery operating in Ireland at prices fixed by the competent Irish ministry. Thus, the Irish legislation gave preference to domestic products.

Held:

The ECJ held that the Irish legislation was in breach of Article 28 EC [Article 34 TFEU] but could be justified under Article 30 EC [Article 36 TFEU] on the basis of public security and public policy exceptions.

Another example is provided by Case 192/84 *Commission v Greece*.[1390]

THE FACTS WERE:

The Greek Government imposed on the Agricultural Bank of Greece an obligation not to finance any purchase of imported agricultural machinery unless there was proof that no similar machinery was manufactured in Greece.

Held:

The ECJ regarded this measure as an MEQR.

Similarly, in Case 263/85 *Commission v Italy*,[1391] Italian legislation which made provision of state aid to Italian public bodies conditional upon the purchase of vehicles made in Italy was held in breach of Article 28 EC [Article 34 TFEU], since it modified the flow of vehicles from other Member States and thus constituted a hindrance to the free movement of goods.

20.8.3 Restrictions relating to the price of goods

Price control may take various forms: price freezes, imposition of maximum or minimum prices, imposition of minimum or maximum profit margins, and resale price maintenance.

1389. [1984] ECR 2727.
1390. [1985] ECR 3967.
1391. [1991] ECR 1991.

In periods of high inflation governments may use a prices policy in order to stabilise the national economy and may impose a maximum selling price for a particular product in order to artificially limit its price. When inflation is low, governments may decide that certain categories of traders should achieve a minimum level of receipts. To achieve this objective a Member State may impose minimum prices for some goods.

The imposition of a maximum price was examined in Case 65/75 *Tasca*.[1392]

THE FACTS WERE:

The Italian authorities imposed a maximum price on both imported and domestic sugar. Tasca ignored this restriction and tried to sell sugar above the maximum price. When criminal prosecutions were commenced against him, he argued that the Italian law was contrary to Article 28 EC [Article 34 TFEU]

Held:

The ECJ held that while national legislation blocking price increases on sugar did not in itself constitute a measure having equivalent effect as it applied indistinctly to imported and domestic sugar, it may, in certain circumstances, be in breach of Article 28 EC [Article 34 TFEU]. This happens where a maximum selling price is fixed at such a low level that the sale of imported products becomes, if not impossible in the sense that the importer can trade only at a loss, at least, more difficult or costly than the disposal of domestic production.

The imposition of a minimum price was examined in Case 82/77 *Openbaar Ministerie v Van Tiggele*.[1393]

THE FACTS WERE:

Criminal proceedings were brought against Van Tiggele for selling gin below the national fixed price.

Held:

The ECJ stated that the fixing of a minimum price for both imported and domestic products was not in breach of Article 28 EC [Article 34 TFEU] provided it did not impede imports. The breach will occur "when a national authority fixes prices or profit margins at such a level that imported products are placed at a disadvantage in relation to identical domestic products either because they cannot profitably be marketed in the conditions laid down or because the competitive advantage conferred by lower prices is cancelled out". In this case the ECJ held that the Dutch law was in breach of Article 28 EC [Article 34 TFEU].

1392. [1976] ECR 291.
1393. [1978] ECR 25.

Joined Case 80/85 and 159/85 *Nederlandse Bakkerij Stichting and Others v Edah BV*,[1394] provides another example of national legislation fixing a minimum price.

THE FACTS WERE:

Dutch legislation imposed a minimum retail price for domestic and imported bread but added to the price of imported bread a compulsory distribution margin equal to the distribution costs of well-organised and efficiently operated distributors in The Netherlands.

Held:

The ECJ held that the Dutch legislation was an MEQR because the distribution margin was compulsory, even when the resulting selling price was higher than the minimum price applicable to domestically produced bread. The ECJ ruled that such a scheme would be lawful if the distribution margin for the sale of imported bread were the same as that taken into account in determining the fixed minimum price for domestic bread and was not compulsory for imported bread sold at or above that minimum price.

It is to be noted that in the light of the ECJ's judgment in *Keck* (see section 20.9), national rules relating to the price of goods are considered as being selling arrangements and thus outside the scope of Article 34 TFEU if they satisfy the criteria set out in *Keck*.

20.8.4 Import licences and other similar procedures applicable to imported products

The ECJ held that import licences and other similar procedures, even if they are only formalities, constitute MEQRs in so far as they intend to limit or delay importations.[1395] This is exemplified in Case 40/82 *Commission v UK [Re Imports of Poultry Meat]*.[1396]

THE FACTS WERE:

The UK introduced a licensing system for poultry imported from all Member States except Denmark and Ireland. This amounted in practice to a ban, in breach of Article 28 EC [Article 34 TFEU]. The UK argued that the system was necessary to protect the health of animals, in particular to prevent the spread of a highly contagious disease affecting poultry known as Newcastle disease.

Held:

The ECJ rejected this argument for a number of reasons. It appeared that the measure was introduced to respond to pressure by domestic poultry breeders concerned about the increased volume of imports of poultry from other Member States (especially from France);

1394. [1986] ECR 3359.
1395. Joined Cases 51–54/71 *International Fruit Company* [1971] ECR 1107; Case 68/76 *Commission v France* [1977] ECR 515; Case 41/76 *Donckerwolcke* [1976] ECR 1921.
1396. [1982] ECR 2793.

was imposed before Christmas (when consumers traditionally buy poultry, especially turkey); and there had been no outbreak of Newcastle disease in France for five years! All these reasons convinced the ECJ that the UK introduced the licensing system in order to safeguard commercial interests, in particular in the light of massive state aid granted to French poultry breeders by the French Government.

National measures which require that only persons established within a national territory may apply for a licence to sell products coming from other Member States are unlawful per se. In Case 155/82 *Commission v Belgium*,[1397] the ECJ condemned Belgian legislation restricting the right to apply for approval of pesticides for non-agricultural use and phytopharmaceutical products to persons established in Belgium. In Case 247/81 *Commission v Germany*,[1398] the ECJ condemned German law requiring that only undertakings having their headquarters in Germany were allowed to sell pharmaceutical products in Germany.

Prior authorisation procedures for importation of goods are not unlawful per se as they may be justified on the grounds of the protection of public health. However, such procedures must not impose unreasonable burdens on an applicant, must be readily accessible, capable of being brought to completion within a reasonable time, and if the procedure leads to a rejection of an application, that rejection must be open to challenge before national courts.[1399] This is exemplified in Case C-212/03 *Commission v France*.[1400]

THE FACTS WERE:

The French Government imposed a requirement of prior authorisations for the importation of homeopathic medicinal products for personal use, not effected by personal transport, in three types of situation as follows:

▪ *When such a product was authorised in France and in the Member State of purchase. The French Government argued that although the requirement was burdensome, in practice only 1 per cent of applications were made annually by nationals of Member States.*

Held:

The ECJ held that the requirement created an obstacle to the free movement of goods and that the mere fact that it existed, not the number of authorisations, was decisive in establishing the infringement.

Comment:

Indeed, Article 28 EC [Article 34 TFEU] does not recognise the de minimis rule and therefore the potential effect of the measure on the free movement of goods suffices to establish that it constitutes an unlawful restriction.

1397. [1983] ECR 531.
1398. [1984] ECR 1111.
1399. Case C-263/03 *Commission v France* [judgment of 12/10/2004] unpublished.
1400. [2005] ECR I-4213, see also Case C-244/06 *Dynamic Medien Vertriebs GmbH v Avides Media AG* [2008] ECR I-505.

> ▪ When a product was registered in another Member State in accordance with Directive 92/73 on the approximation of provisions relating to medicinal products and laying down additional provisions on homeopathic products.[1401] The Commission argued that the product at issue was registered in accordance with the Directive and thus presented no risk to health. The French Government claimed that Directive 92/73 did not lay down a mutual recognition procedure, but a simple obligation for Member States to take due account of registrations or authorisations already issued by another Member State. For that reason the view could not be taken that the Directive had established a sufficient degree of harmonisation of EC law to release the Member State of importation from responsibility for the persons concerned.
>
> *Held:*
>
> The ECJ upheld the argument of the Commission stating that since the product was registered in accordance with the Directive which guaranteed its safety, there was no necessity for further clinical tests and that in any event the French Government did not demonstrate that grounds of health protection required a prior authorisation procedure in respect of that product.
>
> ▪ When a product was not authorised in France but was authorised in the Member State of purchase.
>
> *Held:*
>
> The ECJ held that national authorities were free to require authorisation for such product but restated the requirements for the relevant procedures as mentioned above and emphasised that those procedures must comply with the principle of proportionality. In this case the authorisation procedure applied by the French authorities was found to be disproportionate because the same procedure was applied to both imports for personal use and imports for commercial purposes.

It is well established in EU law that the requirement of prior authorisation in respect of products which are authorised in one Member State and which are identical to ones that have already been authorised in a Member State of importation is in breach of Article 34 TFEU.[1402]

As to similar products, in Case C-201/94 *R v The Medicines Control Agency, ex parte Smith & Nephew Pharmaceutical*[1403] the ECJ held that a drug that was manufactured using the same formulation, the same active ingredient and having the same therapeutic effect as one that had already been authorised in the Member State of importation should be treated as being covered by the previous authorisation of the Member State of importation. The ECJ emphasised that the two drugs are not required to be "identical in all respects". The concept of similarity was further explained in Case C-74/03 *SmithKline Beecham plc*,[1404] in which the ECJ held that in order to assess similarity, the emphasis should be placed on the therapeutic effect of the product rather than on the precise molecular structure of the active ingredients. Accordingly, an unauthorised

---

1401. [1992] OJ L297/8.
1402. Case C-368/96 *Generics (UK) and Others* [1998] ECR I-7967.
1403. [1996] ECR I-5819.
1404. [2005] ECR I-595.

product is not to be found similar to an authorised product if it shows significant difference from the authorised product as regards its safety or efficacy.

It is important to note that in respect of authorisation procedures for medicinal products and homeopathic products there are harmonising measures at EU level which provide for simplified procedures or exemption of such products from any requirement of authorisation.[1405]

20.8.5 Phytosanitary inspections

Phytosanitary inspections constitute an effective way of excluding imported products from national markets, or at least of making imports or exports more difficult or more costly. Nevertheless, phytosanitary inspections may be justified under Article 36 TFEU. This occurred in Case 4/75 *Rewe-Zentralfinanz eGmbH v Landwirtschaftskammer*.[1406]

THE FACTS WERE:

Apples imported into Germany were subject to systematic sanitary inspections designed to control a pest called San José Scale that was not to be found in domestic apples.

Held:

The ECJ held that such inspections constituted MEQRs, although in this case they were justified as there was a genuine risk of spreading the disease to domestic apples if no inspection was carried out on imported apples.

Provided there is no discrimination against imported products and thus inspections are not arbitrary, they may be justified under Article 36 TFEU. However, systematic inspections, whether performed inside the national territory or at the borders, are arbitrary and result in making imports more difficult or costly.[1407] This happened in Case 35/76 *Simmenthal v Italian Minister for Finance*.[1408]

THE FACTS WERE:

Germany imposed mandatory health inspections on meat at its frontiers, for which inspection charges were imposed on importers.

Held:

The ECJ held that systematic health inspections carried out at frontiers are in breach of Article 28 EC [Article 34 TFEU], in particular the delays inherent in the inspections and the additional costs which the trader may incur are likely to make imports more difficult and more costly.

1405. For example Directive 2001/83/EC on the Community Code relating to Medicinal Products for Human Use [2001] OJ L311/67]; Directive 65/65/EEC relating to Proprietary Medicinal Products (amended many times) ([1965–1966] OJ, English Special Edition: Series I Chapter 1965–1966, p. 24); Directive 92/73/EEC, examined above in Case C-212/03 *Commission v France* [2005] ECR I-4213.

1406. [1975] ECR 843.

1407. Case C-272/95 *Dt. Milchkontor II* [1997] ECR I-1905.

1408. [1976] ECR 1871.

In Case 42/82 *Commission v France [Re Italian Table Wine]*,[1409] the issue of double inspections was examined by the ECJ.

THE FACTS WERE:

Italian wine imported into France was subject to a double control: first it was tested by the Italian authorities, then by the French authorities. Inspections conducted at the French frontier were systematic. The Italian wine was delayed at the French frontier for an excessive period of time pending the results of analyses carried out by French authorities.

Held:

The ECJ condemned these inspections for three reasons: they were carried out on a systematic basis, they caused excessive delay and they were discriminatory taking into account that domestic wine was not tested in a similar manner.

In Case C-293/94 *Brandsma*,[1410] the ECJ held that it would not be necessary to carry out technical analyses or laboratory tests on imported goods if they had already been conducted by another Member State.

In respect of inspections of foodstuffs Directive 93/99 of 29 October 1993[1411] lays down general principles governing such inspections. It applies to inspection of foodstuffs, namely food additives, vitamins, mineral salts, trace elements and to materials coming into contact with foodstuffs. Its main objective is to ensure that foodstuffs present no risks to public health and that no double inspections are conducted.

20.8.6   National measures relating to the protected geographical indication (PGI) and the protected designation of origin (PDO)

Under EU law PGI and PDO are symbols affixed to agricultural products or foodstuffs identifying their geographical origin and certifying that the products possess distinctive qualities, or reputation or other characteristics resulting from that specific geographical origin. PGIs and PDOs are distinct from indications of source, which merely specify that a product originates in a specific geographical region (for example: "Made in Germany", "Product of Poland") without any "quality" function. For producers PGIs and PDOs are valuable assets because consumers understand these symbols as conveying an assurance of quality and distinctiveness of products.

Protection of geographical indications (GIs) and of designations of origin (DOs) is necessary for both producers and consumers. With regard to producers they need to be protected against false use of PGIs and PDOs by unauthorised persons. Usurpation not only takes away business from original producers but mainly damages the established reputation of the products and thus erodes their value. As to consumers, they must not be misled. When they are buying a protected product, they must be certain that the product is genuine and not a worthless imitation.

1409. [1983] ECR 1013/14.
1410. [1996] ECR I-3159.
1411. [1993] OJ L290 14.

Protection afforded to GIs and DOs, whether under national law, EU law or international law, is similar to that afforded to trademarks and indeed in some countries (for example, the USA) GIs are protected through the trade mark system (a collective trademark is granted to producers in a particular region). PGIs and PDOs like trademarks give a monopoly right to their owners and serve the same purposes as trademarks: they identify the products, guarantee their quality and constitute an important business asset. The main difference is that a trademark is granted to a specific company/person to distinguish its products from those of other companies (for example, Christian Dior for perfumes and beauty products) while a PGI/PDO is given to all producers who make their products in the place indicated by a PGI/PDO and whose products share typical qualities. Accordingly, PGIs/PDOs highlight the geographical region of origin of goods and the characteristics which are derived from that region while trademarks focus on the producer or manufacturer of a product.

It is important to note that generic names are not protected under national or international law, including EU law, and thus any producer is free to use a generic name for its goods/services. A "generic" name is a geographical term used to designate a kind of product rather than indicate its origin. For example the term "Dijon mustard" is used to indicate a certain kind of mustard, regardless of its place of production.

The rules of the internal market relevant to intellectual property rights (IPRs) also apply to products protected under PGIs/PDOs, as both are IPRs.

The protection of GIs and DOs is ensured by Regulation 510/2006 of 20 March 2006.[1412] The Regulation applies to foodstuffs and agricultural products, whether or not processed, but not to alcoholic beverages which are protected by other EU legislation. The Regulation covers the following:

- PGIs refer to the name of a region, specific place or, in exceptional cases, a country from which a product originates; the product must possess a quality or reputation attributed to the geographical origin; and at least one of the stages of preparation/production/processing must take place in that defined geographical area. The raw material used in the production may come from another region.

- PDOs refer to the name of a region, specific place, or country from which a product originates; the quality or other characteristics of the product are essential or exclusively due to a particular geographical environment; and all stages of food production must take place in that defined geographical area.

The main distinction between PDOs and PGIs is that the geographical connection is stronger for PDOs than for PGIs, that is, for DOs the entire production must take place in the defined geographical area.

Under the Regulation only a group may submit an application for a PGI or a PDO. A group is described as any association of producers or processors working with the same agricultural product/foodstuffs. A natural or legal person is also regarded as a group. Such a group must have an appropriate interest to register the above names in order to protect their products against the sale of competing imitation products seeking to use the reputation of the name of origin.

An application for registration must be sent to the Member State in which the geographical

---

1412. [2006] OJ L93/12, which replaced Regulation 2081/92 of 14 July 1992.

area in which the product originates is located. The Member State must then ensure that the requirements for registration are satisfied and that if it adopts a favourable decision, such a decision is made public and can be subject to appeal.

The relevant Member State is required to forward its favourable decision to the Commission, which, if it agrees with that decision, will publish it in the OJ. If no objection is raised within six months of publication by any Member State or a third state or any natural or legal person having a legitimate interest, including those residing in a third country, the name of the product is entered into a register kept by the Commission and published in the OJ. If an objection is raised and is admissible according to the Commission, the Commission shall invite the interested parties to engage in consultations. If the parties reach an agreement within six months, the Commission, after ensuring that the agreement conforms to the requirements set out in the Regulation, registers the name and publishes its decision to that effect in the OJ. If no agreement is reached, the Commission decides whether or not to enter the name in the register, having regard to fair and traditional usage and the actual likelihood of confusion. Its decision is published in the OJ.

The case law on this topic shows that:

- The Regulation applies only where there is a direct link between both a specific quality, reputation or other characteristic of the product and its specific geographical origin;[1413]

- If the name of the product, although it relates to the place where it was originally produced or marketed, has become a common name for an agricultural product or a foodstuff (thus it has become a generic name), the registration will be refused;[1414]

- The use of PDO may be made conditional on certain operations, such as slicing, grating or packing of the relevant product, being carried out in the region of production. However, those operations are prohibited to third parties outside the region of production only if a condition to that effect is expressly provided for in the specification or registration. In Case C-108/01 *Consorzio del Prosciutto do Parma and Others v Asda Stores and Hygrade Foods Ltd*,[1415] such a condition had not been brought to the attention of Hygrade, which had purchased Parma ham from the claimants but was slicing and packaging it in the UK. The ECJ held that the principle of legal certainty requires that adequate publicity be given to those prohibitions and in the absence of such publicity, those prohibitions cannot be relied on before a national court;

- A Member State is prevented from adopting national laws which alter a designation of origin registered under the Regulation.[1416]

In Case C-132/05 *Commission v Germany*[1417] the ECJ clarified a number of issues concerning Regulation 2081/92/EC.

1413. Case C-312/98 *Shutzverband* [2000] ECR I-9187.
1414. Article 3 of the Regulation.
1415. [2003] ECR I-5121.
1416. Joined Cases C-129/97 and C-130/97 *Chiciak and Fromagerie Chiciak* [1998] ECR I-3315.
1417. [2008] ECR I-957.

THE FACTS WERE:

The Commission commenced proceedings against Germany under Article 226 EC [Article 258 TFEU] for breach of Regulation 2081/92/EC on the ground that Germany refused to take action on its own to stop the marketing of products sold under the name "Parmesan" in Germany which do not comply with the specification for the PDO "Parmigiano Reggiano".

Held:

The ECJ dismissed the infringement proceedings brought by the Commission against Germany on the grounds that "Reggiano" in located in Italy, not in Germany and therefore the responsibility for monitoring compliance with the specification for the PDO "Parmigiano Reggiano" lies with Italy, the Member State from which the PDO originates, not with Germany.

Comment:

The important points in this case were:

First, the ECJ noted that the term PDO "covers a situation where the term used to designate a product incorporates part of a protected designation, so that when the consumer is confronted with the name of the product, the image brought to his mind is that of the product whose designation is protected".[1418] With regard to "Parmesan" and "Parmigiano Reggiano" it is obvious that there is a phonetic and visual similarity between the two names as well as a similarity in the appearance of both products which are hard cheeses grated or intended to be grated.

Second, the ECJ rejected the argument submitted by Germany that the name "Parmesan" had become generic. Indeed, the onus of proof was on Germany which failed to convince the Court to that effect.

Third, once it was established that "Parmesan" was not a generic product, its commercialisation in Germany was in breach of Regulation 2081/92. Germany submitted that the interests of holders of PDOs, producers and consumers were sufficiently protected under German law as the interested parties could bring proceedings before German courts relying on direct effect of Regulation 2081/92 and further they could also base their claims on other relevant German legislation such as the law against unfair competition (Gesetz gegen den unlauteren Wettbewerb) of 7 June 1909 and the law on trade marks and other distinctive signs. Although the ECJ rejected the justification based on direct effect of Community law as exempting a Member State from taking necessary measures it held, nevertheless, that a Member State is not obliged to take on its own initiative measures required in order to penalise the infringement in its territory of PDOs originating from another Member State.

20.8.7   National measures relating to the use of generic names

Abusive restrictions on the use of generic names are regarded as MEQRs. This was examined in Case 286/86 *Ministère Public v Deserbais*.[1419]

1418.   Case C-87/97 *Consorzio per la tutela del formaggio Gorgonzola* [1999] ECR I-1301.

1419.   [1988] ECR 4907.

THE FACTS WERE:

French law stated that only cheese containing a minimum 40 per cent fat could use the name "Edam". Deserbais imported Edam cheese from Germany which was lawfully produced there but contained only 35 per cent fat. When criminal proceedings were brought against Deserbais, he argued that French law was contrary to Article 28 EC [Article 34 TFEU].

Held:

The ECJ held that French law was disproportionate to the objectives it sought to achieve. Consumers would be adequately protected by appropriate labelling informing them about the fat content of German Edam cheese.

A similar situation arose in Case 182/84 *Miro BV*.[1420]

THE FACTS WERE:

Under Dutch law a generic name "jenever" was used for gin containing a minimum 35 per cent alcohol. Criminal proceedings were brought against Miro BV for selling Belgian jenever which contained only 30 per cent alcohol in the Netherlands.

Held:

The ECJ held that the Dutch law was in breach of Article 28 EC [Article 34 TFEU], given that Belgian jenever was lawfully produced and marketed in Belgium and appropriate labelling of Belgian jenever in respect of its alcohol content would be sufficient to protect consumers. The ECJ so decided despite the fact that a higher tax was imposed in The Netherlands on Dutch jenever and thus it would be placed at a comparative disadvantage as compared to Belgian jenever.

In Case C-14/00 *Commission v Italy*,[1421] the generic name "chocolate" was at issue.

THE FACTS WERE:

Italian legislation prohibited the marketing in Italy of cocoa and chocolate products containing vegetable fats other than cocoa butter under the sales name "chocolate". Such products could only be marketed under the name "chocolate substitute". However, the marketing of products containing vegetable fats other than cocoa butter under the name of "chocolate" was permitted in other Member States. Accordingly, the Commission argued that the Italian legislation was an MEQR.

1420. [1985] ECR 3731.
1421. [2003] ECR I-513.

> **Held:**
>
> The ECJ held that the name "chocolate substitute" could discourage consumers from buying the product as the word "substitute" suggests an inferior product as compared to the original product. Accordingly, the Italian legislation was in breach of Article 28 EC [Article 34 TFEU].

20.8.8 National measures imposing restrictions on use of certain ingredients in foodstuffs

The question of permissible ingredients in foods has arisen in a significant number of cases: for instance, in respect of pain brioché,[1422] bread,[1423] alcoholic beverages,[1424] pasta, cheese, and so on.

The position of the ECJ on the matter is that in the absence of EU rules, a Member State is allowed to regulate these matters provided that its rules do not discriminate against imported products or hinder their importation. Thus, it is for a Member State concerned to produce scientific data supporting its claim that prohibited ingredients constitute danger to health. If no such evidence is provided, then national rules are in breach of the principle of proportionality given that a Member State, by prescribing suitable labelling, could have given consumers the desired information regarding the composition of the product.

There are many EC directives and regulations regulating the use of certain ingredients in foodstuffs. Among them are:

- Directive 2002/46/EC on the approximation of the laws of the Member States relating to food supplements,[1425] which covers a wide range of vitamins and minerals which might be present in food supplements. In its annex there is a list of vitamins and minerals that may be used for the manufacture of food supplements;[1426]

- Regulation 258/97 concerning novel foods and novel food ingredients;[1427] and

- Regulation 178/2002 laying down the general principles and requirements of food law, establishing the European Food Safety Authority and laying down procedures in matters of food safety.[1428]

With regard to additives, since 1985, under the new approach towards technical harmonisation and standards, the conditions relating to their use have been unified by Framework Directive 89/

1422. Case 130/80 *Kelderman* [1981] ECR 527 dealing with a particular sort of French bread.
1423. Case C-17/93 *Van der Veldt* [1994] ECR I-3537; Case C-123/00 *Bellamy and English Shop Wholesale* [2001] ECR I-2795. In both cases Belgian legislation prohibiting the marketing of bread and other bakery products whose salt content by reference to dry matter exceeds the maximum permitted level of 2 per cent was condemned by the ECJ as an MEQR.
1424. Case 27/80 *Fietje* [1980] ECR 3839.
1425. [2002] OJ L183/51.
1426. The validity of the Directive was confirmed by the ECJ in Joined Cases C-154/04 and C-155/04 *The Queen, on the application of: Alliance for Natural Health, Nutri-Link Ltd v Secretary of State for Health* (Case C-154/04) and *The Queen, on the application of: National Association of Health Stores and others v Secretary of State for Health and National Assembly for Wales* (Case C-155/04) [2005] ECR I-6451.
1427. [1997] OJ L43/1.
1428. [2002] L31/1.

107/EEC.[1429] EU measures are based on the "positive list" of additives that enumerate those which are permitted in food. All other additives are prohibited. In order to be on the positive list an additive must satisfy stringent criteria:

- From a technical point of view there must be a sufficient need for such an additive;

- The pursued purpose of using an additive must not be capable of being achieved by using other means which are economically or technically practicable;

- The additive must present no danger whatsoever to health; and

- Use of the additive should not confuse consumers.

20.8.9 National measures imposing an obligation to use the national language

In Case C-33/97 *Colim NV v Bigg's Continent Noord NV*,[1430] the ECJ restated its case law on linguistic requirements. The ECJ made a distinction between linguistic requirements imposed by Community law and information required by national law to appear on imported products. A Member State cannot impose additional language requirements if a Community measure fully harmonises language requirements. However, in the absence of full harmonisation of language requirements applicable to information appearing on imported products, a Member State may adopt national measures requiring such information to be provided in the language of the area in which the products are sold or in another language which may be readily understood by consumers in that area. In order to decide whether the language is easily understood by the consumers account should be taken of such factors as "the possible similarity of words in different languages, the widespread knowledge amongst the population concerned of more than one language, or the existence of special circumstances such as a wide-ranging advertising campaign or widespread distribution of the product, provided that it can be established that the consumer is given sufficient information".[1431] In the light of those factors it was not surprising that in Case C-366/98 *Geffroy and Casino France SNC*,[1432] the ECJ held that an importer of Coca-Cola who bought it in the UK labelled in English and then sold it in France, contrary to the French law requiring all labels to be in French, did not need to make any changes to the English label given that the product was well known worldwide.

In Case C-33/97 *Colim*, the ECJ held that imposition of linguistic requirements in the pre-sale stage, i.e. on a producer in respect of importers, wholesalers and retailers, is in breach of Article 34 TFEU. They are not necessary given that persons involved in the distribution of goods are familiar with them or can always ask the producers for more information.

1429. [1989] OJ L40/27. The Directive was replaced by Regulation 1332/2008 of the European Parliament and of the Council of 16 December 2008 on food additives ([2008] OJ L354/16) which entered into force on 10 January 2010. The Regulation provides a common basis for controls on food additives, food flavouring and food enzyme.

1430. [1999] ECR I-3175, see Case C-85/94 *Piageme* [1995] ECR-I-2955; C-369/89 *Piageme* [1991] ECR I-2971 and Case C-51/93 *Meyhui* [1994] ECR I-3879.

1431. Case C-85/94 *Piageme and Others v Peeters NV* [1995] ECR I-2955.

1432. [2000] ECR I-6579.

20.8.10 National measures restricting distance selling (e.g. via the internet or by mail order)

The ECJ held national measures restricting distance selling concern selling arrangements[1433] (see section 20.9).

20.8.11 National measures restricting advertisement

The judgment of the ECJ in Joined Cases C-267 and 268/91 *Criminal Proceedings against Keck and Mithouard*[1434] changed the way in which the compatibility of national rules relating to the advertising of products with Article 28 EC [Article 34 TFEU] should be assessed.

One of the consequences of the *Keck* judgment is that a distinction must be made between advertisement on the label and other forms of advertisement. The ECJ regards advertisement on the label as being incorporated into the product and thus to concern the product itself[1435] and as such is within the scope of Article 34 TFEU, while other forms of advertisement, such as advertisement on TV, on the radio or in the press, are considered by the Court as being selling arrangements. This was examined in Case C-368/95 *Vereinigte Familiapress Zeitungsverlags- und Vertriebs GmbH v Henrich Bauer Verlag*.[1436]

THE FACTS WERE:

Austrian legislation prohibited the sale of periodicals containing games or competitions for prizes. On the basis of this legislation an order was issued against Henrich Bauer Verlag, the German publisher of the weekly magazine "Laura", which was distributed in Germany and Austria and which contained a crossword puzzle offering readers sending the correct solution the opportunity to enter a draw for prizes of DM500, to cease to sell "Laura" in Austria. The publisher claimed that the Austrian law was a QR contrary to Article 28 EC. The Austrian Government argued that the prohibition concerned a method of promoting sales and as such was a selling arrangement outside the scope of Article 28 EC [Article 34 TFEU].

Held:

The ECJ held that:

"Even though such legislation is directed against a method of sales promotion, it bears on the actual content of the products, in so far as the competitions in question form an integral part of the magazine in which they appear, and cannot be concerned with a selling arrangement."

The above case shows the difficulty of drawing a clear line between product characteristics and selling arrangements. This issue is examined below.

1433. Case C-244/06 *Dynamic Medien Vertriebs GmbH v Avides Media AG* [2008] ECR I-505.
1434. [1993] ECR I-6097.
1435. Case C-470/93 *Mars* [1995] ECR I-1923.
1436. [1997] ECR I-3689.

20.9   Article 34 TFEU: national measures relating to selling arrangements

The *Cassis de Dijon* case gave a new impetus to the exercise of the right to the free movement of goods within the Community. Following this judgment, any national rule indistinctly applicable, regardless of whether it concerned the product itself or the way it was marketed was prohibited, save in the exceptional circumstances set out in the rule of reason and in Article 30 EC [Article 36 TFEU]. Further, the rule of recognition, which requires a Member State to respect the manner in which a product was manufactured and commercialised in another Member State, created a presumption that once a product has been lawfully produced and marketed in one Member State, it is entitled to free circulation within the Community. Following the *Cassis de Dijon* case traders were vigorously enforcing their rights under Article 28 EC [Article 34 TFEU] by challenging any national rule restricting their commercial freedom, even though the rule affected general conditions of trading in a Member State and had little effect on the integration of the internal market. The above is exemplified by the long-running saga of the cases dealing with the compatibility of the UK Sunday trading laws with Article 28 EC [Article 34 TFEU].

In the Sunday trading laws cases Section 47 of the Shops Act 1950 prohibited the opening of shops in England and Wales on Sundays except for the sale of certain "essential" items. The owners of shops were prosecuted by their local authorities for opening their shops on Sundays contrary to this statute. In their defence, they claimed that the prohibition was contrary to Article 28 EC [Article 34 TFEU] because it entailed a restriction on trade which had a discriminatory effect on the sale of goods from other Member States, and they evidenced this by showing the reduction in their total weekly sales, including imported goods, resulting from the application of the Shops Act.

The ECJ's answers to the Sunday Trading cases lacked clarity and direction. In Case 145/88 *Torfaen Borough Council v B & Q plc*,[1437] the ECJ's judgment was so unclear that national courts used it both to justify[1438] and to reject[1439] the compatibility of the Shops Act with Article 28 EC [Article 34 TFEU]. In Case C-169/91 *Council of the City of Stoke-on-Trent and Norwich City Council v B & Q plc*,[1440] the ECJ delivered a very short judgment stating that the statute was compatible with Article 28 [Article 34 TFEU] as it had a legitimate socio-economic function which was recognised under Community law. This case by case approach did not offer any guidelines to national courts. However, those judgments indicated that the ECJ was, on the one hand, reluctant to limit the scope of Article 28 EC [Article 34 TFEU], but on the other hand, was not immune to criticism that its case law should be reassessed given that it went beyond market integration into the realms of national laws that affected the volume of trade of all goods, whether domestic or imported, to an equal extent.

A reassessment of the pre-existing case law on Article 28 EC [Article 34 TFEU] and a new strategy for regulating the internal market came from the ECJ in Joined Cases C-267 and 268/91 *Criminal Proceedings against Keck and Mithouard*,[1441] in which the ECJ moved away from the

---

1437.   [1989] ECR 3851.

1438.   E.g. the *Torfean* case, ibid, and *Wellingborough Borough Council v Payless* [1990] 1 CMLR 773.

1439.   *B&Q v Shrewsbury BC* [1990] 3 CMLR 535.

1440.   [1992] ECR I-6635.

1441.   [1993] ECR I-6097.

wide application of the *Dassonville* formula and thus set new limits on Article 28 EC [Article 34 TFEU].

THE FACTS WERE:

The French authorities commenced criminal proceedings against Keck and Mithouard for selling goods at a price lower than they had paid for them (resale at a loss), which was in breach of a French law of 1963 as amended in 1986, although that law did not ban sales at a loss by manufacturers. Both alleged offenders argued that the law in question was contrary to fundamental freedoms under the EC Treaty, that is, to the free movement of goods, persons, services and capital, as well as being in breach of EC competition law. The French court referred to the ECJ.

Held:

The ECJ dismissed all the arguments except one based on the free movement of goods. The Court held that the Dassonville formula did not apply to selling arrangements if national rules, which prima facie appear to be contrary to Article 28 EC [Article 34 TFEU], satisfy two conditions:

■ They apply indistinctly to all traders operating within the territory of a Member State; and

■ They affect in the same manner, in law and in fact, the marketing of both domestic and imported products even though they may have some impact on the overall volume of sales.

Once these two conditions are satisfied, such national rules fall outside the scope of Article 28 EC [Article 34 TFEU]. This is so, even though the national rule may have some negative impact on the overall volume of sales of imported products.

Keck does not modify the principles laid down in *Cassis de Dijon*; it relates to the *Dassonville* formula. In particular, it excludes from the scope of Article 28 EC [Article 34 TFEU] indistinctly applicable measures which relate to selling arrangements.

20.9.1 The scope of application of *Keck*: the distinction between measures relating to the product itself and to the selling arrangements

There is neither a definition of "measures relating to the product itself" (that is, the characteristics of the product), nor of "measures relating to selling arrangements". However, some useful indications have been provided by the ECJ allowing a distinction to be made between them.

20.9.1.1 *National measures relating to characteristics of the product*

In *Keck* the ECJ gave some examples of national measures relating to products themselves. Such measures concern name, designation, form, size, weight, composition, presentation, labelling and packaging of goods. Other measures can be identified from the post-*Keck* case law of the ECJ. They are:

■ Requirements relating to formalities concerning the act of importation, such as the issue of a licence prior to the carrying-on of certain economic activity[1442] and licensing requirements relating to the characteristics of the products;[1443]

■ Requirements relating to the manufacturing/growing of the product in question.

The last-mentioned requirements were examined in Case C-158 and 159/04 *Alfa Vita Vassilopoulos AE*.[1444] The case concerned requirements imposed by a Greek regulation on supermarkets, where "bake-off" products were only briefly thawed and reheated. The requirements were that such supermarkets must have "a flour store, an area for kneading equipment and a solid-fuel store", these being requirements normally imposed on traditional bakeries. The ECJ held that the requirements were related to the process of final production and baking of bread and therefore affected the nature of the product itself, and accordingly could not be regarded as a selling arrangement such as contemplated in *Keck*. Therefore, they were MEQRs.

The *Alfa Vita* case should be distinguished from Case C-416/00 *Morellato*,[1445] which also concerned "bake-off" products. In *Morellato*, Italian law required a trader or distributor to package bread baked from frozen or non-frozen part-baked bread before offering it for sale. Both the Commission and the AG in his opinion in this case argued that such a requirement related to the characteristics of the product (that is, the packaging). The ECJ disagreed. It held that the requirement was imposed after the production process had been completed including the final baking prior to offering for sale, which took place in the Member State of importation. Accordingly, the requirement for prior packaging related only to the marketing of the bread and as such was outside the scope of Article 28 EC [Article 34 TFEU]. This was provided that the requirement did not, in reality, constitute discrimination against imported products, which matter was left to the referring court to assess.

The two above cases illustrate the difficulties in distinguishing between national measures relating to the characteristics of the product and those relating to the selling arrangements.

Another example is provided in Case C-147/04 *De Groot en slot Allium BV*[1446] which concerned two different varieties of a type of onion known as shallots. One was produced by vegetative propagation in France, that is, by direct reproduction from the roots; the other was grown from seed in The Netherlands. The ECJ found French legislation permitting only shallots produced by vegetative propagation to be marketed as shallots in France, and thus preventing the marketing of Dutch shallots in France, to be in breach of Article 28 EC [Article 34 TFEU]. It constituted an MEQR because it concerned the propagation of the product and thus related to its characteristics. The final product, irrespective of the way it was reproduced, was identical.

1442. Case C-120/95 *Decker* [1998] ECR I-1831; Case 124/81 *Commission v United Kingdom [UHT Milk]* [1983] ECR 203; Case C-304/88 *Commission v Belgium* [1990] ECR I-2801; Case C-212/03 *Commission v France* [2005] ECR I-4213; Case 434/04 *Jan-Erik Anders Ahokainen and Mati Leppik* [2006] ECR I-9171.

1443. For example, Case C-389/96 *Aher-Waggon* [1998] ECR I-4473; Case C-189/95 *Franzén* [1997] ECR I-5909; C-390/99 *Canal Satélite Digital* [2002] ECR I-607.

1444. [2006] ECR I-8135.

1445. [2003] ECR I-9343.

1446. [2006] ECR I-245.

20.9.1.2   *National measures relating to selling arrangements*

The concept of selling arrangements is difficult to define. On the basis of the case law of the ECJ subsequent to *Keck*, the national measures, examined below, were found to relate to selling arrangements.

20.9.1.2.1 National rules relating to resale at a loss and national rules relating to the fixing of prices

In Case C-63/94 *Belgapom v ITM Belgium SA and Vocarex SA*,[1447] the ECJ confirmed its ruling in *Keck*. In this case the scenario was very similar to *Keck* as it concerned the Belgian law on Commercial Practices and Consumer Protection (1991) which prohibited resale at a loss.

THE FACTS WERE:

The Belgian law defined resale at a loss as taking place when "the price is not at least equal to the price at which the product was invoiced at the time of supply". Also under that legislation any sale yielding very low profit margins was considered as being within its scope. When Vocarex, a franchisee of ITM, bought a consignment of potatoes at BF27 per 25 kg and resold them at BF29 per 25 kg, it was accused by Belapom of selling at a loss, taking into account that all other Belgian outlets had agreed to sell at BF89 per 25 kg. Vocarex argued that the Belgian law was in breach of Article 28 EC [Article 34 TFEU].

Held:
The Court held that Article 28 EC [Article 34 TFEU] did not apply to this situation as it concerned selling arrangements.

In Case C-531/07 *Fachverband der Buch- und Medienwirtschaft v LIBRO Handelsgesellschaft mbH*,[1448] the ECJ held that national rules which fix prices are to be regarded as selling arrangements. In this case Austrian legislation imposed an obligation on importers of German-language books to sell books at prices fixed in the country of publication (Germany). Although the ECJ ruled that the Austrian law was a selling arrangement it also found that since Austrian law put importers at a disadvantage in comparison with local publishers, who could freely fix the price, the legislation was within the scope of Article 28 EC [34 TFEU]. The Austrian legislation could not be justified on the ground of the protection of cultural diversity under Article 30 EC [Article 36 TFEU] because this justification does not come within the "protection of national treasures possessing artistic, historic or archaeological value". Nevertheless, the protection of books as cultural objects could be considered as an overriding requirement in the public interest capable of justifying measures restricting the free movement of goods, but in this case Austrian law was in breach of the principle of proportionality as the objectives it pursued could have been achieved by less intrusive means.

1447. [1995] ECR I-2467.
1448. [2009] ECR I-3717.

20.9.1.2.2 National rules relating to advertising

In Case C-292/92 *Hünermund v Landesapothekerkammer Baden-Württemberg*,[1449] the ECJ examined national rules on advertising.

THE FACTS WERE:

German rules established by a professional body imposed a partial ban on advertising by pharmacists in order to restrict excessive competition among them. Pharmacists were not allowed to advertise on the radio, on TV or at the cinema. They were allowed to advertise in newspapers and magazines but only to state their address, the name and phone number of the practice and the name of the proprietor. Hünermund challenged these rules.

Held:

The ECJ held that the German rules applied to all pharmacists and thus were indistinctly applicable. Further, the ECJ confirmed that advertisement as a method of sales promotion was a selling arrangement and as such was outside the scope of Article 28 EC [Article 34 TFEU].

The application of *Keck* to advertising was confirmed in Case C-412/93 *Société d'Importation Eduard Leclerc-Siplec v TFI Publicité SA and M6 Publicité SA*,[1450] in which French legislation prohibiting the broadcasting of televised advertisements for the distribution sector (in this case advertisements concerning the "distribution of fuel" in Leclerc supermarkets) was held by the ECJ to relate to selling arrangements and thus was outside the scope of Article 28 EC [Article 34 TFEU].

20.9.1.2.3 National rules regarding business opening hours including closing of shops on Sundays and bank holidays

In Joined Cases 69 and 258/93 *Punto Case SpA v Sindaco del Commune di Capena*,[1451] an Italian law requiring a total closure of shops on Sundays and public holidays was regarded as relating to selling arrangements.

20.9.1.2.4 National rules conferring a monopoly right to distribute certain products to a specific group of people

In Case 391/92 *Commission v Greece [Re Processed Milk for Infants]*,[1452] Greek legislation reserved to pharmacists the distribution of pharmaceutical products. The ECJ, contrary to its previous decision in Case 369/88 *Delattre*,[1453] considered that the Greek legislation related to selling arrangements and thereby was outside the scope of Article 28 EC [Article 34 TFEU].

1449. [1993] ECR I-6787.
1450. [1995] ECR I-179.
1451. [1994] ECR I-2355. See also: Joined Cases 401–402/92 *Tankstation't Heukske and Boermans* [1994] ECR I-2199; Joined Cases 418–421/93, 460–462/93, 464/93 and 9–11/94, 14 and 15/94, 23 and 24/94, 332/94 *Semeraro* [1996] ECR I-2975.
1452. [1995] ECR I-1621.
1453. [1991] ECR I-1487 and Case 60/89 *Monteil and Sammani* [1991] ECR I-1561.

20.9.1.2.5 National rules relating to distance selling, e.g. via the internet or by mail order

In Case C-322/01 *Deutscher Apothekerverband*,[1454] German legislation restricted the sale of most medicinal products for human use to pharmacies located in Germany, and thus prevented their importation by way of mail order through pharmacies approved in other Member States in response to individual orders placed by consumers over the internet. The ECJ held that the German legislation related to a selling arrangement but nevertheless was within the scope of Article 28 EC [Article 34 TFEU], because for pharmacies not established in Germany the internet provided a significant way to gain direct access to the German market. Thus, the prohibition had a greater impact on them and could impede access to the German market for their products more than it impeded access for domestic products.

20.9.1.2.6 National rules governing "itinerant" sales

In Case C-254/98 *TK-Heimdienst*,[1455] the requirement imposed on traders, who were operating sales rounds of foodstuffs in a specific administrative district of Austria, to trade from permanent establishments in that district or in any municipality adjacent thereto was regarded as relating to selling arrangements. Door-to-door sales were categorised as selling arrangements in Case C-20/03 *Burmanjer*[1456] (sale of national periodicals) and in Case C-441/04 *A-Punkt Schmuckhandels GmbH v Claudia Schmidt*[1457] (sale of silver jewellery).

20.9.1.2.7 Assessement

It is submitted that national measures fall within the category of a selling arrangement if they relate to any of the following:

- Conditions and methods of marketing of goods;
- The times and places of the sale of goods;
- Advertisement of goods.

20.9.2 *Keck*: Its legal consequences

The legal consequences of *Keck* are examined below.

20.9.2.1 Obsolete judgments

The most obvious consequence is that a number of previous judgments of the ECJ are obsolete, in particular in the areas examined above.

20.9.2.2 Exclusion, from the scope of Article 34 TFEU, of national rules relating to selling arrangements which do not discriminate against imported goods

National rules relating to selling arrangements which satisfy the conditions set out in *Keck* are excluded from the scope of application of *Cassis de Dijon*. As a result the principle of

---

1454. [2003] ECR I-14887.
1455. [2000] ECR I-151.
1456. [2005] ECR I-4133.
1457. [2006] ECR I-2093.

proportionality cannot be applied to them. This means that the CJEU has no jurisdiction to control whether a national measure that applies to selling arrangements, is necessary and appropriate to the objective pursued by a Member State.

20.9.2.3 Difficulty in determining whether a particular national rule concerns the nature of the product itself or the selling arrangements

The question of how to determine whether a particular national rule concerns the nature of the product itself or the selling arrangements poses considerable difficulty.[1458] In this respect *Keck* has introduced a false dichotomy between the rules relating to selling arrangements and the rules relating to the characteristics of the product. The cases of *Morellato* and *Alfa Vita* (see above) are some of many in which even the AG and the Commission, not mentioning the national courts, had doubts as to the correct categorisation of national measures at issue. This also occurred in Case C-244/06 *Dynamic Medien Vertriebs GmbH v Avides Media AG*.[1459]

THE FACTS WERE:

Avides Media, a German company, imported from the UK to Germany Japanese cartoons called "Animes" in DVD or video cassette format. Prior to the importation the cartoons were classified by the British Board of Film Classification ("the BBFC") under the relevant provisions of British legislation relating to the protection of young persons as being "suitable only for 15 years and over". The image storage media bore a BBFC label stating that they may be viewed only by persons aged 15 years or older. Dynamic Medien, a competitor of Avides Media, asked the competent German court for an interim measure prohibiting Avides Media from selling such image storage media by mail order in Germany on the ground that German law on the protection of young persons prohibits the sale by mail order of image storage media which has not been examined in Germany in accordance with that Law, and which do not bear an age-limit label corresponding to a classification decision from the competent German authority.

Held:

German law constituted a MEQR and could only be justified under Article 30 EC [Article 36 TFEU] or under the rule of reason laid down in the *Cassis de Dijon* case.

The ECJ found that German law was justifiable on a number of grounds and was proportionate to the objective it pursued.

Comment:

Advocate-General Mengozzi in his Opinion concluded that the national measure constituted a selling arrangement because the German law did not appear to impose an obligation for image storage media, whether imported or not, to be examined and classified by the competent German authority, and to be labelled accordingly. The ECJ disagreed. It held that under

---

1458.   Case C-368/95 *Familiapress* [1997] ECR I-3689.
1459.   [2008] ECR I-505.

German law there was the need to adapt the products in question to the rules in force in the Member State. Therefore the German law was a MEQR because the importers needed to alter the labelling of their products.

It emerges from the case law of the ECJ that some rules, which at first glance relate to selling arrangements, in due course were found by the ECJ as relating to the characteristics of the product. For example, national rules on advertisement are categorised as selling arrangements but advertisements on the label, as illustrated by Case C-470/93 *Mars*,[1460] relate to the product itself, because, as the ECJ held in that case, such measures can:

"compel the importer to adjust the presentation of his products according to the place where they are to be marketed and consequently to incur additional packaging and advertisement costs."

Further, in some cases, the ECJ did not apply the distinction between product related restrictions and those concerning selling arrangements and instead focused only on the effects of the challenged national rules.[1461]

20.9.2.4 The undermining of the fundamental importance of selling arrangements

Another consequence of *Keck* can be appreciated when consideration is given to the fundamental importance that selling arrangements, especially advertising, have acquired in the developed market economy rooted on competition. Without carrying out any sophisticated economic analysis it is obvious that products imported into one Member State from other Member States, especially products new to the market in a Member State and those intended for a mass market, will always be more affected by national rules prohibiting or restricting advertisement, or otherwise restricting or banning their marketing, than will domestic products. This is factual discrimination. Therefore, a straightforward exclusion of national rules relating to selling arrangements from the scope of Article 28 EC [Article 34 TFEU] does not take into account the fact that such measures are not only capable of creating serious obstacles to the free movement of goods but, in fact, always restrict marketing opportunities for imported goods as compared with domestic goods. The factual discrimination may either be insignificant or indeed so serious as to constitute a substantial barrier to access to the market in a Member State. In order to determine the magnitude of the barrier to market access represented by national rules, the best approach is to assess them in the light of the principles of proportionality. Unfortunately, under *Keck* this principle cannot be applied.

In the above context, the question arises on what basis should it be decided whether or not *Keck* applies to a particular situation. The ECJ has never identified the criteria required for the application of *Keck*, which criteria would, if known, provide clear guidance as to the means of:

1460. [1995] ECR I-1923, see also Case C-368/95 *Familiapress*, supra note 1458.
1461. See Case C-323/93 *Centre d'Insémination de la Crespelle* [1994] ECR I-5077, para 29, concerning French rules requiring economic operators importing semen from another Member State to deliver it to a centre enjoying an exclusive concession, and Case C-189/95 *Franzén* [1997] ECR I-5909, para 71, concerning the Swedish rules on import and marketing of alcoholic beverages.

- Verifying in practice whether or not national rules affect the marketing of imported products and of domestic products in the same manner; and

- Assessing the degree of impediment that national rules represent for imported products in terms of their access to the market in a Member State.

20.9.2.5 Difficulty in the application of Article 34 TFEU

The *Keck* approach calls into question the simplicity and uniformity of the application of Article 34 TFEU. In *Keck* the ECJ explained that a new approach to Article 28 EC [Article 34 TFEU] was necessary in order to clarify its case law and to curtail the growing tendency of traders to rely on Article 28 EC [Article 34 TFEU] in order to challenge national rules restricting their commercial freedom, even though such rules were not aimed at producers from other Member States.

It is submitted that in the light of the post-*Keck* decisions emanating from the ECJ this explanation is less than convincing. Indeed, instead of clarifying the application of Article 34 TFEU, *Keck* has become a source of confusion and controversy. It is also submitted that the application of *Keck* is contrary to the philosophy of Article 34 TFEU which, in order to ensure unfettered access to national markets for goods coming from other Member States, requires the abolition of any measure which constitutes an obstacle to the free movement of goods.

20.9.3 The access to the market test – the case of *Gourmet*

The growing unease in relation to the application of *Keck* to selling arrangements was acknowledged by the ECJ in Case 405/98 *Konsumentombudsmannen (KO) v Gourmet International Products AB (GIP)*.[1462]

THE FACTS WERE:

Swedish legislation totally banning the advertisement on radio, television and in periodicals and other publications of alcoholic beverages containing more than 2.25 per cent alcohol by volume, but allowing such advertisement in the specialist press (that is, the press addressed to manufacturers and restaurateurs, and publications distributed solely at the point of sale of such beverages), was challenged by Gourmet International Products AB (Gourmet), a Swedish publisher of a magazine entitled "Gourmet", as being in breach of EC law, inter alia, of Article 28 EC [Article 34 TFEU]. Gourmet published in "Gourmet" three pages of advertisements for alcoholic beverages, one for red wine and two for whisky. These pages did not appear in the edition sold in shops but in the edition addressed to subscribers of the magazine, 90 per cent of whom were manufacturers and retailers and 10 per cent private individuals. The Swedish Consumer Ombudsman applied to the Stockholm District Court for an injunction restraining Gourmet from placing advertisements for alcoholic beverages in magazines and for the imposition of a fine in the event of failure to comply. The Stockholm District

---

1462. [2001] ECR I-1795.

Court referred to the ECJ the question of whether or not national rules imposing an absolute prohibition on certain advertisements might be regarded as measures having equivalent effect to a quantitative restriction and if so, whether or not they might be justified under Article 30 EC.

Held:

The ECJ held that given the nature of the product, the consumption of which is linked to traditional social practices and to local habits and customs, a prohibition of all advertising directed at consumers was liable to impede access to the market by products from other Member States more than it impedes access by domestic products with which consumers are instantly more familiar.

Comment:

This new, more realistic approach by the ECJ means that national rules prohibiting or severely restricting advertisement are not automatically excluded from the scope of Article 28 EC [Article 34 TFEU], (unlike the approach of the ECJ to selling arrangements before its judgment in *Gourmet*), but must be assessed in the context of their effect on imported goods. If they affect the marketing of imported products more heavily than the marketing of domestic products (which will always be the case in respect of new imported products, since only by means of advertising can consumers be induced to buy them), they will constitute MEQRs unless justified under the rule of reason or Article 36 TFEU.

The ECJ based its reasoning on the "market access" test. In paragraph 18 of the judgment the ECJ stated that in order to escape the application of Article 28 EC [Article 34 TFEU], national rules prohibiting certain selling arrangements "must not be of such a kind as to prevent access to the market by products from another Member State or to impede access any more than they impede the access of domestic products".

Therefore in the determination of factual discrimination between domestic and imported products the "market access" test must be applied, but this is not an easy task given that the way in which the test should be used has neither been indicated by the ECJ nor clearly addressed in other post-*Keck* cases. Nevertheless, it is submitted that from the post-*Keck* case law and the reasoning of the ECJ in *Gourmet* some conclusions may be drawn:

- A reduction in the volume of sales of a particular product after the introduction of a national measure is not decisive in assessing whether or not such a measure is preventing or impeding access of that product to the market of the Member State any more than it is for domestic products;[1463]

- In the assessment of the degree of severity of a restriction imposed by national rules, a decisive criterion is whether or not other forms of marketing/advertising of the imported

---

1463. In Case C-441/04 *A-Punkt Schmuckhandels* ([2006] ECR I-2093) the ECJ rejected the argument submitted by Mrs Schmidt that her method of sale (prohibited under Austrian legislation and consisting of organising a "jewellery party" in private homes in order to sell silver jewellery of low value), being more efficient and profitable than sale in a fixed commercial structure, was likely to increase the volume of intra-community trade. The Court stated that this was not "enough" to classify the Austrian legislation as a MEQR.

products are available to importers, and if so, to what extent, if any, these alternatives will make the marketing/advertisement of the product more onerous and more expensive for importers than if the restriction had not been imposed.

The access to the market test, as described above, has been applied to many cases.[1464] One is Case C-71/02 *Herbert Karner*,[1465] in which the ECJ had to determine whether or not Austrian legislation prohibiting any information which stated that goods on sale originated from an insolvent estate was outside the scope of Article 28 EC [Article 34 TFEU]. The ECJ applied the two conditions set out in *Keck*. The first condition was met given that the Austrian legislation applied without any distinction to all the operators concerned who carried on their business on Austrian territory, regardless of whether they were Austrian nationals or foreigners.

The issue of whether the second condition was also satisfied was more controversial. In particular, the Advocate General grappled with the issue of the additional costs that an importer must bear in order to adjust its advertisements to the requirements imposed by the Austrian legislation. Indeed, bearing in mind the lack of familiarity of the public with them, advertising imported goods is more expensive than advertising domestic goods, but does the additional expenditure alone suffice to make access to the national market more difficult for foreign goods than for domestic goods? The Advocate General answered this question on the basis of the judgment in *Gourmet*. According to him three factors demonstrated that the second condition set out in *Keck* was met.

- First, the challenged rule did not impose a total ban on advertisements but prohibited only advertisements which made reference to the fact that the goods advertised came from an insolvent estate;

- Second, alternative means of advertising the marketed goods were available to importers; and

- Third, there was no evidence provided by the parties that the challenged rule made it more difficult for goods from other Member States to gain access to the Austrian market.

The ECJ confirmed the conclusion reached by the Advocate General. The Court held that the prohibition on advertising contained in the Austrian law was outside the scope of Article 28 EC [Article 34 TFEU]. However, in the light of new case law of the ECJ (see below) it is uncertain whether the above test will survive or whether it will be replaced by a new access to the market test applicable to all national rules irrespective of whether they are product related or concern selling arrangements.

20.10 New limits of Article 34 TFEU – Can the Keck approach survive?

Two judgments of the ECJ seem to have changed the emphasis in the assessment of national measures under Article 34 TFEU in that in their examination the criterion of the access to the market seems to become essential with the consequence that the distinction based on the type of

---

1464. Case C-322/01 *Deutscher Apothekerverband* [2003] ECR I-14887; Case C-20/03 *Burmanjer* [2004] ECR I-4133.
1465. [2004] ECR I-3025.

rules, i.e. whether they are product related or concern selling arrangements, may lose its importance. In the cases concerned the ECJ had to decide whether national rules prohibiting the use of certain products on the territory of a Member State constituted MEQRs or whether they were outside the scope of Article 34 TFEU on the grounds of the criteria laid down in *Keck*.

These cases are:

Case C-110/05 *Commission v Italy*.[1466]

THE FACTS WERE:

Under Italian legislation two-wheeled or three-wheeled vehicles (mainly motorcycles) were not permitted to tow a trailer. The Commission considered that the Italian legislation was a MEQR because Italian consumers knowing that they could not use trailers in Italy were not interested in buying them.

Held:

The ECJ held that Italian law prohibiting the use of trailers specifically designed for motorcycles constituted a MEQR because it prevented the existence of any demand. The ECJ made a distinction between trailers which were specially designed for motorcycles and other types of trailers, i.e. those which may be towed by automobiles or other types of vehicle. With regard to the second mentioned, the ECJ found that the Commission failed to prove that the Italian law hindered access to the market for that type of trailer. However, the Court found that the prohibition was justified because it aimed at ensuring road safety. It was necessary and proportionate to the objective that the Italian legislation sought to achieve taking into account that the circulation of a combination composed of a motorcycle and a trailer could be dangerous.

Case C-142/05 *Åklagaren v Percy Mickelsson and Joakim Roos*.[1467]

THE FACTS WERE:

The issue was whether a Swedish restriction on the use of jet-skis to generally navigable waterways (which in Sweden simply do not exist in much of the country, and those in existence are generally not suitable for the use of jet-skis on safety grounds) was a MEQR or a selling arrangement. The restriction on use of jet-skis resulted in consumers being not interested in buying jet-skis knowing that they could not use them. The restriction was justified by Sweden on the grounds of the protection of the environment and the protection of health and life of animals, humans and plants.

1466. [2009] ECR I-519.
1467. Judgment of 4/6/2009 (nyr).

Held:

The ECJ held that that the Swedish legislation was a MEQR. It might be justified by the objective of the protection of the environment and the protection of life of animals, humans and plants but was disproportionate given that a general prohibition on using jet-skis on waters other than general navigable waterways constituted a measure going beyond what was necessary to achieve the aim of protection in the light of the fact that in Sweden there were waterways other than general navigable waterways on which jet-skis could be used without giving rise to risks or pollution deemed unacceptable for the environment.

The above cases seem to change the law on the application of Article 34 TFEU. The ECJ seems to say that the access to the market test has become a fundamental principle applicable to Article 34 TFEU alongside the principles of non-discrimination and the principle of mutual recognition (para 34 of the judgment in Case C-110/05 *Commission v Italy*). It also seems that the ECJ followed the suggestion made by A-G Bot in his Opinion in Case C-110/05 *Commission v Italy* that the access to the market test should become a general criterion under Article 34 TFEU to be applied to all measures irrespective of whether they concern the product itself or relate to selling arrangement. The two above cases raise many issues:

- In Case C-142/05 *Åklagaren* the ECJ held that a non-discriminatory national rule may impose restrictions on the use of a product which may "depending on its scope, have a considerable influence on the behaviour of consumers, which may, in turn, affect the access of that product to the market of that Member State". This statement seems to suggest that the market access test should be based on the attitudes of consumers. If a national rule has a considerable influence on the behaviour of consumers (para 26 of the judgment) it will impede access to the market with the consequence that such a national rule will be in breach of Article 34 TFEU. However, if the access to the market test is linked to consumer behaviour, i.e. the behaviour has to be of substantial influence, then, first, this would amount to the application of the de minimis rule which, the ECJ has, with some exceptions, refused to apply to the free movement of goods.[1468] Second, the test based on substantial influence on the behaviour of consumers is difficult to apply in practice. How is this to be measured? In this context arguably any selling arrangement will come within the scope of Article 34 TFEU given that even a national rule which regulates the opening hours of shops may have substantial influence on customers behaviour.

- Professor Snell, having analysed the case law of the ECJ on the application of the access to the market test to the four freedoms, points out its lack of coherence and consistency.[1469] He challenges the use of the access to the market test and questions the reasons for which it is used. He asks "If the concern is that imports are affected more than domestic products, would it not be preferable to speak simply of factual, indirect or material discrimination?, or refer to differential impact if the term discrimination is seen as too loaded, rather than

1468. Joined Cases 177–178/82 *Van de Haar* [1984] ECR 1797; Case C-461/01 *Commission v Germany* [2004] ECR I-11705, see section 20.5.

1469. J. Snell, "The Notion of Market Access: A Concept or a Slogan?", (2010) 47 CMLRev 437.

resort to a vague notion of market access?" Indeed, the meaning of "access to the market" in the light of the case law of the ECJ is elusive and, as Professor Snell stated, the lack of a precise meaning of the concept puts the ECJ in a comfortable position in that "it grants it the maximum freedom of manoeuvre. As the term lacks a clear content, the Court may use it freely either to approve or to condemn measures that it happens to like or dislike";[1470]

- In *Åklagaren* the ECJ held that a case-by-case analysis is required to decide whether a national measure hinders access to the market. This is not of great help to national courts and risks undermining uniformity of application of Article 34 TFEU.

It can be said that national rules relating to arrangements for the use of products clearly show the artificiality of a distinction between product related restrictions and selling arrangements. Indeed, arrangements for the use of products are neither. In Case C-110/05 *Commission v Italy* the Commission's position was that national rules imposing an absolute prohibition on the use of certain products constituted MEQRs on imports and that the criteria set out in *Keck* were not applicable, in particular, because this would lead to the creation of an additional category of measures to which Article 34 TFEU would not apply. Some Member States, e.g. Germany, considered that some national rules prohibiting the use of certain products may be regarded as selling arrangements and consequently the principles concerning selling arrangements should apply to them in so far as national rules were non-discriminatory, ensured fair competition between imported products and domestic products and did not hinder, completely, or almost completely, access to the market in the State of importation. A-G Bot in his Opinion in Case C-110/05 *Commission v Italy* argued that the Italian law was a MEQR[1471] whilst A-G Kokott in *Åklagaren* considered that it "appears logical to extend the Court's Keck case-law to arrangements for use" of the products[1472] because restrictions imposed on jet-skis did not require any modification of jet-skis themselves. The ECJ chose to follow the Opinion of A-G Bot. However, the implications of that choice are still uncertain, in particular the question of whether the *Keck* approach will survive remains. It is submitted that its disappearance will not be regretted given that the ECJ's approach on a case-by-case basis has neither clarified the scope of Article 34 TFEU nor facilitated the use of the *Keck* criteria as exemplified by the controversial case law on selling arrangements.

Further, Article 34 TFEU should ensure that not only unequal access to the market in the importing Member State but also the unequal effect of "marketing rules" in that State should be condemned. This reflects the vision of the internal market presented by A-G Jacobs in his Opinion in Case C-412/93 *Société d'Importation Edouard Leclerc-Siplec v TF1 Publicité SA and M6 Publicité SA*[1473] when he said that: "the main concern of the Treaty provisions on the free movement of goods is to prevent unjustified obstacles to trade between Member States. If an obstacle to inter-State trade exists, it cannot cease to exist simply because an identical obstacle affects domestic trade ... Restrictions on trade should not be tested against local conditions which happen to prevail in each Member State, but against the aim of access to the entire Community market".[1474] However, uniformity in the application of Article 34 TFEU can only be ensured if the

---

1470. Ibid, 469.
1471. Supra note 1466, para 159.
1472. Supra note 1467, para 55.
1473. [1995] ECR I-179, paras 39–40.
1474. Ibid.

market access test is well defined and consistently applied by the ECJ. In *Leclerc-Siplec* A-G Jacobs proposed the application of the access to the market test to both product related measures and selling arrangements based on the significance of the hindrance to trade between Member States, i.e. in fact he proposed the introduction of the de minimis rule. In respect of product related measures he suggested that any national rule which requires the modification of imported products would amount to a substantial restriction on access to the market in the importing State. For selling arrangements, the assessment of whether a national rule constitutes a substantial impediment would depend on such factors as whether it "applies to certain goods . . . or to most goods . . . or to all goods, . . . on the extent to which other selling arrangements remain available, and on whether the effect of the measure is direct or indirect, immediate or remote, or purely speculative and uncertain".[1475]

20.11   Article 35 TFEU: Prohibition of QRs and MEQRs on exports

Article 35 TFEU prohibits quantitative restrictions and measures having equivalent effect on exports. The ECJ explained in Case 15/79 *Groenveld*[1476] that national measures are considered as MEQRs on exports if they "have as their specific object or effect the restriction of patterns of exports and thereby the establishment of a difference in treatment between the domestic trade of a Member State and its export trade in such a way as to provide a particular advantage for national production or for the domestic market of the State in question at the expense of the production or of trade of other Member States". However, the test, as just quoted from the *Groenveld* case, has been abandoned by the ECJ in Case C-205/07 *Criminal Proceedings against Lodewijk Gysbrechts and Santurel Inter BVBA*.[1477]

THE FACTS WERE:

Belgian law on distance-selling contracts prohibited a seller from requiring a deposit, or form of payment from the consumer, or even a consumer's payment credit card number, before the expiry of the mandatory period of seven working days for withdrawal. The claimant argued that the Belgian legislation was in breach of Article 29 EC [Article 35 TFEU]. The Belgian Government submitted that national law was justified on the ground of the protection of consumers. This was because the prohibition on requiring from the consumer an advance, or payment, or a consumer's payment credit card number before expiry of the period for withdrawal sought to ensure that the consumer could exercise his right of withdrawal effectively.

1475.   Ibid, para 45.
1476.   [1979] ECR 3409; Case C-3/91 *Exportur SA v LOR SA and Confiserie du Tech SA* [1992] ECR I-5529.
1477.   [2008] ECR I-9947.

Held:

The ECJ held that:

1. A national measure prohibiting a supplier in a distance sale from requiring an advance or any payment before expiry of the period for withdrawal constituted a MEQR but could be justified by the overriding requirements based on the protection of the consumer. The measure was also necessary and proportionate to the objective sought by the Belgian legislation;

2. A national measure prohibiting a supplier from requiring that consumers provide their payment card number, even if the supplier undertakes not to use it to collect payment before expiry of the period for withdrawals, was a MEQR, and could be justified by the necessity to protect consumers. However, it went beyond what was necessary to protect consumers. National law was disproportionate to the objective of protecting consumers because the uncertainty of the seller, who was not allowed to require the consumer to provide a credit card number, as to whether he would receive the payment might lead the seller to stop exporting goods sold over the internet or to reduce the volume of such exports.

In this case the ECJ decided to harmonise, to some extent, the criteria for determining whether a national measure is a MEQR under Articles 34 and 35 TFEU.

Prior to the judgment, a MEQR under Article 35 TFEU was assessed on the basis of the criteria set out in *Groenveld*, i.e. a measure was a MEQR if it had as its specific object or effect the restriction of patterns of exports and thereby the establishment of a difference in treatment between the domestic trade of a Member State and its export trade in such a way as to provide a particular advantage for national production or for the domestic market of the State in question, at the expense of the production or of the trade of other Member States. The definition of a MEQR under Article 35 TFEU was more restrictive than the definition of a MEQR under Article 34 TFEU which is encompassed in the *Dassonville* formula and which classifies any measure which hinders directly or indirectly, actually or potentially, trade between Member States as a MEQR.

A-G Trstenjak, in her Opinion in the commented case, applied the above criteria to the prohibition established under Belgian law. She concluded that there was no breach of Article 29 EC [Article 35 TFEU]. However, it was obvious that the Belgian law had a greater effect on goods intended for export than on goods marketed domestically in so far as the imposition on a supplier of a prohibition on requiring that a consumer provide his payment credit card number in cross-border distance selling was concerned. This was one of the reasons why the A-G proposed a modification of the test for the determination of MEQRs under Article 35 TFEU. Among other reasons mentioned by the A-G, probably the most convincing was that if certain goods are only produced for export in a Member State the test in *Groenveld* is useless in that it will never be possible to determine whether there are differences in treatment between domestic trade and export trade because the goods in question are not traded on the domestic market. As a result, it will never be possible, either, to determine whether a certain measure confers an advantage on national production or on the domestic market of the Member State concerned.

The A-G proposed two possible ways to modify the *Groenveld* test:

- The first consisting of harmonising law on Articles 28 and 29 [Articles 34 and 35 TFEU], i.e. applying all the definitions and case law relating to Article 34 TFEU to Article 35 TFEU; and

▪ The second consisting of establishing a new definition of MEQRs under Article 35 TFEU which would be narrower than that contained in the *Dassonville* formula, and which might perhaps justify non-application of the criteria set out in *Keck* to exports. However, under a new definition there would be a possibility for justifying national measures by the imperative requirements set out in *Cassis de Dijon*.

The ECJ's response to the A-G's propositions was provided in para 43 which states: "even if a prohibition such as that at issue in the main proceedings is applicable to all traders active in the national territory, its actual effect is none the less greater on goods leaving the market of the exporting Member State than on the marketing of goods in the domestic market of that Member State".

In the above passage one has the impression of "déjà vu", i.e. one recognises some similarity between para 43 above and the criteria laid down in *Keck*. However, the ECJ in the commented case did not apply the *Keck* approach to exports. It has used the access to the market test to define a MEQR under Article 35 TFEU. The Court stated that in order to determine whether a national measure constitutes a MEQR under Article 35 TFEU the basic criterion will be to determine its effect on marketing of products leaving a Member State. Therefore, the Court focused on de facto discrimination, i.e. it found that the actual effect of national law on exports was greater than on the marketing of the goods in the domestic market.

Notwithstanding the lack of explanation from the ECJ of the meaning of the new definition[1478] of a MEQR under Article 35 TFEU, it can be said that the new definition is, on the one hand, well adapted to the characteristics of exports and, on the other, avoids complications which would have appeared had the ECJ applied the *Keck* approach to exports.

20.12 The Rapid Intervention Mechanism (RIM)

In order to enable the Commission to intervene efficiently to restore the free movement of goods when normal procedures are not sufficient, Regulation 2679/98 of 7 December 1998 on the functioning of the internal market in relation to the free movement of goods among the Member States[1479] sets up a rapid intervention mechanism (RIM).

Under the Regulation, where there are "clear unmistakable and unjustified obstacles to the free movement of goods" within the meaning of Articles 34–36 TFEU, which may result in the serious disruption of the free movement of goods and cause serious loss to natural or legal persons, the Commission may, by way of formal decision addressed to the Member State concerned, require that Member State to take all appropriate measures to remove the obstacle within a time limit fixed by the Commission.

The Regulation specifies that the Commission is obliged to act within five days following the day on which the Commission becomes aware of all the facts. The right to defence in respect of the Member State concerned is protected under the procedure. The Member State is given three to

---

1478. See Roth, W-H., "Case C-205/07, *Lodewijk Gysbrechts, Santurel Inter BVBA*, Judgment of the Court of Justice (Grand Chamber) of 16 December 2008", (2010) 47 CMLRev, pp 514–15.
1479. [1998] OJ L337/1.

five working days from the date on which the Commission brings the matter to the attention of the Member State to submit its defence. Once the Commission adopts a formal decision, the Member State concerned must comply with it within the prescribed time limit. If it fails to comply, the Commission is required to notify the Member State concerned that it has three days to submit its observations, failing which the Commission will immediately issue a reasoned opinion requiring it to comply. If the Member State still refuses to comply, the Commission may bring proceedings before the ECJ. However, the RIM does not prejudice the Article 258 TFEU procedure and does not constitute a precondition for commencement of the pre-litigation procedure under Article 258 TFEU. It is up to the Commission to decide which of the two procedures is most appropriate to use in the light of the circumstances of the case.[1480]

The Regulation has important consequences in relation to the Member State which is in breach, since under the RIM that Member State can be promptly brought before the ECJ.

The clear beneficiaries from the RIM are natural or legal persons suffering damage resulting from obstacles to the free movement of goods:

- First, in the event of non-compliance an individual may immediately start proceedings under national law against the relevant Member State and the formal decision of the Commission will facilitate the proceedings;

- Second, an individual may seek remedy against the Commission under Article 340(2) TFEU in the event that the Commission fails to bring proceedings against a defaulting Member State;

- Third, the Regulation permits an individual to bring an action against the Commission under Article 265 TFEU in the case of Commission passivity in respect of serious breaches of Articles 34–36 TFEU by Member States.

In the 2001 Report[1481] the Commission recognised that it had not taken full advantage of the RIM (the mechanism was used only four times in 1999 and 18 times in 2000). The Report also highlighted the main shortcoming of the RIM, being the absence of efficient means to ensure the compensation of the losses sustained by the operators affected. Since 2001 the Commission has improved its record by adopting appropriate measures and using the RIM more energetically.[1482] Further, the Member States adopted a Resolution[1483] in 1998, promising to do everything in their power to remove speedily any serious obstacle to the free movement of goods.

1480. Case C-320/03 *Commission v Austria* [2005] ECR I-9871; Case C-394/02 *Commission v Greece* [2005] ECR I-4713.

1481. Report from the Commission to the Council and the European Parliament on the implementation of Regulation (EC) No 2679/98 [COM(2001) 160 final].

1482. See the official website of the Commission (http://ec.europa.eu/enterprise.regulation/goods/reg267998_en.htm (accessed 11/12/09).

1483. [1998] OJ L337/1.

Article 34 TFEU: prohibits quantitative restrictions (QRs) and measures having equivalent effect to quantitative restrictions (MEQRs).

Definition of QRs: classical bans and quotas, prohibiting or limiting importation by amount or by volume.

Definition of MEQRs: any national rule which directly or indirectly, potentially or actually hinders trade between Member States. This is known as the Dassonville formula.

Definition of distinctly applicable measures: Distinctly applicable measures are those which make a distinction between imported and domestic products in such a way that they "hinder imports which could otherwise take place, including measures which make importation more difficult or costly than disposal of domestic goods" (Article 2(1) of the Directive). They may only be justified under Article 36 TFEU which contains an exhaustive list of justifications. Any justification must be assessed in the light of the principle of proportionality.

Definition of indistinctly applicable measures: Indistinctly applicable measures are those which apply to imported and domestic products alike, but their restrictive effect on the free movement of goods "exceeds the effect intrinsic to trade rules" (Article 3 of the Directive), that is, in fact they are more burdensome for imports. The principle of mutual recognition, which was introduced in *Cassis de Dijon*, requires that goods lawfully marketed and distributed in one Member State can be introduced to any other Member State without restriction. It is for a Member State of importation to prove that national restrictions indistinctly applicable to domestic and imported goods are justified under either Article 36 TFEU or the mandatory requirements developed under the rule of reason set out in *Cassis de Dijon* or both. Any justification must be assessed in the light of the principle of proportionality.

Distinction between product related rules and those concerning selling arrangments. In Joined Cases C-267 and 268/91 *Criminal Proceedings against Keck and Mithouard* the ECJ introduced a distinction between product related measures, i.e. concerning the product itself such as its name, weight, composition, packaging, labelling, presentation, and those concerning selling arrangements. The ECJ has not defined the notion of selling arrangements but identified them on a case-by-case basis. On the basis of the ECJ's case law the following national rules relate to selling arrangements, i.e. those concerning conditions and methods of marketing of goods, the times and places of the sale of goods and advertisement of goods.

Selling arrangements. According to the *Keck* case, selling arrangements in order to fall outside the scope of Article 34 TFEU must "apply to all relevant traders operating within the national territory" and "affect in the same manner in law and in fact the marketing of domestic and imported goods". Accordingly, selling arrangements are indistinctly applicable measures, which may have an effect on the overall volume of trade, but because they are not protectionist and because they affect imported and domestic goods in the same manner in law and in fact, i.e impose the same burden on both, are outside the scope of Article 34 TFEU. The access to the market test established in *Gourmet* determines whether there is factual discrimination between domestic products and imported products. If a national measure passes the access to the market test it is outside the scope of Article 34 TFEU. If a national measure fails the access to the market test it must be assessed in the light of justifications set out either in Article 36 TFEU or under the rule of reason established in the *Cassis de Dijon* case or both. Any justification must also pass the test of proportionality.

New limits on Article 34 TFEU. In the light of Case C-110/05 *Commission v Italy* and Case C-142/05 *Åklagaren* the access to the market test seems to become essential in the assessment of national measures under Article 34 TFEU irrespective of whether they are product related or concern selling arrangements. Although the legal implications of the above cases are still uncertain it seems that the access to the market test set out in *Gourmet* will be modified and indeed, the distinction between product related restrictions and those concerning selling arrangements may lose its importance or even disappear.

Article 35 TFEU. The definition of MEQRs in Article 35 TFEU is more restrictive than that under Article 34 TFEU. This is because it is rare that a Member State restricts its exports rather than promotes them. In Case C-205/07 *Gysbrechts*, the ECJ has broadened the scope of application of Article 35 TFEU. According to *Gysbrechts* it is no longer necessary to prove that a national measure has protective effects, i.e provides a particular advantage for national products at the expense of domestic products intended for exports. What is relevant is whether a national measure discriminates in fact against exported products and thus has a greater "actual effect" on export of goods than on the marketing of the goods in the domestic market.

RECOMMENDED READING

Books

Barnard, C., *The Substantive Law of the EU. The Four Freedoms*, 2nd edition, 2007, Oxford: Oxford University Press

Davies, G., *European Union Internal Market Law*, 2006, London: Routledge Cavendish

MacMaolain, C., *EU Food Law: Protecting Consumers and Health in a Common Market*, 2007, Oxford: Hart Publishing

Shuibhne, N., (ed.), *Regulating the Internal Market*, 2006, Cheltenham: Edward Elgar

Articles

Arnull, A., "What Shall we Do on Sunday?" (1991) 16 ELRev, p 112

Connor, T., "Accentuating the Positive: the 'Selling Arrangement', the first Decade and Beyond", (2005) 54 ICLQ, p 127

Davies, G., "Can Selling Arrangements be Harmonised?", (2005) 30 ELRev, p 37

Garde, A., "EU Food Law – Protecting Consumers and Health in a Common Market", (2008) 14 EPL, p 440

Roth, W-H., "Case C-205/07, *Lodewijk Gysbrechts, Santurel Inter BVBA*, Judgment of the Court of Justice (Grand Chamber) of 16 December 2008", (2010) 47 CMLRev, pp 509–20

Snell, J., "The Notion of Market Access: A Concept or a Slogan?", (2010) 47 CMLRev, p 437

Szajkowska, A., "The Impact of the Definition of the Precautionary Principle in EU Food Law", (2010) 47 CMLRev, p 173

Tryfonidou, A., "Was Keck A Half-Baked Solution After All?" [2007] 34(2) Legal Issues of Economic Integration, p 167

21

ARTICLE 36 TFEU

CONTENTS

SUMMARY

1. Article 36 TFEU contains an exhaustive list of derogations from the principle of free movement of goods. It applies when there is no EU harmonising legislation. It allows Member States, on the grounds set out in Article 36 TFEU, to justify national rules distinctly and indistinctly applicable (although the latter would normally be considered under the *Cassis de Dijon* rule of reason) which are in breach of Articles 34 and 35 TFEU, provided that those national rules:

- Are proportionate to the objectives set out in Article 36 TFEU. This means that a Member State must choose a measure which is necessary to ensure the safeguarding of an overriding consideration embodied in Article 36 TFEU, which is proportionate to the objective pursued, and which must ensure that the objective sought could not have been achieved by a measure less restrictive of trade between Member States;

- Do not constitute a means of arbitrary discrimination or disguised restrictions on trade between Member States;

- Are not of a purely economic nature.

An important feature of Article 36 TFEU is that distinctly applicable measures can only be justified on the grounds set out in that article (so they cannot be justified under the *Cassis de Dijon* rule of reason). The onus for justification is on a Member State, not on a trader.

2. The derogations set out in Article 36 TFEU relate to:

A. Public morality. A Member State enjoys a margin of discretion to define the requirements of public morality in its territory but it is prohibited from applying double morality standards.

B. Public policy. This refers to the protection of the fundamental interests of society. This is potentially a very broad derogation but has rarely been successful.

C. Public security. This concerns the safeguarding of the institutions of a Member State, its essential public services and the survival of its population. This ground has rarely been relied upon by Member States.

D. Protection of the health and life of humans, animals and plants. In order to successfully rely on this derogation a Member State must show that there is a genuine risk to health and life. Additionally, a Member State may invoke the precautionary principle when the potentially dangerous effects of a phenomenon, product or process have been identified by a scientific and objective evaluation, and this evaluation does not allow the risk to be determined with sufficient certainty. However, the risk assessment must not be based on purely hypothetical considerations but on the most reliable scientific data and the most recent results of international research.

E. Protection of national treasures which possess artistic, historic or archaeological value. This derogation can be relied upon if a treasure or work of art is in the public domain but not if such a work is on the market or the subject of a private sale. As at the time of writing this derogation has never been successfully relied upon.

F. Protection of industrial and commercial property. Article 30 EC recognises that IPRs may constitute measures having equivalent effect to quantitative restrictions (MEQRs) and thus a Member State is allowed to adopt measures contrary to the prohibition set out in Article 36 TFEU on the grounds of IPRs; such measures are not, however, to constitute a means of arbitrary discrimination or a disguised restriction on trade between Member States. To ensure this, the ECJ made a distinction between the existence of IPRs, which is protected under Article 345 TFEU, and their exercise, which is subject to the requirements set out in Articles 34 and 36 TFEU, depending upon the specific subject matter of the IPRs. The benefit of the specific subject-matter was described in Case 15/74 *Centrafarm v Sterling Drug* as the exclusive right of a holder of IPRs to first marketing of the protected product, whether this marketing is direct or by means of the grant of licences to third parties, in more than one Member State of the EEA (the EEA comprises all Member States of the EU and three of the EFTA states: Norway, Iceland and Liechtenstein). Once a holder has had the benefit of the specific subject-matter of the IPR, his right is exhausted. Consequently, he cannot rely on the protection of IPRs provided for under the national law of a Member State to prevent parallel imports of the protected goods which have lawfully been marketed in any other Member State of the EEA by him or with his consent. However, the principle of exhaustion does not apply to parallel imports of protected products coming from outside the EEA.

21.1   Introduction

Article 36 TFEU states:

"The provisions of Articles 34 and 35 shall not preclude prohibitions or restrictions on imports, exports or goods in transit justified on grounds of public morality, public policy or public security; the protection of health and life of humans, animals or plants; the protection of national treasures possessing artistic, historic or archaeological value; or the protection of industrial and commercial property. Such prohibitions or restrictions shall not, however, constitute a means of arbitrary discrimination or a disguised restriction on trade between Member States."

The list provided in Article 36 TFEU is exhaustive. All exceptions must be interpreted strictly; otherwise they will undermine the general rule set out in Articles 34 and 35 TFEU.[1484] Distinctly applicable measures can only be justified under Article 36 TFEU. Indistinctly applicable measures can be justified under both Article 36 TFEU and the rule of reason set out in the *Cassis de Dijon* case.

Article 36 TFEU applies only to non-harmonised areas of EU law on the free movement of goods. Accordingly it cannot be invoked to justify a national measure contrary to EU harmonised legislation.[1485] This is because all relevant interests and concerns of the Member States are duly taken account of when harmonising legislation is adopted. When there is only a partial harmonisation Member States are allow to adopt national measures in non-harmonised areas and thus can rely on Article 36 TFEU to defend their national rules.

Examination of the case law regarding the application of Article 36 TFEU reveals the points discussed next.

21.1.1   Distinctly applicable measures can never be justified under the rule of reason[1486]

This was clearly stated by the ECJ in Case 113/80 *Commission v Ireland [Re Irish Souvenirs]*.[1487]

THE FACTS WERE:

Under Irish law souvenirs which were considered as typically Irish (for example, Irish round towels and shamrocks) but imported from other Member States should be stamped either with the indication of their place of origin or with the word "foreign". As a result, importers of Irish souvenirs were discriminated against as compared to Irish producers of Irish souvenirs as they were burdened with an additional requirement imposed by Irish legislation and suffered a reduction in sales since tourists wanted to buy "original" souvenirs. Irish law was clearly discriminatory. The Irish Government argued that national measures were necessary to protect consumers and to ensure the fairness of commercial transactions.

1484. For example, Case 29/72 *Marimex* [1972] ECR 1309.
1485. Case C-5/94 *Hedley Lomas* [1996] ECR I-2553 and Case C-473/98 *Kemikalieinspektionen v Toolex Alpha AB* [2000] ECR I-5681.
1486. Case 229/83 *Associations des Centres Distributeurs E. Leclerc and Others v Sarl "Au Blé Vert"* [1985] ECR 1.
1487. [1981] ECR 1626.

> *Held:*
>
> The ECJ held that as the grounds argued by the Irish Government were not mentioned in Article 30 EC [Article 36 TFEU], it could not rely on that Article.

21.1.2 Justification of economic objectives

Purely economic objectives such as the necessity of ensuring the balance of payments, the reduction of public spending, or the survival of an undertaking cannot be justified under Article 36 TFEU.[1488]

21.1.3 The principle of proportionality

The pursuit of the objectives set out in Article 36 TFEU is not in itself sufficient to justify national measures restricting trade between Member States. Such measures must satisfy the requirements imposed by the principle of proportionality,[1489] which involves a three-stage inquiry:

1. A Member State must choose a measure which is necessary in order to attain the objective of protection referred to in Article 36 TFEU.

    In order to determine whether national measures are necessary the ECJ will examine their restrictive effects – direct, indirect, actual and potential – on trade between Member States.[1490] For example, in Case C-293/94 *Brandsma*[1491] the ECJ held that it would not be "necessary" to carry out technical analyses or laboratory tests on imported goods taking into account that these tests had already been conducted in another Member State.

2. A Member State must choose a measure which is suitable to achieve the objective pursued. When deciding to adopt a measure a Member State must ensure that the objective sought could not have been achieved by a measure less restrictive of trade between Member States, that is, if it has a choice between different measures capable of attaining the same objective, it must choose the one which least hinders the free movement of goods.[1492]

3. A Member State must choose a measure which does not impose a burden on the individual which is excessive as compared to the objective that the Member State seeks to achieve (this is known as proportionality in the strict sense). The third stage of investigation is rarely carried out because normally the first two stages are sufficient to determine whether a measure is disproportionate.

1488. Case 7/61 *Commission v Italy* [1961] ECR 317; Case 104/75 *De Peiper* [1976] ECR 613; Case 95/81 *Commission v Italy* [1982] ECR 2189; Case 238/82 *Duphar* [1984] ECR 523; Case C-324/93 *Evans Medical* [1995] ECR I-563.

1489. See G de Búrca, "The Principle of Proportionality and its Application in EC Law", (1993) 13 YBEL, p 105.

1490. Joined Cases 418–421/93, 460–462/93, 464/93, 9–11/94 14–15/94, 23 and 24/94, 332/94 *Semeraro* [1996] ECR I-2975.

1491. [1996] ECR I-3159.

1492. For example, Case C-17/93 *Van der Veldt* [1994] ECR I-3537.

In Case 104/75 *De Peiper*,[1493] the ECJ held that national measures intended to facilitate the task of the public authorities or to reduce public expenditure could only be justified if alternative arrangements would impose unreasonable burdens on the administration.

21.1.4 Arbitrary discrimination

Article 36 TFEU provides that national measures permitted under Article 36 TFEU must not constitute a means of arbitrary discrimination or a disguised restriction on trade between Member States, i.e must not be protectionist. In Case 34/79 *Henn and Darby*,[1494] the ECJ emphasised that the purpose of this prohibition on arbitrary discrimination and disguised restriction is to:

> ". . . prevent restrictions on trade based on the grounds mentioned in the first sentence of Article [30 EC, now Article 36 TFEU] from being diverted from their proper purpose and used in such a way as either to create discrimination in respect of goods originating in other Member States or indirectly to protect certain national products."

In order to determine whether a national measure that discriminates against imported goods is arbitrary or constitutes a disguised restriction aimed at protecting domestic goods, a comparison between the treatment of domestic goods and imported goods is necessary. The differentiation must be justified on objective grounds, that is, it must be genuine.[1495]

21.1.5 Burden of proof

It is for national authorities to prove that a national measure which restricts trade between Member States is justified under Article 36 TFEU. In Case 227/82 *Leendert van Bennekom*,[1496] the ECJ held that "it is for the national authorities to demonstrate in each case that their rules are necessary to give effective protection to the interests referred to in Article [30 EC now Article 36 TFEU]". Consequently, a Member State is required to supply the appropriate evidence; a mere statement that the measure is justified is not sufficient.[1497] However, in Case C-110/05 *Commission v Italy*,[1498] the ECJ held that the burden of proof "cannot be so extensive as to require the Member State to prove, positively, that no other conceivable measure could enable that objective to be attained under the same conditions".

21.2 Public morality

In principle, it is for each Member State to determine, in accordance with its own scale of values and in the form selected by it, the requirements of public morality in its territory. Thus, Article 36 TFEU permits a Member State to establish it own concept of "public morality". The use of the

---

1493. [1976] ECR 613.
1494. [1979] ECR 3795.
1495. The concept of "disguised restrictions" was examined in Case 40/82 *Commission v UK* [1984] ECR 283.
1496. [1983] ECR 3883.
1497. Case C-265/06 *Commission v Portugal* [2008] ECR I-2245.
1498. [2009] ECR I-519.

words "in principle" is important as it allows the EU to interfere, in particular in order to prevent a Member State from imposing double standards of morality, one applicable to domestic goods and another to imported goods, and thus discriminate against the latter on the ground of public morality.

In this respect it is interesting to contrast Case 34/79 *R v Henn and Darby*[1499] with Case 121/85 *Conegate Limited v HM Customs & Excise.*[1500]

THE FACTS WERE:

In Henn and Darby the defendants imported a number of consignments of obscene films and publications into the UK from The Netherlands. They were caught by Customs officials and were charged with the criminal offence of being "knowingly concerned in the fraudulent evasion of the prohibition of the importation of indecent or obscene articles". In their defence, the defendants claimed that the prohibition on the importation of pornographic material was contrary to Article 28 EC [Article 34 TFEU], as it constituted a MEQR.

Held:

The ECJ held that Article 28 EC [Article 34 TFEU] is subject to a number of exceptions, one of which is contained in Article 30 EC [Article 36 TFEU] and relates to restrictions intended to protect public morality. The British legislation fell within the scope of this exception and consequently the criminal charges were consistent with Community law.

Comment:

The ECJ upheld the arguments of the UK Government, even though the UK applied double standards in that in the UK only pornographic materials likely to "deprave or corrupt" were prohibited while it was lawful to trade in "indecent or obscene" literature. This meant that the UK imposed more stringent conditions on imported goods than on domestic goods, contrary to the principle of non-discrimination based on nationality.

The above situation was rectified in Case 121/85 *Conegate Limited v HM Customs & Excise.*[1501]

THE FACTS WERE:

A British company set up a business importing inflatable dolls from Germany into the UK. A number of consignments of the products were seized by Customs officials on the ground that the dolls were "indecent and obscene", and accordingly subject to the prohibition on imports contained in the Customs Consolidation Act 1876. Although national rules prohibited the importation of these dolls, no regulation prevented their manufacture in the United Kingdom. The company brought an action for recovery of the dolls.

1499. [1979] ECR 3795.
1500. [1986] ECR 1007.
1501. Ibid.

Held:

The ECJ held that the UK could not rely on Article 30 EC [Article 36 TFEU] to prohibit the importation of products when no internal provisions had been enacted to prevent the manufacture and distribution of the offending products within the UK. To allow a Member State to prevent the importation of particular goods, while simultaneously allowing nationals to manufacture such products, would amount to discrimination on the ground of nationality. The argument of the UK, based on the fact that no articles comparable to those imported by Conegate were manufactured in the UK territory, was rejected. The ECJ stressed that as long as UK law did not exclude the possibility of manufacturing such articles, importation from another Member State could not be prevented.

Thus, in the above case, the ECJ abolished "double morality standards".

21.3   Public policy and public security

Member States have rarely invoked derogations based on public policy and public security. The assessment of national measures necessary to ensure public security and public order is left to the Member States, which have to find the right balance between the extent of rights conferred on individuals and the requirements of public policy or public security.

Public policy refers to the fundamental interests of society. Public security concerns the safeguarding of the institutions of a Member State, its essential public services and the survival of its inhabitants. Both derogations have been treated by the ECJ as exceptions of last resort. This is exemplified by the following cases.

THE FACTS WERE:

In Case 231/83 Cullet v Centre Leclerc,[1502] the French Government imposed minimum prices for fuel, arguing that the setting of those prices was necessary to avoid civil disorder, including the violent reactions which would have to be anticipated by retailers affected by unrestricted competition on the fuel market.

Held:

The ECJ rejected this argument on the ground that the French Government did not show that it would be unable to deal with potential disturbances.

Therefore, national measures may be justified on the ground of public policy only if a Member State shows that in their absence, civil unrest would be more than the national authorities could be expected to cope with.

1502. [1985] ECR 305.

In Case 154/85 Commission v Italy,[1503] an Italian Ministerial Decree concerning the registration of vehicles, which set out more stringent requirements for registration of used imported vehicles which had already been registered in the country of exportation than for new cars, was considered as an MEQR. The Italian Government tried to justify the decree on the ground of public order, in particular the necessity to combat the trafficking of stolen vehicles.

Held:

The ECJ stated that under the decree the registration of imported used cars took longer, was more complex and was more expensive than that of new cars. This could not be justified on the ground of public order, taking into account that the multiplication of requirements relating to registration did not constitute an efficient manner of detecting and preventing the trafficking of stolen vehicles.

There are, however, a number of cases in which the requirements of public security were successfully invoked.

Case 7/78 R v Thompson, Johnson and Woodiwiss.[1504]

The case concerned UK legislation prohibiting import of gold coins, export of silver UK coins minted before 1947, which were no longer in circulation, and their destruction and melting. Export and import of coins was allowed only under a licence granted by the Board of Trade. Criminal proceedings were commenced against a number of British citizens who, despite the ban and without obtaining the required licence, imported gold coins into the UK from Germany and exported silver coins from the UK to Germany.

Held:

The ECJ held that the ban was a MEQR but was justified on the ground of public policy because it stemmed from the need to protect the right to mint coinage, which is traditionally regarded as involving the fundamental interests of the State.

Case 72/83 Campus Oil Ltd v Minister for Industry and Energy.[1505]

1503. [1987] ECR 2771.
1504. [1978] ECR 2247.
1505. [1984] ECR 2727.

The public security exception has been successfully relied upon by Member States in respect of national legislation regulating transport of dangerous substances. In Case C-367/89 *Richardt*,[1506] the introduction of a requirement for special authorisation in respect of the transit of strategic material was justified on the ground of public security. However, it is not necessary for national legislation to provide for penal sanctions in order to be considered as being concerned with public policy within the meaning of Article 36 TFEU.[1507]

21.4   Protection of the health and life of humans, animals and plants

The approach of the EU to the protection of the health of its citizens, animals and plants acquired a new dimension in the light of the epidemic of bovine spongiform encephalopathy (BSE), commonly known as mad-cow disease which in the 1990s affected cattle in the UK. On 27 March 1996 the Commission imposed a complete ban on exports of all kinds of bovine products from the UK to other Member States and third countries. This decision was adopted following the discovery of a probable link between a form of Creutzfeldt-Jakob disease in humans and BSE in cattle which, at that time, was quite widespread in the UK. Under the decision the Commission was monitoring the situation in the UK and had decided to lift the ban. The saga of the refusal of the French Government to comply with the decision of the Commission to lift the ban is well known and had its epilogue before the ECJ, which, not surprisingly, found France in breach of Article 28 EC [Article 34 TFEU].[1508] What emerged from the case is that neither the Community institutions nor the French Government reacted with proper consideration when facing BSE:

▪ At the Community level a scheme set up by virtue of Decision 98/692/EC based on the animal's date of birth (DBES) was inadequate;

▪ At the national level, the French Government's conduct was confusing and erratic. In particular, the French authorities did not prevent the import to France of beef and veal and other meat-based products from other Member States which did not bear the distinct mark

---

1506.   [1991] ECR I-4621.
1507.   Case 16/83 *Prantl* [1984] ECR 1299.
1508.   Case C-1/00 *Commission v France* [2001] ECR I-9989.

of products subject to the DBES scheme, although there was a strong possibility that certain consignments of meat or meat products of UK origin could have been processed or rewrapped in other Member States.

However, both the EU and the Member States drew proper conclusions from the above situation. This is illustrated by the adoption of Regulation 178/2002,[1509] which laid down the General Principles and Requirements of Food Law, established the European Food Safety Authority and laid down Procedures in Matters of Food Safety. The Regulation constitutes a main tool for the EU and for the Member States to speedily react to any emergencies where human health, animal health or the environment is at risk. The Regulation:

- Underlines the general principles of food law including the precautionary principle;

- Sets up a new EU body: The European Food Safety Authority;

- Establishes the rapid alert system, a network for exchange of information concerning a food-related risk; and

- Specifies measures available to the Commission and to Member States to deal with emergencies.

The basic principle underpinning the derogation based on the protection of health and life of humans, animals and plants is that a Member State must, in order to justify national measures on these grounds, demonstrate that there is a genuine risk to health and life.[1510] Therefore, national measures must not serve as a pretext for introducing disguised discrimination against imported products. This happened in Case 124/81 *Commission v UK [Re UHT Milk]*.[1511]

THE FACTS WERE:

The UK Government imposed a requirement that UHT milk should be marketed only by approved dairies or distributors. This involved repackaging and retreatment of all imported milk. The UK Government argued that the measure was necessary to ensure that the milk was free from bacterial or viral infections.

Held:

The ECJ held that there was evidence that milk in all Member States was of similar quality and subject to equivalent controls. For that reason the requirement, although it applied to both domestic and imported goods, was considered as disguised discrimination and therefore examined and rejected under Article 30 EC [Article 36 TFEU].

The derogation based on the protection of the health and life of humans, animals and plants has been successfully relied on in a number of cases. For example:

1509. The Regulation has been complemented by a number of items of secondary legislation, see the official website of the Commission at http//ec.europa.eu/food/food/foodlaw/index_en.htm (accessed 13/12/09).

1510. Case 238/82 *Duphar* [1984] ECR 523.

1511. [1983] ECR 203.

■ In Case C-324/93 *R v Secretary of State for Home Department, ex parte Evans Medical Ltd and Macfarlan Smith Ltd,*[1512] in which the refusal to grant an importation licence for diamorphine, a heroin substitute for medical purposes, was justified in order to ensure the reliability of supply of diamorphine in the UK and to avoid risk of unlawful traffic in diamorphine;

■ In Case C-320/93 *Ortscheit,*[1513] German law prohibiting the advertising of medical products which had not yet been authorised in Germany was justified on the ground of public heath. However, these products, which were lawfully on sale in other Member States, could be imported by individual consumers.

Two principles are of utmost importance when a Member State exercises its discretion relating to the protection of public health: the principle of proportionality and the precautionary principle.

21.4.1   The principle of proportionality

This requires a Member State to choose only measures which (1) are necessary to ensure the safeguarding of public health, (2) are suitable to achieve the objective pursued, in that the object-ive sought could not have been achieved by a measure less restrictive of trade between Member States, and (3) do not impose a burden on the individual that is excessive in relation to the objective sought (that is, proportionality in the strict sense).

Its application is illustrated in Case C-366/04 *Schwarz.*[1514]

THE FACTS WERE:

Austrian legislation prohibited the sale of unwrapped chewing-gum and other sugar con-fectionary products from vending machines.

Held:

The ECJ held that although the Austrian legislation was a MEQR, it was justified on the ground of the protection of public health as it was adequate and proportionate, given that non-packaged goods were capable of being impaired by moisture or insects, in particular ants, within vending machine containers.

The requirements of the principle of proportionality were satisfied in Case C-67/97 *Bluhme [Brown Bees of Læsø].*[1515]

1512.   [1995] ECR I-563.
1513.   [1994] ECR I-5243.
1514.   [2005] ECR I-10139.
1515.   [1998] ECR I-8033.

THE FACTS WERE:

Criminal proceedings were instituted against Ditlev Bluhme for breach of Danish law prohibiting the keeping on the island of Læsø of bees other than those of the subspecies Apis mellifera mellifera (brown bees of Læsø). Mr Bluhme argued that the prohibition constituted a MEQR while the Danish authorities claimed that such legislation, even if in breach of Article 28 EC [Article 34 TFEU], was justified on the ground of the protection of the health and life of animals.

Held:

The ECJ held that Danish legislation prohibiting the keeping of any species of bee other than the subspecies *Apis mellifera mellifera* on the island of Læsø constituted a MEQR, but was justified under Article 30 EC [Article 36 TFEU] on the ground of the protection of the health and life of animals. The ECJ recognised that the threat of the disappearance of the Læsø brown bee was, by reason of the recessive nature of the genes of the brown bee, undoubtedly genuine in the event of mating with golden bees. The establishment by the national legislation of a protection area within which the keeping of bees other than Læsø brown bees was prohibited, for the purpose of ensuring the survival of Læsø brown bees, therefore constituted an appropriate measure in relation to the aim pursued.

Comment:

The ECJ failed to fully explain the relationship between national measures and the protection of the health and life of animals within the meaning of Article 30 EC [Article 36 TFEU]. Such an explanation would have been welcome, taking into account that in previous cases in this area the justifications based on the protection of the health and life of animals were made in the context of the prevention of propagation of animal diseases,[1516] or the prevention of unnecessary suffering by animals.[1517] In this case the ECJ stated that such national measures "contribute to the maintenance of biodiversity" and "by so doing, they are aimed at protecting the life of those animals and are capable of being justified under Article 30 of the Treaty [Article 36 TFEU]". The relationship between the maintenance of biodiversity and the protection of environment, which is outside the scope of Article 30 EC [Article 36 TFEU], should have been more clearly explained by the ECJ, taking into account that the ECJ has always emphasised that exceptions to Article 28 EC [Article 34 TFEU] must be strictly interpreted.

In Case 178/84 *Commission v Germany [Re German Beer Purity Laws]*,[1518] one of the leading cases on the application of the principle of proportionality, Germany failed to convince the ECJ that its national law was proportionate to the objective it sought to achieve.

1516. Case C131/93 *Commission v Germany* [1994] ECR I-3303.

1517. Case C-1/96 *Compassion in World Farming* [1998] ECR I-1251.

1518. [1987] ECR 1227.

THE FACTS WERE:

Under German law the use of additives in beer was banned and the marketing in Germany of beer containing additives was prohibited. In other Member States the use of additives was authorised. The Commission brought proceedings against Germany for breach of Article 28 EC [Article 34 TFEU]. The German Government argued that the prohibition was necessary, taking into account that beer was consumed in "considerable quantities" in Germany.

Held:

The ECJ held that there was no scientific evidence, in particular taking into account research conducted by the FAO (Food and Agriculture Organisation) and the WHO (World Health Organisation) and the Community's own Scientific Committee for foods, that additives constituted a danger to public health. Under Article 30 EC [Article 36 TFEU] it was for a Member State to submit convincing evidence based on scientific research. However, the ECJ agreed that the drinking habits of the German population might have justified the prohibition of certain additives, but not all of them. As a result the German Beer Purity Laws were disproportionate as they went far beyond what was necessary to protect public health.

21.4.2   The precautionary principle

The precautionary principle was, for the first time, applied in Case C-157/96 *National Farmers' Union and Others.*[1519] Its meaning was explained in the Communication of the Commission of 2 February 2000.[1520] According to the Communication:

"... the precautionary principle may be invoked when the potentially dangerous effects of a phenomenon, product or process have been identified by a scientific and objective evaluation, and this evaluation does not allow the risk to be determined with sufficient certainty."

It means in effect that a Member State must act with the potentially harmful consequences of a proposed course of action in mind. The application of the precautionary principle does not change dramatically the application of the derogation based on the protection of the health of humans, animals and plants, but certainly emphasises that any national measures must be based on the fullest possible scientific evaluation and the careful assessment of the potential consequences of action or inaction. Member States have relied on the precautionary principle in a number of cases.[1521] In Case C-236/01 *Monsanto Agricoltura Italia,*[1522] the ECJ emphasised that the risk assessment must not be based on purely hypothetical considerations but on the most reliable scientific data and the most recent results of international research. In Case C-333/08

1519.   [1998] ECR I-2211.

1520.   COM(2000) 1 final.

1521.   Case C-236/01 *Monsanto Agricoltura Italia and Others* [2003] ECR I-8105; Case C-192/01 *Commission v Denmark* [2003] ECR I-9693; Case T-177/02 *Malagutti-Vezinhet v Commission* [2004] ECR II-827; Case C-132/03 *Ministero della Salute v Coordinamento delle associazioni per la difesa dell'ambiente e dei diritti degli utenti e dei consumatori* (Codacons)[2005] ECR I-4167.

1522.   Case C-236/01, Ibid.

Commission v France[1523] the ECJ provided guidance on the correct application of the precautionary principle; first a Member State should identify all negative consequences deriving from the potentially dangerous effects of a phenomenon, product or process and then make a comprehensive assessment of the risk they represent based on the most reliable scientific data available and the most recent results of international research. When this assessment shows that it is "impossible to determine with certainty the existence or extent of the alleged risk because of the insufficiency, inconclusiveness or imprecision of the results of studies conducted, but the likelihood of real harm to public health persists should the risk materialise, the precautionary principle justifies the adoption of restrictive measures, provided they are non-discriminatory and objective".

21.5 Protection of national treasures possessing artistic, historic or archaeological value

This exception can be relied upon if a treasure or work of art is in the public domain, but not if such a work is on the market or the subject of a private sale.

Member States are free to determine their national treasures possessing artistic, historic or archaeological value. By virtue of Article 36 TFEU they may also impose restrictions on exports of such national treasures.

The scope of this derogation is uncertain as there is no case law in this respect. However, in Case 7/68 *Commission v Italy [Re Export Tax on Art Treasures]*,[1524] the ECJ held that the desire to protect national treasures could not justify charges under Article 25 EC [Article 30 TFEU]. Therefore, the imposition of QRs seems to be the only way to protect national treasures. This was recognised by the French Conseil d'Etat (highest administrative court in France), which held that French legislation prohibiting export of objects of art or objects of historic value was justified on the ground of Article 30 EC [Article 36 TFEU].[1525]

The completion of the internal market prompted the EU to adopt certain more specific measures ensuring that the free movement of goods would not increase illegal exports of national treasures of a Member State. These measures are: Directive 93/7/EEC on the Return of Cultural Objects Unlawfully Removed from the Territory of a Member State[1526] and Regulation 3911/92/EEC on the Control of the Export of Cultural Goods.[1527]

21.6 Protection of intellectual property rights (IPRs)

The essence of IPRs is that they create a form of monopoly for holders in order to either reward their creativity and investment in terms of time and money, or to protect their commercial reputation and goodwill. Intellectual property rights include patents, trade marks, copyrights, registered designs, and so on.

Under national law holders of intellectual property rights are protected against others copying

---

1523. Judgment of 28/1/10 (nyr).
1524. [1968] ECR 423.
1525. CE 7 November 1987: Receuil Lebon 304; CE 25 March 1994, Syndicat National de la Librairie Ancienne et Moderne.
1526. [1993] OJ L74/74.
1527. [1992] OJ L395/19.

or taking unfair advantage of their work or reputation. The period of protection varies depending on the national law of the Member State and the type of intellectual property. In the UK, in respect of patents, the patentee or holder enjoys exclusive rights for a period of 20 years. For trademarks in the UK, the protection is indefinite, that is, it lasts as long as goods and services are supplied under that trade mark. For copyrights the author of a work (literary work, artistic work, musical work, sound recordings, films, and broadcasts) is protected either until the expiry of 70 years after his death or for 50 years after the creation of the protected work, depending on the type of work.

However, the relationship between intellectual property rights and EU law is not easy. The fundamental objectives of EU law are in conflict with the very nature of IPRs. They might affect two areas of EU law in particular: the free movement of goods and the provisions of the Treaties regarding competition law, especially Articles 101 and 102 TFEU.

In respect of the free movement of goods Article 34 TFEU prohibits the imposition of any QRs and MEQRs. This provision clashes with the territorial protection granted to a holder of intellectual property rights who may use national law to partition the internal market alongside national lines in many ways. For example, he may charge different prices for the protected product in different Member States; he may restrict imports from one Member State to another; he may totally prevent any imports, since without his consent the protected product cannot be sold in another Member State. Thus, the exercise of a holder's rights may seriously hinder the free movement of goods. Article 36 TFEU recognises that intellectual property rights may constitute MEQRs. It provides a derogation from Article 34 TFEU subject to a very important limitation, which is that national measures based on IPRs must not constitute a means of arbitrary discrimination or a disguised restriction on trade between Member States.

The derogation from the free movement of goods contained in Article 36 TFEU applies to industrial and commercial property rights. The ECJ extended the scope of application of this derogation to copyrights and neighbouring rights in Case 78/70 *Deutsche Grammophon GmbH v Metro-SB-Grössmarkte GmbH*.[1528]

21.6.1 Patents

In order to ensure, on the one hand, economic integration within the internal market and, on the other, that the protection afforded to IPRs under national laws of the Member States does not partition the internal market along national lines, the ECJ made a distinction between the existence of intellectual property rights and their exercise. Article 345 TFEU refers to the existence of such rights while Articles 34, 35 and 36 TFEU relate to their exercise.

Article 345 TFEU states:

"The Treaties shall in no way prejudice the rules in Member States governing the system of property ownership."

Accordingly, under Article 345 TFEU EU law must not interfere with the existence of IPRs, but may restrict their exercise by virtue of Articles 34–36 TFEU. This means that the granting of IPRs and the content of such rights is governed by national law, while EU law supervises their

---

1528. [1971] ECR 487.

exercise. The extent of protection granted by national laws which EU law is prepared to tolerate was defined by the ECJ in Case 15/74 *Centrafarm v Sterling Drug*.[1529]

THE FACTS WERE:

Sterling Drug Inc, a holder of the UK and Dutch patents for a drug called Negram, had marketed that drug itself or via its licensees in both the UK and The Netherlands. Centrafarm, a Dutch company, bought Negram in the UK and Germany, it being less expensive there, and resold it in The Netherlands. Sterling Drug Inc brought proceedings against Centrafarm before a Dutch court to prevent Centrafarm from marketing Negram in The Netherlands.

Held:

The ECJ held that:

■ Article 30 EC [Article 36 TFEU] justifies a derogation from the free movement of goods only "for the purposes of safeguarding rights which constitute the specific subject matter of this property" and the specific subject matter of the intellectual property in respect of patents is:

" . . . the guarantee that the patentee, to reward the creative effort of the inventor, has the exclusive right to use an invention with a view to manufacturing industrial products and putting them into circulation for the first time, either directly or by grant of licences to third parties, as well as the right to oppose infringements".

Comment:

■ The specific subject-matter is protected under EU law. Once a holder has had the benefit of the specific subject-matter, its rights are exhausted and consequently, it cannot rely on IPRs provided for under national law of a Member State to prevent parallel imports of the protected goods, which by the holder, or with its consent, have lawfully been marketed in any other Member State of the EEA.

■ Bearing in mind that there is no full harmonisation of patent law and that slightly different patents for the same invention may be granted in different Member States to the holder, the ECJ decided that all patents that protect the same invention granted to the same holder are to be regarded as parallel patents.

From the judgment of the ECJ in Case 15/74 *Centrafarm v Sterling Drug* a distinction can be made between three situations:

■ Patentee A holds a patent in Member State A. It has manufactured and marketed the protected products in Member State A. B, who has manufactured products protected by A's patent in Member State B, without the consent of A, wants to export these products from Member State B to Member State A. Patentee A is entitled to prevent their importation into Member State A.

1529. [1974] ECR 1147.

■ Patentee A holds a patent in Member State A; patentee B holds a patent in Member State B. The patented products are similar in all respects. A and B are legally and economically independent of each other. Patentee A is entitled to prevent importation of B's products into Member State A and vice versa, in that patentee B can use its patent to keep A's products out of Member State B.

■ Patentee A holds a patent in Member State A and has granted a licence to B to manufacture protected products in Member State B. C, a parallel importer (who has no economic or legal links with A or B), decides to export the protected products manufactured in Member State B by B to Member State A (C hopes to make a profit because in Member State A the protected products sell for higher prices than in Member State B). Patentee A cannot prevent importation by C of the protected products from Member State B to Member State A. Patentee A, by giving its consent (by granting a licence to B), has put the protected product into circulation for the first time. His rights are exhausted.

The first two situations concern the existence of intellectual property rights. In both situations the obstacle to the free movement of goods which arises from the existence of national legislation concerning IPRs is justified under EU law. However, the third situation concerns the exercise of IPRs. EU law will not tolerate any obstacle to the free flow of goods between Member States in that situation, and so in this way EU law has achieved a compromise between the competing interests at stake – national IPRs and EU free movement principles.

The doctrine of the exhaustion of rights applies even though the protected products have been put into circulation in a Member State where the invention is not patentable. This occurred in Case 187/80 *Merck and Co. Inc v Stephar BV*.[1530]

THE FACTS WERE:

Merck held a Dutch patent relating to a drug used mainly in the treatment of high blood pressure. Merck was selling its drug in Italy. Under Italian law drugs were not patentable. Stephar bought the drug in Italy and imported it into The Netherlands where its price was much higher than in Italy. Merck brought proceedings against Stephar to prevent the latter from marketing the drug in The Netherlands. Merck argued that the impossibility of patenting its product in Italy deprived its creative effort from being rewarded.

Held:

The ECJ held that the right to reward for the patent holder was not guaranteed in all circumstances. It is for the holder of the patent to decide under what circumstances it will market its product including the possibility of marketing it in a Member State in which its product is not patentable. If the proprietor of the patent decides to market the product in a Member State where its product is not patentable, it must accept the consequences of its choice. In such circumstances its consent to put the product into circulation for the first time is presumed and it cannot rely on its patent to prevent parallel importation of its products.

1530. [1981] ECR 2063.

Comment:

In Joined Cases C-267 and C-268/95 *Merck and Beecham*[1531] the ECJ qualified its judgment in Case 187/80 *Merck*. The ECJ held that consent is presumed unless the proprietor of the patent proves that it is subject to a real and actual duty to market its product (that is, a legal duty) in a Member State in which its product is not patentable. In this case the argument submitted by Merck that it was its moral duty as a manufacturer of drugs to market them even in countries where there was no patent protection, was rejected by the ECJ.

At the centre of the concept of the exhaustion of rights is the consent of the owner of IPRs. Consent is presumed when the protected product is put into the market by its owner, or through its subsidiary, or when the owner and the undertaking that has first put the protected product into circulation are under common control.

The concept of exhaustion of rights, because there is no consent of the holder of the patent, does not apply in three situations:

- If the protected product has been put into circulation under compulsory licence. This was established in Case 19/84 *Pharmon BV v Hoechst AG*.[1532]

THE FACTS WERE:

Hoechst held a patent in Germany, The Netherlands and the UK for the process to manufacture a drug called Frusemide. In the UK Frusemide was manufactured under a compulsory licence by an undertaking named DDSA. Under UK law the consent of the holder of the patent to manufacturing, and so on, is not required under a compulsory licence although royalties on sales are paid to it. Pharmon, a Dutch undertaking, bought Frusemide in the UK and resold it in The Netherlands where Frusemide was more expensive. Hoechst brought proceedings against Pharmon to prevent the latter from marketing Frusemide in The Netherlands.

Held:

The ECJ held that Hoechst was entitled to rely on its patent to prevent Pharmon from marketing Frusemide. The ECJ emphasised that under a compulsory licence the patentee could not be deemed to have consented to the marketing of its product by a third party and thereby it is deprived of its rights to determine freely the conditions under which its product is marketed.

- If the patent is not exploited in the territory of a Member State where it was granted but patented goods are manufactured in another country by the patentee, or on his behalf, and then imported into the patent-granting Member State.[1533]

1531. [1996] ECR I-6285.
1532. [1985] ECR 2281.
1533. Case C-235/89 *Commission v Italy* [1992] ECR I-777; Case C-30/90 *Commission v UK* [1992] ECR I-829.

■ If patented goods are in transit in any Member State irrespective of their final destination.[1534] The case law confirms the view that transit (which consists of transporting goods lawfully manufactured in one Member State to another Member State or to a non-member country by passing through one or more Member States) does not involve any marketing of the goods in question and is therefore not liable to infringe the specific subject-matter of IPRs.

While the rules examined above in respect of patents apply to most types of intellectual property rights, some types of IPRs have peculiarities. These are examined below.

21.6.2 Trade mark rights

Directive 89/104/EEC of 21 December 1988 designed to approximate the Laws of the Member States relating to Trade Marks, which was implemented in the UK in the Trade Mark Act 1994, has brought important changes and clarification to the previous law in the trade marks area.

In particular, the directive clarified the application of the principle of exhaustion to advertisement of the protected products and the meaning of the concept of confusion of consumers. These topics are dealt with below.

In Case 16/74 *Centrafarm v Winthrop*,[1535] the specific subject-matter of a trade mark was defined in terms similar to those regarding patents. The ECJ held that the specific subject-matter is the guarantee to the owner of the trade mark that he has the exclusive right to use that trade mark, for the purpose of putting products protected by the trade mark into circulation for the first time (either directly or by the grant of licences to third parties). Until he does this, he is protected against competitors wishing to take unfair advantage of the status and reputation of the trade mark by illegally selling products bearing it. However, once the owner has put the trade-marked products into circulation for the first time in more than one Member State his exclusive right is lost and consequently he cannot prevent import of protected goods from other Member States into his own Member State. He has exhausted his right. In Case 16/74 *Centrafarm v Winthrop*, the same drug as in *Centrafarm v Sterling*, "Negram" was at issue but Centrafarm relied on the trade mark for this drug rather than the patent to prevent its import from the UK to The Netherlands.

For parallel importers who intend to sell protected products at lower prices than those fixed by the owner of the trade mark or his distributors, the vital issue is whether they can advertise the protected products. This is examined below.

21.6.2.1 The exhaustion of rights with regard to advertisement of protected products

In Case C-337/95 *Parfums Christian Dior SA and Parfums Christian Dior BV v Evora BV*,[1536] the ECJ decided that the principle of exhaustion applies to advertisement of the protected products.

1534. Whether within the EU: Case C-23/99 *Commission v France* [2000] ECR I-7653); or outside the EU: C-115/02 *Administration des Douanes et Droits Indirect v Rioglass SA, and Transremar SL* [2003] ECR I-12705.
1535. [1974] ECR 1183.
1536. [1997] ECR I-6013.

THE FACTS WERE:

The French company, Parfums Christian Dior SA (Dior France), and the Dutch company, Parfums Christian Dior BV (Dior Netherlands), brought an action against the Dutch company Evora, which operated a chain of chemist shops under the name of its subsidiary Kruidvat, for infringement of Dior trade marks and copyrights, and for an order to stop Evora from advertising Dior products in a manner which damaged the luxurious image of Dior products. In a Christmas promotion in 1993 Kruidvat advertised some Dior products. Evora advertising leaflets depicted the packaging and bottles of some Dior products, and according to the judgment of the referring court that depiction related clearly and directly to the goods offered for sale. The advertisement itself was carried out in a manner customary to retailers in this market sector. Kruidvat was neither a distributor of Dior France nor of Dior Netherlands. Dior products sold by the Kruidvat shops were supplied by Evora, which obtained them by means of parallel imports.

Held:

The ECJ held that Articles 5 to 7 of Directive 89/104 requires that when trade-marked goods have been put in the Community market by or with the consent of the owner of the trade mark, a reseller is entitled not only to resell those goods but also to make use of the trade mark to bring to the public's attention their further commercialisation. In other words, an owner of a trade mark cannot prevent a reseller from advertising the protected goods and using the trade mark in so doing. However, the ECJ held that in some circumstances relating to the content of the advertising the owner of a trade mark may stop a reseller from advertising the further commercialisation of goods. The legitimate interests of the trade mark owner must be protected, especially when a reseller is using the trade mark for advertising in a manner which could damage its reputation. This requirement was particularly difficult to satisfy, taking into account the fact that the reseller was not an authorised distributor of Dior products. Under EU law a reseller has to advertise the trade mark protected goods using methods which are customary to its sector of trade, in a manner which will not damage the reputation of the trade mark in question, and must avoid associating luxury products with other non-luxury products it sells.

Further clarification of the concept of exhaustion of trade mark rights in the context of advertisement of protected products was provided in Case C-63/97 *Bayerische Motorenwerke AG (BMW) and BMW Netherlands BV v Ronald Karel Deenik*,[1537] which concerned unauthorised use of the BMW trade mark in an advertisement for a garage business in the light of Articles 5 and 7 of Directive 89/104.

1537. [1999] ECR I-905.

THE FACTS WERE:

A German car manufacturer, BMW, and its Dutch branch, BMW Netherlands, brought an action against Mr Deenik, an independent owner of a garage specialising in the sale of second-hand BMW cars and repairs and maintenance of BMW cars, for using the BMW trade mark in advertisements for his business. The Hoge Raad (the Supreme Court of The Netherlands) considered that some of the advertisements might be unlawful, as they suggested that Mr Deenik's business was affiliated to the trade mark proprietor's distribution network, while other uses of the trade mark – such as "repairs and maintenance of BMW", "BMW specialist" – did not constitute infringement of that mark. The Hoge Raad asked the ECJ to interpret Articles 5 to 7 of Directive 89/104/EEC.

Held:

In relation to Article 5 of Directive 89/104/EEC the ECJ held that both the sale of second-hand BMW cars and services such as repair and maintenance of BMW cars were within the scope of Article 5 of the Directive. In order to determine whether the use of a trade mark is lawful for advertisement purposes, the Court distinguished between the sale of goods covered by that trade mark and their repair and maintenance.

With regard to the sale of goods, the ECJ confirmed its decision in Case C-337/95 *Parfums Christian Dior*,[1538] that is, that a reseller is entitled to make use of a trade mark to bring to the public's attention the further commercialisation of the protected products. However, the owner of a trade mark may stop a reseller from using its trade mark if advertisements by the reseller damage the reputation of the trade mark.

In respect of the advertisement for repair and maintenance of BMW cars, the ECJ held that the principle of the "exhaustion of rights" does not apply as there is no further commercialisation of goods.

Comment:

It should be noted that even if a reseller advertises the goods covered by a trade mark in a manner customary to its sector of trade, the owner of a trade mark may, in special circumstances, invoke Article 7(2) of Directive 89/104/EEC to prohibit the use of its mark by a reseller. This occurs when a reseller advertises in such a manner as to induce the public into believing that there is a commercial connection between the two undertakings. This kind of advertisement is dishonest, unfair and harms the legitimate interests of the trade mark owner. If there is no risk that the public will have the impression that there is a commercial connection between the two undertakings, the reseller is permitted to derive advantage from using the trade mark in the advertisement, in particular to enhance the quality of its business.

As to the advertisement for repair and maintenance of BMW cars, the principle of the "exhaustion of rights" does not apply as there is no further commercialisation of goods. In this context Article 6(1)(c) of the Directive lays down the conditions for using a trade mark. A third party is entitled to use a trade mark to inform the public about the intended purpose of

---

1538. [1997] ECR I-6013.

products or services, and in particular with regard to items such as accessories or spare parts, unless the mark is used in a way that may create the impression that there is a commercial connection between the two undertakings, and in particular that the reseller's business is affiliated to the trade mark proprietor's distribution network or that there is a special relationship between the two undertakings. Accordingly, the use of a trade mark is lawful provided there is no risk that the public will be induced to believe that there is a commercial link between the two undertakings.

21.6.2.2   The concept of confusion

Very often proprietors of trade marks try to prevent the import from other Member States of goods bearing a similar trade mark to their own and relating to similar products on the ground that this may give rise to confusion for consumers in the Member State of importation.

Before the entry into force of Directive 89/104 the ECJ provided some clarifications in a number of cases as to the meaning of the concept of confusion. One of the first cases was Case 119/75 *Terrapin (Overseas) Ltd v Terranova Industrie C.A. Kapferer*.[1539]

THE FACTS WERE:

A German undertaking, proprietor of the trade mark "Terranova", sought to prevent an English company from registering its trade name "Terrapin" in Germany, on the grounds that both undertakings dealt in building materials and the similarity of their name would lead to confusion among consumers.

Held:

The ECJ held Terranova could rely on Article 30 EC [Article 36 TFEU] to prevent the import of goods marketed under a trade mark giving rise to confusion provided that the trade mark rights were acquired by different proprietors under different national laws. However, the usual proviso of Article 30 EC [Article 36 TFEU] applied, that is, the prevention of imports must not constitute arbitrary discrimination or a disguised restriction on trade between Member States.

In Case C-317/91 *Deutsche Renault AG v Audi AG*,[1540] the ECJ held that Audi could rely on its German trade mark "Quattro" to prevent the use of the trade mark "Quadra" in Germany by a Renault subsidiary established in Germany for a four-wheel drive vehicle marketed under this name in France and other countries, if the use of that trade mark gave rise to confusion for German consumers. It was the task of the German court to determine whether that was the case on the basis of German law.

1539.   [1976] ECR 1039.
1540.   [1993] ECR I-6227.

Under Directive 89/104, in particular its Article 4(1)(b), in Case C-251/95 *Sabel BV v Puma AG, Rudolf Dassler Sport*,[1541] the ECJ further clarified the meaning of the concept of confusion.

THE FACTS WERE:

Puma AG, a German company, brought proceedings against a Dutch company, Sabel BV, opposing the registration of a trade mark of Sabel in Germany under the international registration system of the Madrid Arrangement, on the basis that ideas conveyed by the pictorial elements of the mark consisting of the name of Sabel and the representation of a running leopard conflicted with its trade mark of a running puma. Both companies were selling similar goods, that is, leather and imitation leather products. The German Supreme Court (the Bundesgerichtshof) referred to the ECJ for a preliminary ruling a question on the interpretation of Article 4(1)(b) of First Council Directive 89/104. This sets out the grounds on which registration of a trade mark may be refused, or a registered mark declared invalid if, due to similarity of identity to an earlier registered trade mark with the trade mark to be registered (or already registered but later than the first trade mark) there is a likelihood of confusion of both trade marks on the part of the public, which includes the likelihood of association between the two marks. The German court asked the ECJ to clarify the meaning of the criterion "likelihood of confusion . . . which includes the likelihood of association with the earlier trade mark".

The question asked by the German court was whether the simple likelihood of association between the two trade marks on the part of the public, excluding any likelihood of confusion, constituted a sufficient reason to refuse the registration of the second trade mark.

Held:

The ECJ referred to the preamble of the Directive which provides that the likelihood of confusion should be assessed on the basis of a number of factors such as the recognition of the trade mark in the market, the association which can be made with the used or registered sign, and so on. As a result, in order to decide whether in a particular case there is a likelihood of confusion, all relevant factors should be taken into account, that is, an overall impression given by the marks would indicate whether there is visual, aural or conceptual similarity between them.

Comment:

Resulting from the above, the likelihood of confusion between the two marks depends upon the distinctiveness of the earlier mark either per se or because of the reputation it enjoys with the public. The ECJ emphasised that in this case, because the earlier mark was not especially well known to the public and that the idea conveyed by the pictorial element of the two trade marks was of little imaginative content, there was little risk that the public would confuse the two marks, although consumers may associate them in the sense that one would simply bring the other to mind without the likelihood of confusion about the origin of the goods. The

---

1541. [1997] ECR I-6191.

ECJ held that the criterion of "likelihood of confusion which includes the likelihood of association with an earlier mark" means that the mere association which the consumers might
make between two trade marks with analogous semantic content does not constitute in itself
a sufficient ground for concluding that there is a likelihood of confusion. So for the ECJ,
likelihood of confusion is a narrower concept than likelihood of association; association
between two things in the public mind does not mean the public will necessarily confuse
the two.

The concept of confusion was further considered by the ECJ in Case C-342/97 *Lloyd Schuhfab-
rik Meyer & Co GmbH V Klijsen Handel BV*,[1542] in which Article 5(1)(b) of Directive 89/104
concerning the risk of confusion was at issue. In this case the ECJ indicated the criteria which a
referring court should take into consideration in order to assess the likelihood of confusion.

THE FACTS WERE:

*Lloyd Schufabrik Meyer, a German manufacturer of shoes distributed under the trade mark
"Lloyd", sought an order restraining Klijsen Handel BV, a Dutch manufacturer of shoes distributed under the name "Loint's", from using the trade mark "Loint's" in Germany on the
ground that "Loint's" was likely to be confused with "Lloyd" because of the aural similarity
between them. Lloyd emphasised that its trade mark had a particularly distinctive character
arising from the absence of descriptive elements, was well recognised in the market and had
been used consistently and extensively since 1927.*

*The referring court, the Landgericht München I (Munich I Regional Court) doubted the
likelihood of confusion on the part of the public on the ground that there was only aural
similarity between the trade marks.*

Held:

The ECJ repeated that the likelihood of confusion must be assessed globally, taking into
account all factors relevant to the circumstances of the case, that is, does the overall impression given by the trade marks indicate whether there is visual, aural or conceptual similarity
between them.

Comment:

The likelihood of confusion between the two trade marks depends upon the distinctiveness
of the earlier mark either per se or because of the reputation it enjoys with the public.[1543]
Thus, the greater the similarity between the goods or services covered by the trade marks
and the greater the distinctiveness of the earlier mark, the greater would be the likelihood of
confusion. In determining the distinctiveness of a trade mark it is necessary to take into
consideration the greater or lesser capacity of the mark to identify the goods and services for

---

1542. [1999] ECR I-3819.
1543. See Case C-251/95 *Sabel* [1997] ECR I-6191 and Case C-39/97 *Canon* [1998] ECR I-5507.

which it has been registered as coming from a particular undertaking. In this respect, important factors are: the inherent characteristic of the mark including that it does or does not contain an element descriptive of the goods and services for which it has been registered; the consistent and extensive use of the trade mark over a very long period; its geographic market, and so on. However, it was not possible to state in general terms, for example by referring to given percentages relating to the degree of recognition attained by the mark within the relevant section of the public, whether it had a strong distinctive character.

The ECJ held that, taking into consideration all these factors, it was possible that mere aural similarity between trade marks could create a likelihood of confusion in the light of Article 5(1)(b) of Directive 89/104.

To summarise EU law on the concept of confusion, it can be said that:

- The concept of likelihood of confusion includes the likelihood of association with the earlier trade mark, but the likelihood of association does not entail the likelihood of confusion;

- The likelihood of confusion between two trade marks depends upon the distinctiveness of the earlier mark either per se or because of the reputation it enjoys with the public;

- Visual, aural and conceptual similarity of allegedly conflicting trade marks is part of a global assessment;

- When assessing the overall impression given by allegedly conflicting trade marks, their distinctive and dominant components must be taken into account;[1544]

- The assessment is made from the perspective of an average consumer of the EU who is reasonably well-informed and reasonably observant and circumspect. He/she normally perceives a mark as a whole, not its details, and his/her level of attention is likely to depend on the category of goods or services in question;

- The overall assessment takes account of the perception of the conflicting marks by an average EU consumer and of all factors relevant to the circumstances of the case;[1545]

- The existence of a risk that an average consumer (referred to in the Directive as the "public") might believe that the goods or services under consideration come from the same undertakings, or from economically-linked undertakings, shows a likelihood of confusion.[1546]

21.6.2.3   The doctrine of common origin of a trade mark

It may occur that, for various reasons, the right to use the original trade mark has been split. As a result, undertakings independent from each other and operating in different countries are lawfully

---

1544. Case T-292/01 *Phillips Van Heusen v OHIM – Pash Textilvertrieb und Einzelhandel (BASS)* [2003] ECR II-4335.

1545. Case T-185/02 *Ruiz-Picasso and Others v OHIM – DaimlerChrysler* [2004] ECR II-1739, upheld by the ECJ in Case C-361/04P [2006] ECR I-643.

1546. Case T-6/01 *Matratzen Concord v OHIM – Hukla Germany* [2002] ECR II-4335 and Case T-129/01 *Alejandro v OHIM – Anheuser-Busch* [2003] ECR II-2251, para 37.

using the same trade mark. There is an issue as to whether under EU law undertakings using a trade mark of common origin may rely on their trade mark rights to prevent each other from importing protected goods into each other's territory. The ECJ addressed this issue in Case 192/73 *Van Zuylen Frères v Hag AG (No.1)*.[1547]

THE FACTS WERE:

A German undertaking was the proprietor of the "Kaffee Hag" trade mark in Germany, Belgium and Luxembourg. After World War II its rights to the mark in Belgium and Luxembourg were sequestrated and assigned to Van Zuylen. When the German undertaking subsequently exported its "Kaffee Hag" coffee to Belgium, Van Zuylen sought to rely on its trade mark rights to prevent the importation.

Held:

The ECJ held that Van Zuylen was not entitled to rely on its trade mark to prevent the marketing in one Member State of a product lawfully made in another Member State under an identical mark, but the ECJ reversed this judgment in *Hag II* (see below).

The Hag (No. 1) decision was much criticised, in particular because the German undertaking had never consented to the marketing of its product in Belgium by Van Zuylen and therefore the principle of exhaustion of rights was not applicable. The ECJ reached an opposite decision in Case C-10/89 *CNL Sucal v Hag (Hag II)*,[1548] in which the then owner of the trade mark "Kaffee Hag" in Belgium sought to sell its product in Germany and the German proprietor of "Kaffee Hag" tried to prevent the importation. The ECJ allowed the German holder to rely on its trade mark to exclude products made by a third party but bearing a trade mark with a common origin to its own, in a manner that would partition the common market. The likelihood of confusion between both products was an essential factor in deciding the case. However, the ECJ did not justify the change of its approach in *Hag II*.

The approach in *Hag II* was confirmed in Case C-9/93 *IHT Internationale Heiztechnik GmbH v Ideal Standard GmbH*.[1549]

THE FACTS WERE:

The trade mark "Ideal Standard" for sanitary fittings and heating equipment was held by two subsidiaries of an American company, one in France and another in Germany. The trade mark having belonged to the parent company, it had (in the hands of the subsidiaries) a common origin. The French subsidiary assigned the trade mark for France to an undertaking named SGT, which was an independent undertaking. When a German undertaking (IHT) sought to

---

1547. [1974] ECR 731.
1548. [1990] ECR I-3711.
1549. [1994] ECR I-2789.

import heating equipment made by SGT and bearing the trade mark "Ideal Standard" from France to Germany, the German subsidiary successfully relied on its German trade mark to prevent the import of the offending products to Germany.

Held:

The ECJ held that the principle in *Hag II* applied irrespective of whether the splitting of the original trade mark was due to an act of a public authority or a contractual assignment.

21.6.2.4   Repackaging and rebranding of the protected product

The term "repackaging" in EU law is used to refer to the practice of removing the original packaging of trade-marked products and displaying the original trade mark on new packaging.

"Rebranding" involves the replacement of the original packaging and trade mark, so that a new trade mark appears on the new packaging.

Repackaging and rebranding are often used by distributors of products such as pharmaceuticals in order to sell them at different prices in different Member States. Very often a third party takes advantage of the price difference by buying such products in a Member State where they are cheaper, repackaging and/or rebranding them and then reselling them in a Member State where they are generally more expensive.

Under EU law, a parallel importer is not allowed to repackage/rebrand at will. Repackaging and rebranding is allowed only if such action is necessary for the product to be marketed in the Member State of importation. In Case C-443/99 *Merck, Sharp & Dohme GmbH v Paranova Pharmazeutika Handels GmbH*,[1550] the ECJ elucidated the concept of "necessity" of repackaging/rebranding. The Court stated that such necessity exists, for example, where:

- A parallel importer cannot place pharmaceutical products on the market in the Member State of importation because national law requires their repackaging;

- National sickness insurance rules make reimbursement of medical expenses conditional upon certain packaging;

- Well-established medical prescription practices are based, inter alia, on standard sizes recommended by professional bodies or by sickness insurance institutions.

The mere fact that a substantial proportion of consumers in the Member State of importation will refuse to buy relabelled foreign packs is not sufficient to be considered as a necessity to the repackaging/rebranding of pharmaceutical products. In such circumstances a finding of necessity would depend on whether resistance to relabelled pharmaceutical products constitutes a real impediment to effective access to the market concerned. If so, the repackaging is necessary. It is a question of fact and the task of a national court to ascertain whether a strong resistance from a significant proportion of consumers in the Member State of importation constitutes an impediment to effective market access for the products concerned. The ECJ emphasised that a trade

---

1550. [2002] ECR I-3703.

mark owner will succeed in opposing repackaging/rebranding in a situation where a parallel importer, by repackaging, is seeking to secure a commercial advantage.

It emerges from the case law[1551] of the ECJ that, provided it is necessary as above, repackaging is allowed so long as:

- It does not adversely affect the original condition of the product;

- The new packaging clearly states the name of the manufacturer and the person who has repackaged the product;

- The repackaging is not such as to damage the trade mark's reputation;

- The repackager gives notice of its intention to the trade mark owner and supplies samples if requested.

In Case C-143/00 *Boehringer Ingelheim KG and Others v Swingward Ltd and Downelhurst Ltd*,[1552] the ECJ confirmed the requirement of prior notice in all circumstances. The parallel importer must give notice and provide a sample of the repackaged product to the trade mark owner. It is not sufficient that the owner is notified by other sources. If the parallel importer fails to give notice, the trade mark owner may oppose the marketing of the repackaged product. As to the period of notice given to the owner to react to the intended repackaging, the ECJ stated that the proprietor of the trade mark must have a reasonable time to react. What should be considered as a reasonable time depends upon all the relevant circumstances to be assessed by a national court in the event of a dispute. Due attention must be paid to the interests of the parallel importer who will want to put the product concerned on the market in the Member State of importation as soon as possible after completing the necessary formalities in that Member State.

Remedies available to a holder of a trade mark are governed by national rules subject to limitations imposed by EU law as to the requirements of equivalence, effectiveness and pro-portionality. However, in Case C-348/04 *Boehringer Ingelheim KG v Swingward Ltd and Others*[1553] the ECJ held that failure to give prior notice by a parallel importer would give the trade mark holder the right to claim financial remedies on the same basis as if the goods had been spurious.

It is for a parallel importer to prove that the condition of necessity and the further four conditions set out above are satisfied.[1554] If one of them is not satisfied, the holder of a trade mark will be allowed to oppose the further commercialisation.

21.6.3 Copyright

With regard to a copyright a distinction is made between:

- Non-performance copyrights such as those in literary and artistic works (for example, books, paintings, sound-recordings); and

- Performance copyrights concerning plays and films and their performance.

1551. Case 102/77 *Hoffmann-la Roche v Centrafarm* [1978] ECR 1139; Case 3/78 *Centrafarm v American Home Product* [1978] ECR 1823; Cases C-427/93, C-429/93 and C-436/93 *Bristol-Myers Squibb and Others* [1996] ECR I-3457; Case C-379/97 *Pharmacia and Upjohn SA v Paranova* [1999] ECR I-6927.

1552. [2002] ECR I-3759.

1553. [2007] ECR I-3391.

1554. Case C-405/03 *Class International* [2005] ECR I-8735.

In respect of non-performance copyrights EC law has always distinguished between those rights which by their nature may be "exhausted", for instance the marketing of a book in another Member State with the consent of the owner,[1555] and those which cannot be "exhausted" such as rental rights. Rental right cannot be exhausted by the marketing of the protected product in another Member State.[1556] In this respect Article 4(2) of Directive 2001/29/EC harmonising certain aspects of copyright and related rights in the information society[1557] provides that:

> "the distribution right shall not be exhausted within the Community in respect of the original or copies of the work, except where the first sale or other transfer of ownership in the Community of that object is made by the rightholder or with his consent."

Performance copyrights are to be viewed in the context of the provision of services rather than of the free movement of goods, as the exploitation of these works occurs through public exhibitions which can be repeated an indefinite number of times. In Case 62/79 *Coditel SA v Ciné Vog Films*,[1558] the ECJ held that Article 49 EC [Article 56 TFEU] did not preclude "an assignee of the performing right in a cinematographic film in a Member State from relying upon his rights to prohibit the exhibition of that film in that State, without his authority, by means of cable diffusion if the film so exhibited is picked up and transmitted after being broadcast in another Member State by a third party with the consent of the original owner of the right".

The above position is restated in Article 3(3) of Directive 2001/29/EC which provides that the right of communicating to the public and the right to the making available to the public of protected works will not be exhausted by any act of communication to the public or of making available to the public. As a result, the Directive provides authors, during the protection period fixed under national law, with the exclusive right to authorise or prohibit any communication to the public of originals and copies of their works whether by wired or wireless means. The meaning of the concept "communication to the public" (Article 3(1) of Directive 2001/29/EC) was interpreted by the ECJ in Case C-306/05 *Sociedad General de Autores y Editores de España (SGAE) v Rafael Hoteles SA*.[1559]

THE FACTS WERE:

SGAE, the Spanish body responsible for the management of intellectual property rights in Spain, brought proceedings against Rafael Hoteles SA claiming that the use of television sets to play ambient music within a hotel owned by Rafael involved communication to the public of works belonging to the repertoire which SGAE managed. The Spanish court decided that the use of television sets in the hotel's rooms did not involve communication to the public of works managed by SGAE but their use in the public areas of the hotel did. Both parties appealed and the Spanish court dealing with their appeal decided to refer the matter to the ECJ under Article 234 EC.

1555. Joined Cases 55/80 and 57/80 *Musik-Vertrieb v GEMA* [1981] ECR 147.
1556. Case 158/86 *EMI Electrola, Warner Brothers Inc v Christiansen* [1988] ECR 2605.
1557. [2001] OJ L167/10.
1558. [1980] ECR 881.
1559. [2006] ECR I-11519.

Held:

The ECJ held that the concept of "communication to the public" must be interpreted broadly. First, based on the interpretation given by the ECJ to the term "public", which refers to an indeterminate number of potential television viewers,[1560] the Court held that not only guests at a hotel but also customers in public areas of a hotel who were able to make use of television sets taken together constituted "public".

Second, the mere existence of facilities (TV sets) that make public access to broadcast works technically possible does not amount to "communication to the public". However, if by means of television sets the hotel distributes the signal to customers, irrespective of whether they are staying in rooms or in public areas of the hotel, this constitutes communication to the public within the meaning of Article 3(1) of that Directive.

The specific subject matter of the right to rent, perform or show works in public allows the holder of such a right to control each and every use and thus to be paid fees for each and every use. The holder's right is not exhausted by the first showing, or the first performance or the lending of the relevant works in another Member State.

21.6.4 Design rights

The design of a product relates to the appearance of a product, in particular, the shape, texture, colour, materials used, contours and ornamentation.

In Case 144/81 *Keurkoop BV v Nancy Kean Gifts BV*,[1561] the ECJ extended the application of Article 30 EC [Article 36 TFEU] to design rights.

THE FACTS WERE:

A Dutch company Nancy Kean Gifts, which registered a design for a ladies' handbag with the Benelux Design Office and which obtained supplies of handbags from Taiwan, sought to prevent another Dutch company, Keurkoop, from selling in the Benelux countries ladies handbags, which had originally come from Taiwan but were imported from another Member State, and which were identical in appearance to those sold by Nancy Kean.

Held:

The ECJ held that Nancy Kean was allowed to rely on its national intellectual property rights to prevent Keurkoop from selling the product in the Benelux countries. This was because neither Nancy Kean nor a person legally or economically dependent on it had put the product in question into circulation in another Member State.

1560. Case C-89/04 *Mediakabel* [2005] ECR I-4891 and Case C-192/04 *Lagardère Active Broadcast* [2005] ECR I-7199.
1561. [1982] ECR 2853.

The application of the principle of exhaustion of rights in respect of design rights was confirmed in subsequent cases.[1562]

21.6.5 Parallel imports of goods from outside the European Economic Area (EEA)

The principle of the exhaustion of intellectual property rights does not apply to imports from outside the EEA. The holder of intellectual property rights is entitled to prevent parallel import of protected products coming from non-Member States to a Member State, even if the holder was first responsible for putting its goods into circulation. This was confirmed by the ECJ in Case C-355/96 *Silhouette International Schmied GmbH & Co Kg v Hartlauer Handelsgesellschaft MbH.*[1563]

THE FACTS WERE:

Silhouette, a well-known manufacturer of top-quality fashion spectacles, used its trade mark "Silhouette" registered in Austria and most countries in the world to sell its product. In October 1995 Silhouette sold 21,000 out-of-fashion spectacle frames to a Bulgarian company. Silhouette instructed its representative to inform the purchaser that the frames were to be resold only in Bulgaria (at that time Bulgaria was not a member of the EU or the EEA) and the states of the former Soviet Union, and not in the territory of the EU. However, this restriction was not inserted into the contract, and it was not clear whether in fact the purchaser was aware of such a restriction. In December 1995 the frames were resold to Hartlauer, a retailer in Austria that sells spectacles and frames for low prices. Hartlauer offered frames bearing Silhouette's trade mark for sale in Austria. Silhouette never supplied spectacles or frames to Hartlauer because Silhouette considered that distribution of its products by Hartlauer would be harmful to its image as a manufacturer of top-quality fashion spectacles. Silhouette brought an action for interim relief before the Landesgericht Steyr, seeking an injunction restraining Hartlauer from offering spectacles or spectacle frames for sale in Austria under its trade mark, as the sale of cut-price and outmoded spectacle frames would damage its brand reputation within the EU. Silhouette argued that its trade mark rights were not exhausted within the meaning of Directive 89/104/EEC, as they are exhausted only when the goods have been put on the market in the EEA by the proprietor or with its consent. Hautlauer's answer was that Silhouette had not sold the frames subject to any prohibition of, or restriction on, reimportation and that the Austrian law implementing the Directive did not grant a right to seek prohibitory injunctions. Silhouette's action was dismissed by the Landesgericht Steyr and, on appeal, by the Oberlandesgericht Linz. Silhouette appealed to the Oberster Gerichtshof on a point of law.

The Austrian Oberster Gerichtshof (Supreme Court) referred to the ECJ for a preliminary ruling under Article 234 EC [Article 267 TFEU] two questions concerning the interpretation of Article 7(1) of Directive 89/104. In particular, the Austrian court asked whether the holder

---

1562. Case 53/87 *Consorzio Italiano della Componentistica di Ricambio per Autoveicoli and Maxicar v Régie Nationale des Usines Renault* [1988] ECR 6039 and Case 238/87 *AB Volvo v Eric Veng (UK) Ltd* [1988] ECR 6211.
1563. [1998] ECR I-4799.

of a trade mark who has consented to market the protected products in the Community and in the EEA can prevent a third party from using the trade mark outside the EEA, or whether it has exhausted its rights when the goods have been put in circulation, by or with its consent, in the Community and in the EEA.

At the time of the dispute Austria was a Member of the EEA only – not of the EU. Its national law prior to the implementation of Directive 89/104 recognised the principle of inter-national exhaustion, according to which once goods have been marketed anywhere by, or with the consent of the owner, its rights are exhausted and therefore it has no control over the goods. Austrian rules implementing the Directive restricted the exhaustion principle to the time of first marketing within the EEA. For that reason Hautlauer argued that the Directive applied only to the EEA, and the question of international exhaustion was left to the national law of Member States.

Held:

The ECJ rejected the argument submitted by Hautlauer. The Court stated that Article 7 of the Directive had comprehensively resolved the question of exhaustion in the sense that it har-monised law in this area in all Member States. This solution ensures uniformity, and is in conformity with the objectives of the Directive. The ECJ emphasised that if some Member States recognised the principle of international exhaustion while others did not, the result might be the existence of barriers to the free movement of goods and services within the EEA.

Comment:

Silhouette had not exhausted its IPR and was able to stop Hautlauer from selling the pro-tected products in the EEA. For consumers in the EEA the decision of the ECJ means that they are no longer able to buy branded goods imported from outside the EEA and obtained from unauthorised sources at a low price.

The decision of the ECJ in the above case reinforces the protection conferred under EU law upon the owner of a trade mark. He is entitled to stop parallel imports from outside the EEA. As a result, there is nothing to prevent him from setting up whatever differing commercial arrange-ments he likes inside and outside the EEA.

In Case C-173/98 *Sebago Inc v Unic SA*,[1564] the ECJ clarified the concept of consent under Article 7(1) of Directive 89/104. The ECJ held that the concept of consent must relate to each individual item of the product in respect of which exhaustion is pleaded.

THE FACTS WERE:

This case concerned proceedings jointly brought by Sebago Inc, a company incorporated in the USA, the proprietor of two trade marks in the name of "Docksides", and three trade

---

1564.   [1999] ECR I-4103.

marks in the name of "Sebago" for shoes, all registered in the Benelux countries, and Ancienne Maison Dubois et Fils SA, an exclusive distributor in the Benelux countries of shoes bearing Sebago's trade marks. The proceedings were brought against GH-Unic SA for infringement of Sebago's trade mark rights by the marketing of Sebago shoes in the Community without Sebago's consent. GB-Unic SA advertised and sold in its Maxi-GB hypermarkets in Belgium 2,561 pairs of "Docksides" Sebago shoes manufactured in El Salvador, which it purchased from a Belgian company specialising in parallel importation. Sebago did not contest the fact that the shoes so sold were genuine Sebago shoes.

Held:

The ECJ restrictively interpreted the conditions under which the trade mark owner's consent is deemed to have been given for the purposes of the exhaustion of its trade mark rights. Such consent must relate to each individual item of the product in respect of which exhaustion is pleaded. Therefore, the consent of Sebago to the marketing in the EEA of one batch of shoes bearing the mark did not exhaust its trade mark rights in relation to the marketing of other batches of identical or similar shoes bearing the same mark, to the marketing of which in the EEA Sebago had not consented.

Comment:

The above judgment means that a particular product sold by, or with the consent of the trade mark proprietor within the EEA can be resold freely within the territory of the EEA under the exhaustion principle. However, a particular product sold by, or with the consent of the trade mark proprietor outside the EEA cannot be resold freely within the EEA, even if the trade mark proprietor authorises the sale within the EEA of identical products.

In Joined Cases C-414/99 to C-416/99 *Zino Davidoff SA v A & G Imports Ltd*[1565] the issue was whether the express consent of a trade mark holder is required for parallel importation of protected goods from outside the EEA into the EEA. The ECJ answered in the affirmative, adding that unequivocal consent would equal express consent.

AIDE-MÉMOIRE

ARTICLE 36 TFEU

The list of derogations is exhaustive. All derogations have been narrowly construed. Distinctly applicable measures can only be justified under Article 36 TFEU (Case 113/80 *Commission v Ireland [Re Irish Souvenirs]*). Indistinctly applicable measures can be justified under both Article 36 TFEU and the rule of reason set out in the *Cassis de Dijon* case.

- Purely economic measures cannot be justified under Article 36 TFEU (Case 7/61 *Commission v Italy*);

1565. [2001] ECR I-8691.

- Measures taken under Article 36 TFEU must comply with the requirements of the principle of proportionality (C-366/04 *Schwarz*);

- Measures under Article 36 TFEU must not constitute a means of arbitrary discrimination or disguised restrictions on trade between Member States (Case 124/81 *Commission v UK [Re UHT Milk]*);

- It is incumbent on a Member State to prove that a national measure which restricts trade between Member States is justified under Article 36 TFEU (Case 227/82 *Leendert van Bennekom*) but a Member State is not required to prove that no other conceivable measure could enable it to attain the objective sought under the same conditions (Case C-110/05 *Commission v Italy*).

DEROGATIONS UNDER ARTICLE 36 TFEU

1. Public morality: Case 121/85 *Conegate Limited v HM Customs & Excise*;

2. Public policy: Case 154/85 *Commission v Italy*;

3. Public security: Case 72/83 *Campus Oil Ltd v Minister for Industry and Energy*;

4. Protection of the health and life of humans, animals and plants: Case 238/82 *Duphar BV*; Case C-366/04 *Schwarz*;

5. Protection of national treasures possessing artistic, historic or archaeological value: there is no case law on this point;

6. Protection of industrial and commercial property.

Existence of IPRs

This is governed by national law and is not subject to any interference by EU law (Article 345 TFEU).

Exercise of IPRs

Exercise of IPRs falls within the derogation to free movement of goods in Article 36 TFEU in so far as such exercise relates to the **specific subject matter** of the relevant intellectual property.

The specific subject matter varies according to the type of IPR, but its bare essential is that it protects holders of IPRs until they put the protected product into circulation for the first time, in another Member State, themselves or by making appropriate arrangements with a third party. The term "**putting into circulation**" means the marketing by IPR holders, or their consenting to the marketing of the protected product, in more than one Member State. Once IPR holders have marketed or have consented to the marketing of their product in another Member State of the EEA, their **intellectual property rights are exhausted**. They cannot invoke them subsequently to prevent parallel imports of the protected products.

Patents

For patents the specific subject matter of IPRs protected under EU law is:

"... the guarantee that the patentee, to reward the creative effort of the inventor, has the exclusive right to use an invention with a view to manufacturing industrial products and putting them into circulation for the first time, either directly or by grant of licences to third parties, as well as the right to oppose infringements" (Case 15/74 *Centrafarm v Sterling Drug*)."

To be noted:

The principle of exhaustion:

- **Applies** when the patent holder has put the protected product into circulation in a Member State where the product is of a class which is not patentable in that Member State (Case 187/80 *Merck*). However, the principle of exhaustion does not apply if that Member State imposes a legal obligation (not merely an ethical or a moral obligation) on the patent holder to market the product (Cases C-267 and C-268/95 *Merck and Beecham*).

- **Does not apply** in three circumstances:
  - When the protected product has been put into circulation under compulsory licence (19/84 *Pharmon*);
  - When a patent is not exploited in the territory of a Member State where it was granted but patented goods are manufactured in another country and then imported into the patent-granting Member State (Case C-235/89 *Commission v Italy*); and
  - When patented goods are in transit in any Member State irrespective of their final destination (inside or outside the EU) (Case C-23/99 *Commission v France*).

Trade marks

For trade marks the specific subject matter is:

"... the guarantee that the owner of the trade mark has the exclusive right to use that trade mark, for the purpose of putting products protected by the trade mark into circulation for the first time, either directly, or by the grant of licences to third parties and thus to protect him against competitors wishing to take unfair advantage of the status and reputation of the trade mark by selling products illegally bearing his trade mark" (Case 16/74 *Centrafarm v Winthrop*).

The definition of the specific subject matter of a trade mark is largely the same as that for patents.

The principle of exhaustion of trade marks covers the advertisement of the protected products by parallel importers (Case C-337/95 *Parfums Christian Dior*).

The concept of confusion

The likelihood of confusion between two trade marks depends upon the distinctiveness of the earlier mark either per se or because of the reputation it enjoys with the public (Case C-251/95 *Sabel BV v Puma AG*).

The doctrine of common origin of a trade mark

A holder can rely on its trade mark to prevent the importation into its own Member State of products made by a third party but bearing a trade mark with a common origin to its own (Case C-10/89CNL *Sucal v Hag (Hag II)*).

Rebranding and repackaging of the protected product

Rebranding and repackaging, provided it is necessary, is allowed if:

- It does not adversely affect the original condition of the product;

- The new packaging clearly states the name of the manufacturer and the person who has repackaged the product;

- The repackaging is not such as to damage the trade mark's reputation;

- The repackager gives notice of its intention to the trade mark owner and supplies samples if requested (Case C-443/99 *Merck, Sharp & Dohme GmbH*).

Copyright

There is a distinction between non-performance copyrights and performance copyrights.

- Non-Performance copyrights (books, paintings, and so on). The subject matter is similar to patents except that there is an additional distinction between those rights which by their nature may be "exhausted" (for example, the marketing of a book in another Member State with the consent of the owner) and those which cannot be "exhausted" (for example, rental rights which cannot be exhausted by the sale of the protected product in another Member State).

- Performance copyrights (plays, films and their performance). This is related to the provision of services. The specific subject matter of the right to rent, perform and show the works in public allows the holder of such rights to control each and every use and thus to be paid fees for each and every use. Its right is not exhausted by first showing, performing or lending of the relevant works in another Member State (Case C-306/05 *SGAE v Rafael Hoteles SA*).

Design rights

The principle of exhaustion applies (Case 144/81 *Keurkoop BV v Nancy Kean Gifts BV*).

Parallel import from outside the EEA

The principle of the exhaustion of intellectual property rights **does not apply** to imports from outside the EEA (Case C-355/96 *Silhouette*). The consent of a holder of an IPR to parallel importation of protected goods to the EEA must be express or unequivocally demonstrated (Joined Cases C-414/99 to C-416/99 *Zino Davidoff SA*).

RECOMMENDED READING

Books

Barnard, C., *The Substantive Law of the EU. The Four Freedoms*, 2nd edition, 2007, Oxford: Oxford University Press

Oliver, P. assisted by M. Jarvis, *Free Movement of Goods in the European Community: Under Articles 28 and 30 of the EC Treaty*, 4th edition, 2003, London: Sweet & Maxwell

Scott, J., "Mandatory or Imperative Requirements in the EU and the WTO", in Barnard, C, and Scott, J (eds), *The Law of the Single European Market, Unpacking the Premises*, 2002, Oxford: Hart Publishing, Chapter 10

Articles

de Bùrca, G., "The Principle of Proportionality and its Application in EC Law", (1993) 13 YBEL, p 105

Harlander, L., "Exhaustion of Trademark Rights beyond the European Union in Light of Silhouette International Schmied v Hartlauer Handelsdesellschaft. Towards Stronger Protection of Trademark Rights and Eliminating the Grey Market", (2000) 28 Ga J Int'l & Comp L, p 267

Hays, T., "Paranova v Merck and Co-branding of Pharmaceuticals in the European Economic Area", (2004) 94 Trademark Rep, p 821

22

CITIZENSHIP OF THE EU

CONTENTS

SUMMARY

1. This chapter examines the concept of EU citizenship, which was established by the Treaty of Maastricht. The ToL emphasises the importance of creating closer ties between the EU and its citizens and that of ensuring that they fully participate in the democratic life of the Union. In particular, Part Two of the TFEU on "Non-discrimination and Citizenship of the Union" lists the most important rights attached to EU citizenship whilst Title II of the TEU on "Provisions on Democratic Principles" acknowledges that the participation of EU citizens in the decision making process in the EU is central to the creation of a democratic Union.

2. EU citizenship flows from national citizenship: every person holding the nationality of a Member State is an EU citizen. EU citizenship is thus derivative, rather than a right independent of, or autonomous from, national law. Member States have exclusive competence to determine who are to be considered their nationals, and such a determination cannot be challenged either by the EU or by other Member States. However, this is subject to the proviso that Member States must, when exercising their powers in the sphere of nationality, have due regard to EU law, i.e. take it into account when nationality matters are within the scope of the Treaties.

3. In Case C-184/99 *Grzelczyk* the ECJ emphasised that EU citizenship "is destined to be the fundamental status of nationals of the Member States, enabling those who find themselves in the same situation [as nationals of a host Member State] to enjoy the same treatment in law irrespective of their nationality, subject to such exceptions as are expressly provided for". The concept of EU citizenship reinforces the prohibition of discrimination based on nationality embodied in Articles 18 TFEU in a situation where EU citizens are exercising their fundamental freedoms guaranteed under the Treaties. The ECJ has contributed to the development of the content of EU citizenship by deriving far-reaching consequences from the link between the principle of non-discrimination on the ground of nationality and the rights granted by the Treaties to EU citizens. Accordingly, on the basis of citizenship alone, EU citizens, who reside lawfully in a host Member State, are able to claim important social, cultural and other rights. Article 21(3) TFEU, for the first time, brings social security and social welfare matters within the scope of EU citizenship and thus offers the opportunity of creating a social dimension to EU citizenship.

4. Part Two of the TFEU on "Non-discrimination and Citizenship of the Union" lists the most important rights attached to EU citizenship.

A. Article 21(1) TFEU guarantees EU citizens and their families the right to move freely and reside within the territory of the Member States provided they are engaged in the internal market economic activity and/or are financially self-sufficient. The ECJ has broadly interpreted Article 18(1) EC [Article 21(1) TFEU] to the extent that it is now first, directly effective and second, a source of free-standing (though somewhat limited) rights that can be relied upon by EU citizens because they are EU citizens. Directive 2004/38, which entered into force on 30 April 2006, constitutes a response to problems encountered by EU citizens wishing to exercise the rights guaranteed under Article 21(1) TFEU. It comprehensively deals with the scope of these rights, describes administrative procedures relating to obtaining residence documents in a host Member State and defines the rights of family members of EU citizens.

B. Article 22(1) TFEU confers on EU citizens the right to vote and stand for municipal elections in the host Member State, under the same conditions as nationals of that Member State. However, Directive 94/80/EC, which implements what is now Article 22(1) TFEU, provides for two derogations: first, a Member State may decide that only its own nationals are eligible to hold the office of elected head of the executive body of a basic local government unit and second, it may require that non-nationals who are EU citizens must reside in the national territory for a specific period of time in order to benefit from this right. The second derogation may be granted only if the proportion of non-national EU citizens eligible to vote in a Member State exceeds 20 per cent of the total eligible population.

C. Article 22(2) TFEU confers on EU citizens passive and active voting rights in the host Member State for elections to the EP. The word passive simply refers to the right to vote while the word active indicates the right both to vote and to stand as a candidate in elections to the EP.

D. Under Article 23 TFEU, EU citizens have the right to obtain diplomatic and consular protection in a third state, where their own Member State is not represented by a permanent consular post or a diplomatic mission, from any other EU Member State having a diplomatic establishment there, on the same conditions as nationals of that Member State. This right is confirmed in Article 46 of the Charter of Fundamental Rights of the European Union. Decisions 95/553/EC and 96/409/CFSP implement this right but, at the time of writing, both are under review. The Commission considers that new common arrangements should be put in place with a view to strengthening this right. Further, the creation of the European Union External Action Service (see Chapter 5.2.2) may improve the protection of EU citizens abroad bearing in mind that under Article 35 TEU the new EU body is required to co-operate closely with diplomatic missions of the Member States to ensure, inter alia, the implementation of the right of EU citizens guaranteed under Article 23 TFEU.

E.   Article 24(1) TFEU sets out the procedure for implementing the right of EU citizens (i.e. at least one million citizens who are between them nationals of a significant number of Member States) to invite the European Commission to bring forward legislative proposals in areas where the Commission has the power to do so (see Chapter 7).

F.   Article 24(2) and (3) TFEU, which concerns the right to petition the EP and to complain to the EU Ombudsman, does not distinguish between EU citizens and non-EU citizens. Anyone living within the territory of the EU or operating a business there can rely on this right. A petition to the EP must relate to a subject falling within the sphere of activity of the EU and concern the petitioner directly, while a complaint to the Ombudsman must relate to a matter of "mal-administration" by an EU institution, body, office or agency other than the CJEU, but it is not necessary that the complainant is personally affected by it. Article 24(4) TFEU, which provides that every citizen of the EU has the right to write to any EU institution, body, office or agency in one of the official languages of the EU and to receive an answer in the same language, should be read in a broader perspective in that it gives EU citizens the right to information and thus enhances the principle of transparency.

5. Article 25 TFEU emphasises that EU citizenship is a dynamic concept. Indeed, since its establishment it has evolved from a not very coherent bundle of rights into a more meaningful concept.

22.1   Introduction

Citizenship of the EU was established by the Treaty of Maastricht[1566] and has, since then, evolved considerably. In particular, the ECJ has contributed to its evolution by deriving far-reaching consequences from the link between the principle of non-discrimination on the ground of nationality and the rights granted by the Treaties to EU citizens so that EU citizenship has become "the

---

1566. For the historical background see D. O'Keeffe, "Union Citizenship", in *Legal Issues of the Maastricht Treaty*, D. O'Keeffe and P. M. Twomey (eds.) 1994, London: Wiley Chancery, pp 87–9.

fundamental status of nationals of the Member States".[1567] On the basis of this status alone, EU citizens, who reside lawfully in a host Member State, are able to claim important social, cultural and other rights (see section 22.2.1).

The ToL contains numerous provisions which aim at creating closer ties between the EU and its citizens and ensuring that they fully participate in the democratic life of the Union. Article 1 TEU, which contains the over-reaching objectives of the EU, states that "This Treaty marks a new stage in the process of creating an ever closer union among the peoples of Europe, in which decisions are taken as openly as possible and as closely as possible to the citizen". The new approach to EU citizenship is emphasised in the Preamble to the Charter of Fundamental Rights, which has the same binding force as the Treaties (see Chapter 9), and which states that "the individual is at the heart of" the Union. Further, the Treaties ensure that fundamental human rights of EU citizens are respected and promoted (e.g. Articles 2 and 6 TEU). Probably, the most striking feature of the ToL is that many of its provisions are no longer addressed to the Member States but to citizens of the EU, e.g. Article 3(2) TEU offers to its citizens the area of FSJ, and Article 9 TEU ensures equal treatment of its citizens, who shall receive equal attention from EU institutions, bodies, offices or agencies.

Part Two of the TFEU on "Non-discrimination and Citizenship of the Union" lists the most important rights attached to EU citizenship whilst new Title II of the TEU on "Provisions on Democratic Principles" acknowledges that EU citizens' participation in the decision making process in the EU is central to the creation of a democratic Union.

With regard to "Provisions on Democratic Principles" they refer to the principle of equality (Article 9 TEU), the principle of representative democracy (Article 10 TEU) and the principle of participatory democracy (Article 11 TEU) which includes the right of "citizens' initiative", i.e. the possibility for at least one million citizens, who are between them nationals of a significant number of Member States, to ask the Commission to prepare a proposal for a legal act necessary to implement the Treaties.[1568] Further, Article 11 acknowledges the importance of a dialogue between EU citizens, civil society and the EU institutions and ensures transparency in the working of EU institutions.

22.1.1 EU citizenship as a complement to citizenship of a Member State

EU citizenship is based on nationality of a Member State. Article 20(1) TFEU states that "Every person holding the nationality of a Member State shall be a citizen of the Union. Citizenship of the Union shall be additional to and not replace national citizenship." This point is enhanced in Declaration 2 on Nationality of a Member State attached to the Treaty of Maastricht, which provides that:

"... wherever in the Treaty establishing the European Community reference is made to nationals of the Member State, the question whether an individual possesses the nationality of a Member State shall be settled solely by reference to the national law of the Member State concerned."

Consequently, matters relating to nationality are within the exclusive prerogative of a Member

---

1567. Case C-184/99 *Grzelczyk* [2001] ECR I-6193 and Case C-413/99 *Baumbast and R* [2002] ECR I-7091.
1568. For the latest developments on the right of citizens' initiative see the Communication from the Commission IP/10/397.

State. This was confirmed by the ECJ in Case C-369/90 *Micheletti*,[1569] where the ECJ held that the determination of conditions governing the acquisition and loss of nationality were, according to international law, matters which fell within the competence of each Member State, whose decision must be respected by other Member States. However, in *Micheletti*, the ECJ also stated that the Member States must, when exercising their powers in the sphere of nationality, have due regard to EU law. This statement was the subject of a preliminary reference in Case C-135/08 *Janko Rottmann v Freistaat Bayern*,[1570] in which the ECJ was asked whether Article 20 TFEU allows a Member State to withdraw from a citizen of the Union the nationality of that State acquired by naturalisation when that nationality was obtained by deception. In the referred case, the result of withdrawal would have been that the person concerned would become a stateless person, i.e. without nationality. The Austrian and German governments, supported by the Commission, argued that the situation was purely internal, i.e. it concerned a German national, living in Germany, who as a result of his deception (he did not mention in the naturalisation procedure that criminal investigations were commenced against him in his native country, Austria, on account of alleged serious fraud which caused him to move to Germany and subsequently apply for German nationality, the acquisition of which resulted in the automatic loss of his Austrian nationality) was facing the withdrawal of naturalisation. The ECJ found that the link between the situation of the person concerned and EU law was based on the citizenship of the EU and not on the fact that the person concerned had exercised his right to free movement when moving from Austria to Germany. The Court held that because the withdrawal of naturalisation would entail the loss of EU citizenship, and therefore the loss of important rights attached to the status of EU citizenship such withdrawal was within the scope of the Treaties and could only be effected if the requirements of the principle of proportionality were satisfied. In this respect the ECJ held:

> "it is necessary, therefore, to take into account the consequences that the decision entails for the person concerned and, if relevant, for the members of his family with regard to the loss of the rights enjoyed by every citizen of the Union. In this respect it is necessary to establish, in particular, whether that loss is justified in relation to the gravity of the offence committed by that person, to the lapse of time between the naturalisation decision and the withdrawal decision and to whether it is possible for that person to recover his original nationality."

It can be said that although a Member State has to accept as an EU national anyone who has nationality of another Member State regardless of the conditions of acquisition of that nationality,[1571] the fundamental importance that EU law attaches to the status of EU citizenship allows EU law to interfere in nationality laws of the Member States when a situation under consideration is within the scope of the Treaties.

The requirement of nationality of a Member State as a prerequisite of EU citizenship means that nationals of third countries, refugees and stateless persons legally residing in a Member State do not acquire any rights under Article 20 TFEU. To remedy this situation two directives were adopted:

- Directive 2003/109/EC of 25 November 2003 Concerning the Status of Third-Country

---

1569. [1992] ECR I-4239.
1570. Judgment of 20/3/10 (nyr).
1571. Case C-192/99 *Kaur* [2001] ECR I-1237; Case C-200/02 *Zhu and Chen* [2004] ECR I-9925.

Nationals who are Long-term Residents in the EU.[1572] Under the Directive a Member State of residence of non-EU nationals and dependent members of their families is required to confer on such persons a set of rights which are as near as possible to those enjoyed by EU citizens. The status of a long-term resident can be claimed by those who have lawfully and continuously resided in the territory of a Member State concerned for a period of at least five years, are not a burden on that Member State's social assistance system, have appropriate medical insurance and represent no threat to its public policy, public security and public health. Students, asylum seekers, diplomats and other persons who have not been granted permanent leave to remain in a Member State are excluded. The status confers the entitlement to settle in another EU state in order to work. However, both a home Member State and a host Member State may impose some limitations, in particular in respect of access to social benefits or, in the case of a host Member State, of access to employment.

▪ Directive 2003/86/EC of 22 September 2003 on the Right to Family Reunification.[1573] By virtue of Article 3 of the Directive this right is conferred on any national of a third country who "is holding a residence permit issued by a Member State for a period of validity of one year or more who has reasonable prospects of obtaining the right of permanent residence" in that Member State. Under the Directive such a person is entitled to be reunited with members of his/her nuclear family if they are also third-country nationals – in other words, the Member State must allow the person's family members to join them in that Member State. In addition, refugee children or children otherwise in need of protection shall also be entitled to be granted residence permits for family reunion, if the parents and children are third-country nationals. A permit may, however, be refused if the third-country national is considered to represent a threat to public order or security and on certain other grounds.

22.1.2 Specific rights conferred on EU citizens by Part Two of the TFEU entitled "Non-discrimination and Citizenship of the Union"

Part Two of the TFEU entitled "Non-discrimination and Citizenship of the Union" lists specific rights conferred on EU citizens. It also confirms a close relationship between EU citizenship and the prohibition of discrimination not only based on nationality (Article 18 TFEU) but also on other factors mentioned in Article 19 TFEU such as sex, racial or ethnic origin, religion, belief, disability, age or sexual orientation. It is important to note that rights of EU citizens are not limited to Articles 18–25 TFEU but are also contained in other provisions of the Treaties and become relevant in situations where EC citizens are taxpayers, welfare recipients, consumers, workers, recipients of services, etc. Further, secondary legislation details and expands the rights contained in the Treaties.

The issue of whether EU law imposes any duties on EU citizens, bearing in mind that Article 20(2) TFEU states that "Citizens of the Union shall enjoy the rights and be subject to the duties

---

1572. [2004] L16/44.
1573. [2003] L251/12. The Directive was unsuccessfully challenged by the EP in Case C-540/03 *EP v Council* ([2006] ECR I-5769). The EP agued that some of its provisions, e.g. allowing a Member State to verify whether a child aged 12, who arrives independently from the rest of the family, meets an integration criteria set out in the Directive, and the requirement that an application for family reunification must be submitted before the child has reached the age of 15, were in breach of fundamental human rights.

provided for in the Treaties", has to be answered in the negative. It seems that apart from an implied civic duty to vote in the elections to the EP, there are no duties imposed on EU citizens, i.e. they are not required to pay taxes to the EU, or perform compulsory military service for the EU, or have any duty of loyalty towards the Union. As Kadelbach stated:

> ". . . despite surrounding itself with attributes of statehood, such as a flag or an anthem, the Union does not expect personal duties of loyalty. The Union courts its citizens not because it expects them to perform duties but because it wishes to be accepted as a body politic for which everyone feels a sort of ethical responsibility."[1574]

22.2 The right of free movement and residence within the territory of the Member States

Article 21(1) TFEU states:

> "Every citizen of the Union shall have the right to move and reside freely within the territory of the Member States, subject to the limitations and conditions laid down in the Treaties and by the measures adopted to give them effect."

It is to be noted that the right to free movement of a member of an EU national's family is not an independent right but derives from the right conferred upon the EU national, unless the family member himself/herself has rights as a national of a Member State. A member of an EU citizen's family who is a national of a third country cannot exercise the right to free movement unless this is done in parallel with the EU national.[1575]

Under Article 21(2) TFEU the Council acting in accordance with the ordinary legislative procedure, may adopt measures facilitating the exercise of the above rights. The ToL changed the procedure for adoption of the measures under Article 21(2) TFEU in that no longer is a unanimous vote of the Council required, i.e. the QMV is applied, and the EP became a co-legislator (previously its consent was required).

The ToL added a new paragraph 3 to Article 21 TFEU which reads as follows:

> "For the same purposes as those referred to in paragraph 1 and if the Treaties have not provided the necessary powers, the Council, acting in accordance with a special legislative procedure, may adopt measures concerning social security or social protection. The Council shall act unanimously after consulting the European Parliament."

The main importance of Article 21(3) TFEU it that, for the first time, social security and social welfare matters are within the scope of EU citizenship. So far, EU social law has been mainly concerned with co-ordinating social security schemes and social protection measures to ensure that migrant workers, self-employed persons and EU citizens in general are not discriminated against in a host Member State. Under Article 21(3) TFEU, Member States may, if they so decide, create a social dimension of EU citizenship beyond that which has been developed by the ECJ in

---

1574. P. S. Kadelbach, "Union Citizenship", in A. Von Bogdandy and J. Bast (eds), *Principles of European Constitutional Law*, 2nd edition, 2010, Worcester: Hart Publishing, p 467

1575. Cases C-297/88 and 197/89 *Dzodzi* [1990] ECR I-3763; Joined Cases C-64 and 65/96 *Uecker & Jacquet* [1997] ECR I-3171.

its case law under Article 18(1) EC [21(1) TFEU]. Indeed in some instances, the ECJ found that important social welfare rights have derived from the concept of EU citizenship (see below). However, Article 21(3) TFEU is not as revolutionary as it may appear given that any measure adopted under Article 21(3) TFEU requires a unanimous vote in the Council and therefore Member States have ensured that no social welfare rights will be granted to nationals from other Member States solely on the basis that they are EU citizens (as opposed to being EU workers, or self-employed persons) when any Member State expresses its opposition. This is an important safeguard for the Member States which alone are competent to decide whether they can afford to extend certain social benefits to EU nationals who are not their own citizens.

The ECJ has greatly contributed to the development of Article 18(1) EC [Article 21(1) TFEU]. It allowed EU citizens lawfully residing in a host Member State to rely on their citizenship alone to claim important social welfare rights, cultural rights and other rights. The Council's contribution was the adoption of Directive 2004/38/EC of 29 April 2004 on the Right of Citizens and Their Family Members to Move and Reside Freely within the Territory of the Member States.[1576]

22.2.1 Judicial development of Article 18(1) EC [Article 21(1) TFEU]

After initial hesitation the ECJ has made extensive use of Article 18(1) EC [Article 21(1) TFEU], although it is well established that there is no need to examine the applicability of Article 21(1) TFEU if other, more specific articles of the Treaties are applicable, for example, Articles 49 or 45 TFEU, unless they only cover some aspects and not the whole matter under consideration.[1577]

In Case C-413/99 *Baumbast and R v Secretary of State for the Home Department*,[1578] the ECJ for the first time explicitly recognised that Article 18(1) EC [Article 21(1) TFEU] is directly effective. Until this judgment it was uncertain whether or not Article 18(1) EC [Article 21(1) TFEU] was directly effective, although the interpretation of various judgments referring to this article seemed to point towards such recognition.[1579]

THE FACTS WERE:

In 1990 Mrs Baumbast, a Colombian national, married Mr Baumbast, a German national, in the UK where they decided to establish a family home. They had two daughters; the elder was a natural daughter of Mrs Baumbast and possessed Colombian nationality, and the younger had dual German and Colombian nationality. The British authority granted a residence permit to the Baumbast family in 1990 valid for five years.

From 1990 to 1993 Mr Baumbast worked in the UK, initially as an employed person and subsequently he worked as head of his own company. Following the failure of his company he tried to obtain employment in the UK to no avail. From 1993 onwards he was employed by German companies in China and Lesotho.

1576. [2004] OJ L 229/1.
1577. Case C-193/94 *Skanavi and Chryssanthakopoulos* [1996] ECR I-929; Case C-470/04 *N v Inspecteur van de Belastingdienst Oost/kantoor Almelo* [2006] ECR I-7409.
1578. [2002] ECR I-7091.
1579. Case C-85/96 *Martínez Sala* [1998] ECR I-2691; Case C-356/98 *Kaba* [2000] ECR I-2623.

During the relevant period the Baumbast family owned a house in the UK and the daughters went to a UK school. The family did not receive any social benefit and was covered by comprehensive medical insurance in Germany, to which country they travelled for medical treatment when necessary.

In May 1995 Mrs Baumbast applied for indefinite leave to remain in the UK for her family. In January 1996 the Secretary of State refused to renew a residence permit for the Baumbast family. His decision was challenged by the Baumbast family before the UK Immigration Adjudicator, who decided that:

- *Mr Baumbast had no right to reside in the UK as he was neither a worker nor a person entitled to reside in the UK under Directive 90/364;*

- *the daughters had independent rights of residence in the UK under Article 12 of Regulation 1612/68;*

- *Mrs Baumbast's right to reside in the UK derived from her children's rights and consequently she was allowed to stay in the UK for a period coterminous with that during which her daughters were benefiting from rights of residence under Article 12 of Regulation 1612/68.*

Mr Baumbast appealed against the Adjudicator's decision to the Immigration Tribunal, which asked the ECJ for guidance under the preliminary ruling procedure, in particular on the question whether a citizen of the European Union who has ceased to be a migrant worker in a host Member State is still entitled to reside there because of his citizenship of the EU, that is, on the basis of Article 18(1) EC [Article 21(1) TFEU].

Held:

The ECJ confirmed the decision of the UK Immigration Adjudicator in respect of Mrs Baumbast and the children but held that Mr Baumbast should not be refused a residence permit in the UK. In this respect the Court stated that:

"... the right to reside within the territory of the Member States under Article 18(1) EC [Article 21(1) TFEU], ... is conferred directly on every citizen of the Union by a clear and precise provision of the EC Treaty. Purely, as a national of a Member State, and consequently a citizen of the Union, Mr Baumbast therefore has the right to rely on Article 18(1) EC [Article 21(1) TFEU]."

Comment:

Notwithstanding the above, it remains that in order to produce direct effect, a provision of EU law must not only be clear and precise but must also be unconditional in that it must not require the taking of any implementing measures by EU institutions or by Member States. On this point the ECJ acknowledged that the right granted under Article 18(1) EC [Article 21(1) TFEU] was conditional on the limitations and conditions laid down by the EC Treaty and by measures adopted to give it effect. According to the ECJ Article 18(1) EC [Article 21(1) TFEU] is directly effective, notwithstanding the fact that some implementing measures are still necessary, and therefore, in their absence, Article 18(1) EC [Article 21(1) TFEU] can only be directly effective to some extent! The ECJ tackled this problem in the following manner:

"... respect of the exercise of that right of residence is subject to judicial review. Consequently, any limitations and conditions imposed on that right do not prevent the provisions of Article 18(1) EC [Article 21(1) TFEU] from conferring on individuals rights which are enforceable by them and which the national courts must protect."

Consequently all limitations and conditions set out in Article 18(1) EC [Article 21(1) TFEU] must be applied in compliance with EC law and in accordance with the general principles of law, in particular the principle of proportionality. The ECJ, when assessing the situation of Mr Baumbast in the light of the principle of proportionality, took into account the facts that:

- He had sufficient resources within the meaning of Directive 90/364;

- He had worked and resided for a number of years in the UK;

- His family resided with him during his stay in the UK as a worker and subsequently as a self-employed person;

- He had remained there even after his activities as an employed and self-employed person came to an end;

- Neither Mr Baumbast nor his family had ever become burdens on the public finances of the host Member State;

- The Baumbast family including Mr Baumbast had comprehensive sickness insurance in Germany.

In those circumstances the refusal of the UK to grant Mr Baumbast a residence permit was considered by the ECJ as being disproportionate.

On the basis of the above case law it is apparent that important rights have been conferred on EU citizens exclusively because they are EU citizens. The broad interpretation of Article 18 EC [Article 21(1) TFEU] is exemplified in Case C-200/02 *Zhu and Chen*.[1580]

THE FACTS WERE:

Mr and Mrs Chen, both Chinese nationals, deliberately took advantage of Irish law which granted Irish citizenship to a child born in Ireland if such a child was not entitled to citizenship of any other country. Mr Chen often travelled to the UK for business purposes. His wife joined him in the UK when she was six months pregnant and two months later travelled to Ireland to give birth to her daughter Catherine in order for her child to acquire Irish citizenship and, consequently, to secure for herself and her daughter the right to reside in the UK. When Catherine was eight months old Mrs Chen, who resided in the UK, applied for a long-term residence permit in the UK. It was clear from the submission of Mrs Chen that she and her child had the necessary financial resources and the relevant health insurance so as not to be a

---

1580. [2004] ECR I-9925.

burden on the social assistance system of the UK. The application was refused by the UK Secretary of State for the Home Department. Mrs Chen appealed to the Immigration Appellate Authority, which referred the matter to the ECJ.

Held:

The ECJ held that:

▪ Children can exercise the right of free movement;

▪ It is not necessary that an EU citizen possesses personally sufficient resources to avoid being a burden on the social assistance system of the Member State of residence. What is required is that such a person has the necessary resources whatever their origin (but obviously not of criminal origin!);

▪ There was no abuse of EC law when Mrs Chen deliberately went to Ireland in order to enable the child she expected to acquire Irish nationality, and consequently to enable her to acquire the right to reside with her child in the UK;

▪ Mrs Chen could not be regarded as a dependent relative within the meaning of EC law, bearing in mind that her child was dependent on her;

▪ Mrs Chen, as a primary carer for Catherine to whom EC law granted a right of residence in a host Member State, was entitled to reside with her child in the host Member State.

On the basis of Article 21(1) TFEU, EU citizens are entitled to numerous rights. Examples where EU citizens were successful in claims are:

▪ A Spanish national, residing in Germany without being a worker there within the meaning of Article 45 TFEU, obtained a child-raising allowance in Germany;[1581]

▪ Two German nationals, while travelling and staying temporarily in the Italian province of Bolzano, were entitled to use their mother tongue (German) in judicial and administrative proceedings in the circumstances where only a German-speaking minority living in the province was permitted to use German in respect of such proceedings;[1582]

▪ A Greek national, residing lawfully in Belgium, obtained a "tide-over" allowance for young people seeking their first employment in Belgium;[1583]

▪ A French national, who lawfully resided in the UK as a student, obtained financial assistance in the form of a subsidised study loan in the UK;[1584]

▪ Parents (he was Spanish, she was Belgian) living in Belgium (in circumstances where their children, holders of dual Belgian–Spanish nationality residing with them in Belgium, according to Belgian law could use only the surname of the father), were able to have the

---

1581. Case C-85/96 *Maria Martínez Sala* [1998] ECR I-2691.

1582. Case C-274/96 *Bickel and Franz* [1998] ECR I-7637.

1583. Case C-258/04 *Ioannidis* [2005] ECR I-8275; see also Case C-224/98 *D'Hoop* [2002] ECR I-6191.

1584. Case C-209/03 *Bidar* [2005] ECR I-2119.

patronymic surname of their children changed to reflect well-established usage in Spanish law according to which the surname of children of a married couple consists of the first surname of the father followed by that of their mother;[1585]

■ Dutch nationals, who lawfully resided in Spain, obtained a war pension, although Dutch legislation required applicants for the war pension to be actually resident in The Netherlands at the time when their application was submitted;[1586]

■ A German national, who took up residence in Poland on his retirement, obtained reduction of the income tax on his pension taxable in Poland which reduction was equal to the amount of heath insurance contributions paid in Germany. This reduction was only applicable to contributions paid to a Polish health insurance institution.[1587]

It results from some of the above examples that the provisions on citizenship have been used to make some limited inroads on the requirement of economic self-sufficiency imposed on EU citizens.

The question of how far the ECJ will go in the broad construction of Article 21(1) TFEU was partially answered in Case C-215/03 *Salah Oulane*,[1588] in which the ECJ decided that a host Member State (The Netherlands) was not obliged to assume that a national of another Member State (France) staying in the host Member State for a period in excess of six months, who was unable to give the address of a fixed abode or residence in the host Member State and had no money or luggage, was a "recipient of tourist services". The Court ruled that it is for nationals of a Member State residing in another Member State to provide evidence that they are recipients of services. If no evidence is given, a host Member State may undertake deportation of such persons, subject to the usual limits imposed by EU law. Thus, the ECJ chose not to impose a burden of proof on a host Member State.

22.2.2   Directive 2004/38/EC

An important piece of legislation (which merged into one instrument all the legislation – consisting of two regulations and nine directives – on the right of entry and residence for EU citizens) is Directive 2004/38/EC of 29 April 2004 on the right of citizens and their family members to move and reside freely within the territory of the Member States.[1589] The Directive brings together the piecemeal measures found in the complex body of legislation that had previously governed this matter, and reiterates the case law in this area. Its main objective is to simplify and to improve rules in this area, in particular by:

■ Reducing administrative formalities to the bare essentials;

■ Providing a clear definition of the status of family members;

1585. Case C-148/02 *Garcia Avello* [2003] ECR I-11613.
1586. Case C-192/05 *Tas-Hagen and Tas* [2006] ECR I-10451.
1587. Case C-544/07 *Uwe Rüffler v Dyrektor Izby Skarbowej we Wrocławiu Ośrodek Zamiejscowy w Wałbrzychu* (judgment of 24 April 2009 nyr).
1588. [2005] ECR I-1215.
1589. [2004] OJ L 229/1.

- Limiting the scope for refusing entry and terminating the right of residence (see Chapter 25);

- Introducing the right of permanent residence.

The main features of Directive 2004/38 are examined below.

22.2.2.1   Persons covered by the Directive

The Directive applies to all EU citizens and their family members. Article 2(2) provides a definition of family members. They are the EU's citizen's:

- Spouse;

- Partner with whom an EU citizen has contracted a registered partnership, on the basis of the legislation of a Member State if the legislation of a host Member State treats a registered partnership as equivalent to marriage;

- Direct descendants who are under the age of 21 or are dependent and those of the spouse or partner;

- Direct dependent ascendants and those of the spouse or partner.

Article 3 concerns the right of entry and residence of other members of the family who are not mentioned in Article 2(2). With regard to them a host Member State is required to examine the personal circumstances of such persons and must justify any denial of entry of residence. Three categories of persons are mentioned:

- Those who were dependents or members of a household of an EU national in the country from which they have come;

- Those who require personal care by the Union citizen on serious health grounds; and

- A partner with whom the Union citizen has a durable relationship, duly attested.

It is well established in EC law that the status of dependency is not linked to the entitlement to maintenance because such a requirement would result in defining the status of dependency or otherwise on the basis of national law, which varies from one Member State to another. Further, the broad interpretation of provisions on the free movement of workers entails that neither the reason for recourse to financial support nor the assessment of whether the person concerned is able to support himself/herself by taking up employment are relevant in determining the status of dependency.[1590] However, the issue of how to prove the relationship of dependency is more controversial. In Case C-1/05 *Yunying Jia v Migrationsverket*,[1591] the ECJ provided some useful clarification. It held that:

- The same criteria apply when assessing the relationship of dependency, whether the EC national is a worker or a self-employed person;

- A host Member State is required to assess whether the person concerned is in a position to

---

1590. Case 316/85 *Lebon* [1987] ECR 2811.
1591. [2007] ECR I-1.

support himself/herself in the light of his/her financial and social conditions in the Member State of origin or the Member State from whence he/she came (or perhaps this should be expressed as the Member State where he/she was residing) at the time when the application to join the EU national was made. This clearly excludes the assessment of his/her financial and social conditions in the host Member State;

■ Evidence of dependency may be adduced by any appropriate means. On the one hand, it is not necessary to require a document of the competent authority of the Member State of origin, or the Member State from which the applicant came, attesting the existence of a situation of dependency, although this kind of proof is particularly appropriate for that purpose. On the other hand, an undertaking from an EC-national or his/her spouse to support a family member may not be sufficient.

22.2.2.1.1 Spouses/partners

Article 2(2) of Directive 2004/38 expressly mentions a spouse of an EU national. In Case 267/83 *Diatta*,[1592] the ECJ held that it is not necessary for spouses to live under the same roof. This decision was delivered in the context of spouses living separately and intending to obtain a divorce (the wife was of Senegalese nationality, her husband was a French national working in Germany). However, the marriage must be genuine and not a marriage of convenience.[1593]

Directive 2004/38 regulates, for the first time, the issue of the right of residence of a spouse/partner who is not an EC national in the event of divorce, annulment of marriage or termination of registered partnership. Provided that such a person is a worker or a self-employed person (Article 7(a)); or has sufficient resources to avoid becoming a burden on the social security system of the host Member State and has appropriate sickness insurance cover (Article 7(b)); or is a student enrolled at an establishment accredited by the host Member State (Article 7(c)); or is a family member accompanying or joining an EU citizen who satisfies the conditions set out in Article 7 (a), (b) or (c), he/she retains the right of residence in a host Member State if:

■ The relationship specified above has lasted at least three years, including one year in a host Member State; or

■ By agreement or court order, he/she has custody of the EU citizen's children; or

■ This is warranted by particularly difficult circumstances, such as having been a victim of domestic violence while the marriage or registered relationship was subsisting; or

■ By agreement or by court order he/she has a right of access to a minor child, provided that the court has ruled that such access must be in the host Member State. In this case the right of residence is retained for as long as it is required.

The death of an EU citizen should not affect the right of residence of non-EU members of his/her family if they have resided in the host Member State as family members for at least one year before his/her death and can satisfy the conditions set out in Article 7(1)(a), (b), (c) or (d).

In the case of the death or departure of an EU citizen from a host Member State, Article 12(3)

1592. [1985] ECR 567.
1593. Case C-109/01 *Secretary of State for Home Department v Hacene Akrich* [2003] ECR I-9607 and Case C-127/08 *Blaise Baheten Metock and Others v Minister for Justice, Equality and Law Reform* [2008] ECR I-6241.

of Directive 2004/38 states that this should not entail loss of the right of residence by his/her children or by the parent who has actual custody of the children, regardless of their nationality, if the children reside in the host Member State and are enrolled at an educational establishment there. They, as well the parent, retain the right to reside in a host Member State until the completion of their studies.

In respect of partners of EU nationals the content of the Directive mirrors the judgment in Case 59/85 *Reed*,[1594] in which the ECJ held that by virtue of the principle of non-discrimination, a Member State cannot refuse a cohabitee of a worker who is an EU national the right to reside with the worker in so far as national law provides this possibility for its own nationals. As a result, Miss Reed, a British national, was allowed to remain in The Netherlands with her English cohabitee of five years.

22.2.2.2   The right of residence

The right of nationals of a Member State to enter the territory of another Member State and reside there is conferred directly by the Treaties. This was decided by the ECJ in Case 48/75 *The State v Jean Noël Royer*.[1595] Secondary legislation determines the scope of and provides detailed rules for the exercise of the rights conferred directly by the Treaties.

Directive 2004/38 reiterates the principle that failure to comply with formalities regarding entry and residence cannot justify a decision ordering expulsion from the territory of a host Member State[1596] or temporary imprisonment. In respect of sanctions that a Member State may impose on nationals from other Member States for failure to comply with administrative requirements regarding entry and residence, such sanctions are subject to the principle of proportionality. In Case 265/88 *Messner*,[1597] a requirement under Italian law imposing on all immigrants the obligation to register with the police within three days of their arrival, sanctioned by criminal penalties, was considered as disproportionate. Any national measures which are disproportionate to the objectives of the Treaties in the area of free movement of persons will be struck down by the ECJ as contrary to EU law.[1598]

Directive 2004/38 makes a distinction between residence of an EU national in a host Member State for up to three months and for more than three months.

22.2.2.2.1 Right of residence for up to three months

All EU citizens are entitled to enter another Member State on the basis of a valid identity document or passport. If they do not have these travel documents, the host Member State must afford them every facility in obtaining the requisite documents or having them sent. In Case C-215/03 *Salah Oulane*,[1599] the ECJ stated that a Member State may not refuse to recognise the right of residence on the sole ground that a person did not present one of these documents. Any document or evidence proving unequivocally that a person is a EU national should be accepted by a host Member State.

1594. [1986] ECR 1283.
1595. [1976] ECR 497.
1596. See Case 118/75 *Watson and Belmann* [1976] ECR 1185; Case 157/79 *R v Pieck* [1980] ECR 2171.
1597. [1989] ECR 4209.
1598. Case 30/77 *Bourchereau* [1977] ECR 1999.
1599. [2005] ECR I-1215.

A Member State is prohibited from requiring either an entry or an exit visa. A family member who is a non-EU national accompanying an EU national may be required to have a short-stay visa as specified by Regulation 539/2001.

Under Article 8 of Directive 2004/38 EU citizens and members of their families may be required to register their presence in the territory of a host Member State within a reasonable and non-discriminatory period of time after their arrival, but any penalty for breach of the requirement must be proportionate and comparable to those which apply to similar national infringements.[1600]

The question whether a host Member State may restrict the residence of an EU citizen to part of the national territory was examined by the ECJ in Case 36/75 *Roland Rutili v Minister of the Interior*.[1601]

THE FACTS WERE:

Rutili was an Italian national who resided in France, and between 1967 and 1968 he actively participated in political and trade union activities. The French authorities grew increasingly concerned with his activities, and issued a deportation order. This was subsequently altered to a restriction order requiring him to remain in certain provinces of France. In particular, the order prohibited him from residing in the province in which he was habitually resident and in which his family resided.

Rutili challenged the legality of these measures on the ground that they interfered with his right of freedom of movement. The question was referred to the ECJ for a preliminary ruling.

Held:

The ECJ interpreted the right of a Member State to limit the free movement of workers on the ground of public policy and concluded that this right must be construed strictly. In particular, a Member State cannot, in the case of a national of another Member State, impose prohibitions on residence which are territorially limited except in circumstances where such prohibitions may be imposed on its own nationals. Consequently, if a Member State has no power to restrict the residence of its own nationals to a specific area, then it has only two options in relation to an EU migrant worker: either to refuse entry or to permit residence anywhere in the national territory.[1602] This solution has been incorporated into Article 22 of Directive 2004/38.

22.2.2.2.2 Right of residence for more than three months

The right of residence for a period exceeding three months is granted to three categories of persons:

- Workers or self-employed persons (Article 7(1)(a)), including those who are temporarily

---

1600. Case C-378/97 *Wijsenbeek* [1999] ECR I-6207; Article 8(2) of Directive 2004/38.
1601. [1975] ECR 1219.
1602. See Case C-100/01 *Olazabal* [2002] ECR I-10981.

unable to work due to illness or accident, or are involuntarily unemployed and registered as job-seekers with the relevant employment office, or are embarking on vocational training;

- Economically inactive persons and their families (Article 7(1)(b)) where they have sufficient resources to avoid being a burden on the social security system of the host Member State. Further, they must be covered by sickness insurance in respect of all risks in the host Member State;

- Students (Article 7(1)(c)). They must be enrolled at a private or public establishment accredited or financed by the host Member State and must have sufficient resources to avoid becoming a burden on the social security system of the host Member State. As a result they must have health insurance and adequate means of support. In addition only the spouse or the registered partner and dependent children are regarded as family members for the purposes of the Directive.

In the light of crises in many Member States regarding the financing of their social security systems, the Directive leaves it to each Member State to decide whether it will grant social assistance to EU nationals and their families during the first three months of residence, or for a longer period in the case of job-seekers. Also Article 24(2) provides that Member States are not obliged, prior to acquisition of the right of permanent residence, to grant any maintenance aid for study consisting of student grants or student loans to persons other than workers and self-employed persons and their families.

The issue of what constitutes "sufficient resources" is of utmost importance for EU citizens exercising their right to free movement. In this respect Article 8(4) of the Directive specifies that in each case the personal situation of the person concerned should be assessed by a host Member State. It also states that a Member State is not allowed to set a fixed amount, and in any case the amount must not be higher than the threshold below which nationals of the host Member State become eligible for social assistance or, alternatively, not higher than the minimum social security pension paid by the host Member State.

In Case C-408/03 *Commission v Belgium*,[1603] the ECJ reiterated its case law on this topic. It held that the origin of resources, whether personal or belonging to third persons, including those with whom the EC national has no legal link (for example, a partner), are irrelevant. The ECJ found Belgium in breach of Article 18 EC [Article 21 TFEU] and Directive 90/364 for refusing to take account of the income of a long-standing Belgian partner of a Portuguese woman, who came to Belgium with her three daughters to live with him, in the absence of an agreement concluded before a notary and containing an assistance clause. According to the ECJ, an undertaking given by the Belgian partner in a form which was not legally binding was sufficient.

Directive 2004/38 abolished the requirement of residence permits for EU nationals but Member States are still allowed to require them to register with the competent authorities within a period of no less than three months of their date of arrival. A registration certificate must be issued immediately on the presentation of:

- A valid identity card or valid passport;

- Proof that the EU citizen meets the requirements set out by the Directive, e.g. a confirmation of engagement from the employee, a certificate of employment or any other relevant evidence.

1603. [2006] ECR I-2647.

Family members who are non-EU nationals, however, are still required to obtain a residence permit, which must be delivered within six months of the date of submitting the application and is valid for five years from the date of issue.[1604]

The right of residence expires if the persons concerned break any of the conditions of their residence as prescribed by the Directives. Such persons may be deported on the grounds of public policy, public security and public health (see Chapter 25).

22.2.2.3 Permanent residence

Directive 2004/38 has introduced the right of permanent residence. This is granted to EU nationals and members of their families, irrespective of their nationality, after a five-year period of uninterrupted and legal residence in a host Member State, provided that no expulsion decision has been enforced against them. The right of permanent residence is lost only in the event of an absence from the host Member State of more than two successive years. In some circumstances described in Article 17 of the Directive EU nationals and members of their families are entitled to become permanent residents of the host Member State before completion of a continuous period of five years of residence (for example, these who reach the age of retirement, or take early retirement or become unable to work due to an accident at work or an occupational disease).

22.2.2.4 Equal treatment

Article 24 of Directive 2004/38 provides that EU citizens and their family shall enjoy equal treatment with nationals of the host Member State. This is extended to family members who are non-EU nationals and who have the right of residence or permanent residence in the host Member State. They are entitled to take up employment or self-employment in the host Member State and have their professional qualifications recognised.

22.2.2.5 Internal situations

The ECJ has confirmed, on many occasions, that Article 21 TFEU does not apply to wholly internal situations.[1605].

22.3 The right to participate in municipal elections and in elections to the EP

Article 22 TFEU confers both active rights (the right to stand as a candidate) and passive rights (the right to vote) in respect of municipal[1606] and EP[1607] elections on an EU national residing in a Member State of which he/she is not a national under the same conditions as nationals of that Member State. Further measures (mentioned below) were necessary to implement those rights.

1604. Case C-157/03 *Commission v Spain* [2005] ECR I-2911.
1605. Case C-299/95 *Kremzow v Austria* [1997] ECR I-2629.
1606. Article 22(1) TFEU.
1607. Article 22(2) TFEU.

22.3.1 The right to participation in municipal elections

Participation in municipal elections for EU nationals residing in a Member State of which they are not nationals is important as it contributes to their integration into the society of a host Member State. It is also in line with the Council of Europe Convention of 5 February 1992 on the Participation of Foreigners in Public Life at Local Level provided they fulfil the requirement of residence.

The adoption of an EU measure in this area posed three problems:

- First, the matter of the determination of the local government unit;

- Second, the question of the determination of the public offices which nationals of other Member States may hold;

- Third, the issue of the granting of local election rights in a Member State with a very high percentage of residents from other Member States.

All the above problems were addressed in Council Directive 94/80 of 19 December 1994, which conferred on citizens of the Union the right to vote and stand as candidates in local elections in their Member State of residence under the same conditions as nationals of that Member State.[1608]

The first matter was partially solved by Directive 94/80, which in Article 2(1) provides a definition of the basic local government unit, and partially by the Member States, which in the Annex to the Directive listed the types of administrative entity. Article 2(1) defines the basic local governmental unit as "certain bodies elected by direct universal suffrage and . . . empowered to administer, at the basic level of political and administrative organisation, certain local affairs on their own responsibility". However, the reference to national law in determination of those bodies has resulted in wide diversity in the levels of local government accessible to EU citizens. In the UK, Ireland and Denmark EU citizens residing in these countries are entitled to both passive and active voting rights in respect of all levels of government below national government, while in France, Belgium and The Netherlands non-national EU citizens are limited to the lowest level. The list of administrative entities provided by the UK encompasses "counties in England, counties, county boroughs and communities in Wales, regions and Islands in Scotland, districts in England, Scotland and Northern Ireland, London boroughs, parishes in England, the City of London in relation to ward elections for common councilmen".[1609]

The second issue relating to access to certain offices elected by direct universal suffrage, such as the post of mayor or alderman (a member of the local executive), is regulated in Article 5(3) of Directive 94/80 which states that "the office of elected head, deputy or member of the governing college of the executive of a basic local government unit if elected to hold office for the duration of his mandate" may be reserved to nationals of a Member State. This situation is contrary to European integration but in line with Article 45(4) and Article 51 TFEU, which exclude nationals of Member States resident in other Member States from holding public office and from activities which involve the exercise of official authority. As a result, Directive 94/80 strengthens the limitations already existing under the Treaties instead of abolishing any difference in treatment between nationals and non-nationals being EU citizens residing in a host Member State!

1608. [1994] OJ L368/38.
1609. Annex to Directive 94/80.

The third issue was solved by allowing derogations from the Directive to accommodate Member States with a very high percentage of resident nationals from other Member States. If more than 20 per cent of foreign residents are nationals of the EU without being nationals of that Member State, the exercise of their electoral rights may be subject to the requirement of a certain period of residence in that Member State. This derogation concerns mostly Luxembourg where approximately 30 per cent of the population are foreign residents and more than 90 per cent of them are EU nationals.

Other features of the Directive are:

- It allows multiple voting. For example, a French national residing in England and in Belgium is entitled to exercise his/her voting rights in both countries;

- It gives no definition of residence. It only provides that the owners of holiday homes are not considered as residents in the Member State where their holiday homes are situated unless they are allowed to participate in municipal elections on the basis of reciprocity.[1610] To illustrate reciprocity, an Englishman who owns a holiday home in Barcelona in Spain will be allowed to vote and stand at municipal elections in Spain only if a Spanish national who owns a holiday home in Southampton in England has the same rights in England.

Directive 94/80 is very modest. It confers passive and active voting rights in municipal elections which are of little importance in the political life of any Member State.[1611] The grant of voting rights in national parliamentary elections, in direct presidential elections or in referenda would give real meaning to citizenship of the EU.

22.3.2   The right to participate in elections to the European Parliament

Article 22(2) TFEU confers on citizens of the EU the right to vote and to stand in elections to the European Parliament in the Member State of their residence under the same conditions as nationals of that Member State. The content of this right is examined in Chapter 6.5.1.

22.4   The right to diplomatic and consular protection

Article 23 TFEU states that an EU national is entitled to the diplomatic and consular protection of any Member State, under the same conditions as nationals of that Member State, in the territory of a third country in which the Member State of which he/she is a national is not represented. This right is confirmed in Article 46 of the Charter of Fundamental Rights of the European Union.

In international practice when a Member State has no representation in the territory of another state, it often conducts diplomatic relations, including protection of its nationals, indirectly with the assistance of other Member States which have permanent diplomatic offices there. Many countries cannot afford embassies, even in the most strategic places. Also, diplomatic

---

1610. Article 4(2) of Directive 94/80.

1611. In the UK the Representation of the People Act (2000) enacted on 9 March 2000 governs the right to vote or to stand in both municipal and European Parliamentary elections.

relations between two countries can be suspended or terminated, which often requires third countries to act on their behalf.[1612]

Before the entry into force of the ToL, the procedure provided for enactment of further measures in the area of diplomatic and consular protection was based on inter-governmental co-operation. Pre-ToL measures included the "Guidelines for the Protection of Unrepresented EC Nationals by EC Missions in Third Countries" on the basis of which the Council adopted the following binding measures, which are still in force at the time of writing:

- Decision 95/553/EC[1613] on the protection of EU citizens in territories where their own Member State or the state which permanently represents their Member State maintains no accessible permanent mission or relevant consulate. Under the Decision EU citizens can obtain assistance, relief and, if needed repatriation, in most distressing circumstances, e.g. when they are victims of violent crimes, when they have serious accidents, when they are arrested, or in detention, etc.

- Decision 96/409/CFSP[1614] on the Emergency Travel Document, which provides for the issue by Member States of a common format emergency travel document to citizens of the EU in places where their Member State has no permanent diplomatic or consular representation or in other specific circumstances.

Under the ToL, measures relating to the protection of EU citizens outside the EU in the circumstances described in Article 23 TFEU are within the scope of the Treaties. Such measures may be adopted by the Council in accordance with a special legislative procedure and after consulting the EP. At the time of writing, measures adopted under Article 23 TFEU are under review. The Commission considers that, as EU nationals make more than 180 million journeys outside the EU per year, consular and diplomatic protection needs to be strengthened.[1615] In November 2006, the Commission adopted a Green Paper[1616] on diplomatic and consular protection of Union citizens in third countries which set out ideas to be considered for strengthening this right for Union citizens. The Green Paper, following a public consultation, served as a basis for the Commission Action Plan presented in December 2007[1617] which outlined a programme of work for 2007–2009. In order to inform and assist EU citizens the Commission is in the process of preparing a dedicated website on consular protection.[1618]

It can be said that the achievements of the EU so far as the protection of EU citizens outside the EU is concerned in a situation where they are in a third country in which their home Member State is not represented is not impressive. However, it is expected that some improvement may come out of the establishment of the European Union External Action Service (see Chapter 5.2.2)

1612. For example, when Fidel Castro came to power the USA cut off all diplomatic relations with Cuba. The Swiss and Czechoslovakian embassies in Havana acted respectively on behalf of the USA and Cuban governments for many years.

1613. [1995] OJ L314/73.

1614. [1996] OJ L168/4.

1615. On 28 November 2006 the Commission published its Green Paper on Diplomatic and Consular Protection of Union Citizens in Third Countries. COM/2006/0712 final.

1616. COM(2006)712.

1617. COM(2007)767.

1618. See http://ec.europa.eu/justice_home/fsj/citizenship/diplomatic/fsj_citizenship_diplomatic_en.htm.

which, under Article 35 TEU is required to co-operate closely with diplomatic missions of the Member States to ensure, inter alia, the implementation of the right of EU citizens guaranteed under Article 23 TFEU.

22.5 The right of EU citizens' initiative

Article 24(1) TFEU sets out the procedure for implementing the right of citizens' initiative, i.e. the possibility for at least one million EU citizens, who are from a substantive number of Member States, to invite the European Commission to bring forward legislative proposals in areas where the Commission has the power to do so (see Chapter 7.2).

22.6 The right to petition the EP

Article 24(2) TFEU states that a citizen of the Union may petition the EP in accordance with Article 227 TFEU. The right, however, is not limited to EU citizens. It has been granted to any natural or legal person residing or having its registered office in a Member State. There are certain limitations under Article 227 TFEU:

- The matter must come within the fields of activity of the EU; and

- The matter must affect the petitioner directly.

The Committee on Petitions, a special committee which was set up to deal with petitions, decides on the admissibility of petitions. If a petition is admissible the Committee may ask the Commission or other body to provide information. Once there is enough information the petition is put on the agenda of the Committee. At its meeting a representative from the Commission is invited to make an oral statement and comments on its written reply in respect of the matter raised in the petition. Depending on the case a further action may be taken by the Committee:

- If the petition is a special case requiring individual treatment, the Commission will get in touch with relevant authorities or submit the case to the permanent representative of the Member State concerned. In some cases the Committee may ask the president of the EP to make representations to the national authorities in person;

- If the petition is of general interest, that is, a Member State is in breach of EU law, the Commission may start proceedings against the offending Member State;

- If the petition concerns a political matter, the EP or the Commission may use it as the basis for a political initiative, in which case the individual case is not taken up but the petition may result in initiating or prompting an action at EU level.

In each case an applicant is informed of the result of the action taken on the basis of his/her petition.

22.7   The right to submit complaints to the EU Ombudsman

Article 24(3) TFEU states that every EU citizen has the right to make a complaint to the EU Ombudsman. His general duties are set out in Article 228 TFEU and further specified in Council Decision 94/262 of 9 March 1994.[1619]

The Ombudsman is elected by the EP after its own elections, holds office for the duration of the term of the EP and may be reappointed. The Ombudsman must be a citizen of the EU, chosen from persons whose independence is beyond doubt and who must possess the qualifications required for appointment to the highest judicial offices in their own Member State, or have the experience and the competences recognised as necessary for the exercise of the functions of Ombudsman.

The Ombudsman may be removed from office by the ECJ at the request of the EP if he/she no longer satisfies the conditions required for the performance of his/her duties or no longer meets the obligations resulting from his/her office, or is guilty of serious misconduct. The Ombudsman may not hold any office of an administrative or political nature, nor engage in any additional occupation or profession, paid or unpaid, during his/her term of office. The Ombudsman's role is to act independently, in the general interests of the EU, and thus the Ombudsman must neither seek nor take instructions from anybody.

The Ombudsman is empowered to receive complaints from citizens of the EU as well as any natural or legal person residing or having its registered office in a Member State.[1620] The Ombudsman's competences ratione materiae are limited to maladministration in the activities of EU institutions, bodies, offices or agencies.[1621] The Ombudsman cannot investigate complaints of maladministration in the activities of the CJEU acting in its judicial role. The limitation of the Ombudsman's competences to the investigation of maladministration of the EU institutions, bodies, offices or agencies is very disappointing since complaints regarding maladministration by national bodies pursuant to or in violation of EU law are most important and vital to ordinary people. This limitation has been recognised by the EU Ombudsman. According to the Ombudsman in 2008, 55 per cent of the complaints received were outside the Ombudsman's mandate because they concerned the activities of national authorities.[1622] In order to assist EU citizens the European Ombudsman works in close co-operation with national ombudsmen.

The Ombudsman may make investigations on his/her own initiative as well as in response to complaints from individuals, or submitted to him/her through members of the European Parliament, except if the alleged facts are, or have been, the subject of legal proceedings.

If the Ombudsman decides that a complaint is well founded, it is referred to the institution

---

1619. [1994] OJ L113/15. This decision was amended by Decision 2008/587/EC ([2008] OJ L189/587) which increases the powers to the EU Ombudsman, in particular with regard to two issues:

> First, EU institutions, bodies, offices and agencies are not allowed to refuse the EU Ombudsman access to information on the ground of confidentiality. The only exception concerns confidential information supplied by a Member State and classified as such by law or regulation. Its consent is required before the relevant information is sent to the Ombudsman. No such option is available in respect of confidential information provided by a third country. However, as a third country has no duty to co-operate with the EU institutions and bodies it is unlikely that its vital interests will be affected by the Decision. Second, the Ombudsman has been granted the right to co-operate with bodies entrusted with the protection of fundamental human rights.

1620. See the EU Ombudsman website http://www.ombudsman.europa.eu/home/en/default.htm (accessed 18/4/10).
1621. Apart from the CJEU acting in its judicial role.
1622. See Annual Report on the Activities of the EU Ombudsman for the year 2008, http://www.ombudsman.europa.eu.

concerned, which has three months to express its views. After the expiry of that period if the institution in question has not taken appropriate measures to resolve the matter, the Ombudsman must draft a report (which may include recommendations) and forward it to the EP and the institution concerned. However, the Ombudsman may then only inform the complainant of this process; the Ombudsman provides no legal remedy.

Even if the existence of the Ombudsman may seem superfluous taking into account that the competences of the EP Committee on Petitions and the Ombudsman overlap and that the remedies for maladministration by EU institutions, bodies, offices or agencies are already provided by the Treaties, and are more adequate and more efficient than any resulting from the successful intervention of the Ombudsman, it is an important institution protecting rights of EU citizens. For example, in 2008, he was able to help the complainants in almost 80 per cent of cases processed (i.e. 2,643 cases).[1623] Even if the number of complaints is not impressive, i.e. in 2008 he received 3,406 complaints, it is steadily growing and the Ombudsman's existence certainly enhances the democratic nature of the EU.

22.8 The right to use one's own language in correspondence with EU institutions, bodies, offices and agencies

Article 24(4) TFEU provides that every citizen of the EU has the right to write to any EU institution, body, office or agency in one of the official languages of the EU (see Chapter 6.1.2) and to receive an answer in the same language. This provision seems to entail more than a simple right to use one's own language in correspondence with the EU institutions which under Article 13 TEU are required, inter alia, to serve interests of EU citizens and therefore to communicate with them in the language that they can understand. Indeed, Article 24(4) TFEU enhances the principle of transparency including the right of EU citizens to have access to information (see Chapter 7.1.2.2.1).

22.9 The evolving nature of EU citizenship

The most important aspect of Union citizenship is its dynamic character. Its evolution should mirror the progress achieved by the EU. So far, the rights of EU citizenship have mainly been developed by the ECJ, as evidenced by its broad interpretation of Article 18(1) EC [Article 21(1) TFEU]; by the Commission, which has taken many initiatives to strengthen and enhance the European identity and enable European citizens to participate in the EU integration process in an increasingly intense way;[1624] and obviously by the EP, which, being the democratic servant of EU citizens, has always promoted their interests. It is submitted that its development has been stifled by the requirements set out in Article 25 TFEU, which remains in essence the same as its predecessor, Article 22 EC, relating to the adoption of measures aimed at adding to or strengthening the rights of EU citizens. Article 25 TFEU states:

1623. See the 2008 European Ombudsman Report available at http://www.ombudsman.europa.eu/activities/annualreports.faces (accessed 18/4/10).

1624. See the Commission's "Europe for Citizens Programme 2007–2013". See http://ec.europa.eu/citizenship/index_en.html (accessed 17/11/09).

"... the Council, acting unanimously in accordance with a special legislative procedure and after obtaining the consent of the European Parliament, may adopt provisions to strengthen or to add to the rights listed in Article 20(2). These provisions shall enter into force after their approval by the Member States in accordance with their respective constitutional requirements."

As a result, any progress was and remains very slow. It is, however, to be noted that the Council may only increase the list of rights granted to EU citizens and not reduce them.

Article 25(2) TFEU provides that the Commission is obliged to prepare every three years a report on the application of the provisions concerning citizenship of the EU and to forward such a report to the EP, the Council, and the Economic and Social Committee.

AIDE-MÉMOIRE

CITIZENSHIP OF THE EU

The Treaty of Maastricht established citizenship of the EU which complements but does not replace national citizenship. Only nationals of the Member States are citizens of the EU. A Member State has exclusive competence to decide who its nationals are and its decision must be respected by other Member States (Case C-369/90 *Michelletti*; Case C-192/99 *Kaur*; Case C-200/02 *Chen*) but this is subject to a proviso that when a situation under consideration is within the scope of the Treaties Member States must pay due regard to EU law (Case C-135/08 *Janko Rottmann*).

Part Two of the TFEU (Articles 18 to 25 TFEU) entitled "Non-discrimination and Citizenship of the Union" lists specific rights conferred on EU citizens whilst Title II of the TEU on "Provisions on Democratic Principles" (Articles 9 to 11 TEU) ensures EU citizens' participation in the decision making process in the EU. It is important to note that rights of EU citizens are also contained in other provisions of the Treaties and become relevant in situations where EC citizens are taxpayers, welfare recipients, consumers, workers, recipients of services, etc. Further secondary legislation details and expands the contents of the rights set out in the Treaties.

Rights conferred on EU citizens under Article 18–25 TFEU are listed below:

1. Under Article 18 TFEU any discrimination on the ground of nationality is prohibited. This is without prejudice to any special provisions of the Treaties providing otherwise. The ordinary legislative procedure is used for adoption of measures under this Article.

2. Under Article 19 TFEU discrimination based on sex, racial or ethnic origin, religion, belief, disability, age or sexual orientation is prohibited. This is without prejudice to other provisions of the Treaties providing otherwise. However, a unanimous vote in the Council is required and the consent of the EP for the adoption of measures under this Article.

3. Article 21 TFEU confers the right to free movement and residence within the territory of the Member States. The article is directly effective (Case C-413/99 *Baumbast*) and confers important social welfare, cultural and other rights on EU citizens by virtue of

their being EU citizens (Case C-85/96 *Maria Martínez Sala*; Case C-209/03 *Bidar*; Case C-258/04 *Ioannidis*, Case C-148/02 *Garcia Avello*; Case C-200/02 *Chen*).

The most important secondary legislation implementing what is now Article 21 TFEU is Directive 2004/38/EC of 29 April 2004 on the Right of Citizens and their Family Members to Move and Reside Freely within the Territory of the Member States.

4. Article 22(1) TFEU confers the right to vote and stand for municipal elections in a host Member State, under the same conditions as nationals of that Member State.

5. Article 22(2) TFEU confers passive and active voting rights in a host Member State for elections to the European Parliament.

6. Article 23 TFEU confers on every citizen of the EU the right to protection by the diplomatic or consular authorities of any Member State, on the same conditions as the nationals of that Member State, in the territory of a third country in which the Member State of which the EU citizen is a national is not represented (Decision 95/553/EC and Decision 96/409/CFSP[1625]). This right is confirmed in Article 46 of the Charter of Fundamental Rights of the European Union. It is expected that the creation of the EU External Action Service will be instrumental in the implementation of this right (Article 35 TEU).

7. Article 24(1) TFEU sets out the procedure for the implementation of the right conferred on EU citizens (at least one million citizens who are nationals of a substantive number of Member States) embodied in Article 11 TEU to request the European Commission to bring forward legislative proposals in areas where the Commission has the power to do so.

8. Article 24(2) TFEU confers the right to petition the EP.

9. Article 24(3) TFEU confers the right to submit complaints to the Ombudsman.

10. Article 24(4) TFEU confers the right to use one's own language in correspondence with EU institutions, bodies, offices and agencies.

Article 25 TFEU emphasises that EU citizenship is a dynamic concept. It allows the Council, acting unanimously in accordance with the special legislative procedure and after obtaining the consent of the EP, to adopt measures strengthening or adding to the rights listed above. Such measures can enter into force after their approval by the Member States in accordance with their respective constitutional requirements.

It is to be noted that Article 21(3) TFEU, for the first time, brings social security and social welfare matters within the scope of EU citizenship and thus offers the opportunity to Member States to create a social dimension of EU citizenship.

1625. [1996] OJ L168/4.

RECOMMENDED READING

Books

Kadelbach, P. S., "Union Citizenship", in A. Von Bogdandy and J. Bast (eds), *Principles of European Constitutional Law*, 2nd edition, 2010, Worcester: Hart Publishing, p 467

Shaw, J., *The Transformation of Citizenship in the European Union: Electoral Rights and the Restructuring of Political Space*, 2007, Cambridge: Cambridge University Press

Articles

Besson, S., and Utzinger, A., "Introduction: Future Challenges of European Citizenship – Facing a Wide-Open Pandora's Box", (2007) 13/5 ELJ, p 573

Hailbronner, K., "Union Citizenship and Access to Social Benefits", (2005) 42 CMLRev, p 1245

Jacobs, F. G., "Citizenship of the European Union – A Legal Analysis", (2007) 13/5 ELJ, p 1591

Jacqueson, C., "Union Citizenship and the Court of Justice: Something New under the Sun? Towards Social 'Citizenship' ", (2002) 27 ELRev, p 260

Mather, J. D., "The Court of Justice and the Union Citizen", (2005) 11/6 ELJ, p 722

Reich, N., "The Constitutional Relevance of Citizenship and Free Movement in an Enlarged Union", (2005) 11/6 ELJ, p 675

Slot, P. J. and Bulterman, M., "Harmonization of Legislation on Migrating EU Citizens and Third Country Nationals: Towards a Uniform Evaluation Framework", (2006) 29 Fordham Int'l LJ, p 747

Stalford, H., "Concepts of Family under EU law – Lessons from the ECHR", (2002) International Journal of Law, Policy, and the Family, p 410

23

FREE MOVEMENT OF WORKERS

SUMMARY

1. The free movement of workers and their families is governed by Article 45 TFEU, which has been implemented by secondary legislation, in particular:

- Regulation 1612/68 of 15 October 1968 on the free movement of workers within the Community, which governs access to and conditions of employment;

- Directive 2004/38/EC of 29 April 2004 on the right of citizens of the European Union and their family members to move and reside freely within the territory of the Member States; and

- Regulation 1408/71 of 14 June 1971 on the application of social security schemes to employed persons, to self-employed persons and to members of their families moving within the Community.

2. The right granted under Article 45 TFEU is not absolute. It suffers two exceptions expressly mentioned in that Article. By virtue of Article 45(4) TFEU employment in the public service may be reserved to nationals of a host Member State and under Article 45(3) TFEU some limitations may be imposed on the grounds of public policy, public security and public health (see Chapter 25). Some further exceptions are provided for in secondary legislation, for example, under Article 3(1) of Regulation 1612/68 a Member State is allowed to impose genuine linguistic requirements. The case law of the ECJ establishes a category of exceptions to national measures which are indirectly discriminatory or which constitute non-discriminatory obstacles to the free movement of workers. These exceptions are based on overriding reasons of public interest and are allowed if they pursue legitimate aims compatible with the Treaties and do not go beyond what is necessary and appropriate to achieve those aims.

3. Article 45 TFEU is both vertically and horizontally directly effective.

4. The scope of application ratione personae of Article 45 TFEU is very broad, as not only workers and their families can rely on it, but so can employers and even, in certain circumstances, private sector recruitment agencies.

5. Resulting from the enlargement of the EU in May 2004 and in January 2007, the territorial scope of Article 45 TFEU has become rather complex, as the "old" Member States were allowed to impose transitional measures restricting access to their labour markets for workers from "new" Member States. In any event, the transitional measures for those countries which joined the EU on 1 May 2004 must end on 30 April 2011, and for Bulgaria and Romania (which joined the EU on 1 January 2007) on 31 December 2013. Nationals of states belonging to the European Economic Area, that is, Iceland, Liechtenstein and Norway, are also beneficiaries of Article 45 TFEU.

6. The concept of "worker" has been broadly interpreted by the ECJ and has an autonomous EU meaning. The essential feature of the concept of a worker is that a person must perform services of some economic value for and under the direction of another person, in return for which she/he receives remuneration. This definition has two elements. The first relates to the requirement that the activities performed by a worker must be real and genuine, to the exclusion of activities on such a small scale as to be regarded as purely marginal and ancillary. The second concerns the requirement that a worker must perform activities of an economic nature.

7. Some rights guaranteed to EU migrant workers survive the termination of an employment relationship, e.g. in the field of financial assistance for university education or in respect of entitlement to social assistance or upon a worker's return to a home Member State of which he is a national, to be joined by a family member being a third country national, who had not resided in the home Member State of the worker but who lived with him/her in a host Member State.

8. The rights of family members of a worker are parasitic on or derivative from those of the worker. Directive 2004/38/EC defines who are to be regarded as members of a worker's family. Regardless of their nationality, they are entitled to move with a worker, reside with him/her in a host Member State, take up employment as employees or self-employed persons, and be treated in the same way as nationals of a host Member State. In Case C-127/08 *Metock* the ECJ held that a non-EU spouse of an EU citizen benefits from the right to free movement irrespective of when and where the marriage may have taken place and of how he/she entered the host Member State. This means that non-EU spouses are entitled to remain on the territory of a host Member State even if prior to the marriage they were unlawfully residing there.

9. Article 45 TFEU prohibits all forms of discrimination, whether direct or indirect, and (as interpreted by the ECJ) any national provisions which create a substantial obstacle to access to a labour market in a Member State. Directly discriminatory national provisions can only be justified if permitted under the Treaties. National provisions which are indirectly discriminatory or those which are not discriminatory but nevertheless substantially affect access to the labour market of a host Member State, can be justified only if they pursue a legitimate aim compatible with the Treaties, can be justified by overriding reasons in the public interest and do not go beyond what is necessary and appropriate to achieve that aim.

10. Regulation 1612/68 provides a list of rights to which EU migrant workers and their families are entitled once they have settled in a host Member State. Regulation 1612/68 states:

A. Under Article 1, EU migrant workers have the right to take up employment in a host Member State under the same conditions as its nationals.

B. Under Article 2, all discrimination against migrant workers is prohibited with regards to the conclusion and performance of their employment contracts.

C. Under Articles 3 and 4, all directly and indirectly discriminatory law, regulations and administrative practices are prohibited. National quota systems which provide for a limit to the percentage or number of EU migrant workers in a particular area, which restrict advertising of vacancies, or which set a special recruitment or registration procedure are prohibited. However, some genuine linguistic requirements may be imposed upon EU migrant workers.

D. Under Article 5, where assistance in finding employment is granted to nationals of a host Member State, it must equally be offered to EU migrant workers.

E. Under Article 6, discriminatory vocational or medical criteria for recruitment and appointment are prohibited.

F. Under Article 7(1), any discrimination concerning conditions of employment or work is prohibited.

G. Under Article 7(2), EU migrant workers and their families are entitled to the same social and tax advantages as nationals of the host Member State. The broad interpretation of this provision by the ECJ has significantly enhanced the rights of workers and their families in a host Member States:

(a) Social advantages. In Case 207/78 *Even* the ECJ defined social advantages as "those which, whether or not linked to a contract of employment, are generally granted to national workers primarily because of their status as workers or by virtue of the mere fact of their residence on the national territory". It is impossible to give a list of social advantages because each Member State determines what advantages are to be regarded as such, and thus they vary from one Member State to another – the basic principle is that workers from other Member States and their families are entitled to benefit on equal terms. The case law of the ECJ shows that EU migrant workers and their families, even after the worker's death, have been entitled to a vast range of social advantages.

In Case 39/86 *Lair* the ECJ held that entitlement to higher education study finance is to be regarded as a social benefit under Article 7(2). However, the entitlement is subject to the requirement of continuity between the previous occupational activity and the studies pursued, except where a migrant worker involuntarily becomes unemployed and, as a result, is obliged by conditions of the labour market to undertake occupational retraining.

(b) Tax advantages refer mainly to tax deductions which reduce taxable income, for example deductions for private sickness insurance premiums, or for contributions to an occupational pension scheme. A host Member State is required to make deductions in relation to contributions paid in the worker's home Member State.

H.   Under Article 8, EU migrant workers are entitled to equal treatment in respect of the exercise of trade union rights, including the right to vote and to be eligible for the administration and management posts of a trade union.

I.   Under Article 9, EU migrant workers have the same access to all rights and benefits in matters of housing and house ownership as do nationals of a host Member State.

J.   Under Article 12, children of an EU worker are to be treated in the same way as children of a national worker. Once children are settled in a host Member State, they have an independent right of residence there until they terminate their education there. Further, Article 12 confers the right to reside in a host Member State not only on children, but also on a parent, who is a non-EU citizen if he/she is the primary carer of children in a situation where his/her EU spouse divorced him/her, or departed from a Member State or died. In Case C-310/08 *Ibrahim* and Case C-480/08 *Teixeira*, the ECJ held that the right of such a parent to reside in a host Member State is not conditional on the parent having sufficient means to avoid becoming a burden on the social welfare system of the host Member State.

23.1   Introduction

Article 45 TFEU provides:

"1.   Freedom of movement for workers shall be secured within the Union.

2.   Such freedom of movement shall entail the abolition of any discrimination based on nationality between workers of the Member States as regards employment, remuneration and other conditions of work and employment.

3.   It shall entail the right, subject to limitations justified on grounds of public policy, public security or public health:

    (a)   to accept offers of employment actually made;

    (b)   to move freely within the territory of Member States for this purpose;

    (c)   to stay in a Member State for the purpose of employment in accordance with the provisions governing the employment of nationals of that State laid down by law, regulation or administrative action;

    (d)   to remain in the territory of a Member State after having been employed in that State, subject to conditions which shall be embodied in regulations to be drawn up by the Commission.

4.   The provisions of this Article shall not apply to employment in the public service."

Under Article 46 TFEU the Council and the EP in accordance with the ordinary legislative procedure and after consulting the Economic and Social Committee are empowered to adopt measures implementing Article 45 TFEU. Article 46 TFEU particularly refers to measures

    ◾ ensuring liberalisation of the movement of workers, e.g. the abolition of administrative procedures, practices and those qualifying periods in respect of eligibility for available employment whether resulting from national legislation or from agreements previously concluded between Member States;

- restricting free choice of employment by EU workers apart from restrictions imposed on national workers;

- ensuring close co-operation between national employment services;

- ensuring the harmonious development of the EU employment market.

Article 47 TFEU is addressed to the Member States which shall take measures encouraging the exchange of young workers.

The most important pre-ToL secondary legislation adopted to give effect to the principle of the free movement of workers, which is still in force at the time of writing, is:

- Regulation 1612/68 of 15 October 1968 on the free movement of workers within the Community, which governs access to and conditions of employment;[1626]

- Directive 2004/38/EC of 29 April 2004 on the right of citizens of the European Union and their family members to move and reside freely within the territory of the Member States.[1627] The Directive, which is examined in detail in Chapters 22 and 25, consolidates much secondary legislation and introduces new solutions;

- Regulation 1408/71 of 14 June 1971 on the application of social security schemes to employed persons, to self-employed persons and to members of their families moving within the Community.[1628] The Regulation co-ordinates national legislation on social security rights of persons who move within the EU in order to guarantee that all migrants have an adequate level of social protection and do not lose social security benefits when they move to another Member State.

    Article 48 TFEU brought an important change to the manner in which harmonising legislation in social security matters for migrant workers and their dependants is adopted in that the ordinary legislative procedure is applicable with the result that a unanimous vote in the Council has been replaced by QMV and the EP is a co-legislator. However, as legislation in social security matters may have important financial implications for Member States an "emergency brake" procedure is provided for in Article 48 TFEU. Accordingly, any Member State may request that a proposed measure be referred to the European Council if a Member State considers that it would affect important aspects of its social security system. The referral entails the suspension of the ordinary legislative procedure and gives the European Council four months to decide whether to refer the proposal back to the Council (in which case the suspension of the ordinary procedure ends) or take no action, or request the Commission to prepare a new proposal. In the latter two cases, the proposed measure is deemed not to have been adopted.

1626. [1968] OJ L 257/1 as amended many times.
1627. [2004] OJ L158/77. It should be noted that this Directive has been repeated (probably by error) with the number 2004/58 ([2004] OJ L229/26). For completeness it is mentioned that the OJ contains another Directive referenced 2004/58/EC on a totally different topic ([2004] OJ L120/26). In this book the reference will be to Directive 2004/38/EC.
1628. [1971] OJ L149/2, as amended many times.

The right of free movement of workers is not absolute. It suffers two exceptions expressly provided for in Article 45 TFEU, exceptions introduced in secondary legislation implementing Article 45 TFEU and exceptions developed by the ECJ. The exceptions provided for in Article 45 TFEU are:

- First, restrictions on the free movement of workers may be justified on the grounds of public policy, public security and public health (Article 45(3) TFEU);

- Second, employment in the public service may be reserved to nationals of a host Member State (Article 45(4) TFEU).

Secondary legislation contains some further exceptions: for example, Article 3(1) of Regulation 1612/68 allows a Member State to impose genuine linguistic requirements on EU migrant workers.

The third exceptions are based on the case law of the ECJ. They concern national measures which are indirectly discriminatory or which constitute non-discriminatory obstacles to the free movement of workers but substantially affect access to the labour market in a host Member State. These exceptions are based on overriding reasons of public interest, and are allowed if they pursue legitimate aims compatible with the Treaties and do not go beyond what is necessary and appropriate to achieve those aims.

23.2　Vertical and horizontal direct effect of Article 45 TFEU

Article 45 TFEU has been directly effective since the entry into force of Regulation 1612/68 on 15 October 1968.[1629] In Case 36/74 *Walrave and Koch*,[1630] the ECJ held that Article 39 EC [Article 45 TFEU] is also horizontally directly effective.

THE FACTS WERE:

The rules of the Union Cycliste Internationale, an international sporting association which was neither a public body nor part of the state, imposed nationality requirements in respect of "pacemakers" and "stayers" in the world cycling championships.

Held:

The ECJ ruled that a nationality requirement was contrary to Article 39 EC [Article 45 TFEU] since the prohibition of discrimination "does not only apply to the action of public authorities but extends likewise to rules of any nature aimed at regulating in a collective manner gainful employment and the provision of services".[1631]

Since the judgment in *Walrave and Koch* it has been clear that an individual can rely on

---

1629.　Case 48/75 *The State v Jean Noël Royer* [1976] ECR 497; Case 167/73 *Commission v France [Re French Merchant Seamen]* 1974 ECR 359.

1630.　[1974] ECR 359.

1631.　This was confirmed in Case C-415/93 *Bosman* [1995] ECR I-4921 and Case C-176/96 *Jyri Lehtonen* [2000] ECR I-2681.

Article 45 TFEU against public bodies, and bodies such as the Union Cycliste Internationale when they adopt rules regulating "in a collective manner gainful employment" but it was, for many years, unclear whether it could be relied upon against private persons. All doubts as to the horizontal direct effect of Article 45 TFEU were removed in Case C-281/98 *Angonese v Casa di Risparmio di Bolzano SpA*.[1632]

THE FACTS WERE:

Mr Angonese, an Italian national whose mother tongue was German and who was resident in the province of Bolzano (Italy), when applying for a job in a private bank in Bolzano was required to submit a certificate of bilingualism issued by the local authorities. When Mr Angonese's application was rejected because he did not submit the particular certificate even though he was totally bilingual and had other relevant linguistic qualifications, he argued that the requirement to evidence his linguistic knowledge solely by means of one particular certificate issued in a single province of a Member State was contrary to Article 39 EC [Article 45 TFEU].

Held:

The ECJ held that the requirement imposed by the private bank was in breach of Article 39 EC [Article 45 TFEU]. The ECJ held that: "Limiting application of the prohibition of discrimination based on nationality to acts of a public authority risks creating inequality in its application." Thus, the prohibition of discrimination applies to both agreements intended to regulate paid labour collectively and agreements between individuals.

23.3 The scope of application ratione personae of Article 45 TFEU

The ECJ has given a broad interpretation to the personal scope of Article 45 TFEU. It applies not only to EU migrant workers and their families but also to other natural and legal persons. In Case C-350/96 *Clean Car Autoservice*,[1633] the ECJ held that employers can rely on Article 39 EC [Article 45 TFEU] to employ workers in accordance with the rules governing freedom of movement of workers.

In Case C-208/05 *ITC Innovative Technology Center*,[1634] the issue was whether a private sector recruitment agency could rely on Article 39 EC [Article 45 TFEU].

THE FACTS WERE:

Under German legislation persons entitled to claim unemployment benefit who had not found a job after three months of collecting such benefit were entitled to a recruitment

---

1632. [2000] ECR I-4139.
1633. [1998] ECR I-2521.
1634. [2007] ECR I-181.

voucher, which constituted an undertaking made by the German Government to pay a private sector recruitment agency the amount stated on the voucher in a situation where the agency found employment for the voucher-holder. The voucher specified that the holder must be placed in employment subject to compulsory social security contributions for a minimum of 15 hours per week. Under this scheme Mr Halacz, a voucher-holder, instructed a German private sector recruitment agency, ITC, which found him employment in The Netherlands subject to compulsory social security contributions in The Netherlands and for more than 15 hours a week. When ITC asked the relevant German authority for payment under the recruitment voucher, this was rejected on the ground that Mr Halacz had not been placed in employment subject to compulsory social security contributions in Germany. ITC challenged the refusal before the German Social Court in Berlin, which referred for a preliminary ruling to the ECJ the question of compatibility of the German legislation with Articles 39 and 49 EC [Articles 45 and 56 TFEU]. One of the main issues was whether a private sector recruitment agency could rely on Article 39 EC [Article 45 TFEU].

Held:

The ECJ held that a private sector recruitment agency may, in some circumstances, rely on Article 39 EC [Article 45 TFEU].

Comment:

The ECJ, first, gave consideration to the natural and ordinary meaning of Article 39 EC [Article 45 TFEU] and stated that nothing in the wording of that article indicates that persons other than workers may not rely upon it. This was not very convincing, since there was equally no mention of the possibility of persons other than workers relying on it. Consequently, the Court turned to schematic and teleological interpretation. It stated that bearing in mind that ITC acted as a mediator and intermediary between jobseekers and employers, and thus represented the applicant and sought employment on his behalf, it is possible that it may, in certain circumstances, rely on Article 39 EC [Article 45 TFEU]. Consequently, the ECJ did not extend the scope of Article 39 EC [Article 45 TFEU] to all activities of private sector recruitment agencies, but stated that in some circumstances they may rely on the rights granted directly to workers by Article 39 EC [Article 45 TFEU] – exactly how far the principle goes will depend on future case law.

It is to be noted that Article 45 TFEU does not apply to purely internal situations. This is exemplified in Joined Cases 35 and 36/82 *Morson and Jhanjan [Re Surinam Mothers]*.[1635]

THE FACTS WERE:

Two Dutch nationals working and residing in The Netherlands wanted to bring their mothers of Surinamese nationality to reside with them in The Netherlands. Under Dutch law they were not permitted to do so.

1635. [1982] ECR 3723.

Held:

The ECJ held that EU law did not apply to cases which have no factor connecting them with any of the situations governed by EU law. Accordingly, as the matter was of a purely internal nature, EU law was not applicable.

23.4   The territorial scope of application of Article 45 TFEU

With the accession to the EU of 12 "new" Member States, which occurred in two stages, the first on 1 May 2004 (10 Member States) and the second on 1 January 2007 (Bulgaria and Romania), the territorial application of Article 45 TFEU became complex:

- Within and between the territories of the 15 "old" Member States plus Cyprus and Malta[1636] no restrictions are imposed on the nationals of these 17 Member States exercising the right of freedom of movement under Article 45 TFEU;

- All "new" Member States (apart from Hungary, which imposed some conditions) have opened access to their labour markets to nationals of the "old" Member States.

Nationals from 8 of the 10 "new" Eastern and Central European Member States (Bulgaria, the Czech Republic, Estonia, Hungary, Latvia, Lithuania, Poland, Romania, Slovakia and Slovenia) have restricted access to labour markets in the 15 "old" Member States and in Cyprus and Malta.

As mentioned in Chapter 3.3.6, the "old" Member States were allowed to impose restrictions on the free movement of workers from eight "new" Member States (but not Cyprus and Malta) which acceded in 2004. A transitional scheme know as the "2+3+2 year arrangement" was put in place, under which each of the "old" Member States was required to declare in May 2006, and again in May 2009, willingness or otherwise to give access to their labour markets to workers from the eight "new" Member States. In any event, all restrictions must be removed on 30 April 2011. In respect of the eight "new" Member States only Austria and Germany decided to continue the transitional measures after May 2009.

The situation of Bulgaria and Romania is different. A similar "2+3+2" scheme applies to them, however, all restrictions must be removed by 1 January 2014. Apart from Sweden and Finland, all the "old" Member States, Cyprus and Malta decided to impose transitional measures on workers from Bulgaria and Romania. In December 2006 France decided to include workers from these two countries in its scheme of the gradual lifting of restrictions. Italy will consider opening its labour market to Romanians and Bulgarians after the adoption of a European agreement on combating organised crime.

It is to be noted that Article 45 TFEU applies to nationals from the states of the European Economic Area, that is, to Iceland, Liechtenstein and Norway.

1636. Malta obtained a seven-year transitional period, during which, in some circumstances, it can restrict access to its labour market for workers from other Member States. Maltese citizens, however, have the right to seek work in all EU Member States.

23.5   The concept of a worker

There is no definition of a "worker" in the Treaties although Regulation 1408/71 defines a worker as a person insured under a social security scheme.[1637] The ECJ has broadly interpreted the concept of a worker[1638] and has given it an autonomous EU meaning.

23.5.1   The objective criteria characterising the employment relationship

In Case 66/85 *Lawrie-Blum v Land Baden-Württemberg*,[1639] the ECJ held that a "worker" is a person who performs services of some economic value for and under the direction of another person, in return for which she/he receives remuneration.

THE FACTS WERE:

Deborah Lawrie-Blum, a British national, after successfully passing her examination for the teaching profession, was refused admission to the period of probationary service which had to be completed in order to become a teacher in Germany. During the probationary period a trainee teacher is considered as a civil servant and receives remuneration for conducting classes. Under the German law of Land Baden-Württemberg only German nationals were admitted to probationary service. Deborah Lawrie-Blum challenged the decision of the German authorities on the basis of Article 12 EC and Article 39(2) EC [Articles 18 and 45(2) TFEU]. In response, the Land contended, inter alia, that a trainee teacher was not a "worker" within the meaning of Article 39 EC [Article 45 TFEU].

Held:

The ECJ held that a trainee teacher who, under the direction and supervision of the school authorities, is undergoing a period of service in preparation for the teaching profession, during which she/he provides services by conducting classes and receives remuneration, is regarded as a "worker" under Article 39(1) EC [Article 45 TFEU] irrespective of whether her/his employer is a private entity or a public body.[1640]

In the context of the organisation of an undertaking, the personal and property relations between spouses resulting from marriage do not exclude the existence of a relationship of subordination which is characteristic of an employment relationship. The ECJ held in Case C-337/97 *Meeusen*[1641] that a person who is related by marriage to the director and sole shareholder of the company for which she pursues an effective and genuine activity is classified as a "worker" within the meaning of Article 45 TFEU.

1637.   [1971] OJ L149/2.
1638.   Case 53/81 *Levin* [1982] ECR 1053.
1639.   [1986] ECR 2121.
1640.   Case C-71/93 *Guido Van Poucke* [1994] ECR I-1101.
1641.   [1999] ECR I-3289.

23.5.2   Two elements of the definition of a "worker"

Two elements of the definition of a "worker" are provided by the ECJ:

23.5.2.1   *Genuine and effective activity*

The first relates to the requirement that the activity performed by a worker must be genuine and effective.

The ECJ stressed in a number of cases that provided the activities performed are effective and genuine, a person should be considered as a worker even though such a person is not employed full-time or receives pay at a rate lower that for full-time employment. This is illustrated in Case 139/85 *Kempf*.[1642]

THE FACTS WERE:

Mr Kempf, a German part-time music teacher working in The Netherlands from 1981 to 1982, whose income was below the national minimum salary, received supplementary benefit in the form of sickness benefit and general assistance. When he applied for a residence permit in The Netherlands, his application was refused on the ground that his income was insufficient to meet his needs and that he was not a worker.

Held:

The ECJ held that Kempf should be regarded as a worker, irrespective of the fact that he was employed on a part time-basis. The ECJ held that if the activity performed is effective and genuine, a person is a worker even though his salary is insufficient to support him and he has to rely on some other means to bring his income to subsistence level.[1643]

It is also irrelevant whether the money used to supplement the income is obtained from the individual's private means or from public funds.[1644] Further, a person who works occasionally, according to the needs of the employer[1645] or within the framework of an apprenticeship contract[1646] or a training contract,[1647] should be considered as a worker for the purposes of Article 45 TFEU.

In Case 3/87 *Agegate*,[1648] the ECJ held that fishermen paid only when the caught fish were sold were considered as workers as they performed activities which were effective and genuine.

If a person's work is so limited as to be marginal or ancillary,[1649] she/he will not be regarded as

---

1642. [1986] ECR 1741.
1643. Case 53/81 *Levin* [1982] ECR 1035.
1644. Case C-188/00 *Kurz* [2002] ECR I-10691.
1645. Case C-357/89 *Raulin* [1992] ECR I-1027.
1646. Case C-27/91 *Le Manoir* [1991] ECR I-5531.
1647. Case 66/85 *Lawrie-Blum* [1986] ECR 2121; Case C-109/04 *Kranemann* [2005] ECR I-2421; Case C-10/05 *Mattern and Cikotic* [2006] ECR I-3145.
1648. [1989] ECR 4459.
1649. Case 197/86 *Brown* [1988] ECR 3205.

a worker. In order to distinguish between genuine and effective and marginal or ancillary employment, a national court should take into account the duration and the regularity of the activity concerned[1650] and factors, such as those set out by the ECJ in Case C-188/00 *Kurz*,[1651] are irrelevant. In *Kurz* the ECJ held that: "neither the *sui generis* nature of the employment relationship under national law, nor the level of productivity of the person concerned, the origin of the funds for which the remuneration is paid or the limited amount of remuneration can have any consequence in regard to whether or not the person is a worker".

23.5.2.2   Economic nature of activity

The second element concerns the requirement that a worker must perform activities of an economic nature.

In Case 344/87 *Bettray*,[1652] the ECJ held that participation in a drug rehabilitation scheme for which its participants were paid did not involve performance of economic activities and therefore was outside the scope of Article 39 EC [Article 45 TFEU]. However, a plumber working for a religious community who did not receive any remuneration but worked for his keep and some pocket money qualified as a worker, since he performed an effective and genuine activity of an economic nature.[1653]

In Case C-456/02 *Trojani*,[1654] the ECJ provided some indications as to how to decide whether the activities in question are of an economic nature.

THE FACTS WERE:

A destitute French national was given accommodation in a Salvation Army Hostel in Brussels and performed for the Salvation Army (SA), and under its direction, various jobs for approximately 30 hours a week, as part of a personal reintegration programme run by the SA, in return for which he received benefits in kind and some pocket money.

Held:

The ECJ decided that the referring court was better placed to answer the question whether Mr Trojani was a worker. However, the ECJ identified a number of factors which a national court should take into account when ascertaining whether the services actually performed by Mr Trojani were capable of being regarded as forming part of the normal labour market, in particular:

- The status and practices of the hostel;

- The content of the social reintegration programme; and

- The nature and details of performance of the services.

1650. Case C-357/89 *Raulin* [1992] ECR I-1027.
1651. [2002] ECR I-10691.
1652. [1989] ECR 1621.
1653. Case 196/87 *Steymann* [1988] ECR 6159.
1654. [2004] ECR I-7573.

In respect of activities involving sport only those which are of an economic nature are within the scope of Article 45 TFEU. As a result, a professional football player[1655] or a cyclist or a coach[1656] are regarded as workers, while the selecting of national representatives did not involve any economic activities.[1657]

23.5.3   Persons sentenced to prison

With regard to persons sentenced to prison in a host Member State, in particular those who had worked before their conviction, the fact that they are not employed during their detention does not necessarily mean that they lose their status of workers. Indeed, they should continue to be regarded as workers within the meaning of Article 45 TFEU provided they find employment within a reasonable time after the end of their detention.[1658] In Joined Cases C-482/01 and C-493/01 *Georgios Orfanopoulos and Others v Land Baden-Württemberg and Raffaele Oliveri v Land Baden-Württemberg*,[1659] the ECJ applied the above reasoning to Mr Orfanopoulos. He had worked in Germany before serving his prison sentence and was a worker within the meaning of Article 39 EC [Article 45 TFEU] when in prison.

23.5.4   Persons who work for international organisations

When an EU national works in a host Member State for an international organisation, he/she is regarded as a worker.[1660]

23.5.5   Termination of relationship of employment

The termination of relationship of employment does not necessarily extinguish all the rights of a worker or his/her family. Some of them are linked to the status of a worker even after the termination of an employment relationship, for example, in the field of financial assistance for university education[1661] or in respect of other forms of social assistance.[1662] With regard to a family of an EU worker, in Case C-291/05 *Minister voor Vreemdelingenzaken en Integratie v R.N.G. Eind*,[1663] the ECJ held that a third country national who was a member of the family of an EU worker, and who had not resided in the home Member State of the worker but joined him in a host Member State had the right, in the event of the worker returning to the home Member State

---

1655.   Case C-415/93 *Bosman* [1995] ECR I-4921.

1656.   Case 36/74 *Walrave* [1974] ECR 1405.

1657.   Case 13/76 *Donà* [1976] ECR 1333; Case 36/74 *Walrave* ibid.

1658.   Case C-340/97 *Ömer Nazli, Caglar Nazli and Melike Nazli v Stadt Nürnberg* [2000] ECR I-957.

1659.   [2004] ECR I-5257.

1660.   Joined Cases 389/87 and 390/87 *Echternach and Moritz* [1989] ECR 723; Case C-209/01 *Schilling and Fleck-Schilling* [2003] ECR I-13389; Case C-293/03 *My* [2004] ECRI-12013; Case C-185/04 *Öberg* [2006] ECR I-1453; Case C-392/05 *Alevizos* [2007] ECR I-3505.

1661.   Case 39/86 *Lair v Universität Hannover* [1988] ECR 3161, see section 23.9.

1662.   Case C-35/97 *Commission v France* [1998] ECR I-5325, in this case Belgian frontier workers who had been placed in early retirement were entitled to receive a similar supplementary retirement pension to that granted to French workers.

1663.   [2007] ECR I-10719.

of which he was a national, to entry and residence in the home Member State of the EU worker. This is even when the former EU worker did not carry on effective and genuine economic activities in the home Member State and even if he/she was a recipient of social assistance in the home Member State. It should also be noted that children and non-EU spouses of EU workers who have settled in a host Member State, in circumstances where an EU worker dies or departs the host Member State or divorces a non-EU spouse, have been granted important rights under Article 12 of Regulation 1612/68 (see section 23.6.2).

23.5.6   Unemployed persons

In Case 48/75 *The State v Jean Noel Royer*,[1664] the ECJ held that Article 39(3) EC [Article 45(3) TFEU] included the right to enter a host Member State in search of work, although it did not fix any time-limit for such a search.[1665] It seems that a six-month period can be considered as a reasonable time for the purpose of seeking employment. This was implied from the ECJ decision in Case C-292/89 *R v Immigration Appeal Tribunal, ex parte Antonissen*,[1666] in which the ECJ accepted that if after a six-month stay in a host Member State for the purpose of seeking employment an EU migrant had failed to find employment, a deportation order could be issued unless the migrant provided evidence that he/she was actively seeking employment and had a genuine chance of being employed. The law as stated in the above case is now enshrined in Article 14(4)(b) of Directive 2004/38.

Temporary unemployment does not change the status of "worker" of a migrant EC national who lost his/her job due to illness or accident.[1667]

23.6   The family of a worker

The rights of family members of a worker are parasitic on those of the worker. A member of a family of an EU national cannot rely on Article 45 TFEU until that EU national exercises his/her right to work in another Member State,[1668] and then only in a Member State where that national is employed. This is exemplified in Case C-10/05 *Mattern and Cikotic v Ministre du Travail et de l'Emploi*.[1669]

THE FACTS WERE:

Mrs Mattern, a national of Luxembourg, and her husband Mr Cikotic, a national of a third country, were residing in Belgium where Mrs Mattern was taking a professional course,

---

1664. [1976] ECR 497.
1665. In Case C-344/95 *Commission v Belgium* ([1997] ECR I-1035) deportation of an unemployed person who had been seeking a job for only three months was regarded as contrary to Article 39 EC.
1666. Case 75/63 *Hoekstra v BBDA* [1991] ECR I-745.
1667. [1964] ECR 177.
1668. Cases C-297/88 and 197/89 *Dzodzi* [1990] ECR I-3763; Joined Cases C-64 and 65/96 *Uecker and Jacquet* [1997] ECR I-3171.
1669. [2006] ECR I-3145.

which, according to the ECJ, might have conferred on her the status of worker (it was for a national court to decide whether in the course of her professional training she was pursuing a genuine and effective activity). When Mr Cikotic applied for a work permit in Luxembourg, his application was refused.

Held:

The ECJ held that a national of a third country married to an EU national may rely on Article 39 EC [Article 45 TFEU] only in a Member State where that EU national pursues an activity as an employed or self-employed person. Thus, whilst Mr Cikotic would have been entitled to a work permit in Belgium, he was not entitled to obtain it in Luxembourg when his wife was working in Belgium.

23.6.1 The spouse of a worker

A spouse is entitled to move and reside with a worker in a host Member State, regardless of the spouse's nationality, and to take up and pursue activities as an employed or a self-employed person in the territory of a host Member State under the same conditions as a national worker. If the spouse's profession is regulated within the meaning of EU secondary legislation (see Chapter 24.5.2.2.1), and the spouse of an EU worker satisfies the conditions for taking up or pursuing a professional activity in a regulated profession, a host Member State must recognise the professional qualification of the spouse.[1670]

The rights of spouses under EU law have been interpreted broadly by the ECJ. However, EU law is not applicable to a situation where a non-EU spouse wishes to enter and remain in the home Member State of his/her spouse. For EU law to be applied there must be a cross-border, EU element.

It can be said that the objectives of the immigration rules of each Member State and of the objectives of EU rules on the free movement of persons are opposed to each other:

- Under domestic law. A non-EU national who wishes to marry and thereafter live with a national of a Member State would have no automatic right of entry to the home Member State of his or her spouse. The non-EU national will only be granted the right to enter and remain in the territory of a Member State after an individual assessment by the competent national immigration authorities, which assessments are often based on very stringent national criteria. However, when an EU migrant worker returns to the Member State of his nationality with a family member who is not an EU national the *Eind* judgment applies (see section 23.5.5) under which the right of residence of such a person in a Member State of nationality of an EU worker depends on the existence of either dependency or marriage (or partnership so far as it is recognised by that State). If a relationship of dependency or marriage terminates, the right of residence of a non-EU national will be assessed in the light of national rules.

- Under EU law. If an EU citizen settles himself/herself in a Member State other than that of

---

1670. Case 131/85 *Gül* [1986] ECR 1573.

his/her nationality, his/her spouse, regardless of his/her nationality, has an automatic right to join him/her and the national immigration rules of a host Member State do not apply. In these circumstances a host Member State may only refuse entry to a third country national who is a spouse of an EU citizen on the grounds of public policy, public security and public health. Further, unlawful residence of a non-EU national in a host Member State prior to marrying an EU migrant worker living in that host Member State is not sufficient to refuse that non-EU spouse residence in the territory of the host Member State. This is exemplified in Case C-127/08 *Blaise Baheten Metock and Others v Minister for Justice, Equality and Law Reform*,[1671] in which the ECJ was asked to interpret Directive 2004/38 EC to assist the Irish High Court to decide whether Irish legislation implementing the Directive was compatible with EU law. The Irish legislation provided that a national of a third country who is a family member of a EU citizen may reside with or join that citizen in Ireland only if that family member lawfully resided in another Member State immediately before residing with/joining the EU citizen in Ireland.

THE FACTS WERE:

The Irish High Court referred to the ECJ four cases. In each of the four cases, a non-EU national had entered Ireland and lodged an asylum application, which was refused. Subsequent to arrival in Ireland, each non-EU national married a national of another Member State who was living and working in Ireland. All marriages were genuine marriages, not marriages of convenience. After the marriage, the non-EU nationals applied for a residence card, which the Irish Minister for Justice refused. This refusal in three of the four cases was solely based on the fact that each applicant was not in a position to provide evidence that he had been lawfully resident in another Member State prior to arrival in Ireland. In the fourth case concerning Mr Igboanusi, a Nigerian national, who had married Ms Batkowska, a Polish national, subsequent to the final decision refusing his application for political asylum, a deportation order was made prior to his marriage. Therefore, when Mr Igboanusi married Ms Batkowska he was unlawfully residing in Ireland. In execution of the deportation order Mr Igboanusi was arrested on 16 November 2007, and following a decision of the Irish High Court refusing to grant an injunction restraining the Minister for Justice from deporting Mr Igboanusi, deported to Nigeria in December 2007.

Held:

The ECJ held that:

1. Under Directive 2004/38 a host Member State is not allowed to impose a condition requiring a national of a non-member country, who is the spouse of an EU citizen residing in that Member State but not possessing its nationality, to have previously been lawfully resident in another Member State before arriving in the host Member State. The ECJ held that no such condition is provided for in Directive 2004/38 and that Article 2 of Directive 2004/38 makes no distinction between, on the one hand, those

---

1671. [2008] ECR I-6241.

family members who have already resided lawfully in another Member State prior to their arrival in a host Member State and, on the other hand, those who joined an EU national in a host Member State without previously residing in any Member State or whose residence in another Member State was unlawful prior to their arrival in a host Member State. The ECJ emphasised that this broad interpretation of Directive 2004/38 is in conformity both with its case law and with secondary legislation concerning freedom of movement for persons existing prior to the adoption of Directive 2004/38.

2.   The ECJ confirmed that the EU has exclusive powers to regulate, as it did by Directive 2004/38, the entry (and subsequent residence there) of nationals of non-member countries who are family members of an EU citizen into the Member State in which that citizen has exercised his right of freedom of movement, including a situation where the family members were not already lawfully resident in another Member State.

3.   The ECJ held that non-EU nationals who are family members of an EU citizen benefit from the right to free movement irrespective of whether they have entered the host Member State before or after becoming family members of that EU citizen and irrespective of when and where their marriage may have taken place and of how they entered the host Member State. Obviously, in any event, under Article 27 of Directive 2004/38 a Member State is allowed to penalise a national of a non-Member State for, prior to becoming a family member of an EU citizen, entering into and/or residing in its territory in breach of the national rules on immigration. However, any punishment must be in conformity with EU law in that it must be proportionate.

Comment:

With regard to point 2, the ECJ made an important clarification bearing in mind that the Irish Government and many other governments of the Member States submitted that they retained exclusive competence, subject to Title IV of Part Three of the Treaty, to regulate the first access to the EU territory of family members of an EU citizen who are nationals of non-member countries. Recognition of the exclusive competence of Member States in respect of the free movement of persons would have had very serious consequences on the effectiveness of the right to free movement of EU nationals and the uniformity of the application of EU law in this area. An argument in favour of the exclusive competences of Member States based on the necessity to control immigration at the external borders of the EU, which presupposes an individual examination of all the circumstances surrounding a first entry into EU territory, was rejected by the ECJ. The Court rightly stated first, that only non-EU nationals who are family members of EU nationals benefit from the right of entry into and residence in a Member State and second, that a Member State retains its power to refuse entry and residence to both EU citizens and non-EU family members of EU citizens on grounds of public policy, public security or public health.

In the light of the above judgment and the judgment of the ECJ in Case 291/05 *Eind*, the controversial judgment of the ECJ in Case C-109/01 *Secretary of State for the Home Department v Hacene Akrich*[1672] has lost its importance. In *Akrich* the issue was whether a national

---

1672. [2003] ECR I-9607.

of a Member State, who is married to a third-country national who does not qualify under national legislation to enter and reside in that Member State, when he or she moves to another Member State with the non-national spouse with the intention of working there for only a limited period of time as an employee, can take advantage of EU law by securing the right of residence for the non-national spouse when returning to the Member State of nationality. The ECJ held that Mr Akrich could not rely on EU law to enter and remain in the home Member State of his spouse because he resided unlawfully there before he and his wife had moved to another Member State. The only remedy which might have been available to him is based on Article 8 of the ECHR. In this case the ECJ strongly emphasised the importance of the right to family life, referring to its own case law and the judgments of the ECtHR, but did not rule on the point. It is to be noted that in the light of the judgments of the ECJ in *Metock* and in *Eind*, Mr Akrich would have had no problem to return to his spouse's home Member State. However, in *Akrich* the ECJ made two important clarifications:

- That the marriage must be a genuine marriage and not a marriage of convenience;

- That the intention of EU migrant workers (including the intention to use rights conferred under EU law to evade the application of national rules which are unfavourable to them) when exercising their right to free movement has no impact on their entitlement under EU law.

23.6.2 Children of a worker

Under Article 12 of Regulation 1612/68 children of a worker are entitled to admission to general education, apprenticeship and vocational training courses under the same conditions as nationals of a host Member State. In Case 76/72 *Michel S. v Fonds National de Reclassement Social des Handicapés*,[1673] the ECJ ruled that the list of educational arrangements for such children was not exhaustive. In this case a mentally handicapped son of an Italian worker, who was employed in Belgium before his death, was entitled to rehabilitation benefits from a fund set up to assist people whose employment prospects were seriously affected by handicap. The ECJ based its ruling on Articles 7 and 12 of Regulation 1612/68.

Children of workers are entitled to general measures of support such as grants and loans.[1674] This is exemplified in Case C-308/89 *Di Leo v Land of Berlin*[1675] In which the ECJ held that Germany was in breach of the principle of non-discrimination in a situation where German authorities refused a daughter of an Italian worker employed in Germany financial support provided under German law on the ground that the daughter studied in Italy.

In Case 42/87 *Commission v Belgium*,[1676] the ECJ held that children of migrant workers (including workers who have retired or died) are to be treated on an equal footing with children of national workers in respect of access to all forms of state education.

1673. [1973] ECR 457.
1674. Case 9/74 *Casagrande* [1974] ECR 773; Case 68/74 *Alaimo* [1975] ECR 109.
1675. [1990] ECR I-4185.
1676. [1988] ECR 5445.

In Case C-413/99 *Baumbast and R*[1677] the ECJ held that, on the ground of Article 12 of Regulation 1612/68, children of an EU worker who have installed themselves in a host Member State are entitled to reside there in order to attend general educational courses irrespective of the fact that the parents of the children concerned have meanwhile divorced, the fact that only one parent is a citizen of the Union, and the fact that that parent has ceased to be a migrant worker in the host Member State. As a result, children of EU migrant workers have an independent right to residence in a host Member State until they terminate their education there. This is so even though a child has interrupted his/her study in a host Member State and subsequently returns because it is impossible to continue studying in the home Member State.[1678]

In Case C-7/94 *Gaal*,[1679] the ECJ held that Article 12 of Regulation 1612/68 applies also to children who are over 21 years of age and independent. The ECJ emphasised that it would be contrary to the letter and to the spirit of Article 12 to construe it in such a manner as to render students already at an advanced stage in their education ineligible for the financial assistance available in a host Member State as soon as they reach 21 years or are no longer dependent on their parents.

In Case C-310/08 *London Borough of Harrow v Nimco Hassan Ibrahim and Secretary of State for the Home Department*[1680] the issue was whether a parent, who is a non-EU national and the primary carer of children, and whose spouse ceased to be a worker in a host Member State and who, on the authority of the *Baumbast* case, is allowed to reside in a host Member State during the period of his/her children's education, is required under EU law to have sufficient resources to avoid being a burden on the social support system of the host Member State. The ECJ held that solely on the basis of Article 12 of Regulation 1612/68 a parent can claim a right of residence in the host Member State without such a right being conditional on him/her having sufficient resources and comprehensive sickness insurance cover in the host Member State. In Case C-480/08 *Maria Teixeira v London Borough of Lambeth, and Secretary of State for the Home Department*[1681] the issue was whether a non-EU parent and primary carer of a child of a migrant worker who derived her right to residence in a host Member State from Article 12 of Regulation 1612/68 retains her right when the child reaches the age of 18, thus coming of age under the law of the host Member State. The ECJ held that there is no age limit for the rights conferred on a child under Article 12 of Regulation 1612/68. As to the parent who is the primary carer, he/she retains the right of residence until the child has completed his or her education provided that the child continues to need the parent's presence and care after attaining the age of majority. The above two cases have important implications on social welfare systems of the Member States. In both cases the reference was made to the ECJ in a situation where the relevant national authorities refused to grant to non-EU nationals, primary carers social welfare benefits. In Case C-310/08 *Ibrahim*, the parent, who had never worked and who, after the departure of her husband from the host Member State, had been entirely dependent on social assistance and had no comprehensive sickness insurance cover for herself and for her four children applied for housing assistance for herself

---

1677. [2002] ECR I-7091.
1678. Joined Cases 389 and 390/87 *Echternach and Moritz* [1989] ECR 723. See also Case 63/76 *Inzirillo* [1976] ECR 2057.
1679. [1996] ECR I-1031.
1680. Judgment of 23/2/10 (nyr).
1681. Judgment of 23/2/10 (nyr).

and her children. In Case C-480/08 *Teixeira*, the parent applied for housing assistance for home-less persons. It is clear from the ECJ judgments in *Ibrahim* and *Teixeira* that in both cases the parents, as primary carers for children, will be entitled to the social benefits they sought.

23.7   The principle of non-discrimination and beyond

The legal situation of EU nationals working in a host Member State results not only from Article 45 TFEU and secondary legislation implementing that article, but also from a broad interpretation by the ECJ of the principle of non-discrimination which is expressly mentioned in Article 45(2) TFEU and which increases the strength of the general prohibition of discrimination set out in Article 18 TFEU. The main role of the principle of non-discrimination is to ensure equality in treatment between a national worker and a migrant worker as regards employment, remuneration and other conditions of work and employment.

23.7.1   The prohibition of direct and indirect discrimination

Not only direct discrimination based on nationality but also indirect discrimination based on other factors is prohibited. This was examined by the ECJ in Case 15/69 *Württembergische Milchverwertung-Südmilch v Ugliola*.[1682]

THE FACTS WERE:

Ugliola an Italian national employed in Germany challenged German legislation which pro-vided that military service in the Bundeswehr should be taken into account in calculating his seniority with his employment. Ugliola performed his military service in Italy. He argued that by not including similar provision for services in other armies of other Member States, German legislation was in breach of the principle of non-discrimination. The German Govern-ment submitted that its legislation was not discriminatory since it applied to any national of any Member State who served in the Bundeswehr and did not apply to any German national who performed his military service in other Member States.

Held:

The ECJ held that the likelihood of a national of other Member States serving in the Bundeswehr was more hypothetical than real. Consequently, German legislation indirectly discriminated against nationals from other Member States working in Germany.

The principle of non-discrimination requires not only that the same rules are applicable to similar situations but also, conversely, that different situations are treated differently. The case law of the ECJ shows that Article 45(2) TFEU prohibits all forms of indirect discrimination which, by applying distinguishing criteria other than nationality (such as residence), have in practice the

---

1682.   [1969] ECR 363.

same discriminatory result. However, in certain circumstances such rules may be justified as was the Case 152/73 *Sotgiu v Deutsche Bundespost.*[1683]

THE FACTS WERE:

Indirect discrimination in respect of a separation allowance was invoked by an Italian worker whose family lived in Italy but who was employed by the German postal service in Germany. Under German law a separation allowance of DM10 per day was paid (if relevant) to workers residing within Germany at the time of their recruitment, while workers of German nationality as well as workers from other Member States received an allowance of DM7.50 per day if at the time of their recruitment they resided abroad. Sotgiu relied on Article 7(1) of Regulation 1612/68 and the principle of non-discrimination. During the proceedings it became clear that workers residing in Germany at the time of their recruitment received a larger allowance under two conditions: the payment was conditional upon their willingness to move to their place of work and it was limited to the first two years of employment. Neither condition applied to workers who resided abroad at the time of their recruitment.

Held:

The ECJ held that the application of criteria other than nationality, in this case the place of residence at the time of recruitment, could in certain circumstances have a discriminatory result in practice. This would not be the case when the payment of a separation allowance was made on conditions which took into consideration objective differences in the situations of workers, which differences could concern the place of residence of workers at the time of their recruitment. The Court also stated that the difference in amount paid to both groups of workers could be objectively justified, taking into account that one group of workers received an allowance temporarily while for the other group it was of unlimited duration.

Rules of national law, which although indistinctly applicable to both national workers and migrant EU workers (that is, they make no distinction based on nationality) which essentially affect only migrant workers[1684] or the majority of them,[1685] are considered as indirectly discriminatory.

23.7.2 Beyond discrimination

In Case C-415/93 *Bosman,*[1686] the ECJ examined national rules which were not discriminatory directly or indirectly, but which constituted an obstacle to the free movement of workers.

1683. [1974] ECR 153.
1684. Case 41/84 *Pinna* [1986] ECR 1; Case 33/88 *Allué* [1989] ECR 1591.
1685. Case C-272/92 *Spotti* [1993] ECR I-5185.
1686. [1995] ECR I-4921.

> ### THE FACTS WERE:
>
> *Belgian football transfer rules, which were in conformity with the rules of international football organisations, provided that a club which sought to engage a player had to pay a specified sum of money to the player's existing club. The rules applied irrespective of the nationality of a player and irrespective of whether the transfer took place between clubs in the same country or between clubs located in different countries. Bosman, a Belgian player, wished to move from a Belgian club to a French club but was prevented from doing this because his Belgian club refused to accept a transfer fee from the French club.*
>
> *Held:*
>
> The ECJ held that the Belgian rules:
>
> 1. Constituted an obstacle to freedom of movement of workers;
>
> 2. Directly affected players' access to the labour market in other Member States and thus were capable of impeding freedom of movement of workers;
>
> 3. Could not be objectively justified.

The ECJ confirmed this approach in Case C-18/95 *Terhoeve*.[1687] In this case the ECJ stated that it was not necessary to examine whether the challenged Dutch legislation (requiring higher social security contributions to be paid by workers who transfer their residence in the course of a year from one Member State to another in order to take up employment there, as compared to contributions which would be payable by workers who have continued to reside throughout the year in the same Member State) was indirectly discriminatory. It constituted an obstacle to the free movement of workers because it had deterred a national of a Member State from leaving his country of origin in order to exercise his right to freedom of movement in another country.

National rules which are not discriminatory but nevertheless restrict access to the labour market of a Member State can be justified only if they are based on objective considerations, which are independent of nationality and are proportionate to the aim legitimately pursued by the national law.[1688] It is to be noted that the concept of objective justification was developed by the ECJ itself, in the absence of any explicit provision in the Treaties.

The prohibition of all national provisions which hinder the free movement of workers, even if these provisions apply without discrimination, raises the question of whether there is a need to impose some limitations on the scope of application of Article 45 TFEU in order to avoid it becoming a "catch all" provision. This matter was clarified in Case C-190/98 *Volker Graf and Filzmoser Maschinenbau GmbH*.[1689]

1687. [1999] ECR I-345.

1688. Case C-15/96 *Schöning-Kougebetopoulou* [1998] ECR I-47; Case C-224/01 *Köbler v Austria* [2003] ECR I-10239; Case C-464/02 *Commission v Denmark* [2005] ECR I-7929; Case C-109/04 *Kranemann* [2005] ECR I-2421; Case C-208/05 *ITC Innovative Technology Center* [2007] ECR I-181.

1689. [2000] ECR I-493.

THE FACTS WERE:

Mr Graf, an Austrian national who had been employed by Filzmoser since 1992, terminated his contract of employment in 1996 in order to move to Germany to take up new employment. Filzmoser refused to pay Mr Graf compensation equal to two months' salary on termination of employment. Filzmoser relied on Article 23(7) of the Austrian Law on Employees (Angestelltengesetz) under which an employee is not entitled to compensation if he gives notice, leaves prematurely for no important reason or bears responsibility for premature dismissal. Mr Graf challenged this provision as contrary to Article 39(2) [Article 45(2) TFEU], which prohibits national rules precluding or deterring a worker from ending his contract of employment in order to take a job in another Member State, and invoked Article 23(1) of the above-mentioned Austrian law providing that: "If the employment relationship has continued uninterruptedly for three years, the employee shall be entitled to a compensation payment on termination of that relationship." The referring court was uncertain as to the application of the decision of the ECJ in Bosman to the above situation.

Held:

The ECJ confirmed its decision in *Bosman*. It held that Article 39 EC [45 TFEU] applies to national rules which impede the free movement of persons and are indistinctly applicable to both national workers and migrant EC workers. In this respect, the Austrian court clearly established that Article 23(7) of the Austrian Law on Employees was not discriminatory as it neither restricted cross-border mobility to a greater extent than mobility within Austria, nor was the loss of compensation equal to two months' salary on termination of employment such as to result in a perceptible restriction on the freedom of movement for workers.

Comment:

The conclusion of the ECJ concerning the scope of application of Article 45 TFEU to such situations is of great importance because it is necessary to impose limitations on the application of Article 45 TFEU in order to avoid the ECJ's previous experiences regarding the provisions on the free movement of goods (see Chapter 20.9). Article 45 TFEU must not be allowed to become a "catch all" provision, whereby any conceivable national rule could potentially violate EU law. In this respect the ECJ had two options: first, to apply the *Keck* approach to national indistinctly applicable rules and thus to refer to the criterion based on the objective of national rules, or second, to focus on the effect of national rules.[1690] The ECJ decided to combine both approaches.

At first the ECJ seemed to favour the solution in *Keck* by stating that national rules indistinctly applicable, which preclude or deter a national of a Member State from leaving his/her Member State of origin to enter the territory of another Member State in order to take up employment there, constituted an obstacle to the free movement of workers. Thus, the ECJ focused on the discriminatory or non-discriminatory nature of national rules. However, the ECJ qualified this by emphasising that "in order to be capable of constituting such an

---

1690. See Case C-44/98 *BASF* [1999] ECR I-6269.

obstacle, they [national rules] must affect access of workers to the labour market". By stating this, the ECJ applied the second approach consisting of the assessment of the effect of the contested Austrian legislation on access to the labour market. In *Bosman* the impact of the rules of the Belgian Football Association on access to the labour market was considerable, taking into account the amount of penalty payment. In this case the situation was different. As the ECJ pointed out, not only the small amount of compensation but also the fact that the entitlement to compensation was not dependent on the worker's choosing whether or not to continue his employment, but on a future and hypothetical event (namely the subsequent termination of his contract without such termination being at his own initiative or attributable to him) led the ECJ to conclude that "such an event is too uncertain and indirect a possibility for legislation to be capable of being regarded as liable to hinder freedom of movement of workers where it does not attach to termination of a contract of employment by the worker himself the same consequences as it attaches to termination which was not at his initiative or is not attributable to him".

This solution avoids all inconveniences deriving from the application of the *Keck* approach to the area of free movement of workers. Thus, non-discriminatory national rules are outside the scope of Article 45 TFEU when they do not substantially hinder access to the labour market, but they are within the scope of this provision where they do substantially hinder the free movement of workers, as evidenced by Case C-415/93 *Bosman*.

23.8   Rights granted to workers and their families under Regulation 1612/68

The principle of equal treatment laid down in Article 45 TFEU applies to all aspects of employment including eligibility for employment, conditions of work, remuneration and other conditions of work and employment. Regulation 1612/68 gives substance to the requirements of Article 45 TFEU.

23.8.1   Eligibility for employment

Articles 1 to 6 of Regulation 1612/68 prohibit any discrimination against EU migrant workers in respect of access to employment.

Article 1 guarantees to EU migrant workers the right to take up available employment, and pursue it, in the territory of a host Member State under the same conditions as nationals of that Member State.

Article 2 prohibits all discrimination against EU migrant workers with regard to the conclusion and performance of their employment contracts.

Article 3 provides that national provisions and practices which limit the right to seek or to pursue employment, or which impose conditions not applicable to nationals on migrant EU workers, are inapplicable. However, Article 3(1) allows a Member State to impose conditions "relating to linguistic knowledge required by reason of the nature of the post to be filled". Article 3(1) was relied upon by the Irish Government in Case 379/87 *Groener*.[1691]

1691. [1989] ECR 3967.

THE FACTS WERE:

Irish legislation required that appointment to a permanent full-time post as a lecturer in public vocational schools in Ireland was conditional upon proficiency in Gaelic. On this basis Mrs Groener, a Dutch national, was refused a full-time post as an art teacher after she had failed a test intended to assess her knowledge of the Gaelic language.

Held:

The ECJ held that although knowledge of Gaelic was not required for the performance of the duties of teaching art in Ireland, the requirement was not in breach of Article 3(1) of Regulation 1612/68 as it was a part of a national policy for the promotion of the national language and therefore constituted a means of expressing national identity and language in the Irish Republic. It was also non-discriminatory, and not disproportionate to the objective pursued.

Under Article 4 of Regulation 1612/68 Member States must not restrict the employment of EC migrant workers by number or percentage. The leading case on this is Case 167/73 *Commission v France [Re French Merchant Seamen]*.[1692]

THE FACTS WERE:

The 1926 French Maritime Code set a ratio of three French to one non-French nationals for the employment of merchant seamen in the crew of French merchant ships. The justification submitted by the French Government was that the requirement was not used in practice, as oral instructions were given to appropriate national authorities not to apply it.

Held:

The ECJ condemned the French Maritime Code. It ruled that non-application of the requirement was a matter of grace, not of law, and thereby created uncertainty for all parties concerned.

Under Article 5 of Regulation 1612/68 Member States must offer EU migrant workers the same assistance in seeking employment as is available to nationals.

Article 6 of the Regulation provides that the engagement or recruitment of a national of one Member State for a post in another Member State should not depend on medical, vocational or other criteria which are discriminatory as compared with those applied to national workers. However, when an employer actually offers a job to a national of another Member State, it may be on the express condition that the candidate undergoes a vocational test (Article 6(2)).

1692. [1974] ECR 359.

23.8.2 Employment and equality of treatment

Articles 7–9 of Regulation 1612/68 require a host Member State to ensure that EU migrant workers:

■ Are treated in the same way as national workers in respect of any condition of employment and work, in particular as regards remuneration, dismissal and, should they become unemployed, reinstatement or re-employment (Article 7(1));

■ Should enjoy the same social and tax advantages (Article 7(2)) as its nationals. This provision has been broadly interpreted by the ECJ so as to become a source of important rights conferred on EU migrant workers, their families and job seekers;

■ Should have the same access to vocational training as its nationals (Article 7(3));

■ Should enjoy the same treatment as its nationals as regards membership of and participation in trade unions (Article 8);

■ Should have the same access to all rights and benefits in matters of housing as its nationals (Article 9).

Article 7(4) provides that any provision in collective or individual employment agreements or in any other collective regulation concerning eligibility for employment, employment, remuneration and other conditions of work and dismissal which discriminates against EU migrant workers shall be null and void (Article 7(4)).[1693]

23.8.2.1 *Social and tax advantages*

Article 7(2) of Regulation 1612/68 provides that a migrant worker "shall enjoy the same social and tax advantages as national workers".

23.8.2.1.1 Social advantages

The ECJ defined social advantages in Case 207/78 *Even*[1694] as covering all advantages:

"which, whether or not linked to a contract of employment, are generally granted to national workers primarily because of their objective status as workers or by virtue of the mere fact of their residence in the national territory."

Social advantages are different from social security benefits.[1695] An entitlement to social security benefits is governed by Regulation 1408/71. The ECJ has consistently held that Member States are competent to define the conditions for granting social security benefits, provided that the conditions are not directly or indirectly discriminatory against EU migrant workers.[1696]

Each Member State determines what benefits should be regarded as social advantages. For that

---

1693. See Case C-400/02 *Merida* [2004] ECR I-8471.

1694. [1979] ECR 2019.

1695. Case 1/72 *Frilli v Belgium* [1972] ECR 457.

1696. Case C-12/93 *Drake* [1994] ECR I-4337; Case C-320/95 *Ferreiro Alvite* [1999] ECR I-951; Case C-306/03 *Cristalina Salgado Alonso* [2005] ECR I-705).

reason they vary from one Member State to another. The case law of the ECJ shows that Article 7(2) has bestowed a wide range of benefits upon workers and their families. Some examples are:

- In Case 65/81 *Reina*,[1697] an Italian couple residing in Germany obtained an interest-free discretionary loan on the birth of their child, which was payable only to German nationals living in Germany. These loans were an incentive to increase the birth rate in Germany and were granted by a credit institution set up under public law;

- In Case 249/83 *Hoeckx*,[1698] an unemployed worker was entitled to a minimum subsistence allowance;

- In Case 137/84 *Mutsch*,[1699] the use of one's own language in judicial proceedings was considered as being a social benefit;

- In Case 157/84 *Frascogna*,[1700] an Italian widow, living with her son in France, was entitled to an old-age pension falling outside the scope of the national social security rules;

- In Case C-237/94 *O'Flynn*, an Irish national working in the UK successfully claimed expenses incurred in connection with the costs of burying his son in Ireland. Under UK legislation the funeral payment was granted to workers and EC migrant workers alike if the burial or cremation took place within the UK. The ECJ held that this condition was indirectly discriminatory and could not be objectively justified. However, the Court agreed with the UK that the cost of transporting the coffin to Ireland had to be met by the applicant given that this benefit was not available to UK workers;[1701]

- In Case C-85/96 *Maria Martínez Sala*,[1702] a Spanish national living in Germany was entitled to a child-raising allowance;

- In Case 94/84 *Deak*,[1703] an unemployed Hungarian national living with his mother, an Italian national working in Belgium, obtained unemployment benefits for school leavers;

- In Case 32/75 *Christini*,[1704] an Italian widow living in France claimed the special fare reduction card issued by the French Railways to the parents of large families. The ECJ held that since the family was entitled to remain in France after the worker's death and that the card was available to the families of deceased French workers, it should not be denied to the families of deceased workers from other Member States;

- In Case 63/76 *Inzirillo*,[1705] an Italian national working in France obtained a disability allowance for his adult son;

1697. [1982] ECR 33.
1698. [1985] ECR 973.
1699. [1985] ECR 2681.
1700. [1985] ECR 1739.
1701. [1996] ECR I-2617.
1702. [1998] ECR I-2691.
1703. [1985] ECR 1873.
1704. [1975] ECR 1085.
1705. [1976] ECR 2057.

- In Case 261/83 *Castelli*,[1706] an Italian widow living with her retired son in Belgium obtained a guaranteed income paid to old people in Belgium;

- In Case 3/90 *Bernini*,[1707] the ECJ held that a study grant should be classified as a social benefit within the meaning of Article 7(2) of Regulation 1612/68. As a result, a dependent child of a migrant EC worker is entitled to obtain study finance under the same conditions as are applicable to children of national workers;

- In Case 235/87 *Matteucci*,[1708] the ECJ ruled that a scholarship to study abroad, which was a part of a reciprocal agreement between Belgium and Germany, should be granted to the son of an Italian worker employed in Belgium who wanted to study in Germany.

As to the entitlement of jobseekers to social advantages in a host Member State, the case law of the ECJ has evolved. The initial position of the ECJ was stated in Case 316/85 *Centre Public de l'Aide Sociale de Courcelles v Lebon*.[1709]

THE FACTS WERE:

A French national, who was living in Belgium, applied for the Belgian minimex (a minimum income allowance). She was not a worker within the meaning of Article 39 EC [Article 45 TFEU] but she was seeking a job.

Held:

The ECJ made a distinction between workers already in employment and those who are in search of work. Only the former were entitled to the minimex.

With the development of EU law the decision in *Lebon* ceased to be good law. In Case C-138/02 *Collins*,[1710] the ECJ held that in the light of the establishment of the concept of EU citizenship, it was no longer possible to exclude from the scope of Article 39(2) EC [Article 45(2) TFEU] a benefit of a financial nature intended to facilitate access to employment in the labour market of a Member State in a situation where there is a genuine link between the person seeking work and the employment market of that Member State. A residence requirement is, in principle, appropriate for the purpose of ensuring such a connection, if it is proportionate and does not go beyond what is necessary in order to attain that objective. This far-reaching interpretation of the entitlement to social benefits, in particular those aimed at young people to assist them in finding their first employment, was confirmed in Case C-258/04 *Ioannidis*.[1711]

1706. [1984] ECR 3199.
1707. [1992] ECR I-1071.
1708. [1988] ECR 5589.
1709. [1987] ECR 2811.
1710. [2004] ECR I-2703.
1711. [2005] ECR I-8275.

THE FACTS WERE:

Mr Ioannidis, a Greek national, who was lawfully resident in Belgium and who had studied for three years there, was refused a tide-over allowance for young people seeking their first employment on the ground that he had completed his secondary education elsewhere than in Belgium.

Held:

The ECJ held that Mr Ioannidis was entitled to rely on Article 39 EC [Article 45 TFEU] and that the Belgian legislation was indirectly discriminatory as it placed nationals of other Member States lawfully residing in Belgium at a disadvantage as compared to Belgian nationals. Such a difference in treatment can only be justified on objective criteria, independent of the nationality of the persons concerned and proportionate to the aim legitimately pursued by national law. In the case of Mr Ioannidis the condition of the completion of secondary education imposed by Belgian law was too general and exclusive in nature to be justified.

The ECJ emphasised in Case C-209/03 *Bidar*[1712] that what is important in deciding whether or not a person is entitled to social benefits is whether a condition imposed under national law is representative of the real and effective degree of connection between the applicant and the host Member State. A condition concerning the place where an EU national completed his/her secondary education was certainly not, but in the case of *D'Hoop*, a condition requiring a degree of connection between the applicant and the geographic employment market was.[1713]

It is to be noted that in contrast to the general public service exception governing access to public sector employment under Article 45(4) TFEU, once employed in the public sector, EU migrant workers are entitled to social benefits.[1714]

23.8.2.1.2 Tax advantages

Bearing in mind that there is no harmonisation of direct taxation at EU level, EU migrant workers may find themselves bearing a greater burden of taxation as a result of moving to another Member State. In Case C-387/01 *Weigel*,[1715] the ECJ acknowledged that the EC Treaty provided no guarantee to a worker that transferring his/her activities to a Member State other than the one in which he/she previously resided would be neutral as regards indirect taxation. As long as the national legislation of the host Member State does not place the EU migrant worker at a disadvantage as compared to workers who are already subject to that legislation, there will be no breach of Article 45(2) TFEU – so to the extent that higher taxation in a host Member State could be considered a non-discriminatory obstacle to free movement, it is in general outside the general principles as to prohibited national measures developed by the ECJ. In the case of Mr and Mrs Weigel the challenged Austrian legislation applied to all workers who wanted to register a car in Austria without any distinction as to their nationality. Thus, the ECJ did not take account of

---

1712. [2005] ECR I-2119.
1713. Case C-224/98 *D'Hoop* [2002] ECR I-6191.
1714. Case 152/73 *Sotgiu* [1974] ECR 153.
1715. [2004] ECR I-4981, for facts see Chapter 19.3.2.

the situation of Mr and Mrs Weigel prior to the transfer as compared to their situation after the transfer, but compared their situation in the host Member State to the situation of workers already working there.

In Case C-279/93 *Finanzamt Köln-Altstadt v Roland Schumacker*[1716], the ECJ emphasised that differences in treatment of taxpayers are allowed under EU law, provided that the situations of the taxpayers are not the same as each other. This means that if a situation of an EU migrant worker is objectively comparable to a situation of a national worker, an EU migrant worker should enjoy the same tax benefits as that national worker. In *Schumacker* the ECJ held that the situation of Mr Schumacker (a Belgian national who lived in Belgium but worked in Germany and who was denied certain tax benefits which were available to taxpayers resident in Germany) was comparable to the situation of a German resident taxpayer given that Mr Schumacker received all or almost all of his income in Germany.

If the situations of an EU migrant worker and a national worker are objectively comparable, according to the case law of the ECJ (rather than principles set out explicitly in the Treaties) a national taxation system which discriminates indirectly against an EU migrant worker may be justified only if it pursues a legitimate aim compatible with the Treaties, is justified by overriding reasons in the public interest and does not go beyond what is necessary and appropriate to achieve that purpose.

In this connection Member States have submitted various justifications, most of which were rejected by the ECJ. For example, the ECJ has consistently rejected the following justifications:

- Based on reduction in tax revenue;[1717]

- Based on practical difficulties in determining the tax actually paid in another Member State;[1718]

- Based on necessity to prevent tax evasion.[1719]

The ECJ has accepted an argument based on the cohesion of the national tax system, but for this argument to succeed it is necessary to establish a direct link between the discriminatory tax rule and the compensatory tax advantage.[1720] In Case C-204/90 *Bachmann v Belgian State*[1721] such a link was established.

THE FACTS WERE:

Under Belgian law the cost of life insurance premiums could not be deducted from taxable income in circumstances where the premiums were paid in other Member States. Mr Bachmann challenged this.

1716. [1995] ECR I-225.
1717. Case C-136/00 *Rolf Dieter Danner* [2002] ECR I-8147; Case C-436/00 *X and Y* [2002] ECR I-10829.
1718. Case C-319/02 *Petri Manninen* [2004] ECR I-7477.
1719. Case C-464/02 *Commission v Denmark* [2005] ECR I-7929.
1720. Case C-484/93 *Svensson and Gustavsson v Ministre du Logement et de l'Urbanisme* [1995] ECR I-3955; Case C-107/94 *Asscher v Staatssecretaris van Financiën* [1996] ECR I-3089; Case C-55/98 *Skatteministeriet v Bent Vestergaard* [1999] ECR I-7641; Case C-436/00 *X and Y* [2002] ECR I-10829.
1721. [1992] ECR I-249.

Held:

The ECJ held that the Belgian legislation was justified by the fact that the insured person had a choice of either having tax deducted on the premiums and then not paying tax on future benefits or not having tax deducted on the premiums and then paying tax on future benefits. In other words, the Belgian system, on the one hand, allowed natural persons to deduct insurance contributions from their taxable income but, on the other hand, when the capital constituted by such exonerated contributions was paid by the insurer to the taxpayer at the expiry of the insurance contract, it was then subject to taxation.

In the case of Mr Bachmann, if he had been allowed to deduct tax on premiums paid in Germany from his income earned in Belgium, the Belgian tax authorities would have been unable to tax the capital paid at the expiry of the insurance contract, which would be payable in Germany. Consequently "cohesion of the tax system necessarily required that, if the Belgian tax authorities were to allow the deductibility of life assurance contributions from taxable income, they had to be certain that the capital paid by the assurance company at the expiry of the contract would in fact subsequently be taxed".

23.8.2.2 Trade union rights

Article 8 of Regulation 1612/68 regarding equality of treatment covers equal trade union rights. An EU migrant worker is entitled to equal treatment in respect of the exercise of trade union rights, including the right to vote and to be eligible for the administration and management posts of a trade union.

The ECJ ruled that Article 8 of the Regulation applies to organisations similar to trade unions, that is, whose objective is the protection of workers. Consequently, in a situation where EU migrant workers are mandatory members of professional associations and have to pay compulsory contributions, national legislation cannot deny them the right to vote in elections to choose members of their professional associations.[1722]

An EU migrant worker has the right of eligibility to serve on workers' representative bodies within the undertaking where he/she works.[1723]

23.8.2.3 Equal treatment in matters of housing and house ownership

Article 9 of Regulation 1612/68 ensures equal treatment of EU migrant workers in matters of housing and house ownership. This is exemplified in Case 305/87 *Commission v Greece*[1724] in which Greek legislation prohibiting foreign nationals from owning immovable property located in certain regions of Greece (namely, in areas close to Greece's external borders), which applied to approximately 55 per cent of Greek territory, and was condemned by the ECJ.

1722. Case C-213/90 *ASTI* [1991] ECR I-3507; Case C-118/92 *Commission v Luxembourg* [1994] ECR I-1891.
1723. Case C-465/01 *Commission v Austria* [2004] ECR I-8291.
1724. [1989] ECR 1461.

23.9   Entitlement to study finance for EU migrant workers

By virtue of Article 7(3) of Regulation 1612/68 EU migrant workers are entitled to access to training in vocational schools and retraining centres under the same conditions as national workers.

The ECJ has restrictively interpreted this provision. In Case 39/86 *Lair v University of Hanover*,[1725] the ECJ held that "the concept of vocational training is a more limited one and refers exclusively to institutions which provide only instruction either alternating with or closely linked to an occupational activity, particularly during apprenticeship. That is not true of universities".

Luckily for Lair the narrow construction of Article 7(3) was compensated for by the ECJ's generous approach to Article 7(2), causing the Court to rule in the above case that entitlement to study finance is to be regarded as a social benefit under Article 7(2) of the Regulation. Consequently, a person who has kept his/her status as a worker can rely on Article 7(2) to obtain means of financial support from a host Member State to take courses to improve his/her professional qualifications and social advancement.

The above rule is subject to limitations imposed by the ECJ in respect of workers who voluntarily become unemployed in order to undertake a course of study and workers who enter a host Member State and take up employment for a short period of time with a view to subsequently undertaking studies. There are two different situations.

The first situation occurred in the case of *Lair* mentioned above.

THE FACTS WERE:

Lair was a French national who had worked in Germany as a bank clerk for two and a half years. She was then made redundant and for the next two and half years was working, but had spells of involuntary unemployment. She was considered as a worker and therefore entitled to retain that status when she decided to study languages and literature at the University of Hanover. However, when she applied for a maintenance grant, her application was refused. She challenged the refusal.

Held:

The ECJ ruled that although she was a worker "some continuity between the previous occupation and the course of study" was required in order to obtain a grant for university education. In her case there was no link between her previous job and her subsequent studies. Consequently, she was entitled to the payment of registration and tuition fees but not to assistance given in the form of maintenance grants. However, if a worker becomes involuntarily unemployed and is "obliged by conditions of the job market to undertake occupational training in another field of activity", he/she will be entitled to general measures of support such as grants and loans.

The second situation occurred in Case 125/87 *Brown v Secretary of State for Scotland*.[1726]

1725. [1988] ECR 3161.
1726. [1988] ECR 1619.

THE FACTS WERE:

Brown was a holder of dual nationality – French and British. He was employed as a trainee engineer with Ferranti Plc in Edinburgh for nine months with a view to studying engineering at Cambridge. His work was a form of pre-university industrial training as it was a pre-requisite for his admission to university. He would not have been employed by his employer if he had not already been accepted by the university. When he applied for a grant, his application was refused on the ground that he had not been a resident of the UK during the previous three years as required by UK legislation. He challenged this decision.

Held:

The ECJ held that Brown was a worker as he fulfilled the three criteria laid down in the *Lawrie-Blum* case, that is, he was engaged in genuine and effective economic activity. However, the ECJ decided that Brown was not entitled to a grant despite his status of a worker because he "acquired that status exclusively as a result of his being accepted for admission to undertake the studies in question".

Comment:

It can be seen that if employment is merely ancillary to studies, migrant workers are not entitled to financial assistance, unless they can show (as did Danny Bidar[1727]) a real and effective degree of connection with the host Member State based on factors other than ancillary employment.

The rules established by the ECJ with regard to entitlements or otherwise of EC migrant workers to study finance in a host Member State are not easy to apply. This is exemplified in Case C-413/01 *Ninni-Orasche*.[1728]

THE FACTS WERE:

In 1993 Mrs Ninni-Orasche, an Italian national, married an Austrian national and moved with him to Austria. In September 1995 she found employment as a waitress/cashier in an Austrian catering company. The employment contract was, from the outset, for a fixed term. In October 1995 in Italy she successfully sat an examination, thus completing her secondary education in the form of evening classes which required her attendance only at the examinations. Between October 1995 and March 1996 she was looking for a job in Austria. Being unsuccessful, she began studying Romance languages and literature at a university in Austria. When she applied for study finance, her application was refused. She challenged the refusal before an Austrian court, which referred a number of questions to the ECJ, in particular asking the ECJ whether she was a worker within the meaning of Article 39 EC [Article 45 TFEU]

1727. [2005] ECR I-2119.
1728. [2003] ECR I-13187.

bearing in mind her very short period of employment in Austria (two and a half months), and if so, whether her unemployment was voluntary or involuntary.

Held:

The ECJ held that the concept of a worker must be interpreted broadly and in accordance with objective criteria characterising the employment relationship. In determining whether or not she was a worker, neither the fact that employment was of short duration, not her conduct before and after the period of employment was relevant. What counted was whether her work was genuine and effective or whether it was ancillary and marginal. It was for a referring court to decide this matter on the basis of objective criteria and the factual context of the case.

The ECJ held that the fact that an employment contract is concluded for a fixed period of time is, in itself, not conclusive when deciding whether unemployment is voluntary or involuntary. Such a contract should be assessed in the light of other factors such as:

▪ Practices in the relevant sector of economic activity;

▪ The chances of finding employment in that sector which is not fixed-term;

▪ Whether there was an interest in entering into only a fixed-term employment relationship;

▪ Whether there was a possibility of renewing the contract of employment.

Comment:

The facts that Mrs Ninni-Orasche obtained a diploma entitling her to enrol at a university as soon as her employment contract had expired, and that she was actively looking for employment and of the kind of employment she sought were not relevant in deciding whether her unemployment was voluntary or involuntary. However, the Court stated, those facts might be relevant when examining the question of whether she took up short-term employment with the sole aim of benefiting from the system of student finance in Austria. Although this matter was left to the referring court to decide, the ECJ emphasised that the facts were suggesting that she had not entered Austria with the sole aim of taking advantage of the Austrian study finance system, but to live there with her husband.

Obviously, it is difficult to comment on Mrs Ninni-Orasche's case without knowing all the facts at the disposal of the referring court. However, it seems that she was a worker as her employment was not ancillary or marginal. If she was voluntarily unemployed, she would not have been entitled to a study grant because there was no connection between her previous work and the studies pursued. If she was involuntarily unemployed, could not find another job and thus was forced by the labour market conditions to undertake training in another field, then she would have been entitled to a study grant.

THE FREE MOVEMENT OF WORKERS – ARTICLE 45 TFEU

Important secondary legislation:
- Regulation 1612/68 on access to, and conditions of employment.

- Directive 2004/38/EC on the right of citizens of the EU and their families to move and reside freely within the territory of the Member States.

- Regulation 1408/71 on the application of social security schemes to employed persons, to self-employed persons and to members of their families moving within the Community.

Article 45 TFEU is both **vertically** (Case 48/75 *Jean Noël Royer*) and **horizontally** (Case C-281/98 *Angonese*), directly effective.

The scope of application ratione personae of Article 45 TFEU. Not only can workers and their families rely on Article 45 TFEU, but so too can employers (Case C-350/96 *Clean Car Autoservice*), and in certain circumstances so can private sector recruitment agencies (Case C-208/05 *ITC Innovative Technology Center*).

The territorial scope of application of Article 45 TFEU. This is complex as a result of transitional arrangements with the new Member States subsequent to the fifth enlargement of the EU.

The definition of a worker

A person who performs services of some economic value for and under the direction of another person, in return for which she/he receives remuneration (Case 66/85 *Lawrie-Blum*). Two elements of the definition of a worker:

- The activity performed by a worker must be genuine and effective (Case 139/85 *Kempf*; Case 53/81 *Levin*)

- The activity performed by a worker must be of an economic nature (Case 344/87 *Bettray*; Case C-456/02 *Trojani*).

Unemployed persons

EU nationals can enter the territory of a host Member State to seek employment. They cannot be expelled from the host Member State as long as they can provide evidence that they:

- Are continuing to seek employment; and

- Have a genuine chance of being employed (Case C-292/89 *Antonissen*; Article 14(4)(b) of Directive 2004/38/EC).

Persons in prison: should continue to be regarded as workers provided they find employment within a reasonable time after the end of their imprisonment (Case C-482/01 *Orfanopoulos*).

Family of EU migrant workers

The definition of the persons who are considered to be members of an EU migrant worker's family is provided in Directive 2004/38 (see Chapter 22.2.2.1). Their rights are parasitic on those of the worker (Cases C-297/88 and 197/89 *Dzodzi*). A non-EU spouse of an EU citizen benefits from the right to free movement irrespective of when and where the marriage may have taken place and of how he/she entered the host Member State, including a situation where a non-EU spouse had resided unlawfully in a host Member State prior to the marriage (Case C-127/08 *Metock*). However, a marriage must be a genuine marriage, not a marriage of convenience (Case C-109/01 *Akrich*).

A non-EU spouse can rely on her/his spouse's right to free movement only in a Member State where the worker is employed (Case C-10/05 *Mattern and Cikotic*). However, a third country national who is a member of a family of an EU worker, and who had not resided in the home Member State of the worker but joined him in a host Member State has the right, in the event of the worker returning to the home Member State of which he is a national, to enter and reside in the home Member State of the EU worker. This is even where a former EU worker does not carry on effective and genuine economic activities in the home Member State and even if he/she is a recipient of social assistance in the home Member State (Case C-291/05 *Eind*).

Members of the family of an EU migrant worker have the same rights as the EU worker.

Prohibition of discrimination against EU migrant workers and beyond

Direct discrimination (based on nationality of the worker) **can only be justified under derogations set out in the Treaties**.

Indirectly discriminatory rules (based on factors other than nationality, for example, the place of recruitment (Case 152/73 *Sotgiu*)) and all national rules indistinctly applicable to both national workers and migrant EC workers, which **substantially** affect access to the labour market or exercise of the right of free movement of workers **can be justified** under principles developed by the ECJ, if based either on derogations set out in the Treaties or on **objective considerations that are independent of nationality** and **proportionate to the legitimate aim** pursued by the national provisions (Case C-415/93 *Bosman*).

Rights granted to workers and their families are set out in Directive 2004/38 (see Chapter 22), Regulation 1408/71 and Regulation 1612/68

Under Regulation 1612/68 EU migrant workers are entitled to be treated in the same manner as workers who are nationals of the host Member State with regard to:

- Access to employment: any restriction by number or percentage is prohibited (Case 167/73 *Commission v France [Re French Merchant Seamen]*) but genuine linguistic requirements are allowed (Case 379/87 *Groener*);

- Conditions and terms of their employment;

- Entitlements to social advantages which are defined as all advantages "which, whether or not linked to a contract of employment, are generally granted to national workers primarily because of their objective status as workers or by virtue of the mere fact of their residence in the national territory" (Case 207/78 *Even*);

- Entitlements to tax advantages (Case C-279/93 *Schumacker*; Case C-204/90 *Bachmann*);

- Access to vocational training;

- The exercise of trade union rights;

- Housing and house ownership matters;

- Access to education and financial support relevant to education of their children.

Entitlements to study finance for EU migrant workers who become students in a host Member State

Such an entitlement is a social advantage under Article 7(2) of Regulation 1612/68 (Case 39/86 *Lair*).

If previous employment is merely ancillary to the current studies, a migrant worker is not entitled to financial assistance (Case 125/87 *Brown*).

If a worker has become voluntarily unemployed, he/she is entitled to study finance if there is a link between the previous occupation and the current course of study (*Lair*).

If a worker has become involuntarily unemployed and is obliged by conditions of the labour market to undertake occupational retraining, he/she is entitled to study finance (*Lair*).

RECOMMENDED READING

Books

Spaventa, E., *Free Movement of Persons in the EU: Barriers to Movement in their Constitutional Context*, 2007, The Hague: Kluwer Law International

White, R., *Workers, Establishment, and Services in the European Union*, 2004, Oxford: Oxford University Press

Articles

Briggs, L. V., "UEFA v The European Community: Attempts of the Governing Body of European Soccer to Circumvent EU Freedom of Movement and Antidiscrimination Labor Law", (2005) 6 Ch.J.Int'l L., p 439

Costello, C., "*Metock*: Free movement and 'Normal Family Life' in the Union", (2009) 46 CMLRev, p 587

Golynker, O., "Student Loans: The European Concept of Social Justice According to Bidar", (2006) 31 ELRev, p 390

Trimikliniotis, N., "Exceptions, Soft Borders and Free Movement of Workers", in P. Minderhoud and N. Trimikliniotis (eds), *Rethinking the Free Movement of Workers: The European Challenges Ahead*, 2009, Nijmegen: Wolf Legal Publishers, p 135

24

THE RIGHT OF ESTABLISHMENT (ARTICLES 43–48 TFEU) AND THE RIGHT TO SUPPLY AND RECEIVE SERVICES (ARTICLES 49–55 TFEU)

SUMMARY

1. The right of establishment is guaranteed under Article 49 TFEU while the right to supply and receive services is enshrined in Article 56 TFEU. There is a close connection between both freedoms, bearing in mind that barriers to the provision of services affect operators who wish to become established in host Member States as well as those who provide services but are not established there. The Treaties prohibit a Member State from imposing any restriction on which freedom an economic operator can choose. The choice should be free and based on the best strategy for the growth and development of the business. Consequently, the approach of the EU is to create a legal framework to ensure that barriers to both freedoms are removed.

2. Three stages in the development of both freedoms can be identified. The first was based on general programmes for abolition of restrictions on freedoms and resulted in the adoption of a number of directives regulating a specific profession or a sector of economy. During that stage the progress in the elimination of restrictions on both freedoms was very slow.

The judgments of the ECJ in *Reyners*, in the context of the freedom of establishment, and *Van Binsbergen*, in the context of the provision of services, establishing the direct effect of both Articles, marked the beginning of the second stage, following which the ECJ gradually refined the use of Articles 43 and 49 EC [Articles 49 and 56 TFEU] to condemn all discrimination, direct and indirect, as well as all indistinctly applicable measures which hinder the access to or the exercise of either freedom. For national rules which are directly discriminatory the only exceptions are those allowed by the Treaties. With regards to indirectly discriminatory and non-discriminatory measures when they constitute obstacles to freedom of establishment/provision of services, the case law of the ECJ and Directive 2006/123 shows that they can be justified if they satisfy the following four conditions:

- They apply in a non-discriminatory manner;

- They are justified by imperative requirements in the general interest;

- They are suitable for securing the attainment of the objective which they pursue;

- They are proportionate to the objective sought.

In the third stage, based on the Lisbon strategy adopted by the EU in 2000, Directive 2006/123/EC on Services in the Internal Market was adopted on 12 December 2006. It came into force in December 2009. The Directive greatly impacts on the exercise of both freedoms. It introduces novel solutions while confirming the existing case law of the ECJ in these areas. Its importance is highlighted by the fact that although both workers and self-employed persons participate in the life of a host Member State on a stable basis, there is no secondary legislation defining the rights of self-employed persons in a way similar to that contained in Regulation 1612/68 relating to workers. For that reason self-employed persons have relied heavily on the principle of non-discrimination embodied in Article 12 EC [Article 18 TFEU]. Directive 2006/123 will certainly help to fill the gap, although in many instances all persons, irrespective of whether they are economically active, derive important rights from the fact that they are EU citizens (see Chapter 22).

3. EU rules on the right of establishment and the right to provide services have many common features, to a point where in some circumstances it is not easy to determine which provisions should apply to a situation at issue. However, each freedom is distinct. The concept of "service" is defined as any self-employed economic activity which is provided for remuneration. The provision of services normally involves temporary and occasional pursuit of economic activities in a host Member State. Establishment involves participation, on a permanent and continuous basis, in the economic life of a host Member State, although for legal persons even an office managed by the enterprise's own staff or by a person who is independent but is authorised to act on a permanent basis for the enterprise suffices to show establishment. In order to decide whether Article 49 TFEU (establishment) or Article 56 TFEU (services) applies, account must be taken of the regularity, periodicity and continuity of the service provided in a host Member State. Generally, services are short-term while establishment is more long-term, but it results from the ECJ judgment in *Schnitzer* that services may be provided over an extended period of time, even over several years. In such a situation, in order to determine whether an undertaking or a person has ceased to be a provider of services and has become established in a host Member State, account must be taken of all available criteria and each case should be assessed individually.

It is important to determine whether a person/enterprise comes under the rules of provision of services or of establishment because this determination indicates which overall legal regime such a person/enterprise must respect in its activity, that of its home Member State or that of the host Member State.

4. The beneficiaries of both freedoms are natural and legal persons. Natural persons are EU citizens. Legal persons are companies or firms created in accordance with the law of a Member State.

5. Under both freedoms reverse discrimination is allowed. This means that, in some situations, nationals of a Member State are treated less favourably than EU migrants. This is because EU law does not apply to wholly internal situations. However, EU nationals may rely on EU law, even against the Member State whose nationality they possess, when they are in situations which are within the scope of application of EU law, that is, if there is a cross-border element.

6. The beneficiaries of the right of establishment are entitled to leave their home Member State without any hindrance (although for companies, bearing in mind strict national rules relating to transfer of their seat, this is still problematic); establish themselves in a host Member State (in the case of a company establish a branch, agency or subsidiary, whichever form better suits its strategy of growth) without any obstruction from either a host Member State or a home Member State, even if they set up a secondary establishment in order to circumvent incorporation requirements in a host Member State; and take up and pursue the relevant economic activities and benefit from various general facilities which are of assistance in the pursuit of these activities.

7. Under Article 49(2) TFEU the freedom of establishment is to be exercisable under the same conditions by EU migrants as those laid down for nationals of a host Member State. This means that a natural or legal person must comply with the rules relating to, inter alia, requirements of their profession. Refusal by a host Member State or a professional body to recognise qualifications acquired in another Member State excludes access to the relevant profession or economic activity and thus divests the right of any practical meaning. To remedy this, the Council, adopted Directive 2005/36/EC on the Recognition of Professional Qualifications.

Mutual recognition of educational/professional qualifications is more important with regard to the provision of services/right of establishment than the free movement of workers because the provision of services/establishment involves self-employed persons presenting themselves as capable of performing a service.

8. Directive 98/5/EC governs the right of establishment for lawyers who have obtained professional qualifications in their home Member State and wish to practise their profession on a permanent basis in any other Member State, and is one of a number of sector/profession specific directives on mutual recognition of qualifications.

9. Recognition of qualifications obtained outside the EU is not within the scope of EU law. However, if EU nationals who have obtained their qualification in a non-Member State exercise their right of establishment in a host Member State and subsequently seek to practise in another Member State, that Member State must take account not only of professional experience acquired in the host Member State and other Member States but also of all relevant diplomas and other evidence of formal qualifications acquired in a non-Member State.

10. A precondition for the application of Article 56 TFEU is the cross-border nature of the services. Article 56 TFEU applies to both providers and recipients of services. In the context of the provision of services the principle of non-discrimination, direct or indirect, ensures that rules which are normally applicable in a host Member State to providers of services established in that Member State are not applicable in their entirety, and in the same way, to activities of a temporary nature pursued by persons established in another Member State. Further, as mentioned in paragraph 6 above, indistinctly applicable measures which are liable to prohibit or otherwise impede the activities of a provider of services are prohibited unless objectively justified. Finally, the principle of mutual recognition requires a host Member State to take into consideration rules of the home Member State of a provider of services in order to determine whether the public interest which a host Member State wants to protect is not already protected by rules applying to the service provider in the Member State where he/she is established. The freedom to receive services constitutes an essential corollary to the freedom to provide services. Recipients of services must be treated in a host Member State on the same basis as nationals of that Member State.

11. Publicly funded services, such as education or health, are within the scope of Article 56 TFEU.

This means that EU nationals have access to vocational training courses, including most higher education courses, on terms equivalent to those granted to the nationals of a host Member State and may be entitled not only to grants and scholarships, but also, depending upon the circumstances, to non-contributory social advantages on the ground of Article 21 TFEU. With regard to health care services, under Article 56 TFEU and under Regulation 1408/71, all EU citizens and lawful residents of the EU insured under national sickness insurance schemes are entitled to obtain effective and speedy medical treatment from any other Member State, if this is not available in their own Member State.

24.1 Introduction

Article 49 TFEU confers the right of establishment whilst Article 56 TFEU grants the right to supply and receive services. These rights are conferred on both natural persons who are nationals of Member States and legal persons established in Member States. Article 49 TFEU[1729] and Article 56 TFEU[1730] are directly effective.[1731]

The current approach to both freedoms is based on the strategy approved by the Lisbon European Council (March 2000), which aimed at making the EU the most competitive and dynamic knowledge-driven economy in the world by 2010, capable of sustainable economic growth with more and better jobs and greater social cohesion.[1732] One of the key elements of the Lisbon strategy is the creation of a single market in services. According to the Commission, services account for between 60 per cent and 70 per cent of economic activity in the European Union of 25 Member States and for a similar proportion of overall employment, but account only for 20 per cent of EU cross-border trade![1733] Thus the completion of the internal market for the remaining 70 per cent of the EU economy is crucial to the achievement of goals set by the European Council in Lisbon. A concrete step leading to the creation of an internal market for services and the removal of all existing barriers to the exercise of the right of establishment was the adoption of Directive 2006/123[1734] on Services in the Internal Market which entered into force in December 2009.

1729. Case 2/74 *Jean Reyners v the Belgian State* [1974] ECR 631.

1730. Case 33/74 *Van Binsbergen* [1974] ECR 1299.

1731. Case 2/74 *Jean Reyners* [1974] ECR 631 and Case 33/74 *Van Binsbergen* [1974] ECR 1299.

1732. Commission Communication "Working together for Growth and Jobs – A New Start for the Lisbon Strategy", COM(2005) 24 of 2/02/2005.

1733. The report prepared by the Commission on "The Extended Impact Assessment of Proposal for a Directive on Services in the Internal Market", SEC (2004) 21, p 9.

1734. [2006] OJ L376/36.

24.2 Stages in the development of the right of establishment and of the right to provide services: from sectorial harmonisation to the adoption of Directive 2006/123 on Services in the Internal Market

Articles 49 and 56 TFEU provide for the abolition of the restrictions on the freedom of establishment and on the freedom to provide services by progressive stages. Three stages in the development of both rights can be identified.

24.2.1 First stage

In the course of the transitional period (it ended on 31 December 1969) the Council was required to draw up a general programme for the abolition of existing restrictions in these areas. On 18 December 1961[1735] the Council adopted two general programmes for the abolition of restrictions, the first concerning the freedom of establishment and the second relating to the provision of services. Both programmes set out the general conditions necessary to achieve the freedom of establishment and freedom to provide services in respect of each type of activity by progressive stages.

A major consequence of the programmes was the adoption by the Council of a number of directives covering various sectors of the economy, such as mining and quarrying, forestry, energy, coal, the film industry, food and beverage manufacturing industries, and so on. However, the task assigned to the Council by virtue of Articles 43 and 49 EC [Articles 49 and 56 TFEU] was far from being completed at the end of the transitional period. This was because not only were Member States dragging their feet in implementing the programmes, but also many important areas remained outside the harmonising measures; for example, with regard to the right of establishment there were no harmonisation measures relating to conditions of entry and residence for self-employed persons and their families, or social security provisions similar to those applicable to workers under Regulation 1408/71, or rules relating to access to social housing or acquisition of immovable property. In these circumstances two decisions delivered by the ECJ dramatically changed the approach of the Community towards the removal of the restrictions.

24.2.2 Second stage

The principles of freedom of establishment and free movement of services have been developed and clarified over the years through the case law of the ECJ. The leading case in each area is examined below.

24.2.2.1 *The right of establishment: Case 2/74 Reyners v Belgium*[1736]

THE FACTS WERE:

Jean Reyners, a Dutch national born and raised in Belgium, a holder of the Belgian doctorate in law (docteur en droit), sat the necessary examinations to become an advocate in Belgium.

1735.   [1962] OJ 2.
1736.   Case 2/74 *Jean Reyners v the Belgian State* [1974] ECR 631.

The Belgian legislation provided that only Belgian nationals could be called to the Belgian Bar. Reyners challenged the compatibility of this legislation with Article 43 EC [Article 49 TFEU]. The Belgian Conseil d'Etat referred the matter to the ECJ under the preliminary ruling procedure. During these proceedings, the Belgian Bar and the Government of Luxembourg submitted that the profession of advocate was excluded from Article 43 EC [Article 49 TFEU] as its activities were connected with the exercise of official authority within the meaning of Article 45 EC [Article 51 TFEU]. In Belgium an advocate may be called upon to sit as a judge in certain cases, and a judge exercises official authority.

Held:

The ECJ established three principles:

- First, the ECJ held that the fact that Article 43 EC [Article 49 TFEU] stated that the restrictions on the freedom of establishment "shall be abolished by progressive stages in the course of the transitional period" [these words have not been included in Article 49 TFEU] did not affect the right of nationals of one Member State wishing to establish themselves in another Member State to enjoy immediate protection. The ECJ held that Article 43 EC Treaty [Article 49 TFEU] imposed an obligation to attain a precise result that was not conditional upon the implementation of a programme of progressive measures. Such a programme would only facilitate the attainment of the prescribed objectives. As a result, after the expiry of the transitional period Article 43 EC [Article 49 TFEU] became directly applicable despite the absence of implementing measures.

- Second, the ECJ held that Article 43 EC [Article 49 TFEU] had to be interpreted in the light of the whole scheme of the EC Treaty, including Article 12 EC [Article 18 TFEU] which prohibits any discrimination on the grounds of nationality.

- Third, the ECJ stated that the exception to freedom of establishment contained in Article 45 EC [Article 51 TFEU] did not apply to the profession of advocate as it was restricted to activities which involved a direct and specific connection with the exercise of official authority.

24.2.2.2   The right to provide services: Case 33/74 Van Binsbergen v Bestuur Van De Bedrijfsvereniging Voor De Mataalnijverheid[1737]

THE FACTS WERE:

Mr Van Binsbergen was represented before the Dutch social security court by Kortmann, a Dutch national. During the proceedings Mr Kortmann, a legal adviser and representative in social security matters, moved from The Netherlands to Belgium and from there he corresponded with the Dutch court. He was informed by the court registrar that only persons

---

1737. [1974] ECR 1299.

established in The Netherlands were permitted to represent clients before the Dutch social security court, and as a permanent resident of Belgium he could no longer act for Mr Van Binsbergen. Mr Kortmann challenged this provision of the relevant Netherlands statute on procedure in social security matters as incompatible with Article 49 EC [Article 56 TFEU].

Held:

The ECJ established four principles in this case:

▪ Articles 49 and 50 EC Treaty [Articles 56 and 57 TFEU] are directly effective.

▪ Both provisions are subject to the principle of non-discrimination based on the ground of nationality.

▪ National rules which are directly discriminatory can only be justified on the grounds set out in the EC Treaty. However, non-discriminatory rules can be justified in some circumstances. In this respect the ECJ held that:

"taking into account the particular nature of the services to be provided, specific requirements imposed on the person providing the service cannot be considered incompatible with the Treaty where they have as their purpose the application of professional rules justified by the general good – in particular rules relating to organisation, qualifications, professional ethics, supervision and liability – which are binding upon any person established in the State in which the service is provided, where the person providing the service would escape from the ambit of those rules by being established in another Member State" (paragraph 12).

▪ National rules imposing restrictions on the provision of services will be compatible with Articles 49 and 50 EC [Articles 56 and 57] if they are objectively justified by the need to ensure observance of professional rules of conduct provided such rules are non-discriminatory, objectively justified and proportionate.

Comment:

In this case the requirement of permanent residence applied without discrimination to nationals and non-nationals, and it was objectively justified by the general good, that is, by the need to ensure observance of professional rules of conduct, especially those connected with the administration of justice and those relating to professional ethics. As to the third principle, the ECJ held that the requirement of permanent residence was disproportionate as the objective of the proper administration of justice could be achieved by less restrictive measures, such as the choosing of an address in the Member State in which the service is provided. The fourth principle has clear parallels with the test set out in the *Cassis de Dijon* case (see Chapter 20.7). Having said this, the ECJ has always refused to adopt the *Keck* approach to limit the scope of the right to provide services.[1738]

The judgments of the ECJ in *Reyners* and *Van Binsbergen*, as further developed in the case law of the ECJ, have important implications with regard to the application of the provisions of the Treaties relating to the freedom of establishment and the provision of services. These implications are:

1738. Case C-384/93 *Alpine Investments* [1995] ECR I-1141.

▣ Articles 49 and 56 TFEU are directly effective and therefore they can be relied upon by individuals in proceedings before national courts.

▣ The Treaties provisions prohibiting discrimination, Article 18 TFEU (as well as Articles 49 and 56 TFEU themselves), may be invoked to challenge a national rule, whether in the form of a nationality or a residence requirement, which is discriminatory. The principle of non-discrimination has been broadly interpreted in the context of the right of establishment and the right to provide services. Both direct and indirect discrimination is prohibited.

Indirect discrimination is based on factors other than nationality, such as the place of birth, language, the place of residence, and so on. In respect of the right of establishment, initially the ECJ refused to condemn national measures which were non-discriminatory.[1739] However, in *Gebhard*[1740] the ECJ held that any national measure which is indistinctly applicable and which is liable to hinder or to make less attractive the exercise of the freedoms of establishment as guaranteed by the Treaties can be justified only if it satisfies the four conditions set out in the *Binsbergen* case, that is, the measure:

- must be applied in a non-discriminatory manner;
- must be justified by imperative requirements in the general interest;
- must be suitable for securing the attainment of the objective which it pursues;
- must not go beyond what is necessary in order to attain that objective.

These above four points are the same as those used in the four-point *Cassis de Dijon* test. They apply to both freedoms: the freedom to provide services and the freedom of establishment. All indistinctly applicable measures which affect access to, or exercise of these freedoms must be regarded as restrictions.[1741] For example in Case C-518/06 *Commission v Italy [Re Motor Insurance]*,[1742] the ECJ held that Italian legislation which imposed:

- an obligation to contract on all insurance companies (including those which have their head offices in another Member State but which pursue their business in Italy) offering third-party liability motor insurance to any potential customers under terms and rates published in advance;
- limitations on the freedom of the companies to set their premiums;
- heavy fines on companies which breached the above obligations;

interfered with the freedom to contract and thus affected market access of companies from other Member States. The obligation to contract was non-discriminatory as it applied to all insurance companies wherever established which provided services in Italy. The ECJ agreed that both restrictions, i.e. relating to the obligation to cover any risks which were proposed to an insurance company and to moderate premium rates meant that many undertakings wishing to enter the Italian market under conditions which complied with Italian legislation "will be required to re-think their business policy and strategy, inter alia, by considerably expanding the range of insurance services offered". As a result, Italian legislation involved

---

1739. Case 221/85 *Commission v Belgium* [1987] ECR 719.
1740. Case 55/94 [1995] ECR I-4165.
1741. Case C-384/93 *Alpine Investments* [1995] ECR I-1141; Case C-403/03 *Schempp* [2005] ECR I-6421, paragraph 45, and Case C-79/01 *Payroll Data Services* [2002] ECR I-8923.
1742. [2009] ECR I-3491.

changes and costs, in particular for small companies, with the consequences that their access to the Italian market was less attractive and once on the market, their competitiveness against companies traditionally established in Italy was greatly reduced. However, although the Italian legislation was in breach of Articles 44 and 49 EC [49 and 56 TFEU] it was justified by the social objective sought by the legislation, i.e that victims of road accidents were fully compensated, and proportionate in that it ensured that every owner of a vehicle was able to take out third-party insurance for a premium that was not excessive.

■ A distinction must be made between the application of the principle of non-discrimination in respect of the exercise of the right of establishment and the exercise of the right to provide services. With regard to the freedom of establishment the principle of non-discrimination requires that nationals of other Member States are treated in a host Member State in the same manner as nationals of that Member State because they are in exactly the same situation. However, the application of "national treatment" to the providers of services from other Member States is unfair. They are not in the same situation as nationals established in the host Member State. They have already complied with all requirements relating to access to and the exercise of the relevant economic activity in their home Member State. They should not be subjected to the same requirements as are imposed on persons who are established in a host Member State and provide services there. Thus, the principle of non-discrimination seeks to eliminate discrimination which arises not only through the application of different rules to comparable situations, but also results from the application of the same rule to different situations.[1743]

■ The principle of non-discrimination covers both the taking-up of, and the pursuit of a particular activity, including also rules relating to various general facilities which are of assistance in the pursuit of these activities. For example, in Case 63/86 *Commission v Italy [Re Housing Aid]*,[1744] the ECJ held that a cheap mortgage facility available only to Italian nationals should also have been available to all EC providers of services in Italy, so long as the nature of the service provided was such as to require a permanent dwelling in Italy.

■ The right of establishment and the right to provide services are not absolute. The exercise of both rights is subject to important limitations. One is based on the Treaties: Article 51 TFEU provides that the chapter on the freedom of establishment does not apply to activities which are connected, even occasionally, with the exercise of official authority, while Article 52(1) TFEU states that limitations may be imposed on the grounds of public policy, public security and public health by a host Member State (see Chapter 25).

■ The principle of mutual recognition plays a crucial role in the removal of obstacles to the exercise of both freedoms.

24.2.3   Directive 2006/123/EC on services in the Internal Market[1745]

In order to create a genuine single market in services, on 13 January 2004 the Commission submitted a proposal for a Directive on Services in the Internal Market, which was fiercely

---

1743.   C-279/93 *Schumacker* [1995] ECR I-225; Case C-391/97 *Gschwind* [1999] ECR I-5451.
1744.   [1988] ECR 29.
1745.   [2006] OJ L376/36.

attacked by some Member States and their trade unions. The proposed Directive was called the "Frankenstein" Directive (previously it was often named as a Bolkestein Directive, after the former internal market commissioner Bolkestein, who originally proposed it) and played a major role in the French rejection of the proposed EU Constitution.

On 21 March 2005 nearly 100,000 people marched through the streets of Brussels to protest against the Directive. Trade unions of Belgium, France, Germany, Italy and The Netherlands organised the protest. They described the Directive as a declaration of war on working men and women and regarded it as destroying the achievements of two centuries of struggle of workers in social welfare, health care and educational matters. The main criticism concerned the establishment of the principle of origin under which a provider of services was to be subject only to the national provisions of its Member State of origin, that is, it would operate under the home Member State's rules as to, for example, working time, minimum wages, holidays and the right to strike. Any supervision of a provider of services could only be carried out by the authorities of the home Member State. Trade unions argued that the application of the principle of origin would lead to a "race to the bottom", with firms relocating to countries with lower wages and the weakest consumer and environmental protection, employment and health and safety rules. Resulting from this the opponents of the Directive argued that it would lead to competition between workers, reduction of wages, closure of many companies operating in Member States with high standards of social protection given that they could not compete with cheaper, foreign competitors, lower standards of social and environmental protection and an influx of foreign workers. Further, it was argued that a home Member State of a service provider would have no interest and often no resources to supervise businesses registered in that Member State but doing business in another Member State. The trade unions were successful in challenging the proposed directive. The European Council of March 2005 asked the Commission to redraft the Directive. A watered-down version of the original directive was adopted by the Council on 12 December 2006 as Directive 2006/123/EC. The Directive entered into force on 28 December 2009.

24.2.3.1   Main features of Directive 2006/123/EC

24.2.3.1.1 Objective

The objective of the Directive is to make progress towards the creation of a genuine internal market by removing obstacles to both the freedom of establishment and the freedom to provide services. This "big picture" approach is rare (in particular bearing in mind that the Directive applies to numerous economic sectors) but not without precedent, as evidenced by secondary legislation adopted in respect of financial services. Does it suggest that, in the long run, the EU seeks to establish the same legal regime with regard to both freedoms? The "big picture" approach to fundamental freedoms is present in Case C-390/99 *Canal Satélite Digital*,[1746] in which the ECJ examined restrictions imposed by Spanish law simultaneously in the light of both Article 34 and Article 56 TFEU. However, the Directive's contribution to the "big picture" approach to both freedoms is not a "wide screen" approach in that it clearly distinguishes between the right to establishment and the right to provide services, and provides definitions of the concept of "establishment" and the concept of "services" based on the case law of the ECJ.

1746. [2002] ECR I-607.

24.2.3.1.2 Scope of application

The Directive applies to a wide range of services, including legal and tax advice, management consultancy, real estate services, construction, trade services, tourism and leisure services.

The following services have been excluded from its scope of application:

▪ Non-economic services of general interest, that is, services which are not provided for remuneration, for example, services in the areas of primary and secondary education. Such services are not subject to EU competition law. However, services of general economic interest, such as those in the electricity, gas and waste treatment sectors, and the postal service are within the scope of the Directive and EU competition law. Whether a particular service of general interest (SGI) is of an economic or non-economic nature is determined in the light of the case law of the ECJ.[1747] Under the ToL, SGIs are within the competences shared between the EU and the Member States. Article 14 TFEU emphasises the importance of SGIs and their contribution to achievement of social and territorial cohesion. Under Article 14 TFEU, the Council and the EP are empowered to adopt regulations in accordance with the ordinary legislative procedure to ensure that the SGIs "operate on the basis of principles and conditions, particularly economic and financial conditions, which enable them to fulfil their missions". However, Protocol 26 on SGIs attached to the Treaties emphasises that that in the exercise of legislative powers the EU must recognise "the essential role and the wide discretion of national, regional and local authorities in providing, commissioning and organising services of general economic interest". Further Article 2 of Protocol 26 ensures that Member States retain exclusive competence in regulating the provision, commission and organisation of non-economic SGIs. It is submitted that the ToL does not make any great impact on SGIs. Further, the lack in the ToL of criteria which would make it possible to distinguish between SGIs of an economic nature and a non-economic nature is regrettable;

▪ Financial services including banking services, credit services, securities and investment funds, insurance and pension services and services covered by Directive 2006/48/EC relating to the taking-up and pursuit of the business of credit institutions;[1748]

▪ Health care and pharmaceutical services provided by health professionals to patients consisting of assessing, maintaining or restoring their state of health where those activities are reserved to a regulated health profession in the Member State where the services are provided. However, services provided to health professionals or related to enhancing wellness or to providing relaxation are covered by the Directive;

▪ Electronic communication services and network and associated services. They are excluded to the extent that they are not covered by other secondary legislation, for example, the five EU directives forming the so-called "telecoms package";[1749]

1747. See section 24.3.1.
1748. [2006] OJ L 177/1.
1749. Directive 2002/19/EC on access to, and interconnection of, electronic networks and associated facilities [2002] OJ L108/7; Directive 2002/20/EC on the authorisation of electronic communications networks and services [2002] OJ L108/21; Directive 2002/21/EC on the common regulatory framework for electronic communications networks and services [2002] OJ L108/33; Directive 2002/22/EC on universal service and users' rights relating to electronic communications networks and services [2002] OJ L108/51; Directive 2002/58/EC concerning the

- Transport services relating to air, road, rail, maritime and inland waterways transport. Urban transport, such as buses, taxis and ambulances, is however included, but excluded are driving school services, removal services and funeral services;

- Social services relating to social housing, childcare and support of families and persons permanently or temporarily in need if they are provided by the Member State, by providers mandated by the Member State or charities recognised as such by the Member State. If those services are provided by providers other than those mentioned above, they are within the scope of the Directive;

- Activities connected with the exercise of official authority. This relates to the exclusion set out in Article 51 TFEU (see Chapter 25.2);

- Temporary work agencies concerning the service of hiring out workers, but other services carried out by them, such as placement or recruitment of workers, are covered by the Directive;

- Private security services;

- Gambling services;

- Audiovisual and radio broadcasting services;

- Services provided by notaries and bailiffs who are appointed by an official act of government, irrespective of whether they are connected to the exercise of official authority as set out in Article 51 TFEU;

- Tax matters.

The Directive does not affect:

- Criminal law;

- Labour law and social security legislation;

- Fundamental human rights;

- Private international law;

- The posting of workers in another Member State.

24.2.3.1.3 Principle of origin
The Directive rejects the principle of origin.

24.2.3.1.4 The approach to prohibited requirements
The Directive approaches them in two ways: first it gives a broad general definition of prohibited requirements based on the case law of the ECJ, and second, it deals with particular requirements that are prohibited in respect of each freedom.

Requirements are defined as any obligation, prohibition, condition or any other limitation

---

processing of personal data and the protection of privacy in the electronic communications sector [2002] OJ L201/37 as amended by Directive 2006/24/EC [2006] OJ L105/54.

imposed on service providers or recipients of services which affect the access to, or the exercise of a service activity (Articles 14 and 16 of the Directive). On this point the Directive confirms the case law of the ECJ, which prohibits not only direct and indirect discrimination but also any measures which affect access to and exercise of a service activity. As to particular requirements, the Directive sets out separate lists of prohibited requirements relating to each freedom. Both lists contain requirements which had previously been condemned by the ECJ.

The list of prohibited requirements relating to the freedom to provide services is set out in Article 16(2) of the Directive. Member States are prohibited from imposing the following requirements on a provider:

(a)   Having an establishment in their territory;

(b)   Obtaining an authorisation from the competent authorities, including entry into a register or registration with a professional body or association in their territory, unless otherwise provided in the Directive or other EU measures;

(c)   The setting-up of a certain form or type of infrastructure in their territory;

(d)   The application of specific contractual arrangements between the provider and the recipient which prevent or restrict service provision by self-employed persons;

(e)   Possession of an identity document issued by a host Member State's authorities specific to the exercise of a service activity;

(f)   Conditions affecting the use of equipment and material which are an integral part of the service provided other than those necessary for health and safety at work.

Prohibited requirements in respect of recipients of services are listed in Article 19.

The prohibited requirements with regard to the freedom of establishment are divided into those which should be evaluated by a Member State (Article 15) and those which are prohibited (Article 14).

24.2.3.1.4.1 Requirements which should be evaluated

Under Article 15 a Member State is required to evaluate requirements which constitute obstacles to the freedom of establishment in the light of the criteria of non-discrimination, necessity and proportionality to decide whether they can be replaced by less restrictive means. Member States are required to submit an evaluation report to that effect within the framework of the review and mutual evaluation procedure set out in Article 39 of the Directive. Each report will be forwarded not only to the Commission but also to all Member States.

24.2.3.1.4.2 Requirements which are prohibited

They are listed in Article 14 and consist of:

(a)   Directly or indirectly discriminatory requirements based on nationality, or in the case of companies the location of the registered office;

(b)   Prohibition on having an establishment in more than one Member State or on being entered in the registers or enrolled with professional bodies or associations of more than one Member State;

(c)   Restrictions on the freedom of a provider to choose between a principal and secondary establishment, in particular an obligation imposed on it to have its principal establishment in the territory of a particular Member State, or to choose between establishment in the form of an agency, branch or subsidiary;

(d) Conditions of reciprocity with a Member State in which the provider already has an establishment;

(e) The case-by-case application of an economic test making the granting of authorisation subject to proof of the existence of an economic need or market demand, an assessment of the potential or current economic effects of the activity or an assessment of the appropriateness of the activity in relation to economic planning objectives set by the objective pursued;

(f) Direct or indirect involvement of competing operators in the granting of authorisations or in the adopting of other decisions of the competent authorities;

(g) An obligation to provide or participate in a financial guarantee or to take out insurance from a provider or body established in the territory of a Member State;

(h) An obligation to have been pre-registered, for a given period, in the national registers or to have previously exercised the activity for a given period in the same Member State.

24.2.3.1.5 Derogations

The Directive imposes stricter requirements as to justifications that a Member State may rely upon with regard to the provision of services than those relating to the freedom of establishment.

(a) Freedom of establishment. By virtue of Article 15 of the Directive only requirements which are non-discriminatory, necessary (that is, based on an overriding reason relating to the public interest) and proportional can be successfully invoked by a Member State. The list of overriding reasons relating to the public interest is not exhaustive and is to be interpreted in accordance with the case law of the ECJ.

(b) Freedom to provide services. By virtue of Article 16(1) and (3) of the Directive only requirements which are indistinctly applicable, justified by reasons of public policy, public security, public health or the protection of the environment and proportionate can be imposed on incoming service providers. Thus, the list of justifications is exhaustive. This strict approach taken to derogations relating to the freedom to provide cross-border services can be explained by the fact that first, the scope of the Directive has been greatly narrowed as compared to its original version and second, additional justifications for specific sectors is provided for in Article 17 (and also that, given services are short-term, the host Member State has less of an interest in regulating services compared to establishment).

24.2.3.1.6 Novel solutions introduced by the Directive

These can be divided into two categories: those which relate to providers and recipients of services, and those aimed at enhancing co-operation between the Member States.

24.2.3.1.7 Novel solutions relating to providers and recipients of services

24.2.3.1.7.1 The right to obtain information

The Directive creates a new right for providers and recipients of services, that is, the right to obtain information.

Member States are required to take necessary measures to ensure that information is easily accessible, provided in simple, unambiguous language, presented in a coherent and structured manner and available via the internet. Article 21 of the Directive lists information which a Member State must make available to recipients of services. The list encompasses general information on requirements applicable to service providers in their home Member State, on the means of redress available in the event of a dispute between a provider and a recipient, and the contact details of associations and organisations from which the recipient may obtain practical assistance.

It is for Member States to designate the bodies which will be in charge of providing information to consumers. With regard to the providers "points of single contact" (see below) will be the places where they can obtain all necessary information.

24.2.3.1.7.2 Simplification of administrative procedures

For providers of services the greatest innovation introduced by the Directive relates to simplification of administrative procedures.

- First, national authorisation procedures must be simplified and modernised. Member States are required to assess the existing procedures and formalities from the provider's perspective with a view to simplifying or abolishing them. The Commission proposes that many documents and forms should be harmonised at the EU level, so relieving providers from supplying a multitude of different forms. An application, also available in an electronic form, should be processed as quickly as possible, and, if within a reasonable time to be fixed by each Member State, no response is given to the applicant, the authorisation will be deemed to have been granted to the applicant;

- Second, each Member State must establish a "point of single contact" (PSC), that is, set up a single body which will provide all relevant information to a provider and through which the provider can complete all procedures and formalities needed for access and exercise of its service activity in that Member State. The PSCs deal not only with providers established in another Member State but also with providers established in its territory.

In order to promote the high quality of services, the Directive imposes on providers two important requirements:

- The first relates to transparency. Under Article 22(1) a provider is obliged to supply general information relating to its business and its services to recipients, who, under Article 22(3), at their request are entitled to receive information additional to that specified in Article 22(1);

- The second concerns measures which a Member State may impose on a provider in order to protect recipients of services. Where services present a direct and particular risk to the health or safety of a recipient or a third person, or to the financial security of a recipient, a Member State may require the provider to subscribe to professional liability insurance or to make other similar arrangements.

24.2.3.1.7.3 Novel solutions enhancing co-operation between Member States

The Directive imposes a duty on the Member States to assist each other, in particular to reply to information requests and to conduct, if necessary, investigations and inspections (Articles 28 to 36). To ensure speedy and efficient exchange of information the Commission, in co-operation with the Member States, set up an electronic system – the Internal Market Information System (IMI). The obligation of assistance also encompasses an obligation on a Member State to alert other

Member States if it becomes aware of acts of a service provider which could cause serious damage to health or safety of persons or the environment.

24.2.3.1.8 Implementation of Directive 2006/38

At the time of writing, the Directive has been in force for five months. Its impact on the economy of the EU is difficult to assess given the shortness of time of its legal existence. According to the information cited by the Commission the EU wide economic gains of the Directive could range from €60 billion to €140 billion.[1750]

So far as the implementation of the Directive is concerned, an Information Note issued by the Commission following the meeting of the Competitiveness Council on 1 and 2 March 2010[1751] provides the following details:

- The Review of the legislative framework applicable to the services sector covered by the Directive: The review was a huge task involving not only central but also regional and local authorities in Member States. At the time of writing, almost all Member States have finalised the screening of their legislation. The Member States have communicated almost 16,000 requirements imposed on establishment of service providers and 19,000 requirements imposed on cross-border provision of services. The information will serve as a basis of assessment of any future measures on removal of restrictions in respect of both freedoms.

- The adoption of implementing measures: Almost all Member States have adopted a "horizontal act", i.e. framework legislation covering all services covered by the Directive. So far as amendments to specific legislation, i.e. concerning specific sectors of service, are concerned, in nine Member States there are substantive delays. Nevertheless, so far about 6,000 legislative acts have been modified in the Member States.

- The establishment of the PSCs. In 21 Member States PSCs' websites have been set up. Further, in January 2010 the Commission set up an EU portal which identifies the PSCs in all Member States and provides direct links to all national PSCs' websites. Finally, the Member States have decided to develop a "common branding" and logo for their PSCs and many provide information in other languages than their own.

24.2.3.1.9 Conclusion

It is submitted that the Directive, being a compromise, does not revolutionise EU law in respect of both freedoms. It largely confirms the existing case law of the ECJ in both areas. However, it contains some innovations, which, on the one hand, will certainly facilitate access to and exercise of both freedoms, and on the other hand will improve co-operation between Member States. Additionally, it introduces a new approach to harmonisation of EU law. Member States, through the review of the existing administrative procedures, are required to take a proactive approach to the implementation of the Directive. Finally, the Directive has responded to concerns of trade unions and does not erode the European social model. It is to be noted that the Directive applies

---

1750. "Expected Economic Benefits of the European Services Directive" Netherlands Bureau for Economic Policy Analysis, November 2007, available at: http:www.cpb.nl/eng/pub/cpbreeksen/notitie/14nov2007/notitie.pdf (accessed 21/4/10).

1751. See http://ec.europa.eu/internal_market/services/docs/services-dir/implementation/20100301_council_en.pdf (accessed 21/4/10).

in addition to the existing EU law. Services not covered by it do, of course, remain subject to EU law.

24.3 The distinction between the right of establishment and the right to provide services

The distinction is very important because a natural or legal person regarded as "established" in a host Member State will be burdened with complying with all rules for establishment in that Member State. If, however, a person supplies services, such regulatory burden does not apply as that person is required to comply with the rules of the home Member State with regard to access to the relevant activity and the manner in which it is exercised, although a host Member State may impose restrictions based on derogations set out in the Treaties or justified on overriding reasons of general interest.

24.3.1 Provision of services

In Case C-55/94 *Gebhard*,[1752] the ECJ emphasised that the regularity, periodicity and continuity of the service should be taken into consideration in order to decide whether Article 49 TFEU or Article 56 TFEU applies.

The provision of services normally involves temporary and occasional pursuit of economic activities in a host Member State and therefore does not require, as a matter of principle, a person to reside in the host Member State, even for the duration of the service.[1753] However, providers of services may equip themselves with some form of infrastructure in a host Member State in so far as such infrastructure is necessary for the purpose of performing the service in question. To be regarded as a "service", an activity has to be a self-employed activity, that is, it has to be provided outside the ties of a contract of employment by a natural or legal person.[1754]

In Case C-215/01 *Schnitzer*,[1755] one of the issues was whether services provided by an undertaking established in Portugal, consisting of carrying out large-scale plastering works in Germany from November 1994 to November 1997, should, given the long duration of the activity, be examined under Article 43 EC [49 TFEU] rather than Article 49 EC [56 TFEU].

THE FACTS WERE:

Criminal proceedings were commenced against Mr Bruno Schnitzer for an alleged infringement of the German legislation against black-market work. Mr Schnitzer had engaged a Portuguese undertaking to carry out large-scale plastering work in Germany, which it did without being entered on the German Skilled Trades Register. The Portuguese undertaking was carrying out works in Germany from November 1994 to November 1997. The

---

1752. [1995] ECR I-4165.
1753. However, in certain circumstances this may be required: see *Van Binsbergen* case 33/74 [1974] ECR 1299.
1754. Case 36/74 *Walrave and Koch* [1974] ECR I-1405.
1755. [2003] ECR I-14847.

requirement of entry on the skilled trades register (including the requirement to pay subscriptions to the chamber of skilled trades) would apply without restriction had the Portuguese undertaking's activity ceased to be temporary, that is, had it ceased to provide services and in fact became established in Germany.

Held:

The ECJ held that:

- With regard to providers of services, as previously held in Case C-58/98 *Corsten*,[1756] the requirement for entry on the trades register of the host Member State must neither delay nor complicate exercise of the rights of persons established in another Member State. Accordingly such an entry should be automatic and cannot constitute a condition precedent for the provision of services, result in administrative expense for the person providing them or give rise to an obligation to pay subscriptions to the chamber of trades.

- The fact that a service was provided over several years did not necessarily, and certainly not on its own, mean that an undertaking was established in another Member State. The ECJ emphasised that no provision of the EC Treaty "affords a means of determining, in an abstract manner, the duration or frequency beyond which the supply of services or of a certain type of service in another Member State can no longer be regarded as the provision of services within the meaning of the Treaty" and that, indeed, services covered by the EC Treaty may be provided over an extended period of time, even over several years.

Comment:

It is submitted that the above judgment has further obscured the distinction between establishment and freedom to provide services. It results from the above judgment that each case should be assessed in the light of all the relevant factors, and that there is no decisive factor which will determine whether the case involves establishment or provision of services.

Article 57 TFEU refers to services as being "normally provided for remuneration".[1757] Remuneration may be provided by a third party[1758] and encompass payments that bear indirect relation to the service provided, as in the case of payments for medical services covered by a social security scheme of a home Member State provided to a person insured under that scheme in a host Member State. The ECJ refused to make any distinction between national health care systems based on benefit in kind and those based on refund. In Case C-157/99 *Geraets-Smits and Peerbooms*,[1759] the ECJ held that:

"Payments made by the sickness insurance funds . . . albeit set at a flat rate are indeed the consideration for the hospital services and unquestionably represent remuneration for the hospital which receives them and which is engaged in an activity of an economic character."

1756. [2000] ECR I-7919.
1757. Case 263/86 *Belgian State v Humbel* [1988] ECR 5365.
1758. Case 352/85 *Bond van Adverteerders* [1988] ECR 2085.
1759. [2001] ECR I-5473.

In Case C-109/92 *Wirth*,[1760] the ECJ held that a teaching or enrolment fee, which pupils or their parent must sometimes pay under a national education system, does not constitute remuneration if the system is essentially financed out of public funds. However, if an educational establishment is financed essentially out of private funds, in particular by students and their parents, and seeks to make an economic profit, courses offered in such an establishment are regarded as services. The consequence of the above judgment was emphasised in Case C-76/05 *Herbert Schwarz, Marga Gootjes-Schwarz v Finanzamt Bergisch Gladbach*,[1761] in which the ECJ ruled that German tax law which precluded the granting of tax relief in respect of fees paid by German taxpayers to private schools situated in other Member States but granted relief where schools were situated in Germany, was in breach of Article 49 EC [56 TFEU].

24.3.2 The right of establishment

The ECJ defined the concept of establishment broadly. Exercise of the right of establishment involves having a permanent and continuous presence in the host Member State which allows "a Community national to participate on a stable and continuous basis in the economic life of a Member State other than his own". In respect of legal persons, in Case 205/84 *Commission v Germany [Re Insurance Services]*,[1762] the ECJ held that an enterprise (in this case an insurance company) was established in a host Member State "even if its presence is not in the form of a branch or agency but consists merely of an office managed by the enterprise's own staff or by a person who is independent but is authorised to act on a permanent basis for the enterprise".

Article 49 TFEU covers a wide range of activities. In Case C-268/99 *Jany and Others v Staatssecretaris van Justitie*,[1763] the ECJ regarded Polish and Czech women working as prostitutes in The Netherlands as being self-employed persons. They were entitled to establish themselves in The Netherlands on the basis of association agreements between the EU and Poland and the Czech Republic [at the relevant time Poland and the Czech Republic were not Member States], their activities were not contrary to the requirements of public morality of The Netherlands given that prostitution is legalised there and they were duly paying the relevant tax on their income.

24.3.3 A choice between the right of establishment and the right to provide services

It is for economic operators to decide, depending on their business strategy, whether they wish to establish themselves in a Member State or whether they prefer to provide services. Consequently they should be able to choose between those two freedoms and their choice should be restricted neither by bureaucratic obstacles nor by legal barriers. Consequently, a Member State is prohibited from requiring that a service provider has its principal establishment[1764] or a registered office[1765] in that Member State, or in the case of vessels that they are registered in that Member

---

1760. [1993] ECR I-6447.
1761. [2007] ECR 1-6849.
1762. [1986] ECR 3755.
1763. [2001] ECR I-8615.
1764. Case C-162/99 *Commission v Italy* [2001] ECR I-541; Case C-212/97 *Centros* [1999] ECR I-1459.
1765. Case C-101/94 *Commission v Italy* [1996] ECR I-2691.

State.[1766] If an operator decides to establish itself (rather than merely provide services) in a host Member State, it should choose what type of secondary establishment, that is a branch, agency or other form, is the most appropriate for conducting its business activity in that Member State and a host Member State is prohibited from giving more favourable treatment to one type of secondary establishment to the detriment of others.[1767]

24.4 Beneficiaries of the right of establishment and of the right to provide services

Under the Treaties EU nationals and their families, and companies formed according to the law of one of the Member States, are beneficiaries of both freedoms.

24.4.1 Natural persons

Nationals of a Member State are entitled to exercise the right of establishment irrespective of whether or not they reside within the territory of the EU. However, nationals of a third country lawfully residing in a Member State cannot rely on Article 49 TFEU in order to establish themselves in another Member State,[1768] unless they are covered by Directive 2003/109/EC of 25 November 2003 concerning the status of third-country nationals who are long-term residents[1769] (see Chapter 22.1.1) or if they come within the definition of a family member of an EU citizen exercising one of the four freedoms.

It should be noted that third-country nationals lawfully residing and working in a Member State can be temporarily sent by their employers to provide services in another Member State. This situation is covered by Directive 96/71/EC of 16 December 1996 concerning the Posting of Workers in the Framework of the Provision of Services.[1770]

The right to provide services is restricted to EU citizens who are established in a Member State.

If a national of a Member State has dual nationality, the nationality most favourable to the exercise of his/her right of establishment/provision of services will be taken into account. In Case 292/86 *Gullung*,[1771] a lawyer, who was a holder of both French and German nationality, was allowed to rely on his German nationality in France and thereby rely on EU law, whereas he could not have done this as a French national in France.

24.4.2 Legal persons

The right of establishment and the right to provide services are granted to companies and firms. Article 54 TFEU contains a definition of "companies and firms". It covers companies or firms constituted under civil or commercial law including co-operative societies, and other legal persons governed by public or private law. Only companies and firms fulfilling the following conditions are entitled to exercise the right to freedom of establishment:

1766. Case C-62/96 *Commission v Greece* [1997] ECR I-6725; Case C-334/94 *Commission v France* [1996] ECR I-1307; Case C-221/89 *Factortame (No 1)* [1991] ECR I-3905.
1767. Case 270/83 *Commission v France* [1986] ECR 273; Case C-307/97 *Saint Gobain* [1999] ECR I-6161.
1768. Case 65/77 *Razanatsimba* [1977] ECR 2229.
1769. [2004] OJ L16/44
1770. [1997] OJ L18/1.
1771. [1988] ECR 111.

- They must be formed in accordance with the law of a Member State;

- They must have their registered office, central administration or principal place of business within the EU. In the context of the provision of services, if a company's central administration or principal place of business is located outside the EU, the company's activities must have an effective and continuous link with the economy of a Member State, other than a link based on nationality, that is, links based on the nationality of the partners or the members of the managing or supervising bodies, or of persons holding the capital stock, are insufficient;

- A legal person must pursue economic activities for remuneration. Non-profit making undertakings are excluded from the scope of Article 54 TFEU. However, this does not mean that other provisions of the Treaties are not applicable to non-profit making undertakings.[1772]

24.4.3 Reverse discrimination

Reverse discrimination is permitted under EU law relating to the freedom of establishment and the provision of services. In this respect two situations should be distinguished: wholly internal situations to which national law is applicable[1773] and situations in which nationals of a Member State are denied the benefit of more favourable provisions of EU law because they are nationals of that Member State, even though their circumstances are ones to which EU law applies.

24.4.3.1 A wholly internal situation

In this situation, a national of a Member State is placed in a less advantageous position than a national of another Member State who has established himself/herself in that Member State. For example, under Directive 82/489/EEC laying down measures to facilitate the effective exercise of the right of establishment and freedom to provide services in hairdressing, six years' professional experience as a hairdresser is sufficient to exercise that profession in a host Member State. However, for a French national to work in France as a hairdresser, a French diploma in hairdressing is required. A French hairdresser who fails an examination to become a hairdresser cannot rely on his/her six years experience in France in order to practise the profession and is thereby reversely discriminated against. The explanation is that Directive 82/489/EEC did not harmonise the conditions of access to the profession of hairdressers in Member States. It merely established the conditions for the exercise of the right of establishment in a host Member State for members of that profession from another Member State.

24.4.3.2 A situation where a national of a Member State relies on EU law against his/her Member State in matters within the scope of the Treaties

In this situation there is some connection between the matter in issue and EU law. This is exemplified in Case 115/78 *Knoors v Secretary of State for Economic Affairs*.[1774]

1772. See C-172/98 *Commission v Belgium* [1999] ECR I-3999.
1773. See, for example, Case C-332/90 *Volker Steen* [1992] ECR I-341; Joined Cases C-29–35/94 *Aubertin* [1995] ECR I-301.
1774. [1979] ECR 399, see also Case 136/78 *Auer I* [1979] ECR 437 and Case 271/82 *Auer II* [1983] ECR 2727.

THE FACTS WERE:

Mr Knoors, a Dutch national who worked as a plumber in Belgium, was refused permission to work as a plumber in The Netherlands, even though Directive 64/427 governing certain trade skills was applicable to him as it covered the training and experience he had acquired in Belgium. The Dutch authorities argued that Knoors was trying to evade the application of national rules and that Directive 64/427 did not apply to nationals seeking to establish themselves in their own Member State.

Held:

The ECJ held that Mr Knoors was allowed to rely on Directive 64/427.[1775]

It flows from the above cases that when a situation is within the scope of the Treaties, it is irrelevant whether the nationality of the "home" Member State is by birth or has been acquired subsequently.

24.5 The right of establishment

Article 49 TFEU provides:

"Within the framework of the provisions set out below, restrictions on the freedom of establishment of nationals of a Member State in the territory of another Member State shall be prohibited. Such prohibition shall also apply to restrictions on the setting-up of agencies, branches or subsidiaries by nationals of any Member State established in the territory of any Member State.

Freedom of establishment shall include the right to take up and pursue activities as self-employed persons and to set up and manage undertakings, in particular companies or firms within the meaning of the second paragraph of Article 54, under the conditions laid down for its own nationals by the law of the country where such establishment is effected, subject to the provisions of the Chapter relating to capital."

Article 49 TFEU confers on EU citizens and EU companies a bundle of rights consisting of: the (implicit) right to leave a Member State of establishment; the right to establish themselves in a host Member State and, for companies, the right to have their principal or secondary establishment there; the right to have access to the relevant economic activity and to exercise it under the same conditions as nationals or national companies of that Member State.

24.5.1 Legal persons

24.5.1.1 *The right to leave a Member State of establishment: transfer of the seat of a company*

It is unlikely that in reality somebody conducting a successful business in one Member State will want to move it to another Member State. For any organisation contemplating such a move

---

1775. See also Case 246/80 *Broekmeulen* [1981] ECR 2311.

(perhaps believing it to be tax beneficial) the example of the *Daily Mail's* experience[1776] may be highly dissuasive.

THE FACTS WERE:

Daily Mail, an investment company incorporated in the UK, wanted to avoid paying UK tax when selling a significant part of its assets. Daily Mail decided to transfer its central management to The Netherlands but retain its legal status as a UK company. Before its relocation Daily Mail had to apply to the UK Treasury for permission to leave the UK. Daily Mail went ahead with the relocation without waiting for the Treasury's consent. Subsequently, it argued that the requirement to obtain consent was in breach of the principle of equal treatment as embodied in Articles 43 and 48 EC [Article 49 and 56 TFEU].

Held:

The ECJ held that the right to freedom of establishment is not unconditional. Accordingly, a home Member State is allowed to impose restrictions on businesses wishing to move to another Member State. However, such restrictions are assessed in the light of Article 43 EC [Article 49 TFEU] and should not be liable to hinder or render less attractive the transfer of a business. The Court noted that not every aspect of the regulation of businesses was subject to EC law and that there were legitimate national variations as to the requirements for the making of such a move, subject to the underlying basic principle in the Treaty.

In Case C-210/06 *Cartesio Oktató és Szolgáltató bt*[1777] the ECJ has further clarified the scope of the right of a company to move its seat to a Member State other than that in which it has been incorporated.

THE FACTS WERE:

Under Hungarian law a company incorporated under Hungarian law may not transfer its seat to another Member State and, at the same time, continue to operate under Hungarian law. A change of company's registered seat to a foreign country required a liquidation procedure in order to re-incorporate in another Member State. Cartesio, a Hungarian company, wanted, as the Daily Mail, to transfer its de facto head office to Italy while continuing to operate under Hungarian law. The compatibility of the Hungarian law with Articles 43 EC and 48 EC was examined by the ECJ [Articles 49 and 56 TFEU].

Held:

The ECJ held that as companies are creatures of national law and bearing in mind that company law has not been harmonised at the EU level, the matter is within the competence

---

1776. Case 81/87 *The Queen v H. M. Treasury and Commissioners of Inland Revenue, ex parte Daily Mail and General Trust plc* [1988] ECR 5483.
1777. [2008] ECR I-9641.

of each Member State. That competence includes the possibility for that Member State not to permit a company governed by its law to retain that status if the company intends to reorganise itself in another Member State by moving its seat to the territory of the latter, thereby breaking the connecting factor required under the national law of the Member State of incorporation. Accordingly, the Hungarian law was not in breach of EU law.

Comment:

The ECJ distinguished between two situations:

■ The situation where the seat of a company incorporated under the law of one Member State is transferred to another Member State with no change regarding the law which governs that company. This was what *Cartesio* wanted, i.e. to transfer its real seat from Hungary to Italy whilst remaining a company governed by Hungarian law, i.e. no change in the application of national law to the company in question. To this situation national law of incorporation is relevant and determines the conditions of incorporation and other relevant matters concerning the functioning of companies.

■ The situation where a company governed by the law of one Member State moves to another Member State with the consequence that the company has become a company which is governed by the law of the Member State to which it has moved. To this situation EU law applies, and therefore, it would be an obstacle to the freedom of establishment to require the winding-up or liquidation of the company, which could only be justified by overriding requirements in the public interest.[1778]

The loss of substantial value resulting from relocation expenses combined with payments of taxation liability that a company or its shareholders, or both, are likely to incur, shows that the relocation of businesses is not a realistic option, unless harmonising measures at the EU level are adopted allowing a company to retain its legal personality in a home Member State while transferring its seat to another Member State. Obviously, it makes more sense for a company to set up a secondary establishment in a host Member State or to take advantage of Regulation 2157/2001 on the Statute for a European Company.[1779]

24.5.1.2   *Merger of companies*

A less restrictive approach than in *Daily Mail* was taken by the ECJ in Case C-411/03 *Sevic Systems AG*,[1780] where two companies merged.

1778.   Case C-442/02 *CaixaBank France* [2004] ECR I-8961.
1779.   [2001] OJ L294/1.
1780.   [2005] ECR I-10805.

THE FACTS WERE:

Sevic, a German company, and Security Vision, a company established in Luxembourg, concluded a merger contract providing for the dissolution without liquidation of the latter company and the transfer of the whole of its assets to Sevic, without any change in the latter's company name. When Sevic applied for registration in the German commercial register of the merger, its application was rejected on the ground that the German law on company transformations provides only for mergers between companies established in Germany.

Held:

The ECJ held that:

- Cross-border merger operations constituted particular methods of exercise of the freedom of establishment;

- The German legislation was in breach of Articles 43 and 48 EC [Articles 49 and 56 TFEU];

- Even if in some circumstances imperative reasons in the public interest, such as protection of the interests of creditors, minority shareholders and employees and the preservation of the effectiveness of fiscal supervision and the fairness of commercial transactions, may justify a measure restricting the freedom of establishment, this was not the case. The prohibition was too general and thus went beyond what was necessary to protect such interests.

24.5.1.3   Establishment of a branch, agency or subsidiary in another Member State

The establishment of a branch, agency or subsidiary in a host Member State may be hindered by laws and regulations not only of the host Member State but also of the home Member State of a parent company. Case C-446/03 *Marks & Spencer plc v David Halsey (Her Majesty's Inspector of Taxes)* [1781] provides a good example of this.

THE FACTS WERE:

UK tax law provided that a parent company established in the UK was charged corporation tax in respect of the profits attributable only to its branches or agencies established in the UK. Similarly, it allowed a parent company to deduct losses made by its subsidiaries established in the UK but precluded a parent company from deducting from its taxable profits any losses made by subsidiaries in other Member States. Marks and Spencer (M&S), a company established in the UK, challenged the decision of the UK tax authorities rejecting its claim for tax relief. M&S sought to deduct from its taxable profits in the UK losses incurred by its subsidiaries established in Belgium, Germany and France.

1781.   [2005] ECR I-10837. German tax law similar to the UK law was condemned by the ECJ in Case C-347/04 *Rewe Zentralfinanz* [2007] ECR I-2647.

Held:

The ECJ held that:

- The UK tax law hindered the exercise by a parent company of its freedom of establishment by deterring it from setting up subsidiaries in other Member States.

- The UK tax law was justified by overriding reasons of public interest such as:
  - It ensured a balanced allocation of the power to impose taxes between Member States. The ECJ accepted the UK's argument that tax matters must be treated symmetrically in the same tax system, that is, in respect of profits and losses. Consequently, to allow a company to decide in which Member State to have its losses taken into account, that is, either in a Member State where a parent company is established or in a Member State where subsidiaries are established, could lead to a situation where the taxable base would be increased in the first Member State and reduced in the second to the extent of the losses transferred;
  - It ensured that losses were not deducted twice, once in the Member State of establishment of a parent company and once in the Member State of establishment of its subsidiaries;
  - It prevented tax avoidance. Indeed, the possibility of transferring losses incurred by a non-resident company to a resident company entails the risk that within a group of companies losses would be transferred to companies established in the Member States which apply the highest rates of taxation and in which the tax value of the losses is therefore the highest.

- The UK tax law was disproportionate because it precluded a parent company from deducting losses suffered by its subsidiaries in all circumstances. In this respect the ECJ stated that if a parent company provides evidence to the relevant tax authorities that its non-resident subsidiary has exhausted the possibilities available in its Member State of residence of having the losses taken into account for the present, previous and future tax periods, a parent company should be allowed to make a claim for tax relief.

24.5.1.4 Setting up a company in one Member State and then exercising the right to set up a secondary establishment in another Member State in order to circumvent incorporation requirements in the host Member State of the secondary establishment

Under Article 49 TFEU a company is allowed to take advantage of more lenient rules of company law relating to its registration in a Member State other than the Member State where it intends to do business. This was examined in Case C-212/97 *Centros Ltd v Erhvervsog Selsstyrelsen.*[1782]

1782. [1999] ECR I-1459.

THE FACTS WERE:

Mrs Bryde, a Danish national, registered her company Centros in the UK in May 1992, taking advantage of the UK law which did not impose any requirement on limited liability companies as to the paying-up of a minimum share capital.

During the summer of 1992 Mrs Bryde requested the Danish Trade and Companies Board to register a branch of Centros in Denmark. The Board refused on the grounds that Centros had never traded since its formation and that Mrs Bryde was, in fact, seeking to establish in Denmark not a branch but a principal establishment by circumventing Danish rules concerning the paying-up of a minimum share capital fixed at DKK200,000.

Centros challenged the decision of the Danish Trade and Companies Board.

Held:

The ECJ held that it was contrary to Articles 43 and 49 EC [Articles 49 and 56 TFEU] for a Member State to refuse, on the above-mentioned grounds, to register a branch of a company formed in accordance with the law of another Member State in which it had its registered office but in which the company itself was not engaged in any business activities.

Comment:

The ECJ confirmed its liberal approach towards freedom of establishment by stating that national rules regarding the prevention of fraud cannot justify restrictions which impair the freedom of establishment of companies. This was not surprising given that the ECJ had, in previous cases, applied a restrictive approach to national measures intended to fight fraud, which measures imposed restrictions on the freedom of establishment.[1783]

The ECJ did not "look behind the veil" of a company; it applied the provisions relating to the right of establishment. Therefore, the fact that Mrs Bryde was taking advantage of more lenient company law in the UK that permitted her to avoid paying the capital required by Danish law for the establishment of a company and that the main purpose of establishing her company in the UK was to open a branch in Denmark, which actually was intended to be a principal establishment, did not constitute an abuse of the right of establishment.

In Case C-167/01 *Inspire Art Ltd*,[1784] the situation was very similar to that in *Centros*.

THE FACTS WERE:

Inspire Art was registered in England in order to avoid the application of Netherlands law on company formation as to minimum capital and directors' liability. Inspire Art carried on its

---

1783. Case 270/83 *Commission v France* ([1986] ECR 273), in which the right of establishment was exercised in order to benefit from tax advantages in another Member State and Case 79/85 *Segers v Bestuur van de Bedrijfsvereniging voor Bank- en Verzekeringswezen* [1986] ECR 2375 concerning social security benefits.
1784. [2003] ECR I-10155.

business exclusively through a branch in The Netherlands where the branch was duly registered. The company challenged the Dutch law imposing on it an obligation to record, through its registration in the Dutch commercial register, its description as a foreign company and to use that description in all its business dealings.

Held:

The ECJ held that the requirement was in breach of the 11th Company Directive and there were no overriding reasons related to public policy which could justify such restrictions. The ECJ held that:

"The reasons for which the company was formed in that other Member State, and the fact that it carries on its activities exclusively or almost exclusively in the Member State of establishment, do not deprive it of the right to invoke the freedom of establishment guaranteed by the Treaty, save where abuse is established on a case-by-case basis."

24.5.1.5   The exercise of the right of establishment

Most cases that have been decided by the ECJ in this area have concerned restrictions and disadvantages imposed on branches and subsidiaries established in a Member State as compared to companies and firms having their principal establishment in that Member State.[1785] The issue of indirect discrimination often emerges in respect of those host Member States' taxation systems that tend to favour companies and firms having their seat in that Member State. One example is provided by Case C-264/96 *Imperial Chemical Industries v Colmar [Inspector of Taxes]*,[1786] which illustrates how the ECJ deals with discriminatory taxation systems in the Member States.

THE FACTS WERE:

ICI together with another company, both resident in the UK, formed a consortium through which they beneficially owned Coopers Animal Health (Holdings) Ltd (CAH (Holdings)). The sole business of the latter was to hold shares in 23 trading companies which were its subsidiaries. Some of the subsidiaries were resident in the UK (4), some in other Member States (6) and some outside the territory of the EU. Within the subsidiary companies residing in the UK was Coopers Animal Health Ltd (CAH). ICI applied for tax relief under sections 258 to 264 of the UK Income and Corporation Taxes Act 1970 in order to offset losses incurred by CAH. This was refused on the ground that CAH (Holdings) was not a holding company within the meaning of section 258(7) of the Act since the majority of its subsidiaries were not resident in the UK. ICI challenged that decision and argued that the residence requirement under the Act

1785.   Case C-250/95 *Furura Participations SA and Singer v Administration des Contributions* [1997] ECR I-2471; Case C-324/00 *Lankhorst-Hohorst GmbH v Finanzamt Steinfurt* [2002] ECR I-11779; Case C-442/02 *CaixaBank France* [2004] ECR I-8961.
1786.   [1998] ECR I-4695.

was contrary to Articles 43 and 48 EC [Articles 49 and 56 TFEU]. The House of Lords referred two questions to the ECJ: the first being as to whether the residency requirement under the Income and Corporation Taxes Act 1970 was in conformity with Articles 43 and 49 EC [Articles 49 and 56 TFEU], and the second concerning the scope of application of EU law where subsidiaries were established in non-Member States.

Held:

The ECJ held that:

■ Although direct taxation was in principle within the competence of a Member State, that State must, nevertheless, exercise its powers of direct taxation in conformity with Community law.[1787]

■ National legislation hindered the freedom of establishment since it set up differential tax treatment for consortium companies established in the UK as compared with those established in other Member States.

■ The UK justifications based on the risk of tax avoidance and on the maintenance of cohesion of the national tax system were rejected as neither satisfying the conditions established in Case C-204/90 *Hans-Martin Bachmann v Belgian State*[1788] nor fulfilling the criterion of proportionality.

■ While a particular provision of national law must be disapplied in relation to a situation covered by EU law, the same provision could be applied in a situation falling outside the scope of EC law. The ECJ held that Article 10 EC [Article 4(3) TEU] did not require the national court to interpret its legislation in conformity with EC law or to disapply the legislation to situations falling outside the scope of EU law. However, this may create legal uncertainty which a Member State should avoid in so far as it might affect rights deriving from EU law.

24.5.2 Natural persons

24.5.2.1 The right to leave a home Member State

EU citizens and their families are entitled to leave their home Member State and establish themselves in a host Member State. Their freedom should not be hindered. However, in Case C-9/02 *Hughes Lasteyrie du Saillant*[1789] it had been hindered by the French "exit tax".

1787. See Case C-279/93 *Schumacker* [1995] ECR I-225; Case C-319/02 *Manninen* [2004] ECR I-7477.
1788. [1992] ECR I-249.
1789. [2004] ECR I-2409.

THE FACTS WERE:

When Mr de Lasteyrie du Saillant left France in order to reside in Belgium, the French tax authorities charged him a tax on an unrealised increase in the value of securities, which was due in the event of taxpayers transferring their residence outside France for tax purposes.

Held:

The ECJ held that a tax charged on an unrealised increase in the value of securities, which is due in the event of a taxpayer transferring his residence from France to another Member State for tax purposes, was in breach of Article 43 EC [Article 49 TFEU] given that the taxpayer who had transferred his establishment was subjected to disadvantageous treatment in comparison with a person who retained his residence in France, that is, had the taxpayer stayed in France, he would not have been liable to tax on values which had not yet been realised and which he did not have. Had he stayed in France the increases in value would have become taxable only when, and to the extent that, the securities were actually realised.

The ECJ held that the French legislation was likely to discourage a taxpayer from transferring his tax residence and could not be justified by imperative reasons including the prevention of fraud and tax avoidance. The ECJ emphasised that the transfer of a tax residence, in itself, does not imply tax avoidance and cannot justify fiscal measures which compromise the exercise of the freedom of establishment.[1790]

Comment:

The interesting argument presented by the French Government was that the challenged legislation was introduced with a view to preventing temporary transfers of the tax residence of certain French taxpayers outside France, exclusively for tax reasons before they sold securities. This was rejected by the ECJ.

24.5.2.2   *Right of access to the relevant economic activity*

National rules as well as rules of professional bodies, associations or organisations relating to access to a particular economic activity differ greatly. They may, in some cases, completely prevent access to the relevant economic activity. Obviously all directly and indirectly discriminatory rules are prohibited, as are indistinctly applicable rules which prohibit, hinder or render less attractive the exercise of the freedom of establishment. However, indirectly discriminatory rules and indistinctly applicable rules may be justified by overriding reasons of public interest. This entails that in some areas national barriers remain lawful and that in those areas the market can be integrated only through a legislative initiative. One of such areas concerns the recognition of diplomas and qualifications.

24.5.2.2.1 Mutual recognition of diplomas and qualifications

The main limitations on the exercise of the right of establishment (as well as the right to provide services or to have access to employment in a host Member State as a worker) concern the

---

1790. Case C-478/98 *Commission v Belgium* [2000] ECR I-7587.

conditions relating to admission to a particular profession. Indeed, whether EU migrants work as a worker, as a self-employed person or as a provider of services, the exercise of their professional activities is conditional upon recognition by a host Member State of the fact that they are adequately qualified to carry them out. In order to implement the free movement of economically active persons within the EU, the continuing harmonisation of rules on the recognition of diplomas and professional qualifications is of vital importance.

There are two approaches to harmonisation of the rules relating to the mutual recognition of diplomas and professional qualifications.

The first consists of the harmonisation of the rules in respect of individual professions or a particular sector of the economy by use of "sectorial" directives, one by one. The frequency of use of this approach has declined. This approach was applied under the general programme adopted in 1961 during the transitional period. Progress under the sectorial directives was slow and this approach was not appropriate to the requirements of the internal market, although it resulted in the adoption of a number of directives covering many professions, such as architects, dentists, doctors, midwives, nurses, veterinary surgeons, hairdressers, and so on, and a variety of economic sectors.

The second approach relates to Directive 89/48/EEC,[1791] which provides for a general system for the recognition of higher education diplomas awarded on completion of professional education and training of at least three years' duration. The Directive covered all regulated professions for which university diplomas awarded for a course of at least three years' duration are required. This directive was supplemented by additional directives which created a system which was complex, rigid and lacked transparency. The Stockholm European Council (March 2001) requested the Commission to undertake a major reform of that system. This resulted in the adoption of Directive 2005/36/EC of 7 September 2005[1792] on the Recognition of Professional Qualifications which repeals and replaces three directives that set up a general system for recognition (Directives 89/48/EEC, Directive 92/51/EEC and Directive 1999/42/EC) and 12 sectorial directives covering the seven professions of doctors, nurses, dentists, veterinary surgeons, midwives, pharmacists and architects. The Directive came into force in October 2007.

The recognition of a lawyer's qualifications is covered by Directive 2005/36/EC but Directive 98/5/EC, which concerns the right of establishment of lawyers, and Directive 77/249/EEC, which concerns the provision of services by lawyers, are unaffected by it, given that they concern the authorisation to practice, not the recognition of professional qualifications.

Directive 2005/36/EC sets out rules concerning recognition by a Member State of professional qualifications acquired in other Member States, i.e. its relates to the methodologies and procedures for evaluating credentials for work purposes and not for academic purposes such as the pursuit or continuation of higher education on the basis of qualifications obtained in a home Member State. It is neither concerned with the recognition of decisions adopted by other Member States pursuant to this Directive, nor with the recognition of qualifications obtained outside the EU.

Its main features are:

1. Its applies to an EU citizen exercising his/her right to free movement and members of his/her family irrespective of whether they are EU citizens or nationals of third

---

1791. [1989] OJ L19/16.
1792. [2005] OJ L255/22.

countries, nationals of EEA and Switzerland and persons who have refugee status in a Member State when they move to another Member State.

2. It leaves unchanged the mechanism of recognition established by Directive 89/48/EEC as amended by Directives 92/51/EEC and Directive 1999/42/EC. In respect of the recognition of diplomas awarded by another Member State the above Directives set the following rules.

A host Member State is required to carry out a comparative examination of diplomas:

- If there is no substantial difference between them, a diploma awarded by another Member State must be recognised as equivalent;
- If there is a substantial difference between them, a host Member State must give the applicant the opportunity to demonstrate that he has acquired the knowledge and skill which were lacking. He is entitled to choose between an adaptation period and an aptitude test. A Member State may limit the choice when:
  - The practice of the profession requires precise knowledge of national law; and
  - The provision of advice and/or assistance concerning national law is an essential and constant aspect of the professional activity.

The above conditions are cumulative and were further explained by the ECJ in Case C-149/05 *Harold Price v Conseil des Ventes Volontaires de Meubles aux Enchères Publiques*.[1793]

THE FACTS WERE:

Mr Price, a holder of a UK degree in Fine Arts Valuation, wished to pursue the profession of director of voluntary public auctions in France, which under French law required substantial knowledge of law. He was required to take an aptitude test. His preference was for an adaptation period (not surprisingly as he had actually practised the profession for seven years in France).

Held:

The ECJ held that a Member State can limit the choice of an applicant in a situation where advice and/or assistance concerns a specialised area of law and constitutes an essential and constant element of that activity. The ECJ left it to a national court to decide this issue, but from the judgment it was quite clear that Mr Price's preference would not be accommodated.

The application for recognition should be examined within the shortest possible time and must be completed within four months of its submission. The decision given by a competent national authority, or the absence of such decision, is subject to appeal.

In respect of the recognition of professional qualifications on the basis of professional experience acquired in another Member State, Directive 1999/42/EC divides the

---

1793. [2006] ECR I-7691.

activities mentioned in Part One of its Annex A into six categories (there are six lists). The number of years and the capacity in which the applicant was employed, that is, as a manager, self-employed person or employee, are taken into consideration for each category of activities. Directive 1999/42/EC also deals with such requirements as proof of good character, financial standing, insurance, and so on.

3.   The Directive applies to all professions which are "regulated" by the Member States. The concept of a "regulated profession" is defined in its Article 1(a).

4.   It makes a distinction between the provision of services and the freedom of establishment.

A.   Provision of services:

When a professional service is provided on a temporary and occasional basis for a period of not more than 16 weeks per year, a provider of services is not required to apply for recognition of his qualifications. He can provide services under his original professional title, subject to certain conditions imposed with a view to protecting service users. In particular he may be required to comply with certain obligations to provide the recipients of the services and the national administration with information. With regards to health professionals, where public safety concerns are particularly important, those obligations would include advance declarations to host Member State authorities and, in some cases, pro forma registration.

B.   Establishment:

The Directive provides for:

(i)   Automatic recognition of training qualifications on the basis of the minimum training conditions in the cases previously covered by individual directives, that is, in respect of doctors, nurses responsible for general care, dental practitioners, veterinary surgeons, midwives, pharmacists and architects;

(ii)   Automatic recognition of qualifications attested by professional experience in the case of the industrial, craft and commercial activities listed in the annexes to the Directive;

(iii) Application of the general system of recognition to all other professions and to situations not covered by other harmonising measures (see below).

5.   In respect of the general system for the recognition of qualifications, the Directive introduces a more flexible, automatic procedure based on common platforms established by professional associations at European level, stemming from increased co-operation between the public and private sectors. This is intended to ensure speedy processing of requests for recognition of qualifications.

6.   It establishes a network of contact points (one being located in each Member State) which have the task of providing EU citizens with information and assistance in respect of recognition procedures and resolving any difficulties they might encounter in obtaining recognition of their professional qualifications. The network enhances co-operation between national administrations and between them and the Commission.

7.   The Directive provides for the introduction of professional "cards" by professional

associations and organisations with a view to monitoring the career of professionals. Such cards would contain specified information relating to professional qualifications, legal establishment of the holder, any disciplinary measures taken against him and details of the relevant competent national authority.

24.5.2.2.2 Distinction between regulated and unregulated professions

As stated above the mechanism of recognition established by Directives 89/48/EEC as amended remains unchanged under Directive 2005/36/EC. In this respect a distinction should be made between a situation where a profession is regulated and one where it is not.

- A regulated profession: Article 1(c) and (d) of Directive 89/48/EEC defines this concept. A profession is regarded as regulated when national rules (whether legislation, regulations or administrative provisions) which govern the conditions for taking up or pursuing a professional activity impose the possession of a diploma or other certificate of qualification as a precondition to the exercise of that profession. In particular, the use of a professional title limited by such rules to holders of a given professional qualification constitutes a mode of pursuit.[1794]

- An unregulated profession: this is not covered by Directive 2005/36.[1795] The person concerned is not required to apply for recognition, i.e. he/she can freely pursue his/her profession, but the principles established in Case C-340/89 *Vlassopoulou*[1796] apply, if relevant.

The difference between the recognition of professional qualifications in regulated and unregulated professions is well illustrated in Case C-234/97 *Teresa Fernández De Bobadilla v Museo Nacional Del Prado, Comité De Empresa Del Museo Nacional Del Prado, Ministerio Fiscal.*[1797]

THE FACTS WERE:

Ms Fernández de Bobadilla, a Spanish national residing in Madrid, after obtaining her Bachelor of Arts degree in History of Art at the University of Boston, USA, obtained a Master of Arts degree in fine arts restoration at Newcastle upon Tyne Polytechnic in the United Kingdom in 1989. A grant from the Prado museum had helped her to study in the UK. From 1989 to 1992 she worked for the Prado in Spain under a temporary contract as a restorer of works of art on paper. Under the terms of a collective agreement concluded in 1988 by the Prado and staff representatives, the post of restorer was reserved to persons possessing qualifications awarded by the restoration department of the Faculty of Fine Arts or by the School of Arts in Spain, or any other foreign qualification recognised by the competent authorities. In October 1992 Ms de Bobadilla applied to the relevant department of the Ministry of Education to have

---

1794. Article 3 of Directive 2005/36/EC.
1795. Case C-285/01 *Burbaud* [2003] ECR I-8219; in Case C-586/08 *Angelo Rubino v Ministero dell'Università e della Ricerca* [judgment of 17/12/09 (nyr)] the ECJ held that the profession of lecturer in Italy does not constitute a regulated profession given that no specific educational qualification is required to be a lecturer in Italy. In that country lecturers are recruited by means of a selection procedure.
1796. [1991] ECR I-2357.
1797. [1999] ECR I-4773.

the degree obtained in the UK officially recognised as equivalent to a Spanish degree in the conservation and restoration of cultural assets. She was given notice that in order for her English diploma to be recognised, she would have to demonstrate sufficient knowledge of the 24 subjects listed in the notice through an examination arranged in two parts. On 17 November 1992 the Prado organised a competition for a permanent post of a restorer of works of art on paper. The application of Ms de Bobadilla was rejected on the ground that she did not satisfy the requirements laid down in the collective agreement. Ms de Bobadilla brought an action for annulment of such requirements as contrary to the Spanish Constitution and Article 39 EC [Article 45 TFEU].

Held:

The ECJ focused on the issue of whether the collective agreement had a general scope of application, that is, whether in a general way it governed the right to take up or pursue a profession, or whether it governed relations only between the employer and the employees within a single public body. It was for the national court to determine the scope of the collective agreement.

Comment:

The ECJ held that if the collective agreement had a general scope of application, then it might be classified as rules regulating a professional activity for the purposes of Directives 89/48 and 92/51 and therefore one or other of Directives 89/48 and 92/51 would apply to the proceedings commenced by Ms Fernández de Bobadilla. Consequently, if either of these two Directives applied in order to establish whether she could apply for a permanent post as restorer of cultural assets, the national court would have to examine whether the applicant satisfied the conditions laid down in the Directive concerned. Also, if one or other of Directives 89/48 or 92/51 was applicable, a public body could not require that a candidate's qualifications be granted official recognition by the competent national authorities other than according to the conditions set out in those two Directives. However, if the collective agreement had a limited scope of application and therefore governed relations only between the employer and the employees within a single body, the profession of restorer of cultural assets was not regulated within the meaning of Directives 89/48 and 92/51.

When a profession is unregulated, the procedure for granting official recognition must comply with requirements set out by the ECJ in Case C-340/89 *Vlassopoulou*[1798] and C-164/ 94 *Arantis v Land of Berlin.*[1799] In such a case the competent authorities of the Member State in which the recognition is sought must take into account the diplomas, certificates and other evidence of qualifications of the applicant acquired in order to practise that profession in another Member State and compare them with the qualifications required by the host Member State. If the comparison reveals that the knowledge and qualifications certified by the foreign diploma correspond to those required by the national provisions, the diploma should be recognised by the host Member State. If there is a partial equivalence, the host

---

1798. [1991] ECR I-2357.

1799. [1996] ECR I-135.

Member State is entitled to require the person concerned to demonstrate that he/she has acquired the additional knowledge and qualifications needed. However, where there is no general procedure for official recognition laid down by the Member State, or where that procedure does not comply with the requirements of EU law, it is for the public body advertising a particular post to investigate whether the diploma awarded in another Member State, together with practical experience where appropriate, is to be considered as equivalent to the qualification required. In this case, the Museum of Prado, as it advertised the post, was particularly well placed to assess the candidate's actual knowledge and abilities for two reasons: first, it had already employed the candidate and second, it made a grant to the candidate to help her to obtain a diploma in the UK.

In Case C-311/06 *Consiglio Nazionale degli Ingegneri v Ministero della Giustizia and Marco Cavallera*,[1800] the ECJ clarified the meaning of "diploma" under Directive 89/48/EEC.

THE FACTS WERE:

In this case an Italian national, who was awarded a mechanical engineering qualification in Italy after three years' education and training, obtained homologation of his Italian qualification in Spain. As a result he could enroll in Spain in the Register of Engineers. When he applied to the Italian Ministry of Justice for the recognition of the Spanish certificate for the purpose of his enrolment in the register of engineers in Italy, his application was successful. However, the Italian National Council of Engineers challenged the decision of the Ministry of Justice on the ground that the claimant had never worked professionally outside Italy and that he had not taken the State examination provided for under Italian legislation for the purpose of being entitled to pursue the profession of engineer in Italy. The matter went before the ECJ within the preliminary ruling proceedings.

Held:

The Court held that a diploma does not include a certificate issued by a Member State attesting professional qualifications obtained in another Member State. However, if qualifications were acquired, wholly or in part, under the education system of the Member State which issues the certificate in question then such a certificate will be regarded as a "diploma".

Comment:

The ECJ emphasised that the Spanish homologation did not provide evidence of any additional qualification as neither homologation nor enrolment in the register of engineers in Spain in Catalonia was based on an examination of the qualifications or professional experience acquired by the claimant. The ECJ held that in the light of the fact that there was no evidence that the claimant had obtained an additional qualification or professional experience

---

1800. [2009] ECR I-415.

in Spain it would be contrary to the principle enshrined by Directive 89/48, according to which Member States reserve the option of fixing the minimum level of qualification necessary to guarantee the quality of services provided in their territory, to consider the Spanish certificate of homologation as a "diploma".

Further important clarifications regarding the concept of "a diploma" were provided in Case C-151/07 *Theologos-Grigorios Khatzithanasis v OEEK*[1801] and in Case C-84/07 *Commission v Greece.*[1802]

THE FACTS WERE:

Mr Khatzithanasis, a Greek national, after completing a two-year course in optical studies in Italy, was awarded a diploma in optometry and optical studies by the Vinci Regional Institute for Optical Studies and Optometry. That diploma authorised him to pursue the profession of optician in Italy. However, part of his study was completed in Greece in an establishment not recognised as an educational establishment by Greek legislation. Mr Khatzithanasis never practiced the profession in Italy. When he applied to the relevant Greek authorities for the recognition of his Italian diploma, they refused on the ground that he had received education, in whole or in part, at an establishment located in Greece which, according to the Greek legislation, was not recognised as an educational establishment.

Both the Commission and Mr Khatzithanasis submitted that Greece was in breach of Council Directive 92/51/EEC as amended by Directive 2001/19/EC.

Held:

The ECJ held that Greece was in breach of the relevant directive and that subject to the application of Article 4 of that directive, was obliged to recognise a diploma awarded by a competent authority in another Member State.

Comment:

The ECJ provided the following clarifications concerning the recognition of diplomas under Directive 92/51/EEC:

- It is for the institution which awards the diploma alone to decide whether education and training that a person received in another Member State is adequate for the purpose of awarding a diploma. Therefore, the claimant's diploma was within the scope of the Directive;

- Directive 89/48 does not contain any limitation as regards the Member State in which an applicant must have acquired his professional qualifications;

- With regard to Article 4 of Directive 92/51/ECC, this article allows a Member State to take

---

1801. [2008] ECR I-9013.
1802. [2008] ECR I-171.

account of the fact that considerable differences may exist between the training and education required in that Member State and the Member State where the diploma was awarded for taking up the same regulated profession and indeed it allows a Member State where the recognition is sought to require that the applicant either complete an adoption period or take an aptitude test. Greece did not give any choice to applicants. It imposed on them the requirement of completing an adoption period. This was in breach of Article 4 (Case C-84/07 *Commission v Greece*).

24.5.2.2.3 Recognition of qualifications obtained by EU nationals outside the EU

The situation when EU nationals obtain their qualification in a non-Member State, exercise their right of establishment in a host Member State and subsequently seek to practise in another Member State was examined by the ECJ in Cases C-154/93 *Tawil-Albertini v Ministre des Affaires Sociales*[1803] and C-319/92 *Haim v Kassenzahnärtzliche Vereinigung Nordrhein*.[1804]

THE FACTS WERE:

In Tawil-Albertini a French national, Tawil-Albertini, obtained a dental qualification in Lebanon which was subsequently recognised in Belgium where he practised as a dentist. When he applied for authorisation to practise in France, he was refused on the ground that his qualification was obtained in a non-Member State and therefore Directive 78/686/EEC concerning the mutual recognition of diplomas, certificates and other evidence of the formal qualifications of practising of dentistry did not apply to him. Tawil-Albertini argued that he was covered by the Directive since his qualification was recognised in Belgium.

Held:

The ECJ ruled that in respect of qualifications obtained in a non-Member State the recognition is based on agreements between the states in question. In the absence of such an agreement any Member State could recognise the equivalence of qualifications obtained in a non-Member State but was not required to do so, as Directive 78/686/EEC did not cover such situations.

THE FACTS WERE:

In Haim, a German national, Mr Haim, who obtained his qualification in a non-Member State and subsequently practised for eight years in Belgium (he was also admitted to practise in Germany), was refused permission to work on a social security scheme in Germany unless he

---

1803. [1994] ECR I-451.
1804. [1994] ECR I-425.

> completed a further two-year preparatory training course. He argued that his professional experience in Belgium should be taken into account by the German authorities.
>
> *Held:*
>
> The ECJ held:
>
> "The competent national authority, in order to verify whether the training period requirement pre-scribed by the national rules is met, must take into account the professional experience of the plaintiff in the main proceedings, including that which he has acquired during his appointment as a dental practitioner of a social security scheme in another Member State."

It can be seen from the above cases that although there is no obligation imposed on a Member State to recognise qualifications obtained in third countries, the ECJ in *Haim* showed willingness to extend the scope of the EC Treaty to cover situations where a person has acquired some professional experience in a Member State. This approach was further developed in Case C-238/98 *Hocsman*.[1805] In this case the ECJ held that when harmonised EU rules are not applicable, all of the diplomas, certificates and other evidence of formal qualifications acquired in a non-Member State, which are broadly equivalent to those under national law, must be taken into consideration by the relevant authorities when they compare the specialised knowledge and abilities certified by those diplomas and experience with the knowledge and qualifications required by their national rules. As a result, all qualifications, wherever acquired, must be assessed in the light of principles established in the Case C-340/89 *Vlassopoulou*.[1806] This approach is in line with Council recom-mendation 89/49[1807] encouraging the Member States to recognise diplomas and other evidence of formal qualifications obtained in non-Member States by EU nationals.

24.5.2.2.4 Rules established by professional bodies

Professional bodies in a host Member State may impose various formalities necessary to become a member of the profession and have power to impose rules of professional conduct. The ECJ's position on this subject is that national rules imposing restrictions on the right of establishment must fulfil four criteria in order to be justified:[1808]

- They must apply without distinction to nationals and non-nationals;

- They must be justified by imperative requirements in the general interest;

- They must be suitable for the attainment of the objective which they pursue; and

- They must be proportionate to the objective sought.

1805. [2000] ECR I-6623; see also Case C-110/01 *Tennah-Durez* [2003] ECR I-6239.
1806. [1991] ECR I-2357.
1807. [1989] OJ L19/24.
1808. Case C-351/90 *Commission v Luxembourg [Re Access to the Medical Profession]* [1992] ECR I-3945.

24.5.2.2.5 The exercise of the right of establishment

Directive 2004/38/EC on the Right of Citizens of the Union and their Family Members to Move and Reside Freely within the Territory of the Member States[1809] and Directive 2006/123 are the main secondary legislation applicable to the exercise of the right of establishment by self-employed persons. Unlike workers they are not carrying out their activities in the context of a relationship of subordination. They bear the risk of success or failure of their business and they are not paid directly and in full.[1810] There is no secondary legislation similar in scope to Regulation 1612/68. As a result, in many areas self-employed persons established in a host Member State must rely on the principle of non-discrimination.[1811]

The prohibition of direct and indirect discrimination and of all indistinctly applicable national measures applies to access to and the pursuit of economic activities, including various general facilities which are of assistance in the pursuit of these activities. This was first decided by the ECJ in Case 197/84 *Steinhauser v City of Biarritz*.[1812]

THE FACTS WERE:

A German national, who was a professional artist and who resided in Biarritz, applied to the local authorities to rent a "crampotte" (a kind of a fisherman's hut used locally for the exhibition and sale of works of art). His application was refused on the grounds that only French nationals were allowed to rent a "crampotte". Steinhauser challenged this decision.

Held:

The ECJ held that the principle of non-discrimination applies not only to the taking-up of activity as a self-employed person but also the pursuit of that activity in the broadest sense.

In Case 63/86 *Commission v Italy*,[1813] the ECJ provided other examples of such facilities: the right to purchase, exploit and transfer real and personal property, and the right to obtain loans and to have access to various forms of credit.

24.5.2.3 Lawyers' rights of establishment

In 1998 the EP and the Council adopted Directive 98/5/EC on the right of establishment for lawyers who have obtained professional qualifications in their home Member State and wish to practise their profession on a permanent basis in any other Member State.[1814] The Directive applies to employed and self-employed lawyers and in the UK encompasses solicitors, barristers and advocates. The main features of Directive 98/5/EC are that:

1809. See Chapter 25.
1810. Case C-268/99 *Jany and Others* [2001] ECR I-8615.
1811. Case C-337/97 *Meeusen* [1999] ECR I-3289.
1812. [1985] ECR 1819.
1813. [1988] ECR 29.
1814. [1998] OJ L77/36.

▪ Lawyers establishing themselves in another Member State must use the professional title which they have obtained in their home Member State. This restriction was deemed necessary in order to avoid confusion between the lawyers' home Member State qualification and the qualification required in the host Member State. The professional title must be expressed in the official language of the home Member State.

▪ Lawyers who wish to establish themselves in another Member State must register with the competent authorities of the host Member State (see below).

▪ Lawyers can give legal advice on both the law of the host and home Member States as well as EU law and international law.

If a host Member State reserves some activities, such as the preparation of deeds, the administration of estates or the creation and transfer of interests in land for certain categories of lawyers, and in other Member States those activities are performed by non-lawyers, a host Member State is permitted to exclude lawyers practising under a home-country professional title obtained in a home Member State from carrying out those activities. This restriction is explained by the fact that the Directive does not affect notaries who, in many EU countries, have exclusive rights in these two areas. Further, the Directive requires lawyers to be accompanied in court by a local lawyer in situations where only a lawyer can appear before the court in question.

▪ The rules of personal conduct and etiquette of both a home and a host Member State apply to lawyers wishing to practise in a host Member State.

▪ The competent authorities of a host Member State are entitled to bring disciplinary proceedings against lawyers from another Member State registered in the host Member State who fail to meet the professional standards required by that Member State under the same conditions as apply to lawyers qualified in the host Member State.

▪ The Directive has substantially revised the conditions under which lawyers from another Member State may qualify as lawyers in a host Member State. There are two different ways:

  ● First, if they effectively and regularly pursue their practice in the law of the host Member State for three years; and
  ● Second, even if they practise the law of their home Member State or EU law or international law, they may obtain the host Member State's qualification provided they carry out their professional activities in a host Member State for three years and satisfy the host Member State's authorities as to their competence with regard to that Member State's law.

The Directive constitutes a complete harmonisation of conditions for the exercise of the right of establishment for lawyers. Consequently, a Member State is not allowed to impose further conditions in the area covered by the Directive. This was clearly stated in Case C-506/04 *Graham J. Wilson v Ordre des Avocats du Barreau de Luxembourg*,[1815] where lawyers from Member States other than Luxembourg were required to take a linguistic test as a precondition of registration. The ECJ was very clear on the point and stated that the only condition for registration is the

---

1815. [2006] ECR I-8613.

presentation by the applicant to the competent authorities of the host Member State of a certificate attesting to registration with the competent authorities of the home Member State. In this case the ECJ further clarified that the appellate body against decisions refusing registration should be considered as a court or tribunal, within the meaning of Article 234 EC [Article 267 TFEU].

Obviously, Luxembourg was very unhappy with the Directive as it had already unsuccessfully challenged its legality[1816] and, in Case C-193/05 *Commission v Luxembourg*,[1817] was found in breach of EU law for imposing the following requirements on lawyers from other Member States wishing to practise in Luxembourg:

- Requirements concerning language knowledge;

- A prohibition on being a person authorised to accept service on behalf of companies; and

- The obligation to produce each year a certificate attesting to registration with the competent authority in the home Member State.

24.6 The right to provide and receive services

Article 56 TFEU provides:

"Within the framework of the provisions set out below, restrictions on freedom to provide services within the Union shall be prohibited in respect of nationals of Member States who are established in a Member State other than that of the person for whom the services are intended.

The European Parliament and the Council, acting in accordance with the ordinary legislative procedure, may extend the provisions of the Chapter to nationals of a third country who provide services and who are established within the Union."

Services are defined in Article 57 TFEU as being normally provided for remuneration and not covered by the provisions of the Treaties relating to the free movement of persons, capital and goods. In Case C-55/94 *Gebhard*,[1818] the ECJ stated that the provisions of the EC Treaty relating to the supply of services are applicable only if the provisions on the right of establishment are not applicable. Accordingly, the former will apply in so far as the latter are not applicable.

Article 57 TFEU provides a non-exhaustive list, which includes activities of an industrial character, of a commercial character, of craftsmen and of the professions.

The freedom to provide services differs from the freedom of establishment, in that the former involves the legislation of two Member States: the Member State of establishment of the provider of services and the Member State where the service is provided. It would inhibit free movement if short-term provision of services meant that the service provider had to comply with all of the regulatory system of the host Member State. For that reason only some and not all rules relating to the right of establishment apply to the provision of services.

A prerequisite for the application of Article 56 TFEU is the cross-border nature of the service.[1819] If a supplier of the service and its recipient are established in different Member States,

---

1816. Case C-168/98 *Luxembourg v EP and Council* [2000] ECR I-9131.
1817. [2006] ECR I-8673.
1818. [1995] ECR I-4165.
1819. Case 352/85 *Bond van Adverteerders* [1988] ECR 2085.

Article 56 TFEU applies wherever the service is supplied within the EU.[1820] Based on the cross-border nature of the service Article 56 TFEU applies in the following situations:

- When a provider of services established in one Member State travels to another Member State to provide services in that Member State;

- When a recipient travels to another Member State to receive services there;[1821]

- When both a provider and a recipient are established in the same Member State but the provider travels to a host Member State to offer services there and the recipient seeks services from the provider in the host Member State;[1822]

- When neither a provider established in one Member State nor a recipient established in another Member State travel, as services are provided by post or by telecommunication means (phone, fax, the internet[1823] or television[1824]).

There are two particularly surprising aspects of Article 56 TFEU. The first is that its application was extended to services publicly funded such as education and medical services (for example, services provided within a framework of national health care systems of the Member States – see below) and that it applies to situations which at first glance seem purely internal. The second is exemplified by Case C-60/00 *Mary Carpenter v Secretary of State for the Home Department*.[1825]

THE FACTS WERE:

Mary Carpenter, a Philippine national, overstayed her leave to enter the UK as a visitor. Subsequently, she married Peter Carpenter, a British national. From 1995 onwards they lived together and she became the main carer for his children from a previous marriage.

Mr Carpenter ran a business selling advertising space in medical and scientific periodicals and offered the editors of those periodicals various administrative and publication services relating to advertisements. His company was established in the UK, but a significant proportion of his business was carried out with customers established in other Member States. Often Mr Carpenter travelled to those countries for the purposes of his business.

When Mrs Carpenter applied to the Secretary of State for leave to remain in the UK as the spouse of a British national, her application was refused. Her appeal was based on the argument that her deportation would hinder the provision of services by her husband because when her husband travelled to other Member States for the purposes of his business, she took care of his children.

1820. Case C-17/92 *Federación de Distribuidores Cinematográficos v Estado Español et Unión de Productores de Cine y Televisión* [1993] ECR I-2239.
1821. Joined Cases 286/82 and 26/83 *Luisi and Carbone* [1984] ECR 377.
1822. Case C-154/89 *Commission v France* [1991] ECR I-659.
1823. Case C-243/01 *Gambelli* [2003] ECR I-13031.
1824. Case 155/73 *Sacchi* [1974] ECR 409, Joined Cases 34–36/95 *De Agostini and TV-Shop* [1997] ECR I-3843.
1825. [2002] ECR I-6279.

Held:

The ECJ held that Mrs Carpenter could rely on Article 49 EC [Article 56 TFEU], read in the light of the fundamental right to respect for family life, to remain in the UK.

Comment:

The UK Government and the European Commission argued that the situation of Mrs Carpenter must be classified as an internal situation within the meaning of the ECJ's judgment in Joined Cases 35/82 and 36/82 *Morson and Jhanjan*.[1826] Therefore her right to reside in the UK, if it existed, depended exclusively on United Kingdom law. They submitted that since Mr Carpenter had provided services from his home Member State, his non-national spouse could not derive a right of entry or residence in the UK from EU law.

The ECJ approached the issue in a different manner. The Court examined Directive 73/148/EEC of 21 May 1973 on the abolition of restrictions on movement and residence within the Community for nationals of Member States with regard to establishment and the provision of services[1827] in order to decide whether or not it could be applied to the circumstances of the above case.

The ECJ concluded that the Directive granted rights of entry and residence to non-national spouses of EU nationals in the situation where EU nationals, accompanied by their spouses, had left their Member State of origin and moved to another Member State in order to establish themselves there, or to provide or to receive services in that Member State. However, the Directive did not govern the right of residence of members of the family of a provider of services in his/her Member State of origin. Thus the ECJ discovered that there was a gap in the Directive, as it did not regulate a situation such as that in the main proceedings. In order to fill the gap the ECJ relied on the general principles of EU law, in particular the right to family life. The Court concluded that the separation of Mr and Mrs Carpenter would be detrimental to their family life and would constitute an obstacle to the provision of services by Mr Carpenter.

Although the ECJ recognised that a Member State may rely on reasons of public interest to justify national measures likely to hinder the exercise of the freedom to provide services, it pointed out that such measures must be compatible with the fundamental rights protected in EU law. The ECJ referred to Article 8(1) of the ECHR and its interpretation by the ECtHR. The Court noted that although Article 8(1) of the ECHR does not confer on an alien the right to enter and reside in a particular country, the removal of such a person from a country where his/her close family lives may, in some circumstances, amount to an infringement of the right to respect for family life. In this context the decision of the British authorities to deport Mrs Carpenter constituted such an unjustified interference as it was disproportionate to the objective pursued by the UK, taking into account that the marriage of Mr and Mrs Carpenter had been genuine, that since 1996 the spouses had led a true family life and that Mrs Carpenter's conduct since her arrival in the UK in September 1994 had not given any indication that she might in the future constitute a danger to public order or public safety.

1826. [1982] ECR 3723.
1827. [1973] OJ 1973 L172/14.

24.6.1 Freedom to supply services

Article 58 TFEU provides that, without prejudice to the provisions on establishment, persons providing a service may, in order to do so, temporarily pursue their activity in the Member State where the service is provided under the same conditions as are imposed by the Member State on its own nationals.

However, national legislation is normally applicable to providers of services established in the national territory and not to providers of services established in another Member State. It would be unfair to providers of services established in another Member State to be treated in the same manner as providers of services established in the Member State where the service is to be provided. This is because providers have already complied with many regulatory rules in their home Member State. There are three key principles that ensure the proper application of the Treaties in respect of the free movement of services.

24.6.1.1 The principle of non discrimination

EU law prohibits all discrimination based on nationality or on the residence of a provider of services unless otherwise provided in the Treaties. All discrimination whether direct or indirect[1828] on the ground of nationality is prohibited.

A priori a requirement of residence is also prohibited, taking into account that such a requirement would deprive the provisions guaranteeing the freedom to provide services of all practical effectiveness.[1829] However, the prohibition of requirements relating to residence is less absolute than that relating to nationality. Theoretically, a residence requirement can be justified if it is essential to the attainment of a legitimate objective (*Van Binsbergen*) although so far the ECJ has never regarded it as objectively justified.[1830]

24.6.1.2 The prohibition of indistinctly applicable measures which are liable to prohibit or otherwise impede the activities of a provider of services

In Case C-76/90 *Säger*,[1831] the ECJ held that restrictions on the free movement of services, even those indistinctly applicable, are in breach of EU law if they are of such a nature as to prohibit or render more difficult the exercise of activities of a provider of services in a host Member State as compared to a person established in that Member State. This means that for a provider of services in a host Member State it should not be more difficult to reach potential customers than for a person established in that Member State and providing similar services.

Restrictions imposed by a Member State in a situation where an enterprise is established in one Member State and provides services to other Member States are included. In Case C-384/93

1828. Case C-360/89 *Commission v Italy* [1992] ECR I-3401.

1829. Case 205/84 *Commission v Germany* [1986] ECR 3755.

1830. Case 205/84 *Commission v Germany* [1986] ECR 3755. However in Case C-300/90 *Commission v Belgium* [1992] ECR I-305 and Case C-204/90 *Bachman* [1992] ECR I-249 the ECJ accepted that some advantages could be given only to companies established in a Member State.

1831. [1991] ECR I-4221; as confirmed in subsequent cases: Case C-272/94 *Guiot* [1996] ECR I-1905; Case C-3/95 *Reisebüro Broede v Sandker* [1996] ECR I-6511; Case C-222/95 *Parodi v Banque H. Albert de Bary* [1997] ECR I-3899.

Alpine Investment,[1832] a Dutch prohibition on "cold calling" by providers of financial services established in The Netherlands was considered as an obstacle to the free movement of services. In Case C-39/04 *Laboratoires Fournier*,[1833] the ECJ condemned French tax legislation under which undertakings established in France were refused the benefit of a tax credit for medical research if the research was carried out in another Member State.

Obstacles take various forms, for example, the requirement of authorisations, an obligation to register on a trade register in a host Member State,[1834] an obligation to have an establishment in the territory of a host Member State,[1835] more favourable rules on taxation in respect of providers of services established in a host Member State than for providers of services not established in a host Member State, or requirements of a host Member State relating to social protection of temporarily deployed workers for the purpose of providing services in a host Member State.[1836]

24.6.1.3   The principal of mutual recognition

The concept of mutual recognition requires a host Member State to take into consideration the rules of a home Member State of providers of services in order to determine whether the public interest which a host Member State wants to protect is not already protected by rules applying to the service providers in a Member State where they are established.[1837]

24.6.1.4   Justification for national restrictions

Any restriction imposed by national law which is liable to prohibit, impede or render less advantageous the activities of a provider of services who is established in another Member State may only be justified if the following conditions are met:

- There is no harmonising EU legislation in the area concerned;

- Any national restricting measures are adopted in the general interest;

- The measures apply indistinctly, thus they do not discriminate against providers who are established in other Member States but provide services in a host Member State;

- The national restricting measures are objectively necessary, proportionate and respect the principle of mutual recognition, which (in the context of the provision of services) means that a host Member State must take into consideration whether the interest in question is not safeguarded by the rules to which providers of such a service are subject in the Member State of their establishment.

As with the rule of reason laid down in the *Cassis de Dijon* case in relation to free movement of goods there is no exhaustive list of imperative requirements in the general interest. The case law of

---

1832. [1995] ECR I-1141. However, restrictions other than those relating to access to the market or to modalities of the exercise of activities are outside the scope of Article 49 EC.
1833. [2005] ECR I-2057.
1834. Case C-58/98 *Corsten* [2000] ECR I-7919; Case C-215/01 *Schnitzer* [2003] ECR I-14847.
1835. Case C-279/00 *Commission v Italy* [2002] ECR I-1425.
1836. Cases C-369/96 and C-376/96 *Arblade* [1999] ECR I-8453.
1837. Case 279/80 *Webb* [1981] ECR 3305.

the ECJ indicates that the following imperative requirements in the general interest have been accepted:

- Protection of the reputation of national markets;[1838]

- The requirements of the rules of professional conduct and the good administration of justice;[1839]

- The protection of: consumers,[1840] persons proposing for life assurance policies,[1841] workers,[1842] receivers of certain services,[1843] holders of intellectual property rights,[1844] the environment,[1845] a particular language or culture,[1846] and so on.

- The requirements of fundamental values laid down in a national constitution.[1847]

24.6.1.5   Posting of workers temporarily to another Member State in the framework of the provision of services

Matters relating to the posting of workers temporarily to another Member State, whether or not they are EU citizens, have been harmonised at the EU level. Directive 96/71/EC of 16 December 1996 concerning the Posting of Workers in the Framework of the Provision of Services removes many uncertainties in this area while ensuring that posted workers are not exploited. The Directive defines the working conditions applicable to posted workers.[1848]

24.6.2   Freedom to receive services

In Joined Cases 286/82 and 26/83 *Luisi and Carbone v Ministero del Tesoro*,[1849] the ECJ held that the freedom to provide services includes the freedom for the recipient of the services to go to another Member State in order to receive a service there without being obstructed by restrictions. In such a situation a national of a Member State should be treated in the same manner as nationals of the host Member State. This was established by the ECJ in Case 186/87 *Cowan v Trésor Public*.[1850]

1838.   Case C-384/93 *Alpine Investments* [1995] ECR I-1141.

1839.   Case 33/74 *Van Binsbergen* [1974] ECR 1299; Case C-294/89 *Commission v France* [1991] ECR I-3591.

1840.   Case 220/83 *France v Commission* [1986] ECR 3663; tourists Case C-180/89 *Commission v Italy* [1991] ECR I-709; gamblers Case C-275/92 *Schindler* [1994] ECR I-1039; customers of a bank Case C-222/95 *Sci Parodi v Bangue Albert de Bary* [1997] ECR I-3899.

1841.   Case 205/84 *Commission v Germany* [1986] ECR 3755.

1842.   Case 279/80 *Webb* [1981] ECR 3305.

1843.   Cases 110 and 111/78 *Van Wesemael* [1979] ECR 35.

1844.   Case 62/79 *Coditel v Ciné Vog Films* [1980] ECR 881; Case 262/81 *Coditel II* [1982] ECR 3381.

1845.   Case C-379/92 *Matteo Peralta* [1994] ECR I-3453.

1846.   Case C-17/92 *Federación de Distributares Cinematográficas* [1993] ECR I-2239; Case C-473/93 *Commission v Luxembourg* [1996] ECR I-3207.

1847.   Case C-36/02 *Omega* [2004] ECR I-9609.

1848.   Case C-164/99 *Portugaia Construções* [2002] ECR I-787; Case C-341/02 *Commission v Germany* [2005] ECR I-2733; Case C-244/04 *Commission v Germany* [2006] ECR 885; Case C-168/04 *Commission v Austria* [2006] ECR I-9041. Before the entry into force of the Directive the leading cases on the matter were Joined Cases C-369/96 and C-376/96 *Arblade* [1999] ECR I-8453.

1849.   [1984] ECR 377.

1850.   [1989] ECR 195.

THE FACTS WERE:

A British national, Ian Cowan, was violently assaulted outside a Metro station in Paris. The perpetrators of the offence were never apprehended. Mr Cowan applied to the Commission d'Indemnisation des Victimes d'Infraction, the French equivalent of the UK Criminal Injuries Compensation Board, for compensation for his injuries. The French Code of Criminal Procedure allows compensation to be paid to victims of assaults if physical injury has been sustained and compensation cannot be sought from another source. However, the same Code of Criminal Procedure restricted the payment of compensation to French nationals and holders of French residence permits. On these grounds Mr Cowan's application for compensation was refused by the French Treasury. Mr Cowan challenged this decision, relying on Article 12 EC [Article 18 TFEU].

Held:

The ECJ held that since the right to receive services was embodied in the EC Treaty, it was subject to the prohibition of discrimination on the grounds of nationality as prescribed by Article 12 EC [Article 18 TFEU]. Laws and regulations which prevent the exercise of this right were declared to be incompatible with Community law and, in the circumstances of this case, the requirement of French nationality or of a French residence permit in order to claim compensation for criminal injuries constituted unjustifiable discrimination. The ECJ held that tourists, among others, must be regarded as recipients of services.

24.6.2.1   Publicly funded service

In the context of the freedom to receive services the most controversial matter is whether a national of another Member State is entitled to be treated in a host Member State, in respect of such services as education and health, in the same way as nationals of that Member State, given that these are not commercial activities but public services (the right to study finance for workers is examined in Chapter 23.9).

24.6.2.1.1 Education

The content of teaching curricula and the organisation of a Member State's educational system are within the exclusive competence of each Member State. However, as stated by the ECJ, this exclusive competence must be exercised in compliance with EU law, in particular with the freedom of movement of citizens of the EU.[1851] On this ground the ECJ has gradually established a right to education for EU citizens, although only in some circumstances are they entitled to financial assistance for studies in a host Member State, either to be granted by a host Member State or a home Member State.

1851.   Case C-308/89 *di Leo* [1990] ECR I-4185; Case C-337/97 *Meeusen* [1999] ECR I-3289; Case C-147/03 *Commission v Austria* [2005] ECR I-5969; and Case C-76/05 *Schwarz and Gootjes-Schwarz* [2007] ECR I-6849.

*24.6.2.1.1.1   Access to education and entitlement to financial assistance from a host
              Member State*

The matter of education was considered by the ECJ in Case 293/83 *Gravier v City of Liège*.[1852]

THE FACTS WERE:

*Miss Gravier, a French national, was accepted by the Liège Académie des Beaux-Arts in
Belgium for a four-year course in the art of strip cartoons. She was considered as a foreign
student and charged a special fee, known as a "minerval", which Belgian nationals, irrespective of their place of residence, and EU nationals and their families working in Belgium, were
not required to pay. She challenged the fee as discriminatory. She argued that the minerval
constituted an obstacle to her freedom to receive services and that, as the ECJ recognised in
Case 152/82 Forcheri,[1853] vocational education was within the scope of the EC Treaty.*

Held:

The ECJ decided in favour of Miss Gravier. The ECJ held that Article 12 EC [Article 18 TFEU]
prohibited any discrimination based on nationality and applied to all areas covered by the EC
Treaty. The minerval was discriminatory and was therefore in breach of that Article.

Comment:

This decision raised many controversies in Member States. One of them was the definition of
vocational training, which the ECJ defined very broadly in *Gravier* as including all forms of
teaching that prepares for and leads directly to a particular profession, trade or employment.
Furthermore, contrary to the Opinion of Advocate General Sir Gordon Slynn in this case, the
ECJ refused to discuss the organisation and financing of such courses. Member States which
financed university courses from public funds (in Belgium the minerval covered only 50 per
cent of the cost of the course, the remaining 50 per cent coming from public funds) were
deeply concerned.

In Case 24/86 *Blaizot*,[1854] the ECJ clarified the definition of vocational training. In this case
Blaizot, following the decision of the ECJ in *Gravier*, sought reimbursement of the minerval
charged for his university course in veterinary science. The ECJ held that university education
constituted vocational training "not only where the final exam directly provides the required
qualification but also insofar as the studies provide specific training (i.e. where the student needs
the knowledge so acquired for the pursuit of his trade or profession), even if no legislative or
administrative provisions make the acquisition of such knowledge a prerequisite".

Therefore all courses other than those which are intended to improve the general knowledge of
students rather than prepare them for an occupation are considered as vocational courses.

The establishment of the concept of EU citizenship and its interpretation by the ECJ brought
a new perspective regarding, on the one hand, the entitlement of EU citizens/students to

---

1852.   [1985] ECR 593.
1853.   [1983] ECR 2323.
1854.   [1988] ECR 379.

non-contributory social benefits, and on the other hand, the entitlement to general measures of support such as study grants and loans. In effect, the ECJ has used the citizenship provisions to make some inroads into the principle that citizens exercising free movement must be economically independent.

The first topic was examined by the ECJ in Case C-184/99 *Rudy Grzelczyk*.[1855]

THE FACTS WERE:

Mr Grzelczyk, a French national, studied in Belgium. During the first three years of his study in Belgium he supported himself by working, but in his final year of study he applied to the Belgian authorities for payment of the minimex. He was granted the allowance but later denied it on the basis that he was not a Belgian national. This was a clear breach of Article 12 EC [Article 18 TFEU] prohibiting any discrimination based on nationality. The national court decided that he was not a worker and thus not entitled to the minimex under Article 7(2) of Regulation 1612/68. In addition it was clear from the previous judgment of the ECJ in Brown that students who worked for the purpose of their studies were not entitled to any non-contributory benefits.

Held:

The ECJ held that Mr Grzelczyk was entitled to the minimex.

Comment:

The ECJ examined the situation of Mr Grzelczyk in light of the concept of EU citizenship under Articles 17 and 18 EC [Articles 20 and 21 TFEU] and under Directive 93/96 on the right of residence for students.

The Court noted that whilst Article 1 of Directive 93/96 required students to have sufficient resources to avoid becoming a burden on the social security system of a host Member State, the Directive did not contain any provisions precluding students from receiving social security benefits. The ECJ stated that Articles 17 and 18 EC [Articles 20 and 21 TFEU] read in conjunction with Article 12 EC [Article 18 TFEU] precluded Belgium from requiring EU nationals from other Member States to be workers before they could claim the minimex when no such condition was applied to Belgian nationals. Further the ECJ interpreted the preamble to Directive 93/96 as meaning that a person to whom it applied should not become an "unreasonable" burden. Mr Grzelczyk, appeared not to be in this category. Accordingly, the ECJ decided that Mr Grzelczyk, a French student in Belgium, was entitled to a non-contributory minimum subsistence allowance in Belgium. This judgment specified the entitlement of students to financial assistance. The Court ruled that while maintenance loans and grants were outside the scope of the EC Treaty (but see the case of *Bidar* below), non-contributory social benefits were within its scope. It flows from this judgment that the principle of non-discrimination applies to non-contributory social benefits such as income support, housing benefit, child support, and other social benefits that are available to national students.

1855. [2001] ECR I-6193.

The second topic was examined by the ECJ in Case C-209/03 *Bidar*.[1856]

THE FACTS WERE:

In 1998 Mr Bidar, a French national, moved with his mother to the UK where she was to undergo medical treatment. Subsequently she died, after which Mr Bidar lived in the UK with his grandmother as her dependant and completed his last three years of secondary education without ever having recourse to social assistance. In September 2001 he enrolled at University College London and applied to the relevant English authority for financial assistance. He was granted assistance with tuition fees but refused a maintenance loan on the ground that he was not "settled" in the UK.

Under English legislation a person is considered as being "settled" in the UK if he/she has been resident in the UK for the three years prior to commencing their course, but it is impossible to become "settled" if one resides in the UK solely to study.

Mr Bidar challenged the decision before the English High Court on the basis that the requirement to be "settled" constituted discrimination based on nationality in breach of the EC Treaty. The High court referred the matter to the ECJ.

Held:

The ECJ held that Mr Bidar, having been a lawful resident in the UK during his secondary studies, had established a genuine link with the society of his host Member State and was, consequently, entitled to obtain study finance in the UK.

Comment:

The ECJ's starting point was that a citizen of the EU lawfully resident in another Member State could rely on the prohibition of discrimination on grounds of nationality in all situations within the scope of the EC Treaty. The ECJ held that the situation of Mr Bidar was within the scope of the Treaty as a result of developments in Community law. In this respect the ECJ held that since the judgments in Case 39/86 *Lair v Universität Hannover*[1857] and Case 197/86 *Brown v Secretary of State for Scotland*[1858] the EU had introduced the concept of EU citizenship and had made amendments to the EC Treaty consisting of including education and vocational training within its scope.

However, the ECJ then had to consider Article 3 of Directive 93/96 which excludes any right to receipt of maintenance grants by students covered by its provisions and therefore excludes students like Mr Bidar from receiving a maintenance loan. The ECJ solved this problem by stating that Article 3 of Directive 93/96 did not preclude students like Mr Bidar, who are lawfully resident in a Member State in order to pursue their studies, from relying on the principle of non-discrimination enshrined in Article 12 EC [Article 18 TFEU]. However, the application of this principle is limited given that the Member States remain competent to determine the conditions of granting assistance to cover students' maintenance costs. These

---

1856.   [2005] ECR I-2119.
1857.   [1988] ECR 3161.
1858.   [1988] ECR 3205.

conditions, however, must be based on objective criteria independent of nationality and proportionate to the objectives pursued by national legislation. In respect of the English legislation the ECJ found that it was indirectly discriminatory because it was placing nationals of other Member States at a disadvantage as compared to UK nationals. Indeed, the English legislation precluded any possibility of a national of another Member State obtaining settled status as a student in these circumstances. The justifications provided by the UK Government were accepted by the ECJ. A Member State is allowed to ensure that the grant of assistance to cover the maintenance costs of students from other Member States does not become an unreasonable burden which could have consequences for the overall level of assistance which may be granted by that Member State. Thus, it is legitimate for a Member State to grant assistance to cover maintenance costs only to students who have demonstrated a certain degree of integration into the society of that Member State. Previously in Case C-138/02 *Collins*[1859] the ECJ accepted that a certain length of residence in the host Member State can be recognised as an appropriate factor in establishing the degree of integration between the student and the host Member State. In the case of Mr Bidar his lawful residence in the UK for a substantial part of his secondary studies showed that he had established a genuine link with the society of the host Member State. Consequently, the British legislation precluding him from obtaining the status of a settled person as a student was incompatible with EU law.

It is submitted that the judgment of the ECJ in *Bidar*, commendable as a matter of principle, has important implications for all Member States:

- First, it leaves it to national courts to decide whether or not an EU migrant student has established a genuine and sufficient link with a host Member State allowing him/her to claim maintenance costs for his/her studies in that Member State. In making this decision Case C-158/07 *Jacqueline Förster v Hoofddirectie van de Informatie Beheer Groep*[1860] is of assistance. In that case the ECJ found that the requirement of five years' uninterrupted residence is appropriate for the purpose of finding that an applicant has indeed achieved the necessary level of integration into the society of a host Member State to be entitled to a maintenance grant. However, it is submitted that *Förster* is an example, not a rule, as to the assessment of whether a person has established a sufficient level of integration with a host Member State. It should not exclude taking into consideration the particular circumstances of each case.

- Second, important financial consequences flow from the judgment in *Bidar* for all Member States. They are required to grant assistance to students from other Member States who have established the existence of a sufficient degree of integration into the society of the host Member State.

24.6.2.1.1.2 Entitlement to financial assistance from a home Member State
A student who wishes to pursue his/her education in a host Member State may be deterred from so doing by rules relating to financial assistance imposed by a home Member State. This is

---

1859. [2004] ECR I-2703.
1860. [2008] ECR I-8507.

exemplified by Joined Cases C-11/06 *Rhiannon Morgan v Bezirksregierung Köln* and Case C-12/06 *Iris Bucher v Landrat des Kreises Düren*.[1861]

THE FACTS WERE:

In Case C-11/06 Ms Morgan, a German national, moved to the UK where she worked for one year as an au pair. Subsequently, she commenced studies in applied genetics at the University of Bristol. When she applied to the relevant German authorities for a study grant, her application was refused on the ground that she had failed to satisfy the conditions set out under German law relating to awards of education and training grants for studies outside Germany, which required that the course of study outside Germany should constitute a continuation of education or training pursued for at least one year in a German establishment.

In Case C-12/06 Ms Bucher, a German national, moved from Bonn to Düren, a German town on The Netherlands border, in order to take a course of study in ergotherapy in The Netherlands town of Heerlen (which is located very close to the German border). When she applied to the relevant German authorities for a study grant, her application was refused on the ground that she was not "permanently" resident near a border as required by the German law.

Both claimants submitted that the courses being taken in host Member States were not offered in Germany. Both challenged the decisions of the relevant German authorities. The referring courts asked the ECJ to rule on the compatibility of the German legislation with Articles 17 and 18 EC [Articles 20 and 21 TFEU].

Held:

The ECJ held that the German legislation was in breach of Articles 17 and 18 EC [Articles 20 and 21 TFEU] as it constituted an unjustified restriction on the free movement of EU citizens.

Comment:

The Court stated that the challenged legislation was disproportionate because, first, it forced the claimants to choose between abandoning the education they had planned to receive in a host Member State and pursuing it but losing their entitlement to an education grant. Second, the requirement that a student must first study for at least one year in a home Member State was too general and exclusive because: "It unduly favours an element which is not necessarily representative of the degree of integration into the society of that Member State at the time the application for assistance is made."

24.6.2.1.2 Medical services

The ECJ has gradually developed a new right for all EU citizens and lawful residents of the EU, insured under national sickness insurance schemes, which is the right to obtain effective and speedy medical treatment from their own Member State, or if this is not available, from any other Member State.

1861. [2007] ECR I-9161.

The ECJ has achieved this by, on the one hand, finding a "cross-border element" when persons who are insured under a national health care system, but are unable to obtain adequate medical treatment in their home Member State, have exercised their right under Article 56 TFEU or under Article 22 of Regulation 1408/71 and have sought such treatment in another Member State and, on the other hand, applying the rules of the internal market, in particular Articles 56 and 57 TFEU, to health care services covered by national health insurance schemes.

In the development of the new right to effective and speedy medical treatment available to all insured persons living within the EU, three stages can be identified:

In the first stage, the ECJ applied the internal market rules to health care services. This resulted in the inclusion of such services, even if they are provided in the context of social security schemes, within the scope of application of Articles 49 and 50 EC [Articles 56 and 57 TFEU].[1862]

In the second stage, the ECJ examined the system of prior authorisation set out in Article 22 of Regulation 1408/71, which authorisation is required when a national of one Member State seeks medical treatment covered by a home Member State's national health care scheme in another Member State.[1863]

The ECJ found that this system whereby prior authorisation is a prerequisite of receipt in one Member State of medical treatment covered by a national health care scheme in another Member State constitutes an obstacle to freedom to provide services. However, the ECJ acknowledged the existence of at least three overriding considerations which could justify barriers to freedom to provide services in the sphere of hospital treatment:

■ A national social security system's financial balance;

■ The maintenance in a Member State of balanced medical and hospital services open to all; and

■ The maintenance of treatment capacity or medical competence on national territory essential for the public health, and even the survival, of the population.

When the ECJ assessed whether the prior authorisation system exceeded what was objectively necessary for the purpose for which it was set up and whether the same result could be achieved by less restrictive rules,[1864] the Court found:

■ In respect of substantial requirements, the system of prior authorisation must be based on objective, non-discriminatory criteria which must be known in advance and must be applied in such a manner as to prevent the national authorities from taking arbitrary decisions;

■ As to procedural requirements, that the procedure for authorisation must be easily accessible and capable of ensuring that a request for authorisation will be dealt with objectively and impartially within a reasonable time and any refusal must be capable of being challenged in judicial or quasi-judicial proceedings.

The ECJ also elucidated a number of issues relating to the granting of an authorisation.

1862. Case C-158/96 *Kohll* [1998] ECR I-1931.

1863. Case C-157/99 *B.S.M. Geraets-Smits v Stichting Ziekenfonds VGZ and H.T.M. Peerbooms v Stichting CZ Groep Zorgverzekeringen* [2001] ECR I-5473.

1864. Case 205/84 *Commission v Germany* [1986] ECR 3755; Case C-180/89 *Commission v Italy* [1991] ECR I-709; Case C-106/91 *Ramrath* [1992] ECR I-3351.

■ First, concerning the requirement that the proposed treatment be "normal in the professional circles concerned". In this respect the ECJ stated that in order to determine what is considered as normal, reference should be made to the state of international medical science and the medical standards generally accepted at international level. Otherwise, forms of treatment habitually carried out on national territory and scientific views prevailing in national medical circles would always be preferred in practice, which would make it extremely difficult to obtain a grant of prior authorisation. The ECJ stated that where treatment is sufficiently tried and tested by international medical science, it should be regarded as "normal".

■ Second, concerning the requirement of the necessity of the proposed treatment. The ECJ stated that the authorisation to receive treatment in another Member State may be refused only if the same or equally effective treatment can be obtained without undue delay from an establishment in a home Member State.

■ Third, the meaning of "undue delay". This was explained by the ECJ in the case of *Muller-Fauré*.[1865] In a situation where there is a waiting time for medical treatment, each case should be assessed individually in order to decide whether or not the treatment has been offered without undue delay. Many factors should be taken into consideration when national authorities are dealing with a request for authorisation. Examples are: the patient's medical condition, medical history and, where appropriate, the degree of pain or the nature of the patient's disability and whether this might make it impossible or extremely difficult for the patient to carry out a professional activity.

In Case C-372/04 *Yvonne Watts*,[1866] the ECJ refined its position on the waiting time. This must not exceed the period which is medically acceptable in the light of an objective medical assessment of the clinical needs and the medical condition of the patient. That is, the assessment must be strictly based on medical considerations without taking account of the economic and financial implications for the relevant national health care system. Further, the setting of waiting times should be done flexibly and dynamically, so that if the state of health of the patient deteriorates after the first request for authorisation, the initially fixed waiting time can and should be reconsidered. The above case confirms that a Member State cannot refuse authorisation on either of the following grounds:

(i) Simply that the patient is on a waiting list. The method of prioritising on waiting lists must be based on the medical condition of the patient. Other considerations, such as the effects on the position of other patients on the waiting lists or the reallocation of resources within the national health care system, are irrelevant. The UK system, based on the criterion that treatment be provided within NHS Plan targets and which did not take the individual needs of patients sufficiently into account, was in breach of Article 49 EC [Article 56 TFEU].

(ii) On purely budgetary or economic considerations such as the cost involved in obtaining treatment from another Member State in comparison with the cost of its local equivalent, or that hospital treatment is free of charge and thus there is no mechanism

---

1865. Case C-385/99 *V.G. Muller-Fauré v Onderlinge Waarborgmaatschappij OZ Zorgverzekeringen UA and E. E. M van Riet v Onderlinge Waarborgmaatschappij ZOA* [2003] ECR I-4509.
1866. [2006] ECR I-4325.

for reimbursement of costs incurred abroad. In the latter situation, a Member State is required to make available specific funds to reimburse the cost of treatment to be provided in another Member State.

◾ Fourth, the necessity for the authorising Member State to be responsible for the costs incurred as a result of not only the initial referral to another Member State but also of a referral by the authorities of that Member State to another State, including a non-Member State. This was decided in Case C-145/03 *Heirs of Annette Keller*.[1867]

THE FACTS WERE:

Mrs Keller, a German national residing in Spain, obtained an authorisation from Spanish authorities for treatment in Germany, but the German doctors decided that she would receive the most appropriate treatment in Switzerland, to where she subsequently went.

Held:

The ECJ stated that a Member State where the patient is insured is bound by a finding of a need for immediate treatment to be provided in a third country made by doctors of a Member State in which the treatment had been authorised to be carried out. Accordingly, the Spanish authorities were required to pay for treatment received in Switzerland.

◾ Fifth, national legislation which excludes the reimbursement of the costs of hospital treatment in a host Member State, except in the case of treatment provided to children under 14 years of age, is in breach of Article 56 TFEU. This was decided in Case C-444/05 *Aikaterini Stamatelaki v NPDD Organismos Asfaliseos Eleftheron Epangelmation (OAEE)*.[1868] The ECJ held that the absolute nature of the prohibition (with exception of children under 14 years of age) was not appropriate to achieve the objectives of Greek legislation, which consisted of maintaining treatment capacity and medical competence on national territory and of safeguarding the financial balance of the national social security system. The Court stated that those objectives could be achieved by less restrictive means, such as a prior authorisation system or, if appropriate, the determination of scales for reimbursement of the costs of treatment.

◾ Sixth, the reimbursement of costs depends on whether a patient receives treatment in another Member State under Article 22 of Regulation No 1408/71 or under Article 56 TFEU.

    A.   Treatment provided under Article 22 of Regulation No 1408/71.

        This relates to a situation where a patient was granted authorisation under the above provision or received a refusal to authorise which was subsequently found to be unjustified. The ECJ held that the reimbursement should be calculated according to the legislation of the Member State providing the treatment. The home

---

1867. [2005] ECR I-2529.
1868. [2007] ECR I-3185.

Member State must reimburse the cost of treatment. The facts that hospital treatment in that Member State is free of charge, for example, in the UK, and that there are no tariffs for reimbursement, are irrelevant.

B.   Treatment provided under Article 56 TFEU.

In such a case the reimbursement is calculated according to the legislation of the home Member State of the patient.

As to reimbursement of accommodation and subsistence costs (outside a medical institution), travel and other related expenses, these matters are outside the scope of Regulation 1408/71, which applies only to costs linked to the health care received in a host Member State. These matters are governed by national law of the home Member State of the patient. Consequently, where national law provides for the reimbursement of these additional expenses in respect of medical treatment provided on national territory, it follows from Article 56 TFEU that reimbursement should be available under the same limits and conditions for treatment received in another Member State.[1869]

In the third stage, the ECJ removed the requirement for prior authorisation in respect of all treatment provided outside a hospital environment in a host Member State.[1870]

The right to obtain effective, speedy and free-of-charge medical treatment has many important implications for the national health and insurance systems in EU countries, for the development of the free movement of medical services in the EU and, the most important, for patients living in Member States with the worst performing national health systems in the EU. Good health is the most treasured possession of any being. By providing every EU citizen and every insured lawful resident of the EU with the right to access the best national health care service available in the EU in circumstances where his/her own national health care system has failed, the ECJ has given him/her the most valuable service available anywhere.

AIDE-MÉMOIRE

THE RIGHT OF ESTABLISHMENT AND THE RIGHT TO SUPPLY AND RECEIVE SERVICES

1. Stages in the abolition of restrictions on both freedoms:

- First: under the 1961 General Programmes directives aimed at harmonising rules in sectors of economy or in respect of professions were adopted;

- Second: the case law of the ECJ, starting with judgments in Case 2/74 *Reyners* (Article 43 EC – Article 49 TFEU) and Case 33/74 *Van Binsbergen* (Article 49 EC – Article 56 TFEU) expanded and clarified the content of both freedoms;

- Third: the Lisbon European Council (March 2000) adopted a new strategy aimed at making the EU the most competitive and dynamic knowledge-driven economy in the world by 2010. A step in this direction was the adoption of Directive 2006/123/EC which

---

1869.   Case C-466/04 *Acereda Herrera* [2006] ECR I-5341.
1870.   Case C-385/99 *V.G. Muller-Fauré* [2003] ECR I-4509.

contributes to the creation of a genuine internal market by removing obstacles to both the freedom of establishment and the freedom to provide services.

2. Prohibition of discrimination and beyond

Direct discrimination is prohibited and can be justified only under derogations contained in the Treaties (Case 2/74 *Reyners* and Case 33/74 *Van Binsbergen*).

Indirect discrimination and all national measures liable to hinder or to make less attractive the exercise of the freedom of establishment (Case 55/94 *Gebhard*) and the freedom to provide and receive services (Case 33/74 *Van Binsbergen*) can be justified either under the derogations contained in the Treaties, or if four conditions are satisfied, as set out in the case law of the ECJ. These conditions require that national measures:

- must be applied in a non-discriminatory manner;

- must be justified by imperative requirements in the general interest;

- must be suitable for securing the attainment of the objective which they pursue;

- must not go beyond what is necessary in order to attain that objective.

3. The right of establishment

Legal persons

An undertaking is established in a host Member State "even if its presence is not in the form of a branch or agency but consists merely of an office managed by the enterprise's own staff or by a person who is independent but is authorised to act on a permanent basis for the enterprise" (Case 205/84 *Commission v Germany [Re Insurance Services]*).

Natural persons

The right involves a permanent and continuous presence in the host Member State which allows "an EU citizen to participate on a stable and continuous basis in the economic life of a Member State other than his own" (Case 55/94 *Gebhard*).

Recognition of diplomas and qualifications

This is regulated by Directive 2005/36/EC on the Recognition of Professional Qualifications and by previous secondary legislation.

Under the Directive the rules for recognition are as follows: a host Member State is required to carry out a comparative examination of diplomas:

- If there is no substantial difference between them a diploma awarded by another Member State must be recognised as equivalent;

- If there is a substantial difference between them, a host Member State must give applicants the opportunity to demonstrate that they have acquired the knowledge and skill of which evidence was lacking. However, they are entitled to choose between an adaptation period and an aptitude test, but when the profession requires knowledge of national law of a host Member State, applicants must take an aptitude test (Case C-149/05 *Harold Price*).

The Directive makes a distinction between regulated and unregulated professions. The first mentioned are within the scope of the Directive; the second mentioned are still subject to EU law (Case C-340/89 *Vlassopoulou*) but are outside the scope of the Directive (Case C-234/97 *Teresa Fernández De Bobadilla*).

Right of establishment for lawyers

This is regulated by Directive 98/5/EC, which constitutes a complete harmonisation of prior conditions for the exercise of the right of establishment for lawyers (Case C-506/04 *Wilson*).

4. The right to provide services

The provision of services involves temporary and occasional pursuit of economic activities in a host Member State (Case 55/94 *Gebhard*) but a service may be provided over a long period of time, even over several years (Case C-215/01 *Schnitzer*).

5. The right to receive services

The freedom to provide services includes the freedom for the recipient of the services to go to another Member State in order to receive a service there without being obstructed by restrictions (Joined Cases 286/82 and 26/83 *Luisi and Carbone*). Recipients of services should be treated in the same manner as nationals of the host Member State (Case 186/87 *Cowan*).

Publicly funded services

They are within the scope of the Treaties.

Education: (Case 293/83 *Gravier*; Case 24/86 *Blaizot*). On the basis of Article 21 TFEU, citizens of the EU may be entitled, depending on the circumstances, to:

- Claim non-contributory social benefits (Case C-184/99 *Grzelczyk*).

- Claim entitlement to finance studies in the form of grants and loans for studies (Case C-209/03 *Bidar*).

Medical services: Persons who are insured under a national health care system but are unable to obtain adequate medical treatment in their home Member State may exercise their right under Regulation 1408/71 or Article 56 TFEU and seek such treatment in another Member State at the expense of their national insurer (Case C-157/99 *B.S.M. Geraets-Smits*; C-372/04 *Yvonne Watts*).

RECOMMENDED READING

Books

Nascimbene, B., and Bergamini, E., *The Legal Profession in the European Union*, 2009, London: KLI

See recommended books on the internal market in Chapter 17.

Articles

Acierno, S., "The Carpenter Judgment: Fundamental Rights and the Limits of the Community Legal Order", (2003) 28 ELRev, p 398

Barnard, C., "Unravelling the Services Directive", (2008) 45 CMLRev, p 323

Jørgensen, S., "The Right to Cross-Border Education in the European Union", (2009) 46 CMLRev, p 1567

Rich, R. F. and Merrick, K. R., "Cross Border Health Care in the European Union: Challenges and Opportunities", (2006) 23 J. Contemp. Health L. & Pol'y, p 64

White, R., "Conflicting Competences: Free Movement Rules and Immigration Laws", (2004) 29 ELRev, p 385

25

EXCEPTIONS TO THE FREE MOVEMENT OF PERSONS

SUMMARY

1. There are two main Treaties-based exceptions to the free movement of persons. The first allows a host Member State to impose restriction on the access of EU migrant workers to "employment in the public service" (under Article 45(4) TFEU) and of self-employed persons to posts where it is necessary for the holder to "exercise official authority" (under Article 51 TFEU). The second applies to all persons exercising their right to free movement within the EU and is based on the grounds of public policy, public security and public health.
2. The ECJ has interpreted the first exception as meaning that only high profile posts connected with the vital interests of a Member State can be reserved to nationals of a host Member State, for example, that of a judge or other posts in the higher echelons of the civil service, or the police or the armed forces. It is submitted that the main difference between Article 45(4) TFEU and Article 51 TFEU is that under Article 51 TFEU a Member State is allowed to rely on the exception when holders of the post carry out activities connected with the exercise of official authority "occasionally" while under Article 45(4) TFEU holders of a post are required to exercise the official authority on a regular basis and the exercise of official authority must constitute a major part of their activities.

3. The second exception concerns derogations based on public policy, public security and public health. None are defined in EU law. All have been restrictively interpreted by the ECJ so that Member States' discretion, when denying an EU national the right to move freely and reside in a host Member State, can only be exercised within the limits allowed by EU law, in accordance with the requirements of the principle of proportionality. This restrictive approach in the case law was confirmed and clarified by the conditions set out in Directive 2004/38/EC of 29 April 2004 on the Right of Citizens of the Union and their Family Members to Move and Reside Freely within the Territory of the Member States. Most articles of the Directive are directly effective.

4. Derogations based on public policy and public security. The concepts of public security and public policy are interrelated and often public security is invoked as an alternative to public policy, for example, terrorist or other criminal activities pose a threat to both public security and public policy. The concept of public policy is vague and bearing in mind that a wide range of activities may be found by a Member State as jeopardising its public policy (such as organising demonstrations, or walking nude in public places, or being a member of a religious sect), it is the most controversial. For that reason Member States are not allowed to determine the scope of either derogation unilaterally. Directive 2004/38/EC and the case law of the ECJ set the following limitations on the use of public policy and public security derogations:

- Such measures must be based on the personal conduct of the individual concerned. It does not have to be illegal, but a Member State must provide evidence that it has taken repressive or other effective measures to combat such conduct in order to rely on the derogation. What constitutes personal conduct was clarified by the ECJ in Case 41/74 *Van Duyn* in which the Court held that past association with an organisation does not count as personal conduct, although present association does.

- Previous criminal convictions are not in themselves sufficient grounds for relying on derogations, but past conduct may constitute a present threat to public policy where there is evidence that the individual concerned has a propensity to act in the same way in the future as he/she did in the past. Whilst an individual deterrence may be acceptable, a general deterrence is not, that is, a Member State is not allowed to take measures against an individual for reasons of a general preventive nature when it is clear that the individual concerned would not commit further offences.

- Personal conduct of the individual concerned must represent a genuine, present and sufficiently serious threat affecting one of the fundamental interests of the host Member State in order to justify any measure adopted on the grounds of public policy or public security.

- Derogations cannot be relied upon to serve economic ends.

- Non-compliance with administrative formalities in respect of entry and residence never justify an expulsion from the territory of a host Member State.

5. Derogations based on public health. Article 29 of Directive 2004/38/EC provides that only diseases with epidemic potential and other infectious or contagious parasitic diseases, if they are the subject of protection provisions applying to nationals of the host Member State, may justify restrictions on entry and residence. However, health problems arising from the above-mentioned diseases after a person has resided in another Member State for three months cannot be used to justify expulsion.

6. Article 28 of Directive 2004/38/EC provides additional safeguards against expulsion from a host Member State for EU nationals who have resided in that Member State for a considerable length of time or are minors. Those who have obtained permanent residence in that Member State can only be deported on the grounds of serious requirements of public policy, while deportation of those who have resided in a Member State for more than 10 years or who are minors can only be justified on the grounds of imperative requirements of public policy.

7. Articles 31–33 of Directive 2004/38/EC set out important procedural rights for EU citizens who are refused the rights of entry and residence in a host Member State.

25.1   Introduction

The two exceptions to the fundamental principle of the Treaties guaranteeing the free movement of persons have been construed narrowly by the ECJ to ensure that the exceptions do not undermine the principle. Under Articles 45(4) and 51 TFEU a host Member State may reserve access to employment in the public service to its own nationals. This is the first exception. The second is based on the protection of public policy, public security and public health.

25.2   The concept of "employment in the public service" and "the exercise of official authority"

Article 45(4) TFEU provides that Article 45 TFEU "shall not apply to employment in the public service" and Article 51 TFEU states that provisions relating to the freedom of establishment "shall not apply, so far as any given Member State is concerned, to activities which in that State are connected, even occasionally, with the exercise of official authority". By virtue of Article 62 TFEU, which states that the provisions on the right to establishment (Articles 51 to 54 TFEU) apply to the matters covered by Chapter 3 on services (Articles 56–62 TFEU), Article 51 applies to providers of services.

Different terms used in Articles 45(4) and 51 TFEU led some Member States to interpret the derogation from the free movement of workers and that applicable to self-employed persons differently. The ECJ rejected this approach.[1871] It has interpreted both derogations restrictively and often referred to one of them when interpreting the other. In Case 149/79 *Commission v Belgium (No 1)*[1872] the ECJ held that employment in the public service within the meaning of Article 39(4) EC [Article 45(4) TFEU] concerned:

> "posts which involve direct or indirect participation in the exercise of powers conferred by public law and duties designed to safeguard the general interests of the State or other public authorities. Such posts in fact presume on the part of those occupying them the existence of a special relationship of allegiance to the State and reciprocity of rights and duties which form the foundation of the bond of nationality."

In the above case the ECJ made a distinction between tasks "belonging to the public service properly so called" and activities of "an economic and social nature which are typical of the

---

1871.   Case 152/73 *Sotgiu* [1974] ECR 153 at 156, and Cases 149/79 *Commission v Belgium (No.1) and (No. 2)* [1980] ECR 3881, [1982] ECR 1845.

1872.   Case 149/79 (No. 1). Ibid.

public service yet which by their nature still come under the sphere of application of the Treaty". Only the first are within the scope of the derogation. Three elements are necessary in order to invoke the exception embodied in Article 45(4) TFEU:

- The post concerned must require a special relationship of allegiance to the Member State on the part of the person occupying it, which the bond of nationality seeks to safeguard;

- The post involves the exercise of rights under powers conferred by public law;

- The holder of the post is entrusted with responsibility for the general interest of the Member State.

The above requirements are concurrent.

In respect of the exercise of powers conferred by public law the ECJ held in Case 2/74 *Reyners*[1873] that Article 45(1) EC [Article 51(1) TFEU] must be restricted to those activities which in themselves involve a direct and specific connection with the exercise of official authority. This refers to authority emanating from the sovereignty of the Member State and involves the exercise of powers granted by the Member State to require compliance, by coercion if necessary.[1874]

In Case C-283/99 *Commission v Italy*,[1875] the ECJ held that the concept of employment in the public service does not encompass employment by a private natural or legal person, whatever the duties of the employees. In this case Italy argued that private security guards employed by private companies were within the exception because they exercised their duties in the public interest, such duties consisting of preventing and restraining the commission of criminal offences, and they were required to swear before the Italian judicial authority to be loyal to the Italian Republic. The ECJ disagreed. However, in Case C-47/02 *Anker and Others v Germany*,[1876] the ECJ qualified the above judgment.

THE FACTS WERE:

Dutch nationals employed as seamen of private fishing vessels flying the German flag and engaged in small-scale deep-sea fishing, all holders of a Dutch diploma entitling them to captain the type of vessels on which they were serving, were denied permission to serve as masters on such vessels on the ground that the activity of a master in small-scale deep-sea fishing falls within the sphere of public service within the meaning of Article 39(4) EC [Article 45(4) TFEU]

Held:

The ECJ held that the activity of masters of a small-scale deep-sea fishing vessel did not come within the scope of Article 39(4) EC [Article 45(4) TFEU], given that the public functions

---

1873. [1974] ECR 631.
1874. The concept of "official authority" under Article 45 EC was defined by the Advocate General in his Advisory Opinion in Case 2/74 *Reyners* [1974] ECR 631 in the following terms: "Official authority is that which arises from the sovereignty of the State, for him who exercises it, it implies the power of enjoying the prerogatives outside the general law, privileges of official power and powers of coercion over citizens".
1875. [2001] ECR I-4363.
1876. [2003] ECR I-10447.

they exercise are sporadic and represent a very minor part of their activities (the maintenance of safety, the exercise of police powers particularly in the case of danger on board and the registration of births, marriages and deaths). The core of a master's duty consists of the command of the vessel and the management of its crew.

Comment:

The ECJ held that the fact that a person is employed by a private natural or legal person is not, as such, sufficient to exclude the application of Article 39(4) EC [Article 45(4) TFEU]. What is important is to establish whether a person acts as a representative of public authority in the service of the general interests of the Member State. In order to determine this, the ECJ examined powers which were conferred on holders of these posts by public law. According to the judgment in Case C-4/91 *Bleis*,[1877] the exercise of rights under powers conferred by public law must constitute the core of the activity. Thus, when a holder of the post occasionally exercises rights under powers conferred by public law, such a post is outside the scope of Article 39(4) EC [Article 45(4) TFEU].

The concept of "exercise of official authority" under Article 51 TFEU has been construed by reference to Article 45(4) TFEU. This is not surprising given that a person who exercises rights under powers conferred by public law for the purposes of safeguarding the general interests of the Member State acts, in fact, as a representative of public authority. However, Article 51 TFEU has its own peculiarity in that under Article 51 TFEU the activity in question must be directly and specifically connected with the exercise of official authority[1878] with the consequence that merely auxiliary and preparatory functions as against an entity which effectively exercises official authority by taking the final decision, are outside its scope of application.[1879] This is well illustrated in Case C-438/08 *Commission v Portugal*.[1880]

THE FACTS WERE:

Portugal argued that the activity of the technical inspection of vehicles resulting in either certifying that a vehicle passes a roadworthiness test, in which case a badge is affixed to the vehicle, or, conversely, refusing such certification, was directly linked to the exercise of public authority. The activity of vehicle inspection was organised in two stages. In the first stage technical inspections were carried out consisting of verifying whether the vehicles inspected complied with the relevant technical standards and drawing up a report of the inspection. The second stage related to the certification which resulted either in the taking of a decision to certify or a refusal to certify a vehicle's compliance with technical standards. In Portugal, both stages of the procedure, i.e. the technical inspection and the certification, were carried out by

1877. [1991] ECR I-5627.
1878. See Case 2/74 *Reyners* [1974] ECR 63; Case C-42/92 *Thijssen* [1993] ECR I-4047 and Case C-283/99 *Commission v Italy* [2001] ECR I-4363
1879. Case C-42/92 *Thijssen*, ibid; Case C-393/05 *Commission* v *Austria* [2007] ECR I-10195.
1880. Judgment of 22/10/09 (nyr).

private bodies. The procedure was subject to the control of the public authority but in the Portuguese system the decisions regarding certification were taken without any intervention by the public administrative authority. Portugal submitted that these decisions, because of the effects they had on the legal rights of the owner of the vehicle, were connected with the exercise of public power.

Held:

The ECJ held that neither the first stage of the activity consisting of technical inspections nor the second stage of the activity, consisting of certification, was connected with the exercise of public power.

Comment:

With regard to the first activity, technical inspections, by their nature, have no link with the exercise of powers by a public authority.[1881] The second activity, however, contained some elements of the prerogatives of public authority in so far as legal consequences are drawn from technical inspections. Notwithstanding this, the second activity could not be considered as being "connected directly and specifically with the exercise of official authority" within the meaning of Article 51 TFEU because the private body to which the certification function had been delegated by the State:

- had no decision-making powers as it essentially recorded the results of the roadworthiness test;

- lacked the decision-making independence inherent in the exercise of public authority powers as it acted under the direct control of a public authority;

- had no power of coercion as the right to impose penalties for failure to comply with the rules on vehicle inspection was exercised by the police and judicial authorities.

It is submitted that the main difference between Article 45(4) and Article 51 TFEU is that under Article 51 TFEU a Member State is allowed to rely on the exception when the holder of the post carries out activities connected with the exercise of official authority "even occasionally", an expression used in Article 51 TFEU, but not in Article 45(4) TFEU. This is not the case under Article 45(4) TFEU. In *Anker* the ECJ held that, regarding Article 39(4) EC [Article 45(4) TFEU]:

"It is . . . necessary that such rights are in fact exercised on a regular basis by those holders and do not represent a very minor part of their activities."[1882]

The concept of the safeguard of the general interest of the Member State is more difficult to define. In this respect the Commission Notice published in 1988[1883] is particularly helpful. The Notice reviewed certain sectors of employment which are for the most part considered to be "sufficiently remote from the specific activities of the public sphere as defined by the European

---

1881. Case C-3/88 *Commission v Italy* [1989] ECR 4035,

1882. C-47/02 [2003] ECR I-10447.

1883. [1988] OJ C72/02. See also Communication of the Commission on this matter in Com (2002) 694.

Court that they would only in rare cases be covered by the exception to Article [39(4) EC]". These are:

- Public health care services;

- Teaching in Member State educational establishments;

- Research for non-military purposes in public establishments;

- Employment in public bodies responsible for administering commercial services.

It emerges from the case law of the ECJ that Article 45(4) TFEU covers only high-level posts, the holders of which owe a special allegiance to the Member State based on the bond of nationality (for example, members of the armed forces, police, judiciary, and so on). The connection between Article 45(4) and Article 51 TFEU is that holders of these posts normally perform functions which are directly and specifically connected with the exercise of official authority. However, in some circumstances, persons other that those who hold high profile posts may perform, occasionally or on a permanent basis, tasks which are directly and specifically connected with the exercise of official authority.

In a number of cases[1884] the Member States have tried unsuccessfully to challenge the restrictive approach of the ECJ. In Case 307/84 *Commission v France*,[1885] the ECJ held that the post of a nurse in French public hospitals is not within the scope of Article 39(4) EC [Article 45(4) TFEU]. Similarly neither a researcher employed by the Italian National Council of Research[1886] nor a teacher in a secondary school,[1887] nor a trainee teacher during probationary service[1888] should be regarded as employed in the public sector within the meaning of Article 45(4) TFEU. Furthermore the ECJ has, in a number of cases, condemned some Member States for reserving employment in the following sectors to their nationals: distribution of gas and electricity, health, education, all modes of transport including municipal and regional transport, civil research, telecommunications and postal services, radio and television, opera and municipal orchestras.[1889]

25.3 Derogations justified on the grounds of public policy, public security and public health

The right to freedom of movement is subject to limitations based on the grounds of public policy, public security and public health. The derogation in respect of workers is expressly provided for in Article 45(3) TFEU and in respect of self-employed persons in Article 51(1) TFEU. The derogation also applies to members of their families who have acquired free movement rights under the Treaties.

1884. Case 225/85 *Commission v Italy* [1987] ECR 2625; Case 149/79 *Commission v Belgium (No.1) and (No.2)* [1980] ECR 3881, [1982] ECR 1845.

1885. [1986] ECR 1725.

1886. Case 225/85 *Commission v Italy* [1987] ECR 2625.

1887. Case C-4/91 *Bleis* [1991] ECR I-5627.

1888. Case 66/85 *Lawrie-Blum* [1986] ECR 2121.

1889. Case C-473/93 *Commission v Luxembourg* [1996] ECR I-3207; Case C-173/94 *Commission v Belgium* [1996] ECR I-3265; Case C-290/94 *Commission v Greece* [1996] ECR I-3285.

Council Directive 2004/38/EC of 29 April 2004 on the Right of Citizens of the Union and their Family Members to Move and Reside Freely within the Territory of the Member States[1890] regulates the application of the three derogations from the right to freedom of movement conferred on EU nationals by EU law.

No EU definition is provided in respect of these three derogations. The Directive permits a Member State some discretion in the application of these derogations, provided its exercise is within the limits of the Treaties. Furthermore, the Directive provides procedural safeguards for EU nationals from other Member States seeking to enforce their rights of entry and residence in a Member State.

25.3.1 Public policy and public security

The ECJ has developed the following principles in respect of public policy, public security and public health exceptions:

- All derogations from the free movement of persons must be interpreted strictly;[1891]

- All national measures must be proportional to the objective pursued by them;[1892]

- The concept of public policy, public security and public health cannot be determined unilaterally by Member States. Although a Member State is free to determine the requirements of public policy and public security in the light of its national needs, the ECJ has jurisdiction to ensure, from the perspective of EU law, that a Member State exercises its discretion within the limits of the Treaties;[1893]

- The majority of the provisions of the Directive are directly effective.[1894]

Under Article 27(3) of Directive 2004/38/EC, when deciding whether or not a person concerned represents a danger to public policy or public security, a host Member State may request the home Member State of the person concerned, or any other Member State, to provide information concerning any police records of the person concerned. Such a request shall not be a matter of routine. The Member State consulted shall give its reply within two months. A requesting Member State is obliged to give its decision within a very strict time limit: three months either from the date of arrival of the person concerned in its territory or from the date of reporting of his/her presence within the territory, or from the submission of an application for registration or for a residence card by that person.

Directive 2004/38/EC imposes limitations on a Member State in respect of the application of the public policy and public security exceptions. Article 27(2) of Directive 2004/38/EC provides that "measures taken on grounds of public policy or of public security must be based exclusively on the personal conduct of the individual concerned". Further, the personal conduct of the individual concerned must represent a genuine, present and sufficiently serious threat affecting

---

1890. [2004] OJ L229/35.
1891. Case 41/74 *Van Duyn* [1974] ECR 1337; Case 36/75 *Rutilli* [1975] ECR 1219; Case 30/77 *Bouchereau* [1977] ECR 1999.
1892. Case 352/85 *Bond Van Adverteerders* [1988] ECR 2085.
1893. Supra note 1891.
1894. Case 41/74 *Van Duyn* [1974] ECR 1337; Case 131/79 *Santillo* [1980] ECR 1585.

one of the fundamental interests of the host Member State. These concepts require more detailed examination.

25.3.1.1 Personal conduct of the individual concerned

The ECJ emphasised that measures adopted on grounds of public policy and for the maintenance of public security against the nationals of Member States cannot be justified on grounds extraneous to the individual case. Only the "personal conduct" of those affected by the measures is to be regarded as determinative. This was explained by the ECJ in Case 67/74 *Bonsignore v Oberstadtdirektor der Stadt Köln*.[1895]

THE FACTS WERE:

An Italian national permanently residing in Germany, Carmelo Bonsignore, shot his brother by accident. The weapon he used was a pistol he had illegally acquired. He was fined for this offence but no punishment was imposed for the accidental killing of his brother. The German authorities ordered his deportation for "reasons of a general preventive nature" based on "the deterrent effect which the deportation of an alien found in illegal possession of a firearm would have in immigration circles having regard to the resurgence of violence in the large urban cities". The German court referred to the ECJ a question whether Article 3(1) of Directive 64/221/EEC [now Article 27(2) of Directive 2004/38] prohibits deportation for reasons of a general preventive nature when it is clear that the individual concerned would not commit further offences.

Held:

The ECJ held that a Member State should base the decision on deportation exclusively on the personal conduct of the individual concerned. Future behaviour is only relevant in so far as there are clear indications that the individual would commit further offences. Article 3(1) of Directive 64/221/EEC prevents the deportation of a national of a Member State if such deportation is ordered for the purpose of deterring other aliens, that is, if it is based on reasons of a general preventive nature.

The concept of personal conduct was further clarified in Case 41/74 *Van Duyn*.[1896]

THE FACTS WERE:

Miss Van Duyn, a Dutch national, was a member of the Church of Scientology. She wanted to enter the UK to take up employment with the Church of Scientology in the UK but was refused entry. She brought an action against the UK Home Office. The High Court referred,

---

1895. [1975] ECR 297.
1896. [1974] ECR 1337.

inter alia, the following questions to the ECJ: whether membership of organisations should be considered as "personal conduct" within the meaning of Article 3(1) of Directive 64/221/ EEC [Article 27(2) of Directive 2004/38] and if so, whether such conduct must be illegal in order to justify the application of the public policy exception.

Held:

The ECJ answered that past association cannot count as personal conduct but present membership of an organisation, being a voluntary act of the person concerned, counts as "personal conduct". The activities of the Church of Scientology were not illegal in the UK. However, the UK Government considered them as socially harmful.

The ECJ held that it is not necessary that the conduct in question is illegal in order to justify exclusion of EU nationals from other Member States in so far as a Member State makes it clear that such activities are "socially harmful" and has taken some administrative measures to counteract the activities.

Van Duyn was a controversial judgment because it meant that a Member State was allowed to refuse entry to an EU national while allowing its own nationals, although with reluctance and disapproval, to be employed by the Church of Scientology. The justification provided by the UK Government was not very convincing in the context of this case. It submitted that under international law a state has a duty to admit its nationals to the national territory and not to expel them from that territory. This aspect of the *Van Duyn* Case was further clarified in Joined Cases 115 and 116/81 *Andoui and Cornuaille v Belgian State.*[1897]

THE FACTS WERE:

Andoui and Cornuaille were French women who were refused a residence permit in Belgium on the grounds that they were "waitresses in a bar which was suspect from the point of view of morals" (that is, they were prostitutes).

Held:

The ECJ held that a Member State may only justify restrictions on the admission to or residence within its territory of nationals of another Member State if it has adopted, with respect to the same type of conduct on the part of its own nationals, repressive measures or other genuine and effective measures intended to combat such conduct.

25.3.1.2   *Previous criminal convictions*

Article 27(2) of Directive 2004/38/EC provides that "previous criminal convictions shall not in themselves constitute grounds for the taking of such measures".

The matter of previous convictions was examined by the ECJ in Case 30/77 *R v Bouchereau.*[1898]

1897. [1982] ECR 1665.
1898. [1977] ECR 1999.

Mr Bouchereau, a French national, was convicted in the UK of possession of illegal drugs in January 1976 and again in June 1976. He challenged a deportation order made against him on the grounds of Article 39 EC and Article 3(2) of Directive 64/221 [Article 27(2) of Directive 2004/38].

Held:

The ECJ held that a likelihood of reoffending may be found in past conduct although previous criminal convictions do not in themselves constitute grounds for taking measures on the basis of public policy or public security. The Court stated that it is possible that past conduct alone may constitute a threat to the requirements of public policy when the individual concerned has a "propensity to act in the same way in the future" as he did in the past.

25.3.1.3 *Present, genuine and sufficiently serious threat to requirements of public policy affecting one of the fundamental interests of society*

In order to justify any measure adopted on the grounds of public policy or public security, personal conduct of the individual concerned must represent a genuine, present and sufficiently serious threat affecting one of the fundamental interests of the host Member State.

In Joined Cases C-482/01 and C-493/01 *Orfanopoulos and Oliveri*,[1899] the ECJ provided important clarifications in respect of the meaning of "present threat". The Court stated that "the requirement of the existence of a present threat must, as a general rule, be satisfied at the time of the expulsion". This judgment was confirmed and expanded in Article 32 of Directive 2004/38/EC, which provides that if an expulsion order is enforced more than two years after it was issued, the Member State must check whether or not the person concerned is currently and genuinely a threat to public policy or public security, and in order to do this it shall take into consideration whether there has been any material change in circumstances since the expulsion order was issued.

In the Case of Mr Oliveri there were important changes in his personal circumstances since the issuing of the expulsion order by German authorities:

- First, he claimed that the risk of reoffending did not exist any more, as he had changed and had become a responsible adult as a result of difficulties he had to endure in prison;

- Second, he suffered from full-blown Aids and despite the medical treatment received, he was dying from Aids.

25.3.1.4 *Non-compliance with formalities regarding entry and residence in a host Member State*

Non-compliance with administrative formalities imposed on EU migrant workers and their

---

1899. [2004] ECR I-5257.

families in respect of entry and residence never justify an expulsion from the territory of a host Member State.[1900]

25.3.1.5   Economic considerations

Article 27(1) of Directive 2004/38/EC provides that Member States are not allowed to invoke public policy derogations for economic purposes. The judgment of the ECJ in Case 139/85 *Kempf*[1901] confirms that a Member State cannot refuse entry and residence on economic grounds.

When EU migrant workers exercise effective and genuine activity of an economic nature in the territory of a host Member State, the fact that their remuneration is not sufficient to satisfy their needs, and that they receive social security benefits or social assistance from a host Member State, are not sufficient to deny them the right to reside in the territory of that Member State. This is subject to the principle that the migrant worker must not become an unreasonable burden on the social security system of a host Member State (Article 1 of Directive 2004/38/EC) – so it is a matter of interpretation of what is unreasonable.

25.3.1.6   Public health

Article 29 of Directive 2004/38/EC provides that only diseases with epidemic potential, as defined by the relevant instruments of the World Health Organisation, and other infectious or contagious parasitic diseases, if they are the subject of protection provisions applying to nationals of the host Member State, may justify restrictions on entry and residence.

Diseases occurring after a three-month period from the date of arrival shall not constitute grounds for expulsion from the territory of the host Member State.

25.4   Protection against expulsion for long-term residents and minors in a host Member State

Article 28 of Directive 2004/38/EC provides safeguards against expulsion on the grounds of public policy and public security. It incorporates and expands the judgment delivered by the ECJ in Case C-482/01 *Georgios Orfanopoulos and Others v Land Baden-Württemberg*.[1902]

THE FACTS WERE:

Mr Orfanopoulos, a Greek national born in 1959 in Greece, joined his parents in Germany in 1972. Since then he had been living in Germany, apart from a two-year period during which he was completing his military service in Greece. In 1981 he married a German national. Three children had been born to the marriage.

During his residence in Germany Mr Orfanopoulos had been given residence permits of a

---

1900.   Case 48/75 *Royer* [1976] ECR 497.
1901.   [1986] ECR 1741.
1902.   [2004] ECR I-5257.

limited duration. In November 1999 he submitted a request for renewal of his residence permit.

Mr Orfanopoulos had no professional qualifications. Since 1981 he had had various jobs but periods of employment had been interrupted by extended periods of unemployment.

Mr Orfanopoulos was a drug addict. He had been convicted nine times for various offences relating to possession and use of unlawful drugs and for violent assaults. In 1999 he was condemned to six months in prison. In January 2000 he had been admitted to a hospital for detoxification treatment and subsequently had tried to take detoxification cures in specialised institutions, but had been expelled from these institutions for disciplinary reasons. From September 2000 to March 2002 he was in prison serving terms of imprisonment imposed by earlier judgments. In March 2002 his remaining sentence was suspended as a result of his good behaviour while in prison and his willingness to accept detoxification treatment.

The German authorities warned Mr Orfanopoulos on a number of occasions about the serious consequences of his conduct on his residence status in Germany. In February 2001 the German authorities rejected his request for renewal of his residence permit and issued a deportation order against him. Mr Orfanopoulos was informed that he would be deported at the end of his prison sentence.

The German authorities justified the deportation order by the number and seriousness of offences committed by Mr Orfanopoulos and the high risk of his reoffending in the future given his drug and alcohol addictions.

On 21 March 2002 Mr Orfanopoulos and his children appealed against the deportation order before the German court. Mr Orfanopoulos argued that the decision of expulsion was not based on his personal conduct but was taken as a general preventive measure and that this decision was disproportionate and in breach of Article 8 of the ECHR.

Held:

In respect of the issue of compatibility of the expulsion order with the principles of EU law, the ECJ stated that the situation of the individual concerned should be assessed in the light of the general principles of EU law, including the fundamental rights contained in the ECHR which are protected in the Community legal order.[1903] Both EU law and the ECHR recognise the right to respect for private and family life. Article 8(2) of the ECHR sets out the limits of permissible interference with the enjoyment of these rights by a Member State. Any interference in family life of the individual concerned must be necessary in a democratic society, in accordance with law, and proportionate to the legitimate aims pursued by a Member State. In connection with the proportionality test it is necessary to weigh up in each particular case the interests of the Member State taking the measure terminating residence of the person concerned and the interests of that individual. In respect of Mr Orfanopoulos the ECJ stated it was necessary for the referring court to take account of the following factors: the nature, seriousness and frequency of offences that he had committed; the period of time that had

---

1903. C-260/89 *Elliniki Radiophonia Tiléorassi AE and Panellinia Omospondia Syllogon Prossopikou v Dimotiki Etairia Pliroforissis and Sotirios Kouvelas and Nicolaos Avdellas and others* [1991] ECR I-2925; C-368/95 *Familiapress* [1997] ECR I-3689; C-60/00 *Mary Carpenter v Secretary of State for the Home Department* [2002] ECR I-6279.

> elapsed since his last conviction; the extent of his integration into the host Member State, socially, professionally and in terms of family relations; and the seriousness of difficulties for him and his wife to live together as a family should the expulsion order be carried out.

Article 28 of Directive 2004/38/EC adds a new gloss to the judgment in *Orfanopoulos*. It distinguishes between, on the one hand, serious requirements and on the other hand, imperative requirements of public policy and public security of a Member State. As a matter of principle the host Member State is not allowed to make an expulsion order against EU citizens and members of their families who have acquired permanent residence in a host Member State, except on serious grounds of public policy or public security. In respect of persons who have resided in a host Member State for 10 years or are minors, only imperative grounds of public policy or public security will justify an expulsion order.

25.5   Procedural safeguards under Directive 2004/38/EC

Directive 2004/38/EC provides procedural safeguards for EU nationals seeking to enforce their rights of entry and residence in a host Member State. Articles 31–33 set out important procedural rights for individuals who are refused the rights of entry and residence granted by the Treaties and by secondary legislation.

The procedural safeguards are as follows:

A.   The persons concerned must be notified of any decision of expulsion in writing, in such a manner that they are able to comprehend its content and the implications for them. The notification must specify, precisely and in full, the relevant national authority which deals with appeals from such a decision, the time limit for the appeal, the grounds on which the decision was taken, unless this is contrary to the interests of state security, and the time allowed to leave the territory which, apart from duly substantiated cases of urgency, shall be no less than one month from the date of notification (Article 30).

B.   The persons concerned are entitled to seek judicial review of the expulsion decision or, when appropriate, lodge an appeal against it before the administrative authorities of the host Member State. The case law of the ECJ has clarified many aspects of appeal proceedings before administrative bodies of the Member States.[1904] Such bodies must:

▪ be independent of the administrative authority which adopts the decision, or if no such body has been established, then an administrative court must deal with the appeal; and

▪ must examine all the facts and circumstances, including the expediency of the expulsion decision, before the final decision is taken by the appropriate administrative authority, save in cases of emergency.[1905]

1904. Joined Cases C-297/88 and C-197/89 *Dzodzi* [1990] ECR I-3763; Case C-357/98 *R v Secretary of State for the Home Department, ex parte Yiadom* [2000] ECR I-9265.

1905. Case 131/79 *Santillo* [1980] ECR 1585; Joined Cases 115/81 and 116/81 *Adoui and Cornuaille v Belgian State* [1982] ECR 1665; Joined Cases C-482/01 *Georgios Orfanopoulos and Others v Land Baden-Württemberg* (C-482/01) and C-493/01 *Raffaele Oliveri v Land Baden-Württemberg* [2004] ECR I-5257.

When the applicant has, at the same time, challenged the expulsion decision and applied for an interim order to suspend its enforcement, then, save in the cases specified in Article 31(2), he/she should not be removed from the territory of the host Member State until such time as the decision on an interim order has been taken. Pending the redress procedure Member States may exclude the applicant from their national territory but may not prevent him/her from submitting his/her defence in person, except when his/her appearance may cause a serious threat to the requirements of public policy or public security, or when the procedure concerns a denial of entry to the territory.

C. Article 32 introduced the right for persons excluded on grounds of public policy or public security to lodge an application for the lifting of the exclusion order after a reasonable time, depending on the circumstances, and in any event after three years from enforcement of the final expulsion decision. It is for the applicant to submit evidence that there has been a material change in the circumstances that justifies the revision of the previous decision. The applicant is entitled to have an answer within six months of the submission of his/her application but has no right of entry to the territory of the host Member State while his/her application is being considered.[1906]

It is important to note that a Member State is not allowed to expel for life from its territory a national of another Member State. This issue was examined by the ECJ in Case C-348/96 *Criminal Proceedings Against Calfa*.[1907]

THE FACTS WERE:

Donatella Calfa, an Italian national, went on holiday to Crete where she was convicted of the possession and use of prohibited drugs. She was sentenced by a Greek court to three months' imprisonment and expulsion for life from Greek territory. Under Greek penal law, foreign nationals convicted of certain drug offences were automatically subject to an expulsion order for life unless for some compelling reason, particularly family matters, their continued residence in Greece was allowed. Donatella Calfa challenged the expulsion order as contrary to a number of provisions of the EC Treaty, especially Articles 39, 43 and 49 EC [Articles 45, 49 and 56 TFEU] and Directive 64/221/EEC.

Held:

The ECJ held that Donatella Calfa, as a tourist, was a recipient of services in another Member State and as such within the scope of application of Article 49 EC [Article 56 TFEU]. The ECJ emphasised that although national legislation in criminal matters is within the competence of a Member State, the requirements of EC law set limitations on Member States' powers. Such legislation should not limit the fundamental freedoms guaranteed by Community law. The ECJ held that expulsion for life from a territory of a Member State was an obstacle to the

---

1906. Joined Cases C-65 and 111/95 *R v Secretary of State for the Home Department, ex parte Mann Singh Shingara, R v Secretary for the Home Department, ex parte Abbas Radiom* [1997] ECR I-3343.
1907. [1999] ECR I-11.

freedom to receive services under Article 49 EC [Article 56 TFEU] as well as the freedom of establishment under Article 43 EC [Article 49 TFEU] and the free movement of workers contained in Article 39 EC [Article 45 TFEU]. It could not be justified on the ground of public policy since Greek legislation provided for an automatic expulsion for life following a criminal conviction without taking into account the personal conduct of the offender or whether that conduct created a genuine and sufficiently serious threat affecting one of the fundamental interests of society.

AIDE-MÉMOIRE

EXCEPTIONS TO THE FREE MOVEMENT OF PERSONS

1. Exception based on Articles 45(4) and 51 TFEU

Article 45(4) TFEU: the concept of "employment in the public service" applies to workers.
"Employment in the public service" is within the scope of Article 45(4) TFEU if:

- The post concerned requires a special relationship of allegiance to the Member State on the part of the person occupying it, which only the bond of nationality ensures;

- The post involves the exercise of powers conferred by public law;

- The holder of the post is entrusted with responsibility for the general interest of the Member State.

  The above requirements must be concurrent (Case C-47/02 *Anker*).

Article 51 TFEU : the concept of "exercise of official authority" applies to self-employed persons (Case 2/74 *Reyners*). Article 51 TFEU has been construed by reference to Article 45(4) TFEU. The difference between Article 45(4) TFEU and Article 51 TFEU is that under Article 51 TFEU a Member State may rely on the exception when the holder of the post carries out activities connected with the exercise of official authority "even occasionally".

2. The exceptions based on the grounds of public policy, public security and public health – Directive 2004/38/EC

A. Any measure taken by the host Member State restricting freedom of movement on the grounds of **public policy and public security**:
   - Must be based on personal conduct of the individual concerned. If relevant, this includes present membership of organisations but not past membership (Case 41/74 *Van Duyn*);
   - Must not be based on previous criminal convictions of the person concerned unless they show that the individual concerned has the propensity to act in the future as he/she did in the past (Case 30/77 *R v Bouchereau*);
   - Must not be a penalty or legal consequence of a custodial penalty unless it conforms with the requirements of Articles 27, 28, 29 of Directive 2004/38/EC;
   - Must show that the personal conduct of the individual concerned represents a

genuine, present and sufficiently serious threat affecting one of the fundamental interests of society of the host Member State (Case 131/79 *Santillo*; C-493/01 *Raffaele Oliveri*);

- Must not be based on reasons of a general preventive nature (Case 67/74 *Bonsignore*);
- Must not be based on economic considerations (Case 139/85 *Kempf*);
- Must comply with the principle of proportionality (Case 352/85 *Bond Van Adverteerders*);
- Must be supported by evidence that a Member State has taken repressive or other effective measures to combat conduct such as that of the individual concerned with regard to its own nationals (Joined Cases 115 and 116/81 *Andoui and Cornuaille*).

B.   Any measure restricting freedom of movement on the ground of public health may be taken by the host Member State:
- In respect of diseases with epidemic potential (as defined by the World Health Organisation); and
- In respect of other infectious or contagious parasitic diseases if they are the subject of protection provisions applying to nationals of the host Member State **but not if diseases occur after a three-month period from the date of arrival of the person concerned**.

Safeguards

The person concerned:

- Must be notified in writing of any decision taken on the grounds of public policy, public security and public health. Such notification must contain all information specified in Article 30;

- Has the right of access to judicial or administrative redress procedures to appeal against the decision or to seek its judicial review under the conditions set out in Article 31;

- Has the right to re-examination of the exclusion decision after a reasonable time has elapsed or, in any event, after three years from enforcement of the final exclusion decision if he/she can show that there has been a material change in circumstances since the adoption of the expulsion decision.

RECOMMENDED READING

Books

O'Keeffe, D., "Judicial Interpretation of the Public Exception to the Free Movement of Workers", in Curtin, D., and O'Keeffe D. (eds), *Constitutional Adjudication in European Community and National Law*, 1992, Dublin, Butterworths Ireland, p 89

Spaventa, E., *Free Movement of Persons in the EU: Barriers to Movement in their Constitutional Context*, 2007, The Hague: Kluwer Law International

26

INTRODUCTION TO EU COMPETITION LAW

SUMMARY

1. This chapter focuses on some general features common to all EU competition rules. It briefly outlines the main objectives of EU competition law, which are:

- To maintain openness and unify the internal market;

- To ensure economic efficiency in the marketplace;

- To ensure the conditions of effective competition and competitiveness; and

- To protect consumers.

The reform of EU competition law enhances the above objectives and streamlines its application. However, views differ as to whether the objectives of EU competition law under the ToL have changed given that Article 3(1)(g) EC which provides that the maintenance of competition is one of the main activities of the EC was deleted and its content transferred to Protocol 27 on "The Internal Market and Competition".

2. The relationship between EU competition law and the national competition laws of the

Member States is regulated by Article 3 of Regulation 1/2003, which decentralised the enforcement of EU competition law and which emphasises the federal nature of EU competition law. Although competition laws of the Member States may differ from EU competition law, any conflict between the two is resolved in favour of EU competition law. Whatever the situation and circumstances may be, the EU law, being federal in nature, supersedes national competition laws.

3. The ECJ in the *Wood Pulp Cartel* cases endorsed the extraterritorial application of EU competition law. Consequently, EU competition law applies to anti-competitive activities of undertakings established outside the EU in a situation where such activities affect competition in the EU.

4. One result of globalisation is the necessity for international co-operation in competition matters. The EU's contribution is twofold, first, through international organisations such as the World Trade Organisation (WTO), the Organisation for Economic Co-operation and Development (OECD) Competition Committee, and the International Competition Network (ICN) and, second, through bilateral agreements and other forms of co-operation with countries and groups of countries outside the EU.

5. For the purposes of EU competition law any natural or legal person is regarded as an undertaking if such a person is engaged in any economic activity and enjoys some autonomy in determining its course of action in the relevant market.

6. The concept of activity which "may affect trade between Member States" establishes a jurisdictional limitation on the scope of application of Articles 101 and 102 TFEU. According to this concept EU competition law applies only where anti-competitive conduct of an undertaking has an appreciable effect on trade between Member States.

26.1 Introduction

Only a perfect market does not need any correction by rule of law, since it constitutes a self-balancing system. A perfect market is one:

- Tilting toward low prices consistent with the cost of manufacture and supply;

- In which undertakings compete with each other for customers (which is good for both buyers and sellers alike, as it promotes innovation and choice while keeping the economy efficient);

- In which for a particular product there are an infinite number of buyers and sellers;

- In which undertakings can freely enter and leave the market and consumers have complete access to information allowing for free and rational decision-making.

However, the ideal market based on the neo-classical economic theory[1908] does not exist. As a result, the considerations as to what constitutes anti-competitive conduct and what kind of conduct on the part of undertakings requires control by competition policy and law are subject to political, social and economic objectives.

Competition policy is a broad term that refers to a set of economic policies designed to

---

1908. The economic theories on competition are outside the scope of the book. On this topic see: A. Jones and B. Sufrin, *EC Competition Law*, 2007, Oxford: Oxford University Press, pp 22–35.

promote competition in the economy of a country or region. Competition law is the main expression of a competition policy and can be viewed as its cornerstone.

Within the objectives of the European Community, the objectives of EC competition law were set out in Article 3(1)(g) EC which provided that "the activities of the Community shall include . . . the institution of a system ensuring that competition in the common market is not distorted" and Article 4 EC (Article 119 TFEU) which provided that the Community and its Member States are to adopt a co-ordinated economic policy based on "an open market economy with free competition". The ToL repealed Article 3(1)(g) but Protocol 27 attached to the Treaties states that the establishment of the international market includes "a system ensuring that competition is not distorted". It is unclear whether the transfer of the substance of Article 3(1)(g) EC from the opening articles of the EC Treaty to Protocol 27 will have any impact on the interpretation and enforcement of EU competition law. According to the European Commission the change will enhance the position of the Commission as an enforcer of EU competition law.[1909] Some commentators, however, stress that the change will weaken the position of the Commission and may result in competition policy considerations being no longer treated as prevailing when they conflict with other EU policies.[1910]

It is submitted that the position of the European Commission is correct. Protocol 27, as any EU Protocol, has the same legal value as a treaty itself. Further, it seems unlikely that the objectives of EU competition policy, which were reconsidered by the European Commission at the time of the reform of EU competition law, will be changed and that competition law will be interpreted by the ECJ as a lower rank policy within the EU on the basis of the transfer of the essence of Article 3(1)(g) EC to Protocol 27 which transfer was effected as a concession to President Sarkozy of France rather than an intended overhaul of EU competition law.

The objectives of EC/EU competition law have never been clearly stated. However, the aims of achieving economic welfare (referred to as economic efficiency) and the strengthening of the internal market have always been considered as the main objective of competition policy. With the reform of EU competition law (see below) new objectives have been set. Economic efficiency, consumer welfare and competitiveness are now the fundamental objectives of competition policy.[1911] Thus, stimulation of sustained economic growth, competitiveness and employment are at the heart of competition policy as it encourages the optimal allocation of resources and stimulates research and development, innovation and investment. Through this mechanism of effective competition resources and employment are moved from one sector to another to help maximise economic benefit.

The 2000 Guidelines on Vertical Restraints, although they do not deal with all aspects of competition law, confirm the above objectives by stating that "the protection of competition is the primary objective of EC competition law, as this enhances consumer welfare and creates an efficient allocation of resources. In applying the EC competition rules, the Commission will adopt an economic approach which is based on the effects on the market . . . Market integration is an

---

1909. The view expressed by Commissioner Kroes see "Making Waves: Interview with EU Competition Commissioner Neelie Kroes" [2008] 22 Antitrust 2, 47.

1910. Riley, "The EU Reform Treaty and the Competition Protocol: undermining EC Competition Law", [2001] ECLR 703.

1911. See The XXIII Annual Report on Competition Policy, The European Commission, Brussels, 1994, pp 24–5; The White Paper on Modernisation of Rules Implementing Articles 81 and 82 of the EC Treaty [1999] OJ C132/1.

additional goal of EU competition law. Market integration enhances competition".[1912] However, the competitiveness, as one of the objectives of the EC competition policy, is emphasised in the 2004 Commission's Report on Competition Policy. It states: "In 2006, competition policy continued to safeguard and create the conditions which allow markets to function competitively to the benefit of European consumers and businesses."[1913].

It can be said that EU competition policy embraces many objectives and greatly contributes to the establishment of the internal market.

The key provisions of EU competition law that are examined in this book are:

- Article 101 TFEU which prohibits and renders null and void, subject to some exceptions, any agreements between undertakings, decisions by associations of undertakings and concerted practices which may affect trade between Member States and which have as their object or effect the prevention, restriction or distortion of competition within the EU;

- Article 102 TFEU which prohibits any abuse, by one or more undertakings, of a dominant position within the internal market or any substantial part of it in so far as such abuse may affect trade within the EU;

- Merger Regulation 139/2004,[1914] which applies to concentrations which have an EU dimension; and

- Regulation 1/2003 which provides the mechanisms for the enforcement of Articles 101 and 102 TFEU.

It is important to note that a substantial programme of legislative reform of competition law is being undertaken by the Commission. In the White Paper on Modernisation[1915] the Commission explained that modernisation of EU competition law was necessary, taking into account the globalisation of economy, the enlargement of the EU and the existence of a single market and single currency. Some objectives of the reform have already been achieved; others are, as at the beginning of 2010,[1916] still in progress. Overall the programme of reform dramatically alters EU competition law. Its main objective is to strengthen the enforcement of EU competition law in an enlarged EU and at the same time focuses on the importance of economic analyses in competition cases. The main features of the reform are examined in detail in the relevant chapters of this book. The three main pieces of legislation which have modernised EU competition law are:

- Regulation 1/2003 on the Implementation of the Rules on Competition laid down in Articles 101 and 102 TFEU which entered into force on 1 May 2004.[1917] The regulation decentralises the enforcement of EU competition law, abolishes the system of notification and authorisation, renders Article 101(3) TFEU directly effective and sets up a system for co-operation between the Commission on the one hand and national competition authorities

---

1912. [2000] OJ C291/1, para 7.

1913. COM (2007) 358 final, p 1.

1914. [2004] OJ L 24/1.

1915. The White Paper on Modernisation of Rules Implementing Articles 81 and 82 of the EC Treaty [Articles 101 and 102 TFEU] [1999] OJ C132/1.

1916. For example, the proposal relating to the elimination of restrictions on competition in the area of professional services and the approach of the Commission to damages actions for breach of the EU antitrust rules.

1917. [2002] OJ L1/1.

(NCAs) and national courts on the other, and sets up clear rules on the relationship between EU competition law and national competition law. The Commission adopted a package of Notices and Guidelines to help apply the new regime.

■ A new type of block exemption regulations (see Chapter 27.8). They together with the accompanying Notices and Guidelines assist undertakings in the application of Article 101 TFEU and with regard to the application of Article 102 TFEU, the Commission's Guidelines on enforcement priorities in applying Article 102 TFEU to abusive exclusionary conduct by dominant undertakings is of relevance.[1918]

■ Merger Regulation 139/2004[1919] which entered into force on 1 May 2004 and which recast Merger Regulation 4064/89. Subsequently the Commission adopted a new implementing Regulation and a package of Notices and Guidelines on the assessment of horizontal mergers.

26.2 The federal nature of EU competition law

EU competition law does not replace the national competition law of Member States. Undertakings are required to comply with both national and EU competition law.

Article 3 of Regulation 1/2003 sets out clear rules on the relationship between Articles 101 and 102 TFEU and national competition laws. They can be summarised as follows:

1. Under Article 3(1) NCAs and national courts, when applying national law to conduct which constitutes an agreement, decision or concerted practice within the meaning of Article 101 TFEU or an abusive conduct within the meaning of Article 102 TFEU which affects trade between Member States, are also obliged to apply Articles 101 and 102 TFEU.

2. Under Article 3(2) NCAs or national courts may apply national laws which are stricter than Article 102 TFEU, but they are not allowed to do this in respect of an agreement that is permitted under Article 101 TFEU. This latter means that an agreement authorised under Article 101 TFEU cannot be prohibited under national law. The main reasons why Article 3(2) allows the application of a stricter approach to Article 102 while excluding it in respect of Article 101 TFEU is that when an agreement is authorised under Article 101 TFEU (either because it does not restrict competition or because it fulfils the criteria set out in Article 101(3) and therefore its pro-competitive effects prevail over its anti-competitive effects, or it satisfies the conditions of a block exemption), its condemnation at national level would undermine the basic objectives of Article 101 TFEU, which would be entirely inappropriate.

    The Regulation does not address the situation where conduct is unlawful under Article 101 or 102 but lawful under national law. Perhaps this is because the solution is simple: the application of the principle of supremacy means that such conduct cannot be regarded as lawful under national law.

1918.   [2009] OJ C45/7.
1919.   [2004] OJ L24/1.

3.   Article 3(3) precludes the application of paragraphs 1 and 2 of Article 3 to national merger control rules or national provisions that predominately pursue objectives which are not competition objectives, such as social objectives.

26.3   Extraterritorial application of EU competition law

Extraterritorial jurisdiction was developed to respond to the internationalisation of criminal activities at the end of the nineteenth century. It has also found its application in antitrust cases, especially in the US antitrust laws[1920] and EU competition rules. The ECJ endorsed the extraterritorial application of EU competition law in the *Wood Pulp Cartel* cases. All doubts as to the extraterritorial application of EU competition law were dispelled with the entry into force of Merger Regulation 4064/89 which clearly states that in certain circumstances it applies to undertakings from outside the EU.

26.4   International co-operation in the field of competition law in the era of globalisation

The extraterritorial application of EU competition law creates many problems. In particular, the investigation outside the territory of the EU of alleged breaches of EU competition law often necessitates the co-operation of competent authorities of a third state. While this is challenging enough, the actual enforcement outside the EU of decisions of EU competition authorities is even more difficult because a third state, where the offending undertaking is located, has no obligation, unless there is some arrangement to this effect, to co-operate, to assist foreign authorities or to recognise and enforce their decisions. In this respect it is often left to offending undertakings to plead guilty and pay the fine. Accordingly, the undertaking concerned is unlikely to co-operate in investigations and to pay compensation unless forced by powerful countries or blocks of countries.[1921]

Extraterritorial application of EU competition law is contrary to international comity and fairness and encourages confrontation rather than co-operation between countries in resolving competition issues. The EU has recognised the importance of international co-operation in competition matters and has devoted substantial efforts and energy towards both, expanding multilateral co-operation and ensuring basic co-operation with its main trading partners based on bilateral agreements.

26.4.1   Multilateral co-operation in the field of competition law

Multilateral co-operation has been pursued within the framework of such international organisations as the World Trade Organisation (WTO), the United Nations Commission on Trade and

---

1920. *Hartford Fire Insurance Co. v California* 509 U.S. 764,113 S.Ct.2891, 125 L.Ed.2d 612 (1993).

1921. See for example the proceedings of US antitrust authorities against Hoffmann-La Roche and other pharmaceutical giants participating in a conspiracy to eliminate competition in the pharmaceutical sector worldwide. *Hoffmann-La Roche Ltd v Empagran SA* 542 U.S.155, 124 S.Ct.2359, 159 L.Ed.2d 226 (2004). In the EU substantial fines were imposed: see Commission's decision in *Vitamins* [2003] OJ L6/1, [2003] 4 CMLR 1030.

Development (UNCTAD) and the Organisation for Economic Co-operation and Development (OECD), and on an informal basis within the International Competition Network (ICN).

26.4.2 Bilateral co-operation

The EU has entered into many bilateral competition co-operation agreements. They increase the effectiveness of enforcement of competition law and reduce the risk of conflicting or incompatible decisions being reached.

The bilateral agreements may take various forms. They may be:

1. So called dedicated co-operation agreements, which ensure the most extensive co-operation between EU competition authorities and the relevant competition authorities of a third state. A typical dedicated bilateral co-operation agreement provides for:

    - Notification of cases being investigated by either authority, where they may affect the important interests of the other party;
    - Co-operation and co-ordination by the authorities concerned of their enforcement activities, as well as of rendering assistance to each other;
    - The possibility for one party to request the other to take enforcement action, and for one party to take into account the important interests of the other party in the course of its enforcement activities;
    - The exchange of information between the parties, subject to confidentiality obligations with respect to such information;
    - Regular meetings to share information on current enforcement activities and priorities of each party.

    As at the time of writing, the EU has concluded dedicated agreements with the USA,[1922] Canada,[1923] Japan[1924] and the Republic of Korea (i.e. South Korea).[1925]

2. Agreements under which provisions on co-operation in competition matters are inserted into trade agreements between the EU and its trading partners, in particular into free trade agreements, for example, EuroMed Agreements, and Partnership and Co-operation Agreements.

3. Special memoranda of understanding on competition matters. signed between the EU and a non-EU country. A memorandum of understanding establishes a dialogue between competition authorities and provides for exchange of views on enforcement of competition law and non-confidential information on individual cases.[1926]

4. Special agreements concluded with candidate states and states which are members of the European Economic Area.

It is to be noted that the EU agreed on a structured dialogue with China involving sharing experience and views on competition matters and providing technical and capacity-building assistance to China.

1922. [1995] OJ L95/45.
1923. [1999] OJ L175/1.
1924. [2003] OJ L183/1.
1925. [2009] OJ 202/35–41.
1926. See for example a Memorandum of Understanding signed between the EU and Brazil on 9/10/09: IP/09/1500.

Even dedicated co-operation agreements, however useful, do not solve all problems. For example in the *Microsoft* case, although both the Commission and the US antitrust authorities fully co-operated during investigations, on the West side of the Atlantic the case against *Microsoft* was settled in 2001,[1927] whilst on the East side the Commission found *Microsoft* in breach of Article 102 TFEU and the biggest ever fine was imposed on *Microsoft*.[1928] Similarly, the case of *Boeing-McDonnell Douglas* was the subject of acrimonious disagreement between the US and the EU[1929] as was the case of *GE/Honeywell*,[1930] in which the European Commission prohibited a merger between two US multinationals while the US antitrust authorities had no objection to the creation of the biggest merger in corporate history.

The above confirms that the perceptions of national enforcement authorities differ as to what behaviour constitutes a breach of competition law, or is likely to pose a threat to it, in particular when very large firms established in the relevant State are involved, and thus the matter becomes subject to political pressure.

26.5   Definition of an undertaking

Competition law applies only to undertakings. For that reason it is necessary to define this concept. Neither the Treaties nor secondary legislation provide a definition of undertakings. However, the well established case law indicates that under EU competition law any natural or legal person:

- Engaged in any economic activity; and

- Enjoying some autonomy in determining its conduct on the relevant market;

should be regarded as an undertaking.

26.5.1   The meaning of "economic activity"

In Case C-41/90 *Höfner and Elser v Macroton GmbH*, the ECJ stated that the concept of an "undertaking" covers any entity engaged in an economic activity, regardless of its legal status and the way in which it is financed, and any activity consisting of offering goods and services in a given market is an economic activity.[1931]

The case law suggests that the term "economic activity" refers to:

- An activity consisting of provision of goods and services on the market;[1932] and

---

1927. *US v Microsoft Corp.* 253 F.3d 34 (D.C. Cir. 2001) (en banc).

1928. Case T-201/04 *Microsoft v Commission* [2007] ECR II-3601. The CFI [the General Court] upheld the Commission decision and confirmed the totality of the fine imposed, which amounted to €497 million.

1929. H. Greenberg, "Trade Feuds Between US, Europe Rise", *Wall Street Journal*, PA2 (25 July 1997).

1930. The decision of the Commission was confirmed in Joined Cases T-209/01 and T-210/01 *Honeywell and GE v Commission* [2005] ECR II-5527.

1931. [1991] ECR I-1979. The ECJ has confirmed this definition in numerous cases, for example see: Case C-218/00 *Cisal di Battistello Venezio and Co v Instituto Nazionale per Assicurazione Contro Gli Fortuni Sul Lavoro* (INAIL) [2002] ECR I-691.

1932. Case C-205/03P *FENIN v Commission* [2006] ECR I-6295.

■ An activity which can be carried out by private undertakings in order to make profit and therefore if such an activity is carried out by a public body this does not change the nature of the activity, i.e. it remains an economic activity.[1933]

The second above bullet point emphasises that the concept of an undertaking is a relative concept because an entity may be an undertaking under EU competition law with regard to some of its activities and a non-undertaking within the meaning of EU competition law with regard to the remaining activities. This is of crucial importance in respect of activities carried out by a public body in that its different activities must be examined separately in order to establish which of them are of an economic nature and thus within the scope of EU competition law and which are of a non-economic nature and consequently outside the scope of EU competition law. In this respect the ECJ has excluded two types of activities from the scope of EU competition law:

■ Those relating to the management of compulsory social security schemes and provision of insurance services. Bodies in charge of such activities are not undertakings because they fulfil an exclusively social function and perform an activity based on the principle of national solidarity which is entirely non-profit-making;[1934]

■ Those which are connected with the exercise of powers which are typically those of a public authority.

However, these above broad exclusions have been restrictively interpreted by the ECJ.

26.5.1.1 Activities relating to the management of compulsory social security schemes

In Joined Cases C-264, 306 and 355/01 *AOK Bundesverband and Others*[1935] the ECJ explained the basis on which the classification of bodies managing compulsory social security schemes as undertakings under EU competition law or otherwise should be carried out. The ECJ held that a body which fulfils an exclusively social function, is founded on the principle of national solidarity, is entirely non-profit-making, and cannot influence the amount of contributions, the use of assets or the fixing of the level of benefit, should not be regarded as an undertaking for the purposes of EU competition law.[1936]

It emerges from the ECJ's case law that a body managing a compulsory social security scheme will not be classified as an undertaking under EU competition law if it satisfies three criteria:

■ It is a non-profit-making entity which pursues purely social objectives;

■ It manages an insurance scheme based on the principle of solidarity. This principle entails that benefits paid to insured persons are not strictly proportionate to the contributions paid by them;[1937]

■ The essential elements of the scheme are subject to State supervision.

1933. See Case C-113/07P *SELEX Sistemi Integrati SpA v Commission and European Organisation for the Safety of Air Navigation (Eurocontrol)* [2009] ECR I-2207.

1934. See Joined Cases C-159 and C-160/91 *Poucet and Pistre* [1993] ECJ I-637.

1935. [2004] ECR I-2493.

1936. Joined Cases C-159/91 and C-160/91 *Poucet and Pistre* [1993] ECR I-637 and Case C-218/00 *Cisal* [2002] ECR I-691.

1937. Case C-218/00 *Cisal* [2002] ECR I-691.

The ECJ applied the above criteria:

■ In Case C-244/94 *Fédération Française des Sociétés d'Assurance and Others*.[1938] It found that a body managing a supplementary old-age insurance scheme was engaged in economic activity because it was in competition with life assurance companies, given that its members could opt for other schemes which guaranteed better returns, the body applied the principle of capitalisation and the benefits depended solely on the amount of the contributions paid by the beneficiaries and on the financial results of the investments made by the managing organisation;

■ In Case C-67/96 *Albany*.[1939] It found that a body in charge of managing a supplementary pension fund did not fulfil the criteria mentioned above as it could itself determine the amount of contributions of its members and their benefits and operate in accordance with the principle of capitalisation; thus it was engaged in competition with insurance companies and therefore was an undertaking within the meaning of EU competition law.

■ In *AOK Bundesverband*. The ECJ had to determine whether the latitude given to the German sickness funds to determine the fixed maximum amounts payable in respect of medicinal products constituted an activity of an economic nature unrelated to the sickness funds' functions. The ECJ held that the following factors indicated that the sickness insurance funds were not engaged in economic activities and therefore were not undertakings. The factors were:

(a)   That determination of the fixed maximum amounts constituted a task imposed upon them by statute;

(b)   That the procedure for determination was established by statute; and

(c)   That the sickness funds had a limited discretion in this area, that is, they could only determine the maximum amounts and if they could not determine these amounts, the competent minister had to decide them.

■ In Case C-350/07 *Kattner Stahlbau GmbH v Maschinenbau- und Metall-Berufsgenossenschaft (MMB)*.[1940] The ECJ found that a body which provided insurance against accidents at work and occupational diseases in Germany was not an undertaking. It satisfied the three criteria as:

● It pursued social objectives consisting of preventing, by all appropriate means, accidents at work and occupational diseases, and, on the occurrence of accidents or occupational diseases, restoring, by all appropriate means, the health and the capacity to work of insured persons and by providing financial compensation to insured persons or their dependants. Further, it was a non-profit-making body, governed by public law to which affiliation of undertakings established within a specific geographical area was mandatory;

● It was based on the principle of solidarity because, inter alia, amounts of benefits paid under the German insurance scheme were not necessarily proportionate to the insured person's contributions;

1938.   [1995] ECR I-4013.
1939.   [1999] ECR I-5751.
1940.   [2009] ECR I-1513.

● The essential elements of the scheme were subject to State supervision. In this respect the ECJ held that although the MMB had some latitude, i.e. it could decide on factors to be taken into consideration when calculating amounts of contributions and benefits payable under the scheme, this latitude was established and strictly delimited by law.

26.5.1.2 Activities which are connected with the exercise of powers which are typically those of a public authority

The issue of how to determine which activities are connected with the exercise of public powers was examined, first by the CFI [the General Court] in Case T-155/04 *SELEX Sistemi Integrati SpA v Commission*,[1941] and, second, on appeal by the ECJ in Case C-113/07P *SELEX Sistemi Integrati SpA v Commission and Eurocontrol*.[1942]

THE FACTS WERE:

SELEX Sistemi Integrati SpA, an Italian undertaking operating in the sector of air traffic management systems, submitted a complaint to the Commission alleging that Eurocontrol, an international organisation developing a uniform system of air traffic management in Europe, was in breach of Article 82 EC [Article 102 TFEU] when carrying out its standardisation tasks in relation to the creation of a uniform system of Air Traffic Management (ATM) equipment and systems. When the Commission rejected the complaint, SELEX Sistemi brought proceedings before the CFI [the General Court] for annulment of the Commission's decision. In particular three areas of activity of Eurocontrol were at issue:

■ *The first area concerned the activity of regulation, standardisation and validation;*

■ *The second area concerned research and development tasks, which involved, inter alia, the acquisition of and development of prototypes of ATM equipment and systems, for example radar control systems;*

■ *The third activity concerned the assistance provided to the administrations of the Member States by Eurocontrol, when requested, particularly in the field of planning, specification and creation of ATM services and systems. In that context Eurocontrol could, inter alia, be called upon to assist national air traffic control authorities to establish tendering procedures for the supply of ATM equipment and systems.*

The main argument of the Commission was based on the ECJ's judgment in Case C-364/92 SAT Fluggesellschaft,[1943] in which the ECJ held that the activities of Eurocontrol were connected with the exercise of public functions and thus were not of an economic nature. Accordingly, the Commission argued that Eurocontrol was not an undertaking within the meaning of EU competition law.

1941. [2006] ECR II-4797
1942. [2009] ECR I-2207.
1943. [1994] ECR I-43.

Held:

The CFI [the General Court] held that:

Activities of an entity must be considered individually and the fact that some of them are connected to the exercise of public powers does not mean that the others are not economic in nature. Consequently, each activity, if it can be severed from those in which the entity engages as a public authority, must be assessed separately with a view to deciding whether or not it is of an economic nature.[1944]

The ECJ confirmed the CFI reasoning on this point but stated that each activity should be assessed in the light of the mission of Eurocontrol, i.e. its pursuit of public service objectives.

The first activity

The CFI [the General Court] held that the first activity consisting of technical standardisation was not of an economic nature because there was no market for technical standardisation services in the sector of ATM equipment, as the only purchasers of such services can be Member States in their capacity as air traffic control authorities. The purchase of prototypes necessary for producing technical standards did not change the nature of Eurocontrol's activity given that Eurocontrol purchased them for non-economic activities, that is, research. The CFI restated its judgment in T-319/99 *FENIN v Commission*[1945] that being a purchaser in a particular market cannot, in itself, imply an economic activity. The decisive factor is the purpose for which goods are acquired, that is, for the purpose of offering goods and services as part of an economic activity or as part of some other activity such as social or research activity.

The ECJ agreed with the CFI on the above point but found that the CFI [the General Court] was incorrect when it made a distinction between the preparation or production of standards, a task which is undertaken by the Agency of Eurocontrol as the executive organ of that organisation, and their adoption by the Council of Eurocontrol. The ECJ held that the preparation of technical standards could not be dissociated from their adoption. Both activities were performed by Eurocontol as part of its integral task of technical standardisation and thus in the exercise of its public powers. However, as this error in law on the part of the CFI [the General Court] did not affect its final conclusion, i.e. the activity was considered as being of non-economic nature, the ECJ did not set aside the CFI's judgment.

The second activity

The second area of activity consisting of research and development, in particular the purchase of prototypes (which raised intellectual property rights issues) was not considered as being of an economic nature given that prototypes were acquired as a part of Eurocontrol's task as a public authority. They were offered to researchers for non-commercial purposes and licences were granted free of charge. The CFI [the General Court] once again emphasised that such activities were not economic in nature because they did not involve the offer of goods and services in a given market.

The ECJ agreed with the conclusion of the CFI [the General Court].

1944. Case 107/84 *Commission v Germany* [1985] ECR 2655 and Case T-128/98 *Aéroports de Paris v Commission* [2000] ECR II-3929.
1945. [2003] ECR II-357.

The third activity

The CFI [the General Court] decided that the third activity consisting of providing assistance to national administrations in the implementation of tendering procedures for the acquisition of air traffic management systems or equipment was of an economic nature. The Court stated that this activity, which is not indispensable to ensuring the safety of air navigation, can be carried out by private undertakings and the fact that such task was conferred upon a public body to be carried out free of charge did not change the nature of the activity. The CFI [the General Court] found that there was a market for advice in this area and that private undertakings specialised in this area could also very well offer their services.

The ECJ held that the CFI [the General Court] made an error of law in classifying this activity as being of an economic nature. The ECJ emphasised that the provision of assistance constitutes one of the tasks of Eurocontrol as defined in Article 1 of the Convention on the Safety of Air Navigation under which Eurocontol was established. According to the ECJ, the provision of assistance plays "a direct role in the attainment of the objective of technical harmonisation and integration in the field of air traffic with a view to contributing to the maintenance of and improvement in the safety of air navigation". Therefore this activity was connected with the exercise of public powers by Eurocontrol and the fact that the assistance was provided only at the request of the national administration was irrelevant so far as the classification of this activity was concerned. What mattered was that the activity was connected with the maintenance and development of air navigation safety, i.e. connected with the exercise of public powers by Eurocontrol. However, the ECJ stated that the error in law made by the CFI [the General Court] did not justify the setting aside of the judgment given that the CFI [the General Court] did not annul the Commission's decision. Indeed, the CFI [the General Court] held that even if Eurocontrol's activity consisting of providing assistance to national administrations was to be considered as being of an economic nature Eurocontrol was not in breach of Article 82 EC [Article 102 TFEU].

Comment:

Both judgments emphasise that the existence of a competitive or potentially competitive market in the relevant area will be decisive in determining whether a specific activity can be classified as being of an economic nature and thus within the scope of EU competition law.

The definition of an "undertaking" being based on economic activity means that for the application of EU competition law the following are immaterial.

26.5.1.3   The legal personality or form of the body in question

The definition of undertaking has included a Committee organising the World Cup,[1946] professional sports clubs,[1947] members of learned professions,[1948] private individuals engaged in any form

---

1946. *The Distribution of Package Tours During the 1990 World Cup* [1992] OJ L326/31.

1947. *UEFA's Broadcasting Regulations,* OJ [2001] L171/12.

1948. See the Commission Communication of 5 September 2005 on "Professional Services – Scope for More Reform". The Commission has initiated a review of professional rules with a view to eliminating those which have a

of business, commerce or profession, partnerships and co-operatives.[1949] In Case C-35/96 *Commission v Italy*,[1950] the ECJ confirmed the Commission's decision that customs agents in Italy, who in exchange for fees were carrying out customs formalities in respect of export, import and goods in transit, were undertakings. Other examples are:

■ In Case C-180–184/98 *Pavlov v Stichting Pensioen fonds Medische Specialisten*,[1951] the ECJ held that self-employed medical specialists who were contributing to their own individual supplementary pension schemes were undertakings.

■ In Case C-309/99 *Wouters v Algemene Raad van de Nederlandse Orde van Advocaten*, the ECJ held that individual members of the Dutch Bar carried out economic activities when they offered "for a fee, services in the form of legal assistance consisting of drafting of opinions, contracts and other documents and representing of clients in legal proceedings"[1952] and thus were undertakings under EC competition law.

26.5.1.4   The economic purpose of the body in question

The making of profit is not important. For that reason a non-profit-making organisation which is carrying out some economic activity is within the scope of EU competition law.[1953] It is apparent from the case law that the fact that a body is non-profit-making is a relevant factor for the purpose of determining whether or not an activity is of an economic nature but it is not in itself conclusive.[1954]

26.5.1.5   A change of legal form or name

In Joined Cases 29 and 30/83 *CRAM*,[1955] the ECJ held that the successor to an undertaking being investigated may be considered to be the same undertaking for competition law purposes. The decisive factor is "whether there is a functional and economic continuity between the original infringer and the undertaking into which it was merged".[1956]

---

restrictive effect on competition. See the official site of the EU's competition policy – news, legislation, cases at http://ec.europa.eu/competition/index_en.html (accessed 10/12/09).

1949. E.g. *RAI/United* [1978] OJ L157/39 (opera singers); *Reuter/BASF* [1976] OJ L254/40 (an inventor); Case C-250/92 *Gøttrup-Klim Grovvareforening and Others v Dansk Landbrugs Grovvareselskab AmbA* [1994] ECR I-5641 (agricultural co-operatives).

1950. [1998] ECR I-3851, also see *CNSD* [1993] OJ L203/27 confirmed by the CFI in Case T-513/93 *CNSD v Commission* [2000] ECR II-1807.

1951. [2000] ECR I-6451.

1952. [2002] ECR I-1577, para 64.

1953. Joined Cases 209/15 and 218/78 *Van Landewyck* [1980] ECR 3125.

1954. Case C-244/94 *Fédération française des sociétés d'assurance and Others* [1995] ECR I-4013; Case C-67/96 *Albany* [1999] ECR I-5751; and Case C-237/04 *Enirisorse* [2006] ECR I-2843.

1955. [1984] ECR 1679.

1956. *PVC Cartel*, [1990] 4 CMLR 345 para 43.

26.5.2 Autonomy in determining conduct on the market

In order to be regarded as an undertaking an entity must enjoy some autonomy in determining its course of action in the market irrespective of whether or not it has a separate legal personality. This is considered below, first in respect of a corporate body.

A subsidiary will not be regarded as a separate undertaking if both the parent undertaking and its subsidiary "form a single economic unit within which the subsidiary has no real freedom to determine its course of action on the market".[1957] This means that if a parent and its subsidiary, which is not capable of independent policy-making, enter into an agreement which would in other circumstances be prohibited under Article 101 TFEU, there will not be a breach of that provision since that agreement (or concerted practice) will reflect the allocation of functions within the corporate body. This is known under EU competition law as the "group economic unit" doctrine.[1958] On the basis of this doctrine when a subsidiary established within the EU abuses its dominant position, its behaviour is imputable to the parent company, irrespective of whether or not the parent company is established within the EU.[1959]

In Case C-97/08P *Akzo Nobel NV v Commission*[1960] the ECJ confirmed that where a parent company has a 100 per cent shareholding in its subsidiary there is a rebuttable presumption that that parent company exercises a decisive influence over the conduct of its subsidiary and thus will be held responsible for the conduct of its subsidiary. When a parent company's shareholding in its subsidiary is less than 100 per cent the matter of "decisive influence" or otherwise is assessed according to the facts: e.g whether the parent company appoints the board of directors, whether it imposes its commercial policy on the subsidiary.[1961]

If a subsidiary, prior to its acquisition by another undertaking, had carried out anti-competitive activities and the former parent company still exists, that parent company will be liable for the offending conduct of its former subsidiary prior to the acquisition.[1962]

26.5.2.1 *A commercial agent*

The Commission in its 1962 Notice, as confirmed in its Guidelines on Vertical Restraints,[1963] considers that the true commercial agent who acts on behalf of a principal is not considered as an undertaking within the meaning of EU competition rules. However, the situation is different if the commercial agent acts not as an auxiliary but enjoys a degree of independence, permitting it to enter into agreements prohibited under Article 101 TFEU.

In Case 40/73 *Suiker Unie*,[1964] undertakings concerned acted both as agents for each other and as principals on their own account in the sugar market. The ECJ held that taking into consideration the ambiguous relationships between them, they should be regarded as independent under-

---

1957. Case 22/71 *Beguelin Import v GL Import Export* [1971] ECR 949.

1958. Case C-73/95P *Viho Europe* [1996] ECR I-5457.

1959. Case 15/74 *Centrafarm v Sterling Drug Inc* [1974] ECR 1147.

1960. Judgment of 10/09/09 (nyr).

1961. Case T-102/92 *Viho Europe BV v Commission* [1995] ECR II-117.

1962. In Joined Cases T-109/02, T-118/02, T-122/02, T-125/02, T-126/02, T-128/02, T-129/02, T-132/02 and T-136/02 *Bolloré SA and others v Commission* [2007] ECR II-947. See also Case C-49/92P *Commission v Anic Partecipazioni* [1999] ECR I-4125; and Case C-297/98P *SCA Holding v Commission* [2000] ECR I-10101.

1963. Paras 12–21, SEC(2010) 411.

1964. [1975] ECR 1663.

takings. It seems that in each case the Commission will assess the economic functions carried out by the agent in order to decide to what degree it acts as a genuine agent, that is, whether the activities it carries out are associated with a commercial risk. If it bears no such risk or bears only a minimal risk on the contracts negotiated, it will be considered as a "genuine" agent[1965] and therefore not considered as an undertaking within the meaning of EU competition law.

26.5.2.2 An employee

In Case C-22/98 *Jean Claude Becu*,[1966] the ECJ held that employees, whether taken individually or collectively, cannot be regarded as undertakings given that they are incorporated into an undertaking which employs them and thus form an economic unit with it. However, an ex-employee who carries on an independent business would be considered as an undertaking.[1967]

In Case T-325/01 *DaimlerChrysler AG v Commission*,[1968] the CFI [the General Court] decided that commercial agents of DaimlerChrysler AG in Germany should be categorised as employees of DaimlerChrysler given that they did not bear any commercial risk when acting for Daimler-Chrysler either when soliciting orders for sales of new cars or providing other services such as repairs and after-sales services. Indeed, it appeared from the facts that they negotiated sales contracts for new vehicles in the name of DaimlerChrysler with a view to transmitting them to DaimlerChrysler, but they neither purchased new vehicles nor stocked them. In addition, they had neither the authority to fix their own prices for new vehicles nor to grant discounts on them. Further, the terms and conditions of their agency contracts were unilaterally determined by DaimlerChrysler. Consequently they could not be classified as independent undertakings.

26.5.2.3 A public body

Articles 101 and 102 TFEU apply to public bodies if they do not conduct commercial or economic activities in the exercise of "official authority"[1969] or when acting "as public authority" (see above the case of *Eurocontrol*).

A private company acting in the capacity of a public authority cannot be regarded as an undertaking.[1970] Public bodies entrusted with the operation of services of general economic interest or having the character of a revenue-producing monopoly are subject to EU competition rules "in so far as the application of such rules does not obstruct the performance in law or in fact of the particular tasks assigned to them"[1971] and provided that their activities do not affect trade between Member States to such an extent as would be contrary to the interests of the EU.

1965. Case 311/85 *ASBL* [1987] ECR 3801; Case C-266/93 *Volkswagen et VAG Leasing* [1995] ECR I-3477; Case C-217/05 *Confederación Española de Empresarios de Estaciones de Servicio v Compañía Española de Petróleos SA* [2006] ECR I-11987.
1966. [1999] ECR I-5665.
1967. *Reuter/BASF* [1976] OJ L 254/40.
1968. [2005] ECR II-3319.
1969. Case 30/87 *Corinne Bodson v SA Pompes Funèbres des Régions Libérées* [1988] ECR 2479.
1970. Case C-343/95 *Diego Cali v SEPG* [1997] ECR I-1547.
1971. Article 106(2) TFEU.

26.5.3 The doctrine of "State compulsion"

When an undertaking is required by national legislation to act in breach of EU competition law or when the national legal framework is such as to eliminate any possibility of competitive activity on the part of an undertaking, EU competition law will not apply.[1972] The justification is that in these circumstances it cannot be said that the undertaking concerned has freely participated in anti-competitive conduct. However, for the doctrine to apply the legislation in question must have a "decisive influence" on the undertaking's conduct. This is not the case when a State simply encourages an undertaking to adopt anti-competitive conduct without compelling it (see Chapter 27).

26.6 The concept of activity which "may affect trade between Member States"

In order to breach Article 101 and 102 TFEU agreements, decisions, concerted practices or abuses of a dominant position must have an effect on trade between Member States.

The concept of an activity which "may affect trade between Member States" establishes the jurisdictional limitation on the scope of application of Articles 101 and 102 TFEU.

26.6.1 The meaning of the concept of activity which "may affect trade between Member States"

This was explained in Case 56/65 *Société Technique Minière v Maschinenbau Ulm*,[1973] in which the ECJ held that:

> "For this requirement to be fulfilled, it must be possible to foresee with a sufficient degree of probability on the basis of a set of objective factors of law or fact that the agreement in question may have an influence, direct or indirect, actual or potential, on the pattern of trade between Member States."

This definition shows that the ECJ has taken the same approach to EU competition law as to Article 34 TFEU, that is, it applies the *Dassonville* formula in the context of competition law. It is a broad test that brings within the scope of EU competition law even matters that potentially may affect trade between Member States, although that effect must not be purely hypothetical (see below).

The reform of EU competition law prompted the Commission to publish its Guidelines on the Effect on Trade Concept Contained in Articles 81 and 82 of the Treaty [Articles 101 and 102 TFEU].[1974] The Guidelines reiterate the previous case law. They provide that the requirement mentioned above constitutes "an autonomous Community law criterion, which must be assessed separately in each case" (paragraph 19). The taking into account of potential effect means that even if an undertaking concerned does not in fact carry out a prohibited agreement or a decision, its conduct will, nevertheless, fall under the prohibition of EU law as being capable of constituting a threat to freedom of trade between Member States.

1972. Case T-4/96 *Commission v Bayer* [2000] ECR II-3383.
1973. [1966] ECR 235.
1974. [2004] OJ C101/81.

In Case T-77/92 *Parker Pen*,[1975] a clause prohibiting exports was ignored by a distributor but despite this, the potential effect of the clause on the pattern of trade was considered as sufficient to condemn the agreement.

The Commission Guidelines provide that to be in breach of the EU competition rules, any effect must have been sufficiently probable. This confirms the judgment of the CFI in Case T-374/94 *European Night Services v Commission*,[1976] in which the Court ruled that there must be "a real, concrete possibility" not just hypothesis and speculations unsupported by any evidence or any analysis of the structure of the relevant market.

The broad interpretation of the requirement entails that it is irrelevant whether the prohibited conduct will affect trade favourably or not, as this will be assessed later in order to determine the possible exemption under Article 101(3) TFEU. Consequently, the argument that an agreement encourages an increase in the volume of trade between Member States is not sufficient to exclude the possibility that it may affect trade between Member States.[1977]

The prohibition in Articles 101 and 102 applies when the effect on trade between Member States of unlawful conduct is appreciable. The Guidelines on the Effect on Trade Concept Contained in Articles 81 and 82 of the EC Treaty [Articles 101 and 102 TFEU] explain that the appreciability threshold is to be determined by reference to the position and importance of an undertaking in the relevant product market in the light of the circumstances of each individual case.[1978] In paragraph 52 of the Guidelines the Commission sets out quantitative criteria, which when applied cumulatively, may indicate in principle that agreements entered into by the parties do not affect trade. This is an equivalent concept to the de minimis principle developed in the case law of the ECJ (see below).

The criteria are as follows:

- The aggregate market share of the relevant parties does not exceed 5 per cent;

- For horizontal agreements, the aggregate community turnover of the parties does not exceed €40 million; and

- For vertical agreements, the turnover of the supplier of the product does not exceed €40 million.

Paragraph 52 of the Guidelines provides a short-term exemption for parties who have exceeded the above figures in terms of turnover by up to 10 per cent and of market share by up to 2 per cent in no more than two successive calendar years.

26.6.2   Agreements confined to one Member State

It should be noted that an agreement between undertakings in a single Member State may affect trade between Member States if it creates or reinforces partitioning of the internal market in accord with national borders[1979] or limits the capacity of production in a Member State by, for

1975. [1994] ECR II-549.
1976. [1998] ECR II-3141, paras 139–47.
1977. Cases 56 and 58/64 *Consten v Grundig* [1966] ECR 299.
1978. [2004] OJ C101/81.
1979. Case 8/72 *Vereeniging van Cementhandelaren* [1972] ECR 977; Case 246/86 *Belasco* [1989] ECR 2117.

example, fixing prices to be charged in that Member State[1980] or by creating a common subsidiary there responsible for production and commercialisation of their products.[1981]

In Joined Cases T-259–264/02 and T-271/02 *Raiffeisen Zentralbank Österreich AG and Others v Commission [The Lombard Club]*,[1982] the CFI [the General Court] held that in a situation where an agreement/concerted practice covers the whole of the territory of a Member State, there is a strong presumption that such an agreement/concerted practice by its very nature has the effect of reinforcing the compartmentalisation of national markets, and thus is capable of affecting trade between Member States. In this case the Austrian credit establishments involved in a cartel did not rebut this presumption, given that almost all Austrian banks were involved and their agreement covered a wide range of banking products and services, in particular deposits and loans. Thus it was capable of affecting trade between Member States.

In the context of the requirement that to be in breach of Article 101(1) TFEU conduct of undertakings must affect trade between Member States, it is important to emphasise that the agreement as a whole must be taken into consideration, not just every clause restricting competition.[1983] If there is a network of agreements, the actual circumstances, both economic and legal, in which each agreement was made must be taken into consideration.[1984] In the case of abuse of a dominant position, it is necessary to take into account the entirety of the commercial activities of an undertaking, including those outside the internal market.[1985] Even if an abusive practice is principally directed towards imports from a non-Member State, Article 102 TFEU still applies.[1986]

Obviously, if an agreement is confined to one Member State and it does not affect intra-community trade, such an agreement will be outside EU jurisdiction.[1987]

26.6.3 The de minimis rule

Under the de minimis rule some agreements prima facie in breach of Article 101(1) TFEU are outside its scope of application where the market share of the parties is so minimal that their agreement has no effect on trade between Member States. The de minimis rule has developed as a logical complement to the concept of appreciable effect. It was first established in Case 5/69 *Völk v Vervaecke*.[1988]

1980. *Flat Glass* [1989] OJ L33/44.
1981. *Fiat-Hitachi* [1993] OJ L20/10.
1982. [2006] ECR II-5169. This was confirmed by the ECJ in Joined Cases C-125/07P, C-133/07P and 135/07P *Erste Group Bank and Others v Commission* [judgment of 24/09/10] (nyr).
1983. Case 193/83 *Windsurfing International* [1986] ECR 611.
1984. Case 23/67 *Brasserie de Haecht v Wilkin- Janssens (No 1)* [1967] ECR 407.
1985. Cases 6 & 7/73 *Commercial Solvents* [1974] ECR 223 and Case 22/79 *Greenwich Film* [1979] ECR 3275.
1986. *Solvay* [1991] OJ L152/21.
1987. See para 60 of the Guidelines and Case C-215/96 *Carlo Bagnasco v BPN* [1999] ECR I-135, in which the ECJ held that an agreement concerning retail banking services had no appreciable effect on intra-community trade as the potential in trade in the sector concerned (being guarantees for current account credit facilities) was very limited, and undertakings from other Member States would not consider the restrictions imposed by the agreement as important factors in deciding whether or not to establish themselves in the relevant Member State.
1988. [1969] ECR 295.

> **THE FACTS WERE:**
>
> *Völk, a small undertaking manufacturing washing machines, concluded an exclusive distribution agreement with Vervaecke, a Dutch distributor. Völk's share of the market in washing machines was less than 1 per cent. When a dispute arose between the parties, a Dutch court referred to the ECJ a question whether Article 81(1) EC [Article 101(1) TFEU] should apply, taking into account the small share of the market held by Völk.*
>
> *Held:*
>
> The ECJ held that the exclusive distributorship agreement ensuring absolute territorial protection was outside the scope of Article 81(1) EC [Article 101(1) TFEU] as the effects produced on trade between Member States were not appreciable (the agreement concerned only 600 units).

The de minimis rule applies also in the context of Article 102 TFEU.[1989]

26.6.4 Notice on Agreements of Minor Importance

In order to help businesses to assess whether the de minimis rule applies to their agreement, the Commission first published a Notice on Agreements of Minor Importance in 1970.[1990] The version of the Notice current at the time of writing was published in 2001.[1991]

The Notice is not binding on anyone, even on the Commission, but is very useful for undertakings since if their agreement falls below the fixed thresholds, they can reasonably assume that their agreement is outside the scope of EU competition rules. The Commission states in its Notice that no infringement proceedings will be commenced in respect of any such agreement.

The 2001 Notice, contrary to the previous notices on the topic, does not formally distinguish between horizontal and vertical agreements. It refers to agreements between competitors (horizontal) and non-competitors (vertical). The Notice quantifies, by using market share thresholds, what constitutes an appreciable effect on trade between Member States within the meaning of Article 101(1) TFEU in the following manner:

- Agreements between competitors (actual or potential). In the case of undertakings operating at the same level of production or marketing, the threshold is fixed at 10 per cent, that is, the aggregate market share held by an undertaking participating in any of the relevant market must not exceed 10 per cent;
- Agreements between non-competitors. Agreements between undertakings operating at different economic levels in the distribution process are within the scope of the Notice if the aggregate market share of participating undertakings does not exceed a threshold of 15 per cent in any of the relevant markets;
- Mixed agreements. For a mixed horizontal/vertical agreement (or in the event that the classification of an agreement is difficult) a threshold of 10 per cent is applicable;

1989. Case 22/78 *Hugin* [1979] ECR 1869.
1990. [1970] OJ C64/1.
1991. Commission Notice on Agreements of Minor Importance [2001] OJ C368/13.

▪ Networks of agreements. Paragraph 8 relates to networks of agreements. It provides that where competition in the relevant product market is restricted by the cumulative effect of agreements entered into by different suppliers and distributors, a reduced threshold of 5 per cent applies. The matter being addressed by paragraph 8 is that the cumulative effect of agreements may lead to foreclosure of the market. Paragraph 9 states that foreclosure is unlikely to occur if the cumulative effect of parallel networks of agreements affects less than 30 per cent of the relevant market.

The Commission will treat agreements as being within the scope of the Notice if they exceed the fixed threshold by no more that 2 per cent in relation to the market share over two successive financial years.

The Notice does not apply to agreements containing the so-called "hard-core restrictions", for example, those blacklisted in Regulation 330/2010 (see Chapter 27.8.2). Thus, horizontal agreements which are within the scope of the de minimis rule but have as their object price fixing, restriction of production or sales or market sharing, being per se contrary to Article 101(1) TFEU, are excluded from the scope of the Notice (paragraph 11). However, the Commission will usually not commence proceedings in respect of such agreements unless the interests of the EU require it. This will be the case if an undertaking participates in a cartel.[1992] Similar treatment is applied to vertical agreements which fix resale prices, or confer absolute territorial protection upon the participating undertakings or third undertakings.

The Notice acknowledges that agreements between small and medium sized undertakings, that is undertakings which have fewer than 250 employees and have either an annual turnover not exceeding €40 million or an annual balance sheet total net worth not exceeding €27 million,[1993] are unlikely to have appreciable effect on trade between Member States.

26.6.5 The concept of "trade"

The concept of "trade" has been broadly interpreted by the EU institutions. It covers all economic activities including the provision of commercial services such as banking,[1994] insurance[1995] and financial services.[1996] It also encompasses other activities of a commercial nature such as the provision of exhibitions and trade fairs[1997] and the granting of aid to exporters by a professional body in order to finance promotion of their products abroad.[1998]

The concept includes not only import and export between Member States but also between

---

1992. In Case T-56/99 *Marlines SA v Commission (Greek Ferries Cartel)* ([2003] ECR II-5225) the CFI [the General Court] confirmed the Commission's decision that even if an undertaking is small and its market share is below the threshold of 10 per cent (in this case the ferry company operated between the Ports of Patras and Ancons, carrying a very small number of passengers and vehicles and had no ship of its own) but is a member of a cartel, it is not immune from the application of Article 81 EC [Article 101 TFEU]. Marlines argued, inter alia, that because of its limited size and very limited commercial influence it was not in a position to conclude price agreements with its competitors and thus did not participate in a cartel. The CFI [the General Court] replied that the fact that, despite its size, the other undertakings participating in the cartel perceived it as an undertaking whose opinion should be ascertained in order to establish a common position, constituted a factor indicating its participation in the cartel.

1993. Para 3 of the Notice.

1994. Case 172/80 *Züchner* [1981] ECR 2021.

1995. Case 45/85 *Verband Der Sachversicherer* [1987] ECR 405.

1996. [1985] *LSFM* OJ L369/25.

1997. [1975] *UNIDI* OJ L228/17.

1998. [1985] *Milchförderungsfonds* OJ L35/35.

Member States and a non-Member State as, for example, the case of an agreement limiting export of Japanese cars to the United Kingdom.[1999]

The Commission published Guidelines on the Effect on Trade Concept Contained in Articles 81 and 82 of the EC Treaty [Articles 101 and 102 TFEU] which, relying on the case law of the EU courts, state that "the concept of trade is not limited to traditional exchanges of goods and services across borders. It is also a wider concept, covering all cross-border economic activity, including establishment. This interpretation is consistent with the fundamental objectives of the Treaty to promote free movement of goods, services, persons and capital".[2000]

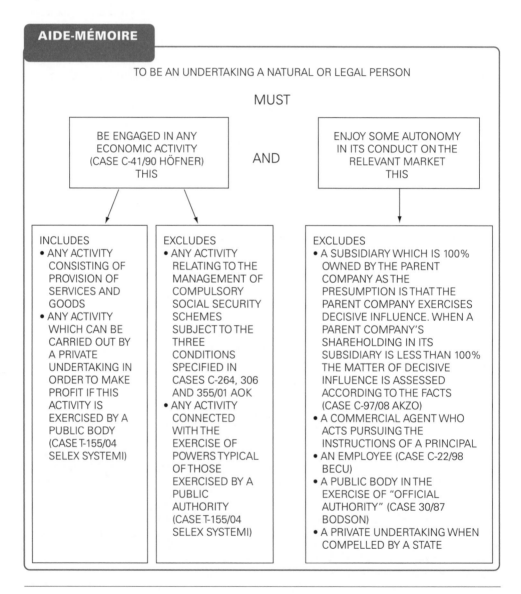

AIDE-MÉMOIRE

TO BE AN UNDERTAKING A NATURAL OR LEGAL PERSON

MUST

BE ENGAGED IN ANY ECONOMIC ACTIVITY (CASE C-41/90 HÖFNER) THIS

AND

ENJOY SOME AUTONOMY IN ITS CONDUCT ON THE RELEVANT MARKET THIS

INCLUDES
• ANY ACTIVITY CONSISTING OF PROVISION OF SERVICES AND GOODS
• ANY ACTIVITY WHICH CAN BE CARRIED OUT BY A PRIVATE UNDERTAKING IN ORDER TO MAKE PROFIT IF THIS ACTIVITY IS EXERCISED BY A PUBLIC BODY (CASE T-155/04 SELEX SYSTEMI)

EXCLUDES
• ANY ACTIVITY RELATING TO THE MANAGEMENT OF COMPULSORY SOCIAL SECURITY SCHEMES SUBJECT TO THE THREE CONDITIONS SPECIFIED IN CASES C-264, 306 AND 355/01 AOK
• ANY ACTIVITY CONNECTED WITH THE EXERCISE OF POWERS TYPICAL OF THOSE EXERCISED BY A PUBLIC AUTHORITY (CASE T-155/04 SELEX SYSTEMI)

EXCLUDES
• A SUBSIDIARY WHICH IS 100% OWNED BY THE PARENT COMPANY AS THE PRESUMPTION IS THAT THE PARENT COMPANY EXERCISES DECISIVE INFLUENCE. WHEN A PARENT COMPANY'S SHAREHOLDING IN ITS SUBSIDIARY IS LESS THAN 100% THE MATTER OF DECISIVE INFLUENCE IS ASSESSED ACCORDING TO THE FACTS (CASE C-97/08 AKZO)
• A COMMERCIAL AGENT WHO ACTS PURSUING THE INSTRUCTIONS OF A PRINCIPAL
• AN EMPLOYEE (CASE C-22/98 BECU)
• A PUBLIC BODY IN THE EXERCISE OF "OFFICIAL AUTHORITY" (CASE 30/87 BODSON)
• A PRIVATE UNDERTAKING WHEN COMPELLED BY A STATE

1999. Case T-37/92 *BEUC and National Consumer Council* [1994] ECR II-285.
2000. [2004] OJ C101/81, para 19.

RECOMMENDED READING

Books for Chapters 26–30

Bishop, S., and Walker, M., *The Economics of EC Competition Law: Concepts, Application and Measurement*, 2nd edition, 2002, London: Sweet and Maxwell

Furse, M., *Competition Law of the EC and UK*, 6th edition, 2008, Oxford: OUP

Jones, A. and Sufrin, B., *EC Competition Law: Text, Cases and Materials*, 3rd edition, 2007, Oxford: OUP

Korah, V., *An Introductory Guide to EC Competition Law and Practice*, 9th edition, 2007, Oxford: Hart Publishing

Lianos, I. and Kokkoris, I., *The Reform of EC Competition Law: New Challenges* 2009, London: KLI

Monti, G., *EC Competition Law*, 2007, Cambridge: Cambridge University Press

Prosser, T., *The Limits of Competition Law: Markets and Public Services*, 2005, Oxford: Oxford University Press

Whish, R., *Competition Law*, 6th edition, 2008, Oxford: Oxford University Press

Articles

Crutchfield, George B., "Increasing Extraterritorial Intrusion of European Union Authority into US Business Mergers and Competition Practices: US Multinational Businesses Underestimate the Strength of the European Commission From G.E.-Honeywell to Microsoft", (2004), 19 Conn. J. Int'l L., p 571

Howard, A., "Modernisation – a Brave New World?", (2007) 6/1 Comp. L.J., p 33

Nihoul, P. and Lübbig, T., "What Competition Policy after Lisbon?", Journal of European Competition Law & Practice, 2010, p 91

Weitbrecht, A., "From Freiburg to Chicago and Beyond – the First 50 years of European Competition Law", (2008) 29/2 ECLR, p 81

27

ARTICLE 101 TFEU

CONTENTS

SUMMARY

1. Article 101(1) TFEU prohibits commercial arrangements consisting of agreements between undertakings, decisions of associations of undertakings, and concerted practices which may affect trade between Member States and which have as their object or effect the prevention, restriction or distortion of competition. Article 101(1) TFEU provides a non-exhaustive list of prohibited arrangements. Examples of these are agreements among competitors to fix prices, share markets or limit production. All such arrangements are void by virtue of Article 101(2) TFEU. However, arrangements which fall within the scope of Article 101(1) TFEU may escape the prohibition if they meet the criteria set out in Article 101(3) TFEU.

2. Article 101(1) TFEU applies not only to commercial arrangements between rival undertakings, known as horizontal agreements, but also to vertical agreements, that is, agreements between undertakings which do not compete with each other because they operate at different levels of the market. Amongst them distribution agreements, franchising agreements, purchasing agreements and sales agreements are the most popular.

3. The concept of an agreement encompasses not only legally enforceable written contracts which are normally concluded in respect of vertical agreements such as distribution agreements, or in respect of horizontal agreements such as joint venture agreements, but also any oral, informal or clandestine arrangements between the parties. In Case T-56/02 *Bayerische*, the CFI stated that the concept of an agreement "centres round the existence of a concurrence of wills between at least two parties, the form in which it is manifested being unimportant so long as it constitutes the faithful expression of the parties' intention". Genuinely unilateral conduct, without the express or implied participation of another undertaking, is outside the scope of Article 101(1) TFEU.

4. The concept of an association of undertakings and the concept of a decision of associations of undertakings have been broadly interpreted. Also the concept of undertaking itself has been interpreted broadly – see Chapter 26.5). The concept of an association encompasses not only a formal association of undertakings such as a trade association but also an informal one such as a gathering of representatives of undertakings in a particular sector to deal with a particular situation or a particular competitor. The term decision refers to associations of undertakings' constitutions, bye-laws, decisions which can be formal (such as a code of conduct) or informal (such as recommendations, circular letters, and so on).

5. The concept of a concerted practice refers to collaboration between at least two undertakings which falls short of an agreement proper. Such co-ordination or co-operation must have been established as a result of direct or indirect contact between them for the purpose of eliminating uncertainties related to a competitor's behaviour or to affect their commercial behaviour in the relevant market. There must be conduct in the market pursuant to the relevant collusive practices, and a relationship of cause and effect between them. Tacit collusion is usually very difficult to prove, but the ECJ has adopted an approach whereby subtle forms of co-ordinated behaviour come within the concept (for example, public announcements of price increases in advance of the actual increase, as a way of "tipping off" other players in the market who then follow suit, could amount to a concerted practice). It can, however, be the case that parallel behaviour may simply reflect the nature of the market rather than any attempt to restrict competition (for example, in an oligopolistic market). Therefore, even if the only logical explanation for parallel conduct of undertakings is that they are engaged in a concerted practice, this must be corroborated by evidence.

6. The purpose of Article 101(1) TFEU is to catch different forms of co-ordination and collusion between undertakings. Accordingly, as the ECJ stated in *Commission v Anic*, "from the subjective point of view, they [agreements and concerted practices] are intended to catch forms of collusion having the same nature and are only distinguishable from each other by their intensity and the forms in which they manifest themselves". However, from a theoretical point of view it is important to distinguish between them because a concerted practice requires the existence of the three above mentioned elements. Notwithstanding this, the case law shows that, in practice, the distinction is blurred. First, in Case C-199/92 *Hüls AG v Commission* the ECJ established a rebuttable presumption that concertation is followed by conduct if the undertaking taking part in the concertation remains active on the relevant market. Second, in *Interbrew and Alken-Maes*,[2001] the Commission stated that a concerted practice is within the scope of Article 101(1) TFEU even in

---

2001. [2003] OJ L200/1.

the absence of actual anti-competitive effects on the competition, i.e potential negative impact on competition will suffice.

7. In Case 56/65 *Société Technique Minière*, the ECJ held that the words "object" and "effect" must be read disjunctively and thus these concepts are not cumulative but alternative. If an agreement, decision, or a concerted practice restricts competition by its object, its effect is irrelevant. It is presumed that it has such a high potential of negative effects that it is not necessary to show any actual effects on the relevant market. If an agreement is not restrictive by object, it must be determined whether it has restrictive effects on competition. Not only are actual and direct effects taken into account but also potential effects and indirect effects on competition in the relevant market. An assessment takes account of the economic and legal setting of the relevant agreement, decision or concerted practice. Only those which have or are likely to have an appreciable adverse effect on competition in the relevant market are caught by Article 101(1) TFEU.

8. Article 101(1) contains a sweeping prohibition that, if interpreted literally, could render almost all commercial arrangements with European dimensions unlawful. For that reason, Article 101(3) TFEU provides for exemption of arrangements which confer sufficient benefit to outweigh their anti-competitive effects. Until the entry into force of Regulation 1/2003 the Commission was the only body entitled to grant exemptions under Article 101(3) TFEU. This was subject to strong criticism, as was the fact that initially Article 101(1) TFEU was interpreted literally (the per se approach), that is, illegality was presumed when an agreement, decision or a concerted practice was in breach of Article 101(1) TFEU by falling within one of the examples of anti-competitive behaviour listed. The response of the Community was to adopt an economic approach to the interpretation of Article 101(1) TFEU consisting of placing the relevant agreement in its economic and legal context in order to determine its compatibility with Article 101(1) TFEU, sometimes referred to as the rule of reason approach. However, the EU courts rejected the approach of the US version of the rule of reason (under which, if the pro-competitive consequences of a challenged arrangement outweigh its anti-competitive effects then the prohibition can be overcome) to the interpretation of Article 101(1) TFEU. This is because the inquiry into pro and anti-competitive effects of a restriction is assessed in the light of Article 101(3) TFEU.

9. When an agreement, decision or a concerted practice is found to be restrictive of competition, it may, nevertheless, be exempted under Article 101(3) TFEU if it satisfies the four cumulative conditions, two positive and two negative, set out in that provision. The positive conditions are:

- Agreements, decisions or concerted practices must contribute to improving the production or distribution of goods or contribute to promoting technical or economic progress;

- They must allow consumers a fair share of the resulting benefit.

The negative criteria are:

- They must not impose on the undertakings concerned restrictions which are not indispensable to the attainment of these objectives;

- They must not afford such undertakings the possibility of eliminating competition in respect of a substantial proportion of the products in question.

10. Block exemptions have been issued in the form of EU regulations (which are thus legally binding). These make agreements, decisions and concerted practices, which are within their scope of application and which conform to their provisions, valid and enforceable even if they are restrictive of competition within the meaning of Article 101(1) TFEU. Within the framework of modernisation of EU competition law the Commission has adopted new style block exemption regulations. The best example is provided by Regulation 330/2010 on the application of Article 101(3) of the TFEU to categories of vertical agreements and concerted practices.

11. Under Article 101(2) TFEU any agreements or decisions prohibited under Article 101(1) TFEU which do not qualify for exemption under Article 101(3) TFEU are automatically void. However, if it is possible to sever the offending clause from an agreement or a decision, then such a clause will be void and the remainder of the agreement or decision may remain in force. Concerted practices are not mentioned in Article 101(2) TFEU since they are informal arrangements and as such cannot be rendered void.

12. Only agreements, decisions and concerted practices which have appreciable effect on trade between Member States are within the scope of Article 101 TFEU. The de minimis rule has developed as a logical complement to the concept of appreciable effect (see Chapter 26.6.3).

27.1 Introduction

Article 101 TFEU states:

"1. The following shall be prohibited as incompatible with the internal market: all agreements between undertakings, decisions by associations of undertakings, and concerted practices which may affect trade between Member States and which have as their object or effect the prevention, restriction or distortion of competition within the common market, and in particular those which:

    (a) directly or indirectly fix purchase or selling prices or any other trading conditions;

    (b) limit or control production, markets, technical development, or investment;

    (c) share markets or sources of supply;

    (d) apply dissimilar conditions to equivalent transactions with other trading parties, thereby placing them at a competitive disadvantage;

    (e) make the conclusion of contracts subject to acceptance by the other parties of supplementary obligations which, by their nature or according to commercial usage, have no connection with the subject of such contracts.

2. Any agreements or decisions prohibited pursuant to this Article shall be automatically void.

3. The provisions of paragraph 1 may, however, be declared inapplicable in the case of:

    – any agreement or category of agreements between undertakings;

    – any decision or category of decisions by associations of undertakings;

    – any concerted practice or category of concerted practices,

which contributes to improving the production or distribution of goods or to promoting technical or economic progress, while allowing consumers a fair share of the resulting benefit, and which does not:

    (a) impose on the undertakings concerned restrictions which are not indispensable to the attainment of these objectives;

    (b) afford such undertakings the possibility of eliminating competition in respect of a substantial part of the products in question."

Breach of the prohibition embodied in Article 101(1) TFEU occurs when an entity identified as an undertaking (see Chapter 26.5) behaves in a manner capable of affecting the pattern of trade between Member States by entering into an unlawful arrangement with another undertaking.

Such an arrangement must have as its object or effect the prevention, restriction or distortion of competition within the internal market.

The concept of an undertaking is not defined in the TFEU but its meaning has emerged from the case law of the ECJ. It has been interpreted broadly so as to maximise the EU competences in competition matters. An entity, whether a natural or a legal person, and regardless of its legal status, the way in which it is financed and irrespective of whether it pursues profit, is regarded as an undertaking if it is engaged in an economic activity and enjoys some autonomy in determining its conduct on the relevant market. The concept of an undertaking is also a relative concept because an entity may be an undertaking under EU competition law with regard to some of its activities and not an undertaking within the meaning of that law with regard to the remaining activities (see Chapter 26.5).

However, in the circumstances set out in Article 101(3) TFEU arrangements which are prima facie in breach of Article 101(1) TFEU may fall outside the Article 101(1) TFEU prohibition. Agreements and decisions which infringe Article 101(1) TFEU and which are not eligible for exemption under Article 101(3) TFEU are, by virtue of Article 101(2) TFEU, void from inception and as such unenforceable.

Horizontal and vertical agreements are within the scope of Article 101 TFEU. The difference between them is explained below.

27.1.1   A horizontal agreement

This is an agreement entered into by undertakings that compete with each other at the same level of the production/distribution chain, for example, agreements between producers, manufacturers or retailers.

Horizontal agreements which are in breach of Article 101 TFEU are the most harmful to competition because rival undertakings, instead of competing with each other, collude and therefore can act as one undertaking in the relevant market. An arrangement between rival undertakings is called a cartel. In a cartel participating undertakings considerably increase their market power and, in some cases, can monopolise the relevant market. As a result, they can reduce output to increase prices and are not subjected to pressure to improve the products they sell, to create new products or to find new ways of commercialisation of such products. Thus, cartels stifle creative innovation, impose higher prices for lower quality goods, and narrow the choice of products. Additionally, they harm consumers, who have to pay cartel prices. Further, they dampen opportunities for new undertakings to enter the relevant market. In short, the existence of cartels runs counter to the objectives of competition law and adversely affects the competitiveness of the economy as a whole.

27.1.2   A vertical agreement

This occurs when two or more undertakings which operate at different levels of the production/distribution chain enter into an agreement, for example, agreements between producers and retailers. The undertakings involved do not in any event compete with each other because they operate at different levels of the market. The most popular vertical agreements are distribution agreements and franchising agreements.

Under EU competition law vertical agreements are treated less severely than horizontal agreements. They are in general less obviously anti-competitive than horizontal agreements. This is because each party to such an agreement exercises its power independently of any rivals. If any party is in a dominant position and abuses such a position, the matter is dealt with under Article 102 TFEU. Usually, the only anti-competitive effect of such agreements is when there is insufficient inter-brand-competition.[2002] Many economists (in particular those allied to the Chicago School[2003]) emphasise that vertical agreements offer many pro-competitive benefits. This is also the current view of the Commission, which under Regulation 330/2010 introduced a rebuttable presumption of compatibility with Article 101(1) TFEU of vertical agreements where the parties to a vertical agreement have a share in the relevant product market of less than 30 per cent. This is subject to some exceptions and subject to a limited number of "hard core" restrictions set out in the Regulation (see section 27.8.2).

27.2   The application of Article 101 TFEU to vertical agreements

There were some doubts as to whether Article 101 applies to vertical agreements, taking into consideration that the parties to such agreements are not on an equal footing. This question was examined by the ECJ in Joined Cases 56 and 58/64 *Établissements Consten Sarl and Grundig-Verkaufs-GmbH v Commission.*[2004]

THE FACTS WERE:

Grundig, a large German manufacturer of electrical equipment, entered into an exclusive distribution agreement with a French distributor, Consten, according to which Consten was appointed as Grundig's exclusive distributor in France, Corsica and the Saar region. Under the contract Consten agreed not to sell outside its territory. Grundig undertook not to compete itself, nor to deliver to third parties, even indirectly, products intended for the territory assigned to Consten and to obtain assurances from its distributors in other Member States that they would not sell to buyers from outside their exclusive territories. This "airtight" exclusive distribution agreement was reinforced by a clause allowing Consten to use the Grundig trade mark "GINT" and emblem in its promotions. On the basis of this authority, Consten registered the Grundig trade mark in France.

A French competitor imported a number of Grundig products from Germany and attempted to sell these in the French market. Consten raised an action for trade mark infringement against this rival, relying on the earlier registration of the trade mark. The Commission objected to these proceedings and commenced an investigation into the functioning of the exclusive distribution agreement. The Commission found that the agreement was contrary to Article 81(1) EC [Article 101(1) TFEU], being an agreement which had the object of distorting competition within the Community by restricting trade. Consten brought an action before the ECJ contesting these findings.

2002. Inter-brand competition refers to competition between suppliers of competing brands. Intra-brand competition concerns competition between distributors of the same brand.

2003. W. S. Comanor, "Vertical Price-Fixing, Vertical Market Restrictions, and the New Antitrust Policy", (1985) 98 Harvard Law Review p 986.

2004. [1966] ECR 299.

Held:

The ECJ confirmed that vertical agreements are within the scope of Article 81 EC [Article 101 TFEU] in the following words:

"Article [Article 101 TFEU] refers in a general way to all agreements which distort competition within the Common Market and does not lay down any distinction between those agreements based on whether they are made between competitors operating at the same level in the economic process or between non-competing persons operating at different levels. In principle, no distinction can be made where the Treaty does not make any distinction."

The ECJ held that it is irrelevant that parties to such an agreement are not equal as regards their position and function in the economy.

Comment:

The ECJ restrictively interpreted Article 81 EC [Article 101 TFEU]. It held that the agreement between Consten and Grundig as well as agreements concluded between Grundig and its other distributors would stifle parallel imports. Although those agreements did not explicitly exclude parallel imports, they discouraged them. Such agreements were intended to isolate the national markets for Grundig products and therefore partition the internal market along national lines, which in itself distorted competition in the internal market. For that reason (without examining other factors such as economic data which indicated that the agreement had increased the volume of trade between France and Germany in Grundig products, the correctness of the criteria which the Commission had applied in order to compare the French market with the German market, and so on) the ECJ held that the agreement was in breach of Article 81(1) EC [Article 101(1) TFEU] and upheld the Commission's position in this matter.

In relation to the trade mark, the ECJ held that the registration of the trade mark which gave Consten an additional protection based on the law of intellectual property rights against the risk of parallel imports into France of Grundig products constituted an abusive use of IPR, because no third party could import Grundig products from other Member States for resale in France without running the serious risk of being liable for breach of trade mark rights, and thus the use of the mark "GINT" was for the purpose of partitioning the internal market along national lines and as such in breach of Article 81(1) EC [Article 101(1) TFEU].[2005]

27.3   Agreements, decisions and concerted practices

Article 101(1) TFEU prohibits all arrangements between undertakings capable of distorting competition within the internal market. It lists three types of arrangement:

- Agreements between undertakings;

- Decisions by associations of undertakings; and

- Concerted practices.

2005.   However, in some exceptional situations absolute territorial protection may be permitted, see Case C-262/81 *Coditel* [1982] ECR 3381; Case 258/78 *Nungesser* [1982] ECR 2015.

Concerted practices are conceptually distinct from the other two types of arrangement. Nevertheless, in fact it is difficult to distinguish between the three types of arrangements mentioned because they are often interrelated. The ECJ, in Case C-8/08 *T-Mobile Netherlands BV, and others v Commission*,[2006] emphasised that "the definitions of 'agreement', 'decisions by associations of undertakings' and 'concerted practice' are intended, from a subjective point of view, to catch forms of collusion having the same nature which are distinguishable from each other only by their intensity and the forms in which they manifest themselves".

In Case C-49/92P *Commission v Anic SpA*,[2007] the ECJ held that although Article 101 distinguishes between "concerted practices", "agreements between undertakings" and "decisions by associations of undertakings", its objective is to catch different forms of co-ordination and collusion between undertakings, and therefore the CFI [the General Court] was correct in considering that "patterns of conduct by several undertakings were a manifestation of a single infringement, corresponding partly to an agreement and partly to a concerted practice". Therefore the two concepts are not incompatible and certain conduct may be qualified as being in the first place a concerted practice and in the second place an agreement, or as being at the same time an agreement and a decision of associations.[2008]

The joint classification is especially useful in respect of a complex infringement of considerable duration involving many undertakings. As the Commission stated in *British Sugar*,[2009] in such circumstances it would be artificial and unrealistic to subdivide continuous conduct, having one and the same overall objective, into several distinct infringements. From a theoretical point of view, however, the distinction between agreements and concerted practice is of importance because:

- For a concerted practice to exist three conditions must be proved by the Commission, i.e. there must be contact between undertakings which has resulted in undertakings concerting together, subsequent conduct on the market pursuant to the agreed course of action and a causal link between the contact and the course of conduct (see section 27.3.3). Accordingly, if there is contact between undertakings but the other conditions are not met the Commission will be unable to prove the existence of a concerted practice. With regard to agreements, this concept emphasises the element of "joint intention" of the parties to conduct themselves on the market in a specific way, irrespective of the form in which the joint intention is expressed (see section 27.3.1). G. Monti explains the difference as follows:

  - If two competitors enter into a contract to fix prices, this is an unlawful agreement;
  - If two competitors meet and exchange information on their intended conduct on the market, this is a concerted practice only when they take this information into consideration in devising their future conduct on the relevant market;[2010]

- The concept of "concerted practice" cannot be used by the Commission as a surrogate for an unproven anti-competitive agreement;

- The concept of "concerted practice" allows the Commission to: investigate and punish

---

2006. [2009] ECR I-4529.

2007. [1999] ECR I-4125, also see Case T-62/98 *Volkswagen AG v Commission* [2000] ECR II-2707.

2008. *Visa International* [2002] OJ L318/17.

2009. *British Sugar plc, Tate and Lyle plc, Napier Brown and Co Ltd, James Budgett Sugars Ltd* [1999] OJ L76/1.

2010. G. Monti, *EC Competition Law, Law in Context*, 2007, Cambridge: CUP, pp 325 et seq.

collusive arrangements which have not taken the form of "agreement" within the meaning of the law of contract, as well as punish certain illicit collective action of undertakings on the basis of indirect evidence.

Notwithstanding the above, the important difference between the concept of an agreement and the concept of a concerted practice (i.e. that the latter requires that anti-competitive conduct must be implemented on the market in order to be caught by Article 101(1) TFEU) has been blurred. First, in Case C-199/92 *Hüls AG v Commission*[2011] the ECJ established a rebuttable presumption that concertation is followed by anti-competitive conduct if the undertaking taking part in the concertation remains active on the relevant market. Second, in *Interbrew and Alken-Maes*,[2012] the Commission stated that a concerted practice is within the scope of Article 101(1) TFEU even in the absence of actual anti-competitive effects on the competition, i.e. its potential negative impact on competition will suffice.[2013]

27.3.1 Agreements between undertakings

The concept of agreements refers mainly to contracts concluded between undertakings. This is particularly evident in the context of vertical agreements.

In respect of horizontal agreements it is very unlikely that undertakings would enter into a formal contract. For that reason EU institutions apply a pragmatic approach in the identification of an agreement within the meaning of Article 101(1) TFEU. Agreements have been defined as consensual arrangements between undertakings irrespective of whether or not they are formally binding contracts and as involving the acceptance of an obligation irrespective of whether the obligation is legally binding.

Consequently, an agreement will fall within the scope of Article 101(1) TFEU, irrespective of whether it is:

- Written, or oral;[2014]

- Signed or not by or on behalf of an undertaking;[2015]

- Legally binding.[2016]

The following were regarded as agreements within the scope of Article 101(1) TFEU: standard sale conditions;[2017] out-of-court settlements; correspondence between undertakings and conversations between representatives of those undertakings;[2018] rules adopted by a trade association when they are binding on its members (such rules are considered as agreements with regard to the

---

2011. [1999] ECR I-4287.

2012. [2003] OJ I200/1.

2013. Case C-209/07 *Beef Industry Development Society and Barry Brothers* [2008] ECR I-0000.

2014. Case T-43/92 *Dunlop Slazenger International* [1994] ECR II-441.

2015. *BP-Kemi-DDSF* [1979] OJ L286/32 [1979] 3 CMLR 684. In *BP Kemi* the agreement was implemented by the parties although not formally signed by them.

2016. Joined Cases T-217/03 and T-245/03 *Fédération Nationale de la Coopération Bétail et Viande (FNCBV)* [2006] ECR II-4987, appeal pending C-110/07.

2017. Case C-277/87 *Sandoz* [1990] ECR I-45; Case T-168/01 *GlaxoSmithKline Services Unlimited v Commission* [2006] ECR II-2969.

2018. Case T-7/89 *Hercules Chemicals NV v Commission* [1991] ECR II-1711.

members and as a decision with regard to the association).[2019] An informal agreement such as a "gentlemen's agreement" also falls within the scope of Article 101(1) TFEU. This was exemplified in the *Quinine Cartel* cases.[2020]

THE FACTS WERE:

In 1958 undertakings from France, Germany and The Netherlands selling quinine (quinine is mainly used for making medicines to treat malaria but also in synthetic quinidine, which is an ingredient in other pharmaceuticals) decided to form a cartel in order to stabilise the quinine market which (due to the sale of surpluses of quinine by the Government of the US and to new sources of supply established in Congo and Indonesia) was falling dramatically. The undertakings involved fixed prices for the bark, from which both quinine and synthetic quinidine are made, allocated purchases of the stock which was disposed of by the US Government, allocated national markets to individual members of the cartel, allocated export markets outside the EC to the undertakings involved and decided on which markets undertakings were allowed to compete in while allocating to them quotas in relation to these markets. The agreement was concluded for a period of five years. In order to supervise its implementation, each party had to notify each other of its quarterly sales and prices. Also compensatory sales were organised for undertakings unable to reach their export sales quotas. With the entry into force of the EC Treaty, the participating undertakings decided not to notify their agreements to the Commission. When investigated by the German Bundeskartellamt, the undertakings concerned concluded a new agreement which fixed prices and allocated quotas and markets outside the EC. However, it was supplemented by a gentlemen's agreement in writing extending its application to the internal market, and containing a clause providing that breach of its provisions would be considered a breach of the formal written agreement and enforceable by arbitration. The "gentlemen's agreement" contract was unsigned and secret.

Held:

The ECJ held that both agreements and others implementing oral and written agreements amounted to "agreements" within the meaning of Article 81(1) EC [Article 101(1) TFEU]. The Court stated that it suffices that an agreement "amounted to the faithful expression of the joint intention of the parties to the agreement with regard to their conduct in the Common Market" to be within the scope of Article 81(1) EC [Article 101(1) TFEU.

In Case T-56/02 *Bayerische Hypo und Vereinsbank v Commission*,[2021] the CFI [the General Court] defined the concept of an agreement, which is relevant to both horizontal and vertical agreements, in the following terms:

".. the concept of an agreement within the meaning of Article 81(1) EC [Article 101(1) TFEU], as interpreted by the case-law, centres round the existence of a concurrence of wills between at least

---

2019. *Nuovo Cegam* [1984] OJ L 99/29.
2020. Case 41/69 *Chemiefarma* [1970] ECR 661.
2021. [2004] ECR II-3495.

two parties, the form in which it is manifested being unimportant so long as it constitutes the faithful expression of the parties' intention."

Even if a contract is contrary to the economic interests of one of the parties,[2022] or was legally terminated but still produces unlawful effects,[2023] or was concluded subject to a condition,[2024] it is regarded as an agreement within the meaning of Article 101(1) TFEU. Further, the legal nature of an agreement is determined by the EU institutions/national competition authorities in the light of factual considerations and not by the parties to it.[2025] It was confirmed by the CFI [the General Court] in Case T-99/04 *AC-Treuhand AG v Commission*[2026] that the concept of "agreement" should be interpreted broadly. In that case the CFI classified conduct of a consultancy company, which was not active on the relevant market but which contributed to the implementation of a cartel by, inter alia, organising meetings for the three producers of organic peroxides which set it up and by covering up evidence of its existence, as an agreement between undertakings within the meaning of Article Article 81 EC [Article 101 TFEU]. The Court held that although the consultancy company was only an accessory and not a party to the cartel, the element of "joint intention" which is essential to the existence of an "agreement" does not require the relevant market, on which the undertaking which is the "perpetrator" of the restriction of competition is active, to be exactly the same as the one on which that restriction is deemed to materialise.

There is no concurrence of wills between the parties at the stage of negotiations, preparatory discussions, and so on,[2027] as at that stage no agreement has been reached.

It is to be noted that collective bargaining agreements between workers and employers are not regarded as agreements within the meaning of Article 101(1) TFEU in so far as their objective is to improve conditions of work and employment.[2028]

27.3.1.1   The limit of the concept of an agreement: unilateral conduct of an undertaking

One undertaking acting alone cannot be in breach of Article 101(1) TFEU. However, until the judgment of the CFI [the General Court] in Case T-41/96 *Bayer AG v Commission*,[2029] the concept of an agreement was open to being broadly interpreted so that even unilateral conduct could conceivably have come within it, for example, unilateral anti-competitive measures adopted by a manufacturer vis-à-vis its dealers without account being taken of the actual conduct of the dealers with regard to those measures. The signature of the dealership contract was open to being regarded as tacit acquiescence in subsequent anti-competitive initiatives of the manufacturer regardless of subsequent conduct adopted by the dealers.[2030] Even when anti-competitive

---

2022. *Johnson and Johnson* [1980] OJ L377/16; [1981] 2 CMLR 287, Case T-48/98 *Acerinox v Commission* [2001] ECR II-3859.

2023. Case 51/75, Case 86/75 and Case 96/75 *EMI Records* [1976] ECR 811, 871 and 913.

2024. *SAS/Maersk Air* [2001] OJ L265/15.

2025. *Auditel and AGB Italia SpA* [1993] OJ L306/50.

2026. [2008] ECR II-1501.

2027. Case T-60/02, *Deutsche Verkehrsbank AG* [unpublished].

2028. Case C-67/96 *Albany International BV v Stichting Bedrijfspensioenfonds Textielindustrie* [1999] ECR I-5751.

2029. [2000] ECR II-3383. The ECJ confirmed the above judgment in Joined Cases C-2/01P and C-3/01P *Bundesverband der Arzneimittel-Importeure EV v Commission* [2004] ECR I-23.

2030. [1983] ECR 3151.

initiatives were to the disadvantage of dealers, they were regarded as forming part of an agreement. This is exemplified in Case C-277/87 *Sandoz*.[2031]

THE FACTS WERE:

Sandoz, a pharmaceutical company, put on its invoices for the supply of pharmaceuticals the words "export prohibited" in order to prevent parallel imports of its products to Italy, where prices were controlled by Sandoz and as a result were much higher than in other Member States. The invoices were sent to its distributors.

Held:

The ECJ held that the unilateral act of Sandoz was part of the distribution agreement between Sandoz and its distributors, irrespective of the actual adherence to it by the distributors.[2032]

The consequences of this approach for distributors and dealers in similar circumstances were twofold: first they were in breach of Article 101 TFEU and thus could be fined by the Commission, and second they were liable for damages to anyone who had suffered losses as a result of their conduct.

Doubtless distributors and dealers welcomed the judgment of the CFI [the General Court] in Case T-41/96 *Bayer AG v Commission*.[2033] In that case the CFI [the General Court] stated that unilateral behaviour of an undertaking would be considered as being an agreement only if a concurrence of wills of at least two parties could be established. The mere existence of an agreement and a measure imposed unilaterally does not suffice. The Commission must establish to the requisite legal standard that such a measure has the express or implicit acquiescence of the other party.

THE FACTS WERE:

Bayer AG, one of the most important chemical and pharmaceutical groups in Europe, which has subsidiaries in all the Member States, brought proceedings before the CFI challenging Decision 96/478/EC of the Commission in Adalat ([1996] OJ L201/1) in which it was found in breach of Article 81(1) EC {Article 101(1) TFEU}.

Under the trade mark "Adalat" or "Adalate" Bayer AG had manufactured and marketed a range of medicinal preparations designed to treat cardio-vascular disease. In a number of Member States the price for "Adalat" was directly determined by the national health authorities. Between 1989 and 1993 in France and Spain the price was 40 per cent lower than the price in the United Kingdom. The price difference had encouraged parallel imports of "Adalat"

2031. [1990] ECR I-45.
2032. Similar conclusions were reached by the ECJ in Joined Cases 32 and 36–82/78 *BMW Belgium SA v Commission* [1980] ECR 2435.
2033. [2000] ECR II-3383. The above judgment was confirmed in Case T-208/01 *Volkswagen AG V Commission* [2003] ECR II-5141.

from France and Spain to the UK. According to Bayer, sales of "Adalat" by its British subsidiary fell by almost half between 1989 and 1993. In order to recover the lost profit Bayer AG decided to cease fulfilling all of the increasingly large orders placed by wholesalers in Spain and France with its Spanish and French subsidiaries. Some French and Spanish wholesalers complained to the Commission. Following its investigations the Commission found that Bayer AG was in breach of Article 81(1) EC [Article 101(1) TFEU]. The Commission decided that the prohibition of the export to other Member States of "Adalat" from France and Spain agreed between Bayer France and its wholesalers since 1991 and between Bayer Spain and its wholesalers since 1989 constituted a breach of Article 81(1) EC [Article 101(1) TFEU]. Bayer AG argued that the Commission went too far in its interpretation of the concept of an agreement and that in fact Bayer's unilateral conduct was outside the scope of that Article.

Held:

The CFI [General Court] ruled that in order to establish whether or not there was an agreement between the parties two elements should be considered:

■ the intention of Bayer to impose an export ban; and

■ the intention of the wholesalers to adhere to Bayer's policy designed to reduce parallel imports.

In the light of the evidence submitted the CFI held that the Commission had failed to prove to the requisite legal standard that an agreement existed.

The CFI emphasised that:

"The proof of an agreement between undertakings within the meaning of Article 81(1) [Article 101(1) TFEU] must be founded upon the direct or indirect finding of the existence of the subjective element that characterises the very concept of an agreement, that is to say a concurrence of wills between economic operators on the implementation of a policy, the pursuit of an objective, or the adoption of a given line of conduct on the market, irrespective of the manner in which the parties' intention to behave on the market in accordance with the terms of that agreement is expressed."

27.3.2 Decisions by associations of undertakings

This concept refers to decisions of trade associations and of any economic interest grouping of undertakings as defined in Joined Cases T-39 and 40/92 *Groupement des Cartes Bancaires CB and Europay International*,[2034] irrespective of their legal form.

The distortion of competition may result from either a written constitution of an association which imposes certain rules of conduct on its members[2035] or decisions of its managing body which are binding and thus must be complied with by all its members.

Although the concept of "associations" under Article 101(1) TFEU is mainly concerned with trade associations of undertakings, the ECJ has given it a broad interpretation. As a result, it

---

2034. [1994] ECR II-49
2035. *National Sulphuric Acid Association* [1980] OJ L 260/24; [1980] 3 CMLR 429.

encompasses professional associations[2036] including a body set up by statute with public functions, members of which are appointed by the government,[2037] international organisations such as the International Railways Union,[2038] groupings such as the European Broadcasting Union[2039] which co-ordinates the Eurovision system, and even a maritime conference.[2040]

In Case 123/83 *BNIC v Clair*,[2041] the ECJ held that an agreement concluded between two groups of traders must be regarded as "an agreement between undertakings or associations of undertakings". A decision adopted by a federal type association, that is, its members are themselves associations, is also within the Article 101(1) TFEU prohibition.[2042]

The question of whether non-binding decisions of associations are within the scope of Article 101(1) TFEU was answered by the ECJ in Case 8/72 *Vereeniging van Cementhandelaren*.[2043]

THE FACTS WERE:

A Dutch trade association, of which most Dutch cement dealers were members, recommended the prices at which cement should be sold in The Netherlands. The trade association actually controlled the Dutch cement industry given that it imposed detailed trading rules on its members (for example, the obligation to notify any change in management), supervised its members accounts, required that they sell to each other and thus eliminated the possibility of the building-up of stocks of cement by third parties, and was empowered to expel its members for non-compliance with these rules.

Held:

The ECJ held that a non-binding recommendation would amount to a decision in so far as its acceptance by undertakings actually influenced their conduct in the market. The Cementhandelaren's decision recommending target prices had great impact on the level of prices: first, its members were actually complying with the recommendation and second, it removed to a great extent the uncertainty as to prices, as almost all dealers were charging the same as each other. Consequently, the recommendation was regarded as a decision within the meaning of Article 81(1) EC [Article 101(1) TFEU].

2036. *COAPI* [1995] OJ L 122/37, including professional bodies such as the Bar of The Netherlands: Case C-309/99 *Wouters v Algemene Raad van de Nederlandse Orde van Advocaten* [2002] ECR I-577.

2037. E.g. the examination committee of the Italian Bar: Case C-250/03 *Mauri* (Ord) [2005] OJ C115/8.

2038. Case T-14/93 *UIC* [1995] ECR II-1503; or the International Olympic Committee, the supreme authority of the Olympic Movement, which brings together the various international sporting federations Case C-519/04 P *Meca-Medina and Majcen v Commission* [2006] ECR I-6991.

2039. Joined Cases T-528, 542, 543/93 and 546/93 *Metropole Télévision SA and Reti Televisive Italiane SpA and Gestevisión Telecinco SA and Antena 3 de Televisión v Commission* [1996] ECR II-649.

2040. Joined Cases C-395 and 396/96P *Compagnie Maritime Belge Transport SA* [1996] ECR I-1365.

2041. [1985] ECR 391.

2042. *Milchförderungsfonds* [1985] OJ L35/35.

2043. [1972] ECR 977.

27.3.2.1 Exchange of information systems allowed to be set up by a trade or other association

Trade and other associations provide a comprehensive range of services to their members, are guardians of professional standards for the benefit of their members and their customers, provide professional training and support, and lobby on behalf of their members. However, as they provide a forum for discussion and exchange of their members' views, they may facilitate collusion between their members. They may either actively participate in the collusive actions of members,[2044] or may be used as a means by which members exchange information on prices, outputs and other conditions of the industry, which will enable undertakings to be aware of the market position and strategy of their rivals and thus increase the probability of collusion, or even facilitate it. They may act in such a way as to control entry to a given market and block potential competitors.

The issue of what kind of information exchange system an association is allowed to put in place was examined in Case C-7/95P *John Deere Ltd v Commission*.[2045] The ECJ held that the compatibility of an exchange of information system with competition law must be assessed in the context of the economic conditions of the market and the particular characteristics of the system in question. However, it seems that the following three factors will decide whether such a system is compatible with EU law:

- The degree of concentration of the market. For example, in an oligopolistic market[2046] competition is already greatly reduced and thus any exchange of information substantially risks impairing the competition which exists between traders;

- Whether such a system reveals to all the competitors the market positions and strategies of the various individual competitors. Thus, an exchange of information system must not reduce or remove uncertainty regarding the conduct of competitors in the relevant market;

- Whether non-discriminatory access to the system is available, in law and in fact, to all operators in the relevant area.

It results from the case law that any scheme for the exchange of information will be permitted if it is carried out where the market is question is not highly concentrated and in such a manner as to exclude any information from which the behaviour of individual producers can be identified and ensure all operators have access to the system. Such a system will be helpful and neutral while assisting undertakings, and often consumers, in making informed choices.

27.3.2.2 The limit of the concept of an agreement or a decision – the "State compulsion doctrine"

By virtue of Article 4(3) TEU read in conjunction with Articles 101 and 102 TFEU, a Member State is prohibited from introducing or maintaining national rules which may render EU competition law ineffective.[2047]

2044. Case 246/86 *Belasco v Commission [Re Belgian Roofing Felt Cartel]* [1989] ECR 2117.
2045. [1998] ECR I-3111. This was confirmed in Case C-238/05 *ASNEF-EQUIFAX* [2006] ECR I-11125.
2046. An oligopoly is a market dominated by a small number of undertakings, usually more than two.
2047. Joined Cases 209–15 and 218/78 *Van Landewyck* [1980] ECR 3125.

If a trade association is forced by a government through a mandatory act, whether legislative or administrative, to regulate industry in a manner contrary to Article 101(1) TFEU, the association will not be in breach of Article 101(1) TFEU.[2048] However, if a government merely encourages undertakings to impose anti-competitive restrictions, such encouragement will not constitute a defence for the association concerned.[2049]

27.3.3 Concerted practices

It derives from the very nature of a concerted practice that it does not have all the elements of a contract, but it constitutes a form of informal co-ordination between undertakings.

Concerted practices are difficult to evidence, taking into account that:

- They are implicit, secret arrangements which the participating undertakings will try to hide from the public view at all costs. This is exemplified in *Graphite Electrodes Cartel*.[2050]

THE FACTS WERE:

The Graphite Electrodes Cartel was a worldwide cartel aimed at fixing prices and sharing markets for graphite electrodes. The participating undertakings from Europe, the USA and Japan, knowing that they were acting in breach of antitrust law, took great pains to conceal their meetings in Switzerland. All expenses for hotel and travel were paid in cash with no explicit reference to those meetings being made in the expense claims of those attending. The participants also took great care to avoid keeping any written evidence of meetings, and agreements and in such documents as did exist code names were used to refer to cartel participants (for example, "BMW" for Germany's SGL Carbon AG, "Pinot" for the USA-based UCAR and "Cold" for the group of Japanese companies).

Held:

When the cartel was discovered, the Commission imposed fines totalling €218 million on the participating undertakings.

- When there is no direct evidence, for example, minutes of meeting, plans, and so on, indirect evidence, for instance, parallel conduct, may indicate that an undertaking is engaged in a concerted practice. However, even in a case where the only logical explanation for parallel behaviour is concerted practice, this must be corroborated by evidence.[2051] Parallel

---

2048. Case 123/83 *BNIC v Clair* [1985] ECR 391.

2049. Case C-35/99 *Arduino* [2002] ECR I-1529; Case C-198/01 *CIF* [2003] ECR I-8055; Case C-198/01 *Consorzio Industrie Fiammiferi (CIF) v Autorità Garante della Concorrenza e del Mercato* [2003] ECR I-8055; Joined Cases T-217/03 and T-245/03 *Fédération Nationale de la Coopération Bétail et Viande (FNCBV) and Others v Commission* [2006] ECR II-4987.

2050. COMP/E-2/37.667. The CFI largely confirmed the Commission's decision but reduced the amount of fines for some participants: Joined Cases T-71, 74, 87 and T-91/03 *Tokai Carbon and Others v Commission* [15/06/2005 (unpublished)].

2051. See Commission Decision IP/02/1603 dated 04/11/202 *(Carlsberg-Heineken)*.

behaviour of undertakings may be justified by other factors such as a high degree of market transparency or the oligopolistic tendencies of the market, in which situation the market is dominated by a small number of large undertakings. In this context it is extremely difficult to establish collusive practices as it is expected that when one producer changes its prices/policies, others will follow.

27.3.3.1 Meaning of a concerted practice

Three cases decided by the Community courts have defined the meaning of a concerted practice. They are discussed below.

27.3.3.1.1 Case 48/69 *Imperial Chemical Industries Ltd v Commission (Dyestuffs)*[2052]

THE FACTS WERE:

ICI was one of several undertakings which manufactured aniline dyestuffs. The leading producers of aniline dyestuffs increased their prices almost simultaneously on three occasions: in 1964 by 10 per cent, in 1965 by 10 to 15 per cent and in 1967 by 8 per cent. The Commission decided that these three general and uniform increases in prices indicated that there had been a concerted practice between the undertakings concerned contrary to Article 101(1) TFEU and imposed fines on them. The undertakings challenged the Commission's decision on the grounds that the price increase merely reflected parallel behaviour in an oligopolistic market and did not result from concerted practices.

Held:

The ECJ upheld the Commission's decision and provided a definition of a concerted practice. The Courts held that a concerted practice refers to a form of co-operation between undertakings which, without having been taken to the stage where an agreement properly so-called has been concluded, knowingly substitutes for the risk of competition practical co-operation between them. Therefore, co-ordination and co-operation between undertakings constituted an essential feature in determining whether or not they had been engaged in a concerted practice.

27.3.3.1.2 Cases 40–48/73, 50/73, 54–56/73, 111/73, 113–114/73 *Suiker Unie*[2053]
The ECJ held:

■ That "the criteria of co-ordination and co-operation must be understood in the light of the concept inherent in the provision of the Treaty relating to competition that each economic operator must determine independently the policy which he intends to adopt on the Common Market". The ECJ emphasised that the autonomy of an undertaking must not be altered. This autonomy is called into question when competing undertakings intentionally exchange information, directly or indirectly, in order to influence the conduct of actual or

---

2052. [1972] ECR 619.
2053. [1975] ECR 1663.

potential competitors or to disclose to such a competitor the adopted or envisaged course of conduct;

▪ That no actual plan is required, but for the practice to exist it is necessary that undertakings have direct or indirect contact, the object or effect of which is to either influence the conduct of an actual or potential competitor or to disclose to such a competitor the course of action that the colluding undertakings have agreed to adopt or envisage adopting in the relevant market.

27.3.3.1.3 Joined Cases T-25 to 104/95 *Cimenteries CBR and Others v Commission* ([2000] ECR II-491)

The CFI [the General Court]:

▪ First, made a distinction between passive reception of information and active reception of information. It stated that, to amount to a concerted practice there must be an intention to communicate information to the other party and the latter must be aware that it is receiving such communication not accidentally, but on purpose. The exchange of information must go beyond mutual awareness of what the other party is doing based on normal sources of information such as the terms and conditions quoted to customers, which are easy to obtain and which will influence prices and policies adopted by competitors;

▪ Second, held that: "a concerted practice implies, besides undertakings' concerting together, conduct on the market pursuant to those collusive practices, and a relationship of cause and effect between the two".

The above case law can be summarised as follows:

For there to be a concerted practice there must be direct or indirect contact between competitors which must have effect on the undertaking's future conduct and the relationship of cause and effect between the concertation and the market conduct.

▪ Direct or indirect contact

Any direct or indirect contact between competitors which undermines the requirement of independence, i.e. the requirement according to which each economic operator must determine independently the policy which it intends to adopt on the relevant market, is prohibited.[2054] In this respect the issue of the participation of undertakings in meetings arises. Under EU law there is a presumption that when an undertaking participates in a meeting during which its competitor discloses its future policy regarding the relevant market, that undertaking takes account of such information for the purpose of determining its conduct on the market.

In *Cimenteries*, the CFI held that an undertaking could not argue that it was merely a passive recipient of information when it received information at a meeting about the future conduct of a competitor and failed to raise objections or express its reservations.[2055] The way for an undertaking,

---

2054. See *Suiker Unie and Others v Commission*, para 173; Case 172/80 *Züchner* [1981] ECR 2021, para 13; *Ahlström Osakeyhtiö and Others v Commission*, para 63; and Case C-7/95 P *Deere* v *Commission* [1998] ECR I-3111, para 86.

2055. [2000] ECR II-491; Cases T-202/98 *Tate and Lyle Plc, British Sugar Plc and Napier Brown Plc v Commission* [2001] ECR II-2035.

which finds itself participating in this type of meeting to protect itself, is to prove by means of corroborated evidence[2056] that it participated in the meeting "in a spirit that was different" from the other participants,[2057] i.e. the undertaking concerned must publicly distance itself from what was discussed at the meeting or must report the unlawful initiative to the relevant administrative authorities.

Non-implementation by an undertaking of any unlawful policy discussed at a meeting will not be sufficient to exclude it from liability under Article 101(1) TFEU. In Case T-334/94 *Sarrió SA v Commission*,[2058] the CFI [the General Court] rejected the argument of Sarrió that despite its participation in an agreement which co-ordinated prices, it applied its own prices to each individual transaction. The CFI [the General Court] held that the agreement had an impact on transaction prices as it provided the basis for price negotiation in each transaction and that solely by participating in the agreement Sarrió had infringed Article 81(1) EC [Article 101(1) TFEU]. The CFI [the General Court] rejected Sarrió's argument concerning no implementation of the agreement. The CFI [the General Court] stated that a serious anti-competitive intent is contrary to Article 81(1) EC [Article 101(1) TFEU] whether or not the agreement is in fact implemented.

In *Industrial and Medical Gases*,[2059] two undertakings which were participating in anti-competitive meetings, Air Liquide and Westfalen, tried to convince the Commission that their conduct in the market subsequent to meetings (which consisted of pursuing an "aggressive commercial policy" towards their competitors) provided sufficient evidence that they neither participated in the agreements nor implemented them. This argument was rejected by the Commission.

In Case C-8/08 *T-Mobile Netherlands BV and Others v Commission*,[2060] the ECJ held that the finding of a concerted practice does not require that competitors meet regularly over a period of time. A single meeting between competitors may constitute a sufficient basis for them to concert their market conduct. Accordingly, the number, frequency and form of meetings is irrelevant. What counts is whether a meeting or meetings allow the participating undertaking to take account of information exchanged with its competitors so as to influence its future conduct on the relevant market.

■ Conduct pursuant to direct or indirect contact and the relationship of cause and effect between concertation and market conduct

The ECJ in Case C-199/92 P *Hüls v Commission*[2061] set out a presumption according to which an undertaking which takes part in a concerted action and remains active on the relevant market is presumed to take account of the information exchanged with its competitors for the purpose of determining its conduct on the relevant market. This presumption is almost impossible to rebut, unless the undertaking ceases to exist, because in order to establish a concerted practice, it is not necessary for the Commission to prove the actual anti-competitive effect of a concerted practice, if its object is to restrict competition. Therefore even potential anti-competitive impact of a

---

2056. Case T-14/89 *Montedipe v Commission* [1992] ECR II-1155.
2057. Cases C-204/00, C-205/00, C-211/00, C-213/00, C-217/00, C-219/00 *Aalborg Portland AS v Commission* [2004] ECR I-123.
2058. [1998] ECR II-1439.
2059. [2003] OJ L84/1.
2060. [2009] ECR I-4529.
2061. [1999] ECR I-4287.

concerted practice on competition is sufficient to be regarded as having an anti-competitive object (see section 27.4).

27.3.3.1.4 Intelligent conduct

Under Article 101(1) TFEU intelligent conduct of an undertaking based on current and anticipated conduct of its competitors is not prohibited.

The Commission considers that the exchange of price information between undertakings is in breach of Article 101(1) TFEU if the information exchanged concerns individual data of an undertaking relating directly to the prices charged or to the elements of a pricing policy, including discounts, costs, terms of trade, rates and dates of change. In Case T-334/94 *Sarrió SA v Commission*,[2062] the CFI [the General Court] provided some clarification relating to the exchange of information between undertakings. It held that the exchange of statistical data is not in itself an infringement of Article 81(1) EC [Article 101(1) TFEU]. The mere fact that a system for the exchange of statistical information might be used for anti-competitive purposes does not make it contrary to Article 101(1) TFEU, since in such circumstances it is necessary to establish its actual anti-competitive effect.

27.3.3.2   *Parallel behaviour in an oligopolistic market*

When there is no direct evidence of any contact, direct or indirect, between undertakings but they exhibit parallel conduct over a period of time, the question arises whether their conduct constitutes sufficient evidence of a concerted practice. This is of particular relevance in a situation where the relevant market is oligopolistic. This issue was examined in Joined Cases 89, 104, 114, 116, 117 and 125–129/85 *Ahlström and Others [Re Wood Pulp Cartel] v Commission*.[2063]

THE FACTS WERE:

The Commission found more than 40 suppliers of wood pulp in violation of EC competition law despite the fact that none of these companies was resident within the EC. Fines were imposed on 36 of these companies for violation of Article 81(1) EC [Article 101(1) TFEU]. A number of these companies appealed against the decision to the ECJ. They challenged the Commission's finding that they breached Article 81(1) EC [Article 101(1) TFEU] through concertation of prices for their products by means of a system of quarterly price announcements. The factors that the Commission took into account, inter alia, were the system of early announcements of prices which made prices transparent, the uniform fluctuation of prices and the uniform approach to prices which could be explained in a narrow oligopolistic situation where undertakings had to follow a market leader. However, at that time there were more than 50 producers of wood pulp. On this basis the Commission had concluded that the market was not oligopolistic and that the uniform market behaviour could be explained only by a concerted practice.

2062.   [1998] ECR II-1439.
2063.   [1993] ECR I-1307.

Held:

The ECJ annulled the decision of the Commission on the ground that the Commission had not provided a firm, precise and consistent body of evidence of infringement.

The ECJ held that parallel conduct could not be regarded as furnishing proof of concertation unless concertation constituted the only plausible explanation.

Comment:

The ECJ appointed its own experts to analyse the market. Their findings convinced the ECJ that there may be explanations of parallel behaviour other than concertation, such as the natural structure of the market. In the present case the market was cyclical. In respect of transparency of prices, the early announcements were requested by customers; taking into account the cyclical nature of the market, they wanted to know the price for wood pulp as soon as possible. The ECJ held that: "it must be stated that, in this case, concertation is not the only plausible explanation for the parallel conduct. To begin with, the system of price announcements may be regarded as constituting a rational response to the fact that the pulp market constituted a long-term market and to the need felt by both buyers and sellers to limit commercial risks. Further, the similarity in the dates of price announcements may be regarded as a direct result of the high degree of market transparency, which does not have to be described as artificial. Finally, the parallelism of prices and the price trends may be satisfactorily explained by the oligopolistic tendencies of the market and by the specific circumstances prevailing in certain periods. Accordingly, the parallel conduct established by the Commission does not constitute evidence of concertation."

However, even if concertation constitutes the only plausible explanation, this must be corroborated by evidence.

27.3.3.3   Limited participation of an undertaking in an anti-competitive practice

The question of collective responsibility attributed to individual undertakings for breach of Article 101(1) TFEU was explained by the ECJ in Case C-49/92 P *Commission v Anic SpA*.[2064] Anic argued that the Commission was confusing the concept of a single infringement with collective responsibility. It submitted that when various actions amount to a single infringement, the Commission must show that the undertaking concerned had participated in all aspects of the infringement, that is, in all actions forming the infringement in order to make it responsible for all aspects of the conduct of all the undertakings charged during the relevant period. As Anic participated in only some concerted actions, not all of them, it argued that it was held responsible for actions of other undertakings that participated in the infringement.

The ECJ emphasised that, taking into account the nature and degree of the ensuing penalties, responsibility for infringements of Article 81(1) EC [Article 101 TFEU] is personal in nature. However, it flows from Article 101 TFEU that the anti-competitive conduct results from collaboration by several undertakings and therefore each undertaking is a co-perpetrator of the

---

2064. [1999] ECR I-4125.

infringement, even if it participates in different ways depending on a number of factors such as its position in the market, the characteristics of the market itself, the objectives pursued and the means of implementation of anti-competitive practices chosen or envisaged by it. The ECJ held that an undertaking may be held responsible for the conduct of other undertakings which have participated in the same infringement:

> "... where it is proved that the undertaking in question was aware of the unlawful conduct of the other participants, or could reasonably foresee such conduct, and was prepared to accept the risk. Such a conclusion is not at odds with the principle that responsibility for such infringements is personal in nature, nor does it neglect individual analysis of the evidence adduced, in disregard of the applicable rules of evidence, or infringe the rights of defence of the undertakings involved."

However, the Commission gives due regard to the extent to which the undertaking concerned participated in the infringement when it determines the amount of the fine to be imposed.

In Case T-334/94 *Sarrió SA v Commission*,[2065] the CFI [the General Court] explained the conditions under which an undertaking may be held liable for an overall cartel, that is, for all anti-competitive activities of the cartel. Sarrió argued that it had participated only in some, not all, aspects of the infringement. It held that it was possible for a member of a cartel to be held liable for the overall cartel once it had become aware of the overall plan of the cartel.

Accordingly, for an undertaking to be held liable for the whole infringement, that is for conduct put into effect by other undertakings, even though it has participated only in some of its aspects, it must be established that the undertaking concerned was aware of the offending conduct of the other participating undertakings, that it could reasonably have foreseen it and that it was ready to take the risk. However, the degree of participation in the infringement is taken into consideration in the determination of the fine.

27.3.3.4   The burden of proof

The Commission is always required to prove the infringement. It must demonstrate to the requisite legal standard the existence of circumstances constituting an infringement.[2066] The test is based on the balance of probabilities.[2067]

In respect of the burden of proof, in Case C-199/92P *Hüls v Commission*[2068] (one of the *Cartonboard Cartel* cases) the ECJ held that it was the task of the Commission to establish that Hüls participated in the meetings at which price initiatives were decided, organised and monitored. However, it was incumbent on Hüls to prove that it had not subscribed to those initiatives if that was the case. Consequently, there was no reversal of the burden of proof.

The ECJ emphasised that the principle of the presumption of innocence constitutes one of the fundamental principles of the Community legal order and as such applies to competition procedures. However, in the above case the Commission was not in breach of that principle.

It is well established that statements made by an undertaking participating in a cartel which run counter to its interests are regarded as particularly reliable evidence.[2069] However, if an

---

2065.   [1998] ECR II-1439.
2066.   Case C-185 /95P *Baustahlgewebe v Commission* [1998] ECR I-8417, para 58.
2067.   See Article 2 of Regulation 1/2003.
2068.   [1999] ECR I-4287.
2069.   Joined Cases T-67/00, T-68/00, T-71/00 and T-78/00 *JFE Engineering v Commission* [2004] ECR II-2501.

undertaking makes self-incriminating statements that are contested by several other participants in a cartel, such statements are not regarded as constituting adequate proof of a breach committed by that undertaking unless corroborated by other evidence.[2070]

27.4 Object or effect of an agreement, decision or a concerted practice

Article 101(1) TFEU is intended to catch all anti-competitive agreements between undertakings that have as their object or effect the prevention, restriction or distortion of competition. There is a very close connection between an anti-competitive object or effect and the effect of such an arrangement on trade between Member States. If an agreement, decision or a concerted practice restricts, prevents or distorts competition, its effect on trade between Member States is obvious.

In Case 56/65 *Société Technique Minière v Maschinenbau Ulm GmbH*,[2071] the ECJ stated that the terms "object" and "effect" are to be read disjunctively. As a result, the Commission must:

- In the first place, establish whether or not an agreement, decision or concerted practice has as its object the restriction of competition. The restriction of competition by object entails a rebuttable presumption that the collusive conduct has anti-competitive market effects. Not only actual but also potential negative effects are sufficient to trigger the application of the presumption. In Case 8/08 *T-Mobile Netherlands BV*,[2072] the ECJ clarified the meaning of the concept of an anti-competitive object. It set out the criteria to be applied to decide whether a concerted practice (this also applies to agreements and decisions) has as its object restriction of competition. These are: the content and the objective of concerted practice which should be assessed in the light of the circumstances of the case, i.e. its legal and economic considerations. Further, the intent of the parties is relevant although not an essential factor in determining whether a concerted practice is restrictive. The ECJ stated that "the distinction between 'infringements by object' and 'infringement by effect' arises from the fact that certain forms of collusion between undertakings can be regarded, by their very nature, as being injurious to the proper functioning of normal competition" (para 29). As a result, when the restriction of competition is an inevitable consequence of an agreement, decision or a restrictive practice, e.g. a ban on export, it will be regarded as having anti-competitive object irrespective of whether it has actually restricted competition or whether it has only the potential to have negative effect on competition;

- In the second place, if an agreement is not intended to restrict competition by object, e.g. a standard distribution agreement, the Commission must assess whether an agreement, decision or concerted practice has restrictive effects on competition. In Case 7/95P *John Deere*, the ECJ held: "in order to determine whether an agreement is to be considered to be prohibited by reason of the distortion of competition which is its effect, the competition in question should be assessed within the actual context in which it would occur in the absence

---

2070. *JFE Engineering v Commission* ibid. See also: Case T-337/94 *Enso-Gutzeit v Commission* [1998] ECR II-1571; Joined Cases T-109/02, T-118/02, T-122/02, T-125/02, T-126/02, T-128/02, T-129/02, T-132/02 and T-136/02 *Bolloré SA and Others (Carbonless Paper Cartel)* [2007] ECR II-947.

2071. [1966] ECR 235.

2072. Supra note 2006.

of the agreement in dispute".[2073] However, not only the actual and direct effect but also the potential and indirect effects of the restriction are taken into account.[2074] Negative effects of an agreement must be established with reasonable probability. Further, it is necessary that an agreement has appreciable or potentially appreciable effects on trade between Member States (see Chapter 26.6).

There are a number of factors which should be taken into consideration in order to assess the effect of an agreement on the particular market. These are:

- The parties' combined share of the relevant market. The combined market share may be assessed in percentage terms[2075] or on a quantitative basis.[2076] However, in Case 19/77 *Miller*[2077] the ECJ considered that an agreement in which the parties' combined share of the relevant market was only 5 per cent had an appreciable effect on trade between Member States;

- The type of agreement. Some agreements are capable of having appreciable effect even where the combined market share is not significant. These are mainly agreements which directly or indirectly fix prices, share markets, impose bans on export, or are one of a network of similar agreements which have a cumulative effect in the relevant market;

- The position in the relevant market and the size of the parties concerned;

- The nature and the quantity of the product concerned;

- The number of undertakings competing within the relevant geographical and product market;

- The general economic and legal context of the agreement.

The Commission's Guidelines on the Interpretation of Article 81(3) of the Treaty [Article 101(3) TFEU] explain the factors to be taken into account when assessing whether or not an agreement restricts competition by effect.[2078]

The issue of whether an agreement is restrictive of competition by its effect is the most controversial in competition law. This is because eventually everything boils down to economic matters, that is, how, why and in the light of what general objectives an economic assessment is carried out. Thus expert economic evidence plays a very important role in the fact-finding part of proceedings.

27.5 Prevention, distortion and restriction of competition

Each of the words "prevention", "distortion" and "restriction" imply a manipulation of the market in a manner which is improper or unlawful and refer to the situation in which a restraint is imposed on competition.

2073. [1998] ECR I-3111.

2074. Case 56/65 *Société Technique Minière* [1966] ECR 235 and Case 31/80 *L'Oréal v De Nieuwe AMCK* [1980] ECR 3775.

2075. In *Vimpoltu* a 90 per cent share of the relevant market [1983] OJ L200/44, in *Continental Michelin* 70 per cent of the relevant product market [1981] OJ L143/1.

2076. *Kawasaki* [1979] OJ L16/9.

2077. [1978] ECR 131.

2078. [2004] OJ C101/97, para 24.

Article 101(1) TFEU provides a non-exhaustive list of agreements which will generally fall within a prohibition but subject to the de minimis rule, and subject to the legal exception in Article 101(3) TFEU. There will be other additional agreements not listed which are prohibited because of their particular conditions or restrictions. The list sets out the most common types of anti-competitive agreement. These are dealt with below.

27.5.1 Agreements which directly or indirectly fix purchase or selling prices or other trading conditions – Article 101(1)(a) TFEU

Both horizontal and vertical agreements are within the scope of this prohibition.

Normally, market forces determine the price for a particular product. However, in some circumstances undertakings may decide to interfere with market forces. They may agree to raise, lower, maintain or stabilise prices, set a "target price",[2079] impose minimum or maximum prices,[2080] and so on. Agreements which fix purchase or selling prices may do so directly, that is, an agreement may expressly and directly state prices, or indirectly, that is, by providing for discounts,[2081] by granting allowances,[2082] by providing for favourable credit terms or the terms of guarantees, by exchanging information on prices,[2083] and so on.

There are many examples of price fixing by cartels, the more recent (at the time of writing) being in the graphite electrodes sector,[2084] in vitamin products,[2085] in lysine,[2086] in the beef sector by the French federation of beef producers,[2087] in food flavour enhancers,[2088] in industrial thread,[2089] in the carbonless paper market,[2090] and in the gas insulated switchgear market.[2091]

With regard to vertical agreements fixing prices is prohibited; however, the imposition by the supplier of a maximum sale price or a recommended price is allowed provided that those prices do not amount to fixed or minimum sale prices. In Case 161/84 *Pronuptia*,[2092] the ECJ held that recommended prices within the framework of a franchising agreement would not be unlawful if such recommendations were not binding on the franchisees. Thus, if franchisees are free to fix their own price despite the franchisor's recommendation, the recommended price will not cause the agreement to be in breach of Article 101(1) TFEU.

2079. *Cartonboard Cartel* [1986] OJ 1230/1.

2080. *Assurance Incendie* [1985] OJ L35/20; *Vitamines* [2003] OJ L6/1; *Hennessy/Henkell* [1980] OJ L383/11.

2081. Case 311/85 *ASBL Vereniging van Vlaamse Reisbureaus v ASBL Sociale Dienst van de Plaatselijke en Gewestelijke Overheidsdiensten* [1987] ECR 3801.

2082. *IFTRA* [1974] OJ L160/1.

2083. *Hasselblad* [1982] OJ L161/18.

2084. [2000] OJ L100/1.

2085. [2003] OJ L6/1.

2086. [2001] OJ L152/24.

2087. [2003] OJ L38/18.

2088. [2004] OJ L75/1.

2089. See Press Releases, EC Commission, IP/05/1140 of 14/10/2005.

2090. Joined Cases T-109/02, T-118/02, T-122/02, T-125/02, T-126/02, T-128/02, T-129/02, T-132/02 and T-136/02 *Bolloré SA and Others* [26/04/07].

2091. IP/07/80 of 24/01/07.

2092. [1986] ECR 353.

27.5.1.1   Other trading conditions

Other trading conditions refer to agreements which per se restrict access to the market, in particular exclusive and selective distribution and franchising agreements. These types of vertical restraints or agreements are not prohibited under Article 101(1) TFEU, although certain requirements imposed by them are considered as being in breach of Article 101(1)(a) (see section 27.6.4).

Other trading conditions refer to, for example, export/import bans,[2093] whether or not applied in practice,[2094] and other export/import deterrents and inducements. The Commission will always impose heavy penalties on an undertaking which imposes an export ban. This occurred in Case 19/77 *Miller International v Commission.*[2095]

THE FACTS WERE:

Miller International was a German subsidiary of an American undertaking which produced cheap records and tapes and specialised in "bargain offers". This subsidiary imposed an export ban on its French distributors in order to prevent parallel imports to Germany where prices were higher. Miller was heavily fined notwithstanding that it had only 2.5 per cent of the total German record market.

Held:

The ECJ held that Miller International was in breach of Article 81(1)EC [Article 101 TFEU].

The ECJ took into account the potential effect of the ban on trade between Member States and the fact that if the effect had not been appreciable, the imposition of a ban on its distributors would not have been necessary.

In general export bans are not capable of exemption, although in the context of intellectual property rights even an agreement ensuring absolute territorial protection was considered by the ECJ as not infringing Article 101(1) TFEU.[2096]

Prohibitions imposed on distributors from one Member State against selling their products in another Member State without manufacturer/supplier consent have been condemned.[2097]

A prohibition imposed on distributors against selling to customers likely to engage in parallel import[2098] was regarded as breaching Article 101(1) TFEU.

Export deterrents and export boosters are both in breach of the Article 101(1) prohibitions. In *Cimbel,*[2099] Belgian cement producers decided to collectively subsidise exports by "equalising receipts from domestic sales and from exports". The ECJ held that this arrangement artificially reinforced the competitive position of the participating undertakings in export markets, taking

---

2093. There are many examples: Case 28/77 *Tepea* [1978] ECR 1391; Case T-49/95 *Van Megen Sports Group* [1966] ECR II-1799; *JCB* [2002] OJ L69/1.

2094. Case T-77/92 *Parker Pen* [1994] ECR II-549.

2095. [1978] ECR 131.

2096. Case 27/87 *Erauw-Jacquéry v La Hesbignonne* [1988] 4 CMLR 576.

2097. *GERO-fabriek* [1977] OJ L16/8; *Windsurfing International* [1983] OJ L229/1; *Viho/Toshiba* [1991] OJ L287/39; *Eco System/Peugeot* [1992] OJ L66/1.

2098. *Tipp-Ex* [1987] OJ L222/1.

2099. [1973] CMLR D 167, [1972] OJL 303/24.

into account that undertakings in other Member States had to compete with all the members of Cimbel and not with each Belgian undertaking separately.

27.5.2 Agreements which control production, markets, technical developments or investments – Article 101(1)(b) TFEU

Normally horizontal agreements are capable of breaching Article 101(1)(b) TFEU. However in some circumstances they may qualify for exemption. Further, many specialisation agreements and research and development agreements are within the scope of block exemptions (see section 27.8).

27.5.2.1 Agreements which control production

This prohibition concerns agreements which are designed to reduce actual and potential production. Any agreement that intends to control production is anti-competitive, taking into account that such an agreement might lead to the elimination of small and medium-sized undertakings and the monopolisation of a particular market to the detriment of consumers. Cartels have often used a system of allocating production quotas to participating undertakings as an alternative,[2100] or a complement to a common pricing policy.[2101]

When there is dramatic over-capacity in an industry, undertakings are tempted to enter into agreements limiting their production. The economic and social consequences of major reduction in demand in certain industries have changed the approach of the Community institutions to agreements between undertakings aimed at limiting production. In the XIIth Annual Report on Competition Policy the Commission provided its view on the reconstruction of industries in crisis. The Commission is prepared to accept agreements limiting production if it is shown that:

■ Structural over-capacity has affected all the undertakings concerned, over a prolonged period of time;

■ The over-capacity has resulted in a significant reduction in undertakings' rate of capacity utilisation, leading to a drop in output accompanied by substantial operating losses;

■ There is no expectation of lasting improvement in the medium term.

The Commission will grant exemption for such agreements provided that the reduction in over-capacity provided for by the agreements is permanent and irreversible and of an amount which will enable the existing undertakings in the industry to compete at this lower level of capacity. The reduction must facilitate specialisation by the undertakings concerned, and the timetable for the reduction in capacity must minimise the social consequences of that reduction, for example, resulting unemployment.[2102]

27.5.2.2 Agreements which control technical developments or investments

These agreements may qualify for exemption under Article 101(3) TFEU provided that the restrictions which they impose are ancillary to some desirable pro-competitive objectives which they

---

2100. *BELASCO* [1986] OJ L232/15, *Zink Phosphate Cartel* (2003) OJ L153/1.

2101. *The Quinine Cartel*, supra note 2020. *The Polypropylene Cartel* [1986] OJL 230/1.

2102. See *Synthetic Fibres* [1984] OJ L207/17, [1985] 1 CMLR 787.

intend to achieve. Such agreements are encouraged by the Commission when made between small and medium-sized undertakings.

27.5.3 Agreements to share markets or sources of supply – Article 101(1)(c) TFEU

The main objective of this prohibition is to avoid the partition of the internal market along national boundaries. It concerns both horizontal and vertical agreements.

One of the best-known examples of an agreement designed to share the market and the sources of supply was provided in the *Quinine Cartel* cases[2103] (for facts see section 27.3.1). More recent examples are:

- In the *Pre-Insulated Pipes Cartel*, the "directors club", consisting of the chairmen or managing directors of the participating undertakings, allocated quotas of the European market to each participating undertaking, both at European and national level;[2104]

- In the *Seamless Steel Tubes Cartel*, four European companies and four Japanese companies producing seamless steel tubes were fined for participating in an illegal market sharing cartel;[2105]

- In the *Needles Cartel*, three companies were fined by the Commission for sharing the product and geographical market.[2106]

In respect of vertical agreements the most obvious examples of agreements contravening Article 101(1)(c) TFEU are exclusive distributorship agreements and exclusive purchasing agreements (but see section 27.6.4). In Cases 56 and 58/64 *Consten and Grundig*,[2107] the ECJ held that an exclusive distributorship agreement intended to isolate the French market for Grundig products and therefore partition the common market along national lines, in itself distorted competition in the internal market.

27.5.4 Agreements which apply dissimilar conditions to equivalent transactions with other trading parties, thereby placing them at a competitive disadvantage – Article 101(1)(d) TFEU

Article 101(1)(d) TFEU imposes an obligation on a manufacturer/producer to treat all its customers equally, that is, to apply the same conditions to equivalent transactions. The principle of non-discrimination is at the centre of this provision. However, the prohibition of discrimination is neither absolute nor general. Some agreements in breach of the principle of non-discrimination may be capable of exemption if the difference in treatment is objectively justified.[2108] For example "quantity" discounts (discounts for bulk purchase) are allowed if they represent a genuine cost saving.

2103. Case 45/69 *Boehringer Mannheim v Commission* [1970] ECR 769.
2104. [1999] OJ L24/1.
2105. Joined Cases C-403/04P and C-405/04P, Case C-407/04 and Case C-411/04P *Sumitomo Metal Industries Ltd and Others v Commission* [2007] ECR I-729.
2106. Case T-30/05 and T-36/05 *Prym and Others v Commission* [2007] ECR II-107.
2107. [1966] ECR 299.
2108. Case 26/76 *Metro* [1977] ECR 1875.

In Case 96/82 *JAZ International Belgium*,[2109] the requirements imposed by a Belgian trade association that only washing machines and dryers which had a certificate of conformity with Belgian standards could be installed in Belgium was found to be discriminatory because:

- First, membership of the association was restricted to manufacturers of such machines and sole importers of foreign manufactured machines, thereby excluding parallel importers;

- Second, it was easy for its members to obtain certificates of conformity while non-members had to ask for an individual certificate of conformity for each machine concerned; and

- Third, only the trade association was entitled to deliver certificates of conformity!

27.5.5 Agreements which make conclusion of contracts subject to acceptance by other parties of supplementary obligations which, by their nature and/or according to commercial usage, have no connection with the subject-matter of such contracts – Article 101(1)(e) TFEU

This prohibition concerns "tying" agreements whereby the acceptance of an obligation not related to the substance of the agreement is a precondition of its conclusion. This kind of obligation is often imposed by undertakings which are in a dominant position under Article 102, although it also occurs in the context of Article 101(1) EC.

In *IFTRA Rules on Glass Containers*,[2110] the members of a trade association of glass container manufacturers were obliged by the rules of the association, inter alia, to supply glass containers on the basis that they were delivered and thus their customers could not save costs by organising their own transport.

In *Vaessen/Morris*[2111] the Commission condemned a clause which required a licensee to buy from the patent holder not only a patented device for packing sausage meat into a casing to create saucissons de Boulogne but also the casing itself.

27.6 The evolution of the interpretation of Article 101(1) TFEU: the per se rule v the rule of reason?

The US antitrust law, first enacted in 1890, has served as a model for competition law in many countries, including some of the Member States of the EU. It has also influenced interpretation of competition law around the world.

US antitrust law and EU competition law have much in common but they differ in respect of the objective they seek to achieve, and in the way competition rules are enforced. Comparison between US antitrust law and EU law is beyond the scope of this book. However, the main differences can be summarised as follows:

- The main objective of US antitrust law has been defined as consisting of "maintaining public confidence in the market mechanism by deterring and punishing instances of

---

2109. [1983] ECR 3369.
2110. [1974] OJ L160/1, [1974] 2 CMLR D50.
2111. [1979] OJ L19/32, [1979] 1 CMLR 511.

economic oppression".[2112] The EU certainly shares this objective with the US, but the perspective is different. The EU's objective of integrating the markets of the Member States, even if no longer the prime objective of EU competition law, entails that any conduct which results in the partition of the internal market along national borders or the imposition of discriminatory prices in different Member States without any objective justification is prohibited. This is not the case in the US.

■ The treatment of undertakings with market power is quite different in the US and in the EU. Section 1 of the Sherman Act prohibits monopolisation and attempts to monopolise, while Article 102 TFEU contains no such prohibition but forbids abuses of a dominant position. In the US mere exploitation of market power which was innocently achieved by charging monopoly (that is, excessive) prices or discriminatory prices is not unlawful and it is left to market forces to correct such irregularities. Charging excessive prices or discriminatory prices is an abuse under Article 102 TFEU. A further difference between Article 102 TFEU and Section 1 of the Sherman Act is a different approach to, inter alia, predatory prices, refusal to deal, exclusive contracts and loyalty rebates (see Chapter 28).

■ The enforcement of competition law differs in the US and in the EU in terms of:

  ● Methods of enforcement, for example, in the US private enforcement, including class actions, is very popular while in the EU private enforcement is rare (see Chapter 30.3);
  ● Sanctions: under EU law, contrary to USA law, there is no criminal enforcement of competition rules;
  ● Procedures: in the US the Federal Trade Commission enforces competition rules mainly by bringing proceedings before ordinary federal courts (although it has some administrative powers as well), while in the EU the Commission acts as prosecutor, jury and decision-maker/judge in competition matters.

US and EU competition laws have influenced each other. For example, EU competition law has endorsed, more or less, the American "effects doctrine" (see Chapter 26), while the US antitrust system has become more sensitive to social policy and environmental issues.

US antitrust law uses two methods to analyse conduct under Section 1 of the Sherman Act, which prohibits contracts, combinations and conspiracies in restraint of trade.

■ Under the per se rule, certain conduct of companies, such as price fixing and other hard core horizontal restraints, is inherently illegal, that is, if a company has been found engaging in illegal conduct, it will automatically be deemed to have breached competition law. There will be no chance of justifying the measure. Illegality follows as a matter of law. No consideration is given to such factors as the market share of the defendant, the pro-competitive aspects of its conduct, and so on.

■ Under the rule of reason an inquiry is carried out in all circumstances before determining the legality or otherwise of particular conduct. Under Section 1 of the Sherman Act there is no possibility for exemption. All contracts, combinations and conspiracies in restraint of trade are prohibited. This excessive rigidity had to be attenuated. The rule of reason has

---

2112. L. A. Sullivan and W. S. Grimes, *The Law of Antitrust: An Integrated Handbook*, 2006, St Paul: Thomson/West, p 10. See § 18.6 for Similarities and Differences between US and EU Antitrust, pp 1040 et seq.

become the main tool for adjusting Section 1 of the Sherman Act to changing economic conditions. Its content has evolved according to economic reality. Under the rule of reason US courts are required to consider the overall impact of an agreement on competition within the relevant market. In order to do so, they have to identify and weigh the anti-competitive and pro-competitive effects it produces. If pro-competitive effects prevail, the agreement is regarded as not being restrictive of competition. As a result, an economic analysis is required in each case.

The difference between the way in which antitrust analysis is conducted under EU law and under Section 1 of the Sherman Act is substantial. As Goyder stated:

"The United States Courts may take into account all the positive and negative features of the restraint, as well as the context in which it is applied, remaining as free from statutory restrictions as the courts of common law in assessing the local validity of contractual restraints between vendor and purchaser or employer and employee. By comparison, the Commission must operate within a rigid conceptual framework which allows less freedom of manoeuvre and requires the restriction to pass, not one single balancing test, but a cumulative series of four separate tests."[2113]

The debate concerning the alleged application of the US rule of reason in the context of Article 101(1) TFEU has its origin in the judgment of the ECJ in Case 56/65 *Société Technique Minière (STM) v Maschinenbau*[2114] (see section 27.6.2).

Until that judgment, Article 81(1) EC [Article 101(1) TFEU] was interpreted by the Commission and by the ECJ literally, that is, the per se method was applied to the interpretation of Article 101(1) TFEU. The Commission tended to regard both any restriction on a party's conduct and any agreement which interfered with the objectives of the internal market as restricting competition, while an assessment on the basis of an economic analysis would often have shown that neither had any serious restrictive effect on competition.

The per se interpretation was understandable, given that Article 81(3) EC [Article 101(3) TFEU] provides a mechanism under which the Commission could scrutinise an agreement from the point of view of its effect on competition by applying an economic-based approach consisting of weighing the pro and anti-competitive aspects of an agreement which was apparently in breach of Article 101(1). The problems with this two-tier analysis (first applying Article 81(1) EC [Article 101(1) TFEU] and then Article 81(3) EC [Article 101(3) TFEU]) were twofold:

- First, many agreements which were eligible for exemption had to be notified to the Commission, as the Commission alone was empowered to grant exemptions. Given that the notification procedure was time-consuming and burdensome, the Commission started adopting block exemption regulations (see section 27.8). This resulted in many businesses either not proceeding with their business projects or tailoring their agreements in conformity with the relevant block exemption regulation, which often meant that the agreements did not accurately reflect the true intention of the parties;

- Second, for years the Commission was trying to find the right balance between paragraphs (1) and (3) of Article 81 EC [Article 101(1) TFEU]. This was necessary given that the literal interpretation of Article 81(1) EC [Article 101(1) TFEU] would result in its scope of

---

2113. D. G. Goyder. *EC Competition Law*, 3rd Edition, 1998, Oxford University Press, p 145.
2114. [1966] ECR 235.

application being such that almost all transactions with a European dimension could be unlawful. To find a way out of these difficulties, the EU institutions have adopted a more flexible approach consisting of assessing any given conduct in its economic setting, and thus, to some extent, weighing the pro and anti-competitive effects of an agreement under Article 81(1) EC [Article 101(1) TFEU], instead of examining such effects under Article 81(3) EC [Article 101(3) TFEU]. This approach is similar to the application of the rule of reason under the US Sherman Act. Because of this it has been submitted that the rule of reason has a place under Article 101(1) TFEU. This reflected a mixed approach, where the per se categories under Article 81(1) EC [Article 101(1) TFEU] were subject to a rule of reason-type analysis under Article 81(3) EC [Article 101(3) TFEU].

It is to be noted that the debate relating to the application of the US-style rule of reason has lost much of its practical importance with the entry into force of Regulation 1/2003, which abolished the system of notification. Under that Regulation businesses have to make their own assessment of an intended agreement and national courts and national competition authorities, on the basis of the existing case law, have to determine if the matter is in issue, and whether the agreement is in conformity with EU competition rules.

27.6.1 The rejection of the rule of reason by the CJEU

The issue of the existence or otherwise of the rule of reason under Article 101(1) TFEU was addressed in Case T-112/99 *Métropole Télévision (M6) and Others v Commission*,[2115] in which the CFI [the General Court] expressly rejected the application of the rule of reason to Article 81(1) EC [Article 101(1) TFEU]. The Court held that:

> "... the existence of such a rule has not, as such, been confirmed by the Community courts. Quite to the contrary, in various judgments the Court of Justice and the Court of First Instance have been at pains to indicate that the existence of a rule of reason in Community competition law is doubtful."[2116]

The CFI [the General Court] emphasised that the pro and anti-competitive effects of an agreement should be assessed in the light of Article 101(3) TFEU, which Article "would lose much of its effectiveness if such an examination had to be carried out under Article 101(1) of the Treaty". However, the Court acknowledged that Article 81(1) EC [Article 101(1) TFEU] has, for some time, been interpreted in a more flexible manner by the EU institutions.

The above judgment has not ended the debate. Indeed, the judgment in Case C-309/99 *Wouters v Algemene Raad van de Nederlandse Orde van Advocaten*[2117] reinvigorated it.

2115. [2001] ECR II-2459. This judgment was confirmed two years later in Case T-65/98 *Van den Bergh Foods Ltd v Commission* [2003] ECR II-4653.

2116. Case T-112/99 *Métropole Télévision (M6)*, [2000] ECR II-2459.

2117. [2002] ECR I-1577.

THE FACTS WERE:

Mr Wouters challenged a rule adopted by the Dutch Bar prohibiting lawyers in The Nether-lands from entering into partnership with non-lawyers.

Held:

The ECJ held that the challenged rule was liable to limit production and technical development within the meaning of Article 81(1) EC [Article 101(1) TFEU], but held that:

"... For the purpose of the application of [Article 101(1)] to a particular case, account must first of all be taken of the overall context in which the decision of the association of undertakings was taken or produces its effect. More particularly, account must be taken of its objectives, which are here connected with the need to make rules relating to organisation, qualifications, professional ethics, supervision and liability, in order to ensure that the ultimate consumer of legal services and the sound administration of justice are provided with the necessary guarantees in relation to integrity and experience ... It has then to be considered whether the consequential effects restrictive of competition are inherent in the pursuit of those objectives."[2118]

The ECJ found that the rule, being necessary in order to ensure the proper practice of the legal profession in The Netherlands, did not infringe Article 81(1) EC [Article 101(1) TFEU].

Comment:

The reasoning of the Court clearly takes into consideration the pro and anti-competitive aspects of the challenged rule and concludes that as the pro-competitive aspects prevailed, the rule was not in breach of Article 101(1) TFEU. The judgment in *Wouters* has been commented as meaning:

- First, that the US-style rule of reason is alive and well under Article 101(1) TFEU;[2119]

- Second, that a European-style rule of reason finds its place under Article 101(1) TFEU. The European-style rule is similar to and indeed based on the *Cassis de Dijon* rule, under which a national measure which is indistinctly applicable to both domestic and imported goods will not breach the prohibition of Article 34 TFEU if it is necessary to satisfy mandatory requirements. This transposition of the *Cassis de Dijon* rule to competition cases means that: "an anti-competitive agreement necessary to preserve a domestic mandatory requirement of public policy is allowed to escape the application of Article 81 [Article 101 TFEU]."[2120]

- Third, that the doctrine of regulatory ancillarity is recognised under Article 101(1) TFEU.[2121]

It is submitted that whatever position is taken in the debate, it is undeniable that the per se

---

2118. Ibid, para 97.
2119. N. Korah, "Rule of Reason; Apparent Inconsistency in the Case Law under Article 81", (2002) 1 Competition Law Insight, p 24.
2120. G. Monti, "Article 81 EC and Public Policy", (2002) CML Rev, p 1057, in particular p 1088.
2121. R. Whish, *Competition Law*, 5th edition, 2003, London: Butterworths, pp 119–22.

interpretation of Article 101(1) has been replaced by the economic-based interpretation of Article 101(1) TFEU.[2122] This topic is examined below.

27.6.2 The economic-based approach to the interpretation of Article 101(1) TFEU

For the first time in Case 56/65 *Société Technique Minière (STM) v Maschinenbau*[2123] the ECJ relaxed its rigorous interpretation of Article 81(1) EC [Article 101(1) TFEU] and applied a more flexible approach, taking into account the economic and legal context of the agreement under consideration.

THE FACTS WERE:

STM, a French undertaking supplying equipment for public works, and Maschinenbau, a German producer of heavy grading machinery, entered into an exclusive distribution agreement under which Maschinenbau agreed not to supply to any other distributor in France and not to sell there itself any large earth levellers of the type in which STM dealt. STM agreed to buy a large number of machines from Maschinenbau over a period of two years but could not then find a sufficient number of purchasers for them. When Maschinenbau did not receive payment, it sued STM in France. STM argued that the agreement, or at least some clauses in it, were in breach of Article 101(1) TFEU.

Held:

The ECJ held that exclusivity was essential to the setting-up of a distribution system in the context of the high commercial risks taken by STM when entering into the agreement, as the product was highly specialised and expensive.

The ECJ emphasised that:

"The competition in question must be understood within the actual context in which it would occur in the absence of the agreement in dispute. In particular it may be doubted whether there is an interference with competition if the said agreement seems really necessary for the penetration of a new area by an undertaking."

The ECJ identified a number of factors which should be taken into consideration in assessing whether or not an exclusive distribution agreement is within the scope of Article 81(1) EC [Article 101(1) TFEU]. They are:

■ The nature of the product and its volume, that is whether the supply was limited or unlimited in amount;

2122. The Commission in its Modernisation White Paper emphasised that it has already adopted an approach similar to that applied under the rule of reason consisting of assessing the pro- and anti-competitive aspects of an agreement under Article 101(1), but stated that the structure of that Article prevents it from making greater use of this approach.
2123. [1966] ECR 235.

> The importance of both the supplier and the distributor with respect to the relevant market;
>
> Whether the agreement was one of or a part of a network of agreements covering at least a substantial area or region of a Member State;
>
> The degree of territorial protection afforded by the agreement, in particular whether it provides for absolute territorial protection and whether it allows parallel imports.

Following the judgment in *STM*, every transaction must be considered in its economic and legal context. Accordingly, in order to assess whether an agreement is restrictive of competition within the meaning of Article 101(1) TFEU, it is necessary:[2124]

- First, to examine what would be the state of competition, actual and potential, in the relevant market if the agreement with its alleged restrictions did not exist. In this respect, the assessment of the impact of the agreement on first, inter-brand competition and second, intra-brand competition is required. Further, account must be taken of internal competition, that is, between the parties to the agreement under consideration, and external, that is from third parties or between the third parties. Special attention is given to the so-called "cumulative effect" on competition of several vertical agreements forming a network of agreements[2125] (see section 27.6.4.3).

- Second, to determine whether the agreement under consideration has an appreciable effect on competition (see Chapter 26.6), that is, whether it is within the scope of the de minimis rule. In respect of vertical agreements Regulation 330/2010 sets up thresholds by reference to the market power of the undertaking concerned (its market share in the relevant product market) and provides a blacklist of hard core restrictions, actual and potential, which restrict competition by object.

- Third, to decide whether in order to determine the question dealt with in the paragraph immediately above, that is, whether an agreement has an appreciable effect on competition, it is necessary to examine the pro and anti-competitive effects of the agreement and thus use the criteria set out in Article 101(3) TFEU, or whether individual restraints contained in the agreement are to be treated as ancillary to the agreement (see section 27.6.3) and, therefore, analysed together with that agreement. Ancillary restraints follow the treatment applied to the agreement. If the agreement in its main parts does not have as its object or effect the restriction of competition and thus falls outside the scope of Article 101(1) TFEU, then ancillary restraints, being directly necessary for its implementation, also are outside the ambit of Article 101(1) TFEU. However, if the agreement is within the scope of Article 101(1) TFEU, so are any of its ancillary restraints, and thus the entire agreement must be examined in the light of Article 101(3) TFEU.

2124. See Guidelines on the Application of Article 81(3) EC [Article 101(3) TFEU], paras 17–27.
2125. Case 23/67 *SA Brasserie de Haecht v Consorts Wilkin-Janssen* [1967] ECR 407; T-88/92 *Groupement d'Achat Édouard Leclerc v Commission* [1996] ECR II-1961; Case C-234/89 *Stergios Delimitis v Henninger Bräu AG* [1991] ECR I-935.

▪ Fourth, in some cases, to determine whether a restriction on competition can be justified by considerations of general interest. For example, a Member State may delegate certain powers to undertakings or associations which do not pursue economic activities.[2126] Also, professional associations and similar organisations, which are not exercising public powers delegated by a Member State, may adopt rules which, while they restrict competition, seek to achieve other objectives. This was the case in *Wouter*, in which rules adopted by the Dutch Bar prohibiting its members from practising in full partnership with accountants were regarded as necessary to ensure the proper practice of the legal profession. If a restriction can be justified by considerations of general interest, an agreement is outside the scope of Article 101(1) TFEU.

By applying the analytical framework set out above, even a clause providing for absolute territorial protection may be exempted from the scope of Article 101(1) TFEU if it is seen as necessary from an economic point of view. This was confirmed in Case 258/78 *Nungesser v Commission*,[2127] in which it was held that an "open" exclusive licensing agreement (that is, one that affects neither the position of third parties such as parallel importers nor that of licensees for other territories) for the exploitation of plant breeders' rights did not infringe Article 101(1) TFEU.

The ECJ defined an "open" exclusive licence as relating solely to a contractual relationship between a licensor and licensee whereby the licensor undertakes not to grant other licences in respect of the same territory and not itself to compete with the licensee in that territory. Consequently any limitation of the licensee's freedom, apart from an obligation not to produce (as opposed to sell which is normally permitted, but see below[2128]) outside its allocated territory will transform an "open" exclusive licence (which is allowed) into a "closed" exclusive licence (which is prohibited).

Further, the ECJ held in paragraph 58 of *Nungesser* that in order to decide whether the grant of an open exclusive licence was outside the scope of Article 81(1) EC [Article 101(1) TFEU], the nature of the product in question was a decisive factor. If the product is particularly fragile and the investment made by the licensor was considerable, the ECJ is prepared to justify even a clause which prohibits the licensee selling, assigning or exporting the product outside the assigned territory. This was confirmed in Case 27/87 *SPRL Louis Erauw-Jacquery v La Hesbignonne SC*.[2129] In both *Nungesser* and *Erauw-Jacquery* the product itself was decisive as to the validity or otherwise of the clause granting absolute territorial protection. In *Nungesser* the object of the licence was hybrid maize seed intended to be used by a large number of farmers for the production of maize. This was referred to as basic seed. The licence agreement would have been outside the scope of Article 101 TFEU if it was an "open" agreement, but as it prohibited parallel imports, it was a "closed" agreement that was in breach of Article 101(1) TFEU and was also denied the benefit of exemption under Article 101(3) TFEU. In *Nungesser* the seed was so-called "certified seed" that is, it was placed at the disposal of the licensee only for the purpose of propagation. The ECJ held that the licence agreement which prohibited licensees from selling, assigning and exporting seed outside their assigned territory did not infringe Article 101(1) TFEU.

2126. Case C-519/04 *Meca-Medina and Majcen* [2006] ECR I-6991.

2127. [1982] ECR 2105.

2128. *Boussois/Interpane* [1987] OJ L50/30.

2129. [1988] ECR 1919.

The *Nungesser* principle is not confined to plant breeders' rights but, on the authority of the subsequent case law of the ECJ, applies to licences relating to other intellectual property rights, for example, patents and know-how.

In contrast, in Cases 56 and 58/64 *Consten and Grundig*,[2130] the clause ensuring absolute territorial protection for Consten was aimed at isolating the French market. For that reason the ECJ held that the agreement was in breach of Article 81(10 EC [Article 101(1) TFEU] and upheld the Commission's position.

27.6.3 Ancillary restraints

The ECJ has applied the concept of ancillary restraints, which is akin to the US rule of reason, to the interpretation of EU competition law.

Under US antitrust law a distinction is made between "naked restraints" and "ancillary restraints":

- ▪ "Naked restraints" refer to those restraints which are always anti-competitive and unlawful, for example, fixing prices by means of a cartel (even if the prices fixed are reasonable);

- ▪ Ancillary restraints may be justified under the rule of reason. In *US v Addyston Pipe and Steel Co.*[2131] Judge Taft described ancillary restraints as being restrictions necessary to some transactions in order to make them viable. Ancillary restraints which would otherwise be unlawful can become acceptable if used to support pro-competitive transactions. The example given by Judge Taft concerned non-competition clauses normally contained in a business sale agreement and in particular in respect of partners who retire.

Ancillary restraints under EU competition law have been defined as covering "any alleged restriction of competition which is directly related and necessary for the implementation of a main non-restrictive transaction and proportionate to it".[2132]

In order to decide whether a particular restraint is ancillary or not, the Commission Notice on Ancillary Restraints in the context of concentrations may be of assistance (see Chapter 29.4.5). Further, with regard to vertical agreements the ECJ found the following restraints as being ancillary:

- ▪ In Case 42/84 *Remia BV*,[2133] a non-compete clause inserted into a contract of sale of a business, provided such restriction was necessary for the successful transfer of an undertaking;

- ▪ In Case C-250/92 *Gøttrup-Klim e.a. Grovvareforeninger v Dansk Landbrugs Grovvareselskab AmbA*,[2134] a clause in a statute of a Danish co-operative association, which distributed farm supplies, prohibiting its members from participating in other forms of organised co-operation in direct competition with that association. The Court held that such dual

---

2130. [1966] ECR 299.
2131. 85 F.271 (6th Cir.1897), aff'd, 175 U.S. 211, 20 S.Ct.96, 44 L.Ed.136 (1899).
2132. Guidelines on Application of Article 81(3) EC [Article 101(3) TFEU], para 29.
2133. [1985] ECR 2545.
2134. [1994] ECR I-5641.

membership would jeopardise both the proper functioning of the co-operative and its contractual power in relation to producers;

- In Case 161/84 *Pronuptia*,[2135] the ECJ found that the protection of the franchisor's knowhow was necessary for the successful operation of a franchising agreement (see section 27.6.4.2).

However, in Case T-112/99 *Métropole Télévision (M6)*[2136] the ECJ refused to classify the exclusivity clause under which the appellant would be allowed the exclusive broadcasting of general-interest channels for an initial period of 10 years as being ancillary to the creation of TPS.

27.6.4 The application of the economic-based approach to vertical agreements

The economic-based interpretation of Article 101(1) TFEU has been carried out mainly in respect of vertical restraints. The concept of vertical restraints has been defined by the Commission in its Guidelines on vertical restraints as "agreements or concerted practices entered into between two or more companies each of which operates, for the purposes of the agreement, at a different level of the production or distribution chain, and relating to the conditions under which the parties may purchase, sell or resell certain goods or services".

The most common vertical restraints are: single branding, exclusive distribution, exclusive customer allocation, selective distribution, franchising, exclusive supply, tying, and recommended and maximum resale prices.

27.6.4.1 *Selective distribution agreements*

In selective distribution agreements the supplier sells the goods or services either directly or indirectly only to distributors selected on the basis of specific criteria and the distributors undertake not to sell such goods or services to unauthorised distributors.

Selective distribution agreements are normally used by producers of branded high technology or luxury products. The very nature of distribution agreements entails that such agreements may adversely affect the competitive conditions of the market by facilitating collusive behaviour between suppliers and distributors, by reducing or eliminating intra-brand competition (this refers to competition among the distributors of a given brand, for example, between distributors of Rolex watches), by foreclosing access to the market, and by increasing the price of the goods/ services to the detriment of consumers. However, selective distribution agreements can also have pro-competitive effects, for example, they may ensure greater efficiency in distribution and thus provide benefits to all parties concerned including consumers.

The application of Article 101(1) TFEU to selective distribution agreements was examined by the ECJ in Case 26/76 *Metro SB-Großmärkte GmbH & Co. KG v Commission*.[2137]

2135. [1986] ECR 353.
2136. Supra note 2116.
2137. [1977] ECR 1875.

THE FACTS WERE:

Saba, a producer of electric and electronic equipment, refused Metro's request for access to its selective distribution network in Germany. Outside Germany Saba's products were sold directly to sole distributors dealing exclusively with approved specialist dealers who were serving the public. The German selective distribution system was open to wholesalers who were reselling goods purchased from Saba to approved specialist dealers, whose turnover had to be obtained from the sale of electric and electronic products. Metro, as a cash and carry self-service business established in Germany, served retailers and the public. This was the main reason for Saba's refusal, although Metro did not fulfil other requirements of Saba's in that neither its trading premises nor its turnover nor the technical qualifications of its staff were appropriate to handle highly sophisticated electronic goods. Metro complained to the Commission, which decided that in general the Saba system of selective distribution did not breach Article 81(1) EC [Article 101(1) TFEU]. Saba was entitled to prohibit direct supplies by wholesalers or sole distributors to consumers although particular clauses, for example prohibiting its wholesalers, sole distributors and specialised dealers from exporting to other EU countries or prohibiting "cross-supplies" (wholesaler to wholesaler or retailer to retailer), were condemned. Metro sought to annul the Commission's decision.

Held:

The ECJ held that a selective distribution system such as that put in place by Saba was justified in so far as resellers were selected "on the basis of objective criteria of a qualitative nature relating to the technical qualifications of the reseller and his staff and the suitability of his trading premises and that such conditions are laid down uniformly for all potential resellers and are not applied in a discriminatory fashion".

From this statement it is clear that a limitation of competition based on price alone in favour of competition relating to factors other than price is allowed. This is of course provided that the supplier does not enjoy a dominant position in the relevant product market (that is, distributors are able to obtain supplies from other sources) and the supplier's selective distribution system is not discriminatory (that is, it is open to all undertakings), and where conditions are laid down uniformly for all potential dealers and the distribution system seeks to achieve a legitimate objective of improving competition in relation to factors other than price.[2138]

Thus, purely qualitative selective distribution is, in general, outside the prohibition of Article 101(1) TFEU, provided three conditions are satisfied:

- First, the nature of the product in question must necessitate a selective distribution system (but this is no longer required under Regulation 330/2010);

- Secondly, resellers must be chosen on the basis of objective criteria of a qualitative nature;

- Thirdly, the criteria laid down must not go beyond what is necessary.

With regard to the first condition the ECJ stated in *Metro* that selective distribution

---

2138. Case 107/82 *AEG-Telefunken* [1983] ECR 3151.

agreements were justified in "the sector covering the production of high quality and technically advanced consumer durables". The ECJ in subsequent cases confirmed that, apart from technically sophisticated products,[2139] other types of products such as luxury or branded products[2140] and newspapers (given their extremely short life)[2141] justified selective distribution. It is important to note that Regulation 330/2010 abolished the requirement to establish that the product concerned merits a selective distribution system (see section 27.8.2).

In respect of the second condition, qualitative criteria may be defined as relating to the selection of dealers based on their objective suitability to distribute a particular kind of goods, while quantitative restrictions "more directly limit the potential number of dealers by, for instance, requiring minimum or maximum sales, by fixing the number of dealers, etc".[2142] The distinction between qualitative and quantitative was of importance until the entry into force of Regulation 2790/99 (now replaced by Regulation 330/2010),[2143] given that qualitative restrictions which met the criteria stated above were not in breach of Article 101(1) TFEU while quantitative criteria were in breach of Article 101(1) TFEU unless justified under Article 101(3) TFEU.

In *Metro* the ECJ found that restrictions relating to the technical qualifications of the reseller and its staff and to the suitability of the reseller's premises were of a qualitative nature.

With regard to quantitative restrictions the following clauses were considered as such and accordingly were in breach of Article 101(1) TFEU: in *Metro* a clause requiring dealers to maintain specific amounts of stock, to promote the manufacturer's product and to stock an entire range of products; in Case 31/80 *L'Oréal*[2144] and in *Givenchy*[2145] the requirement that the distributor should guarantee a minimum turnover; in *Hasselblad*[2146] a clause prohibiting distributors from selling to each other; in *Kodak*[2147] a clause prohibiting distributors from selling to customers in other Member States.

With regard to the third condition, in *Metro* the ECJ made it clear that "qualitative criteria" should not go beyond what is necessary to maintain the quality of the goods or to ensure they are sold under proper conditions. What is necessary depends on the nature of the product. This is illustrated in Case T-19/91 *Vichy*,[2148] where the requirement that its cosmetics should be sold in retail pharmacies in which a qualified pharmacist was present in all EU countries but France (where this was not required) was considered as being disproportionate, taking into account that the objectives which Vichy wanted to achieve outside France (that is, improving the quality both of its product and the service, as well as enhanced competition with other cosmetic

---

2139. Personal computers: *IBM* [1984] OJ L 118/24; cameras: *Hasselblad* [1982] OJ L 161/18.

2140. *Parfumes (Parfums Givenchy)* [1992] OJ L236/11, high quality gold and silver products: *Murat* [1983] OJ L348/20.

2141. Case 126/80 *Maria Salonia v Giorgio Poidomani* [1981] ECR 1563; Case 243/83 *Binion v Agence et Messageries de la Presse* [1985] ECR 2015.

2142. Guidelines on Vertical Restraints [2000] OJ C291/1, para 185.

2143. Under Regulation 2790/99 it is not required that members of the network are selected only by reference to qualitative criteria. Quantitative criteria may also be used to select distributors. Further, the manufacturer/supplier may use a combination of selective distribution and exclusive distribution. See Guidelines on Vertical Restraints, [2000] OJ C291/1 para 53.

2144. [1980] ECR 3775.

2145. [1992] OJ L236/11.

2146. [1982] OJ L161/18.

2147. [1970] OJ L142/24.

2148. [1992] ECR II-415.

manufacturers) could be achieved by less restrictive measures. In *Ideal-Standard*,[2149] the requirements imposed on wholesalers that they specialise in the sale of plumbing fittings and sanitary ware and had a specialised department for their sale was considered as unjustified on the ground of the nature of the product, that is, plumbing fitting devices were not sufficiently technically advanced.

27.6.4.2   Franchising agreements

The nature of franchising agreements is that they contain licences of intellectual property rights relating to trade marks or signs or know-how for the use and distribution of goods and services, and that the franchisor provides technical and commercial assistance to the franchisee during the life of the agreement. The franchisee gets to exercise the rights in question and, in exchange, the franchisee pays a franchise fee for the use of the particular business method. Franchising agreements usually contain a combination of different vertical restraints relating to the manner in which the products must be distributed.

In respect of franchising agreements the leading case is Case 161/84 *Pronuptia de Paris GmbH v Pronuptia de Paris Irmgard Schillgallis*.[2150]

THE FACTS WERE:

Pronuptia de Paris, which specialised in selling wedding dresses and other wedding accessories, entered into a franchise agreement with Mrs Schillgalis. In exchange for the exclusive right to use the trade mark "Pronuptia de Paris" in three areas in Germany – Hamburg, Oldenburg and Hanover – Mrs Schillgalis was required to purchase 80 per cent of dresses intended to be sold by her directly from Pronuptia and a certain percentage of other dresses from suppliers approved by the franchisor, to make the sale of wedding dresses her main business activity, to advertise in a manner approved by the franchisor, to sell in shops decorated and equipped according to the franchisor's requirements, to fix prices in conformity to recommendations of the franchisor, to pay "entry" fees of DM15,000 for the know-how and thereafter a "royalty" of 10 per cent on her initial sales of Pronuptia products, to refrain from transferring her shop to another location without the approval of the franchisor, and to refrain (both during the agreement and for one year afterwards) from competing in whatever way with Pronuptia outside the territory assigned in the franchise agreement. Pronuptia promised to refrain from opening any other Pronuptia shop in the territory covered by the agreement and to offer its assistance in all aspects of the business from staff training to marketing.

When Pronuptia sued Mrs Schillgalis for non-payment of "royalties", she argued that the franchise agreement was void as contrary to Article 81(1) EC [Article 101(1) TFEU]. The German Supreme Court referred to the ECJ a preliminary question concerning the application of Article 81(1) EC [Article 101(1) TFEU] to franchise agreements.

2149.   [1985] OJ L20/38.
2150.   [1986] ECR 353.

Held:

The ECJ held that restrictions imposed by the franchisor are outside the scope of Article 81(1) EC [Article 101(1) TFEU] if they satisfy two conditions:

- First, the legitimate interests of the franchisor should be protected under Community law, that is, the franchisor should be protected from a risk that the know-how and assistance provided by it to the franchisees would be used to benefit its competitors. As a result, a clause preventing the franchisee, during and after termination of the agreement, from opening a shop selling the same or similar items outside her territory and the requirement for the franchisor's approval of a proposed transfer of the shop to another party were not in breach of Article 81(1) EC [Article 101(1) TFEU];

- Second, the franchisor is entitled to protect the reputation and the identity of its network and therefore to retain some measure of control in this respect. In particular the requirements concerning the location of the shop, the lay-out and decoration of the shop, the percentage of dresses purchased and sources of supplies were legitimate.

Price recommendations were not in breach of Article 81(1) EC [Article 101(1) TFEU] if the franchisee was able to fix her own prices and thus there was not a concerted practice between the parties on prices.

A clause restricting the franchisee from opening a second shop within her exclusive territory without the consent of the franchisor was in breach of Article 81(1) EC [Article 101(1) TFEU], taking into account that it might lead to the division of a Member State's territory into a number of closed territories. In addition this restriction would prevent the franchisee from benefiting from her investment, taking into account that "... a prospective franchisee would not take the risk of becoming part of a chain, investing its own money, paying a relatively high entry fee and undertaking to pay a substantial annual royalty, unless he could hope, thanks to a degree of protection against competition on the part of the franchisor and other franchisees, that his business would be profitable". Consequently, such a clause should be examined under Article 81(3) EC [Article 101(3) TFEU].

The EU institutions have taken a liberal approach to restrictions imposed by franchising agreements by considering their overall beneficial effect on trade and the advantages they offer to both the franchisor and the franchisee. Even a clause condemned in *Consten and Grundig* ensuring absolute territorial protection may fall outside the Article 101(1) TFEU prohibition if it is considered as necessary to induce the franchisee to enter into the agreement.[2151]

27.6.4.3   The cumulative effect of exclusive purchasing agreements

Exclusive purchasing agreements in many ways closely resemble exclusive distribution agreements. Under exclusive purchasing agreements the buyer is required to purchase goods from the manufacturer. Both parties potentially benefit from that arrangement. Manufacturers are able to calculate the demand for their product for the duration of the agreement, and adjust their production

---

2151. See: Commission's decision in *Computerland Europe SA* [1987] OJ L222/12, [1989] 4 CMLR 259.

accordingly; buyers, in exchange for their commitment, receive more advantageous prices, technical assistance, preference in supply, and so on. In dealing with exclusive purchasing agreements the Commission takes into consideration whether the agreement in question forms part of a network of similar agreements. If so, the cumulative effect of such agreements on trade between Member States is assessed. This was illustrated in Case 23/67 *Brasserie de Haecht v Wilkin-Janssens (No.1)*.[2152]

THE FACTS WERE:

The proprietors of a café in Esneux, Belgium, promised, in exchange for a loan made by a brewery in Belgium, to buy all their requirements for beer, lemonade and other drinks from the brewery for the duration of the loan and two further years. When the café proprietors were sued by the brewery for breach of the contract, they argued that the agreement infringed Article 81(1) EC [Article 101(1) TFEU] as it restricted trade between Member States by limiting the outlets in Belgium for breweries from other Member States.

Held:

The ECJ held that the agreement should be assessed in its economic and legal context, in particular whether there was only one agreement or whether the agreement was a part of a network of similar agreements. If it was a separate agreement, its effect on trade between Member States was insignificant. However, if it formed part of a network of agreements, its overall impact might result in making it difficult or even impossible for new undertakings to enter the market through the opening of new outlets.

Comment:

Exclusive purchasing agreements will not fall within the scope of Article 101(1) TFEU if the effect of such an agreement, either individually or as a part of a network of several similar agreements, does not have a "blocking" effect on potential competitors.[2153]

27.7 From exemption to legal exception: Article 101(3) TFEU

Exemptions to the prohibition in Article 101(1) TFEU may be granted under the conditions laid down in Article 101(3) TFEU. With the coming into force of Regulation 1/2003, Article 101(3) exemptions became legal exceptions.[2154] Regulation 2003/1 renders Article 101(3) directly effective, whereas previously it was not directly effective and thus could not be relied on by individuals in national courts, and abolishes the system of notification of envisaged agreements to the Commission which alone had the power to grant exemptions under Article 81(3) EC [Article 101(3) TFEU].

2152. [1967] ECR 407.

2153. This line of reasoning was continued in Case C-234/89 *Delimitis v Henninger Bräu* [1991] ECR 1935; Joined Cases T-374, 375, 384 and 388/94 *European Night Services v Commission* [1998] ECR II-3141.

2154. However, commentators, including the author, continue to refer to them as exemptions.

Under Article 101(3) an agreement, decision or concerted practice will qualify for exemption provided the benefit from it outweighs the disadvantage resulting from the restriction that it imposes on competition and provided it fulfils two positive and two negative criteria.

The positive criteria are:

- It must contribute to improving the production or distribution of goods or the promotion of technical or economic progress;

- It must allow consumers a fair share of the resulting benefit.

The negative criteria are:

- It must not impose on the undertakings concerned restrictions which are not indispensable to the attainment of the objectives set out in the agreement;

- It must not afford an undertaking the possibility of eliminating competition in respect of a substantial proportion of the products in question.

The principles which guide the Commission in deciding whether or not an agreement might qualify for exemption are embodied in Guidelines to the Application of Article 81(3) of the EC Treaty [Article 101 TFEU].[2155] The guidelines indicate, inter alia, that:

- No agreement, even if it seriously restricts competition, can be a priori excluded from the benefit of exemption. In Case T-17/93 *Matra Hachette*,[2156] the CFI [the General Court] held that as a matter of principle there is no anti-competitive practice which cannot qualify for exemption provided that the criteria laid down in Article 81(3) EC [Article 101(3) TFEU] are satisfied;

- An economic assessment of the agreement should be carried out in each case. Article 101(3) provides a forum for the analysis of the pro and anti-competitive aspects of an agreement.[2157] Notwithstanding this, there is an ongoing debate whether aspects other than economic efficiency such as wider socio-political considerations should play any role in the assessment of an agreement. While the Commission takes the position that only economic factors should be taken into consideration,[2158] the case law provides examples where account has been taken of non-competition factors, such as the creation of employment in one of the poorest regions of the EU[2159] or the protection of environment,[2160] as being relevant to the exemption decisions;

- All four criteria laid down in Article 101(3) TFEU must be satisfied. If one of them is not

---

2155. [2004] OJ C101/1.

2156. [1994] ECR II-595.

2157. Case T-65/98 *Van den Berg Foods v Commission*, [2003] ECR II-4653. See also the Guidelines on the Application of Article 81(3) EC [Article 101(3) TFEU], para 33.

2158. In the Guidelines the Commission stated that the objective of Article 81(3) EC [Article 101(3) TFEU] is "to provide a legal framework for the economic assessment of restrictive practices and not to allow the application of the competition rules to be set aside because of political considerations", para 33.

2159. *Ford/Volkswagen* [1993] OJ L20/14.

2160. *European Council of Manufacturers of Domestic Appliances (CECED)* [2000] OJ L 187/47, *DSD* [2001] OJ L319/1.

fulfilled, the agreement will not be exempted.[2161] The exemption ceases to apply if any of the criteria ceases to be satisfied, but in some circumstances the assessment will be made on the basis of the facts existing at the time of implementation of an agreement.[2162]

▪ Article 101(3) TFEU may apply to individual agreements or categories of agreements by way of block exemption regulation (see section 27.8).

The criteria set out in Article 101(3) TFEU are examined below.

27.7.1 First criterion: economic benefit

The first positive criterion requires that agreements, decisions or concerted practices must contribute "to improving the production or distribution of goods or to promoting technical or economic progress". The criterion does not require that all four possibilities are present; it is sufficient if only one of them occurs. In applying the first criterion, advantages flowing from the agreement must be compared with disadvantages resulting from the restriction that it imposes on competition. The advantages must prevail over the disadvantages. The advantages are objectively assessed and refer to the general interest, and not to the benefit which the parties to the agreement may derive for themselves in production or distribution.[2163]

27.7.1.1 *Improvements in production*

Improvements in production will be foreseen if the agreement will result in an increase of productivity, a greater capacity of production, the possibility of making a wider range of products, or the reduction of prices. Specialisation and joint-venture agreements are most likely to contribute to improvements in production.

In *Amersham Buchler*,[2164] the Commission granted exemption on the ground that without the agreement the participating undertakings would hardly be able to offer such a wide range of products as they would with it. Agreements which reduce over-capacity of production in an industry in crisis may qualify for exemption.

In *Synthetic Fibres*,[2165] an agreement concluded between 10 major producers of synthetic fibres intended to reduce over-capacity of production by 18 per cent was granted exemption as it eased the financial burden of keeping under-utilised capacity open, allowed specialisation in the development of products offered to customers, raised the profitability of participating undertakings and alleviated the social consequences of restructuring by making arrangements for retraining and redeployment of redundant workers.

In *Clima Chappé/Buderus*,[2166] under a specialisation agreement a French undertaking Clima Chappé, supplying air-conditioning apparatus, and a German undertaking Buderus, new to the air-conditioning market, agreed to allocate to each other the production of different air-conditioning products. For non-allocated products each was to give preference to the other when

---

2161. Joined Cases T-528, 542, 543 and 546/93 *Métropole Télévision* [1996] ECR II-649; Case T-395/94 *Atlantic Container Line AB v Commission* [2002] ECR II-875.
2162. Guidelines on the Application of Article 81(3) EC, para 45.
2163. Cases 56 and 58/64 *Consten and Grundig* [1966] ECR 299.
2164. [1982] OJ L314/34, [1983] 1 CMLR 619.
2165. [1984] OJ 1984, L 207/17.
2166. [1970] CMLR D7.

buying, provided the price and quality were equal. Buderus agreed not to sell in France (apart from selling to Clima Chappé), while Clima Chappé promised not to sell in Germany (apart from selling to Buderus). There were no restrictions on sales in other Member States. The Commission granted exemption to the agreement on the ground that it would eliminate unnecessary duplication of effort.

In *Prym/Beka*,[2167] under an agreement Prym, in return for shares in Beka, sold its plant which manufactured needles to Beka, who also manufactured needles, and Prym agreed to buy all its future requirement for needles from Beka. Although the agreement lacked reciprocity, the Commission granted exemption, taking into account that it would bring reductions in the price of the needles.

In *Bayer Gist-Brocades*,[2168] the Commission granted exemption to a long-term research and development project regarding production of penicillin between a German and a Dutch undertaking. Each undertaking agreed to give up part of its production in favour of the other, allowing one party to specialise in the production of one particular penicillin product and the other in a different penicillin product.

27.7.1.2 Distribution

Improvements in distribution may result from selective distribution agreements, exclusive dealership networks and the organisation of trade fairs and exhibitions. By virtue of Regulation 330/2010 (see section 27.8.2) most distribution agreements will be exempted under Article 101(3) TFEU.

27.7.1.3 Technical or economic progress

Technical or economic progress concerns the improvement of the quality of products or services, introduction of new technology, the development of new and safer products and the making of a wider range of products. It also includes protection of the environment[2169] and protection of employment.[2170] Specialisation agreements involving common research and development usually qualify for exemption.[2171]

Agreements to co-operate in order to establish a common standard which results in the standardisation of a product are eligible for exemption. In *X/Open Group*,[2172] exemption was granted to computer manufacturers co-operating in order to produce a common standard which would enable users to connect hardware and software from different sources. In *Re ABI*,[2173] an agreement between Italian banks was exempted on the ground that although it restricted competition in respect of charges imposed for their services, it simplified and standardised banking procedures.

2167.   [1973] OJ L296/24.
2168.   [1976] 1 CMLR D98.
2169.   *BBC Brown Boveri* [1988] OJ L301/68.
2170.   Case 26/76 *Metro* [1977] ECR 1875.
2171.   *ACEC-Berliet* [1968] CMLR D35, [1984] OJ L201/7.
2172.   [1987] OJ L35/36.
2173.   [1988] OJ L143.

27.7.1.4   Economic progress

This possibility is rarely invoked as a ground for exemption. However, it was a main factor in granting exemption to an agreement concluded between Iveco and Ford concerning the establishment of a common undertaking for manufacturing and selling cars.[2174]

27.7.2   Second criterion: benefit to consumers

The second positive criterion requires that an agreement, decision or concerted practice must not only contribute to improving the production or distribution of goods or to promoting technical or economic progress, but must also allow consumers a fair share of the resulting benefit.

The term "consumers" applies to final consumers, including wholesalers and retailers, who purchase products in the course of their trade and business.[2175] The Commission takes into consideration the interests of the majority of consumers. In *VBBB/VBVB*,[2176] the Commission refused to grant exemption to an agreement between associations of booksellers and publishers in The Netherlands and Belgium imposing collective prices on books in the Dutch language to be sold in Belgium and in The Netherlands. Under this agreement less popular books on specific subjects published in a limited number of copies were to be subsidised by more popular books. The Commission condemned the agreement on the ground that it would be unfair to the majority of consumers, taking into account that they prefer popular books rather than specialised books which have a limited number of readers.

As to the term "benefit" it covers not only the reduction of purchase prices but also improvement in the quality of products, improvement of after-sales service, the possibility of a greater range of products, an increase in the number or quality of outlets from which the products may be purchased and quicker delivery.[2177]

27.7.3   Third criterion: indispensable restrictions

This first negative criterion requires that an agreement, decision or concerted practice must not impose on the undertakings concerned restrictions which are not indispensable to the attainment of the objectives of the agreement.[2178] This requires that the agreement must not go beyond what is absolutely necessary to achieve the objectives regarded as beneficial. The applicant must prove that this is the case.[2179] In order to assess whether the restriction is indispensable, the Commission will apply the principle of proportionality. This is exemplified in the following cases:

2174.   *Iveco/Ford* [1988] OJ L230/39.
2175.   *Kabel und Metallwerke Neumeyer/Luchaire* [1975] OJ L222/34, [1975] 2 CMLR D40.
2176.   [1982] OJ L54/36; [1982] 2 CMLR 344.
2177.   See Guidelines on the Application of Article 81(3) of the Treaty [Article 101(3) TFEU], para 88 et seq.
2178.   Ibid., paras 73 and 74.
2179.   Case 71/74 *Frubo* [1975] ECR 563; Case 42/84 *Remia* [1985] ECR 2545.

The Rennet case[2180]

THE FACTS WERE:

A co-operative at Leeuwaden producing animal rennet and colouring agents for cheese failed to satisfy the indispensability condition, although it met the two positive criteria. The co-operative which accounted for 100 per cent of the Dutch national output of rennet (of which 94 per cent went to its members) and 90 per cent of the output of colouring agents (of which 80 per cent went to its members) imposed on its members the obligation to purchase all their requirements from the co-operative. If they refused or withdrew from the co-operative, it imposed heavy pecuniary sanctions on them.

Held:

The Commission and the ECJ decided that the economic advantage consisting of greater efficiency in rennet production in The Netherlands was outweighed by the restrictions that the co-operative imposed on its members and that the same result could have been achieved by less restrictive measures.

Case T-17/93 Matra Hachette[2181]

THE FACTS WERE:

An agreement was concluded between Ford of Europe Inc. and Volkswagen AG ("the founders") for a joint venture known as AutoEuropa, to be set up in Setúbal, Portugal, for the production of a multi-purpose vehicle, the VX62. The central question was whether the joint venture was indispensable to enable the founders to penetrate the market in question. If answered in the affirmative, it would ipso facto be established that the restrictions of competition deriving from the agreement were indispensable in order to achieve the two positive objectives set out in Article 81(3) EC [Article 101(3) TFEU].

Held:

The CFI [the General Court] held that the agreement between Ford and Volkswagen satisfied the negative criterion (that is, it was indispensable), taking into account that even if the undertakings concerned had had sufficient financial and technical means to penetrate the market for the multi-purpose vehicle concerned separately, each would have lost a lot of money as a result of the technical and economic difficulties they would have had to face.

With regard to the first positive criterion (that is, the agreement must contribute to improving the production or distribution of goods or to promoting technical or economic progress), the ECJ held that given that the manufacturing process to be used was highly recommended

---

2180. Case 61/80 *Coöperative Stremsel- en Kleurselfabriek v Commission [Re Rennet]* [1981] ECR 851.
2181. [1994] ECR II-595.

by many researchers, in particular those from the Massachusetts Institute of Technology, and that the new technology would optimise the manufacturing process, it satisfied the first of the four criteria laid down by Article 81(1) EC [Article 101(3) TFEU], namely it would contribute to improving production and it would promote technical progress. The agreement, according to the ECJ, would also contribute to technical improvement as it would bring together in a single vehicle model production techniques which, prior to the agreement, were used in isolation on different vehicle models.

With regard to the second positive criterion (that is, the agreement must benefit consumers), the ECJ held that European consumers would benefit from the agreement in that they would have a greater availability of a wider range of multi-purpose vehicles of high quality and at a reasonable price.

In many cases the Commission has granted exemption only if the parties remove from their agreement certain clauses which do not comply with the third criterion.

27.7.4 Fourth criterion: no possibility of eliminating competition

The second negative criterion requires that an agreement, decision or restrictive practice must not result in eliminating competition in respect of a substantial part of the relevant product market.[2182] This situation exists if the undertakings concerned do not have an important share of the relevant market. In order to apply this criterion, the Commission must determine the relevant geographic and product markets.[2183] However, an agreement for joint research may qualify for exemption even if the undertakings concerned have a substantial share of the relevant product market.[2184]

In assessing the fourth criterion, competition between similar competing products (inter-brand competition) rather than competition between rival distributors of the same brand of products (intra-brand competition) is taken into account. The major factor in deciding whether to exempt an agreement under the fourth criterion will be the retention of reasonable competition between the different brands and the absence or otherwise of any restriction on parallel import of these brands.

27.8 Block exemption regulations

Article 101 TFEU does not specify the body which is empowered to grant or refuse individual exemption under Article 101(3) TFEU. However, this task was assigned to the Commission under Article 9 of Council Regulation 17/62.[2185] It was decided that the exclusive competence of the Commission to grant individual exemptions would ensure uniformity in the application and interpretation of Article 81(1) EC [Article 101(1) TFEU].

2182. Commission's Guidelines on the Application of Article 81(3) EC [Article 101(3) TFEU], paras 105–16.

2183. *Lightweight Paper* [1972] OJ L182; Joined Cases 19 and 20/74 *Kali und Salz v Commission* [1975] ECR 499. See Chapter 28.3).

2184. *Michelin* [1981] OJ L353/33.

2185. OJ (1959–62) Spec.ED.87.

Soon after Regulation 17/62 was adopted, the Commission received about 30,000 notifications of exclusive distribution agreements alone. In order to ease the Commission's workload, the Council under Regulation 19/65 empowered it to adopt block exemption regulations exempting classes of agreements (that is why they are called "block" exemption regulations) such as exclusive distribution agreements, purchasing agreements and agreements licensing intellectual property rights so long as the agreements conform to any exemption regulations so adopted. The first regulation adopted by the Commission under the said powers concerned exclusive distribution agreements and was embodied in Regulation 67/67.

Each block exemption is contained in a separate regulation and is, of course, legally binding. If an agreement strictly complies with every condition and term of a block exemption regulation, it enjoys the same protection as used to be afforded to an agreement exempted on an individual basis under Article 101(3) TFEU. Thus parties to an agreement may decide to tailor its terms to ensure it matches those of the relevant block exemption regulation, and in doing so they must, of course, ensure that the envisaged agreement does not contain any restriction not permitted by the block exemption. The EU courts interpret agreements based on block exemption regulations restrictively.[2186] Any doubt as to the legality of any restriction not set out in the relevant block exemption regulation is decided to the detriment of the parties with the result that the agreement is unlawful.

Apart from easing the workload of the Commission, block exemptions offer an important benefit to undertakings. Before the reform of the application of Article 81 EC [Article 101 TFEU] it was not essential to notify the Commission of an agreement which conformed to the terms of a block exemption regulation. Thus, parties could avoid the delays and uncertainty of the procedure for individual exemption. The result of the reform is that the usefulness of block exemption regulations remains, but now the parties themselves are compelled to determine for themselves (rather then having the option of obtaining negative clearance from the Commission) whether their agreement conforms to any relevant block exemption regulation and, if necessary, defend their position before national competition authorities or national courts.

The number of block exemption regulations adopted either by the Council or by the Commission under delegated authority from the Council has considerably increased over the years. This proliferation of block exemption regulations was highly criticised. This and other factors, which are discussed elsewhere in this book (see Chapter 30.1), resulted in the adoption of a new approach to block exemption regulations, forming part of the reform of EU competition law. Following the Commission's Green Paper on Vertical Restraints in Competition Policy,[2187] the first piece of legislation reforming EU competition law was Regulation 2790/99 on the Application of Article 81(3) of the Treaty [Article 101(3) TFEU] to Categories of Vertical Agreements and Concerted Practices,[2188] which entered into force on 1 June 2000 and which has been replaced by Regulation 330/2010[2189] (see section 27.8.2).

The Commission explained that the reform of competition law would increase the freedom to contract, especially for small and medium-sized companies and generally for companies without

---

2186. See Case C-234/89 *Delimitis* [1991] ECR I-935 in which a single clause which was not set out in the white list, although it was not on the black list, was held by the ECJ as depriving the agreement of the benefit of the block exemption.

2187. COM(96) 721 final, 22 January 1997.

2188. [1999] OJ L336/21.

2189. [2010] OJ L142/1.

market power, as well as take away the straitjacket imposed by previous block exemption regulations.

27.8.1 The main features of the new-type block exemption regulations

These are as follows:

■ They are less formalistic. They contain only a black list as opposed to the previous regulation which set out a white list of permitted restrictions and a black list of prohibited restrictions;

■ Their material scope of application has been extended so that the compatibility with EU law or otherwise of the vast majority of agreements is easy to assess. In relation to paragraphs 1 and 3 of Articles 101(1) TFEU, the Commission has issued guidelines and notices as to their respective scope of application. The most relevant are: Guidelines on Vertical Restraints (2010),[2190] Guidelines on the Application of Article 81 [Article 101 TFEU] to Horizontal Agreements (2001),[2191] and Guidelines on the Application of Article 81 of the EC Treaty [Article 101 TFEU] to Technology Transfer Agreements (2004);[2192]

■ The presumption that a restrictive agreement is contrary to Article 101(1) has been abolished;

■ Small and medium-sized undertakings are largely excluded from the scope of Article 101(1) as the regulations set out market share thresholds which range from 30 per cent for vertical agreements to 20 per cent for specialisation and transfer of technology agreements;

■ New mechanisms are set up to increase co-operation between the Commission and national authorities and national courts (see Chapter 30.3 and 30.4).

Regulation 1/2003 gives the Commission and the Member States the power to withdraw the benefit of all block exemptions. Previously the possibility of withdrawal was provided for in each individual block exemption. The Commission may withdraw the benefit of any block exemption where it finds that in any particular case an agreement, decision or concerted practice produces effects which are incompatible with Article 101(3) TFEU. As to national competition authorities, they may withdraw the benefit of a block exemption in a situation where an agreement has "certain effects which are incompatible with the conditions laid down in Article 81(3 [Article 101(3) TFEU]) . . . in the territory of a Member State, or in part thereof, which has all the characteristics of a distinct market".

2190. SEC(2010) 411.
2191. [2001] OJ C3/2.
2192. [2004] OJ C101/2.

27.8.2   Commission Regulation 330/2010 of 20 April 2010 on the application of Article 101(3) of the Treaty on the Functioning of the European Union to categories of vertical agreements and concerted practices[2193]

The above Regulation replaces Regulation 2790/99 on the Application of Article 81(3) of the Treaty [Article 101(3) TFEU] to categories of Vertical Agreements and Concerted Practices,[2194] which in turn replaced the earlier regulations on the block exemptions for exclusive distribution agreements, exclusive purchasing agreements and franchising agreements. Regulation 330/2010 entered into force on 1 June 2010 and and is expected to expire on 31 May 2022. It is accompanied by Commission Gudelines.[2195]

It applies in the following cases:

1.   To all vertical agreements between non-competitors where the supplier of goods or services under the agreement has a share in the relevant product market of less than 30 per cent and the market share of the buyer does not exceed 30 per cent of the relevant market.

2.   To vertical agreements entered into between an association of undertakings and its members, or between such an association and its suppliers if:

(i)   all the members of the association are retailers (i.e. they sell to final consumers) of goods (not services); and

(ii)   each member has a turnover not exceeding € 50 million.

3.   To vertical non-reciprocal agreements between competitors[2196] within the market share threshold specified in point 1 above but only if:

(i)   the supplier is a manufacturer and a distributor of goods while the buyer is only a distributor and not a competing undertaking at the manufacturing level; or

(ii)   the supplier supplies services at several levels of trade while the buyer does not provide competing services at the same level at which it purchases the contract services.

4.   To vertical agreements containing provisions relating to the assignment /use of IPRs and which are within the market share threshold specified in point 1 where five conditions are satisfied:

(i)   The IPRs provisions must be part of a vertical agreement;

(ii)   The IPRs must be assigned to, or licensed for use by, the buyer;

(iii)   The IPRs provisions must not be the primary object of the agreement;

(iv)   The IPRs provisions must be directly related to the use, sale or resale of goods by the buyer or its customer;

(v)   The IPRs provisions concerning goods or services must not contain restrictions of competition having the same object as vertical restraints which are not exempted under the Regulation.

2193.   [2010] OJ L142/1.
2194.   [1999] OJ 336/21.
2195.   SEC(2010) 411.
2196.   A competitor is defined in Article 1(1)(c) of the Regulation as "an actual or potential competitor on the same relevant market, irrespective of whether or not they operate in the same geographic market".

The Commission considers that, in principle, vertical agreements do not have an adverse effect on competition. However, the market share test was introduced to make sure that when the parties to a vertical agreement have market power, the agreement will not produce anti-competitive effects (see Chapter 28.3).

Under Regulation 330/2010 the hard core restrictions are as follows:

- Resale price maintenance, except the setting of maximum resale prices or of recommended resale prices provided that they do not, in practice, amount to fixed or minimum resale prices;

- Restrictions of the territory into which, or of the customers to whom, a buyer may sell apart from:

    (i)   active[2197] resales into the exclusive territory which are allocated by the supplier to another buyer;
    (ii) resales to unauthorised distributors by members of a selective distribution scheme; and
    (iii) resales of goods or services which are supplied for the purpose of incorporation into other products;

- The prevention or restriction of active or passive sales to users, whether professional end users or final customers, by members of a selective distribution scheme;

- The prevention or restriction of cross-supplies between distributors within a selective distribution scheme;

- Restrictions (agreed between a supplier of those spare parts and a buyer who incorporates and resells them) on sales of spare parts to independent repairers and service providers.

The above hard core restrictions are contained in Article 4 of Regulation 2790/99. The insertion of any one of them will result in the entire agreement being excluded from the benefit of block exemption.

Article 5 of the Regulation concerns non-compete clauses which, although prohibited, are severable from the agreement. This means that such clauses will be invalid while the remainder of the agreement can benefit from the block exemption. The following are prohibited:

- Any direct or indirect obligation imposed on members of a selective distribution scheme to sell or not to sell "specified brands" of competing suppliers;

- A non-competition obligation on the buyer exceeding five years in duration, unless the goods to which the agreement relates are resold by the buyer from premises owned or leased by the supplier, provided that the duration of the non-competition obligation does not exceed the period of occupancy of the premises by the buyer; and

- Non-compete obligations in relation to the "contract" goods of any preceding distribution contracts that extend beyond the duration of the agreement unless they relate to competing goods or services, are limited to the premises and land from which the buyer has operated

---

2197. The terms "active" and "passive" sales are defined in para 51 of the Guidelines on Vertical Restraints.

during the agreement, are indispensable to protect know-how transferred by the supplier under the agreement, and are limited to a period of one year.

27.8.3 Other block exemption regulations adopted as a part of the reform of EU competition law

In addition to Regulation 2790/99 the following are the main block exemptions as at March 2010:

- Regulation 1400/2002 on Vertical Agreements and Concerted Practices in the Motor Vehicle Sector;[2198]

- Regulation 772/2004 on Technology Transfer Agreements;[2199]

- Regulation 2658/2000 on Specialisation Agreements;[2200]

- Regulation 2659/2000 on Research and Development Agreements;[2201]

- Regulation 1459/2006 on Passenger Tariffs and Slot Allocations.[2202]

27.9   Civil consequences of breaches of Article 101(1) TFEU

Article 101(2) TFEU states that agreements and decisions in breach of Article 101(1) TFEU which do not qualify for exemption under Article 101(3) TFEU are automatically void from their inception.

The term "automatically" means that no decision to that effect is required from EU institutions or national courts.[2203]

Concerted practices are not mentioned in Article 101(2) TFEU since they are informal arrangements and as such cannot be rendered void.

It is not necessary for the entire agreement or decision to be declared null and void if it is possible to sever offending clauses without destroying the substance of the agreement. Whether or not it is possible to do so is a matter for national courts to decide.[2204] Sometimes, EU institutions assist national courts in this task. For example, in Joined Cases 56 and 58/64 *Consten and Grundig*[2205] the ECJ severed the offending clauses of the agreement, which were those giving absolute territorial protection.

Since the entry into force of Regulation 1/2003 national courts have jurisdiction to apply Article 101(3) TFEU.

Private enforcement of EU competition law is discussed in Chapter 30.

2198. [2002] OJ L203/30.
2199. [2004] OJ L123/18.
2200. [2000] OJ L304/3.
2201. [2000] OJ L304/7.
2202. [2006] OJ L272/3.
2203. Case 22/71 *Beguelin* [1971] ECR 949, Article 1 of Regulation 17/62.
2204. Case 319/82 *Société de Vente de Ciments et Béton de L'Est v Kerpen and Kerpen GmbH and CO KG* [1983] ECR 4173.
2205. [1966] ECR 299.

AIDE-MÉMOIRE

ARTICLE 101 TFEU
Applies to both:

Horizontal agreements: agreements entered into by undertakings that compete with each other at the same level of the production/distribution chain (for example, agreements between producers, or between manufacturers or between retailers); and

Vertical agreements: agreements entered into by undertakings that operate at different levels of the production/distribution chain and do not compete with each other (for example, franchising and distribution agreements) (Cases 56 and 58/64 *Consten and Grundig*).

ARTICLE 101(1) TFEU
Breach of the prohibition embodied in Article 101(1) TFEU occurs when an entity identified as an undertaking behaves in a manner capable of affecting the pattern of trade between Member States by entering into an unlawful arrangement with another undertaking. Such an arrangement must have as its object or effect the prevention, restriction or distortion of competition within the internal market.

Article 101(1) TFEU contains the following essential elements:

1. The definition of an undertaking
Any natural or legal person engaged in any economic activity is regarded as an undertaking for the purposes of EU competition law if it enjoys some autonomy in determining its conduct on the relevant market. The concept of an undertaking is also a relative concept because an entity may be an undertaking under EU competition law with regard to some of its activities and a non-undertaking within the meaning of competition law with regard to its remaining activities (Case C-41/90 *Höfner*; Case T-155/04 *SELEX Sistemi* and see Chapter 26.5.1.2).

2. Agreements, decisions or concerted practices
Agreements between undertakings refer to binding contracts (mainly vertical agreements), and all consensual arrangements between undertakings irrespective of whether or not they are formally binding contracts (Case 41/69 *Chemiefarma [Quinine Cartel]*). The concept of an agreement centres round the existence of a concurrence of wills between at least two parties, the form in which it is manifested being unimportant so long as it constitutes the faithful expression of the parties' intention (Case T-56/02 *Bayerische Hypo*).

Unilateral conduct of an undertaking adopted in the context of contractual relationships with its dealers amounts to an agreement if that conduct receives express or tacit acquiescence by dealers. Such acquiescence cannot be inferred from the mere fact that the dealers entered into the distribution network (Case T-56/02 *Bayerische Hypo*; Case T-208/01 *Volkswagen*).

Decisions by associations of undertakings refer to either a written constitution or decisions of a managing body of a trade association or of any economic interest grouping of undertakings irrespective of their legal form (Case 8/72 *Vereeniging van Cementhandelaren*).

Concerted practices

These refer to a form of informal co-ordination or co-operation between at least two undertakings falling short of an agreement or a decision within the meaning of Article 101(1) TFEU. The conditions required for proof of a concerted practice are: there must be direct or indirect contact between competitors, which must have effect on their future conduct on the relevant market, and a relationship of cause and effect between collusion and market conduct (Case 48/69 *Imperial Chemical Industries [Dyestuffs]*; Cases 40–48/73 etc. *Suiker Unie*; Cases T-25 etc. *Cimenteries*). However, there are the following rebuttable presumptions which alleviate the Commission's burden of proof:

▪ Where undertakings exchange information concerning their commercial policies it is presumed that the recipient of the information cannot fail to take that information into account when formulating its policy on the market.

▪ In Case C-199/92 *Hüls* the ECJ established a presumption that concertation is followed by conduct if an undertaking taking part in the concertation remains active on the relevant market.

Additionally, in Case *Interbrew and Alken-Maes*, the Commission stated that a concerted practice is within the scope of Article 101(1) TFEU even in the absence of actual anti-competitive effects on the competition, i.e. its potential negative impact on competition will suffice.

Parallel behaviour of undertakings in an oligopolistic market cannot be regarded as furnishing proof of concertation **unless concertation constitutes the only plausible explanation of such behaviour** (Cases 89/85 etc. [*Re Wood Pulp Cartel*]). However, even in such a situation some corroborating evidence is required.

The purpose of Article 101(1) TFEU is to catch different forms of co-ordination and collusion between undertakings (C-49/92P *Anic*). Accordingly, the distinction between agreements, decisions and concerted practices is somewhat blurred in practice given the above rebuttable presumptions, although they are distinct concepts.

3. "which have as their object or effect"

The terms "object" and "effect" are to be read disjunctively (Case 56/65 *Société Technique Minière*), so there is a breach if either of them is present:

▪ **"object"** refers to the content and the objective of an agreement, decision or concerted practice which should be assessed in the light of the circumstances of the case, i.e. its legal and economic considerations. Further, the intent of the parties is relevant, although not an essential factor, in determining whether an agreement, decision or concerted practice has anti-competitive object (Cases T-305/94 etc. *Limburgse Vinyl*). The restriction of competition by object entails a rebuttable presumption that the collusive conduct has anti-competitive market effects. Not only actual but also potential negative effects are sufficient to trigger the application of the presumption (Case 8/08 *T-Mobile Netherlands BV*).

■ "**effect**", whether an agreement is anti-competitive or not is assessed only if the object is lawful. In order to determine whether an agreement, decision or concerted practice is restrictive of competition, its actual, direct, indirect and potential effects are taken into account and assessed within the economic and legal context in which they occur. However, the adverse impact on competition of an agreement, decision or concerted practice must be appreciable in order for it to be caught by the prohibition set out in Article 101(1) TFEU (Case 7/95P *John Deere*).

4. Prevention, distortion or restriction of competition

All three words imply a manipulation of the market in a manner which is improper or unlawful. All three words are adequately represented by one, that is, "restraint" on competition.

5. Examples of prohibited arrangements set out in Article 101(1) TFEU

Agreements, decisions and concerted practices are prohibited if they:

(a)   directly or indirectly fix purchase or selling prices or any other trading conditions;

(b)   limit or control production, markets, technical development, or investment;

(c)   share markets or sources of supply;

(d)   apply dissimilar conditions to equivalent transactions with other trading parties, thereby placing them at a competitive disadvantage;

(e)   make the conclusion of contracts subject to acceptance by the other parties of supplementary obligations which, by their nature or according to commercial usage, have no connection with the subject of such contracts.

6. The evolution of interpretation of Article 101(1) TFEU from the per se approach to the economic based approach also referred to as the effects based approach

The effects based approach to the interpretation of Article 101(1) TFEU consisting of taking into account the economic and legal context of the agreement under consideration was initiated in *Société Technique Minière*. This approach has been mainly applied to vertical agreements (Case 26/76 *Metro*; Case 161/84 *Pronuptia*; Case 23/67 *Brasserie de Haecht*).

Although the EU courts explicitly rejected application of the US-style rule of reason to the interpretation of Article 101(1) TFEU (Case T-112/99 *Métropole Télévision (M6)*), they, nevertheless, replaced the per se approach by the effects based approach.

ARTICLE 101(3) TFEU

Article 101(3) TFEU provides an escape from the prohibition set out in Article 101(1). In order to qualify for an exemption, an agreement, a decision or a concerted practice must satisfy four criteria.

The positive criteria are:

■ it must contribute to improving the production or distribution of goods or the promotion of technical or economic progress;

■ it must allow consumers a fair share of the resulting benefit.

The negative criteria are:

- it must not impose on the undertakings concerned restrictions which are not indispensable to attainment of the objectives pursued by it;

- it must not afford such undertakings the possibility of eliminating competition in respect of a substantial proportion of the products in question.

Block exemption regulations: They are EU regulations. They remove uncertainty about the validity of agreements covered by the relevant block exemption regulation. If an agreement benefits from a block exemption, the parties are relieved of their burden to prove under Article 2 of Regulation 1/2003 that their agreement satisfies the four requirements set out in Article 101(3) TFEU.

ARTICLE 101(2) TFEU

Agreements and decisions in breach of Article 101(1) TFEU which do not qualify for exemption under Article 101(3) TFEU are automatically void from their inception. The term "automatically" means that they are prohibited per se and no decision to that effect is required from EU institutions or national courts. Concerted practices are not included in Article 101(2) TFEU since they are informal arrangements and as such cannot be rendered void.

RECOMMENDED READING

Books

Odudu, O., *The Boundaries of EC Competition Law: The Scope of Article 81*, 2006, Oxford: Oxford University Press

Wijckmans, F., Tuytschaever, F. and Vanderelst, A., *Vertical Agreements and the EC Competition Rules*, 2006, Oxford: Oxford University Press

Articles

Albors-Llorens, A., "A Horizontal Agreement and Concerted Practices in EC Competition Law: Unlawful and Legitimate Contacts between Competitors", (2006) 51 Antitrust Bulletin, p 837

Bailey, D., "Single, Overall Agreement in EU Competition Law", (2010) 47 CMLRev, p 473

Bailey, D., " 'Publicly Distancing' Oneself from a Cartel", (2008) 31 World Competition, p 177

Lianos, I., "Collusion in Vertical Relations under Article 81 EC", (2008) 45 CMLRev, p 1027

Meyring, B., "T-Mobile: Further Confusion on Information Exchanges between Competitors: Case C-8/08 T-Mobile Netherlands and others [2009] ECR 0000", Journal of European Competition Law & Practice Advance, 2009, 30.

28

ARTICLE 102 TFEU

SUMMARY

1. Article 102 TFEU prohibits the abuse of a dominant position by a single undertaking or by a number of undertakings, which abuse affects trade between Member States.

2. The concept of dominance was defined by the ECJ in Case 85/76 *Hoffmann-La Roche* as referring to such a position of market power being held by an undertaking as to enable it to act independently from its competitors and consumers and thus not subjecting it to normal competitive forces. The degree of dominance does not have to amount to a monopoly.

3. In order to ascertain dominance and also for the purposes of enforcement of any competition law, it is vital to determine whether an undertaking has market power. This concept has been defined as the seller's ability to raise and sustain a price increase without losing so many sales that it must rescind the increase. The usual method of assessing whether an undertaking has market power is to:

- First, define the relevant market, which has three components: the relevant product market (RPM), the relevant geographical market (RGM) and if appropriate, the relevant temporal market (RTM). In order to identify the relevant market three factors are taken into consideration:

- demand substitutability – this involves identifying products that consumers will substitute for the product under consideration in response to a Small but Significant and Non-transitory Increase in Price (the SSNIP test) in order to include those products within the relevant market;
- supply substitutability – this is to identify all producers that currently produce a relevant product and all producers that could easily and economically produce and sell the relevant product in a short period of time in response to a small increase in price in order to include them within the relevant market; and
- potential competition. This is in fact often assessed at the third stage (see below).

■ It should be noted that the greater the substitutability, the less likely it is that an undertaking has market power.

■ Second, the Commission identifies three main factors as essential to the assessment of market power, i.e:

- constraints imposed by the existing supplies firms, and the position on the market of the actual competitors (the position of the undertaking concerned and its rivals);
- constraints imposed by the credible threat of future expansion by actual competitors or entry by potential competitors to the relevant market (expansion and entry);
- constraints imposed by the bargaining power of the dominant undertaking's customers (countervailing buyer power).

4. In the context of dominance two new concepts have emerged: the concept of "super-dominance" and the concept of "collective dominance".

A. The concept of "super-dominance" refers to a situation where an undertaking enjoys a monopoly or a quasi-monopoly in the relevant product market. However, the practical implications deriving from an undertaking holding such a position, as opposed to simply being dominant, are unclear taking into account that all undertakings in a dominant position, irrespective of "how dominant" they are, have a special responsibility under EU competition rules, but EU law does not impose upon them different obligations according to the degree of their dominance.

B. The concept of "collective dominance" concerns the situation where the relevant market is oligopolistic and undertakings, through tacit parallel conduct, can act in a similar way to a cartel or a monopoly. However, tacit parallel conduct is not sufficient to establish collective dominance. To prove collective dominance three conditions must be met. These are:

■ Transparency, that is, each member of the dominant oligopoly must have the ability to know how the other members are behaving in order to monitor whether or not they are adopting the common policy;

■ Sustainability, that is, there must be a retaliatory mechanism in place which secures unity within an oligopoly and thus dissuades its members from deviating from their common policy adopted in the relevant market; and

■ An absence of competitive constraints, so allowing undertakings within a dominant oligopoly to act independently of their customers and consumers, actual or potential.

It is to be noted that tacit collusion is caught by Article 102 TFEU while explicit collusion between undertakings in an oligopolistic market is caught byArticle 101 TFEU.

5. The concept of abuse is an objective concept. It has been interpreted broadly to encompass not only conduct by which a dominant undertaking exploits its position, that is, conduct which may cause damage to purchasers or consumers directly, but also conduct which affects the structure of the market, that is, conduct which excludes competitors, strengthens the dominant position of the undertaking concerned and weakens competition in the market, and thus is detrimental to purchasers and consumers through its impact on an effective competition structure of the relevant market.

6. Article 102(a)–(d) TFEU sets out a non-exhaustive list of abusive practices. This raises the issue of interpretation, that is, whether the per se rule or the rule of reason (i.e the effects-based approach) should be applied to decide whether an undertaking in a dominant position has abused that position. The per se approach has been rejected by the Commission in its Guidance on Enforcement Priorities in Applying Article 82 of the EC Treaty [Article 101 TFEU] to Abusive Exclusionary Conduct by Dominant Undertakings adopted in December 2008. As a result, the qualification of a unilateral practice will depend on the anti-competitive effects it produces on the relevant market. Further, the Guidance has generalised the possibility for a dominant undertaking to rely on objective justifications to exempt a practice which the Commission has found abusive. The dominant undertaking may justify its conduct by demonstrating that:

- It is objectively necessary, e.g. justified by imperative considerations such as health and safety reasons related to the nature of the product concerned;

- It produces substantial efficiencies which outweigh any anti-competitive effects on consumers. The test here is similar to that set out in Article 101(1) TFEU.

On the basis of Article 102(a)–(d) abuses can be classified as follows:

- Exploitative abuses – these occur when an undertaking is, at the expense of customers or consumers, using its economic power to obtain benefits or to impose burdens, which are unobtainable or imposable within normal competition on the merits. An example of this type of abuse is the imposition of excessively high prices;

- Discriminatory abuses – these occur when a dominant undertaking treats its customers in a dissimilar manner without costs based or legally acceptable justification;

- Exclusionary abuses – these are aimed at foreclosing the relevant market. They are especially harmful to competition. They are always anti-competitive and some, for example discriminatory pricing, may be both discriminatory and exploitative. Further some abuses, for example refusal to supply, may, at the same time, be reprisary, exploitative and discriminatory.

- Reprisal abuses – these occur when the conduct of an undertaking in a dominant position is directed at injuring another undertaking in order to punish it, usually for what the undertaking in a dominant position considers as "disloyal" conduct towards it. They may consist, for example, of refusals to deal or of the use of predatory prices as a reprisal weapon.

28.1 Introduction

Article 102 TFEU states:

"Any abuse by one or more undertakings of a dominant position within the internal market or in a substantial part of it shall be prohibited as incompatible with the internal market in so far as it may affect trade between Member States.

Such abuse may, in particular, consist in:

(a)   directly or indirectly imposing unfair purchase or selling prices or other unfair trading conditions;

(b)   limiting production, markets or technical development to the prejudice of consumers;

(c)   applying dissimilar conditions to equivalent transactions with other trading parties, thereby placing them at a competitive disadvantage;

(d)   making the conclusion of contracts subject to acceptance by the other parties of supplementary obligations which, by their nature or according to commercial usage, have no connection with the subject of such contracts."

Within the framework of modernisation of EU competition law, and in line with the reform that has taken place regarding Article 101 TFEU and the Merger Regulation,[2206] the European Commission commenced revising its enforcement approach to Article 102 TFEU. The main objective is to develop a much stronger economic-based approach, often referred to as the effects-based approach (that is, the rule of reason approach), to the interpretation of EU law on the abuse of a dominant position, focusing on the promotion of economic efficiency and consumer welfare. As a result, instead of giving undue attention to the list of examples of presumptively abusive conduct contained in Article 102 TFEU, the Commission should concentrate on the actual anti-competitive effects caused by the conduct. It should therefore concentrate on the substance, i.e. the actual effect that the conduct has (or has not) had rather than the form of a particular practice.

The task of reform of Article 102 TFEU is not easy given that a per se or rigid interpretation would hinder pro-competitive and pro-consumer conduct of dominant undertakings, while a lax policy or effects-based interpretation would jeopardise the competitiveness of the relevant market.

In order to further the debate on the topic the Commission asked the Economic Advisory Group for Competition Policy to prepare a report on the revision of Article 102 EC. The Report entitled "An Economic Approach to Article 82 [Article 102 TFEU]" was submitted to the Commission in July 2005.[2207] The Report supports an economics-based approach to Article 102 TFEU, focusing on the anti-competitive effects of the actions of undertakings rather than the form these actions may take. The Report emphasises that the main objective of competition policy is the satisfaction of consumers' needs. The application of an economic approach (that is, the rule of reason approach) entails that a careful examination of how competition works in each particular market is required in order to assess how specific actions of an undertaking affect consumer welfare, if at all. This implies that if a competitive harm is identified, its pro and anti-competitive effects must be assessed in order to decide whether or not the negative effects on consumer welfare are outweighed by efficiency gains. The Report, because it embraces the economic approach to the point of challenging the principle of certainty in the application of Article 102 TFEU, in particular, by rejecting the need for a separate assessment of dominance has, so far, not greatly influenced

---

2206.   See Chapter 29.

2207.   See the Official site of the EU's competition policy – news, legislation, cases at http://ec.europa.eu/competition/index_en.html.

the Commission. However, the Guidance on the Commission Enforcement Priorities in Applying Article 82 of the EC Treaty [Article 102 TFEU] to Abusive Exclusionary Conduct by Dominant Undertakings[2208] (hereafter referred to as the Guidance) confirms that the Commission intends to apply the effects-based approach to exclusionary conduct under EU competition law. The Guidance covers only exclusionary conduct as opposed to exploitative and discriminatory conduct.

Two main innovations have been introduced so far as the new approach is concerned:

▪ The Guidance officially recognises the applicability of the effects-based approach to the establishment of abuses under Article 102 TFEU. As a result, the Commission is expected to use a more refined economic analysis than it did in the past;

▪ The Guidance establishes a generalised system of justifications for abusive practices.

Under Article 102 TFEU a dominant position is not prohibited. What is unlawful and therefore prohibited, is the abuse of a dominant position. In order to show a breach of the prohibition set out in Article 102 TFEU, it is necessary to establish that:

▪ One or more undertakings;

▪ In a dominant position within the internal market or in a substantial part of it;

▪ Has a dominant position which it has abused;

▪ The abuse has affected trade between Member States (see Chapter 26.6).

The TFEU does not define any of the above terms. Their meanings have gradually been clarified by the Commission and CJEU.

28.2   The concept of dominance

The ECJ defined the concept of dominance in Case 27/76 *United Brands v Commission*[2209] as being

"a position of economic strength enjoyed by an undertaking which enables it to prevent effective competition being maintained on the relevant market by giving it the power to behave to an appreciable extent independently of its competitors, customers, and ultimately of its consumers."

This definition was further explained in Case 85/76 *Hoffmann-La Roche*,[2210] in which the ECJ restated the above-mentioned definition and added that:

". . . such a position does not preclude some competition which it does where there is a monopoly or quasi-monopoly but enables the undertakings which profit by it, if not to determine, at least to have an appreciable influence on the conditions under which that competition will develop, and in any case to act largely in disregard of it so long as such conduct does not operate to its detriment."

Accordingly, an undertaking is in a dominant position when it can act independently from its competitors and consumers and thus is not subject to normal competitive forces. In Case T-219/99

2208.   [2009] OJ C45/7–20.
2209.   [1978] ECR 207.
2210.   [1979] ECR 461.

British Airways plc v Commission,[2211] the CFI confirmed that a dominant position may exist not only in the supplier market but also in the buyer market. In this case British Airways was found to be in a dominant position as a purchaser of services in the UK from travel agents.

The Commission's Guidance on the enforcement priorities in applying Article 102 TFEU confirms the above definition of dominance. The Commission considers that "an undertaking which is capable of profitably increasing prices above the competitive level for a significant period of time does not face sufficiently effective competitive constraints and can thus generally be regarded as dominant" (para 11).

28.3   Establishing dominance: market power, market definition, assessing the existence of market power

The determination that an undertaking has market power is vital for the enforcement of any competition law. This is because only undertakings which have market power can distort the competitive process. Market power is usually linked to the elasticity of supply and demand;[2212] however, in some cases it may be inferred from the conduct of the undertaking concerned (see section 28.3.1.1.4).

Market power can be exercised by a seller or by a buyer. However, economists generally refer to the position of a seller rather than a buyer to define market power.[2213] In a perfectly competitive market, no undertaking has market power because no undertaking has the ability to individually affect either the total quantity of goods on the market or the prevailing prices in the market. As there is no such market an undertaking has market power when it has those abilities. Usually economists refer to "market power" to describe the ability of a seller to profitably impose prices above competitive prices for a sustainable period of time. The crucial issue is how to assess whether an undertaking has market power. Competition enforcement authorities, including the Commission, usually determine whether market power exists by first, defining the relevant market, second, determining the market share which the relevant undertaking holds on the market and third, considering other relevant factors. In this respect the Commission's Guidance confirms the effects-based approach. The Commission intends to abandon the mechanical calculation of dominance based on a market shares threshold and instead take into account the competitive structure of the market. In particular, the Commission identifies three main factors as essential to the assessment of market power (see Chapter 28.3.2):

- constraints imposed by the existing supplies firms, and the position on the market of the actual competitors (the position of the undertaking concerned and its rivals);

- constraints imposed by the credible threat of future expansion by actual competitors or entry by potential competitors (expansion and entry);

- constraints imposed by the bargaining power of the undertaking's customers (countervailing buyer power).

2211. [2003] ECR II-5917. Upheld by the ECJ in Case C-95/04P *BA v Commission* [2007] ECR I-2331.

2212. On the economic aspects of competition law see: S. Bishop and M. Walker, *The Economics of EC Competition Law: Concepts, Application and Measurement*, 2002, London: Sweet and Maxwell.

2213. W. Landes and R. Posner, "Market Power in Antitrust Cases", (1981) 94 Harv.L.Rev, p 939.

28.3.1 Market definition

Only in the context of the relevant market can dominance or otherwise be ascertained. Thus, identification of the relevant market is of crucial importance and is the first step for the application of Article 102 TFEU and the Merger Regulation (see Chapter 29). It is also relevant for the application of Article 101 TFEU given that undertakings with low market shares, that is, below 30 per cent, are within the scope of Regulation 330/2010 (see Chapter 27.8.2).

The main purpose of market definition has been explained by the Commission in its Discussion Paper on the Application of Article 82 [Article 102 TFEU] to Exclusionary Abuses[2214] in the following words:

"The objective of defining a market in both its product and geographic dimension is to identify all actual competitors of the undertaking concerned that are capable of constraining its behaviour."

The relevant market has three components:

- The relevant product market (RPM). The determination of the RPM is the most important and the most common issue in every case which raises competition concerns but poses a great challenge because of the interchangeability of many products (see below).

- The relevant geographical market (RGM). The definition of the RGM is necessary as Article 102 TFEU only applies if an undertaking abuses its dominant position "within the internal market or in a substantial part of it".

- The relevant temporal market (RTM).

The Notice on the Definition of the Relevant Market for the Purposes of Community Competition Law[2215] issued by the Commission in 1997 is very helpful in understanding the concept of the relevant market. The Notice sets out the means (which are based on the practices of both the Commission and the CJEU) of assessing the relevant product and geographical market.

The Commission identifies three main factors of competitive constraints to which undertakings are subject and which are used to identify the three relevant markets: RPM, RGM and RTM. They are:

- Demand substitutability;

- Supply substitutability; and

- Potential competition.

With regard to potential competition, it should be noted that this factor, although of relevance when supply substitutability is assessed, is essentially taken into consideration by the Commission subsequent to definition of the relevant market, when it examines other factors relevant to the assessment of the market power of the undertaking concerned.

2214. Available at http://ec.europa.eu/comm/competition/antitrust/art82/discpaper2005.pdf, para 12 (accessed on 20/12/07).
2215. [1997] OJ C372/5.

28.3.1.1   The relevant product market (RPM)

The 1997 Commission Notice provides the following definition of the RPM:

> "a relevant product market comprises all those products and/or services which are regarded as interchangeable or substitutable by the consumers, by reason of the products' characteristics, their prices and their intended uses."[2216]

The identification of the RPM depends on the determination of which products are substitutable one for another. In order to determine whether products are or can be substitutes for one another, and thus to identify the RPM, two main factors of competitive constraints are taken into consideration:

- Demand substitutability; and

- Supply substitutability.

The above definition, however, focuses on demand substitutability because, according to the Commission: ". . . from an economic point of view, for the definition of the relevant market, demand substitutability constitutes the most immediate and effective disciplinary force on the suppliers of a given product, in particular in relation to their pricing decision."[2217] The Commission explained in its Notice that an undertaking cannot hold a dominant position in the relevant market, and consequently cannot have market power, if consumers can easily switch to available substitute products or to suppliers offering the same product located within the same geographical market. The focus on demand substitutability has been subject to criticism given that the consequence of ignoring other constraints, such as supply substitutability and potential competition, is that the relevant market will be too narrowly defined, and consequently, an undertaking's apparent position on the relevant market will not reflect its actual position, that is, it may be found to be in a dominant position by the Commission but, in fact, may have no market power.[2218]

Divergences between the Commission and the undertaking under investigation in the determination of the RPM usually follow a similar pattern, bearing in mind that undertakings always seek a broad definition and the Commission always seeks the opposite. The narrower the definition of a product market, the greater the market power of any one undertaking and thus the more likely it is that the undertaking will have to bear the extra responsibilities that go with being in a dominant position.

28.3.1.1.1 Demand substitutability

To assess demand substitutability the test is based on the question of whether consumers of the relevant product would switch to substitute products if prices for the relevant product were raised by a small but significant amount (between 5 and 10 per cent) above competitive levels (this is known as the SSNIP test – a Small but Significant Non-transitory Increase in Price). If so, the relevant product market should include the substitutes. It would be unrealistic to expect that all or even the majority of customers would switch. The decisive factor is whether, if prices were raised

---

2216. [1997] OJ C37, para 7.
2217. [1997] OJ C37, para 13.
2218. S. Bishop and M. Walker, *The Economics of EC Competition Law: Concepts, Application and Measurement*, 2002, London: Sweet and Maxwell, p 112.

as mentioned above, a sufficiently large number of consumers would be likely to switch to substitutes and so dissuade an undertaking in a dominant position from charging prices above competitive levels.

The identification of the RPM was at issue in Case 27/76 *United Brands v Commission.*[2219]

THE FACTS WERE:

United Brands, a multinational corporation registered in New Jersey (USA), was the main supplier of bananas to many Member States. Identification of the relevant product market was crucial to the outcome of the case. United Brands argued that bananas were interchangeable with other fruits such as apples and oranges from the perspective of the consumer, and thus it did not enjoy a dominant position as it was not free from competitive pressures, taking into account that any producers of other fruits were able to challenge its performance. Further, United Brands argued that the banana market was seasonal and thus affected by the availability of other fresh fruits in the summer. The Commission decided that bananas were not part of a wider product market encompassing other fruits because of their unique characteristics. The effect of this decision was that the percentage share in the relevant market held by United Brands was greatly increased above the percentage share that it would have held if the relevant product had included many other fruits.

Held:

The ECJ upheld the Commission's decision. It ruled that bananas were not substitutable by other fruits because a "banana has certain characteristics, appearance, taste, softness, seedlessness, easy handling, and a constant level of production which enable it to satisfy the constant needs of an important section of the population consisting of the very young, the old and the sick". In addition, the arrival on the market of seasonal fruits such as apples did not have any impact on the consumption of bananas and there was almost no fluctuation of prices for bananas. Therefore, there was no substitutability as the consumers of bananas were not likely to switch to other fruits in order to satisfy their needs, even if an increase in the price of bananas was substantial.

Case T-30/89 *Hilti AG v Commission*[2220] provides another example of the manner in which the Commission determines demand substitutability.

THE FACTS WERE:

Hilti manufactured nail guns, and the nails and cartridge strips for such equipment. After an investigation by the Commission Hilti was found to have abused its dominant position within

---

2219. [1978] ECR 207.
2220. [1990] ECR II-163.

the internal market for each of these products, namely the market in nail guns, the market in cartridge strips and the market in nails.

The Commission stated that Hilti abused its position, inter alia, by pursuing a policy of supplying cartridge strips to certain end users or distributors only when such cartridge strips were purchased with the necessary complement of nails ("tying" of cartridge strips and nails), by blocking the sale of competitors' nails, by pursuing a policy of reducing discounts for orders of cartridges without nails (the reduction of discounts was based essentially on the fact that the customers were purchasing nails from Hilti's competitors), by exercising pressure on independent distributors (mainly in The Netherlands) not to fulfil certain export orders (notably to the UK), and by refusing to supply cartridges to independent nail manufacturers (mainly to the undertakings that complained to the Commission).

Hilti challenged the Commission's definition of the relevant product market. Hilti argued that the alleged three markets for the three products must be regarded as constituting a single indivisible market because none of the products could be used by consumers without the others.

Held:

The CFI [the General Court] upheld the decision of the Commission. The Court stated that the Commission was correct in identifying three separate product markets because all the products could be manufactured separately and could be purchased by consumers without them having to buy the other products. There were, therefore, three distinct product markets.

28.3.1.1.2 The cellophane fallacy

The SSNIP test does not work in a situation where current prices are above competitive prices. Indeed, if current prices are monopoly prices, that is, above competitive prices, it would be unprofitable for a monopoly to increase prices further since its product would probably be replaced by its closest substitutes as there is a limit to what consumers are likely to pay. Therefore, if current prices are above competitive prices, a small increase of 5 per cent will force a switch to a product outside the relevant market. For example, if prices for railway tickets rise to that point, a significant number of consumers will drive their own vehicle or take a coach. Thus it may appear that there are many substitutes (private cars and coaches) but they are not in the same product market as the monopolist product (trains). This problem is known as the cellophane fallacy after a US case involving cellophane products.[2221]

In this case the US Supreme Court accepted erroneously that cellophane was not a separate relevant market but formed part of a market for flexible packaging materials such as aluminium foil, polythene and wax paper. As a result, the Court failed to recognise that the price charged for cellophane was already a monopoly price.

The 1997 Notice recognises that the application of the SSNIP test may be inappropriate where the price of the relevant product has been determined in the absence of competition. Bearing in

---

2221. *US v El Du Pont de Nemours & Co* [1956] 351 US 377. This problem was acknowledged by the UK Office of Fair Trading in Case CA98/14/2002 *Aberdeen Journals Ltd v Office of Fair Trading* [2002] UKCLR 740 and in Case CA98/20/2002 *BSkyB Investigation: Alleged Infringement of the Chapter II Prohibition* [2003] UKCLR 240.

mind that the SSNIP test may not be reliable in a situation where the current price is already a monopoly price, in order to identify the relevant product market, the EU institutions have to take into account other factors such as excessive profit made by an undertaking and past price fluctuations, together with other evidence on market power and of the undertaking's conduct. As the UK's Guideline on Market Definition published by the Office of Fair Trading emphasised, the market definition is only a tool for assessing whether undertakings possess market power, not an end in itself.[2222]

28.3.1.1.3 Supply substitutability

Supply substitutability (the supply-side substitution) refers to substitutability of products or otherwise as assessed from the point of view of suppliers. The question to be asked is whether suppliers, who do not currently supply the relevant products, would be able to switch production to the relevant products and market them in the short term without incurring significant additional costs or risk in response to small and permanent changes in prices in respect of the relevant product. If this occurs, according to the 1997 Notice, "the additional production that is put on the market will have a disciplinary effect on the competitive behaviour of the companies involved" and will be taken into consideration when defining the relevant product market, given that its effect in terms of effectiveness and immediacy is equivalent to the demand substitution effect.[2223]

The important factor in assessing supply substitutability is time. If supply-side substitution would take place within a short time (usually one year, but it depends on the product), the supply-side substitution will be relevant to the definition of the RPM. Further, if a substantial investment would be needed, or undertakings which might be involved in substitution had no spare capacity, or there would be substantial costs involving the advertisement or distribution of a substitute product, that product would not normally be included in the relevant product market.

Supply substitutability was examined by the Commission in *Torras/Sarrió*.[2224]

THE FACTS WERE:

The case concerned the supply of paper for use in publishing. Only the coating used for paper determines the grade of the paper and, consequently, it is very simple to switch production from one grade to another as the same raw materials and the same plant can be used. Following from this there was, in this case, a great measure of supply substitutability given that if an undertaking increased prices for a particular grade of paper above competitive levels, other undertakings could easily and quickly change their production in order to produce that grade.

Held:

The Commission decided that the existence of supply substitutability would undermine any potential market power in that particular grade of paper. Therefore, the relevant product

---

2222. Para 5.14.
2223. The Notice on the Definition of the Relevant Market for the Purposes of Community Competition Law [1997] OJ C37, para 20.
2224. [1992] 4 CMLR 341.

market was that in publishing paper generally and not that in any particular grade of publishing paper.

The assessment of supply-side substitutability was at issue in Case 6/72 *Europemballage Corporation and Continental Can Company Inc. [Continental Can] v Commission.*[2225]

THE FACTS WERE:

Continental Can, a multinational corporation engaged in packing operations worldwide, acquired 86 per cent of the shares in Schmalbach-Lubeca-Werke AG (SLW), a maker in Germany of light metal containers for meat and fish and of bottle-sealing machines. A year later, Continental Can set up a new corporation in Delaware, Europemballage, which opened an office in Brussels and subsequently acquired 91.7 per cent of the shares of a Dutch company, TDV, which was a leading manufacturer of packaging material in the Benelux countries. Continental Can wanted to transfer the ownership of its shares in SLW to Europemballage and thus indirectly control large market shares. The Commission claimed that Continental Can, through its shares in SLW, was in a dominant position in three product markets, i.e:

- *for light containers for canned meat products;*

- *for light containers for canned seafood;*

- *for metal closures for glass containers.*

Held:

The ECJ annulled the Commission's decision on the ground that the Commission did not assess supply-side substitutability. It held that in order to ascertain the relevant product market, the products in question must be individualised "not only by the mere fact that they are used for packing certain products, but by particular characteristics of production which make them specially suitable for this purpose. Consequently, a dominant position in the market for light metal containers for meat and fish cannot be decisive, as long as it has not been proved that competitors from other sectors of the market for light metal containers are not in a position to enter this market, by a simple adoption, with sufficient strength to create a serious counterweight".

28.3.1.1.4 The RPM inferred from the conduct of an undertaking

The identification of the RPM may also be inferred from the conduct of an undertaking. This is exemplified in Case C-62/86 *AKZO Chemie BV v Commission*[2226] where the ECJ defined the RPM not by reference to demand and supply substitutability but by focusing on AKZO's behaviour.

2225. [1973] ECR 215.
2226. [1991] ECR I-3359.

THE FACTS WERE:

Benzoyl peroxide is a chemical that is used both for bleaching flour and as a catalyst in the manufacture of plastics. Engineering and Chemical Supplies Ltd (ECS), an English undertaking producing benzoyl peroxide which had mainly operated in the flour additive sector, decided to expand its sales into the plastics sector in the United Kingdom and Ireland. This sector was dominated by AKZO, a producer of organic peroxide. When one of the largest customers of AKZO in its plastics sector became a customer of ECS, AKZO threatened to reduce prices in the UK flour sector. ECS complained to the Commission. The Commission ordered interim measures under which AKZO's branch in the UK was to stay within its profit levels existing prior to ECS's expansion into the plastics sector. The Commission found a memo prepared by one of AKZO's directors stating that ECS's managing director was informed that "aggressive commercial action would be taken on the milling [that is, flour] side unless he refrained from selling his products to the plastics industry".

The Commission found that AKZO had abused its dominant position in the market for organic peroxides by threatening to engage in predatory pricing in order to eliminate ECS. AKZO challenged the methodology employed by the Commission in assessing the existence of a dominant position, in particular in the determination of the RPM and the RGM, and claimed that its prices were not abusive as they always included an element of profit and thus should not be considered predatory.

Held:

The ECJ upheld the Commission's assessment of the relevant product market and relevant geographical market. In respect of identification of the RPM the ECJ stated that AKZO applied price reductions in the sector of flour additives, which was vital to ECS, but only of limited importance to itself. Furthermore, AKZO was able to set off any losses that it incurred in the flour additives sector against profits from its activity in the plastics sector, a possibility not available to ECS. In respect of the flour market, the charging of predatory prices by AKZO in that market would not have been financially viable had AKZO not been in a dominant position in that market. Therefore, by its action AKZO defined the RPM.

28.3.1.1.5 Small undertakings and narrow product markets

An undertaking can fall foul of Article 102 TFEU without being a powerful multinational and without the relevant product market being very large.

In *British Brass Band Instruments v Boosey & Hawkes*,[2227] the RPM was defined very narrowly as it concerned instruments for British-style brass bands in which Boosey & Hawkes held a 90 per cent share.[2228] In this case the Commission emphasised that the important factor was whether the market, or in this case the sub-market, "was sufficiently distinct in commercial reality". In making this finding the Commission was influenced, inter alia, by advertising material published by Boosey & Hawkes claiming that the market for brass band instruments for British-style brass

---

2227. [1987] OJ L286/36.
2228. Ibid.

bands was distinct from that for brass instruments generally. However, in Case T-5/02 *Tetra Laval v Commission*,[2229] the CFI [the General Court] held that statements made by undertakings as to how they perceived the RPM not supported by any other evidence have no probative value.

The fact that some activities of an undertaking are insignificant in terms of quantity does not necessarily stop them from being caught by Article 102 TFEU. This can be seen in Case 26/75 *General Motors Continental (GMC)*,[2230] in which, under Belgian law, GMC was the only undertaking allowed to provide test certificates for imports of second-hand Opel cars and was held to be in a dominant position in relation to issuing such certificates, even though it delivered merely five of them in 1973!

28.3.1.1.6 Power in aftermarkets

For many products a customer will need to purchase spare parts or repair/maintenance services or other supplementary (for example, cartridges for a laser printer) or complementary products (for example, nails for use with nails guns) at a later date. The market for those products/services is referred to as an aftermarket. The issue here is that an undertaking may not be in a dominant position with regard to its original product, but may, nevertheless, be regarded as being in a dominant position in respect of aftermarket products/services. Accordingly, if the RPM is defined as being confined to aftermarket products/services rather than the original products, the RPM may be very narrow and the undertaking concerned will be found to be in a dominant position in that market. This was at issue in Case 22/78 *Hugin Kassaregister AB v Commission*.[2231]

THE FACTS WERE:

Hugin, a Swedish manufacturer of cash machines, supplied spare parts to Liptons Cash Registers and Business Equipment Ltd (a British undertaking specialising in reconditioning and repairing used Hugin cash registers) in the UK through its British subsidiary. Hugin held only 12 per cent of the cash registers market within the EU. However, it had a monopoly with regard to supply of its own spare parts to its cash machines. Hugin refused to continue the supply of spare parts to Liptons. The reason was that Hugin intended to enter the downstream market for servicing. Hugin argued that spare parts and maintenance services were not a separate market but formed part of the market for cash registers as a whole. The Commission decided that Hugin was in a dominant position in respect of its own spare parts as they were not interchangeable with those of other cash machines, and that Hugin abused its dominant position in the spare parts market by refusing to supply them to Liptons.

Held:

The ECJ upheld the Commission's finding with regard to the definition of the RPM, although it annulled the decision on the ground that the Commission failed to show that Hugin's conduct was capable of affecting trade between Member States.

2229. [2002] ECR II-4381.
2230. [1975] ECR 1367.
2231. [1979] ECR 1869.

The ruling of the ECJ in *Hugin* was followed in subsequent judgments. In Case 238/87 *AB Volvo v Erik Veng (UK) Ltd*[2232] and Case 53/87 *CICRA v Régie Nationale des Usines Renault*[2233] the ECJ confirmed that spare parts can form a market separate from that relating to the original product. Also complementary products, such as nails for use with nail guns[2234] and cartons for use with filling machines[2235] were defined as forming a separate market from that of the original product. It is important to note that the RPM in aftermarkets can only be determined after a factual inquiry into all circumstances of the case. This is because a consumer may have already taken account of high prices of products/services in the aftermarkets when purchasing the original products. Accordingly, the high prices charged for spare parts or other supplementary or complementary products/services may constitute competitive restraints with regard to the original product market. In such a situation there is only one RPM, not two separate product markets. This was recognised in paragraph 56 of the Commission's Notice on Market Definition.[2236]

28.3.1.2 The Relevant Geographic Market (RGM)

In order to establish dominance it is necessary to determine the RGM, given that Article 102 TFEU requires that an undertaking must hold the alleged dominant position "within the internal market or in a substantial part of it".

The main purpose of the requirement that an undertaking must hold a dominant position "within the internal market or in a substantial part of it" is to determine whether the matter is of relevance to the EU, that is, within the scope of Article 102 TFEU, or whether it is of a local/ national interest, that is, subject to national competition rules. Only conduct of undertakings which has appreciable effect on competition within the internal market can threaten the EU objectives (see Chapter 26.6).

Geographic markets are defined using the same criteria as those used to define the RPM. The demand side and the supply side are the main factors in determining the RGM. If customers will or can travel in order to obtain a different product in response to a 5 per cent increase in price, a hypothetical monopolist would not initiate a price increase as this would lead to a large reduction in its sales, and consequently its profit would fall.

According to the Notice a major factor in determining the geographic market is that within that market the cost and feasibility of transporting products are similar for all traders. Accordingly, when the cost of the product is low as compared with its transportation cost, for example, potatoes, the RGM is likely to be narrow, and when the cost of the product is high as compared to its transportation cost, for example, cameras, the RGM is likely to be wide. This was taken into consideration in Case T-30/89 *Hilti*,[2237] in which the CFI [the General Court] upheld the Commission's decision that the RGM for Hilti's nails was the entire EU for two reasons: first, there were large differences in the price of Hilti products between the Member States and, second, transport costs for nails were low. The CFI [the General Court] held that:

2232. [1988] ECR 6211.
2233. [1988] ECR 6039.
2234. Case T-30/89 *Hilti AG v Commission* [1990] ECR II-163.
2235. Case T-83/91 *Tetra Pak International SA v Commission* [1994] ECR II-755.
2236. [1997] OJ C372/5, see also *Kyocera/Pelikan*, XXVth Report of Competition Policy (1995), point 87.
2237. [1990] ECR II-163.

"Those two factors make parallel trading highly likely between the national markets of the Community [the EU]. It must therefore be concluded that the Commission was right in taking the view that the relevant geographic market in this case is the Community [the EU] as a whole."

In Case 27/76 *United Brands*,[2238] the ECJ held that the geographic market is an area in which "the conditions of competition are sufficiently homogeneous for the effect of the economic power of the undertaking to be able to be evaluated". In this case the ECJ stated, in particular, that the RGM encompassed all Member States except France, Italy and the UK. The reason for this finding was that in all Member States except those three countries the conditions of competition were homogeneous, taking into account that in those markets there was free competition in respect of banana imports while residents of the UK, France and Italy preferred bananas coming from their former colonies.

In Case T-229/94 *Deutsche Bahn v Commission*,[2239] the CFI [the General Court] held that it is not necessary for the purposes of defining the RGM that the conditions of competition are homogeneous. It is sufficient that they are "similar" or "sufficiently homogeneous". This is a question of fact to be decided in each case.

In respect of the meaning of a substantial part of the internal market under Article 102 TFEU, the emphasis is put not on an area by measurement but on the economic importance of the market located in a particular part of the internal market. In Joined Cases 40–48, 50, 54–56, 111, 113 and 114/73 *Suiker Unie and Others v Commission*,[2240] the ECJ held that: "For the purpose of determining whether a specific territory is large enough to amount to 'a substantial part of the Common Market' [the internal market] within the meaning of Article 86 of the Treaty [102 TFEU] the pattern of volume of the production and consumption of the said product as well as the habits and economic opportunities of vendors and purchasers must be considered". Following from this, it should be noted that if the internal market in the relevant product is small in absolute terms, it may, nevertheless, be within the scope of Article 102 TFEU.

In Case 322/81 *NV Nederlandsche Banden Industrie Michelin (Michelin I) v Commission*[2241] the RGM was confined to the territory of The Netherlands, whereas in *B & I Line v Sealink Harbours*[2242] the Commission decided that the RGM was the port of Holyhead, which although confined to a small geographical area was, nevertheless, found to be a substantial part of the internal market as it was an important corridor for ferry services between Ireland and the UK.

It can be seen that in order to determine whether the RGM constitutes a substantial part of the internal market, every case will be assessed on the basis of the facts. Furthermore, the 1997 Commission Notice is very useful. In this Notice the Commission provided the following definition of relevant geographic markets:

"the area in which the undertakings concerned are involved in the supply and demand of products or services, in which the conditions of competition are sufficiently homogeneous and which can be distinguished from neighbouring areas because the conditions of competition are appreciably different in those areas."

2238. [1978] ECR 207.
2239. [1997] ECR II-1689.
2240. [1975] ECR 1663.
2241. [1983] ECR 3461.
2242. [1992] 5 CMLR 255.

In order to identify the RGM, criteria very similar to those used to define the RPM will be applied, although not all of them will be relevant in any one case. The criteria are:

- Past evidence of diversion of orders to other areas;

- Basic demand characteristics, that is whether there are local preferences based on brand, language, culture and the need for a local presence;

- Views of customers and retailers;

- The current geographic pattern of purchases;

- The trade flow/pattern of shipment when ascertaining the actual geographical pattern in the context of a large number of customers;

- Barriers and costs associated with switching orders to companies situated in other areas.

28.3.1.3 The Relevant Temporal Market (RTM)

The third dimension of the relevant market is that of the RTM. The existence of a temporal market affects the position of an undertaking in the market because in order to be considered as being in a dominant position, an undertaking must be capable of sustaining such position for a considerable time.

Temporal markets may refer to seasonal variations, such as summer months and winter months. *United Brands* argued that the banana market was seasonal as it was affected by the availability of other fresh fruits in the summer. Both the Commission and the ECJ disagreed.

The risk of customers changing their preferences according to seasons or the time of the day, for example in relation to peak and off-peak services (different charges being made for consumption of electricity or water or gas or telephone services during the day as against during the night), must be taken into consideration when identifying the relevant temporal market as it may concern, for example, off-peak supply of electricity only.

The temporal market should be assessed both from the point of view of consumers, for example, they may not consider bananas and apples as substitutes for each other, and from the point of view of suppliers' capacity, for example, they may not be able to supply fresh strawberries in winter.

28.3.2 Assessment of market power

There are different economic methods for measuring market power. The most common and used by the Commission was through determining market shares in the RPM of the undertaking under consideration. Although holding a high percentage of the market is likely to indicate that an undertaking has market power, the opposite may also be true. Some undertakings with high market shares may have relatively little market power if, for example, entry barriers are low. Similarly in an oligopolistic market, an undertaking may have market power while having a relatively low market share as a result of high brand differentiation. For these reasons using the size of the market share for measuring market power is a highly contested issue, full treatment of which is outside the scope of this book. In accordance with the effects-based approach to the enforcement of Article 102 TFEU, the Commission's Guidance identifies three factors which the Commission will take into consideration when assessing the market power of an undertaking:

▓ Constraints imposed by the existing supplies from, and the position on the market of, actual competitors;

▓ Expansion and entry constraints;

▓ Constraints imposed by the bargaining power of the undertaking's customers.

28.3.2.1   Market position of the dominant undertaking and its competitiors

In Case T-30/89 *Hilti v Commission*,[2243] the CFI [the General Court] held that a very large share of the relevant market is in itself evidence of a dominant position. In this case it was established that Hilti had a share of between 70 and 80 per cent of the relevant market. According to the CFI [the General Court], this constituted in itself a clear indication of the existence of a dominant position.

In Case 27/76 *United Brands*,[2244] the ECJ held that market shares of between 40 and 45 per cent did not automatically indicate that an undertaking held a dominant position.

With the reform of EU competition rules entailing an effects-based approach to the enforcement of Article 102, the issue of what weight should be given to the existence of a very large market share in the determination of dominance has become highly debated. On the one hand, it can be said that even if an undertaking holds an 80 per cent share of the relevant market, it is still in competition with the undertakings holding the remaining 20 per cent share of the relevant market and therefore to focus on a very large market share in establishing dominance is to fail to take account of the degree to which competitors can constrain the conduct of the allegedly dominant undertaking. On the other hand, the existing case law clearly indicates that high market shares have been regarded as conclusive in proving dominance. The Commission's Guidance has not completely eliminated the relevance of market shares as indicative of dominance. It reiterates the Commission's view that market shares constitute an important indicator of the market structure, but, at the same time, removes the rebuttable presumption that a high market share is, on its own, a conclusive factor in establishing a dominant position. Consequently, the Commission will conduct a comprehensive economic analysis of the relevant product market even in situations where an undertaking holds a very large market share.

28.3.2.2   Barriers to expansion and entry

Market shares indicate the current situation in the market. An undertaking may not have market power if existing competitors could easily expand or potential competitors could easily enter the relevant market. The Commission's Guidance confirms this view. As a result, the Commission will take account of whether there are barriers to expansion or entry into the market.

The definition of barriers to entry has been debated at length by lawyers and economists. There is no definition under EU competition law. Relying on the UK Office of Fair Trading's guidelines on the Assessment of Market Power[2245] three types of barrier to entry can be identified. The Guidelines describe the barriers in terms of advantages of an "existing" undertaking over new entrants. The three are:

2243. [1990] ECR II-163.
2244. [1978] ECR 207.
2245. OFT 415, paras 5.1–5.29.

- "Absolute advantage" which refers to a situation in which a new undertaking does not have equal access to important assets (for example, raw materials or intellectual property rights);

- "Strategic advantage" which refers to a situation in which a new entrant will have to incur "sunk costs", that is, those which are necessary to enter the market but cannot be recovered on exit. If a new entrant expects to recover the entry costs, it will be tempted to enter a new market. However, if an undertaking already active in a market would fiercely compete with a new entrant, sunk costs may be irrecoverable and therefore prohibitive for a new entrant;

- "Exclusionary behaviour". This refers to the exclusionary behaviour of an undertaking already active in a market such as predatory pricing and refusals to supply, and the extent to which that undertaking is "tying up" its distributors or retailers.

An additional important consideration in connection with barriers to entry into the market is the rate of innovation which exists in the particular market under consideration. If that rate is very high, it will be relatively easy for an undertaking to enter into a new market.

The question of barriers to entry into a market was examined in Case 85/76 *Hoffmann-La Roche v Commission*.[2246] Hoffmann-La Roche (a Swiss pharmaceutical giant) had no potential competitors in the vitamins market. Barriers to entry to that market were very high principally because of the considerable amount of capital investment necessary. Further, in assessing the barriers to entry to the vitamins market, the Commission took into consideration any unused manufacturing capacity capable of creating potential competition between manufacturers established in that market. This factor reinforced the conclusion of the Commission as to Hoffmann-La Roche's dominant position. Hoffmann-La Roche admitted that during the period covered by the contested decision, its manufacturing capacity was sufficient to meet world demand without surplus capacity placing the company in a difficult economic or financial situation.

In *Eridania/ISI*,[2247] the Commission took into consideration the potential competition when deciding that the merger between Italian undertakings operating in the industrial sugar market did not create a risk of the merged undertaking occupying a dominant position in the market. It took into account the likelihood of imports of sugar at a lower price from neighbouring areas and the low cost of transport.

In contrast, in Case T-228/97 *Irish Sugar plc v Commission*,[2248] Irish Sugar argued that the Commission failed to take into account potential competition in the industrial sugar market in Ireland. It claimed that due to the overproduction of sugar in the EU, there were many potential competitors that could supply the Irish market many times over without suffering any economic or financial difficulties. The CFI [the General Court] rejected this argument. The Court held that the Commission had identified the applicant's residual and potential competitors in the industrial sugar market. The Commission determined that residual competition was very weak as only one undertaking had actually tried to import industrial sugar to Ireland and had demonstrated that potential competition was unlikely to develop, taking into account the impact of the cost of transport on imports of industrial sugar to Ireland "particularly in the absence of a load travelling in the opposite direction". So the Commission and the CFI [the General Court] look to the economic reality rather than purely hypothetical entrants to the market.

2246. [1979] ECR 461.
2247. [1991] OJ C204.
2248. [1999] ECR II-2969.

28.3.2.3 Countervailing buyer power

The Commission's Guidance provides that the Commission will take account of the bargaining power of customers of a dominant undertaking, including a situation where such an undertaking holds a high market share. This development should be welcome given that when a buyer can easily switch to competing suppliers, to promote new entry or to vertically integrate its power, important constraints are imposed on the market power of a dominant undertaking.

28.4 The concept of super-dominance

In a number of cases a new concept of "super-dominance" or "overwhelming dominance" has been mentioned.[2249] This refers to a situation where an undertaking enjoys a monopoly or a quasi-monopoly in the relevant market.

Advocate General Fennelly in his opinion in Joined Cases C-395 and 396/96P *Compagnie Maritime Belge and Others v Commission*[2250] introduced this concept and explained that where an undertaking enjoys a position of such overwhelming dominance, "it would be consonant with the particularly onerous special obligation affecting such a dominant undertaking not to impair further the structure of the feeble existing competition".

It is a matter of speculation what is the difference between an undertaking "just" dominant and an undertaking "overwhelmingly dominant" in terms of their treatment under Article 102 TFEU.

It is submitted that the new concept, unless further refined and clearly defined, should not have a place in EU competition law. This is because:

- All undertakings in a dominant position, irrespective of "how dominant" they are, have a special responsibility under EU competition rules, but EU law does not impose upon them different obligations according to the degree of their dominance;

- It results from the definition of an abuse of a dominant position that a dominant undertaking is prohibited from eliminating its existing or potential competitors and thereby reinforcing its position by methods which are incompatible with competition on the merits. However, an undertaking in a dominant position is allowed to take reasonable and appropriate steps to protect its commercial interests irrespective of whether the undertaking concerned is "just" dominant or "overwhelmingly dominant".[2251]

It seems that the distinction between "dominance" and "overwhelming dominance" has no practical implications.

28.5 The concept of collective dominance

The question whether in an oligopolistic market (that is, when two or more undertakings independent from each other hold a dominant position) Article 102 TFEU applies was examined,

---

2249. For example, *Microsoft* was found overwhelmingly dominant in the client PC operating systems market.
2250. [2000] ECR I-1365.
2251. *BBI-Boosey and Hawkes* [1987] OJ L286/36.

for the first time, by the CFI [the General Court] in Cases T-68/89, 77/89 and 78/89 *Società Italiana Vetro [Re Italian Flat Glass] v Commission.*[2252]

The Commission followed the CFI's [the General Court] above advice and in Cases T-24–26, 28/93 *Compagnie Maritime Belge and Others v Commission*[2254] addressed separately breaches of Article 81(1) EC [Article 101(1) TFEU] and infringements of Article 82 EC [Article 102 TFEU]. The CFI [the General Court] confirmed the cumulative application of Articles 81(1) and 82 EC [Articles 101(1) and 102 TFEU]. The Court held that a joint dominant position consists of a number of undertakings being able together, in particular because of factors giving rise to a connection between them, to adopt a common policy in the market and to act to a considerable extent independently of their competitors, their customers and ultimately consumers.

In Case T-228/97 *Irish Sugar plc,*[2255] the CFI [the General Court] confirmed that a joint dominant position could apply to vertical relationships. At the time of the decision in that case, this concept was rather confusing; no definition was contained in the relevant legislation. It was also unclear what kind of structural or economic links between undertakings were necessary to

---

2252. [1992] ECR II-1403.
2253. [1989] OJ L33/44.
2254. [1996] ECR II-1201, upheld by the ECJ in Joined Cases C-395/96P and C-396/96P *Compagnie Maritime Belge Transports SA v Commission* [2000] ECR I-1365. See also Cases C-68/94 and C-30/95 *France and Others v Commission (Kali and Salz)* [1998] ECR I-1375.
2255. [1999] ECR II-2969; Case T-374/00 *Verband der Freien Rohrwerke and Others v Commission* [2003] ECR II-2275, para 121.

establish collective dominance. It was clear, however, that introduction of the concept of joint dominance was to assist the Commission in tackling the problem of oligopolistic markets in which undertakings, without entering into prohibited agreements or concerted practices, adjust their conduct with their competitors in a manner advantageous to both parties but disadvantageous to their customers and to consumers generally.

The uncertainty was partially resolved when it became apparent that the concept of collective dominance has the same meaning under Article 102 TFEU as it has under the Merger Regulation[2256] (see Chapter 29.3.2). It is important to note, however, that under Article 102 TFEU collective dominance is assessed retrospectively while under the Merger Regulation a prospective analysis of the relevant market is required in order to decide whether the envisaged merger will lead to the creation or strengthening of a collective dominance. Consequently, it is more difficult to assess prospective collective dominance in the market post-merger than to evaluate it on facts that already exist.

As at the time of writing, the most important judgment on collective dominance is that delivered by the CFI [the General Court] in Case T-342/99 *Airtours/First Choice.*[2257] In paragraph 62 of the judgment the Court agreed with the applicants that three conditions are necessary for a finding of collective dominance:

▪ "first, each member of the dominant oligopoly must have the ability to know how the other members are behaving in order to monitor whether or not they are adopting the common policy." With regard to this condition the CFI [the General Court] found that there was insufficient transparency to permit such monitoring and consequently the four tour operators were not able to adopt a common policy so as to face consumers as a single entity.

▪ "second, the situation of tacit coordination must be sustainable over time, that is to say, there must be an incentive not to depart from the common policy on the market." As the Commission observed, "it is only if all the members of the dominant oligopoly maintain the parallel conduct that all can benefit. The notion of retaliation in respect of conduct deviating from the common policy is thus inherent in this condition."

The CFI [the General Court] decided that the Commission did not provide sufficient evidence of existence of a retaliatory mechanism and rejected the Commission's argument that "it is not necessary to show that there would be a strict punishment mechanism".

▪ "third, to prove the existence of a collective dominant position to the requisite legal standard, the Commission must also establish that the foreseeable reaction of current and future competitors, as well as of consumers, would not jeopardise the results expected from the common policy."

The CFI [the General Court] found that the Commission did not provide sufficient evidence demonstrating that small competitors would be unable to expand adequately to serve consumers in response to a price increase by the oligopolists.

Collective dominance thus defined is based on tacit co-ordination between the undertakings concerned and not on any structural[2258] or economic links[2259] between them, although when such

---

2256. See: Joined Cases C-68/94 and C-30/95 *France and Others v Commission (Kali & Salz)* [1998] ECR I-1375 and Case T-102/96 *Gencor Ltd v Commission* [1999] ECR II-753.
2257. [2002] ECR II-2585.
2258. Supra note 2252.
2259. Supra note 2255.

links exist they facilitate a finding of collective dominance. Putting the three conditions set out by the CFI [the General Court] that must be satisfied for a finding of collective dominance into concise language, they are:

▪ Mutual awareness of the colluding parties concerning the adoption and execution of the common policy;

▪ Sustainability, which means that there must be a retaliatory mechanism put in place which secures unity within an oligopoly and thus dissuades its members from deviating from their common policy adopted in the relevant market; and

▪ An absence of competitive constraints, so allowing undertakings within a dominant oligopoly to act independently of their customers and consumers, actual or potential.

On the basis of the case law, it can be said that the conditions set out in *Airtours/First Choice* will rarely be met. The CFI [the General Court] annulled the Commission's Decision in *Airtours/First Choice* on the ground that the Commission failed to provide convincing evidence supporting its conclusion that a proposed hostile acquisition by Airtours of First Choice would create a collective dominance of three undertakings (Airtours/First Choice, Thompson Travel Group and Thomas Cook) in the market for short-haul package holidays from the UK. In subsequent cases the Commission, after its serious reprimand by the CFI in *Airtours/First Choice*,[2260] has cautiously applied the definition of a collective dominance set out in that case.

In Case T-193/02 *Laurent Piau v Commission*,[2261] the CFI [the General Court] found that the Commission was wrong in deciding that the Fédération Internationale de Football Association (FIFA), a Swiss-based association whose members are national associations of professional and amateur football clubs, did not hold a collective dominant position in the market for players' agents' services. Although the CFI [the General Court] decided that the three conditions set out in *Airtours/First Choice* were satisfied,[2262] it did not find that FIFA abused its position of collective dominance.

It appears from the recent case law that the General Court has set the requisite standard of proof in respect of both the finding of a position of collective dominance (and of its abuse, discussed next) at a very high level. This is appropriate given that the burden of proof against an undertaking in an oligopolistic market should not be lower than that against an undertaking in a non-oligopolistic market.

It is to be noted that undertakings in an oligopolistic market structure are at the same time independent from each other and interdependent. If one of them increases prices, it will lose the clear benefit it enjoys from the mirroring conduct of its competitors. It is also aware that any action to increase its share of the relevant market by, for example, dramatically reducing prices would result in a similar action taken by its competitors. Accordingly, oligopolists know that they would derive no benefit from such an action because they will all be affected by the collective reduction in price levels. In order to ensure high profits, they maintain a tacit understanding that

---

2260. E.g. in *UPM-Kymmenne/Haindl* COMP/M2498 [2002] OJ L233/38 and *Ernst and Young France/Anderson France* COMP/M 2816 the Commission refrained from an adverse finding, that is, that there was or would be the possibility of tacit co-ordination.

2261. [2005] ECR II-209.

2262. [2002] ECR II-2585, paras 111–16.

they will take no action changing the existing situation in the relevant market. However, this will not be sufficient to breach Article 102 TFEU as there are further requirements under the *Airtours/ First Choice* test.

If there is explicit collusion, the matter is dealt with under Article 101 TFEU.

28.6   The concept of abuse

In the early years of the Community the issue of whether the concept of abuse covered only exploitative abuses or whether it also applied to conduct which had structural effects on the competition conditions in the relevant market was controversial.[2263] This was settled by the ECJ in Case 6/72 *Europemballage Corp and Continental Can Inc v Commission*,[2264] in which, in the context of a merger, the Court rejected the narrow interpretation of Article 102 TFEU in which only exploitative behaviour was caught by Article 102 TFEU. The ECJ interpreted Article 102 TFEU teleologically and concluded that in the light of Article 3(g) EC (which set out the objectives of EC competition policy but was repealed by the ToL) and Article 2 EC (which emphasises the importance of harmonious development of economic activities – replaced in substance by Article 3 TEU), Article 102 TFEU prohibits not only practices which may cause damage to consumers directly, but also those:

> "... which are detrimental to them through their impact on an effective competition structure. ... Abuse may therefore occur if an undertaking in a dominant position strengthens such position in such a way that the degree of dominance reached substantially fetters competition."

The ECJ ruled that in the circumstances of the case, where there was no monopolistic exploitation of the market, an undertaking in a dominant position, by merging with its rival and thus strengthening its position to the possible extent of eliminating any competition in that market, was in breach of Article 102 TFEU.

It is important to note that under Article 102 TFEU it is the competitive process which is protected, not the competitors of an undertaking in a dominant position.

The ECJ's definition of an abuse under Article 82 EC [Article 102 TFEU] was provided in Case 85/76 *Hoffmann-La Roche*,[2265] where the ECJ emphasised that the concept refers to conduct of an undertaking in a dominant position:

> "... which is such as to influence the structure of a market where, as the result of the very presence of the undertaking in question, the degree of competition is weakened and which, through recourse to methods different from those which condition normal competition in products or services on the basis of the transactions of commercial operators, has the effect of hindering the maintenance of the degree of competition still existing in the market or the growth of that competition."

One obvious implication of the above definition is that the very presence of an undertaking in a dominant position weakens the degree of competition in a particular product or services market and thus such an undertaking should be very careful in its business conduct not to abuse its dominant position. It is inherent in the system set up by Article 102 TFEU that an undertaking in

---

2263. R. Joliet, *Monopolisation and Abuse of Dominant Position*, 1970, Dordrecht: Nijhof, pp 250–52.
2264. [1973] ECR 215.
2265. [1979] ECR 461.

a dominant position may breach Article 102 TFEU by engaging in conduct which, if carried out by its competitors rather than by it, would be lawful. Even a small reduction in competition may infringe Article 102 TFEU. In Case 85/76 *Hoffmann-La Roche* a reduction of 5 per cent was regarded as sufficient to hold that undertaking responsible for a breach of Article 102 TFEU. The same percentage reduction in competition in respect of a dominant undertaking which holds "only" 50 per cent of the relevant market would probably not have such a dramatic effect on its competitors. In the last mentioned case the ECJ came close to saying that dominance could automatically be abusive.[2266] However, the per se approach has been rejected by the Commission in its Guidance with the result that the qualification of a unilateral practice will depend on the anti-competitive effect it has on the relevant market. Further, under the effects-based approach undertakings in a dominant position will be allowed to submit justifications based on objective and proportionate considerations.

Under Article 102 TFEU a dominant undertaking is allowed to compete on merits, but is not allowed to use methods which are different from those governing normal competition in products and services based on traders' performance,[2267] and in particular the practices set out in Article 102(a)–(d) TFEU are prohibited.

In *Hoffmann-La Roche* the ECJ held that the concept of abuse is an objective concept. This means that, in general, a subjective intent of a dominant undertaking to distort competition is irrelevant for the application of Article 102 TFEU, although in some particular cases the intention is of relevance.

28.7 The categories of abuses

There is a traditional nomenclature, mainly used by economists, which provides a convenient categorisation of abuses. Article 102 (a)–(d) TFEU sets out a non-exhaustive list of various types of prohibited behaviour but neither categorises them nor equates them with the traditional nomenclature. However, both the Commission and the CJEU use the traditional nomenclature/categorisation as set out below:

- Exploitative abuses: these occur when an undertaking is, at the expense of customers or consumers, using its economic power to obtain benefits or to impose burdens which are not obtainable, or imposable, within normal competition on the merits;

- Discriminatory abuses: these occur when a dominant undertaking treats its customers in a dissimilar manner without cost based or legally acceptable justifications;

- Exclusionary abuses: these are aimed at foreclosing the relevant market;

- Reprisal abuses: these occur when the conduct of an undertaking in a dominant position is directed at injuring another undertaking in order to punish it, usually for what the undertaking in a dominant position considers as "disloyal" conduct towards it. They may consist, for example, of refusals to deal or of the use of predatory prices as a reprisal weapon.

2266. In Case 6/72 *Continental Can* [1973] ECR 215, the ECJ seemed to suggest that a merger might necessarily entail abuse where it results in a high level of dominance.

2267. Ibid. See also Case 322/81 *NV Nederlandsche Banden Industrie Michelin (Michelin I) v Commission* [1983] ECR 3461.

28.7.1 Exploitative abuses

Examples of exploitative abuses are examined below.

28.7.1.1 Excessively high prices

Prices may be considered as excessive if they allow an undertaking to sustain profits higher than it could expect to earn in a competitive market.

The definition of excessively high prices was provided by the ECJ in Case 26/75 *General Motors Continental NV v Commission*.[2268] In this case the ECJ held that "charging a price which is excessive because it has no reasonable relation to the economic value of the product supplied is . . . an abuse".

This definition was also applied by the ECJ in Case 27/76 *United Brands*,[2269] although the Commission's finding of excessive prices was rejected by the ECJ. In *United Brands* the ECJ set out a test to be applied in order to determine whether or not the price was excessive. The test is contained in paragraph 252 of the judgment, which states that: ". . . the questions therefore to be determined are whether the difference between the costs actually incurred and the price actually charged is excessive, and if the answer to this question is in the affirmative, whether a price has been imposed which is either unfair in itself or when compared to competing products". The Court insisted that the evidence of excessive price must be obtained objectively by means of an analysis of the relevant factors such as the cost structure and the amount of the profit margin, established by comparison to the selling price of the product in question with the cost of production.

The *United Brands* test was explained by the Commission in *Sundbusserne v Port of Helsingborg*.[2270]

THE FACTS WERE:

A Danish company, Sundbusserne, which provided ferry services for passengers between Helsingborg (Sweden) and Elsinore (Denmark), complained to the Commission that HHAB, a Swedish company owned by the City of Helsingborg, responsible for the provision of facilities and services to vessels using the port and for the determination of the fees for users, was, inter alia, charging excessive prices to ferry operators. This conclusion was based on the answer to the first question in the United Brands test. The Commission, contrary to the submission of Sundbusserne, stated that both questions set out in the United Brands test must be answered and therefore even if it appeared that the difference between the revenue derived from the ferry operations through the port charge and the costs incurred by HHAB was "excessive",[2271] this was not conclusive as regards the existence of an abuse. The second question also had to be answered, that is, the Commission had to decide whether or

---

2268. [1975] ECR 1367.

2269. [1978] ECR 207.

2270. COMP/A.37.792/DS of 23 July 2004; [2005] 4 CMLR 965.

2271. It is interesting to note that according to the assessment of cost allocation submitted by HHAB to the Commission, the ferry operations were not profitable! This assessment was rejected by the Commission as being unrealistic.

not the prices charged to the ferry operators were unfair, either when compared to other ports or in themselves. The comparison was very difficult given that HHAB held a monopoly position in the port of Helsingborg. Nevertheless, the Commission referred to various points of comparison.

First, based on Case 30/87 Bodson v Pompes Funèbres des Regions Liberées,[2272] the Commission tried to compare the prices charged by HHAB with prices charged in other ports. This approach failed because the Commission could not find a substitute product or service provided by competitors on the same relevant market. In each port conditions were different from those in the Port of Helsingborg in terms of services provided, activities and the repartition between the ship fee and the goods fee.

Second, the Commission made a comparison between the port fees charged by HHAB to the ferry operators and those charged to cargo vessel operators. This failed as the services provided to the ferry operators and the cargo vessel operators markets were not equivalent, and therefore it was impossible to compare the level of the charges to ferry operators and cargo vessel operators.

Third, the Commission compared the Port of Elsinore with the Port of Helsingborg in terms of fees charged to ferry operators. Sundbusserne argued that this was an ideal point of comparison while the Commission disagreed on the ground that the infrastructure in Elsinore, being much less developed than that in Helsingborg, explained the different cost structure of both ports.

Fourth, the Commission returned to the first point of comparison. It decided to compare the fees charged by HHAB with the fees charged by other European ports to ferry operators. The Commission admitted that any meaningful comparison was difficult, but nevertheless this was the best it could achieve in terms of comparison. The Commission's comparison was based on the official tariff published by several European ports relating to their port charges to ferry operators.

Held:

The conclusion drawn by the Commission, on the above shaky basis, was that the difference between the costs actually incurred by HHAB and the price charged by it was not excessive. Subsequently, the Commission proceeded to the assessment of whether the port charges were unfair in themselves. The Commission took account of the relevant economic factors in the determination of the economic value of the services and facilities provided to ferry operators by HHAB. The conclusion reached by the Commission was that there was insufficient evidence to establish that the port charges had no reasonable relation to the economic values of the services provided by HHAB and, consequently, the Commission did not find prices charged by HHAB as being unfair in themselves.

It can be said that in some circumstances prices may, at first glance, seem excessive but in fact may be justified by objective considerations. Such objective considerations include a temporary increase of demand, greater efficiency of an undertaking than that of its competitors in the

---

2272. [1988] ECR 2479.

relevant market, the introduction of an innovation where the profits earned are necessary in order to provide a fair return on the cost of the development of the innovation and a fair reward for the risks taken by an undertaking in developing and introducing the innovation to the market. For these reasons, in many instances it is not easy to assess whether high prices are excessive and thus amount to an abuse.

28.7.2 Discriminatory abuses

Case 27/76 *United Brands*[2273] is the leading case on discriminatory abuses.

THE FACTS WERE:

United Brands (UB), a multinational US corporation, shipped bananas from its own plantations in South America to Rotterdam and Bremerhaven using its own fleet. In both ports unloading costs were almost identical. From those ports bananas were resold to distributors from different Member States, on a "free on rail basis" at prices which differed substantially. UB explained that it fixed the prices taking into account what the market in a particular Member State would bear.

Held:

The ECJ held that United Brands' prices were discriminatory because "bananas unloaded in two Community ports on practically identical terms as regards costs, quality and quantity were sold to the customers at prices which differed considerably – by between 30 and 50 percent – from one Member State to another, although the services offered were identical in each case". The ECJ rejected the explanation submitted by UB and stated that differences in prices can only be justified on the basis of objective criteria such as differences in transport costs, taxation, customs duties, labour wages, and so on.

Price discrimination may take two forms:

- First, an undertaking may charge different customers different prices for the same product without any objective justification; and

- Second, an undertaking may charge different customers the same price even though the costs of supplying the product are very different, taking into account objective criteria such as different transport costs.

The circumstances of each case should be examined in order to decide whether an undertaking abuses its dominant position by charging different prices to different sets of customers.[2274]

2273. [1978] ECR 207.
2274. Case C-53/92P *Hilti AG v Commission* [1994] ECR I-667 and Case C-62/86 *AKZO Chemie BV v Commission* [1991] ECR I-3359.

28.7.2.1   Other terms or conditions

"Other terms or conditions" refers to discrimination on terms other than price. In *United Brands* the ban on the resale of unripened bananas was considered as an abuse because it confined the ripeners to the role of suppliers of the local market, limited sales outlets to the prejudice of consumers and isolated national markets.

28.7.3   Exclusionary abuses

The Commission's Guidance defines anti-competitive foreclosure as a situation "where effective access of actual or potential competitors to supplies or markets is hampered or eliminated as a result of the conduct of the dominant undertaking whereby the dominant undertaking is likely to be in a position to profitably increase prices to the detriment of consumers" (para 19).

This definition encompasses two elements:

■ Foreclosure. The concept of foreclosure is understood as a situation where "access of actual or potential competitors to supplies or markets is hampered or eliminated". To prove anti-competitive foreclosure the Commission must establish that foreclosure has actually occurred or is likely to occur. Paragraph 20 of the Guidance states that in deciding whether the allegedly abusive conduct is likely to lead to anti-competitive foreclosure the Commission must submit cogent and convincing evidence. Paragraph 20 lists factors which will be taken into account in the determination of a credible risk of foreclosure. Those factors are:

   ● The position, on the relevant market, of the dominant undertaking;
   ● The conditions on the relevant market;
   ● The position of the dominant undertaking's competitiors;
   ● The position of the customers or input suppliers, i.e. those with which the dominant undertaking has concluded exclusive supplies arrangements;
   ● The extent of the alleged abusive conduct;
   ● Possible evidence of actual foreclosure;
   ● Direct evidence of any exclusionary strategy.

However in some situations, i.e. where anti-competitive conduct may be inferred, the Commission will not carry out a detailed assessment of the likely consumer harm caused by anti-competitive conduct based on the factors mentioned in para 20. This occurs in particular, "if it appears that the conduct can only raise obstacles to competition and that it creates no efficiencies". The Guidance provides two examples of conduct that it considers to be within this category. First, when a dominant undertaking prevents its customers from testing the products of competitors (either by making this a condition of sale or by offering payment not to test competitors' products). Second, when a dominant undertaking pays a distributor or a customer to delay the introduction of a competitor's product.

■ Consumer harm. This occurs when conduct of the dominant undertaking "is likely to be in position to profitably increase prices, to the detriment of consumers" once its competitors are eliminated. The concept of "consumer harm" is the main factor distinguishing anti-competitive foreclosure from foreclosure arising from competition "on merits". The exclusion of competitors, being a preliminary step, to the exploitation of consumers, is therefore a key element in the assessment of adverse impact on consumer welfare.

The Guidance distinguishes between "price based" and "non-price based" exclusionary conduct (see below) of a dominant undertaking.

The Commission in its Guidance has generalised the possibility for a dominant undertaking to rely on objective justifications to exempt a practice which it has found abusive. The dominant undertaking may justify its conduct by demonstrating that:

▪ it is objectively necessary, e.g. justified by imperative considerations such as health and safety reasons related to the nature of the product concerned;

▪ it produces substantial efficiencies which outweigh any anti-competitive effects on consumers. The test set out on para 30 of the Commission's Guidance is similar to that contained in Article 101(3) TFEU (see Chapter 27.7).

28.7.3.1   Price-based exclusionary conduct and the "as efficient competitor" test

The Guidance states that the Commission will intervene "where the conduct concerned has already been or is capable of hampering competition from competitors which are considered to be as efficient as the dominant undertaking" (para 23). As a result, the Commission will use the test of hypothetical rivals that are "as efficient" (the AEC test) as the dominant undertaking in order to determine whether the "price-based" conduct of a dominant undertaking leads to foreclosure. If a rival is less efficient the Commission will normally assume that foreclosure results from mere competition on merits and thus is not anti-competitive. However, this is subject to an exception. In some circumstances the Commission will depart from the AEC test, i.e. when the relevant market is one in which network and/or learning effects are important. In such a situation the AEC test will use the hypothetical prospective entrant standard. Departures from the AEC test have been criticised as introducing uncertainty in that a dominant undertaking will not be able to assess whether its conduct is potentially exclusionary and this may lead to its overly cautious response to competition. This could result in higher prices to consumers. Further, some authors have criticised the use of AEC on the basis that a failure to protect a less efficient rival may have negative effects on consumers, in particular the presence of a less efficient rival on the market may constitute a competitive constraint on the market power of a dominant undertaking and thus prevent it from raising prices and reducing consumer surplus.[2275]

In order to determine whether a hypothetical rival is "as efficient" as the dominant undertaking the Commission will examine economic data relating to cost and sales prices. This will require detailed analyses of sufficiently reliable data. Paragraph 25 of the Guidance states that "where available, the Commission will use information on the costs of the dominant undertaking itself".

The Guidance identifies two cost benchmarks in order to determine whether a dominant undertaking's pricing should be regarded as exclusionary. These are:

▪ average avoidable cost (AAC);[2276]

▪ long-run average incremental cost (LRAIC).[2277]

2275. I. Lianos, "The EU Commission's Guidance on Exclusionary Abuses: A Step Forward or a Missed Opportunity", available at http:/ssm.com/Abstract=1398943 (27/02/10).

2276. AAC is the average of the costs that could have been avoided if the undertaking had not produced a discrete amount of (extra) output which is allegedly the subject of abusive conduct. In most cases AAC and the average variable cost (AVC) are the same.

2277. LRAIC is the average of all the (variable and fixed) costs that an undertaking incurs to produce a particular product.

Paragraph 26 of the Guidance explains that failure to cover AAC indicates that the dominant undertaking is sacrificing profits in the short term and that an equally efficient rival could not serve the targeted customers without incurring a loss. Failure to cover LRAIC indicates that the dominant undertaking is not recovering all the (attributable) fixed costs of producing the good or service and that an equally efficient competitor could be foreclosed from the market.

28.7.3.1.1 Predatory prices

Predatory pricing refers to a situation where a dominant undertaking sets prices below cost over a long enough period of time in order to drive competitors out of the market or obstruct potential competitors from entering the market, with the objective of solidifying its market position and obtaining long-term profit. The practice is profitable because a dominant undertaking after predation can recoup its short-term lost profits (referred to as "sacrifice") and obtain a long-term profit by raising and maintaining anti-competitive prices, thereby causing consumer harm.

The leading case on predatory prices is Case C-62/86 *AKZO v Commission* (the facts are set out in section 28.3.1.1.4).[2278] In this case the ECJ established the following test in order to discover whether an abuse in the form of predatory prices existed:

- Where variable costs are not covered by the selling price, an abuse is "automatically" presumed;

- Where variable costs are covered, but total costs are not, the pricing is deemed to constitute an abuse if it forms part of a plan to eliminate rivals from the relevant market.

A good example of the application of the test set out in *AKZO* is provided in the *Wanadoo* case.[2279]

THE FACTS WERE:

Wanadoo Interactive, a subsidiary of France Telecom, was charging retail prices below cost for its ADSL-based Internet access service from the end of 1999 to August 2002 in order to pre-empt the highly profitable market for high-speed Internet access. Wanadoo had every intention of eliminating rivals and was aware of the level of losses it suffered. After the initial period of selling its services at a loss, during which the main competitors were eliminated and any potential new competitors were dissuaded from entering the market (given the level of losses they could expect to suffer in order to compete with Wanadoo), Wanadoo's market share rose spectacularly. From January 2001 to September 2002 it increased from 46 per cent to 72 per cent of the market, which market multiplied five times during that period.

Held:

The Commission found that Wanadoo charged predatory prices. They were below variable costs until August 2001 and subsequently, although the variable costs were covered in full, Wanadoo's pricing policy formed part of a plan to pre-empt the market in high-speed Internet

---

2278. [1991] ECR I-3359.
2279. COMP/38.223 of 16/07/2003, [2005] 5 CMLR 120.

access during a key phase in its development. The Commission imposed a fine of €10.35 million on Wanadoo.

The CFI [the General Court] upheld the Commission's decision in Case T-340/03 *France Télécom SA v Commission*.[2280] It is interesting to note that the ECJ in Case C-202/07 *France Telecom SA v Commission*[2281] upheld the decision of the CFI [the General Court] and, contrary to the effects-based approach stated in the Guidance (see below), held that the possibility for a dominant undertaking to recoup losses "is not a necessary precondition for a finding of predatory pricing" (para 113).

The Commission's Guidance abandons the test established in *AKZO* in favour of the effects-based approach. The Guidance provides that the Commission will take AAC as a starting point in the assessment of whether the dominant undertaking incurred or is incurring losses. Charging prices below AAC will be indicative of sacrifice. However, this will not be enough to show predation. In this respect, the Commission will have to show that by charging predatory prices, the dominant undertaking is susceptible to force its competitor "as efficient" as itself to leave the market, or to prevent entry of potential competitors. Normally only pricing below LRAIC is capable of foreclosing "as efficient" competitors from the market. So far as harm to consumers is concerned, they are likely to be harmed if the dominant undertaking will be able to benefit from sacrifice.

28.7.3.1.2 Rebates

Rebates granted by a dominant undertaking are not in themselves in breach of Article 102 TFEU. They constitute a form of price competition and encourage a customer to do business with a supplier on a long-term basis. A rebates system which seeks to tie dealers to an undertaking in a dominant position by granting advantages which are not based on a countervailing economic advantage and to prevent those dealers from obtaining their supplies from the undertaking's competitors infringes Article 102 TFEU. Such rebates are loyalty-inducing rebates and have exclusionary effect. Thus, under Article 102 TFEU the grant of a discount must be based on economic considerations.[2282]

Article 102 TFEU is breached by the giving of rebates only if they are anti-competitive, that is, if they tend to remove or restrict the buyers' freedom to choose their sources of supply, or to bar competitors from access to the market, or to apply dissimilar conditions to equivalent transactions with other trading partners, or to strengthen a dominant position by distorting competition.[2283] A discount system must also be non-discriminatory. This was explained in Case C-163/99 *Portugal v Commission (Landing Fees at Portuguese Airports)*.[2284]

2280. [2007] ECR II-107.
2281. Judgment of 2/4/09 (nyr).
2282. Case 322/81 *Michelin v Commission* [1983] ECR 3461.
2283. Ibid.
2284. [2001] ECR I-2613.

> **THE FACTS WERE:**
>
> *Portugal set up a scheme for granting discounts on landing fees to airlines depending on the number of planes they landed. In fact only two airlines, both Portuguese, qualified for the highest rate discount.*
>
> *Held:*
>
> The ECJ held that a non-abusive rebates system must be non-discriminatory in fact. The Court emphasised that while it was inherent in any quantity rebates system that the largest buyers obtained the highest price reduction, nevertheless the system could be discriminatory if it set out thresholds that only a few very large users could reach and which gave them disproportionate rewards.

The very strict approach to the treatment of discounts and rebates under Article 102 TFEU, which has been widely criticised as not taking account of economic reality, was confirmed and expanded by the CFI [the General Court] in *Michelin II*[2285] and in *British Airways*.[2286] In *Michelin II* the CFI [the General Court] found Michelin in breach of Article 82 EC [Article102 TFEU] by applying to its dealers a complex system of rebates, discounts and various financial benefits whose main objective was to tie resellers to it and to entrench its dominant position.

The Commission's Guidance responds to the criticism. The Commission makes clear that it will intervene if rebates are likely to lead to anti-competitive foreclosure of actual or potential competitors as "efficient" as the dominant undertaking. The Commission lists factors which it will take into account when analysing potential anti-competitive foreclosure (paras 38 et seq). In general, the higher the rebate as a percentage of the total price, the higher and more individualised its threshold the greater likelihood of foreclosure of actual or potential competitors.

The likelihood of anti-competitive foreclosure will be stronger in respect of retroactive rebates than incremental rebates. Both are conditional rebates given to the customer, if its purchases over a defined reference period exceed a certain threshold. Retroactive rebates are given on all purchases whilst incremental rebates are given on purchases made in excess of those required to achieve the threshold. In respect of retroactive rebates, they are more likely to have a potential foreclosing effect given that they may make it less attractive for customers to switch small amounts of demand to an alternative supplier. The concept of the "relevant range" (para 40), i.e. the part of the demand that the buyer is likely to switch or the proportion that the rival might offer to supply, of the tranch offered by the dominant undertaking will be of importance in assessing the likelihood of anti-competitive foreclosure. The Commission will intervene if the "effective price" (i.e. the price including the rebate for previous purchases (paras 41–44)) for the relevant range is below its LRAIC.

28.7.3.1.3 Margin or price-squeeze

A "margin-squeeze" leads to anti-competitive foreclosure when a dominant undertaking in an upstream market which supplies goods or services to its rivals, who use them to compete with

---

2285. Case T-203/01 *Michelin v Commission* [2003] ECR II-4071.
2286. Case T-219/99 *British Airways v Commission* [2003] ECR II-5917.

the dominant undertaking in one or more downstream market, squeezes its downstream rivals by charging prices which do not allow as efficient rivals as the dominant undertaking to make a living profit. As a result of the upstream price (which is set by a dominant undertaking) the prevailing price in the downstream market is such that a rival or potential rival is forced out the downstream market.

The Guidance treats the issue of margin squeeze and that of refusal to contract together (see section 28.7.3.2.3). Thus it seems that a margin squeeze is not a stand-alone abuse. This is despite the fact that the Commission in its Deutsche Telekom decision[2287] considered the margin-squeeze as a separate abuse in its own right.

28.7.3.2   Non-price based exclusionary conduct

Examples of non-price exclusionary conduct are examined below.

28.7.3.2.1 Tying and bundling

In tying arrangements an undertaking makes customers purchase not only one product/service which they want to purchase but obliges them to buy an additional item, or items, or service whether they want to do this or not. Thus, the purchase of the main product/service (the tying product) is conditional upon the purchase of another product/service (the tied product).

In bundling the additional product is already incorporated in the main product.

In both tying and bundling the customer has no choice other than to buy both products/services or not to buy at all.

Tying, in the context of Article 82 EC [Article 102 TFEU], was examined in depth in Case C-333/94P *Tetra Pak II*.[2288] In this case the ECJ held that when an undertaking in a dominant position makes the purchase of one product (the tying product) conditional on the purchase of a second product (the tied product), this may amount to an abuse, even though such sales are in conformity with commercial usages and even though the two products are closely associated, unless the "natural link" between them can be objectively justified. Tetra Pak argued that both products (that is, the carton-filling machinery and the requisite cartons for milk products) constituted an "integrated service". The ECJ rejected this argument. It held that it would be justified to consider the manufacturing equipment and the cartons as forming a natural link, and thus being treated as an integrated service only if there was no other independent manufacturer specialising in the production of non-aseptic cartons or if it was impossible for other manufacturers to start producing non-aseptic cartons for reasons relating to intellectual property rights.

This was confirmed in Case T-30/89 *Hilti AG v Commission*,[2289] in which the CFI [the General Court] held that Hilti abused its dominant position by requiring the end users or distributors of its patented cartridge strips to buy nails, thus "tying" cartridge strips and nails. The argument submitted by Hilti that its tying arrangement was necessary for the protection of users against injury was rejected by the CFI [the General Court] as not sufficient to objectively justify the tie. In

---

2287.   COMP/C1/37.451, 37.578, 37.579 upheld by the CFI in Case T-271/03 *Deutsche Telecom AG v Commission* [2008]. See also, Case T-5/97 *Industrie des Poudres Sphériques SA v Commission* [2000] ECR II-3755.
2288.   [1996] ECR I-5951.
2289.   [1990] ECR II-163 and upheld by the ECJ in Case C-53/92P *Hilti AG v Commission* [1995] ECR I-667.

many tying arrangements the owner of the "tying" product refuses to supply a customer who wishes to buy the tying product but not the "tied" product.

In the *Microsoft* case,[2290] the Commission clarified its approach to the matter of tying. The Commission found that Microsoft by tying/bundling Windows Media Player (WMP) to desktop operating systems (OS) was in breach of Article 82(d) EC [Article 102(d) TFEU].

The decision in *Microsoft* is of great importance for the following reasons:

■ While tying had always been condemned under Article 82(d) EC [Article 102(d) TFEU], it was in this case that this Article was applied for the first time to the bundling together of products;

■ The Commission set out the criteria (which criteria apply to both tying and bundling) which have to be satisfied for an abuse under Article 82(d) EC [Article 102(d) TFEU] to be established. These criteria are:

  (i) The tying and tied goods must not be within the same product market. In *Microsoft* the Commission found that there were two separate product markets, one for OS and one for WMP;

  (ii) The undertaking concerned must be in a dominant position in the tying product market. In this respect Microsoft was in a position of "super-dominance" in the OS market;

  (iii) The undertaking concerned does not give customers a choice to obtain the tying products without the tied product. WMP was sold as a package with OS. Users could not get OS without WMP. Therefore, as the Commission stated, the issue was not whether users were forced to use WMP, but whether they had the choice to get OS without WMP. As WMP was a built-in feature of OS, obviously consumers had no choice. The argument of Microsoft that the customers were not required to pay separately for WMP was rejected;

  (iv) The tying must foreclose competition. The Commission stated that:

  > ". . . tying WMP with the dominant Windows makes WMP the platform of choice for complementary content and applications which in turn risks foreclosing competition in the market for media players. This has spillover effects on competition in related products such as media encoding and management software (often server-side), but also in client PC operating systems for which media players compatible with quality content are an important application. Microsoft's tying practice creates a serious risk of foreclosing competition and stifling innovation."

The Commission established that the above criteria were met in *Microsoft*. It was left to Microsoft to show that the efficiencies of tying prevailed over harm to competition. The argument of Microsoft was that the pro-competitive effects of tying, that is, distribution efficiency, platform efficiency, the desirability of one unique media player worldwide, and so on, outweighed the harm to competition. The Commission stated that these argued benefits of tying could be achieved in the absence of Microsoft tying WMP with OS. The major benefit, according to the Commission was "Microsoft's own profitability" which, being disproportionate to the anti-competitive effect

---

2290. COMP/C3/37.792, [2005] 4 CMLR, p 965.

of tying could not be accepted as an objective justification. It is to be remembered that the burden of proof to establish an objective, proportional justification is on the undertaking concerned.

Finally, the Commission (relying on the judgments in *Michelin II*[2291] and *British Airways*[2292]) assessed the potential effect of tying in the light of the probability of, and the possible magnitude of, harm to competition and established that there was a reasonable likelihood that tying WMP with OS would lead to a lessening of competition, so that if the tying were to continue, the maintenance of an effective competition structure in the relevant product market would not be ensured in the foreseeable future.

Microsoft was ordered:

- To prepare and market a version of its OS without WMP, although it was allowed to continue selling OS bundled with WMP.

- To reveal to server software rivals complete interface information that would allow the interconnection of server terminals with a central computer using Microsoft's OS. Accordingly this would allow rivals to design compatible products.

- To pay a record fine of €500 million.

The Commission's decision was upheld by the CFI [the General Court] in T-201/04 *Microsoft Corp. v Commission*.[2293]

The Commission's Guidance confirms the criteria used in *Microsoft* as decisive in the determination of anti-competitive foreclosure. It is interesting to note that the Guidance sets out the distinct products test as follows: "Two products are distinct if, in the absence of tying or bundling, a substantial number of customers would purchase or would have purchased the tying product without also buying the tied product from the same supplier, thereby allowing stand-alone production for both the tying and the tied product" (para 51).

In order to show that products are distinct the Commission will use direct evidence, i.e. based on the choice of customers in that when they have a choice to purchase the tying and the tied product from different sources of supply they will choose to do this, and indirect evidence such as the presence on the market of undertakings which manufacture and sell the tied product without the tying product, or the fact that undertakings with little market power, particularly in a competitive market, tend not to tie or not to bundle such products.

28.7.3.2.2 Exclusive dealing

Exclusive sales or exclusive purchasing agreements aim at creating an obligation or an incentive as a result of which the buyer makes all of its purchases on the relevant market from one dealer alone. The imposition of an exclusive dealing requirement by a dominant undertaking is exemplified in Case 85/76 *Hoffmann-La Roche*.[2294]

2291. Case T-203/01 *Manufacture Française des Pneumatiques Michelin [Michelin II] v Commission* [2003] ECR II-4071.

2292. Case T-219/99 *BA v Commission* [2003] ECR II-5917.

2293. [2207] ECR II-3601.

2294. [1979] ECR 461. Similar conclusions were reached by the Commission in *Soda-Ash-ICI* [2003] OJ L10/33, para 142, in which the obligation or promise by customers to obtain the whole or substantially the whole of their requirements from Soda-Ash-ICI constituted an abuse.

Indeed, exclusive purchasing or dealing agreements may lead to the foreclosure of a market if purchasers are tied to an undertaking enjoying a dominant position. In such circumstances the ability of new competitors to enter the market is restricted as well as the ability of the existing competitors to expand their market share. The Guidance states that the Commission will concen-trate on cases where consumers as a whole do not benefit as a result of an exclusive purchasing obligation. This will, in particular, occur where there are many customers and the exclusive purchasing, taken together, will have the effect of preventing the entry or expansion of competi-tors. Other factors (mentioned in para 20 of the Guidance) will also be taken into account. In general, the likelihood of anti-competitive foreclosure will increase the longer the duration of the exclusive purchasing agreement. However, in a situation where the dominant undertaking is an unavoidable trading partner for all or most customers, even an exclusive purchasing obligation of short duration can lead to anti-competitive foreclosure.

28.7.3.2.2.1 *"Freezer exclusivity"*

This relates to a practice whereby frozen goods suppliers provide retail outlets with freezers free of charge, but require that no other supplier's brand can be stored in the freezers so provided. This practice leads to the same effect as an exclusive purchasing obligation (see above).

The leading case on this topic is Case T-65/98 *Masterfoods Ltd v HB Ice Cream Ltd. and HB Ice Cream Ltd v Masterfoods Ltd.*[2295]

THE FACTS WERE:

HB (a wholly-owned subsidiary of the Unilever group), which was a leading manufacturer of ice cream in Ireland, for a number of years supplied its ice cream retailers free of charge with freezer cabinets on the proviso that they were used exclusively for HB products. Further, a condition was imposed that no other freezer cabinets could be used in the retailers'

2295. [2003] ECR II-4653.

premises. In 1989 Masterfoods, a subsidiary of the US corporation Mars Inc, entered the Irish ice cream market. From that time a number of HB's retailers began to stock and display Masterfoods products in the freezer cabinets belonging to HB. HB insisted that its retailers comply with the exclusivity clause contained in the agreements for the supply of its freezer cabinets. Masterfoods commenced proceedings against HB before the High Court in Ireland, challenging the validity of the exclusivity clause on the grounds of Articles 81 and 82 EC [Articles 101 and 102 TFEU]. HB answered by bringing proceedings for an injunction to restrain Masterfoods from inducing retailers to breach the exclusivity clause. Both parties sought damages.

On 28 May 1992 the High Court dismissed the action brought by Masterfoods and granted HB a permanent injunction, but dismissed HB's claim for damages.

On 4 September 1992 Masterfoods appealed against that decision to the Irish Supreme Court. In parallel with these proceedings Masterfoods lodged a complaint against HB with the Commission. On 29 July 1993 the Commission in its statement of objections found HB in breach of Articles 81 and 82 EC [Articles 101 and 102 TFEU]. In response HB submitted a proposal to alter the distribution agreements (which proposal was never implemented).

On 11 March 1998 the Commission adopted Decision 98/531/EC (OJ (1998) L 246), which found HB in breach of Article 81(1) EC [Article 101(1) TFEU] for imposing the exclusivity clause requiring that its retailers must have one or more freezer cabinets supplied by HB in their retail outlets and must not have freezer cabinets procured by themselves or provided by another ice-cream manufacturer, and in breach of Article 82 EC [Article 102 TFEU] for inducing its retailers to enter into the above freezer cabinet agreements.

HB, which in the meantime had changed its name to Van Den Berg Foods Ltd, brought an action under Article 263 TFEU for annulment of that decision (Case T65/98 van den Berg v Commission) and an action for the suspension of the application of Decision 98/531 until the CFI had given a ruling on the substance.

Held:

The CFI [the General Court] upheld the Commission's decision.

In respect of Article 81 EC [Article 101 TFEU] it ruled that the effect of the agreement as a whole was to restrict competition in the market given the specific conditions of the market, the popularity of HB ice creams, HB's dominant position in the market, and the fact that retailers were unlikely to stock ice creams from various manufacturers if they were not allowed to do so in one and the same freezer. In addition, the exclusivity clause constituted a barrier to entry for new suppliers given that retailers were not inclined to accept freezers that were not free, and thus the supplier had to acquire a stock of cabinets, which represented a large investment and could dissuade it from entering the market.

With regard to Article 82 EC [Article 102 TFEU] the CFI [the General Court] found that in the context of a competitive market the provision of freezer cabinets on a condition of exclusivity constitutes a standard practice and does not restrict competition, but the situation is different in respect of a market dominated by one trader where competition is already restricted. In a market dominated by one undertaking the exclusivity clause "has the effect of preventing the retailers concerned from selling other brands of ice cream, even though there is a demand for such brands, and of preventing competing manufacturers from gaining access to the relevant market". Therefore, by inducing retailers by those means to obtain supplies exclusively from HB, HB abused its dominant position in the market.

28.7.3.2.3 Refusal to deal or continue to deal with existing and potential customers and the doctrine of essential facility

It is important to make a distinction between the situation when a dominant undertaking refuses to deal with existing customers and the situation when such an undertaking decides to deny access to an essential facility, that is, when a dominant undertaking is in possession of a scarce resource or facility which cannot be duplicated, for example, access to a port, or a railway station, or other facility protected by intellectual property rights.

This is because if there is a duty imposed on a dominant undertaking to deal or continue to deal with its customers, such a duty will go beyond the duty imposed under the doctrine of essential facility, which prohibits, in certain well-defined circumstances, a dominant undertaking from denying access to an essential facility.

28.7.3.2.3.1 Refusal to deal or to continue to deal on a non-discriminatory basis with existing or potential customers

The principle of the freedom of contract entails that an undertaking, whether dominant or not, should be free to decide with whom it wants to do business. The importance of preserving the freedom of contract was recognised by the CFI in *Bayer*[2296] when the Court held that "refusal to supply, even where it is total, is prohibited only if it constitutes an abuse". Based on the case law it seems that a refusal will constitute an abuse if a dominant undertaking refuses to supply either its existing or new customers without some objective justification.[2297] This occurred in Joined Cases 6 and 7/73 *Commercial Solvents v Commission*.[2298] In this case the facts were as follows.

THE FACTS WERE:

Commercial Solvents, the world's only large-scale producer of raw materials from which the drug ethambutol could be made (and as such holding a dominant position in that sector), refused to supply raw materials to Zoja, one of the three makers of ethambutol in the EC. The circumstances of the case were that Commercial Solvents' refusal to supply Zoja was intended to eliminate Zoja from the secondary market for Commercial Solvents (the down-stream market for Commercial Solvents) where ICI, a subsidiary of Commercial Solvents, was emerging as a competitor to Zoja. The main market, that is, the upstream market of Commercial Solvents was the market for the raw materials. The secondary or downstream market was the market for the manufacture of drugs for the treatment of tuberculosis, in which market Zoja was the main competitor of Commercial Solvents' subsidiary, ICI.

Held:

The ECJ held that Commercial Solvents was in breach of Article 82 EC [Article 102 TFEU] as its refusal to supply a competitor in a downstream market would result in the elimination of all competition in the downstream market.

2296. Case T-41/96 *Bayer AG v Commission* [2000] ECR II-3383.
2297. *BP v Commission* [1978] ECR 1513, the refusal to supply occasional customers over regular customers was objectively justified in the time of oil shortage resulting from the OPEC oil boycott in 1973.
2298. [1974] ECR 223.

In Case 22/78 *Hugin Kassaregister AB and Hugin Cash Registers Ltd v Commission*,[2299] Hugin refused to supply spare parts for Hugin's cash register machines to Liptons, a UK-based undertaking that services cash registers. The reason was that Hugin intended to enter the downstream market for servicing. The Commission found Hugin in breach of Article 82 EC [Article 102 TFEU]. The ECJ did not depart from the Commission's finding that the refusal to supply was abusive, but annulled the decision on the ground that the Commission failed to show that Hugin's conduct was capable of affecting trade in the EU.

It the light of the above cases it is clear that refusals to supply an existing or a new customer,[2300] unless objectively justified, will constitute an abuse where the refusal would result in eliminating or weakening competition in the downstream market.[2301]

In *BBI/Boosey and Hawkes*[2302] and in Case 27/76 *United Brands*[2303] the refusal to supply was a retaliatory measure against an existing customer, in the first case because a distributor wanted to start a rival business, and in the second, because the distributor's conduct was considered as disloyal with regard to UB. Such refusals constitute abuses.

In Case T-65/89 *BPB Industries Plc and British Gypsum Ltd v Commission*[2304] the ECJ condemned BPB for giving priority to "loyal" customers in a time of shortage, that is, those who were almost exclusively buying BPB's products over those who marketed plasterboard imported and produced by BPB's competitors, and in Case 7/82 *GVL v Commission*[2305] the refusal of GVL (the only undertaking in Germany entitled to manage services relating to secondary rights vested in performing artists and manufacturers) to conclude management agreements, that is, to admit to its membership undertakings and persons residing outside Germany, constituted an abuse. The above cases confirm that a dominant undertaking has a duty to deal with customers on a non-discriminatory basis unless such action is objectively justified.

28.7.3.2.3.2 Refusal to deal in the pharmaceutical sector

Competition in the pharmaceutical market is of great importance to EU citizens. This is because, first, the pharmaceutical sector is a vital part of national health care systems in the Member States, and second, the market's potential for growth is increasing as EU citizens consume ever greater volumes of pharmaceutical products at a time when the average life span of these citizens

---

2299. [1979] ECR 1869.

2300. *London-European-Sabena* [1988] OJ L317/47.

2301. *Napier Brown v British Sugar* [1990] 4 CMLR 196. In this case British Sugar refused to supply Napier and used other unlawful practices to weaken Napier's position in the market for consumer retail one-kilogram sugar bags, in which market Napier was a rival of British Sugar.

2302. · In *BBI/Boosey and Hawkes: Interim Measures* [1987] OJ L286/36.

2303. Supra note 2219.

2304. [1993] ECR II-389.

2305. [1983] ECR 483.

is increasing in parallel with demand for a wider choice of those products at affordable prices. The market, however, has two characteristics which differentiate it from other sectors of the economy:

■ The price of patented and new drugs tends to be regulated by the Member States. Often Governments are the only buyers. This entails that pharmaceutical companies cannot freely set prices or, indeed, increase them;

■ The structure of the market is peculiar in that the ultimate consumer (the patient) differs from the decision maker (the doctor) and often from the payer (the national insurance service or private health insurer). The decision of a doctor is not based on the price but on the therapeutic effect of the relevant drug.

In the light of the above, the issue of whether the refusal by a dominant undertaking to supply its wholesalers in circumstances where those wholesalers could benefit from parallel trading raised many concerns and controversies. The ECJ in Joined Cases C-468 to C-478/06 *Sot. Lelos Kai Sia EE (C-468/06) and Others v GlaxoSmithKline AEVE Farmakeftikon Proionton*[2306] stated the position of EU competition law on the matter.

THE FACTS WERE:

GlaxoSmithKline plc, a pharmaceutical research and manufacturing company established in the UK, both warehoused products in Greece and distributed them there through its subsidiary GSK AEVE ("GSK"). Until November 2000 GSK met in full orders from Greek pharmacists and wholesalers for three drugs (Imigran, for migraine, Lamictal, for epilepsy, and Serevent, for asthma). The wholesalers for a number of years had supplied these products both to the Greek and to other markets, particularly Germany and the UK where prices were higher than in Greece. After November 2000 GSK alleged that, as a result of a shortage in Greece of the three products due to their export by Greek wholesalers, it was forced to change its system of distribution in Greece. Under the new system GSK refused to supply the products to its wholesalers and decided to supply the products itself to hospitals and pharmacies in Greece. In February 2001 GSK resumed its supplies to wholesalers but it limited them in terms of quantity. Greek wholesalers and pharmacists started proceedings against GSK for abuse of its dominant position on the Greek market. During the proceedings the Greek Court of Appeal decided that it needed an answer from the ECJ on the compatibility of the practices of GSK with Article 82 EC [Article 102 TFEU].

Held:

The ECJ held that Article 82 EC [Article 102 TFEU] applies in the same manner to the pharmaceutical sector as to other sectors of the economy. As a result, it confirmed that there is no justification under EU competition law for various anti-competitive practices used by the pharmaceutical industry, such as supply quotas, dual-pricing and direct-to-pharmacy distribution schemes.

The Court found that parallel trade in medical products is pro-competitive, benefits the

---

2306. [2008] ECR I-7139.

final consumers, constitutes an important factor in market integration, and that in cases where it would result in a shortage of medical products on a given national market, it would not be for an undertaking in a dominant position, but for the relevant national authorities to resolve the situation by taking appropriate and proportionate steps. However, an undertaking in a dominant position is entitled to protect its own commercial interests and if it is confronted with orders that are out of the ordinary in terms of quantity, it may refuse to meet such orders but if the orders are ordinary any refusal to meet them will constitute an abuse prohibited by Article 82 EC [Article 102 TFEU]. To decide whether orders are ordinary, factors such as the previous relations between the pharmaceutical company and the wholesalers concerned, and the size of the orders in relation to the requirements of the market in the Member State concerned must be taken into account.[2307] The ECJ held that it was the task of the referring court to decide whether, in the light of the above mentioned factors. a restriction of supply by GSK was abusive.

28.7.3.2.3.3 *The doctrine of essential facility*

To understand the doctrine of essential facility it is necessary to determine what facilities should be considered as essential. This is done on a case-by-case basis. Advocate General Jacobs, in his opinion in Case C-7/97 *Oscar Bronner GmbH & Co. KG v Mediaprint Zeitungs- und Zeitschriftenverlag GmbH & Co. KG*,[2308] stated that a facility is considered as essential if access to it is indispensable in order to compete in a related market, and duplication of that facility is impossible or extremely difficult owing to physical, geographic or legal constraints, or is highly undesirable for reasons of public policy.

Examples of essential facilities are ports,[2309] bus stations, and intellectual property rights. One of the most commented cases was the *Magill* case,[2310] which concerned intellectual property rights. In *Magill* the Irish television companies refused to supply information, which was protected by copyright under Irish law, regarding the weekly schedules of certain television channels to Magill. The ECJ held that in "exceptional circumstances" the refusal to supply was in breach of Article 102 TFEU. These "exceptional circumstances" were that the refusal prevented the introduction of a new product, that is, a general television guide, for which there was a potential consumer demand, the refusal was not based on any objective justification, and was likely to have the effect of excluding all competition in the market for television guides. Further clarifications were provided by the ECJ in Case C-7/97 *Oscar Bronner GmbH & Co. KG v Mediaprint Zeitungs- und Zeitschriftenverlag GmbH & Co. KG.*

2307. *United Brands and United Brands Continentaal v Commission* [1978] ECR 207 and Case 77/77 *Benzine en Petroleum Handelsmaatschappij and Others v Commission* [1978] ECR 1513.

2308. [1998] ECR I-7791.

2309. E.g. the port of Holyhead in *B&I Line v Sealink Harbours* [1992] 5 CMLR 255.

2310. Cases C-241 and C-242/91P *RTE and ITP v Commission* [1995] ECR I-743 on appeal from Cases T-69–70/89 *RTE, ITP, BBC v Commission* [1991] ECR II-485, on appeal from *Magill TV Guide* [1989] OJ L78/43.

THE FACTS WERE:

A dispute had arisen between two Austrian undertakings. They were: Oscar Bronner, editor, publisher, manufacturer and distributor of the daily newspaper Der Standard, which in 1994 held 3.6 per cent of the Austrian daily newspaper market in terms of circulation and 6 per cent in terms of advertising revenues, and Mediaprint Zeitungs, publisher of two daily newspapers which in 1994 held 46.8 per cent of the Austrian daily newspaper market in terms of circulation and 42 per cent in terms of advertising revenues. Mediaprint Zeitungs' two newspapers reached 53.3 per cent of the population above the age of 14 in private households and 71 per cent of all newspaper readers. Mediaprint set up a nationwide delivery system consisting of delivering the newspapers directly to subscribers in the early hours of the morning. Oscar Bronner (for financial reasons) was not able to set up a similar system of delivery on its own and had to use a postal service for delivery of its newspaper, which occurred late in the morning. Bronner sought an order requiring Mediaprint to cease abusing Mediaprint's alleged dominant position in the market by including Bronner's newspaper, Der Standard, in its home-delivery service against payment of reasonable remuneration. Mediaprint refused to do this voluntarily.

Held:

The ECJ specified four conditions (which must all pertain simultaneously) under which the refusal of the dominant undertaking (Mediaprint) could not be justified:

- First, if the refusal would be likely to eliminate all competition in the downstream market;

- Second, if such a refusal was incapable of being objectively justified;

- Third, if access was indispensable to carrying on business by the person requesting access;

- Fourth, if there was no actual or potential substitute for the facility to which the person requested access.

These four conditions were not satisfied in this case and, therefore, the ECJ held that there was no abuse of a dominant position on the part of Mediaprint. The Court emphasised that in all normal circumstances undertakings are free to decide who is to have access to their facilities and assets. Only in exceptional cases can an undertaking rely on EC Competition law to gain access to such facilities. The burden of proof lies with the alleged victim.

The Commission's Guidance states that the Commission is likely to intervene in the following circumstances:

- the refusal relates to a product or service that is objectively necessary to be able to compete effectively on a downstream market; and

- the refusal is likely to lead to the elimination of effective competition on the downstream market; and

- the refusal is likely to lead to consumer harm.

The notable omission is that the Guidance does not state that a duty of a dominant undertaking to contract should arise only in "exceptional circumstances".

28.7.4 Reprisal abuses

The best example is provided in Case 27/76 *United Brands*,[2311] in which United Brands decided to punish its Danish distributor Olesen, who promoted a competitive brand of banana, by refusing to supply it with its "Chiquita" banana. The ECJ held that the punitive action of United Brands was out of proportion to the alleged "disloyal" conduct of Olesen and decided that an undertaking in a dominant position was not allowed to refuse to supply a long-standing distributor, so long as the distributor's orders placed with the supplier remained within the normal range.

AIDE-MÉMOIRE

ARTICLE 102 TFEU

Under Article 102 TFEU a dominant position is not prohibited. What is unlawful is the abuse of a dominant position (although in the past the ECJ comes close to suggesting that a very dominant position might of itself be abusive). The effects-based approach to the determination of whether a unilateral practice is abusive has been confirmed in the Commission's Guidance on its enforcement priorities in applying Article 102 TFEU to abusive exclusionary conduct by dominant undertakings. To prove breach of the prohibition set out in Article 102 TFEU it is necessary to establish that:

- One or more undertakings;

- In a dominant position within the internal market or in a substantial part of it;

- Has abused that dominant position;

- Which abuse has affected trade between Member States.

DOMINANCE

An undertaking is in a dominant position when it can act independently from its competitors and consumers and thus is not subject to normal competitive forces.

Establishing dominance

The determination of whether an undertaking has market power involves two stages:

A.   **Stage one**: the relevant market must be defined. This has three aspects:
   - The relevant product market (RPM);
   - The relevant geographical market (RGM). In Case 27/76 *United Brands* the ECJ held that the geographic market is the area in which "the conditions of

---

2311.   [1978] ECR 207.

competition are sufficiently homogeneous for the effect of the economic power of the undertaking to be able to be evaluated"; and

▪ The relevant temporal market (RTM).

(See the 1997 Notice on the Definition of the Relevant Market for the Purposes of Community Competition Law.)

The RPM is the central concept (it is always a controversial issue and arises in every case). The RGM in many cases is obvious. The RTM is rarely at issue. All three are defined by reference to:

Demand substitutability

To assess demand substitutability (the demand-side substitutability), the test is based on the question of whether consumers of the relevant product would switch to substitute products if prices for the relevant product were raised by a small but significant amount above competitive levels (this is known as the SSNIP test – a Small but Significant Non-transitory Increase in Price). (Case 27/76 *United Brands v Commission*.)

Supply substitutability (*Torras/Sarrió* Case)

Supply substitutability (the supply-side substitutability) refers to substitutability of products or otherwise as assessed from the point of view of suppliers. The question to be asked is whether suppliers, who do not currently supply the relevant products, would be able to switch production to the relevant products and market them in the short term without incurring significant additional costs or risk in response to small and permanent changes in prices in respect of the relevant product. Consequently, all producers that currently produce the relevant product and all producers that could easily and economically produce and sell the relevant product in a short period of time in response to a small increase in price will be included in the relevant product market.

Potential competition

This is normally examined in stage two below.

The relevant product market may be inferred from the conduct of an undertaking (Case C-62/86 *AKZO*)

B. **Stage two**: consists of the determination of the market power of the allegedly dominant undertaking. The Commission in its Guidance identifies three main factors as essential to the assessment of market power:

▪ Constraints imposed by the existing supplies from, and the position on the market of, the actual competitors (the position of the undertaking concerned and its rivals);

▪ Constraints imposed by the credible threat of future expansion by actual competitors or entry by potential competitors (expansion and entry);

▪ Constraints imposed by the bargaining power of the undertaking's customers (countervailing buyer power).

Collective dominance

The CFI [the General Court] in Case T-342/99 *Airtours/First Choice* established three conditions necessary for a finding of collective dominance.

These are:

- Transparency, that is, each member of the dominant oligopoly must have the ability to know how the other members are behaving in order to monitor whether or not they are adopting the common policy;

- Sustainability, that is, there must be a retaliatory mechanism put in place which secures unity within an oligopoly and thus dissuades its members from deviating from their common policy adopted on the relevant market; and

- An absence of competitive constraint, so allowing undertakings within a dominant oligopoly to act independently of their customers and consumers, actual or potential.

Abuse

The concept of abuse is an objective concept. It refers to conduct of an undertaking in a dominant position "which is such as to influence the structure of a market where, as the result of the very presence of the undertaking in question, the degree of competition is weakened and which, through recourse to methods different from those which condition normal competition in products or services on the basis of the transactions of commercial operators, has the effect of hindering the maintenance of the degree of competition still existing in the market or the growth of that competition" (Case 85/76 *Hoffmann-La Roche*).

Categories of abuses

A. **Exploitative abuses**: these refer to conduct of an undertaking in a dominant position which is prejudicial to the interests of its customers or consumers. An example of exploitative abuse is the imposition of excessively high prices by a dominant undertaking (Case 27/76 *United Brands*).

B. **Discriminatory abuses** (Case 27/76 *United Brands*).

C. **Exclusionary abuses**: these are aimed at foreclosing the relevant market.

The dominant undertaking may justify its conduct by demonstrating that:

- It is objectively necessary, e.g. justified by imperative considerations such as health and safety reasons related to the nature of the product concerned.

- It produces substantial efficiencies which outweigh any anti-competitive effects on consumers. The test here is similar to that set out in Article 101(3) TFEU.

There is a distinction between "price based" and "non-price based" exclusionary conduct.

Price-based exclusionary conduct

The Commission will use the test of hypothetical rivals that are "as efficient" (AEC) as the dominant undertaking in order to determine whether the "price-based" conduct of a dominant undertaking leads to foreclosure. If a rival is less efficient the Commission will normally assume that foreclosure results from mere competition on merits and thus is not anti-competitive. However, this is subject to an exception. In some circumstances the Commission will depart from the AEC test, i.e. when the relevant market is one in which network and/or learning effects are important. In such a situation the AEC test will use the hypothetical prospective entrant standard.

Examples of exclusionary abuses are:

▪ Predatory prices (Case C-62/86 *AKZO; Wanadoo*). The Commission's Guidance abolishes the test established in *AKZO* in favour of the AEC test;

▪ Discounts: the grant of a discount must be based on economic considerations (Case T-203/01 *Michelin II*) and must be non-discriminatory in fact (Case C-163/99 *Portugal*). According to the Guidance the Commission will intervene if rebates are likely to lead to anti-competitive foreclosure of actual or potential competitors "as efficient" as the dominant undertaking;

▪ A margin-squeeze: this leads to anti-competitive foreclosure when a dominant undertaking in an upstream market which supplies goods or services to rivals who use them to compete with the dominant undertaking in one or more downstream market squeezes its downstream rivals by charging prices which do not allow as efficient rivals as the dominant undertaking to make a living profit.

Non-price-based exclusionary conduct

▪ Tying-in and bundling agreements (Case T-30/89 *Hilti*; Case T-201/04 *Microsoft*). The Guidance confirms the *Microsoft* test.

▪ Exclusive Contracts (Case 85/76 *Hoffmann-La Roche* and Case T-65/98 *Masterfoods*). According to the Guidance, the likelihood of anti-competitive foreclosure will increase the longer the duration of an exclusive purchasing agreement. However, in a situation where the dominant undertaking is an unavoidable trading partner for all or most customers, even a short duration of an exclusive purchase obligation can lead to anti-competitive foreclosure.

▪ Refusal to supply.

The Guidance states that the Commission is likely to intervene in the following circumstances:

▪ the refusal relates to a product or service that is objectively necessary to be able to compete effectively on a downstream market; and

▪ the refusal is likely to lead to the elimination of effective competition on the downstream market; and

▪ the refusal is likely to lead to consumer harm.

D. **Reprisal abuses**: these occur when the conduct of an undertaking in a dominant position is directed at injuring another undertaking in order to punish it, usually for what the undertaking in a dominant position considers as "disloyal" conduct towards it (Case 27/76 *United Brands*).

RECOMMENDED READING

Books

Lovdahl Gormsen, L., *A Principled Approach to Abuse of Dominance in European Competition Law*, 2010, Cambridge: Cambridge University Press

O'Donoghue, R. and Padilla, J. A., *The Law and Economics of Article 82 EC*, 2006, Oxford: Hart Publishing

Articles

Mezzanotte, F. E., "Using Abuse of Collective Dominance in Article 102 TFEU to Fight Tacit Collusion: The Problem of Proof and Inferential Error", (2010) 33 World Competition, p 77

Monti, G., "Article 82 EC: What Future for the Effects-Based Approach?", 2010, Journal of European Competition Law & Practice, p 2

Petit, N., "From Formalism to Effects? The Commission's Communication on Enforcement Priorities in Applying Article 82 EC", (2009) 32 World Competition, p 485

29

MERGER CONTROL

CONTENTS

SUMMARY

1. The 1957 Treaty of Rome did not include merger control provisions. This omission had serious consequences for competition conditions in the Community given that undertakings could circumvent the prohibitions set out in Articles 101 and 102 TFEU by merging. Although most mergers (which under the Merger Regulation are called "concentrations") have pro-competitive effects, some may be harmful to competition given that they reduce the number of competitors in the relevant market and thus increase the merging undertakings' joined market power, and at the extreme can create a monopoly and thus increase the potential for abuse of that power. The necessity of introducing legislation at the Community level controlling the potential distortive effect of mergers on trade between Member States was increased by the fact that the application of Articles 101 and 102 TFEU proved to be inadequate to control mergers, and that the creation of the internal market prompted many undertakings to engage in cross-border mergers. The first Merger Regulation (Regulation 4064/89) was adopted in 1989. This regulation was amended by Regulation 1310/97 and subsequently replaced by Regulation 139/2004 (MR), which entered into force on 1 May 2004.

2. Concentrations are classified as horizontal when they occur between direct competitors, vertical when they involve undertakings in a customer–supplier relationship, and conglomerate when they neither involve direct competitors nor customer–supplier relationships, that is, they are neither horizontal nor vertical in nature. There are three types of conglomerate concentrations:

■ Product-line extension, where one undertaking adds a new product to its existing products by merging with another undertaking;

■ Market extension, where, prior to their merger, undertakings operated in the same product market but in different geographical markets; and

■ Pure conglomerates, where there is no functional connection between the merged undertakings, that is, they involve neither a market extension concentration nor a product-line extension concentration.

3. Article 3(1) of the MR identifies two types of concentration:

■ Those which occur when previously independent undertakings merge; and

■ Those arising from an acquisition of control.

A third type, being a full-function joint venture, is defined in Article 3(4) as a joint venture performing on a lasting basis all the functions of an autonomous economic entity. A joint venture which satisfies this definition is within the scope of the MR, otherwise it is dealt with under Article 101 TFEU.

4. Only concentrations which have an EU dimension are within the scope of the MR. Article 1 of the MR sets out two sets of thresholds, expressed in terms of turnover of the undertakings concerned worldwide and within the EU, to establish whether the relevant operation has an EU dimension. The thresholds determine the jurisdiction of the Commission or of national competition authorities to deal with the intended concentration.

5. Article 2(2) of the MR contains the substantive test for assessment of compatibility of the intended concentration with the requirements of the internal market. According to this test a concentration may be prohibited first, if it strengthens or creates a dominant position, and second, when it takes place in the context of a non-collusive oligopoly and does not lead to a single or joint dominance but produces effects which significantly impede effective competition in the internal market or a substantial part of it.

6. All concentrations which are within the scope of the MR must be notified to the Commission within seven days of the acceptance of an offer, the announcement of a public bid, or the acquisition of a controlling interest. If a concentration is implemented either before notification or before it is cleared by the Commission, the parties concerned may be fined by the Commission. Further, Article 7(1) of the MR provides that no concentration may come into legal effect until the Commission has delivered a compatibility decision or failed to make such a decision. The Commission (in what is known as the Phase I Investigation) is required to take an initial decision within 25 working days of receipt of complete notification (however, this period may be extended to 35 working days in the circumstances described in Article 9 of the MR). At the end of this procedure the Commission may decide that the concentration under consideration:

■ Is compatible with the internal market subject to some conditions which it attaches to the decision, or without any conditions;

■ Falls outside the scope of the MR, in which case national laws may apply to the concentration;

■ Requires more investigation as it raises serious doubts about its compatibility with the internal market. In that case the Phase II Investigation commences.

If the Commission takes no decision, the concentration is deemed to be compatible with the internal market.

The Phase II Investigation must be concluded in principle within 90 working days of commencement (there are some exceptions). At the end of this phase the Commission may declare the concentration:

■ Compatible with the internal market, with or without conditions. Such a decision also covers ancillary restraints; or

■ Incompatible with the internal market.

7. Under the MR the Commission has important enforcement powers: to revoke approved concentrations, to request information and to search and to fine for breaches of the MR.
8. The Commission's exclusive jurisdiction with regard to concentrations with an EU dimension is subject to some exceptions as set out in the MR.

29.1 Introduction

The Treaty of Rome was totally silent on the topic of mergers. This omission had serious consequences for competition conditions within the EU. Undertakings were able to circumvent the application of Articles 101(1) and 102 TFEU. Instead of entering into agreements prohibited by virtue of Article 101(1) TFEU, they could achieve the same objectives by merging with other undertakings. In respect of Article 102 EU an undertaking in a dominant position (the existence of which per se weakens competition within the relevant market) could lawfully increase its market power by acquiring or merging with its competitors and thus further reduce competition to the detriment of its customers/consumers, although the merged entity might then be subject to Article 102. The Commission was powerless to prevent such mergers between, and acquisitions by, undertakings having market power, and could only act afterwards under Article 102.

29.1.1 Application of Article 102 TFEU to mergers

The first attempt to bring mergers within the realm of EU competition law was made by the Commission in Case 6/72 *Europemballage and Continental Can v Commission*.[2312] Although the Commission failed to prove that Continental Can held a dominant position in the German market,[2313] the ECJ recognised for the first time that Article 102 TFEU was, in principle, applicable to mergers. The ECJ interpreted Article 102 TFEU teleologically and concluded that it would be contradictory to prohibit certain agreements and practices by virtue of Article 101(1) TFEU while allowing undertakings in a dominant position in the relevant market to merge and thus strengthen their position to the possible extent of eliminating any competition in that market. Allowing such a course would call into question the proper functioning of the internal market.

2312. [1973] ECR 215 (for facts and further comments see Chapter 28.3.1.1.3).
2313. The Commission failed to assess the supply-substitutability of the relevant product market.

Shortly after the decision in *Continental Can* the Commission prepared its first draft Merger Regulation, but the Council did not choose to endorse it. As a consequence it took many years before the reluctance of the Member States to deal with mergers at EU level was overcome.

29.1.2 Application of Article 101 TFEU to mergers

The ECJ for the first time applied Article 101(1) TFEU in Cases 142 and 156/84 *British-American Tobacco Company Ltd (BAT) and R. J. Reynolds Industries Inc. v Commission and Philip Morris.*[2314]

THE FACTS WERE:

In April 1981 two leading cigarette manufacturers, Rembrandt and Philip Morris, entered into an agreement under which Philip Morris acquired 50 per cent equity interest in and joint management of Rothmans Holdings, until then a subsidiary of Rembrandt. BAT, a competitor, and other undertakings complained to the Commission. As a result, a new agreement was made under which Philip Morris acquired 30 per cent equity interest in Rothmans and 24.9 per cent voting rights in Rothmans International, a subsidiary of Rothmans Holdings.

The second agreement together with other complementary arrangements made sure that Philip Morris would neither be represented on the Rothmans International board nor have any managerial influence upon it. This agreement was exempted by the Commission under Article 101(3) TFEU. BAT and others challenged the Commission decision under Article 263 TFEU.

Held:

The ECJ upheld the Commission decision on the grounds that the limited voting rights and the lack of managerial representation would prevent Philip Morris from restricting competition. The ECJ did, however, make important statements in this case:

- First, confirming the application of Article 101 TFEU to mergers; and

- Second, holding that although the acquisition by one undertaking of an equity interest in its competitor does not in itself necessarily restrict competition, such an acquisition *may* restrict or distort competition in the relevant market. The ECJ emphasised that "this will be true, in particular, where by the acquisition of a shareholding, or through subsidiary clauses in the agreement, the investing company obtains legal or de facto control of the commercial conduct of the other company or where the agreement provides for commercial co-operation between the companies or creates a structure likely to be used for such co-operation. This may also be the case where the agreement gives the investing company the possibility of reinforcing its position at a later stage and taking effective control of the other company".

The above decision showed:

- First, that Article 101 TFEU was not an appropriate tool to deal with mergers, taking into

---

2314. [1987] ECR 4487.

account the nullity sanction under Article 101(2), the possibility of the revocability of exemption under Article 101(3) and the lack of thresholds triggering its application to mergers;

▣ Second, that the ECJ, by interpreting Article 101 TFEU broadly, had in effect extended the scope of the Treaty and thus judicially revised it;

▣ Third, that in order to avoid further judicial developments by the ECJ on the control of mergers and the uncertainty of whether or not the Commission would exercise its discretion, a wise option for the Member States would be to adopt legislation on merger control, especially in the light of the then forthcoming completion of the internal market.

29.1.3 Adoption of Regulation 4064/89 and its replacement by Regulation 139/2004 (MR)

In March 1988 a draft Regulation was submitted to the Council which, after a number of amendments, was adopted on 21 December 1989 as Merger Regulation 4064/89 and came into force on 21 September 1990.[2315] It was updated on 26 June 1997 by Regulation 1310/97/EC which entered into force on 1 March 1998.[2316] Merger Regulation 4064/89 was supplemented by a number of implementing and interpretative instruments. However, the reform of EU competition law encompassed Regulation 4064/89 which resulted in the adoption of Regulation 139/2004[2317] (MR) adopted on 20 January 2004. It entered into force on 1 May 2004.

The MR is accompanied by an implementing Regulation,[2318] Notices (including the long-awaited Notice on the Appraisal of Horizontal Mergers) and guidelines (including Best Practice Guidelines on the Conduct of EU Merger Regulation Proceedings).[2319]

In order to strengthen the economic approach to the assessment of intended concentrations and to respond to criticism expressed by the CFI [General Court] regarding the failure of the Commission to provide good quality evidence to satisfy the requisite standard of proof,[2320] the Commission appointed a chief competition economist, working with a team of economists, and set up, within the Phase II investigation, arrangements for a peer review panel to scrutinise the conclusions reached in that Phase by the investigating team.

Particularly helpful in the interpretation of the MR is the Commission's Consolidated Jurisdictional Notice[2321] adopted on 10 July 2007, which replaced the four previous jurisdictional Notices.[2322] The new Notice is user-friendly, takes account of the existing case law in the area and

2315. [1989] OJ L395/1.

2316. [1997] OJ L180/1.

2317. [2004] OJ L24/1.

2318. Regulation 802/2004 [2004] OJ L133/1.

2319. [2004] OJ C31/5.

2320. The CFI [the General Court] overturned the Commission's decisions in many important more recent cases, e.g. Case T-342/99 *AirTours/First Choice* [2002] ECR II-2585; Case T-310/01 *Schneider Electric SA* [2002] ECR II-4071; and Case T-5/02 *Tetra Laval BV* [2002] ECR II-4381, confirmed by the ECJ in Case C-12/03P *Commission v Tetra Laval BV* [2005] I-1113.

2321. Found at http://ec.europa.eu/comm/competition/mergers/legislation/jn_en.pdf (accessed 28/12/09).

2322. These are: the Notice on the concept of concentration; the Notice on the concept of full-function joint ventures; the Notice on the concept of undertakings concerned; and the Notice on calculation of turnover.

of the practices of the Commission, and reflects the changes that the MR has introduced in respect of jurisdictional matters in merger control.

29.2   The scope of application of the Merger Regulation (MR)

The MR does not prohibit concentrations. Unlike Articles 101 and 102 TFEU the repressive element is absent. The emphasis is on the structure of the relevant market, not on the anti-competitive conduct of an undertaking. On the one hand, many concentrations are necessary in order to reinforce the competitiveness of EU undertakings, but on the other, concentrations may have damaging effects on the competitive structure of the market. Concentrations can be classified as horizontal, vertical and conglomerate.

- **Horizontal.** This occurs when a concentration takes place between undertakings which are competing in the same product and geographical market and at the same level of production/distribution. Such concentrations have great impact on the market, given that after the concentration the number of undertakings in the relevant market is reduced, at least by one, and ordinarily the new, merged undertaking has a larger market share than either undertaking had previously. Horizontal mergers are the most likely to adversely affect the structure of the relevant market in terms of its competitiveness. The Commission's Guidelines on the Assessment of Horizontal Mergers[2323] are of great help to parties who are actual or potential competitors in the same relevant market when they intend to merge;

- **Vertical.** This refers to a concentration between undertakings operating at different levels of the economy (for example, between a manufacturer and its supplier of raw material). They do not increase concentration of the relevant product market but they "can give rise to a number of competition issues, including the possibility of foreclosure or of creating a more favourable environment for collusive behaviour. As with vertical restraints, anti-competitive effects are likely to occur only if there is horizontal market power at one or more of the vertical levels";[2324]

- **Conglomerate.** This refers to a concentration between undertakings that are not competing with each other in any product market and which does not result in any vertical integration. Three types of conglomerate merger may be identified:

  - Product line extension, where one undertaking adds a new product to its existing products by merging with another;
  - Market extension, where prior to their merger undertakings operated in the same product market but in different geographical markets; and
  - Pure conglomerates, where there is no functional connection between the merged undertakings, that is, they involve neither a market extension concentration nor a product-line extension concentration.

Ordinarily conglomerate effects are neutral, or even beneficial for competition. While US

2323. [2004] OJ C31/5.

2324. S. Bishop and M. Walker, *The Economics of EC Competition Law: Concepts, Application and Measurement*, 2nd edition, 2002, London: Sweet and Maxwell, para 7.61.

antitrust law is not interested in conglomerate mergers, the position of EU competition law is different, as exemplified in the *Tetra Laval* case.[2325]

The MR applies to all sectors of the economy, to both public and private undertakings, and to undertakings which are established within and outside the EU.

Concentrations are within the scope of the MR if they satisfy two conditions:

▓ They are "concentrations" as defined by the MR; and

▓ They have "an EU dimension" within the meaning of the MR.

Concentrations with an EU dimension must be notified to the Commission in conformity with the requirements laid down in Form "CO". The Commission is required to deal with notifications as soon as they are received and must adopt relevant decisions within a very strict, legally binding timetable. Business operators greatly appreciate this feature of the MR. Unlike cases examined under Articles 101 and 102 TFEU (where there are no binding deadlines for the Commission), in concentration cases they have certitude that whatever the decision of the Commission, at least it will be adopted within a well-defined time frame.

An appeal from the decision of the Commission can be lodged with the General Court.

The concept of concentration and the concept of EU dimension are vital for the application of the MR.

29.2.1 The concept of concentration

Article 3(1) of the MR states that the MR applies only to concentrations which permanently modify the structure of the undertakings concerned. The concept of concentration is defined in Article 3 of the Regulation and covers two types of concentration:

▓ First, the case where two or more previously independent undertakings merge; and

▓ Second, the case where one or more undertakings already controlling at least one or more undertakings, acquire direct or indirect control of the whole or parts of one or more other undertakings, whether by purchase of securities or assets, by contract or by any other means.

A third type of concentration is a full-function joint venture (JV) defined in Article 3(4) of the MR as a joint venture performing on a lasting basis all the functions of an autonomous economic entity. A joint venture which satisfies the above definition is within the scope of the MR, otherwise it is dealt with under Article 101 TFEU.

29.2.1.1   Merger[2326]

This first type of concentration is not very complex. There is no definition of a "merger". Merger may occur in two ways:

2325. In Case C-12/03P *Commission v Tetra Laval BV* [2005] I-1113 the ECJ stated that the CFI was correct in requiring the same standard of proof in respect of conglomerate effects of a merger as in cases of vertical and horizontal mergers (para 40). US antitrust law is not interested in conglomerate effects of a merger, considering them as being, at the worst, neutral for competition. See R. Whish, *Competition Law*, 5th edition, 2003, London: LexisNexis Butterworths, p 780 and pp 841–2.

2326. It is important to note that the term "merger" is commonly used to describe what the MR defines as "concentration". This first type of concentration seems to refer to a merger in the technical sense of "fusion" see: C. J. Cook and C. S. Kerse, *EC Merger Control*, 3rd edition, 2000, London: Sweet and Maxwell, pp 27 and 29.

■ Legal merger where two or more undertakings cease to be legally distinct and independent from each other and form a single separate legal entity;

■ De facto merger where two or more undertakings create a permanent economic management while continuing to exist as separate legal entities. In fact, they act on the relevant market as a single economic unit.

Perhaps for the sake of clarity this type of concentration should be referred to as a fusion.

29.2.1.2 Acquisition

The second type of concentration refers to acquisition, by whatever means, of control over the whole or part of other undertakings. The situation of "acquisition of control" is more complex than that of merger. Further, a distinction is made between:

■ Sole control, a situation where one undertaking alone can exercise de facto or de jure decisive influence on another undertaking;[2327] and

■ Joint control, which exists where two or more undertakings are able to exercise decisive influence over another undertaking. As Article 62 of the Jurisdictional Notice explains: "Decisive influence normally means the power to block actions which determine the strategic commercial behaviour of an undertaking." As in the case of sole control, the acquisition of joint control may be established on a de facto or on a de jure basis.

The MR also covers situations where the acquisition of sole or joint control leads to a change in the quality of control. Article 83 of the Notice explains that changes in the quality of control occur:

■ When there is a change from sole to joint control and vice versa; and

■ With regard to a change in joint control, if there is a reduction in the number or a change in the identity of the controlling shareholders.

Acquisition of control is defined in Article 3(1)(b) of the MR in the following terms:

"Control shall be constituted by rights, contracts or any other means which, either separately or in combination, and having regard to the considerations of fact or law involved, confer the possibility of exercising decisive influence on an undertaking, in particular by:
(a)   ownership or the right to use all the assets of an undertaking;
(b)   rights or contracts which confer decisive influence on the composition, voting or decisions of the organs of an undertaking."

The definition of control is broad. In many cases the existence of control is easy to determine, for example, on the basis of ownership. In other cases an economic analysis will be necessary to establish the existence of control. For example, minority shareholders may have sole control on a de facto basis in a situation where at a shareholders' meeting they are highly likely to achieve a majority vote for any proposal put forward by them because the remaining shares are widely

---

2327.   See The Consolidated Jurisdictional Notice para 54 et seq.

dispersed. In such cases the Commission has consistently based its assessment on the actual participation in shareholders' meetings in previous years.[2328]

In Cases 142 and 156/84 *BAT and Reynolds v Commission*,[2329] it was established that control was exercised by a minority shareholding, as in fact no other shareholder or group of shareholders could combine to oppose that minority shareholder. Even a shareholding of 25 per cent may amount to control. In *CCIE/GTE*, by acquiring 19 per cent of the voting rights in EDIL, CCIE had acquired control over EDIL given that the remaining shares were held by independent banks whose approval of important business decisions was not necessary.[2330]

In Case No COMP/M3330 *RTL/M6*,[2331] RTL, a Luxembourg TV channel (which already owned a 48.4 per cent shareholding), acquired sole control of M6, a French TV channel, without acquiring any additional shares in M6. This occurred when Suez Lyonnaise des Eau (Suez) sold its shares in M6. Before the divestment Suez held 37.6 per cent and RTL held 48.4 per cent of shares in M6. Under a decision of the French Conseil Supérieur de l'Audiovisuel, which supervises ownership of French TV channels, the voting rights held by any shareholder or group of shareholders in this sector were limited to 34 per cent. Although RTL held 48.4 per cent of M6 shares, its voting rights were limited to 34 per cent. The divestment of Suez's shares led to passive acquisition of sole control by RTL because the remaining shares, other than the 48.4 per cent owned by RTL, with their maximum 34 per cent voting power became widely dispersed among a large number of small shareholders who were unlikely to coalesce to reach a majority in future shareholders' meetings.

There may be acquisition of control even if this is not the declared intention of the parties.[2332]

By virtue of Article 3(3)(b) indirect control, that is, the situation where title to the assets or contract conferring control is "divorced" from the ability to benefit from such rights, is within the scope of the MR. This can be illustrated by the following example: when undertaking A acquires a controlling interest in undertaking B that has subsidiaries C and D, undertaking A will have direct control over B and indirect control over C and D. A is not a holder of the rights to shares in C and D but as a result of its control over B, it exercises indirect control over C and D. In order to decide whether the change of control has amounted to a concentration, all relevant factual and legal considerations are taken into account.[2333]

An acquisition of control must result in a lasting change in the control of the undertaking concerned. Agreements which provide for a definite end-date are within the scope of the MR if the period envisaged is sufficiently long to result in a lasting change. The Commission considers that 10–15 years constitute a sufficient period but not a period of three years.[2334]

2328. Cases No.IV/M 343 *Société Generale de Belgique/Generale de Banque* of 3/08/1993; No.IV/M/754 *Anglo American Corporation/Lonrho* of 23/04/1997 and No. IV/M.1157 *Skanska/Scancam* of 11/11/1998; Case COM/M 2574 *Pirrelli/Edizione/Olivetti/Telecom Italia* of 20/09/2001.

2329. [1987] ECR 4487.

2330. No. IV/M 258.

2331. Decision of 12/03/2004. See the official site of the EU's competition policy – news, legislation, cases at http://ec.europa.eu/competition/index_en.html (accessed in December 2007). The Commission cleared the concentration.

2332. Case No. IV/M/157 *Air France/Sabena* [1994] 5 CMLR M1.

2333. Case T-102/96 *Gencor Ltd v Commission* [1999] ECR II-753.

2334. See para 28 of the Consolidated Jurisdictional Notice.

29.2.1.3   Joint ventures

This third type of concentration refers to joint ventures (JVs). These can be described as commercial arrangements between two or more undertakings to create a new entity by contributing equity and then sharing the profit/losses, expenses and control of the new entity. JVs are created in order to achieve a particular commercial goal. The term JV covers a wide variety of business arrangements, ranging from merger-like operations to co-operation for a particular function such as R&D, production, distribution, and so on. The difference between mergers and JVs is that in a JV there is no transfer of ownership. Some JVs are within the scope of the MR, others are dealt with under Article 101 TFEU. This is because the majority of competition laws, including EU competition law, treat mergers and agreements between undertakings differently. The difference rests on the theory that mergers affect the structure of the relevant market while agreements between undertakings relate to behaviour of undertakings in the relevant market. As a JV can have both behavioural and structural aspects, either the MR or Article 101 TFEU may apply depending upon whether it is a full-function or a non-full-function joint venture.

Only a full-function JV having a Community dimension is within the scope of the MR, such a JV should be notified by the parties to the Commission. Article 3(4) of the MR defines a full-function JV as a concentration where a joint venture performing on a lasting basis all the functions of an autonomous economic entity is created. The Commission's Consolidated Jurisdictional Notice explains in Chapter IV[2335] the definition set out in Article 3(4) of the MR. Three requirements must be satisfied for a JV to be within the scope of Article 3(4) of the MR:

- The first requirement is that there must be joint control by two or more entities over another entity. The concept of joint control is defined in Article 3 of the MR (see section 29.2.1.2).

- The second requirement refers to full-functionality.[2336] In this respect paragraph 93 of the Notice states that:

  > "Full function character essentially means that a joint venture must operate on a market, performing the functions normally carried out by undertakings operating on the same market. In order to do so the joint venture must have a management dedicated to its day-to-day operations and access to sufficient resources including finance, staff, and assets (tangible and intangible) in order to conduct on a lasting basis its business activities within the area provided for in the joint-venture agreement."

  Accordingly, it is essential for a JV to operate as an autonomous economic entity. Substantial dependency on parent companies will disqualify it from being "full-function". However, during the first three years of its existence support from the parent companies is allowed, for example, during that period a JV may rely almost entirely on sales to or purchases from its parent companies.

- The third requirement is that a JV must be intended to operate on a lasting basis. The period for which it has been created must be sufficiently long to bring about a lasting change in the structure of the parent undertakings. Accordingly, if a JV is created for a short finite period, it will not be considered as operating on a lasting basis. An example of this is provided in

---

2335. http://ec.europa.eu/comm/competition/mergers/legislation/jn_en.pdf.

2336. See para 92 of the Consolidated Jurisdictional Notice.

paragraph 104 of the Notice in relation to a JV established in order to construct a power plant, which excludes any involvement of the JV in the operation of the plant once the construction has been completed.

Under Article 2(4) of the MR if a joint venture falls within that definition but has as its object or effect the co-ordination of the competitive behaviour of undertakings that remain independent, such co-ordination is assessed in the light of Article 101(1) TFEU.

The MR excludes joint ventures between a parent and its subsidiary when the former uses the latter in order to co-ordinate its business practices to the detriment of fair competition in the particular market. These kinds of situation are within the realm of Articles 101 and 102 TFEU.

29.2.2 The EU dimension

The MR applies to all concentrations having an EU dimension. This occurs when they exceed either of the following thresholds (known as the quantitative jurisdictional tests):

- The combined aggregate worldwide turnover of all participating undertakings is over €5 billion and the aggregate EU-wide turnover of each of at least two of the undertakings concerned is more than €250 million, unless each of the undertakings concerned achieves more than two-thirds of its aggregate EU-wide turnover within one and the same Member State (Article 1(2) of the MR);

    This is a primary test. If the requirement for the turnover set out in Article 1(2) of the MR is satisfied but each of the undertakings concerned achieves more than two-thirds of its aggregate EU-wide turnover within one and the same Member State, the concentration has no EU dimension and thus it should be dealt with by the relevant NCA. When the primary test is not satisfied, there is a secondary test contained in Article 1(3) of the MR which may bring the intended concentration within the scope of the MR.

- The combined aggregate worldwide turnover of all the undertakings concerned is more than €2.5 billion and an aggregate EU-wide turnover of €100 million or more is spread between not fewer than three Member States, and

    (i)   Each of at least two of the undertakings concerned generates at least €25 million turnover in each of the Member States over which the above-mentioned €100 million or more turnover is spread; and

    (ii) The aggregate EU-wide turnover of each of at least two of the undertakings concerned is more than €100 million.

    However, if each of the undertakings concerned achieves more than two-thirds of its aggregate EU-wide turnover within one and the same Member State, the MR will not apply (Article 1(3) of the MR).

Article 1(3) provides for a "one-stop-shop" EU notification procedure for cross-border merger agreements which in any way involve at least three Member States and meet a slightly lower turnover criteria than those set out in Article 1(2) of the MR. The lower threshold was set out in Article 1(3) of the MR in order to bring more concentrations within the scope of the MR. It offers a substantial advantage to undertakings involved in merger agreements stretching across at least three Member States and falling short of having an EU dimension as defined in Article 1(2) of the MR. Instead of notifying their intended deal to the competent authorities in the three or more Member States concerned and being subject to investigations in all those Member States (which would impose considerable hardship on them and be very time-consuming), such undertakings can obtain a decision from the Commission within a time limit specified in the Regulation.

Article 5 of the MR provides detailed rules on how the turnover of the relevant parties is to be calculated and the Commission's Consolidated Jurisdictional Notice[2337] provides further assistance in this respect.

The thresholds in the MR are much higher than those that the Commission expected. The Commission's attempts to lower the thresholds failed. Nevertheless, the MR provides that the Commission is required to report on the operation of thresholds criteria by 1 July 2009 and may present proposals to have the thresholds amended (Article 1(4) and (5) of the MR). The Commission submitted its Report on 30 June 2009[2338] in which it concluded that the threshold criteria in Articles 1(2) and 1(3) had, in the light of corrective mechanisms, i.e. the referral mechanism, operated during the relvant period overall, in a satisfactory way in allocating jurisdiction between the Commission and NCAs. However, the Report noted that the efficiency of the merger control system across the EU could be enhanced by, inter alia, improving the pre-notification referral mechanism and by increasing the coming together of the national and EU rules on merger control.

29.2.3 Extraterritorial application of the MR

The MR has an extraterritorial scope of application.[2339] While the Commission enjoys a large measure of discretion in relation to the enforcement of Articles 101 and 102 TFEU and has used it to avoid international disputes, this is not the case in relation to the control of concentrations. It seems that once an envisaged concentration satisfies the threshold requirements, the Commission must act, or at least assess the proposed concentration from the point of view of the interests of the EU.

In order to justify the extraterritorial application of the MR, the CJEU relies on the effects doctrine (see Chapter 26.3). Its jurisdiction is justified "when it is foreseeable that a proposed concentration will have an immediate and substantial effect in the Community [in the EU]". This was stated by the CFI [the General Court] in Case T-102/96 *Gencor Ltd v Commission*.[2340]

29.3   Substantial appraisal of concentration

29.3.1   The substantive test

Provided that the intended concentration has an EU dimension within the meaning of the MR, the Commission has to assess whether it is compatible with the internal market. The substantive test for the assessment of concentration has been reworded. Article 2(2) of the MR states that:

"a concentration which would significantly impede effective competition in the common market or in a substantial part of it, in particular as a result of strengthening of a dominant position, shall be declared incompatible with the common market."

2337. Paras 157–220.
2338. The Staff Working Paper Accompanying the Communication from the Commission to the Council, Report on the Functioning of Regulation No 139/2004 [COM (2009) 281 final].
2339. See recital 10 of the preamble to the MR.
2340. [1999] ECR II-753.

The previous test under Regulation 4064/89 was exclusively related to dominance while the new test goes beyond dominance. It has two objectives: first, as before, to prohibit a concentration which strengthens or creates a dominant position, and second, to block a concentration which takes place in the context of a non-collusive oligopoly, and does not lead to a single or joint dominance, but, nevertheless, produces effects which significantly impede effective competition in the internal market or a substantial part of it.[2341]

Under Article 2(1) of the MR the Commission, in assessing whether a concentration is compatible with the internal market, should take into consideration:

- ▪ The necessity to maintain and develop effective competition within the internal market in the light, inter alia, of the structure of all the markets concerned and the actual or potential competition from undertakings established either within or outside the EU;

- ▪ The market position of the undertakings concerned, and their economic and financial power based on the following factors:

  - ● Market share;
  - ● The alternatives available to suppliers and users and their access to supplies and markets;
  - ● Any legal barriers to entry to the relevant market;
  - ● Supply and demand trends for the relevant product market;
  - ● The interests of intermediate and ultimate consumers;
  - ● The development of technical and economic progress which must bring advantages to consumers but must not constitute an obstacle to competition.

The Commission, before assessing the compatibility of a concentration with the internal market, must identify the relevant product market and the relevant geographic market.[2342]

29.3.2 The concept of collective dominance

The concept of collective dominance has the same meaning under Article 102 TFEU and under the MR. This topic is examined in Chapter 28. It is important to note that the assessment of a collective dominance under the MR is prospective. In Case C-12/03P *Commission v Tetra Laval BV*[2343] the ECJ emphasised that a prospective analysis "does not entail the examination of past events – for which often many items of evidence are available which make it possible to understand the causes – or of current events, but rather a prediction of events which are more or less likely to occur in future if a decision prohibiting the planned concentration or laying down the conditions for it is not adopted."[2344]

2341. For example, in *Linde/BOC* (COMP/M4141) Decision of 6/06/06, the Commission applied the above test to an intended concentration between two undertakings active in the helium market. The Commission prohibited the concentration on the ground that the effect of the concentration would be to significantly impede effective competition in the relevant market, although the merged entity would not become the market leader.

2342. Both concepts are examined in Chapter 28.

2343. [2005] ECR I-987.

2344. Ibid., para 42. On the standard of proof in merger control see G Drauz, "Conglomerate and Vertical Mergers in the Light of the Tetra Judgment", (2005) Competition Policy Newsletter, Nr. 2, pp 35–9.

29.4   The procedure under the MR

The basic rule is that any intended concentration satisfying the criteria laid down by the MR should be notified to the Commission after the conclusion of the agreement, announcement of the public bid, or the acquisition of a controlling interest. A concentration can neither be implemented before its notification[2345] nor until it has been cleared by the Commission as compatible with the internal market, otherwise the Commission may impose fines on the undertakings concerned.

Further, Article 7(1) of the MR provides that no concentration may come into legal effect until the Commission has delivered a compatibility decision or has failed to do this. However, this is qualified by the other provisions of Article 7.

In practice, it is unlikely that parties will fail to notify, given the adverse consequences which may result from such a situation. First, if a concentration is implemented without being notified to the Commission, the Commission may declare it incompatible with the internal market and consequently require undertakings or assets brought together to be separated or the cessation of joint control.[2346] Second, the Commission may impose fines not exceeding 10 per cent of the aggregate turnover of the undertaking concerned for intentional or negligent failure to notify a concentration in accordance with Articles 4 and 22(3) prior to its implementation.

Under Article 4(1) of the MR notification can be made where the undertakings demonstrate to the Commission a good faith intention to enter into an agreement or, in the case of a public bid, where they have publicly announced an intention to make such a bid, in a situation where their intended agreement or bid would result in a concentration with an EU dimension.

29.4.1   Pre-notification reasoned submissions

The MR introduced a pre-notification system whereby parties to a concentration are allowed to make pre-notification reasoned submissions to the Commission or the relevant NCA. This is to settle jurisdictional issues in a situation where the application of numerical turnover thresholds set out in Regulation 139/2004 may result, in a limited number of cases, in jurisdiction being assigned wrongly either to the Commission or to an NCA. A request for referral of an intended concentration to an NCA is dealt with under Article 4(4) of the MR and a request for referral to the Commission under Article 4(5) of the MR.

- Under Article 4(4) parties to a concentration with an EU dimension may ask the Commission to refer it, or some aspects of it, to an NCA of a Member State where the intended concentration may significantly affect competition in a distinct market of that Member State.

- Article 4(5) concerns a situation where a concentration does not have an EU dimension but is likely to affect at least three Member States and thus the parties are required to make multiple notifications. In this situation, the parties may ask the Commission to assess the concentration, but this request will be rejected if any of the Member States concerned disagree with the giving of jurisdiction to the Commission.

2345. There are some exceptions to this rule: see Art. 7 (2) and (3) of the MR.
2346. Para 114 of the Notice states that the parties must re-establish the status quo ante.

29.4.2   The Phase I Investigation

The Commission takes an initial decision (that is, whether the Commission has serious doubts as to the compatibility of the concentration with the internal market) within 25 working days following receipt of complete notification. This period is extended to 35 working days when a Member State, relying on Article 9 of the MR, informs the Commission that a concentration has an undesirable impact on competition within that Member State or in cases where commitments are made by the parties aimed at making the concentration compatible with the internal market. At the end of that period the Commission may:

- Declare the concentration as being outside the scope of the MR;

- Declare the concentration compatible with the internal market;

- Declare the concentration as compatible with the internal market subject to the acceptance of commitments by the parties;

- Declare that the Commission has serious doubts as to the compatibility of the concentration with the internal market.

If no decision is taken within the prescribed time limit, the concentration is deemed to be compatible with the internal market.

The Commission clears between 90 and 95 per cent of concentrations at the end of Phase I, but usually makes its authorisation subject to conditions.

29.4.3   The Phase II Investigation

If the Commission considers that the intended concentration raises serious concern, the Commission must open the Phase II Investigation, which must be concluded within 90 working days and which involves consultation with third parties. The time limit may be extended by the Commission by 15 working days where commitments (that is, adjustments to the concentration) are offered by the parties in order to satisfy the Commission's reservations on competition grounds. Further, this period may be extended to 20 working days at the request of either party, or of the Commission with the consent of the parties. In complex cases the time limit may be extended up to a maximum of 125 working days. The Commission may also "stop the clock" if it has obtained insufficient information from the undertaking concerned.[2347] If no decision is taken within the prescribed time limit, the concentration is deemed to be compatible with the internal market.

At the end of the Phase II proceedings the Commission may:

- Declare the concentration compatible with the internal market;

- Declare the concentration compatible with the internal market but impose conditions to ensure that the parties comply with the commitments they have offered. If the parties breach the commitments, the decision of compatibility can be revoked;

- Declare that the concentration is incompatible with the internal market.

2347. See Case COMP/M.2282 *Schneider/Legrand* of 10/10/2001.

The Advisory Committee on Concentrations must be consulted before a final decision is taken and when the Commission intends to impose pecuniary sanctions on an undertaking. Under the MR the Commission's powers to fine undertakings are similar to those under Regulation 1/2003 (see section 29.5).

The MR contains provisions for oral hearings and for informal and confidential discussions of proposals. The undertakings concerned are permitted to comment on any objections to the proposals by the Commission.

In order to guarantee the right of the parties, and of third parties whose interests are likely to be affected by an intended concentration, to be heard and to have access to the files of the Commission, the post of Hearing Officer was created in 1984. He/she is an independent person experienced in competition matters whose task is to ensure that the right to be heard is respected in all competition proceedings including proceedings under Articles 101 and 102 TFEU.[2348]

29.4.4 Commitments and remedies

During the examination of a notification parties are free to propose adjustments to the concentration so as to avoid a negative decision. The Commission codified its practices regarding the assessment, acceptance and implementation of commitments in Phases I and II of merger investigations in its 2001 Notice.[2349]

The Commission is very clear that promises not to abuse dominance are not sufficient. It insists upon commitments which will ensure a specific, lasting and appropriate solution to any problems created by the envisaged concentration.

The implementation of commitments must occur within a short period of time and be speedy and effective. The notice sets out deadlines for the submission of commitments in Phase I (20 working days from the submission of the notification) and in Phase II (within 65 working days of the date of the commencement of the Phase II investigation[2350]).

29.4.5 Ancillary restraints

The concept of restraints is explained in Article 10 of the Commission's 2005 Notice on Restrictions Directly Related and Necessary to Concentrations[2351] in the following terms: "In addition to these arrangements and agreements [which carry out the main object of the concentration, such as the sale of shares or assets of an undertaking] the parties to the concentration may enter into other agreements which do not form an integral part of the concentration but can restrict the parties' freedom of action in the market." Examples of restraints are non-competition clauses and restrictions imposed in licence agreements (see Chapter 27.6.3).

Restraints are part of the merger and therefore they are not separately assessed in the context of Article 101 TFEU, which is the case where restraints occur outside the context of a related

---

2348. On this topic, see Chapter 30.2.4.
2349. The Remedies Notice [2001] OJ C6/3.
2350. When commitments are offered in the Phase I Investigation, the time period for examination of a concentration is extended by 10 days. If offered in the Phase II Investigation, the time period may be extended by 15 working days. Also in the Phase II Investigation in respect of complex cases a further extension of up to 20 days may be agreed.
2351. [2005] OJ C56/3.

concentration. The Notice makes a distinction between restraints "directly related" (meaning subordinate in importance to the main object of concentration) and "necessary" (meaning that in the absence of such restraints the proposed concentration could not be implemented or could only be implemented under more unsatisfactory conditions, for example at higher cost).

The 2005 Notice provides very useful guidance on the interpretation of the notion of restraints given that it is for the parties to assess whether or not their agreement can be regarded as ancillary to a concentration. The Notice provides that if there is a genuine uncertainty as to the assessment of a restraint, that is, the case presents "novel or unresolved questions", the parties may ask the Commission to elucidate the issue (Article 3 of the 2005 Notice).

29.4.6 Simplified procedure

Reliance on the quantitative jurisdictional tests (see section 29.2.2) means that many undertakings must notify their intended concentration even though that concentration does not significantly impede effective competition in the internal market. This involves costs and inconvenience for the undertakings.

In order to alleviate this problem, the Commission issued a Notice on Simplified Procedures in 2005.[2352] According to the Notice the parties to a concentration, which is eligible for the simplified procedure, do not have to submit a full-form notification. On receipt of notification the Commission will, if appropriate, publish a notice in the Official Journal that the concentration is eligible for the simplified procedure. The purpose of the notice is to give interested parties the opportunity to make representations to the Commission, in particular on circumstances which may require an investigation. If the Commission is satisfied that the concentration meets the criteria for the simplified procedure, it will normally, within 25 working days from the date of notification, adopt a short-form clearance decision declaring the concentration compatible with the internal market, which decision will be published in the Official Journal.

Concentrations likely to be eligible for the simplified procedure are:

- Joint-ventures which have no, or negligible actual or foreseeable activities within the EEA, that is where the turnover of the joint venture or the turnover of the activities contributing to the joint venture is less than €100 million in the EEA and the total value of assets transferred to the joint venture is less than €100 million in the EEA;

- Mergers and acquisitions where none of the merging undertakings are involved in business activities in the same product and/or geographical market, or in any markets which are upstream or downstream of a product market in which any other party is engaged;

- Mergers and concentrations where two or more undertakings are involved in a horizontal relationship (that is, the same product and geographical market) provided that their combined market share is less than 15 per cent, or mergers and concentrations where two or more undertakings are involved in a vertical relationship (markets upstream or downstream of a product market) provided their combined market share is less than 25 per cent;

- Where a party is to acquire sole control of an undertaking.

2352. [2005] OJ C56/4.

However, in some circumstances, even when the above criteria are satisfied, the Commission may decide not to apply the simplified procedure, namely where:

- The intended concentration has conglomerate aspects, especially where one or more undertakings hold a market share of 25 per cent or more in any product market and particularly where there is no horizontal or vertical relationship;

- The assessment of the market share poses difficult problems, for example, the market is new or not developed;

- The market is characterised by high entry barriers, a high degree of concentration or poses other serious competition problems;

- A full-function joint venture risks the co-ordination of competitive behaviour within the meaning of Article 2(4) of the MR;

- A Member State or a third party has objected within 15 working days of receipt of a copy of the notification.

29.5   Enforcement and investigating powers of the Commission under the MR

The MR contains its own rules on investigations and on the enforcement powers of the Commission, which are broadly similar to those under Regulation 1/2003. The Commission is entitled to request information (Article 11) and to carry out on-the-spot investigations (Article 13). The Commission may also interview any natural or legal person, but only with that person's consent (Article 11(7)) but has no power to conduct "dawn raids" or any other sort of raids on the homes of directors of the undertakings concerned.

Under the MR the Commission is empowered to impose fines and pecuniary sanctions in the event of failure to notify or to co-operate.

The Commission is empowered to impose fines if the undertakings concerned fail to supply relevant information or supply incorrect or misleading information. In *Sanofi/Synthélabo*, the Commission imposed a fine of €50,000 on each of two undertakings for being grossly negligent and for supplying incorrect information when notifying their intended merger.[2353] In *Mitsubishi*,[2354] for the first time the Commission imposed a fine on a third party not involved in a concentration for failure to provide required information. In respect of procedural infringements a fine of up to 1 per cent of turnover of the undertaking or undertakings concerned may be imposed. In respect of substantial infringements a maximum fine of 10 per cent of the total worldwide turnover of the undertaking concerned achieved in the preceding business year may be imposed.

29.6   The role of Member States in the enforcement of the MR

Under the MR the Commission has exclusive power to deal with concentrations which have an EU dimension, subject to the exception mentioned below. The Commission and NCAs have a

---

2353. [2000] OJ L95/34.
2354. [2001] OJ L4/31.

duty to co-operate with each other and indeed there are situations where cases are referred from the Commission to NCAs or vice versa. The MR contains exceptions to the principle of exclusive competence of the Commission to deal with concentrations with an EU dimension. These are set out below:

 ▪ First, Article 9 (known as the German clause) provides for a referral, at the initiative of either a particular Member State or the Commission, of a concentration (this is known as a total referral) or of aspects of a concentration (this is known as a partial referral) to a NCA of a Member State where a concentration threatens to significantly affect competition in a "distinct" market in that Member State. Article 9 therefore provides a safeguard that the interests of a Member State will be taken into consideration in the assessment of a concentration either by the requesting Member State itself, when the Commission agrees to refer to the relevant NCA, or the Commission when it deals with the case.

 ▪ Second, by virtue of Article 21(4) the Commission may refer a concentration with an EU dimension to a Member State if the Commission perceives that there may be a need for a Member State to protect "legitimate interests" which are not protected by the MR. "Legitimate interests" refer to public security, plurality of media and prudential rules of a Member State. This provision is rarely used.

 ▪ Third, under Article 22 (known as the Dutch clause) a Member State may, on its own initiative or at the invitation of the Commission, refer to the Commission a concentration which does not have an EU dimension, but "affects trade between Member States and threatens to significantly affect competition within the territory of the Member State or Member States making the request". This provision is rarely used.

 ▪ Fourth, under Article 346 TFEU, when essential interests of security of a Member State are at stake, the Member State may instruct the parties to a concentration not to notify the military aspects of a concentration to the Commission.[2355] Article 346 TFEU is distinct from Article 21(4) of the MR and as a Treaty provision is hierarchically superior to the MR in terms of a ranking of the sources of EU law. When Article 346 TFEU is relied upon by a Member State, the Commission will normally assess only the non-military aspects of a concentration.

In order to rationalise the system of referral, the Commission has published a Notice on Case Allocation under the Referral rules of the Merger Regulations.[2356]

2355. See Case IV/M 1438 *British Aerospace/GEC Marconi* [1999] OJ C241/8.
2356. [2005] OJ C56/2.

AIDE-MÉMOIRE

MERGER CONTROL

The concept of concentration

There are three types of concentration:

- Where two or more previously independent undertakings merge;

- Where one or more persons already controlling at least one or more undertakings, acquire, whether by purchase of securities or assets, by contract or by any other means, direct or indirect control of the whole or parts of one or more other undertakings;

- Full-function joint ventures.

The concept of an EU dimension

A concentration has an EU dimension when it exceeds either of the following thresholds:

- The combined aggregate worldwide turnover of all participating undertakings is over €5 billion and the aggregate EU-wide turnover of each of at least two of the undertakings concerned is more than €250 million, unless each of the undertakings concerned achieves more than two-thirds of its aggregate EU-wide turnover within one and the same Member State (Article 1(2) of the MR);

- The combined aggregate worldwide turnover of all the undertakings concerned is more than €2.5 billion and an aggregate EU-wide turnover of €100 million or more is spread between not fewer than three Member States, and
  (i)   Each of at least two of the undertakings concerned generates at least €25 million turnover in each of the Member States over which the above-mentioned €100 million or more turnover is spread; and
  (ii)   The aggregate EU-wide turnover of each of at least two of the undertakings concerned is more than €100 million.
  However, if each of the undertakings concerned achieves more than two-thirds of its aggregate EU-wide turnover within one and the same Member State, the MR will not apply (Article 1(3) of the MR).

Substantial appraisal of concentration

The substantive test for the assessment of concentrations provides that:

"a concentration which would significantly impede effective competition in the common market or in a substantial part of it, in particular as a result of strengthening of a dominant position, shall be declared incompatible with the common market."

The test has two objectives:

- First, to prohibit a concentration which strengthens or creates a dominant position; and

■ Second, to block a concentration which takes place in the context of a non-collusive oligopoly, and does not lead to a single or joint dominance, but still produces effects which significantly impede effective competition in the internal market or a substantial part of it.

The procedure under the MR
Any intended concentration must be notified to the Commission after the conclusion of the agreement, announcement of the public bid, or the acquisition of a controlling interest.

Phase I Investigation
The Commission takes an initial decision (that is, whether the Commission has serious doubts as to the compatibility of the concentration with the internal market) within 25 working days following receipt of complete notification (but the time limit may be extended).

Phase II Investigation
If the Commission considers that the intended concentration raises serious concern, the Commission must open a Phase II investigation, which must be concluded within 90 working days (but the time limit may be extended) and which involves consultation with third parties.

Enforcement and investigation powers of the Commission under the MR
The MR contains its own rules on investigations and on the enforcement powers of the Commission, which are broadly similar to those under Regulation 1/2003. The Commission is entitled to:

■ Request information (Article 11);

■ Carry out on-the-spot investigations (Article 13);

■ Interview any natural or legal person, but only with their consent (Article 11(7));

■ Impose fines for failure to notify or co-operate;

but has no power to conduct "dawn raids" or any other sort of raids on the homes of directors of the undertakings concerned.

The role of the Member States in the enforcement of the MR
The exceptions to the principle of exclusive competence of the Commission to deal with a concentration with an EU dimension are set out below:

■ First, Article 9 (known as the German clause) provides for a referral, at the initiative of either a particular Member State or the Commission, of a concentration (this type of referral is known as a total referral) or aspects of a concentration (this is known as a partial referral) to the NCA of a Member State where a concentration threatens to significantly affect competition in a "distinct" market in that Member State;

■ Second, by virtue of Article 21(4) the Commission may refer a concentration with an

EU dimension to a Member State if the Commission perceives that there may be a need for a Member State to protect its "legitimate interests" which are not protected by the MR;

- Third, under Article 22 (known as the Dutch clause) a Member State may, on its own initiative or at the invitation of the Commission, refer to the Commission a concentration which does not have an EU dimension, but "affects trade between Member States and threatens to significantly affect competition within the territory of the Member State or Member States making the request";

- Fourth, under Article 346 TFEU, when essential interests of security of a Member State are at stake, the Member State may instruct the parties to a concentration not to notify the military aspects of a concentration to the Commission.

RECOMMENDED READING

Books

Furse, M., *The Law of Merger Control in the EC and the UK*, 2007, Oxford: Hart Publishing

Ilzkovitz, F. and Meiklejohn, R. (eds), *European Merger Control: Do We Need an Efficiency Defence?*, 2006, Cheltenham: Edward Elgar

Kekelekis, M., *EC Merger Control Regulation: Rights of Defence*, 2006, The Hague: Kluwer Law International

Articles

Gerard, D., "Protectionist Threats against Cross-border Mergers: Unexplored Avenues to Strengthen the Effectiveness of Article 21 ECMR", (2008) 45 CMLRev, p 987

Howarth, D., "The Court of First Instance in GE/Honeywell", (2006) ECLR, p 485

Reeves, T., and Dodoo, N., "Standards of Proof and Standards of Judicial Review in European Commission Merger Law", (2006), 29 Fordham Int'l L.J., p 1034

Riesenkampff, A., "The New EC Merger Control Test under Article 2 of the Merger Control Regulation", (2004) 24 Nw. J. Int'l L. & Bus., p 715

30

ENFORCEMENT OF ARTICLES 101 AND 102 TFEU

CONTENTS

SUMMARY

1. This chapter examines the enforcement of Articles 101 and 102 TFEU by the Commission, by national courts and by NCAs and the manner in which all competition law enforcement bodies within the EU are required to co-operate in order to ensure the uniform application of EU competition law.

2. A process of modernisation and simplification of EU competition law has resulted in the major overhaul of the enforcement of Articles 101 and 102 TFEU. Its main components are:

■ First, prior to the overhaul (which decentralised the enforcement of EU competition law) national courts could apply Articles 101(1) and 102 TFEU, as both have direct effect, but not Article 101(3) TFEU. As a result of Regulation 1/2003 the Commission has relinquished its exclusive power to grant exemptions under Article 101(3) TFEU. This article has become directly effective and can be applied by NCAs and national courts. The major implication for undertakings is that the previous system of notification under Article 101(3) TFEU has been abolished. If an agreement satisfies the requirements of Article 101(3) TFEU, it is valid and enforceable ab initio. It is for the undertaking concerned to assess whether this is the case and, if necessary, to defend its assessment before national courts and NCAs.

- Second, under Regulation 1/2003 the Commission shares its enforcement powers with NCAs and national courts. The decentralisation of the enforcement of Articles 101 and 102 TFEU means that when the jurisdictional threshold concerning effect on trade between Member States is met, the relevant NCA is required to apply Articles 101 and 102 TFEU alone or together with relevant national competition rules. However, based on the supremacy of EU law, agreements which are not in breach of Article 101(1) TFEU cannot be challenged under national law, although a stricter national law than EU competition law is allowed to be applied to unilateral conduct of undertakings. The new system allows the Commission to concentrate its resources on the most serious infringements of EU competition law which have appreciable effect on trade between Member States.

3. The Commission may become aware of an infringement of EU competition law through many sources; one of them is via a complaint lodged by a Member State or any natural or legal person who can show a legitimate interest. The Commission is required to reply to the complainant. Failure to do this may result in an action under Article 265 TFEU. The first stage in the Commission's investigation concerns the gathering of information. This may take various forms: from issuing of a "simple" request for information which the undertaking concerned may ignore as there is no penalty for failure to respond (although a false or misleading response may be subject to a fine) to including entering any premises of the undertaking, as well as homes of individual directors, managers and staff, on a reasonable suspicion that important documents are likely to be found there.

In the next stage of proceedings the Commission must decide whether to send a Statement of Objections (SO) to the undertaking concerned; if it does so, that undertaking's right to defence must be respected. Further, the undertaking has the right to have access to the Commission's file, except to confidential documents and documents which do not form part of the investigation (internal documents of the Commission and the NCAs).

4. The Commission may adopt final decisions and procedural decisions during investigations. These decisions may concern:

- A finding and termination of infringements;

- Interim measures;

- Commitments;

- Findings of inapplicability.

5. The Commission can impose the following fines on undertakings (but not on individuals):

- Substantive fines for:

  - Infringements of Articles 101 and 102;
  - Failure to comply with an interim measures decision; and
  - Failure to comply with a binding commitment made under Article 9 of Regulation 1/2003.

  These can be as high as 10 per cent of the undertaking's global turnover in the preceding business year.

- Procedural fines up to 1 per cent of an undertaking's global turnover in the preceding business year when the undertaking has committed offences in relation to requests for information or inspections.

■ Periodic penalty payments for defiance of the Commission of up 5 per cent of the average daily turnover in the preceding business year at a daily rate.

6. The Commission runs a leniency programme, first started in 1996 and subsequently revised in 2002 and 2006, which aims at combating cartels. It offers undertakings participating in a cartel immunity or reduction of fines which would have been imposed had the Commission discovered the cartel, in exchange for self-reporting and co-operation in the Commission's investigation.

7. National courts have an important role to play in the enforcement of EU competition law having been empowered to apply Article 101 TFEU in its entirety since the entry into force of Regulation 1/2003. The basic rules on co-operation between the Commission and national courts are defined in the 2004 Commission's Notice on Co-operation between the Commission and the Courts of the EU Member States.

Enforcement of EU competition law before national courts has been regarded by the Commission as vital. In 2008 the Commission published a White Paper on antitrust damages actions by private claimants, a follow-up to its 2005 Green Paper.

8. In order to ensure consistency and uniformity in the parallel enforcement of Articles 101 and 102 TFEU (by NCAs and by the Commission), Regulation 1/2003 sets out basic rules on co-operation between the Commission and the NCAs and between NCAs themselves. These rules mainly concern matters relating to allocation of cases, exchange of information and consultation. To foster co-operation between NCAs, an informal "European Competition Network" (ECN), consisting of all NCAs and the Commission, was set up. The ECN has no legal status. It provides a forum for discussions and exchange of information on best practices. At the time of writing the main achievement of the ECN is the adoption of a Model Leniency Programme with a view to improving the handling of parallel leniency applications in the ECN.

30.1 Introduction

Under Article 103 TFEU the Council is empowered to adopt any appropriate measures in order to give effect to Articles 101 and 102 TFEU. The first and the most important implementing measure was Council Regulation 17/62[2357] adopted by the Council in 1962 which set out detailed rules for the application of Articles 81 and 82 EC [Articles 101 and 102 TFEU]. Regulation 17/62 provided for a centralised enforcement system in which the Commission was in charge of the notification procedure under Article 81(3) EC [Article 101(3) TFEU].

When Regulation 17/62 was adopted the Community had only six Member States and the internal market was at the nascent stage. With the development and expansion of the EU a new approach was needed. The Commission recognised this and in May 1999 published a White Paper which proposed a profound reform of the rules implementing Articles 81 and 82 EC [Articles 101 and 102 TFEU].[2358] The Commission explained that there was a need for modernisation of EU competition law taking into account the following external factors:

■ The enlargement of the EU;

■ The existence of a single market and single currency; and

2357. [1959–61] OJ Spec. Ed, 87.
2358. [1999] OJ C132/1.

▪ The globalisation of economy;

and the following internal factors:

▪ The limited resources available to the Commission;

▪ The requirements of the principle of subsidiarity; and

▪ The need for coherent application of competition rules at national and at EU levels entailing the avoidance of parallel proceedings before the Commission and national authorities.

With regard to the enforcement of Articles 81 and 82 EC [Articles 101 and 102 TFEU], the reform culminated with the adoption of Regulation 1/2003,[2359] which entered into force on 1 May 2004. The Regulation is accompanied by Regulation 773/2004[2360] on the Conduct of Proceedings by the Commission Pursuant to Articles 81 and 82 of the EC Treaty [Articles 101 and 102 TFEU] (which gives "flesh to the bare bones" of Regulation 1/2003 – the implementing regulation) and a number of notices and guidelines forming the so-called "Modernisation Package".[2361]

The two main themes of the modernisation were simplification and decentralisation. This was achieved by the following:

A. The replacement of the notification and authorisation system by a "legal exception" system.

Under the legal exception system, agreements, decisions and concerted practices are lawful from the outset if they do not breach Article 101(1) TFEU or if they meet the conditions set out in Article 101(3) TFEU. According to Article 1 of Regulation 1/2003, commercial arrangements within the meaning of Article 101(1) TFEU need no longer be notified to the Commission in order to obtain exemption. Undertakings themselves must assess whether their agreements, decisions or concerted practices meet the criteria set out in Article 101(3) TFEU and be ready to defend their assessment before national courts and NCAs.

B. Direct applicability of Article 101(3) TFEU

Article 101 TFEU became directly applicable in its entirety, whereas previously only the first two paragraphs were directly applicable. This means that national courts and NCAs are empowered to apply directly not only Articles 101(1) and (2) TFEU and 102 TFEU but also Article 101(3) TFEU.

C. Decentralisation of enforcement

Under Regulation 1/2003 the Commission shares its enforcement powers with NCAs and national courts. The decentralisation of the enforcement of Articles 101 and 102 TFEU means that when the jurisdictional threshold concerning effect on trade between Member States is met (see Chapter 26.6), the relevant NCA is required to apply Articles 101 and 102 TFEU alone or together with relevant national competition rules. The Commission supervises the system and will intervene whenever necessary to ensure that EU competition law is applied consistently and uniformly in the Member States.

2359. [2003] OJ L1/1. It replaced Regulation 1/17.
2360. [2004] OJ L123/18.
2361. Detailed examination of the modernisation "package" is provided in this chapter.

This system allows the Commission to concentrate its limited resources on important matters and the most serious infringements of EU law, leaving less important tasks to NCAs and national courts. The Commission alone is empowered to initiate legislation at EU level in competition matters as well as to draw up further notices and guidelines to assist national authorities in the application of EU competition rules and policies. In order to make the system work properly, a mechanism entitled the European Competition Network (ECN) was set up to increase co-operation between the Commission and NCAs.

D.   Increase of the Commission's investigatory powers
The Commission's investigatory powers were increased, particularly with regard to obtaining information from undertakings under investigation. Regulation 1/2003 also provides for additional fines for failure to co-operate with the Commission.

E.   Confirmation of the application of EU law over national law
In order to ensure uniformity in the application of EU competition law Article 3 of Regulation 1/2003 sets out the relationship between Articles 101 and 102 TFEU and national competition law. Under Article 3(1) national courts and NCAs are required to apply EU competition law alongside national law whenever a case falls within the scope of Articles 101 and 102 TFEU. They may also apply Articles 101 and 102 TFEU exclusively. Further, in order to ensure the supremacy and the effectiveness of EU competition law Article 3(2) provides that any commercial arrangement which is lawful under Article 101 EC is also lawful under national competition law. However, Member States are not precluded from adopting and applying on their territory stricter national laws which prohibit or sanction unilateral conduct engaged in by undertakings, that is, national competition rules which are stricter than Article 102 TFEU. Accordingly, when conduct of an undertaking does not amount to an abuse as understood under Article 102 TFEU but constitutes an abuse under national competition law, the relevant NCA is allowed to prohibit or sanction such conduct in conformity with national rules.

It seems that the ECN system is working well.[2362]

30.2   Enforcement of Articles 101 and 102 TFEU by the Commission

Within the Commission the Directorate General for Competition (DG Competition) is in charge of competition policy and enforcement of EU competition law. DG Competition comprises 10 directorates covering management, antitrust and merger policy, cartel enforcement, sectoral expertise (four directorates) and state aid (three directorates). A Director General, who is a career manager, is responsible for DG Competition and reports directly to the Commissioner for Competition.

2362.   According to P. Lowe, the Director General of DG Competition: ". . . we can only be impressed with the way that the European Competition Network is functioning", in "Anti-trust Reform in Europe: A Year in Practice", a paper delivered at the European Commission Conference held in Brussels on 11 March 2005. See also the Commission's Report on Competition Policy 2006, p 19. Both are available at the official site of the EU's competition policy – news, legislation, cases at http://ec.europa.eu/competition/index_en.html (accessed in December 2009).

DG Competition employs a chief economist, who works with a team to provide independent advice on economic issues in the application of EU competition law, in general and in respect of particular cases, and who co-ordinates the activities of the Economic Advisory Group on Competition Policy. The post of chief economist is of great importance given that enforcement of competition law is inextricably linked with economics, in particular with its branch called industrial organisation. Its creation was the Commission's response to criticism that it neglected the importance of economic analyses to the application of competition law.

There are two hearing officers who are independent of DG Competition and who report directly to the Commissioner for Competition (see section 30.2.4).

The procedures and powers of the Commission in competition matters are dealt with below.

30.2.1 The initiation of proceedings: complaints to the Commission in respect of infringements of Articles 101 and 102 TFEU

The Commission may become aware of the infringement of EU competition law through any source, for example, the press, TV, complaints from competitors and the general public. It may act ex officio, or upon an application from a Member State, or from "any natural or legal person who can show a legitimate interest" (Article 7 of Regulation 1/2003). It is not difficult to show such an interest. Complainants must demonstrate that their interest is, or is likely to be, adversely affected by the anti-competitive conduct of an undertaking.[2363]

Under Regulation 1/2003 a complaint may be made to both the Commission and the relevant NCA. The Commission's 2004 Notice on the Handling of Complaints by the Commission under Articles 81 and 82 of the Treaty[2364] [Articles 101 and 102 TFEU] provides guidance to a potential complainant. According to the Notice a complaint should be lodged with the authority which is best placed to deal with it. In this respect the Commission's Notice on Co-operation (see section 30.4.1) is helpful as it sets out criteria for identifying the best placed authority in respect of allocation of cases between the Commission and the Member States. Article 23 of the 2004 Notice on the Handling of Complaints provides that the members of the ECN will endeavour to determine within the time limit of two months which NCA is best placed to deal with the complaint, and that complainants must be informed of the location at which their complaint is being dealt with and of any change in that location. Under Article 25 of the 2004 Notice the Commission may reject a complaint on the ground that a NCA is dealing with, or has dealt with the case. The Commission must inform the complainant without delay of the NCA which is dealing with or has dealt with the case.

Any letter of complaint must be written on the official form ("Form C").

The Commission is under a duty to reply to a complainant.[2365] Failure so to do may result in an action under Article 265 TFEU for failure to act.

A complainant should take into consideration many factors when choosing whether to bring an action based on Article 101 or Article 102 before national authorities, national courts or before the Commission. The factors include:

2363. See Case T-144/92 *BEMIM v Commission* [1995] ECR II-147, where it was accepted that a trade association had standing in a situation where its members were likely to be adversely affected by the conduct complained of.

2364. [2004] OJ C101/65.

2365. Case 210/81 *Demo-Studio Schmidt* [1983] ECR 3045.

▪ The inability of the Commission to award damages to an aggrieved party or to provide the remedy of restitution;

▪ The powers of the Commission to investigate the alleged infringement, which are more extensive than those of national authorities;

▪ The cost of proceedings before national courts whereas proceedings before the Commission are free;

▪ The possibility for the Commission to impose substantial fines;

▪ The length of time likely to be taken to achieve the desired result.

In Case T-24/90 *Automec (II)* [2366] the CFI [the General Court] stated that the procedure concerning individual complaints before the Commission could be divided into three stages:

▪ First stage: the submission of the complaint, which is followed by the gathering of information by the Commission and involves informal contact with the parties;

▪ Second stage (if appropriate): notification by the Commission of its intention not to pursue the complaint, specifying the reasons for the Commission's decision and inviting complainants to submit their observations within a fixed time limit;

▪ Third stage: following receipt of observations from the complainants, if any (or in the absence of the second stage), the Commission has a duty[2367] either to initiate a procedure against the subject of the complaint or to adopt a definitive decision rejecting the complaint.

In Case C-282/95P *Guérin*,[2368] the ECJ specified that at the end of the third stage the Commission is required to take a definitive position as to whether to proceed with the complaint within a reasonable time.[2369] If the Commission adopts a final decision on rejection or acceptance of a complaint, the complainant has locus standi to seek judicial review of that decision under Article 263 TFEU.[2370]

30.2.1.1   The meaning of "EU interest"

The Commission may reject a complaint on the ground that it does not raise sufficient EU interest. The concept of "EU interest" was clarified by the CFI in Case T-24/90 *Automec II*.[2371] In that case the CFI [the General Court] stated that the Commission is entitled to prioritise cases and assess on a factual and legal basis whether a case raises significant EU interest, in particular as regards the functioning of the internal market, the probability of establishing the existence of an

---

2366. [1992] ECR II-2223.
2367. Case C-282/95P *Guérin* [1997] ECR I-1503.
2368. Ibid.
2369. Case T-127/98 *UPS Europe SA v Commission* [1999] ECR II-2633.
2370. Case 26/76 *Metro v Commission* [1977] ECR 1875.
2371. [1992] ECR II-2223. The definition of "EU interest" provided in *Automec* rather than that provided in Article 44 of the 2004 Notice was applied by the CFI in Case T-458/04 *Au Lys de France SA* [2007] ECR II-71.

infringement and the required scope of the investigation. Thus, the Commission is not required to start an investigation in each case, although it is obliged to reply to the complainant.

Some helpful guidelines as to the criteria to be applied in order to assess whether a particular case has an EU interest are provided by Article 44 of the 2004 Notice on Handling Complaints. These are:

- Whether or not complainants can bring action to enforce their rights before a national court;

- The seriousness, duration, and effect within the EU of the alleged infringement on competition;

- The significance of the alleged infringement as regards the functioning of the internal market, the probability of establishing the existence of the infringement and the scope of the investigation to be carried out;

- The stage of investigation if the investigation has already commenced;

- Whether or not the infringement has ceased and if so whether its anti-competitive effects are serious and persistent;

- Whether the undertaking concerned, as a result of the complaint, has agreed to change its conduct in such a way that it can be considered that there is no longer a sufficient EU interest to intervene.

30.2.2 The first stage of the procedure: obtaining information

Under Article 18 of Regulation 1/2003 the Commission has power to compel undertakings to provide "all necessary information". In Case 374/87 *Orkem*,[2372] the ECJ held that it is up to the Commission to decide what information is "necessary" and that "necessary information" relates to anything which is connected to or has some relationship to the information requested and the infringement under investigation.

In Case C-36/92P *Samenwerkende Elektriciteits Produktiebedrijven (SEP) NV v Commission*,[2373] the ECJ further explained that information should be regarded as necessary if it has some connection with the alleged infringement, assists detection of, or confirmation of, the alleged infringement or confirms evidence already gathered by the Commission.

The request for information may take two forms. Under Regulation 1/2003 the Commission can choose which is the most appropriate in the light of the circumstances of the case.

- A simple request. The Commission may ask the competent authorities of the Member States, their officials and other servants, undertakings and associations of undertakings for information. There is no duty to comply with a simple request. However, if incorrect or misleading information is supplied, the Commission may impose a fine up to 1 per cent of the undertaking's turnover in the preceding business year.

- A formal decision requiring the information to be provided. If the Commission adopts a

---

2372. [1989] ECR 3283.
2373. [1994] ECR I-1911.

decision requesting information and the undertaking concerned fails to comply within a time limit specified in that decision, the Commission may impose periodic penalties under Article 24 (up to 5 per cent of the average daily turnover). The Commission has a duty to send a copy of a decision to the NCA in the place of the seat of the undertaking and to the Member States which are affected. Often when an addressee of a simple request for information fails to provide it within a fixed time limit or supplies incomplete or inexact information, the Commission adopts a formal decision requiring the supply of information.

Each of the above requests for information must specify the legal basis and the reason for the request, the information requested, the consequences of an incorrect or misleading response and a deadline for response.

30.2.2.1 Incriminating information

In Case 27/88 *Solvay*[2374] and in Case 374/87 *Orkem SA*[2375] the issue was whether an undertaking under investigation could refuse to supply the relevant information by relying on the right not to incriminate oneself. The ECJ held that it is the task of the Commission to evidence the infringement of Article 81(1) and 82 EC [Articles 101(1) or 102 TFEU] and that an undertaking cannot be compelled to admit an infringement, as this would undermine its rights to defence, but added that an undertaking is obliged to co-operate with the Commission and thus to supply documents required by the Commission even though these might serve to establish the infringement.[2376]

It follows from the above that the ECJ, on the one hand, recognises the right not to self-incriminate by admitting the infringement but, on the other, refuses the right not to provide evidence against oneself. This position is contrary to the case law of the European Court of Human Rights (ECtHR), which has developed subsequent to the judgment of the ECJ in *Orkem*. The ECtHR in, inter alia, *Funke v France*,[2377] *Saunders v UK*[2378] and *J.B. v Switzerland*[2379] ruled that the right to remain silent and not to contribute to incriminating oneself applies to undertakings and is therefore covered by Article 6 of the ECHR.

In *PVC Cartel II*,[2380] the undertakings concerned argued that EC competition law should adjust to the case law of the ECtHR. The ECJ held that the developments in the ECtHR jurisprudence since *Orkem* did not change the position of EC law on these matters. The ECJ in *PVC Cartel II* stated that the right of undertakings not to be compelled by the Commission to admit an infringement of EC competition law is to be understood as meaning that: "in the event of a dispute as to the scope of a question, it must be determined whether an answer from the undertaking to which the question is addressed is in fact equivalent to the admission of an infringement, such as to undermine the rights of the defence." In this judgment the ECJ emphasised that the case law of the ECtHR requires:

2374. [1989] ECR 3355.

2375. [1989] ECR 3283.

2376. This was confirmed in Case C-301/04P *Commission v SGL Carbon* [2006] ECR I-5915.

2377. (1993) 16 EHRR 297. The ECtHR held that anyone charged with a criminal offence has the right to remain silent and not to contribute to incriminating himself. This includes the right not to supply incriminating documents.

2378. (1997) 23 EHRR 313.

2379. [2001] 12/5–6 Human Rights Case Digest p 281.

2380. Cases C-238, 244–245, 247, 250–252 and 254/99P *Limburgse Vinyl Maatschappij NV and Others v Commission* [2002] ECR I-8375.

- First, the exercise of coercion against the suspect in order to obtain information from him or her; and

- Second, establishment of an actual interference with the protected right

in order for there to be a violation of Article 6 (see section 30.2.8).

30.2.2.2   Legal profession privilege (LPP)

The principle of lawyer–client confidentiality is recognised under EU law, but a distinction is made between communications between a client and its in-house lawyer and a client and its independent lawyer.[2381]

At the time of writing, only communications between a client and an independent lawyer, which are made for the purpose and in the interests of the client's rights of defence, are privileged. The explanation is that an in-house lawyer is bound to his client by an employment relationship and that in some Member States there are differing rules of ethics with regard to independent lawyers and in-house lawyers.

It was expected that this position might change as a result of the order in Case T-125/03 and T-253/03 *Akzo Nobel Chemicals Ltd and Akcros Chemicals Ltd v Commission*, in which the president of the CFI [General Court] stated in his Order[2382] of 30 October 2003 that the arguments presented by Akzo regarding the extension of professional privilege to cover communications with in-house lawyers were not unfounded, in particular (as was the situation in this case) when an in-house-lawyer is subject to professional rules equivalent to those imposed on an independent lawyer. However, on 17 September 2007 the CFI [the General Court][2383] rendered a judgment maintaining the pre-existing position. The Court held that there was no valid reason to reconsider that position given that comparative examination of national laws of the Member States shows that a large number of them exclude in-house lawyers from the benefit of LPP, and that the principle of equal treatment in the context of the right of establishment and the right to provide services has not been infringed, given that the situation of an independent lawyer and an in-house lawyer are different due to the functional, structural and hierarchical integration of in-house lawyers within the undertakings that employ them.

In the above case the CFI [the General Court] made important statements regarding privileged documents:

- It held that during investigations the Commission is not allowed to take even a cursory look at documents which are claimed by the undertaking concerned as being privileged;

- The Commission is not entitled to read such documents before it adopts a decision refusing to classify such documents as privileged, and before a challenge, if any, to that decision by the undertaking concerned has been rejected by the CFI [the General Court];

- Documents which were drafted exclusively for the purpose of seeking legal advice from an independent lawyer in the exercise of the rights of defence, even if they have not been communicated with a lawyer, may be classified as privileged;

2381. Case 155/79 *AM and S Ltd v Commission* [1982] ECR 1575.

2382. [2003] ECR II-4771.

2383. [2007] ECR II-3523.

■ Documents which were discussed with an independent lawyer are not necessarily covered by LPP. This depends on whether they were prepared for the purpose of seeking legal advice.

30.2.2.3   *Power to take statements*

Article 19 of Regulation 1/2003 gives the Commission a new power to interview any natural or legal persons, with their consent, in order to collect information relating to the investigation. An NCA in whose territory the interview is taking place must be informed and is entitled to be present during interviews.

30.2.2.4   *Sector enquiries*

Under Article 17 of Regulation 1/2003 the Commission is empowered to conduct general enquiries into any economic sector if there is a suspicion that competition conditions in that sector are restricted or distorted. The Commission is entitled to request information from undertakings in the sector under investigation.

The objective of sector enquiries is to study the functioning of the relevant sector and to decide what measures, if any, should be taken to improve conditions of competition in that sector. Since the entry into force of Regulation 1/2003 this provision has often been used. The Commission has launched enquiries into, inter alia, the retail banking sector, the energy sector, the pharmaceutical industry and the financial services sector. Accordingly, the reform of the enforcement of EU competition law allows the Commission to be more proactive in the enforcement of that law, and sector enquiries, which were very rarely carried out under the old regulation, are the best example of this.

30.2.3   Inspections

Article 20 of Regulation 1/2003 defines the Commission's powers of investigation.

Article 20(2) authorises the Commission to undertake all necessary investigations into undertakings and associations of undertakings including:

■ Examination of books and other business records;

■ Taking copies of or extracts from the books and business records;

■ Asking for oral explanations on the spot;

■ Entering any premises, land and means of transport belonging to undertakings;

■ Sealing any business premises and books or records for the period and to the extent necessary for the inspection. If seals are broken, the Commission may impose a fine on the undertaking of up to 1 per cent of its total turnover in the preceding year.

Investigations may be carried out under a "simple" written authorisation given by the Commission or under a formal decision adopted by the Commission, and with or without prior notification to the undertaking concerned.

In Case 136/79 *National Panasonic v EC Commission*,[2384] the ECJ held that the Commission

---

2384. [1980] ECR 2033.

may choose between a simple written authorisation and a formal decision in the light of the special features of each case. Both the written authorisation and the formal decision must specify the subject-matter and purpose of the investigation.

An undertaking is not obliged to submit to investigation under a "simple authorisation". Due notice of its refusal is, however, taken by the Commission's officials. In such a situation the Commission may adopt a formal decision to inspect. Also, when the Commission fears that vital evidence may be destroyed, it adopts a formal decision. Refusal of an undertaking to submit to an investigation ordered by way of a decision was examined in Cases 46/87 and 227/88 *Hoechst AG v Commission*.[2385]

THE FACTS WERE:

The plaintiff objected to the conduct of the search on the ground that this had infringed general principles of Community law [EU law] and the need to respect due process of law as enshrined in the ECHR.

Held:

The ECJ held that certain rights of the defence, such as the right to legal representation and the privileged nature of correspondence between an independent lawyer and his client, must be respected as from the preliminary inquiry stage. Other rights of defence which relate to the contentious proceedings which follow the delivery of the statement of objections could be overridden during the investigations stage, taking into account that inspections may be decisive in providing evidence of the unlawful nature of conduct engaged in by undertakings.[2386]

Commission officials may decide to carry out a so-called "dawn raid" – that is, arrive at the undertaking's premises without warning (at any time of day!). In such event, the undertaking under investigation is legally obliged to submit to an investigation ordered by the Commission's decision under Article 20(4) of Regulation 1/2003. However, if it refuses to admit the Commission staff, under EU law alone the Commission's officials are not entitled to enter the premises of the undertaking under investigation. They have to respect the relevant procedural guarantees laid down in the national law of the undertaking under investigation.

Under Article 20(5), at the request of the Commission, officials of the relevant NCA shall actively assist the Commission with inspections. Article 20(6) provides that when an undertaking refuses to submit to investigations, NCAs are required to provide necessary assistance to enable the Commission to make its investigation. Article 20(7) states that if judicial authorisation is required, such authorisation should be applied for. Article 20(8) incorporates the principle emanating from Case C-94/00 *Roquette Frères SA v Commission*,[2387] in which the ECJ held that when judicial authorisation is required, a national court is neither entitled to call into question the need for the investigations (since only the ECJ can review the acts of the Commission) nor demand to

---

2385. [1989] ECR 2859.
2386. Case 322/81 *NV Nederlandsche Banden Industrie Michelin (Michelin I) v Commission* [1983] ECR 361.
2387. [2002] ECR I-9011.

be supplied with all the information in the Commission's possession. A national court is empowered to verify whether the Commission's decision is authentic and whether the coercive measures sought are arbitrary or excessive. If in doubt, a national court may ask the Commission to provide further clarification.

It is also clear that the Commission is not permitted to carry out "fishing expeditions". The subject of the investigations must be specified in an authorisation or decision, that is, the suspicion which the Commission is seeking to verify must be clearly indicated, but, as the ECJ held in *Hoechst*, the Commission is not obliged to provide the addressee with all information at its disposal in relation to the alleged infringement.

30.2.3.1 Inspections in premises other than those of an undertaking under investigation

Incriminating documents may be kept at other premises including private homes.[2388] Article 21 of Regulation 1/2003 gives the Commission power to search private homes, subject to prior judicial authorisation, if such documents are likely to be kept there.

30.2.4 The second stage of the procedure: hearings

Under both Article 27 of Regulation 1/2003 and Article 10(1) of Regulation 773/2004 the Commission is required to give undertakings concerned the opportunity to be heard before adopting any decision finding an infringement, taking interim measures or imposing fines or periodic payments.

The first step of the contentious procedure starts when the Commission sends a written letter to the undertaking concerned specifying the objections raised against it. This "statement of objections" (SO) must set forth clearly all the essential facts upon which the Commission relies against the undertaking. In the final decision the Commission must repeat only objections set out in the statement of objections and cannot add any new matters. This is to ensure that the undertaking concerned is aware of the allegations to which it will wish to respond and to protect the undertaking's right to be heard.[2389] The Commission specifies a time limit for a written submission which an undertaking concerned may submit in response to the statement of objections. An undertaking is not obliged to reply,[2390] although this is necessary if the undertaking wishes to have the opportunity to submit its arguments orally at an oral hearing.

The Commission will offer the parties the opportunity to attend an oral hearing. In order to ensure that the rights of the parties are respected, hearings are conducted by persons appointed by the Commission and referred to as "hearing officers". This post was created in 1982[2391] to respond to criticism that the Commission acts as prosecutor, jury and judge and uses biased evidence against the defendant. The powers of hearing officers were greatly extended by Commission

---

2388. In *SAS/Maersk Air* [2001] OJ L265/15 the Commission discovered incriminating documents relating to a market sharing agreement in individuals' homes.

2389. Joined Cases C-89/85, C-114/85, C-116/85, C-117/85 and C-125/85 to C-129/85 *Ahlström [Re Wood Pulp Cartel]* [1993] ECR I-1307.

2390. Case T-30/89 *Hilti* [1991] ECR II-1439.

2391. [1982] OJ C251/2 and the Commission Decision 94/810 [1994] OJ L330/67.

Decision 2001/462.[2392] The hearing officer, an independent person (although appointed by the Commission and attached to the commissioner in charge of competition) experienced in competition matters and of high moral standing, is familiar with the file, and ensures that the hearing is properly conducted and that the requirements of due process are respected. On the one hand, hearing officers ensure that the Commission, when preparing a decision in the matter under consideration, is aware of all factual aspects of the case irrespective of whether they are favourable or unfavourable to the party, and, on the other hand, have authority to decide on procedural matters such as the granting of extensions with regard to responses to the SO, further access to the Commission's file and the admission to a hearing of third parties interested in the outcome of the case.

Hearing officers may organise meetings with the parties concerned before the formal hearing. They are entitled to get in touch with the member of the Commission in charge of the case and they submit a final report to the commissioner in charge of competition, which report is attached to the final decision of the Commission and published in the Official Journal. The parties summoned to attend the hearing must appear either in person or be represented by their legal or duly authorised representatives.[2393] They may be assisted by lawyers or other qualified persons admitted by the Hearing Officer.[2394] At hearings lawyers can only assist the parties and not represent them. The reason is that only factual matters are discussed at hearings, and not legal arguments. Hearings are conducted in private and often last no more than one day, but their duration depends upon the complexity of the case.

30.2.5 Access to documents

Access to documents relevant to the case is of vital importance to the parties concerned. The extent to which a party can have access to documents has been specified in a number of cases decided by the EU judicature, and further explained by the Commission in its Notice on the internal rules of procedure for processing requests for access to the file in competition matters.[2395] The principle that interested parties should have access to all files held by the Commission is subject to two exceptions:[2396]

■ The first concerns access to documents which the Commission considers to be confidential. Article 245 TFEU imposes a duty of confidentiality on the members of the Commission. This general duty of confidentiality is reinforced by Article 28 of Regulation 1/2003 which provides that information collected for the purposes of investigation in competition matters must only be used for the purposes for which it was acquired. Two kinds of documents may be identified: those concerning business secrets and those relating to other confidential documents.

2392. [2001] OJ L162/21.
2393. Article 14(4) of Regulation 773/2004.
2394. Article 14(5) of Regulation 773/2004.
2395. [1997] OJ C25/3.
2396. Case T-7/89 *Hercules* [1991] ECR II-1711; Case C-185/95P *Baustahlgewebe GmbH v Commission* [1999] ECR I-8417; Cases C-204–205/00P, C-211/00P, C-231/00P, C-217/00P and C-219/00P *Aalborg Portland A/S and Others v Commission* [2004] ECR I-123.

● Documents which relate to business secrets. In Case 53/85 *AKZO*,[2397] the ECJ emphasised that undertakings have a legitimate interest in protecting their business secrets, taking into account the extremely serious damage which could result from improper communication of documents to a competitor. In *AKZO*, the ECJ held that it is for the Commission to judge whether or not a particular document contains business secrets. If there is a request from a third party to consult a particular document, the Commission must inform the undertaking from which this document was taken. If the undertaking concerned identifies that this document is of a confidential nature, the Commission has two options. First, it may agree with the undertaking concerned, whereupon this document will not be communicated to a third party. Second, the Commission may disagree, in which case it must give the undertaking an opportunity to state its views. If the Commission still disagrees, it is required to adopt a decision in that connection which contains an adequate statement of the reasons on which it is based and which must be notified to the undertaking concerned. The Commission must, before implementing its decision, give the undertaking an opportunity to bring an action before the General Court with a view to having the decision reviewed by it and to prevent disclosure of the document in question. The right of an undertaking to protect documents containing business secrets is contained in Article 27(2) of Regulation 1/2003 and Article 15(2) of Regulation 773/2004 (for exchange of information between the Commission and NCAs and between NCAs themselves see section 30.4).

● Other confidential documents. The Commission will refuse access to other documents in order to protect the identity of an informer, or if documents were supplied to the Commission subject to a condition of non-disclosure, or if documents relate to military secrets.

■ The second exception concerns documents which do not form part of the investigation. These are internal documents of the Commission and the NCAs (for example, draft notices, projects, correspondence within the ECN, and so on). These documents are not binding but their disclosure may prejudice the confidentiality of the deliberations of the Commission in respect of the case in hand. Access to them is not permitted. In order to make them truly inaccessible they are not placed in the main file, although in *NMH Stahlwerke*[2398] the CFI [the General Court] held that a list of those documents together with a short description of their content should be attached to the main file in order to allow the parties to decide whether those documents were of any relevance to them and if so, to apply for their disclosure. This exception has been codified in Article 27(2) of Regulation 1/2003 and Article 15(2) of Regulation 773/2004.

By way of the above exceptions the Commission tries to reconcile the opposing obligations of safeguarding the right of the defence and of protecting confidential information.

If the Commission refuses access to documents in its possession without sufficient reasons, its final decision may be annulled by the CJEU.[2399] In Case C-51/92P *Hercules Chemicals NV v Commission*,[2400] the appellant, an undertaking which had participated in a cartel, challenged the

---

2397.   [1986] ECR 1965.
2398.   Case T-134/94 [1999] ECR II-239.
2399.   Cases T-10 to 12 and 15/92 *Cimenteries* [1992] ECR II-2667.
2400.   [1998] ECR I-8417.

Commission's refusal to allow access to the replies of the other undertakings to the statement of objections. The ECJ held that a refusal to grant access would have led to annulment of the contested decision only if the relevant documents were capable of having some influence on the procedural or substantive outcome of the case, that is, only if the defence of the undertaking concerned had actually been prejudiced. This was not the case, taking into account that although Hercules was granted access at a later stage following joinder of the case, it did not draw from those replies any exonerating evidence and therefore was not in fact prejudiced.

The matter of access to documents relating to ECJ proceedings was examined in Case C-185/95P *Baustahlgewebe GmbH v Commission*.[2401] On appeal from the CFI [the General Court] the appellant argued that he was entitled to consult such documents. The ECJ held that although the right of access to documents constitutes a fundamental principle of EU law, "contrary to the appellant's assertion, the general principles of Community law [EU law] governing the right of access to the Commission's file do not apply, as such, to court proceedings, the latter being governed by the EC Statute of the Court of Justice and by the Rules of Procedure of the Court of First Instance". However, the appellant was entitled to ask the CFI [the General Court] to order the Commission to produce certain documents in its possession. In this respect it was for the CFI [the General Court] to determine whether it was necessary to order the production of those documents. Further, the party requesting production had to identify the documents which it wished to inspect, and provide the CFI [the General Court] with at least minimum information indicating the utility of those documents for the purposes of the proceedings. In this case the appellant did not sufficiently identify the documents in the file which it wanted produced and therefore the CFI [the General Court] was right to reject its request for the production of documents.

30.2.6 Decisions of the Commission

Under Regulation 1/2003 the Commission is empowered to adopt the following decisions:

1. A finding and termination of infringement. When the Commission, acting on a complaint or on its own initiative under Article 7, finds an infringement of Articles 101 or 102 TFEU, it may adopt a decision requiring the undertaking concerned to end an infringement and the Commission may impose on undertakings behavioural or structural remedies proportionate to the infringement and necessary to bring the infringement to an end.

2. Interim measures. Under Article 8 the Commission is empowered to order interim measures. In Case 792/79R *Camera Care Ltd v Commission*,[2402] the ECJ held that the Commission may grant interim relief in urgent cases where there is immediate danger of irreparable damage to the complainant, or where there is a situation which is intolerable for the public interest.

3. Commitments. Under Article 9 of Regulation 1/2003 when the Commission intends to adopt a decision requiring the parties to terminate infringements, the parties may offer

---

2401. [1999] ECR I-4235.
2402. [1980] ECR 119.

commitments to meet the concerns expressed to them by the Commission. In such a situation the Commission may adopt a decision making these commitments binding on the undertakings. Commitment decisions may be reopened by the Commission if there has been a material change in facts, or if the undertakings breach their commitments, or if the decision was based on incomplete, incorrect or misleading information provided by the parties. Recital 13 of Regulation 1/2003 states that commitment decisions are not appropriate when the Commission intends to impose a fine. Further, Recital 13 says that commitment decisions are without prejudice to the powers of NCAs and national courts to decide a case. Perhaps this is because, as Recital 13 specifies, commitment decisions are not conclusive as to whether or not there has been or still is an infringement.

4.   A finding of inapplicability. Under Article 10, where the public interest of the EU requires, the Commission, acting on its own, may find that Article 101 TFEU is not applicable to agreements, decisions or concerted practices either because these commercial arrangements are outside the scope of Article 101(1) or because they satisfy the conditions of Article 101(3). The Commission may likewise make such a finding with reference to Article 102 TFEU. Recital 14 states that such a finding should only be adopted in "exceptional circumstances", that is, to clarify "the law and ensuring its consistent application throughout the Community, in particular with regard to new types of agreements or practices that have not been settled in the existing case-law and administrative practice". Decisions of a finding of inapplicability are not intended to be for the benefit of the parties and are of a declaratory nature.

If parties are confronted by issues raising genuine uncertainty because they present novel or unresolved questions, they may ask the Commission for informal guidance. If appropriate, the Commission will provide such guidance in a written statement called a guidance letter.[2403] These letters are not binding on national courts or NCAs but their value will certainly depend on the procedure the Commission follows in adopting such decisions. If a decision is adopted subsequent to an investigation carried out by the Commission, the status of such "informal guidance letter" should be similar to that of a qualified comfort letter[2404] and therefore unlikely to be overruled by national courts and NCAs.

Under Article 14 of Regulation 1/2003 the role and powers of the Advisory Committee on Restrictive Practices and Dominant Positions (AC), which was first established under Regulation 17/62, were reinforced. The AC is made up of representatives of the NCAs. The 2004 Commission Notice on Co-operation within the Network of Competition Authorities[2405] states that the AC provides a forum "where experts from various national authorities discuss individual cases and general issues of Community competition law [EU competition law]". Under Article 14 of

---

2403. The Commission issued a Notice on Informal Guidance Relating to Novel Questions Concerning Articles 81 and 82 [Articles 101 and 102 TFEU] that Arise in Individual Cases [2004] OJ C101/78.

2404. Prior to the entry into force of Regulation 1/2003 the Commission had often sent a comfort letter in response to an application for individual exemption under Article 81(1) EC [Article 101(3) TFEU]. In such a letter the Commission stated that it had no intention of pursuing the matter and was closing the file because the notified agreement was not in breach of Article 81(1) EC [Article 101(1) TFEU], either because it was outside its scope, or because it was covered by a block exemption regulation, or would merit an individual exemption under Article 81(3) EC [Article 101(3) TFEU]. Comfort letters had no binding force, but in fact national courts never disputed their content.

2405. [2004] OJ L123/18.

Regulation 1/2003, the AC must be consulted before the Commission adopts any important decision, including any of a type mentioned above. Further, an NCA may, when the Commission decides to relieve it from taking a case under Article 11(6) of Regulation 1/2003, request that the AC be consulted.

30.2.7 Fines that can be imposed by the Commission

In order to enforce EU competition law the Commission is empowered to impose pecuniary sanctions on undertakings. Financial penalties can be imposed for infringements that have already ceased (subject to the limitation period) as well as for ongoing infringements. There are three kinds of penalty:

- Procedural fines up to 1 per cent of the undertaking's total turnover in the preceding business year. These may be imposed on an undertaking which refuses to supply information, or when it provides incorrect or misleading information intentionally or negligently, or in other circumstances set out in Article 23(1) of Regulation 1/2003;

- Periodic penalty payments not exceeding 5 per cent of the undertaking's average daily turnover in the preceding business year and calculated from the date fixed by the Commission decision. These may be imposed at a daily rate during the continued defiance of the Commission decision. Article 24 provides a list of circumstances in which the Commission may impose periodic penalty payments, for example, when an undertaking has not terminated an infringement despite a decision adopted by the Commission to that effect, or has not complied with a decision ordering interim measures.

- "Substantive" fines. Under Article 23(2) of Regulation 1/2003 the Commission is empowered to impose fines for substantive infringements (either intentional or negligent) of Articles 101 or 102 TFEU, of a decision ordering interim measures under Article 8, or for failure to comply with a commitment made binding by a decision pursuant to Article 9. To find intention or negligence it is not necessary that the partners or principal managers of an undertaking have themselves acted negligently or with intent, or have even been aware of an infringement. It suffices that the prohibited action was performed by a person authorised to act on behalf of the undertaking.[2406] Intentional infringement has been defined by the ECJ as an act deliberately committed with the intention of achieving some object prohibited by the Treaties.[2407] A negligent infringement occurs when an undertaking knew or ought to have known that its action would result in infringement of the prohibition.[2408] An undertaking may be regarded as having acted intentionally or negligently even though it participated in an infringement under pressure.[2409] This factor will be considered when fixing the fine. The amount of the fine is:

  - Up to 10 per cent of the undertaking's total turnover in the preceding business year for each undertaking and association of the undertaking participating in the infringement;

2406.   Joined Cases 100–103/80 *SA Musique Diffusion Française and Others v Commission* [1983] ECR 1825.

2407.   Case 172/80 *Gerard Züchner v Bayerische Vereinsbank AG* [1981] ECR 2021.

2408.   Case 27/76 *United Brands v Commission* [1977] ECR 207.

2409.   *Tipp-ex* [1987] OJ L2221.

● Where an infringement by an association relates to the activities of its members, the fine should not exceed 10 per cent of the sum of the total turnover of each member active in the market affected by the association's infringement.

The fining policy of the Commission has changed over the years. Initially, the Commission imposed relatively light fines. However, in *Pioneer Hi-Fi Equipment*[2410] the Commission indicated a change in its policy. It stated that fines should be a real deterrent and should be of sufficiently greater amounts in cases of serious infringements. On appeal,[2411] the ECJ confirmed that the Commission was entitled to change its approach and to impose heavier fines than previously. The ECJ held that "the proper application of the Community [EU] competition rules requires that the Commission may at any time adjust the levels of fines to the needs of that policy." As a result the Commission has, over the years, refined its fining policy with a view to not only punishing past conduct of an undertaking but to ensuring that fines constitute sufficient deterrent.

In Case C-185/95P *Baustahlgewebe GmbH v Commission*,[2412] the ECJ held that the CFI [the General Court] has unlimited jurisdiction to determine the amount of fines imposed on undertakings for infringements of EC [EU] competition law and that if the ECJ becomes involved by virtue of its appellate capacity, it can only rule on questions of law and therefore has no jurisdiction, even on grounds of fairness, to substitute its assessment of the amount of fines for that of the CFI [the General Court]. Obviously, the relevant Guidelines for setting fines in competition cases adopted by the Commission contain limitations as to the setting of maximum fines. In practice, on appeal the General Court quite often reduces the amount of fines imposed by the Commission.

In 1998, with a view to ensuring the transparency and impartiality of its decisions, the Commission published a Notice regarding its fining policy under Articles 81 and 82 EC [Articles 101 and 102 TFEU].[2413] The 2006 Guidelines on the Method of Setting Fines imposed pursuant to Article 23(2)(a) of Regulation No 1/2003 replaced that Notice.[2414] The main purpose of the Guidelines is to make fines a real deterrent by setting a basic amount at a much higher level than under the 1998 Notice, although fines must not exceed the limits specified in the Regulation, that is, 10 per cent of the undertaking's total turnover in the preceding business year.

The Notice is not binding. The Commission enjoys a wide discretion in the determination of the amount of fine in each case.

The Guidelines provide that the Commission's first task in assessing the amount of fine is to determine the basic amount. This is based on up to 30 per cent of the undertaking's annual sales, multiplied by the number of years of participation in the infringement. Irrespective of the duration of infringement, a so-called "entry fee" may be imposed to punish the undertaking's participation in a cartel – from 15 to 25 per cent of its annual sales in the relevant sector. An entry fee may also be imposed in other types of infringements.

The next step consists of adjusting the basic amount in the light of two sets of circumstances, that is, it is increased by reference to aggravating circumstances or reduced by reference to attenuating circumstances.

2410. [1980] OJ L60/1.
2411. Supra note 2406.
2412. [1998] ECR I-8417.
2413. [1998] 3 CMLR 472.
2414. [2006] OJ C210/2.

Aggravating circumstances refer to a situation where:

- An undertaking is either a first-time repeat offender or a multiple repeat offender. The basic amount may be increased by up to 100 per cent for each previous infringement established. The Commission will take into account not only its own previous decisions but also those of the relevant NCA;

- An undertaking refused to co-operate with the Commission during investigations;

- An undertaking was a leader in, or instigator of the infringement, or coerced other undertakings to participate in the infringement, or took retaliatory measures against other undertakings in order to enforce its own anti-competitive conduct.

The above list is not exhaustive.

The list of extenuating circumstances (also not exhaustive) refers to a situation where:

- An undertaking terminated its infringement as soon as the Commission intervened (except when it participated in secret agreements and practices, in particular, cartels);

- An undertaking's infringement was unintentional or negligent;

- An undertaking did not implement an anti-competitive agreement or practice;

- An undertaking terminated an infringement as soon as the Commission so requested;

- An undertaking actively co-operated with the Commission outside the scope of the Leniency Notice and beyond its legal obligation to do so;

- An undertaking's anti-competitive conduct was authorised or encouraged by public authorities or by legislation.

The Commission will take into consideration the economic context of the infringement and the ability of an undertaking to actually pay the fine.

30.2.8   Enforcement of EU competition law in the light of accession of the EU to the ECHR

Two issues are particularly controversial:

- First, the determination of whether an infringement of EU competition law constitutes a criminal offence. With regard to this issue, it is vital to decide whether an infringement of EU competition law constitutes a criminal offence, given that under Article 6(2) and (3) of the ECHR criminal defendants enjoy rights additional to those specified in Article 6(1) of the ECHR which sets out general requirements for "fair trial" in criminal and civil proceedings. Among more specific and additional rights relating only to criminal trials, Article 6(2) of the ECHR guarantees the rights to remain silent and not to incriminate oneself. So far as EU law is concerned, Article 23(5) Regulation 1/2003 states that decisions imposing fines "shall not be of a criminal law nature";

- Second, that the Commission combines investigating and judicial functions which may be in breach of Article 6(1) of the ECHR which requires that a court, tribunal, etc determining civil rights and obligations or a criminal charge must be and must appear to be "independent and impartial".

As at the time of writing, the ECtHR has not ruled on either of the above issues but its judgment in *Dubus SA v France*[2415] delivered on 11 June 2009 has the potential of substantially changing the way in which EU competition law will be enforced by the Commission.

THE FACTS WERE:

Dubus SA, an investment company registered in France argued that the French Banking Commission, the supervisory authority responsible for credit and investment establishments, chaired by the Governor of the Bank of France, which conducted disciplinary proceedings against Dubus SA, was in breach of Article 6(1) ECHR. This was because the French Banking Commission was all, at the same time, a prosecuting, investigating and judicial authority. Therefore, the simultaneous exercise of investigation powers and judicial functions infringed the right of Dubus SA to an independent and impartial tribunal guaranteed under Article 6(1) ECHR.

Held:

The ECtHR held that France was in breach of Article 6(1) ECHR on the ground that the French Banking Commission in conducting disciplinary proceedings against Dubus SA, showed a lack of independence and impartiality.

Comment:

There are two aspect of *Dubus SA v France* which may be of great relevance to the enforcement of EU competition law by the Commission. These are:

1. The ECtHR held that although it was not, in itself, incompatible with Article 6(1) of the ECHR for a body to combine investigation and judicial functions this was subject to their being no "prejudgment" on the part of that body. In *Dubus SA* the Court noted that the applicant company "might reasonably have had the impression that it had been prosecuted and tried by the same people, and had doubts about the decision of the Commission, which, in its various capacities, had brought disciplinary proceedings against it, notified it of the offences and pronounced the penalty."

    It is important to note that the procedure used by the French Banking Commission is not very dissimilar to that used by the European Commission. In *Dubus SA* the ECtHR emphasised the lack of precision of the texts governing proceedings before the French Banking Commission and the lack of any clear distinction between the functions of prosecution, investigation and adjudication in the exercise of its judicial power. Is Regulation 1/2003 less bad?

    There have been many complaints about the fact that the European Commission combines investigatory and judicial functions. At the time of writing, the applicant in Case T-56/09 *Saint-Gobain Glass France and Others v Commission* has submitted that its right to an independent and impartial tribunal and its right to respect for the presumption of innocence were breached in so far as a fine was imposed by an administra-

---

2415. Application No 5242/04, available at the official website of the ECrHR at http://www.echr.coe.int.

tive authority which holds simultaneously powers of investigation and sanction, and that Regulation 1/2003 is unlawful in so far as it does not provide for the right to an independent and impartial tribunal.

2. The ECtHR, without spending much time on this issue, stated that the penalties in the form of fines were penal in nature taking into account that high fines could be imposed on the applicant. This statement is very relevant in so far as the current fining policy of the European Commission is concerned. For example, the European Commission in May 2009 imposed a record fine on Intel of €1.06 billion for abusing its dominant position by engaging in illegal anti-competitive practices to exclude competitors from the market for computer chips called "x86 central processing units (CPUs)" by awarding conditional rebates and payments to major computer manufacturers in respect of its x86 CPUs.[2416]

30.2.9   The EU Leniency Programme

The main objective of leniency programmes is to provide an incentive to an undertaking participating in an unlawful cartel to come forward and to expose the cartel by offering immunity from, or a reduction of the fines that would have been applicable to the undertaking had the cartel been discovered by the relevant competition enforcement authorities without the undertaking's assistance. However, the immunity/reduction is only available if the undertaking crosses certain thresholds in respect of evidence provided by it.

The Commission established the first Leniency Programme in 1996.[2417] Although effective, it had many flaws but these were, to a large extent, remedied by the 2002[2418] and 2006 Leniency Programmes.[2419]

The 2006 Leniency Programme, which is outlined in the 2006 Notice on Immunity from Fines and Reduction of Fines in Cartels Cases, improves the transparency and certainty of the conditions on which the immunity and the reduction of fines is granted.

The evidential thresholds for immunity have been clarified by the Notice. In order to obtain immunity the undertaking has to provide sufficient evidence for the Commission to commence an investigation, or must be the first to enable the Commission to establish an infringement of Article 101 TFEU (Articles 8, 9 and 10 of the Notice).

Article 12 specifies the extent of the duties imposed on an applicant for immunity, inter alia, it must promptly supply the Commission with any evidence in its possession or available to it, remain at the Commission's disposal to answer any relevant questions, not have destroyed, falsified or concealed any evidence before or after making an application and subsequently, not disclose the fact of, or any of the content of its application before the Commission has issued a

---

2416. IP/09/745.

2417. [1996] OJ C207/4.

2418. [2002] OJ C45/3.

2419. [2006] OJ C298/17. Under the 1996 Programme, the Commission received over 80 leniency applications; under the 2002 Programme, from 2002 to the end of 2005, it received 167 applications. J. S. Sandhu, "The European Commission's Leniency Policy: A Success?", (2007) ECLR, Issue 3, p 148.

statement of objections, unless otherwise agreed. It must also terminate its participation in the cartel unless otherwise agreed between the Commission and the applicant.

The 2006 Notice introduced a marker system, whereby an applicant can, first, know where it stands with respect to other applicants in the line for immunity, and second, when it is first in the queue, keep its place while it gathers necessary information and evidence in order to meet the evidential threshold requirements. The Notice specifies the kind of information the applicant is required to provide, including the identity of the applicant and some details of the cartel. This distinguishes it from a hypothetical application, whereby an application can be made in such a way as to preserve the anonymity of the applicant who wishes to know whether evidence in its possession meets the relevant evidential immunity threshold.

The Notice states that an undertaking which has coerced any other undertaking into participating in the infringement or remains in it does not qualify for immunity, although it may qualify for a reduction of fines.

When an applicant does not qualify for immunity, it may nevertheless be eligible for a reduction of fines. The first applicant who provides the Commission with evidence that represents significant added value with respect to the evidence already in the Commission's possession will receive a reduction in fines between 30 per cent and 50 per cent. The next, a reduction between 20 per cent and 30 per cent, and any subsequent applicant a reduction of up to 20 per cent.

Article 25 of the Notice specifies that evidence which needs little or no corroboration is considered as significantly adding value. In addition, this kind of evidence will be rewarded outside the normal bands for reduction of fines when its assists the Commission in establishing any additional facts increasing the gravity or duration of the infringement. The extent of the duty of co-operation for applicants for a reduction of fines is similar to that imposed on applicants for immunity.

The Programme does not protect an undertaking that has come forward from civil claims. Therefore there is nothing to prevent parties who have suffered damage as a result of the cartel operation starting separate proceedings in national courts. The 2006 Leniency Notice introduces a procedure aimed at protecting corporate statements given by an undertaking to the Commission from discovery in civil damage proceedings. In this respect the Commission can take oral corporate statements at its premises. The Commission will record and transcribe the statements and no one else will have a copy. Such statements will form part of the Commission's file, access to which is limited to the addressees of a statement of objections in the same case and under strict conditions specified in paragraph 34 of the Notice.

The 2006 Notice is aligned with the Model Leniency Programme of the ECN, and consequently it is hoped that many controversial and unresolved issues will disappear in the future and that both the EU and national programmes will become more attractive to potential whistle-blowers (see section 30.4.3.1).

30.3 Enforcement of Articles 101 and 102 TFEU before national courts and co-operation between the Commission and national courts

This section examines, first, the enforcement of Articles 101 and 102 TFEU before national courts, and second, the manner in which the Commission and national courts co-operate in order to ensure the proper enforcement of EU competition law.

30.3.1 Enforcement of EU competition law before national courts

In Case 127/73 *BRT v SABAM*,[2420] the ECJ held that Articles 81(1) and 82 EC [Articles 101(1) and 102 TFEU] are directly effective. They are both horizontally and vertically directly effective. As a result of entry into force of Regulation 1/2003 Article 101(3) TFEU is also directly effective, both horizontally and vertically. .

In Case C-453/99 *Courage Ltd v Crehan*,[2421] the ECJ confirmed the existence of the right to damages based on Articles 81 and 82 EC [Articles 101 and 102 TFEU].

The decision of the ECJ in *Crehan* has far-reaching consequences so far as private enforcement of EU competition law is concerned because:

- Even parties to a contract that is liable to restrict or distort competition within the meaning of Article 101(1) TFEU are entitled to rely on breach of that provision before a national court. Their participation in an unlawful contract does not deprive them of the right to bring an action;

- Parties to a contract liable to restrict or distort competition cannot, on the sole ground that they are a party to an unlawful contract, be deprived of the right to seek compensation from the other party for loss caused by such a contract. Only the fact that such parties bear significant responsibility for the distortion of competition may deprive them of the right to obtain damages;

- In order to determine whether a party bears significant responsibility for the distortion of competition, and therefore to assess the merits of a claim for damages, a national court must take into account the economic and legal context in which the parties find themselves and their respective bargaining power and conduct.

30.3.2 Factors encouraging private enforcement of Articles 101 and 102 TFEU before national courts

Among factors which encourage private enforcement of Articles 101 and 102 before national courts, the following can be mentioned:

1. The right to claim damages based on Article 101 or 102 TFEU as set out in the *Crehan* judgment. This was confirmed in Joined Cases C-295/04 and C-298/04 *Vincenzo Manfredi v Lloyd Adriatico Assicurazioni SpA*,[2422] in which the ECJ held that:
    - Any individual is entitled to rely on the invalidity of an agreement or practice prohibited under Article 81 EC [Article 101 TFEU] in order to seek damages for the harm suffered where there is a causal link between that agreement or practice and the harm;
    - The right to seek compensation includes not only compensation for actual loss (damnum emergens) but also for loss of profit (lucrum cessans) plus interest.

2. Only national courts can:

2420. [1974] ECR 313.
2421. [2001] ECR I-6297.
2422. [2006] ECR I-6619.

- Award damages to individuals or undertakings for loss suffered as a result of the infringement of Articles 101 and 102 TFEU;
- Rule on claims for payment or fulfilment of contractual obligations based on an agreement under Article 101 TFEU;
- Apply the civil sanction of nullity of contracts based on Article 101(2) TFEU;
- Award legal costs to a successful claimant.[2423]

3. With the entry into force of Regulation 1/2003, Article 81 EC [Article 101 TFEU] became, in its entirety, both vertically and horizontally directly effective and thus major problems previously encountered by national courts in its application (see Chapter 27.9) were solved.

    The rationale for this solution seems to be that EU competition law has become well established. Consequently, decentralisation is less likely to undermine uniformity of enforcement than it would have been in the early days of the European Community.

4. The Commission's policy is to encourage private enforcement of EU competition law. On 2 April 2008, the Commission adopted a White Paper on Damages Actions for Breach of the EU Antitrust Rules.[2424] This is a follow-up to a Green Paper on damages actions for breach of EU competition rules, which stirred a debate across Europe on the need for legal reform that would encourage private plaintiffs to claim compensation for losses suffered as a result of the anti-competitive conduct of undertakings.

A new approach to enforcement is necessary because:

- First, the number of successful damages claims for infringement of EU competition law has been few; and

- Second, in the absence of EU rules governing this area, the principle of national procedural autonomy, although subject to the requirements of equivalence, effectiveness and pro-portionality (see Chapter 14.6), has a great impact on private enforcement. National pro-cedural rules (which govern, for example, matters relating to locus standi, methods of proof of damage, types of damage for which compensation is recoverable, the principles of dam-age calculation), which differ greatly from one Member State to another, often not only determine the outcome of the case but also encourage or discourage private enforcement. For example, in *Vincenzo Manfredi* the ECJ held that it is for a Member State to decide whether to recognise the award of punitive damages as this matter falls within the scope of the procedural autonomy of each Member State. Obviously, the possibility for a claimant to be awarded punitive damages would constitute an important incentive to start proceedings before a national court.

The matter of private enforcement of EU competition law is very delicate because on the one hand, private enforcement of competition law offers many advantages (that is, it ensures that those who have suffered a loss resulting from anti-competitive conduct are compensated, involves

---

2423. Para 14 of the 2004 Notice on the Handling of Complaints by the Commission ([2004] OJ L101/65) specifies the advantages resulting from bringing claims before national courts.
2424. COM(2008) 165.2.4.2008. This should be read together with the Commission's Staff Working Paper SEC(2008) 404.2.4.3008.

consumers and undertakings in the enforcement of EU competition law, and thus makes the enforcement of EU competition law more relevant to EU citizens and undertakings) but, on the other hand, it may create a US-style private litigation culture, in particular if punitive damages are accepted as an important part of private enforcement and class actions are allowed. Such perverse incentives may lead to a situation where undertakings choose to forgo legitimate competitive initiatives and this may, in the long run, be harmful to the economy and to consumers.[2425] Consequently, the right balance should be struck between private enforcement and the needs of undertakings.

The 2008 White Paper states that its recommendations reconcile the need to overcome the existing over-deterrence in private enforcement of competition law with the necessity to avoid excessive litigation. The recommendations concern:

- The possibility of class action. The recommendation is that redress should be available via representative action, for example, by recognised consumer protection groups, and actions for which victims can choose to participate;

- The necessity to ensure equivalent access to the evidence by both parties to the proceedings. The Commission proposes to achieve this by a "form of judge-controlled" pre-trial disclosure of relevant evidence rather than by recommending an automatic right to wide pre-trial discovery which may lead to procedural abuses, i.e. settlement of cases in order to avoid costly proceedings;

- The granting of locus standi not only to direct customers but also to indirect customers;

- The possibility for the infringer to rely on the passing-on defence whilst facilitating the proof of the passing-on by the eventual victims;

- The probative value of final infringement decisions of NCAs. In actions for damages they should constitute sufficient proof of the infringement in question.

A legislative act based on the White Paper is expected to be proposed by the Commission after wide public consultation in respect of the White Paper.

30.3.3 Co-operation between the Commission and national courts

The 2004 Commission Notice on Co-operation between the Commission and the Courts of the EU Member States in the Application of Articles 81 and 82 EC [Articles 101 and 102 TFEU][2426] sets out general rules aimed at ensuring that EU competition law is applied uniformly. The Notice expands and clarifies the principles of co-operation set out in Articles 15 and 16 of Regulation 1/2003.

Under Article 15(1) of Regulation 1/2003 national courts are entitled to obtain from the Commission information in its possession with a view to applying Articles 101 and 102 TFEU. They may also ask for the Commission's opinion in this area.

Article 15(3) introduces the right for the Commission to make submissions to national courts

---

2425. W. Breit and K. G. Elzinga, "Antitrust Enforcement and Economic Efficiency: The Uneasy Case for Treble Damages", (1974) 17 J.L.& Econ., p 329.

2426. [2004] OJ C101/54.

in written and oral forms acting in the interest of the EU (as amicus curiae) but not in favour of one of the parties. Such submissions will not be binding on the national court. The main objective of submissions is to draw the attention of national courts to certain issues of considerable importance for the uniform application of EU competition rules. Additionally, national courts will, at the specific request of the Commission, be obliged to supply information concerning national proceedings. This will allow the Commission to decide whether it should make a submission in a particular case.

Article 16 of Regulation 1/2003 deals with the uniform application of EU competition law. It sets out general rules aimed at avoiding the taking of conflicting decisions in the same proceedings at national and EU level. As a principle, national courts must use every effort to avoid such conflict; in particular they should, if appropriate, refer a case to the ECJ for a preliminary ruling and if a decision adopted by the Commission is pending before the CJEU, national courts should suspend their own proceedings. This was endorsed in Case C-344/98 *Masterfoods Ltd v HB Ice Cream Ltd.*[2427]

30.4 Enforcement of Articles 101 and 102 TFEU by national competition authorities (NCAs), co-operation between the Commission and NCAs, and co-operation between NCAs within the European Competition Network (ECN)

Article 5 of Regulation 1/2003 provides that NCAs are empowered, and (in situations described in Article 3 of Regulation 1/2003) obliged to apply both Article 101 TFEU in its entirety and Article 102 TFEU. Under Article 3 of Regulation 1/2003 NCAs may make the following decisions:

- Order an infringement to be brought to an end;

- Order interim measures;

- Accept commitments from the parties concerned;

- Impose fines or other penalties provided for in their national laws.

The basic rules on co-operation between the Commission and the NCAs are contained in Chapter IV of Regulation 1/2003 and further explained in a Joint Statement of the Council and the European Commission on the Functioning of the Network of Competition Authorities[2428] and in the 2004 Commission's Notice on Co-operation within the network of competition authorities.[2429]

30.4.1 Co-operation between the Commission and the NCAs

The main features of the co-operation relate to:

1. **Allocation of cases**. This is a very important issue given an infringement of EU competition law may involve a single NCA, several NCAs acting in parallel or the Commission.

2427. [2000] ECR I-11369.

2428. See the official site of the EU's competition policy – news, legislation, cases at http://ec.europa.eu/comm/competition/index_en.html (accessed 21/11/2009).

2429. [2004] OJ C101/43.

The principles upon which the cases are allocated are set out in the 2004 Notice. This indicates that the determination of the competition authority which is best placed to deal with a case is based on the following three criteria:

- The agreement or practice has substantial direct and actual or foreseeable effects on competition within an NCA territory, is implemented or originates from its territory;
- The authority is able to effectively bring to an end the entire infringement;
- It can gather, possibly with the assistance of other authorities, the evidence to prove the infringement.

The allocation of cases should be determined speedily, normally within a period of two months (paragraph 18 of the 2004 Notice).

2. **Exchange of information**. Under Article 11(3) of Regulation 1/2003 an NCA is required to inform the Commission and other NCAs "before, or without delay after, commencing the first formal investigative measures". Further the Commission is obliged to send to the relevant NCA copies of documents in its possession relating to the case. The relocation of a case should be avoided but this may occur when the circumstances of the case change materially during the proceedings (paragraph 19 of the 2004 Notice).

The Commission and the NCAs keep each other informed when acting under Articles 101 and 102 TFEU. An NCA is obliged to inform the Commission at the latest 30 days before adopting any of the following decisions:

- Requiring that an infringement be terminated;
- Accepting commitments;
- Withdrawing the benefit of a block exemption regulation.

The NCA is required to provide a summary of the case and of the intended decision, or (in the absence of any decision) of any other relevant document indicating the proposed course of action, or at the request of the Commission any other relevant document necessary for the assessment of the case. The information may also be made available to other NCAs (Article 11(4) of Regulation 1/2003).

3. **Consultations**. Under Article 11(5) of Regulation 1/2003 an NCA may consult the Commission on any case involving the application of EU competition law.

An NCA may ask the Commission to place any case or cases that are being dealt with by it on the agenda of the Advisory Committee. The Commission may also do this on its own initiative. In particular, such request or placing on the agenda is likely to occur in a situation where the Commission intends to take over a case which has already been started by the requesting NCA, either because the case presents "EU interest" or because the Commission, in the light of a draft decision submitted under Article 11(6) Regulation 1/2003, disapproves of the manner in which the NCA intends to deal with the case.

30.4.2 Co-operation between NCAs

Regulation 1/2003 provides for co-operation between NCAs in respect of:

1. **Allocation of cases**. By virtue of Article 13 the fact that two or more NCAs are dealing with the same case or complaint constitutes a sufficient ground for all but one to suspend their proceedings or to reject the complaint. The purpose of this provision is to avoid a

number of decisions emanating from various NCAs in the same case, which decisions may contradict each other.

2.   **Exchange of information.** Under Article 11(3) and (4) the NCAs are required to inform each other of the commencement of proceedings and in respect of decisions they intend to adopt (see below). In a situation where an NCA suspends national proceedings or rejects a complaint because another NCA is better placed to deal with the case, the first NCA is permitted to transfer information, including confidential information, to the other NCA.

In this context it is very important that individuals and undertakings are protected against the misuse of exchanged information. In this respect paragraph 28 of the 2004 Notice provides for the following safeguards:

- The competition authorities are bound by the obligation of professional secrecy;
- The information exchanged can only be used for the purposes of Articles 101 and 102 TFEU and in respect of the subject-matter for which it was collected;
- The information can only be used to impose sanctions on natural persons in two sets of circumstances: first, where the law of the receiving authority provides for sanctions of a similar kind to the law of the transmitting authority; second, where the rights of defence as regards the collection of evidence have been respected by the transmitting authority to the same standard as is guaranteed by the receiving authority. The Notice makes a distinction between sanctions which result in custody and other sanctions, for example, fines. Whether or not an NCA can impose sanctions and the kind of sanctions it is allowed to impose depends on its national law. For example, the UK's authority (the Office of Fair Trading (OFT)) is not entitled to impose sanctions on individuals and therefore will not be allowed to transfer information to an NCA which is allowed to impose sanctions unless the required information has been collected by the OFT in a manner which protects the individual's right to defence to the same standard as is protected under the rules of the receiving NCA. It should not be forgotten that custodial sanctions can only be imposed if both the receiving and the transmitting authorities have the power to impose such sanctions. This does not, however, apply if the information will be used in proceedings against an undertaking, not an individual.

30.4.3   The European Competition Network (ECN)

The NCAs and the Commission form a network of public authorities, which co-operate in order to protect competition within the internal market. The network, which was established in 2002, is called the European Competition Network (ECN). It is made up of representatives of all NCAs. It constitutes a forum for discussion, inter alia, on issues that arise in the enforcement of competition law and on the improvement of the existing enforcement system. Additionally, it provides a flexible mechanism for increasing co-operation between NCAs.

The ECN does not take decisions and cannot compel an NCA to act in a particular way or to expel its members. At the time of writing, the biggest achievement of the ECN was the adoption of a Model Leniency Programme in 2006.

30.4.3.1   The ECN Model Leniency Programme

Decentralisation of enforcement of Articles 101 and 102 TFEU introduced by Regulation 1/2003[2430] brought some undesirable consequences as to the EU Leniency Programme's consistency, uniformity and efficacy. The ECN Model Leniency Programme[2431] which was launched by the ECN on 29 September 2006 tries to deal with them. Its main features are:

30.4.3.1.1 Scope of application of the MP

A.   The scope of application ratione personae.

The MP applies to "secret cartels", which are the most difficult first to discover, and then to investigate without the co-operation of at least one of their participants. In particular it applies to agreements and/or concerted practices between two or more competitors aimed at restricting competition through fixing prices, the allocation of production or the sharing of markets, including bid-rigging. Other categories of agreements, decisions and concerted practices, both vertical and horizontal, are excluded from the benefit of the MP as being less harmful to the competition process and easier to detect. However, it should be noted that national leniency programmes may be more extensive and thus encompass other forms of anti-competitive conduct violating Article 101 TFEU.

In the MP the NCAs agreed to exclude from immunity an undertaking which has coerced another undertaking to participate in a cartel. However, two NCAs, German and Greek, expressly stated that only the "sole ringleader" would not be eligible for immunity from fines in their countries. This divergence is regrettable given that, on the one hand, in practice it is very difficult to decide who the "ringleader" is and, on the other hand, such an undertaking is likely to supply the most valuable information leading to dismantling the cartel. While it is fair to withhold the benefit of immunity from an undertaking which has coerced other undertakings to participate in a cartel, it is unfair to do this is respect of the ringleader, unless the latter has acted as a coercer.

B.   The scope of application ratione materiae.

The MP distinguishes between applications for immunity from fines (Type 1) and applications for reduction of fines (Type 2).

(a)   Applications for immunity from fines.

The MP establishes two types of immunity – Type 1A and Type 1B – as follows:

▪ Type 1A, which relates to a situation where the applicant is the first to submit evidence on the basis of which the NCA will be able to carry out targeted inspections but where, at the time the NCA assesses the application, it does not have sufficient evidence in its possession to adopt an inspection decision or to seek a court warrant for an inspection. Thus, the evidential threshold for immunity is quite low given that the targeted inspection may be unsuccessful, or the relevant NCA may decide not to carry out targeted inspections. Article 6 of the MP sets out the kind of information that an applicant is required to submit.

2430. [2003] OJ L1/1.
2431. Available at http://ec.europa.eu/comm/competition/ecn/documents.html (accessed on 5/12/07).

■ Type 1B, which relates to a situation where the applicant is the first to submit evidence to the relevant NCA which will enable it to find a breach of Article 101 TFEU, and at the time of application the NCA did not have sufficient evidence to establish such a breach and no undertaking has been granted immunity. The evidential threshold for immunity is very high since the applicant must provide the NCA with sufficient information to establish the infringement of Article 101 TFEU.

(b) Applications for reduction of fines – Type 2.

An undertaking which does not qualify for immunity, either because it does not meet the relevant evidential threshold or because of the role it played in the cartel, may nevertheless apply for a reduction of a fine that would otherwise have been imposed. This is called T2 Immunity. A reduction will be granted only if the information provided adds significant "added value" to the investigation. The concept of significant added value is defined in Article 10 of the MP as referring to the extent to which the evidence provided strengthens, by its very nature and/or its level of detail, the NCA's ability to prove the existence of the cartel. The undertaking concerned does not know whether its contribution will "add value" while the NCA can see all the cards. This may seem unfair to the applicant, but is compensated by the fact that the relevant NCA will inform the applicant as early as possible of the status of its application. However, the reward given for providing significant added value should not result in the reduction of a fine by more than 50 per cent. The distinction between the reward given to immunity applicants and the reward which applicants for reduction of fines may expect is fair and justified, bearing in mind that the main purpose of any leniency programme is to award the "first-at-the door" undertaking and thus enable the relevant competition authorities to detect an unlawful cartel. Once they are aware of its existence, it is no longer necessary to show any leniency to undertakings involved in illegal activities, although it may be useful in terms of gathering evidence.

30.4.3.1.2 Conditions attached to leniency

A. Termination of an infringement.

Under Article 13(1) of the MP, an applicant must terminate its participation in the alleged cartel immediately following filing of its application, save to the extent that its participation would, according to the relevant NCA, be reasonably necessary to preserve the integrity of the NCA's investigations. This provision emphasises that the basic rule is that an applicant is required to terminate its participation at the time it submits its application for immunity and accordingly there is now less likelihood than previously of conflicting requirements being imposed on an applicant by different NCAs. However, exceptionally, termination of participation may be delayed to safeguard the integrity of investigation. This is reasonable because some flexibility is needed, given that the sudden disappearance of the applicant from regular cartel meetings or its refusal to communicate with other members of the cartel will suggest that something is wrong and may prompt concealment or destruction of vital evidence.

B. The obligation to co-operate.

Article 13(2) of the MP not only states that the applicant must co-operate genuinely, fully and on a continuous basis with the relevant NCA from the time of its application until the conclusion of the case, but also specifies in detail the meaning of this obligation. This obligation also applies to the pre-application stage – the applicant being required not to destroy evidence or disclose directly or indirectly either that it is contemplating making an application or any likely content of the contemplated application.

30.4.3.1.3 Procedural matters

A. The marker system.
    The MP introduced a discretionary marker system, similar to that set out under the 2006 Commission Leniency Notice (see section 30.2.9).

B. Oral evidence.
    Oral evidence is allowed under the MP in all cases where this would be justified and proportionate. This is to be applauded given that this ensures that the applicant will not, as a result of its application, be in a worse position than other members of a cartel when litigants in civil damage proceedings seek discovery of documents lodged with the relevant NCA. Additionally, the MP provides for safeguards for any records of oral statements, that is, no access will be granted to them before the statement of objections has been issued. Further, the exchange of records of oral statements between NCAs is limited to cases where the protection afforded to such records by the receiving NCA is equivalent to that afforded by the transmitting NCA.

C. Summary applications.
    To create a "one-stop-shop" for multiple leniency applications in Type 1A cases the MP introduced the summary applications system. Under this system, in cases where more than three NCAs are competent to take action against the cartel and a full leniency application has been made to the Commission, an NCA can accept the application temporarily (so protecting the applicant's first place in the queue) on the basis of very limited information as set out in Article 22 of the MP. The relevant NCA will not process a summary application. It will only confirm that the applicant is first in the queue, if this is the case. If the NCA decides to start investigations, the applicant will be given a specific time limit to make a full submission of all relevant evidence and information.

30.4.3.1.4 Conclusions

The MP has no binding force. It is perceived as a first step in the harmonisation of national leniency programmes and contains substantial procedural rules that the NCAs consider should be incorporated into any leniency programme. The heads of Member States' national competition authorities have agreed to use their best efforts to align their leniency programmes with the MP within the shortest possible time. The first review of the MP, in terms of the progress it had made towards convergence of national programmes, took place in 2008. The Report on Assessment of the State of Convergence covered the period ending on 31 December 2008.[2432] It assessed the state of convergence of national leniency programmes with the EU leniency programme as satisfactory emphasising that many Member States had either replaced or amended their national rules in order to make them compatible with the EU Leniency Programmme. At the time of writing 26 Member States have implemented national leniency programmes.

2432. The Report can be found at http://ec.europa.eu/competition/ecn/model_leniency_programme.pdf (6/3/10).

It is submitted that if the NCAs live up to their political commitment and model their national leniency programmes on the MP, this will have a very positive impact on the dynamics of these programmes and the EU Leniency Programme itself. The MP clarifies many issues, makes the procedural and substantive requirements more transparent for applicants, removes useless and burdensome constraints resulting from discrepancies between different national leniency programmes and thus enhances the confidence of applicants in the fairness of the leniency policy at both EU and national levels.

AIDE-MÉMOIRE

I. ENFORCEMENT OF ARTICLES 101 AND 102 TFEU

The main themes of the reform of the enforcement of Articles 81 and 82 EC [Articles 101 and 102 TFEU] were simplification and decentralisation. This has been achieved by the following:

- The replacement of the notification and authorisation system under Article 81(3) EC [Article 101(3) TFEU] by a "legal exception" system;

- Direct applicability of Article 101(3) TFEU;

- Decentralisation of enforcement of Articles 101 and 102 TFEU;

- Increase of the Commission's investigatory powers;

- Confirmation by national courts and national competition authorities of the application of EU competition law over national law.

II. ENFORCEMENT OF ARTICLES 101 AND 102 TFEU BY THE COMMISSION

Under Regulation 1/2003 the Commission is empowered to adopt the following decisions:

- A finding and termination of infringement;

- Interim measures;

- Commitments;

- A finding of inapplicability.

If parties to an agreement are confronted by issues raising genuine uncertainty because they present novel or unresolved questions, they may ask the Commission to provide guidance in a written statement called a guidance letter.

1. Complaints to the commission in respect of infringements of Articles 101 and 102 TFEU

The Commission may act ex officio or upon an application from a Member State, or from "any natural or legal person who can show a legitimate interest" (Case T-144/92 *BEMIM*). A complaint may be rejected if it does not raise sufficient EU interest (Case T-24/90 *Automec*). The Commission is not obliged to start investigations but is obliged to reply to the complainant within a reasonable time (Case C-282/95P *Guérin*).

2. Obtaining information

The request for information may take two forms:

- A simple request. There is no duty to comply, but if inexact or misleading information is supplied, the Commission may impose a fine up to 1 per cent of the undertaking's turnover in the preceding business year;

- A formal binding decision requiring the information to be provided. For failure to comply the Commission may impose periodic penalties of up to 5 per cent of the undertaking's average daily turnover.

Incriminating information

The ECJ, on the one hand, recognised the right not to self-incriminate by admitting the infringement but, on the other, refused the right not to provide evidence against oneself (Case 27/88 *Solvay*; Case C-301/04P *Commission v SGL Carbon*).

Legal professional privilege (LPP)

The principle of lawyer–client confidentiality is recognised under EU law, but only communications between a client and an independent lawyer (permitted to practise in at least one Member State) are privileged (not those between a client and an in-house lawyer) (T-125/03 and T-253/03 *Akzo*).

Power to take statements (Article 19 of Regulation 1/2003)

The Commission may interview any natural or legal person, with their consent, in order to collect information relating to the investigation.

3. Inspections (Article 20 of Regulation 1/2003)

The Commission is authorised to undertake all necessary investigations into undertakings and associations of undertakings including:

- Examination of books and other business records;

- Taking copies of or extracts from the books and business records;

- Asking for oral explanations on the spot;

- Entering any premises, land and means of transport owned by undertakings;

- Sealing any business premises and books or records for the period of, and to the extent necessary for the inspection. If seals are broken, the Commission may impose a fine on the undertaking of up to 1 per cent of its total turnover in the preceding year.

An undertaking is obliged to submit to an investigation ordered by way of a decision (Cases 46/87 and 227/88 *Hoechst AG v Commission*) but co-operation of the relevant NCA is required and, if necessary, judicial authorisation must be obtained (Case C-94/00 *Roquette Frères*).

Inspections at premises other than those of an undertaking under investigation (Article 21 of Regulation 1/2003)

If incriminating documents are likely to be kept in private homes, the Commission is empowered to search those homes, subject to prior judicial authorisation.

4. Hearing (Article 27(1) of Regulation 1/2003 and Article 10(1) of Regulation 773/2004)

The Commission is required to give undertakings the opportunity to be heard before adopting any decision finding an infringement, taking interim measures or imposing fines or periodic payments. Hearings are conducted by a hearing officer.

5. Access to documents (Article 27(2) of Regulation 1/2003 and Articles 15 and 16 of Regulation 773/2004) (C-51/92 Hercules)

The principle that interested parties should have access to all files held by the Commission is subject to three exceptions concerning:

- Documents which relate to business secrets (Case 53/85 *AKZO*);

- Documents which do not form part of the investigation (internal documents of the Commission and the NCAs);

- Confidential documents (to protect the identity of an informer, or because the relevant documents were supplied to the Commission subject to a condition of non-disclosure, or because they relate to military secrets).

6. Fines

There are three kinds:

- Procedural fines up to 1 per cent of the undertaking's total turnover in the preceding business year. These may be imposed on an undertaking which refuses to supply information, or when it provides incorrect or misleading information intentionally or negligently, or in other circumstances set out in Article 23(1) of Regulation 1/2003;

- Periodic penalty payments not exceeding 5 per cent of the average daily turnover in the preceding business year and calculated from the date fixed by the Commission decision. These may be imposed at a daily rate during the continued defiance of the Commission decision. Article 24 provides a list of circumstances in which the Commission may impose the periodic penalty payments;

- "Substantive" fines. Under Article 23(2) of Regulation 1/2003 the Commission is empowered to impose fines for substantive infringements (either intentional or negligent) of Articles 101 or 102 TFEU, of a decision ordering interim measures under Article 8, or for failure to comply with a commitment made binding by a decision pursuant to Article 9.

2006 EU Leniency Programme

The main objective of the Programme is to provide an incentive to an undertaking participating in an unlawful cartel to come forward and to expose the cartel. The incentive is to offer immunity from, or a reduction in, the fine that would be applicable to the undertaking had the cartel been discovered without the undertaking's assistance.

III. ENFORCEMENT OF EC COMPETITION LAW BEFORE NATIONAL COURTS AND CO-OPERATION BETWEEN THE COMMISSION AND NATIONAL COURTS

1. Enforcement of EU competition law before national courts

Only national courts can:

- Award damages to individuals or undertakings for loss suffered as a result of the infringement of Articles 101 and 102 TFEU;

- Rule on claims for payment or fulfilment of contractual obligations based on an agreement under Article 101;

- Apply the civil sanction of nullity under Article 101(2);

- Award legal costs to the successful claimant.

2. Co-operation between the Commission and national courts

This is provided for in Articles 15 and 16 of Regulation 1/2003 and in the 2004 Commission Notice on Co-operation between the Commission and the Courts of the EU Member States in the Application of Articles 81 and 82 EC [Articles 101 and 102 TFEU].

IV. ENFORCEMENT OF ARTICLES 101 AND 102 BY NCAs, CO-OPERATION BETWEEN THE EUROPEAN COMMISSION AND NCAs, AND CO-OPERATION BETWEEN NCAs WITHIN THE EUROPEAN COMPETITION NETWORK (ECN)

1. Enforcement of EU competition law by NCAs

NCAs may make the following decisions:

- Order an infringement to be brought to an end;

- Order interim measures;

- Accept commitments from the parties concerned;

- Impose fines or other penalties provided for in their national laws.

2. Co-operation between NCAs and the Commission

This concerns:

- Allocation of cases;

- Exchange of information;

- Consultations.

3. Co-operation between NCAs

This is in respect of:

- Allocation of cases;

- Exchange of information, but there are safeguards aimed at protecting individuals and undertakings against the misuse of exchanged information.

4. The European Competition Network (ECN)

The NCAs and the Commission form a network called the European Competition Network, which constitutes a forum for discussion on issues that arise in the enforcement of competition law. Its main achievement was the adoption of a Model Leniency Programme in 2006.

RECOMMENDED READING

Books

Basedow, J. (ed.), *Private Enforcement of EC Competition Law*, 2007, The Hague: Kluwer Law International

Möllers, T.M. and Heinemann, A., (eds) *The Enforcement of Competition Law in Europe*, 2008, Oxford: Oxford University Press

Articles

Berghe, P. and Dawes, A., " 'Little Pig, Little Pig, Let Me Come In': An Evaluation of the European Commission's Powers of Inspection in Competition Cases", (2009) 30/9 ECLR, p 407

Boylan, P., "Privilege and In-house Lawyers", (2007) 6/10 Comp. L.J., p 15

De Broca, H., "The Commission Revises its Guidelines for Setting Fines in Antitrust Cases", (2006) 3 EC Competition Policy Newsletter, p 1

Kortman, J.S., and Swaak, CH.R.A., "The EC White Paper on Antitrust Damage Actions: Why the Member States are (Right to be) Less Than Enthusiastic", (2009) 30/7 ECLR, p 340

Parlak, S., "Passing-on Defence and Indirect Purchaser Standing: Should the Passing-on Defence Be Rejected Now the Indirect Purchaser Has Standing after *Manfredi* and the White Paper of the European Commission?", (2010) 33 World Competition, p 31

Wouter P.J. Wils, "The Increased Level of EU Antitrust Fines, Judicial Review and the ECHR", (2010) 33 World Competition, p 5

INDEX